Lecture Notes in Artificial Intelligence   10313

Subseries of Lecture Notes in Computer Science

LNAI Series Editors

Randy Goebel
University of Alberta, Edmonton, Canada
Yuzuru Tanaka
Hokkaido University, Sapporo, Japan
Wolfgang Wahlster
DFKI and Saarland University, Saarbrücken, Germany

LNAI Founding Series Editor

Joerg Siekmann
DFKI and Saarland University, Saarbrücken, Germany

More information about this series at http://www.springer.com/series/1244

Editors
Lech Polkowski
Polish-Japanese Academy of Information
  Technology
Warsaw
Poland

Yiyu Yao
University of Regina
Regina, SK
Canada

Piotr Artiemjew
University of Warmia and Mazury
Olsztyn
Poland

Davide Ciucci
University of Milano-Bicocca
Milan
Italy

Dun Liu
Southwest Jiaotong University
Chengdu
China

Dominik Ślęzak
Warsaw University
Warsaw
Poland

Beata Zielosko
Silesian University
Sosnowiec
Poland

ISSN 0302-9743   ISSN 1611-3349 (electronic)
Lecture Notes in Artificial Intelligence
ISBN 978-3-319-60836-5   ISBN 978-3-319-60837-2 (eBook)
DOI 10.1007/978-3-319-60837-2

Library of Congress Control Number: 2017944319

LNCS Sublibrary: SL7 – Artificial Intelligence

Printed on acid-free paper

This Springer imprint is published by Springer Nature
The registered company is Springer International Publishing AG
The registered company address is: Gewerbestrasse 11, 6330 Cham, Switzerland

Lech Polkowski · Yiyu Yao
Piotr Artiemjew · Davide Ciucci
Dun Liu · Dominik Ślęzak
Beata Zielosko (Eds.)

Rough Sets

International Joint Conference, IJCRS 2017
Olsztyn, Poland, July 3–7, 2017
Proceedings, Part I

 Springer

Preface

The two-volume set of proceedings of IJCRS 2017, the 2017 International Joint Conference on Rough Sets, contains the results of the meeting of the International Rough Set Society held at the University of Warmia and Mazury in Olsztyn, Poland, during July 3–7, 2017.

Conferences in the IJCRS series are held annually and comprise four main tracks relating the topic rough sets to other topical paradigms: rough sets and data analysis covered by the RSCTC conference series from 1998, rough sets and granular computing covered by the RSFDGrC conference series since 1999, rough sets and knowledge technology covered by the RSKT conference series since 2006, and rough sets and intelligent systems covered by the RSEISP conference series since 2007. Owing to the gradual emergence of hybrid paradigms involving rough sets, it was deemed necessary to organize Joint Rough Set Symposiums, first in Toronto, Canada, in 2007, followed by Symposiums in Chengdu, China in 2012, Halifax, Canada, 2013, Granada and Madrid, Spain, 2014, Tianjin, China, 2015, where the acronym IJCRS was proposed, continuing with the IJCRS 2016 conference in Santiago de Chile.

The IJCRS conferences aim at gathering together experts from academia and industry representing fields of research in which theoretical and applicational aspects of rough set theory already find or may potentially find usage. They also provide a venue for researchers wanting to present their ideas before the rough set community, or for those who would like to learn about rough sets and find out whether they could be useful for their problems.

This year's conference, IJCRS 2017, celebrated the 35th anniversary of the seminal work by Prof. Zdzisław Pawlak published in 1982, in which the notion of a rough set emerged.

Professor Zdzisław Pawlak (1926–2006) contributed to computer science with many achievements such as addressless Pawlak machines, a random number generator, a participant in the design and production of the Polish computing machine UMC-2, and a proposition of the first genomic grammar (1965).

The emergence of the rough set idea owes much to Prof. Pawlak's deep interest in the foundations of logics and mathematics — in the 1960s he conducted seminars with the eminent logician and mathematician Prof. Andrzej Ehrenfeucht at the Mathematical Institute of the Polish Academy of Sciences. At the root of the idea of a rough set lie the mathematical notions of the lower and the upper approximation known in geometry and analysis, and the idea of an inexact concept as possessing a boundary that consists of things belonging neither in the concept nor in its complement, going back to Gottlob Frege.

The second motive for celebration was the 50th anniversary of the dissemination in the scientific world by Prof. Solomon Marcus (1924–2015) of the Pawlak model of the DNA grammar, published in 1965 in Polish, in a small popular monograph on grammar theory, intended for high schoolers. This grammar, constructed also visually by means of chains of triangles, was the precursor of visual and mosaic grammars.

The conference commemorated Prof. Pawlak with a special session on "Zdzisław Pawlak — Life and Heritage" with Prof. Grzegorz Rozenberg as the honorary chair and Professor Andrzej Skowron as the chair; there were also commemorative talks by Prof. Grzegorz Rozenberg, Sankar Kumar Pal, Lech Polkowski, Roman Słowiski, Shusaku Tsumoto, Guoyin Wang, Zbigniew Ras, and Urszula Wybraniec-Skardowska. The essay by Prof. Wybraniec-Skardowska opens the proceedings.

The conference included six keynote lectures by Prof. Rakesh Agrawal, Jan Komorowski, Eric Matson, Sankar Kumar Pal, Grzegorz Rozenberg, and Guoyin Wang as well as four plenary lectures by Profs. Tianrui Li, Son Hung Nguyen, Pradipta Maji, Amedeo Napoli, and Zbigniew Ras.

For the process of submission, review, acceptance, updating, and compilation of the proceedings, the EasyChair Pro system was used that allowed for subdivision of submissions into tracks: Rough Sets (68 submissions), Special Session on Vagueness, Rough Sets and Mereology (11 submissions), Special Session on Trends in Multi-Agent Systems (five submissions), Special Session on Formal Concept Analysis, Rough Set Theory and Their Applications (five submissions), Special Session: Software and Systems for Rough Sets (four submissions), Workshop Three-Way Decisions, Uncertainty, Granular Computing (The 5th International Workshop on Three-way Decisions, Uncertainty, and Granular Computing, TWDUG 2017; 17 submissions), Workshop: Recent Advances in Biomedical Data Analysis (three submissions), and one invited submission to the Special Session "Zdzisław Pawlak — Life and Heritage." In all, 114 (130 with invited talks) submissions were received. Submissions were allowed to be regular at 10–20 long length and short at 6–8 pages. They were reviewed by members of Program Committee (PC) and invited reviewers, each submission reviewed by at least three reviewers in certainly positive cases and by four or five reviewers in cases of conflicting reviews by the first three reviewers. Finally, the most complex cases were decided by the conference and PC chairs.

Of 114 (130) submissions, after positive reviews and decisions, 74 papers were selected to be included as regular papers and 16 as short papers in the proceedings, which comprise two volumes. Section 1, Invite Talks, contains the essay by Urszula Wybraniec Skardowska in remembrance of Prof. Pawlak, abstracts of the keynote, plenary, IRSS fellow talks and tutorials, as submitted by respective speakers, making up 16 chapters. Section 2 on "General Rough Sets" contains papers devoted to the rough set theory in its foundational and decision-theoretic aspects, collected in 44 chapters. Section 3 on "Software and Systems for Rough Sets" contains papers submitted and accepted to the special session with this title. These sections constitute the first volume of proceedings.

The second volume of proceedings opens with Section 4, which collects papers submitted and accepted to the special session on "Vagueness, Rough Sets, Mereology" is devoted to foundational concept-theoretical and logical analysis of the rough set idea, as well as papers on applications of mereology in intelligent methods of computer science, containing ten chapters. Section 5, "Workshop on Three-Way Decisions, Uncertainty, Granular Computing," comprises 17 chapters. In these papers, the classic trichotomy introduced by Prof. Pawlak into data objects with respect to a given concept as belonging certainly in the concept, certainly not belonging in the concept, and belonging into the boundary of the concept is extended to soft computing with these regions; the topic of granular computing fits naturally in this section since rough sets, from their very inception, are computed with elementary granules defined by attribute-value descriptors. In Section 6 on "Recent Advances in Biomedical Data Analysis, Trends in Multi-Agent Systems, Formal Concept Analysis, Rough Set Theory and Their Applications," we find submitted and accepted regular papers on these topics that are strongly tied to the rough set domain. Section 6 contains 13 chapters; 24 papers were rejected, i.e., 21% of submissions. In the "General Rough Sets" track, 22 papers were rejected, i.e., 32% of submissions to this track.

In addition to the proceedings, participants of the conference found in the conference sets a booklet, "The Polish Trace," consisting of four chapters dedicated to the little known yet spectacular achievements of Polish scientists in the area of computer science: on the work by Jan Czochralski, "the forefather of the silicon era"; on achievements of cryptologists Jan Kowalewski and professors of Warsaw University Stanisł aw Leśniewski, Stefan Mazurkiewicz, and Wacław Sierpiński in deciphering codes of the Red Army during the Polish–Russian war of 1918–1920; on cryptologists Marian Rejewski, Jerzy Różycki, and Henryk Zygalski, who broke the German Enigma code in the 1930s; and on the contributions of Stanisław Leśniewski, Jan Łukasiewicz, and Alfred Tarski to the theory of concepts, computing, and soft computing.

An additional booklet contained texts of talks in the Special Session devoted to the memory of Prof. Zdzisław Pawlak.

We acknowledge the acceptance of our proposal of organizing IJCRS 2017 in Poland at the University of Warmia and Mazury by authorities of the International Rough Set Society, the owner of rights to the series.

Honorary patronage of the conference was accepted by Gustaw Marek Brzezin, Marshal of the Province of Warmia and Mazury, Prof. Ryszard Górecki, Rector of the University of Warmia and Mazury, and by Dr. Piotr Grzymowicz, President of the City of Olsztyn.

Scientific patronage was given by the International Rough Set Society and by the Committee on Informatics of the Polish Academy of Science.

Many eminent scientists offered us their kind help by accepting our invitations. Thanks go to the honorary chairs of the conference, Profs. Ryszard Górecki, Sankar Kumar Pal, Roman Słowiński, Andrzej Skowron, and Jerzy Nowacki as well as Wojciech Samulowski, Director of the Olsztyn Park of Science and Technology, to Guoyin Wang, to the keynote speakers Profs. Rakesh Agrawal, Jan Komorowski, Eric Matson, Sankar Kumar Pal, Grzegorz Rozenberg, and Guoyin Wang, and to the plenary speakers, Profs. Tianrui Li, Nguyen Hung Son, Pradipta Maji, Amedeo Napoli, and Zbigniew Ras. The Steering Committee members are gratefully acknowledged for their support.

We express our gratitude to the organizers and chairs of special sessions and workshops: Profs. Mani A-, Andrzej Pietruszczak, Rafał Gruszczyński, Duoqian Miao, Georg Peters, Chien Chung Chan, Hong Yu, Bing Zhou, Nouman Azam, Nan Zhang, Sushmita Paul, Jan G. Bazan, Andrzej Skowron, Pradipta Maji, Dominik Ślęzak, Julio Vera, Grzegorz Rozenberg, Sankar Kumar Pal, Roman Słowiński, Shusaku Tsumoto, Guoyin Wang, Zbigniew Ras, Urszula Wybraniec-Skardowska, Andrzej Zbrzezny,

Agnieszka M. Zbrzezny, Magdalena Kacprzak, Jakub Michaliszyn, Franco Raimondi, Wojciech Penczek, Bożena Woźna-Szczęśniak, Mahdi Zargayouna, Jaume Baixeries, Dmitry Ignatov, Mehdi Kaytoue, Sergei Kuznetsov, Tianrui Li, Jarosław Stepaniuk, and Hung Son Nguyen.

We thank the following for the tutorials: Jan Komorowski, Piero Pagliani, Andrzej Zbrzezny, Ivo Duentsch, and Dimiter Vakarelov. Our special thanks go to Program Committee members and Program Committee chairs: Profs. Piotr Artiemjew, Davide Ciucci, Dun Liu, Dominik Ślęzak, and Beata Zielosko, for their dedicated work in reviewing and selecting papers to be accepted, and to the members of the Organizing Committee: Dr. Przemysław Górecki, Dr. Paweł Drozda, Dr. Krzysztof Sopyła, Dr. Piotr Artiemjew, Dr. Stanisław Drozda, Dr. Bartosz Nowak, Łukasz Żmudzinski, Dr. Agnieszka Niemczynowicz, Hanna Pikus, Dr. Marek Adamowicz, and Beata Ostrowska. Special thanks for their dedicated and timely work to Mr Łukasz Żmudziński, for his work on the conference website, Dr. Paweł Drozda, for taking care of the administration of conference finances, and to Dr. Przemysław Górecki, for liaising with the hosting university's administrative offices. Student volunteers should be mentioned for their help in running the conference. Thanks go to our material sponsors: the Olsztyn Park of Science and Technology, the Marshal of the Province of Warmia and Mazury, Billennium. For moral support we would like to mention the co-organizers, the Polish-Japanese Academy of Information Technology and the Polish Information Processing Society. Our host, the University of Warmia and Mazury in Olsztyn, provided ample space for the conference sessions, secured the participation of the Kortowo ensemble, and the professional help of the university services: the financial and international exchange offices and the Foundation "ŻAK" that provided the catering. Thanks go to Park Hotel in Olsztyn for hosting the participants.

Special thanks go to Alfred Hofmann of Springer, for accepting to publish the proceedings of IJCRS 2017 in the LNCS/LNAI series, and to Anna Kramer and Elke Werner for their help with the proceedings. We are grateful to Springer for the grant of 1,000 euro for the best conference papers.

April 2017

Lech Polkowski
Yiyu Yao
Piotr Artiemjew
Davide Ciucci
Dun Liu
Dominik Ślęzak
Beata Zielosko

Organization

Honorary Patronage

Gustaw Marek Brzezin   Marshal of the Warmia and Mazury Province, Olsztyn, Poland

Ryszard Górecki   Rektor, University of Warmia and Mazury in Olsztyn, Olsztyn, Poland

Piotr Grzymowicz   President of the City of Olsztyn, Olsztyn, Poland

Scientific Patronage

International Rough Set Society
Committee for Informatics of the Polish Academy of Science

Conference Committees

Honorary Chairs

Ryszard Górecki   University of Warmia and Mazury in Olsztyn, Poland
Jerzy Nowacki   Polish-Japanese Academy of IT, Poland
Sankar Kumar Pal   Indian Statistical Institute, India
Wojciech Samulowski   Olsztyn Park of Science and Technology, Poland
Roman Słowiński   Poznań University of Technology, Poland
Andrzej Skowron   Warsaw University, Poland
Guoyin Wang   Chongqing University of Posts and Telecommunications, China

Conference Chairs

Lech Polkowski   University of Warmia and Mazury in Olsztyn, Poland
Yiyu Yao   University of Regina, Canada

Steering Committee

Jerzy Grzymala-Busse (Chair)   University of Kansas at Lawrence, USA
Chien-Chung Chan   University of Akron, USA
Chris Cornelis   Ghent University, Belgium
Qinghua Hu   Tianjin University, China
Masahiro Inuiguchi   Osaka University, Japan
Tianrui Li   Southwest Jiaotong University, China
Pawan Lingras   St. Mary's University, Canada
Ernestina Menasalvas   Universidad Politecnica de Madrid, Spain
Duoqian Miao   Tongji University, China
Sushmita Mitra   Indian Statistical Institute, India

Marian Noga	AGH University of Science and Technology, Poland
Nguyen Hung Son	Warsaw University, Poland
Jerzy Stefanowski	Poznań University of Technology, Poland
Jarosław Stepaniuk	Białystok University of Technology, Poland
Zbigniew Suraj	Rzeszów University, Poland
Marcin Szczuka	Warsaw University, Poland
Shusaku Tsumoto	Matsue University, Japan
Richard Weber	Universidad de Chile, Chile
Weizhi Wu	Zhejiang Ocean University, China
Jingtao Yao	University of Regina, Canada

Chairs and Organizers of Special Sessions, Workshops, Tutorials

Special Session on Foundations of Vagueness, Rough Sets and Mereology

Mani A.	University of Calcutta, India
Rafał Gruszczyński	Nicolaus Copernicus University in Toruń, Poland
Andrzej Pietruszczak	Nicolaus Copernicus University in Toruń, Poland
Lech Polkowski	University of Warmia and Mazury in Olsztyn, Poland

Special Plenary Session: Zdzisław Pawlak Life and Heritage

| Grzegorz Rozenberg | Leiden Universiteit, The Netherlands; University of Colorado at Boulder, USA |
| Andrzej Skowron | Warsaw University, Poland |

Special Session: Trends in Multi-Agent Systems

Andrzej Zbrzezny	Jan Długosz Academy, Poland
Agnieszka M. Zbrzezny	Jan Długosz Academy, Poland.
Magdalena Kacprzak	Białystok University of Technology, Poland
Jakub Michaliszyn	University of Wrocław, Poland
Wojciech Penczek	IPI PAN, Poland
Franco Raimondi	Middlesex University, UK
Bożena Woźna-Szcześniak	Jan Długosz Academy, Poland
Mahdi Zargayouna	Ifsttar Institute, University of Paris-Est, France

Special Session on Formal Concept Analysis, Rough Set Theory and Their Applications

Jaume Baixeries	Universidad Politecnica de Catalunya, Spain
Dmitry Ignatov	National Research University, School of Economics, Russia
Mehdi Kaytoue	Institut National des Sciences Appliques de Lyon, France
Sergei Kuznetsov	National Research University, School of Economics, Russia

Special Session: Software and Systems for Rough Sets

Tianrui Li	Southwest Jiaotong University, Chengdu, China
Jarosław Stepaniuk	Białystok University of Technology, Poland
Hung Son Nguyen	Warsaw University, Poland

TWDUG 2017: The 5th Workshop on Three-Way Decisions, Uncertainty and Granular Computing

Duoqian Miao	Tongji University, China
Georg Peters	University of Applied Sciences, Germany
Chien Chung Chan	Akron University, USA
Nouman Azam	National University of Computer and Emerging Sciences, Pakistan
Hong Yu	Chongqing University of Posts and Telecommunications, China
Bing Zhou	Sam Houston State University, USA
Nan Zhang	Tianjin University, China

Workshop on Recent Advances in Biomedical Data Analysis

Sushmita Paul	Indian Institute of Technology Jodhpur, India
Jan G. Bazan	University of Rzeszów, Poland
Pradipta Maji	Indian Statistical Institute, Kolkata, India
Andrzej Skowron	Warsaw University, Poland
Lech Polkowski	University of Warmia and Mazury in Olsztyn, Poland
Dominik Ślęzak	Warsaw University, Poland
Julio Vera	Friedrich Alexander University of Erlangen-Nürnberg, Germany

Tutorial Chairs

Ivo Düntsch	Brock University, Canada
Jan Komorowski	Uppsala University, Sweden
Piero Pagliani	Rome, Italy
Andrzej Zbrzezny	Jan Długosz Academy, Poland
Dimiter Vakarelov	Sofia University, Bulgaria

Organizing Committee

Przemysław Górecki (Chair)	University of Warmia and Mazury in Olsztyn, Poland
Marek Adamowicz	Polish Information Processing Society, Poland
Piotr Artiemjew	University of Warmia and Mazury in Olsztyn, Poland
Paweł Drozda	University of Warmia and Mazury in Olsztyn, Poland
Stanisław Drozda	University of Warmia and Mazury in Olsztyn, Poland
Agnieszka Niemczynowicz	University of Warmia and Mazury in Olsztyn, Poland

Bartosz Nowak	University of Warmia and Mazury in Olsztyn, Poland
Beata Ostrowska	Polish Information Processing Society, Poland
Hanna Pikus	Polish Information Processing Society, Poland
Sławomir Popowicz	University of Warmia and Mazury, Poland
Krzysztof Ropiak	University of Warmia and Mazury, Poland
Krzysztof Sopyła	University of Warmia and Mazury in Olsztyn, Poland
Łukasz Żmudziński	University of Warmia and Mazury in Olsztyn, Poland

Sponsoring Institutions

Marshal of the Warmia and Mazury Province
Olsztyn Park of Science and Technology
University of Warmia and Mazury in Olsztyn, Poland
Billennium

Program Committee

Mani A.	Calcutta University, India
Mehwish Alam	Université de Paris, Laboratoire d'Informatique de Paris-Nord, France
Natasha Alechina	University of Nottingham, UK
Piotr Artiemjew	University of Warmia and Mazury in Olsztyn, Poland
Nouman Azam	National University of Computer and Emerging Sciences
Jaume Baixeries	Universitat Politècnica de Catalunya, Spain
Mohua Banerjee	Indian Institute of Technology Kanpur, India
Jan Bazan	University of Rzeszów, Poland
Rafael Bello	Universidad Central de Las Villas, Cuba
Nizar Bouguila	Concordia University, Canada
Aleksey Buzmakov	National Research University Higher School of Economics
Jerzy Błaszczyński	Poznań University of Technology, Poland
Mihir Chakraborty	Jadavpur University, India
Shampa Chakraverty	Netaji Subhas Institute of Technology, Dwarka, India
Chien-Chung Chan	University of Akron, USA
Mu-Chen Chen	National Chiao Tung University, Taiwan
Giampiero Chiaselotti	Università della Calabria, Italy
Costin-Gabriel Chiru	Politehnica University of Bucharest, Romania
Davide Ciucci	University of Milano-Bicocca, Italy
Victor Codocedo	Laboratoire lorrain de recherche en informatique et ses applications, France
Chris Cornelis	University of Granada, Spain
Zoltán Ernö Csajbók	University of Debrecen, Hungary
Jianhua Dai	Tianjin University, China
Martine De Cock	University of Washington Tacoma, USA
Dayong Deng	Zhejiang Normal University, China

Gabriela Lindemann-Von Trzebiatowski	Humboldt University of Berlin, Germany
Pawan Lingras	Saint Mary's University, UK
Caihui Liu	Gannan Normal University, China
Dun Liu	Southwest Jiaotong University, China
Guilong Liu	Beijing Language and Culture University, China
Pradipta Maji	Indian Statistical Institute, Kolkata, India
Krzysztof Marasek	Polish-Japanese Academy of Information Technology, Poland
Benedetto Matarazzo	University of Catania, Italy
Jesús Medina Moreno	University of Cádiz, Spain
Ernestina Menasalvas	Universidad Politecnica de Madrid, Spain
Claudio Meneses	Universidad Católica del Norte, Chile
Duoqian Miao	Tongji University, China
Marcin Michalak	Silesian University of Technology, Poland
Jakub Michaliszyn	University of Wroclaw, Poland
Tamás Mihálydeák	University of Debrecen, Hungary
Fan Min	Southwest Petroleum University, China
Boris Mirkin	School of Data Analysis and Artificial Intelligence, Moscow, Russia
Pabitra Mitra	Indian Institute of Technology Kharagpur, India
Sadaaki Miyamoto	University of Tsukuba, Japan
Jesús Medina Moreno	University of Cádiz, Spain
Mikhail Moshkov	KAUST
Michinori Nakata	Josai International University, Japan
Amedeo Napoli	LORIA Nancy, France
Hung Son Nguyen	Institute of Mathematics, Warsaw University, Poland
Sinh Hoa Nguyen	Polish-Japanese Academy of Information Technology, Poland
M.C. Nicoletti	FACCAMP and UFSCar
Vilem Novak	University of Ostrava, Czech Republic
Jerzy Nowacki	Polish-Japanese Academy of Information Technology, Poland
Bartosz Nowak	University of Warmia and Mazury in Olsztyn, Poland
Hannu Nurmi	University of Turku, Finland
Ewa Orlowska	Institute of Telecommunication, Warsaw, Poland
Piero Pagliani	Research Group on Knowledge and Information, Rome, Italy
Sankar Kumar Pal	Indian Statistical Institute, Kolkata, India
Krzysztof Pancerz	University of Rzeszow, Poland
Vladimir Parkhomenko	St. Petersburg State Polytechnical University, Russia
Sushmita Paul	Indian Institute of Technology, Jodhpur
Andrei Paun	University of Bucharest, Romania
Witold Pedrycz	University of Edmonton, Canada
Wojciech Penczek	ICS PAS and Siedlce University
Tatiana Penkova	Institute of Computational Modelling SB RAS

Li-Shiang Tsay	North Carolina A&T State University, USA
Dimiter Vakarelov	Sofia University, Bulgaria
Dmitry Vinogradov	Federal Research Center for Computer Science and Control RAN, Russia
Guoyin Wang	Chongqing University of Posts and Telecommunications, China
Thomas Wilcockson	Lancaster University, UK
Szymon Wilk	Poznan University of Technology, Poland
Arkadiusz Wojna	Warsaw University, Poland
Marcin Wolski	Maria Curie-Sklodowska University, Poland
Bożena Wozna-Szczesniak	Jan Dlugosz University in Czestochowa, Poland
Wei-Zhi Wu	Zhejiang Ocean University, China
Yan Yang	Jiaotong University, China
Jingtao Yao	University of Regina, Canada
Yiyu Yao	University of Regina, Canada
Dongyi Ye	Fuzhou University, China
Hong Yu	Chongqing University of Posts and Telecommunications, China
Mahdi Zargayouna	Université Paris Est, Ifsttar, France
Agnieszka M. Zbrzezny	Jan Dlugosz University, Poland
Andrzej Zbrzezny	Jan Dlugosz University, Poland
Bo Zhang	Chinese Academy of Sciences, China
Nan Zhang	Yantai University, China
Qinghua Zhang	Institute of Computer Science and Technology, Chongqing University of Posts and Telecommunications, China
Yan Zhang	University of Regina, Canada
Ning Zhong	Maebashi Institute of Technology, Japan
Bing Zhou	Sam Houston State University, USA
William Zhu	Minnan Normal University, China
Wojciech Ziarko	University of Regina, Canada
Beata Zielosko	University of Silesia, Poland

Additional Reviewers

Azam, Muhammad
Boldak, Cezary
Chen, Yewang
Czajkowski, Marcin
Garai, Partha
Jana, Purbita
Keith, Brian
Kopczynski, Maciej

Krzeszowski, Tomasz
Melliti, Tarek
Mondal, Ajoy
Nayak, Losiana
Szreter, Maciej
Tripathy, B.K.
Vluymans, Sarah

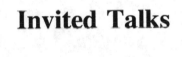

Invited Talks

Structure and Interpretation
of Classifiers – The Rule Networks

Jan Komorowski[1,2]

[1] Program in Bioinformatics and Computational Biology,
Department of Cell and Molecular Biology,
Uppsala University, Uppsala, Sweden
jan.komorowski@icm.uu.se
[2] Institute of Computer Science, PAN, Warsaw, Poland

Research in machine learning and in particular in supervised machine learning has been over focused on numerical measures of the classification quality of the classifiers. Although classification quality is, of course, of interest, this preoccupation shadowed other important aspects such as interpretation of classifiers. Understanding the structure of classifiers and, consequently, the ability to explain the classification in terms comprehensible to the user are particularly important in several applications in Life Sciences. For example, a molecular engineer does not only want to know whether a protein will have a given function as predicted by the classifier, but also needs to know how the function arises or is lost. Likewise, classifying an avian influenza virus into high or low pathogenicity is helpful, but it does not elucidate the mechanisms of the pathogenicity. And in precision medicine, the prediction of drug applicability must be trusted, i.e. be explainable.

We have pioneered the research into interpretable classifiers by studying interactions. In 2004 we published the first model of G-Protein Coupled Receptor-ligand interactions that explained the reasons for strong versus weak bindings [1] and [2]. This work was followed by a number of results in the world of transcriptomics, virology, proteomics, (e.g. [3–5]) as well as in the now important field of discovering interactions between an environment and organisms such as, for instance, allergy [6].

Recently, we have expanded our investigations to the issue of discovery if interactions in living systems from rule-based classifiers, which lead us, among others, to a development of the notion of rule networks. Essentially, a rule network is a graph constructed from the rules of a classifier. Two nodes are connected by an edge if the nodes are conjuncts in the IF-part of one rule. The strength of the edge is the sum for all rules of the support for a rule multiplied by its accuracy. The construction of rule networks was inspired by our earlier development of literature networks of genes [7].

We have developed two display formalisms to visualize interactions Ciruvis [8] and VisuNet [9]. These networks often display unexpected properties that help understand the modelled systems. It appears that rule networks are functional in that the interactions do often represent true interaction in the living systems.

The rule networks are a supervised counterpart of co-expression networks that use similarity of nodes: two genes are connected by an edge if the they are similarly expressed [10] Co-expression networks are based on unsupervised learning, usually hierarchical clustering. In contrast, rule networks are applicable to any study domain, not only gene expressions, and since they are based on classifiers, they (a) are predictive of the decision class, (b) can discover much more complex relationships than co-expression nets. Possibly the most important property of rule networks is that separate networks are constructed for each decision class (or outcome), which is not possible for co-expression networks.

In the talk I shall introduce the concept of rule networks and illustrate their applications in a number of Life Science applications. Our methodology is applicable to big data. Using Monte Carl feature selection [11] or Random Reducts [12] we can effectively preprocess decision systems of even 1 million features and reduce them to several hundreds of significant features, but usually much fewer. We then apply ROSETTA to generate rough set models [13, 14] and finally study the networks displayed by Ciruvis or VisuNet. Selected case studies in transcriptomics, virology, proteomics both published and unpublished ones will be presented [15, 16].

Research into rule networks has just started and there is a number of interesting issues to be explored one of them the all important data integration, another the relationship of the mechanism to other approaches to discovering interactions.

References

1. Strmbergsson, H., et al.: Proteochemometrics modeling of receptor-ligand interactions using rough sets. In: Proceedings of the German conference on Bioinformatics, pp. 4–6 (2004)
2. Strombergsson, H., et al.: Rough set-based proteochemometrics modeling of G-protein-coupled receptor-ligand interactions. Proteins 63(1), 24–34 (2006)
3. Kontijevskis, A., Wikberg, J.E., Komorowski, J.: Computational proteomics analysis of HIV-1 protease interactome. Proteins 68(1), 305–312 (2007)
4. Kierczak, M., et al.: A rough set-based model of HIV-1 reverse transcriptase resistome. Bioinform. Biol. Insights 3, 109 (2009)
5. Kierczak, M., et al.: Computational analysis of molecular interaction networks underlying change of HIV-1 resistance to selected reverse transcriptase inhibitors. Bioinform. Biol. Insights 4, 137 (2010)
6. Bornelv, S., et al.: Rule-based models of the interplay between genetic and environmental factors in childhood allergy. PLoS One (2013)
7. Jenssen, T.K., et al.: A literature network of human genes for high-throughput analysis of gene expression. Nat. Genet. 28(1), 21–28 (2001)
8. Bornelv, S., Marillet, S., Komorowski, J.: Ciruvis: a web-based tool for rule networks and interaction detection using rule-based classifiers. BMC Bioinform. 15(1), 1 (2014)
9. Omondi, S.: VisuNet (2016). http://bioinf.icm.uu.se/~visunet/
10. Childs, K.L., Davidson, R.M., Buell, C.R.: Gene coexpression network analysis as a source of functional annotation for rice genes. PloS one 6(7), e22196 (2011)
11. Draminski, M., et al.: Monte Carlo feature selection for supervised classification. Bioinformatics 24(1), 110–117 (2008)
12. Kruczyk, M., et al.: Random reducts: a Monte Carlo rough set-based method for feature selection in large datasets. Fundamenta Informaticae 127(1), 273–288 (2013)
13. Komorowski, J., Hrn, A.: ROSETTA – A rough set toolkit for analysis of data. In: Fifth International Workshop on Rough Sets and Soft Computing. Springer Verlag, Tokyou (1997)

14. Komorowski, J., Hrn, A., Skowron, A.: Rosetta and other software systems for rough sets. Handbook of Data Mining and Knowledge Discovery, pp. 554–559 (2000)
15. Khaliq, Z., et al.: Identification of combinatorial host-specific signatures with a potential to affect host adaptation in inuenza A H1N1 and H3N2 subtypes. BMC Genomics **17**(1), 529 (2016)
16. Moghadam, B.T., et al.: Combinatorial identification of DNA methylation patterns over age in the human brain. BMC Bioinform. **17**(1), 393 (2016)

Realizing Applied, Useful Self-organizing Cyber-physical Systems with the HARMS Integration Model

Eric T. Matson

M2M Lab, Purdue University, West Lafayette, IN, USA
ematson@purdue.edu

Abstract: The future in the enhancement of cyber-physical system and robotic functionalities lies not only in the mechanical and electronic improvement of the robots' sensors, mobility, stability and kinematics, but also, if not mostly, in their ability to connect to other actors (human, agents, robots, machines, and sensors HARMS). The capability to communicate openly, to coordinate their goals, to optimize the division of labor, to share their intelligence, to be fully aware of the entire situation, and thus to optimize their fully coordinated actions will be necessary. Additionally, the ability for two actors to work together without preference for any specific type of actor, but simply from necessity of capability, is provided by a requirement of indistinguishability, similar to the discernment feature of rough sets.

Once all of these actors can effectively communicate, they can take on group rational decision making, such as choosing which action to take that optimizes a group's effectiveness or utility. Given group decision making, optimized capability-based organization can take place to enable human-like organizational behavior. Similar to human organizations, artificial collections with the capability to organize will exhibit emergent normative behavior. In this session, we will show how these models are applied to real world problems in security, first response, defense and agriculture.

Biography: Eric T. Matson, Ph.D., is an Associate Professor in the Department of Computer and Information Technology in the College of Technology at Purdue University, West Lafayette. Prof. Matson is also an International Faculty Scholar in the Department of Electrical Engineering at Kyung Hee University, Yongin City, Korea. He was also formerly a Visiting Professor with the LISSI, University of Paris et Creteil (Paris 12), Paris, France, Visiting Professor, Department of Computer Science and Engineering, Dongguk University, Seoul, South Korea and in the School of Informatics at Incheon National University in Incheon, South Korea. He is the Director of the Robotic Innovation, Commercialization and Education (RICE) Research Center, Director of the Korean Software Square at Purdue and the co-founder of the M2M Lab at Purdue University, which performs research at the areas of multiagent systems, cooperative robotics, wireless communication. The application areas are focused on safety and security robotics and agricultural robotics and systems.

Prior to his position at Purdue University, Prof. Matson was in industrial and commercial software development as a consultant, software engineer, manager and director for 14 years. In his software development experience, he developed and lead numerous large software engineering projects dealing with intelligent systems, applied artificial intelligence, distributed object technologies, enterprise resource planning and product data management implementations. Prof. Matson has a Ph.D. in Computer Science and Engineering from the University of Cincinnati, M.B.A in Operations Management from Ohio State University and B.S. and M.S.E. degrees in Computer Science from Kansas State University.

Granular Data Mining and Uncertainty Modeling: Concepts, Features and Applications

Sankar K. Pal

Center for Soft Computing Research, Indian Statistical Institute, Kolkata, India
http://www.isical.ac.in/~sankar

The talk has two parts. First it describes the

- Role of pattern recognition in data mining and machine intelligence
- Features of granular computing
- Significance of fuzzy sets and rough sets in granular computing
- Characteristics of fuzzy sets and rough sets in handling uncertainties arising from overlapping regions/concepts, and granularity in domain respectively
- Relevance of defining the generalized rough sets and entropy by embedding fuzzy sets into rough sets; providing a stronger paradigm for uncertainty modeling

The second part deals with various mining applications such as in

- Video tracking in ambiguous situations
- Bioinformatics (e.g., selection of miRNAs for cancer detection)
- Social network analysis (e.g., community detection)

The applications demonstrate the roles of different kinds of granules, rough lower approximation, and various information measures. Granules considered range from crisp, fuzzy, 1-d, 2-d, 3-d, and regular shape to arbitrary shape. While the concept of rough lower approximation in temporal domain provides an initial estimate of object model in video tracking, it enables in determining the probability of definite and doubtful regions in cancer classification.

Several examples and results would be provided to explain the aforesaid concepts. The talk concludes mentioning their relevance in handling Big data, the challenging issues and the future directions of research.

A Framework for Exploring Disciplines of Science: Dynamic Processes Within a Static Depository of Knowledge

Grzegorz Rozenberg[1,2]

[1] Leiden University, Leiden, The Netherlands
[2] University of Colorado in Boulder, Boulder, USA

In this lecture we present a framework for exploring disciplines of science. This framework takes into account the knowledge about the given discipline as well as dynamic processes (computations) taking place within this knowledge. We illustrate this approach by considering a framework for exploring biology.

This framework, called exploration systems, consists of two parts:

A *static* part which is a depository of knowledge formalized by the notion of a zoom structure. The integrating structure of such a depository allows one to deal with the hierarchical nature of biology.

A *dynamic* part is given by reaction systems. They originated as models for processes instigated by the functioning of living cells and they address two important aspects of biology: non-permanency of its entities and open system aspect of biological units such as living cells.

In this setup the depository of static knowledge given by a zoom structure is explored by computations/processes provided by reaction systems, where this exploration can use/integrate knowledge present on different levels (e.g., atomic, cellular, organisms, species, ... levels).

Rescarch topics in this framework are motivated by considerations originating in the modelled discipline of science as well as by the need to understand the underlying structure of knowledge and the structure of computations exploring this knowledge. The framework we discuss turned out to be novel and attractive also from the theory of computation as well as from the modelling points of view.

The lecture is of interest to mathematicians and computer scientists interested in models of computation and/or in modelling processes taking place in nature as well as to bioinformaticians interested in foundational/formal understanding of biological processes. The lecture is of a tutorial style and self-contained. In particular, no prior knowledge of biochemistry or cell biology is required.

The presented framework was developed jointly with A. Ehrenfeucht from University of Colorado at Boulder.

Big Data Analysis by Rough Sets and Granular Computing

Tianrui Li

School of Information Science and Technology,
Southwest Jiaotong University, Chengdu 611756, China
trli@swjtu.edu.cn

Abstract. Enormous amounts of data are generated every day with the rapid growth of emerging information technologies and application patterns in modern society, e.g., Internet, Internet of Things, and Cloud Computing [1, 2]. It leads to the advent of the era of Big Data. Big Data is often characterized by using five V's, e.g., Volume, Velocity, Variety, Value and Veracity [3]. Volume refers to the very huge amount of data that needs to be managed; Velocity implies that the very high speed of data update; Variety means that the nature of data is varied and there are many different types of data that need to be properly fused to make the most of the analysis; Value signifies high yield will be achieved by handling the big data correctly and accurately; Veracity means the data is full of uncertainty and ambiguity. Exploring efficient and effective knowledge discovery approaches to manage Big Data with rich information has become a hot research topic in the area of information science [4]. This talk aims to show our recent work on big data analysis by rough sets and granular computing. It covers the following seven aspects. (1) A hierarchical entropy-based approach is demonstrated to evaluate the effectiveness of data collection [5], the first step of knowledge discovery from data, which is vital because it may affect mining results and its cost is generally huge [6]. (2) A multi-view-based method is illustrated for filling missing data since it is very common phenomenon in Big Data due to communication or device errors, etc [7]. (3) A unified framework is outlined for Parallel Large-scale Attribute Reduction, termed PLAR, to manage Big Data with high dimension through applying a granular computing-based initialization [8, 9]. (4) A MapReduce-based parallel method together with three parallel strategies are presented for computing rough set approximations [10–13], which is a fundamental part in rough set-based data analysis similar to frequent pattern mining in association rules. (5) Incremental learning-based approaches are shown for updating approximations and knowledge in dynamic data environments, e.g., the variation of objects, attributes or attribute values, which improve the computational efficiency by using previously acquired learning results to facilitate knowledge maintenance without re-implementing the original data mining algorithm [14–17]. (6) A composite rough set model to deal with multiple different types of attributes is developed, which provides a novel approach for complex data fusion [18, 19]. (7) The uncertainty information processing under three-way decisions for the veracity of data is discussed [20–22].

Keywords: Big data · Rough set · Granular computing · Incremental learning · Knowledge discovery

References

1. Li, T.R., Lu, J., Luis, M.L.: Preface: Intelligent techniques for data science. Int. J. Intell. Syst. **30**(8), 851–853 (2015)
2. Dealing with data. Science **331**(6018), 639–806 (2011)
3. Li, T.R., Luo, C., Chen, H.M., Zhang, J.B.: PICKT: A solution for big data analysis. In: Ciucci, D., Wang, G., Mitra, S., Wu, W.Z. (eds.) Rough Sets and Knowledge Technology. LNCS, vol. 9436, pp. 15–25. Springer, Cham (2015)
4. Li, T.R., Luo, C., Chen, H.M., Zhang, J.B.: The Principles and Methodologies of Big Data Mining—From the Perspectives of Granular Computing and Rough Sets, pp. 1–176. Science Press (In Chinese) (2016)
5. Ji, S.G., Zheng, Y., Li, T.R.: Urban sensing based on human mobility. In: Proceedings of ACM International Joint Conference on Pervasive and Ubiquitous Computing. UbiComp 2016, pp. 1040–1051 (2016)
6. Li, T.R., Ruan, D.: An extended process model of knowledge discovery in database. J. Enterp. Inf. Manage. **20**(2), 169–177 (2007)
7. Yi, X.W., Zheng, Y., Zhang, J.B., Li, T.R.: ST-MVL: filling missing values in geo-sensory time series data. In: Proceedings of International Joint Conference on Artificial Intelligence. IJCAI 2016, pp. 2704–2710 (2016)
8. Zhang, J.B., Li, T.R., Pan, Y.: PLAR: parallel large-scale attribute reduction on cloud systems. In: Proceedings of International Conference on Parallel and Distributed Computing, Applications and Technologies. PDCAT 2013, pp. 184–191 (2013)
9. Zhang, J.B., Li, T.R., Pan, Y.: Parallel large-scale attribute reduction on cloud systems. arXiv preprint. arXiv: 1610.01807 (2016)
10. Zhang, J.B., Li, T.R., Ruan, D., Gao, Z.Z., Zhao, C.B.: A parallel method for computing rough set approximations. Inf. Sci. **194**, 209–223 (2012)
11. Zhang, J.B., Wong, J.S., Li, T.R., Pan, Y.: A comparison of parallel large-scale knowledge acquisition using rough set theory on different MapReduce runtime systems. Int. J. Approx. Reason. **55**(3), 896–907 (2014)
12. Zhang, J.B., Li, T.R., Pan, Y., Luo, C. Teng, F.: Parallel and incremental algorithm for knowledge update based on rough sets in cloud platform. J. Softw. **26**(5), 1064–1078 (2015) (in Chinese)
13. Zhang, J.B., Wong, J.S., Pan, Y., Li, T.R.: A parallel matrix-based method for computing approximations in incomplete information systems. IEEE Trans. Knowl. Data Eng. **27**(2), 326–339 (2015)
14. Li, T.R., Ruan, D., Geert, W.: A rough scts based characteristic relation approach for dynamic attribute generalization in data mining. Knowl.-Based Syst. **20**(5), 485–494 (2007)
15. Chen, H.M., Li, T.R., Ruan, D., Lin, J.H., Hu, C.X.: A rough-set based incremental approach for updating approximations under dynamic maintenance environments. IEEE Trans. Knowl. Data Eng. **25**(2), 274–284 (2013)
16. Chen, H.M., Li, T.R., Luo, C., Horng, S.J., Wang, G.Y.: A rough set-based method for updating decision rules on attribute values' coarsening and refining. IEEE Trans. Knowl. Data Eng. **26**(12), 2886–2899 (2014)
17. Chen, H.M., Li, T.R., Luo, C., Horng, S.J., Wang, G.Y: A decision-theoretic rough set approach for dynamic data mining. IEEE Trans. Fuzzy Syst. **29**(6), 2365–2371 (2015)
18. Zhang, J.B., Li, T.R., Chen, H.M.: Composite rough sets for dynamic data mining. Inf. Sci. **257**, 81–100 (2014)
19. Zhang, J.B., Zhu, Y., Pan, Y., Li, T.R.: Efficient parallel boolean matrix based algorithms for computing composite rough set approximations. Inf. Sci. **329**, 287–302 (2016)

20. Fujita, H, Li, T.R., Yao, Y.Y.: Advances in three-way decisions and granular computing. Knowl.-Based Syst. **91**, 1–3 (2016)
21. Luo, C., Li, T.R., Chen, H.M.: Dynamic maintenance of three-way decision rules. In: Miao, D., Pedrycz, W., Ślęzak, D., Peters, G., Hu, Q., Wang, R. (eds.) RSKT 2014. LNCS, vol. 8818, pp. 801–811. Springer, Cham (2014)
22. Luo, C., Li, T.R.: Incremental three-way decisions with incomplete information. In: Cornelis, C., Kryszkiewicz, M., Ślęzak, D., Ruiz, E.M., Bello, R., Shang, L. (eds.) RSCTC 2014. LNCS, vol. 8536, pp. 128–135. Springer, Cham (2014)

Exploratory Knowledge Discovery and Approximations: An FCA Perspective

Extended Abstract

Amedeo Napoli

LORIA (CNRS – Inria Nancy Grand Est – Université de Lorraine)
Orpailleur Team, BP 239, 54506 Vandoeuvre les Nancy, France
Amedeo.napoli@loria.fr
https://members.loria.fr/ANapoli/

Abstract. Knowledge discovery (KD) in complex datasets can be considered as a problem solving process, which can be either data-directed (most of the time) or goal-directed [6]. Moreover, KD can be procedural when based on a specific solver or declarative when based on a general-purpose solver (as in declarative data mining approaches [4, 15]). These various dimensions have a direct impact on the way of making KD an exploratory process (e.g. how to explore a pattern space).

In this presentation, we will discuss the process of Exploratory Knowledge Discovery (EKD) in the framework of Formal Concept Analysis (FCA) [12]. FCA starts with a binary context and outputs a concept lattice, which can be visualized and navigated by human agents [2], and which can be processable by software agents as well. In a concept lattice, each concept is made of an "intent", i.e. the description of the concept in terms of attributes, and an "extent" (i.e. the objects instances of the concept). Intents and extents are two dual facets of a concept that naturally apply in knowledge representation and ontology engineering. Moreover, the structure of a concept lattice can be visualized – whole or in part– allowing a suggestive interpretation by human agents while being processable by software agents.

Plain FCA applies to binary data and can be extended to Pattern Structures [11], based on description similarity, for dealing with more complex data such as numbers, sequences, graphs and Linked Data (RDF) [1, 5, 14]. Pattern Structures allow to solve various problems among which text mining [16], information retrieval [10], biclustering and recommendation [9, 13], definition mining [1] and discovery of functional dependencies [3, 8]...

For lowering computational costs, "approximations" can be introduced such as similarity thresholds and description projections [7]. We will discuss and illustrate the potential of approximations within Pattern Structures with the discovery of definitions in Linked Data [1] and the discovery of crisp and soft functional dependencies in numerical datasets [8].

References

1. Alam, M., Buzmakov, A., Codocedo, V., Napoli, A.: Mining definitions from RDF annotations using formal concept analysis. In: Yang, Q., Wooldridge, M. (eds.) Proceedings of IJCAI 2015, pp. 823–829. AAAI Press (2015)
2. Alam, M., Le, T.N.N., Napoli, A.: Latviz: A new practical tool for performing interactive exploration over concept lattices. In: Huchard, M., Kuznetsov, S. (eds.) Proceedings of CLA 2016, pp. 9–20. CEUR Workshop Proceedings 1624 (2016)
3. Baixeries, J., Napoli, A., Kaytoue, M.: Characterizing functional dependencies in formal concept analysis with pattern structures. Ann. Math. Artif. Intell. **72**, 129–149 (2014)
4. Blockeel, H.: Data mining: from procedural to declarative approaches. New Gener. Comput. **33**(2), 115–135 (2015)
5. Buzmakov, A., Egho, E., Jay, N., Kuznetsov, S.O., Napoli, A., Raïssi, C.: On mining complex sequential data by means of FCA and pattern structures. Int. J. Gen. Syst. **45**(2), 135–159 (2016)
6. Buzmakov, A., Kuznetsov, S.O., Napoli, A.: Fast Generation of best interval patterns for nonmonotonic constraints. In: Appice, A., Rodrigues, P.P., Costa, V.S., Gama, J., Jorge, A., Soares, C. (eds.) ECML-PKDD 2015 (Part II). LNCS, vol. 9285, pp. 157–172. Springer, Cham (2015)
7. Buzmakov, A., Kuznetsov, S.O., Napoli, A.: Revisiting pattern structure projections. In: Baixeries, J., Sacarea, C., Ojeda-Aciego, M. (eds.) ICFCA 2015. LNAI, vol. 9113, pp. 200–215. Springer, Cham (2015)
8. Codocedo, V., Baixeries, J., Kaytoue, M., Napoli, A.: Characterization of order-like dependencies with formal concept analysis. In: Huchard, M., Kuznetsov, S. (eds.) Proceedings of CLA 2016, vol. 1624, pp. 123–134. CEUR Workshop Proceeding (2016)
9. Codocedo, V., Napoli, A.: Lattice-based biclustering using partition pattern structures. In: Schaub, T., Friedrich, G., O'Sullivan, B. (eds.) 21st European Conference on Artificial Intelligence. ECAI 2014, pp. 213–218. IOS Press (2014)
10. Codocedo, V., Napoli, A.: Formal concept analysis and information retrieval – a survey. In: Baixeries, J., Sacarea, C., Ojeda-Aciego, M. (eds.) ICFCA 2015. LNCS, vol. 9113, pp. 61–77. Springer, Cham (2015)
11. Ganter, B., Kuznetsov, S.O.: Pattern structures and their projections. In: Delugach, H.S., Stumme, G. (eds.) ICCS 2001. LNCS, vol. 2120, pp. 129–142. Springer, Cham (2001)
12. Ganter, B., Wille, R.: Formal Concept Analysis. Springer, Berlin (1999)
13. Kaytoue, M., Kuznetsov, S.O., Macko, J., Napoli, A.: Biclustering meets triadic concept analysis. Ann. Math. Artif. Intell. **70**(1–2), 55–79 (2014)
14. Kaytoue, M., Kuznetsov, S.O., Napoli, A., Duplessis, S.: Mining gene expression data with pattern structures in formal concept analysis. Inf. Sci. **181**(10), 1989–2001 (2011)
15. van Leeuwen, M.: Interactive data exploration using pattern mining. In: Holzinger, A., Jurisica, I. (eds.) Interactive Knowledge Discovery and Data Mining in Biomedical Informatics. LNCS, vol. 8401, pp. 169–182. Springer, Berlin (2014)
16. Leeuwenberg, A., Buzmakov, A., Toussaint, Y., Napoli, A.: Exploring pattern structures of syntactic trees for relation extraction. In: Baixeries, J., Sacarea, C., Ojeda-Aciego, M. (eds.) ICFCA 2015. LNCS, vol. 9113, pp. 153–168. Springer, Cham (2015)

More with Less - A New Paradigm in Modern Machine Learning

Hung Son Nguyen

Institute of Computer Science, University of Warsaw,
Banacha 2, 02-097 Warsaw, Poland
son@mimuw.edu.pl

Extended Abstract

A significant progress that Machine Learning has made in recent years is related to the research and development of deep neural network. The first successful application of deep neural network was achieved on image recognition where the model was trained exhaustively on GPUs: a garden-variety parallel computing hardware used for video-games. Similar advances were then quickly reported for speech recognition and later for machine translation and natural language processing. In short order, big companies like Google, Microsoft and Baidu established large machine learning groups, quickly followed by essentially all other big tech companies. Since then, with the combination of big data and big computers, rapid advances have been reported, including the use of machine learning for self-driving cars, and consumer-grade real-time speech-to-speech translation. Human performance has even been exceeded in some specialised domains. It is no exaggeration to say that at present, machine learning allows for many more applications than there are engineers capable of implementing them.

However, most of deep learning approaches rely on the availability of huge amounts of data, often requiring millions of correctly labelled examples. We will discuss the newest learning techniques for the case when we have a huge amount of data but very little amount of labelled data. Such challenging learning problems occurs, for example, in the health care data, robotic applications or streaming data. In the existing techniques, statistical methods and domain knowledge management play a crucial role.

Micro-Data learning approaches is an application of this learning paradigm in robotics where they can often only use a few dozen training examples because acquiring them involves a process that is expensive or time-consuming. There are few percepts of macro-data learning. As the examples we can refer to active learning, control and strategy learning and learning to use the right prior knowledge in decision making [2]. Bayesian optimisation [5] is such a data-efficient algorithm that has recently attracted a lot of interest in the machine learning community. Using the data acquired so far, this algorithm creates a probabilistic model of the function that needs to

---

[1] This research is in frame of the project "Parking space in rest and service areas (RSA)" financed by NCBiR/GDKKiA as a part of common undertaking "RID", under the contract DZP/RID-I-44/8/NCBR/2016.

be optimised. It then exploits this model to identify the most promising points of the search space. This micro-data learning algorithm makes it possible to learn a complex task in only a few trials.

Combining graphical models with deep learning is another example of learning techniques that can be applied for large unlabeled data sets. The authors of [4] proposed a comprehensive framework called Variational Auto Encoders. The main idea in this approach is based on a double modelling process, i.e. (1) learning generative model to simulate the data generation process, and (2) learning classification models, such as deep learning, where measurements are directly mapped to class labels. The advantage of this approach i based on the observation that Bayesian networks do not necessarily represent the causal relationships, but they can express the expert knowledge and can be interpreted as the "structural equation models". If we know that one set of variables causes another set of variables then we can simply insert that relation into the model. Relations that we do not know will need to be learned from the data. Incorporating expert knowledge (e.g., the laws of physics) into models is the everyday business of scientists. They build sophisticated simulators with relatively few unidentified parameters, for instance implemented as a collection of partial differential equations (PDEs). Variational Auto Encoders are a framework for unsupervised learning. However, they can be extended to semi-supervised learning by incorporating labels in the generative model.

Rough set theory offers a couple of methods for data reduction, i.e. a smaller part of data that make it possible to solve the learning task at the same, or even higher accuracy level, as using the whole data set. The natural question for Rough Set Society is does rough set theory can propose some new and accurate methods for big data. We will present the most recent data reduction techniques in rough sets including feature reduction, feature selection, object selection as well as the data decomposition.

As an example, we present an applications of the tolerance rough set model (TRSM) in concept learning for scientific document repositories. In fact, this is a general framework incorporating semantic indexing and semi-supervised machine learning. In this approach, a semantic interpreter, which can be seen as a tool for automatic tagging of textual data, is interactively updated based on feedback from the users, in order to improve quality of the tags that it produces. As an illustration, we presented an improved method for the Explicit Semantic Analysis (ESA) method [3]. In RSA algorithm, an external knowledge base is used to measure relatedness between words and concepts, and those assessments are utilized to assign meaningful concepts to given texts The improvement is based on learning the weights expressing relations between particular words and concepts using the interaction with users or by employment of expert knowledge [6].

The other ongoing research is to discover the link between the one working example of intelligence, the brain, and learning principles. This relates to such diverse questions as "How can goals be selected in an autonomous fashion?" and "How can we optimise over many different learning problems with one system?", but also in reverse: "What can the success of deep neural networks tell us about the brain?".

The last example is a part of our research investigation on interactive computations based on the so called complex granules for dealing with the biggest challenges in machine learning. In particular, this concerns control problems over such computations.

We also investigate the special class of learning algorithm called *ecorithms* (propose by Valiant) [7]. Unlike most algorithms, they can be run in environments unknown to the designer, and they learn by interacting with the environment how to act effectively in it. After sufficient interaction they will have expertise not provided by the designer, but extracted from the environment.

References

1. Bohte, S., Nguyen, H.S.: Modern machine learning: more with less, cheaper and better. ERCIM News **107**, 16–17 (2016)
2. Cully, A., Clune, J., Tarapore, D., Mouret, J.-B.: Robots that can adapt like animals. Nature **521**, 503–507
3. Gabrilovich, E., Markovitch, S.: computing semantic relatedness using wikipedia-based explicit semantic analysis. In: Proceedings of The 20th International Joint Conference on Artificial Intelligence, Hyderabad, India, 2007
4. Kingma, P.D., Welling, M.: Auto-encoding variational bayes. In: The International Conference on Learning Representations (ICLR), Banff (2014)
5. Shahriari, B., Swersky, K., Wang, Z., Adams, R.P., de Freitas, N.: Taking the human out of the loop: a review of bayesian optimization. In: Proceedings of the IEEE, vol. 104, no. 1, pp. 148–175 (2016)
6. Swieboda, W., Krasuski, A., Nguyen, H.S., Janusz, A.: Interactive method for semantic document indexing based on explicit semantic analysis. Fundamenta Informaticae. **132**(3), 423–438 (2014)
7. Valiant, L.: Probably Approximately Correct. Natures Algorithms for Learning and Prospering in a Complex World. Basic Books, A Member of the Perseus Books Group, New York (2013)

A Tutorial on Mereotopology: Contact Structures, Crisp and Rough

Ivo Düntsch

Brock University, St. Catharines, ON L2S 3A1, Canada
duentsch@brocku.ca

In this tutorial I shall present the main concepts and tools of mereotopology for reasoning with both crisp and approximated regions.

Contemporary qualitative spatial reasoning is based largely on the relational and topological properties of regions instead of points. A basic role is played by the binary "part – of" and "contact" relations, from which many more meaningful relations can be defined. The formal study of the "part – of" relation goes back to Stanisław Leśniewski, a Polish mathematician, who, together with Twardowsky, Łukasiewicz, and his sole doctoral student Tarski, formed the core of the Lwów – Warsaw school of Logic and Philosophy, which, at the time, could be considered as the world's foremost research centre for the foundations of Mathematics. Mereology[1], the "Science of parts", is a part of S. Leśniewski's work on the foundations of Mathematics, developed from about 1915 onwards. Leśniewski's works were mainly in Polish [5] or in German [6]. An English translation of [6] appeared in [7], and a comprehensive overview of his work can be found in [13].

Extending mereological structures by a relation of "contact" among regions leads to what today is called "mereotopology" or "region based theory of space". Its objects are Boolean algebras (or more general structures) enhanced with a binary relation C which satisfies some axioms. The objects of the algebra are considered to be regions, the Boolean order as the mereological "part of" relation, and C as a relation of "contact" between regions. These go back as far as the works of de Laguna [4], Nicod [9], and Whitehead [14], Standard models are Boolean algebras of regular closed sets of a topological space, where two regular closed sets are said to be in contact if they have a nonempty intersection. The recent books [1] and [8] provide an extensive view of the current state mereotopology.

It is not always the case that spatial regions can be determined up to their true boundaries, if, indeed, they have such boundaries; in many cases, we can only observe regions up to a certain granularity. Often, this is a desirable feature, since too much detail can disturb the view, and we will not be able to see the wood for the trees, if our desire is to see the wood. Thus, one aims for a language with models which can express concepts as "approximated region", "approximate contact", and "approximate part of".

[1] Ivo Düntsch gratefully acknowledges support by the Natural Sciences and Engineering Research Council of Canada Discovery Grant 250153 and by the Bulgarian National Fund of Science, contract DN02/15/19.12.2016.

[2] Τὸ μέρεος = The Part

Such concepts can be obtained with the tools provided by Pawlak's rough set theory: The "part of" relation between regions is "rough inclusion" (also called "rough mereology") [10, 11] by measuring the degree to which a set is contained in another one. An approximated region may be described by its lower and upper approximation; approximated regions may be in possible contact or in certain contact [2, 12]. An appropriate logic for contact relations in the style of Rasiowa and Sikorski was presented in [3].

References

1. Aiello, M., Pratt-Hartmann, I., van Benthem, J. (eds.): Handbook of Spatial Logics. Springer (2007)
2. Düntsch, I., Orłowska, E., Wang, H.: Algebras of approximating regions. Fundamenta Informaticae **46**, 71–82 (2001) (MR2009801)
3. Düntsch, I., Orłowska, E., Wang, H.: A relational logic for spatial contact based on rough set approximation. Fundamenta Informaticae **148**, 191–206 (2016)
4. de Laguna, T.: Point, line and surface as sets of solids. J. Philos. **19**, 449–461 (1922)
5. Leśniewski, S.: O podstawach matematyki. Przeglad Filozoficzny 30–34 (1927–1931)
6. Leśniewski, S.: Grundzüge eines neuen Systems der Grundlagen der Mathematik. Fundamenta Mathematicae 14, 1–81 (1929)
7. Leśniewski, S.: On the foundation of mathematics. Topoi **2**, 7–52 (1983)
8. Ligozat, G.: Qualitative Spatial and Temporal Reasoning. Wiley (2012)
9. Nicod, J.: Geometry in a sensible world. Doctoral thesis, Sorbonne, Paris (1924), English translation in Geometry and Induction, Routledge and Kegan Paul (1969)
10. Polkowski, L.: Approximate Reasoning by Parts, Intelligent Systems Reference Library, vol. 20. Springer Verlag, Heidelberg (2011)
11. Polkowski, L., Skowron, A.: Rough mereology: a new paradigm for approximate reasoning. Int. J. Approx. Reason. **15**, 333–365 (1996)
12. Roy, A.J., Stell, J.G.: Spatial relations between indeterminate regions. Int. J. Approx. Reason. **27**(3), 205–234 (2001)
13. Urbaniak, R.: Leśniewski's Systems of Logic and Foundations of Mathematics, Trends in Logic, vol. 37. Springer Verlag, Heidelberg (2014)
14. Whitehead, A.N.: Process and Reality. MacMillan, New York (1929)

Rough Sets for Big Data – A Tutorial on Applications in Life Sciences

Klev Diamanti[1], Mateusz Garbulowski[1], and Jan Komorowski[1,2]

[1] Program in Bioinformatics and Computational Biology,
Department of Cell and Molecular Biology,
Uppsala University, Uppsala, Sweden
[2] Institute of Computer Science, PAN, Warsaw, Poland

In this tutorial we shall show how rough sets can be effectively used to generate models from big data collections as exemplified with applications in Life Sciences (Komorowski 2014). The tutorial is based on our successful applications in, for instance, methylome analysis in the human brain (500K features), gene expression analysis and avian inuenza virus pathogenicity.

Prerequisites: High school knowledge of molecular biology; general acquaintance with machine learning principles, supervised and unsupervised ones; basic knowledge of rough sets.

The attendees are recommended to download the ROSETTA (Komorowski and Hrn 1997; Komorowski et al. 2002) and rMCFS systems (Draminski et al. 2008) and install the systems on their laptops, as well as sample data sets from bioinf.icm.uu.se and CRAN, respectively.

Syllabus

1. Introduction to ROSETTA with Graphical User Interface
2. Introduction to the scripting in ROSETTA
3. Big data: rMCFS for feature selection
4. Integrated scripting: from rMCFS to ROSETTA
5. Refinement and interpretation of rule sets
6. Introduction to rule networks

Basic facts needed to understand the fundamentals of the analyzed biomedical phenomena will be provided.

Lecture notes will provide detailed instructions on how to develop the classifiers and interpret their structure. Research articles, data sets and manuals will be downloadable from the web. (Available after 15 June 2017).

References

Draminski, M., Rada-Iglesias, A., Enroth, S., Wadelius, C., Koronacki, J., Komorowski, J.: Monte Carlo feature selection for supervised classification. Bioinformatics **24**(1), 110–117 (2008)

Komorowski, J.: Learning rule-based models-the rough set approach. Comprehensive Biomedical Physics, vol. 6, pp. 19–39. Elsevier, Amsterdam (2014)

Komorowski, J., Hrn, A., Skowron, A.: ROSETTA rough sets. In: Klsgen, W., Zytkow, J. (eds.) Handbook of data mining and knowledge discovery, pp. 554–559. Oxford University Press, Inc., New York (2002)

Komorowski, J., Hrn, A.: ROSETTAA rough set toolkit for analysis of data. In: Fifth International Workshop on Rough Sets and Soft Computing. Tokyou, Springer Verlag (1997)

Mereotopology: Static and Dynamic

(A survey talk)

Dimiter Vakarelov

Department of Mathematical Logic with applications,
Faculty of Mathematics and Computer Science, Sofia University,
blvd James Bouchier 5, 1126 Sofia, Bulgaria
dvak@fmi.uni-sofia.bg

This talk presents a formalization of some ideas of Alfred North Whitehead about space and time. Alfred North Whitehead (February 15, 1861 – December 30, 1947) was an English mathematician and philosopher. He is well-known as the co-author with Bertrand Russell of the famous book "Principia Mathematica" and also as the founder of the contemporary Process philosophy. The main part of his philosophical system is related to his view on an integrated theory of space and time which should be put on a relational base, which means that it has to be extracted from natural spatio-temporal relations between real things. His early view on this subject can be found in his book "The Organization of Thought" [8], page 195, where he claims that the theory of space and time should be "point-free" in a sense that neither space points nor time points (instances of time, moments) have to be put on the base of the theory, because they are abstract things having no separate existence in reality. This does not mean that space points, as well as time points should be disregarded at all - they should be defined in a later stage of the theory on the base of the other primitives. A more detailed program of how to rebuilt the theory of space on relational base is given in his famous book Process and reality [10]. The primitive notions are the notion of a **region** as a formalization of physical body and some relations between regions as **part-of, overlap** and **contact**. Note that part-of and overlap are ones of the base relations of mereology (see [3]), so the approach is also known as the **mereological approach to geometry**. Since the contact relation between regions has a certain topological nature which can not be expressed in mereology, the extension of mereology with some contact-like relations is called now **mereotopology**. Witehead's approach to the theory of space is also known as a **Region-Based Theory of Space** (RBTS). Survey papers on RBTS and mereotopology are, for instance, [1, 2, 4].

Whitehead's theory of time, named in his books [9, 10] **Epochal Theory of Time** (ETT), is a quite unusual and interesting theory aiming to explain difficult and old problems concerning the nature of time. It is called "epochal" because one of its main notions is the notion of **epoch** considered as an atomic region of time. However, while one can find in [10] a detailed program how to develop RBTS as a mathematical theory, Whitehead did not present such a program for ETT and developed it in an informal manner and on a quite complicated philosophical terminology. Influenced by the Relativity theory, Whitehead claims that the theory of time should not be separated from the theory of space and they both have to be presented as an integrated point free theory of space-time, developed on a relational base. The first steps in formalization of Whitehead's ideas on an integrated theory of space and time are the papers by the present author [5–7], based on some systems of **dynamic mereotopology**. Shortly speaking dynamic mereotopology is an extension of mereotopology studying spatial regions changing in time, called also **dynamic regions**. In this context standard mereotopology which does not consider time will be called **"static mereotopology"**. This terminology makes a parallel to the two main parts of the classical physics: **Statics** and **Dynamics**.

The aim of this talk is to sketch a version of dynamic mereotopology based on the paper [7]. For that purpose a survey of facts for static mereotopology needed in the building of a version of dynamic mereotopology will also be given. We, first, build a concrete point-based dynamic model of space based on the **"snapshot construction"**, which to each moment of time associates a "snapshot" of the static picture of dynamic regions at the corresponding moment of time. Then we define a suitable spatio-temporal relations between dynamic regions. Finally we take some properties of these relations as axioms and in this way we define the abstract dynamic mereotopology, which is a point free in the above described sense. The main mathematical result is a representation theorem of the abstract system into a concrete snapshot model, which fact shows that the axiomatization is successful.

References

1. Bennett, B., Düntsch, I.: Axioms, algebras and topology. In: Aiello, M., Pratt, I., van Benthem, J. (Eds.) Handbook of Spatial Logics, pp. 99–160. Springer (2007)
2. Hahmann, T., Gröuninger, M.: In: Hazarika, S. (ed.) Region-based Theories of Space: Mereotopology and Beyond, in Qualitative Spatio-Temporal Representation and Reasoning: Trends and Future Directions, pp. 1–62. IGI Publishing (2012)
3. Simons, P.: A Study in Ontology. Clarendon Press, Oxford (1987)
4. Vakarelov, D.: Region-based theory of space: algebras of regions, representation theory and logics. In: Gabbay, D., et al. (Eds.) Mathematical Problems from Applied Logics. New Logics for the XXIst Century. II, pp. 267–348. Springer (2007)
5. Vakarelov, D.: Dynamic mereotopology: a point-free theory of changing regions. I. Stable and unstable mereotopological relations. Fundamenta Informaticae **100**(1–4), 159–180 (2010)
6. Vakarelov, D.: Dynamic mereotopology II: Axiomatizing some Whiteheadian type space-time logics. In: Bolander, Th., Braüner, T., Ghilardi, S., Moss, L. (eds.) Advances in Modal Logic, vol. 9, pp. 538–558. College Publications (2012)
7. Vakarelov, D.: Dynamic mereotopology III. Whiteheadean type of integrated point free theories of space and tyme. Part I, Algebra and Logic, vol. 53, No. 3, pp. 191–205 (2014). Part II, Algebra and Logic, vol. 55, No. 1, pp. 9–197 (2016). Part III, Algebra and Logic, vol. 55, No. 3, pp. 181–197 (2016)
8. Whitehead, A.N.: The Organization of Thought. London (1917)
9. Whitehead, A.N.: Science and the Modern World. MacMillan, New Work (1925)
10. Whitehead, A.N.: Process and Reality. MacMillan, New York (1929)

Revisiting Indiscernibility as the foundation of Rough Sets

Mihir Kumar Chakraborty

Jadavpur University, Kolkata, India

At the root of rough sets there lies an indiscernibility. This is true for rough sets of any kind. I have been arguing for this position for a long time. After so much of development in this area, it seems necessary to re-evaluate this position both philosophically and mathematically. My first task would be to make a brief survey of the literature on rough sets that have dealt with indiscernibility. During this survey, focus would be cast on the various ways an indiscernibility crops up and on the various types of indiscernibility thus created. Relationship between indiscernibility and granulation would be taken up. It may be realised that in any kind of rough set approach granulation of the universe remains the starting point. Finally I will argue that indiscernibility and corresponding granulation, though necessary, are not sufficient to address the basic essence of rough sets.

Contents – Part I

Software and Systems for Rough Sets

Contents – Part II

Three-Way Decisions, Uncertainty, Granular Computing

Recent Advances in Biomedical Data Analysis, Trends in Multi-Agent Systems, Formal Concept Analysis, Rough Set Theory and Their Applications

Invited Talks

Zdzisław Pawlak: Man, Creator and Innovator of Computer Sciences
Personal Memories

Urszula Wybraniec-Skardowska[✉]

Faculty of Christian Philosophy, The Cardinal Wyszyński University,
ul. Wóycickiego 1/3, 01-938 Warsaw, Poland
skardowska@gmail.com

The first test of a great man is his humility.
John Ruskin

An attempt at reaching the past, extracting the essence of humanity, creative achievements and making them real from already partially obliterated traces is not an easy task from the personal perspective. Thus, it is only crumbs of thoughts and words which have been available to compose the picture of the existence and output of Professor Zdzisław Pawlak, presented here. The intention behind the writing of the present paper excludes application of a regular – with reference to scientific works – research procedure.

For me to be able to say who Zdzisław Pawlak was – as a man, creator and innovator of computer science – from the personal perspective in current and contemporary time, I need to go back to the past which my recollection of him emerges from; and an outline of his portrait comes out in a sort of freeze-frame, reflecting his conceptual profile.

1. Let me begin with a memory belonging to the rather distant past – equally real as the present time and equally important as contemporary reality.

My first meeting with Professor Pawlak took place many years ago, when shortly after my completing the procedure of earning the title of Associate Professor in the field of logic and philosophy of language, I still belonged to the Polish generation of the pre-IT era and to the circle of propagators of formal logic. The meeting took place in Nieborów, in the Palace of the Radziwiłł Family, where – in the autumn of 1986 – the 9th School of Logic was held. It was organized by Professor Ryszard Wójcicki then. I fell ill there, rather seriously, and had difficulty in getting back home. Opole, where I was living at that time, lies quite a distance away from Nieborów. It was then, that Professor Wiesław Szczerba and another man of athletic build offered to take me in their car to Warsaw, find a doctor and provide me with accommodation until I would recover and could return home. That other man turned out to be Zdzisław Pawlak, presented to me as a professor of computer science. This rather unexpected offer initially raised my astonishment and distrust, although I had known Professor Szczerba fairly well by that time and both men assured me of their absolutely pure intentions. However, I did not accept their kind offer. It was not until some time later that I found out I should not have declined it, as it was absolutely an act of goodwill.

© Springer International Publishing AG 2017
L. Polkowski et al. (Eds.): IJCRS 2017, Part I, LNAI 10313, pp. 3–12, 2017.
DOI: 10.1007/978-3-319-60837-2_1

Being at home, where in the then – Teacher's Training College (later transformed into Opole University) I managed the freshly-established Chair of Computer Science and Applied Logic, I was invited on the telephone to participate in seminars devoted to computer science, which were run by Professor Pawlak at the Polish Academy of Sciences in Warsaw. Since I had already made scientific contacts with well-known logicians, but not with computer scientists I was only too happy to accept the invitation; besides, my daughter was just beginning her studies at the Academy of Music in Warsaw.

I remember I used to go to the seminars, mainly with Edward Bryniarski, a colleague of mine, with whom we discussed questions pertaining to information systems and Pawlak's theory of rough sets. During his seminars, which disseminated the theses of his theory and information systems, Professor Pawlak always managed to excellently extract and draw the participants' attention to the main and the most interesting aspects and conclusions in the lecture which he delivered.

My first observation related to the basic notions of the rough sets theory: approximation space, approximations – the upper and the lower ones of a subset of the given *universum* – concerned their relation with certain so-called unit operations, which I had dealt with partially in my doctoral dissertation. I noticed first of all, that the operation of upper approximation of a set, determined by a certain equivalence relation R is an operation of the R-image of the set, and that – in turn – it is a certain unit operation. I shared my suggestions with Professor Pawlak at the beginning of 1988. He was quick to ask me to present them in his seminar and to write a relevant article for publication in *Bulletin of the Polish Academy of Sciences in Mathematics* series. In this way, the inspiration of Professor Pawlak and his rough sets theory gave rise to my first work in the field of *Theoretical Computer Science*, entitled "On a Generalization of Approximation Space" (published in the *Bulletin* in 1989). The same issue of the *Bulletin* also included Edward Bryniarski's first work on rough-sets, which came out under the title "Calculus of Rough Sets of the First Order". That was the beginning of taking up the problem of rough sets by a group of scientists in the Chair managed by me in Opole at that time. Following, the history of rough sets came into being at Opole University, since in the Chair I managed there emerged a group of scientists, who were being honoured by Profesor's invitation to cooperate. Those contacts were indeed fruitful, resulting in completion of three doctoral dissertations and a number of publications.

My second observation concerned the possibilities of using relations between the rough sets theory and the problem area of vagueness in the logical theory of language. This was connected with the change in the line of my scientific interests and formulating them in the form of themes: (1) Knowledge and its representation, incomplete information, vague information and logic; (2) Logical and computer-science aspects of information and communication. The result of these interests were about 10 publications, some co-authored with Zbigniew Bonikowski.

The harmonious cooperation of computer science and logic, which was developed by the Opole Group, was possible owing to strong dedication and integration around the common research goal realized within a scientific project in the framework of Professor Pawlak's grant. Our cooperation within the grant showed Professor to be a man eager for knowledge, full of enthusiasm and imaginativeness, open to new ideas and trends as well as research perspectives; a friendly man who was straightforward while being with others, consistently setting the direction of further research which took into account progress of science, not related solely to computers; a man of courage who perceived new perspectives and ways of reaching for them, at the same time displaying a positive attitude towards good co-existence and co-partnership.

Afterwards, in my eyes, Zdzisław Pawlak appeared as a man worthy of trust, somebody who could offer support in difficult moments, a man of natural goodness, warmth, tolerance; yet demanding and deserving respect, sensitive to new trends emerging in computer science, a scholar of a wide spectrum of scientific interests.

He was able to concentrate around himself a circle of young researchers who felt no barrier of fear separating them from him. He influenced their intellectual lives and scientific advancement. He created favourable conditions for creative activity. He offered advice, set an example and provided substantive help. We were full of respect and admiration for him for his modesty and dedication. He was a reviewer of many doctoral and postdoctoral dissertations and the author of scientific opinions. He was always a model of simplicity – a feature which earned him appreciation with all who worked together with him and with everybody who knew him. He was an intellectually dynamic person, this valuable trait enabling him to perceive new vistas and to make them real. His scholarly and organizational activities were dynamic, too. He was able to combine them with an exceptional communicative skill.

2. Zdzisław Pawlak, beyond any doubt, was not the type of a scholar-loner. His seminars at Warsaw University of Technology were attended by computer scientists, engineers and logicians, including Professor Helena Rasiowa and her students, among others Ewa Orłowska, Cecylia Rauszer, Grażyna Mirkowska, and also Damian Niwiński, Andrzej Skowron, Henryk Rybiński. The atmosphere of warmth, which was present during those meetings, favoured exchange of scientific experience and making valuable friendly contacts, which in the case of myself and my students invested our journeys from the land on the Oder (Opole) to the land on the Vistula (Warsaw) with sense. And not only the journeys.

An astonishing feature of Zdzisław Pawlak's scholarly activity was his opening to international cooperation and directing intellectual efforts towards strengthening the position of Polish computer science. He initiated cyclical scientific meetings and international conferences at home and abroad. I took part in some of them myself or my students attended them, meeting well-known computer scientists, e.g., Lotti Zadech – the creator of the fuzzy sets theory. The two men entered into a particular friendship and scientific exchange. Professor Pawlak's pioneering and innovatory works attracted a lot of scientists from all over the world. He enjoyed high esteem abroad and was frequently invited to deliver lectures and, in this way, disseminated many notions related to computer science. As a scientist he was endowed with the ability to think both theoretically and practically. He also carried out an unusually broad and effective cooperation with scientific institutions abroad, among others located in Canada, the United States, Russia, China, India. It was thanks to his widespread contacts that many outstanding computer scientists visited Poland and many Polish scientists were able to go on shorter or longer visits to scientific centres of world renown. The visible effects of the international cooperation are numerous publications.

3. I have always looked at Zdzisław Pawlak's activity more from the position of a distanced observer rather than that of somebody who would wholly approve of it or understand it completely, although my contacts with the Professor and his family grew closer due to my frequent stays in Warsaw, where my daughter, a pianist by then, lived and where I took the opportunity of taking part in seminars and conferences on logic or computer science.

With time I found out that Zdzisław Pawlak was not only a great scholar, but also a helpful man, very sociable, full of jolly sense of humour, and an individual of a very rich and many-sided personality.

I remember very well our meetings and visits to Professor's private house, where he lived with his wife and daughter. I felt moved by Mr. and Mrs. Pawlak's unique kindness and hospitality, afternoon teas prepared by Professor's wife, Danuta, sometimes also for my husband and daughter. The natural and pleasant atmosphere during the visits allowed me to gradually shorten the distance on the professional ground and feel closer to his home space, and also some nooks of his likings and creativity – not only that connected with his scientific activity.

He loved classical music (himself studied to play the violin in his youth) and in the quiet of his home, he used to play the instrument and also the ocarina. He, too, liked (as I learned from his daughter, Mrs Dorota Rybnik) slightly jazzy standards performed by Edith Piaf, Frank Sinatra or Louis Armstrong. Moreover, he used to listen to ABBA, was keen on humour, style and cabaret pieces of the Cabaret of Elderly Men, once greatly popular in Poland. He adored beauty, the world and nature, was keen on sport (he used to swim regularly in the nearby swimming-pool). He simply loved life. He loved people. He was highly tolerant of them. Confronted with an instance of stupidity or ugliness, he would express his criticism by exclaiming: "Atrocity!", which was to be a manifestation of lack of acceptance. He then usually rounded it off with a joke. He was characterized by buoyancy and wisdom of life.

He had in his home a small study, where he created his works: not only dealing with scientific material on computer science and technological innovations, but also revealing his artistic interests. He painted. Mainly landscapes which reflected the beauty of nature he saw. His pictures were full of life and peculiar charm, as well as bowing down to the beauty of nature. He reflected his creative vision of the world also through abstract pieces of art, which were rich in clear, lively colours and content, often making use of combinations of circular techniques. He also wrote poetry.

4. The years of Zdzisław Pawlak's life can be described as a series of intensive creative explorations intended to work out positive forms of scientific and organizational progress, as well as modes of self-realization. His artistic and cognitive passion, his humbleness and reaching beyond the frames of temporariness by taking up intellectual challenges, creation of space in which many entrants to computer science were able to successfully develop scientifically and implement their research projects, can be truly astonishing.

Zdzisław Pawlak is multidimensional person – a creator-theoretician and practician, a model of fulfilled humanity. Meeting such a man must be significant and no wonder that it yielded numerous achievements of his co-workers and students in the form of a host of scientific publications.

I will still remember him as a man of great stature, creative, worthy of admiration for his activity, for revealing his intellectual potential; a warm-hearted, sociable man, friendly to people, a modest scholar, sensitive to beauty and curious of the world and open to it.

To me Zdzisław Pawlak remains a man of realized and creative being, lasting in the living memory of new generations.

Now, I would like to present to you some of Zdzisław Pawlak's paintings from the family archives of his daughter, Małgorzata Dorota and his son-in-law Janusz Rybnik.

Data-Driven Granular Cognitive Computing

Guoyin Wang[✉]

Chongqing Key Laboratory of Computational Intelligence,
Chongqing University of Posts and Telecommunications, Nan'an District,
Chongqing 400065, People's Republic of China
wanggy@ieee.org

Abstract. Many artificial intelligence (AI) theoretical models are inspired by human/natural/social intelligence mechanisms. Three main schools of artificial intelligence have been formed, that is, symbolism, connectionism and behaviorism. Cognitive computing is one of the key fields of AI. It is a critical task for AI researchers to develop advanced cognitive computing models. Cognitive computing is the third and the most transformational phase in computing's evolution, after the Tabulating Era and Programming Era. Inspired by human's granularity thinking based problem solving mechanism and the cognition law of "global precedence", a data-driven granular cognitive computing model (DGCC) is proposed in this paper. It integrates two contradictory mechanisms, namely, human's cognition mechanism of "global precedence" which is a cognition process of "from coarser to finer" and the information processing mechanism of machine learning systems which is "from finer to coarser". According to DGCC, deep learning is taken as a combination of symbolism and connectionism, and named hierarchical structuralism in this paper.

Keywords: Granular cognitive computing · Cognitive computing · Granular computing · Data-driven · Hierarchical structuralism · Artificial intelligence · DGCC

1 Introduction

Artificial intelligence (AI) was born at a conference at Dartmouth College in 1956. Since then, many intelligent computing models with inspiration of various human/natural/social intelligence mechanisms have been developed. Three main schools of artificial intelligence (symbolism, connectionism and behaviorism) are formed.

In the middle 1950s, AI researchers began to explore the possibility that human intelligence could be reduced to symbol manipulation. It is the symbolism of AI. Newell and Simon introduced the physical symbol system hypothesis in 1976 [38]. Feigenbaum introduced expert systems [23]. The connectionism of AI was established by McClelland and Rumelhart in the 1980s [36]. It largely resulted from various dissatisfactions with the symbolism of AI. It models mental or behavioral phenomena as the emergent processes of interconnected networks

© Springer International Publishing AG 2017
L. Polkowski et al. (Eds.): IJCRS 2017, Part I, LNAI 10313, pp. 13–24, 2017.
DOI: 10.1007/978-3-319-60837-2_2

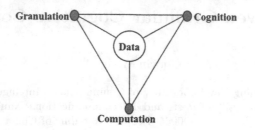

Fig. 1. Triangular structure of DGCC

of simple units. A lot of artificial neural network models were developed, for example, BP neural network [17], Hopfield neural network [22], Kohonen self-organizing maps [27], Boltzmann machine [1], radial basis function network [32], et al. In the behaviorism of AI, "Perception-action" model is used, which considers that intelligence depends on the perception and behavior [39]. In 1988, Brooks developed the Hexapod Walking Robot, which was composed of 150 sensors and 23 actuators [6].

In the recent 20 years, AI has more and more great achievements. Deep Blue became the first computer chess-playing system to beat Garry Kasparov, a reigning world chess champion, in 1997. Watson defeated two greatest Jeopardy champions, Brad Rutter and Ken Jennings in 2011. In 2016, AlphaGo defeated Sedol Lee, a professional Go player. The development of AI has been accompanied with the development of computer science in the past 60 years. Kelly introduced the three phases in computing's evolution: Tabulating Era, Programming Era, and Cognitive Era [26]. AI is entering the cognitive era too.

A data-driven granular cognitive computing model (DGCC) is proposed in this paper. Its triangular structure is shown in Fig. 1. It integrates the traditional data-driven bottom-up information computing mechanism of machine learning/data mining systems, and the top-down "global precedence" law of human cognition [8,16].

Deep learning [20,21,29] has great advances in machine learning and perception in recent 10 years. According to DGCC, the intelligence learning mechanism of deep learning is a new artificial intelligence mechanism called hierarchical structuralism in this paper.

2   Cognitive Computing

Cognitive science [33,40] includes research on intelligence and behavior, especially focusing on how information is represented, processed, and transformed within nervous systems and machines. Cognitive computing aims to develop a coherent, unified, universal mechanism inspired by the mind's capabilities [34]. Cognitive computing is based on the scientific disciplines of artificial intelligence and signal processing. Many intelligent computing models and machine learning models have been developed to address complex real-world problems inspired by some specific intelligence observation of brain/mind law, biological law, natural law, and social law. Fuzzy logic enables a computer to understand natural language and reason in a similar way to human being [51]. Artificial neural networks learn experiential data by operating like the biological/human brain [1,17,22,27,32]. Evolutionary computing is based on the process of natural selection and evolution [11]. Swarm intelligence is inspired by biological systems [5]. Artificial immune systems are inspired by theoretical immunology and observed immune functions, principles and models [10]. Granular computing mimics a way of thinking that relies on the human ability to perceive the real world under various levels of granularity [47,52]. Some researchers are trying to design a unified computational theory of the mind, and a set of mechanisms for all cognitive behaviors [34]. Cognitive-based systems could build knowledge and learn, understand natural language, and reason and interact more naturally with human beings than traditional systems [2].

3   Granular Computing

Granular computing has emerged as a quick growing intelligent computing paradigm in the domain of cognitive intelligence and artificial intelligence [47]. It is often regarded as an umbrella term to cover theories, methodologies, techniques, and tools that make use of granules in complex problem solving [48]. Bargiela and Pedrycz consider granular computing as a conceptual and algorithmic platform for analyzing and designing human-centric intelligent systems [3]. Zadeh considers granular computing as a basis for computing with words [51]. Skowron uses rough approximations to model syntax, semantics, and operations of information granules [25]. Multilevel granulation structures could be induced by hierarchies of the universe and neighborhood systems. Zhang proposes a quotient space theory for problem solving inspired by the human thinking ability of perceiving the real world under various levels of granularity in order to abstract and consider only those things that serve a specific interest and switching among different granularities [52]. Formal concept analysis could be adopted to automatically derive ontology from a set of objects [45]. The granular structure of concept lattices in formal concept analysis is useful for knowledge reduction [9,47]. Yao views granular computing as a complementary and dependent triangle shown in Fig. 2, which integrates three important perspectives [49,50]. Wang proposes a bidirectional cognitive computing model (BCC) based on a qualitative and quantitative mapping model for expressing and processing of uncertain concepts [31]. It uses 3 parameters (expected value, entropy, hyper entropy) to describe the intension of a concept, while a set of samples to describe its extension. A multiple granularity concept generation model was developed for generating hierarchical concept trees as shown in Fig. 3 [31]. Xu and Wang develop an adaptive hierarchical clustering approach to generate a hierarchical tree as shown in Fig. 4 [46].

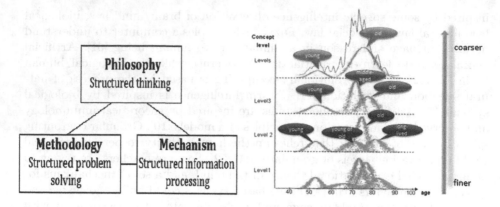

Fig. 2. GrC triangle   Fig. 3. Hierarchical concept tree

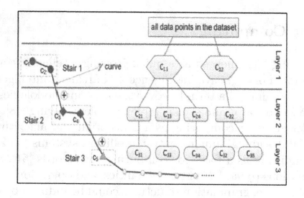

Fig. 4. Hierarchical clustering

4 Data-driven Granular Cognitive Computing

In classical intelligent information systems, original data is collected from environment at first, useful information is extracted through analyzing the input data then, and it is used to solve problems at last. In traditional machine learning, data mining and knowledge discovery models, knowledge is always transformed (extracted) from data. It is a unidirectional transformation from finer granularity to coarser granularity as shown in Fig. 5.

There is a human cognition law called "global precedence" [7,8,16]. In Fig. 6(a) [16,35], there are 4 large characters (the global level) made out of 2 small characters (the local level). People always recognize the large characters in the global level at first and then the small characters in the local level. It is easy to draw and recognize a people, as shown in Fig. 6(b), through his/her caricature, which has just a few lines, without analyzing detailed pixels. It shows the cognition law of the information processing in human visual perception. It is a process from coarser to finer.

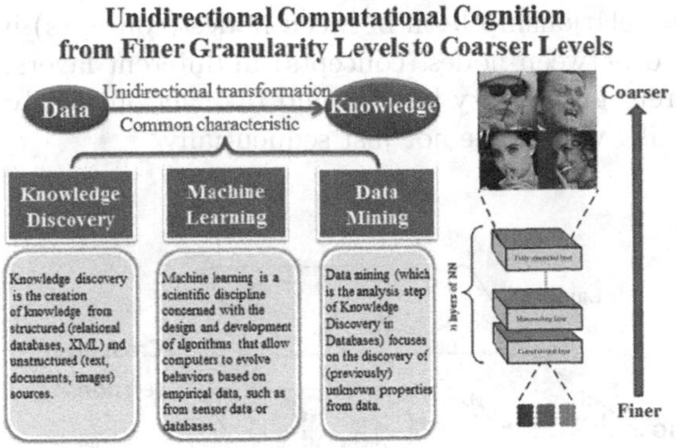

**Unidirectional Computational Cognition
from Finer Granularity Levels to Coarser Levels**

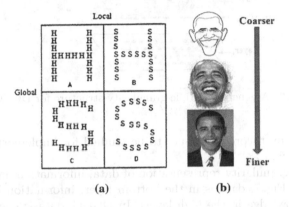

Fig. 5. Unidirectional transformation from finer to coarser

Fig. 6. Human cognition: from coarser to finer

There is a contradiction between the unidirectional transformation mechanism "from finer granularity to coarser granularity" of traditional intelligent information systems with the global precedence law of human cognition. A data-driven granular cognitive computing model (DGCC) is proposed to integrate them. Its triangular structure is shown in Fig. 1. Computation emphasizes the data science which includes all efficient computing models and methods for processing big data; cognition emphasizes the smart understanding of big data and the intelligent interaction between users and information systems; granulation emphasizes the multiple granularity thinking and modeling for dealing with big data. Computation, cognition and granulation are all implemented in a data-driven manner. Wang developed a general multiple granularity structure for DGCC as shown in Fig. 7 [44]. DGCC has the following key features.

- In DGCC, data is considered to be knowledge in the lowest granularity level, and knowledge is considered to be the abstraction of data in different granularity layers.

- There could be relationship both between nodes (concepts) in a same granularity layer, and between nodes (concepts) in different layers.
- Nodes in different granularity layers could take action jointly and simultaneously in a parallel way, while not just sequentially.

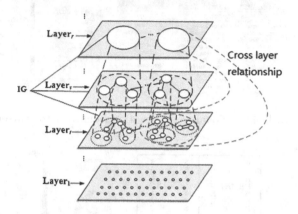

Fig. 7. A general multiple granularity structure for DGCC

There are many theoretical issues to be studied for implementing a DGCC model.

(1) Multiple granularity representation of data, information and knowledge.

As shown in Fig. 7, data is in the bottom layer, information in the middle layers, while knowledge in the high layers. In DGCC, data is considered to be the knowledge represented in the lowest granularity layer. In other words, data is viewed as the extension of concepts (knowledge in a higher granularity layer), while a concept is viewed as the intension (abstraction) of some data. The idea of taking data as a format for encoding knowledge was introduced in our early work about domain-oriented data-driven data mining (3DM) [43]. Data, information and knowledge are encoded in a hierarchical multiple granularity space together. A general multiple granularity structure needs to be set up for expressing data, information and knowledge.

(2) Integration of the human cognition of "from coarser to finer" and the information processing of "from finer to coarser".

In DGCC, there are two kinds of transformation operators, namely, upward operators and downward operators. An upward operator transforms the data/information/knowledge in a low granularity layer to a high granularity layer, while a downward operator transforms the data/information/knowledge in a high granularity layer to a low granularity layer. Downward operators mimic the human cognition of "from coarser to finer", while upward operators mimic the information processing of "from finer to coarser".

(3) Transformation of the uncertainty of big data in a multiple granularity space.

Generally speaking, concepts (information and knowledge) in a higher granularity layer would be more uncertain than the ones in a lower granularity layer. A concept in a higher granularity layer is the abstraction of some objects (data or concepts in a lower granularity layer). Exceptionally, some concepts in a lower granularity layer could also be more certain than the ones in a higher granularity layer, since there is more detailed information in a lower layer.

(4) Multiple granularity joint computing model and problem solving mechanism.

Data, information and knowledge are encoded in a multiple granularity space together. They could be used in problem solving simultaneously in a parallel way. As shown in Fig. 8, decisions in a manufacturing industry group are being made at several different layers simultaneously every day. Decisions in different layers might be either dependent or independent. Mechanisms for joint computing and decision making in a multiple granularity space is required.

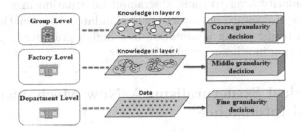

Fig. 8. Joint decision making in a multiple granularity space

(5) Dynamical evolution mechanism in a multiple granularity knowledge space.

Most real life systems are dynamical. The data, information and knowledge of an intelligent information system would also be dynamical, while not static. Dynamic evolution mechanisms need to be developed to deal with the dynamic data, information and knowledge in a multiple granularity knowledge space.

(6) Affective progressive variable granularity computing method.

Usually, coarser answers could be generated in a higher granularity layer with less time cost, while finer answers in a lower granularity layer with more time cost. Affective progressive variable granularity computing method should be developed. Some kinds of coarser answers are generated in a higher granularity layer at first, and more exact answers will be available in lower granularity layers later.

(7) Calculation goes ahead of some perception.

In some real life applications, not all input information (data) is available simultaneously in the beginning. It would be better to make a draft decision according to some partial inputs available at first, while not wait for all inputs. In some problem solving tasks, we do not need all inputs. In such cases, in order to take efficient actions, an answer (decision) in a lower granularity layer could be generated based on partial inputs at first, and then an improved answer (decision) could be generated in a higher granularity layer after more inputs are available. A decision (answer) will be generated according to partial inputs in a lower granularity layer if it is impossible to have all inputs.

(8) Distributed multiple granularity machine learning method.

Since data, information and knowledge are encoded in a multiple granularity space together, a parallel and distributed learning process would be possible. It is not needed to learn layer by layer.

(9) Multiple granularity mechanism of associative memory with forgetting.

The information storage mechanism of computers is a mechanical one. Information (data, knowledge) could be either stored in a memory system or not. It will be unavailable after being removed. However, there is an association mechanism in human brain. The bidirectional cognitive computing model in [34] might be used to implement such an association mechanism of human brain. Upward operators could simulate a forgetting process through transforming information in a lower granularity layer to some abstracted information in a higher granularity layer, while downward operators could simulate an associating (recalling) process through transforming information in a higher granularity layer to some detailed information in a lower granularity layer.

5   Hierarchical Structuralism: A New Mechanism for Artificial Intelligence

Various deep learning architectures like deep neural networks [4,37], convolutional deep neural networks [30], deep belief networks [20] and recurrent neural networks [14] have been applied in many fields such as image recognition [28], speech recognition [12], et al., successfully. Deep Learning architecture built from artificial neural networks (ANN) could date back to the Neocognitron in 1980 [13]. The challenge of ANN study is to train a network with multiple layers. In 1989, LeCun applied the standard BP algorithm to a deep neural network with the purpose of recognizing handwritten ZIP codes [30]. In 1995, Hinton trained a network containing six fully connected layers and several hundred hidden units using the wake-sleep algorithm [19]. However, the time cost was too high, making it impractical for general applications.

It is always very difficult and time consuming to train a traditional ANN with multiple layers. The inner structure of a traditional ANN is always considered as a black box. Thus, there is no observable, understandable structure or feature in a trained network. The more hidden layers an ANN has, the more difficult and time cost to train it. This is the reason that almost all ANN researchers usually used networks with only 3 layers before deep learning was developed.

In 2006, Hinton effectively pre-trained a many-layered feed forward neural network one layer at a time, treated each layer in turn as an unsupervised restricted Boltzmann machine, and then fine-tuned it using supervised back propagation [18]. It has become part of many state-of-the-art systems in various disciplines in recent years. Deep learning is a branch of machine learning

based on a set of algorithms attempting to model high-level abstractions in data
by using a deep graph with multiple processing layers of linear or non-linear
transformations [15].

In fact, there were some ANN researchers who had also implemented such
ideas in their many-layered neural networks in 1990s. Wang developed a neuro-
fuzzy network (FCN) for bucket motion control with 9 layers in 1992 [41]. As
shown in Fig. 9(a), it is composed of 3 structured sub networks. Jang developed
an adaptive-network-based fuzzy inference system (ANFIS) in 1993 [24], which
is a neural network with 5 layers as shown in Fig. 9(b). Wang developed a triple-
valued or multiple-valued logic neural network (TMLNN) in 1996 [42]. As shown
in Fig. 9(c), each neuron of TMLNN is a triple-valued or multiple-valued logic
neuron. A TMLNN with 5 layers could implement any logic function like XOR
(Exclusive OR).

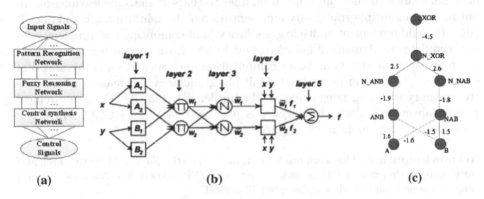

Fig. 9. Many-layered neural networks. (a) FCN; (b) ANFIS; (c) TMLNN for XOR

It is easy to train an FCN, ANFIS and TMLNN with a low time cost since
they have clear logical structures. Unfortunately, both computation power and
data were very limited in 1990s. It was impossible to use them to solve large
scale complex real life problems at that time.

From the above discussion, it could be found that FCN, ANFIS and TMLNN
have the same idea of deep learning. A concept in a higher layer is learned from
the ones in a lower layer. It is a kind of multi-granularity representation structure
discussed in Sect. 4. The inner structure of these multi-level ANN models is
not a black box. Neurons in each layer have distinct logic meaning. The links
between neurons correspond to their logic relationship. This kind of ANNs could
be considered as a kind of logic reasoning networks of symbolism systems. It is a
special case of DGCC, and called hierarchical structuralism. It has the following
HD³ characteristics.

- Hierarchical. The knowledge and information are encoded in a hierarchical
  system. The inner structure of a hierarchical system is understandable.

- Distributed. The knowledge and information are encoded in a distributed manner.
- Data-driven and training based. It is set up based on training in a data-driven manner.
- Dynamical. The inner structure of a hierarchical system could be dynamically adjusted in an adaptive and evolutionary way.

6   Conclusion

Inspired by human's granularity thinking based problem solving mechanism and the cognition law of "global precedence", a data-driven granular cognitive computing model (DGCC) is proposed. It integrates two contradictory mechanisms, human's cognition mechanism of "global precedence" which is a cognition process of "from coarser to finer" and the "from finer to coarser" machine learning mechanism. It is a multiple granularity representation of data, information and knowledge. It could implement multiple granularity joint computing and problem solving, simulate the dynamical knowledge evolution. Both computing mechanisms of progressive variable granularity computation and calculation going ahead of some perception could be realized. Multiple granularity mechanism of associative memory with forgetting could also be implemented in DGCC. A hierarchical structuralism for artificial intelligence is proposed based on DGCC, which is a combination of symbolism and connectionism.

Acknowledgments. This work has been supported by the National Key Research and Development Program of China under grant 2016YFB1000905, the National Natural Science Foundation of China under grant 61572091.

References

1. Ackley, D.H., Hinton, G.E., Sejnowski, T.J.: A learning algorithm for Boltzmann machines. Cogn. Sci. **9**(1), 147–169 (1985)
2. B, J.: What's the future of cognitive computing? http://www.forbes.com/sites/ibm/2015/02/23/whats-the-future-of-cognitive-computing-ibm-watson/#768939e51fef, forbes BrandVoice. Accessed 23 Feb 2015
3. Bargiela, A., Pedrycz, W.: Toward a theory of granular computing for human-centered information processing. IEEE Trans. Fuzzy Syst. **16**(2), 320–330 (2008)
4. Bengio, Y.: Learning deep architectures for AI. Found. Trends Mach. Learn. **2**(1), 1–127 (2009)
5. Beni, G., Wang, J.: Swarm intelligence in cellular robotic systems. In: Dario, P., Sandini, G., Aebischer, P. (eds.) Robots and Biological Systems: Towards a New Bionics?, vol. 102, pp. 703–712. Springer, Heidelberg (1993). doi:10.1007/978-3-642-58069-7_38
6. Brooks, R.A.: Intelligence without representation. Artif. Intell. **47**(1–3), 139–159 (1991)
7. Chen, L.: Topological structure in visual perception. Science **218**, 699–700 (1982)

8. Chen, L., Zhang, S., Srinivasan, M.V.: Global perception in small brains: topological pattern recognition in honey bees. Proc. Natl. Acad. Sci. **100**(11), 6884–6889 (2003)
9. Chou, G., Ma, J., Yang, H., Zhang, W.: Mathematic model of concept granular computing system. Sci. China Ser. F-Inf. Sci. **39**(12), 1239–1247 (2009). (in Chinese)
10. De Castro, L., Timmis, J.: Artificial Immune Systems: A New Computational Approach. Springer, Heidelberg (2002)
11. De Jong, K.A.: Evolutionary Computation: A Unified Approach. MIT Press, Cambridge (2006)
12. Deng, L., Hinton, G., Kingsbury, B.: New types of deep neural network learning for speech recognition and related applications: an overview. In: 2013 IEEE International Conference on ICASSP, pp. 8599–8603. IEEE (2013)
13. Fukushima, K.: A self-organizing neural network model for a mechanism of pattern recognition unaffected by shift in position. Biol. Cybern. **36**, 193–202 (1980)
14. Goller, C., Kuchler, A.: Learning task-dependent distributed representations by backpropagation through structure. In: IEEE International Conference on Neural Networks, vol. 1, pp. 347–352. IEEE (1996)
15. Goodfellow, I., Bengio, Y., Courville, A.: Deep Learning. MIT Press, Cambridge (2016)
16. Han, S.H., Chen, L.: The relationship between global properties and local properties-global precedence. Adv. Psychol. Sci. **4**(1), 36–41 (1996)
17. Hinton, G.E., Rumelhart, D.E., Williams, R.J.: Learning internal representations by back-propagating errors. Nature **323**(99), 533–536 (1986)
18. Hinton, G.E.: Learning multiple layers of representation. Trends Cogn. Sci. **11**(10), 428–434 (2007)
19. Hinton, G.E., Dayan, P., Frey, B.J., Neal, R.M.: The wake-sleep algorithm for unsupervised neural networks. Science **268**(5214), 1158 (1995)
20. Hinton, G.E., Osindero, S., Teh, Y.W.: A fast learning algorithm for deep belief nets. Neural Comput. **18**(7), 1527–1554 (2006)
21. Hinton, G.E., Salakhutdinov, R.R.: Reducing the dimensionality of data with neural networks. Science **313**, 504–507 (2006)
22. Hopfield, J.J.: Neural networks and physical systems with emergent collective computational abilities. Proc. Natl. Acad. Sci. **79**(8), 2554–2558 (1982)
23. Jackson, P.: Introduction to Expert Systems, 3rd edn. Addison Wesley, Boston (1998)
24. Jang, J.S.: ANFIS: adaptive-network-based fuzzy inference system. IEEE Trans. Syst. Man Cybern. **23**(3), 665–685 (1993)
25. Jankowski, A., Skowron, A.: Toward rough-granular computing. In: An, A., Stefanowski, J., Ramanna, S., Butz, C.J., Pedrycz, W., Wang, G. (eds.) RSFDGrC 2007. LNCS, vol. 4482, pp. 1–12. Springer, Heidelberg (2007). doi:10.1007/978-3-540-72530-5_1
26. Kelly, J.E.: Computing, cognition and the future of knowing. http://www.research.ibm.com/software/IBMResearch/multimedia/Computing_Cognition_WhitePaper.pdf
27. Kohonen, T.: Self-organized formation of topologically correct feature maps. Biol. Cybern. **43**(1), 59–69 (1982)
28. Krizhevsky, A., Sutskever, I., Hinton, G.E.: ImageNet classification with deep convolutional neural networks. In: Advances in neural information processing systems, pp. 1097–1105 (2012)

29. LeCun, Y., Bengio, Y., Hinton, G.: Deep learning. Nature **521**, 436–444 (2015)
30. LeCun, Y., Boser, B., Denker, J.S., et al.: Backpropagation applied to handwritten zip code recognition. Neural Comput. **1**(4), 541–551 (1989)
31. Liu, Y., Li, D., He, W., Wang, G.: Granular computing based on gaussian cloud transformation. Fundamenta Informaticae **127**(1–4), 385–398 (2013)
32. Lowe, D.: Multivariable functional interpolation and adaptive networks. Complex Syst. **2**(3), 321–355 (1988)
33. Miller, G.A.: The cognitive revolution: a historical perspective. Trends Cogn. Sci. **7**(3), 141–144 (2003)
34. Modha, D.S., Ananthanarayanan, R., Esser, S.K., et al.: Cognitive computing. Commun. ACM **54**(8), 62–71 (2011)
35. Navon, D.: Forest before trees: the precedence of global features in visual perception. Cogn. Psychol. **9**(3), 353–383 (1977)
36. Rumelhart, D.E., McClelland, J.L.: Parallel distributed processing: explorations in the microstructures of cognition (1986)
37. Schmidhuber, J.: Deep learning in neural networks: an overview. Neural Netw. **61**, 85–117 (2015)
38. Simon, H.A.: Computer science as empirical inquiry: symbols and search. Commun. ACM **19**(3), 113–126 (1976)
39. Skinner, B.F.: About Behaviorism. Vintage, New York City (2011)
40. Thagard, P.: Cognitive Science. The Metaphysics Research Lab Center for the Study of Language and Information, Stanford University (2011)
41. Wang, F.: Building knowledge structure in neural nets using fuzzy logic (1992)
42. Wang, G., Shi, H.: TMLNN: triple-valued or multiple-valued logic neural network. IEEE Trans. Neural Netw. **9**(6), 1099–1117 (1998)
43. Wang, G., Wang, Y.: 3DM: domain-oriented data-driven data mining. Fundamenta Informaticae **90**(4), 395–426 (2009)
44. Wang, G., Yang, J., Xu, J.: Granular computing: from granularity optimization to multi-granularity joint problem solving. Granul. Comput. (2016). doi:10.1007/s41066-016-0032-3
45. Wille, R.: Restructuring lattice theory: an approach based on hierarchies of concepts. In: Rival, I. (ed.) Ordered Sets, vol. 83, pp. 445–470. Springer, Heidelberg (1982). doi:10.1007/978-94-009-7798-3_15
46. Xu, J., Wang, G., Deng, W.: DenPEHC: density peak based efficient hierarchical clustering. Inf. Sci. **373**, 200–218 (2016)
47. Yao, J., Vasilakos, A.V., Pedrycz, W.: Granular computing: perspectives and challenges. IEEE Trans. Cybern. **42**, 1977–1989 (2013)
48. Yao, Y.: Perspectives of granular computing. In: 2005 IEEE International Conference on Granular Computing, vol. 1, pp. 85–90. IEEE (2005)
49. Yao, Y.: Three-way decisions and cognitive computing. Cogn. Comput. **8**(4), 543–554 (2016)
50. Yao, Y.: A triarchic theory of granular computing. Granular Comput. **1**(2), 145–157 (2016)
51. Zadeh, L.A., Klir, G.J., Yuan, B.: Fuzzy Sets, Fuzzy Logic, and Fuzzy Systems: Selected Papers. World Scientific, Singapore (1996)
52. Zhang, L., Zhang, B.: Quotient Space Based Problem Solving: A Theoretical Foundation of Granular Computing. Morgan Kaufmann, Burlington (2014)

Advances in Rough Set Based Hybrid Approaches for Medical Image Analysis

Pradipta Maji[✉]

Biomedical Imaging and Bioinformatics Lab, Machine Intelligence Unit,
Indian Statistical Institute, 203 B.T. Road, Kolkata, West Bengal, India
pmaji@isical.ac.in

Abstract. Recent advancement in the area of medical imaging produces a huge amount of image data. Automatic extraction of meaningful information from these data has become necessary. In this regard, different image processing techniques provide efficient tools to extract and interpret meaningful information from the medical images, which, in turn, provide valuable directions for medical diagnosis. One of the major problems in real-life medical image data analysis is uncertainty. Among other soft computing techniques, rough sets provide a powerful tool to handle uncertainties, vagueness, and incompleteness associated with data, while fuzzy set and probabilistic paradigm serve as analytical tools for dealing with uncertainty that arises due to the overlapping characteristics and/or randomness in data. Hence, they can be integrated judiciously to develop efficient algorithms for automatic analysis of medical image data. In this regard, the paper presents a brief review on recent advances of rough set based hybrid intelligent approaches for medical image analysis.

Keywords: Rough sets · Medical imaging · Hybrid intelligent systems

1 Introduction

Medical image analysis plays an important role in improving public health, by introducing a number of complementary diagnostic tools such as x-ray computer tomography, magnetic resonance imaging, position emission tomography, and so on. A huge amount of medical imaging data has been generated due to the improvement in the area of medical imaging. However, the manual extraction of meaningful information from these huge data has become an insurmountable problem. In this regard, several automatic image analysis tools are being developed to process these medical image data for diagnostic and treatment purposes [31].

In recent years, there has been a growing interest towards the realization of computer aided diagnostic systems for the analysis of medical images. Results produced by these techniques can be used to support the scientists' manual/subjective analysis, leading to test results being more reliable and consistent

© Springer International Publishing AG 2017
L. Polkowski et al. (Eds.): IJCRS 2017, Part I, LNAI 10313, pp. 25–33, 2017.
DOI: 10.1007/978-3-319-60837-2_3

across laboratories. In this background, there is a growing interest in both scientific and industrial societies for automatic medical image pattern analysis due to the following benefits:

- reducing high labor costs;
- increasing the reliability;
- avoiding ambiguous results caused by subjective analysis;
- providing more efficient analysis report; and
- increasing the test repeatability.

Pattern recognition and image processing techniques are widely used in the field of medicine for the development of computer aided diagnostic system. Such systems may support the physician in many ways: they can be adopted as a second reader, thus augmenting the physician's capabilities and reducing errors; they allow to perform a pre-selection of the cases to be examined, enabling the physician to focus his/her attention only on the most relevant cases, making it easier to carry out mass screening campaigns; they may aid the physician while he/she carries out the diagnosis; finally, they can be used as a tool for training and education of specialized medical personnel. These issues can be addressed by contributing to different aspects of the analysis of medical images such as cell or tumor detection, image segmentation, intensity classification, and texture pattern recognition [13].

In the analysis of medical images for computer-aided diagnosis and therapy, segmentation is often required as a preliminary stage. However, medical image segmentation is a complex and challenging task due to intrinsic nature of the images. For example, the brain has a particularly complicated structure and its precise segmentation is very important for detecting tumors, edema, and necrotic tissues, in order to prescribe appropriate therapy [31]. Conventionally, the medical images are interpreted visually and qualitatively by radiologists. Advanced research requires quantitative information, such as the size of the brain ventricles after a traumatic brain injury or the relative volume of ventricles to brain. Fully automatic methods sometimes fail, producing incorrect results and requiring the intervention of a human operator. This is often true due to restrictions imposed by image acquisition, pathology and biological variation. So, it is important to have a faithful method to measure various structures in the brain. One of such methods is the segmentation of images to isolate objects and regions of interest.

One of the major problems in real-life medical image data analysis is uncertainty. Some of the sources of this uncertainty include incompleteness and vagueness in tissue class definition. The theory of rough sets [22] can deal with uncertainty, vagueness, and incompleteness successfully. One of the key advantages of using rough set theory is that it is capable of expressing vagueness, not by means of membership, like fuzzy sets, but by employing a boundary region of a set. If the boundary region of a set is empty, the set is crisp; otherwise the set is rough (inexact). Nonempty boundary region of a set denotes that the present knowledge about the set is not sufficient to define the set precisely. The theory of rough set offers reasonable structures to model overlapping boundaries of image classes depending on some domain knowledge; and hence, it has been widely used in image segmentation tasks. In this regard, the paper presents a brief review on existing and recent advances of rough set based hybrid intelligent approaches for medical image analysis.

2 Image Analysis Using Rough Sets

The rough set theory has been hybridized with other techniques of computational intelligence such as neural networks, support vector machines, fuzzy sets, wavelets, mathematical morphology, Bayesian inference, and probabilistic models for image segmentation [5,6]. A method for image segmentation, based on rough set theory and neural networks, is proposed in [9]. Sinha and Laplante [30] developed a method to detect binary objects using rough sets by constructing a gray-scaled (or, fuzzy) template for correlation-based matching. Pal et al. [21] demonstrated the application of rough sets and granular computing for object extraction from gray scale images. They described different object regions as rough sets with upper and lower approximations to handle the uncertainty due to overlapping class boundaries. Petrosino and Salvi [23] presented a multi-scale method, based on the notion of rough-fuzzy sets, incorporating two models of uncertainty, namely, vagueness and coarseness for multi-class image segmentation. Borkowski and Peters [4] introduced an approach for matching 2D image segments using genetic algorithms and approximation spaces.

The segmentation of color images using the concept of histon, based on rough set theory, is presented in [18,19]. An integration of rough set theoretic knowledge extraction, expectation-maximization algorithm, and minimal spanning tree clustering is described in [20] to solve the problem of segmentation of multispectral satellite images. Sen and Pal [29] described the application of rough set theory and its certain generalizations for quantifying ambiguities in images and demonstrated the performance using image processing operations such as segmentation, edge detection, and enhancement evaluation.

A hybrid approach to MR image segmentation, using unsupervised clustering and the rules derived from approximate decision reducts, has been proposed in [32]. Widz et al. [35] introduced an automated multispectral MR image segmentation technique based on approximate reducts derived from the theory of rough sets. The theory of rough sets has also been employed to automatically identify partial volume effects from image voxels for segmentation of MR images [33]. Widz and Ślęzak utilized a classification approach for MR image segmentation based on the attribute reduction, derived from the data mining paradigm of rough set theory [34]. Hirano and Tsumoto [7,8] developed a medical image segmentation method based on rough set theory, where the region of interest is approximated using positive, boundary, and negative regions, depending on multiple types of expert knowledge. Mao et al. [17] introduced the rough set reasoning into the fuzzy Hopfield model for segmentation of multispectral MR images. The rough-fuzzy clustering algorithms, introduced in [10–14], have been shown to yield significantly more accurate results compared to fuzzy clustering in image segmentation tasks. It can avoid the noise sensitivity problem of fuzzy clustering based segmentation algorithms. The rough-fuzzy clustering algorithm has been used in [12] for segmentation of brain MR images.

3   Recent Advances of Rough Sets in Medical Imaging

This section presents some recent developments in the areas of medical imaging, based on the theory of rough sets. The rough set based hybrid intelligent systems, as depicted in Fig. 1, have been successfully applied to address several important problems related to medical imaging as follows:

1. Skull stripping for brain MR volumes [15, 25];
2. Correction of bias field or intensity inhomogeneity from brain MR images [1];
3. Introduction of new probability distribution for tissue class modeling [2, 3];
4. Segmentation of healthy brain MR volumes [27];
5. Detection of brain tumor from MR volumes [16];
6. Segmentation of HEp-2 cell IIF images [26, 28].

Each of these problems is briefly described next one by one.

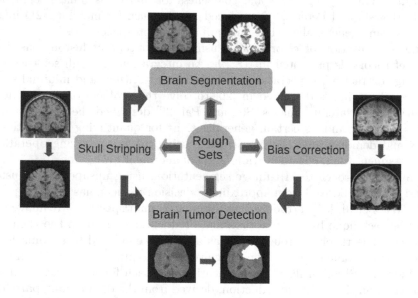

Fig. 1. Some applications of rough set based intelligent systems in medical imaging

3.1 Skull Stripping for 3-D Brain MR Images

The skull stripping is an important area of study in brain image processing applications. It acts as preliminary step in numerous medical applications as it increases the speed and accuracy of diagnosis in manifold. It removes non-cerebral tissues like skull, scalp, and dura from brain volumes. In this regard, a simple skull stripping algorithm has been described in [15,25], which is based on brain anatomy and image intensity characteristics. The method is unsupervised and knowledge based. It uses adaptive intensity thresholding followed by morphological operations, for increased robustness, on brain MR volumes. The threshold value is adaptively calculated based on the knowledge of intensity distribution in brain MR volumes.

3.2 Bias Field Correction in MR Images

One of the challenging tasks for MR image analysis is to remove the intensity inhomogeneity artifact present in MR images, which often degrades the performance of an automatic image analysis technique. In this regard, the theory of rough sets has been used in [1] for bias field correction in MR images. The method judiciously integrates the merits of rough sets and contraharmonic mean. While the contraharmonic mean is used in low-pass averaging filter to estimate the bias field in multiplicative model, the concept of lower approximation and boundary region of rough sets deals with vagueness and incompleteness in filter structure definition. A theoretical analysis has been presented in [1] to justify the use of both rough sets and contraharmonic mean for bias field estimation. The integration enables the algorithm to estimate near optimum bias field.

3.3 New Probability Distribution for Tissue Class Modeling

Image segmentation is an essential prerequisite for any automatic medical image analysis technique. It is useful for clinical analysis of medical images to visualize human tissues as manual segmentation is labor intensive, time consuming, and difficult task. The finite Gaussian mixture model is one of the popular models for parametric model based image segmentation. However, the normality assumption of this model induces certain limitations as a single representative value is considered to represent each class. In this regard, a new probability distribution, called stomped normal distribution, has been introduced in [2,3] to model each tissue class. The intensity distribution of a tissue class is represented by the new distribution, where each class consists of a crisp lower approximation and a probabilistic boundary region. The intensity distribution of an image is modeled as a mixture of finite number of new distributions. A new approach for segmentation of medical images has been described, which integrates judiciously the concept of rough sets and the merit of the new distribution. The method incorporates both the expectation-maximization and hidden Markov random field frameworks to provide an accurate and robust segmentation.

3.4   Segmentation of Brain MR Volumes

The clustering in fuzzy approximation spaces provides an effective mean for image segmentation by handling overlapping partitions and uncertainty in cluster definition. However, the existing rough-fuzzy clustering algorithms [10,11,13,14] assign pixels to the clusters depending on the distribution of pixels, without considering their spatial distribution in the image. In this regard, a novel segmentation algorithm has been introduced in [27,28] for brain MR volumes, integrating judiciously local contextual information and the merits of rough-fuzzy clustering, which are very much effective for image segmentation. The algorithm assigns the label of a pixel depending on the labels of its local neighbors. The effect of immediate neighbors acts as a regularizer. Each cluster in this approach consists of a cluster representative or prototype, a lower approximation, and a boundary region. The lower approximation of each cluster is possibilistic in nature, while the boundary region is probabilistic or fuzzy. The cluster prototype depends on the lower approximation, boundary region, and neighborhood regularizer.

3.5   Brain Tumor Detection

One of the important problems in medical diagnosis is the segmentation and detection of brain tumor in MR images. The accurate estimation of brain tumor size is important for treatment planning and therapy evaluation. In this regard, Maji and Roy described a method in [16] for segmentation of brain tumor from MR images. It integrates judiciously the merits of rough-fuzzy computing and multiresolution image analysis technique. To extract the scale-space feature vector for each pixel of brain region, the dyadic wavelet analysis has been used, while an unsupervised feature selection method, based on maximum relevance-maximum significance criterion, has been used to select relevant and significant textural features for brain tumor segmentation [15]. To address the uncertainty problem of brain MR image segmentation, the brain tumor detection method uses the robust rough-fuzzy clustering [14]. After the segmentation process, asymmetricity is analyzed by using the Zernike moments of each of the tissues segmented in the brain to identify the tumor. Finally, the location of the tumor is searched by a region growing algorithm based on the notion of rough sets [24].

3.6   Segmentation of HEp-2 Cell IIF Images

Human epithelial type-2 (HEp-2) cell is currently the most recommended substrate in indirect immunofluorescence (IIF) tests to diagnose various connective tissue disorders. The IIF test identifies the presence of antinuclear antibody (ANA) in patient serum. However, the proper detection of HEp-2 cells from the IIF images is an important prerequisite for the recognition of staining patterns of ANAs. The characteristics of HEp-2 cell images, due to fluorescence intensity, make the segmentation process more challenging. Recently, rough-fuzzy clustering algorithms have been shown to provide significant results for HEp-2 cell IIF image segmentation by handling different uncertainties present in the images [26]. But, the neighborhood information is completely ignored in these algorithms. However, the spatial information is useful when the image is distorted by different imaging artifacts. In this regard, a rough-fuzzy segmentation algorithm has been introduced in [28], by incorporating the neighborhood information into rough-fuzzy clustering algorithm.

Acknowledgement. This work is partially supported by the Department of Electronics and Information Technology, Government of India (PhD-MLA/4(90)/2015-16). The author would like to thank Ms. Shaswati Roy and Dr. Abhirup Banerjee of Indian Statistical Institute, Kolkata, India for providing helpful and valuable criticisms.

References

1. Banerjee, A., Maji, P.: Rough sets for bias field correction in MR images using contraharmonic mean and quantitative index. IEEE Trans. Med. Imaging **32**(11), 2140–2151 (2013)
2. Banerjee, A., Maji, P.: Rough sets and stomped normal distribution for simultaneous segmentation and bias field correction in brain MR images. IEEE Trans. Image Process. **24**(12), 5764–5776 (2015)
3. Banerjee, A., Maji, P.: Rough-probabilistic clustering and hidden markov random field model for segmentation of HEp-2 cell and brain MR images. Appl. Soft Comput. **46**, 558–576 (2016)
4. Borkowski, M., Peters, J.F.: Matching 2D image segments with genetic algorithms and approximation spaces. In: Peters, J.F., Skowron, A. (eds.) Transactions on Rough Sets V. LNCS, vol. 4100, pp. 63–101. Springer, Heidelberg (2006). doi:10.1007/11847465_4
5. Hassanien, A.E., Abraham, A., Peters, J.F., Schaefer, G.: An overview of rough-hybrid approaches in image processing. In: Proceedings of the IEEE World Congress on Computational Intelligence, pp. 2135–2142 (2008)
6. Hassanien, A.E., Abraham, A., Peters, J.F., Schaefer, G., Henry, C.: Rough sets and near sets in medical imaging: a review. IEEE Trans. Inf. Technol. Biomed. **13**(6), 955–968 (2009)
7. Hirano, S., Tsumoto, S.: Segmentation of medical images based on approximations in rough set theory. In: Alpigini, J.J., Peters, J.F., Skowron, A., Zhong, N. (eds.) RSCTC 2002. LNCS, vol. 2475, pp. 554–563. Springer, Heidelberg (2002). doi:10.1007/3-540-45813-1_73
8. Hirano, S., Tsumoto, S.: Rough representation of a region of interest in medical images. Int. J. Approx. Reason. **40**(1–2), 23–34 (2005)
9. Jiang, J., Yang, D., Wei, H.: Image segmentation based on rough set theory and neural networks. In: Proceedings of the 5th International Conference on Visual Information Engineering, pp. 361–365 (2008)
10. Maji, P., Pal, S.K.: RFCM: a hybrid clustering algorithm using rough and fuzzy sets. Fundamenta Informaticae **80**(4), 475–496 (2007)
11. Maji, P., Pal, S.K.: Rough Set based generalized fuzzy c-means algorithm and quantitative indices. IEEE Trans. Syst. Man Cybern. Part B: Cybern. **37**(6), 1529–1540 (2007)
12. Maji, P., Pal, S.K.: Maximum class separability for rough-fuzzy c-means based brain MR image segmentation. LNCS Trans. Rough Sets IX **5390**, 114–134 (2008)

13. Maji, P., Pal, S.K.: Rough-Fuzzy Pattern Recognition: Applications in Bioinformatics and Medical Imaging. Wiley-IEEE Computer Society Press, New Jersey (2012)
14. Maji, P., Paul, S.: Rough-fuzzy clustering for grouping functionally similar genes from microarray data. IEEE/ACM Trans. Comput. Biol. Bioinf. **10**(2), 286–299 (2013)
15. Maji, P., Roy, S.: Rough-fuzzy clustering and unsupervised feature selection for wavelet based MR image segmentation. PLoS ONE **10**(4), e0123677 (2015). doi:10.1371/journal.pone.0123677
16. Maji, P., Roy, S.: SoBT-RFW: rough-fuzzy computing and wavelet analysis based automatic brain tumor detection method from MR images. Fundamenta Informaticae **142**(1–4), 237–267 (2015)
17. Mao, C.W., Liu, S.H., Lin, J.S.: Classification of multispectral images through a rough-fuzzy neural network. Opt. Eng. **43**(1), 103–112 (2004)
18. Mohabey, A., Ray, A.K.: Rough set theory based segmentation of color images. In: Proceedings of the 19th International Conference of the North American Fuzzy Information Processing Society, pp. 338–342 (2000)
19. Mushrif, M.M., Ray, A.K.: Color image segmentation: rough-set theoretic approach. Pattern Recogn. Lett. **29**(4), 483–493 (2008)
20. Pal, S.K., Mitra, P.: Multispectral image segmentation using the rough-set-initialized EM algorithm. IEEE Trans. Geosci. Remote Sens. **40**(11), 2495–2501 (2002)
21. Pal, S.K., Shankar, B.U., Mitra, P.: Granular computing, rough entropy and object extraction. Pattern Recogn. Lett. **26**(16), 2509–2517 (2005)
22. Pawlak, Z.: Rough Sets: Theoretical Aspects of Reasoning about Data. Kluwer Academic, Dordrecht, The Netherlands (1991)
23. Petrosino, A., Salvi, G.: Rough fuzzy set based scale space transforms and their use in image analysis. Int. J. Approx. Reason. **41**(2), 212–228 (2006)
24. Roy, S., Maji, P.: A new post-processing method to detect brain tumor using rough-fuzzy clustering. In: Kryszkiewicz, M., Bandyopadhyay, S., Rybinski, H., Pal, S.K. (eds.) PReMI 2015. LNCS, vol. 9124, pp. 407–417. Springer, Cham (2015). doi:10.1007/978-3-319-19941-2_39
25. Roy, S., Maji, P.: A simple skull stripping algorithm for brain MRI. In: Proceedings of the 8th International Conference on Advances in Pattern Recognition (ICAPR2015), Kolkata, India, pp. 1–6 (2015)
26. Roy, S., Maji, P.: A modified rough-fuzzy clustering algorithm with spatial information for hep-2 cell image segmentation. In: Proceedings of 10th IEEE International Conference on Bioinformatics and Biomedicine (BIBM 2016), China, pp. 383–388 (2016)
27. Roy, S., Maji, P.: Partitioning spatially constrained fuzzy approximation spaces for image segmentation. IEEE Trans. Syst. Man Cybern.: Syst. **SMCA−17−02−0196**, 1–14 (2017)
28. Roy, S., Maji, P.: Rough-fuzzy segmentation of HEp-2 cell indirect immunofluorescence images. Int. J. Data Mining Bioinf. **IJDMB−173484**, 1–20 (2017)
29. Sen, D., Pal, S.K.: Generalized rough sets, entropy, and image ambiguity measures. IEEE Trans. Syst. Man Cybern. - Part B: Cybern. **39**(1), 117–128 (2009)
30. Sinha, D., Laplante, P.: A rough set-based approach to handling spatial uncertainty in binary images. Eng. Appl. Artif. Intell. **17**(1), 97–110 (2004)
31. Suetens, P.: Fundamentals of Medical Imaging. Cambridge University Press, Cambridge (2002)

32. Widz, S., Revett, K., Ślęzak, D.: A hybrid approach to MR imaging segmentation using unsupervised clustering and approximate reducts. In: Ślęzak, D., Yao, J.T., Peters, J.F., Ziarko, W., Hu, X. (eds.) RSFDGrC 2005. LNCS, vol. 3642, pp. 372–382. Springer, Heidelberg (2005). doi:10.1007/11548706_39
33. Widz, S., Revett, K., Ślęzak, D.: A rough set-based magnetic resonance imaging partial volume detection system. In: Pal, S.K., Bandyopadhyay, S., Biswas, S. (eds.) PReMI 2005. LNCS, vol. 3776, pp. 756–761. Springer, Heidelberg (2005). doi:10.1007/11590316_122
34. Widz, S., Ślęzak, D.: Approximation degrees in decision reduct-based MRI segmentation. In: Proceedings of the Frontiers in the Convergence of Bioscience and Information Technologies, pp. 431–436 (2007)
35. Widz, S., Ślęzak, D., Revett, K.: Application of rough set based dynamic parameter optimization to MRI segmentation. In: Proceedings of the IEEE Annual Meeting of the Fuzzy Information Processing, vol. 1, pp. 440–445 (2004)

User Friendly NPS-Based Recommender System for Driving Business Revenue

Zbigniew W. Ras[1,2,3](✉), Katarzyna A. Tarnowska[1], Jieyan Kuang[1],
Lynn Daniel[4], and Doug Fowler[4]

[1] Department of Computer Science, University of North Carolina,
Charlotte, NC 28223, USA
{ras,ktarnows,jkuang1}@uncc.edu
[2] Institute of Computer Science, Warsaw University of Technology,
00-665 Warsaw, Poland
[3] Polish-Japanese Academy of IT, Warsaw, Poland
[4] The Daniel Group, Charlotte, NC, USA
{LynnDaniel,DougFowler}@thedanielgroup.com

Abstract. This paper provides an overview of a user-friendly NPS-based Recommender System for driving business revenue. This hierarchically designed recommender system for improving NPS of clients is driven mainly by action rules and meta-actions. The paper presents main techniques used to build the data-driven system, including data mining and machine learning techniques, such as hierarchical clustering, action rules and meta actions, as well as visualization design. The system implements domain-specific sentiment analysis performed on comments collected within telephone surveys with end customers. Advanced natural language processing techniques are used including text parsing, dependency analysis, aspect-based sentiment analysis, text summarization and visualization.

Keywords: NPS · Recommender system · Actionable knowledge mining · Semantic similarity · Sentiment analysis · Visualization

1 Introduction

The main idea behind this system is based on today's standard metric for measuring customer satisfaction called Net Promoter Score (NPS)[1]. It was designed to evaluate and improve the performance of a company's growth engine. The NPS metric is a concept based on the assumption that each customer can be labeled as either Promoter, Passive or Detractor. Promoters are loyal enthusiasts who are buying from a company and recommend others to do so. Passives are satisfied but unenthusiastic customers who are open to offers from competitors, while

---

[1] NPS®, Net Promoter® and Net Promoter® Score are registered trademarks of Satmetrix Systems, Inc., Bain and Company and Fred Reichheld.

© Springer International Publishing AG 2017
L. Polkowski et al. (Eds.): IJCRS 2017, Part I, LNAI 10313, pp. 34–48, 2017.
DOI: 10.1007/978-3-319-60837-2_4

detractors are the least loyal customers who may urge others to avoid that company. The total Net Promoter Score is computed as %Promoters - %Detractors, where percentage is understood as the total number of promoters/detractors divided by the total number of surveys. The goal here is to maximize NPS, which in practice is a difficult task to achieve especially when a company has already quite high NPS. Nowadays most businesses, whether small, medium-sized or enterprise-level organizations with hundreds or thousands of locations collect their customers' feedback on products or services.

The data we worked on was collected by telephone surveys on customer's satisfaction. There are about 400,000 records in the dataset collected in the years 2011–2016, and the data is continued to be collected. The dataset represents questionnaires sent to a randomly chosen group of customers and consists of features related to customer's details (localization, type of work done, invoice, etc.), survey details (date, survey type, etc.), and benchmark questions on which service is being evaluated. Benchmarks include numerical scores (0–10) on different aspects of service. For example, if the job is done correctly, are you satisfied with the job, likelihood to refer, etc. All the responses from customers are saved into a database with each question (benchmark) as one feature in the dataset. The entire dataset consists of 38 companies, located in different sites across the United States as well as several parts of Canada. Based on overall benchmark scores, the Net Promoter Status (Promoter, Passive or Detractor) is determined for a client, which is a decision attribute in the dataset.

2   Semantic Similarity

The dataset was divided into single-client subsets (38 in total). Additional attributes were developed, including spacial and temporal attributes. More detailed description of data pre-processing techniques is provided in Kuang [1].

In the first place, classification experiments were conducted for each single dataset in order to determine the predictive capability of standard classifier

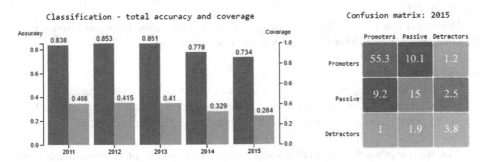

Fig. 1. Javascript-based visualization for depicting the results (accuracy, coverage and confusion matrix) of classification experiments on service data.

model and the same ability to discern and recognize different types of customers (promoters, passives and detractors). It was discovered that the classifier's accuracy/coverage was high for the category "Promoters", but low for the two other categories "Passives" and "Detractors".

We have used *RSES* (Rough Set Exploration System) to conduct initial experiments. The results of the classification experiments - accuracy, coverage and confusion matrix, for Service data for each client were implemented into a visualization system. The view for a sample client is shown in Fig. 1. The confusion matrix updates for a chosen year is displayed right after placing a mouse over the corresponding bar on the first chart.

Following the classification experiments, the notion of semantic similarity was defined [1]. Assuming that RC[1] and RC[2] are the sets of classification rules extracted from the single-client datasets (of clients *C1* and *C2*), and also:

$RC[1] = RC[1, Promoter] \cup RC[1, Passive] \cup RC[1, Detractor]$, where the above three sets are collections of classification rules defining correspondingly: "Promoter", "Passive" and "Detractor":

$RC[1, Promoter] = \{r[1, Promoter, i] : i \in I_{Pr}\}$
$RC[1, Passive] = \{r[1, Passive, i] : i \in I_{Ps}\}$
$RC[1, Detractor] = \{r[1, Detractor, i] : i \in I_{Dr}\}$

In a similar way we define:
$RC[2] = RC[2, Promoter] \cup RC[2, Passive] \cup RC[2, Detractor]$.
$RC[2, Promoter] = \{r[2, Promoter, i] : i \in J_{Pr}\}$
$RC[2, Passive] = \{r[2, Passive, i] : i \in J_{Ps}\}$
$RC[2, Detractor] = \{r[2, Detractor, i] : i \in J_{Dr}\}$

By $C1[1, Promoter, i], C1[1, Passive, i], C1[1, Detractor, i]$ we mean confidences of corresponding rules in a dataset for client $C1$.

We define $C2[1, Promoter, i], C2[1, Passive, i], C2[1, Detractor, i]$ as confidences of rules extracted from $C1$ calculated for $C2$.

Analogously, $C2[2, Promoter, i], C2[2, Passive, i], C2[2, Detractor, i]$ are confidences of rules extracted from $C2$, and $C1[2, Promoter, i], C1[2, Passive, i], C1[2, Detractor, i]$ are confidences of rules extracted from client $C2$ calculated for client $C1$.

Based on the above, the concept of semantic similarity between clients $C1$, $C2$, denoted by $SemSim(C1, C2)$ was defined as follows:

$$SemSim(C1, C2) =$$
$$\frac{\sum \{C1[1,Promoter,k]-C2[1,Promoter,k] | k \in I_{Pr}\}}{card(I_{Pr})} + \frac{\sum \{C1[1,Passive,k]-C2[1,Passive,k] | k \in I_{Ps}\}}{card(I_{Ps})} +$$
$$\frac{\sum \{C1[1,Detractor,k]-C2[1,Detractor,k] | k \in I_{Dr}\}}{card(I_{Dr})} + \frac{\sum \{C2[2,Promoter,k]-C1[2,Promoter,k] | k \in I_{Pr}\}}{card(J_{Pr})} +$$
$$\frac{\sum \{C2[2,Passive,k]-C1[2,Passive,k] | k \in I_{Ps}\}}{card(J_{Ps})} + \frac{\sum \{C2[2,Detractor,k]-C1[2,Detractor,k] | k \in J_{Dr}\}}{card(J_{Dr})}$$

The metric is used to find clients similar to a current client in semantic terms. It calculates the distance between each pair of clients–the smaller the distance is, the more similar the clients are. The resulting distance matrix serves as an input to the hierarchical clustering algorithm. The output of the algorithm is a structure, called dendrogram.

3 Hierarchical Agglomerative Method for Improving NPS

Hierarchical Agglomerative Method for Improving NPS (HAMIS) was proposed in Kuang et al. [2] as a strategy for improving NPS of a company based on its local knowledge and knowledge collected from other semantically similar companies operating in the same type of industry. The strategy is based on the definition of semantic similarity introduced in the previous section. HAMIS is a dendrogram built by using agglomerative clustering strategy and semantic distance between clients.

The dendrogram was visualized in our web-based system by means of a node-link diagram that places leaf nodes of the tree at the same depth (see Fig. 2).

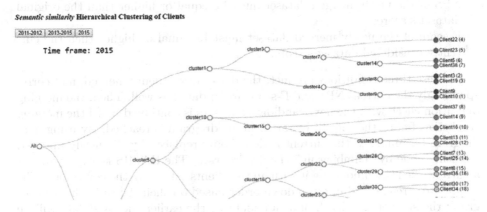

Fig. 2. Javascript-based visualization of the dendrogram showing semantic similarity between clients in 2015: chosen Client9 with highlighted semantically similar clients ordered by numbers.

The clients (leaf nodes) are aligned on the right edge, with the clusters (internal nodes) - to the left. The data shows the hierarchy of client clusters, with the root node being "All" clients. The visualization facilitates comparing the clients by means of similarity. The nodes that are semantically closest to the chosen client are the leaf nodes on the sibling side. The diagram is interactive: after clicking on the client node, all the semantically similar clients are highlighted with numbers in parentheses denoting sequence of the most similar clients (with 1 - denoting the first most similar client, 2 - the second similar, etc.), and the color strength corresponding to the similarity.

The dendrogram was used to construct new "merged" datasets for further data mining (in particular, action rule mining, described in the next section). The merged datasets replace a current client's dataset expanded by adding datasets of better performing clients who are semantically similar to it. So, besides semantic similarity, NPS efficiency rating is another primary measure considered when "merging" two semantically similar clients [2]. As a result of this strategy, the NPS rating of the newly merged dataset will be higher than, or at least equal to, the dataset before its extension. This way, we can offer recommendations to the company with a lower NPS based on the data collected by companies with a higher NPS assuming that these two are semantically similar (that is, their customers understand the concepts of promoter, passive and detractor in a similar way). The second factor considered in the merging operation, besides the NPS, is the quality and consistency of the newly merged data. It is checked by means of F-score calculated for a classifier extracted from the newly merged dataset. The F-score was chosen for keeping track of datasets quality as it combines two other important metrics: accuracy and coverage of the classifier. In summary, three conditions have to be met for the two datasets to be merged:

- merged clients have to be semantically similar within defined threshold;
- NPS of the newly merged dataset must be equal or higher than the original dataset's score;
- F-score of the newly merged dataset must be equal or higher then the currently considered dataset's score.

If these three conditions are met, the datasets are being merged, and correspondingly the current NPS and F-score are updated as well. Then, the merging operation check with the next candidate datasets is continued, until the merging conditions fail or the root of hierarchical dendrogram is reached. By using dendrogram terminology, the current node is being replaced by the newly updated resulting node by "climbing up" the dendrogram. The HAMIS keeps expanding a current client by unionizing it with all the clients satisfying the conditions. The candidates are checked in a top down order based on their depth in the dendrogram: the smaller the depth of a candidate is, the earlier the candidate will be checked. The detailed algorithm for HAMIS and experiments on example runs with it are described in [1,2]. An example of expanding datasets of 36 clients based on Service 2016 data is shown in Fig. 4. Half of the clients were extended by applying the HAMIS procedure, and a client was extended on average by about 3 other datasets. It can be observed that generally clients with lower NPS were extended by a larger number of datasets. It shows that their NPS can be improved more by using additional knowledge from semantically similar, better performing clients. For example, in Fig. 4, Client20 with the worst NPS (of 63%) was extended by 10 other datasets and Client33 with the second worst NPS (69%) was extended by 11 other datasets. Expanding the original, single-client datasets was followed by action rule mining–the action rules mined from the extended datasets are expected to be better in quality and quantity. Recommender system based on action rules extracted from the extended datasets can give more promising suggestions for improving clients' NPS score. The more extended the datasets, the better recommendations for improving NPS can be given by the system Fig. 3.

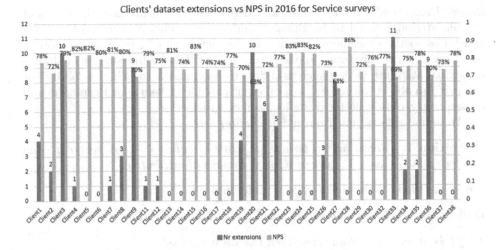

Fig. 3. Results of running HAMIS procedure on 38 datasets representing clients for Service survey data from 2016: the number of clients by which a client was extended and its original NPS.

4   Action Rules

The whole system is built from the knowledge extracted from the preprocessed dataset in the form of action rules. The knowledge is in actionable format and collected not only from the customers using certain business, but also from customers using semantically similar businesses having a higher NPS score.

Action rule concept was firstly proposed by Ras and Wieczorkowska in [11], and since then investigated further in application areas such as business, healthcare, music automatic indexing and retrieval. Action rules present a new way in machine learning domain that solve problems that traditional methods, such as classification or association rules cannot handle. The purpose is to analyze data to improve understanding of it and seek specific actions (recommendations) to enhance the decision-making process. An *action* shows a way of controlling or changing some of the attribute values for a given set of objects to achieve desired results [5]. An *action rule* is defined [11] as a rule that describes a transition that may occur within objects from one state to another, with respect to decision attribute, as defined by the user. Decision attribute is a distinguished attribute [11], while the rest of the attributes are partitioned into stable and flexible attributes.

In nomenclature, action rule is defined as a term: $[(\omega) \wedge (\alpha \rightarrow \beta) \Rightarrow (\Phi \rightarrow \Psi)]$, where ω denotes conjunction of fixed condition attributes often called the header of the rule, $(\alpha \rightarrow \beta)$ are proposed changes in values of flexible features, and $(\Phi \rightarrow \Psi)$ is an expected change of a decision attribute value (action effect).

So, in our domain, decision attribute is *PromoterStatus* (with values *Promoter, Passive, Detractor*). Let us assume that Φ means 'Detractors' and Ψ

means 'Promoters'. The discovered knowledge would indicate how the values of flexible attributes need to be changed under the condition specified by stable attributes so the customers classified as detractors should become promoters. So, an action rule discovery applied to customer data would suggest a change in flexible attribute values, such as different benchmarks to help "reclassify" or "transit" an object (customer) to a different category (Passive or Promoter) and consequently, obtain better overall customer satisfaction.

An action rule is built from *atomic action sets*.

Definition 1. *Atomic action term is an expression* $(a, a_1 \rightarrow a_2)$, *where* a *is an attribute, and* $a_1, a_2 \in V_a$, *where* V_a *is a domain of attribute* a.

If $a_1 = a_2$ then attribute a is called stable on a_1.

Definition 2. *By action sets, we mean the smallest collection of sets such that:*

1. *If* t *is an atomic action term, then* t *is an action set.*
2. *If* t_1, t_2 *are action sets, then* $t_1 \wedge t_2$ *is a candidate action set.*
3. *If* t *is a candidate action set and for any two atomic actions* $(a, a_1 \rightarrow a_2)$, $(b, b_1 \rightarrow b_2)$ *contained in* t *we have* $a \neq b$, *then* t *is an action set. Here* b *is another attribute* $(b \in A)$, *and* $b_1, b_2 \in V_b$.

Definition 3. *By an action rule, we mean any expression* $r = [t_1 \Rightarrow t_2]$, *where* t_1 *and* t_2 *are action sets.*

The interpretation of the action rule r is, that by applying the action set t_1, we would get, as a result, the changes of states in action set t_2. So, action rule suggests the smallest set of necessary actions needed for switching from current state to another within the states of the decision attribute. We need to extract these kind of actions, so that we can build an effective recommender system that provides actionable suggestions for improving a client's performance.

The first step to extract action rules from the dataset by our recommender system is to complete the initialization of the mining program by setting up all the variables. This process consists of selecting stable attributes, flexible attributes and the decision attribute. We also need to set up the favorable state and the unfavorable state for the decision attribute, as well as minimum support of the rule and its minimum confidence. *PromoterScore* is set as the decision attribute, with *Promoter* value to be the target state (most favorable one) and *Detractor* the most undesirable state. For the stable attributes, all features related to the general information about clients and customers are considered; the final choice of stable attributes includes:

- *ClientName* - since rules should be client-oriented,
- *Division* - specific department,
- *SurveyType* - type of service: field trips, in-shop, parts, etc.
- *ChannelType*

Initially, as the flexible attributes, all features denoting numerical benchmark questions were chosen, as it is believed that representing them areas of service/parts can be changed by undertaking certain actions. This set of benchmarks has been reduced to smaller set of benchmarks, which we can call critical. We used them for mining action rules. The choice of critical benchmarks was preceded by an analysis of decision reducts, which are visualized in a user-friendly interface built for our recommender system.

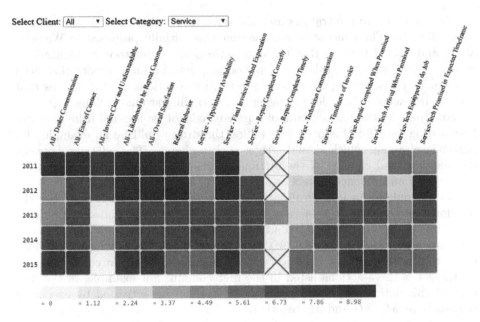

Fig. 4. Javascript-based visualization supporting an analysis of features related to survey benchmarks. The color of the cell corresponds to an occurrence of the associated benchmark in reducts of a corresponding dataset (for a client in a year). (Color figure online)

According to the definition, *reducts* are minimal subsets of attributes that keep the characteristics of the full dataset. In the context of action rule discovery, an *action reduct* is a minimal set of attribute values distinguishing a favorable object from another.

For our domain, decision reducts were extracted using Rough Set Exploration System (RSES). We also kept track of how the importance (or criticality) of particular benchmarks changed year by year and by client. The resulting visualization is depicted as a heatmap with colors denoting the importance of a benchmark (relative frequency of occurrence in decision reducts), rows representing years (2011–2015) and columns representing benchmarks occurring in decision reducts.

5   Meta Actions and Triggering Mechanism

Our recommender system is driven by action rules and meta-actions to provide proper suggestions to improve the revenue of companies. Action rules, described in the previous section, show minimum changes needed for a client to be made in order to improve its ratings so it can move to the Promoter's group. Action rules are extracted from the client's dataset expanded by HAMIS procedure, explained in the previous sections.

Meta-actions are the triggers used for activating action rules [4] and making them effective. The concept of *meta-action* was initially proposed in Wang et al. [9] and later defined in Ras [6]. Meta-actions are understood as higher-level actions. While an action rule is understood as a set of atomic actions that need to be made for achieving the expected result, meta-actions are the actions that need to be executed in order to trigger corresponding atomic actions.

For example, the temperature of a patient cannot be lowered if he does not take a drug used for this purpose - taking the drug would be an example of a higher-level action which should trigger such a change. The relations between meta-actions and changes of the attribute values they trigger can be modeled using either an influence matrix or ontology.

An example of an influence matrix is shown in Table 1 [1]. It describes the relations between the meta-actions and atomic actions associated with them. Attribute a denotes stable attribute, b - flexible attribute, and d - decision attribute. $\{M_1, M_2, M_3, M_4, M_5, M_6\}$ is a set of meta-actions which hypothetically triggers action rules. Each row denotes atomic actions that can be invoked by the set of meta-actions listed in the first column. For example, in the first row, atomic actions $(b_1 \rightarrow b_2)$ and $(d_1 \rightarrow d_2)$ can be activated by executing meta-actions M_1, M_2 and M_3 together.

Table 1. Sample meta-actions influence matrix

	a	b	d
$\{M_1, M_2, M_3\}$		$b_1 \rightarrow b_2$	$d_1 \rightarrow d_2$
$\{M_1, M_3, M_4\}$	a_2	$b_2 \rightarrow b_3$	
$\{M_5\}$	a_1	$b_2 \rightarrow b_1$	$d_2 \rightarrow d_1$
$\{M_2, M_4\}$		$b_2 \rightarrow b_3$	$d_1 \rightarrow d_2$
$\{M_1, M_5, M_6\}$		$b_1 \rightarrow b_3$	$d_1 \rightarrow d_2$

In our domain, we assume that one atomic action can be invoked by more than one meta-action. A set of meta-actions (can be only one) triggers an action rule that consists of atomic actions covered by these meta-actions. Also, some action rules can be invoked by more than one set of meta-actions.

If the action rule $r = [\{(a, a_2), (b, b_1 \rightarrow b_2)\} \Rightarrow \{(d, d_1 \rightarrow d_2)\}]$ is to be triggered, we consider the rule r to be the composition of two association rules

r_1 and r_2, where $r_1 = [\{(a, a_2), (b, b_1)\} \Rightarrow \{(d, d_1)\}]$ and $r_2 = [\{(a, a_2), (b, b_2)\} \Rightarrow \{(d, d_2)\}]$. The rule r can be triggered by the combination of meta-actions listed in the first and second row in Table 1, as meta-actions $\{M_1, M_2, M_3, M_4\}$ cover all required atomic actions: (a, a_2), $(b, b_1 \to b_2)$, and $(d, d_1 \to d_2)$ in r. Also, one set of meta-actions can potentially trigger multiple action rules. For example, the mentioned meta-action set $\{M_1, M_2, M_3, M_4\}$ triggers not only rule r, but also another rule, such as $[\{(a, a_2), (b, b_2 \to b_3)\} \Rightarrow \{(d, d_1 \to d_2)\}]$, according to the second and fourth row in Table 1, if such rule was extracted.

The goal is to select such a set of meta-actions which would trigger a larger number of action rules and the same bring greater effect in terms of NPS improvement. The effect is quantified as following [1]: supposing a set of meta-actions $M = \{M_1, M_2, ..., M_n : n > 0\}$ triggers a set of action rules $\{r_1, r_2, ..., r_m : m > 0\}$ that covers objects in a dataset with no overlap. We defined the coverage (support) of M as the summation of the support of all covered action rules. That is, the total number of objects that are affected by M in a dataset. The confidence of M is calculated by averaging the confidence of all covered action rules:

$$sup(M) = \sum_{i=1}^{m} sup(r_i)$$
$$conf(M) = \frac{\sum_{i=1}^{m} sup(r_i) \cdot conf(r_i)}{\sum_{i=1}^{m} sup(r_i)}$$

The effect of applying M is defined as the product of its support and confidence: $(sup(M) \cdot conf(M))$, which is a base for calculating the increment of NPS rating.

6   Text Mining

Triggers aiming at different action rules are extracted from respectively relevant comments left by customers in our domain [4]. Text comments are a complementary part of structured surveys. For example, for a rule described by: $r = [(a, a_2) \land (b, b_1 \to b_2)] \Rightarrow (d, d_1 \to d_2)]$, where a is a stable attribute, and b is a flexible attribute, the clues for generating meta-actions are in the comments of records matching the description: $[(a; a2) \land (b; b1) \land (d; d1)] \lor [(a; a2) \land (b; b2) \land (d; d2)]$.

Mining meta-actions consists of four characteristic steps involving sentiment analysis and text summarization [3]:

1. Identifying opinion sentences and their orientation with localization;
2. Summarizing each opinion sentence using discovered dependency templates;
3. Opinion summarizations based on identified feature words;
4. Generating meta-actions with regard to given suggestions.

The whole process of mining customers' comments uses sentiment analysis, text summarization and feature identification based on guided folksonomy (domain specific dictionaries are built). It also generates appropriate suggestions, such as meta-actions, which is important for the purpose of recommender system.

The schema of the presented aspect-based sentiment mining was inspired by a process described in [10]. *Sentiment analysis* is generally defined as analyzing people's opinions, sentiments, evaluations, attitudes, and emotions from written language. *Aspect-based sentiment analysis* is based on the idea that an opinion consists of a sentiment (positive or negative) and a *target* of the opinion, that is, a specific aspect or feature of the object. It offers more detailed and fine-grained analysis than document-level or sentence-level sentiment analysis.

Consequently, the first step in text mining consists of identifying an opinion sentence, based on the occurrence of an opinion word. A dictionary (list) of positive and negative words (adjectives) were used for that purpose. Context (localization) was also taken into account. For example, in the comment *"the charge was too high"*, "high" is recognized according to the adjective lists as neither positive nor negative. However, the comment still presents an insightful opinion about discontent when it comes to pricing. Therefore, "high" was added to the list as a negative in the context of pricing.

In the next step, sentences with opinion words identified are shortened into segments. Feature-opinion pairs are generated based on grammatical dependency relationships between features and opinion words. The foundation of this step is the grammatical relations defined by Stanford Typed Dependencies Manual [8] and generated by Stanford Parser. A dependency relationship describes a grammatical relation between a governor word and a dependent word in a sentence. Given the wide definition of dependency templates (about 50 defined dependencies in [8]), all the necessary relations associated with opinion words can be identified. On top of it, negation and 'but'-clauses are identified.

Having extracted segments, feature words are identified using the supervised pattern mining method (similarly as described in [7]). The Parts-of-Speech tags (POS) help in the process of recognizing the features.

Opinion summarizations are used in many sentiment analysis works (first in [10]) to generate a final review summary about the discovery results on feature and opinions mining and also rank them according to their appearances in the reviews. In our work, we also focused on removing the redundancy of extracted segments and clustering segments into different classes. The feature clustering was based on the pre-defined list of seed words or phrases. To cluster a segment into the corresponding class, its feature word or the base form of its feature is checked whether it exists in any list of the seed words.

For the purpose of generating meta-actions, each feature class has been divided into several subclasses. Each subclass is related to the specific aspect of that feature. The aspects have been defined based on the domain knowledge.

The last step is generating meta-actions and providing them to the end business user along with the comments from which they were mined. The recommendations are divided into positive and negative recommendations. Negative opinions show the undesirable behaviors that should be fixed, while the positive segments indicate which areas should be continued.

7   Visualization

For review summarization purposes, often a variety of visualization methods are deployed in the literature. We have developed an interactive user-friendly web-based interface for the recommender system. The interaction was divided into three basic steps:

1. Selecting the entity (client) the business user would like to analyze (see Fig. 5);
2. Rating feasibility of improvements (drop-down lists in Fig. 6);
3. Exploring the recommended improvement options (bubble chart in Fig. 6) and comments from raw data related to the chosen option (data table in Fig. 7).

Fig. 5. Javascript-based visualization for depicting clients' locations and their semantic neighbors. Also, it serves as an interface for further analysis of a chosen entity. (Color figure online)

The map in Fig. 5 serves as an interface for further analysis of the chosen client (amongst 38 in total). The current version of the interface allows for choosing recommendations based on the datasets from the years 2016 or 2015 and surveys on Service or Parts. The clients are represented as points (dots) placed in their headquarters' locations. The size of the dot informs about how many other clients were added to the original client's dataset to mine for actionable knowledge (see section on semantic similarity and HAMIS procedure). The connecting lines show the semantic neighbors. After clicking the client's dot, it changes color from blue to red and the corresponding semantic neighbors are highlighted in a red scale as well. The color scale corresponds to the strength of semantic similarity. Additionally, the number in parentheses denotes the sequence of semantic similarity to the current client. We have hidden client labels (text next to the dots) on the grounds of data confidentiality.

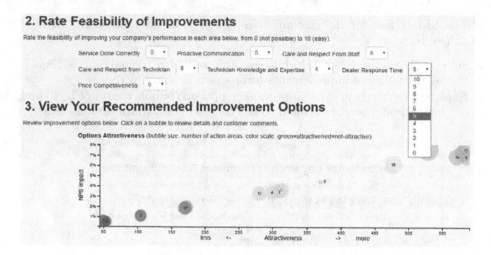

Fig. 6. Javascript-based interactive visualization for exploring recommendations options and their attractiveness based on chosen feasibility. (Color figure online)

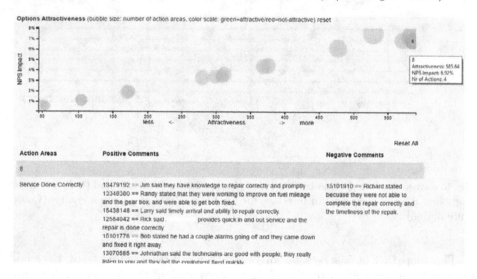

Fig. 7. Javascript-based dynamic data table for exploring raw data comments associated with the analyzed recommendation option.

The next step of interaction with the business user is exploring the recommendation options. The displayed options correspond to the extracted meta-actions (see the previous section) mined from text comments and summarized into aspect categories. The user (business consultant) can assign a feasibility score to each option based on dialogue with the currently analyzed client. For some clients some options might be more feasible that the others. For example, it might be quite difficult to change pricing, while it might relatively easier to change technician knowledge (for example, by introducing appropriate training).

The option's attractiveness depends on both factors: NPS improvement (calculated as described in the previous section based on the action rule and meta action mining) and feasibility chosen by the user. Each bubble (identified by an ordering number) corresponds to a different set of improvement options and they are ordered on the X-axis and the Y-axis according to their attractiveness (see Fig. 6). The most attractive options lie in the top right corner of the chart. The attractiveness is also denoted by the color scale - from red scale (unattractive) to green scale (attractive).

The user can choose the option and analyze it further (see Fig. 7): the highlighted bubble shows details on:

- number of actions included in the option;
- the quantified attractiveness (calculated as combination of feasibilities and NPS impact of single actions in the option);
- the combined overall NPS impact.

Furthermore, the data table shows raw text comments from customers associated with the particular areas (aspects), divided into negative and positive columns (see Fig. 7). Each comment can be investigated further by analyzing the whole survey and context in which it was expressed, as each comment is identified with Work Order ID.

8   Future Work

Currently, the system is driven by the knowledge extracted from questionnaires. Our plan is to make it adaptive to text-only data, as the structured forms of surveys will be replaced by open ended questionnaires in the future. Another challenge lies in the system's efficiency of mining processes and we need to develop new methods of optimizing them by using distributed environment.

In general, there are many industrial solutions developed in recent years that are based on aspect-based sentiment analysis and text analytics. However, we recognized that although a lot of work has been done in the research community in this area, the problem is still far from being solved. Also, the research focus has been mainly on electronic products, hotels and restaurants. There are still novel ideas needed to study different ranges of domains. Domain and context-dependent sentiments remain to be highly challenging. There is a need to build integrated systems that try to deal with different problems together in an interactive way. As of now, a completely automated and accurate solution is nowhere in sight. On the other hand, there is still a huge and real demand in industry for such systems because every business wants to know how customers perceive their services or products.

References

1. Kuang, J.: Hierarchically structured recommender system for improving NPS. The University of North Carolina at Charlotte, ProQuest Dissertations Publishing (2016)
2. Kuang, J., Raś, Z.W., Daniel, A.: Hierarchical agglomerative method for improving NPS. In: Kryszkiewicz, M., Bandyopadhyay, S., Rybinski, H., Pal, S.K. (eds.) PReMI 2015. LNCS, vol. 9124, pp. 54–64. Springer, Cham (2015). doi:10.1007/978-3-319-19941-2_6
3. Kuang, J., Raś, Z.W., Daniel, A.: Personalized meta-action mining for NPS improvement. In: Esposito, F., Pivert, O., Hacid, M.-S., Raś, Z.W., Ferilli, S. (eds.) ISMIS 2015. LNCS (LNAI), vol. 9384, pp. 79–87. Springer, Cham (2015). doi:10.1007/978-3-319-25252-0_9
4. Kuang, J., Raś, Z.W.: In search for best meta-actions to boost businesses revenue. Flexible Query Answering Systems 2015. AISC, vol. 400, pp. 431–443. Springer, Cham (2016). doi:10.1007/978-3-319-26154-6_33
5. Im, S., Ras, Z., Tsay, L.-S.: Action reducts. In: Kryszkiewicz, M., Rybinski, H., Skowron, A., Raś, Z.W. (eds.) ISMIS 2011. LNCS (LNAI), vol. 6804, pp. 62–69. Springer, Heidelberg (2011). doi:10.1007/978-3-642-21916-0_7
6. Tzacheva A., Ras Z.W.: Association action rules and action paths triggered by meta-actions. In: Proceedings of 2010 IEEE Conference on Granular Computing, Silicon Valley, CA. IEEE Computer Society, pp. 772–776 (2010)
7. Liu, B.: Sentiment analysis and subjectivity. In: Handbook of Natural Language Processing, vol. 2, pp. 627–666 (2010)
8. Marneffe M.D., Manning C.: Stanford typed dependencies manual. Technical report, Stanford University (2008)
9. Wang, K., Jiang, Y., Tuzhilin, A.: Mining actionable patterns by role models. In: Proceedings of the 22nd International Conference on Data Engineering. IEEE Computer Society, pp. 16–25 (2006)
10. Hu, M., Liu, B.: Mining and summarizing customer reviews. In: Proceedings of the Tenth ACM SIGKDD International Conference on Knowledge Discovery and Data Mining (KDD 2004), pp. 168–177, New York (2004)
11. Ras, Z.W., Wieczorkowska, A.: Action-rules: how to increase profit of a company. In: Zighed, D.A., Komorowski, J., Żytkow, J. (eds.) PKDD 2000. LNCS, vol. 1910, pp. 587–592. Springer, Heidelberg (2000). doi:10.1007/3-540-45372-5_70

The Multi-purpose Role of the Relational Approach to Classic and Generalized Approximation Spaces. A Tutorial

Piero Pagliani[✉]

Research Group on Knowledge Models, Roma, Italy
pier.pagliani@gmail.com

1 Introduction

Rough Set Theory is inherently connected with relations.

In its classical form, the theory is based on the intuition that objects (entities, observables) are linked by indiscernibility relations (equivalence relations) induced by the properties that are fulfilled by the objects.

This approach reflects the more general fact that the world is made of relations or, otherwise stated, that things and events are sheaves of relations. Indeed, since inception, classical Rough Set Theory was generalised using arbitrary binary relations, other than equivalence relations, and fuzzy relations as well.

In the tutorial we shall try and reconstruct most of Rough Set Theory on the basis of a very limited set of operations between relations. This setting makes it possible to achieve a number of goals, easily:

1. Comparing various approaches and generalisations.
2. Connecting Rough Set Theory and Logical Theories, especially Modal Logics.
3. Straightforwardly deriving the properties of a number of approximation operators.
4. Setting Rough Set Theory and its generalisations into the framework of pretopology and topology.
5. Easily describing functions for computing approximations and functional dependencies.
6. Expanding the scope of the approximation operators from simple sets to relations.

Since the proposed set of relational operations are easily implemented by programming languages, the tutorial will provide the audience with both a theoretically and practical framework to deal with rough sets.

2 Binary Relations and Their Basic Operations

Let $R \subseteq A \times B$ be a binary relation. From now on we shall denote the Boolean matrix corresponding to a relation R by $\mathbf{R}$.

© Springer International Publishing AG 2017
L. Polkowski et al. (Eds.): IJCRS 2017, Part I, LNAI 10313, pp. 49–57, 2017.
DOI: 10.1007/978-3-319-60837-2_5

Definition 1. *Let $R \subseteq A \times B$, $X \subseteq A$ and $Y \subseteq B$,*

1. $-R = \{\langle a, b \rangle : \langle a, b \rangle \notin R\}$ *is called the* complement *of R.*
2. $R^\smile = \{\langle b, a \rangle : \langle a, b \rangle \in R\}$ *is called the* reverse relation *of R.*
3. $R(X) = \{b \in B : \exists x(x \in X \wedge \langle x, b \rangle \in R)\}$ *is called the* left Peirce product *of R and X. Vice-versa, $R^\smile(Y)$ is called the* right Peirce product *of R and Y (or the* left Peirce product *of $R^\smile$ and Y).*

We call (A, B, R) a *relational system*. If $A = B$, then we call (A, A, R) (or simply (A, R)) a *square relational system, SRS*.

Definition 2. *Let $R \subseteq A \times B$ and $S \subseteq A' \times B'$ be such that $|B| = |A'|$, where $|...|$ is the cardinality of a set. Let ϕ be a bijection between B and A. Then,*

$$R \otimes_\phi S = \{\langle x, y \rangle \in A \times B' : \exists z(\langle x, z \rangle \in R \text{ and } \langle \phi(z), y \rangle \in S)\}.$$

$R \otimes_\phi S$ *is called the* composition *of R and S.*

Composition is simply the Boolean multiplication of matrices. Thus, to obtain $\mathbf{R} \otimes \mathbf{S}$ we multiply pointwise row i with column j; if the pointwise Boolean multiplication gives 1 for at least one point, then element at row i and column j of $\mathbf{R} \otimes \mathbf{S}$ is 1. It is 0 otherwise.

If $B = A'$ then we intend the identity as ϕ and omit the subscript of $\otimes$. Anyway, the bijection ϕ will be generally understood and omitted.

EXAMPLE 1. Let $A = \{a, b, c, d\}$, $B = \{e, f, g\}$, $A' = \{\alpha, \beta, \gamma\}$, $B' = \{\delta, \epsilon, \theta, \mu, \nu\}$, $\phi(e) = \alpha, \phi(f) = \beta, \phi(g) = \gamma$.

$\mathbf{R}$	e	f	g
a	1	1	1
b	0	1	1
c	0	0	1
d	1	0	0

$\mathbf{S}$	δ	ϵ	θ	μ	ν
α	1	1	1	0	0
β	0	0	0	1	1
γ	0	1	0	0	1

$\mathbf{R} \otimes \mathbf{S}$	δ	ϵ	θ	μ	ν
a	1	1	1	1	1
b	0	1	0	1	1
c	0	1	0	0	1
d	1	1	1	0	0

Definition 3. *Let $X \subseteq A$. Then $X^C = X \times B = \{\langle x, a \rangle : x \in X \wedge a \in B\}$ is called the* right cylinder *of X.*

Right cylinders will be used in SRS in order to represent sets in a relational guise.

Now we can introduce two fundamental operations.

Definition 4. *Assume $R \subseteq A \times B$ and $S \subseteq A' \times B'$.*

$$R \longrightarrow S = -(R^\smile \otimes -S), \text{ right residuation of } S \text{ with respect to } R. \tag{1}$$

$$S \longleftarrow R = -(-S \otimes R^\smile), \quad \text{left residuation of } S \text{ with respect to } R. \tag{2}$$

The operation (1) is defined only if $|A| = |A'|$; (2) is defined only if $|B| = |B'|$. In particular, if R and S are binary relations on a set U, then (see [10]):

$$R \longrightarrow S = \{\langle a, b \rangle \in U \times U : \forall c \in U(\langle c, a \rangle \in R \Longrightarrow \langle c, b \rangle \in S)\} \tag{3}$$

$$S \longleftarrow R = \{\langle a, b \rangle \in U \times U : \forall c \in U(\langle b, c \rangle \in R \Longrightarrow \langle a, c \rangle \in S)\} \tag{4}$$

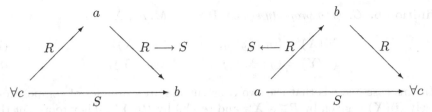

It can be shown that $R \longrightarrow S$, is the largest relation Z on U such that $R \otimes Z \subseteq S$, while $S \longleftarrow R$, is the largest relation Z such that $Z \otimes R \subseteq S$.

3   Intensional and Extensional Constructors

Suppose now that $R \subseteq G \times M$ is a relation connecting objects in G with properties in M. That is, if $\langle g, m \rangle \in R$, then g fulfils m. We call $\mathbf{P} = \langle G, M, R \rangle$ a *property system.*

Given a subset X of G it is important to know the properties which *necessarily* and *exclusively* are fulfilled by the elements of X. They are the properties which are fulfilled at most by the elements of X. Vice-versa, given a subset Y of properties, one is interested to the set of the objects which fulfil at most the properties from Y:

Definition 5. *Let* $\mathbf{P} = \langle U, M, R \rangle$ *be a property system,* $X \subseteq G, Y \subseteq M$:

$$[i](X) = \{m : \forall g(\langle g, m \rangle \in R \Longrightarrow g \in X)\} \tag{5}$$

$$[e](Y) = \{g : \forall m(\langle g, m \rangle \in R \Longrightarrow m \in Y)\} \tag{6}$$

$[i](X)$ is the necessary intension of X, while $[e](Y)$ is the necessary extension of Y. It is straightforward to see that they are cases of right residuations.

EXAMPLE 2. Consider the relation R of Example 1. Let $X = \{a, b, c\}$. Let us denote by $\mathbf{X^C}$ the matrix representing its right cylinder[1]. Here is how $[i](X)$ is computed:

$\mathbf{X^C}$	e f g		$-\mathbf{X^C}$	e f g		$R^\smile$	a b c d		$R^\smile \otimes -\mathbf{X^C}$	e f g
a	1 1 1		a	0 0 0		e	1 0 0 1		e	1 1 1
b	1 1 1		b	0 0 0		f	1 1 0 0		f	0 0 0
c	1 1 1		c	0 0 0		g	1 1 1 0		g	0 0 0
d	0 0 0		d	1 1 1						

Therefore the right cylinder of $[i](X)$ is $-(\mathbf{R^\smile} \otimes -\mathbf{X^C})$ which represents the set $\{f, g\}$.

A couple of dual constructors can be defined to compute the properties which *possibly* are fulfilled by the elements of $X \subseteq G$, that is, the properties such that are fulfilled by at least an element from X. Conversely, one can compute the entities which fulfil at least one property from a set $Y \subseteq M$:

---

[1] If the cylindrification of X is given by $X \times M$, then $[i](X)$ is a right cylinder subset of $M \times M$. If the cylindrification of X is $X \times G$, then $[i](X)$ is a right cylinder subset of $M \times G$. Similar considerations apply to $[e](X)$.

Definition 6. *Given a property system* $\mathbf{P} = \langle G, M, R \rangle$, $X \subseteq G, Y \subseteq M$:

$$\langle i \rangle(X) = \{m : \exists g(\langle g, m \rangle \in R \wedge g \in X)\} \tag{7}$$
$$\langle e \rangle(Y) = \{g : \exists m(\langle g, m \rangle \in R \wedge m \in Y)\} \tag{8}$$

In this case one has that the two constructors are examples of composition. Namely $\langle i \rangle(X)$ is given by $R^\smile \otimes X^C$ and $\langle e \rangle(Y)$ by $R \otimes Y^C$. They represent the left Peirce product $R(X)$ and $R^\smile(Y)$, respectively.

EXAMPLE 3. Consider again the relation R of Example 1. Let $X = \{c, d\}$ and $Y = \{e, f\}$. We have:

$\mathbf{X}^C$	e f g		$\mathbf{R}^\smile \otimes \mathbf{X}^C$	e f g		$\mathbf{Y}^C$	a b c d		$\mathbf{R} \otimes \mathbf{Y}^C$	a b c d
a	0 0 0		e	1 1 1		e	1 1 1 1		a	1 1 1 1
b	0 0 0		f	0 0 0		f	1 1 1 1		b	1 1 1 1
c	1 1 1		g	1 1 1		g	0 0 0 0		c	0 0 0 0
d	1 1 1								d	1 1 1 1

Therefore, $\langle i \rangle(X) = \{e, g\}$ while $\langle e \rangle(Y) = \{a, b, d\}$.

4   Duality and Adjointness

It is evident that $\langle e \rangle$ and $[e]$, on the one side, and $\langle i \rangle$ and $[i]$ on the other side, are dual, in that $\langle e \rangle(X) = -[e](-X)$ and $\langle i \rangle(Y) = -[i](-Y)$. This can be easily proved by means of the logical equivalences $\neg \exists \equiv \forall \neg$ and $\neg(A \wedge \neg B) \equiv A \Longrightarrow B$. But one can also verify the duality by means of the equation $\langle e \rangle(X) = --(R^\smile \otimes --X^C) = -[e](-X^C)$, and so on.

But these constructors are connected by a more important property. Indeed, given a property system $\mathbf{P} = \langle G, M, R \rangle$, for any $X \subseteq G, Y \subseteq M$:

$$\langle i \rangle(X) \subseteq Y \quad iff \quad X \subseteq [e](Y) \tag{9}$$
$$\langle e \rangle(Y) \subseteq X \quad iff \quad Y \subseteq [i](X) \tag{10}$$

This means that $\langle \uparrow \rangle$ is *lower adjoint* of $[\downarrow]$, where the two arrows signify the opposite direction of the constructors. The proof comes straightforwardly from the following important logical considerations:

$$\langle \cdot \rangle \ \ has \ the \ form \ \exists \wedge. \tag{11}$$
$$[\cdot] \ \ has \ the \ form \ \forall \Longrightarrow. \tag{12}$$
$$\exists \ is \ adjoint \ of \ \forall \ and \ \wedge \ is \ adjoint \ of \Longrightarrow \tag{13}$$

In view of the adjoint property, many and various consequences follow:

1. $[\cdot]$ are multiplicative while $\langle \cdot \rangle$ are additive.
2. $[\cdot]$ and $\langle \cdot \rangle$ are monotonic.
3. $[e](M) = G$ (e-co-normality), $[i](G) = M$ (i-co-normality) and $\langle \cdot \rangle(\emptyset) = \emptyset$ (e-i-normality).

4. $\langle \cdot \rangle (A \cap B) \subseteq \langle \cdot \rangle (A) \cap \langle \cdot \rangle (B)$ and $[\cdot](A \cup B) \supseteq [\cdot](A) \cup [\cdot](B)$.
5. The combination $\langle \uparrow \rangle [\downarrow]$ is an interior operator (that is, decreasing, monotonic and idempotent) and $[\uparrow]\langle \downarrow \rangle$ is a closure operator (that is, increasing, monotonic and idempotent).

Let us then define the following operators, for all $X \subseteq G, Y \subseteq M$:

$$(a)\ \ int(X) = \langle e \rangle ([i](X)) \qquad\qquad (b)\ \ cl(X) = [e](\langle i \rangle (X)). \qquad (14)$$
$$(c)\ \ \mathcal{A}(Y) = [i](\langle e \rangle (Y)) \qquad\qquad (d)\ \ \mathcal{C}(Y) = \langle i \rangle ([e](Y)). \qquad (15)$$

Notice that int and cl map $\wp(G)$ on $\wp(G)$, while $\mathcal{A}$ and $\mathcal{C}$ map $\wp(M)$ on $\wp(M)$.

From 5 above we have that int and $\mathcal{C}$ are interior operators, while cl and $\mathcal{A}$ are closure operators. However, in general they are not topological. Indeed, int and $\mathcal{C}$ are not multiplicative, because the external constructor $\langle \cdot \rangle$ is not, and cl and $\mathcal{A}$ are not additive, because the external constructor $[\cdot]$ is not. Moreover, int and $\mathcal{C}$ may fail to be co-normal, while cl and $\mathcal{A}$ may fail to be normal.

EXAMPLE 3. Consider the property system $\langle G, M, R \rangle$ where $G = \{a, b, c\}$, $M = \{\alpha, \beta, \gamma, \delta\}$ and $R = \{\langle b, \alpha \rangle, \langle b, \beta \rangle, \langle b, \gamma \rangle \langle c, \gamma \rangle, \langle c, \delta \rangle\}$. Trivially, $\langle e \rangle (\emptyset) = \emptyset$ and $[e](M) = G$, since for any subset X of G, $X \cap \emptyset = \emptyset$ and, by definition, $X \subseteq G$. A little bit less trivial is, for instance, that $[e](\emptyset) = \{a\} \neq \emptyset$ or $\langle e \rangle (M) = \{b, c\} \neq G$. But $R(a) = \emptyset$, thus $R(a) \subseteq \emptyset$ and $R(a) \cap M = \emptyset$. One can easily verify that: $\langle e \rangle (\{\alpha, \beta, \gamma\}) = \{b, c\}$, $[e](\{\alpha, \gamma, \delta\}) = \{a, c\}$, $[i](\{a, c\}) = \{\delta\}$, $[i](\{b, c\}) = M$, $\langle e \rangle (\{\delta\}) = \{c\}$, $\langle i \rangle (\{b, c\}) = M$. Consequently, $int(\{a, c\}) = \{c\}$, $cl(\{b, c\}) = M$, $\mathcal{A}(\{\alpha, \beta, \gamma\}) = M$ and $\mathcal{C}(\{\alpha, \gamma, \delta\}) = \{\gamma, \delta\}$.

5 Relational Constructors and Operators Vs Approximations

Notice, that in a SRS system $\langle U, R \rangle$, for $x \in U$ the left Peirce product $R(\{x\})$ is what in Rough Set Theory is called a *granule*. We shall denote it by $R(x)$ and call it *R-neighbourhood* of x, too.

Let $\langle U, R \rangle$ be any SRS. As is well-known the generalised lower and upper approximations (lR) and (uR) are defined as follows, for all $X \subseteq U$:

$$(lR)(X) = \{x : R(x) \subseteq X\}; \qquad (uR)(X) = \{x : R(x) \cap X \neq \emptyset\} \qquad (16)$$

In view of (6) and (8) one can easily verify that $(uR)(X) = \langle e \rangle (X)$ and $(lR)(X) = [e](X)$. Thus from the above observations, we know some important basic facts: generalised lower approximation operators are upper adjoints, thus multiplicative, monotonic and co-normal, while generalised upper approximation operators are lower adjoints, thus additive, monotonic and normal.

Indeed, additional properties depend on the properties of the relation R. For instance, if R is reflexive, then (uR) is increasing and (lR) is decreasing.

If R is at least a preorder (transitive and reflexive), then for any $X \subseteq U$, $[e](X) = \mathcal{C}(X)$, $[i](X) = int(X)$, $\langle e \rangle (X) = \mathcal{A}(X)$ and $\langle i \rangle (X) = cl(X)$.

It follows that in this case we are in the presence of topological interior and closure operators. Since (lR) coincides with $[e]$, hence $\mathcal{A}$, and (uR) with $\langle e \rangle$, hence with $\mathcal{C}$, the structure $\langle U, (lR) \rangle$ is a topological space with interior operator (lR) and closure (uR).

In particular, if R is an equivalence relation, the topological space is 0-dimensional, that is, a space made of sets which are closed and open, or clopen. This is the classical situation devised by Z. Pawlak.

EXAMPLE 4. Let the Boolean matrix $\mathbf{R}$ below represent the SRS $\langle U, R \rangle$, where $U = \{a, b, c, d\}$:

$\mathbf{R}$	a	b	c	d
a	1	1	1	1
b	0	1	0	1
c	0	0	1	0
d	0	0	0	1

$$int(\{d, a\}) = \langle e \rangle [i](\{d, a\}) = \langle e \rangle(\{a\}) = \{a\}.$$
$$cl(\{d, a\}) = [e]\langle i \rangle(\{d, a\}) = [e](U) = U.$$
$$\mathcal{C}(\{d, a\}) = \langle i \rangle [e](\{d, a\}) = \langle i \rangle(\{d\}) = \{d\}.$$
$$\mathcal{A}(\{d, a\}) = [i]\langle e \rangle(\{d, a\}) = [i](\{a, b, d\}) = \{a, b, d\}.$$

It is worth noticing that int and cl are the interior, respectively closure operators of the Alexandrov topology induced by the preorder $R^{\smile}$, while $\mathcal{C}$ and $\mathcal{A}$ are the interior, respectively closure operators of the Alexandrov topology induced by the preorder R.

On the contrary, if R is not at least a preorder, one obtains various kinds of *pre-topological spaces*, that is, spaces in which (lR) and (uR) fulfill weaker properties than their topological companions.

However, in Modal Logics with Kripke models the definition of the constructor $\langle e \rangle$ is the same as that of the modalization $\Diamond$ (*possibility*) and $[e]$ is the same as the *necessity* modalization $\Box$. Indeed, given a set of possible worlds W and an accessibility relation between them R, for any formula α:

$$w \models \Box(\alpha) \text{ iff } \forall w'(\langle w, w' \rangle \in R \Longrightarrow w' \models \alpha). \tag{17}$$

$$w \models \Diamond(\alpha) \text{ iff } \exists w'(\langle w, w' \rangle \in R \wedge w' \models \alpha) \tag{18}$$

If one considers instead of the formula α its set of validity $[\![\alpha]\!]$ so that $w' \in [\![\alpha]\!]$ stays for $w' \models \alpha$, one obtains that $[\![\Box(\alpha)]\!] = [e]([\![\alpha]\!])$ and $[\![\Diamond(\alpha)]\!] = \langle e \rangle([\![\alpha]\!])$.

Therefore, the results in Kripkean modal logics may be applied to generalized approximations almost for free, thus avoiding useless efforts.

6 Further Applications

6.1 Covering-Based Rough Sets

A covering of a set U is a family $C \subseteq \wp(U)$ such that $\bigcup C = U$. A family $\mathcal{G}_R(U) = \{R(x) : x \in U\}$ of R-neighbourhoods may form a covering of U (for sure if R is reflexive or if for all $x \in U$ there is an x' such that $\langle x', x \rangle \in R$, that is, if R is onto). Coverings, moreover, may occur from observations without being induced by any binary relation necessarily. This fact launched a long series of studies about covering-based rough sets, which is still a reach vein of research.

Indeed, different lower and upper approximations can be defined from a covering of a set U. In some cases, however, granules are manipulated in order to recover bases for topological spaces, and this manipulations may miss the added value of the granulation at hand, even if they induce operators fulfilling the nice properties of the topological operators.

We shall see how the relational machinery can be helpful in this approach and simplify it. Below we give an example.

If one set for $x \in U$ and $K \in C$, $\langle x, K \rangle \in R$ iff $x \in K$, then one obtains a property system $\mathbf{C} = \langle U, C, R \rangle$. Let int be defined on $\mathbf{C}$. The following operator was introduced in [15] and studied by Bonikowski, Zhu and others: $\underline{C_1}(X) = \bigcup \{ K \in C : K \subseteq X \}$. It is straightforward to prove that $\underline{C_1} = int$. Therefore, its dual operator $\overline{C_1}$ coincides with cl. From this observation all the properties of $\underline{C_1}$ and $\overline{C_1}$ are provided for free by the adjunction properties introduced above[2].

For a comprehensive application to covering-based rough sets of the constructor and operators introduced above, see [8].

6.2   Approximation of Relations

An n-ary *Relational Approximation Space* is a tuple $RA(U) = \langle U, Z, {}^n Z \rangle$, where $U = \{U_i\}_{1 \le i \le n}$ is a family of sets, $Z = \{Z_i\}_{1 \le i \le n}$ is a family of binary relations such that for any $1 \le i \le n$, $Z_i \subseteq U_i \times U_i$ and a modalizing relation ${}^n Z$ is point-wise defined on $\prod_{i=1}^{n} U_i$ by: $\langle \langle x_1, ..., x_n \rangle, \langle y_1, ..., y_n \rangle \rangle \in {}^n Z$ iff $\langle x_i, y_i \rangle \in Z_i$, all i. Thus for any $R \subseteq \prod_{i=1}^{n} U_i$, we set:

$$(l \, {}^n Z)(R) = \{ \langle x_1, ..., x_n \rangle : \forall \langle y_1, ..., y_n \rangle (\langle \langle x_1, ..., x_n \rangle, \langle y_1, ..., y_n \rangle \rangle \in {}^n Z \implies \langle y_1, ..., y_n \rangle \in R \}.$$

In particular, when all Z_i are equivalence relations, under some constraints we obtain the notion introduced in [13]. If, moreover, $U_i = U_j$, and $Z_i = Z_j$ for all i, j, we obtain the *Generalized Approximation Spaces* studied in [6] where a modal relational characterization for the case $n = 2$, was given.

With a slight modification of that result, one can prove that for any binary Relational Approximation Space $\langle U, Z, {}^2 Z \rangle$, for any $R \subseteq U_1 \times U_2$, $(l \, {}^2 Z)(R) = (Z_1^{\smile} \longrightarrow R) \longleftarrow Z_2$ (which is the same as $Z_1^{\smile} \longrightarrow (R \longleftarrow Z_2)$; that is, we can change the temporal but not the spatial application order of the two residuations).

In particular when $\langle U, Z, {}^2 Z \rangle$ is a Generalized Approximation Space, then we have the case discussed in [2] and in [3], for which the following holds (see [6]): for any binary Relational Approximation Space $\langle U, Z, {}^2 Z \rangle$ such that $U_1 = U_2$ and $Z_1 = Z_2$ is an equivalence relation, for any $R \subseteq U_1 \times U_1$:

$$(l \, {}^2 Z)(R) = Z_1 \longrightarrow R \longleftarrow Z_1.$$

---

[2] Our argument proves that the dual of $\underline{C_1}(X)$ is not the operator X^* introduced in [1], in an elementary but analytic way without using counterexamples.

6.3   Dependency Relations

In Rough Set Theory, dependency relations deserve a noticeable role. In an Information System $IS = (U, At, v)$ on a set of items U, with set of attributes At and evaluation function v, if A and B are subsets of attributes, it is important to know whether the indiscernibility relation E_B induced by B functionally depends on that induced by A, E_A. This is the case if the granules of E_A are finer than the granules of E_B, that is, if for any granule $[x]_{E_A}$ there is a granule $[y]_{E_B}$ such that $[x]_{E_A} \subseteq [y]_{E_B}$, for $x, y \in U$. Since we are dealing with equivalence relations, one can set $x = y$. More precisely:

1. An element $u \in U$ is said to fulfil the functional dependency $A \mapsto B$, and we write $A \mapsto_u B$, if and only if $E_A(u) \subseteq E_B(u)$.
2. By $FD(A, B)$ we denote the set $\{u \in U : A \mapsto_u B\}$, that is the set of all the elements of U fulfilling the functional dependency we are dealing with.
3. A subset B of attributes is said to be functionally dependent on A, $A \mapsto B$, if $FD(A, B) = U$.

It is proved that for any Information System $IS = (U, At, v)$, $A, B \subseteq At$

$$(E_A \longrightarrow E_B) \longleftarrow E_A)) \otimes \mathbf{1} = FD(A, B)^c$$

where, we recall, $FD(A, B)^c$ is the right cylindrification of the required set $FD(A, B)$. So we can compute functional dependencies between sets of attributes by means of the fundamental operations of Relation Algebra.

Moreover, approximation of relations can be used to compute functional dependencies between granules from arbitrary binary relations.

References

1. Bonikowski, Z., Bryniarski, E., Wybraniec-Skardowska, U.: Extensions and intensions in the rough set theory. Inf. Sci. **107**, 149–167 (1998)
2. Comer, S.: On connections between information systems, rough sets and algebraic logic. In: Algebraic Methods in Logic and Computer Science, vol. 28. Banach Center Publications (1993)
3. Düntsch, I.: Rough sets and algebras. In: Orlowska, E. (ed.) Incomplete Information: Rough Set Analysis, pp. 95–108. Physica-Verlag, Heidelberg (1997)
4. Düntsch, I., Gegida, G.: Modal-style operators in qualitative data analysis. In: Proceedings of the 2002 IEEE International Conference on Data Mining, pp. 155–162 (2002)
5. Huang, A., Zhu, W.: Topological characterizations for three covering approximation operators. In: Ciucci, D., Inuiguchi, M., Yao, Y., Ślęzak, D., Wang, G. (eds.) RSFDGrC 2013. LNCS, vol. 8170, pp. 277–284. Springer, Heidelberg (2013). doi:10. 1007/978-3-642-41218-9_30
6. Pagliani, P.: A modal relation algebra for generalized approximation spaces. In Tsumoto S., Kobayashi S., Yokomori T., Tanaka H., Nakamura A. (eds.) Proceedings of the Fourth Int. Workshop on Rough Sets, Fuzzy Sets, and Machine Discovery, 6–8 November 1996. The University of Tokyo (1996)

7. Pagliani, P.: A practical introduction to the modal relational approach to Approximation Spaces. In: Polkowski, L., Skowron, A. (eds.) Rough Sets in Knowledge Discovery, pp. 209–232. Physica-Verlag, Heidelberg (1998)
8. Pagliani, P.: Covering rough sets and formal topology – a uniform approach through intensional and extensional constructors. In: Peters, J.F., Skowron, A. (eds.) Transactions on Rough Sets XX. LNCS, vol. 10020, pp. 109–145. Springer, Heidelberg (2016). doi:10.1007/978-3-662-53611-7_4
9. Pagliani, P., Chakraborty, M.K.: Information quanta and approximation spaces. I: non-classical approximation operators. In: Proceedings of the IEEE International Conference on Granular Computing, Beijing, China, 25–27, vol. 2, July 2005, pp. 605–610. IEEE Los Alamitos (2005)
10. Pagliani, P., Chakraborty, M.K.: A geometry of Approximation. Trends in Logic, vol. 27. Springer, Heidelberg (2008)
11. Qin, K., Gao, Y., Pei, Z.: On covering rough sets. In: Yao, J.T., Lingras, P., Wu, W.-Z., Szczuka, M., Cercone, N.J., Ślęzak, D. (eds.) RSKT 2007. LNCS, vol. 4481, pp. 34–41. Springer, Heidelberg (2007). doi:10.1007/978-3-540-72458-2_4
12. Sambin, G., Gebellato, S.: A preview of the basic picture: a new perspective on formal topology. In: Altenkirch, T., Reus, B., Naraschewski, W. (eds.) TYPES 1998. LNCS, vol. 1657, pp. 194–208. Springer, Heidelberg (1999). doi:10.1007/3-540-48167-2_14
13. Skowron, A., Stepaniuk, J.: Approximation of relations. In: Ziarko, W. (ed.) Rough Sets, Fuzzy Sets and Knowledge Discovery, pp. 161–166. Springer, Heidelberg (1994)
14. Yao, Y.Y., Chen, Y.H.: Rough set approximations in formal concept analysis. In: Proceedings of 2004 Annual Meeting of the North American Fuzzy Information Processing Society (NAFIPS 2004), pp. 73–78. IEEE Catalog Number: 04TH8736 (2004)
15. Zakowski, W.: Approximations in the space (U, Π). Demonstratio Mathematic **16**, 761–769 (1983)

General Rough Sets

Heterogeneous Approximate Reasoning with Graded Truth Values

Francesco Luca De Angelis[1], Giovanna Di Marzo Scrugendo[1],
Barbara Dunin-Kęplicz[2], and Andrzej Szałas[2,3(✉)]

[1] Institute of Services Science, University of Geneva, 1227 Carouge, Switzerland
{francesco.deangelis,giovanna.dimarzo}@unige.ch
[2] Institute of Informatics, University of Warsaw,
ul. Banacha 2, 02-097 Warsaw, Poland
{keplicz,andrzej.szalas}@mimuw.edu.pl
[3] Department of Computer and Information Science, Linköping University,
581 83 Linköping, Sweden

Abstract. This paper is devoted to paraconsistent approximate reasoning with graded truth-values. In the previous research we introduced a family of many-valued logics parameterized by a variable number of truth/falsity grades together with a corresponding family of rule languages with tractable query evaluation. Such grades are shown here to be a natural qualitative counterpart of quantitative measures used in various forms of approximate reasoning. The developed methodology allows one to obtain a framework unifying heterogeneous reasoning techniques, providing also the logical machinery to resolve partial and incoherent information that may arise after unification. Finally, we show the introduced framework in action, emphasizing its expressiveness in handling heterogeneous approximate reasoning in realistic scenarios.

Keywords: Graded truth-values · Approximate reasoning · Paraconsistent reasoning · Rule-based languages

1 Introduction and Motivations

Contemporary intelligent systems acquiring data from multiple information sources have to cope with incomplete and potentially inconsistent information of different reliability levels. Also, when heterogeneous techniques are involved in reasoning, their relative strengths may vary: conclusions based on sure facts and certain rules are typically stronger than those obtained from heuristic non-monotonic rules. In addition, perception heavily depends on sensor platforms with different accuracy. Therefore, the resulting model of the environment is an approximation of the perceived reality. Major methodologies addressing such imperfect models are based on approximate reasoning, like those originating from fuzzy sets (see, e.g., [2,3,12–14,23,26,30–32]) or rough sets (see, e.g., [8–10,15,18,19,21,22,24,25,27–29]). Such a variety of methods calls for integration tools resulting in truly heterogeneous approximate reasoning.

© Springer International Publishing AG 2017
L. Polkowski et al. (Eds.): IJCRS 2017, Part I, LNAI 10313, pp. 61–82, 2017.
DOI: 10.1007/978-3-319-60837-2_6

In previous works [7] we have introduced and investigated a paraconsistent and paracomplete logic with graded truth values together with a corresponding family of rule languages, RL^N, with tractable query evaluation. These tools are based on a family of paraconsistent many-valued logics supporting both monotonic and non-monotonic reasoning. The combination of those many-valued logics, together with RL^N, allows both for modelling uncertain and inconsistent information as well as for appropriate aggregation of information originating from multiple sources. The many-valued logic developing paraconsistency in [7] provides several logical values for truthfulness, falseness and inconsistency, selected from a finite but arbitrarily large set of truth-degrees reflecting relative strengths of techniques involved in reasoning.

Given an integer $N \geq 1$, we consider the following truth-degrees:

- degrees of truth: $t_1, \ldots, t_N$, where t_1 is the weakest and t_N the strongest truth;
- degrees of falsity: $f_1, \ldots, f_N$, where f_1 is the weakest and f_N the strongest falsity;
- degrees of inconsistency: $i_{1,1} \ldots, i_{N,N}$, where $i_{i,j}$ is the inconsistency level involving t_i and f_j;
- unknown: u.

RL^N accommodates positive and negative literals both in premises and conclusions of rules and is based on the Open World Assumption. Moreover, introspection operators provide a machinery for non-monotonic reasoning, in particular for closing the world locally and globally and for resolving inconsistent information. Other paraconsistent approaches are discussed, e.g., in [1,4,6,10,17,20].

Our goal is to show that RL^N, presented in [7], and the corresponding family of many-valued logics constitute a powerful tool to encompass various forms of approximate reasoning, simultaneously combining, in a uniform framework, various techniques and methodologies developed for approximate reasoning (see Fig. 1(a)). We demonstrate that many approximate reasoning methods, that have been developed in the literature, can be integrated with RL^N by providing suitable interpretations of values associated with membership of elements in sets (or satisfaction of formulas by such elements). Therefore we argue that the language together with the developed methodology provide a step towards full heterogeneity of approximate reasoning. Let us stress that RL^N is not meant to substitute approximate reasoning techniques. We view the language as an integrating umbrella, gathering results from other reasoning engines and allowing one to derive improved or entirely new conclusions.

Paper Structure

The paper is structured as follows. In Sect. 2, we briefly recall the family of logics introduced in [7] and continue, in Sect. 3, with indicating relationships of graded truth-values to approximate reasoning based on fuzzy sets and rough sets. Section 4 recalls the family of rule languages RL^N. In Sect. 5 we show case studies illustrating the use of our language in heterogeneous approximate reasoning. Finally, Sect. 6 concludes the paper.

While Sects. 2 and 4 mainly recall solutions from [7], Sects. 3 and 5 present a novel material.

2   The Family of Logics

Let us now recall the family of logics introduced in [7].

For $N \geq 1$, $\tau_N \overset{\text{def}}{=} \{0, 1, ..., N\} \times \{0, 1, ..., N\}$. Elements of τ_N denote truth-values. For the sake of clarity, we adopt the following notation, where $1 \leq i, j \leq N$:

$$\boldsymbol{u} \overset{\text{def}}{=} (0,0), \boldsymbol{t}_i \overset{\text{def}}{=} (i,0), \boldsymbol{f}_i \overset{\text{def}}{=} (0,i), \boldsymbol{i}_{i,j} \overset{\text{def}}{=} (i,j). \tag{1}$$

Semantics of rules requires two orderings on truth values on τ_N: the knowledge partial order, to manage information at the level of multiple information sources, and the truth-partial order, to perform computations on the information of a single source.

Definition 1. *Knowledge ordering*, $\leq_k$, is the transitive closure of the binary relation $\leq^k$, defined by:

$$(i, j) \leq^k (p, q) \text{ if } i \leq j \text{ and } p \leq q \tag{2}$$

Truth-ordering, $\leq_t$, is the reflexive and transitive closure of the binary relation $\leq^t$, defined by:

$$
\begin{aligned}
&(0, i) \leq^t (0, j) \leq^t (0, 0) \leq^t (k, l) \leq^t (m, 0) \leq^t (n, 0), \\
&\qquad \text{for } 1 \leq j \leq i \leq N, 1 \leq k, l \leq N, 1 \leq m \leq n \leq N, \\
&(i, j) \leq^t (p, q) \quad \text{if } (i = p + 1 \text{ and } j = q) \text{ or } (i = p \text{ and } j = q + 1).
\end{aligned}
\tag{3}
$$

$\lhd$

With respect to knowledge ordering we obtain: (i) $\boldsymbol{u} \leq_k \tau$ for all $\tau \in \tau_N$ as it represents the absence of information; (ii) $\boldsymbol{t}_i$ and $\boldsymbol{f}_j$ are never comparable in terms of ammount of information; (iii) $\boldsymbol{t}_i \leq_k \boldsymbol{i}_{p,q}$ and $\boldsymbol{f}_j \leq_k \boldsymbol{i}_{p,q}$ for all $i \leq p$ and $j \leq q$ as the inconsistent value contains more information than the true and false truth-degrees.

The definition of truth-ordering states that:

$$
\begin{aligned}
&\boldsymbol{f}_i \leq_t \boldsymbol{f}_j \leq_t \boldsymbol{u} \leq_t \boldsymbol{i}_{p,q} \leq_t \boldsymbol{t}_m \leq_t \boldsymbol{t}_n \\
&\qquad \text{for } 1 \leq j \leq i \leq N, 1 \leq p, q \leq N, 1 \leq m \leq n \leq N, \\
&\boldsymbol{i}_{i,j} \leq_t \boldsymbol{i}_{p,q} \text{ iff } \boldsymbol{i}_{p,q} \leq_k \boldsymbol{i}_{i,j}, \text{ for } 1 \leq p \leq i \leq N \text{ and } 1 \leq q \leq j \leq N.
\end{aligned}
\tag{4}
$$

With respect to truth-ordering we obtain: (i) $\boldsymbol{f}_N$ is less true than $\boldsymbol{f}_{N-1}, \ldots, \boldsymbol{f}_2$, being less true than $\boldsymbol{f}_1$; (ii) *unknown* ($\boldsymbol{u}$) is less false than all $\boldsymbol{f}_i$ and less true than all $\boldsymbol{i}_{i,j}$, $\boldsymbol{t}_k$; (iii) all $\boldsymbol{i}_{i,j}$ are more true than $\boldsymbol{u}$ and less true than $\boldsymbol{t}_k$ (they have a negative component grater than zero); (iv) $\boldsymbol{t}_1$ is less true than $\boldsymbol{t}_2, \ldots, \boldsymbol{t}_{N-1}$ being less true than $\boldsymbol{t}_N$.

Notice that $\langle \tau_N, \leq_k \rangle$ and $\langle \tau_N, \leq_t \rangle$ are complete lattices, in particular:

$$\mathrm{glb}_k\{(i,j),(p,q)\} = (min\{i,p\}, min\{j,q\}),$$
$$\mathrm{lub}_k\{(i,j),(p,q)\} = (max\{i,p\}, max\{j,q\}),$$

where glb stands for the greatest lower bound and lub for the lowest upper bound w.r.t. the specified partial order.

From Definition 1 one can derive specific instances of truth-degrees; for example, Fig. 1(b) and (c) show the lattices for the instance τ_3.

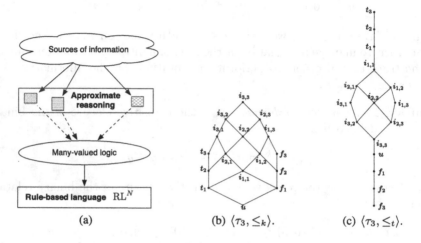

Fig. 1. (a) Presented methodology. (b) and (c): partial orders for τ_3.

Given $\{a_1, ..., a_n\} \subseteq \tau_N$ (with $n \geq 2$), we define the following logical connectives:

$$a_1 \wedge_t \ldots \wedge_t a_n \stackrel{def}{=} \mathrm{glb}_t\{a_1, ..., a_n\}, \quad a_1 \vee_t \ldots \vee_t a_n \stackrel{def}{=} \mathrm{lub}_t\{a_1, ..., a_n\}$$
$$a_1 \wedge_k \ldots \wedge_k a_n \stackrel{def}{=} \mathrm{glb}_k\{a_1, ..., a_n\}, \quad a_1 \vee_k \ldots \vee_k a_n \stackrel{def}{=} \mathrm{lub}_k\{a_1, ..., a_n\}.$$

We also define $\neg(i,j) \stackrel{def}{=} (j,i)$ and the material implication:

$$a \Rightarrow_k b \stackrel{def}{=} \begin{cases} \boldsymbol{t}_N & \text{if } a \leq_k b \\ & \text{or } a = \boldsymbol{f}_i \text{ for some } 1 \leq i \leq N; \\ \boldsymbol{f}_N & \text{otherwise.} \end{cases} \qquad (5)$$

The implication $\Rightarrow_k$ is an extension of the classical two-valued implication connective: it reflects the intuition of gathering new knowledge passing from the antecedent to the consequent. That is, we solely derive conclusions containing a non-zero truth component.

3   Relationship to Approximate Reasoning

RL^N can accommodate several forms of approximate reasoning, depending on the interpretation of the introduced truth-values as a qualitative counterpart of approximate reasoning techniques. Below we introduce some of them, perhaps the most natural ones. In the sequel, U denotes the universe of considered elements.

3.1   Deriving Truth-Degrees from Fuzzy Values

Fuzzy set-based reasoning [30–32] is frequently used as a basis for decision making. It belongs to a larger area of quantitative approaches to reasoning, like those concentrated around models involving probability, credibility and plausibility, possibility and necessity, degrees of belief and disbelief (mass distributions), fuzzy truth-degrees (see [16,23]). In many application areas it is natural to assume that truth-degrees of a property and its complement sum up to 1 [13,14,16,23,31].

A natural way to understand τ_N in the context of fuzzy reasoning, where inconsistencies are not explicitly present, is to select $2*N$ pairwise disjoint subintervals $\iota_N^f, \ldots, \iota_1^f, \iota_1^t, \ldots \iota_N^t$ from the interval $[0,1]$ and then define the mapping:

$$\delta_F : [0,1] \longrightarrow \{f_N, \ldots, f_1, u, t_1, \ldots, t_N\}$$

such that:

$$\delta_F(x) \stackrel{\text{def}}{=} \begin{cases} t_i \text{ when } x \in \iota_i^t; \\ f_i \text{ when } x \in \iota_i^f; \\ u \text{ otherwise.} \end{cases} \qquad (6)$$

Example 1. Let $N = 3$ and let us select six subintervals of $[0,1]$, e.g.,

$$\iota_3^f = [0.0, 0.2], \ \iota_2^f = (0.2, 0.3], \ \iota_1^f = (0.3, 0.4],$$
$$\iota_1^t = [0.6, 0.8], \ \iota_2^t = (0.8, 0.9], \ \iota_3^t = (0.9, 1.0].$$

In this case, for example,

- the interval ι_3^f represents values considered to be "strong" false (f_3);
- the interval ι_2^f represents values considered to be "weaker" false (f_2);
- the interval ι_3^t represents values considered to be "strong" true (t_3);
- the interval $(0.4, 0.6)$ represents values being unknown (u).   ◁

Let $A \subseteq U$ be a fuzzy set. For $a \in U$, by $A(a)$ we understand the fuzzy value of the membership of a in A. The mapping of fuzzy values to $\{f_N, \ldots, f_1, u, t_1, \ldots, t_N\}$ is natural:

$$a \in A \text{ obtains the truth-value } \delta_F(A(a)). \qquad (7)$$

Notice that we no longer deal with the interval $[0,1]$ which might compromise the precision of reasoning. Nevertheless, all the results shown in [7] are valid for any integer $N > 0$, thus the cardinality of $\{f_N, \ldots, f_1, u, t_1, \ldots, t_N\}$ is finite but arbirarly large. On the other hand, the gain is that grades become symbolic entities. In applications of fuzzy sets, precise degrees of membership are frequently less interesting than their interrelationships. For example, in fuzzy decision making one is often more interested in relative reliability or strength of conclusions than in exact fuzzy values associated with them. Fuzzy values are sometimes difficult to interpret, especially when complicated algorithms, requiring large numbers of iterations, are needed to compute them.

3.2   Deriving Truth-Degrees from Intuitionistic Fuzzy Sets

In fuzzy sets the fuzzy measure of a formula and its negation sum up to 1. This assumption is problematic in modelling ignorance. Therefore, generalizations of fuzzy sets have been proposed. In [2], so called, *intuitionistic fuzzy sets* are introduced (see also the discussion in [11] and the most recent book [3]). In that approach, a fuzzy set A is defined by a pair of membership functions $\langle A^+(x), A^-(x) \rangle$, where $A^+(a)$ is the degree of membership of a in A and $A^-(a)$ is its degree of membership in the complement of A. That is, for $a \in U$, $A(a) \in [0,1] \times [0,1]$. It is required that for every $a \in U$, $A^+(a) + A^-(a) \leq 1$. The intuition behind introducing positive and negative characteristics of properties is that in many cases such properties are more naturally modeled by separating positive and negative evidence for concept membership. This is close to ideas underpinning our approach.

In order to integrate intuitionistic fuzzy sets with RL^N, we can select N pairwise disjoint subintervals $\iota^1, \ldots, \iota^N$ from the interval $[0,1]$ and then define the mapping:

$$\delta_I : [0,1] \times [0,1] \longrightarrow \{f_N, \ldots, f_1, u, t_1, \ldots, t_N\}$$

such that:

$$\delta_I(x,y) \stackrel{\text{def}}{=} \begin{cases} t_i & \text{when } x > y \text{ and } x - y \in \iota^i; \\ f_i & \text{when } x < y \text{ and } y - x \in \iota^i; \\ u & \text{otherwise.} \end{cases} \qquad (8)$$

That is, a pair $\langle x, y \rangle$ represents a degree of truth when it contains more truth and a degree of falsity when it contains more falsity. The mapping of fuzzy values to truth values $\{f_N, \ldots, f_1, u, t_1, \ldots, t_N\}$ is again natural, where $A \subseteq U$ and $a \in U$:

$$a \in A \text{ obtains the truth-value } \delta_I(A^+(a), A^-(a)). \qquad (9)$$

Example 2. Let $N = 3$ and $\iota^1 = [0.3, 0.5]$, $\iota^2 = (0.5, 0.8]$ and $\iota^3 = (0.8, 1.0]$. Then:

$$\delta_I(0.7, 0.7) = \delta_I(0.1, 0.2) = u,$$
$$\delta_I(0.7, 0.1) = \delta_I(1.0, 0.3) = t_2,$$
$$\delta_I(0.1, 1.0) = f_3.$$

$\triangleleft$

3.3   Deriving Truth-Degrees from Generalized Fuzzy Sets

In [26] the idea of intuitionistic fuzzy sets is further developed into *paraconsistent intuitionistic fuzzy sets*, applied to model uncertainty, lack of knowledge as well as inconsistency. It is no longer required here that $A^+(x) + A^-(x) \leq 1$. Intuitively, cases when $A^+(x) + A^-(x) > 1$ reflect inconsistencies. In [25] this idea is further generalized, in particular by relaxing the concept of inconsistencies, where all pairs involving non-zero truth and falsity, but not necessarily making $A^+(x) + A^-(x) > 1$, are inconsistent. To address the more general case of [25] we can select N pairwise disjoint subintervals $\iota^1, \ldots, \iota^N$ of the interval $[0,1]$ and then define the mapping:

$$\delta_G : [0,1] \times [0,1] \longrightarrow \tau_N$$

such that:

$$\delta_G(x,y) \overset{\text{def}}{=} \begin{cases} t_i & \text{when } x \in \iota^i \text{ and } \forall j(y \notin \iota^j), \\ f_i & \text{when } \forall j(x \notin \iota^j) \text{ and } y \in \iota^i, \\ i_{i,j} & \text{when } x \in \iota^i \text{ and } y \in \iota^j, \\ u & \text{in all other cases.} \end{cases} \tag{10}$$

The mapping of generalized fuzzy values to truth values of τ_N is the following, where $A \subseteq U$ and $a \in U$:

$$a \in A \text{ obtains the truth-value } \delta_G(A^+(a), A^-(a)). \tag{11}$$

Example 3. Let $N = 3$ and ι^1, ι^2 and ι^3 be as in Example 2. Then $\delta_G(0.9, 0.2) = t_3$, $\delta_G(0.1, 0.7) = f_2$, $\delta_G(0.4, 0.9) = i_{1,3}$, and $\delta_G(0.1, 0.2) = u$.   ◁

3.4   Deriving Truth-Degrees from Rough Sets

In the case of rough sets [8,10,18,19] one defines approximations in terms of a family of elementary sets $\{E_i \mid i \in I\}$ being a partition or a covering of the domain. Intuitively, such sets consist of elements indistinguishable using available information. Here, rather than elementary sets, we shall consider *neighborhoods* of objects, consisting of objects indistinguishable from a given object. The function $E : A \longrightarrow 2^A$, for each $a \in A$, $E(a)$, determines the (unique) neighborhood of a. For technical reasons, we assume that for each $a \in A$, $a \in E(a)$ (meaning that a is indistinguishable from itself).

Example 4. Let $A = [0.0, 50.0]$ consist of temperature measurements in a given environment. If a sensor measures temperature with accuracy up to $0.4°C$ then it is natural to associate for every $a \in A$ the neighborhood $E(a) = [a - 0.4, a + 0.4]$: if the sensor indicates temperature a, then the actual temperature can actually be any value from $E(a)$. E.g., $E(10.3) = [9.9, 10.7]$ contains temperatures indistinguishable from 10.3.   ◁

Approximation operators can be defined by generalizing the corresponding definitions from standard rough sets:

$$A_E \overset{\text{def}}{=} \{a \in U \mid E(a) \subseteq A\} \quad \text{–the lower approximation;}$$
$$A^E \overset{\text{def}}{=} \{a \in U \mid E(a) \cap A \neq \emptyset\} \quad \text{–the upper approximation.}$$

A natural way to define the semantics of rough sets within the framework of many-valued logics is to consider three- or four-valued logics, where classical truth values indicate sure information and the two others, inconsistent and unknown, represent values in boundary regions of relations.

Graded truth values can provide more fine-grained degrees of truth values than three or four. Let $A \subseteq U$ and let, for any $a \in U$, $A(a) \stackrel{\text{def}}{=} (a \in A)$. Then with each $A(a)$ one can associate $\langle R^+(A(a)), R^-(A(a)) \rangle \in [0,1] \times [0,1]$, where:[1]

$$R^+(A(a)) \stackrel{\text{def}}{=} \frac{|A \cap E(a)|}{|E(a)|}, \quad R^-(A(a)) \stackrel{\text{def}}{=} \frac{|(-A) \cap E(a)|}{|E(a)|}. \qquad (12)$$

In this case $A(a)$ can obtain the truth-value as shown in Sect. 3.2.[2] That is, we first select suitable subintervals of $[0,1]$ and then define truth values by δ_I or δ_G, as needed, where δ_I and δ_G are defined by Eqs. (8), (10), respectively. That is,

$$a \in A \text{ (i.e., } A(a)) \text{ obtains the truth-value } \delta_I(R^+(A(a)), R^-(A(a)))$$
$$\text{(respectively} \quad \delta_G(R^+(A(a)), R^-(A(a)))). \qquad (13)$$

Note that $|\ldots|$ in Formula (12) denotes:

- the cardinality of the argument set, when it is finite (see Example 5);
- a suitable measure, like length, area, volume, etc. in the case of one, two-, three- and more dimensional geometric objects (for an example see calculations concerning distance in Sect. 5.2, p. 17).

Example 5. Let $N = 3$ and ι^1, ι^2 and ι^3 be as in Example 2 and let be $U = \{a_1, \ldots, a_{10}\}$. Let the following sets consist of indistinguishable elements:

$$\{a_1, a_2, a_4, a_5\}, \{a_3, a_{10}\}, \{a_6, a_9\}, \{a_7, a_8\}.$$

That is,

$$E(a_1) = E(a_2) = E(a_4) = E(a_5) = \{a_1, a_2, a_4, a_5\}, \ E(a_3) = E(a_{10}) = \{a_3, a_{10}\}, \text{ etc.}$$

Consider a set $p = \{a_5, a_6, a_8, a_9\}$ and the associated relation $p(a) \stackrel{\text{def}}{=} (a \in p)$. Then, e.g.,

- $R^+(p(a_5)) = 0.25$, $R^-(p(a_5)) = 0.75$, so $\delta_I(p(a_5)) = \mathbf{f}_1$ and $\delta_G(p(a_5)) = \mathbf{f}_2$;
- $R^+(p(a_7)) = 0.5$, $R^-(p(a_7)) = 0.5$, so $\delta_I(p(a_7)) = \mathbf{u}$ and $\delta_G(p(a_7)) = \mathbf{i}_{1,1}$;
- $R^+(p(a_6)) = 1.0$, $R^-(p(a_7)) = 0.0$, so $\delta_I(p(a_6)) = \mathbf{t}_3$ and $\delta_G(p(a_6)) = \mathbf{t}_3$. ◁

---

[1] Note that, in the classical setting, $R^+(a) + R^-(a) = 1$. If, however, the values of $A(z)$ may be unknown or inconsistent then these values do not have to sum up to 1.

[2] Of course, one could also adapt here the method for fuzzy sets provided in Sect. 3.1.

3.5   Deriving Truth-Degrees from Graded Rough Sets

Graded rough sets, as defined in [28], also assumes a family of neighborhood functions represents objects not distinguishable from a given object. Rather than a single function E, for every $a \in U$ one considers sets $E_i(a)$ $(i = 1, \ldots, N)$ such that:

$$E_1(a) \subseteq E_2(a) \subseteq \ldots \subseteq E_N(a). \tag{14}$$

That is, E_1 distinguishes more elements than E_2 which distinguishes more than E_3, etc. As shown in [28], if for every $1 \leq i \leq N$ and every $a \in U$, we have that $a \in E_i(a)$ and given that property (14) holds, approximations obtained using E_i's satisfy:

$$A_{E_N} \subseteq \ldots \subseteq A_{E_2} \subseteq A_{E_1} \subseteq A \subseteq A^{E_1} \subseteq A^{E_2} \subseteq \ldots \subseteq A^{E_N}. \tag{15}$$

In this case, graded truth values can be assigned to formulas by simple adaptation of the methods for rough sets presented in Sect. 3.4. For this purpose, we consider the best approximations of a given set, i.e., approximations closest to the approximated set which are given by E_1. That is, E used in Eq. (12) is defined to be $E_1(a)$. Of course, whenever under given circumstances, for $j < N$ one cannot use $E_1, \ldots, E_j$ (e.g., due to a failure of certain sensors) then one uses the best available approximation given by E_{j+1}, i.e., E used in Eq. (12) becomes E_{j+1}.

4   The Family of Rule Languages

4.1   The Basic Rule Language

Let us now recall the family of rule languages, RL^N, of [7].

Definition 2. Given a set of truth-degrees τ_N, a set of predicate symbols *Pred*, a finite set of constants *Cons* and a set of variables *Var*, we define:

$$\mathcal{L}_+ \overset{\text{def}}{=} \{P(t_1, ..., t_n) \mid P \in Pred \text{ and for } 1 \leq i \leq n, t_i \in Cons \cup Var\};$$
$$\mathcal{L}_- \overset{\text{def}}{=} \{\neg P(t_1, ..., t_n) \mid P \in Pred \text{ and for } 1 \leq i \leq n, t_i \in Cons \cup Var\};$$
$$\mathcal{L} \overset{\text{def}}{=} \mathcal{L}_+ \cup \mathcal{L}_- \cup \bigcup_{i=1}^{N} \{true_i\} \cup \bigcup_{1 \leq i \leq N} \{false_i\} \cup \bigcup_{1 \leq i, j \leq N} \{inc_{i,j}\},$$

where each n, called the *arity* of a predicate, is a nonnegative integer $(n \geq 0)$, and *Pred*, *Cons* and *Var* are mutually disjoint. Every element of $\mathcal{L}$ is called a *literal*. $\mathcal{L}_+$ (respectively, $\mathcal{L}_-$) is the set of *positive* (respectively, *negative*) literals. A literal without variables is called *ground*. We identify expressions $\neg\neg l$ with l. ◁

Definition 3. A *rule* R is an expression of the form:

$$H \leftarrow B_1, ..., B_n \tag{16}$$

with $n \geq 0$ and $H \in \mathcal{L}_+ \cup \mathcal{L}_-$ and $B_1, ..., B_n \in \mathcal{L}$. If $n = 0$ and H is ground then R is called a *fact*. We abbreviate R as $H \leftarrow B$, assuming $B = B_1, ..., B_n$. H is called the *head* or a *conclusion* of the rule and B is called its *body* or *premises*. We assume that all the rules are universally quantified. ◁

Definition 4. A *program* P is a finite set of rules. By P' we denote the *ground version of* P, i.e., the program with all the possible ground instances of rules derived from P. $\mathcal{G}_P \stackrel{\text{def}}{=} \mathcal{G}_P^+ \cup \mathcal{G}_P^-$ is the set of all ground literals appearing in P'; $\mathcal{G}_P^+$ (respectively, $\mathcal{G}_P^-$) is the set of *positive* (respectively, *negative*) ground literals of P'.   ◁

The semantics of rules is provided by many-valued Herbrand interpretations.

Definition 5. Let P be a program. A *many-valued Herbrand interpretation* for P is a set $I \subseteq \mathcal{G}_P^+ \times (\tau_N \setminus \{u\})$ such that each positive literal of $\mathcal{G}_P^+$ appears in I in at most one pair. The set of all many-valued Herbrand interpretations is denoted by $\mathcal{V}$.   ◁

Definition 6. Given a many-valued Herbrand interpretation I and a positive ground literal l, we define the *truth-degree associated* to l as follows:

$$I(l) \stackrel{\text{def}}{=} \begin{cases} \tau & \text{if there is (a unique) } \tau \text{ such that } (l, \tau) \in I; \\ u & \text{otherwise.} \end{cases}$$

We extend I to truth constants, negative literals, conjunctions of literals and rules:

$$I(true_i) \stackrel{\text{def}}{=} t_i, I(false_i) \stackrel{\text{def}}{=} f_i, I(inc_{ij}) \stackrel{\text{def}}{=} i_{ij};$$
$$I(\neg l) \stackrel{\text{def}}{=} (q, p) \text{ iff } I(l) = (p, q);$$
$$I(l_1 \wedge_t \dots \wedge_t l_k) \stackrel{\text{def}}{=} I(l_1) \wedge_t \dots \wedge_t I(l_k);$$
$$I(H \leftarrow B) \stackrel{\text{def}}{=} I(B) \Rightarrow_k I(H).$$

If $B = B_1, \dots, B_n$ is a body of a rule and $n \geq 1$ then $I(B) \stackrel{\text{def}}{=} I(B_1) \wedge_t \dots \wedge_t I(B_n)$. If $n = 0$ then $I(B) \stackrel{\text{def}}{=} t_N$.   ◁

Note that negation transforms a true literal (t_i) into a false literal (f_i) and vice versa, whereas it swaps the components of inconsistent literals (from $i_{p,q}$ to $i_{q,p}$). Negation of u remains u.

Definition 7. Let P be a program and P' its ground version. A *many-valued Harbrand model* of P is a many-valued Herbrand interpretation I such that $I(H \leftarrow B) = t_N$ for every ground rule $H \leftarrow B$ of P'.   ◁

The knowledge ordering $\leq_k$ can be extended to interpretations as follows.

Definition 8. Given a program P and many-valued Herbrand interpretations I_1 and I_2, we define:

$$I_1 \leq_k I_2 \text{ iff for every literal } l \text{ in } \mathcal{G}_P, I_1(l) \leq_k I_2(l).$$

                                                                                          ◁

In RL^N, the semantics of programs is given in terms of minimal Herbrand models w.r.t. $\leq_k$, i.e. the semantics of P is a many-valued Herbrand model M of P such that $M \leq_k M'$ for every many-valued Herbrand model M' of P. In [7] the following important theorem is proved.

Theorem 1. *Over finite domains, computing the least many-valued Herbrand model of P can be done in deterministic polynomial time w.r.t. the size of the domain.*   ◁

In [7] it is proven that the least many-valued Herbrand model of a program is defined by the least fixpoint of the operator $T_P : \mathcal{V} \to \mathcal{V}$ defined as follows:

$$T_P(I) \stackrel{\text{def}}{=} \big\{ (l, \tau) \mid l \in \mathcal{G}_P^+ \text{ and }$$
$$\tau = \mathrm{lub}_k \big(\{ (p, q) \mid (l \leftarrow B) \in P' \text{ and } I(B) = (p, q) \geq_k t_1 \} \cup$$
$$\{ (q, p) \mid (\neg l \leftarrow B) \in P' \text{ and } I(B) = (p, q) \geq_k t_1 \} \big)$$
$$\big\}$$

$$(17)$$

4.2 Introspection Operators

In order to resolve inconsistencies and lack of knowledge, in [7] a logical machinery called *introspection operators* is introduced. They empower RL^N rules allowing one to access and compare truth-values of (sets of) literals, generating further truth-degrees as output. Introspection operators generalize *Negation As Failure* and they can be also employed to introduce arbitrary truth orderings for evaluating premises of rules (see [7]).

Definition 9. By an *introspection operator* we mean any function $\mathcal{O}$ mapping sets of literals and truth-values into τ_N.   ◁

Example 6. Let I be a many-valued Herbrand interpretation. A natural operator $\mathcal{O}$ can be defined by:

$$I\big(\mathcal{O}_\in(\{l\}, \{t_1, \dots, t_n\}) \big) \stackrel{\text{def}}{=} \begin{cases} t_N & \text{when } I(l) \in \{t_1, \dots, t_n\}; \\ f_N & \text{otherwise.} \end{cases} \qquad (18)$$

For simplicity we often write $l \in \{t_1, \dots, t_n\}$ rather than $\mathcal{O}_\in(\{l\}, \{l_1, \dots, t_n\})$.   ◁

In [7] we extend rules allowing for introspection operators in their bodies. However, analogically to stratified logic programs where recursion through negation is forbidden, in RL^N recursion through introspection operators is not allowed. This follows from the fact that these operators are non-monotonic; in fact, they allow for rather complicated forms of non-monotonic reasoning. Introspection operators do not affect the complexity computing least Herbrand models, as stated in the following theorem.

Theorem 2. *Over finite domains, computing the least many-valued Herbrand model of programs extended with introspection operators can be done in deterministic polynomial time w.r.t. the size of the domain.* ◁

The least many-valued Herbrand model for programs containing introspection operators can be computed through an extended version of the T_P operator of (17).

4.3 Integrating Approximate Reasoning with Rules

A program used to model a scenario described by an approximate reasoning technique can be decomposed into two parts:

- a set of rules exposing the logical relations among the entities in question;
- a set of facts generated by applying (7), (9), (11), (13), or similar formulas, to obtain truth-degrees of literals involved in the rules of the program.

In order to keep mappings coherent, facts will be generated according to the following rule, where $l \mapsto \tau$ with $\tau \in \tau_N$ is a mapping defined by (7), (9), (11) or (13). Then:

- A fact $l \leftarrow true_i$ is added to the program for every literal l that obtains the truth-degree t_i.
- A fact $\neg l \leftarrow true_i$ is added to the program for every literal l that obtains the truth-degree f_i.
- A fact $l \leftarrow inc_{i,j}$ is added to the program for every literal l that obtains the truth-degree $i_{i,j}$.

Example 7. Let us assume that $A(a)$ obtains the truth-degree $\delta_F(A(a))$ and $A(b)$ obtains $\delta_F(A(b))$, with $\delta_F(A(a)) = t_1$ and $\delta_F(A(b)) = f_2$. Then set of facts added to the program is: $\{A(a) \leftarrow true_1, \neg A(b) \leftarrow true_2\}$. ◁

5 Case Studies

In the sequel we show the benefits of modelling approximate reasoning scenarios with the rule language RL^N. Importantly, the case study presented in Sect. 5.2 is based on a real-world scenario concerning industrial monitoring systems. This is not accidental: for example, defeasible logics [5] can be used to resolve conflicts in program rules implementing applications for embedded systems. Therefore, we argue that the framework we propose might simplify the integration of heterogeneous approximate reasoning techniques in the engineering process of industrial controllers, especially when dealing with contextual sensor data.

In the notation adopted for RL^N, variables are denoted by x and y.

5.1   From Approximate Reasoning to the Rule Language: An Image Recognition Scenario

In the first case study we show how to establish relationships between approximate reasoning techniques and our rule language, using a many-valued logic to draw information from fuzzy values.

We consider a software component used in an image recognition process. The component is used to classify some objects based on their shapes and colors. Its principal behaviour consists in recognizing yellow cups by resorting to two main estimators: (i) estimator for color yellow; (ii) estimator for shape cup. Each estimator is modelled through a fuzzy set $A_i \subseteq U$, where U is the set of objects. In particular, we define A_{col} as the membership function for the fuzzy set of color estimator and A_{sh} for the fuzzy set of shape estimator. $A_{yc} : U \longrightarrow [0,1]$ is the membership function for the fuzzy set in U of yellow cups, which is defined as follows:

$$A_{yc}(x) \stackrel{\text{def}}{=} \begin{cases} 1 & \text{if } A_{col}(x) \in (0.8,1] \text{ and } A_{sh}(x) \in (0.8,1] \\ 0.8 & \text{if } \big(A_{col}(x) \in (0.6,0.8] \text{ and } A_{sh}(x) \in (0.8,1]\big) \\ & \text{or } \big(A_{col}(x) \in (0.8,1] \text{ and } A_{sh}(x) \in (0.6,0.8]\big) \\ & \text{or } \big(A_{col}(x) \in (0.6,0.8] \text{ and } A_{sh}(x) \in (0.6,0.8]\big) \\ 0.3 & \text{if } \big(A_{col}(x) \in (0.2,0.4] \text{ and } A_{sh}(x) \notin [0,0.2]\big) \\ & \text{or } \big(A_{sh}(x) \in (0.2,0.4] \text{ and } A_{col}(x) \notin [0,0.2]\big) \\ 0 & \text{if } A_{col}(x) \in [0,0.2] \text{ or } A_{sh}(x) \in [0,0.2] \\ 0.5 & \text{otherwise} \end{cases} \tag{19}$$

The definition of $A_{yc}(x)$ looks a bit cumbersome. We will show that a more natural way to interpret the same scenario is a logic program expressed in RL^N. In this case, τ_2 provides enough truth-degrees to represent all the cases of (19). We define the following subintervals of $[0,1]$:

$$\iota_2^f \stackrel{\text{def}}{=} [0,0.2], \quad \iota_1^f \stackrel{\text{def}}{=} (0.2,0.4], \quad \iota^u \stackrel{\text{def}}{=} (0.4,0.6], \quad \iota_1^t \stackrel{\text{def}}{=} (0.6,0.8], \quad \iota_2^t \stackrel{\text{def}}{=} (0.8,1].$$

A_{yc} can be translated in the following program:

$$\begin{aligned} \text{YellowCup}(x) &\leftarrow \text{Shape}(x,cup), \text{Color}(x,yellow) \\ \neg\text{YellowCup}(x) &\leftarrow \neg\text{Shape}(x,cup) \\ \neg\text{YellowCup}(x) &\leftarrow \neg\text{Color}(x,yellow) \end{aligned} \tag{20}$$

Literals $\text{Shape}(x,cup)$ and $\text{Color}(x,yellow)$ are associated with the two fuzzy sets:

$$\begin{aligned} \text{Shape}(x,cup) &\quad \text{obtains the truth-degree } \delta_F(A_{sh}(x)); \\ \text{Color}(x,yellow) &\quad \text{obtains the truth-degree } \delta_F(A_{col}(x)). \end{aligned} \tag{21}$$

The first rule of the program reflects the cases for $A_{yc}(x) \in \{0.8,1\}$, while the second and the third one model respectively the cases for $A_{yc}(x) = 0.3$ and $A_{yc}(x) = 0$. YellowCup is the predicate associated with the fuzzy set of yellow cups: YellowCup(x) *in the least Hebrand model of the program obtains the truth-degree* $\delta_F(A_{yc}(x))$. The case $A_{yc}(x) = 0.5$ is reflected by the absence of information about YellowCup in the least Herbrand model of the program. Thus, we can model the scenario as an RL^N program consisting of the three rules (20).

As an example, let us consider $U \overset{\text{def}}{=} \{o_1, o_2, o_3\}$ and the following membership functions for estimators:

$$A_{col}(o_1) \overset{\text{def}}{=} 0.7, \quad A_{col}(o_2) \overset{\text{def}}{=} 0.35 \quad A_{col}(o_3) \overset{\text{def}}{=} 0.75$$
$$A_{sh}(o_1) \overset{\text{def}}{=} 0.9, \quad A_{sh}(o_2) \overset{\text{def}}{=} 0.75, \quad A_{sh}(o_3) \overset{\text{def}}{=} 0.5$$

We notice that $A_{yc}(o_1) = 0.8$, $A_{yc}(o_2) = 0.3$, $A_{yc}(o_3) = 0.5$, thus w.r.t. the fuzzy set of yellow cups, applying (7) we expect that o_1 obtains $\delta_F(0.8) = t_1$, o_2 obtains $\delta_F(0.3) = f_1$ and o_3 obtains $\delta_F(0.5) = u$.

From (21) we have the following mappings:

Color(o_1, *yellow*) obtains t_1 Shape(o_1, *cup*) obtains t_2
Color(o_2, *yellow*) obtains f_1 Shape(o_2, *cup*) obtains t_1
Color(o_3, *yellow*) obtains t_1 Shape(o_3, *cup*) obtains u,

leading to the following program:

$$
\begin{aligned}
&\text{YellowCup}(x) &&\leftarrow \text{Shape}(x, cup), \text{Color}(x, yellow) \\
&\neg\text{YellowCup}(x) &&\leftarrow \neg\text{Shape}(x, sc) \\
&\neg\text{YellowCup}(x) &&\leftarrow \neg\text{Color}(x, yc) \\
&\text{Color}(o_1, yellow) \leftarrow true_1 &&\neg\text{Color}(o_2, yellow) \leftarrow true_1 \\
&\text{Color}(o_3, yellow) \leftarrow true_1 &&\text{Shape}(o_1, cup) \leftarrow true_2 \\
&\text{Shape}(o_2, cup) &&\leftarrow true_1
\end{aligned}
\tag{22}
$$

The least many-valued Herband model of (22) is:

$$
\begin{aligned}
M = \{&(\text{Color}(o_1, yellow), t_1), (\text{Color}(o_2, yellow), f_1), (\text{Color}(o_3, yellow), t_1), \\
&(\text{Shape}(o_1, cup), t_2), (\text{Shape}(o_2, yellow), t_1), (\text{YellowCup}(o_1), t_1), \\
&(\text{YellowCup}(o_2), f_1)\}
\end{aligned}
$$

Therefore, we obtain:

$$M(\text{YellowCup}(o_1)) = t_1, \quad M(\text{YellowCup}(o_2)) = f_1 \text{ and } M(\text{YellowCup}(o_3)) = u.$$

Note that such truth-degrees are the expected ones for the fuzzy set of yellow cups.

5.2 Integration of Heterogeneous Approximate Reasoning Techniques: A Chemical Warehouse Monitoring System

In the previous case study the logical relationship among fuzzy values is mainly captured by the logical connective $\wedge_t$. In a more complex scenario of preventing safety hazards in a chemical warehouse, it may be necessary to handle truth-degrees through non-monotonic operators and to resolve inconsistencies and lack of information. This is needed especially when reasoning is based on data arriving from multiple sources of information associated with different approximate reasoning techniques. Introspection operators (e.g., (18)) provide the logical machinery to perform these tasks. In the sequel we resort to the following definitions.

Let I be a many-valued Herbrand interpretation. We define some useful introspection operators by setting:

$$I(\mathcal{O}_{\notin}(\{l\}, \{t_1, ..., t_n\})) \stackrel{\text{def}}{=} \begin{cases} t_N & \text{when } I(l) \notin \{t_1, ..., t_n\} \\ f_N & \text{otherwise;} \end{cases} \qquad (23)$$

$$I(\mathcal{O}_{\geq_t}(\{l\}, \{t\})) \stackrel{\text{def}}{=} \begin{cases} t_N & \text{when } I(l) \geq_t t; \\ f_N & \text{otherwise.} \end{cases} \qquad (24)$$

$$I(\mathcal{O}_{\Delta_1}(\{l\}, \emptyset)) \stackrel{\text{def}}{=} \begin{cases} t_i & \text{if } I(l) = (p, q), \ i = p - q, \ i > 0 \\ f_N & \text{otherwise.} \end{cases} \qquad (25)$$

$$I(\mathcal{O}_{\Delta_2}(\{l_1, l_2\}, \emptyset)) \stackrel{\text{def}}{=} \begin{cases} t_i & \text{if } I(l_1) = (p_1, q_1), \ I(l_2) = (p_2, q_2), \\ & \quad i = p_1 - p_2, \ i > 0 \\ f_N & \text{otherwise.} \end{cases} \qquad (26)$$

Other useful operators can be defined using the following partial order:

$$(p_1, p_2) <_{truth} (q_1, q_2) \text{ when } (p_1 - p_2) < (q_1 - q_2) \text{ or} \\ (p_1 - p_2) = (q_1 - q_2) \text{ and } p_1 < q_1. \qquad (27)$$

$$(p_1, p_2) \leq_{truth} (q_1, q_2) \text{ when } (p_1, p_2) <_{truth} \text{ or } (p_1, p_2) = (q_1, q_2). \qquad (28)$$

In particular,

$$I(\mathcal{O}_{<_{truth}}(\{l_1, l_2\}, \emptyset)) \stackrel{\text{def}}{=} \begin{cases} t_N & \text{when } I(l_1) <_{truth} I(l_2); \\ f_N & \text{otherwise;} \end{cases} \qquad (29)$$

$$I(\mathcal{O}_{\leq_{truth}}(\{l_1, l_2\}, \emptyset)) \stackrel{\text{def}}{=} \begin{cases} t_N & \text{when } I(l_1) \leq_{truth} I(l_2); \\ f_N & \text{otherwise;} \end{cases} \qquad (30)$$

We will use the more convenient notation $l \notin \{t_1, ..., t_n\}$, $l \geq_t t$, $\Delta_1(l)$, $\Delta_2(l_1, l_2)$, $l_1 \leq_{truth} l_2$. In a similar way, we define the alternative notation for $\mathcal{O}_{>_t}(\{l\}, \{t\})$, $\mathcal{O}_{<_t}(\{l\}, \{t\})$, $\mathcal{O}_{\leq_t}(\{l\}, \{t\})$, $\mathcal{O}_{>_{truth}}(\{l_1, l_2\}, \emptyset)$ and $\mathcal{O}_{\geq_{truth}}(\{l_1, l_2\}, \emptyset)$.

A monitoring system preventing safety hazards in a chemical warehouse considered in this section extends an existing prototype in which logic programs encode legislation constraints that can be updated at run-time by authorized persons.[3] Logic programs reason on contextual-information gathered by heterogeneous sensors and trigger warning signals when they detect dangerous situations. In this scenario we consider an extended version of the system kernel,

---

[3] A video of the prototype is available at:https://www.youtube.com/watch?v=4u_O6-ylhvU.

enriched with approximate reasoning techniques and resorting to the following sources of information: humidity level, temperature, category and distances between shelf units. Every shelf unit is associated with a category that defines the type of chemical compound stored in the container; $C_{at} \overset{\text{def}}{=} \{C_1, C_2, C_3\}$ is the set of all recognized categories. A warning signal is triggered if at least one of the following conditions holds:

- The humidity level and temperature for the environment surrounding a shelf unit are both above a given threshold.
- The distance of two shelf units with categories C_1 and C_2 is below a certain value.

Depending on the strength of the warning signal, the system can perform one of actions: calling an operator, enabling an alarm siren or launching the evacuation signal. In this case study we deal with information generated by several sensors, modelled through different approximate reasoning techniques. The system implements several strategies to manage the inconsistent information that naturally arises during reasoning. Inconsistencies may occur due to the presence of multiple sources of contextual information obtained from non-ideal sensors. The underlying set of truth-degrees is τ_3.

In order to assess the humidity threshold, the system resorts to a low-precision and high-precision sensor. The first one is modelled through a fuzzy set of U with membership function $A_{hl}(x)$, associated with the following decomposition of $[0,1]$:

$$\iota^f_{3,hl} \overset{\text{def}}{=} [0, 0.05], \quad \iota^f_{2,hl} \overset{\text{def}}{=} (0.05, 0.1], \quad \iota^f_{1,hl} \overset{\text{def}}{=} (0.1, 0.15], \quad \iota^u_{hl} \overset{\text{def}}{=} (0.15, 0.85],$$
$$\iota^t_{1,hl} \overset{\text{def}}{=} (0.85, 0.9], \quad \iota^t_{2,hl} \overset{\text{def}}{=} (0.9, 0.95], \quad \iota^t_{3,hl} \overset{\text{def}}{=} (0.95, 1]$$

$$(31)$$

The high-precision humidity sensor is modelled through an intuitionistic fuzzy set of U with membership functions $\langle A^+_{hh}(x), A^-_{hh}(x) \rangle$, associated with the following subintervals of $[0,1]$:

$$\iota_{1,hh} \overset{\text{def}}{=} [0.2, 0.45], \quad \iota_{2,hh} \overset{\text{def}}{=} (0.45, 0.8], \quad \iota_{3,hh} \overset{\text{def}}{=} (0.8, 1] \qquad (32)$$

Also the temperature is estimated through an intuitionistic fuzzy set of U, with membership functions $\langle A^+_t(x), A^-_t(x) \rangle$ and the following subintervals of $[0,1]$:

$$\iota_{1,t} \overset{\text{def}}{=} [0.15, 0.4], \quad \iota_{2,t} \overset{\text{def}}{=} (0.4, 0.7], \quad \iota_{3,t} \overset{\text{def}}{=} (0.7, 1] \qquad (33)$$

The distance among shelf units is estimated through a rough set on the domain of values of measurements with membership functions $\delta_G(R^+(A(d)), R^- A(d))$, associated with the following subintervals of $[0,1]$:

$$\iota_{1,d} \overset{\text{def}}{=} [0.2, 0.5], \quad \iota_{2,d} \overset{\text{def}}{=} (0.5, 0.75], \quad \iota_{3,d} \overset{\text{def}}{=} (0.75, 1] \qquad (34)$$

Since we are interested in evaluating the property that the measured distance d exceeds a given threshold th, we have that $A(d) \overset{\text{def}}{=} d > th$.

Finally, the category of a shelf unit is estimated through a paraconsistent intuitionistic fuzzy set of $U \times C_{at}$, with membership functions $\langle A_{cat}^+(x), A_{cat}^-(x) \rangle$ and the following subintervals of $[0, 1]$:

$$\iota_{1,cat} \overset{\text{def}}{=} [0.4, 0.6], \quad \iota_{2,cat} \overset{\text{def}}{=} (0.6, 0.8], \quad \iota_{3,cat} \overset{\text{def}}{=} (0.8, 1] \qquad (35)$$

The condition on the temperature and humidity level for the environment surrounding a shelf unit are verified by the following program P_1:

$$\text{HumLim}(x) \leftarrow \text{HLimL}(x) \geq_t t_1, \text{HLimH}(x) \geq_t t_1, \text{HLimH}(x)$$
$$\text{HumLim}(x) \leftarrow \text{HLimL}(x) <_t t_1, \text{HLimH}(x) \geq_t t_1,$$
$$\Delta_2(\text{HLimH}(x), \text{HLimL}(x))$$
$$\text{Warning} \quad \leftarrow \text{HumLim}(x), \text{TempL}(x)$$

$\text{HLimL}(x)$ and $\text{HLimH}(x)$ indicates whether the limit of humidity level for shelf unit x is above the threshold respectively according to the low-precision and high-precision sensor. Similarly, $\text{TempL}(x)$ characterizes the threshold for the temperature. The behaviour of P_1 is the following one: if both humidity sensors agree on the threshold ($\text{HLimL}(x) \geq_t t_1$ and $\text{HLimH}(x) \geq_t t_1$) then the truth-degree of the high-precision sensor is finally considered ($\text{HLimH}(x)$). Otherwise, if the low-precision sensor senses a humidity value below the threshold while the high-precision one detects a value above the limit, the final truth-degree is evaluated by the program as the difference between the positive components of the literals $\Delta_2(\text{HLimH}(x), \text{HLimL}(x))$. The third rule produces a warning literal if both the humidity and the temperature are above their thresholds. The truth values of the literals of P_1 are obtained by mapping fuzzy sets and intuitionistic fuzzy sets to truth-degrees, following the strategy applied in (21). Due to the involved techniques, $\text{HLimH}(x)$, $\text{HLimL}(x)$ and $\text{TempL}(x)$ cannot be inconsistent, thus Warning assumes values in $\{u, t_1, t_2, t_3\}$.

The conditions on the categories and distances of shelf units are verified by the program P_2, where $\text{DistL}(x, y)$ indicates whether the distance between shelf units x and y is above the limit:

$$
\begin{aligned}
\text{DistL}(x, y) \quad &\leftarrow \text{DistL}(y, x) \\
\text{DLim}(x, y) \quad &\leftarrow \Delta_1(\text{DistL}(x, y)) \\
\neg\text{DLim}(x, y) \quad &\leftarrow \neg\Delta_1(\text{DistL}(x, y)) \\
\text{C}(x, C_1) \quad &\leftarrow \Delta_1(\text{Cat}(x, C_1)), \text{Cat}(x, C_1) \geq_{truth} \text{Cat}(x, C_2), \\
& \quad \text{Cat}(x, C_1) \geq_{truth} \text{Cat}(x, C_3) \\
\text{C}(x, C_2) \quad &\leftarrow \Delta_1(\text{Cat}(x, C_2)), \text{Cat}(x, C_2) \geq_{truth} \text{Cat}(x, C_1), \\
& \quad \text{Cat}(x, C_2) \geq_{truth} \text{Cat}(x, C_3) \\
\text{C}(x, C_3) \quad &\leftarrow \Delta_1(\text{Cat}(x, C_3)), \text{Cat}(x, C_3) \geq_{truth} \text{Cat}(x, C_1), \\
& \quad \text{Cat}(x, C_3) \geq_{truth} \text{Cat}(x, C_2) \\
\text{Warning} \quad &\leftarrow true_1, \text{Cat}(x, y) \notin \{u\}, \text{C}(x, C_1) \in \{u\}, \text{C}(x, C_2) \in \{u\} \\
& \quad \text{C}(x, C_3) \in \{u\} \\
\text{Warning} \quad &\leftarrow \text{C}(x, C_1), \text{C}(y, C_2), \neg\text{DLim}(x, y)
\end{aligned}
$$

When dealing with an inconsistent truth-degree $i_{p,q}$, p can be considered as an index of the evidence supporting a particular fact, whereas q estimates the evidence against the fact. Given that $\text{DistL}(x, y)$ is obtained from a rough set, its truth-degree may be inconsistent. In this case, the program considers $\Delta_1(\text{DistL}(x, y))$: if there is a stronger evidence supporting the fact that the distance is above the limit (i.e., the positive component is greater than the negative one), then the truth-degree of $\Delta_1(\text{DistL}(x, y))$ is considered as the representative for the distance (with the difference between positive and negative component). Otherwise, the truth-degree of $\neg\Delta_1(\text{DistL}(x, y))$ is kept.

$\text{Cat}(x, C)$ with $C \in \{C_1, C_2, C_3\}$, estimates the category C of the shelf unit x. In P_2 we adopt a different strategy to manage the inconsistent information that may arise in $\text{Cat}(x, C)$: if the difference between positive and negative evidence for a category C is stronger than the ones sustaining the remaining two categories, then C with $\Delta_1(\text{Cat}(x, C))$ is considered as the representative category. In case the evidence does not allow to determine which category is most supported (e.g. $C(x, C) \in \{u\}$ for every category C), then a warning with truth-degree t_1 is generated.

The above strategies guarantee that the truth value of $\text{DLim}(x, y)$ is contained in $\{f_3, f_2, f_1, u, t_1, t_2, t_3\}$, whereas $\text{Cat}(x, C)$ belongs to $\{t_1, t_2, t_3\}$. Thus, all possible inconsistencies are properly managed. The last rule of the program tests the condition on the proximity of two shelf units having categories C_1 and C_2. Once again, the literals of the program are obtained by fuzzy values and rough set values, by applying strategies similar to the one in (21).

The final program P_3 analyses the truth-degree of the warning signal, entailing a proper action depending on the criticality of the detected problem.

$$
\begin{array}{ll}
\text{SafeLevel} & \leftarrow \text{Warning} \in \{u\} \\
\text{CallOperator} & \leftarrow \text{Warning} \in \{t_1\} \\
\text{EnableSiren} & \leftarrow \text{Warning} \in \{t_2\} \\
\text{EvacuationSignal} \leftarrow & \text{Warning} \in \{t_3\}
\end{array}
$$

As a concrete instance of the case study, let us consider $U \overset{\text{def}}{=} \{o_1, o_2\}$ and:

$$
\begin{array}{llll}
A_{hl}(o_1) \overset{\text{def}}{=} 0.04 & A_{hh}^+(o_1) \overset{\text{def}}{=} 0.96 & A_{hh}^-(o_1) \overset{\text{def}}{=} 0.1 & A_{hl}(o_2) \overset{\text{def}}{=} 0.86 \\
A_{hh}^+(o_2) \overset{\text{def}}{=} 0.83 & A_{hh}^-(o_2) \overset{\text{def}}{=} 0.1 & A_t^+(o_1) \overset{\text{def}}{=} 0.3 & A_t^-(o_1) \overset{\text{def}}{=} 0.8 \\
A_t^+(o_2) \overset{\text{def}}{=} 0.4 & A_t^-(o_2) \overset{\text{def}}{=} 0.7 & A_{cat}^+(o_1, C_1) \overset{\text{def}}{=} 0.5 & A_{cat}^-(o_1, C_1) \overset{\text{def}}{=} 0.3 \\
A_{cat}^+(o_1, C_2) \overset{\text{def}}{=} 0.2 & A_{cat}^-(o_1, C_2) \overset{\text{def}}{=} 0.5 & A_{cat}^+(o_1, C_3) \overset{\text{def}}{=} 0.2 & A_{cat}^-(o_1, C_3) \overset{\text{def}}{=} 0.8 \\
A_{cat}^+(o_2, C_1) \overset{\text{def}}{=} 0.5 & A_{cat}^-(o_2, C_1) \overset{\text{def}}{=} 0.7 & A_{cat}^+(o_2, C_2) \overset{\text{def}}{=} 0.5 & A_{cat}^-(o_2, C_2) \overset{\text{def}}{=} 0.9 \\
A_{cat}^+(o_2, C_3) \overset{\text{def}}{=} 0.8 & A_{cat}^-(o_2, C_3) \overset{\text{def}}{=} 0.6
\end{array}
$$

Assume further that distance between objects is measured with the accuracy of $0.5\,\text{m}$ and the threshold $th = 3.0\,\text{m}$. Let the actual measurement of the distance between objects o_1 and o_2 be $d = 3.3\,\text{m}$. We are interested in the truth value of $\text{DistL}(o_1, o_2)$ expressing that the distance between objects o_1 and o_2 exceeds th. Thus, using formula (12), we have

$$
R^+(3.3 > th) = \frac{|\{z \mid z > th\} \cap E(3.3)|}{|E(3.3)|}, \text{ and } R^-(3.3 > th) = \frac{\{z \mid z \le th\} \cap E(3.3)|}{|E(3.3)|},
$$

where $E(3.3)$ is the neighborhood of distances indistinguishable from 3.3, i.e., the interval $[3.3 - 0.5, 3.3 + 0.5]$ being $[2.8, 3.8]$. Of course, $\{z \,|\, z > th\} = (3.0, +\infty)$, $\{z \,|\, z \leq th\} = (-\infty, 3.0]$ and $|E(3.3)| = 1.0$. Therefore:

$$\delta_G(R^+(3.3 > th), R^-(3.3 > th)) = \delta_G(0.8, 0.2) = i_{3,1}.$$

From such values we infer:

HLimL(o_1) *obtains* f_3	HLimL(o_2) *obtains* t_1	HLimH(o_1) *obtains* t_3
HLimH(o_2) *obtains* t_2	DistL(o_1, o_2) *obtains* $i_{3,1}$	
TempL(o_1) *obtains* f_2	TempL(o_2) *obtains* f_1	
Cat(o_1, C_1) *obtains* t_1	Cat(o_1, C_2) *obtains* f_1	Cat(o_1, C_3) *obtains* f_2
Cat(o_2, C_1) *obtains* $i_{1,2}$	Cat(o_2, C_2) *obtains* $i_{1,3}$	Cat(o_2, C_3) *obtains* $i_{2,1}$

Thus, we obtain the following set of facts:

$$
\begin{array}{lll}
\neg\text{HLimL}(o_1) \leftarrow true_3 & \text{HLimL}(o_2) \leftarrow true_1 & \text{HLimH}(o_1) \leftarrow true_3 \\
\text{HLimH}(o_2) \leftarrow true_2 & \text{DistL}(o_1, o_2) \leftarrow inc_{3,1} & \\
\neg\text{TempL}(o_1) \leftarrow true_2 & \neg\text{TempL}(o_2) \leftarrow true_1 & \\
\text{Cat}(o_1, C_1) \leftarrow true_1 & \neg\text{Cat}(o_1, C_2) \leftarrow true_1 & \neg\text{Cat}(o_1, C_3) \leftarrow true_2 \\
\text{Cat}(o_2, C_1) \leftarrow inc_{1,2} & \text{Cat}(o_2, C_2) \leftarrow inc_{1,3} & \text{Cat}(o_2, C_3) \leftarrow inc_{2,1}
\end{array}
\tag{36}
$$

We consider the program obtained from the union of $P_1 \cup P_2 \cup P_3$ and (36). Its least many-valued Herbrand model is:

$$
\begin{aligned}
M = \{ & (\text{HLimL}(o_1), f_3), (\text{HLimL}(o_2), t_1), (\text{HLimH}(o_1), t_3), (\text{HLimH}(o_2), t_2), \\
& (\text{DistL}(o_1, o_2), i_{3,1}), (\text{Cat}(o_1, C_1), t_1), (\text{Cat}(o_1, C_2), f_1), (\text{Cat}(o_1, C_3), f_2), \\
& (\text{Cat}(o_2, C_1), i_{1,2}), (\text{Cat}(o_2, C_2), i_{1,3}), (\text{Cat}(o_2, C_3), i_{2,1}), (\text{TempL}(o_1), f_2), \\
& (\text{TempL}(o_2), f_1), (\text{HumLim}(o_2), t_2), (\text{DistL}(o_2, o_1), i_{3,1}), \\
& (\text{DLim}(o_1, o_2), t_2), (\text{DLim}(o_2, o_1), t_2), (\text{C}(o_1, C_1), t_1), (\text{C}(o_2, C_3), t_1), \\
& (\text{SafeLevel}, t_1) \}
\end{aligned}
$$

Even in the presence of contradictory information about the category of o_2, we obtain $M(\text{SafeLevel}) = t_1$, meaning that both safety constraints are met for shelf units o_1 and o_2. In fact, $(\text{TempL}(o_1), f_2)$ and $(\text{TempL}(o_2), f_1)$ assure that the first constraint is satisfied. Moreover, $(\text{C}(o_2, C_3), t_1)$ is inferred from the rules of P_2 and the truth-degree of $\text{DLim}(o_1, o_2)$ is t_2, which make the second constraint satisfied.

We now consider these new values for the temperature:

$$A_t^+(o_2) \overset{\text{def}}{=} 0.8 \qquad A_t^-(o_2) \overset{\text{def}}{=} 0.5 \qquad \text{TempL}(o_2) \; obtains \; t_1$$

The set of facts becomes:

$$
\begin{array}{lll}
\neg\text{HLimL}(o_1) \leftarrow true_3 & \text{HLimL}(o_2) \leftarrow true_1 & \text{HLimH}(o_1) \leftarrow true_3 \\
\text{HLimH}(o_2) \leftarrow true_2 & \text{DistL}(o_1, o_2) \leftarrow inc_{3,1} & \\
\neg\text{TempL}(o_1) \leftarrow true_2 & \text{TempL}(o_2) \leftarrow true_1 & \\
\text{Cat}(o_1, C_1) \leftarrow true_1 & \neg\text{Cat}(o_1, C_2) \leftarrow true_1 & \neg\text{Cat}(o_1, C_3) \leftarrow true_2 \\
\text{Cat}(o_2, C_1) \leftarrow inc_{1,2} & \text{Cat}(o_2, C_2) \leftarrow inc_{1,3} & \text{Cat}(o_2, C_3) \leftarrow inc_{2,1}
\end{array}
\tag{37}
$$

Computing the least many-valued Herbrand model of the program given from the union of $P_1 \cup P_2 \cup P_3$ and (37) we obtain:

$$M = \{ \big(\mathrm{HLimL}(o_1), \boldsymbol{f}_3\big), \big(\mathrm{HLimL}(o_2), \boldsymbol{t}_1\big), \big(\mathrm{HLimH}(o_1), \boldsymbol{t}_3\big), \big(\mathrm{HLimH}(o_2), \boldsymbol{t}_2\big),$$
$$\big(\mathrm{DistL}(o_1, o_2), i_{3,1}\big), \big(\mathrm{Cat}(o_1, C_1), \boldsymbol{t}_1\big), \big(\mathrm{Cat}(o_1, C_2), \boldsymbol{f}_1\big), \big(\mathrm{Cat}(o_1, C_3), \boldsymbol{f}_2\big),$$
$$\big(\mathrm{Cat}(o_2, C_1), i_{1,2}\big), \big(\mathrm{Cat}(o_2, C_2), i_{1,3}\big), \big(\mathrm{Cat}(o_2, C_3), i_{2,1}\big), \big(\mathrm{TempL}(o_1), \boldsymbol{f}_2\big),$$
$$\big(\mathrm{TempL}(o_2), \boldsymbol{t}_1\big), \big(\mathrm{HumLim}(o_2), \boldsymbol{t}_2\big), \big(\mathrm{DistL}(o_2, o_1), i_{3,1}\big),$$
$$\big(\mathrm{DLim}(o_1, o_2), \boldsymbol{t}_2\big), \big(\mathrm{DLim}(o_2, o_1), \boldsymbol{t}_2\big), \big(\mathrm{C}(o_1, C_1), \boldsymbol{t}_1\big), \big(\mathrm{C}(o_2, C_3), \boldsymbol{t}_1\big),$$
$$\big(\mathrm{Warning}, \boldsymbol{t}_1\big), \big(\mathrm{CallOperator}, \boldsymbol{t}_1\big)\}$$

In this case, the first safety constraint is violated because of $\big(\mathrm{TempL}(o_2), \boldsymbol{t}_1\big)$ and $\big(\mathrm{HumLim}(o_2), \boldsymbol{t}_2\big)$; $\big(\mathrm{Warning}, \boldsymbol{t}_1\big)$ is inferred from P_2 (we notice that $\boldsymbol{t}_2 \wedge_t \boldsymbol{t}_1 = \boldsymbol{t}_1$) and $\big(\mathrm{CallOperator}, \boldsymbol{t}_1\big)$ is obtained from the second rule of P_3.

6   Conclusions

In this paper we have developed a methodology for an integration of important forms of approximate reasoning with a rule language RL^N, based on a family of many-valued logics. This way a framework to encompass and unify heterogeneous reasoning techniques has been obtained. Besides truthfulness and falseness, the underpinning many-valued logic can model unknown, uncertain and inconsistent information. Also, the discrete set of truth-degrees can be parameterized in order to achieve the best granularity required in the application in question. Clearly, the best granularity does not necessarily mean the best accuracy. Importantly, RL^N offers a logical machinery to reason on truth-degrees, paving the way to resolving inconsistencies and to managing the quality level of the inferred information.

We have shown that by selecting the most appropriate underlying logic, information treated through approximate reasoning techniques can be easily integrated with the rule-based language RL^N. This means that the framework can be successfully used as an umbrella unifying several forms of approximate reasoning within the same logical model. This aspect turns out to be particularly interesting when dealing with complex systems interacting with multiple information sources of different credibility and accuracy modelled by heterogeneous approximate reasoning techniques.

Last but not least, the complexity of queries remain tractable even though the cardinality of truth-degrees increases to reach the best level of approximation w.r.t. the adopted reasoning technique. Therefore, the presented framework represents an important step towards heterogeneous approximate reasoning.

Acknowledgments. The last two authors have been supported by the Polish National Science Centre grant 2015/19/B/ST6/02589.

References

1. de Amo, S., Pais, M.: A paraconsistent logic approach for querying inconsistent databases. Int. J. Approximate Reason. **46**, 366–386 (2007)
2. Atanassov, K.: Intuitionistic fuzzy sets. Fuzzy Sets Syst. **20**, 87–96 (1986)
3. Atanassov, K.: On Intuitionistic Fuzzy Sets Theory. Studies in Fuzziness and Soft Computing, vol. 283. Springer, Heidelberg (2012)
4. Bézieau, J.J., Carnielli, W., Gabbay, D. (eds.): Handbook of Paraconsistency. College Publications, London (2007)
5. Covington, M.: Defeasible logic on an embedded microcontroller. Appl. Intell. **13**(3), 259–264 (2000)
6. Damásio, C., Pereira, L.: A survey of paraconsistent semantics for logic programs. In: Besnard, P., Hunter, A. (eds.) Reasoning with Actual and Potential Contradictions, vol. 2, pp. 241–320. Springer, Heidelberg (1998). doi:10.1007/978-94-017-1739-7_8
7. De Angelis, F.L., Di Marzo Serugendo, G., Szałas, A.: Paraconsistent rule-based reasoning with graded truth values. To be published in IfColog Journal of Logics and their Applications (2017)
8. Demri, S., Orłowska, E.: Incomplete Information: Structure, Inference, Complexity. EATCS Monographs. Springer, Heidelberg (2002)
9. Doherty, P., Dunin-Kęplicz, B., Szałas, A.: Dynamics of approximate information fusion. In: Kryszkiewicz, M., Peters, J.F., Rybinski, H., Skowron, A. (eds.) RSEISP 2007. LNCS, vol. 4585, pp. 668–677. Springer, Heidelberg (2007). doi:10.1007/978-3-540-73451-2_70
10. Doherty, P., Łukaszewicz, W., Skowron, A., Szałas, A.: Knowledge Representation Techniques, A Rough Set Approach. Studies in Fuziness and Soft Computing, vol. 202. Springer, Heidelberg (2006)
11. Dubois, D., Gottwald, S., Hájek, P., Kacprzyk, J., Prade, H.: Terminological difficulties in fuzzy set theory - the case of "Intuitionistic Fuzzy Sets". Fuzzy Sets Syst. **156**(3), 485–491 (2005)
12. Dubois, D., Konieczny, S., Prade, H.: Quasi-possibilistic logic and its measures of information and conflict. Fundamenta Informaticae **57**(2–4), 101–125 (2003)
13. Dubois, D., Lang, J., Prade, H.: Fuzzy sets in approximate reasoning, part 2: logical approaches. Fuzzy Sets Syst. **40**(1), 203–244 (1991)
14. Dubois, D., Prade, H.: Fuzzy sets in approximate reasoning, part 1: inference with possibility distributions. Fuzzy Sets Syst. **40**(1), 143–202 (1991)
15. Dunin-Kęplicz, B., Szałas, A.: Agents in approximate environments. In: Eijck, J., Verbrugge, R. (eds.) Games, Actions and Social Software. Multidisciplinary Aspects. LNCS, vol. 7010, pp. 141–163. Springer, Heidelberg (2012). doi:10.1007/978-3-642-29326-9_8
16. Kruse, R., Schwecke, E., Heinsohn, J.: Uncertainty and Vagueness in Knowledge Based Systems. Numerical Methods. Springer, Heidelberg (1991)
17. Małuszyński, J., Szałas, A.: Partiality and inconsistency in agents' belief bases. In: Barbucha et al., D. (ed.) Proceedings of KES-AMSTA. Frontiers of Artificial Intelligence and Applications, vol. 252, pp. 3–17. IOS Press (2011)
18. Pawlak, Z.: Rough Sets. Theoretical Aspects of Reasoning about Data. Kluwer Academic Publishers, Dordrecht (1991)
19. Pawlak, Z., Polkowski, L., Skowron, A.: Rough set theory. In: Wah, B. (ed.) Wiley Encyclopedia of Computer Science and Engineering. Wiley (2008)

20. Pimentel, S.G., Rodi, W.L.: Belief revision and paraconsistency in a logic programming framework. In: Nerode, A., Marek, W., Subrahmanian, V.S. (eds.) Logic Programming and Non-Monotonic Reasoning: Proceedings of the First International Workshop, pp. 228–242. MIT Press (1991)
21. Polkowski, L.: Approximate Reasoning by Parts - An Introduction to Rough Mereology. Intelligent Systems Reference Library, vol. 20. Springer, Heidelberg (2011)
22. Polkowski, L., Semeniuk-Polkowska, M.: Where rough sets and fuzzy sets meet. Fundam. Inform. **142**(1–4), 269–284 (2015)
23. Prade, H.: A quantitative approach to approximate reasoning in rule-based expert systems. In: Bolc, L., Coombs, M. (eds.) Expert System Applications, pp. 199–256. Springer, Heidelberg (1988)
24. Skowron, A., Stepaniuk, J., Swiniarski, R.: Approximation spaces in rough-granular computing. Fundam. Inform. **100**(1–4), 141–157 (2010)
25. Szałas, A.: Symbolic explanations of generalized fuzzy reasoning. In: Neves-Silva, R., Tshirintzis, G., Uskov, V., Howlett, R., Jain, L. (eds.) Smart Digital Futures 2014, pp. 7–16. IOS Press (2014)
26. Wang, H., Sunderraman, R.: A data model based on paraconsistent intuitionistic fuzzy relations. In: Hacid, M.-S., Murray, N.V., Raś, Z.W., Tsumoto, S. (eds.) ISMIS 2005. LNCS (LNAI), vol. 3488, pp. 669–677. Springer, Heidelberg (2005). doi:10.1007/11425274_69
27. Yao, Y., Lin, T.: Generalization of rough sets using modal logics. Intell. Autom. Soft Comput. **2**(2), 103–119 (1996)
28. Yao, Y., Lin, T.: Graded rough set approximations based on nested neighborhood systems. In: Proceedings of the 5th European Congress on Intelligent Techniques and Soft Computing, vol. 1, pp. 196–200 (1997)
29. Yao, Y., Wong, S., Lin, T.: A review of rough set models. In: Lin, T.Y., Cercone, N. (eds.) Rough Sets and Data Mining, pp. 47–75. Springer, New York (1997)
30. Zadeh, L.: From computing with numbers to computing with words - from manipulation of measurements to manipulation of perceptions. Int. J. Appl. Math. Comput. Sci. **12**(3), 307–324 (2002)
31. Zadeh, L.: Fuzzy sets. Inf. Control **8**, 333–353 (1965)
32. Zadeh, L.: Computing with Words - Principal Concepts and Ideas. Studies in fuzziness and soft computing, vol. 277. Springer, Heidelberg (2012)

Computer Certification of Generalized Rough Sets Based on Relations

Adam Grabowski[✉]

Institute of Informatics, University of Białystok,
Konstantego Ciołkowskiego 1M, 15-245 Białystok, Poland
adam@math.uwb.edu.pl

Abstract. The aim of this paper is to describe the issues concerning the full formal translation of a single but important paper devoted to generalized rough sets based on binary relations, authored by William Zhu. Although we started the encoding (using automated proof-assistant Mizar) quite some time ago, we met unexpected difficulties during this task forcing us to refactor the created formal framework. Now, when the work is completed, we can shed some light for lessons learned during the process of encoding of the collection of quite elementary constructions written by means of relatively simple syntactical apparatus.

1 Introduction

Recently, it seems that the main activity at the intersection of rough sets and knowledge technology is discovering knowledge based on rough set methods: granular computing, approximate reasoning or some non-classical logics (at least that is the tradition of the core of rough set conference series). Essentially then, if we deal with incomplete data, we meet the situation when classical logic or classical set theory is just not sufficient. On the other hand, models for rough set theory are often formalized within those above-mentioned traditional mathematical tools [4], but rough set theory itself is relatively rarely treated as a testbed for methods of knowledge discovery. The main reason seems to be that among many automatically generated theorems it is hard to point out those really interesting for a working mathematician. In the same time, among terabytes of data, interesting rules can be discovered and successfully applied. In our opinion, mathematical reasoning is also an important part of the area of information sciences, recently it belongs rather to the part explored by the community of automated reasoning within computer science. We can quote here the words of Dana Scott opening Vienna Summer of Logic in 2014:

> *"Computers and logic have to come together to discover new unexpected facts in mathematics and give their proofs. (...) So, we have to put together all of our technology to really come up with new things."*[1]

---

[1] http://vsl2014.at/livestream/index.html#Recordings.

© Springer International Publishing AG 2017
L. Polkowski et al. (Eds.): IJCRS 2017, Part I, LNAI 10313, pp. 83–94, 2017.
DOI: 10.1007/978-3-319-60837-2_7

In order do achieve this goal, many activities should be done in parallel: the formalization language should not be very artificial to be attractive for mathematician. Also fundamental theorems of the basic areas of mathematics should be provided in a uniform framework, or at least interfaces linking various platforms should be provided; last but not least – not only archival papers, but also those from the so-called research frontier should be encoded. In wide repository of formalized mathematical knowledge we have the possibilities of using various available tools from the area of computerized proof-assistants. The papers should be carefully selected as sometimes the gap between theorems formulated and proven by the author and the current state of the library could be too wide. Our paper was intended a step towards bridging this gap.

The paper is organized as follows: in Sect. 2 we formulate the problem chosen for the formalization, concentrating on basic ideas standing behind the formal development, the next section shows the duality between relational and structural approaches which we used in Mizar. In Sects. 4 and 5 we show that the one exception of a proof from [27] which was hard to follow for us and some solutions of how to lift the formulations from predicative style into the language of adjectives. The next two sections contain the description of chosen mechanisms of automation and some statistical data about the code finally submitted by us to the Mizar Mathematical Library. At the end of the paper, we conclude and draw some hints for future work.

2   Generalized Rough Sets

Generalizations of rough sets [18], practically from their beginnings, attracted much efforts from researchers' side. Now we can treat the work of Skowron and Stepaniuk on tolerance approximation spaces [21] as the foundational paper on how to lift generality of the original (based on equivalence relations) a bit up, but this slightly more general approach really opened new paths of reasoning about incomplete knowledge. Many of these ways can be explored by means of automated reasoning tools. As our software system, we used Mizar proof assistant [1], which together with the Mizar Mathematical Library – the repository of machine-verified mathematical knowledge has already shown its potential in the field of rough sets [11].

As our challenge to do so we have chosen a paper of William Zhu "Generalized rough sets based on relations" [27] published in a leading journal in the field. Immediately we noticed, that many relatively popular notions of a general character quoted by Zhu (e.g. seriality and mediateness of a binary relation), were not defined in MML, so they had to be introduced by us from scratch. Hence, a major part of initial encoding was devoted to various basic properties of binary relations (although some of them seem to be not of a general interest for ordinary mathematician, as positive or negative alliance relations). We were facing lots of tiny decisions of which approach should be formally chosen (a concrete model of a rough set – pairs vs. approximations, application of relational structures, etc.), however Zhu's paper is written quite consistently with mathematical intuitions.

Hence we were prepared for relatively simple formalization, and as informal presentation took 15 pages, it should be of the order of 60 pages in Mizar, a few thousand lines of code (ca. two-three Mizar articles). We already deal with much more complex frameworks, i.e. the formalization of the Jordan Curve Theorem consisted of approx. 100 Mizar articles, and the encoding of *A Compendium of Continuous Lattices* of the same order of complexity. Another case study of ours on formalization of the connections between lattice theory and rough set theory resulted in massive development, e.g. twenty Mizar articles, and as of now, is still not completed [6].

2.1 Listed Characteristic Formulas

The main idea of the considered paper was to establish the connection between basic properties of approximation operators [12,13] and corresponding properties of binary relations; in foundational mathematics it can be considered a preliminary work to *reverse mathematics*. Original list of the common properties considered by Zhu is rather long (16 formulas), we quote here only basic four of them, briefly reflecting the idea of research:

(3L) $R_*(X) \subseteq X$
(4L) $R_*(X \cap Y) = R_*(X) \cap R_*(Y)$
(7L) $R_*(-R_*(X)) = -R_*(X)$
(8LH) $R_*(-X) = -R^*(X)$

Of course, the considerations can be done on the very abstract level – the definition of the approximation operator is quite meaningless and some of the formulas are well known; we can find Kuratowski's closure properties among them. However, if we try to follow Yao [24] method of proving, we can freely accept (8LH) as the definition of the dual approximation operator, so it is more a kind of axiom than the property which should be proven. As in our primary approach both approximation operators are defined separately, it is proven like the remaining theorems. We could also separate properties dealing with algebraic operations or set-theoretic (mainly, the complementation operator).

We were not aware of the adjectives of finiteness and non-emptiness of the universe of discourse U – even if sometimes these assumptions can be avoided, we left them in order to keep proofs simple (based on induction) and faithful to the original. In the future, we will try to attack these proofs with the help of automated theorem provers (from scratch).

2.2 Hidden vs. Visible Arguments

In real mathematics, one rarely uses the syntax of expressing all the arguments explicitly. But to avoid the confusion, Zhu writes

$$L(R)(X \cup Y)$$

to underline that the lower approximation operator depends on the binary relation R or even introduces a notation letting $L = L(R)$ and afterwards he uses naturally-looking

$$L(X \cup Y)$$

instead, which is especially justified taking into account complicated formula from p. 5004 of [27]:

$$(5H'') \ H(R)H(R)(X)(X) \subseteq H(R)(X).$$

Using relational structures we should not give the argument of indiscernibility relation explicitly as the type system recognizes it from the type of the argument. This trick is called a *hidden argument* and it significantly simplifies the notation without any affect of its understandability by the computer. That is the reason of writing `LAp X` (parentheses around the single argument can be omitted) instead of something like `LAp(R)(X)`.

2.3   Refactoring of the Existing Proof

It appeared that old developments can be just reused, in order to do that, we introduced a new object, the Mizar functor called `GeneratedRelation`. It is quite natural to say that we generate a relational structure based on the ordering given by the specific formula, such construction is then formally introduced.

Basic idea is expressed by the formula

$$xRy \Leftrightarrow x \in H(\{y\})$$

```
definition
  let R be non empty RelStr,
      H be Function of bool the carrier of R, bool the carrier of R;
  func GeneratedRelation (R,H) -> Relation of the carrier of R means
:: ROUGHS_3:def 3
      for x,y being Element of R holds [x,y] in it iff x in H.{y};
end;
```

The idea standing behind this definition is justified by Theorem 3 from [24]:

```
theorem :: ROUGHS_3:14   :: Yao Theorem 3
  for A being finite non empty set,
      L, H being Function of bool A, bool A st L = Flip H holds
      (H.{} = {} &
      (for X,Y being Subset of A holds H.(X \/ Y) = H.X \/ H.Y))
      iff
      ex R being non empty finite RelStr st
        the carrier of R = A & LAp R = L & UAp R = H &
        for x,y being Element of R holds
        [x,y] in the InternalRel of R iff x in H.{y};
```

The auxiliary functor `Flip` H constructs from an arbitrary map defined on the powerset of the universe its corresponding map (it takes the the value of the set-theoretic complementation of the argument, and then complements it once more, i.e. returns $(H(x^c))^c$ for every subset x of the universe of discourse). This clearly corresponds with the property (8LH) mentioned in Sect. 2.1.

The Mizar functor described in this subsection plays a role of the interface between an arbitrary map (regardless of its properties) and corresponding relational structure, where approximation operators can be further studied. The use of this lemma saved about 340 lines of Mizar code which was originally spent just on copies of the same parts of proofs under various combinations of properties.

3   Relational vs. Structural View for Rough Sets

The distinction between classical and abstract mathematics (i.e. the one based on ordinary axioms of set theory, and all those using the notion of a structure, respectively) is important from the viewpoint of the organization of the Mizar repository. We had to choose between two paths:

- it is possible to formulate practically all notions as logical predicates, without the use of a structure, and also set theory could be meaningless for that framework, only the classical logic with Mizar predicates is enough (equality plays a special role in the system based on set theory;
- the use of Mizar structures forces us paradoxically to use basics of set theory – defining a signature of any algebraic system needed to give a type of an object, which was set-theoretic (as the Mizar language is typed, and in the earlier case one should also give a type at least to primitive objects, otherwise the most general type `object` is attributed).

The latter was also chosen by us as the theory of posets in MML is written in abstract style (as the majority of MML, as you can read from the numbers: 323 articles are without structures, the rest, i.e. 966 use them at least once) as structures in Mizar are present for a long time. Even if in ordinary mathematical tradition they are considered as ordered tuples, in the implementation in Mizar they are treated rather as partial functions, with selectors as arguments, and ordinary inheritance mechanism (with polymorphic enabled, which will be extensively used in our formalizations).

Another main premise to cope with such an approach was the possibility of further theory merging: rough fuzzy hybridization [5] (as we did fuzzy numbers [26] recently [8]) or variable precision [29] rough set models. Merging with topology [25, 28] is already provided formally as we described in [10].

Such construction is also known in other automated proof-assistants, e.g. in Isabelle under the name *modules*, but their importance and the possibility of its further reuse is not that high as in our case (recently, Isabelle is oriented on programming rather than on mathematics). We were strongly convinced that the structural view provides better readability for at least two reasons:

- hidden arguments are structures, and usually we work within a single fixed approximation space;
- structures are relatively well developed in the Mizar Mathematical Library (at least they offer more flexible syntax than other proof-assistants), furthermore they provide merging theories.

The first added value soon appeared to be a significant drawback: we observed that if we have to deal with two or more approximation spaces at the same time, i.e. we deal with the union and the intersection of two approximation spaces, things get much worse formally. That was the situation with the final theorems of [27] dealing also with a problem of the uniqueness of binary relations to generate rough sets. We have no space here to describe how we successfully coped with this problem, but of course it can be tracked in MML.

4   The Gap

Our original aim is to translate full paper into Mizar formalism, and we almost succeeded formalizing Zhu's paper as a whole. There is one exception, though: the theorem named "Proposition 10", p. 5005, and as a consequence, the single item from Theorem 2, p. 5007, which is in fact, a corollary (7H) are proven in a weaker form, that is only for singletons instead of arbitrary sets. Of course, the other implication (that the alliance relation exists under the assumptions of (2H), (4H), and (7H)) is proven.

```
theorem :: ROUGHS_3:33 :: Proposition 10 (7H') for singletons
  for R being finite positive_alliance non empty RelStr,
     x being Element of R holds
   ((UAp R).{x})' c= (UAp R).(((UAp R).{x})');

::theorem :: Proposition 10 (7H') general case - FAILED
::   for R being finite positive_alliance non empty RelStr,
::      X being Subset of R holds
::    ((UAp R).X)' c= (UAp R).(((UAp R).X)');
```

We left it unproven intentionally (of course, it is not present in the Mizar code as in order to be included in the Mizar Mathematical Library it can contain no errors in the source) just to let the automated theorem provers automatically discover proof for this single inference. Unfortunately, neither of basic methods of automated proving (running basic MPTP, Vampire 4.1, and E prover 2.0) succeeded in this concrete case.

This second theorem was commented out, because otherwise it would be marked by the system as erroneous.

5   Attributes

In a form of a summary, all the characterizations of approximations in terms of the properties of binary relations are collected in Sect. 3.7, page 5007 of [27].

Not to get into details, we can give the simple idea of how this works in Mizar, quoting two conditional registrations of clusters.

```
registration
  cluster positive_alliance -> serial for non empty RelStr;
  cluster transitive serial -> positive_alliance for non empty RelStr;
end;
```

It should be noted that regardless of the use of adjectives, all the summarizing content can be expressed in Mizar in terms of ordinary implications between corresponding formula denoting properties; it is quite straightforward, but registrations of clusters provide the automatic treatment of positive alliance relations as serial ones, and additionally, those which are transitive and serial, are equipped with the property of positive alliance. Similar connection between seriality and totality of a binary relation was automatically discovered before [9].

As a side effect, we can further consider other properties originating in conflict theory: alliance, conflict, and coalition [17]. This quite natural setting within the information system is also well-known in the theory of social choice, when the buyer expresses his opinion about the goods: either he/she expresses his/her preference to this object, or he/she is strongly against that, or is neutral, i.e. none of special opinions are emphasized, or neutrality is stated. Thanks to theory merging mechanism, we can reuse at least some of such theorems.

6   Automatizing Properties

In mathematical papers, there are many phrases like "The proof is obvious" or just theorems are left without the proof (which is considered trivial and marked by the sign "□"). This very informal level of obviousness, which of course varies depending on many circumstances, was considered by Rudnicki in [20], and in the setting of automated proof verifiers describes the "smartness" of the software, or the ability of justification of an inference based on available premises.

For example, the inclusion

$$H(R)((H(R)(\emptyset))^c) \subseteq (H(R)(\emptyset))^c$$

expressed in the Mizar formalism as

```
theorem   :: Obvious due to the mechanism of clusters
  for R being non empty RelStr holds
    UAp ((UAp ({}R))') c= (UAp ({}R))';
```

is obvious because of the mechanism of registrations and reductions formulated by us:

- UAp {}R reduces to the subterm {}R;
- ({}R)' is automatically expanded to set-theoretic difference of the universe of R and the empty set;

- $X \setminus \emptyset$ is automatically unified with X or, in our case, with the universe of a relational structure R;
- that the left hand side term is included in the right hand side term is automatically calculated from the type of the left hand side term (it is just the subset of R), hence an inference is accepted provided the last item;
- the upper approximation operator is properly defined, i.e., for subset of a relational structure R it returns again a subset of R (or, to be formally strict, a subset of the carrier of R).

The mechanism of reductions, i.e. the first item from the above list, was a relatively recently implemented example of the influence of equational theorem provers [1]. The issue of creating the net of such connections as smart as possible is important as mathematicians do not want to cope with very rigorous details of their proofs (also the design of flexary connectives in Mizar, i.e. logical operations with an ellipsis in the list of arguments [15] allows to decrease the rigour on the syntax level).

7   Some Statistics

In total, we have formulated and proven all items[2] from Zhu's paper. The results were accepted for inclusion to the Mizar Mathematical Library and the formalized content is divided into two parts (two files with MML identifiers ROUGHS_2 and ROUGHS_3). First part was finished already a couple of years ago, the second – more problematic – part was finished last year [7] and this paper is a kind of a brief report on it. The Mizar articles are hyperlinked and can be browsed freely online[3]. We decided also to give some data for two other files – ROUGHS_1 contains very basic notions specific to rough set theory, obviously not introduced by Zhu, but heavily used in his paper. The Mizar article ROUGHS_4 contains potentially useful constructions of operators, also not used directly in [27], but improving the readability of the proper code. As we can read from Table 2, the time of both verification and finding irrelevant premises is notably bigger in these auxiliary submissions than in straight translations of Zhu's theorems.

The summary of our work is given in two tables. Table 1 gives the idea of the complexity of the code by some quantitative measures. Four files containing the formal development needed to understand and prove material from considered paper took about 125 pages of fully formal definitions, theorems, proofs and more Mizar-specific constructions allowing for better use of the encoded work. The ratio of the number of theorems and the number of definitions can be slightly disappointing (ca. 2.4 vs. 3–5 claimed to be optimal), but we have to bear in mind that the formalization of this theory is in its early stage, so many new constructions had to be introduced.

---

[2] One exception is described in Sect. 4.

[3] The addresses are http://mizar.org/version/current/html/roughs_2.html and http://mizar.org/version/current/html/roughs_3.html.

Table 1. Basic statistical data on our four main contributions

MML Id	ROUGHS_1	ROUGHS_2	ROUGHS_3	ROUGHS_4	Total
Lines of code	1686	1791	2392	1605	7474
Pages (approx.)	28	30	40	27	125
Core lines	0	848	1645	0	2493
Core pages	0	14	27	0	41
Definitions	19	18	12	28	77
Theorems	61	44	54	23	182
TPTP problems	591	557	858	566	2572
Notations attached	29	19	22	42	51
Used articles	61	39	55	75	83

In the last line we counted all originally attached articles, some of them could bring relatively small percentage of knowledge (it should be remembered that MML is subject to continuous evolution, one of important changes are those increasing the integrity of the library, that is making the library better organized, without much accidental theory placements). Significantly higher value (75 files) in the fourth file is caused by the fact that we reuse general and algebraic topology there, and even a bit of category theory. It should be also mentioned that ROUGHS_4 was completed before ROUGHS_3 and in fact it develops some formal apparatus for the earlier; even if it does not bring any "core" formalization (i.e. directly translating Zhu's paper), it merges known approaches to make the formalization more smooth.

Times measured on a machine with 8 GB of RAM and Intel i7 processor (under Linux operating system by `time` command, in seconds) are contained in Table 2.

Table 2. Running time of selected Mizar commands (in seconds)

Command	ROUGHS_1	ROUGHS_2	ROUGHS_3	ROUGHS_4
Accomodator	0.548	0.327	0.412	0.396
Verifier	6.672	3.817	4.901	6.428
Relprem	15.040	8.486	12.081	13.728

Even if we established the automation at quite high level via tight network of registrations and reductions, the time of checking is reasonable: `relprem` tool discovers potential irrelevant premises (of course, in our case, all such linkages were removed), so the values are approximately three times bigger. The accomodator imports all the needed knowledge previously stored in the MML.

Summarizing, the translation of [27] took slightly over 40 pages of Mizar code. Taking into account only number of pages, not kilobytes, the rough de Bruijn factor [23] (the ratio of the fully formal translation within the computer system and its informal counterpart) is equal to $41/15 \approx 2.73$, which is significantly below 4 claimed as an average value. In our opinion that shows both the high level of formalism used in [27], and relatively high expressive power of the Mizar language applied to rough set theory.

For a broader development, having also lattice theory in mind (see our case study [11]), these numbers are not so optimistic (the value 3.3 is one of the best cases measured for a single section). On the other hand, the nature of textbooks, monographs like [14], and regular papers [27] is different: textbooks provide usually more detailed proofs, and the exposition of the topic is rather elementary. In recent papers from research frontier significant part of proofs is usually sketchy, while monographical publications are somewhere in the middle. Frankly speaking, both abovementioned publications chosen to formalize in Mizar provide very rigorous proofs, which was an exceptional circumstance for us, making the work much easier.

8   Conclusions and Further Work

One of our main objectives was to provide reasonably faithful translation of Zhu's paper to be included as a part of one of the largest repositories of automatically verified mathematical knowledge. This allows for further exploration via TPTP (Thousands of Problems for Theorem Provers) tools.[4]

Of course, this encoding should not be treated as *l'art pour l'art*; the gains can be potentially at least threefold:

- it opens the possibility of further translation into other repositories, as Isabelle's Archive of Formal Proofs [2]; we do not know about formalization of rough sets in any other popular proof-asistant like HOL Light, Isabelle, Coq, and Metamath;
- even if as of now, automated provers offer about 50% of positive hits [22], completed results can serve for machine learning in order to be more successful, also experiments with external SAT solvers are quite successful [16]; this could eventually save a lot of time spent for more time-consuming tedious passages in proofs;
- fully formal, hyperlinked version of proofs can be explored via Semantic Web-type tools. Such computerized, mechanically verified repository is an ideal starting point for further transformations: in fact, Wikipedia was established years after the project of hyperlinking knowledge contained in the Mizar Mathematical Library (started in 1995). The choice of the appropriate formal model just to open an area of research is quite hard – we hope however that our framework allows to attract more people to continue this work (especially because of the open access to the repository of Mizar texts).

---

[4] The set of problems extracted from the Mizar Mathematical Library was used for years at yearly CADE (Conferences on Automated Deduction) conferences.

It should be noted here, that our failure in proving one of the Zhu's propositions had rather unexpected consequence: as we did not provide the proof of the general case (for arbitrary sets), but only in case of singletons, we spent some time to study the so-called *unit operations* proposed by Bonikowski [3]. We hope that more formal interconnections with this method will be shown as in the future. It could allow to do reasonings basically only about singletons, having general theory behind these to justify needed theorems on universal sets. On the other hand, Theorem 3 from [24] is of general character and can be used not only for approximation operators, but also e.g., for maps in topological spaces as the properties are very intuitive.

The next step will be to automatize the proofs [19] and notions as much as possible in order to gain additional linking between various theories. As of now, we see general topology as a promising area of mathematics – well represented in MML, and an important framework for expressing notions of rough set theory.

References

1. Bancerek, G., Byliński, C., Grabowski, A., Korniłowicz, A., Matuszewski, R., Naumowicz, A., Pąk, K., Urban, J.: Mizar: state-of-the-art and beyond. In: Kerber, M., Carette, J., Kaliszyk, C., Rabe, F., Sorge, V. (eds.) CICM 2015. LNCS, vol. 9150, pp. 261–279. Springer, Cham (2015). doi:10.1007/978-3-319-20615-8_17
2. Blanchette, J.C., Haslbeck, M., Matichuk, D., Nipkow, T.: Mining the archive of formal proofs. In: Kerber, M., Carette, J., Kaliszyk, C., Rabe, F., Sorge, V. (eds.) CICM 2015. LNCS, vol. 9150, pp. 3–17. Springer, Cham (2015). doi:10.1007/978-3-319-20615-8_1
3. Bonikowski, Z.: Unit operations in approximation spaces. In: Szczuka, M., Kryszkiewicz, M., Ramanna, S., Jensen, R., Hu, Q. (eds.) RSCTC 2010. LNCS, vol. 6086, pp. 337–346. Springer, Heidelberg (2010). doi:10.1007/978-3-642-13529-3_36
4. Bryniarski, E.: Formal conception of rough sets. Fundam. Informaticae **27**(2/3), 109–136 (1996). doi:10.3233/FI-1996-272302
5. Dubois, D., Prade, H.: Rough fuzzy sets and fuzzy rough sets. Int. J. Gen Syst **17**(2–3), 191–209 (1990). doi:10.1080/03081079008935107
6. Grabowski, A.: Mechanizing complemented lattices within Mizar type system. J. Autom. Reason. **55**(3), 211–221 (2015). doi:10.1007/s10817-015-9333-5
7. Grabowski, A.: Binary relations-based rough sets - an automated approach. Formaliz. Math. **24**(2), 143–155 (2016). doi:10.1515/forma-2016-0011
8. Grabowski, A.: On the computer certification of fuzzy numbers, In: Ganzha, M., Maciaszek, L., Paprzycki, M. (eds.) Proceedings of Federated Conference on Computer Science and Information Systems, FedCSIS 2013, pp. 51–54 (2013)
9. Grabowski, A.: Automated discovery of properties of rough sets. Fundam. Informaticae **128**(1–2), 65–79 (2013). doi:10.3233/FI-2013-933
10. Grabowski, A.: Efficient rough set theory merging. Fundam. Informaticae **135**(4), 371–385 (2014). doi:10.3233/FI-2014-1129
11. Grabowski, A.: Lattice theory for rough sets - a case study with Mizar. Fundam. Informaticae **147**(2–3), 223–240 (2016). doi:10.3233/FI-2016-1406
12. Grabowski, A.: On the computer-assisted reasoning about rough sets. In: Dunin-Kęplicz, B., Jankowski, A., Szczuka, M. (eds.) Monitoring, Security and Rescue Techniques in Multiagent Systems. Advances in Soft Computing, vol. 28, pp. 215–226. Springer, Heidelberg (2005). doi:10.1007/3-540-32370-8_15

13. Grabowski, A., Jastrzębska, M.: Rough set theory from a math-assistant perspective. In: Kryszkiewicz, M., Peters, J.F., Rybinski, H., Skowron, A. (eds.) RSEISP 2007. LNCS, vol. 4585, pp. 152–161. Springer, Heidelberg (2007). doi:10.1007/978-3-540-73451-2_17

14. Järvinen, J.: Lattice theory for rough sets. In: Peters, J.F., Skowron, A., Düntsch, I., Grzymała-Busse, J., Orłowska, E., Polkowski, L. (eds.) Transactions on Rough Sets VI. LNCS, vol. 4374, pp. 400–498. Springer, Heidelberg (2007). doi:10.1007/978-3-540-71200-8_22

15. Korniłowicz, A.: Flexary connectives in Mizar. Comput. Lang. Syst. Struct. 44(Part C), 238–250 (2015). doi:10.1016/j.cl.2015.07.002

16. Naumowicz, A.: Automating boolean set operations in Mizar proof checking with the aid of an external SAT solver. J. Autom. Reason. 55(3), 285–294 (2015). doi:10.1007/s10817-015-9332-6

17. Pawlak, Z.: On conflicts. Int. J. Man-Mach. Stud. 21, 127–134 (1984). doi:10.1016/S0020-7373(84)80062-0

18. Pawlak, Z.: Rough Sets: Theoretical Aspects of Reasoning about Data. Kluwer, Dordrecht (1991). doi:10.1007/978-94-011-3534-4

19. Pąk, K.: Improving legibility of formal proofs based on the close reference principle is NP-hard. J. Autom. Reason. 55(3), 295–306 (2015). doi:10.1007/s10817-015-9337-1

20. Rudnicki, P.: Obvious inferences. J. Autom. Reason. 3(4), 383–393 (1987). doi:10.1007/BF00247436

21. Skowron, A., Stepaniuk, J.: Tolerance approximation spaces. Fundam. Informaticae 27(2–3), 245–253 (1996). doi:10.3233/FI-1996-272311

22. Urban, J., Sutcliffe, G.: Automated reasoning and presentation support for formalizing mathematics in Mizar. In: Autexier, S., Calmet, J., Delahaye, D., Ion, P.D.F., Rideau, L., Rioboo, R., Sexton, A.P. (eds.) CICM 2010. LNCS, vol. 6167, pp. 132–146. Springer, Heidelberg (2010). doi:10.1007/978-3-642-14128-7_12

23. Wiedijk, F.: Formal proof - getting started. Not. AMS 55(11), 1408–1414 (2008)

24. Yao, Y.Y.: Two views of the rough set theory in finite universes. Int. J. Approx. Reason. 15(4), 291–317 (1996). doi:10.1016/S0888-613X(96)00071-0

25. Yao, Y., Yao, B.: Covering based rough set approximations. Inf. Sci. 200, 91–107 (2012). doi:10.1016/j.ins.2012.02.065

26. Zadeh, L.: Fuzzy sets. Inf. Control 8(3), 338–353 (1965). doi:10.1016/S0019-9958(65)90241-X

27. Zhu, W.: Generalized rough sets based on relations. Inf. Sci. 177(22), 4997–5011 (2007). doi:10.1016/j.ins.2007.05.037

28. Zhu, W.: Topological approaches to covering rough sets. Inf. Sci. 177(6), 1499–1508 (2007). doi:10.1016/j.ins.2006.06.009

29. Ziarko, W.: Variable precision rough set model. J. Comput. Syst. Sci. 11, 39–59 (1993). doi:10.1016/0022-0000(93)90048-2

New Algebras and Logic from a Category of Rough Sets

Anuj Kumar More[(⊠)] and Mohua Banerjee

Department of Mathematics and Statistics, Indian Institute of Technology,
Kanpur, Kanpur 208016, India
{anujmore,mohua}@iitk.ac.in

Abstract. In this work, we focus on the study of the algebra of strong subobjects obtained from a category of rough sets that forms a quasitopos. A new algebraic structure called 'contrapositionally complemented pseudo Boolean algebra' is obtained and its basic properties studied. The corresponding logic 'intuitionistic logic with minimal negation' is introduced, and its connection with the intuitionistic and minimal logics is discussed.

Keywords: Rough sets · Quasitopos · Contrapositionally complemented lattices · Pseudo-Boolean algebras · Intuitionistic logic · Minimal logic

1 Introduction

Rough set theory was defined by Pawlak [1] in 1982 to deal with incomplete information. Since then it has been studied from both foundational and application points of view. One of the many directions of study on the foundational side is that involving algebraic studies of rough sets, a summary of which can be found in [2]. Another direction involves the category-theoretic study of rough sets. Our work is an amalgamation of the algebraic and category-theoretic approaches.

Categories $ROUGH$ and ξ-$ROUGH$ of rough sets were first given by Banerjee and Chakraborty in [3]. Further work on categories and rough sets were later done, and can be found in [4–7]. In [8], it was shown that the category RSC [7] is equivalent to $ROUGH$; RSC and ξ-RSC (equivalent to ξ-$ROUGH$) were further investigated. Their generalizations, categories $RSC(\mathscr{C})$ and ξ-$RSC(\mathscr{C})$ over an arbitrary elementary topos $\mathscr{C}$, were defined, such that in the special case when $\mathscr{C}$ is the topos SET, we get RSC and ξ-RSC. The topos-theoretic properties of these categories were studied, and $RSC(\mathscr{C})$ was shown to form a quasitopos. Furthermore, the algebra of strong subobjects of an RSC-object obtained using the internal logic of the quasitopos RSC was studied. 'Contrapositionally $\vee$ complemented' ($c. \vee c.$) lattices were obtained by replacing the

A.K. More—This work is supported by the *Council of Scientific and Industrial Research* (CSIR) India, Research Grant No. 09/092(0875)/2013-EMR-I.

© Springer International Publishing AG 2017
L. Polkowski et al. (Eds.): IJCRS 2017, Part I, LNAI 10313, pp. 95–108, 2017.
DOI: 10.1007/978-3-319-60837-2_8

negation operator in the algebra with Iwiński's *rough difference* operator [9]. In fact, starting with an arbitrary Boolean algebra, a whole class of $c. \lor c.$ lattices was obtained by abstracting the constructions in the algebra of RSC-subobjects (which is a Boolean algebra).

In this work, we study the algebra and logic of the class of strong subobjects of an $RSC(\mathscr{C})$-object. We proceed in a way similar to this study done for RSC in [8]. As the algebra of $RSC(\mathscr{C})$-subobjects is a pseudo-Boolean algebra, here we start with an arbitrary pseudo-Boolean algebra. On abstracting the constructions in the algebra of $RSC(\mathscr{C})$-subobjects, we obtain a class of contrapositionally complemented (*c.c.*) lattices instead of $c. \lor c.$ lattices. In fact, the strong subobjects of an $RSC(\mathscr{C})$-object form a new algebraic structure with two negations which we call 'contrapositionally complemented (*c.c.*) pseudo-Boolean algebra'. We give the representation theorem for this class of algebras. Further we define the corresponding logic which we call 'intuitionistic logic with minimal negation' (ILM). We introduce the definition of 'interpretation' and show that ILM is interpretable in intuitionistic logic (IL). We can further show that ILM is interpretable in minimal logic (ML) as well, using well-known mappings between IL and ML [10,11].

In the next section, we recall the definitions and properties of various categories of rough sets [3,4,8], and also derive a necessary and sufficient condition for the category $\xi\text{-}RSC(\mathscr{C})$ to be a quasitopos. In Sect. 3, the algebra of strong subobjects of an object in $RSC(\mathscr{C})$ is investigated. The *c.c.*-pseudo-Boolean algebras are defined and their representation theorem is obtained. The corresponding logic ILM and its connection with other logics is discussed in Sect. 4. Section 5 concludes the article.

For all basic category-theoretic notions, we refer to [12,13].

2   Categories of Rough Sets

An approximation space is a pair (U, R), where R is an equivalence relation over a set U. For any set $X \subseteq U$, $\overline{X}_R$ denotes the collection of equivalence classes in U properly intersecting X and $\underline{X}_R$ denotes the collection of equivalence classes in U contained in X, that is,

$$\overline{X}_R := \{[x]_R \mid [x]_R \cap X \neq \emptyset\}, \text{ and}$$

$$\underline{X}_R := \{[x]_R \mid [x]_R \subseteq X\}.$$

The R-upper approximation of X is $\overline{X}_R = \bigcup \overline{X}_R$ and the R-lower approximation of X is $\underline{X}_R = \bigcup \underline{X}_R$, where union is taken over the elements of equivalence classes in the respective collections. The suffix R can be dropped from the notation whenever the approximation space is clear from the context. The following two categories of rough sets are defined in [3] and [7] respectively.

Definition 1 (The category *ROUGH* **[3]).** *The category ROUGH has the triples $\langle U, R, X \rangle$ as objects, where (U, R) is an approximation space and $X \subseteq U$. The set functions $f : \overline{X}_R \rightarrow \overline{Y}_S$ are the arrows with domain $\langle U, R, X \rangle$ and codomain $\langle V, S, Y \rangle$ such that $f(\underline{X}_R) \subseteq \underline{Y}_S$.*

The arrows of *ROUGH* thus preserve the lower approximation.

Definition 2 (The category *RSC* [7]). *The category RSC has the pairs (X_1, X_2) as objects, where X_1, X_2 are sets and $X_1 \subseteq X_2$, and the set functions $f : X_2 \to Y_2$ as arrows with domain (X_1, X_2) and codomain (Y_1, Y_2) such that $f(X_1) \subseteq Y_1$.*

The category *ROUGH* is finitely complete but not a topos [3]; the category *RSC* is also not a topos [7]. In fact, the categories *RSC* and *ROUGH* are equivalent [8]. Furthermore, *RSC* forms a weak topos [7] as well as a quasitopos [8], structures that are weaker than a topos. Note that an important feature of a quasitopos distinguishing it from a topos is that the subobject classifier in a quasitopos classifies only the strong monics and not the monics.

Elementary toposes were defined to capture properties of the category *SET* of sets. With a similar goal in mind, in [8] we proposed the following natural generalization $RSC(\mathscr{C})$ of the rough set category *RSC*.

Definition 3 (The category $RSC(\mathscr{C})$ [8]). *The category $RSC(\mathscr{C})$ has the pairs (A, B) as objects, where A and B are objects in $\mathscr{C}$ such that there exists a monic arrow $m : A \to B$ in $\mathscr{C}$. m is said to be a* monic arrow corresponding to the object (A, B).
The pairs (f', f) are the arrows with domain (X_1, X_2) and codomain (Y_1, Y_2), where $f' : X_1 \to Y_1$ and $f : X_2 \to Y_2$ are arrows in $\mathscr{C}$ such that $m'f' = fm$, and m and m' are monic arrows corresponding to the objects (X_1, X_2) and (Y_1, Y_2) in $RSC(\mathscr{C})$ respectively.

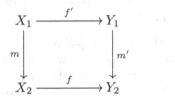

We observe that $RSC(\mathscr{C})$ is just *RSC*, when $\mathscr{C}$ is the topos *SET*. *RSC* forms a quasitopos. Therefore, a natural question is what kind of topos-theoretic structure does $RSC(\mathscr{C})$ form.

Theorem 1 [8]. $RSC(\mathscr{C})$ *is a quasitopos.*

Let us recall one more category of rough sets defined in [3]. In both the definitions of the categories *ROUGH* and *RSC*, the morphisms preserve the upper and lower approximations. Capturing the idea that during 'communications' (being represented by morphisms) between rough sets, the boundary region $(\overline{\mathcal{X}}_R \setminus \underline{\mathcal{X}}_R)$ may be an invariant, the category ξ-*ROUGH* is defined as follows.

Definition 4 (The category ξ-*ROUGH* [3]). *The category ξ-ROUGH has the objects same as ROUGH-objects. An arrow in ξ-ROUGH with domain $\langle U, R, X \rangle$ and codomain $\langle V, S, Y \rangle$ is a map $f : \overline{\mathcal{X}}_R \to \overline{\mathcal{Y}}_S$ such that $f(\underline{\mathcal{X}}_R) \subseteq \underline{\mathcal{Y}}_S$ and $f(\overline{\mathcal{X}}_R \setminus \underline{\mathcal{X}}_R) \subseteq \overline{\mathcal{Y}}_S \setminus \underline{\mathcal{Y}}_S$.*

Similarly, we can define ξ-RSC category having objects same as RSC and arrows satisfying $f(X_1) \subseteq Y_1$ and $f(X_2 \setminus X_1) \subseteq Y_2 \setminus Y_1$. Both ξ-RSC and ξ-$ROUGH$ are equivalent to SET^2, and thus, they form a topos [8]. The generalization of ξ-RSC is also possible over any topos $\mathscr{C}$, as the set difference operation can be abstracted in any topos using the negation $\neg$ operator in the algebra of subobjects of $\mathscr{C}$. Given any monic arrow $f : A \to C$ in $\mathscr{C}$, the negation $\neg f : \neg A \to C$ is obtained by taking the pullback of the morphism $\neg \circ \chi_f$ along the subobject classifier $\top : 1 \to \Omega$ in $\mathscr{C}$. The domain of $\neg f$, that is $\neg A$, is the set difference $C \setminus A$ in the topos SET. Therefore, we can say that $\neg$ abstracts the definition of set difference operation. We are now in a position to define ξ-$RSC(\mathscr{C})$.

Definition 5 (The category ξ-$RSC(\mathscr{C})$ [8]). *Objects of ξ-$RSC(\mathscr{C})$ are same as objects of $RSC(\mathscr{C})$. An arrow (f', f) of $RSC(\mathscr{C})$, where $f' : X_1 \to Y_1$ and $f : X_2 \to Y_2$, is an arrow in ξ-$RSC(\mathscr{C})$ if there exists an arrow $f'' : \neg X_1 \to \neg Y_1$ such that the following diagram commutes,*

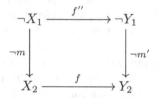

where $m, m', \neg m$ and $\neg m'$ are monics corresponding to the objects (X_1, X_2), (Y_1, Y_2), $(\neg X_1, X_2)$ and $(\neg Y_1, Y_2)$ respectively. Arrows in ξ-$RSC(\mathscr{C})$ are represented as the triple (f'', f', f).

ξ-$RSC(SET)$ is just the category ξ-RSC, which, as mentioned earlier, is a topos. However, for an arbitrary topos $\mathscr{C}$, we are able to show that ξ-$RSC(\mathscr{C})$ is not always a topos (or a quasitopos), and that depends on the Boolean property of the 'base' topos $\mathscr{C}$. By a 'Boolean topos' $\mathscr{C}$, we mean that for any monic $m : A \to B$ in $\mathscr{C}$, we have $(m \cup \neg m) \cong Id_B$ in the subobject lattice of B. Using standard notation [12], we write $C \cong D$ to denote that there is an iso arrow $f : C \to D$ in $\mathscr{C}$.

Theorem 2. *$\xi - RSC(\mathscr{C})$ is a quasitopos if and only if $\mathscr{C}$ is a Boolean topos.*

Proof. We have seen in [8], that if $\mathscr{C}$ is Boolean topos, ξ-$RSC(\mathscr{C})$ is equivalent to $\mathscr{C}^2$ and thus, a topos (and quasitopos).

For the converse, assume $\mathscr{C}$ to be a non-Boolean topos, that is, there exists a monic arrow $m : A \to B$ such that $(m \cup \neg m) \not\cong Id_B$ in the subobject lattice of the object B in $\mathscr{C}$. Consider the arrow $(Id_0, m \cup \neg m, Id_B) : (A \cup \neg A, B) \to (B, B)$ in ξ-$RSC(\mathscr{C})$, where $A \cup \neg A$ is the domain of $m \cup \neg m$, and $m \cup \neg m$ and Id_B are the monic arrows corresponding to the objects $(A \cup \neg A, B)$ and (B, B) respectively in $RSC(\mathscr{C})$. It can be checked that $(Id_0, m \cup \neg m, Id_B)$ is epi and strong monic, but not iso as $(m \cup \neg m) \not\cong Id_B$. However, in any quasitopos, any arrow which is epi and strong monic is iso. Therefore, ξ-$RSC(\mathscr{C})$ is not a quasitopos.   □

Recall the category $RSC(\mathbf{2}\text{-Set})$ defined in [8], where $\mathbf{2}\text{-Set}$ is the category of monoid actions of $\mathbf{2} := \{0, 1\}$ on sets. Since, $\mathbf{2}\text{-Set}$ is a topos but not a Boolean topos, $\xi\text{-}RSC(\mathbf{2}\text{-Set})$ does not form a quasitopos. In general, any topos $\mathbf{M}\text{-Set}$ [12], where $\mathbf{M}$ is a monoid but not a group, is non-Boolean. Therefore, we have

Corollary 1. $\xi\text{-}RSC(\mathbf{M}\text{-Set})$ *is not a quasitopos, where* $\mathbf{M}$ *is any monoid that is not a group.*

Any quasitopos, just like a topos, has an internal logic associated with the class of strong subobjects of its objects. In the next section, we exploit this feature to study the algebras of strong subobjects in the quasitopos(es) of rough sets just discussed.

3 Algebras of Strong Subobjects in RSC and $RSC(\mathscr{C})$

One of our goals of studying the categories of rough sets discussed above, is to investigate the algebraic structures emerging from the internal logic of the categories. In any topos (quasitopos), the class of all the monics (strong monics) with fixed codomain forms a pseudo-Boolean algebra, where one defines the basic operators $\cap$, $\cup$, $\rightarrow$ and $\neg$ on the class by the internal logic associated with the topos (quasitopos) [13]. Let us recall the algebra of strong subobjects of an object in the quasitopos RSC, and its properties [8].

Consider the set $\mathcal{M}(X)$ of all the strong subobjects of an RSC-object $(\underline{\mathcal{X}}, \overline{\mathcal{X}})$. Elements of $\mathcal{M}(X)$ are the pairs (A_1, A_2) such that $A_1 \subseteq A_2 \subseteq \overline{\mathcal{X}}$ and $A_1 = A_2 \cap \underline{\mathcal{X}}$, that is $A_2 \setminus A_1 \subseteq \overline{\mathcal{X}} \setminus \underline{\mathcal{X}}$. In RSC, $(\mathcal{M}(X), (\underline{\mathcal{X}}, \overline{\mathcal{X}}), (\emptyset, \emptyset), \cap, \cup, \rightarrow, \neg)$ forms a pseudo-Boolean algebra, where operations are obtained using pullbacks of specific characteristic morphisms along the RSC subobject classifier $(\top, \top)$: $(1, 1) \rightarrow (2, 2)$. In fact, we have something more.

Proposition 1 [8]. *In RSC, the class of strong subobjects of an RSC-object $(\underline{\mathcal{X}}, \overline{\mathcal{X}})$, $(\mathcal{M}(X), (\underline{\mathcal{X}}, \overline{\mathcal{X}}), (\emptyset, \emptyset), \cap, \cup, \rightarrow, \neg)$ forms a Boolean algebra.*

The class of monics in $\xi\text{-}RSC$ and the class of strong monics in RSC are the same and the algebras of subobjects obtained over the same object in $\xi\text{-}RSC$ and RSC are also identical. Therefore, it is sufficient to study the algebra of subobjects of any one of them.

It is well-known that the algebraic structures formed from rough sets (e.g. cf. [14]) are non-Boolean. The prime reason for the classical behavior of the strong subobjects of an RSC-object lies in the definition of negation $\neg$ of the RSC-object (A_1, A_2). We had noted in [8] that since the complementation $\neg$ is with respect to the object $(\underline{\mathcal{X}}, \overline{\mathcal{X}})$, we actually require the concept of *relative* rough complementation. Iwiński's *rough difference* operator [9] is what we use, and we define a new negation $\sim$ on $\mathcal{M}(X)$ as:

$$\sim: \quad \sim (A_1, A_2) := (\underline{\mathcal{X}} \setminus A_2, \overline{\mathcal{X}} \setminus A_1).$$

Let us note the following definitions from literature.

Definition 6.

1. [15] *The algebra* $(B, 1, \wedge, \vee, \rightarrow, \neg)$ *is a* contrapositionally complemented *lattice (c.c. lattice) if* $(B, 1, \wedge, \vee, \rightarrow)$ *is a relatively pseudo-complemented lattice (r.p.c. lattice) and for any* $x \in B$, $x \rightarrow \neg y = y \rightarrow \neg x$.
   Equivalently, $(B, 1, \wedge, \vee, \rightarrow, \neg)$ *is a c.c. lattice if and only if* $(B, 1, \wedge, \vee, \rightarrow)$ *is an r.p.c. lattice, and for any* $x \in B$, $\neg x = x \rightarrow \neg 1$.
2. [16] *A c.c. lattice* $(B, 1, \wedge, \vee, \rightarrow, \neg)$ *is a* contrapositionally $\vee$ complemented *lattice (c. $\vee$ c. lattice) if for any* $x \in B$, $x \vee \neg x = 1$.

Proposition 2 [8]. *For every RSC-object* $(\underline{\mathcal{X}}, \overline{\mathcal{X}})$, $(\mathcal{M}(X), (\underline{\mathcal{X}}, \overline{\mathcal{X}}), \cap, \cup, \rightarrow, \sim)$ *is a c. $\vee$ c. lattice with the least element* $(\emptyset, \emptyset)$.

We shall see in the sequel that $(\mathcal{M}(X), (\underline{\mathcal{X}}, \overline{\mathcal{X}}), \cap, \cup, \rightarrow, \sim)$, in fact, forms a richer structure.

As $RSC(\mathscr{C})$ is a quasitopos, just as in the case of RSC, the set of strong monics of an $RSC(\mathscr{C})$-object (U_1, U_2) also forms a pseudo-Boolean algebra. Let us recall what the strong monics in $RSC(\mathscr{C})$ are. An arrow $(f', f) : (X_1, X_2) \rightarrow (U_1, U_2)$ is a strong monic if and only if $f : X_2 \rightarrow U_2$ is a monic and the following diagram in a pullback,

$$
\begin{array}{ccc}
X_1 & \xrightarrow{\ f'\ } & U_1 \\
{\scriptstyle m_1}\downarrow & & \downarrow{\scriptstyle m_2} \\
X_2 & \xrightarrow{\ f\ } & U_2
\end{array}
$$

where m_1 and m_2 are the monic arrows corresponding to (X_1, X_2) and (U_1, U_2) respectively. Let $\mathcal{M}((U_1, U_2))$ denote the set of all strong monics in $RSC(\mathscr{C})$ with codomain (U_1, U_2). We can characterize the operations on $\mathcal{M}((U_1, U_2))$ as follows.

Proposition 3. *The operations on* $\mathcal{M}((U_1, U_2))$ *obtained by taking the pullbacks of specific characteristic morphisms along the $RSC(\mathscr{C})$-subobject classifier* $(\top, \top) : (1, 1) \rightarrow (\Omega, \Omega)$ *are*

$$
\begin{aligned}
\cap &: \ (f', f) \cap (g', g) = (f' \cap g', f \cap g), \\
\cup &: \ (f', f) \cup (g', g) = (f' \cup g', f \cup g), \\
\neg &: \ \neg(f', f) = (\neg f', \neg f), \\
\rightarrow &: \ (f', f) \rightarrow (g', g) = (f' \rightarrow g', f \rightarrow g),
\end{aligned}
$$

where (f', f) and (g', g) are strong monics with codomain (U_1, U_2), and $\top : 1 \rightarrow \Omega$ is the subobject classifier of the topos $\mathscr{C}$. The operations on f', g' (f, g) used above are those of the algebra of subobjects of U_1 (U_2) in the topos $\mathscr{C}$.

As noted above, $(\mathcal{M}((U_1, U_2)), (Id_{U_1}, Id_{U_2}), (0, 0), \cap, \cup, \rightarrow, \neg)$ is a pseudo-Boolean algebra. Bringing Iwiński's *rough difference* operator into this generalized scenario as well, we define a new negation $\sim$ on $\mathcal{M}((U_1, U_2))$.

Definition 7. *On the set* $\mathcal{M}((U_1, U_2))$, *define 'rough' negation as:*

$$\sim : \quad \sim (f', f) := (\neg f', \neg(m \circ f')).$$

where (f', f) *is strong monics with codomain* (U_1, U_2) *and* $m : U_1 \to U_2$ *is the corresponding monic arrow associated to* (U_1, U_2).

Simplifying $\sim (f', f)$, we have $\sim (f', f) = (\neg f', \neg(f \cap m)) = (\neg f', f \to (\neg m)) = (f', f) \to (0, \neg m)$ and $\sim (Id_{U_1}, Id_{U_2}) = (\neg Id_{U_1}, Id_{U_2} \to \neg m) = (0, \neg m)$. Therefore, from the definition of a *c.c.* lattice (cf. Definition 6), we have the following.

Theorem 3. $\mathcal{A} := (\mathcal{M}((U_1, U_2)), (U_1, U_2), (0, 0), \cap, \cup, \to, \sim)$ *is a c.c. lattice with the least element* $(0, 0)$.

Moreover, we have

Proposition 4.

1. *The algebra* $\mathcal{A}$ *satisfies the following properties:*
   $\sim (Id_{U_1}, Id_{U_2}) = \neg\neg \sim (Id_{U_1}, Id_{U_2})$, *and*
   $\sim (f', f) = (f', f) \to (\neg\neg \sim (Id_{U_1}, Id_{U_2}))$, *for any* $(f', f) \in \mathcal{M}((U_1, U_2))$.
2. $\sim$ *does not satisfy the semi-negation property: in general,*
   $\sim ((f', f) \to (f', f)) \to (g', g) \neq (Id_{U_1}, Id_{U_2})$,
   for $(f', f), (g', g) \in \mathcal{M}((U_1, U_2))$.
3. $\sim$ *does not satisfy the involution property: in general,*
   $\sim\sim (f', f) \neq (f', f)$ *for* $(f', f) \in \mathcal{M}((U_1, U_2))$, *as the first component of* $\sim\sim (f', f)$ *is* $\neg\neg f'$, *which need not be equal to* f' *in a non-Boolean topos* $\mathscr{C}$.

The properties in Proposition 4(1) are not true in general for an arbitrary *c.c.* lattice. Proposition 4(2) and (3) suggest that the lattice $\mathcal{A}$ is neither pseudo-Boolean nor quasi-Boolean. Therefore the proposition indicates that $\mathcal{A}$ is an instance of a new algebraic structure, involving two negations $\sim$ and $\neg$ and defined as follows.

Definition 8. *An abstract algebra* $\mathcal{A} := (A, 1, 0, \cap, \cup, \to, \neg, \sim)$ *is said to be a* contrapositionally complemented pseudo-Boolean algebra *(c.c.-pseudo-Boolean algebra) if* $(A, 1, 0, \cap, \cup, \to, \neg)$ *forms a pseudo-Boolean algebra and for all* $a \in A$, *the following condition holds:*

$$\sim a = a \to (\neg\neg \sim 1).$$

If, in addition, for all $a \in A$, $a \vee \sim a = 1$, *we call* $\mathcal{A}$ *a c.* $\vee$ *c.-pseudo-Boolean algebra.*

Observation 1.

1. *For each* $RSC(\mathscr{C})$-*object* (U_1, U_2), $(\mathcal{M}((U_1, U_2)), (U_1, U_2), (0, 0), \cap, \cup, \to, \neg, \sim)$ *is a c.c.-pseudo-Boolean algebra.*
2. *For each* RSC-*object* $(\underline{\mathcal{X}}, \overline{\mathcal{X}})$, $(\mathcal{M}(X), (\underline{\mathcal{X}}, \overline{\mathcal{X}}), \cap, \cup, \to, \neg, \sim)$ *is a c.* $\vee$ *c.-pseudo-Boolean algebra.*

Let us compare the algebras defined above with some existing lattices having two different negations. One of the most familiar such structures is the *quasi-pseudo Boolean algebra* [15,17], in which one of the negations satisfies the involution property. However, both the negations in c.c.-pseudo-Boolean and $c. \vee c.$-pseudo-Boolean algebras are non-involutive in general. Another example is from fuzzy logics, where the *strict basic logic (SBL)* with an additional negation and the corresponding algebras $SBL_\sim$ are defined [18]. Again, the additional negation is always taken to be involutive in $SBL_\sim$-algebras.

Starting from the Boolean algebra property of the set $\mathcal{M}(X)$ in the quasitopos RSC, we had obtained a $c. \vee c.$ lattice (cf. Proposition 2). More generally, we have seen in [8] that starting with an arbitrary Boolean algebra, a whole class of $c. \vee c.$ lattices can be obtained by abstracting the constructions in the Boolean algebra $\mathcal{M}(X)$. We proceed in a way similar to this for $RSC(\mathscr{C})$. As the algebra of strong subobjects of an $RSC(\mathscr{C})$-object is a pseudo-Boolean algebra, here we start with an arbitrary pseudo-Boolean algebra $\mathcal{H} := (H, 1, 0, \wedge, \vee, \rightarrow, \neg)$. On abstracting the constructions in the algebra, we find an entire class of c.c.-pseudo-Boolean algebras.

Theorem 4. *Let $u := (u_1, u_2) \in \mathcal{H}^{[2]} := \{(a, b) : a \leq b, a, b \in H\}$. Consider the set $A_u := \{(a_1, a_2) \in \mathcal{H}^{[2]} : a_2 \leq u_2 \text{ and } a_1 = a_2 \wedge u_1\}$. Define the following operators on A_u:*

$$\sqcup : (a_1, a_2) \sqcup (b_1, b_2) := (a_1 \vee b_1, a_2 \vee b_2),$$
$$\sqcap : (a_1, a_2) \sqcap (b_1, b_2) := (a_1 \wedge b_1, a_2 \wedge b_2),$$
$$\rightarrow : (a_1, a_2) \rightarrow (b_1, b_2) := ((a_1 \rightarrow b_1) \wedge u_1, (a_2 \rightarrow b_2) \wedge u_2),$$
$$\sim : \sim (a_1, a_2) := (u_1 \wedge \neg a_1, u_2 \wedge \neg a_1),$$
$$\neg : \neg(a_1, a_2) := (a_1, a_2) \rightarrow (0, 0).$$

Then $\mathcal{A} := (A_u, (u_1, u_2), (0, 0), \sqcap, \sqcup, \rightarrow, \neg, \sim)$ is a c.c.-pseudo-Boolean algebra.

Proof. $(A_u, (u_1, u_2), \sqcap, \sqcup, \rightarrow)$ forms a *r.p.c.* lattice. In fact with the negation $\neg$, $(A_u, (u_1, u_2), (0, 0), \sqcap, \sqcup, \rightarrow, \neg)$ forms a pseudo-Boolean algebra. For $\mathcal{A}$ to be a c.c.-pseudo-Boolean algebra, we must have $\sim (a_1, a_2) = (a_1, a_2) \rightarrow (\neg\neg \sim (u_1, u_2))$ for all $(a_1, a_2) \in A_u$. We have $\sim (u_1, u_2) = (u_1 \wedge \neg u_1, u_2 \wedge \neg u_1) = \neg(u_1, u_1)$ and

$$\sim (a_1, a_2) = (u_1 \wedge \neg a_1, u_2 \wedge \neg a_1) = (a_1, a_2) \rightarrow ((u_1, u_1) \rightarrow (0, 0))$$
$$= (a_1, a_2) \rightarrow (\neg(u_1, u_1)) = (a_1, a_2) \rightarrow (\neg\neg\neg(u_1, u_1))$$
$$= (a_1, a_2) \rightarrow (\neg\neg \sim (u_1, u_2)).$$

$\square$

Corollary 2. *If $\mathcal{H}$ is a Boolean algebra, then $\mathcal{A}_u$ forms a $c. \vee c.$-pseudo-Boolean algebra.*

The class of pseudo-Boolean algebras has a representation theorem [15]. For every pseudo-Boolean algebra $\mathcal{H}$, there exists a monomorphism h from $\mathcal{H}$ into the pseudo-field of all open subsets of a topological space. Using the definition of pseudo-fields of open subsets, we can define the corresponding set lattice for c.c.-pseudo-Boolean algebras.

Definition 9 (Contrapositionally complemented pseudo-fields). *Let* $\mathcal{G}(X) := (\mathcal{G}(X), X, \emptyset, \cap, \cup, \rightarrow, \neg)$ *be a pseudo-field of open subsets of a topological space X. Define*

$$\sim X := \neg\neg Y_0 \quad \text{for some } Y_0 \text{ belonging to } \mathcal{G}(X),$$
$$\sim Z := Z \rightarrow (\neg\neg \sim X).$$

The algebra $(\mathcal{G}(X), X, \emptyset, \cap, \cup, \rightarrow, \neg, \sim)$ *is called the* contrapositionally complemented pseudo-field *(c.c. pseudo-field) of open subsets of X.*

The definition of *c.c.* pseudo-field is motivated by the definition of the *c.c.* set lattice [15]. In *c.c.* set lattice also, the negation of any element is defined using an arbitrary but fixed element Y_0.

We now obtain the representation for the class of *c.c.*-pseudo-Boolean algebras.

Theorem 5 (Representation theorem). *For every c.c.-pseudo-Boolean algebra* $\mathcal{A} := (A, 1, 0, \cap, \cup, \rightarrow, \neg, \sim)$, *there exists a monomorphism h from $\mathcal{A}$ into a c.c. pseudo-field of all open subsets of a topological space X.*

Proof. By the representation theorem for pseudo-Boolean algebras, there exists a monomorphism h from $\mathcal{H} := (A, 1, 0, \cap, \cup, \rightarrow, \neg)$ into the pseudo-field $\mathcal{G}(X) := (\mathcal{G}(X), X, \emptyset, \cap, \cup, \rightarrow, \neg)$ of all open subsets of a topological space X. Fixing $Y_0 := h(\sim 1)$ and defining $\sim$ on $\mathcal{G}(X)$ as in Definition 9, $(\mathcal{G}(X), X, \emptyset, \cap, \cup, \rightarrow, \neg, \sim)$ is a *c.c.* pseudo-field of all open subsets of X. We now have

$$\sim X = \neg\neg Y_0 = \neg\neg h(\sim 1) = h(\neg\neg \sim 1) = h(\sim 1) \qquad (*)$$

because $\neg h(a) = h(\neg a)$ for all $a \in A$, and $\neg\neg \sim 1 = \sim 1$. For h to be a monomorphism from $\mathcal{A}$ into a *c.c.* pseudo-field, we must have $h(\sim a) = \sim a$. Indeed, using (*), we get the following.

$$h(\sim a) = h(a \rightarrow (\neg\neg \sim 1)) = h(a) \rightarrow (\neg\neg h(\sim 1))$$
$$= h(a) \rightarrow (\neg\neg \sim X) = \sim h(a). \qquad \square$$

4   Intuitionistic Logic with Minimal Negation

Since the class of all pseudo-Boolean algebras is equationally definable, the class of all *c.c.*-pseudo-Boolean algebras is also so. We can now define the logic corresponding to *c.c.*-pseudo-Boolean algebras.

Definition 10 (Intuitionistic logic with minimal negation (ILM)). *The language of* ILM, $\mathfrak{L}_5$, *consists of propositional variables* $p, q, r, \ldots,$; *logical unary symbols* $\sim, \neg$; *logical binary symbols* $\wedge, \vee, \rightarrow$; *and the constant symbols* $\top, \bot$; *and parentheses. The class F of well-formed formulas is defined recursively as:*

$$\top \mid \bot \mid p \mid \alpha \wedge \beta \mid \alpha \vee \beta \mid \alpha \rightarrow \beta \mid \neg \alpha \mid \sim \alpha$$

Axiom schemes:

Ax(1). $\alpha \rightarrow (\beta \rightarrow \alpha)$
Ax(2). $(\alpha \rightarrow (\beta \rightarrow \gamma)) \rightarrow ((\alpha \rightarrow \beta) \rightarrow (\alpha \rightarrow \gamma))$
Ax(3). $\alpha \rightarrow (\alpha \vee \beta)$
Ax(4). $\beta \rightarrow (\alpha \vee \beta)$
Ax(5). $(\alpha \rightarrow \gamma) \rightarrow ((\beta \rightarrow \gamma) \rightarrow ((\alpha \vee \beta) \rightarrow \gamma))$
Ax(6). $(\alpha \wedge \beta) \rightarrow \alpha$
Ax(7). $(\alpha \wedge \beta) \rightarrow \beta$
Ax(8). $(\alpha \rightarrow \beta) \rightarrow ((\alpha \rightarrow \gamma) \rightarrow (\alpha \rightarrow (\beta \wedge \gamma)))$
Ax(9). $(\alpha \rightarrow \neg\beta) \rightarrow (\beta \rightarrow \neg\alpha)$
Ax(10). $\neg(\alpha \rightarrow \alpha) \rightarrow \beta$
Ax(11). $\alpha \rightarrow \top$
Ax(12). $\bot \rightarrow \alpha$
Ax(13). $\sim \alpha \rightarrow (\alpha \rightarrow ((\sim \top \rightarrow \bot) \rightarrow \bot))$
Ax(14). $(\alpha \rightarrow ((\sim \top \rightarrow \bot) \rightarrow \bot)) \rightarrow \sim \alpha$

With the modus ponens rule of inference and above formulas as axioms, we define $\Gamma \vdash_{\text{ILM}} \alpha$, *where* $\Gamma \cup \{\alpha\} \subseteq F$.

One can define the semantics $\Gamma \vDash_{\text{ILM}} \alpha$ with respect to the class of *c.c.-*pseudo-Boolean algebras in the standard way, and get the soundness and completeness results.

Theorem 6. ILM *is sound and complete with respect to the class of c.c.-pseudo-Boolean algebras.*

Remark 1. If we add the following axiom Ax(15) in ILM, we obtain the logic corresponding to the class of all *c.* $\vee$ *c.-*pseudo-Boolean algebras.

Ax(15). $\top \rightarrow (\alpha \vee \sim \alpha)$

We have seen that any *c.c.-*pseudo-Boolean algebra is a pseudo-Boolean algebra. In ILM, Ax(1) $-$ Ax(12) are the axioms of intuitionistic logic (IL), the logic corresponding to the class of pseudo-Boolean algebras. Consider $\mathfrak{L}_r$, the language of IL, which is the same as $\mathfrak{L}_5$ but without the negation $\sim$ sign. Then F^*, the set of all IL-formulas on $\mathfrak{L}_r$, is a subset of F. IL is embedded into ILM through the inclusion map from F^* to F, that is, for any $\Gamma \cup \{\alpha\} \subseteq F^*$,

$$\Gamma \vdash_{\text{IL}} \alpha \Leftrightarrow \Gamma \vdash_{\text{ILM}} \alpha.$$

A natural question is whether some 'interpretation' of ILM in IL exists? The answer is in the positive. Let us first formally define the notion of interpretation of one logic in another that is being considered in this work.

Definition 11 (Interpretation). *Consider two formal logics $\mathfrak{L}_1$ and $\mathfrak{L}_2$. The mapping $r : L_1 \rightarrow L_2$, from the set L_1 of formulas in $\mathfrak{L}_1$ to the set L_2 of formulas in $\mathfrak{L}_2$, is called an* interpretation *of $\mathfrak{L}_1$ in $\mathfrak{L}_2$, if for any formula $\alpha \in L_1$, we have the following condition:*

$$\vdash_{\mathfrak{L}_1} \alpha \text{ if and only if } \Delta_\alpha \vdash_{\mathfrak{L}_2} r(\alpha),$$

where Δ_α is a finite set of formulas in $\mathfrak{L}_2$ corresponding to α.

The mapping r is called interpretation *of $\mathfrak{L}_1$ in $\mathfrak{L}_2$ with respect to derivability, if for any set $\Gamma \cup \{\alpha\}$ of formulas in L_1, we have*

$$\Gamma \vdash_{\mathfrak{L}_1} \alpha \text{ if and only if } r(\Gamma) \cup \Delta_\alpha \vdash_{\mathfrak{L}_2} r(\alpha),$$

where Δ_α is a finite set of formulas in $\mathfrak{L}_2$ corresponding to α.

Various definitions of mappings from one formal system to another can be found in literature. The very first studies of logic connections were done by Kolmogorov in 1925 and Glivenko in 1929 (cf. [10]). Some definitions of mappings from one logic into another, called translations, can be found in [11,19]. A detailed study of connections between classical logic (CL), IL and minimal logic (ML) can be found in [10], which has defined the term 'interpretable'. Our definition of interpretation is more general. In the above definition, if Δ_α is empty, both the definitions coincide. Note that we are not requiring the interpretation r to be *schematic* [10].

Let us now prove that ILM can be interpreted in IL, according to Definition 11. The proof is similar to the one used to show the connections between constructive logic with strong negation and IL [15, Chap. XII]. Using axioms (13) and (14) of ILM, we obtain the following proposition.

Proposition 5. *Let $\alpha \in F$ such that $p_1, p_2, \ldots, p_n$ are all the distinct propositional variables in α. Then there exists a formula $\alpha^* \in F$ such that (i) there is no occurrence of $\sim$ sign in α^*, (ii) α^* contains $p_1, p_2, \ldots, p_n$ and a propositional variable q distinct from the p_i's, and (iii) the following condition is satisfied.*

(**) *For any substitution T such that $T(p_i) = p_i$ and $T(q) = \sim \top$ for all $i = 1, \ldots, n$, we have $\vdash_{ILM} \alpha \leftrightarrow T(\alpha^*)$.*

Proof. For the formula α, define α^* by (i) replacing all the occurrences of $\sim \gamma$ by $\gamma \rightarrow \neg\neg \sim \top$, where $\sim \gamma$ is any subformula of α other than $\sim \top$, and (ii) replacing $\sim \top$ by a propositional variable q, where q is distinct from $p_1, p_2, \ldots, p_n$. In the language $\mathfrak{L}_s$, for any $\delta \in F$ and a subformula β of δ, if $\vdash_{ILM} \beta \leftrightarrow \gamma$ for some $\gamma \in F$, then $\vdash_{ILM} \delta \leftrightarrow \bar{\delta}$, where $\bar{\delta}$ is obtained by replacing all the occurrences of β by γ in the formula δ. Since $\vdash_{ILM} (\sim \gamma \leftrightarrow (\gamma \rightarrow \neg\neg \sim \top))$ using the axioms (13)–(14) of ILM, we have $\vdash_{ILM} \alpha \leftrightarrow T(\alpha^*)$ for any substitution T as defined in the condition (**).   □

Using the above proposition and Theorems 5 and 6, we have the following result.

Theorem 7. *For any formula* $\alpha \in F$, *consider* α^* *and a propositional variable* q *as in Proposition 5. Let* $\beta := \neg\neg q \to q$. *Then* $\vdash_{ILM} \alpha$ *if and only if* $\{\beta\} \vdash_{IL} \alpha^*$.

Proof. Let $\nvdash_{ILM} \alpha$. Using Proposition 5, there exists a formula α^* such that for any substitution T, where $T(p_i) = p_i$ for all propositional variables p_i, $i = 1, \ldots, n$, occurring in α and $T(q) =\sim \top$, we have $\nvdash_{ILM} T(\alpha^*)$. Using the completeness, there exists a *c.c.*-pseudo-Boolean algebra $\mathcal{A}$ and a valuation v on $\mathcal{A}$ such that $v(T(\alpha^*)) \neq 1$. Define a valuation Tv on $\mathcal{A}$ such that $Tv(p) := v(T(p))$ for all propositional varibales p. We have, for any formula $\gamma \in F$, $Tv(\gamma) = v(T(\gamma))$. Therefore $Tv(\alpha^*) \neq 1$. For β,

$$Tv(\beta) = Tv(\neg\neg q \to q) = \neg\neg Tv(q) \to Tv(q)$$
$$= \neg\neg v(Tq) \to v(Tq) = \neg\neg v(\sim \top) \to v(\sim \top)$$
$$= v(\neg\neg \sim \top \to \ \sim \top) = 1$$

Therefore, we have $\{\beta\} \nvdash_{IL} \alpha^*$, and by soundness, $\{\beta\} \nvdash_{IL} \alpha^*$.

Let $\{\beta\} \nvdash_{IL} \alpha^*$. By completeness, we have $\{\beta\} \nvDash_{IL} \alpha^*$. Thus, there exists a pseudo-Boolean algebra $\mathcal{H} := (H, 1, 0, \cap, \cup, \to, \neg)$ and a valuation v on $\mathcal{H}$ such that $v(\alpha^*) \neq 1$ and $v(\beta) = 1$. Define a *c.c.*-pseudo-Boolean algebra $\mathcal{B} := (H, 1, 0, \cap, \cup, \to, \neg, \sim)$ such that $\sim 1 := v(q)$ and $\sim a := a \to (\neg\neg \sim 1)$, for any $a \in H$. Note that we have $\neg\neg \sim 1 = v(\neg\neg q) = v(q)$ as $v(\beta) = v(\neg\neg q \to q) = 1$. Therefore the operator $\sim$ is well defined in $\mathcal{B}$. Consider a valuation v' on $\mathcal{B}$ such that $v'(p_i) := v(p_i)$ for all propositional variables p_i occurring in α and $v'(q) := \ \sim 1$. For the valuation v', we have $v'(\alpha^*) = v(\alpha^*)$. Therefore $v'(\alpha^*) \neq 1$ and by soundness, $\nvdash_{ILM} \alpha^*$. Finally using Proposition 5, we have $\nvdash_{ILM} \alpha$. $\square$

Therefore, we have an interpretation of ILM in IL. What about a connection between ILM and ML? We know that ML corresponds to the class of *c.c* lattices [15], and any *c.c.*-pseudo-Boolean algebra is a *c.c.* lattice. In fact, in any *c.c.*-pseudo Boolean algebra $\mathcal{A} := (A, 1, 0, \cap, \cup, \to, \neg, \sim)$, both the negations $\sim$ and $\neg$ satisfy the contraposition law $x \to \neg y = y \to \neg x$. Consider $\mathfrak{L}_m$, the language of ML, which is the same as the language $\mathfrak{L}_{\mathfrak{r}}$ of IL, but without the symbol $\perp$. Therefore, ML is embedded inside ILM. The interpretation of ILM in ML (according to Definition 11) can be obtained by a composition of interpretations. For instance, one can take the mapping r between F^* and $\bar{F}$, the set of formulas of ML, given in [10, Theorem B]: for any $\alpha \in F^*$, $r(\alpha)$ is obtained by induction, by replacing every subformula β of α with $\beta \vee \neg \top$. We then have $\vdash_{IL} \alpha$ if and only if $\vdash_{ML} r(\alpha)$. Composing r with the interpretation of ILM in IL (cf. Theorem 7), we have the following.

Corollary 3. *There exists an interpretation* $t : F \to \bar{F}$ *of* ILM *in* ML.

5   Conclusions

While studying topos and quasitopos properties of categories of rough sets, one finds that the subobjects constitute a new algebraic structure, that we call '*c.c.*

pseudo Boolean algebra'. We obtain an entire class of instances of these algebras. A representation theorem for the algebras is proved. The corresponding logic, 'intuitionistic logic with minimal negation', is then studied and connections with the intuitionistic and minimal logics are presented.

The algebraic structure formed by the subobjects of ξ-$RSC(\mathscr{C})$ when it is a quasitopos, has not yet been investigated. As we saw in the case of RSC and ξ-RSC, the class of monics in ξ-RSC is the same as the class of strong monics in RSC. Proceeding in a similar way, to answer the above question about the algebraic structure, we could first study the relation between the classes of monics and strong monics of the categories ξ-$RSC(\mathscr{C})$ and $RSC(\mathscr{C})$ respectively.

We have also seen some properties of another rough set category ξ-$ROUGH$ [3], which is based on the condition of 'boundary' preservation. There can be other possibilities of defining categories of rough sets depending on the 'regions' of rough sets that are required to be invariant. For instance, one may want the 'negative' region to be preserved, in which case one may refer to Pagliani's definition of rough sets [20] to define the corresponding categories. These studies may give rise to different category-theoretic properties, algebras of subobjects and corresponding logics.

The connections of ILM with IL and ML could also be studied in greater detail. For example, one may check whether some schematic interpretations or translations, based on the definitions in [10,11,19], can be obtained between ILM and IL.

Acknowledgments. We are grateful to the anonymous referees for their valuable remarks.

References

1. Pawlak, Z.: Rough sets. Int. J. Comput. Inform. Sci. **11**(5), 341–356 (1982). doi:10. 1007/BF01001956
2. Banerjee, M., Chakraborty, M.K.: Algebras from rough sets. In: Pal, S.K., Polkowski, L., Skowron, A. (eds.) Rough-Neural Computing. Cognitive Technologies, pp. 157–184. Springer, Heidelberg (2004). doi:10.1007/978-3-642-18859-6_7
3. Banerjee, M., Chakraborty, M.K.: A category for rough sets. Found. Comput. Decis. Sci. **18**(3–4), 167–180 (1993)
4. Banerjee, M., Chakraborty, M.K.: Foundations of vagueness: a category-theoretic approach. Electron. Notes Theor. Comput. Sci. **82**(4), 10–19 (2003). doi:10.1016/ S1571-0661(04)80701-1
5. Banerjee, M., Yao, Y.: A categorial basis for granular computing. In: An, A., Stefanowski, J., Ramanna, S., Butz, C.J., Pedrycz, W., Wang, G. (eds.) RSFDGrC 2007. LNCS, vol. 4482, pp. 427–434. Springer, Heidelberg (2007). doi:10.1007/ 978-3-540-72530-5_51
6. Eklund, P., Galán, M.A.: Monads can be rough. In: Greco, S., Hata, Y., Hirano, S., Inuiguchi, M., Miyamoto, S., Nguyen, H.S., Słowiński, R. (eds.) RSCTC 2006. LNCS, vol. 4259, pp. 77–84. Springer, Heidelberg (2006). doi:10.1007/11908029_9
7. Li, X.S., Yuan, X.H.: The category RSC of I-rough sets. In: Fifth International Conference on Fuzzy Systems and Knowledge Discovery, vol. 1, pp. 448–452 October 2008. doi:10.1109/FSKD.2008.106

8. More, A.K., Banerjee, M.: Categories and algebras from rough sets: new facets. Fundam. Inform. **148**(1–2), 173–190 (2016). doi:10.3233/FI-2016-1429

9. Iwiński, T.B.: Algebraic approach to rough sets. Bull. Pol. Acad. Sci. Math. **35**, 673–683 (1987)

10. Prawitz, D., Malmnäs, P.E.: A survey of some connections between classical, intuitionistic and minimal logic. Stud. Log. Found. Math. **50**, 215–229 (1968). doi:10.1016/S0049-237X(08)70527-5

11. Carnielli, W.A., D'Ottaviano, I.M.L.: Translations between logical systems: a manifesto. Log. Anal. **40**(157), 67–81 (1997)

12. Goldblatt, R.: Topoi: The Categorial Analysis of Logic. Dover Books on Mathematics. Dover Publications, Mineola (2006)

13. Wyler, O.: Lecture Notes on Topoi and Quasitopoi. World Scientific, Singapore (1991)

14. Banerjee, M., Chakraborty, M.K.: Rough sets through algebraic logic. Fundam. Inf. **28**(3,4), 211–221 (1996). doi:10.3233/FI-1996-283401

15. Rasiowa, H.: An Algebraic Approach to Non-classical Logics. Studies in Logic and the Foundations of Mathematics. North-Holland Publishing Company, Amsterdam (1974)

16. Nowak, M.: The weakest logic of conditional negation. Bull. Sect. Log. **24**(4), 201–205 (1995)

17. Gurevich, Y.: Intuitionistic logic with strong negation. Stud. Logica. **36**(1), 49–59 (1977). doi:10.1007/BF02121114

18. Esteva, F., Godo, L., Hájek, P., Navara, M.: Residuated fuzzy logics with an involutive negation. Arch. Math. Log. **39**(2), 103–124 (2000). doi:10.1007/s001530050006

19. Ferreira, G., Oliva, P.: On various negative translations. In: Third International Workshop on Classical Logic and Computation, CL&C 2010, pp. 21–22. Czech Republic, Brno, 21–33 August 2010. doi:10.1007/978-3-7908-1888-8_6

20. Pagliani, P.: Rough set theory and logic-algebraic structures. In: Orłowska, E. (ed.) Incomplete Information: Rough Set Analysis, pp. 109–190. Physica-Verlag HD, Heidelberg (1998)

Rough and Near: Modal History of Two Theories

Marcin Wolski[1]([⊠]) and Anna Gomolińska[2]

[1] Department of Logic and Cognitive Science, Maria Curie-Skłodowska University,
Maria Curie-Skłodowska Sq. 4, 20-031 Lublin, Poland
`marcin.wolski@umcs.lublin.pl`
[2] Faculty of Mathematics and Informatics, University of Białystok,
Konstantego Ciołkowskiego 1M, 15-245 Białystok, Poland
`anna.gom@math.uwb.edu.pl`

Abstract. Near sets were introduced by J.F. Peters in 2007 in the context and within the conceptual framework of rough sets, which were initiated by Z. Pawlak in the early 1980s. However, due to further evolution and development, near set theory has become an independent field of study. For this reason, nowadays, the relationships between near set theory and rough set theory are not easy to spot. In this short paper we would like to re-define near sets and to re-think their foundations and relationships to/bearing on rough sets. To this end we translate the basic concepts of near set theory into the framework of modal logic, which has already been successfully applied to rough sets. The concept of nearness of sets, however, was originally defined globally (that is, with respect to the whole underlying space), but modal logic is intrinsically local: the logical value of a formula is computed with respect to a single point and its neighbourhood. Our approach to near sets is local in the very same sense: we are concerned with nearness of sets seen from the perspective of a single point. Interestingly, this local perspective brings together rough set theory and near set theory, revealing their deep theoretical connections. Therefore, what we offer is a modal and algebraic "shared history" of the two theories at issue.

1 Introduction

Near sets were introduced by J.F. Peters in 2007 papers [22,23]. The main idea stemmed from the 2002 private correspondence between J.F. Peters and Z. Pawlak – the creator of rough set theory [16–21] – and the collaboration between J.F. Peters, A. Skowron, and J. Stepaniuk in 2006 [24]. Thus, near sets were brought in within the context of rough set theory, and primarily regarded as a kind of "young siblings" of rough sets. The next natural context for introduction of near sets is the spatial nearness of sets. The beginning of the study of that type of nearness might be traced back to the address by F. Riesz at the International Congress of Mathematicians in Rome in 1908 [27]. The most fundamental concepts were introduced by Čech during the 1936–1939 Brno seminar series (published in [7]), and V.A. Efremovič in 1933 (published in [8]). In this

© Springer International Publishing AG 2017
L. Polkowski et al. (Eds.): IJCRS 2017, Part I, LNAI 10313, pp. 109–122, 2017.
DOI: 10.1007/978-3-319-60837-2_9

regard, the main novelty of near set theory comes from introduction of descriptive nearness, which is more concerned with descriptions of objects rather than objects alone. Still, a lot of topological results about spatial nearness may be naturally transferred to the descriptive framework. The study of formal connections between spatially near sets and descriptively near sets may be found in papers by J.F. Peters and S.A. Naimpally [15,25]. On the one hand, this topological development is of great importance: it has made near sets an independent framework and field of study. On the other hand, it has also made the formal relationships between near sets and rough sets much harder to notice.

The main goal of this paper is to re-tell the story of near sets and rough sets within the conceptual framework of modal logic and re-build the formal relationships between these two theories. We would like to emphasise once again that our goal is not to define a new modal system, but to use modal logic to reveal some hidden relationships between rough sets and near sets, which are not visible outside that modal frame.

Modal logic is intrinsically local, therefore we need to translate basic concepts of near set theory into the local framework. Surprisingly, this frame reveals many interesting connections between rough sets and nearness collections, which are hardly noticeable from the global standpoint. More importantly, these connections turn out to be a part of a bigger story about modal logic and Kripke frames, on the one hand, and modal coalgebraic logic and relational liftings [12,13], on the other hand. The beginning of interest in coalgebraic modal logic may be traced back to the seminal paper by L. Moss [13]. Since then the so-called cover modality has been studied extensively by many authors. General overview my be found in [12]. The study of proof systems and axiomatisation are discussed in M. Bilkova et al. [5,6]. It is worth recalling that coalgebraic logic is a part of a very important research area of the theory of coalgebras, which was initiated by P. Aczel in the late 1980s [1,2]. Therefore, in the paper we offer a description of formal relationships between rough sets and near sets within the general framework of coalgebras, which is now one of the most important conceptual frameworks in theoretical computer science.

The paper is organised as follows. In the first part we recall rough set theory and its modal counterpart. Then we recall fundamental concepts from topology and near sets. We focus our attention especially on nearness collections and discuss their relationships with rough set approximation operators. Finally, we assign to nearness collections corresponding modal operators and compare them with $\Diamond$ and $\Box$ of **S5** modal logic, which provides the modal counterpart of rough approximations. At the end we embed our study into the coalgebraic framework of modal logic [12,13].

2   Rough Sets: Modal Story

In this section we present the fundamental concepts of rough set theory within the framework of (normal) modal logic. We start with a standard presentation and then discuss its modal counterpart. In the next section we are going to repeat this scheme/method for the case of near set theory, whose modal counterpart has never been discussed before.

In rough set theory *knowledge about a specific domain is construed as a classification of its elements* [21]. For this very reason the fundamental structure of rough set theory, an *approximation space*, is a classification itself.

Definition 1 (Approximation Space). *A pair (U, E), where U is a finite set of objects, and E is an equivalence relation, is called an* approximation space.

As is well known, each equivalence relation E determines a partition U/E of the universe U, which is usually interpreted as a classification of objects (of course, each object x may be classified only to one equivalence class $[x]_E$). Therefore an approximation space expresses the information/knowledge encoded by the underlying information system. Any subset $X \subseteq U$ is called a *concept*, U/E is called a *knowledge basis*, and concepts built up from elements of the knowledge basis are called *definable concepts* or *exact concepts*. Since definable (exact) concepts/sets are supposed to form some algebraic structure (e.g., a topology or an algebra), usually the empty set $\emptyset$ is added to the knowledge basis. An undefinable (not exact) concept/set is then approximated by a pair of exact concepts/sets.

Definition 2 (Set's Approximations). *Let be given an approximation space (U, E). Every subset X of U is given two approximations:*

$$\underline{X} = \{x \in U : [x]_E \subseteq X\},$$

$$\overline{X} = \{x \in U : [x]_E \cap X \neq \emptyset\}.$$

The set $\underline{X}$ is called the lower approximation *of X, and the set $\overline{X}$ is called the* upper approximation *of X.*

Let $\mathcal{P}U$ denote the collection of all subsets of U. By the usual abuse of language and notation, the operator $\underline{\quad} : \mathcal{P}U \to \mathcal{P}U$ sending X to $\underline{X}$ will be called the *lower approximation operator*, whereas the operator $\overline{\quad} : \mathcal{P}U \to \mathcal{P}U$ sending X to $\overline{X}$ will be called the *upper approximation operator*.

If X is a definable concept/set, then $\overline{X} = \underline{X} = X$. A *rough set* is defined as a pair $(\underline{X}, \overline{X})$; in this approach a definable set is also a rough set. It may seem (philosophically) unintuitive, however it is necessary due to mathematical reasons – otherwise rough sets would not form any interesting structure.

Approximation operators might be easily generalised by replacing an equivalence relation E by any reflexive relation $R \subseteq \mathcal{P}U \times \mathcal{P}U$, and equivalence classes $[x]_E$ by $R[x] = \{y \in U : (x, y) \in R\}$ in the body of Definition 2. In Sect. 4 we regard R as a function $R[\ ] : U \to \mathcal{P}U$ sending x to $R[x]$.

What written above may be regarded as a standard "biography" of rough sets; in what follows we would like to translate it into modal language. Our presentation of modal logic is based upon G. Priest book [26].

Definition 3 (Modal Language). *Let be given a set Φ of propositional variables, elements of which are denoted by p, q, r, and so on, constants $\top, \bot$, and* *a modal operator $\Diamond$. Then the formulas of modal language are generated by the following grammar:*

$$\alpha, \beta ::= p \mid \top \mid \bot \mid \neg\alpha \mid \alpha \vee \beta \mid \alpha \wedge \beta \mid \Diamond\alpha \mid \Box\alpha$$

where p ranges over elements of Φ. The set of well-formed formulas is denoted by $\mathcal{F}$. The Boolean part of $\mathcal{F}$ (i.e., the subset of formulae without any occurrence of modal operators) will be denoted by $\mathcal{F}(\text{Boolean})$.

Definition 4 (Kripke Model). *A Kripke model $\mathbb{K}$ is a triple (W, R, v), where W is a non-empty set of worlds, R is a binary relation on W, and $v : W \times \Phi \to \{0, 1\}$ is a function assigning to each pair (w, p) a truth value 1 (truth) or 0 (falsity). We usually write $v_w(p)$ instead of $v(w, p)$ and read as at the world w, p is true. The function v is extended to every formula $\alpha \in \mathcal{F}$ in the standard way:*

- $v_w(\top) = 1$,
- $v_w(\bot) = 0$,
- $v_w(\neg\alpha) = 1$ *if $v_w(\alpha) = 0$, and 0 otherwise,*
- $v_w(\alpha \wedge \beta) = 1$ *if $v_w(\alpha) = 1$ and $v_w(\beta) = 1$, and 0 otherwise,*
- $v_w(\alpha \vee \beta) = 1$ *if $v_w(\alpha) = 1$ or $v_w(\beta) = 1$, and 0 otherwise,*
- $v_w(\Diamond\alpha) = 1$ *if for some $w' \in W$ such that wRw', $v_{w'}(\alpha) = 1$, and 0 otherwise,*
- $v_w(\Box\alpha) = 1$ *if for all $w' \in W$ such that wRw', $v_{w'}(\alpha) = 1$, and 0 otherwise.*

If $v_w(\alpha) = 1$, for $\mathbb{K} = (W, R, v)$ and $w \in W$, then we also write: $\mathbb{K}, w \models \alpha$. This notation is very handy when we need to covert the relation $\models$ into some other form: e.g., to extend $\models$ to $\mathcal{P}W$ and $\mathcal{P}\mathcal{F}$. We shall return to this problem in the last section of this article.

Definition 5 (Semantic Consequence). *Let $\Sigma \subseteq \mathcal{F}$ and $\alpha \in \mathcal{F}$:*

- $\Sigma \models \alpha$ *if and only if for all Kripke models $\mathbb{K} = (W, R, v)$ and all $w \in W$, if $v_w(\beta) = 1$ for all $\beta \in \Sigma$, then $v_w(\alpha) = 1$.*

Along the standard lines, we write $\models \alpha$ if Σ is empty.

Thus the inference is valid if it is truth preserving at all worlds of all Kripke models. The logic which stems from Kripke models, where R is an equivalence relation, is well-known as **S5**.

For every model (W, R, v) let us define: $|\alpha| = \{x \in U : v_x(\alpha) = 1\}$. It is a straightforward observation that:

Proposition 1. *Every approximation space (U, E) and a map $\phi : \Phi \to \mathcal{P}U$ give rise to a Kripke model $\mathbb{K} = (U, E, v)$ of S5, where $v_x(p) = 1$ iff $x \in \phi(p)$. Furthermore:*

$$|\Box\alpha| = \underline{|\alpha|} \quad \text{and} \quad |\Diamond\alpha| = \overline{|\alpha|}.$$

This approach can be easily applied to generalised approximation spaces (U, R), where R is at least a reflexive relation, and to other modal systems like **KT**, **S4**, **K4**, etc., see e.g. [4,28]. It suffices to take other types of Kripke structures $\mathbb{K} = (U, R, v)$, and the corresponding modal operators $\Diamond$, $\Box$ as the upper and lower approximation operators, respectively.

3 Spatially and Descriptively Near Sets

As said in the introduction, the concept of spatial nearness may be traced back to 1908. As the result of its long history, comes its theoretical depth. Actually, its theoretical "range" goes beyond elementary topology. In this section we focus our attention on the very simplest and fundamental examples of nearness relations and structures, along with their bearing on descriptive nearness. An excellent introduction to spatially near sets is given by S.A. Naimpally [14]. The role of nearness in topology, proximity spaces, and uniform spaces is discussed in great detail in [25].

Definition 6 (Topology). *Let U be a set. A topology in U is family τ of subsets such that:*

- *each union of members of τ is a member of τ;*
- *each finite intersection of members of τ is also a member of τ;*
- *U and $\emptyset$ are members of τ.*

If τ is closed under arbitrary intersections, then τ is called an Alexandrov *topology. A couple (U, τ) is called a* topological space; *members of τ are called* open *sets. A set $X \subseteq U$ is* closed *if $U \setminus X \in \tau$.*

As usual, the smallest closed set containing X is denoted by $Cl(X)$, and the largest open set contained in X is denoted by $Int(X)$. Operator $Cl : \mathcal{P}U \to \mathcal{P}U$ sending X to $Cl(X)$ is called a *closure*, whereas an operator $Int : \mathcal{P}U \to \mathcal{P}U$ sending X to $Int(X)$ is called an *interior*. Thus, $Cl(X)$ is called a closure of X and $Int(X)$ is called an interior of X.

Definition 7 (Spatial Nearness). *A spatial nearness relation δ (called a* discrete *proximity) is defined by*

$$\delta = \{(X, Y) \in \mathcal{P}U \times \mathcal{P}U : Cl(X) \cap Cl(Y) \neq \emptyset\}.$$

A pair (U, δ) is called a proximity space.

We need to emphasise, that a discrete proximity defined above is only an example of proximity relations discussed in topology. The theory of nearness spaces [3, 9] is very rich and we discuss here only a small fragment, which is relevant to near set theory.

If two sets X and Y belong to δ, that is $(X, Y) \in \delta$, we will (as usual) write $X \, \delta \, Y$. If sets X and Y are not near, then we say that these sets are *far* from each other (denoted by $X \, \underline{\delta} \, Y$), where

$$\underline{\delta} = \mathcal{P}U \times \mathcal{P}U \setminus \delta.$$

As an example, let us consider an approximation space.

Proposition 2. *Let be given an approximation space (U, E) and the collection σ of all definable sets. Then (U, σ) is an Alexandrov topological space, whose closure operator is an upper approximation operator. Therefore for the corresponding proximity space (U, δ) it holds that:*

$$\delta = \{(X, Y) : X, Y \subseteq U \ \ \& \ \ \overline{X} \cap \overline{Y} \neq \emptyset\}.$$

The next step in unfolding the nearness relation δ it to find nearness collections ξ such that

$$\xi(X) = \{Y \in U : X \delta Y\}.$$

These collections lead to very rich structures: *nearness spaces* [9] and the category **Near** [3].

Definition 8 (Perceptual System). *A* perceptual system *is a pair* $(U, \mathbb{F})$, *where* U *is a non-empty finite set of perceptual objects and* $\mathbb{F}$ *is a finite sequence of probe functions* $\phi_i : U \to \mathbb{R}$.

The probe functions describe physical features of objects and usually are regarded as sensors. We define $\mathbb{F}$ as a sequence in order to assign to each object $x \in U$ a feature vector $\Phi(x)$ over $\mathbb{F}$, i.e., a vector $(\phi_1(x), \phi_2(x), \dots, \phi_n(x))$ of feature values that describe the object x. For a set $X \subseteq U$ let as define:

$$\mathcal{Q}(X) = \{\Phi(x) : x \in X\}.$$

Definition 9 (Descriptive Nearness). *A set* X *is* descriptively near *to* Y *in* $(U, \mathbb{F})$, *denoted by* $X \delta_\Phi Y$, *iff* $\mathcal{Q}(X) \cap \mathcal{Q}(Y) \neq \emptyset$.

It is important to note that descriptively near sets can be spatially far sets. However, we may "produce" the spacial counterpart of descriptive nearness. Firstly, each perceptual system $(U, \mathbb{F})$ gives rise to an approximation space (U, E), where $(x, y) \in E$ iff $\{x\} \delta_\Phi \{y\}$. Thus, secondly, we also have its Alexandrov topological space (U, σ) and the discrete proximity δ_σ.

Proposition 3. *A set* X *is is descriptively near to* Y *in* $(U, \mathbb{F})$ *iff* X *is spatially near to* Y *in the corresponding* (U, σ).

Let us define a nearness collection of X:

$$\xi_\sigma(X) = \{Y \in U : X \delta_\sigma Y\}.$$

It is worth to note the following inverse of standpoints between upper approximations and nearness collections.

Proposition 4. *For a perceptual system* $(U, \mathbb{F})$ *and its approximation space* (U, E) *it holds that:*

$$\overline{X} = \{x : \boxed{[x]_E \cap X \neq \emptyset}\} = \bigcup\{[x]_E : \boxed{[x]_E \cap X \neq \emptyset}\}, \tag{1}$$

$$\xi_\sigma(\{x\}) = \{X \subseteq U : \boxed{[x]_E \cap X \neq \emptyset}\}. \tag{2}$$

This proposition is of pivotal importance: it establishes a connection between rough set and near set perspectives on points, sets, and a granulation of U (in terms of neighbourhoods). In the rough set approach we examine how points are related to a given set X via their minimal neighbourhoods. In the near set approach we examine how sets are related to a given point via the same granulation. It is worth emphasising that Eq. (2) holds only for equivalence relations. If we replace $[x]_E$ by $R[x]$, where R is, e.g., a preorder, then we fail to define the nearness collection $\xi_\sigma(\{x\})$ even for the Alexandrov topological space induced by R. The important consequence of Proposition 4 is the following fact.

Proposition 5. *Let $(U, \mathbb{F})$ be a perceptual system and (U, E) be its approximation space; then*
$$x \in \overline{X} \ iff \ X \in \xi_\sigma(\{x\}).$$

Before we elaborate on that important statement, let us additionally note what follows.

Proposition 6. *For a perceptual system $(U, \mathbb{F})$ and its approximation space (U, E) the following holds: $X \delta_\sigma Y$, for all $X, Y \in \xi_\sigma(\{x\})$ and $x \in U$.*

Thus all elements of $\xi_\sigma(\{x\})$ are near to each other. Let us rewrite $X \delta_\sigma Y$ as $\delta_\sigma(X, Y)$. Then, by Proposition 6, we can extend (the predicate) δ_σ for any (finite) family of sets $\{X_i\}_{i \in I}$ and make it relative to x:

$$\delta_\sigma^x \{X_i\}_{i \in I} \ \text{iff it holds that } X_i \in \xi_\sigma(\{x\}), \text{ for every } i \in I. \tag{3}$$

As already said, Proposition 4 is of special importance. (1) stands that the upper approximation of X is a cover of X by equivalence classes (minimal open neighbourhoods), such that $[x] \cap X \neq \emptyset$. (2) stands that $\xi(\{x\})$ is a maximal cover of $[x]_E$ by $X \subseteq U$, such that $[x] \cap X \neq \emptyset$. Since we want to link these nearness collections to rough set theory, we need to allow them consist of a single set X (in order to compare them with $\overline{X}$ and $\underline{X}$). Therefore we introduce $\mathcal{N}_x \{X_i\}_{i \in I}$, which stands that $\{X_i\}_{i \in I}$ is a subcover of $\xi_\sigma(\{x\})$.

In the next section we discuss $\delta_\sigma^x \{X_i\}_{i \in I}$ and $\mathcal{N}_x \{X_i\}_{i \in I}$ in the modal settings. Let us summarise what we have already discussed with the proposition relating our nearness operators with rough set approximation operators.

Proposition 7. *Let $(U, \mathbb{F})$ be a perceptual system and (U, E) be its approximation space; then*
$$x \in \overline{X} \ iff \ \delta_\sigma^x \{X\},$$
$$x \in \underline{X} \ iff \ \mathcal{N}_x \{X\}.$$

Actually, $\mathcal{N}_x$ is strong enough to define δ_σ^x.

Proposition 8.
$$\delta_\sigma^x (X_i)_{i \in I} \ iff \ \mathcal{N}_x(\{X_i\}_{i \in I} \cup \{U\}).$$

4 Modal Rendering of Nearness

In this subsection we are going to provide modal version of descriptive nearness. As in the case of rough sets, our aim is firstly to show representations of nearness collections in modal language and compare them with rough set modalities. It turns out that nearness collections' modalities are special cases of coalgebraic modalities, which have been extensively studied (including axiomatisations and proof systems) for more than 20 years, e.g. [5,6,12,13]. Thus, as rough sets have the well-defined modal counterpart, near sets have the coalgebraic modal counterpart. However, let us emphasise it again, this strong connection to coalgebraic logic holds only for equivalence relations. Rough sets may be easily generalised to, e.g., a preorder and modal logic **S4**; but any generalisation of near sets "ruins" the connection to coalgebraic modalities.

Let $\mathbb{K} = (U, E, v)$ be a Kripke model for a perceptual system $(U, \mathbb{F})$ and its approximation space (U, E). Thus, we are additionally provided with a map $\phi : \Phi \to \mathcal{P}U$, and $v_x(p) = 1$ iff $x \in \phi(p)$, for $p \in \Phi$. The function ϕ may be further extended to $|\ | : \mathcal{F} \to \mathcal{P}U$, by $|\alpha| = \{x \in X : v_x(\alpha) = 1\}$.

Let us emphasise once again that modal logic is intrinsically local: a given formula/statement $\alpha \in \mathcal{F}$ is always evaluated with respect to the actual world x and we can move only within its neighbourhood, which, in our case, is $[x]_E$. Therefore let us now fix a point x, and rewrite the consequences of Proposition 1:

$$\mathbb{K}, x \models \Diamond\alpha \text{ iff } [x]_E \cap |\alpha| \neq \emptyset \text{ iff } x \in \overline{|\alpha|},$$

$$\mathbb{K}, x \models \Box\alpha \text{ iff } [x]_E \subseteq |\alpha| \text{ iff } x \in \underline{|\alpha|}.$$

Thus, when we translate $\overline{X}$ into the modal language, the set X is replaced by α and the operator $\overline{}$ is represented by $\Diamond$; so we finally obtain $\Diamond\alpha$ in $\mathcal{F}$. In the same way we translate $\underline{X}$ into $\mathcal{F}$ as $\Box\alpha$. Our goal is to make similar translations of $\delta^x_\sigma(X_i)_{i \in I}$ and $\mathcal{N}_x(X_i)_{i \in I}$. Firstly, as X is replaced by α, $(X_i)_{i \in I}$ is replaced by a finite set of formulae Γ. Secondly, we need modal operators to represent δ^x_σ and $\mathcal{N}_x$. Let us write **near**Γ and **Near**Γ, respectively, and define a new language:

$$\alpha, \beta ::= p \mid \neg\alpha \mid \alpha \vee \beta \mid \alpha \wedge \beta \mid \mathbf{near}\Gamma \mid \mathbf{Near}\Gamma$$

where p ranges over the set Φ, and Γ is a finite set of formulae. The set of all formulae of this language will be denoted by $\mathcal{F}_{near}$. In consequence we obtain:

$$\mathbb{K}, x \models \mathbf{near}\Gamma \text{ iff } \delta^x_\sigma\{|\alpha|_i\}_{i \in I}, \text{ where } \Gamma = \{\alpha_i : i \in I\}, \tag{4}$$

$$\mathbb{K}, x \models \mathbf{Near}\Gamma \text{ iff } \mathcal{N}_x\{|\alpha|_i\}_{i \in I}, \text{ where } \Gamma = \{\alpha_i : i \in I\}. \tag{5}$$

Since the main topic of this paper is the story of two theories (rather than a theory incorporating both of them), we will keep rough set theory and near set theory separately "written" in two different modal languages. Thus our task is to show "translations" between $\mathcal{F}$ and $\mathcal{F}_{near}$.

Proposition 9. *Let be given a perceptual system* $(U, \mathbb{F})$ *and its Kripke model* $\mathbb{K} = (U, E, v)$, *where* (U, E) *is an approximation space induced by* $(U, \mathbb{F})$, *and* v *is defined with respect to a map* $\phi : \Phi \rightarrow \mathcal{P}U$. *Then for any* $\alpha \in \mathcal{F}(\texttt{Boolean})$ *the following equivalences hold:*

$$\mathbb{K}, x \models \Diamond\alpha \; iff \; \mathbb{K}, x \models \mathbf{near}\{\alpha\}, \tag{6}$$

$$\mathbb{K}, x \models \Box\alpha \; iff \; \mathbb{K}, x \models \mathbf{Near}\{\alpha\}, \tag{7}$$

$$\mathbb{K}, x \models \Diamond\alpha \; iff \; \mathbb{K}, x \models \mathbf{Near}\{\alpha, \top\}. \tag{8}$$

This proposition describes "translation" of rough set and near set operators on the level of a single formula $\alpha \in \mathcal{F}(\texttt{Boolean})$. The next step is to describe it on the granular level of $\Gamma \subseteq \mathcal{F}(\texttt{Boolean})$. This step however is a bit more complicated. The formula **near**Γ actually means that for every element p of Γ, it is true that $\Diamond p$. Therefore we need to generalise $\wedge$ and $\vee$ for sets of formulae, that is: $\bigwedge \Gamma$ and $\bigvee \Gamma$, respectively. Now, we may write $\bigwedge\{\Diamond p : p \in \Gamma\}$. The formula **Near**$\Gamma$ means that **near**Γ and additionally that $\bigcup\{|p| : p \in \Gamma\}$ covers $[x]_E$, where x is the actual world. Therefore we need to redefine our near set language:

$$\alpha, \beta ::= p \mid \neg\alpha \mid \bigvee \Gamma \mid \bigwedge \Gamma \mid \mathbf{near}\Gamma \mid \mathbf{Near}\Gamma$$

Thus, $\alpha \wedge \beta$ is an abbreviation of $\bigwedge\{\alpha, \beta\}$. Similarly, $\alpha \vee \beta$ stands for $\bigvee\{\alpha, \beta\}$. Let us denote the set of all formulae by $\mathcal{F}_{NEAR}$. The standard Kripke semantics is extended on $\mathcal{F}_{NEAR}$ in the obvious way:

- $v_w(\bigwedge \Gamma) = 1$ if $v_w(\alpha) = 1$ for all $\alpha \in \Gamma$, and 0 otherwise,
- $v_w(\bigvee \Gamma) = 1$ if $v_w(\alpha) = 1$ for some $\alpha \in \Gamma$, and 0 otherwise.

Proposition 10. *Let be given a perceptual system* $(U, \mathbb{F})$ *and its Kripke model* (U, E, v), *defined as above. Then for all* $\Gamma \subseteq \mathcal{F}_{NEAR}(\texttt{Boolean})$:

$$\mathbb{K}, x \models \bigwedge\{\Diamond\alpha : \alpha \in \Gamma\} \; iff \; \mathbb{K}, x \models \mathbf{near}\Gamma,$$

$$\mathbb{K}, x \models \bigwedge\{\Diamond\alpha : \alpha \in \Gamma\} \wedge \Box\bigvee \Gamma \; iff \; \mathbb{K}, x \models \mathbf{Near}\Gamma.$$

The above proposition is of great importance, because it allowed us to notice that the relationships between rough sets and near sets is a part of a bigger story.

In 1995 S. Janin and I. Walukiewicz in the paper [11] extended the syntax of μ-calculus by $a \rightarrow A$, where a is an action and A is a finite set of formulae, and observed that $a \rightarrow A$ is semantically equivalent to $\bigwedge\{<a>\alpha : \alpha \in A\} \wedge [a]\bigvee A$. If we simplify this settings and assume that the set of actions is a singleton, and replace A by our language, that is, $\Gamma \subseteq \mathcal{F}_{NEAR}(\texttt{Boolean})$, then we obtain:

$$a \rightarrow \Gamma \; iff \; \underbrace{\underbrace{\bigwedge\{\Diamond p : p \in \Gamma\}}_{\mathbf{near}\Gamma} \wedge \Box\bigvee \Gamma}_{\mathbf{Near}\Gamma}.$$

S. Janin and I. Walukiewicz also observed that a formula $< a > \alpha$ is equivalent to $a \rightarrow \{\alpha, \top\}$ (compare Proposition 9, Eq. 9) and a formula $[a]\alpha$ is equivalent to $a \rightarrow \{\alpha\} \vee a \rightarrow \emptyset$. Since we deal with equivalence relations (actually, any serial relation would do the job), we may drop out the second part, i.e., $a \rightarrow \emptyset$ (compare Proposition 9, Eq. 8).

Even more interestingly, 4 years later, in 1999, L. Moss in [13] initiated the re-invention of $a \rightarrow A$ in the co-algebraic framework, which further led to the generalisation of this "modality", denoted this time by ∇, from Kripke structures $\mathbb{K} = (W, R, v)$ to coalgebras. The further studies of this modality, proof systems, and axiomatisation may be found, e.g., in [5,6]. The reader is also encourage to consult also [12], which provides a very good overview of this topic. Let us also recall that the theory of coalgebras – initiated by P. Aczel in the late 1980s [1,2] – is a very rich field of study with deep mathematical foundations and interesting applications. The modern introduction to this field may be found in [10]. For the sake of clarity we simplify here coalgebraic results and (instead of discussing the most general cases), we discuss only a case relevant to our study. To make the paper self-contained we firstly recall some basic definitions from category theory and then discuss coalgebras.

Definition 10 (Category). *A category C consists of:*

- *a class of objects denoted by $|C|$,*
- *a class of arrows (or morphisms) from $\mathbf{a}$ to $\mathbf{b}$, denoted by $C(\mathbf{a}, \mathbf{b})$, for all $\mathbf{a}, \mathbf{b} \in |C|$,*
- *a composition operation $\circ : C(\mathbf{b}, \mathbf{c}) \times C(\mathbf{a}, \mathbf{b}) \rightarrow C(\mathbf{a}, \mathbf{c})$, for all $\mathbf{a}, \mathbf{b}, \mathbf{c} \in |C|$,*
- *the identity arrows $id_{\mathbf{a}} \in C(\mathbf{a}, \mathbf{a})$, for all $\mathbf{a} \in |C|$,*

such that, for all $f \in C(\mathbf{a}, \mathbf{b}), g \in C(\mathbf{b}, \mathbf{c}), h \in C(\mathbf{c}, \mathbf{d})$, the following equations are satisfied:

$$h \circ (g \circ f) = (h \circ g) \circ f,$$

$$f \circ id_{\mathbf{a}} = f = id_{\mathbf{b}} \circ f.$$

A standard example of a category is Set which has sets as objects and total functions as arrows. Let us recall that for any topological space (U, τ) its open sets are partially ordered by set inclusion $\subseteq$. Now, we can regard τ as a small category where there is an arrow from $X \in \tau$ to $Y \in \tau$ iff $X \subseteq Y$. Such a category will be denoted by $C(\tau)$.

Definition 11 (Functor). *A functor F from a category A to a category B consists of:*

- *a mapping $|A| \rightarrow |B|$ of objects; the image of $\mathbf{a} \in |A|$ is denoted by $F\mathbf{a}$;*
- *a mapping $A(\mathbf{a}, \mathbf{b}) \rightarrow B(F\mathbf{a}, F\mathbf{b})$ of arrows, for all $\mathbf{a}, \mathbf{b} \in |A|$; the image of function $f \in A(\mathbf{a}, \mathbf{b})$ is denoted Ff;*

such that, for all $\mathbf{a}, \mathbf{b}, \mathbf{c} \in |A|, f \in A(\mathbf{a}, \mathbf{b}), g \in A(\mathbf{b}, \mathbf{c})$, the following conditions are satisfied:

$$F(g \circ f) = Fg \circ Ff \text{ and } Fid_{\mathbf{a}} = id_{F\mathbf{a}}.$$

To give an example, let $\mathbf{C}(\tau_1)$ and $\mathbf{C}(\tau_2)$ be two categories defined above. Then a functor $\mathbf{F} : \mathbf{C}(\tau_1) \to \mathbf{C}(\tau_2)$ is an order preserving function: if $X \subseteq Y$, then $\mathbf{F}(X) \subseteq \mathbf{F}(Y)$, for all $X, Y \in \tau_1$. Another important example is a covariant powerset functor $P : \mathsf{Set} \to \mathsf{Set}$. For objects of Set we have $PX = \mathcal{P}X$, that is, the functor P sends a set X to its powerset. For any function $f : U \to W$, $Pf : PU \to PW$ is defined by $Pf(X) = f[X] = \{f(x) : x \in X\}$, for $X \subseteq U$, that is, $Pf(X)$ is a direct image of X via f.

A T-colagebra is a pair (W, f), where $T : \mathsf{Set} \to \mathsf{Set}$ is a functor (as defined above) and $f : W \to TW$ is a function. In particular, given (U, R) (a generalised approximation space) or $\mathbb{K} = (U, R, v)$, the pair $(U, R[\,])$ is a P-colagebra, where P is the covariant powerset functor, and $R[\,] : U \to \mathcal{P}U$ is a function sending $x \in U$ to $\{y \in U : (x, y) \in R\}$.

In category theory any relation R from U to W determines and is determined by its graph $\mathcal{G}R \subseteq U \times W$ and two projections $\pi_1 : \mathcal{G}R \to U$ and $\pi_1 : \mathcal{G}R \to W$. Therefore, R is construed as:

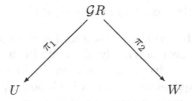

Thus, xRy, for $x \in U$, $y \in W$, means $(x, y) \in \mathcal{G}R$. Now, given an endofunctor $T : \mathsf{Set} \to \mathsf{Set}$, we would like to *lift* R via TR

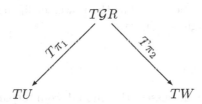

to (a very special relation) $\overline{T}R$.

Definition 12 (Relational Lifting). *Given a set endofunctor* $T : Set \to Set$, *and* $\mathcal{G}R \subseteq U \times W$, *the* T-*lifting* $\mathcal{G}\overline{T}R \subseteq TU \times TW$ *is defined as:*

$$\mathcal{G}\overline{T}R = \{(s, t) \in TU \times TW : there\, exits\, w \in T\mathcal{G}R\; s.t.\; T\pi_1(w) = s,\; T\pi_2(w) = t\}.$$

L. Moss' main (and very significant) idea – in short – was to define a new modality based on the T-relational lifting. Following [12], which is a great overview of this topic, we are going to use the finitary version of Moss' language. Let be given a language $\mathcal{L}$:

$$\alpha, \beta ::= p \mid \neg\alpha \mid \bigvee \Gamma \mid \bigwedge \Gamma \mid \nabla_T \Lambda$$

where $\Gamma \in \mathcal{P}_\omega \mathcal{L}$ and $\Lambda \in T_\omega \mathcal{L}$ (as usual, $\mathcal{P}_\omega$ and T_ω are finitary versions of $\mathcal{P}$ and T, respectively). The key observation of L. Moss is that the truth condition for the modal operator ∇_T with respect to a coalgebra $\zeta : W \to TW$, may be defined by:

$$w \models \nabla_T \Gamma \text{ iff } (\zeta(w), \Gamma) \in \mathcal{G}\overline{T} \models .$$

Now we would like to translate this idea into our framework. For the powerset functor P the definition of relation lifting is given by:

$$\mathcal{G}\overline{P}R = \{(X,Y) \in \mathcal{P}U \times \mathcal{P}W : \text{there exits } w \in \mathcal{P}\mathcal{G}R \text{ s.t. } \pi_1[w] = X, \ \pi_2[w] = Y\},$$

where $\pi_i[w]$ is a direct image of $w \subseteq \mathcal{G}R$ via π_i. In consequence, we obtain the following result.

Proposition 11. *Let be given a perceptual system* $(U, \mathbb{F})$ *along with its Kripke model* $\mathbb{K} = (U, E, v)$, *and the P-colagebra* $(U, E[\ ])$ *of* $\mathbb{K}$. *Then for* $\Gamma \subseteq \mathcal{F}_{NEAR}(Boolean)$ *it holds that:*

$$x \models \mathbf{Near}\Gamma \text{ } iff \text{ } ([x]_E, \Gamma) \in \mathcal{G}\overline{P} \models .$$

Thus, the relationships between rough sets and near sets are theoretically much deeper than we would have previously thought. Both theories bring different yet complementary perspective on the universe U, its objects, and granulation expressed in terms of equivalence classes of relation E, which stands that two objects have exactly the same description. The rough set approach my be construed as (standard) modal **S5** framework, whereas the near set approach as a co-algebraic rendering of this framework. Even more precisely, as a specific and concrete instantiation of L. Moss' significant idea of ∇_T and its T-lifting semantics. Thus near sets may be viewed as the powerset lifting of the main concepts and assumptions of rough set theory.

5 Conclusions

In the paper we have discussed the modal counterpart of near set theory [22, 23, 25], which has not been previously studied. We have firstly discussed topological settings of rough sets [16–21] and near sets and then defined the corresponding modal operators for nearness collections. It has turned that we can mutually translate rough set operators and near set operators. Finally, we have discovered that near set operators may be construed as an instantiation of L. Moss coalgebraic modal operator ∇_T. Thus, the relationships between rough sets and near sets are part of more general scheme of modal and coalgebraic logic. However, all said above holds only for equivalence relations as the underlying descriptive nearness of objects. As noted in Introduction, the idea of near sets (or descriptive nearness) stemmed from the 2002 private correspondence between J.F. Peters and Z. Pawlak. Now we may regard the near set methodology as the powerset lifting of the main concepts and assumptions of Z. Pawlak's theory.

Acknowledgements. We would like to thank anonymous reviewers for careful reading the manuscript, their insightful comments, and corrections.

References

1. Aczel, P.: Non-Well-Founded Sets. CSLI Lecture Notes, vol. 14. CSLI Publications, Stanford (1988)
2. Aczel, P., Mendler, N.: A final coalgebra theorem. In: Pitt, D.H., Rydeheard, D.E., Dybjer, P., Pitts, A.M., Poigné, A. (eds.) Category Theory and Computer Science. LNCS, vol. 389, pp. 357–365. Springer, Heidelberg (1989). doi:10.1007/BFb0018361
3. Adámek, J., Herrlich, H., Strecker, G.: Abstract and Concrete Categories. Wiley-Interscience Publication, London (1990)
4. Banerjee, M., Khan, M.A.: Propositional logics from rough set theory. In: Peters, J.F., Skowron, A., Düntsch, I., Grzymała-Busse, J., Orłowska, E., Polkowski, L. (eds.) Transactions on Rough Sets VI. LNCS, vol. 4374, pp. 1–25. Springer, Heidelberg (2007). doi:10.1007/978-3-540-71200-8_1
5. Bilkova, M., Palmigiano, A., Venema, Y.: Proof systems for the coalgebraic cover modality. Adv. Modal Log. **7**, 1–23 (2008)
6. Bilkova, M., Palmigiano, A., Venema, Y.: Proof systems for Moss' coalgebraic logic. Theor. Comput. Sci. **549**, 36–60 (2014)
7. Čech, E.: Topological Spaces. Wiley, London (1966)
8. Efremovič, V.: The geometry of proximity I. Mat. Sb. **31**, 189–200 (1951). (in Russian) MR 14, 1106
9. Herrlich, H.: A concept of nearness. Gen. Topol. Appl. **4**, 191–212 (1974)
10. Jacobs, B.: Introduction to Coalgebra. Towards Mathematics of States and Observation. Cambridge University Press, Cambridge (2016)
11. Janin, D., Walukiewicz, I.: Automata for the modal μ-calculus and related results. In: Wiedermann, J., Hájek, P. (eds.) MFCS 1995. LNCS, vol. 969, pp. 552–562. Springer, Heidelberg (1995). doi:10.1007/3-540-60246-1_160
12. Kupke, K., Kurz, A., Venema, Y.: Completeness for the coalgebraic cover modality. Log. Methods Comput. Sci. **8**, 1–76 (2012)
13. Moss, L.: Coalgebraic logic. Ann. Pure Appl. Log. **96**, 277–317 (1999)
14. Naimpally, S.: Proximity Approach to General Topology. Lakehead University, Thunder Bay (1974)
15. Naimpally, S., Peters, J.: Topology with Applications. Topological Spaces via Near and Far. World Scientific, Singapore (2013)
16. Pawlak, Z.: Classification of Objects by Means of Attributes. Institute of Computer Science, Polish Academy of Sciences PAS 429, Warsaw (1981)
17. Pawlak, Z.: Rough sets. Int. J. Comput. Inf. Sci. **11**, 341–356 (1982)
18. Pawlak, Z.: Rough sets and decision tables. In: Skowron, A. (ed.) SCT 1984. LNCS, vol. 208, pp. 187–196. Springer, Heidelberg (1985). doi:10.1007/3-540-16066-3_18
19. Pawlak, Z.: Rough logic. Bull. Pol. Acad. Sci. (Tech. Sci.) **35**(5–6), 253–258 (1987)
20. Pawlak, Z.: Rough Sets: Theoretical Aspects of Reasoning about Data. Kluwer Academic Publisher, Berlin (1991)
21. Pawlak, Z.: Wiedza z Perspektywy Zbiorów Przybliżonych. Institute of Computer Science Report 23, Toronto (1992)
22. Peters, J.: Near sets. special theory about nearness of objects. Fundam. Inform. **75**(1–4), 407–433 (2007)
23. Peters, J.: Near sets. General theory about nearness of objects. Appl. Math. Sci **1**(53), 2609–2629 (2007)

24. Peters, J., Skowron, A., Stepaniuk, J.: Nearness in approximation spaces. In: Proceedings of Concurrency, Specification and Programming (CS&P 2006), Humboldt Universitat, pp. 435–445 (2006)
25. Peters, J., Naimpally, S.: Applications of near sets. Am. Math. Soc. Not. **59**(4), 536–542 (2012). doi:10.1090/noti817.
26. Priest, G.: An Introduction to Non-classical Logic. Cambridge University Press, Cambridge (2001)
27. Riesz, F.: Stetigkeitsbegriff und abstrakte mengenlehre. IV Congresso Internazionale dei Matematici II, pp. 18–24 (1908)
28. Yao, Y.Y., Lin, T.Y.: Generalization of rough sets using modal logic. Intell. Autom. Soft Comput. **2**(2), 103–120 (1996)

Multi-stage Optimization of Matchings in Trees with Application to Kidney Exchange

Michal Mankowski[(✉)] and Mikhail Moshkov

Computer, Electrical and Mathematical Sciences and Engineering Division,
King Abdullah University of Science and Technology,
Thuwal 23955-6900, Saudi Arabia
{michal.mankowski,mikhail.moshkov}@kaust.edu.sa

Abstract. In this paper, we propose a method for multi-stage optimization of matchings in trees relative to different weight functions that assign positive weights to the edges of the trees. This method can be useful in transplantology where nodes of the tree correspond to pairs (donor, recipient) and two nodes (pairs) are connected by an edge if these pairs can exchange kidneys. Weight functions can characterize the number of exchanges, the importance of exchanges, or their compatibility.

Keywords: Tree · Matching · Weight function · Multi-stage optimization

1 Introduction

In this paper, we consider problems of matching optimization connected with kidney paired donation [7,13]. This is a novel alternative for living, incompatible (donor, recipient) pairs to get an organ by matching with another incompatible pair. Let G be an undirected graph which edges and nodes have positive weights. Nodes of this graph can be interpreted as pairs (donor, recipient) and two nodes $A = (a_1, a_2)$ and $B = (b_1, b_2)$ are connected by an edge if the donor a_1 can donate a kidney to the recipient b_2, and the donor b_1 can donate a kidney to the recipient a_2. The weight of a node A can be interpreted as an importance of the transplantation for the recipient from the pair A. The weight of an edge connecting nodes A and B can be interpreted as a compatibility of the exchange of kidneys between the pairs A and B.

A matching in G is a set of edges without common nodes. We consider three optimization problems connected with matchings: (c) maximization of the cardinality of a matching, (n) maximization of the sum of weights of nodes in a matching, and (e) maximization of the sum of edges in a matching. The considered problems can be solved in polynomial time [6,10].

Each solution of the problem (c) allows us to help to the maximum number of transplants. It is known [9] that each solution of the problem (n) is also a solution of the problem (c). The situation with the problem (e) is different: a solution of the problem (e) can be not a solution of the problem (c) (see Fig. 1).

© Springer International Publishing AG 2017
L. Polkowski et al. (Eds.): IJCRS 2017, Part I, LNAI 10313, pp. 123–130, 2017.
DOI: 10.1007/978-3-319-60837-2_10

Fig. 1. Matching with maximum weight of edges (a) and matching with maximum cardinality (b)

In such a situation, it is reasonable to consider multi-stage optimization of matchings relative to different criteria, for example, to describe all matchings with maximum cardinality and later to describe among these matchings all matchings with maximum weight of edges. Another possibility is to describe the whole set of matchings with maximum weight of nodes and after that to describe among these matchings all matchings with maximum weight of edges.

The problem (c) can be formulated as the problem (e) when the weight of each edge is equal to 1. The problem (n) can be formulated as the problem (e) when the weight of each edge is equal to the sum of weights of its ends. So we can consider multi-stage optimization of weights of edges in matchings relative to a number of weight functions each of which assigns a positive weight to each edge of the graph G.

The algorithm for weighted matching in trees is very well known [8]. In this paper, we consider an extension of dynamic programming algorithm for multi-stage optimization of matchings in trees. This algorithm can be generalized in a natural way to the forests.

The dynamic programming multi-stage optimization approach was created initially for the decision trees and decision rules [2]. One of the main areas of applications for the approach is the rough set theory [11,12] in which decision trees and rules are widely used. This approach was extended also to some combinatorial optimization problems [1,3–5]. Here we consider one more its application.

This paper consists of four sections. In Sect. 2, we consider a graph $D(G)$ corresponding to the tree G. We use this graph to describe the set of matchings in G and to optimize these matchings. Section 3 is devoted to the multi-stage optimization of matchings in G relative to different weight functions. Section 4 contains short conclusions.

2   Graph $D(G)$ Corresponding to Tree G

Let G be a tree. A matching in G is a set of edges without common nodes. We choose a node in the tree G as a root. It will be useful for us to consider G as a directed graph with the orientation of edges from the root. Now each node v in G defines a subtree $G(v)$ of G in which v is the root.

We describe now a graph $D(G)$ (forest of directed trees) which will be used to describe the set of matchings in G and to optimize these matchings. It contains main nodes from G and auxiliary nodes corresponding to the main ones.

Let v be a terminal node of G – see Fig. 2(a). Then in the graph $D(G)$ there are two nodes v (main) and $v(\emptyset)$ (auxiliary) corresponding to v which are connected by an edge starting in v and entering $v(\emptyset)$ – see Fig. 2(b).

(a)   (b)

Fig. 2. Nodes and edge in $D(G)$ (b) corresponding to terminal node v of G (a)

Let v be a nonterminal node of G which has k outgoing edges $e_1, \dots, e_k$ entering nodes $v_1, \dots, v_k$, respectively – see Fig. 3(a). Then in $D(G)$ there are the main node v, $k+1$ auxiliary nodes $v(e_1), \dots, v(e_k), v(\emptyset)$, and $k+1$ edges starting in v and entering these auxiliary nodes – see Fig. 3(b).

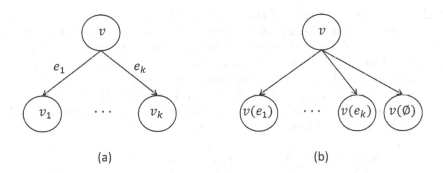

(a)   (b)

Fig. 3. Nodes and edges in $D(G)$ (b) corresponding to nonterminal node v of G (a)

A proper subgraph Δ of the graph $D(G)$ is a graph obtained from $D(G)$ by removal of some edges such that each main node in Δ has at least one outgoing edge. Let v be a main node in $D(G)$ with children $v(e_1), \dots, v(e_k), v(\emptyset)$. We denote by $E_\Delta(v)$ the set of all $\sigma \in \{e_1, \dots, e_k, \emptyset\}$ such that there is an edge in Δ from v to $v(\sigma)$. Proper subgraphs of the graph $D(G)$ can be obtained as results of optimization of matchings in G relative to weight functions.

Let Δ be a proper subgraph of the graph $D(G)$. We correspond a set $M_\Delta(u)$ of matchings in G to each node u of Δ. Let C and D be sets elements of which are also sets. We denote $C \otimes D = \{c \cup d : c \in C, d \in D\}$.

Let v be a terminal node of G. Then $M_\Delta(v) = M_\Delta(v(\emptyset)) = \{\lambda\}$ where λ is the empty matching. Let v be a nonterminal node of G which has k outgoing edges $e_1, \ldots, e_k$ entering nodes $v_1, \ldots, v_k$, respectively. Then, for $i = 1, \ldots, k$,

$$M_\Delta(v(\emptyset)) = \bigotimes_{j \in \{1,\ldots,k\}} M_\Delta(v_j),$$

$$M_\Delta(v(e_i)) = \bigotimes_{j \in \{1,\ldots,k\}\setminus\{i\}} M_\Delta(v_j) \otimes M_\Delta(v_i(\emptyset)) \otimes \{\{e_i\}\},$$

$$M_\Delta(v) = \bigcup_{\sigma \in E_\Delta(v)} M_\Delta(v(\sigma)).$$

Let $\Delta = D(G)$. One can show that, for any node v of G, $M_{D(G)}(v)$ is the set of all matchings in $G(v)$ and $M_{D(G)}(v(\emptyset))$ is the set of all matchings in $G(v)$ which do not use the node v (have no edges with the end v). For any nonterminal node v of G and for any edge e starting in v, $M_{D(G)}(v(e))$ is the set of all matchings in $G(v)$ containing the edge e.

Let G contain n nodes and, therefore, $n - 1$ edges. Then the graph $D(G)$ contains $3n - 1$ nodes and $2n - 1$ edges. It is clear that the graph $D(G)$ can be constructed in linear time depending on n.

3   Multi-stage Optimization of Matchings

Let Δ be a proper subgraph of the graph $D(G)$ and w be a weight function which assigns a positive weight $w(e)$ to each edge e of G. We now describe the procedure of optimization of matchings described by Δ relative to the weight function w. During the work of this procedure, we attach a number $w_\Delta(u)$ to each node u of Δ and, may be, remove some edges from Δ.

Let v be a terminal node of G. Then $w_\Delta(v) = w_\Delta(v(\emptyset)) = 0$. Let v be a nonterminal node of G which has k outgoing edges $e_1, \ldots, e_k$ entering nodes $v_1, \ldots, v_k$, respectively. Then, for $i = 1, \ldots, k$,

$$w_\Delta(v(\emptyset)) = \sum_{j \in \{1,\ldots,k\}} w_\Delta(v_j),$$

$$w_\Delta(v(e_i)) = \sum_{j \in \{1,\ldots,k\}\setminus\{i\}} w_\Delta(v_j) + w_\Delta(v_i(\emptyset)) + w(e_i)$$

$$= w_\Delta(v(\emptyset)) - w_\Delta(v_i) + w_\Delta(v_i(\emptyset)) + w(e_i),$$

$$w_\Delta(v) = \max\{w_\Delta(v(\sigma)) : \sigma \in E_\Delta(v)\}.$$

For each $\sigma \in E_\Delta(v)$ such that $w_\Delta(v(\sigma)) < w_\Delta(v)$, we remove the edge connecting nodes v and $v(\sigma)$ from the graph Δ. We denote by Δ^w the obtained proper subgraph of the graph $D(G)$. It is clear that $E_{\Delta^w}(v) = \{\sigma : \sigma \in E_\Delta(v), w_\Delta(v(\sigma)) = w_\Delta(v)\}$ for each nonterminal node v of the tree G.

One can show that, for each node u of the graph Δ, the number $w_\Delta(u)$ is the maximum total weight of edges in a matching from $M_\Delta(u)$ relative to the weight function w, and the set $M_{\Delta^w}(u)$ is the set of all matchings from $M_\Delta(u)$ that have the total weight of edges $w_\Delta(u)$ relative to the weight function w.

Let G contain n nodes and, therefore, $n-1$ edges. For a terminal node v of the tree G, we do not need arithmetical operations to find values of $w_\Delta(v)$ and $w_\Delta(v(\emptyset))$. Let v be a nonterminal node of G which has k outgoing edges $e_1, \ldots, e_k$ entering nodes $v_1, \ldots, v_k$, respectively. We need $k-1$ additions to compute the value $w_\Delta(v(\emptyset))$, $3k$ additions and subtractions to compute the values $w_\Delta(v(e_1)), \ldots, w_\Delta(v(e_k))$, at most k comparisons to compute the value $w_\Delta(v)$, and at most $k+1$ comparisons to determine edges starting in v that should be removed. As a result, for the node v, the considered algorithm makes at most $6k$ arithmetical operations. To process the tree G, the procedure of optimization makes at most $6n$ arithmetical operations, i.e., has linear time complexity depending on n.

We can use the considered procedure for multi-stage optimization of matchings. Let we have a tree G and weight functions $w_1, w_2, \ldots$ which assign positive weights to the edges of G. We choose a node v of G as the root and construct the graph $\Delta = D(G)$. We know that the set $M_\Delta(v)$ corresponding to the node v of Δ is equal to the set of all matchings in G.

We apply to the graph Δ the procedure of optimization relative to the weight function w_1. As a result, we obtain a proper subgraph Δ^{w_1} of the graph $D(G)$. The set $M_{\Delta^{w_1}}(v)$ corresponding to the node v of Δ^{w_1} is equal to the set of all matchings from $M_\Delta(v)$ which have maximum total weight of edges relative to the weight function w_1.

We apply to the graph Δ^{w_1} the procedure of optimization relative to the weight function w_2. As a result, we obtain a proper subgraph Δ^{w_1,w_2} of the graph $D(G)$. The set of matchings $M_{\Delta^{w_1,w_2}}(v)$ corresponding to the node v of Δ^{w_1,w_2} is equal to the set of all matchings from $M_{\Delta^{w_1}}(v)$ which have maximum total weight of edges relative to the weight function w_2, etc.

In particular, we can maximize the cardinality of matchings and after that among all matchings with maximum cardinality we can choose all matchings with maximum total weight of edges.

It is easy to extend the considered approach to forests: we can apply the optimization procedures to each tree from a forest independently.

4   Example

We consider an example of matching optimization problem for the tree G depicted in Fig. 4(a) which has five nodes v_1, v_2, v_3, v_4, v_5 and four edges e_1, e_2, e_3, e_4 with weights $2, 5, 1, 2$, respectively. There are two matchings with maximum cardinality $\{e_1, e_3\}$ and $\{e_1, e_4\}$, and one matching $\{e_2\}$ with maximum edge weight. Our aim is to find all matchings with maximum edge weight among all matchings with maximum cardinality. To this end, we apply to G a

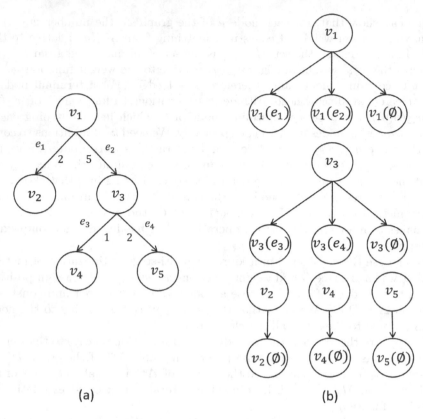

Fig. 4. Graph $D(G)$ (b) corresponding to tree G (a)

multi-stage optimization procedure relative to two cost functions w_1 and w_2: $w_1(e_1) = w_1(e_2) = w_1(e_3) = w_1(e_4) = 1$ and $w_2(e_1) = 2, w_2(e_2) = 5, w_2(e_3) = 1, w_2(e_4) = 2$.

First, we construct the graph $D(G)$ – see Fig. 4(b). We denote $\Delta = D(G)$ and apply to Δ the procedure of optimization relative to the weight function w_1. As a result, we obtain the proper subgraph Δ^{w_1} of the graph $D(G)$ (see Fig. 5(a)). It is easy to see that $M_{\Delta^{w_1}}(v_1) = \{\{e_1, e_3\}, \{e_1, e_4\}\}$. This is exactly the set of all matchings in G with maximum cardinality.

We apply to the graph Δ^{w_1} the procedure of optimization relative to the weight function w_2. As a result, we obtain the proper subgraph Δ^{w_1, w_2} of the graph $D(G)$ (see Fig. 5(b)). The set $M_{\Delta^{w_1, w_2}}(v_1) = \{\{e_1, e_4\}\}$ contains the only matching with maximum edge weight among all matchings with maximum cardinality.

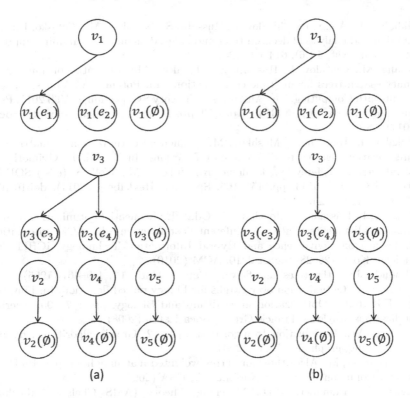

Fig. 5. Graph Δ^{w_1} (a) and graph Δ^{w_1,w_2} (b)

5   Conclusions

In this paper, we proposed a method for multi-stage optimization of matchings in trees relative to a sequence of weight functions. This method can be useful in transplantology if besides of the maximization of transplanted kidneys we would like to maximize the compatibility of the transplantations. In the future, we will try to generalize this method to other classes of graphs.

Acknowledgments. Research reported in this publication was supported by King Abdullah University of Science and Technology (KAUST).

References

1. AbuBekr, J., Chikalov, I., Hussain, S., Moshkov, M.: Sequential optimization of paths in directed graphs relative to different cost functions. In: Sato, M., Matsuoka, S., Sloot, P.M.A., van Albada, G.D., Dongarra, J. (eds.) International Conference on Computational Science, ICCS 2011, Nanyang Technological University, Singapore, 1–3 June 2011. Procedia Computer Science, vol. 4, pp. 1272–1277. Elsevier (2011)

2. Alkhalid, A., Amin, T., Chikalov, I., Hussain, S., Moshkov, M., Zielosko, B.: Optimization and analysis of decision trees and rules: dynamic programming approach. Int. J. Gen. Syst. **42**(6), 614–634 (2013)
3. Alnafie, M., Chikalov, I., Hussain, S., Moshkov, M.: Sequential optimization of binary search trees for multiple cost functions. In: Potanin, A., Viglas, T. (eds.) Seventeenth Computing: The Australasian Theory Symposium, CATS 2011, Perth, Australia, January 2011. CRPIT, vol. 119, pp. 41–44. Australian Computer Society (2011)
4. Chikalov, I., Hussain, S., Moshkov, M.: Sequential optimization of matrix chain multiplication relative to different cost functions. In: Černá, I., Gyimóthy, T., Hromkovič, J., Jefferey, K., Královič, R., Vukolić, M., Wolf, S. (eds.) SOFSEM 2011. LNCS, vol. 6543, pp. 157–165. Springer, Heidelberg (2011). doi:10.1007/978-3-642-18381-2_13
5. Chikalov, I., Hussain, S., Moshkov, M., Odat, E.: Sequential optimization of global sequence alignments relative to different cost functions. In: ACM International Conference on Convergence and Hybrid Information Technology, ICHIT 2010, Daejeon, Korea, 26–28 August 2010. ACM (2010)
6. Edmonds, J.: Paths, trees, and flowers. Can. J. Math. **17**, 449–467 (1965)
7. Gentry, S.E.: Optimization over graphs for kidney paired donation. In: Lim, G.J., Lee, E.K. (eds.) Optimization in Medicine and Biology, pp. 177–195. Auerbach Publications, Taylor & Francis Group, Boca Raton (2008)
8. Goddard, W.: Introduction to algorithms, part 2: Greedy algorithms, dynamic programming, graph algorithms (2004)
9. Halappanavar, M.: Algorithms for vertex-weighted matching in graphs. Ph.D. thesis, Old Dominion University, Norfolk, VA, USA (2009)
10. Lovász, L., Plummer, M.D.: Matching Theory (AMS Chelsea Publishing). Akadémiai Kiadó - North Holland, Budapest (1986)
11. Pawlak, Z.: Rough Sets - Theoretical Aspect of Reasoning About Data. Kluwer Academic Publishers, Dordrecht (1991)
12. Pawlak, Z., Skowron, A.: Rudiments of rough sets. Inf. Sci. **177**(1), 3–27 (2007)
13. Segev, D.L., Gentry, S.E., Warren, D.S., Reeb, B., Montgomery, R.A.: Kidney paired donation and optimizing the use of live donor organs. J. Am. Med. Assoc. **293**(15), 1883–1890 (2005)

A Rough-Set Based Solution of the Total Domination Problem

Anhui Tan[1,2]($^{\boxtimes}$), Yuzhi Tao[1,2], and Chao Wang[1,2]

[1] School of Mathematics, Physics and Information Science,
Zhejiang Ocean University, Zhoushan 316022, Zhejiang,
People's Republic of China
tananhui86@163.com
[2] Key Laboratory of Oceanographic Big Data Mining
and Application of Zhejiang Province, Zhoushan 316022,
Zhejiang, People's Republic of China

Abstract. This paper aims to provide a rough set-based reduction solution for a type of domination problem in graph theory. First, we introduce a decision table to represent the vertices and edges of a graph. Second, we claim that computing a minimal total dominating set of a graph is equivalent to finding a reduct of the induced decision table. Then, a reduction algorithm in rough set theory is designed for finding a suboptimal total dominating set of a graph. In the end, numerical experiments are conducted to examine the effectiveness and efficiency of the proposed algorithm.

Keywords: Attribute reduction · Total dominating set · Graph · Rough set · Information table

1 Introduction

Rough set theory, proposed by Pawlak [3], is a useful mathematical tool for dealing with uncertain and inexact knowledge. It has been widely used in the fields of data analysis, data mining and artificial intelligence [11]. The notion of attribute reductions plays an essential role in rough set theory [9]. An attribute reduct is a minimal subset of attributes, which remains the same classification ability as the entire decision table. Meanwhile, the domination problem is well known in graph theory and combinatorial optimization theory [1,2,5]. A total dominating set of a graph is a minimal subset of vertices, which covers all the vertices of the graph. However, the problems for finding the attribute reducts of a decision table and the minimal dominating sets of a graph are both NP-hard. Subsequently, many approximation algorithms have been proposed [6–8] to calculate a suboptimal solution for the two problems. For instance, Ślęzak [7,8] defined dependencies between attributes, which were used to construct generalized decision functions of decision systems.

It is exciting that the theoretical principles for solving the two problems have been grasped in essence, i.e., all their solutions can be obtained by the Boolean

© Springer International Publishing AG 2017
L. Polkowski et al. (Eds.): IJCRS 2017, Part I, LNAI 10313, pp. 131–139, 2017.
DOI: 10.1007/978-3-319-60837-2_11

algebra theory by using the same Boolean logic operations. Inspired by this idea, this paper aims to connect the two problems and introduce intersectional methods for dealing with these problems. First, for a given graph, we induce a decision information table in rough set theory. Second, we point out that each total dominating set of the graph is exactly the attribute reduct of the induced decision table. Based on our analysis, the methods of attribute reduction in rough set theory can be directly used for solving the domination problem in graph. Especially, a rough set method based on positive region is introduced to compute a total dominating set of a graph. In the end, numerical experiments are conducted to show the efficiency of the proposed method.

2 Preliminaries

In this section, we review some basic concepts related to the problems of attribute reduction in rough set and domination in graph.

2.1 Attribute Reduction in Rough Set Theory

Formally, an information table is a pair $\mathbf{S} = (U, A)$, where U is a nonempty and finite set of objects called the universe, A is a nonempty finite set of attributes. If A is the union of two kinds of attributes, i.e., $A = C \cup D$, where C is the so-called condition attributes set, D is the so-called decision attribute set and $C \cap D = \emptyset$, then $\mathbf{S}$ is called a decision table. Each nonempty subset $B \subseteq A$ determines an indiscernibility relation: $R_B = \{(x, y) \in U \times U | a(x) = a(y), \forall a \in B\}$. Since R_B is an equivalence relation on U, it forms a partition $U/R_B = \{[x]_B | x \in U\}$, where $[x]_B$ is the equivalence class determined by x with respect to B, i.e., $[x]_B = \{y \in U | (x, y) \in R_B\}$.

Let $B \subseteq A$ and $X \subseteq U$, two sets

$$\underline{R_B}(X) = \{x \in U | [x]_B \subseteq X\}, \ \overline{R_B}(X) = \{x \in U | [x]_B \cap X \neq \emptyset\},$$

are called the lower and upper approximation of X w.r.t. B, respectively.

In a decision table $\mathbf{S} = (U, C \cup \{d\})$, suppose $U/\{d\} = \{D_1, D_2, \ldots D_r\}$ are the equivalence classes determined by d. The positive region of the decision table S w.r.t. $B \subseteq A$ is defined as $POS_B(d) = \cup_{i=1}^{r} \underline{R_B}(D_i)$.

In the theory of rough set, the attribute reduction is one of the key processes for knowledge discovery.

Definition 1 [3]. *Let* $\mathbf{S} = (U, C \cup \{d\})$ *be a decision table. An attribute set* $B \subseteq C$ *is called a consistent set of the information table, if* $[x]_B \subseteq [x]_{\{d\}}$ *for all* $x \in U$. *Furthermore, if* B *is consistent and any proper subset of* B *is not consistent, then* B *is called an attribute reduct of the information table.*

Definition 2 [10]. *Let* $\mathbf{S} = (U, C \cup \{d\})$ *be a decision table. For all* $(x, y) \in U \times U$, *the discernibility set of* x, y *in* $\mathbf{S}$ *is referred to as*

$$M_S(x, y) = \begin{cases} \{a \in C | a(x) \neq a(y)\}, & d(x) \neq d(y); \\ \emptyset, & d(x) = d(y). \end{cases}$$

$\mathcal{M}_S = \{M_S(x,y)|(x,y) \in U \times U\}$ is called the discernibility matrix of $\boldsymbol{S}$.

If $M_S(x,y) \neq \emptyset$, then the pair (x,y) is called a discernible object pair.

Definition 3 [10]. Let $\boldsymbol{S} = (U, C \cup \{d\})$ be a decision table with $C = \{a_1, a_2, \ldots a_m\}$. The Boolean expression of $\boldsymbol{S}$ is defined as:

$$f_S(a_1^*, a_2^*, \ldots a_m^*) = \vee\{\wedge M_S(x,y)|M_S(x,y) \in \mathcal{M}_S, M_S(x,y) \neq \emptyset\},$$

where each Boolean variable a_i^* corresponds to each attribute a_i, respectively.

The expression $\vee M_S(x,y)$ is the disjunction of all attributes in $M_S(x,y)$, indicating that the object pair (x,y) can be distinguished by any attribute in $M(x,y)$. The expression $\wedge\{\vee M_S(x,y)\}$ is the conjunction of all $\vee M_S(x,y)$, indicating that the family of discernible pairs can be distinguished by a set of attributes satisfying $\wedge\{\vee M_S(x,y)\}$ [10].

Based on the discernibility matrix and Boolean expression, one can compute the reducts as follows.

Theorem 1 [10]. Let $\boldsymbol{S} = (U, C \cup \{d\})$ be a decision table with $C = \{a_1, a_2, \ldots a_m\}$. An attribute subset $B \subseteq C$ is a reduct of $\boldsymbol{S}$ iff $\wedge_{a_i \in B} a_i^*$ is a prime implicant of the Boolean function f_S.

From Theorem 1, if

$$f_S(a_1^*, a_2^*, \ldots a_m^*) = \wedge\{\vee M_S(x,y)|M_S(x,y) \in \mathcal{M}_S, M_S(x,y) \neq \emptyset\} = \vee_{i=1}^t (\wedge_{j=1}^{s_i} a_j^*),$$

then, $B_i = \{a_j | j \leq s_j\}, i \leq t$, are all the reducts of $\boldsymbol{S}$.

Example 1. Let $\boldsymbol{S} = (U, C \cup \{d\})$ be a decision table as shown in Table 1, where $U = \{x_1, x_2, \ldots, x_6\}$ and $C = \{v_1, v_2 \ldots, v_5\}$.

By Definition 3, the Boolean expression of $\boldsymbol{S}$ is:

$$f_S(v_1^*, v_2^*, \ldots v_5^*) = (v_1 \vee v_2 \vee v_3 \vee v_4) \wedge (v_1 \vee v_2 \vee v_3) \wedge (v_1 \vee v_2 \vee v_3) \wedge (v_4 \vee v_5) \wedge (v_4 \vee v_5)$$
$$= (v_1 \wedge v_4) \vee (v_1 \wedge v_5) \vee (v_2 \wedge v_4) \vee (v_2 \wedge v_5) \vee (v_3 \wedge v_4) \vee (v_3 \wedge v_5).$$

Thus, there exist 6 reducts of $\boldsymbol{S}$: $B_1 = \{v_1, v_4\}$, $B_2 = \{v_1, v_5\}$, $B_3 = \{v_2, v_4\}$, $B_4 = \{v_2, v_5\}$, $B_4 = \{v_3, v_4\}$, $B_6 = \{v_3, v_5\}$.

2.2 The Domination Problem in Graph Theory

In this part, we introduce the domination problem in graph. A graph is a pair $G = (V, E)$ consisting of a set of vertices V and a set of edges E such that $E \subseteq V \times V$. Two vertices $v_1, v_2 \in V$ are adjacent if there is an edge that has them as ends, i.e., $(v_1, v_2) \in E$.

Definition 4 [1,2]. Let $G = (V, E)$ be a graph. For a subset $S \subseteq V$, if for every vertex $v \in V$, there is some $u \in S$ such that $(v, u) \in E$, then S is called a total dominating set(TDS) of the graph. Furthermore, if S is a TDS, and every subset of S is not a TDS any more, then S is a minimal TDS.

Table 1. A decision table **S**

$U/(C \cup \{d\})$	v_1	v_2	v_3	v_4	v_5	d
x_1	2	1	1	1	2	1
x_2	2	1	1	0	2	1
x_3	2	1	1	0	2	1
x_4	2	0	0	1	1	1
x_5	1	0	0	1	1	1
x_6	1	0	0	0	2	0

Given a graph $G = (V, E)$ and $v \in V$, let $N(v)$ denote a set of vertices adjacent to v, i.e., $N(v) = \{v' \in V | (v, v') \in E\}$. We call $N(v$ as the adjacency set of v.

We next use the Boolean logic operations to solve the domination problem.

Definition 5 [5]. *Let $G = (V, E)$ be a graph with $V = \{v_1, v_2, \ldots, v_m\}$. The Boolean expression is defined as $f_{TDS}(v_1^*, v_2^*, \ldots v_m^*) = \wedge\{\vee N(v) | v \in V\}$.*

Theorem 2 [5]. *Let $G = (V, E)$ be a graph. Then, a set of vertices $S \subseteq V$ is a minimal TDS of G iff $\wedge_{v_i \in S} v_i^*$ is a prime implicant of the Boolean function f_{TDS}.*

Theorem 2 shows that if $f_{TDS}(v_1^*, v_2^*, \ldots v_m^*) = \wedge\{\vee N(v) | v \in V\} = \vee_{i=1}^{t}(\wedge_{j=1}^{s_i} v_j^*)$, then $B_i = \{v_j | j \leq s_j\}, i \leq t$, are all the minimal TDSs of **S**.

Example 2. Let $G = (V, E)$ be the graph with $V = \{v_1, v_2, v_3, v_4, v_5\}$ and $E = \{e_1, e_2, e_3, e_4, e_5\}$, where $e_1 = (v_1, v_2), e_2 = (v_2, v_5), e_3 = (v_1, v_3), e_4 = (v_1, v_4)$ and $e_5 = (v_4, v_5)$.

The adjacency sets are listed as:

$$N(v_1) = \{v_2, v_3, v_4\}, \quad N(v_2) = \{v_1, v_3\}, \quad N(v_3) = \{v_1, v_2\},$$
$$N(v_4) = \{v_1, v_5\}, \quad N(v_5) = \{v_4\}.$$

The Boolean expression of G is:

$$f_{TDS}(v_1^*, v_2^*, \ldots v_5^*) = (v_2 \vee v_3 \vee v_4) \wedge (v_1 \vee v_3) \wedge (v_1 \vee v_2) \wedge (v_1 \vee v_5) \wedge (v_4)$$
$$= (v_1 \wedge v_4) \vee (v_2 \wedge v_3 \wedge v_4 \wedge v_5).$$

Thus, there are 2 minimal TDSs of G: $B_1 = \{v_1, v_4\}$, $B_2 = \{v_2, v_3, v_4, v_5\}$.

3 An Induced Decision Table of Graph

In this section, we first induce a decision table from a graph and then discuss the relationship between the attribute reduction problem and domination problem.

First, we introduce the notions of adjacency matrices of a graph. Let $G = (V, E)$ with $V = \{v_1, v_2, \ldots v_m\}$. The adjacency matrix of G is an $m \times m$ matrix $M_{TDS} = (d_{ij})_{m \times m}$ such that $d_{ij} = 1$ if $v_j \in N(v_i)$; otherwise, $d_{ij} = 0$.

Based on the adjacency matrix, we next construct a decision table for representing a graph.

Definition 6. *Let* $G = (V, E)$ *be a graph with* $V = \{v_1, v_2, \ldots v_m\}$ *and* $M_{DS} = (d_{ij})_{m \times m}$ *be the adjacency matrix of* G. $\mathbf{S}_{TDS} = (U, C \cup \{d\})$ *is called the induced decision table of* G, *if it satisfies the following conditions:*

(1) $U = \{x_1, x_2, \ldots x_m, x_{m+1}\}$;

(2) $C = \{v_1, v_2, \ldots v_m\}$;

(3) $v_j(x_i) = \begin{cases} d_{ij}, & 1 \leq i \leq m, 1 \leq j \leq m, \\ 0, & i = m+1, 1 \leq j \leq m; \end{cases}$

(4) $d(x_i) = \begin{cases} 0, & 1 \leq i \leq m, \\ 1, & i = m+1. \end{cases}$

The new decision table has $m + 1$ objects, while the adjacency matrix of the graph is a $m \times m$ matrix. The aim of this idea is to construct an appropriate discernibility matrix, which will be shown in the following.

Example 3. Continue Example 2.

According to Definition 6, we can induce a decision table $\mathbf{S}_{TDS}$ of G is as shown in Table 2.

Table 2. Decision table $\mathbf{S}_{TDS}$

$U/(C \cup \{d\})$	v_1	v_2	v_3	v_4	v_5	d
x_1	0	1	1	1	0	0
x_2	1	0	1	0	0	0
x_3	1	1	0	0	0	0
x_4	1	0	0	0	1	0
x_5	0	0	0	1	0	0
x_6	0	0	0	0	0	1

Property 1. Let $G = (V, E)$ be a graph with $V = \{v_1, v_2, \ldots v_m\}$ and $\mathbf{S}_{DS} = (U, C \cup \{d\})$ the induced decision table. Then the discernibility set of $(x_i, x_j) \in U \times U$ satisfies:

$$M_{S_{TDS}}(x_i, x_j) = \begin{cases} \emptyset, & 1 \leq i \leq m, 1 \leq j \leq m; \\ N(v_i), & 1 \leq i \leq m, j = m+1. \end{cases}$$

Proof. By Definition 6, $d(x_i) = 0$ for any $1 \leq i \leq m$, then $d(x_i) = d(x_j)$ for any $1 \leq i, j \leq m$. By Definition 2, the discernibility set satisfies $M_{S_{TDS}}(x_i, x_j) = \emptyset$ for any $1 \leq i, j \leq m$.

Moreover, with the fact that $v_j(x_{m+1}) = 0$ for any $v_j \in C$. Then for any $1 \leq i \leq m$, we have that $v_j(x_i) \neq v_j(x_{m+1}) \Leftrightarrow v_j(x_i) = 1$. Thus, the discernibility set satisfies $M_{S_{TDS}}(x_i, x_{m+1}) = \{v_j \in C | v_j(x_i) \neq v_j(x_{m+1})\} = \{v_j \in C | v_j(x_i) = 1\}$ for any $1 \leq i \leq m$.

On the other hand, we have that $v_j(x_i) = 1 \Leftrightarrow v_j \in N(v_i)$. The discernibility set satisfies $M_{S_{TDS}}(x_i, x_{m+1}) = \{v_j \in C | v_j \in N(v_i)\} = N(v_i)$ for any $1 \leq i \leq m$. We finish the proof. □

Theorem 3. *Let $G = (V, E)$ be a graph and $\boldsymbol{S}_{TDS} = (U, C \cup \{d\})$ be the induced decision table. Then, $S \subseteq V$ is a minimal TDS of G iff S is an attribute reduct of $\boldsymbol{S}_{TDS}$.*

Proof. It can be concluded from Property 1. □

Theorem 3 shows that the problem of finding a minimal TDS of a graph can be translated into the problem of finding the reduct of a decision table. Based on this analysis, we in the next section introduce the attribute reduction algorithms to solve the domination problem.

4   Algorithms for the Domination Problem Based on Rough Set

Let $\boldsymbol{S} = (U, C \cup \{d\}, V)$ be a decision table. For any $B \subseteq C$ and $a \in C - B$, the significance of a w.r.t. B is

$$Sig(a, B) = \gamma_{B \cup \{a\}}(d) - \gamma_B(d),$$

where $\gamma_B(d) = \frac{|POS_B(d)|}{|U|}$ and $|\cdot|$ denotes the cardinality of a set.

In [4], Qian et al. introduced an attribute reduction method, called positive approximation algorithm, which performs well in saving time consumption. We use this method to construct an approximation algorithm for the domination problem.

Algorithm 1. A rough set-based algorithm for computing a TDS of a graph
Input: A graph $G = (V, E)$
Output: A suboptimal TDS
    1: Generate the decision table $\boldsymbol{S}_{TDS} = (U, C \cup \{d\})$;
    2: $R \leftarrow \emptyset$;
    3: $i = 1$;
    4: **While** $POS_{DS}(d) \neq U$ **do**
    5: $U_i \leftarrow U - POS_{DS}(d)$;
    6: $R \leftarrow R \cup \{v_0\}$, where v_0 satisfies $Sig(v_0, R) = max\{Sig(v, R) | v \in C - R\}$;
    7: $i \leftarrow i + 1$;
    8: **End while**
    9: **Output** A TDS R.

The time complexity of Algorithm 1 is $\mathbf{O}(|U|^2 |V|^2)$.

5   Experiments

To illustrate efficiency of the proposed algorithm, we compare it with some classical algorithms for domination problems in this section. In [7], Sanchis et al. constructed and summarized several algorithms. As shown in [7], greedy-ran algorithm does a good job in reducing time consumption and greedy-rev algorithm works well in finding a TDS with relative small cardinality. So we choose the greedy-ran algorithm and the greedy-rev algorithm for comparison.

These algorithms are tested on randomly generated graphs which are input by adjacency matrices. Density of a graph is the percentage of non-zero entries in the adjacency matrix of the graph. The experiments are performed on a personal computer with Windows XP and an Intel Pentium R Dual (E2140) 3 GHz with 4 GB of memory. The algorithms are implemented using Matlab 7.8. All the algorithms are executed 4 times on random graphs with the same number of vertices and density. We test 16 random graphs which are divided into 4 sets as shown in Table 3.

Table 3. Graphs in the tests

Set	No. of vertices	Density	No. of graphs
A	100	1%	4
B	100	2%	4
C	200	4%	4
D	200	6%	4

Table 4 lists the experiment results of the algorithms. In the table, the column "Time" is the running time (in seconds) of the algorithms and "Value" is the value of a solution found by an algorithm.

As shown in Table 4, greedy-ran algorithm is the most fast, but the vertices found are the most which implies that it does not perform better than greedy-rev algorithm and rough set algorithm. We can also see that when the vertex number is equal to 100, the vertices found by greedy-rev algorithm are less than by rough set algorithm, and their time consumptions are not much different, when the vertex number is equal to 200, the vertices found by rough set algorithm are less than by greedy-rev algorithm and the time consumptions of rough set algorithm are also less than greedy-rev algorithm. So the larger the graph's size is, the better rough set algorithm performs.

Table 4. Results on the three algorithms

Graph	Greedy-ran		Greedy-rev		Rough set	
	Value	Time	Value	Time	Value	Time
A1	94	0.002	58	0.445	60	0.302
A2	95	0.002	60	0.382	62	0.266
A3	93	0.002	54	0.386	63	0.267
A4	96	0.002	59	0.386	62	0.266
B1	84	0.002	40	0.333	42	0.219
B2	85	0.002	36	0.340	42	0.223
B3	87	0.002	44	0.354	43	0.221
B4	84	0.002	38	0.338	41	0.217
C1	81	0.002	43	1.319	37	0.490
C2	93	0.002	43	1.265	33	0.417
C3	90	0.002	45	1.256	33	0.418
C4	91	0.002	45	1.268	32	0.404
D1	69	0.003	37	1.267	25	0.322
D2	68	0.003	38	1.263	23	0.297
D3	67	0.002	36	1.263	24	0.311
D4	67	0.002	38	1.261	22	0.286

6 Conclusions

In this paper, we have transformed the domination problem in graph theory into the attribute reduction problem in rough set theory. Based on our approach, the methods for finding the attribute reducts of a decision table can be used for solving the domination problem. Moreover, a substantial reduction algorithm has been introduced to compute a suboptimal total dominating set of a graph. Experiments have been conducted to examine the efficiency of the proposed algorithm.

Acknowledgements. This work was supported by a grant from the National Natural Science Foundation of China (No. 61602415).

References

1. Haynes, T., Hedetniemi, S., Slater, P.: Fundamentals of Domination in Graphs. Marcel Dekker Inc., New York (1998)
2. Henning, M.: A survey of selected recent results on total domination in graphs. Discret. Math. **309**, 32–63 (2009)
3. Pawlak, Z.: Rough Sets: Theoretical Aspects of Reasoning About Data. Kluwer Academic Publishing, Dordrecht (1991)

4. Qian, Y., Liang, J., Pedrycz, J., Dang, C.: Positive approximation: an accelerator for attribute reduction in rough set theory. Artif. Intell. **174**, 597–618 (2010)
5. Sanchis, L.: Experimental analysis of heuristic algorithms for the dominating set problem. Algorithmica **33**, 3–18 (2002)
6. Skowron, A., Rauszer, C.: The discernibility matrices and functions in information systems, handbook of applications and advances of the rough sets theory. In: Slowinski, R. (ed.) Intelligent Decision Support. Kluwer, Dordrecht (1992)
7. Ślęzak, D.: Association reducts: complexity and heuristics. In: Greco, S., Hata, Y., Hirano, S., Inuiguchi, M., Miyamoto, S., Nguyen, H.S., Słowiński, R. (eds.) RSCTC 2006. LNCS (LNAI), vol. 4259, pp. 157–164. Springer, Heidelberg (2006). doi:10. 1007/11908029_18
8. Ślęzak, D.: On generalized decision functions: reducts, networks and ensembles. In: Yao, Y., Hu, Q., Yu, H., Grzymala-Busse, J.W. (eds.) RSFDGrC 2015. LNCS (LNAI), vol. 9437, pp. 13–23. Springer, Cham (2015). doi:10.1007/ 978-3-319-25783-9_2
9. Wang, G., Yu, H., Yang, D.: Decision table reduction based on conditional information entropy. Chin. J. Comput. **25**, 759–766 (2002)
10. Yao, Y., Zhao, Y.: Discernibility matrix simplification for constructing attribute reducts. Inf. Sci. **179**, 867–882 (2009)
11. Yao, Y., Zhao, Y.: Two bayesian approaches to rough sets. Eur. J. Oper. Res. **251**, 904–917 (2016)

Yet Another Kind of Rough Sets Induced by Coverings

Ryszard Janicki[⊠]

Department of Computing and Software, McMaster University,
Hamilton, ON L8S 4K1, Canada
janicki@mcmaster.ca

Abstract. A new model of rough sets induced by coverings is proposed. In this new model, the elementary sets are defined as set components generated by a given covering of universe. The new model is compared with two other existing models of rough sets induced by covering and with a standard rough sets where elementary sets are defined by a given equivalence relation. The concept of optimal approximation is also introduced and analyzed for all models discussed in the paper. It is shown that, for a given covering of a universe, our model provides better approximations than the other ones.

Keywords: Rough sets induced by coverings · Set components · Lower, upper and optimal approximation

1 Introduction and Motivation

Rough sets [15,16] and fuzzy sets [25] are currently the two most popular mathematical approaches to imperfect knowledge. In the classical Pawlak model of rough sets, the basic observable, measurable, or atomic sets, the building blocks for whatever that can be to expressed, usually called *elementary sets*, are equivalence classes of some given equivalence relation. In other words, elementary sets, i.e. building blocks, are a *partition* of the given universe of objects of our interest. All objects we can describe in a constructive way are called *definable* or *exact sets* and are defined as a union of some elementary sets.

In the classical model each subset of the universe X has two definable approximations, the lower approximation of X, which is the biggest definable set included in X and the upper approximation of X, which the smallest definable set that contains X.

A natural extension is to replace a *partition* of the universe by an arbitrary *covering* of the universe. This idea, first proposed by Żakowski in 1983 [27], discussed later in eighties and nineties among other in [2,17], resulted recently in two refined models, that of [22,26]. An excellent survey of covering based rough sets models (up to 2012) can be found in [24].

The differences between existing different models based on coverings of universe depend and rely on two definitions:

© Springer International Publishing AG 2017
L. Polkowski et al. (Eds.): IJCRS 2017, Part I, LNAI 10313, pp. 140–153, 2017.
DOI: 10.1007/978-3-319-60837-2_12

- how elementary and definable sets are set up,
- how lower and upper approximations are defined.

These definitions must be treated as axiomatic assumptions of the model. Both definable sets and all approximations must be derived from a given covering by using some primitive operations. The choice of these operators and circumstances where and when they are allowed to be used, in principle defines the model.

Lower and upper approximations stem from the fact that empirical numerical data always have errors, so in reality we seldom have the exact value x (even if the measurements are expressible in integers) but usually some interval $\langle x - \epsilon, x + \epsilon \rangle$. In the standard model, the lower approximation is also a kernel and the upper approximation is a closure for the property of being definable set (cf. [1]).

However there are other kind of approximations, as for example the *linear least squares approximation* of points in the two dimensional plane (cf. [3]). It is neither lower nor upper approximation of any kind. This kind of 'optimal' approximations requires a well defined concept of *similarity* (or *distance*) and some techniques for finding maximal similarity (or minimal distance) between entities and their approximations.

Recently, in [10,11], a concept of an *optimal approximation* have been introduced and analyzed for the standard model of rough sets.

Our new model of rough sets induced by coverings follows from the assumption that the *primitive operations* we can use to construct elementary and definable sets are *set union, set intersection and set subtraction* (i.e. $\cup$, $\cap$ and $\setminus$), and we can use them without any restriction. We do not think that any of them is superior to other in any sense, their computational complexities are identical, i.e. quadratic in general case. Such assumption implies that elementary sets are *set components* (as defined and discussed in [12]) generated by the elements of a given covering.

We will show that both lower and upper approximations provided by our model are tighter than that of both [22,26].

We also will define optimal approximation for all three models based on coverings and we will show that optimal approximations in our model are closer to a given set than the ones based on approaches of [22,26], for any similarity measure that satisfies usually required axioms (cf. [10,11]).

Our new model with coverings can be in a very natural way transformed into an equivalent standard model with some equivalence relation.

2   Rough Sets and Approximations

In this chapter we introduce, review, and also adapt for our purposes, some general ideas that are crucial to our approach.

The principles of *rough sets* [15,16] can be formulated as follows.

Let U be a finite and non-empty universe of elements, and let $E \subseteq U \times U$ be an *equivalence relation*. Recall that for each $E \subseteq U \times U$, $[x]_E$ denotes the equivalence class of E containing x, and U/E denotes the set of all equivalence classes of E. Moreover U/E is also a *partition* of U.

The pair $\mathsf{AS} = (U, E)$ is usually referred to as a *Pawlak approximation space*, or just *approximation space*.

The elements of $\mathsf{ESets} = U/E$ (or $\mathsf{ESets(AS)}$, if necessary) are called *elementary sets*[1] and they are interpreted as basic observable, measurable, or atomic sets. They are just building blocks for whatever we want to express in this model. Since the elements of ESets are disjoint, union is the most obvious an natural tool to construct bigger objects from elementary sets.

A set $A \subseteq U$ is *definable* (or *exact*) [16] if it is a union of some equivalence classes of the equivalence relation E. Let DSets (or $\mathsf{DSets(AS)}$, if needed) denote the family of all definable sets defined by the space (U, E). Formally:

Definition 1. $A \in \mathsf{DSets} \iff \exists A_1, \ldots, A_k \subseteq \mathsf{ESets}. \ A = A_1 \cup \ldots \cup A_k.$ □

A non-empty set $X \subseteq U$ is approximated by two definable sets; $\underline{\mathbf{A}}(X) \in \mathsf{DSets}$ and $\overline{\mathbf{A}}(X) \in \mathsf{DSets}$. They are called the *lower* and *upper approximations* of X respectively, and defined as follows:

Definition 2 [15,16]. For each $X \subseteq U$,

1. $\underline{\mathbf{A}}(X) = \bigcup \{A \mid A \in \mathsf{Esets} \wedge A \subseteq X\}$,
2. $\overline{\mathbf{A}}(X) = \bigcup \{A \mid A \in \mathsf{Esets} \wedge A \cap X \neq \emptyset\}$.   □

Clearly $\underline{\mathbf{A}}(X) \subseteq X \subseteq \overline{\mathbf{A}}(X)$. Moreover, with respect to set inclusion, $\underline{\mathbf{A}}(X)$ is the greatest lower bound of X in DSets and $\overline{\mathbf{A}}(X)$ is the least upper bound of X in DSets. Hence, in DSets, $\underline{\mathbf{A}}(X)$ is the best approximation of X from the bottom and $\overline{\mathbf{A}}(X)$ is the best approximation of X from the top.

We may write $\underline{\mathbf{A}}_{\mathsf{AS}}(X)$ and $\overline{\mathbf{A}}_{\mathsf{AS}}(X)$ when more than one approximation space is discussed.

There are many versions and many extensions of this basic model, see for example [9,19,20,23], as well as many various applications (cf. [8,18,20,21]).

Recently, in [10,11], a concept of an *optimal approximation*, has been introduced and analyzed. Assuming that we have a well defined function that measure the numerical similarity between two sets, $sim(A, B)$, we can define *optimal approximations* as follows:

Definition 3 [10,11]. For every set $X \subseteq U$, a definable set $\mathsf{O} \in \mathsf{DSets}$ is an *optimal approximation* of X (w.r.t. a given similarity measure sim) if and only if:

$$sim(X, \mathsf{O}) = \max_{A \in \mathsf{DSets}} (sim(X, A))$$

The *set* of all optimal approximations of X will be denoted by $\mathsf{Opt}_{sim}(X)$ (or $\mathsf{Opt}_{sim,\mathsf{AC}}(X)$, if needed).   □

---

[1] The name *components* is also often used, however this paper we will use the name 'component' in the sense of [12].

Note that in general we might have *more than one* optimal approximation for a given similarity measure *sim*.

In [10, 11] it is shown that any (total) function $sim : 2^U \times 2^U \to [0,1]$ satisfying the following five axioms can be used as a *similarity measure* in Definition 3 above. These axioms are:

$S1 :$ $sim(A,B) = 1 \iff A = B,$
$S2 :$ $sim(A,B) = sim(B,A),$
$S3 :$ $sim(A,B) = 0 \iff A \cap B = \emptyset,$
$S4 :$ if $a \in B \setminus A$ then $sim(A,B) < sim(A \cup \{a\}, B),$
$S5 :$ if $a \notin A \cup B$ and $A \cap B \neq \emptyset$ then $sim(A,B) > sim(A \cup \{a\}, B).$

For *sim* satisfying the above five axioms, we have:

Proposition 1 [10,11]. *For every set $X \subseteq U$, and every $O \in \mathsf{Opt}_{sim}(X)$:*
$$\underline{\mathbf{A}}(X) \subseteq O \subseteq \overline{\mathbf{A}}(X) \qquad \square$$

There are many similarity measures satisfying the axioms $S1$–$S5$ [5], the oldest one was proposed by Jaccard[2] in 1901 [7]. The notion of *consistency* introduced in [10] makes many of different similarity measures equivalent for our purposes.

Definition 4 [10,11]. We say that two similarity indexes sim_1 and sim_2 satisfying axioms $S1$–$S5$ are *consistent* if for all sets $A, B, C \subseteq U$,

$$sim_1(A,B) < sim_1(A,C) \iff sim_2(A,B) < sim_2(A,C). \qquad \square$$

Corollary 1 [10,11]. *If sim_1 and sim_2 are consistent then for each $X \subseteq U$, then*

$$\mathsf{Opt}_{sim_1}(X) = \mathsf{Opt}_{sim_2}(X). \qquad \square$$

An efficient greedy algorithm for finding the set $\mathsf{Opt}_{sim}(X)$ has been proposed in [11] for all similarity measures that are consistent with Marczewski-Steinhaus index[3] [14], which includes such similarity measures as Jaccard, Dice-Sørensen, symmetric Tversky, etc. [5,11]. The complexity of this algorithm is $O(|X|^2)$, i.e. the same as complexities of calculating $\underline{\mathbf{A}}(X)$ and $\overline{\mathbf{A}}(X)$ (cf. [18]). The algorithm relies heavily on the fact that definable sets are unions of *disjoint* elementary sets.

Since an equivalence relation and a partition it generates are dual equivalent notions, an approximation space $\mathsf{AS} = (U, E)$ can equivalently be defined as $\mathsf{AS} = (U, \mathsf{ESets})$. This lead to a natural extension by replacing a *partition* ESets of U by an arbitrary *covering* $\mathbb{C}$ of U. This idea, first considered probably in [2], resulted in two relatively known models, that of [22,26]. Our approach will be based on the concept of *set components* as defined and discussed in [12].

---

[2] Jaccard index is defined as $sim(X,Y) = \frac{|X \cap Y|}{|X \cup Y|}$ [7].

[3] Marczewski-Steinhaus index is defined as $sim(X,Y) = \frac{\mu(X \cap Y)}{\mu(X \cup Y)}$, where μ is a finite measure on U and $X, Y \subseteq U$ [14].

3   Coverings, Components and Definability

Let U be a set and let $\mathbb{C}$ be a family of nonempty subsets of U.

- We say that $\mathbb{C}$ is a *covering* of U if $U = \bigcup_{C \in \mathbb{C}} C$.

In the rest of this section we briefly adapt the results of Chap. 1.7 of [12] for our purposes. We start with the definition of *definable* sets as this concept is crucial in our approach.

Definition 5. Let U be a set and let $\mathbb{C}$ be a nonempty family of nonempty subsets of U. A non-empty set $X \subseteq U$ *definable* by $\mathbb{C}$ if it can be constructed from the elements of $\mathbb{C}$ by means of set operations $\cup$, $\cap$ and $\setminus$.
The family of all sets *definable* by $\mathbb{C}$ will be denoted by $\mathsf{definable}(\mathbb{C})$.   □

We would like to point out that the family of sets $\mathbb{C}$ in Definition 5 *does not have to* be a covering.

The next crucial idea in our approach in the concept of *set components*.

Definition 6 [12]. Let U be set and $\mathbb{C} = \{C_1, \ldots, C_n\}$ be any nonempty family of nonempty subsets of U. For each $i = 1, 2, \ldots, n$, let $C_i^0 = C_i$ and $C_i^1 = U \setminus C_i$. Each intersection

$$C^{(i_1, \ldots, i_n)} = C_1^{i_1} \cap \ldots \cap C_n^{i_n},$$

where $i_k = 0, 1$ and $k = 1, 2, \ldots, n$, is called a *component* of $\mathbb{C}$.
The set of all *nonempty* components of $\mathbb{C}$, will be denoted by $\mathsf{comp}(\mathbb{C})$, i.e.

$$\mathsf{comp}(\mathbb{C}) = \{C^{(i_1, \ldots, i_n)} \mid i_k = 1, 2, \ k = 1, 2, \ldots, n, \ C^{(i_1, \ldots, i_n)} \neq \emptyset\}.   □$$

The above definition is illustrated in Fig. 1. If neither component is empty, we have exactly 2^n components, in general $|\mathsf{comp}(\mathbb{C})| \leq 2^n$.

In the rest of this paper, an arbitrary component will be denoted by $C^{(\alpha)}$. First note that $\mathbb{C}$ is a covering if and only if the component $C^{(1, \ldots, 1)} = U \setminus (C_1 \cup \ldots \cup C_n)$ is empty, i.e. not a member of $\mathsf{comp}(\mathbb{C})$.

Corollary 2. $U = \bigcup_{C \in \mathbb{C}} C \iff C^{(1, \ldots, 1)} = \emptyset \iff C^{(1, \ldots, 1)} \notin \mathsf{comp}(\mathbb{C})$.   □

The basic properties of components are the following.

Theorem 1 [12]. *Let U be a set and $\mathbb{C}$ a covering of U.*

1. $U = \bigcup_{C^{(\alpha)} \in \mathsf{comp}(\mathbb{C})} C^{(\alpha)}$.

2. *For all $C^{(\alpha)}, C^{(\beta)} \in \mathsf{comp}(\mathbb{C})$, we have $C^{(\alpha)} \cap C^{(\beta)} = \emptyset \iff \alpha \neq \beta$.*
3. *Every set $X \in \mathsf{definable}(\mathbb{C})$ is a union of some components of $\mathbb{C}$, i.e.*

$$X \in \mathsf{definable}(\mathbb{C}) \iff \exists C^{(\alpha_1)}, \ldots, C^{(\alpha_k)} \in \mathsf{comp}(\mathbb{C}). \ X = C^{(\alpha_1)} \cup \ldots \cup C^{(\alpha_k)}.$$

□

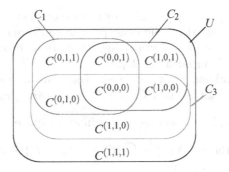

Fig. 1. All eight components for a given U and $\mathbb{C} = \{C_1, C_2, C_3\}$. In this case neither component is an empty set.

Theorem 1 simply says that the set of all components $\mathsf{comp}(\mathbb{C})$ is a partition of U and each definable set is a union of some components. In particular each element of $\mathbb{C}$ is a union of some components, i.e. $\mathbb{C} \subseteq \mathsf{definable}(\mathbb{C})$.

Theorem 1 has a natural interpretation in propositional logic. Let $\mathbb{C} = \{C_1, \ldots, C_n\}$ and assume that all elements of C_i satisfy some property (predicate) π_i, and additionally $\pi_i \neq \pi_j$ if $i \neq j$. Then the elements of $\mathsf{definable}(\mathbb{C})$ correspond to all nonequivalent predicates that can be derived from $\{\pi_1, \ldots, \pi_n\}$ by means of logical operators $\vee, \wedge$ and $\neg$. With this interpretation Theorem 1(3) simply states that each propositional predicate built from $\{\pi_1, \ldots, \pi_n\}$ has its disjunctive normal form [6]. The elements of $C^{(1,\ldots,1)}$ then satisfy the property $\neg(\pi_1 \vee \ldots \vee \pi_k)$.

Since $\mathsf{comp}(\mathbb{C})$ is always a partition of U, we can define the following an *equivalence relation* $E_{\mathbb{C}} \subseteq U \times U$:

Definition 7. Let U be a set and $\mathbb{C}$ be a nonempty family of nonempty subsets of U. We define the relation $E_{\mathbb{C}} \subseteq U \times U$ as follows:

$$\forall a, b \in U.\ a E_{\mathbb{C}} b \iff \exists C^{(\alpha)} \in comp(\mathbb{C}).\ a \in C^{(\alpha)} \wedge b \in C^{(\alpha)}.$$

The relation $E_{\mathbb{C}}$ is called the *equivalence relation induced by a family* $\mathbb{C}$.   □

Clearly $U/E_{\mathbb{C}} = comp(\mathbb{C})$, i.e. the set of all equivalence classes of $E_{\mathbb{C}}$ is equal to the set of all components of the covering $\mathbb{C}$.

While in the next section we will assume that $\mathbb{C}$ is some covering of U, there is not such an assumption for the results of this section. In this section $\mathbb{C}$ is just an arbitrary nonempty family of nonempty subsets of U.

4 Rough Sets Induced by Coverings

In this section we recall two two types of generalized rough sets induced by coverings, one from [22] and another from [26]. Their mutual relationship is discussed in detail in [13]. We will also introduce our new model of rough sets induced by coverings, based on the concept of a *component* from the previous section and show that lower and upper approximations provided by our model are tighter that these from both [22,26].

Let U be a finite and non-empty universe of elements and let $\mathbb{C}$ be its covering. Following [13], we will call the pair $\mathsf{CS} = (U, \mathbb{C})$ a *covering approximation space*.

Definition 8. Let $(U, \mathbb{C})$ a covering approximation space.

1. For every $x \in U$, the set $N(x) = \bigcap\{C \in \mathbb{C} \mid x \in C\}$ is called the *neighborhood* of an element $x \in U$ [13].
2. For every $X \subseteq U$, its *Zhu lower approximation* [26] is defined as:

$$\mathbf{A}_+(X) = \bigcup\{C \in \mathbb{C} \mid C \subseteq X\}$$

and its *Zhu upper approximation* [26] is defined as:

$$\mathbf{A}^+(X) = \mathbf{A}_+(X) \cup \bigcup\{N(x) \mid x \in X \setminus \mathbf{A}_+(X)\}.$$

3. For every $X \subseteq U$, its *Xu-Zhang lower approximation* [22] is defined as:

$$\mathbf{A}_*(X) = \{x \mid N(x) \subseteq X\}$$

and its *Xu-Zhang upper approximation* [22] is defined as:

$$\mathbf{A}^*(X) = \{x \mid N(x) \cap X \neq \emptyset\}. \qquad \square$$

The relationship between $\mathbf{A}_+(X)$ and $\mathbf{A}_*(X)$, and between $\mathbf{A}^+(X)$ and $\mathbf{A}^*(X)$ is discussed in details in [13].

Definition 3 can be used for defining *optimal approximations* in both Zhu and Xu-Zhang models, provided the *definable sets* are well and precisely defined. While definable sets are not explicitly described in [13,22,26] the following definitions are a safe bet for both models: neighborhoods play the role of elementary sets, i.e.

$$\mathsf{ESets}^{+*} = \{N(x) \mid x \in U\},$$

and definable sets are standardly unions of elementary sets, i.e.

$$\mathsf{A} \in \mathsf{DSets}^{+*} \iff \exists N_1, \dots, N_n \subseteq \mathsf{ESets}^{+*}. \ A = N_1 \cup \dots \cup N_n.$$

We may now define an optimal approximation, for both Zhu and Xu-Zhang models as follows.

Definition 9. For every set $X \subseteq U$, a definable set $\mathsf{O} \in \mathsf{DSets}^{+*}$ is an *optimal approximation* of X (w.r.t. a given similarity measure *sim*) if and only if:

$$sim(X, \mathsf{O}) = \max_{\mathsf{A} \in \mathsf{DSets}^{+*}} (sim(X, \mathsf{A}))$$

The *set* of all optimal approximations of X will be denoted by $\mathsf{Opt}^{+*}_{sim}(X)$. $\qquad \square$

We still have (assuming sim satisfies axioms $S1$–$S5$):

Proposition 2. *For every set $X \subseteq U$, and every $O \in \mathsf{Opt}^{+*}_{sim}(X)$:*

1. $\mathbf{A}_+(X) \subseteq O \subseteq \mathbf{A}^+(X)$, and
2. $\mathbf{A}_*(X) \subseteq O \subseteq \mathbf{A}^*(X)$.

Proof

(1) Suppose that $A = \mathbf{A}^+(X) \setminus O \neq \emptyset$. Since $C \subseteq X$, then by axiom $S4$, $sim(O, X) < sim(O \cup A, X)$, so O must not be optimal. Now suppose that $A = O \setminus \mathbf{A}^+(X) \neq \emptyset$. i.e. $A \subseteq O$ but $A \not\subseteq X$. By axiom $S5$, $sim(O \setminus C, X) > sim(O, X)$, so O must not be optimal again.
(2) Identically as (1). $\qquad\qquad\qquad\qquad\qquad\qquad\qquad\qquad\qquad\qquad\qquad\qquad$ □

Unfortunately, the efficient greedy algorithm for finding optimal approximations for standard Pawlak approximation spaces, i.e. $\mathsf{Opt}_{sim}(X)$, described in [11] for large class of similarity measures, does not work for $\mathsf{Opt}^{+*}_{sim}(X)$, and it it not clear how it can be modified or adapted.

While both approaches [22, 26] are mathematically correct and have believable intuitions that support them, the author of this paper thinks that both approaches are missing one important point.

In classical Pawlak's approach, we have:

- *Definable sets are the only sets that can be expressed exactly, everything else must be approximate by some definable set.*
- *The lower approximation of $X \subseteq U$ is defined as the biggest definable (exact) set (or greatest lower bound) included in X, while*
- *The upper approximation is defined as the smallest definable (exact) set (or least upper bound) containing X.*
- *Definable sets can be derived from some class of elementary sets by using a finite number of simple and 'natural' operations.*

We believe that the above mantra should be followed when any extension is considered, so the only differences could be in the definitions of greatest lower bound, least upper bound, and, especially, in the definition of definable and elementary sets.

When we have a classical Pawlak approximation space (U, E), the elementary sets are defined as just equivalence classes of the relation E and definable sets as arbitrary unions of elementary sets.

- However, we can define definable set is a slightly different but equivalent manner, namely, a set is *definable* or *exact* if it can be derived from the elements of U/E by applying operations $\cup$, $\cap$ and $\setminus$ finitely many times.

Since two different equivalence classes are disjoint, the standard definition and this new one are equivalent, so one can replace another. For equivalent classes the operators $\cap$ and $\setminus$ are never used, but they do not any harm either. Furthermore, there is no obvious reason why the operation $\cap$ should only be allowed in a restricted manner (to calculate neighborhoods but not definable sets in the models of [22, 26]). There is no 'natural' advantage of the operator $\cup$ over the operators $\cap$ or $\setminus$, all three are primary operations in set theory and they computational complexities are identical.

All the above lead to the following third model of rough sets induced by coverings. This model utilizes the fact that $comp(\mathbb{C})$ is a partition of U (cf. Theorem 1), so the pattern used in standard Pawlak approximation space can be applied again.

Definition 10. Let $(U, \mathbb{C})$ be a covering approximation space, and let $comp(\mathbb{C})$ be the set of all components of $\mathbb{C}$.

1. ESets $= \mathbb{C}$, i.e. the elements of $\mathbb{C}$ are *elementary sets*.
2. DSets $=$ definable$(\mathbb{C})$, i.e. the elements of definable$(\mathbb{C})$ are *definable sets*.
3. For every $X \subseteq U$, its lower approximation $\underline{\mathbf{A}}^c(X)$ is defined as:

$$\underline{\mathbf{A}}^c(X) = \bigcup \{ C^{(\alpha)} \mid C^{(\alpha)} \in comp(\mathbb{C}) \wedge C^{(\alpha)} \subseteq X \}.$$

4. For every $X \subseteq U$, its upper approximation $\overline{\mathbf{A}}^c(X)$ is defined as:

$$\overline{\mathbf{A}}^c(X) = \bigcup \{ C^{(\alpha)} \mid C^{(\alpha)} \in comp(\mathbb{C}) \wedge C^{(\alpha)} \cap X \neq \emptyset \}.$$

5. For every set $X \subseteq U$, a definable set $O \in$ definable$(\mathbb{C})$ is an *optimal approximation* of X (w.r.t. a given similarity measure sim) if and only if:

$$sim(X, O) = \max_{A \in \text{definable}(\mathbb{C})} (sim(X, \mathbf{A}))$$

The *set* of all optimal approximations of X will be denoted by $\text{Opt}^c_{sim}(X)$. $\square$

The key part of the above definition are the points (1) and (2). They guarantee the below results, which was our initial motivation.

Corollary 3. DSets, *i.e. definable sets, are all subsets of U than can be constructed from the elements of $\mathbb{C}$ by applying the operations $\cup, \cap$ and $\setminus$ finite number of times.*

Proof. From Theorem 1(2). $\square$

We will now show that lower and upper approximations of our model are tighter, and the optimal approximation of our model is closer than appropriate approximations from the previous two models, i.e. approximations of our model are more precise.

Theorem 2

1. *Let $(U, \mathbb{C})$ be a covering space. For every $X \subseteq U$ we have:*

$$\mathbf{A}_+(X) \subseteq \underline{\mathbf{A}}^c(X) \quad and \quad \overline{\mathbf{A}}^c(X) \subseteq \mathbf{A}^+(X)$$
$$\mathbf{A}_*(X) \subseteq \underline{\mathbf{A}}^c(X) \quad and \quad \overline{\mathbf{A}}^c(X) \subseteq \mathbf{A}^*(X)$$

2. *There are coverings* $(U_i, \mathbb{C}_i)$ *and* $X_i \subseteq U_i$, *for* $i = 1, \ldots, 4$ *such that*

$$\mathbf{A}_+(X_1) \neq \underline{\mathbf{A}}^c(X_1) \ \ and \ \ \overline{\mathbf{A}}^c(X_2) \neq \mathbf{A}^+(X_2)$$
$$\mathbf{A}_+(X_3) \neq \underline{\mathbf{A}}^c(X_3) \ \ and \ \ \overline{\mathbf{A}}^c(X_4) \neq \mathbf{A}^+(X_4)$$

3. *Let* $(U, \mathbb{C})$ *be a covering space. For every* $X \subseteq U$, *every* $\mathsf{O} \in \mathsf{Opt}^{+*}_{sim}(X)$ *and every* $\mathsf{O}' \in \mathsf{Opt}^c_{sim}(X)$, *we have:*

$$sim(X, \mathsf{O}) \leq sim(X, \mathsf{O}').$$

4. *There is a covering* $(U, \mathbb{C})$, $X \subseteq U$, $\mathsf{O} \in \mathsf{Opt}^{+*}_{sim}(X)$ *and every* $\mathsf{O}' \in \mathsf{Opt}^c_{sim}(X)$, *such that:*

$$sim(X, \mathsf{O}) \neq sim(X, \mathsf{O}').$$

Proof

(1) Let $x \in \mathbf{A}_+(X)$. Then there is $C \in \mathbb{C}$ such that $x \in C \subseteq X$. By Theorem 1(2), C is a union of some components, so there is $C^{(\alpha)} \in \mathsf{comp}(\mathbb{C})$ and $x \in C^{(\alpha)} \subseteq X$, i.e. $x \in \underline{\mathbf{A}}^c(X)$. Hence $\mathbf{A}_+(X) \subseteq \underline{\mathbf{A}}^c(X)$.

Let $x \in \overline{\mathbf{A}}^c(X)$. If $x \in X$ then clearly $x \in \mathbf{A}^+(X)$, so assume $x \in \overline{\mathbf{A}}^c(X) \backslash X$. This means there is $C^{(\alpha)} \in \mathsf{comp}(\mathbb{C})$ such that $C^{(\alpha)} \cap X \neq \emptyset$, but $x \in C^{(\alpha)} \backslash X$. Assume that $y \in C^{(\alpha)} \cap X$. If $y \in \mathbf{A}_+(X)$ then $C^{(\alpha)} \subseteq \mathbf{A}_+(X)$, so $x \in \mathbf{A}^+(X)$. Nevertheless, always, $\{x, y\} \subseteq C^{(\alpha)} \subseteq \bigcap\{C \mid C \in \mathbb{C} \wedge C^{(\alpha)} \subseteq C\} \subseteq N(y)$, and, if $y \in X \backslash C^{(\alpha)} \cap X$, $\{x, y\} \subseteq N(y) \subseteq \mathbf{A}^+(X)$. Hence $\overline{\mathbf{A}}^c(X) \subseteq \mathbf{A}^+(X)$.

Let $x \in \mathbf{A}_*(X)$. Hence $x \in N(x) = \bigcap\{C \in \mathbb{C} \mid x \in C\} \subseteq X$. By Theorem 1(2), there is $C^{(\alpha)} \in \mathsf{comp}(\mathbb{C})$ such that $x \in C^{(\alpha)} \subseteq N(x)\}$, i.e. $x \in \underline{\mathbf{A}}^c(X)$. Hence $\mathbf{A}_*(X) \subseteq \underline{\mathbf{A}}^c(X)$.

Let $x \in \overline{\mathbf{A}}^c(X)$. If $x \in X$ then clearly $x \in \mathbf{A}^*(X)$, so assume $x \in \overline{\mathbf{A}}^c(X) \backslash X$. This means there is $C^{(\alpha)} \in \mathsf{comp}(\mathbb{C})$ such that $C^{(\alpha)} \cap X \neq \emptyset$, but $x \in C^{(\alpha)} \backslash X$. Assume that $y \in C^{(\alpha)} \cap X$. Since we always have $\{x, y\} \subseteq C^{(\alpha)} \subseteq \bigcap\{C \mid C \in \mathbb{C} \wedge C^{(\alpha)} \subseteq C\} \subseteq N(y)$, we can conclude $\{x, y\} \subseteq N(y) \subseteq \mathbf{A}^*(X)$. Hence $\overline{\mathbf{A}}^c(X) \subseteq \mathbf{A}^*(X)$.

(2) Consider the following example: $U = \{1, 2, 3\}$, $C_1 = \{1, 2\}$, $C_2 = \{2, 3\}$, i.e. $\mathbb{C} = \{C_1, C_2\}$, and $X = \{1\}$. Hence we have: $C^{(0,0)} = \{2\}$, $C^{(1,0)} = \{3\}$, $C^{(0,1)} = \{1\}$, $C^{(1,1)} = \emptyset$, and $\mathsf{comp}(\mathbb{C}) = \{C^{(0,0)}, C^{(0,1)}, C^{(1,0)}\} = \{\{1\}, \{2\}, \{3\}\}$. Moreover: $N(1) = C_1 = \{1, 2\} = C^{(0,1)} \cup C^{(0,0)}$, $N(2) = C_1 \cap C_2 = \{2\} = C^{(0,0)}$, $N(3) = C_2 = \{2, 3\} = C^{(1,0)} \cup C^{(0,0)}$. In this case we have (since $X = \{1\}$):
$\mathbf{A}_+(X) = \mathbf{A}_*(X) = \emptyset \subsetneq \{1\} = \underline{\mathbf{A}}^c(X) = \overline{\mathbf{A}}^c(X) = X$,
$\overline{\mathbf{A}}^c(X) = X \subsetneq \mathbf{A}^*(X) = N(1) = \{1, 2\} \subsetneq \mathbf{A}^+(X) = N(1) \cup N(2) \cup N(3) = \{1, 2, 3\}$.

(3) Since for every $x \in X$, $N(x)$ is a union of some elements from $\mathsf{comp}(\mathbb{C})$, we have $\mathsf{DSets}^{+*} \subseteq \mathsf{definable}(\mathbb{C})$. Hence $sim(X, \mathsf{O}') = \max_{A \in \mathsf{DSets}^{+*}}(sim(X, A)) \leq sim(X, \mathsf{O}) \max_{A \in \mathsf{definable}(\mathbb{C})}(sim(X, A))$.

(4) Consider the same example as in (2). For $X = \{1\}$ we have $\mathsf{Opt}^c_{sim}(X) = \{\{1\}\} = \{X\}$ and $\mathsf{Opt}^{+*}_{sim}(X) = \{\{1,2\}\}$. Hence $sim(X,\{1\}) = 1$ and by axiom $S1$, $sim(X,\{1,2\}) < sim(X,\{1\})$.   □

While occasionally appropriate approximations from above theorem are equal, for most random cases the inclusions and inequality are sharp.

Let $\mathsf{CS} = (U, \mathbb{C})$ be a given covering approximation space. We define the Pawlak approximations space $\mathsf{AS_{CS}} = (U, E_{\mathbb{C}})$, where $E_{\mathbb{C}}$ is an equivalence relation on U given by Definition 7.

- The Pawlak approximations space $\mathsf{AS_{CS}} = (U, E_{\mathbb{C}})$ is called *derived* from the covering approximation space $\mathsf{CS} = (U, \mathbb{C})$.

Proposition 3. *For every covering approximation space* $\mathsf{CS} = (U, \mathbb{C})$, *the Pawlak approximations space* $\mathsf{AS_{CS}} = (U, E_{\mathbb{C}})$ *has the following properties:*

1. $\mathsf{ESets}(\mathsf{AS_{CS}}) = \mathsf{comp}(\mathbb{C})$, *i.e. the elements of* $\mathsf{comp}(\mathbb{C})$ *are also the elementary sets of* $\mathsf{AS_{CS}}$.
2. $\mathsf{DSets}(\mathsf{AS_{CS}}) = \mathsf{definable}(\mathbb{C})$, *i.e. the elements of* $\mathsf{definable}(\mathbb{C})$ *are also definable sets of* $\mathsf{AS_{CS}}$.
3. *For all* $X \subseteq U$, *we have:*

$$\underline{\mathbf{A}}_{\mathsf{AS_{CS}}}(X) = \underline{\mathbf{A}}^c(X)$$
$$\overline{\mathbf{A}}_{\mathsf{AS_{CS}}}(X) = \overline{\mathbf{A}}^c(X)$$
$$\mathsf{Opt}_{sim,\mathsf{AC_{CS}}}(X) = \mathsf{Opt}^c_{sim}(X)$$

Proof. Directly from the properties of the equivalence relation $E_{\mathbb{C}}$.   □

Proposition 3 describes an easy and natural transformation of rough sets induced by coverings into an equivalent standard rough sets, i.e. rough sets induced by partitions. This allows us to apply all methods invented for standard rough sets for our model of rough sets induced by a given covering. Among others, the greedy algorithm from [11] works for $\mathsf{Opt}_{sim,\mathsf{AC_{CS}}}(X)$ (if sim is consistent with Marczewski-Steinhaus index), so it can also be used for $\mathsf{Opt}^c_{sim}(X)$.

This again, was one of the intentions of our model.

The set of components $\mathsf{comp}(\mathbb{C})$ is defined for *any* family $\mathbb{C}$ of subsets of U, i.e. $\mathbb{C}$ does not need to be a covering of U. This allows us to make a generalization of *covering approximation space* to *subset approximation space*.

Let U be a set and let $\mathbb{C}$ be a nonempty family of nonempty subsets of U.

- The pair $(U, \mathbb{C})$ is called a *subsets approximation space*.

If $\mathbb{C}$ is a covering of U, then $(U, \mathbb{C})$ is an covering approximation space, if $\mathbb{C}$ is a partition of U, then $(U, \mathbb{C})$ is a standard Pawlak approximation space.

- Note that Definition 10, Corollary 3 and Proposition 3 are still valid and correct when we replace '*covering approximation space*' with '*subsets approximation space*'.

In other words, from mathematical point of view, covering approximation space is just a special case of subsets approximation space. What is substantially different is an interpretation. Let $\mathbb{C} = \{C_1, \ldots, C_n\}$ and all elements of C_i satisfy some property (predicate) π_i, with $\pi_i \neq \pi_j$ if $i \neq j$. If $(U, \mathbb{C})$ is a covering approximation space then the component $C^{(1,\ldots,1)} = \emptyset$, if $(U, \mathbb{C})$ is a subsets approximation space then the component $C^{(1,\ldots,1)} \neq \emptyset$. All the elements of the component $C^{(1,\ldots,1)}$ satisfy the property $\neg(\pi_1 \vee \ldots \vee \pi_n)$. This might be interpreted as some incomplete information. For the elements of $C^{(1,\ldots,1)}$ all we know if that neither of π_i is satisfied, but we do not have any particular π, different than $\neg(\pi_1 \vee \ldots \vee \pi_n)$, that is satisfied. Every exact set, i.e. an element of $\mathsf{definable}(\mathbb{C})$, that contains $C^{(1,\ldots,1)}$, has also some part with incomplete information.

For subset approximation spaces we can define two types of lower, upper and optimal approximations. We can define $\underline{\mathbf{A}}^s(X)$, $\overline{\mathbf{A}}^s(X)$ and $\mathsf{Opt}_{sim}^s(X)$ just by applying appropriate formulas from Definition 10(3–5). These approximations are built from the components that belong to $\mathsf{comp}(\mathbb{C})$, including the component $C^{(1,\ldots,1)}$, and they might be interpreted as approximations with incomplete information.

We can also replace $\mathbb{C}$ in Definition 10 with $\widehat{\mathbb{C}} = \mathbb{C} \setminus \{C^{(1,\ldots,1)}\}$, and define appropriate approximations $\underline{\mathbf{A}}^{\hat{s}}(X)$, $\overline{\mathbf{A}}^{\hat{s}}(X)$ and $\mathsf{Opt}_{sim}^{\hat{s}}(X)$. While $\overline{\mathbf{A}}^{\hat{s}}(X)$ always exists, it has a standard interpretation, i.e. $X \subseteq \overline{\mathbf{A}}^{\hat{s}}(X)$, only if $X \cap C^{(1,\ldots,1)} = \emptyset$, but in such case $\overline{\mathbf{A}}^{\hat{s}}(X) = \overline{\mathbf{A}}^s(X)$, and also $\underline{\mathbf{A}}^{\hat{s}}(X) = \underline{\mathbf{A}}^s(X)$ and $\mathsf{Opt}_{sim}^{\hat{s}}(X) = \mathsf{Opt}_{sim}^s(X)$.

5 Final Comments

A new model of rough sets induced by coverings has been proposed. The model is based on the assumption that $\cup$, $\cap$ and $\setminus$ are the primitive operations used for deriving elementary and definable sets from a given coverings of a universe. This assumption resulted in representing elementary sets by components (in the sense of [12]) generated by a covering. Both lower and upper approximations of this new model are tighter than the ones from [22,26], two other popular models that use coverings instead of partitions. Optimal approximations, first introduced for standard rough sets in [10] and analyzed in detail in [11], were defined for the new model and for models of [22,26], and it was proven that optimal approximation for the new model is closer to a given set than similar optimal approximations of [22,26] for any similarity measure that satisfies axioms from [10].

It is also shown that our new model can easily be extended from coverings to any arbitrary family of subsets of the universe.

The model introduced in this paper can also be interpreted as an aim to provide a sound semantics foundations of covering based rough sets (in a sense of [4]). The difference is that we use set-theoretic operations instead of operators of logic as in [4]. In terminology of [4] our model corresponds to the case when atomic formulas are predicates $\pi_1, \ldots, \pi_n$, each π uniquely defines $C_i \in \mathbb{C}$, and an *extended descriptive language* (denoted EDL_A in [4]) is just the set of all propositional formulas built from atoms. The latter is due to Theorem 1.

Last, but not least, the model can in a very natural manner be transformed into an equivalent standard rough set, so the whole rich theory of standard rough sets can be used without any restriction, including algorithms for finding optimal approximations [11].

Acknowledgment. The authors gratefully acknowledge four anonymous referees, whose comments significantly contributed to the final version of this paper.

This research was partially supported by a Discovery NSERC grant of Canada.

References

1. Bogobowicz, A.D., Janicki, R.: On approximation of relations by generalized closures and generalized kernels. In: Flores, V., Gomide, F., Janusz, A., Meneses, C., Miao, D., Peters, G., Ślęzak, D., Wang, G., Weber, R., Yao, Y. (eds.) IJCRS 2016. LNCS (LNAI), vol. 9920, pp. 120–130. Springer, Cham (2016). doi:10.1007/978-3-319-47160-0_11
2. Bonikowski, Z., Bryniarski, E., Wybraniec, U.: Extensions and intentions in the rough set theory. Inf. Sci. **107**, 149–167 (1998)
3. Bretcher, O.: Linear Algebra with Applications. Prentice Hall, Englewood Cliffs (1995)
4. D'eer, L., Cornelis, C., Yao, Y.Y.: A semantically sound approach to Pawlak rough sets and covering-based rough sets. Int. J. Approx. Reason. **78**, 62–72 (2016)
5. Deza, M.M., Deza, E.: Encyclopedia of Distances. Springer, Berlin (2012)
6. Huth, M., Ryan, M.: Logic in Computer Science. Cambridge University Press, Cambridge (2004)
7. Jaccard, P.: Étude comparative de la distribution florale dans une portion des Alpes et des Jura. Bulletin de la Société Vaudoise des Sciences Naturalles **37**, 547–549 (1901)
8. Janicki, R.: Approximations of arbitrary binary relations by partial orders. Classical and rough set models. Trans. Rough Sets **13**, 17–38 (2011)
9. Janicki, R.: Property-driven rough sets approximations of relations. In: [20], pp. 333–357
10. Janicki, R., Lenarčič, A.: Optimal approximations with rough sets. In: Lingras, P., Wolski, M., Cornelis, C., Mitra, S., Wasilewski, P. (eds.) RSKT 2013. LNCS, vol. 8171, pp. 87–98. Springer, Heidelberg (2013). doi:10.1007/978-3-642-41299-8_9
11. Janicki, R., Lenarčič, A.: Optimal approximations with rough sets and similarities in measure spaces. Optimal approximations with rough sets. In: Lingras, P., Wolski, M., Cornelis, C., Mitra, S., Wasilewski, P. (eds.) Proceedings of Rough Sets and Knowledge Technology, RSKT 2013. Int. J. Approx. Reason. **71**, 1–14 (2016)
12. Kuratowski, K., Mostowski, A.: Set Theory. North-Holland, Amsterdam (1967)
13. Liu, G., Sai, Y.: A comparison of two types of rough sets induced by coverings. Int. J. Approx. Reason. **50**, 521–528 (2009)
14. Marczewski, E., Steinhaus, H.: On a certain distance of sets and corresponding distance of functions. Colloq. Math. **4**, 319–327 (1958)
15. Pawlak, Z.: Rought sets. Int. J. Comput. Inform. Sci. **34**, 557–590 (1982)
16. Pawlak, Z.: Rough Sets. Kluwer, Dordrecht (1991)
17. Pomykała, J.A.: Approximation operations in approximation space. Bull. Acad. Pol. Sci. **35**, 653–662 (1987)

18. Saquer, J., Deogun, J.S.: Concept approximations based on rough sets and similarity measures. Int. J. Appl. Math. Comput. Sci. **11**(3), 655–674 (2001)
19. Skowron, A., Stepaniuk, J.: Tolarence approximation spaces. Fundam. Inform. **27**, 245–253 (1996)
20. Skowron, A., Suraj, Z. (eds.): Rough Sets and Intelligent Systems. Intelligent Systems Reference Library, vol. 42. Springer, Heidelberg (2013)
21. Słowiński, R., Vanderpooten, D.: A generalized definition of rough approximations based on similarity. IEEE Trans. Knowl. Data Eng. **12**(2), 331–336 (2000)
22. Xu, W.H., Zhang, W.X.: Measuring roughness of generalized rough sets induced by a covering. Fuzzy Sets Syst. **158**, 2443–2455 (2007)
23. Yao, Y.Y., Wang, T.: On rough relations: an alternative formulation. In: Zhong, N., Skowron, A., Ohsuga, S. (eds.) RSFDGrC 1999. LNCS, vol. 1711, pp. 82–90. Springer, Heidelberg (1999). doi:10.1007/978-3-540-48061-7_12
24. Yao, Y.Y., Yao, B.X.: Covering based rough set approximations. Inf. Sci. **200**, 91–107 (2012)
25. Zadeh, L.A.: Fuzzy sets. Inf. Control **8**(3), 338–353 (1965)
26. Zhu, W.: Topological approaches to covering rough sets. Inf. Sci. **177**(6), 1499–1508 (2007)
27. Żakowski, W.: Approximations in the space (U, Π). Demonstr. Math. **16**, 761–769 (1983)

Approximation Operators in Covering Based Rough Sets from Submodular Functions

Mauricio Restrepo[✉]

Department of Mathematics, Universidad Militar Nueva Granada,
Bogotá, Colombia
mauricio.restrepo@unimilitar.edu.co

Abstract. We present a new collection of upper approximation operators for covering based rough sets, obtained from sub modular functions and closure operators. Each non decreasing submodular function defines a closure operator that can be considered as an approximation operator. The construction allows us to define several upper approximation operators. Some properties of these operators are studied.

Keywords: Covering rough sets · Approximation operators · Submodular functions

1 Introduction

The rough set theory was extended to covering based rough sets by many authors to applying in other contexts. In 2012, Yao and Yao [21] introduced a general framework for the study of dual pairs of covering-based approximation operators, distinguishing between element based, granule based and subsystem based definitions. Other approximation pairs have been studied in literature; for instance, in [16], Yang and Li present a summary of seven non dual pairs of approximation operators used by Żakowski [22], Pomykala [6], Tsang et al. [11], Zhu [25], Zhu and Wang [26], Xu and Wang [15]. On the other hand, Restrepo et al. present a general framework of pairs of dual operators and established partial order relation among these operators [7,8]. Deer et al. [3] present a systematic work about neighborhood based operators. Recently Zhao [23] develops approximation operators from a topological point of view.

The concept of submodular function has a relationship with attribute reduction, Matroids theory and closure operators [9]. The relationship with covering rough sets was presented in [10,13,18,27]. Some relationships with binary relation based rough sets were presented in [17,19]. Each non decreasing submodular function defines a closure operator which can be used as an upper approximation operator. In this paper we establish a new way of defining upper approximation operators from submodular functions.

Here we extend this definition to other coverings to define new approximation operators and we show that they are different from the operators in previous

© Springer International Publishing AG 2017
L. Polkowski et al. (Eds.): IJCRS 2017, Part I, LNAI 10313, pp. 154–164, 2017.
DOI: 10.1007/978-3-319-60837-2_13

frameworks. We use some neighborhood operators of covering based rough sets, for defining other sub modular functions and their respectively closure operators. Some properties of these operators also are studied.

The paper is organized as follows. Sections 2 presents preliminary concepts about covering based rough sets, as lower and upper approximations, the main neighborhood operators, and different coverings obtained from a covering $\mathbb{C}$. Section 3 presents the concept of submodular function and the closure operator obtained from a sub modular function. Here we show that using this procedure it is possible to obtain new approximation operators. Section 4 presents a list of new approximation operators. Finally, Sect. 5 presents some conclusions and future work.

2   Preliminaries

2.1   Pawlak's Rough Set Approximations

In Pawlak's rough set model an approximation space is an ordered pair $apr = (U, E)$, where E is an equivalence relation defined on a non-empty set U [5]. In this paper we consider U as a finite set. The set $[x]_E$ represents the equivalence class of x and $\mathscr{P}(U)$ represents the set of parts of U. According to Yao and Yao [20,21], there are three different, but equivalent ways to define lower and upper approximation operators: element based definition, granule based definition and subsystem based definition. For each $A \subseteq U$, the lower and upper approximations are defined by:

$$\underline{apr}(A) = \{x \in U : [x]_E \subseteq A\} = \bigcup\{[x]_E \in U/E : [x]_E \subseteq A\} \tag{1}$$

$$\overline{apr}(A) = \{x \in U : [x]_E \cap A \neq \emptyset\} = \bigcup\{[x]_E \in U/E : [x]_E \cap A \neq \emptyset\} \tag{2}$$

The first equality of Eqs. 1 and 2 and the second parts are called element based and granule based definition, respectively.

Other equivalent sub-system based definition for approximation in covering based rough sets can be seen in [21].

2.2   Covering Based Rough Sets

Covering based rough sets were proposed to extend the range of applications of rough set theory. In rough set theory an element $x \in U$ belongs to an unique set or equivalent class, but in covering based rough sets this same element can belong to many sets, so we need to consider the sets K in $\mathbb{C}$ such that $x \in K$.

Definition 1 [24]. *Let $\mathbb{C} = \{K_i\}$ be a family of nonempty subsets of U. $\mathbb{C}$ is called a covering of U if $\bigcup K_i = U$. The ordered pair $(U, \mathbb{C})$ is called a covering approximation space.*

Definition 2. *Let $(U, \mathbb{C})$ be a covering approximation space and $x \in U$. The set collection of minimal sets $K \in \mathbb{C}$ such that $x \in K$, is called the minimal description of the object $x \in U$ and it is denoted as $md(\mathbb{C}, x)$.*

Similarly, it is possible to define $MD(\mathbb{C}, x)$, the maximal description of $x \in U$. In this case we consider the maximal sets K, with $x \in K$.

Definition 3 [21]. *A mapping $N : U \to \mathscr{P}(U)$, such that $x \in N(x)$ is called a neighborhood operator.*

According to the first parts in Eqs. 1 and 2, each neighborhood operator defines a pair of approximation operators, when we use the neighborhood $N(x)$ instead of the equivalence class $[x]_E$.

$$\underline{apr}_N(A) = \{x \in U : N(x) \subseteq A\} \tag{3}$$

$$\overline{apr}_N(A) = \{x \in U : N(x) \cap A \neq \emptyset\} \tag{4}$$

Equations 3 and 4 give the neighborhood element based definition in covering based rough sets.

From $md(\mathbb{C}, x)$ and $MD(\mathbb{C}, x)$, Yao and Yao define the following neighborhood operators [21]:

1. $N_1^{\mathbb{C}}(x) = \bigcap\{K : K \in md(\mathbb{C}, x)\}$
2. $N_2^{\mathbb{C}}(x) = \bigcup\{K : K \in md(\mathbb{C}, x)\}$
3. $N_3^{\mathbb{C}}(x) = \bigcap\{K : K \in MD(\mathbb{C}, x)\}$
4. $N_4^{\mathbb{C}}(x) = \bigcup\{K : K \in MD(\mathbb{C}, x)\}$

Therefore, we have four lower and upper approximation operators $\overline{apr}_{N_i}$ using Eqs. 3 and 4.

Generalizing the granule based definitions given by the second parts of Eqs. 1 and 2, the following approximation operator based on a covering $\mathbb{C}$ was considered in [21]:

$$\overline{apr}_{\mathbb{C}}(A) = \bigcup\{K \in \mathbb{C} : K \cap A \neq \emptyset\} \tag{5}$$

Other coverings obtained from a covering $\mathbb{C}$ have been used for new definitions of approximation operators.

From a covering $\mathbb{C}$ of U, the following coverings have been defined:

1. $\mathbb{C}_1 = \bigcup\{md(\mathbb{C}, x) : x \in U\}$
2. $\mathbb{C}_2 = \bigcup\{MD(\mathbb{C}, x) : x \in U\}$
3. $\mathbb{C}_3 = \{\bigcap(md(\mathbb{C}, x)) : x \in U\}$
4. $\mathbb{C}_4 = \{\bigcup(MD(\mathbb{C}, x)) : x \in U\}$
5. $\mathbb{C}_{\cap} = \mathbb{C} \setminus \{K \in \mathbb{C} : (\exists \mathbb{K} \subseteq \mathbb{C} \setminus \{K\}) (K = \bigcap \mathbb{K})\}$
6. $\mathbb{C}_{\cup} = \mathbb{C} \setminus \{K \in \mathbb{C} : (\exists \mathbb{K} \subseteq \mathbb{C} \setminus \{K\}) (K = \bigcup \mathbb{K})\}$

Coverings $\mathbb{C}_\cap$ and $\mathbb{C}_\cup$ are called the $\cap$-reduction and the $\cup$-reduction of $\mathbb{C}$, respectively. The main idea is to eliminate the elements K in $\mathbb{C}$ that can be expressed as intersection or union of other sets in the covering.

The following two covering based upper approximation operators were introduced in [14, 26] as $IH_\mathbb{C}$ and $XH_\mathbb{C}$, respectively and they were presented in [7] as follows:

- $H_5^C(A) = \cup\{N_1(x) : x \in A\}$
- $H_6^C(A) = \{x : N_1(x) \cap A \neq \emptyset\} = \overline{apr}_{N_1}(A)$

In [7] a partial order relation, based on the property: $\overline{apr}_1 \leq \overline{apr}_2$ if and only if $\overline{apr}_1(A) \subseteq \overline{apr}_2(A)$, for all $A \subseteq U$, was established among these operators.

The operators H_5^C and H_6^C are minimal elements in the framework of upper approximations. Therefore, for each operator $\overline{apr}$ in this framework we have that $H_5^C \leq \overline{apr}$ or $H_6^C \leq \overline{apr}$.

3   SubModular Functions

Submodular functions, also called rank function [18], are used to connect many theories like rough sets, matroids, attribute reduction and closure operators. Submodular functions are the generalization of *rank* concept in vector spaces of finite dimension. The submodular functions can be employed for both attribute reduction and feature selection simultaneously [27]. They have important applications on graph theory, game theory and optimization.

3.1   Closures

The notion of closure operator usually is used on ordered sets and topological spaces. Some relations between closure operators with upper approximation and matroids are presented in [1, 4].

We present some concepts about ordered structures, according to Blyth [2].

Closure Operators

Definition 4. *A map $C : \mathscr{P}(U) \to \mathscr{P}(U)$ is a **closure operator** on U if it is such that, for all $A, B \subseteq U$:*

1. $A \subseteq C(A)$, (extensive).
2. $A \subseteq B$ implies $C(A) \subseteq C(B)$, (order preserving).
3. $C(A) = C[C(A)]$, (idempotent).

3.2   Submodular Functions from Coverings

Some relationships among submodular functions and covering rough sets was presented in [13].

Definition 5. *If* $\mathbb{C}$ *is a covering of* U, *for all* $A \subseteq U$ *is defined the function* $f_{\mathbb{C}} : \mathscr{P}(U) \to \mathbb{N}$ *(natural numbers):*

$$f_{\mathbb{C}}(A) = |\{K \in \mathbb{C} : K \cap A \neq \emptyset\}| \qquad (6)$$

This function is called upper approximation number of A and it represents the number of sets K in the covering with a nonempty intersection with A.

Proposition 1 [13]. *If* A *and* B *are subsets of* U, *the function* $f_{\mathbb{C}}$ *satisfies:*

1. $f_{\mathbb{C}}(\emptyset) = 0$
2. *If* $A \subseteq B$ *then* $f_{\mathbb{C}}(A) \leq f_{\mathbb{C}}(B)$
3. $f_{\mathbb{C}}(A \cup B) + f_{\mathbb{C}}(A \cap B) \leq f_{\mathbb{C}}(A) + f_{\mathbb{C}}(B)$ *(Sub-modular property).*

Function $f_{\mathbb{C}}$ is sub-modular and non decreasing. For each function $f_{\mathbb{C}}$ is possible to define a closure operator given by:

$$C_f(A) = \{x \in U : f_{\mathbb{C}}(A) = f_{\mathbb{C}}(A \cup x)\} \qquad (7)$$

To establish that C_f is a closure operator we need the following lemma, proved in [12], using induction over the elements of $B - A$.

Lemma 1 [12]. *If* $A, B \subseteq U$ *and for all* $b \in B - A$ *we have* $f_{\mathbb{C}}(A \cup b) = f_{\mathbb{C}}(A)$, *then* $f_{\mathbb{C}}(A \cup B) = f_{\mathbb{C}}(A)$.

Proposition 2. *If* $f_{\mathbb{C}}$ *is a non-decreasing sub modular function such that* $f_{\mathbb{C}}(\emptyset) = \emptyset$, *then the operator* C_f *defined by means Eq. (7) is a closure operator.*

Proof. a. *Clearly* $A \subseteq C_f(A)$, *because* $x \in A$ *implies* $f_{\mathbb{C}}(A) = f_{\mathbb{C}}(A \cup x)$.
b. *For the order preserving property, if* $z \in C_f(A)$, *then* $f_{\mathbb{C}}(A) = f_{\mathbb{C}}(A \cup z)$. *By the property 2 in Proposition 1, we know that* $f_{\mathbb{C}}(B) \leq f_{\mathbb{C}}(B \cup z)$. *To establish the other inequality we will see that for each* $K \in \mathbb{C}$ *such that* $K \cap (B \cup z) \neq \emptyset$ *there exist at least a* $K' \in \mathbb{C}$ *such that* $K' \cap B \neq \emptyset$. *Effectively, for* $K \in \mathbb{C}$ *such that* $K \cap (B \cup z) \neq \emptyset$, *we have that* $K \cap B \neq \emptyset$ *or* $z \in K$. *If* $K \cap B \neq \emptyset$, *then* $K' = K$. *On the other hand, if* $z \in K$ *then* $K \cap (A \cup z) \neq \emptyset$. *Since* $f_{\mathbb{C}}(A) = f_{\mathbb{C}}(A \cup z)$, *there exists a* $K' \in \mathbb{C}$ *such that* $K' \cap A \neq \emptyset$ *and by the inclusion* $A \subseteq B$, *we have that* $K' \cap B \neq \emptyset$. *This shows that* $f_{\mathbb{C}}(B) \geq f_{\mathbb{C}}(B \cup z)$. *Therefore,* $z \in C_f(B)$, *because* $f_{\mathbb{C}}(B) = f_{\mathbb{C}}(B \cup z)$.
c. *Finally, we will see that* $C_f(A) = C_f[C_f(A)]$. *For the extensive property we have* $C_f(A) \subseteq C_f[C_f(A)]$. *Now, if* $x \in C_f[C_f(A)]$ *then* $f_{\mathbb{C}}(C_f(A) \cup x) = f_{\mathbb{C}}(C_f(A))$. *For all* $b \in C_f(A) - A$, $f_{\mathbb{C}}(A \cup b) = f_{\mathbb{C}}(A)$ *and for Lemma 1,* $f_{\mathbb{C}}(A) = f_{\mathbb{C}}(A \cup (C_f(A) - A)) = f_{\mathbb{C}}(C_f(A))$, *thus* $f_{\mathbb{C}}(C_f(A) \cup x) = f_{\mathbb{C}}(A)$ *and therefore* $f_{\mathbb{C}}(A \cup x) = f_{\mathbb{C}}(A)$, *so* $x \in C_f(A)$.

$\square$

According to the properties of C_f, $f_{\mathbb{C}}$ also defines an upper approximation operator denoted as $\overline{apr}_f$. Lower approximation operators can be defined from $\overline{apr}$, for example by means of the relation $\underline{apr}(A) = co(\overline{apr}(co(A)))$ we obtain a dual operator. The Example 1 shows that $\overline{apr}_f$ is different from all operators in the framework of [7], because they are not comparable, by means of the order relation $\overline{apr}_1 \leq \overline{apr}_2$ if and only if $\overline{apr}_1(A) \subseteq \overline{apr}_2(A)$, for all $A \subseteq U$. As was presented in [8], all operators are dominated by $H_5^{\mathbb{C}}$ or $H_6^{\mathbb{C}}$. Therefore we have a new way of defining approximation operators.

Example 1. In this example we show a comparison of $\overline{apr}_f$ and operators $H_5^{\mathbb{C}}$ and $H_6^{\mathbb{C}}$. For the covering $\mathbb{C} = \{\{2\}, \{1,2\}, \{1,3\}, \{2,4\}, \{1,2,3\}\}$ of $U = \{1,2,3,4\}$ we have the information in Table 1.

According to this, $\overline{apr}_f(A)$ is a new approximation operator, different from any operator in the cited framework.

Table 1. Illustration of sub-modular function and a comparison with $H_5^{\mathbb{C}}$ and $H_6^{\mathbb{C}}$.

A	$f_{\mathbb{C}}(A)$	$\overline{apr}_f(A)$	$H_6^{\mathbb{C}}(A)$	$H_5^{\mathbb{C}}(A)$
$\{1\}$	3	$\{1,3\}$	$\{1\}$	$\{1,3\}$
$\{2\}$	4	$\{2,4\}$	$\{2\}$	$\{2,4\}$
$\{3\}$	2	$\{3\}$	$\{1,3\}$	$\{3\}$
$\{4\}$	1	$\{4\}$	$\{2,4\}$	$\{4\}$
$\{1,2\}$	5	$\{1,2,3,4\}$	$\{1,2\}$	$\{1,2,3,4\}$
$\{1,3\}$	3	$\{1,3\}$	$\{1,3\}$	$\{1,3\}$
$\{1,4\}$	4	$\{1,3,4\}$	$\{1,2,4\}$	$\{1,3,4\}$
$\{2,3\}$	5	$\{1,2,3,4\}$	$\{1,2,3\}$	$\{2,3,4\}$
$\{2,4\}$	4	$\{2,4\}$	$\{2,4\}$	$\{2,4\}$
$\{3,4\}$	4	$\{3,4\}$	$\{1,2,3,4\}$	$\{3,4\}$
$\{1,2,3\}$	4	$\{1,2,3,4\}$	$\{1,2,3\}$	$\{1,2,3,4\}$
$\{1,2,4\}$	4	$\{1,2,3,4\}$	$\{1,2,4\}$	$\{2,3,4\}$
$\{1,3,4\}$	5	$\{1,3,4\}$	$\{1,2,3,4\}$	$\{1,3,4\}$
$\{2,3,4\}$	5	$\{1,2,3,4\}$	$\{1,2,3,4\}$	$\{2,3,4\}$

Obviously, different sub modular functions $f_{\mathbb{C}}$ can be obtained from other coverings, for example $\mathbb{C}_1$, $\mathbb{C}_2$, $\mathbb{C}_3$, $\mathbb{C}_4$, $\mathbb{C}_{\cup}$ and $\mathbb{C}_{\cap}$.

Proposition 3. *For the operator $\overline{apr}_f$, we have: $\overline{apr}_f(\emptyset) = \emptyset$ and $\overline{apr}_f(U) = U$.*

Proof. From the property 1 in Proposition 1, $f_{\mathbb{C}}(\emptyset) = 0$. If $x \in \overline{apr}_f(\emptyset)$, then $f_{\mathbb{C}}(x) = 0$. So, there is not exists $K \in \mathbb{C}$ such that $x \in K$, and it is impossible, because $\mathbb{C}$ is a covering of U. The second property is a consequence of the extensive property of a closure operator. □

Some relations between these functions can be established immediately from the order relations in [8]. For example, we have the next proposition.

Proposition 4. *If $\mathbb{C}$ and $\mathbb{C}'$ are coverings of U such that $\mathbb{C} \subseteq \mathbb{C}'$, then $f_{\mathbb{C}} \leq f_{\mathbb{C}'}$.*

Proof. It is easy to show from definition of $f_{\mathbb{C}}$.   □

Example 2. The operator $\overline{apr}_f$ are not a joint morphism. According to values in Table 1, we can see that $\overline{apr}_f(\{2\}) \cup \overline{apr}_f(\{3\}) = \{2,4\} \cup \{3\} \neq \overline{apr}_f(\{2,3\}) = \{1,2,3,4\}$.

Other sub modular functions can be defined from different approximation operators in covering based rough sets.

3.3   Neighborhood Operators

From the neighborhood operators defined above, we have the following coverings:

$$\mathbb{C}_N = \{N(x) : x \in U\} \tag{8}$$

Therefore, using Definition 5 is possible to obtain new approximation operators. In the same way, it is possible to show they are different from $\overline{apr}_{N_i}$.

Example 3. For the covering $\mathbb{C}$ in Example 1, we have the coverings:

1. $\mathbb{C}_{N_1} = \{\{1\}, \{2\}, \{1,3\}, \{2,4\}\}$
2. $\mathbb{C}_{N_2} = \{\{1,2,3\}, \{2\}, \{1,3\}, \{2,4\}\}$
3. $\mathbb{C}_{N_3} = \{\{1,2,3\}, \{2\}, \{2,4\}\}$
4. $\mathbb{C}_{N_4} = \{\{\{2,4\}, \{1,2,3\}, \{1,2,3,4\}\}$

Each covering $\mathbb{C}_{N_i}$ for $i = 1,2,3,4$ defines a non decreasing sub modular function and therefore a closure operator according to Proposition 1, that can be used as an approximation operator. In this case we note this approximation operators as: $\overline{apr}_{f_i}$.
It is possible to see that operators $\overline{apr}_{f_i}$, in general, are different from $\overline{apr}_{N_i}$. The values for the sub modular functions $f_{N_i}(A)$ and the approximations $\overline{apr}_{f_i}$, are presented in Table 2.

From the results in Table 2 is possible to see that the upper approximations $\overline{apr}_{f_i}$ are different from the operators $\overline{apr}_{N_i}$. For example, $\overline{apr}_{N_2}(\{2,4\}) = \{1,2,4\}$, while $\overline{apr}_{f_2}(\{2,4\}) = \{2,4\}$. Similarly, $\overline{apr}_{N_3}(\{1\}) = \{1,3\}$, while $\overline{apr}_{f_3}(\{1\}) = \{1\}$ and $\overline{apr}_{N_4}(\{1\}) = \{1,2,3\}$, while $\overline{apr}_{f_4}(\{1\}) = \{1,3\}$. The values of $\overline{apr}_{N_i}(A)$ were calculated before and they are not shown in this table.

Example 4. The operators $\overline{apr}_{f_i}$ are not joint morphism, they do no satisfy the relation $\overline{apr}(A \cup B) = \overline{apr}(A) \cup \overline{apr}(B)$. For example, according to the values in Table 2, we can see that $\overline{apr}_{f_3}(\{3\}) \cup \overline{apr}_{f_3}(\{4\}) = \{3\} \cup \{4\} = \{3,4\} \neq \{1,3,4\} = \overline{apr}_{f_3}(\{3,4\})$.

Using different concepts in covering rough sets it is possible to define other sub-modular functions. As an alternative way, we use the element approach of neighborhood for defining other type of sub modular functions.

Table 2. Illustration of sub-modular functions from neighborhood operators.

A	$f_{N_1}(A)$	$f_{N_2}(A)$	$f_{N_3}(A)$	$f_{N_4}(A)$	$\overline{apr}_{f_1}$	$\overline{apr}_{f_2}$	$\overline{apr}_{f_3}$	$\overline{apr}_{f_4}$
$\{1\}$	2	2	1	2	$\{1,3\}$	$\{1,3\}$	$\{1\}$	$\{1,3\}$
$\{2\}$	2	3	3	3	$\{2,4\}$	$\{2,4\}$	$\{1,2\}$	$\{1,2,3,4\}$
$\{3\}$	1	2	1	2	$\{3\}$	$\{1,3\}$	$\{3\}$	$\{1,3\}$
$\{4\}$	1	1	1	2	$\{4\}$	$\{4\}$	$\{4\}$	$\{4\}$
$\{1,2\}$	4	4	3	3	$\{1,2,3,4\}$	$\{1,2,3,4\}$	$\{1,2,3\}$	$\{1,2,3,4\}$
$\{1,3\}$	2	2	1	2	$\{1,3\}$	$\{1,3\}$	$\{1,3\}$	$\{1,3\}$
$\{1,4\}$	3	3	2	3	$\{1,3,4\}$	$\{1,3,4\}$	$\{1,3,4\}$	$\{1,2,3,4\}$
$\{2,3\}$	3	4	3	3	$\{2,3,4\}$	$\{1,2,3,4\}$	$\{1,2,3,4\}$	$\{1,2,3,4\}$
$\{2,4\}$	2	3	3	3	$\{2,4\}$	$\{2,4\}$	$\{1,2,3,4\}$	$\{1,2,3,4\}$
$\{3,4\}$	2	3	2	3	$\{3,4\}$	$\{1,3,4\}$	$\{1,3,4\}$	$\{1,2,3,4\}$
$\{1,2,3\}$	4	4	3	3	$\{1,2,3,4\}$	$\{1,2,3,4\}$	$\{1,2,3,4\}$	$\{1,2,3,4\}$
$\{1,2,4\}$	4	4	3	3	$\{1,2,3,4\}$	$\{1,2,3,4\}$	$\{1,2,3,4\}$	$\{1,2,3,4\}$
$\{1,3,4\}$	3	3	2	3	$\{1,3,4\}$	$\{1,3,4\}$	$\{1,3,4\}$	$\{1,2,3,4\}$
$\{2,3,4\}$	3	4	3	3	$\{2,3,4\}$	$\{2,3,4\}$	$\{1,2,3,4\}$	$\{1,2,3,4\}$

Definition 6. *If $(U,\mathbb{C})$ is a covering space and N_i are the neighborhood operators defined above, is possible to define the functions:*

$$\psi_{N_i}(A) = |\{x \in U : N_i(x) \cap A \neq \emptyset\}| \tag{9}$$

Clearly $\psi_{N_i}(\emptyset) = 0$ for N_1, N_2, N_3 and N_4.

Proposition 5. *The functions ψ_{N_i} are non decreasing.*

Proof. It is simple to prove from definition. $\qquad\square$

Proposition 6. *The functions ψ_{N_i} are sub modulars.*

Proof. Using a similar counting method, used in [13] we will show that $\psi_{N_i}(A \cup B) + \psi_{N_i}(A \cap B) \leq \psi_{N_i}(A) + \psi_{N_i}(B)$.

a. If $z \in \underline{apr}_N(A \cup B)$ then $N(z) \cap (A \cup B) \neq \emptyset$, therefore $(N(z) \cup A) \cap (N(z) \cup B) \neq \emptyset$, so $\overline{N(z)} \cap A \neq \emptyset$ or $N(z) \cap B \neq \emptyset$, then $z \in \underline{apr}_N(A)$ or $z \in \underline{apr}_N(A)$.

b. On the other hand, If $z \in \underline{apr}_N(A \cap B)$ then $\overline{N(z)} \cap (A \cap B) \neq \emptyset$, therefore $(N(z) \cap A) \cap (N(z) \cap B) \neq \emptyset$, so $N(z) \cap A \neq \emptyset$ and $N(z) \cap B \neq \emptyset$, then $z \in \underline{apr}_N(A)$ or $z \in \underline{apr}_N(A)$. $\qquad\square$

Each closure operator can be seen as an approximation operator. In this case we will see that the approximation operators $C_{f_i} = \overline{apr}_{\psi_i}$ obtained from the sub modular functions ψ_{N_i} are different from the approximation operators defined before.

Example 5. From the covering $\mathbb{C} = \{\{1,2\},\{1,3\},\{1,2,3\},\{2,4\}\}$ of $U = \{1,2,3,4\}$ in Example 3, we have the coverings obtained from neighborhoods.

The values for the sub modular functions $\psi_{N_1}(A)$, the approximation operators $\overline{apr}_\psi$, $H_6^\mathbb{C}(A)$ and $H_5^\mathbb{C}(A)$ are presented in Table 3. Comparing with values of f_{N_i} in Table 2, it is easy to see that $f_{N_i} \neq \psi_{N_i}$.

Table 3. Illustration of sub-modular function and the approximation operator.

A	$\psi_{N_1}(A)$	$\overline{apr}_{\psi_1}(A)$	$H_6^\mathbb{C}(A)$	$H_5^\mathbb{C}(A)$
$\{1\}$	3	$\{1,3\}$	$\{1\}$	$\{1,3\}$
$\{2\}$	4	$\{2,4\}$	$\{2\}$	$\{2,4\}$
$\{3\}$	2	$\{3\}$	$\{1,3\}$	$\{3\}$
$\{4\}$	1	$\{4\}$	$\{2,4\}$	$\{4\}$
$\{1,2\}$	5	$\{1,2,3,4\}$	$\{1,2\}$	$\{1,2,3,4\}$
$\{1,3\}$	3	$\{1,3\}$	$\{1,3\}$	$\{1,3\}$
$\{1,4\}$	4	$\{1,3,4\}$	$\{1,2,4\}$	$\{1,3,4\}$
$\{2,3\}$	5	$\{1,2,3,4\}$	$\{1,2,3\}$	$\{2,3,4\}$
$\{2,4\}$	4	$\{2,4\}$	$\{2,4\}$	$\{2,4\}$
$\{3,4\}$	4	$\{3,4\}$	$\{1,2,3,4\}$	$\{3,4\}$
$\{1,2,3\}$	4	$\{1,2,3,4\}$	$\{1,2,3\}$	$\{1,2,3,4\}$
$\{1,2,4\}$	4	$\{1,2,3,4\}$	$\{1,2,4\}$	$\{2,3,4\}$
$\{1,3,4\}$	5	$\{1,3,4\}$	$\{1,2,3,4\}$	$\{1,3,4\}$
$\{2,3,4\}$	5	$\{1,2,3,4\}$	$\{1,2,3,4\}$	$\{2,3,4\}$

From results in Table 3 is it easy to see that the closure operators are different from the approximations $\overline{apr}_{N_i}$ given in Eq. 4. (See approximation of $A = \{1,2,4\}$).

4   List of New Approximation Operators

In this section we list the new approximation operators obtained from submodular functions via closure operators.

Approximation operators $\overline{apr}_{\mathbb{C}_i}$ are obtained from submodular functions $f_{\mathbb{C}_i}$, therefore we have seven different operators one for each covering: $\mathbb{C}$, $\mathbb{C}_1$, $\mathbb{C}_2$, $\mathbb{C}_3$, $\mathbb{C}_4$, $\mathbb{C}_\cup$ and $\mathbb{C}_\cap$. Similarly, the four operators, $\overline{apr}_{f_i}$ are obtained from functions $\overline{apr}_{f_i}$ defined from Eq. 6 with the coverings $\mathbb{C} = \{N_1^\mathbb{C}(x)\}, \{N_2^\mathbb{C}(x)\}, \{N_3^\mathbb{C}(x)\}, \{N_4^\mathbb{C}(x)\}$. Finally $\overline{apr}_{\psi_i}$ are obtained from ψ_{N_i} functions with Definition 6. Therefore we have at least eleven new closure operators, which are listed in Table 4.

Table 4. List of sub-modular functions and the approximation operators.

N	Sub-modular	Upper approximation	Element used
1	$f_{\mathbb{C}_i}$	$\overline{apr}_{\mathbb{C}_i}$	$\mathbb{C}, \mathbb{C}_1, \mathbb{C}_2, \mathbb{C}_3, \mathbb{C}_4, \mathbb{C}_\cup, \mathbb{C}_\cap$
2	f_{N_i}	$\overline{apr}_{f_i}$	N_1, N_2, N_3, N_4 (granules)
3	ψ_{N_i}	$\overline{apr}_{\psi_i}$	N_1, N_2, N_3, N_4 (elements)

5 Conclusions

This paper presents new approximation operators obtained from submodular functions via closure operators. The submodular definition given for a covering $\mathbb{C}$ is extended to different coverings. Neighborhood operators can be used for new coverings, therefore they also define operators. A new element based submodular function is introduced and used for new operators. Finally some properties of these operators are studied. As a future work, we will study partial order relation among the new operators and the relationship with matroid theory for attribute reduction.

References

1. Bian, X., Wang, P., Yu, Z., Bai, X., Chen, B.: Characterization of coverings for upper approximation operators being closure operators. Inf. Sci. **314**, 41–54 (2015)
2. Blyth, T.S.: Lattices and Ordered Algebraic Structures. Springer Universitext, London (2005)
3. Deer, L., Restrepo, M., Cornelis, C., Gómez, J.: Neighborhood operators for covering-based rough sets. Inf. Sci. **336**, 21–44 (2016)
4. Li, X., Liu, S.: Matroidal approaches to rough sets via closure operators. Int. J. Approx. Reason. **53**, 513–527 (2012)
5. Pawlak, Z.: Rough sets. Int. J. Comput. Inform. Sci. **11**(5), 341–356 (1982)
6. Pomykala, J.A.: Approximation operations in approximation space. Bulletin de la Académie Polonaise des Sciences **35**(9–10), 653–662 (1987)
7. Restrepo, M., Cornelis, C., Gómez, J.: Duality, conjugacy and adjointness of approximation operators in covering-based rough sets. Int. J. Approx. Reason. **55**, 469–485 (2014)
8. Restrepo, M., Cornelis, C., Gómez, J.: Partial order relation for approximation operators in covering-based rough sets. Inf. Sci. **284**, 44–59 (2014)
9. Roa, L.: Una nueva construcción de los espacios topológicos finitos desde las funciones submodulares. Tesis de Maestría en Matemáticas. Universidad Nacional de Colombia, Bogotá (2012)
10. Tang, J., She, K., Min, F., Zhu, W.: A matroidal approach to rough set theory. Theoret. Comput. Sci. **47**(1), 1–11 (2013)
11. Tsang, E., Chen, D., Lee, J., Yeung, D.S.: On the upper approximations of covering generalized rough sets. In: Proceedings of the 3rd International Conference on Machine Learning and Cybernetics, pp. 4200–4203 (2004)
12. Varela, R.: FD- Relaciones. Tesis de Maestría en Matemáticas. Universidad Nacional de Colombia, Bogotá (2011)

13. Wang, S., Zhu, W., Min, F.: Transversal and function matroidal structures of covering-based rough sets. In: Yao, J.T., Ramanna, S., Wang, G., Suraj, Z. (eds.) RSKT 2011. LNCS, vol. 6954, pp. 146–155. Springer, Heidelberg (2011). doi:10. 1007/978-3-642-24425-4_21
14. Wu, M., Wu, X., Shen, T.: A new type of covering approximation operators. In: IEEE International Conference on Electronic Computer Technology, pp. 334–338 (2009)
15. Xu, Z., Wang, Q.: On the properties of covering rough sets model. J. Henan Normal Univ. (Nat. Sci.) **33**(1), 130–132 (2005)
16. Yang, T., Li, Q.: Reduction about approximation spaces of covering generalized rough sets. Int. J. Approx. Reason. **51**, 335–345 (2010)
17. Liu, Y., Zhu, W.: Relation matroid and its relationship with generalized rough set based on relations. CoRR abs 1209.5456 (2012)
18. Liu, Y., Zhu, W., Zhang, Y.: Relationship between partition matroids and rough sets through k-rank matroids. J. Inf. Comput. Sci. **8**, 2151–2163 (2012)
19. Li, Y., Wang, Z.: The relationships between degree rough sets and matroids. Anals Fuzzy Math. Inform. **12**(1), 139–153 (2012)
20. Yao, Y.Y.: Constructive and algebraic methods of the theory of rough sets. Inf. Sci. **109**, 21–47 (1998)
21. Yao, Y.Y., Yao, B.: Covering based rough sets approximations. Inf. Sci. **200**, 91–107 (2012)
22. Zakowski, W.: Approximations in the space (u, π). Demonstr. Math. **16**, 761–769 (1983)
23. Zhao, Z.: On some types of covering rough sets from topological points of view. Int. J. Approx. Reason. **68**, 1–14 (2016)
24. Zhu, W.: Properties of the first type of covering-based rough sets. In: Proceedings of Sixth IEEE International Conference on Data Mining - Workshops, pp. 407–411 (2006)
25. Zhu, W.: Relationship between generalized rough sets based on binary relation and covering. Inf. Sci. **179**, 210–225 (2009)
26. Zhu, W., Wang, F.: A new type of covering rough set. In: Proceedings of Third International IEEE Conference on Intelligence Systems, pp. 444–449 (2006)
27. Zhu, X.Z., Zhu, W., Fan, X.N.: Rough sets methods in features selection via submodular function. Soft Comput. **21**, 3699–3711 (2017)

Toward Adaptive Rough Sets

Soma Dutta[1] and Andrzej Skowron[2,3(✉)]

[1] Vistula University, Stokłosy 3, 02-787 Warsaw, Poland
somadutta9@gmail.com
[2] Faculty of Mathematics, Informatics and Mechanics, University of Warsaw,
Banacha 2, 02-097 Warsaw, Poland
skowron@mimuw.edu.pl
[3] Systems Research Institute, Polish Academy of Sciences,
Newelska 6, 01-447 Warsaw, Poland

Abstract. In this paper we take an attempt to depart from the closed way of presenting information table characterizing a vague concept with respect to a closed sample of objects, a fixed set of attributes, and a static time point. The aim is rather to have an interactive information system which is open to incorporate new information based on the interactions of an agent with the physical reality. This in turn prepares the ground for the notion of adaptive information system which incorporates the possibility of adapting decision strategies based on the history of making decisions over a period of time through interactions of an agent with the physical reality.

Keywords: Information flow · Interactive information system · Adaptive rough set · Adaptive reasoning

1 Introduction

Natural languages are abundant with imprecise, vague linguistic expressions of different characteristics [2,10]. Relationship of the rough set approach with vague, imprecise concepts has been investigated by many researchers (see, *e.g.*, [3,8,9,17,30,41,42,44,48,49,51,57,59,62,64]). Plenty of other approaches are also existing in the literature (see, *e.g.*, [11–18,29,46,47]). As mentioned in [33], some prefer to have for new ontology for semantics going beyond set theory, and some prefer addressing vagueness by new ways staying inside the framework of set theory.

From the perspective of rough sets [39,40,43] impreciseness, arising from lack of information about a universe, is addressed as follows. A universe U is accessible with respect to properties of the elements of U, expressed through a set of attributes. An indiscernibility relation R, which can only distinguish those objects of the universe which are of different natures with respect to the set of attributes, plays a central role in the theory. This indiscernibility relation represents a perspective of viewing whether for a set of objects a (vague) concept applies or not. Now as the concept under consideration is imprecise because of

© Springer International Publishing AG 2017
L. Polkowski et al. (Eds.): IJCRS 2017, Part I, LNAI 10313, pp. 165–184, 2017.
DOI: 10.1007/978-3-319-60837-2_14

lack of information, perspectives about whether an object satisfies the concept can be different. These differences in perspectives can have different reasons behind.

(i) The same set of objects with respect to the same set of attributes can be viewed differently as satisfying or not satisfying or partially satisfying a concept by different individuals or agents.

(ii) A concept can be differently perceived by a number of agents with respect to different sets of attributes based on the same set of objects.

(iii) A concept can be perceived by a number of agents with respect to different sets of objects and different sets of attributes.

(iv) Perspective about (vague) imprecise concepts can change with respect to time, and appearance of new objects and attributes.

It is not hard to understand that vague concepts cannot be approximated with a satisfactory quality by static constructs such as induced membership/inclusion functions, or models that are derived from a sample. Understanding vague concepts can be only realized in a process, in which the induced models are adapted through matching the concepts in a dynamically changing environment. Thus, our goal in this paper would be to emphasize the role of interactive information systems, *i.e.*, information systems which are open for interactions with the physical reality, and which are changing with time based on those interactions. This requires some modifications in the existing definition of information system. Our approach, in this paper, differs from the existing attempts to interactive information systems, and this formalization is based on the ideas outlined in [23,56,61]. Each information system can be modified, with time, with the change of the perspective of an agent. In contrast to the existing approaches, we propose to consider different parameterized families of attributes together, with one kind influencing the other kind. The values of parameters, characterizing properties of objects, are fixed by some control parameters, which are set by the owner/agent on the basis of her accumulated knowledge. On the basis of interactive information systems we introduce adaptive information systems which are crucial for introducing adaptation strategies, taking care of dynamically changing nature of information.

The content of the paper is organized as follows. In Sect. 2, an introduction to the basic notions from the literature of information systems, rough sets, and complex granules is presented. Section 2.2 presents some intuitions behind complex granules, necessary for modeling computations on granules based on interactions in the physical world. A general background explaining different components and requirements for introducing the notions of interactive information systems and adaptive information systems is presented in Sect. 3. Section 4 presents an outline for a proposal towards adaptive information systems. In Sect. 5 we discuss the further challenges to build a substantially grown-up theory of adaptive information systems.

If $(x, y) \in I\!N\!\mathcal{D}_B$ we will say that x and y are *B-indiscernible*. Equivalence classes of the relation $I\!N\!\mathcal{D}_B$ (or blocks of the partition U/B) are referred to as *B-elementary sets* or *B-elementary granules*. In the rough set approach the elementary sets are the basic building blocks (concepts) of our knowledge about reality. The unions of *B-elementary sets* are called *B-definable sets*.

For $B \subseteq A$ we denote by $Sg_B(x)$ the *B-signature* of $x \in U$, which is represented by the set $\{(a, e(x, a)) : a \in B\}$. Let $Sg_B(U) = \{Sg_B(x) : x \in U\}$. Then for any objects $x, y \in U$ the following equivalence holds: $x \, I\!N\!\mathcal{D}_B \, y$ if and only if $Sg_B(x) = Sg_B(y)$.

This indiscernibility relation is further used to define basic concepts of rough set theory. The following two operations on any set $X \subseteq U$, given by,

$$\mathsf{LOW}_B(X) = \{x \in U : [x]_B \subseteq X\}, \tag{2}$$

$$\mathsf{UPP}_B(X) = \{x \in U : [x]_B \cap X \neq \emptyset\}, \tag{3}$$

assign to every subset X of the universe U respectively to two sets $\mathsf{LOW}_B(X)$ and $\mathsf{UPP}_B(X)$, called the *B-lower* and the *B-upper approximation* of X. The set

$$\mathsf{BN}_B(X) = \mathsf{UPP}_B(X) - \mathsf{LOW}_B(X), \tag{4}$$

will be referred to as the *B-boundary region* of X.

If the boundary region of X is the empty set, *i.e.*, $\mathsf{BN}_B(X) = \emptyset$, then the set X is *crisp* (*exact*) with respect to B; in the opposite case, *i.e.*, if $\mathsf{BN}_B(X) \neq \emptyset$, the set X is referred to as *rough* (*inexact*) with respect to B. Thus any rough set, in contrast to a *crisp set*, has a non-empty boundary region.

Thus a set is *rough* (imprecise) if it has non-empty boundary region; otherwise the set is crisp (precise). Therefore with every rough set we associate two *crisp* sets, called *lower* and *upper approximation*. Intuitively, the lower approximation of a set consists of all elements that *surely* belong to the set, and the upper approximation of the set constitutes of all elements that *possibly* belong to the set. The *boundary region* of the set consists of all elements that cannot be classified uniquely as belonging to the set or as belonging to its complement, with respect to the available knowledge. This is exactly the idea of vagueness proposed by Frege.

Let us also observe that the definition of rough sets start with referring to data (knowledge), and hence it is *subjective*, in contrast to the definition of classical sets which is in some sense an *objective* one.

2.2   Complex Granules

Obtaining a convincingly complete description of a universe of objects, lying in the reality, usually comes through a process of learning which dynamically keeps on changing with time. So, models of computations should be based on learning through interactions with the physical reality. In [63] the need for considering the physical world as the basis for computations is expressed as follows.

further study of this [learning] phenomenon requires analysis that goes beyond pure mathematical models. As does any branch of natural science, learning theory has two sides:

- *The mathematical side that describes laws of generalization which are valid for all possible worlds and*
- *The physical side that describes laws which are valid for our specific world, the world where we have to solve our applied tasks.*

[...] To be successful, learning machines must use structures on the set of functions that are appropriate for problems of our world. [...] Constructing the physical part of the theory and unifying it with the mathematical part should be considered as one of the main goals of statistical learning theory. [...] In spite of all results obtained, statistical learning theory is only in its infancy...

According to Vapnik [63] there are many aspects of this theory that have not yet been analyzed and that are important both for understanding the phenomenon of learning and for practical applications. Surely, one of the aspects should be to consider the necessity of linking the abstract world of mathematics with the physical world. This may be related to the grounding problem investigated in psychology [1, 19, 20, 23]. In this paper, in order to link these two worlds we follow the approach based on complex granules (c-granules, for short) [23, 26, 27, 52–56].

One of the main assumptions in interactive computations on c-granules is that the computations are based on physical objects. These physical objects can be control tools, for following some schemes of measurements, as well as the objects that are to be measured. They interact among themselves. These activities take place in the physical world (*i.e.*, P of Fig. 1). The results of these interactions are recognized (measured) by a given agent ag using so called measurable objects, *i.e.*, objects whose states at a given moment of time t may be measured. The values of measurements are represented as values of attributes (*e.g.*, real numbers) or degrees of satisfiability of some formulas. This pertains to the activity of the abstract world (cf. Fig. 1). Using measurable objects the agent may indirectly recognize properties of other physical objects, which are not-directly measurable, in a given configuration. Prior to that ag must have learned relevant rules of interaction for predicting the states of such objects on the basis of measurement performed on the measurable objects. Information about states of non-directly measurable objects is transmitted to measurable objects through interactions in the considered configuration.

Using the information flow approach by Barwise and Seligman [4], in particular using the definition of infomorphism, one can explain how the abstract part, related to measurable objects, is conjugated to physical objects (see Fig. 1).

In Fig. 1, the abstract world is represented by a set of formulas Σ (*e.g.*, Boolean combinations of descriptors over a given set of attributes A [43]), and the set $Sg_A(U)$ of A-signatures of objects. The satisfiability relation $\models_A$ is defined by $u \models_A \alpha$ iff u satisfies (matches) some of the disjunctive components of α. The abstract world is defined by a classification $(Sg_A(U), \Sigma, \models_A)$ [4]. P denotes the set of physical objects, and SP is the set of states of physical objects. Moreover,

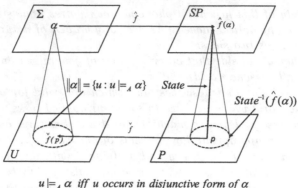

$$u \models_A \alpha \ \text{ iff } \ u \text{ occurs in disjunctive form of } \alpha$$

$$p \models_{State} s \ \text{ iff } \ p \in State^{-1}(s)$$

$$\check{f}(p) \models_A \alpha \ \text{ iff } \ p \models_{State} \hat{f}(\alpha)$$

Fig. 1. Infomorphism from the abstract world to the physical world.

$State : P \rightarrow SP$ is a function assigning a unique state to each physical object lying in the reality. The satisfiability relation for the physical world is defined by $p \models_{State} s$ iff $p \in State^{-1}(s)$ for any $p \in P$ and $s \in SP$. The physical world is represented by a classification $(P, SP \models_{State})$ [4]. A pair of functions $(\hat{f}, \check{f})$ is an infomorphism from the abstract world to the physical world iff the condition at the bottom of the figure holds for all $p \in P$ and $\alpha \in \Sigma$ [4].

3   Towards Adaptive Decision Strategies: Focusing on Different Perspectives of Agents with Time

In the definition presented in this paper, we have observed that the notion of boundary region is defined as a crisp set $\mathsf{BN}_B(X)$. While in [28], it is stressed that boundaries of vague concepts are not crisp. In this context, let us notice the crucial point in the definition of boundary region, as given above, lies in the fact that this definition is relative to the subjective knowledge expressed with respect to a set of attributes B. Different sources of information, may be called agents, may use different sets of attributes for approximating a concept with the basis of the same set of objects (see point (ii) of Introduction). Hence, the boundary region can change when we consider these different views. Another reason behind the change of boundary region could be because of change in information with respect to time. At some point of time, we only have information available for some samples of objects [21]. Hence, when new objects appear again the boundary region may change. This seems to have important consequences for further development of rough set theory, in combination with fuzzy sets and other soft computing paradigms, towards adaptive approximate reasoning.

Let us consider a context when approximations of a vague concept are considered over a family of decision systems $\{Inf_{\mathcal{A}_t}(U_t)\}_{t \in T}$, where T is a set of time points. Hence, we obtain a family of the lower approximations, upper approximations and boundary regions of a considered vague concept which are changing with time (see Fig. 2). As a result, an agent's perception about a vague concept gets adapted with dynamically changing environment and time.

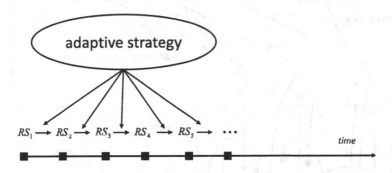

Fig. 2. Adaptive rough sets.

It is worthwhile to mention that the information systems in this family are obtained through interactions with the environment, and that points to the necessity of embedding the adaptive rough set approach in the framework of interactive granular computing and WisTech program [23–25, 27].

In the next section, we shall illustrate a formal way of introducing a prototype of adaptive information system. Here, we present a general perspective in order to prepare a ground for an adaptive information system.

We start with the consideration that the information systems (decision systems) are created on the basis of interactions of an agent with the environment, using some control parameters. In particular, control parameters are used to perform some actions or plans on some distinguished physical objects for predicting different values of parameters about the physical objects. This process of controlling the schemes for obtaining values of attributes by fixing control parameters may be called as *agent's control*. In general, by fixing the control parameters, *e.g.*, space, time, location, position of sensors and/or actuators etc., agent prepares the ground for obtaining an information system describing the properties of real physical objects. These real physical objects along with the set-up of the control tools (*i.e.*, space-time-angle of sensors or cameras) generates a complex granule (c-granule, for short) [23,53]. These c-granules, parts of c-granules and relationships among them, features of parts of the c-granules, and links of the c-granules all together help to transmit the results of interactions with objects to the agent, the owner of the so called information tables (see Fig. 3). The complex c-granule lying in the reality represents the *physical world*, in Fig. 1 which is denoted as P. On the other hand, the information tables basically represent the states of the measurable physical objects lying in the c-granules in terms of values of attributes; this is part of the *abstract world*, information about which is represented by some formulas (cf. Σ in Fig. 1).

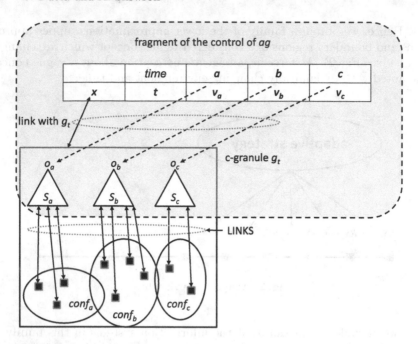

Fig. 3. An illustrative fragment of the control of agent ag for acquiring values v_a, v_b, v_c of attributes a, b, c using interactions of the control of ag with the c-granule g_t created by ag at the local time t of ag.

Figure 3 presents a summary of the idea discussed above. An agent ag at time t initiates some actions for computing values of attributes a, b, c for some objects lying in the reality, and that creates a c-granule g_t. The values v_a, v_b, v_c represent the states of some objects o_a, o_b, o_c at time t. These values are transmitted by a set of links. Configurations of physical objects in g_t, related to the attributes a, b, c, are denoted by $conf_a, conf_b, conf_c$. $LINKS$ is the set of links for transmitting results of interactions, that take place in configurations $conf_a, conf_b, conf_c$ on the measurable objects o_a, o_b, o_c, to the agent ag. That is, the links from g_t to ag are responsible for transmitting values v_a, v_b, v_c of attributes a, b, c corresponding to the states of objects o_a, o_b, o_c at time t. The symbol x is a variable assuming names for objects of g_t together with a pointer to g_t.

The control of an agent works for preparing the granule g_t by setting control parameters in the physical reality as a prior step of constructing the relevant current information system. The prediction regarding how the control parameters are to be set is performed on the basis of knowledge accumulated in the memory of the control. The aim of the control of an agent is to satisfy the needs of the agent by controlling computations on c-granules. The algorithms, called classifiers (or regressors), for predicting the values of parameters are induced on the basis of information dynamically accumulated by the agent in the form of interactive information (decision) systems. These systems are dynamically changing with time due to interactions of the control with the environment. The process of inducing classifiers (or regressors) is often supported using hierarchical learning [7, 23, 60].

Next comes the necessity of developing adaptive strategies on the basis of the history/memory of control regarding how the information was gathered in such interactive systems, as well as how the structures of classifiers (regressors) were used in the past for predicting values of parameters. All these help to induce high quality classifiers (regressors) for predicting values of the parameters for the current situation. The challenge is to develop methods for learning classifiers (regressors) for predicting adaptation of parameters following the agent's available learning about the already perceived changes in situations and in the classifiers (regressors). The induced classifiers (regressors) can be treated as the temporary approximations of decision functions [57, 58].

The fundamental intuition behind the concept of the c-granule g_t is the following:

C-granules are generated by an agent ag depending on the specific configurations of spatio-temporal portions of physical matter (called hunks [22]) related to the ag. The control of an agent ag creates (her/his) c-granules for perceiving and/or accessing fragments of the surrounding of the physical world. Each c-granule consists of three architectural layers:

1. *Soft_suits*, which are configurations of hunks that represent the properties of the ag's environment of activity. That means in the *Soft_suit* all the properties of the present, past, and expected phenomena, as well as the expected properties of interaction plans and/or the results of some interactions, potentially activated by the agent's c-granule, are included.
2. *Link_suits* are the communication channels (links) which transmit the results of interactions among accessible fragments of the agent's environment of activities and the results of interactions among different representations of properties in the soft_suit (i.e., information systems); according to the weight (significance) of the current ag's needs, links may have assigned priorities, which reflect the results of judgment, performed by ag.
3. *Hard_suits* are the configurations of hunks that are accessible by links from the link_suit.

The hard_suits, link_suits, and soft_suits of more compound c-granules are defined using the relevant networks over already defined c-granules. The networks may satisfy some constraints which can be interpreted as definitions for types of networks. The link_suits of such more compound granules are responsible for transmission of interactions between the hard_suits and soft_suits represented by the corresponding networks. The results and/or properties of transmitted interactions are recorded in the soft_suits.

Any c-granule makes it possible to record in its soft_suit what is perceived by the interactions in its hard_suit. The perceived information is transmitted by the link_suit to the soft_suit. This is typical for sensory measurement. On the other hand, a c-granule may cause some interactions in its hard_suit by transmitting through its link-suit some interactions from the soft-suit. However, the c-granule may perceive the results (or properties) of such interactions, caused in the hard-suits, only by using the soft-suit. This is done by transmitting back (through the link-suit) the results of interactions, which take place in the hard-suit, to the soft-suit. These results (or properties) may be different from the predicted ones which can a priori be stored in soft-suit. This is typical for performing actions initiated by c-granules.

It should be underlined that any typical active c-granule is a dynamically changing entity. It means that all components of c-granules (*i.e.*, soft-suite, link-suite and hard-suite) are usually subject to continuous changes.

4   Adaptive Information System: An Outline

The imprecise nature of a concept is often caused due to the unavailability of the information about all possible objects of the discourse. An agent at some point of time t may become able to gauge some part of the reality by accessing some objects, lying in the real world, and certain properties of them. Thus, at time t the agent only becomes able to describe the nature of the real world by a vague/imprecise concept. At some further point of time t' the agent may manage to access some more objects relevant to the concerned fragment of the reality, and learn about their properties. This helps the agent to have a better description of the vague concept, fitting to the reality. The following quote by Noë [32] regarding having a vague perception about reality and thereby generating vague concepts, may be proper here.

> *Think of a blind person tap-tipping his or her way around a cluttered space, perceiving that space by touch, not all at once, but through time, by skillful probing and movement. This is or ought to be, our paradigm of what perceiving is.*

Keeping this in mind, in this section our target would be to develop a set-up for departing from the notion of information system [34, 36–38, 40, 43] to a notion of *Adaptive Information System* (AIS). In order to do so, below, we first present an intuitive background of the proposed formalism.

Let us explain the formal requirements for the notion of adaptive information system through the example of a blind person's way of gauging the real world surrounding her/him, through a process of probing over a passage of time.

(i) Let us assume that at some time point t_0 of starting a walk, the person knows certain things, *e.g.*, where is what, of a local surrounding. So, the person is aware of a certain set of objects and some of its properties (relevant attributes $\mathcal{A}$). Availability of this knowledge at t_0 may be caused due to some earlier process of probing through some sensory tools, like white cane, a stick for blind persons. So, there are two kinds of parameters; parameters for describing the characteristics of the objects, and the parameters like time, space, tools, methods, etc., based on which one can access the information about the former kind of parameters of the objects. The latter kind may be called control parameters as change of these parameters may change the observation about the real attributes of the objects. So, at t_0 the person has an information system specifying values of a set of objects with respect to the attributes $\mathcal{A}$. In fact, the person based on the information system may be aware of the usual decisions to be taken, *e.g.*, moving forward, turning left, in the context of object surrounding her. So, at t_0 the person is aware of some usual set of decisions D which may include all possible functions over control parameters, indicating different actions for modifying control parameters. These are all part of a *knowledge base* KB of the person, and a state of KB at t_0 may be denoted as kb_0.

(ii)   Now at time t_1 ($> t_0$), after starting a walk, with the white cane (*i.e.*, a control tool) the person guesses presence of a new set of objects $U = \{o_1, o_2, \ldots, o_n\}$ in the surrounding. Through an initial probing she may guess that object o_1 is *very close* to her position, object o_2 is on the *left side of* o_1, there is *no object left to* o_2, and so on. We may call this sort of evaluation of properties of the objects as *crude evaluation*. The sense of *close to a position* may have some mental mapping with some exact value, and in that sense each exact value v may be considered to be surrounded by a set of *inexact expressions* having some sense of mapping with v.

(iii)   Now based on this crude evaluation of the objects surrounding her, the person may consider moving towards the left. But while taking a move towards the left he stumbles over an object that he did not expect. So, she needs to change the direction of the control parameter, which might lead to initiate a fresh probing to the left hand side of o_2 (with the white cane) carefully. Thus, with gradual probing the person may come to know about the properties of the objects in real. So, we can think of that at time t_0, at first, the appearance of new objects to an agent's crude sensory level generates some expectation regarding the properties of the objects, then based on that the agent chooses some mode of probing by fixing some control parameters. While fixing the control parameters the agent expects to get some concrete values in order to satisfy her hypothesis about the properties of the objects. In order to get the real values for the attributes of the objects, the agent then needs to make some interactions (e.g., actions) with the reality following the decisions regarding control parameters. Based on how close the real values are to the expected values of the attributes, an agent can decide what is to be changed in the control parameters. That is, at each time point in a sequential manner three kinds of information regarding the parameters are playing role in obtaining an information system; first comes the *expected values for the attributes*, then that expectation pushes the agent for a specific interaction with the physical reality by fixing set-up of the *control parameters*, and finally that process of interaction with physical reality using agent's control helps to get the *real values for the attributes*.

4.1   Formal Counterpart

Below we take an attempt to formalize the above idea in order to develop a framework for *adaptive information system*.

(1) Let us assume that we have a *knowledge base KB*, and at time t_0 the state of the knowledge base is denoted as kb_0.

- kb_0 may contain information about a set of objects with respect to a set of attributes $\mathcal{A}$, and the information regarding some specification of some *control parameters* based on which values for the attributes of $\mathcal{A}$ are obtained. We assume that $V_{\mathcal{A}}$ is the set of values for the attributes of $\mathcal{A}$. It is to be noted that kb_0 is subjective to an agent's perspective.

- kb_0 may also contain information regarding how for a set of objects an initial *crude evaluation* of some attributes from $\mathcal{A}$ works as an guide for selecting specification for control parameters. This crude evaluation might be interpreted as a function which assigns a set of crude values $Cr(V_{\mathcal{A}})$ $(\supseteq V_{\mathcal{A}})$ to the objects of concern. The intuitive idea behind introducing the notion of *crude values*, without entering into much technical details, is that these values are some values lying very closely surrounding the actual set of values $V_{\mathcal{A}}$. One may think of that for each value $v \in V_{\mathcal{A}}$, there is a set of values $N(v)$ containing v, and in some sense similar to v. The set $Cr(V_{\mathcal{A}})$ then can be considered as $\cup_{v \in V_{\mathcal{A}}} N(v)$.

- kb_0 may contain information of a time window, preceding t_0 and ending at t_0. $Fr(kb_0)$ denotes a set of, possibly overlapping, clusters which divides kb_0.

(2) A set of new objects U appeared at time t_0. At the time of appearance there is a crude evaluation function $e_{TA}^{Fr(kb_0)} : U \times \mathcal{A} \mapsto Cr(V_{\mathcal{A}})$. It is to be noted that for some attributes there might be missing values, and that is why we assume possibility of a blank-value, denoted as Λ, in $V_{\mathcal{A}}$. In other words, we have an information system $Inf_{\mathcal{A}}(U)$ where for each object $o \in U$ there is a row, for each attribute $a \in \mathcal{A}$ there is a column, and value that an object o assumes with respect to a is given by $e_{TA}^{Fr(kb_0)}(o, a)$. It is to be noted that this initial crude evaluation of objects with respect to the attributes depends on some clues taken from some fragment of kb_0, and thus the function e_{TA} is suffixed by $Fr(kb_0)$.

(3) Based on the crude evaluation of the objects with respect to the attributes, the agent may consider a set of decisions regarding fixing a set of control parameters. Let us consider D to be the set of decisions, and V_D is the set of values for D. We consider the possibility of having no-values for some decisions, and hence $\Lambda \in V_D$. Agent's decision about which control parameter is to be set with which specification also depends on some previous precedences from kb_0. So, we have an *approximate-decision* function $e_d^{Fr(kb_0)} : Inf_{\mathcal{A}}(U) \mapsto V_D^{|D|}$. It is to be mentioned that $Inf_{\mathcal{A}}(U)$ can be presented as a set of sequences $\{\langle e_{TA}^{Fr(kb_0)}(o, a_1), \ldots, e_{TA}^{Fr(kb_0)}(o, a_n) \rangle : a_i \in \mathcal{A}, o \in U\}$.

(4) While making decisions regarding which control parameters are to be fixed with which specification using the function $e_d^{Fr(kb_0)}$, the agent expects to

have some concrete values, improving the crude values, for the attributes of $\mathcal{A}$. So, we have a *prediction function* $e_p^{Fr(kb_0)} : Inf_{\mathcal{A} \cup D}(U) \mapsto V_{\mathcal{A}}^{|\mathcal{A}|}$. The set $Inf_{\mathcal{A} \cup D}(U) = \{\langle e_{TA}^{Fr(kb_0)}(o, a_1), \ldots, e_{TA}^{Fr(kb_0)}(o, a_n), e_d^{Fr(kb_0)}(o, d_1), \ldots,$ $e_d^{Fr(kb_0)}(o, d_m)\rangle : a_i \in \mathcal{A}, d_j \in D, o \in U\}$, where $\mathcal{A} = \{a_1, \ldots, a_n\}$ and $D = \{d_1, \ldots, d_m\}$.

(5) Based on the decisions, taken regarding fixing control parameters, the agent initiates some interaction with the physical reality at some point of time $t_1 \ (> t_0)$. Outcomes of such interaction is reflected in some part of the configuration of the physical reality, denoted as $CF_U(PR)$. As decisions are regarding the objects of U, the *configuration of the physical reality* also concerns about a set of objects in the physical reality surrounding U. So, $CF_U(PR)$ is the set of all relational structures $Rel(Sr(U))$ where $Sr(U)(\supseteq U)$ represents a neighbourhood of U. $Rel(Sr(U))$ represents a relational structure which includes descriptions of some possible states of the objects of $Sr(U)$. So, the interaction of agent with the physical reality is presented by a function $\overrightarrow{Int} : V_D^{|D|} \mapsto CF_U(PR)$.

(6) As the result of this interaction some actual values are assigned to the attributes, and these values get transmitted to the agent. So, we have another interaction function, may be called *transmission function* $\overleftarrow{Int}$: $CF_U(PR) \mapsto \cup_{\mathcal{A}} V_{\mathcal{A}}^{|\mathcal{A}|}$. In order to explain how this transmission function works we need to refer to some earlier interaction, which has taken place in the process of obtaining the initial information system $Inf_{\mathcal{A}}(U)$ from the physical reality at time t_0 (cf. (1)).

- Let us consider the relational structure $Rel(Sr(U))$ lying in the physical reality, surrounding the objects of U. We can represent such a structure $Rel(Sr(U))$ as a classification $(Sr(U), \{st_i\}_{i=1}^{l}, \models)$ in the sense of Barwise and Seligman [4], where $Sr(U)$ is the set of objects, $\{st_i\}_{i=1}^{l}$ is a collection of states, and $\models$ is a binary relation which specifies which object satisfies which state.

- Now from the initial information table $Inf_{\mathcal{A}}(U)$ let us consider the classification given by $(U, \mathcal{A} \times Cr(V_{\mathcal{A}}), e_{TA}^{kb_0} : U \times \mathcal{A} \mapsto Cr(V_{\mathcal{A}}))$. This is obtained based on some interaction of the agent with the physical reality; that is we have a *flow of information*, in the sense of Barwise and Seligman, from $Rel(Sr(U))$ to $(U, \mathcal{A} \times Cr(V_{\mathcal{A}}), e_{TA}^{kb_0} : U \times \mathcal{A} \mapsto Cr(V_{\mathcal{A}}))$. The direction of information flow indicates presence of an infomorphism [4] $I : (Sr(U), \{st_i\}_{i=1}^{l}, \models) \rightleftarrows (U, \mathcal{A} \times Cr(V_{\mathcal{A}}), e_{TA}^{kb_0} : U \times \mathcal{A} \mapsto Cr(V_{\mathcal{A}}))$ where $\hat{I}(st_i) \in \mathcal{A} \times Cr(V_{\mathcal{A}})$ for each $st_i \in \{st_i\}_{i=1}^{l}$, $\check{I}(o) = o \in Sr(U)$ for each $o \in U$, and $\check{I}(o) \models st_i$ iff $e_{TA}^{kb_0}(o, \Pi_1(\hat{I}(st_i))) = \Pi_2(\hat{I}(st_i))$. It is to be noted that Π_1 and Π_2 represent the projection functions on the first and second components of $\mathcal{A} \times Cr(V_{\mathcal{A}})$ respectively.

- $\overleftarrow{Int}(Rel(Sr(U))) \in V_{\mathcal{A}}^{|\mathcal{A}|}$ if there is an infomorphism from $Rel(Sr(U))$ to $(U, \mathcal{A} \times Cr(V_{\mathcal{A}}), e_{TA}^{kb_0} : U \times \mathcal{A} \mapsto Cr(V_{\mathcal{A}}))$ (see Fig. 4).

(7) We now have a *real evaluation* function based on the interaction with physical reality at time t_1, and the function is given by $e_r^{t_1} = \overleftarrow{Int} \circ \overrightarrow{Int} \circ e_d^{Fr(kb_0)}$ (see Fig. 4).

Figure 4 presents an illustrative basic cycle of the control of agent ag. In order to keep simplicity of the presentation we drop the references of kb_0 from the above mentioned functions.

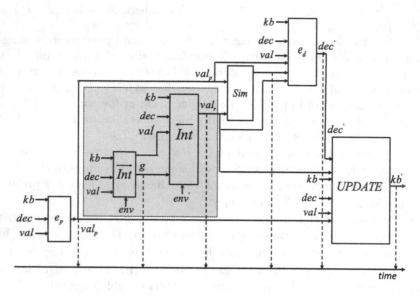

Fig. 4. Basic cycle

First the value of function e_p is computed on the basis of the agent's knowledge base state kb, the row of values for decision attributes, called dec, and values of conditional attributes from A. The predicted valuation val_p of conditional attributes A (i.e., the row of values for each attributes from $\mathcal{A}$) is obtained by e_p. The gray box in Fig. 4 illustrates the process of construction (by operation $\overrightarrow{Int}$) of c-granule g, in particular on the basis of valuation of decision attributes (control parameters). At next step, using the configuration of the c-granule g, through another interaction (operation $\overleftarrow{Int}$) (real) valuation of conditional attributes val_r (which can be different from val_p, the predicted ones) is transmitted to the agent. This box is related to the Vapnik [63] remark:

> [...] further study of this [learning] phenomenon requires analysis that goes beyond pure mathematical models...

Next valuations val_p, val_r are compared by operation Sim and in the result a degree of similarity between val_p and val_r is obtained. Using this degree together with the valuations of conditional attributes val_p, val_r, valuation of control parameters dec, and the control state of knowledge base the function e_d helps to adapt new values for the decision parameters (decision attributes). In the result we obtain the corrected valuation dec' of control parameters. The computed entities are next used to update the contents of knowledge base, and the new state kb' is obtained. This cycle illustrates an idea of adaptation of control parameters.

5   Concluding Remarks

As concluding remarks, we would like to emphasize two basic problems related to the discussed idea of adaptation.

Functions presented in Fig. 4 such as $e_p, e_r, Sim, UPDATE, e_d$ should be learned by the agent. They can be learned on the basis of partial information about these functions stored in the knowledge base. For each of these functions, this information has usually a form of a decision system. Hence, the agent should have strategies to learn from such partial information the models of the functions making it possible to compute their values for new situations not yet stored in the decision systems.

In the case of gray area, the agent should be ready to learn the rules of interactions allowing her to perceive if the c-granule g has been properly constructed, and predict the results of interactions (at least in typical situations) transmitted by g, and transformed into values of conditional attributes. Though for simlicity the role of environment is not included in the formal part, in Fig. 4 we see that obtained values depend also on the state of the environment env, which can change in an unpredictable way. Hence, the conclusions obtained by using interaction rules may be treated only as hypotheses. The interaction rules are related to the above mentioned point view of Vapnik [63] about necessity of the second component of learning consisting of:

The physical side that describes laws which are valid for our specific world, the world where we have to solve our applied tasks.

Iteration of the basic cycle leads to histories. A partial information about histories (*e.g.*, in a form of time windows, or sequences of such windows) may be stored in the knowledge base in the form of decision tables which can be used for inducing more advanced forms of adaptation of decision valuations. The new decisions may depend not only on the current values of decisions but also on the decisions contained in histories, which are treated as objects in these more advanced decision systems. Thus, modeling process of perception adjoined with actions, as mentioned in [32], can be realized. One may observe that this process is related to hierarchical modeling and hierarchical learning and it may be modeled using networks of information systems analogous to Barwise and Seligman's approach [4]. This process is based on reasoning which is called adaptive judgment [23, 26, 27, 52–56] which has some roots not only in logic, but also in psychology and phenomenology [31] (see Fig. 5).

Definitely, the reasoning for adaptation should allow agents to base their reasoning on experience what is the main concept of phenomenology. Hence, it is necessary to have good understanding of this concept for implementation in intelligent systems. This reasoning should allow agents to discover relevant patterns of behavior of other agents or objects what is the subject of studies in psychology.

One can observe that this kind of reasoning is crucial for tasks mentioned above by Vapnik [63], related to the following sentence:

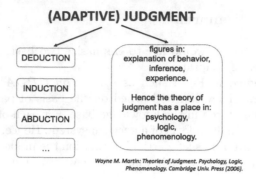

Fig. 5. (Adaptive) judgment

To be successful, learning machines must use structures on the set of functions that are appropriate for problems of our world.

It is worthwhile mentioning that the considered information systems (decision systems) should be considered not as closed objects but in the context of c-granules, these are interacting with the environment. This means that these systems should be treated as open information systems. This requires to develop methods for concept approximation based on networks of information systems changing with time. One of the important changes in such information systems is that instead of value sets of attributes relational structures over the value sets together with set of formulas interpreted over such structures are considered. This makes the process of modeling relevant granules, searching for relevant computational building blocks (patterns) for the approximation of complex vague concept, challenging. These concepts are used as guards for initiating actions performed by agents [23,50].

Apart from that, there is an interesting branch of logic, well known as Adaptive Logic [5,6], where deductive proof techniques are developed based on changing the steps of a proof with the adaptation of new information along the line of the proof. Whether our proposed idea of adaptive information system can serve as a semantics of such a logical system would be a point of future interest too.

Acknowledgments. This work was partially supported by the Polish National Science Centre (NCN) grants DEC-2011/01/D /ST6/06981, DEC-2013/09/B/ST6/01568 as well as by the Polish National Centre for Research and Development (NCBiR) under the grant DZP/RID-I-44 / 8 /NCBR/2016.

References

1. Anderson, J.R.: How Can the Human Mind Occur in the Physical Universe?. Oxford University Press, New York (2007)
2. Baker, G.P., Hacker, P.M.S. (eds.): Wittgenstein: Understanding and Meaning: Volume 1 of an Analytical Commentary on the Philosophical Investigations, Part II: Exegesis, 2nd edn. pp. 1–184. Blackwell, Hoboken (2005)

3. Banerjee, M., Chakraborty, M.K.: Foundations of vagueness: a category-theoretic approach. Electron. Notes Theor. Comput. Sci. **82**(4), 10–19 (2003)
4. Barwise, J., Seligman, J.: Information Flow: The Logic of Distributed Systems. Cambridge University Press, Cambridge (1997)
5. Batens, D.: Inconsistency-adaptive logics. In: Orlowska, E. (ed.) Logic at Work: Essays Dedicated to the Memory of Helena Rasiowa, pp. 445–472. Physica Verlag (Springer), Heidelberg (1999)
6. Batens, D.: Tutorial on inconsistency-adaptive logics. In: Beziau, J.-Y., Chakraborty, M., Dutta, S. (eds.) New Directions in Paraconsistent Logic, Springer Proceedings in Mathematics & Statistics, vol. 152, pp. 3–38. Springer, Heidelberg (2016)
7. Bazan, J.G.: Hierarchical classifiers for complex spatio-temporal concepts. In: Peters, J.F., Skowron, A., Rybiński, H. (eds.) Transactions on Rough Sets IX: Journal Subline. LNCS, vol. 5390, pp. 474–750. Springer, Heidelberg (2008). doi:10. 1007/978-3-540-89876-4_26
8. Bazan, J., Skowron, A., Swiniarski, R.: Rough sets and vague concept approximation: from sample approximation to adaptive learning. In: Peters, J.F., Skowron, A. (eds.) Transactions on Rough Sets V. LNCS, vol. 4100, pp. 39–62. Springer, Heidelberg (2006). doi:10.1007/11847465_3
9. Bonikowski, Z., Wybraniec-Skardowska, U.: Vagueness and roughness. In: Peters, J.F., Skowron, A., Rybiński, H. (eds.) Transactions on Rough Sets IX. LNCS, vol. 5390, pp. 1–13. Springer, Heidelberg (2008). doi:10.1007/978-3-540-89876-4_1
10. Bums, L.C.: Vagueness. In: An Investigation into Natural Languages and the Sorites Paradox. Kluwer, Dordrecht (1991)
11. Dubois, D., Esteva, F., Godo, L., Prade, H.: An information-based discussion of vagueness. In: Proceedings of 10th IEEE International Conference on Fuzzy Systems, Melbourne, Australia, 2–5 December 2001, pp. 781–784. IEEE Computer Science Press (2001)
12. Dubois, D., Godo, L., Prade, H., Esteva, F.: An information-based discussion of vagueness. In: Cohen, H., Lefebvre, C. (eds.) Handbook of Categorization in Cognitive Science, pp. 892–913. Elsevier, Amsterdam (2005)
13. Dubois, D., Lang, J., Prade, H.: Handling uncertainty, context, vague predicates, and partial inconsistency in possibilistic logic. In: Driankov, D., Eklund, P.W., Ralescu, A.L. (eds.) IJCAI 1991. LNCS, vol. 833, pp. 45–55. Springer, Heidelberg (1994). doi:10.1007/3-540-58279-7_18
14. Dubois, D., Prade, H.: Modeling uncertain and vague knowledge in possibility and evidence theories. In: Shachter, R.D., Levitt, T.S., Kanal, L.N., Lemmer, J.F. (eds.) Proceedings of 4th Annual Conference on Uncertainty in Artificial Intelligence (UAI 1988), Minneapolis, MN, USA, 10–12 July 1988, LNCS, vol. 7750, pp. 303–318. North-Holland, Amsterdam (1988)
15. Dubois, D., Prade, H.: Fuzzy sets - a convenient fiction for modeling vagueness and possibility. IEEE Trans. Fuzzy Syst. **2**(1), 16–21 (1994)
16. Dubois, D., Prade, H., Modeling uncertain and vague knowledge in possibility and evidence theories. CoRR abs/1304.2349. http://arxiv.org/abs/1304.2349
17. Dutta, S., Basu, S., Chakraborty, M.K.: Many-valued logics, fuzzy logics and graded consequence: a comparative appraisal. In: Lodaya, K. (ed.) ICLA 2013. LNCS, vol. 7750, pp. 197–209. Springer, Heidelberg (2013). doi:10.1007/ 978-3-642-36039-8_18
18. Goguen, J.A.: The logic of inexact concepts. Synthese **19**, 325–373 (1968–1969)
19. Harnad, S.: Categorical Perception: The Groundwork of Cognition. Cambridge University Press, New York (1987)

20. Harnad, S.: The symbol grounding problem. Physica D **42**, 335–346 (1990)
21. Hastie, T., Tibshirani, R., Friedman, J.H.: The Elements of Statistical Learning: Data Mining, Inference, and Prediction. Springer, Heidelberg (2001)
22. Heller, M.: The Ontology of Physical Objects. Four Dimensional Hunks of Matter. Cambridge Studies in Philosophy. Cambridge University Press, Cambridge (1990)
23. Jankowski, A.: Interactive Granular Computations in Networks and Systems Engineering: A Practical Perspective. LNNS. Springer, Heidelberg (2017, in print)
24. Jankowski, A., Skowron, A.: A wistech paradigm for intelligent systems. In: Peters, J.F., Skowron, A., Düntsch, I., Grzymała-Busse, J., Orłowska, E., Polkowski, L. (eds.) Transactions on Rough Sets VI. LNCS, vol. 4374, pp. 94–132. Springer, Heidelberg (2007). doi:10.1007/978-3-540-71200-8_7
25. Jankowski, A., Skowron, A.: Wisdom technology: a rough-granular approach. In: Marciniak, M., Mykowiecka, A. (eds.) Aspects of Natural Language Processing. LNCS, vol. 5070, pp. 3–41. Springer, Heidelberg (2009). doi:10.1007/978-3-642-04735-0_1
26. Jankowski, A., Skowron, A., Dutta, S.: Toward problem solving support based on big data and domain knowledge: interactive granular computing and adaptive judgement. In: Japkowicz, N., Stefanowski, J. (eds.) Big Data Analysis: New Algorithms for a New Society, Series Big Data, vol. 16, pp. 44–90. Springer, Heidelberg (2015)
27. Jankowski, A., Skowron, A., Swiniarski, R.W.: Perspectives on uncertainty and risk in rough sets and interactive rough-granular computing. Fundamenta Informaticae **129**(1–2), 69–84 (2014)
28. Keefe, R.: Theories of Vagueness. Cambridge Studies in Philosophy. Cambridge University Press, Cambridge (2000)
29. Lawry, J., Dubois, D., A bipolar framework for combining beliefs about vague propositions. In: Brewka, G., Eiter, T., McIlraith, S.A. (eds.) Principles of Knowledge Representation and Reasoning: Proceedings of KR 2012, Rome, Italy, 10–14 June 2012, pp. 530–540. AAAI Press (2012)
30. Marcus, S.: The paradox of the heap of grains in respect to roughness, fuzziness and negligibility. In: Polkowski, L., Skowron, A. (eds.) RSCTC 1998. LNCS, vol. 1424, pp. 19–22. Springer, Heidelberg (1998). doi:10.1007/3-540-69115-4_2
31. Martin, W.M. (ed.): Theories of Judgment. Psychology, Logic, Phenomenology. Cambridge University Press, New York (2006)
32. Noë, A.: Action in Perception. MIT Press, Cambridge (2004)
33. Orłowska, E.: Semantics of vague concepts. In: ICS PAS Reports 450/82, pp. 1–20. Institute of Computer Science Polish Academy of Sciences (ICS PAS), Warsaw, Poland (1982)
34. Orłowska, E., Pawlak, Z.: Expressive power of knowledge representation systems. In: ICS PAS Reports 432/81, pp. 1–31. Institute of Computer Science Polish Academy of Sciences (ICS PAS), Warsaw, Poland (1981)
35. Pal, S.K., Polkowski, L., Skowron, A. (eds.): Rough-Neural Computing: Techniques for Computing with Words. Cognitive Technologies. Springer-, Heidelberg (2004)
36. Pawlak, Z.: Mathematical foundation of information retrieval. In: Proceedings of International Symposium and Summer School on Mathematical Foundations of Computer Science, Strbske Pleso, High Tatras, Czechoslovakia, pp. 135–136. Mathematical Institute of the Slovak Academy of Sciences (1973)
37. Pawlak, Z.: Mathematical foundations of information retrieval. In: CC PAS Reports 101/73, pp. 1–8. Computation Center Polish Academy of Sciences (CC PAS), Warsaw, Poland (1973)

38. Pawlak, Z.: Information systems - theoretical foundations. Inf. Syst. **6**, 205–218 (1981)
39. Pawlak, Z.: Rough sets. Int. J. Comput. Inform. Sci. **11**, 341–356 (1982)
40. Pawlak, Z.: Rough Sets: Theoretical Aspects of Reasoning about Data, System Theory, Knowledge Engineering and Problem Solving, vol. 9. Kluwer Academic Publishers, Dordrecht (1991)
41. Pawlak, Z.: Vagueness and uncertainty: a rough set perspective. Comput. Intell.: Int. J. **11**, 217–232 (1995)
42. Pawlak, Z.: Vagueness — a rough set view. In: Mycielski, J., Rozenberg, G., Salomaa, A. (eds.) Structures in Logic and Computer Science. LNCS, vol. 1261, pp. 106–117. Springer, Heidelberg (1997). doi:10.1007/3-540-63246-8_7
43. Pawlak, Z., Skowron, A.: Rudiments of rough sets. Inf. Sci. **177**(1), 3–27 (2007)
44. Polkowski, L., Semeniuk-Polkowska, M.: Boundaries, borders, fences, hedges. Fundamenta Informaticae **129**(1–2), 149–159 (2014)
45. Polkowski, L., Skowron, A.: Rough mereological calculi of granules: a rough set approach to computation. Comput. Intell.: Int. J. **17**(3), 472–492 (2001)
46. Prade, H.: A two-layer fuzzy pattern matching procedure for the evaluation of conditions involving vague quantifiers. J. Intell. Rob. Syst. **3**, 93–101 (1990)
47. Prade, H., Testemale, C.: Generalizing database relational algebra for the treatment of incomplete/uncertain information and vague queries. Inf. Sci. **34**, 115–143 (1984)
48. Read, S.: Thinking about Logic: An Introduction to the Philosophy of Logic. Oxford University Press, Oxford (1994)
49. Skowron, A.: Rough sets and vague concepts. Fundamenta Informaticae **64**(1–4), 417–431 (2005)
50. Skowron, A., Dutta, S.: From information systems to interactive information systems. In: Wang, G., Skowron, A., Yao, Y., Slezak, D., Polkowski, L. (eds.) Thriving Rough Sets. SCI, vol. 708, pp. 207–223. Springer, Heidelberg (2017). doi:10.1007/978-3-319-54966-8_10
51. Skowron, A., Jankowski, A.: Rough sets and vague concepts. Ann. Univ. Buchar. Inform. Ser. LXI **LXII**(3), 119–133 (2015)
52. Skowron, A., Jankowski, A.: Interactive computations: toward risk management in interactive intelligent systems. Nat. Comput. **15**(3), 465–476 (2016)
53. Skowron, A., Jankowski, A.: Rough sets and interactive granular computing. Fundamenta Informaticae **147**, 371–385 (2016)
54. Skowron, A., Jankowski, A.: Toward W2T foundations: interactive granular computing and adaptive judgement. In: Zhong, N., Ma, J., Liu, J., Huang, R., Tao, X. (eds.) Wisdom Web of Things (W2T), pp. 47–71. Springer, Heidelberg (2016)
55. Skowron, A., Jankowski, A., Dutta, S.: Interactive granular computing. Granul. Comput. **1**, 95–113 (2016). Springer, Heidelberg. doi:10.1007/s41066-015-0002-1
56. Skowron, A., Jankowski, A., Wasilewski, P.: Risk management and interactive computational systems. J. Adv. Math. Appl. **1**, 61–73 (2012)
57. Skowron, A., Jankowski, A., Wasilewski, P.: Rough sets and sorites paradox. In: Schlingloff, H. (ed.) International Workshop on Concurrency, Specification and Programming (CS&P 2016), Rostock, Germany, 28–30 September, CEUR-WS.org 2016, CEUR Workshop Proceedings, vol. 1698, pp. 49–60 (2017)
58. Skowron, A., Nguyen, H.S.: Rough sets: from rudiments to challenges. In: Skowron, A., Suraj, Z. (eds.) Rough Sets and Intelligent Systems. Professor Zdzislaw Pawlak in Memoriam. Intelligent Systems Reference Library, vol. 42, pp. 75–173. Springer, Heidelberg (2013). doi:10.1007/978-3-642-30344-9_3

59. Skowron, A., Swiniarski, R.: Rough sets and higher order vagueness. In: Ślęzak, D., Wang, G., Szczuka, M., Düntsch, I., Yao, Y. (eds.) RSFDGrC 2005. LNCS, vol. 3641, pp. 33–42. Springer, Heidelberg (2005). doi:10.1007/11548669_4
60. Skowron, A., Szczuka, M.: Toward interactive computations: a rough-granular approach. In: Koronacki, J., Raś, Z., Wierzchoń, S., Kacprzyk, J. (eds.) Advances in Machine Learning II: Dedicated to the Memory of Professor Ryszard S. Michalski. SCI, vol. 263, pp. 23–42. Springer, Heidelberg (2009)
61. Skowron, A., Wasilewski, P.: Interactive information systems: toward perception based computing. Theoret. Comput. Sci. **454**, 240–260 (2012)
62. Ślęzak, D., Wasilewski, P.: Foundations of rough sets from vagueness perspective. In: Hassanien, A.E., Suraj, Z., Ślęzak, D., Lingras, P. (eds.) Rough Computing: Theories, Technologies and Applications, pp. 1–37. IGI Global, Hershey (2008)
63. Vapnik, V.: Statistical Learning Theory. Wiley, New York (1998)
64. Wolski, M.: Science and semantics: a note on vagueness. In: Skowron, A., Suraj, Z. (eds.) Rough Sets and Intelligent Systems. Professor Zdzislaw Pawlak in Memoriam. Intelligent Systems Reference Library, vol. 42, pp. 623–643. Springer, Heidelberg (2013)

Optimal Scale Selections in Consistent Generalized Multi-scale Decision Tables

You-Hong Xu[1,2], Wei-Zhi Wu[1,2(✉)], and Anhui Tan[1,2]

[1] School of Mathematics, Physics and Information Science,
Zhejiang Ocean University, Zhoushan 316022, Zhejiang, China
{xyh,wuwz}@zjou.edu.cn, tananhui86@163.com
[2] Key Laboratory of Oceanographic Big Data Mining and Application of Zhejiang
Province, Zhejiang Ocean University, Zhoushan 316022, Zhejiang, China

Abstract. A generalized multi-scale information table is an attribute-value system in which each object under each attribute is represented by different scales at different levels of granulations having a granular information transformation from a finer to a coarser labeled value. In such table, diverse attributes have different numbers of levels of scales. In this paper, information granules and optimal scale selections in consistent generalized multi-scale decision tables are studied. The concept of scale combinations in generalized multi-scale information tables is first reviewed. Representation of information granules in generalized multi-scale information tables is then shown. Lower and upper approximations with reference to different levels of granulations in multi-scale information tables are further defined and their properties are presented. Finally, belief and plausibility functions in the Dempster-Shafer theory of evidence are used to characterize optimal scale selections in consistent generalized multi-scale decision tables.

Keywords: Granular computing · Information tables · Multi-scale decision tables · Optimal scale selections · Rough sets

1 Introduction

Human beings often observe objects or deal with data hierarchically structured at different levels of granulations. Granular computing (GrC), which imitates human being's thinking, is an approach for knowledge representation and data mining. The purpose of GrC is to seek for an approximation scheme which can effectively solve a complex problem at a certain level of granulation. The theory of rough sets, proposed by Pawlak [6], is proved to be well performed for constructing a granulated view of the universe of discourse and for interpreting, representing, and processing concepts in the granulated universe.

Most applications based on rough set theory belong to the attribute-value representation model. It is well-known that, in rough-set data analysis, each object can only take on one value under each attribute in almost all of information tables [1,6,11,17,20]. However, in some real-life applications, one has to

© Springer International Publishing AG 2017
L. Polkowski et al. (Eds.): IJCRS 2017, Part I, LNAI 10313, pp. 185–198, 2017.
DOI: 10.1007/978-3-319-60837-2_15

2 Rudiments of Rough Sets and Complex Granules

2.1 Rough Sets

The rough set (RS) approach was proposed by Professor Zdzisław Pawlak in 1982 [39,40,43] as a tool for dealing with imperfect knowledge. Over the years many methods based on rough set theory, alone or in combination with other approaches, have been developed.

The starting point of rough set theory is the indiscernibility relation, which is generated from the information about objects of interest (defined later in this section as signatures of objects). Through indiscernibility relation it is reflected that due to lack of information (or knowledge) some objects based on the available information (or knowledge) become indiscernible with each other. This entails that, in general, we are unable to deal with each particular object separately; rather we can only consider granules (clusters) of indiscernible objects as a fundamental units of the theory.

From a practical point of view, it is better to define basic concepts of this theory in terms of data. Therefore we will start our considerations from a data set called an *information system*.

Suppose we are given a pair $\mathbb{A} = (U, \mathcal{A})$ of non-empty, finite sets U and $\mathcal{A}$, where U is the *universe* of *objects*, and $\mathcal{A}$ is a set consisting of *attributes*, *i.e.*, functions $a : U \longrightarrow V_a$, where V_a is the set of values of attribute a, called the *domain* of a. The pair $\mathbb{A} = (U, \mathcal{A})$ is called an *information system* (see, *e.g.*, [38]). It is to be noted here that similar to the notion of information system, in [4], Barwise and Seligman have introduced a notion of classification. Drawing analogy with classification [4], an information system $\mathbb{A}$ can be viewed as a triple, $Inf_A(U) = (U, \mathcal{A}, e : U \times \mathcal{A} \mapsto L)$, where $L = \cup_{a \in A} V_a$ and $e(u, a) = a(u)$ for $a \in \mathcal{A}$, $u \in U$. In order to keep the symbols uniform, from now onwards by information system we would refer to a triple of the above kind.

Any information system can be represented by a data table with rows labeled by objects and columns labeled by attributes. Any pair (x, a), where $x \in U$ and $a \in A$ defines the particular entry in the table indicated by the value $e(x, a)$ (or in other words $a(x)$).

Any subset B of $\mathcal{A}$ determines a binary relation $I\!N\!D_B$ on U, called an *indiscernibility relation*, defined by

$$x\ I\!N\!D_B\ y \text{ if and only if } e(x, a) = e(y, a) \text{ for every } a \in B, \tag{1}$$

where $e(x, a)$ denotes the value of attribute a for object x.

Obviously, $I\!N\!D_B$ is an equivalence relation. The family of all equivalence classes of $I\!N\!D_B$, *i.e.*, the partition determined by B, will be denoted by $U/I\!N\!D_B$, or simply U/B; an equivalence class of $I\!N\!D_B$, *i.e.*, the block of the partition U/B, containing x will be denoted as $[x]_B$ (or more precisely $[x]_{I\!N\!D_B}$). Thus in view of the data we are unable, in general, to observe individual object; rather we are forced to reason only about the accessible granules of objects with respect to available knowledge (see, *e.g.*, [35,40,45]).

make decision with different levels of granulations. That is, an object may take on different values under the same attribute, depending on at which scale it is measured. Therefore, some authors proposed multi-granulation rough set models to generalize traditional rough set models (see e.g. [5,7–9,18]). These multi-granulation rough set models are in fact obtained by adding/deleting attributes in information tables.

In [14], Wu and Leung introduced the notion of multi-scale information tables, which was called Wu-Leung model in [4], from the perspective of granular computing, represented the structure of and relationships among information granules, and analyzed knowledge acquisition in multi-scale decision tables under different levels of granularity. In a multi-scale information table, each object under each attribute is represented by different scales at different levels of granulations having a granular information transformation from a finer to a coarser labeled value. Wu and Leung [15] further investigated optimal scale selection for choosing a proper decision table for final decision or classification with an assumption that all attributes are granulated with the same number of levels of granulations. Based on the same assumption, Gu et al. [2,3] and She et al. [12] explored knowledge acquisitions and rule induction in multi-scale decision tables. Recently, multi-scale information tables have been extended to incomplete and ordered information tables [13,16]. However, such assumption may bring some limitations on the applications of multi-scale information tables in real-life world. To overcome this shortcoming, Li and Hu [4] made a generalization of Wu-Leung model in which attributes may have different numbers of levels of granulations. They also developed two methods, called complement model and lattice model, to obtain optimal scale selection of a generalized multi-scale decision table. We found that the definition of optimal scale combinations in the lattice model is not so reasonable. In this paper, we redefine the concept of optimal scale combinations and use belief and plausibility functions in the Dempster-Shafer theory of evidence to characterize optimal scale combinations in consistent generalized multi-scale decision tables.

2   Information Systems and Belief Functions

Throughout this paper, for a nonempty set U, the class of all subsets of U is denoted by $\mathcal{P}(U)$. For $X \in \mathcal{P}(U)$, we denote the complement of X in U as $\sim X$, i.e. $\sim X = U - X = \{x \in U | x \notin X\}$. In this section, we review some basic notions related to information systems, decision tables, and belief and plausibility functions in the Dempster-Shafer theory of evidence.

2.1   Information Systems and Decision Tables

The notion of information systems (also called information tables) provides a convenient tool for the representation of objects in terms of their attribute values [6,20].

Definition 1. *An information system is a 2-tuple (U, A), where $U = \{x_1, x_2, \ldots, x_n\}$ is a non-empty, finite set of objects called the universe of discourse and $A = \{a_1, a_2, \ldots, a_m\}$ is a non-empty, finite set of attributes, such that $a : U \to V_a$ for each $a \in A$, i.e. $a(x) \in V_a, x \in U$, where $V_a = \{a(x)|x \in U\}$ is called the domain of a.*

A *decision table* (sometimes called *decision system*) is a 2-tuple $S = (U, C \cup \{d\})$ where (U, C) is an information system, and $d \notin C$ is a special attribute called the decision. In this case, C is called the conditional attribute set, d is a mapping $d : U \to V_d$ from the universe of discourse U into the value set V_d, we assume, without any loss of generality, that $V_d = \{1, 2, \ldots, r\}$. Define

$$R_d = \{(x, y) \in U \times U | d(x) = d(y)\}.$$

Then we obtain a partition $U/R_d = \{D_1, D_2, \ldots, D_r\}$ of U into decision classes, where $D_j = \{x \in U | d(x) = j\}, j = 1, 2, \ldots, r$.

For any $B \subseteq C$, denote an equivalence relation (also called indiscernibility relation) R_B as

$$R_B = \bigcap_{a \in B} R_a = \{(x, y) \in U \times U | a(x) = a(y), \forall a \in B\}.$$

Since R_B is an equivalence relation on U, it forms a partition $U/R_B = \{[x]_B | x \in U\}$ of U, where $[x]_B$ denotes the equivalence class determined by x with respect to (w.r.t.) B, i.e., $[x]_B = \{y \in U | (x, y) \in R_B\}$.

If $R_C \subseteq R_d$, then the decision table $S = (U, C \cup \{d\})$ is referred to as *consistent*, it is said to be *inconsistent* otherwise.

2.2 Belief Structures and Belief Functions

The Dempster-Shafer theory of evidence, also called the "evidence theory" or the "belief function theory", is treated as a promising method of dealing with uncertainty in intelligence systems. The basic representational structure in the Dempster-Shafer theory of evidence is a belief structure [10].

Definition 2. *Let U be a non-empty finite set, a set function $m : \mathcal{P}(U) \to [0, 1]$ is referred to as a basic probability assignment if it satisfies axioms* (M1) *and* (M2):

$$\text{(M1) } m(\emptyset) = 0, \quad \text{(M2) } \sum_{A \subseteq U} m(A) = 1.$$

The value $m(A)$ represents the degree of belief that a specific element of U belongs to set A, but not to any particular subset of A. A set $A \in \mathcal{P}(U)$ with nonzero basic probability assignment is referred to as a *focal element*. We denote by $\mathcal{M}$ the family of all focal elements of m. The pair $(\mathcal{M}, m)$ is called a *belief structure* on U.

Associated with each belief structure, a pair of belief and plausibility functions can be defined [10].

Definition 3. *Let* $(\mathcal{M}, m)$ *be a belief structure on* U. *A set function* Bel : $\mathcal{P}(U) \to [0, 1]$ *is referred to as a belief function on* U *if*

$$\mathrm{Bel}(X) = \sum_{A \subseteq X} m(A), \ \forall X \in \mathcal{P}(U).$$

A set function Pl : $\mathcal{P}(U) \to [0, 1]$ *is referred to as a plausibility function on* U *if*

$$\mathrm{Pl}(X) = \sum_{A \cap X \neq \emptyset} m(A), \ \forall X \in \mathcal{P}(U).$$

Belief and plausibility functions based on the same belief structure are connected by the dual property

$$\mathrm{Pl}(X) = 1 - \mathrm{Bel}(\sim X), \ \forall X \in \mathcal{P}(U).$$

And furthermore,

$$\mathrm{Bel}(X) \leq \mathrm{Pl}(X), \ \forall X \in \mathcal{P}(U).$$

The following theorem shows that probabilities of lower and upper approximations are a dual pair of belief and plausibility functions [19].

Theorem 1. *Let* (U, R, P) *be a probabilistic approximation space, for any* $X \subseteq U$, *denote*

$$\mathrm{Bel}(X) = P(\underline{R}(X)), \qquad \mathrm{Pl}(X) = P(\overline{R}(X)).$$

Then Bel *and* Pl *are a dual pair of belief and plausibility functions on* U *respectively, and the corresponding basic probability assignment is*

$$m(Y) = \begin{cases} P(Y), \text{ if } Y \in U/R, \\ 0, \qquad \text{otherwise.} \end{cases}$$

3 Knowledge Representations in Generalized Multi-scale Information Tables

In this section, we introduce the concept of multi-scale decision tables from the perspective of granular computation.

3.1 Multi-scale Information Tables

In [14], Wu and Leung proposed a model, which was called Wu-Leung model in [4], to extract rules and discover knowledge in multi-scale decision tables. This model is based on two assumptions, one is that all attributes have the same number of levels of granulations and the other is that the order indexes (superscript) of all single-attributes in any subsystem are the same.

Definition 4. *A multi-scale information table is a tuple $S = (U, A)$, where $U = \{x_1, x_2, \ldots, x_n\}$ is a non-empty, finite set of objects called the universe of discourse, $A = \{a_1, a_2, \ldots, a_m\}$ is a non-empty, finite set of attributes, and each $a_j \in A, j = 1, 2, \ldots, m$, is a multi-scale attribute, i.e., for the same object in U, attribute a_j can take on different values at different scales. Such a multi-scale information table can be represented as a table $(U, \{a_j^k | k = 1, 2, \ldots, I, j = 1, 2, \ldots, m\})$, where $a_j^k : U \to V_j^k$ is a surjective function and V_j^k is the domain of the k-th scale attribute a_j^k. For $1 \le k \le I - 1$, there exists a surjective function $g_j^{k,k+1} : V_j^k \to V_j^{k+1}$ such that $a_j^{k+1} = g_j^{k,k+1} \circ a_j^k$, i.e.*

$$a_j^{k+1}(x) = g_j^{k,k+1}(a_j^k(x)), \quad x \in U,$$

where $g_j^{k,k+1}$ is called a granular information transformation function.

Definition 5. *A multi-scale decision table is a system $S = (U, C \cup \{d\}) = (U, \{a_j^k | k = 1, 2, \ldots, I, j = 1, 2, \ldots, m\} \cup \{d\})$, where $(U, C) = (U, \{a_j^k | k = 1, 2, \ldots, I, j = 1, 2, \ldots, m\})$ is a multi-scale information table and $d \notin \{a_j^k | k = 1, 2, \ldots, I, j = 1, 2, \ldots, m\}$, $d : U \to V_d$, is a special attribute called the decision.*

For $k \in \{1, 2, \ldots, I\}$, denote that $A^k = \{a_j^k | j = 1, 2, \ldots, m\}$, then a multi-scale information table $S = (U, A)$ can be decomposed into I information tables $S^k = (U, A^k), k = 1, 2, \ldots, I$. Similarly, a multi-scale decision table $S = (U, C \cup \{d\})$ can be decomposed into I decision subsystems $S^k = (U, C^k \cup \{d\}), k = 1, 2, \ldots, I$, with the same decision attribute.

However, the Wu-Leung model which assumed that each attribute is granulated by granules with the same number of levels may limit its applications in real-life world. Recently, Li and Hu [4] made a generalization that attributes may have different numbers of levels of granulations. Formally, a generalized multi-scale information table $S = (U, A)$ can be described as a table $(U, \{a_j^k | k = 1, 2, \ldots, I_j, j = 1, 2, \ldots, m\})$, where $a_j^k : U \to V_j^k$ is a surjective function and V_j^k is the domain of the k-th scale attribute a_j^k. For $1 \le k \le I_j - 1$, there exists a surjective function $g_j^{k,k+1} : V_j^k \to V_j^{k+1}$ such that $a_j^{k+1} = g_j^{k,k+1} \circ a_j^k$. Similarly, a generalized multi-scale decision table is a system $S = (U, C \cup \{d\}) = (U, \{a_j^k | k = 1, 2, \ldots, I_j, j = 1, 2, \ldots, m\} \cup \{d\})$, where $(U, C) = (U, \{a_j^k | k = 1, 2, \ldots, I_j, j = 1, 2, \ldots, m\})$ is a generalized multi-scale information table and $d \notin \{a_j^k | k = 1, 2, \ldots, I, j = 1, 2, \ldots, m\}$, $d : U \to V_d$, is a special attribute called the decision. We see that if $I_1 = I_2 = \cdots = I_m = I$, then the generalized multi-scale information table and generalized multi-scale decision table are degenerated to a multi-scale information table and a multi-scale decision table respectively defined by Wu and Leung in [14].

3.2   Scale Combinations in Generalized Multi-scale Information Tables

The main method of knowledge acquisition in a multi-scale information table is to decompose it into several single-scale information systems since a multi-scale attribute can become a single-scale one when it is restricted on a special scale [4,14]. How to obtain an appropriate single-scale information system is an important issue in the knowledge representation in a multi-scale information table. In [4], Li and Hu introduced the concept of scale combination which can be used to describe a single-scale information system from a multi-scale information table.

Definition 6. *Let $S = (U, A) = (U, \{a_j^k | k = 1, 2, \ldots, I_j, j = 1, 2, \ldots, m\})$ be a generalized multi-scale information table, where attribute a_j has I_j levels of granulations, $j = 1, 2, \ldots, m$. Attributes $a_1, a_2, \ldots, a_m$ restricted on their l_j-th scale, $j = 1, 2, \ldots, m$, respectively, form a single-scale information table S^K, where $K = (l_1, l_2, \ldots, l_m)$. The index set $(l_1, l_2, \ldots, l_m)$ is called the scale combination of S^K in S. The family of all scale combinations in S, called the scale collection of S, is denoted as $\mathcal{L}$, i.e. $\mathcal{L} = \{(l_1, l_2, \ldots, l_m) | l_j \in \{1, 2, \ldots, I_j\}, j = 1, 2, \ldots, m\}$.*

For any $K = (l_1, l_2, \ldots, l_m) \in \mathcal{L}$, let $A^K = \{a_1^{l_1}, a_2^{l_2}, \ldots, a_m^{l_m}\}$, then $S^K = (U, A^K)$ is a single-scale information table determined by the scale combination K.

Definition 7. *Let $S = (U, A)$ be a generalized multi-scale information table and $\mathcal{L}$ the scale collection of S. For $K_1 = (l_1^1, l_2^1, \ldots, l_m^1), K_2 = (l_1^2, l_2^2, \ldots, l_m^2) \in \mathcal{L}$, if $l_j^1 \leq l_j^2$ for all $j \in \{1, 2, \ldots, m\}$, then we say that K_1 is weaker than K_2, or K_2 is stronger than K_1, denoted as $K_1 \preceq K_2$. Furthermore, if there exists a $j \in \{1, 2, \ldots, m\}$ such that $l_j^1 < l_j^2$, then K_1 is strictly weaker than K_2, or K_2 is strictly stronger than K_1, denoted as $K_1 \prec K_2$.*

Proposition 1. *Let $S = (U, A)$ be a generalized multi-scale information table and $\mathcal{L}$ the scale collection of S. For $K_1 = (l_1^1, l_2^1, \ldots, l_m^1), K_2 = (l_1^2, l_2^2, \ldots, l_m^2) \in \mathcal{L}$, define $K_1 \wedge K_2 = (l_1^1 \wedge l_1^2, l_2^1 \wedge l_2^2, \ldots, l_m^1 \wedge l_m^2)$ and $K_1 \vee K_2 = (l_1^1 \vee l_1^2, l_2^1 \vee l_2^2, \ldots, l_m^1 \vee l_m^2)$, where $l_j^1 \wedge l_j^2 = \min\{l_j^1, l_j^2\}$ and $l_j^1 \vee l_j^2 = \max\{l_j^1, l_j^2\}$ for all $j \in \{1, 2, \ldots, m\}$. Then*

$$K_1 \preceq K_2 \Leftrightarrow K_1 \wedge K_2 = K_1 \Leftrightarrow K_1 \vee K_2 = K_2.$$

And $(\mathcal{L}, \preceq, \wedge, \vee)$ is a bounded lattice with the maximal element $(I_1, I_2, \ldots, I_m)$ and the minimal element $(1, 1, \ldots, 1)$.

Just as pointed out by Li and Hu in [4], for a generalized multi-scale information table, a scale selection is to determine an appropriate subsystem for decision making. After all, weaker scale combination means higher cost and stronger scale combination may reduce attributes discernibility.

3.3   Information Granules and Rough Approximations in Multi-scale Information Tables

Let $S = (U, A)$ be a generalized multi-scale information table and $\mathcal{L}$ the scale collection of S. For $B \subseteq A$ and $K = (l_1, l_2, \ldots, l_m) \in \mathcal{L}$, denote the limitation of K on B as K_B (for example, if $A = \{a_1, a_2, a_3, a_4\}$, $B = \{a_2, a_4\}$, and $K =$

$(2, 2, 3, 4) \in \mathcal{L}$, then $K_B = (2, 4)$) and let $\mathcal{L}_B = \{K_B | K \in \mathcal{L}\}$. Obviously, $\mathcal{L}_B$ is the scale collection of the multi-scale information sub-table (U, B). Define

$$R_{B^K} = \{(x, y) \in U \times U | b^l(x) = b^l(y), \forall b^l \in B^{K_B}\}.$$

Then R_{B^K} is an equivalence relation on U determined by attribute subset B with the scale level K. For $x \in U$, denote $[x]_{B^K} = \{y \in U | (x, y) \in R_{B^K}\}$, $[x]_{B^K}$ is called the R_{B^K}-equivalence class of x. Denote $U/R_{B^K} = \{[x]_{B^K} | x \in U\}$.

Definition 8. *Let U be a nonempty set, and $\mathcal{A}_1$ and $\mathcal{A}_2$ two partitions of U. If for each $A_1 \in \mathcal{A}_1$, there exists $A_2 \in \mathcal{A}_2$ such that $A_1 \subseteq A_2$, then we say that $\mathcal{A}_1$ is finer than $\mathcal{A}_2$ or $\mathcal{A}_2$ is coarser than $\mathcal{A}_1$, and is denoted as $\mathcal{A}_1 \preceq \mathcal{A}_2$. Furthermore, if there exist $A_1 \in \mathcal{A}_1$ and $A_2 \in \mathcal{A}_2$ such that $A_1 \subset A_2$, then we say that $\mathcal{A}_1$ is strictly finer than $\mathcal{A}_2$, and is denoted as $\mathcal{A}_1 \prec \mathcal{A}_2$.*

Proposition 2. *Let $S = (U, A)$ be a generalized multi-scale information table and $\mathcal{L}$ the scale collection of S. For $B \subseteq A$, and $K_1, K_2 \in \mathcal{L}$, we have*

(1) $K_1 \preceq K_2 \Rightarrow R_{B^{K_1}} \subseteq R_{B^{K_2}}$,
(2) $K_1 \preceq K_2 \Rightarrow [x]_{B^{K_1}} \subseteq [x]_{B^{K_2}}, \forall x \in U$,
(3) $K_1 \preceq K_2 \Rightarrow U/R_{B^{K_1}} \preceq U/R_{B^{K_2}}$,
(4) $B \subseteq C \subseteq A \Rightarrow R_{C^K} \subseteq R_{B^K}$.

For $B \subseteq A$, $X \subseteq U$, and $K \in \mathcal{L}$, the lower and upper approximations of X w.r.t B^K, denoted by $\underline{R_{B^K}}(X)$ and $\overline{R_{B^K}}(X)$ respectively, are defined as follows:

$$\underline{R_{B^K}}(X) = \cup\{[x]_{B^K} | [x]_{B^K} \subseteq X\} = \{x \in U | [x]_{B^K} \subseteq X\},$$

$$\overline{R_{B^K}}(X) = \cup\{[x]_{B^K} | [x]_{B^K} \cap X \neq \emptyset\} = \{x \in U | [x]_{B^K} \cap X \neq \emptyset\}.$$

Proposition 3. *Let $S = (U, A)$ be a generalized multi-scale information table and $\mathcal{L}$ the scale collection of S. If $B \subseteq A$, and $K, K_1, K_2 \in \mathcal{L}$, then: $\forall X, Y \in \mathcal{P}(U)$,*

(1) $\underline{R_{B^K}}(X) = \sim \overline{R_{B^K}}(\sim X)$,
(2) $\overline{R_{B^K}}(X) = \sim \underline{R_{B^K}}(\sim X)$,
(3) $\underline{R_{B^K}}(\emptyset) = \overline{R_{B^K}}(\emptyset) = \emptyset$,
(4) $\underline{R_{B^K}}(U) = \overline{R_{B^K}}(U) = U$,
(5) $\underline{R_{B^K}}(X \cap Y) = \underline{R_{B^K}}(X) \cap \underline{R_{B^K}}(Y)$,
(6) $\overline{R_{B^K}}(X \cup Y) = \overline{R_{B^K}}(X) \cup \overline{R_{B^K}}(Y)$,
(7) $X \subseteq Y \Rightarrow \underline{R_{B^K}}(X) \subseteq \underline{R_{B^K}}(Y)$,
(8) $X \subseteq Y \Rightarrow \overline{R_{B^K}}(X) \subseteq \overline{R_{B^K}}(Y)$,
(9) $\underline{R_{B^K}}(X \cup Y) \supseteq \underline{R_{B^K}}(X) \cup \underline{R_{B^K}}(Y)$,
(10) $\overline{R_{B^K}}(X \cap Y) \subseteq \overline{R_{B^K}}(X) \cap \overline{R_{B^K}}(Y)$,
(11) $\underline{R_{B^K}}(X) \subseteq X \subseteq \overline{R_{B^K}}(X)$,
(12) $K_1 \preceq K_2 \Rightarrow \underline{R_{B^{K_2}}}(X) \subseteq \underline{R_{B^{K_1}}}(X)$,
(13) $K_1 \preceq K_2 \Rightarrow \overline{R_{B^{K_1}}}(X) \subseteq \overline{R_{B^{K_2}}}(X)$,

(14) $B \subseteq C \subseteq A \Rightarrow \underline{R_{B^K}}(X) \subseteq \underline{R_{C^K}}(X),$

(15) $B \subseteq C \subseteq A \Rightarrow \overline{R_{C^K}}(X) \subseteq \overline{R_{B^K}}(X).$

For $B \subseteq A$, $X \subseteq U$, and $K \in \mathcal{L}$, the accuracy of approximation of X w.r.t. B^K is defined as follows:

$$\alpha_{B^K}(X) = \frac{|\underline{R_{B^K}}(X)|}{|\overline{R_{B^K}}(X)|},$$

where $|X|$ is the cardinality of X, and, for the empty set $\emptyset$, we define $\alpha_{B^K}(\emptyset) = 1$. Clearly, if $K_1, K_2 \in \mathcal{L}$ and $K_1 \preceq K_2$, then

$$\alpha_{B^{K_2}}(X) \leq \alpha_{B^{K_1}}(X).$$

By employing Theorem 1 and Proposition 3, we can conclude following:

Proposition 4. *Let $S = (U, A)$ be a generalized multi-scale information table and $\mathcal{L}$ the scale collection of S. For $B \subseteq A$, and $K, K_1, K_2 \in \mathcal{L}$, denote*

$$\mathrm{Bel}_{B^K}(X) = P(\underline{R_{B^K}}(X)) = \frac{|\underline{R_{B^K}}(X)|}{|U|}, \ \forall X \in \mathcal{P}(U),$$
$$\mathrm{Pl}_{B^K}(X) = P(\overline{R_{B^K}}(X)) = \frac{|\overline{R_{B^K}}(X)|}{|U|}, \ \forall X \in \mathcal{P}(U).$$

Then $\mathrm{Bel}_{B^K} : \mathcal{P}(U) \to [0, 1]$ and $\mathrm{Pl}_{B^K} : \mathcal{P}(U) \to [0, 1]$ are a dual pair of belief and plausibility functions on U, and the corresponding basic probability assignment $m_{B^K} : \mathcal{P}(U) \to [0, 1]$ is

$$m_{B^K}(Y) = \begin{cases} P(Y) = \frac{|Y|}{|U|}, & \text{if } Y \in U/R_{B^K}, \\ 0, & \text{otherwise.} \end{cases}$$

Moreover, the belief and plausibility functions satisfy the following properties:

(1) $K_1 \preceq K_2 \Rightarrow \mathrm{Bel}_{B^{K_2}}(X) \leq \mathrm{Bel}_{B^{K_1}}(X) \leq P(X),$
(2) $K_1 \preceq K_2 \Rightarrow P(X) \leq \mathrm{Pl}_{B^{K_1}}(X) \leq \mathrm{Pl}_{B^{K_2}}(X),$
(3) $B \subseteq C \subseteq A \Rightarrow \mathrm{Bel}_{B^K}(X) \leq \mathrm{Bel}_{C^K}(X) \leq P(X) \leq \mathrm{Pl}_{C^K}(X) \leq \mathrm{Pl}_{B^K}(X).$

4   Optimal Scale Selections in Consistent Generalized Multi-scale Decision Tables

Knowledge acquisition in the sense of rule induction from a multi-scale decision table is an important issue. As we know not all decision tables (corresponding to all scale combinations) are consistent with some requirements to the decision table under the finest level of scale. So, it is critical to select the optimal level of details corresponding a suitable decision table before decision rules are produced. In this section, we study optimal scale selections in consistent generalized multi-scale decision tables.

Definition 9. *A generalized multi-scale decision table S is referred to as consistent if the decision table under the finest level of scale $K_0 = (1, 1, \ldots, 1)$, $S^{K_0} = (U, \{a_j^1 | j = 1, 2, \ldots, m\} \cup \{d\}) = (U, C^{K_0} \cup \{d\})$, is consistent, and S is called inconsistent if S^{K_0} is an inconsistent decision table.*

For a consistent generalized multi-scale decision table $S = (U, C \cup \{d\}) = (U, \{a_j^k | k = 1, 2, \ldots, I_j, j = 1, 2, \ldots, m\} \cup \{d\})$, we have $R_{C^{K_0}} \subseteq R_d$. For $K, H \in \mathcal{L}$ with $K \prec H$, if S^H is a consistent decision table, i.e. $R_{C_H} \subseteq R_d$, then, by Proposition 2, it can be observed that $R_{C^K} \subseteq R_{C_H} \subseteq R_d$. Hence, S^K is also a consistent decision table.

In [4], Li and Hu defined the concept of "optimal scales combination" in lattice model as follows:

Definition 10 [4]. *Let S be a consistent generalized multi-scale decision table and $\mathcal{L}$ the scale collection of S. For $K \in \mathcal{L}$, denote $Q(K) = \{K' \in \mathcal{L} | K \preceq K'\}$. K is called optimal scales combination if S^K is consistent and $S^{K'}$ (if there exists $K' \in Q(K)$) is inconsistent.*

Remark 1. If $H, K, K' \in \mathcal{L}$, $K \prec H \prec K'$, both of S^K and S^H are consistent, and $S^{K'}$ is inconsistent, then, according to Definition 10, K and H are all "optimal scales combinations", thus, the concept of an optimal scale combination in Definition 10 is unreasonable and we make a reasonable definition of an optimal scale combination as follows:

Definition 11. *For a consistent generalized multi-scale decision table S and $K \in \mathcal{L}$, if S^K is a consistent decision table and S^H is an inconsistent decision table for all $H \in \mathcal{L}$ with $K \prec H$, then K is said to be an optimal scale combination of S.*

According to Definition 11, we can see that an optimal scale combination of a consistent multi-scale decision table is one of the best scales for decision making or classification in the multi-scale decision table. And K is an optimal scale if and only if K is a maximal scale combination in $\mathcal{L}$ such that S^K is a consistent decision table.

Consider Example 3.3 in [4].

Example 1. Table 1 depicts an example of a consistent generalized multi-scale decision table $(U, C \cup \{d\})$, where $U = \{x_1, x_2, \ldots, x_{12}\}$ and $C = \{a_1, a_2, a_3, a_4\}$, a_1 has two levels of scales while the others have three, where "E", "G", "F", "B", "S", "M", "L", "Y", and "N" stand for, respectively, "Excellent", "Good", "Fair", "Bad", "Small", "Medium", "Large", "Yes", and "No". $V_{a_1^1} = V_{a_1^2} = \{1, 2, 3, 4, 5, 6\}$, $V_{a_1^3} = \{1, 2, 3, 4, 5\}$, $V_{a_1^4} = \{1, 2, 3, 4\}$, $V_{a_2^1} = V_{a_2^2} = \{E, G, F, B\}$, $V_{a_2^3} = V_{a_4^2} = \{S, M, L\}$, and $V_{a_3^3} = V_{a_3^3} = V_{a_4^3} = \{Y, N\}$. Granular information transformation functions can be seen directly from Table 1, for example, $g_1^{1,2}(1) = E$, $g_1^{1,2}(2) = g_1^{1,2}(3) = G$, $g_1^{1,2}(4) = F$, $g_1^{1,2}(5) = g_1^{1,2}(6) = B$, and $g_4^{2,3}(S) = Y$, $g_4^{2,3}(M) = g_4^{2,3}(L) = N$.

Let $K_1 = (2, 2, 3, 3)$, it can be calculated that $R_{C^{K_1}} \subseteq R_d$ and $R_{C^{(2,3,3,3)}} \nsubseteq R_d$, notice that $K = (2, 3, 3, 3)$ is the unique scale combination in $\mathcal{L}$ such that

Table 1. An example of consistent generalized multi-scale decision table

U	a_1^1	a_1^2	a_2^1	a_2^2	a_2^3	a_3^1	a_3^2	a_3^3	a_4^1	a_4^2	a_4^3	d
x_1	1	E	1	E	Y	1	S	Y	1	S	Y	1
x_2	2	G	2	E	Y	1	S	Y	1	S	Y	1
x_3	3	G	3	G	Y	2	S	Y	2	S	Y	1
x_4	4	F	4	F	N	3	M	N	3	M	N	2
x_5	5	B	5	F	N	4	L	N	4	L	N	1
x_6	6	B	6	B	N	5	L	N	4	L	N	1
x_7	4	F	4	F	N	1	S	Y	1	S	Y	2
x_8	5	B	5	F	N	1	S	Y	1	S	Y	2
x_9	6	B	6	B	N	2	S	Y	2	S	Y	1
x_{10}	4	F	4	F	N	3	M	N	1	S	Y	2
x_{11}	5	B	5	F	N	4	L	N	1	S	Y	1
x_{12}	6	B	6	B	N	5	L	N	2	S	Y	1

$K_1 \prec K$, so, by Definition 11, $K_1 = (2,2,3,3)$ is an optimal scale combination of S. Similarly, it can be checked that $K_2 = (1,3,3,3,), K_3 = (2,3,1,3)$, and $K_4 = (2,3,3,1)$ are also optimal scale combinations of S.

Let $K_4 = (2,2,2,2)$, according to Definition 10, it can be seen that K_4 is an optimal scale combination of S. Since $K_4 \prec K_1 = (2,2,3,3)$ and $R_{C^{K_1}} \subseteq R_d$, K_4 is not an optimal scale combination in the sense of Definition 11. Hence, we see that Definition 10 is unreasonable.

The following two theorems show that belief and plausibility functions of Dempster-Shafer theory of evidence can be used to determine an optimal scale combination.

Theorem 2. *Let* $S = (U, C \cup \{d\}) = (U, \{a_j^k | k = 1,2,\ldots,I_j, j = 1,2,\ldots,m\} \cup \{d\})$ *be a consistent generalized multi-scale decision table and* $\mathcal{L}$ *the scale collection of* S. *Then, for* $K = (k_1, k_2, \ldots, k_m) \in \mathcal{L}$, *the following statements are equivalent:*

(1) $S^K = (U, \{a_j^{k_j} | j = 1,2,\ldots,m\} \cup \{d\})$ *is a consistent decision table, i.e.,* $R_{C^K} \subseteq R_d$,

(2) $\sum\limits_{j=1}^{r} \mathrm{Bel}_{C^K}(D_j) = 1$,

(3) $\sum\limits_{j=1}^{r} \mathrm{Pl}_{C^K}(D_j) = 1$.

Proof. "(1) $\Rightarrow$ (2)" For any $j \in \{1,2,\ldots,r\}$, denote

$$\mathcal{J}_{C^K}(D_j) = \{[y]_{C^K} \in U/R_{C^K} | [y]_{C^K} \subseteq D_j\}.$$

Since $R_{C^K} \subseteq R_d$, we see that $\mathcal{J}_{C^K}(D_j)$ forms a partition of D_j. Then we have

$$\mathrm{Bel}_{C^K}(D_j) = \sum\{m_{C^K}(X)|X \subseteq D_j\}$$

$$= \sum\{m_{C^K}([x]_{C^K})|[x]_{C^K} \in U/R_{C^K}, [x]_{C^K} \subseteq D_j\}$$

$$= \sum\{m_{C^K}([x]_{C^K})|[x]_{C^K} \in \mathcal{J}_{C^K}(D_j)\}$$

$$= \sum\{P([x]_{C^K})|[x]_{C^K} \in \mathcal{J}_{C^K}(D_j)\} = P(D_j).$$

It follows that

$$\sum_{j=1}^{r} \mathrm{Bel}_{C^K}(D_j) = \sum_{j=1}^{r} P(D_j) = 1.$$

"(2) $\Rightarrow$ (1)" Assume that $\sum_{j=1}^{r} \mathrm{Bel}_{C^K}(D_j) = 1$. By Proposition 4, we observe that

$$\mathrm{Bel}_{C^K}(D_j) \leq P(D_j) = \frac{|D_j|}{|U|}, \quad \forall j \in \{1, 2, \ldots, r\}.$$

Since $1 = \sum_{j=1}^{r} \mathrm{Bel}_{C^K}(D_j) \leq \sum_{j=1}^{r} P(D_j) = 1$, by Proposition 4 again, we can conclude that

$$\mathrm{Bel}_{C^K}(D_j) = P(D_j), \quad \forall j \in \{1, 2, \ldots, r\}.$$

From which we can see that $\{[x]_{C^K}|[x]_{C^K} \in U/R_{C^K}, [x]_{C^K} \subseteq D_j\}$ forms a partition of D_j. Since $\{D_j|j \in \{1, 2, \ldots, r\}\}$ is a partition of U, we conclude that $\{[x]_{C^K}|[x]_{C^K} \subseteq D_j, j \in \{1, 2, \ldots, r\}\}$ forms a partition of U. Hence, for any $x \in U$, there exists $j \in \{1, 2, \ldots, r\}$ such that $[x]_{C^K} \subseteq D_j$. Evidently,

$$x \in [x]_{C^K} \subseteq D_j \Longleftrightarrow [x]_d = D_j.$$

Thus, $[x]_{C^K} \subseteq [x]_d$ for all $x \in U$, that is, $R_{C^K} \subseteq R_d$.

"(1) $\Rightarrow$ (3)" Since $R_{C^K} \subseteq R_d$, we have $[x]_{C^K} \subseteq [x]_d$ for all $x \in U$. Define

$$\mathcal{J}_{C^K}(D_j) = \{[x]_{C^K} \in U/R_{C^K}|[x]_{C^K} \subseteq D_j\}, \quad j \in \{1, 2, \ldots, r\}.$$

It is easy to see from $R_{C^K} \subseteq R_d$ that $\mathcal{J}_{C^K}(D_j)$ forms a partition of D_j, and moreover,

$$[x]_{C^K} \cap D_j \neq \emptyset \Longleftrightarrow [x]_{C^K} \subseteq D_j, \quad \forall x \in U.$$

Hence

$$\mathrm{Pl}_{C^K}(D_j) = \sum\{m_{C^K}(Y)|Y \cap D_j \neq \emptyset\}$$

$$= \sum\{m_{C^K}([x]_{C^K})|[x]_{C^K} \in U/R_{C^K}, [x]_{C^K} \cap D_j \neq \emptyset\}$$

$$= \sum\{m_{C^K}([x]_{C^K})|[x]_{C^K} \in U/R_{C^K}, [x]_{C^K} \subseteq D_j\}$$

$$= \sum\{P([x]_{C^K})|[x]_{C^K} \in \mathcal{J}_{C^K}(D_j)\}$$

$$= P(D_j), \quad \forall j \in \{1, 2, \ldots, r\}.$$

It follows that

$$\sum_{j=1}^{r} \mathrm{Pl}_{C^K}(D_j) = \sum_{j=1}^{r} P(D_j) = 1.$$

"(3) $\Rightarrow$ (1)" Assume that $\sum_{j=1}^{r} \mathrm{Pl}_{C^K}(D_j) = 1$. Since S is consistent, by Proposition 4, we have $1 = \sum_{j=1}^{r} \mathrm{Pl}_{C^{K_0}}(D_j) \geq \sum_{j=1}^{r} \mathrm{Pl}_{C^K}(D_j) = 1$. Then, by Proposition 4 again, we have $\mathrm{Pl}_{C^K}(D_j) = \mathrm{Pl}_{C^{K_0}}(D_j) = P(D_j)$ for all $j \in \{1, 2, \ldots, r\}$, that is,

$$P(\overline{R_{C^K}}(D_j)) = P(\overline{R_{C^{K_0}}}(D_j)) = P(D_j), \forall j \in \{1, 2, \ldots, r\}.$$

By Proposition 3, we observe that $\overline{R_{C^K}}(D_j) \supseteq \overline{R_{C^{K_0}}}(D_j) \supseteq D_j$, then we conclude that $\overline{R_{C^K}}(D_j) = \overline{R_{C^{K_0}}}(D_j) = D_j$ for all $j \in \{1, 2, \ldots, r\}$. Thus

$$\overline{R_{C^K}}([x]_d) = \overline{R_{C^{K_0}}}([x]_d) = [x]_d, \qquad \forall x \in U.$$

Given $x \in U$ and for any $y \in [x]_{C^K}$, notice that $[y]_{C^K} = [x]_{C^K}$, then $[y]_{C^K} \cap [x]_d = [x]_{C^K} \cap [x]_d \neq \emptyset$, that is, $y \in \overline{R_{C^K}}([x]_d) = [x]_d$, and in turn, $[x]_{C^K} \subseteq [x]_d$. It follows that $R_{C^K} \subseteq R_d$.

According to Theorem 2, we can conclude following:

Theorem 3. *Let $S = (U, C \cup \{d\}) = (U, \{a_j^k | k = 1, 2, \ldots, I_j, j = 1, 2, \ldots, m\} \cup \{d\})$ be a consistent generalized multi-scale decision table and $\mathcal{L}$ the scale collection of S. Then, for $K \in \mathcal{L}$, the following statements are equivalent:*

(1) *K is an optimal scale combination of S,*

(2) *$\sum_{j=1}^{r} \mathrm{Bel}_{C^K}(D_j) = 1$. And for any $H \in \mathcal{L}$ with $K \prec H$,*

$$\sum_{j=1}^{r} \mathrm{Bel}_{C^H}(D_j) < 1.$$

(3) *$\sum_{j=1}^{r} \mathrm{Pl}_{C^K}(D_j) = 1$. And for any $H \in \mathcal{L}$ with $K \prec H$,*

$$\sum_{j=1}^{r} \mathrm{Pl}_{C^H}(D_j) > 1.$$

Example 2. (Continued from Example 1). For the consistent multi-scale decision table $S = (U, C \cup \{d\})$ of Example 1, let $K_1 = (2, 2, 3, 3)$, it can be calculated that

$$\mathrm{Bel}_{C^{K_1}}(D_1) + \mathrm{Bel}_{C^{K_1}}(D_2) = 1,$$
$$\mathrm{Pl}_{C^{K_1}}(D_1) + \mathrm{Pl}_{C^{K_1}}(D_2) = 1,$$

and, for $K = (2, 3, 3, 3)$, it can be conclude that

$\mathrm{Bel}_{C^K}(D_1) + \mathrm{Bel}_{C^K}(D_2) = 10/12 < 1,$
$\mathrm{Pl}_{C^K}(D_1) + \mathrm{Pl}_{C^K}(D_2) = 14/12 > 1.$

Notice that $K = (2,3,3,3)$ is the unique scale combination in $\mathcal{L}$ such that $K_1 \prec K$, so, according to Theorem 3, $K_1 = (2,2,3,3)$ is an optimal scale combination of S. Similarly, it can be checked that $K_2 = (1,3,3,3,)$, $K_3 = (2,3,1,3)$, and $K_4 = (2,3,3,1)$ are also optimal scale combinations of S.

5 Conclusion

Optimal scale selection is a main issue in the study of knowledge representation and knowledge discovery in multi-scale decision tables. In [4], Li and Hu studied optimal scale selection for multi-scale decision tables with an assumption that diverse attributes may have different numbers of levels of granulations. We found that the definition of "optimal scales combinations" of the lattice model in [4] is unreasonable. We have redefined in this paper the concept of optimal scale combinations in generalized multi-scale decision tables. We have also used belief and plausibility functions in the Dempster-Shafer theory of evidence to characterize optimal scale combinations in consistent generalized multi-scale decision tables. In the further study, on one hand, optimal scale selections in various situations for inconsistent generalized multi-scale decision tables are interesting issues. On the other hand, since scale combinations in generalized multi-scale decision tables are very high, study on algorithms to select optimal scale combinations is also an important topics.

Acknowledgement. This work was supported by grants from the National Natural Science Foundation of China (Nos. 61573321, 41631179, and 61602415) and the Open Foundation from Marine Sciences in the Most Important Subjects of Zhejiang (No. 20160102).

References

1. Greco, S., Matarazzo, B., Slowinski, R.: Rough sets theory for multicriteria decision analysis. Eur. J. Oper. Res. **129**, 1–47 (2001)
2. Gu, S.M., Wu, W.Z.: On knowledge acquisition in multi-scale decision systems. Int. J. Mach. Learn. Cybernet. **4**, 477–486 (2013)
3. Gu, S.-M., Wu, W.-Z.: Knowledge acquisition in inconsistent multi-scale decision systems. In: Yao, J.T., Ramanna, S., Wang, G., Suraj, Z. (eds.) RSKT 2011. LNCS, vol. 6954, pp. 669–678. Springer, Heidelberg (2011). doi:10.1007/978-3-642-24425-4_84
4. Li, F., Hu, B.Q.: A new approach of optimal scale selection to multi-scale decision tables. Inf. Sci. **381**, 193–208 (2017)
5. Li, J.H., Ren, Y., Mei, C.L., et al.: A comparative study of multigranulation rough sets and concept lattices via rule acquisition. Knowl.-Based Syst. **91**, 152–164 (2016)
6. Pawlak, Z.: Rough sets. Int. J. Comput. Inform. Sci. **11**, 341–356 (1982)
7. Qian, Y.H., Liang, J.Y., Dang, C.Y.: Incomplete multi-granulation rough set. IEEE Trans. Syst. Man Cybernet. **40**, 420–431 (2010)

8. Qian, Y.H., Liang, J.Y., Yao, Y.Y., et al.: MGRS: a multi-granulation rough set. Inf. Sci. **180**, 949–970 (2010)
9. Qian, Y.H., Zhang, H., Sang, Y.L., et al.: Multigranulation decision-theoretic rough sets. Int. J. Approx. Reason. **55**, 225–237 (2014)
10. Shafer, G.: A Mathematical Theory of Evidence. Princeton University Press, Princeton (1976)
11. Shao, M.W., Zhang, W.X.: Dominance relation and rules in an incomplete ordered information system. Int. J. Intell. Syst. **20**, 13–27 (2005)
12. She, Y.H., Li, J.H., Yang, H.L.: A local approach to rule induction in multi-scale decision tables. Knowl.-Based Syst. **89**, 398–410 (2015)
13. Wu, W.Z., Gu, S.M., Wang, X.: Information granules in multi-scale ordered information systems. In: Proceedings of the 2015 International Conference on Machine Learning and Cybernetics, Holiday Inn, Guangzhou, 12–15 July 2015, pp. 182–187 (2015)
14. Wu, W.Z., Leung, Y.: Theory and applications of granular labelled partitions in multi-scale decision tables. Inf. Sci. **181**, 3878–3897 (2011)
15. Wu, W.Z., Leung, Y.: Optimal scale selection for multi-scale decision tables. Int. J. Approx. Reason. **54**, 1107–1129 (2013)
16. Wu, W.Z., Qian, Y.H., Li, T.J., et al.: On rule acquisition in incomplete multi-scale decision tables. Inf. Sci. **378**, 282–302 (2017)
17. Xu, W.H.: Ordered Information Systems and Rough Sets. Science Press, Beijing (2012)
18. Yang, X.B., Song, X.N., Chen, Z.H., et al.: On multigranulation rough sets in incomplete information system. Int. J. Mach. Learn. Cybernet. **3**, 223–232 (2012)
19. Yao, Y.Y., Lingras, P.J.: Interpretations of belief functions in the theory of rough sets. Inf. Sci. **104**, 81–106 (1998)
20. Zhang, W.X., Leung, Y., Wu, W.Z.: Information Systems and Knowledge Discovery (in Chinese). Science Press, Beijing (2003)

A Framework for Analysis of Granular Neural Networks

Julian Skirzyński[(✉)]

University of Warsaw, Warsaw, Poland
j.skirzynski@student.uw.edu.pl

Abstract. Granular neural networks are neural networks which operate at the level of information granules. Granules, in turn, can be seen as collections of objects that exhibit similar structure or possess similar functionality. In this work we try to provide a comprehensive look at the problem of how granular, feed-forward neural networks conduct their computations, i.e. what is the interpretation for the connections and the neurons of such networks. The paper orbits around the assumption that the networks come from the superposition of their certain subnetworks which emulate membership functions for the granules. The superposition represents an aggregation of a certain number of granules into another one. This interpretation comes from a general granular tree-model that is constructed prior to the network and which describes a particular problem in a semantically understandable form.

Keywords: Framework · Neural networks · Granules · Granular computing · Granular neural networks · Information aggregation

1 Introduction

According to granular computing conceptualization (read more in [1,13,15,20]) all the information taking part in a reasoning process is interpreted, and then processed in terms of information granules. Granules can be seen as possibly non-disjoint collections of objects exhibiting similar structure or behavior, i.e. objects that are close to each other with regards to some measure of similarity. To this date, the most common formal models include intervals, fuzzy sets, rough sets, fuzzy-rough sets, shadowed sets and probability calculus [5,6,8,10–12,16,19].

In this work we are concerned with the interpretation for feed-forward, numerical granular neural networks (GNNs) and the description of processes occurring in the course of their signal propagation. A step-by-step construction of a GNN has not been fully covered yet, though it should be noted Pedrycz and Vukovich [16] or Song and Pedrycz [17] made an attempt to sketch an overall (yet sometimes vague) model. The approach presented herein can be put briefly the following way: A GNN is the lower level of creation of a granular model, a level of implementation. The higher level, depicted as a tree with possibly many roots, is the level of granules which we know in what structure should be aggregated to derive to the goal concept and this constitutes a part of our domain

© Springer International Publishing AG 2017
L. Polkowski et al. (Eds.): IJCRS 2017, Part I, LNAI 10313, pp. 199–206, 2017.
DOI: 10.1007/978-3-319-60837-2_16

knowledge. Besides the initial granules constructed from the data though, we do not know the exact form of other aggregated granules from this tree. A granular neural network then, is a network consisting of subnetworks each of which learns to emulate a function describing each of such granules, i.e. it models how the membership for one of the tree's nodes is computed from the memberships of its sons (for membership value see section below). Ideas similar to those elaborated in this work can be found in [18]. More details regarding hierarchical classifiers are discussed in [2, 9].

The paper is constructed as follows. The Sect. 2 lays some basic assumptions regarding the structure of a GNN. The Sect. 3 introduces common-sense framework for granular aggregation and sketches an example. It is followed by a discussion on framework's strengths and limitations. The work ends with a short summary.

2   GNN Axioms

This section is devoted to introduction of certain propositions regarding GNNs in general. To understand them in full, it should be firstly noted that each of the formalisms for describing information granules presents an entity of a set-alike structure (e.g. each can contain elements). Additionally, the granules are all understood in terms of some functions that can be used as their equivalent definitions. In case of a standard, crisp set it is obviously a characteristic function which describes it and for an information granule it is a membership function.

Remark 1. Further in the text we will use the word membership function (value) as a general name for a function (a value) describing any information granule, whether it is a rough set, a probabilistic set, an interval, etc.

(1) **Axiom of input neurons.** *All the input neurons represent granules created from the original data that was in our possession, and the input values for a GNN are the membership values of those data points to every of the granules.*

(2) **Axiom of subnetworks' homogeneity.** *All the neurons of a granular neural network are used to emulate granules of the same type (same formal model).*

(3) **Axiom of available data.** *For each of the raw data points we start from (input), we are able to determine the correct membership value of the topmost aggregation (output) and a value for an arbitrary, non-ultimate aggregation.*

By **(1)** we actually equate the input level of the network with the leaves level of the granulation tree. In **(2)**, if a GNN was constructed to process information encoded, say, in terms of fuzzy sets, then each subnetwork used in the creation of a GNN also computes the membership function of a fuzzy set. In particular, this assumption guarantees that the network does not generate granules of higher types such that contain other granules in them etc. [14]. By acknowledging **(3)** we make sure that the data we possess enable us to train a subnetwork for the function in each node of the granules' aggregation tree.

3   GNN as a Robust Tool for Information Aggregation

In this section we present the framework for analysis of GNNs in detail. The main idea orbits around the notion that given some task and universe of our raw data X we are able to represent the problem in a granular form by forming some kind of a granulation tree which is a semantic model of the issue at hand (see Fig. 1). By Axiom (3), we can specify membership values for each of the nodes of this tree. In general, finding these numbers is deeply an unobvious task which has been under the scope of many research endeavors in the recent years, e.g. [3,7]. A solution which has been often proposed is to transform linguistic descriptions provided by experts into their numerical counterpart. A different way could be to extrapolate the values for the granules with the help of the data we start from (e.g. with a weighted mean, etc.). Given the abstract model of the problem and a sample of input-output pairs we translate it to a more down-to-earth specification, namely a neural network which performs the task in question robustly. This network is a GNN.

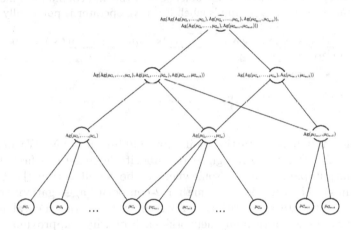

Fig. 1. A tree structure for granular aggregation. Lines connecting the nodes represent the fact that from a given set of granules, another granule emerges through the aggregation operator.

First, consider Fig. 1 which presents a hierarchical model with a tree structure for information granules aggregation. Here, we treat a granule as equivalent to its membership function. Ag (written on top of the nodes) are unknown aggregation operators (possibly different for each node) which transform a given set of granules into another granule keeping the formal model of its components. μ_{G_i}'s (written on top of the input nodes) are membership functions for known granules G_i (the ones we create from the data). The tree itself is generated using rich domain knowledge which enables us to state exactly which notions of higher order that are represented by the granules we need, and what those notions consist of, i.e. which granules are used as arguments to the aggregation operator.

3.1 Overall Framework

Now we can present the framework for a GNN interpretation.

Using the knowledge we possess, we first build the granulation tree. Then, we compose granules $G_1, \ldots, G_l$ that somehow describe the elements in X. Using axioms (1) and (3) we know that for any of their aggregation and all the subsequent aggregations we are able to provide some number of input-output pairs. Let's present our partial data regarding the granules in a table form (Table 1).

Definition 1. *We will call an aggregation n-composite if it has a $n-1$-composite aggregation as one of its arguments. A 1-composite aggregation is just* $\mathrm{Ag}(\ldots)$.

Table 1. Table presenting membership values $(a, b, c, \ldots, z$ labeled by pairs of natural numbers) for all the granules of the granulation tree. We assume there are l leaves, k 1-composite aggregations, ..., p the highest level-composite aggregations (roots of the granulation tree). Each element in the table, besides the first column, is a membership value to a granule given as a column's label. Each Ag operator is potentially different.

X	G_1	...	G_l	$\mathrm{Ag}(\ldots)$	...	$\mathrm{Ag}(\ldots)$	$\mathrm{Ag}(\mathrm{Ag}(\ldots), \ldots, \mathrm{Ag}(\ldots))$	...	$\mathrm{Ag}(\ldots(\mathrm{Ag}(\ldots), \ldots, \mathrm{Ag}(\ldots))\ldots)$
x_1	a_{11}	...	a_{l1}	b_{11}	...	b_{k1}	c_{11}		z_{p1}
x_2	a_{12}	...	a_{l2}	b_{12}	...	b_{k2}	c_{12}		z_{p2}
...	...	...	...	...	...	...	...	...	...
x_n	a_{1n}	...	a_{ln}	b_{1n}	...	b_{kn}	c_{1n}		z_{pn}

This information is a starting point for building a GNN. We begin with training neural networks to recognize 1-composite aggregations first, based on the input-output pairs that are somewhere to be found within the table (G_1 to G_l columns). Then we do the same for 2-composite aggregations, etc. until we reach the ultimate aggregations for which we also train neural networks. After this process we have many networks each of which approximates one of the nodes of the granulation tree. Obviously, each has just one output neuron. We now superpose these networks preserving the structure of the tree, i.e. by "substituting" each tree's node with a trained network and connecting its output neuron to a correct input neuron of the higher aggregation network with an arbitrary weight. The resulting ANN is a GNN. It is later possible to tune it a bit if we have some examples for training left, but even without doing so we already created a granular neural network. Recapitulation of the procedure is presented in Procedure 1 box.

3.2 A Schematic Example

Let's consider an example of a GNN construction in the scheme we developed above. Suppose our problem concerns music genre recognition or equivalently, song classification. Assume the training set consists of songs represented as time series and the main task is to label such an element of a larger information system

Procedure 1. Steps involved in the advent of a granular neural network

1. Based on the problem in question create a granulation tree which represents how to tackle the problem starting from the elements in the universe X.
2. Create basic, leaves granules from the data and set them as input neurons to the network.
3. Create input-output pairs for each of the aggregation nodes of the tree created in 1.
4. Using data points from 3, train neural subnetworks on each of the aggregations represented by nodes of the tree in 1.
5. Superpose resulting subnetworks into a bigger network.
6. (Optionally) refine all the connection weights, or at least the ones which were newly formed, with new examples.

(with possibly thousands of attributes extracted from the series or representing the series itself) with one of the two classes: rock or classic.

First, equipped with a rich, musical knowledge and using help of various sound producers, record producers, musicians, etc., we may construct one possible way of semantic representation of the problem at hand (see Fig. 2). Here, the top-most aggregation is a granule denoting the genre itself, and as our decision is binary we might assume lower membership values indicate rock, and higher, classical music. It is aggregated from granules standing for the tempo, intensity, pleasantness, harmony and structurality, all fairly difficult to describe with the means of the time series attributes' only. Hence, they are decomposed to simpler entities, with all of those also requiring decomposition. Finally, we get the leaves level of the tree with the granules for numeric amount of particular instruments in certain time intervals, e.g. every $\frac{1}{10}$-th of the musical piece. We assume these non-composite granules are of a certain form, e.g. of triangular fuzzy sets form with parameters extracted from the available data or chosen arbitrarily. The construction of a proper membership function is another interesting issue, however, it falls out of the scope of this paper to discuss it thoroughly. Assuming it was manageable to construct those functions, we set the input neurons of our network to receive numerical data from their outputs on the raw time series representing the songs.

Table 2. Table presenting normalized membership values for all the granules of the granulation tree in Fig. 2.

Song	Instrument 1	...	Instrument N	Drums, $\frac{1}{10}$-th	...	Dynamics		Genre
s_1	0.3	...	0	0.44	...	0.9	...	0.38
s_2	0	...	1	0.05	...	0.02	...	0.93
...	...	...	...	...	...	...	...	...
s_n	0.78	...	0.5	0.75	...	0.2	...	0.04

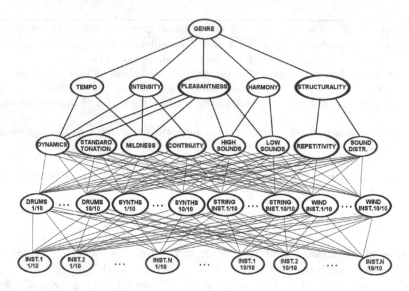

Fig. 2. A tree structure for song's genre recognition. Fractions appearing in some of the nodes denote parts of the song in which we measure a given quantity, e.g. 2/10 means we take time interval that covers the second tenth of the whole recording. There are N instruments. Lines connecting the nodes represent the fact that from a given set of granules, another granule emerges through the aggregation operator.

Now, we ask the experts for their assistance once more and request them to (qualitatively) describe the amount of wind instruments, string instruments, electronics, etc., in a song, (qualitatively) measure its harmony, structurality, continuity, calmful tonation, pleasantness and so on until we get all the data points in our possession labeled. This gives us a linguistic characterization of the granules that shall be now translated to numerical values. This, again, is a tremendous leap to make which nevertheless does not concern the matter of this paper.

After the process of decoding word instructions to quantitative data we might obtain a table as presented in Table 2. The next step is to take a 1-composite granule, e.g. *the amount of string instruments in the first $\frac{1}{10}$-th of the song*, and with the help of the data in Table 2 try to construct a neural network which could learn to emulate the aggregation operator. In this particular case we would look for a network which has $10N$ input nodes, for all the instruments, and one output node. For the *harmony* granule we would take two inputs (*equanimity, structurality*) and one output, etc. After a successfull construction, we take another k-composite aggregations until we "ticked" them all.

Finally, we substitute the nodes of the granulation tree with the subnetworks and superpose them by connecting their outputs accordingly. At the very end, we can test the working of such a GNN with new examples and tune some connection weights if necessary.

4   Discussion

The proposition put forth by this paper is that the new models of numerical granular neural networks should try to follow the steps recapitulated in Procedure 1, as the outcome of this process is a network that is intelligible because of its inspiration in higher level analysis of the problem. Thanks to that, GNNs lose some of their black-box character, in a sense that it becomes apparent what happens to the granules at the input, how they are transformed, etc. A GNN differs from standard ANNs in that it was created as an implementation of a model from non-numerical level. The input neurons represent the granules that are leaves of the granulation tree but later these are whole parts of the network that act similarly. Connections do not have any granular interpretation.

One major drawback of the approach we employed is that there is no place for granules of higher order in that understanding. It still poses a great issue of how to implement higher-order granules into the numerical level (for interval-valued fuzzy sets cf. [4]), which is certainly a huge downside in the case of neural networks. Nevertheless, in GNNs it seems like a natural process for an aggregation operator to return a granule that is more general not only in its interpretation but also in structure. Hence, we could potentially gain a more beneficial insight into the problem if we decided to dismiss Axiom (2).

5   Summary

Throughout this paper we tried to lay foundations for building a framework for analysis of granular feed-forward neural networks. The main idea that was presented in the paper stated that a GNN is a numerical level made from a granular model of the problem which had a form of a tree. Conforming to three axioms the network imitated the tree using subnetworks for training each of its nodes.

On the other hand, an approach which was not discussed in this work is the topic of a GNN and granules of higher types, like interval fuzzy sets, etc. There is still no acknowledged way in which so-called type-n granules could be implemented in an ANN which served as the main reason for omitting deliberations on this issue. For later work however, a careful research on this problem may provide valuable insights into the field of granular computing in general. As the presented scheme is also very general it may be beneficial to specify the construction of the GNN's subnetworks in more detail, tackle the problem of developing quantitative data for training them, and use the framework in a practical application.

References

1. Bargiela, A., Pedrycz, W.: Granular Computing: An Introduction. Kluwer Academic Publishers, Boston (2003). doi:10.1007/978-1-4615-1033-8
2. Bazan, J.G.: Hierarchical classifiers for complex spatio-temporal concepts. In: Peters, J.F., Skowron, A., Rybiński, H. (eds.) Transactions on Rough Sets IX. LNCS, vol. 5390, pp. 474–750. Springer, Heidelberg (2008). doi:10.1007/978-3-540-89876-4_26

3. Dong, Y., Xu, Y., Yu, S.: Computing the numerical scale of the linguistic term set for the 2-tuple fuzzy linguistic representation model. IEEE Trans. Fuzzy Syst. **17**(6), 1366–1378 (2009). doi:10.1109/TFUZZ.2009.2032172

4. Dubois, D., Prade, H.: Interval-valued fuzzy sets, possibility theory and imprecise probability. In: Proceedings of International Conference in Fuzzy Logic and Technology, pp. 314–319 (2005)

5. Ganivada, A., Dutta, S., Sankar, K.P.: Fuzzy rough granular neural networks, fuzzy granules, and classification. Theoret. Comput. Sci. **412**, 5834–5843 (2011). doi:10.1016/j.tcs.2011.05.038

6. Ganivada, A., Ray, S.S., Sankar, K.P.: Fuzzy rough sets, and a granular neural network for unsupervised feature selection. Neural Netw. **48**, 91–108 (2013). doi:10.1016/j.neunet.2013.07.008

7. Herrera, F., Alonso, S., Chiclana, F., Herrera-Viedma, E.: Computing with words in decision making: foundations, trends and prospects. Fuzzy Optim. Decis. Making **8**(4), 337–364 (2009). doi:10.1007/s10700-009-9065-2

8. Hirota, K.: Concepts of probabilistic sets. Fuzzy Sets Syst. **5**, 31–46 (1981). doi:10.1109/CDC.1977.271516

9. Nguyen, S.H., Bazan, J., Skowron, A., Nguyen, H.S.: Layered learning for concept synthesis. In: Peters, J.F., Skowron, A., Grzymała-Busse, J.W., Kostek, B., Świniarski, R.W., Szczuka, M.S. (eds.) Transactions on Rough Sets I. LNCS, vol. 3100, pp. 187–208. Springer, Heidelberg (2004). doi:10.1007/978-3-540-27794-1_9

10. Pawlak, Z.: Rough sets. Int. J. Comput. Inform. Sci. **11**(5), 341–356 (1982). doi:10.1007/BF01001956

11. Pedrycz, W.: Shadowed sets: representing and processing fuzzy sets. IEEE Trans. Syst. Man Cybern. Part B (Cybern.) **28**(1), 103–109 (1998). doi:10.1109/3477.658584

12. Pedrycz, W.: Interpretation of clusters in the framework of shadowed sets. Pattern Recogn. Lett. **26**, 2439–2449 (2005). doi:10.1016/j.patrec.2005.05.001

13. Pedrycz, W.: Granular Computing: Analysis and Design of Intelligent Systems. CRC Press, Boca Raton (2013). doi:10.1201/b14862

14. Pedrycz, W.: Hierarchical granular clustering: an emergence of information granules of higher type and higher order. IEEE Trans. Fuzzy Syst. **23**(6), 2270–2283 (2015). doi:10.1109/TFUZZ.2015.2417896

15. Pedrycz, W., Skowron, A., Kreinovich, V. (eds.): Handbook of Granular Computing. Wiley, New York (2008). doi:10.1002/9780470724163

16. Pedrycz, W., Vukovich, G.: Granular neural networks. Neurocomputing **36**, 205–224 (2001). doi:10.1016/S0925-2312(00)00342-8

17. Song, M., Pedrycz, W.: From local neural networks to granular neural networks: a study in information granulation. Neurocomputing **74**, 3931–3940 (2011). doi:10.1016/j.neucom.2011.08.009

18. Szczuka, M., Skowron, A., Jankowski, A., Ślezak, D.: Granular systems: from granules to systems. In: Webster, J. (ed.) Wiley Encyclopedia of Electrical and Electronics Engineering. Wiley, Hoboken (2016). doi:10.1002/047134608X

19. Zadeh, L.A.: Fuzzy sets. Philos. Psychol. **8**, 333–353 (1965). doi:10.1016/S0019-9958(65)90241-X

20. Zadeh, L.A.: Toward a theory of fuzzy information granulation and its centrality in human reasoning and fuzzy logic. Fuzzy Sets Syst. **2**(1), 111–127 (1997). doi:10.1016/S0165-0114(97)00077-8

Petri Nets over Ontological Graphs: Conception and Application for Modelling Tasks of Robots

Jarosław Szkoła[1] and Krzysztof Pancerz[2(✉)]

[1] University of Information Technology and Management,
Sucharskiego Str. 2, 35-225 Rzeszów, Poland
jszkola@wsiz.rzeszow.pl
[2] Chair of Computer Science, Faculty of Mathematics and Natural Sciences,
University of Rzeszów, Prof. S. Pigonia Str. 1, 35-310 Rzeszów, Poland
kpancerz@ur.edu.pl

Abstract. On the one hand, Petri nets are a powerful graphical and formal tool to model real-life dynamic systems. Special attention in research and applications is focused on the so-called high-level Petri nets enabling us to obtain much more succinct and expressive descriptions than can be obtained by means of low-level Petri nets. On the other hand, ontologies specify the concepts and relationships among them comprising the vocabulary from real-life areas. In the paper, we propose a new model of high-level Petri nets, called Petri nets over ontological graphs. In the new model, we try to combine the graphic power of Petri nets with the semantic power of ontologies. The new type of Petri nets is used by us to model, at the abstract level, some tasks performed by robots.

Keywords: Petri nets · Ontological graphs · Semantics · Behaviour of robots

1 Introduction

Research on the development of autonomous robots is one of the fastest-growing scientific disciplines. In case of a mobile robot, one of the basic functions is moving in relation to its surroundings. The mobile autonomous robot performs its tasks in a specific period of time, without human intervention. One of the basic abilities of the robot is the capacity to independently create and execute action plans on the basis of observation of the environment. A navigation system is a complex control system with the feedback from the environment. Appropriate models are needed in terms of object recognition and control. The control algorithms are based on data recorded in a way that allows the robot to detect an association or aggregation between the objects. For this purpose, domain ontologies seem to be the most suitable choice (cf. [3]). The domain knowledge is stored in ontologies efficiently and unambiguously. The task of the robot is to recognize, in the environment, objects that can be named and next to find associations of these objects with other objects in ontologies. It gives information

© Springer International Publishing AG 2017
L. Polkowski et al. (Eds.): IJCRS 2017, Part I, LNAI 10313, pp. 207–214, 2017.
DOI: 10.1007/978-3-319-60837-2_17

what the abstraction level of recognized objects is. For example, the robot can recognize that the object is a specific plant or, in case of insufficient information, that the object is a plant, but it is unknown which one. Identifying the objects and their abstraction levels can be helpful to select further actions.

As a tool for modeling the robot tasks, we have selected Petri nets. Petri nets were developed by Petri [11] as a graphical and formal (mathematical) tool, among others, for describing information processing systems and modelling dynamic systems with distinguished states and transitions between states. In general, a Petri net structure has two types of nodes, places and transitions, and arcs connecting them. It is a bipartite graph, i.e., arcs cannot directly connect nodes of the same type. Two types of nodes in the Petri net structure are differentiated when it is drawn. The convention is to use circles to represent places and rectangles to represent transitions. There are many different classes of Petri nets extending the basic definition. Special attention in research and applications is focused on the so-called high-level Petri nets [5]. They enable us to obtain much more succinct and expressive descriptions than can be obtained by means of low-level Petri nets (e.g., place-transition nets [12]). The step from low-level nets to high-level nets is often compared to the step from assembly languages to modern high-level programming languages. In low-level nets, there is only one kind of tokens. In high-level nets, each token can carry complex information. In the paper, we propose a new model of high-level Petri nets, called Petri nets over ontological graphs. In the new model, we try to combine the graphic power of Petri nets with the semantic power of ontologies. Each token in Petri nets over ontological graphs corresponds to one concept from ontologies describing objects present in the modeled domain. The information carried by the token is much closer to the human perception. Therefore, analysis of such models is easier. Moreover, it enables us to define the conditions for firing transitions in a coherent way on the basis of linguistic semantics of tokens.

To our knowledge, none of the Petri net models use concepts as tokens and perform actions on the basis of linguistic semantics of tokens directly derived from ontologies. Some combinations of Petri nets and ontologies were earlier considered. In [13], Fuzzy semantic Petri nets were proposed as a subclass of colored Petri nets proposed by Jensen [4]. Fuzziness was introduced by equipping tokens with weights. However, concepts included in ontologies are not directly incorporated into tokens. Moreover, some high-level Petri nets with tokens belonging to the domains defined as abstract data types were considered in [2].

2   Petri Nets over Ontological Graphs

In this section, we recall basic notions concerning ontological graphs and semantic relations. Next, we define our new model called Petri nets over ontological graphs. Finally, we give a simple example explaining an idea of using Petri nets over ontological graphs in modeling some tasks performed by robots.

An ontology specifies the concepts and relationships among them comprising the vocabulary from a given area (cf. [9]). Formally, the ontology can be represented by means of graph structures (cf. [10]). In our approach, the graph representing the ontology $\mathcal{O}$ is called the ontological graph. Let $\mathcal{O}$ be a given ontology. An ontological graph is defined as

$$OG = (\mathcal{C}, E, \mathcal{R}, \rho),$$

where:

- $\mathcal{C}$ is the nonempty, finite set of nodes representing concepts in the ontology $\mathcal{O}$,
- $E \subseteq \mathcal{C} \times \mathcal{C}$ is the finite set of edges representing semantic relations between concepts from $\mathcal{C}$,
- $\mathcal{R}$ is the family of semantic descriptions (in a natural language) of types of relations (represented by edges) between concepts,
- $\rho : E \to \mathcal{R}$ is the function assigning a semantic description of the relation to each edge.

Let $OG = (\mathcal{C}, E, \mathcal{R}, \rho)$ be an ontological graph. We will use the following notation:

- $[c_i, c_j]$ - a simple path in OG between $c_i, c_j \in \mathcal{C}$,
- $\mathcal{E}([c_i, c_j])$ - a set of edges from E belonging to the simple path $[c_i, c_j]$,
- $\mathcal{P}(OG)$ - a set of all simple paths in OG.

In general, ontology can model various semantic relations between concepts. A comprehensive review of the literature concerning semantic relations is given in [8]. In the presented approach, our attention is focused on two fundamental paradigmatic semantic relations (or paradigmatic relations shortly) used in linguistics (cf. [6]), namely, synonymy and hyponymy. For simplicity, we will use the following labels for these paradigmatic relations:

- $R_\sim$ - synonymy,
- $R_\triangleleft$ - hyponymy.

Let $OG = (\mathcal{C}, E, \mathcal{R}, \rho)$ be an ontological graph. We are interested in three relations that can hold between two concepts $c, c' \in \mathcal{C}$:

- An exact meaning relation

$$EMR = \{(c, c') \in \mathcal{C} \times \mathcal{C} : c = c'\}$$

- A synonymous meaning relation

$$SMR = \{(c, c') \in \mathcal{C} \times \mathcal{C} : (c, c') \in E \text{ and } \rho((c, c')) = R_\sim\}.$$

- A generalization relation

$$GR = \{(c, c') \in \mathcal{C} \times \mathcal{C} : \underset{[c,c'] \in \mathcal{P}(OG_a)}{\exists} \underset{e \in \mathcal{E}([c,c'])}{\forall} \rho(e) \in \{R_\sim, R_\triangleleft\}\}.$$

It is worth noting that the relation GR is reflexive, i.e., each concept $c \in C$ is generalized by itself.

In description logics used in ontological modelling, there are two distinguished concepts with useful applications (cf. [1]), namely:

- $\top$ - the top concept, i.e., a concept with every individual as an instance.
- $\bot$ - the bottom concept, i.e., an empty concept with no individuals as instances.

The top concept is a concept that generalizes each concept present in a given ontology. The bottom concept will be called further, the empty concept.

We can build some formulas over the set of concepts C from the ontological graph $OG = (C, E, \mathcal{R}, \rho)$. In the presented approach, we will use formulas collected in Table 1. The semantics of a given formula ϕ built over the set of concepts C from the ontological graph OG, will be denoted by $||\phi||_{OG}$.

Table 1. Formulas built over the set of concepts from the ontological graph

Syntax	Semantics	Description
c	$c \in C$	An individual concept c
$c^=$	$\{c\}$	A set containing just an individual concept c
$c^{\approx}$	$\{c' \in C : (c', c) \in EMR$ or $(c', c) \in SMR\}$	A set containing an individual concept c and all of the synonyms of c
$c^{\leq}$	$\{c' \in C : c' \neq \bot$ and $(c', c) \in GR\}$	A set containing all of the concepts generalized by c (including c but excluding $\bot$)

Definition 1. *A marked Petri net over ontological graphs (PNOG) is a tuple*

$$PNOG = (Pl, Tr, \{OG_p\}_{p \in Pl}, Arc_{in}, Arc_{out}, Form_{in}, Form_{out}, Mark_0),$$

where:

- *Pl is the finite set of places,*
- *Tr is the finite set of transitions,*
- *$\{OG\}_{p \in Pl}$ is the family of ontological graphs associated with places,*
- *$Arc_{in} \subseteq Pl \times Tr$ is the set of input arcs (i.e., arcs from places to transitions),*
- *$Arc_{out} \subseteq Tr \times Pl$ is the set of output arcs (i.e., arcs from transitions to places),*
- *$Form_{in}$ is the input arc formula function mapping each input arc (p, t) to a formula $Form_{in}(p, t)$, such that:*

$$\mathop{\forall}_{(p,t) \in Arc_{in}} ||Form_{in}(p, t)||_{OG_p} \subseteq C_p,$$

– $Form_{out}$ is the output arc formula function mapping each output arc (t, p) to a formula $Form_{out}(t, p)$, such that:

$$\underset{(t,p)\in Arc_{out}}{\forall} \ ||Form_{out}(t, p)||_{OG_p} \in \mathcal{C}_p,$$

– $Mark_0$ is the initial marking function mapping each place p to $\{\bot\} \cup \mathcal{C}_p$,

and $\mathcal{C}_p$ is the set of concepts from the graph OG_p.

The initial marking function $Mark_0$ assigns concepts to places. The dynamics of a marked Petri net over ontological graphs $(PNOG)$ is given by firing enabled transitions causing the movement of concepts through the net. A mapping $Mark : Pl \rightarrow \{\bot\} \cup \mathcal{C}_p$ assigning concepts to places is called a marking of $PNOG$. A transition $t \in Tr$ is said to be enabled if and only if

1. $Mark(p) \in ||Form_{in}(p, t)||_{OG_p}$ for all $p \in Pl$ such that $(p, t) \in Arc_{in}$,
2. $Mark(p) = \bot$ for all $p \in Pl$ such that $(t, p) \in Arc_{out}$.

If, for $t \in Tr$, there is no $p \in Pl$ such that $(p, t) \in Arc_{in}$, then only condition (2) must be satisfied. When a transition $t \in Tr$ is enabled, we say that it can fire. After firing an enabled transition t, we obtain a new marking $Mark'$ of $PNOG$:

– $Mark'(p) = \bot$ for all $p \in Pl$ such that $(p, t) \in Arc_{in}$,
– $Mark'(p) = ||Form_{out}(t, p)||_{OG_p}$ for all $p \in Pl$ such that $(t, p) \in Arc_{out}$.
– $Mark'(p) = Mark(p)$, otherwise.

Now, we will show a simple example explaining an idea of using Petri nets over ontological graphs to model some tasks performed by the robot. Let us consider an agricultural robot intended to perform two basic actions. After recognizing a plant in its environment, the robot should either pull it out if it is a weed or water it if it is a vegetable. A part of the ontological graph $OG_{operations}$ describing operations that can be made by an agricultural robot is shown in Fig. 1(a). A part of the ontological graph OG_{plants} describing plants is shown in Fig. 1(b). It is worth noting that real-life ontological graphs are much more complex. Both ontological graphs are depicted as a hierarchy of classes in Protege. Protege [7] is a free, open source, platform-independent environment for creating and editing ontologies and knowledge bases. The top concept $\top$ is said to be *Thing* in the OWL ontologies created in Protege.

A marked Petri net over ontological graphs $(PNOG)$

$$PNOG = (Pl, Tr, \{OG_p\}_{p \in Pl}, Arc_{in}, Arc_{out}, Form_{in}, Form_{out}, Mark_0),$$

representing actions taken by an agricultural robot is shown in Fig. 2. For the net $PNOG$, we have:

– $Pl = \{pl_1, pl_2, pl_3\}$,
– $Tr = \{tr_1, tr_2, tr_3, tr_4, tr_5, tr_6, tr_7, tr_8, tr_9, tr_{10}\}$,
– $Mark_0(pl_1) = \bot$, $Mark_0(pl_2) = Searching$, $Mark_0(pl_3) = \bot$.

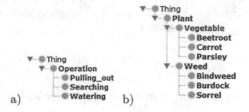

Fig. 1. Hierarchies of classes in Protege for: (a) a part of the ontological graph describing operations that can be made by an agricultural robot, (b) a part of the ontological graph describing plants

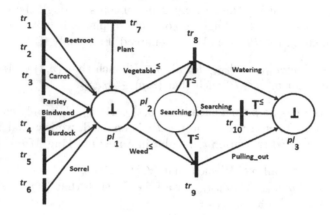

Fig. 2. A marked Petri net representing actions taken in one of tasks of an agricultural robot (an initial state)

An ontological graph associated with place pl_1 is shown in Fig. 1(b). An ontological graph associated with places pl_2 and pl_3 is shown in Fig. 1(a). The set Arc_{in} of input arcs, the set Arc_{out} of output arcs, the values of the input arc formula function $Form_{in}$, and the values of the output arc formula function $Form_{out}$ can be obtained from Fig. 2.

Place pl_1 represents an object recognized in the environment. It can be either a specific plant or a plant, in general, if no suitable information is provided. According to the token (concept) present in pl_1, one of the two actions can be selected. Petri nets over ontological graphs enable us to give succinct conditions for firing transitions. A formula on the input arc of transition tr_8 determines a more general class of plants, i.e., vegetables. For each vegetable, the action *Watering* is performed. Analogously, a formula on the input arc for transition tr_9 determines a more general class of plants, i.e., weeds. For each weed, the action *Pulling out* is performed. Figure 3 shows the marked Petri net representing actions taken in one of tasks of an agricultural robot after firing transition tr_5. At this state, transition tr_9 is enabled to fire. Figure 4 shows the marked Petri net after firing transition tr_9.

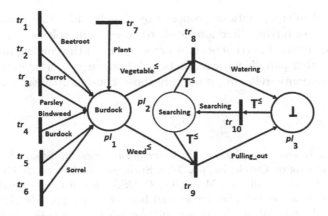

Fig. 3. A marked Petri net representing actions taken in one of tasks of an agricultural robot (after firing transition tr_5)

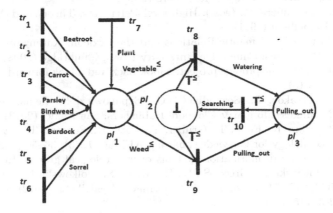

Fig. 4. A marked Petri net representing actions taken in one of tasks of an agricultural robot (after firing transition tr_9)

If the robot cannot recognize a specific kind of a plant, no actions can be performed (transitions tr_8 and tr_9 are not enabled to fire). One can see that both actions, *Watering* and *Pulling out*, are followed by action *Searching*. The formula on the input arc of transition tr_{10} causes that each token in place pl_3 is accepted. $\top^\leq$ means *each concept in the ontological graph excluding the empty concept*.

3   Conclusions

We have proposed a new model of Petri nets, called Petri nets over ontological graphs. This model enables us to deal directly with concepts included in ontologies describing modeled systems. Our approach tries to make Petri nets fit into a general trend in computations proposed by Zadeh and called *computing with words* [14]. One of further directions leads to considering tokens as multi-sets of concepts as in coloured Petri nets [4]. Moreover, one of the challenging problems is to consider other paradigmatic semantic relations (e.g., meronymy/holonymy) or any other semantic relations, especially those non-hierarchical.

References

1. Baader, F., Horrocks, I., Sattler, U.: Description logics. In: Staab, S., Studer, R. (eds.) Handbook on Ontologies, pp. 3–28. Springer, Heidelberg (2004)
2. Battiston, E., De Cindio, F., Mauri, G.: OBJSA nets: a class of high-level nets having objects as domains. In: Jensen and Rozenberg [5], pp. 189–212
3. Hertzberg, J., Saffiotti, A.: Using semantic knowledge in robotics. Robot. Auton. Syst. **56**(11), 875–877 (2008)
4. Jensen, K., Kristensen, L.M.: Coloured Petri Nets: Modelling and Validation of Concurrent Systems. Springer, Heidelberg (2009)
5. Jensen, K., Rozenberg, G. (eds.): High-level Petri Nets: Theory and Application. Springer, Heidelberg (1991)
6. Murphy, M.L. (ed.): Semantic Relations and the Lexicon: Antonymy, Synonymy, and Other Paradigms. Cambridge University Press, Cambridge (2003)
7. Musen, M., et al.: The protege project: a look back and a look forward. AI Matters **1**(4), 4–12 (2015)
8. Nastase, V., Nakov, P., Séaghdha, D.O., Szpakowicz, S.: Semantic Relations Between Nominals. Morgan & Claypool Publishers, San Rafael (2013)
9. Neches, R., Fikes, R., Finin, T., Gruber, T., Patil, R., Senator, T., Swartout, W.: Enabling technology for knowledge sharing. AI Mag. **12**(3), 36–56 (1991)
10. Pancerz, K.: Toward information systems over ontological graphs. In: Yao, J.T., Yang, Y., Słowiński, R., Greco, S., Li, H., Mitra, S., Polkowski, L. (eds.) RSCTC 2012. LNCS, vol. 7413, pp. 243–248. Springer, Heidelberg (2012). doi:10.1007/978-3-642-32115-3_29
11. Petri, C.: Kommunikation mit automaten. Schriften des IIM nr. 2, Institut für Instrumentelle Mathematik, Bonn (1962)
12. Reisig, W.: Petri Nets. Springer, Berlin (1985)
13. Szwed, P.: Video event recognition with fuzzy semantic petri nets. In: Gruca, D.A., Czachórski, T., Kozielski, S. (eds.) Man-Machine Interactions 3. AISC, vol. 242, pp. 431–439. Springer, Cham (2014). doi:10.1007/978-3-319-02309-0_47
14. Zadeh, L.: Fuzzy logic = computing with words. IEEE Trans. Fuzzy Syst. **4**(2), 103–111 (1996)

Fractal Analysis Approaches
to Granular Computing

JingTao Yao[⊠], Oladunni A. Oladimeji, and Yan Zhang

Department of Computer Science, University of Regina, Regina, SK S4S 0A2, Canada
{jtyao,oladimol,zhang83y}@cs.uregina.ca

Abstract. Granular computing has emerged as one of the fastest growing information processing paradigms in computational intelligence and human-centric systems. Fractal analysis has equally gained ground in understanding complex phenomena. This article examines and analyzes fractal analysis and its close relationship with granular computing. We argue that fractal analysis can be viewed as special granular computing approaches especially from methodology and mechanism point of views. In this article, we also bring out the granular structure existing in a fractal analysis application. The aim of this research is to demonstrate fractal analysis as a granular computing approach based on these findings.

Keywords: Granular computing · Fractal analysis · Fractals · Fractal dimension · Information granulation

1 Introduction

The research on granular computing has attracted much attention from various fields in recent years. Granular computing is regarded as an umbrella term which contains theories, methodologies, techniques, and tools that use granules in problem solving precess [21]. Granular computing is geared towards representing and processing granules. Granules are basic building blocks of granular computing, and they are arranged together due to some relationships [20,22]. A granule or information granule is defined as a subset of objects, class or cluster of a universe. Granulation is the operation performed on granules [3,20]. Granulation involves two basic operations: decomposition and construction. Decomposition involves dividing a larger granule into smaller granules. Construction on the other hand, involves forming a larger granule from smaller ones [22].

There are different views and approaches to granular computing [20]. Yao presents a triarchic view which is composed of philosophy of structured thinking, methodology of structured problem solving, and mechanism of structured information processing [21]. Yao argues that the applications are the fourth perspective of granular computing, in addition to triarchic view, and should be a focus of study [18,19]. Bargiela and Pedrycz see granular computing as a conceptual and algorithmic platform supporting analysis and design of human-centric

© Springer International Publishing AG 2017
L. Polkowski et al. (Eds.): IJCRS 2017, Part I, LNAI 10313, pp. 215–222, 2017.
DOI: 10.1007/978-3-319-60837-2_18

intelligent system [4]. Research has identified a need for new tools, theories and methods to granular computing [20]. It is thereby expected that there will be new approaches to granular computing.

Fractal analysis deals with theories, techniques and methodologies that explain, define and offer problem solving solutions to complex phenomena [5]. A fractal is an object that exhibits a repeating pattern displayed at every scale [6]. The underlying principle of fractals is that a simple object that goes through infinite times of iterations becomes a very complex system. Fractals attempt to model the complex system by searching for the simple process underneath. The idea of fractals is originated in naturally existing phenomena that have the ability to replicate themselves while still maintaining a self-similar property [11]. The key feature of fractals is the self-similarity across a range of spatial scales. This means that a part of the fractal is identical or similar to the entire fractal itself without considering the scale. Originally, fractals are proposed to investigate the geometric figures with self-similarity and non-integer dimensions [11]. Nowadays fractal analysis is extended to study the self-similarity from the different perspectives, such as structures, functions, and times. Fractal theory has been widely applied in different areas, such as economics, ecology, physics, image processing, and speech processing [2,5]. Some researchers regard fractal theory as a methodology with which we can understand a whole complex system via a simple part of the system [5].

There are connections between some concepts and processes in granular computing and fractal analysis. Concepts such as similarity, granules, fractals, and granulation are seen to have some things in common. The box-counting, walking-divider and prism-counting method of determining the fractal dimension of fractals employ information granulation [9,12]. In spite of these, not much work has been done to harmonize the fields of granular computing and fractal analysis [12]. In this research, we investigate the connections between granular computing and fractal analysis. We also examine an existing application of fractal analysis and bring out the granular computing structure of the application. This will lead to a proposition of adopting fractal analysis as a granular computing approach.

2   Fractal Analysis and Concepts

Fractal analysis aims at constructing a very complex object or system by infinitely iterating a simple process. Fractals are objects or system that have self-similar and self-repeating patterns across a wide range of scale in the iterative process. They are created by repeating simple processes over and over again. A fractal is a rough or fragmented geometric shape that can be subdivided in parts, each of them is (at least approximately) a reduced copy of the whole [11].

Fractals can be categorized as either artificially created or naturally existing objects. The artificial fractals are usually mathematically generated by an iteration function, i.e., $Z_{k+1} = f(Z_k)$. The fractal Z_{k+1} is obtained by dividing the fractal Z_k, and f represents the iteration function or process. Examples of artificial fractals include Koch curve, Mandelbrot set, Cantor set, Sierpinski

triangle, etc [2]. These mathematically generated fractals are formed from algorithms with repetition of steps. The Sierpinski triangle, for instance, may be
constructed from an equilateral triangle by repeated removal of the central triangles, as shown in the Fig. 1. The algorithm starts with an equilateral triangle
denoted by Z_0. It is further subdivided into four smaller congruent equilateral
triangles and the central one is removed. The geometric figure Z_1 is obtained
and it contains 3 smaller equilateral triangles. Each of the smaller equilateral
triangles in Z_1 is subdivided into four smaller congruent equilateral triangles
and the central ones are removed. The geometric figure Z_2 is obtained and it
contains 9 smaller equilateral triangles. This subdivision step can be repeated
infinite times. The Fig. 1 shows the fractals of Sierpinski triangle after 4 iterations. Similar process of repetition occurs in algorithms for constructing other
types of mathematical fractals [1,11]. Naturally existing fractals are those found
in nature such as mountains, water masses, water drops, lung, blood cells of the
nervous systems, trees, ferns, leaves, coastlines, etc [1].

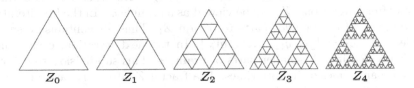

$$Z_0 \qquad Z_1 \qquad Z_2 \qquad Z_3 \qquad Z_4$$

Fig. 1. Sierpinski triangle

Self-similarity means that a part of the fractal is identical to the entire fractal itself except smaller [7]. Self-similarity can be exact or deterministic self-
similarity. The mathematically defined fractals possess an exact similar pattern
at all scales. For example, in the Fig. 1, the fractal Z_1 is obtained by decomposing Z_0 into three disjoint equilateral triangles, each of which is an exact copy
of Z_0. Self-similarity can also be statistical self-similarity. Many natural fractals
such as trees, human lung, leaves, etc. exhibit statistical self-similarity. The fractals are similar in the sense that each portion can be considered a reduced-scale
image of the whole [10,13].

Fractal dimension is used to measure the complexity or space filling capacity
of fractal objects. It is one of the factors in determining whether an object is a
fractal or not. Fractal dimension D is given by the following formula,

$$D = \frac{log(N)}{log(\epsilon)}, \tag{1}$$

where N is the number of self-similar pieces and ϵ is the scaling factor. For
example, Sierpinski triangle is cut in half and 3 similar triangles are obtained,
so we have $N = 3$ and $\epsilon = 2$. The fractal dimension of Sierpinski triangle is
$D = \frac{log(3)}{log(2)} = 1.585$. There are different methods used in determining fractal
dimension of an object, including box-counting method, the divider method, the
triangular prism method, spectral methods and area-based methods [8,9].

3   Connection in Granular Computing and Fractal Analysis

Some concepts in granular computing have certain things in common with concepts in fractal analysis. In this section we will examine some of these concepts and bring out the connection between them.

3.1   Granules and Fractals

The definition of fractals given earlier shows that a fractal can be broken down or divided into smaller parts. These smaller parts are similar to each other, and they also are similar to the whole fractal. When fractals are broken down, they are just like granules of granular systems with some relationships bonding them together. As such, a fractal can be viewed as a granular system and the parts of a fractal are the granules of the system. Assuming an artificial fractal generated by mathematical iteration function $Z_{k+1} = f(Z_k)$. The fractal Z_k is obtained from Z_0 after k iterations. Z_0 can be viewed as a granule g_0. In the first iteration, Z_0 is divided into N smaller parts to obtain Z_1. Thus Z_1 contains N smaller granules, i.e., $Z_1 = \{g_{11}, g_{12}, \ldots \ldots, g_{1N}\}$. In the next iteration, each granule in Z_1 is divided into N smaller parts or granules. This subdivision step can be repeated many times or infinite times. The fractal Z_i after i iterative processes contains N^i finer granules. We have,

$$Z_0 = \{g_0\},$$
$$Z_1 = \{g_{11}, g_{12}, \ldots \ldots, g_{1N}\},$$
$$Z_2 = \{g_{21}, g_{22}, \ldots \ldots, g_{2N^2}\},$$
$$\ldots \ldots$$
$$Z_i = \{g_{i1}, g_{i2}, \ldots, g_{iN^i}\}, \tag{2}$$

where g_{ij} denotes the jth granule in the fractal generated after i iterations. The parts of a fractal are in fact the granules of the granular system constructed based on this fractal.

3.2   Relationships

In granular computing, granules in a certain granular level or in the different granular levels need different relationships to conduct granulation [20]. Similarly, the parts of fractals in the different iterative processes are not independent to each other, and there are some relationships existing between these parts. As we discussed in last subsection, the parts of a fractal and granules correspond to each other. The relationships that used to construct granulation can be used to define the relationships among the parts of a fractal. We consider three relationships, i.e., similarity, refinement and coarsening, and granulations as partitions and coverings.

Similarity. The fractals are self-similar, that is, a fractal is broken down into an arbitrary number of small parts, and each of those parts is a replica of the entire fractal. This means all granules are similar to each other without considering scale. This similarity may be evaluated by different measures according to the different types of fractals. The fractals with exact self-similarity, for example, the mathematically generated artificial fractals, contain the granules which all have same geometric figures. The similarity in this case means the exactly same shapes. Assuming a fractal generated by $Z_{k+1} = f(Z_k)$ and a part is divided into N smaller parts, we can altogether get $\frac{N^{i+1}-1}{N-1} + 1$ granules after i iterations, as shown in Eq. 2. All the granules have geometrical similarity. Any two granules g_{ik} and g_{it} generated in the same iteration are totally same. Any two granules g_{ik} and g_{jt} in generated different iterations are same except for different scale.

Refinement and Coarsening. Refinement and coarsening relationship is defined in granular computing [20]. A granule g_1 is a refinement of another granule g_2, or equivalently g_2 is a coarsening of g_1, which is denoted by $g_1 \preceq g_2$ or $g_2 \succeq g_1$, if g_1 is contained in g_2. The fine relationship is represented by $\preceq$ and the coarse relationship by $\succeq$ [20]. The granular system constructed from a fractal involves refinement and coarsening relationship. The granules generated in a former iteration are coarsening of the granules generated in a latter iteration. The granules contained in fractals Z_i and Z_{i+1} maintain the following relations,

$$g_{(i+1)1}, g_{(i+1)2}, \cdots\cdots, g_{(i+1)N} \preceq g_{i1},$$
$$g_{(i+1)(N+1)}, g_{(i+1)(N+2)}, \cdots\cdots, g_{(i+1)(N*2)} \preceq g_{i2},$$
$$\cdots\cdots$$
$$g_{(i+1)(N^{i+1}-N+1)}, g_{(i+1)(N^{i+1}-N+2)}, \cdots\cdots, g_{(i+1)N^{i+1}} \preceq g_{iN^i}. \tag{3}$$

Granulations as Partitions and Coverings. A partition of a finite universe is a collection of nonempty and pairwise disjoint subsets of the universe whose union is the universe [20]. A covering of a finite universe is a collection of nonempty subsets of the universe whose union is the universe [20]. The granules contained in a fractal Z_i is a partition of the fractal Z_i if the granules meet the following conditions,

$$Z_i = \{g_{i1} \cup g_{i2} \cup \ldots \cup g_{iN^i}\} \text{ and } g_{iu} \cap g_{iv} = \emptyset, 1 \leq u, v \leq N^i \text{ and } u \neq v. \tag{4}$$

The granules contained in a fractal Z_i is a covering of the fractal Z_i if the granules meet the following conditions,

$$Z_i = \{g_{i1} \cup g_{i2} \cup \ldots \cup g_{iN^i}\}. \tag{5}$$

The Fig. 2 shows the granular relationships in Sierpinski triangle. The left side is Z_1 which is generated after the first iteration, and it contains 3 granules, i.e., $Z_1 = \{g_{11}, g_{12}, g_{13}\}$. The three granules form a partition of Z_1. The right side is Z_2 which is generated after the second iteration, and it contains 9 granules,

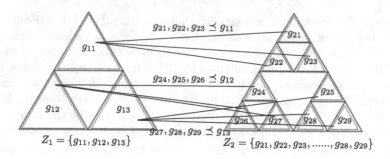

Fig. 2. Granular relationships in Sierpinski triangle

i.e., $Z_2 = \{g_{21}, g_{22}, \ldots\ldots, g_{29}\}$. The nine granules form a partition of Z_2. The granule g_{11} is a coarsening of granules g_{21}, g_{22} and g_{23}, that is, $g_{21}, g_{22}, g_{23} \preceq g_{11}$. The granules g_{12} and g_{13} are coarsening of other smaller granules. All granules in the Fig. 2 are similar to each other, and they are all equilateral triangles.

3.3 Granulation and Fractal Dimension

Pedrycz and Bargiela [12] pointed out a linkage existing between fractal dimension and information granulation. The relationship is explained as a power law existing in the form:

$$M = M_{nominal}^{D}$$

where M is the number of information granules (fuzzy sets) to use, $M_{nominal}$ is the maximal number of fuzzy sets to use in the modelling process and D is the fractal dimension. Therefore, the more complex a phenomena to be modelled, the more information granules one needs to use to construct the model. Pedrycz claimed that fractal analysis is inherently rooted in information granulation [12]. The three methods for determining fractal dimension, i.e., box counting, divider and triangular prism employ the use of objects such as, boxes, dividers and prism to determine fractal dimension [9]. The objects are divided into smaller pieces and sizes each time. The logarithm of the number of divisions to the size of the object is used in calculating fractal dimension. This attempt to divide the measuring objects resembles granulation technique of decomposition. In order words, these measures attempt to granulate the fractal objects into smaller elements. Hence, the claim of fractal dimension having root in granulation [14,15].

4 Fractal Analysis Application and Its Granular Computing Structure

Fractal analysis has been used extensively to address many problems. When some problems are carefully examined, we see their granular computing aspects. We examine image analysis with fractal analysis method in this part. A common process in image analysis is image segmentation. Segmentation is the identification of different regions of an image, it can be used to identify objects and boundaries in images. Image segmentation assigns a label to every pixel in an image such that pixels with the same label share certain characteristics. Fractal analysis approach is one of the methods through which image segmentation can be done. Many disease diagnosis procedures in healthcare rely on image analysis. Squarcina et al. [16] carried out an experiment to diagnose occurrence of schizophrenia and bipolar disorder in patients. Brain images were analysed in this experiment to distinguish healthy brains from pathological brains. The segmentation of the images were done with fractal analysis approach. Fractal dimensions of the brain images were calculated using the box-counting method. The result was proper diagnosis of the brain image using fractal analysis approach [16].

Although the article did not discuss the details of the segmentation with box-counting method, further research on methods of segmentation using box-counting method reveals close relationship to granular computing. Vuduc described image segmentation with box-counting method [17]. A basic procedure was to segment images. For each pixel in the image, fractal dimension of a small window surrounding the pixel is calculated and this is assigned to the pixel. The process is repeated till all pixels of the image have been assigned a fractal dimension. Then a histogram is made of the various fractal dimension values. The image is subsequently color-coded based on the fractal dimension values. The different color-codes represent the different segments of the image. The image segmentation process in this example clearly resembles granulation in granular computing. It involves both decomposition and construction. Segmenting images into different regions is an example of decomposition. Grouping images together based on their fractal dimension values is construction.

5 Conclusion

The aim of this paper is to provide a granular computing view of fractal analysis. We summarize basic concepts in granular computing and fractal analysis. The connections between concepts of granules, fractals, granulation, fractal dimension and some relationships are examined. The analysis shows that fractals can be viewed as granular system and many granules are contained in them. We also examine a real life application of fractal analysis and present the granular computing aspects of the application.

It can be concluded that there are close connections between granular computing and fractal analysis. Fractal analysis indeed can be considered as a granular computing approach. Some fractal analysis applications have granular structures in them. These applications with granular structures are more or less granular systems which have been benefitted from fractal analysis approach.

Acknowledgement. This research was partially supported by an NSERC discovery grant.

References

1. Addison, P.S.: Fractals and Chaos: An Illustrated Course. CRC Press, Boca Raton (1997)
2. Al-Akaidi, M.: Fractal Speech Processing. Cambridge University Press, Cambridge (2004)
3. Bargiela, A., Pedrycz, W.: Granular Computing: An introduction. Springer Science and Business Media, Heidelberg (2002)
4. Bargiela, A., Pedrycz, W.: Towards a theory of granular computing for human-centered information processing. IEEE Trans. Fuzzy Syst. **16**(2), 320–330 (2008)
5. Barnsley, M.: Fractals Everywhere. UK Academic Press, Cambridge (1998)
6. Boeing, G.: Visual analysis of nonlinear dynamical systems: chaos, fractals, self-similarity and the limits of prediction. Systems **4**(4), 37 (2016)
7. Feder, J.: Fractals. Springer Science & Business Media, Heidelberg (2013)
8. Kinsner, W.: A unified approach to fractal dimensions. Int. J. Cogn. Inf. Nat. Intell. **1**(4), 26–46 (2007)
9. Klinkenberg, B.: A review of methods used to determine the fractal dimension of linear features. Math. Geosci. **26**(1), 23–46 (1994)
10. Mandelbrot, B.B.: How long is the coast of britain? Statistical self-similarity and fractional dimension. Science **156**(3775), 636–638 (1967)
11. Mandelbrot, B.B., Pignoni, R.: The Fractal Geometry of Nature. WH freeman, New York (1983)
12. Pedrycz, W., Bargiela, A.: Fuzzy fractal dimensions and fuzzy modeling. Inf. Sci. **153**, 199–216 (2003)
13. Peitgen, H.O., Jürgens, H., Saupe, D.: Chaos and Fractals: New Frontiers of Science. Springer Science & Business Media, Heidelberg (2006)
14. Polkowski, L.: On asymptotic properties of rough—set—theoretic approximations. fractal dimension, exact sets, and rough inclusion in potentially infinite information systems. In: Alpigini, J.J., Peters, J.F., Skowron, A., Zhong, N. (eds.) RSCTC 2002. LNCS, vol. 2475, pp. 167–174. Springer, Heidelberg (2002). doi:10.1007/3-540-45813-1_21
15. Polkowski, L.: On fractal dimension in information systems. Toward exact sets in infinite information systems. Fundamenta Informaticae **50**(3–4), 305–314 (2002)
16. Squarcina, L., DeLuca, A., Bellani, M., Brambilla, P., Turkheimer, F., Bertoldo, A.: Fractal analysis of MRI data for the characterization of patients with schizophrenia and bipolar disorder. J. Theor. Biol. **60**(4), 1697 (2015)
17. Vuduc, R.: Image segmentation using fractal dimension. Report on GEOL 634 (1997)
18. Yao, J.T.: Recent developments in granular computing: a bibliometrics study. In: IEEE International Conference on Granular Computing, pp. 74–79 (2008)
19. Yao, J.T.: Novel Developments in Granular Computing: Applications for Advanced Human Reasoning and Soft Computation: Applications for Advanced Human Reasoning and Soft Computation. IGI Global, Hershey (2010)
20. Yao, J.T., Vasilakos, A.V., Pedrycz, W.: Granular computing: perspectives and challenges. IEEE Trans. Cybern. **43**(6), 1977–1989 (2013)
21. Yao, Y.Y.: Three perspectives of granular computing. J. Nanchang Inst. Technol. **25**(2), 16–21 (2006)
22. Zadeh, L.A.: Towards a theory of fuzzy information granulation and its centrality in human reasoning and fuzzy logic. Fuzzy Sets Syst. **90**(2), 111–127 (1997)

Generating Natural Language Explanations from Knowledge-Based Systems Results, Using Ontology and Discourses Patterns

Víctor Flores$^{(\boxtimes)}$, Yahima Hadfeg, and Claudio Meneses

Department of Computing and Systems Engineering,
Universidad Católica del Norte, Angamos Av. 0610, Antofagasta, Chile
{vflores,Yahima.Hadfeg01,cmeneses}@ucn.cl

Abstract. The understanding of results of Knowledge-based systems (KBS) working on complex Dynamic Systems (DS) requires expert knowledge and interpretation capability in order to make a correct analysis of observations at multiple scales and instants. Normally, these kinds of KBS generate extensive inference-trees before showing a definitive result to final users; these inference-trees are not included in the KBS outputs, but they could provide additional information to understand the functioning of the KBS, and also to understand the overall performance of a DS. This document describes a method to generate natural language explanations, based on the results reached by a KBS in respect to a DS behavior, using a specific ontology and discourse patterns. The input of the method is an intermediate-state tree (the inference-tree) and specific domain knowledge represented on domain ontology. The document describes also the software architecture to generate the explanations and the test cases designed to validate the results in a specific domain.

Keywords: Knowledge-based systems · Automatic natural language generation · Expression generation · Ontology · Automatic generation of explanations · Discourse patterns

1 Introduction

Modern Knowledge-based Systems (KBS) usually produce long inference-trees as intermediate results before presenting final results to users; this is frequently due to the enormous complexity of these systems. Recently, the interest on inference-trees is growing because these inference-trees can help to improve the understanding of KBS results [1]; in addition, the inference-tree can show how a KBS arrived at a final conclusion in respect to a recently Dynamic System (DS) behavior, showing the set of intermediate states concluded during the inference process. In general, the task of presenting the intermediate state to final users is not made because it can be complicated and difficult to show [1].

An example of DS is an industrial copper bioleaching heap, which is divided into lifts and strips. Generally the heaps are built with run-of-mine (ROM) ore, characterized as low-grade sulfide material [2]. Bioleaching is the process that uses ROM and microorganisms populations to obtain valuable metals (e.g. copper) which otherwise

© Springer International Publishing AG 2017
L. Polkowski et al. (Eds.): IJCRS 2017, Part I, LNAI 10313, pp. 223–238, 2017.
DOI: 10.1007/978-3-319-60837-2_19

would not be economically profitable [3, 4]. Various works are presented in the literature that shows results of bacterium incidence on optimum conditions of bioleaching [24].

Actually several intelligent tools (such as KBS), mathematical models or middleware are used for the setting up of data mechanisms interpretations about DS states, in order to monitor DS behavior. Specifically on the copper bioleaching domain, there are several mathematical models used to simulate bacterium activity on simulated bioleaching heaps, but on real heaps they are not adequate due to the complexity and limited knowledge in respect to bacteria population behavior. In this context some KBS can help operators understand the copper bioleaching process and support the decision making process [3].

At the moment, copper mining is the most important economic activity in Chile, generating almost 10% of copper production worldwide [5], bioleaching is gaining ground over the copper mining activity because of the low environmental impact and the profits that it is possible to obtain. The management of a bioleaching heap usually involves operator teams and decision makers [1], and in general the human teams are interested not only in the output of a KBS, but also in the description of possible states of the dynamic system at the time, in order to improve production. A tool that automatically generates descriptions of a heap behavior can help end-users understand and analyze the heap complexity.

In this paper we describe how such textual descriptions can be generated from internal inference-trees that represent intermediate results of a KBS in a specific domain. Our method of text descriptions generation from data brings to a more general problem on the natural language generation community: reference expression generation [23]. Our method uses specific domain ontology [19] and discourse patterns to generate the explanations. Discourse patterns are structures used for automatic text processing applications, among other objectives, to generate coherent text. For a more general overview of discourse patterns approaches, see Wang et al. [32], Sect. 2.

In this paper we describe the results of our recent research in the area of automatic generation of explanation from non textual data. We discuss the facility of using intermediate-state tree (the inference-tree) from a KBS, specific knowledge and pre-defined discourse structures, to automatically construct descriptions in natural language. We present a method that we evaluated using a KBS results with a significant amount of conclusions related to a Dynamic System. In general, the evaluation results on the selected domain show that this approach generates acceptable descriptions.

This paper also describes briefly the bioleaching process and related works; then the software methodology to construct the prototype, and finally the proposal and validation are described; at the end of this paper a discussion on the practical utility, a comparative discussion on the human interpretation of Expert System results, and the automatically generated presentation by the software are made.

2   Bioleaching Process and Work Context

In order to understand the method presented here, the general characteristics of a bioleaching heap should be described. This description is focused on copper bioleaching, and basically, the copper bioleaching process involving dumping a low-grade (otherwise waste) copper-bearing ore in the form of small pieces of rock into vast mounds and irrigating it with diluted H_2SO_4 to enhance the growth and the activity of iron-oxidizing microorganisms [24]. The latest developments on the hydrometallurgical and new engineering techniques have been included in order to optimize the process.

Nowadays a bioleaching heap is divided into lifts and strips and provided of an irrigation line and a data pickup line with PLSs, with a data pick up line with PLSs, and these are provided with multiple sensors; to monitor the performance of bioleaching heaps the use of PLS (Pregnant Leach Solution) is common [24]. The PLS monitoring could be made to assess concentration of microorganisms, microbial activity and physicochemical parameters; this task can generate a huge amount of information [3]. Figure 1 depicts (in a simplified form) a three-floors bioleaching heap.

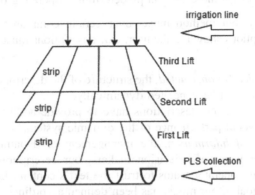

Fig. 1. Schematic design of a Bioleaching heap considering three lifts

2.1 Work Context

Metals are one of the most significant natural resources for humans. The metals are extracted from the rocks using different techniques, and several produce environmental pollution [7, 8]. Actually, there are recent and clear methods of copper extraction such as bioleaching that give the option of obtaining metals such as copper from low-grade material, at a lower cost and at a minimized environmental impact [3].

There are some works that use KBSs to improve mining processes results, for example the "Centro de Biotecnología Alberto Ruiz" is developing an Expert System to improve the actual knowledge on the bioleaching process and the influence of certain parameters on the microbial oxidation (this software is being developed under public funding granted by the government of Chile); also in [26] a predictive mineral potential mapping using neuro-fuzzy and expert knowledge-base is described, and the authors explain in this paper that the mapping could be used (in the future) to create criteria for the exploitation of copper.

2.2 Domain Specifications

Our method needs to know certain characteristics of the domain in order to work properly. This method generates descriptions that describe the behavior of a certain type of dynamic systems; the general characteristics of such a dynamic system should be the following:

- *Interpretability*, the behavior of the system is observed with the help of sensors that periodically measure the value of a number of quantitative properties and these observations are interpreted, using expert knowledge.
- *Complex,* the system has different types of components and relations among components that can be aggregated on different levels or that can be decomposed into small parts. Moreover, this complexity can change due to new elements incorporated in the system.
- *Prefixed goals,* the system are controlled according to prefixed management goals that try to keep certain indicators on predetermined operating objectives.

In the same way, our method must cover certain communicative challenges in respect to the descriptions shown to the user. Our descriptions must have the following characteristics:

- *Discourse dynamically constructed*, the structure of the descriptions is not rigid and these descriptions must be generated dynamically.
- *Relevant descriptions*, our descriptions have to provide additional information to understand the overall performance of the dynamic system.
- *Detail and level of information*, the management of dynamic systems usually involves operator teams and decision makers, our description needs to include evidence that helps operator teams to trust the text's content. In this respect, each communicative goal of our model has been defined according to certain *rhetorical relations* [31] that establish the structure of discourse [27]. The detail of these communicative structures and communicative goals are described later.

2.3   Knowledge-Based Systems

There are many papers about Knowledge-based system (KBS) definition. For example, in [25] a KBS (also known as Expert System) is defined as a software system that contains a significant amount of knowledge in an explicit, declarative form. Another way to describe a KBS can be, a computer system that operates by applying an inference mechanism to obtain results, based on a specific knowledge represented and in which results are similar to those obtained by a human expert [20].

The ideas of KBS or Expert Systems are regularly used in the extensive sense of systems whose main components are a set of production rules and an inference engine that fires these rules in a non-deterministic way. This kind of intelligent system is being used in many domains to support tasks such as decision making or the prediction of behavior in DS [1].

Our interest is focused on Expert systems that use rules to determine the state of a dynamic system. Deterministic rules are commonly used in Expert Systems as a valid form of knowledge representation [8] and to infer Dynamic System states [1, 9]. It is due to the fact that many real complex situations are governed by deterministic rules, and this representation can simplify the problem complexity and generate human-like reasoning. These reasons have contributed to KBS popularity on different domains. The kind of Expert System type considered on this proposal is the Rule-based Expert System (RBES), can have different states over time and those states are measurable with a variety of devices such as electronic devices, specific sensors, etc. There are previous works to summarize behavior or relevant information, for example in [1] a model for automatically generation of presentations is presented.

2.4 Ontology

A formal definition of an ontology proposed by Gruber [17] is that "ontology is an explicit specification of a conceptualization"; ontology models the domain using the elements concepts, attributes and relationships, in order to specify the domain vocabulary. In the literature various ontologies classifications are presented; Mizoughi et al. [18] propose that ontology can be a domain, task or general/common specification.

Ontology representation is comprised of four main elements [21]: concept or class as an abstract group; set or collection of elements; instance, which is the "ground-level" component; relation or slot, used to express relationships between two concepts and axiom, which is used to improve constraints on the values of classes or instances. These elements are combined on tuples in order to generate the structure of ontology [22].

An important function of ontologies for our work is its capacity to represent knowledge. Today there are several techniques to knowledge representation. A classification of knowledge-based modeling techniques is presented on [11], this classification is made based on the fundamental theories of knowledge-based modeling and manipulation. In this classification, the following groups are considered: linguistic knowledge basis [12], expert knowledge basis [13, 14], ontology and cognitive knowledge basis [15, 16]. At present, these knowledge representations are widely used for support Intelligent Systems build applications.

3 Software Methodology

Software has emerged as a means for creating value to products and services in many industries [6] including the copper mining industry. In this context, it is well known that quality software products depend largely on the processes development, final quality [6] and level of knowledge used to build the responses [1]. The methodology corresponds to an incremental process that combines software engineering with artificial intelligence steps in order to generate a prototype. The steps in our methodology can be described as follows:

- In the first step, the task of collecting both information and relevant knowledge related to mining copper domain was made. For this task, experts on bioleaching domain were consulted to identify how to show relevant information on the copper mining domain.
- In the second step, the structure of the inference-tree from the bioleaching heap was identified.
- The specific ontology was built in the third step, using for this the collected knowledge.

- The algorithm of presentation was generated in the fourth step. In order to perform this task, the expert knowledge related to *what* is important to show was modeled.
- The validation cases were achieved in the fifth step; these cases allowed validating our prototype and evaluating its possible practical value.
- The preparation of validation was made in the sixth step. Validation is an important step in Expert Systems, therefore, a real complex domain was selected and test cases were designed.

The core of this proposal is made during the fourth to sixth steps. All the expert knowledge mentioned in the steps of our methodology was modeled on the domain ontology; this process is described below.

4   Proposed Method for Generating Natural Language Explanations

The proposal presented here corresponds to a method for generating natural language explanations on Expert System results; the aim is presenting a tool that helps to understand the results shown by a KBS, working on a Dynamic System (DS). Our method follows a knowledge-based approach with a set of particular inference steps that use domain specific knowledge about what is important to say related to a KBS outputs.

Our method performs two main tasks: abstraction - to both interpret and abstract the intermediate (inference-tree) from the KBS - and planning to generate the explanation plan according to specific communicative objectives (previously identified for the work domain). The final output of our method is the explanation plan; using this explanation plan a natural language explanation of the KBS intermediate-states is generated.

Figure 2 describes the components of our method with two principal tasks: abstraction and planning, inputs/outputs and the domain knowledge. For the abstraction task, the inputs are (1) an XML file containing events triggered by the Drools inference engine and (2) the specific ontology (RDF/XML); and for the planning task the inputs are both a list structure with all the interpretations (the abstraction output) and the ontology.

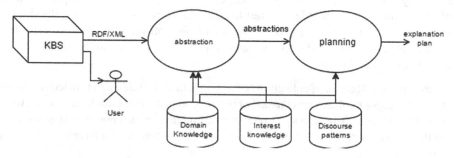

Fig. 2. The general architecture for our method of automatic generation of explanations

Briefly, the method works as follow: the abstraction task uses the XML file to interpret the relevant intermediate-states from the KBS; each of these intermediate-states is characterized by an object of the KBS data-model, then, the inference-tree interpreter relates these objects with elements (concepts) of our ontology. The general structure of each of our abstractions (output of the abstraction task) is: ‹*class*, *object*, *attribute*, *value*›. These abstractions together with the domain ontology are the input to planning. All elements (tasks and knowledge) from the model are described in detail in the following sections.

Our ontology has the relevant knowledge to decide how interpretations (abstractions) could be selected for the explanation plan, so later it can provide the explanations for the process. The explanation generator uses the ontology and the presentation model to produce the explanation plan.

In order to represent the domain knowledge, an ontology scheme has been designed. There are two aims of the ontology construction, the first being to improve a usable representation close to the important dynamic system elements to be described, and the second to ensure that its concepts can be understood by the presentation module.

The knowledge base is composed by three ontologies: domain knowledge, interest knowledge and knowledge related to how and what to present on the final explanation (discourse patterns). The details about the core concepts of these ontologies are aligned with the model given in [1].

4.1   The Domain Knowledge

To support the abstraction task the domain knowledge ontology has been developed using expert knowledge related to structure and behavior of certain kinds of dynamic systems (previously described in the section entitled *domain specifications*). Our approach is based on expert knowledge described in the literature (previous works as [1–5, 24]) and validated by a human expert. The domain representation is focused on the structure and process involved in the production of copper in a bioleaching heap.

The general class is the bioleaching heap. A bioleaching heap is considered here as any physical entity space on the soil's surface. The first level of the hierarchy has two disjoint classes: Microorganisms and Heap; in this document the Microorganism hierarchy is described because it is richer in its number of elements. For the class microorganisms, three disjoint classes are considered. Figure 3 shows some of the main classes and properties of the Microorganisms using UML notation.

Our ontology representation is based on principles of representation of Protégé[1] tool, so the *Thing* class is a superclass of protégé that we use in our representation. As Fig. 3 shows, the domain ontology consists of 6 main classes, a brief description of these elements and their characteristics is: *Gen* represents a biological gene, *Sample* represents a biological sample, *Bacteria* represents a Bacterium, *Arches* represents an Achaea, *Microorganism* represents a microorganism, *Target-sample* represents a target sample and *Target-control* represents a sample that is used to contrast with the Target-sample.

---

[1] www.progete.org.

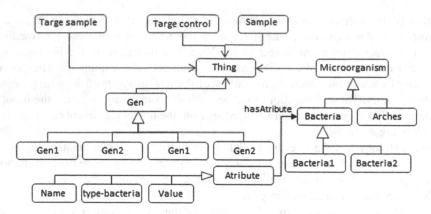

Fig. 3. A subset of the conceptualization of the domain knowledge

The relations between classes are defined as follows: *Gen is-a Thing, Microorganism is-a Thing, Bacteria is-a Thing*. Sample is-related to Gen, Sample contains genes, also Target control and Target sample contains genes, *Bacteria is-a-kind-of Microorganism, Archaea is-a-kind-of Microorganism, Sample-control is-a-kind-of Sample, Target-sample is-a-kind-of Sample*. Axioms on this representation are:

Axiom-1:   If B *is-a* Bacteria and A *is-an* Archaea → A ≠ B and A ∩ B = Ø.

Axiom-2:   If A *is-a* Sample Target, B *is-a* Sample Control → A ≠ B and A ∩ B = Ø.

Axiom-3:   If B *is-a* Bacteria and A *is-an* Archaea → A ⊆ Microorganism and B ⊆ Microorganism and A ∪ B = Microorganism.

Axiom-4:   If C, D *is-a-kind-of* Sample, C *is-a* Target-sample, D *is-a* Target-control → C ≠ D and C £ D, where £ represents an expression of D in respect to C and £ is IN {over-expressed, sub-expressed, non-expressed, equally-expressed}.

Our ontology contains also abstract qualitative values that abstract other qualitative values that correspond to basic elements. When two or more instances of a concept are abstracted by another more general, Functions is-an-abstract-of. For example, if £ is the set of elements {A, B, C} and they are related with other elements, D *is-a* relation, then D represents the set £.

4.2   Interest Knowledge

The interest knowledge represents knowledge about how to generate abstractions and what behavior (what intermediate-states) is relevant to show in the final presentation. Our method simulate is designed to simulate interpretation tasks performed by professional human operators and expert researchers with approximated knowledge about the behavior of the dynamic system. Our representation shares certain elements existing common ontologies used in qualitative physics [1, 17].

The domain ontology includes both single and complex components; we obtain the state value of a single component by both goals, to interpret the abstractions (output of the abstraction task) and to select what information to show. In order to make this task we use qualitative interpretation rules. The following rules are examples of the described above:

$$[value(<Bacteria, bacteria - 1, current - value, n >) \land value(<Bacteria, bacteria - 2, current - value, m >) \land n > m] \rightarrow select-to-show(<Bacteria, bacteria - 1, current - value, n >) \tag{1}$$

$$[value(<control sample, sample1, current - value, n >) \land value(<target sample, sample2, current - value, m >) \land n > m + k] \rightarrow select-to-show(value(<target sample, sample2, current - value, m >)) \tag{2}$$

The rule present on Eq. (1) means: when the current qualitative value of bacteria-1 is greater than the value of bacteria-2, then the relevant abstraction to show is ⟨Bacteria, name- bacteria-1, current-value, n⟩, and the rule present on Eq. (2) means: when the value of the target sample is less than the sum of the control value plus a k value (where k is a differentiator value), then the important value to be displayed is the sample value. A second type of rules is used to abstract single components into more complex ones. The Eq. (3) is an example of this set of rules.

$$[<Bacteria, bacteria - 1, current - value, n >) \land <Bacteria, bacteria - 2, current - value, m >) \land type - bacteria(bacteria - 1) = type - bacteria(bacteria - 2)] \rightarrow select - to - show(<microorganism, name - microorganism, average - value(n, m, p), p >) \tag{3}$$

4.3   Discourse Patterns

The discourse patterns are used to automatically construct description plans. The discourse pattern represents knowledge about strategies that express how to present abstracted information, related to intermediate-states from the KBS. We use discourse patterns similarly as described in [30]; the knowledge base of the patterns contains a set of operators that represents atomic presentation operations. Operators generate natural language descriptions using templates. Each operator includes a set of conditions; these conditions help the inference engine select the appropriate template.

Our operators correspond to communicative objectives (goals) [31, 32] and these were defined in accordance to rhetorical relations that establish a natural structure of discourse [27]. Each operator is linked to one of these communicative objectives; we have selected a subset of rhetorical relations applied in our context of dynamic system. Some of these are: detail, this relation is used to show the value of a quantity (value) that characterize an intermediate-state; list, this relation is used to show sequentially several of the detail relations. Figure 4 shows a set of operators related to abstractions, in these example operators generate text using templates according to rhetorical relations. An example of operator in accordance with the list relation is the following:

Operator: list-2-current-values-bacteria
Goal: detail-quantities-2-bacteria
Conditions: *is-a-kind-of* (Microorganism,bacteria),
               is-a(bacteria, bact-1), *is-a(bacteria, bact-2)*
Input: ⟨*bacteria, bact-1, quantity, 10e4*⟩,⟨*bacteria, bact-2, quantity, 10e2*⟩
Effect: add-text("The Bacterium: " bact-1, bact-2 " are presents with a values:",
               10e4, ", ",10e2)

4.4   Abstraction

To facilitate access to intermediate-states of a KBS to specific users (operators and/or researchers), a solution is to use data-to-text techniques [29, 30]. As mentioned above, the input for abstraction task is an XML file generated for Drools; this file has specifics tags that identify elements of the domain in the inference process. Table 1 describes the tags used to characterize these elements and Fig. 5 shows a segment of this file.

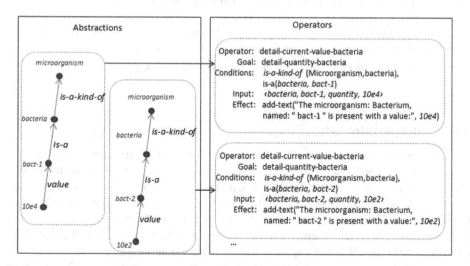

Fig. 4. Examples of operators

Table 1. Tags and their descriptions of the XML file generated by Drools

Tag identifier	Description
<object-stream>	This tag identifies the beginning of the section used to describe the objects that have been placed in the working-memory
</object-stream>	This tag identifies the end of the section <object-stream>
<events>	This tag identifies the beginning of the section used to describe the events that have been placed in the working-memory
</events>	This tag identifies the end of the section <events>
<activationId>	This tag identifies a rule-name that has been placed in the working-memory
</activationId>	This flag identifies the end of the section <activationId>
<objectToString>	This tag identifies an object, its corresponding class and an object attribute that have been placed in the working-memory
</objectToString>	This flag identifies the end of the section <objectToString>
<rule>	This tag identifies a rule that was activated placed in the working-memory
</rule>	

```
<object-stream>
<org.drools.core.audit.WorkingMemoryLog>
<version>6.1</version>
<events>
<org.drools.core.audit.event.ObjectLogEvent>
<type>1</type>
<factId>1</factId>
<objectToString> Object-name [Object-name-1:PLS, tempPLS:
50]</objectToString>
</org.drools.core.audit.event.ObjectLogEvent>
<org.drools.core.audit.event.ActivationLogEvent>
<type>4</type>
<activationId>Rule-name[3, 1, 2, 4]</activationId>
<rule> Rule-name </rule>
<declarations>Object-name=Object-name[Object-
name1:PLS,tempPLS:50](1)</declarations>
<factHandleIds>4,3,1,2</factHandleIds>
</org.drools.core.audit.event.ActivationLogEvent>
</events>
<engine>PHREAK</engine>
</org.drools.core.audit.WorkingMemoryLog>
</object-stream>
```

Fig. 5. Code segment of the XML file generated by Drools (www.drools.org) (using the workingMemoryLogger)

Once the objects and their characteristics have been identified, the process of relating these elements with the concepts of the domain ontology is carried out. Our algorithm to perform the task described above is detailed below:

Algorithm 1. Abstraction
1. **Input:** inference-tree (XML file), ontology.
2. **Var integer** total_events =0
3. **Var list** abstractions[a_I, b_I, c_I, d_I] where a, b, c = **string**, d = **real** and I is an index value.
4. **output:** the abstraction results (abstractions)
5. select <event> from inference-tree & make total_events equal to COUNT(<event>)
6. **If** total_event> 0 then
7.   **For** I=1 to total_events **do**
8. Extract values from tag:<objectToString> and do the assignment: a_I= class-name, b_I= object-name, $c_I$attribute-name and d_I= value.
9. **End-For**
10.   **Else**
11.   abstractions[a_I, b_I, c_I, d_I]=<empty, empty, empty, 0>.
12.   **End-IF**
13.   **If** Count(abstractions[a_I, b_I, c_I, d_I])> 1 **then**
14.   **For each** (abstractions[a_I, b_I, c_I, d_I]) **do**
15.   IFa_I=aI+1 **then**
16.   Abstract bI, bI+1 an another representative object (to do this the abstraction knowledge in the ontology must be used)
17.   **End-If**
18.   **End-For**
19.   Output the result Abstractions = {abstraction[a_1, b_1, c_1, d_1], abstraction [a_2, b_2, c_2, d_2],.., abstraction[a_I, b_I, c_I, d_I]}.

4.5 Planning

The planning process follows a heuristic approach using text templates. Our method defines patterns of natural language descriptions and they are selected and instantiated according to specific strategies formulated with a set of productions rules. The rules help to generate the descriptions taking into account the abstractions (output of the abstraction task) and the constraints generated when the ontology interest knowledge is used. The general format of such rules is the following:

The planning is the one in charge of gathering the criteria that allows to automatically constructing a presentation that shows the information corresponding to the rules fired at the moment of executing the KBS. The purpose of this presentation is to explain "why" a KBS arrives at a particular result; to achieve this goal and generate descriptions that sound natural to final users, a presentation model was built. Our presentation model builds a presentation plan. In practice, this presentation plan is designed as a combination of *elements of presentation* and *presentation strategies.*

The elements of presentation are explanatory elements that we used to show the Expert System status and explain salient events; specifically in this proposal presentation elements are text-template. A text-template combines variables (concept characteristic) and fixed text, and the graphic-directive are commands to build graphics within the explanation.

Presentation strategies are patterns that are schematic of how to articulate the presentation; a presentation strategy establishes relationships between text-template and graphic-directive and indicates which of these are to be used to structure the presentation. Presentation strategies are selected using an inference process based on rules. For example, let us consider the following rule:

The domain ontology includes single and complex components as classes; we obtain the state value of a single component by both goals, to interpret the abstractions (output of the abstraction task) and to select what information to show. In order to make this task we use qualitative interpretation rules. For example, let us consider the following rule: IF *value* (mesophyll) > 10e5, value (thermophile) > 10e6, value (oxid-level) < 5 → select-strategy (strategy-1).

This rule selects strategy-1 that uses a set of operators combined according to the overall discourse goal: highlight the oxidation level value (oxid-level). Thus, the strategy-1 would consist of: show-final-state (oxid-level) ∧ list-2-current-values-bacteria(‹bacteria, thermophile, quantity, 10e6›, ‹bacteria, mesophyll, quantity, 10e5›).

5 Validation

In order to evaluate the proposed model a file that shows the results of an Expert System working on a complex real world domain was used. As we have previously mentioned, the selected domain was a bioleaching heap because this is a real Dynamic System that has certain features as follows: (1) a large and complex amount of physical elements that might also have a significant number of characteristics and connections between them, (2) the real dynamic system has to be managed and supervised by human experts, and (3) these experts can interact with the system in order to change its behavior. To construct the ontology the software Protégé [10] was used (for more details, see Flores et al. [1], Sect. 3).

5.1 Examples

Table 2 shows examples of natural language descriptions generated using our method (descriptions translated into English) for each description. Table 2 also shows the correspondence that exists between the objects and their descriptions. Example number 2 in the Table corresponds to a partial-state description when that state is characterized by the quantity of a bacterium (mesophyll).

Table 2. Examples of generated descriptions

Object	Abstractions	Generated description
bact-1	‹Bacteria, bact-1, quantity, 10e2›	The microorganism: Bacterium, named: bact-1 is present with a value: 10e2
mesophyll	‹Bacteria, mesophyll, quantity, 10e5›	The microorganism: mesophyll is present with a value: 10e5
arque-1	‹Archaea, arche-1, quantity, 10e3›	The microorganism: Achaea, named: arque-1 is present with a value: 10e3

5.2 Practical Utility

Practical utility can be made with the help of an expert and using the post-edition technique [1, 28–30]. Basically, the post-editing technique consists of the following: first the expert uses the descriptions to generate a new text (an expert version), and then both versions are contrasted. Finally, the level of satisfaction is measured in terms of the amount of changes.

Currently this validation is being applied on the results of the explanatory generator. According to the authors' assessment, the use of the post-editing technique has allowed to increase the confidence of the experts on the validity results. Our partial evaluation indicates that the automatically generated texts are easily interpreted and reflect the partial states of the KBS, and this helps to understand these results.

6 Conclusions and Future Work

This work is a step towards the creation of a module that automatically generates explanations in natural language, using ontology and speech patterns. This work is based on previous proposals, but it is different in the sense that it incorporates an ontological representation that contributes more wealth and flexibility to the representation. Our proposal is also distinguished because we generate a relevance model that is able to identify the most relevant behavior that should be shown in the explanation. Our method is also capable of transforming code from an XML file into domain abstractions, which are then transformed into text segments using operators. These operators correspond to communicative goals and discourse strategies that are of interest to a complex domain of a dynamic system.

The prototype that we developed in the copper mining domain showed that our method was able to generate coherent descriptions in natural language by using approximate knowledge that was possible to acquire with acceptable effort. This was possible thanks to the use of paradigms such as the ontologies, discursive structures (from automatic generation of natural language) and recent tools to program Expert Systems. The model was validated in a complex dynamic system, such as a bioleaching heap. As a future line of work, we intend to generate new cases of study in the same domain, but cases with greater complexity in respect to the case described in [1] and mentioned in this document, and then proceed to validate the model in another complex domain.

Acknowledgements. This work was carried out thanks to the authors' participation in a research project in the field of copper bioleaching, Project code: IT13I20042. This project was funded by the Government of Chile through the Fund for the Promotion of Scientific and Technological Development (Fondef).

References

1. Flores, V., Hadfeg, Y., Bekios, J., Quelopana, A., Meneses, C.: A method for automatic generation of explanations from a rule-based expert system and ontology. Trends Appl. Softw. Eng. Adv. Intell. Syst. Comput. **537**, 167–176 (2017)
2. Demergasso, D., Galleguillos, F., Soto, P., Seron, M., Iturriaga, V.: Microbial succession during a heap bioleaching cycle of low grade copper sulfides: does this knowledge mean a real input for industrial process design and control. Hydrometallurgy **104**(3), 382–390 (2010)
3. Soto, P., Galleguillos, P., Seron, M., Zepeda, V., Demergasso, C., Pinilla, C.: Parameters influencing the microbial oxidation activity in the industrial bioleaching heap at Escondida mine. Chile. Hydrometall. **133**, 51–57 (2013)
4. Kaibin, F., Hai, L., Deqiang, L., Wufei, J., Ping, Z.: Comparison of bioleaching of copper sulphides by Acidithiobacillusferrooxidans. Afr. J. Biotechnol. **13**(5), 664–672 (2014)
5. Preliminary Data: ICSG PRESS RELEASE Date Issued: 20th December 2013 Copper: Preliminary Data for September 2013, 00(September 2013) (2013)
6. Flores, V., Quelopana, A.: An intelligent system prototype to support and sharing diagnoses of malignant tumors, based on personalized medicine philosophy. J.: "Revistalberoamericana de Inteligencia Artificial" **19**(58), 17–22 (2017)
7. Abdel-Fattah, T.M., Haggag, S.M.S., Mahmoud, M.E.: Heavy metal ions extraction from aqueous media using nonporous silica. Chem. Eng. J. **175**, 117–123 (2011)
8. Khaliq, A., Rhamdhani, M.A., Brooks, G., Masood, S.: Metal extraction processes for electronic waste and existing industrial routes: a review and Australian perspective. Resources **3**, 152–179 (2014)
9. Green, N., Carenini, G., Kerpedjiev, S., Mattis, J., Moore, J., Roth, S.: AutoBrief: an experimental system for the automatic generation of briefings in integrated text and information graphics. Int. J. Hum. Comput. Stud. **61**(1), 32–70 (2004)
10. Gennari, J.J., Musen, M., Fergerson, R., Grosso, W., Crubezy, M., Eriksson, H., Noy, N., Tu, S.: The evolution of Protégé: an environment for knowledge-based systems development. Int. J. Hum. Comput. Stud. **58**(1), 89–123 (2003)
11. Bimba, A.T., Idris, N., Al-Hunaiyyan, A., Mahmud, R., Abdelaziz, A., Khan, S., Chang, V.: Towards knowledge modeling and manipulation technologies: a survey. Int. J. Inf. Manag. **36**(6), 857–871 (2016)
12. Baker, C.F.: FrameNet: a knowledge base for natural language processing. In: Proceedings of Frame Semantics in NLP: A Workshop in Honor of Chuck Fillmore (2014)
13. Driankov, D., Hellendoorn, H., Reinfrank, M.: An Introduction to Fuzzy Control. Springer Science & Business Media, Heidelberg (2013)
14. Kerr-Wilson, J., Pedrycz, W.: Design of rule-based models through information granulation. Expert Syst. Appl. **46**, 274–285 (2016)
15. Sánchez, D., Moreno, A.: Learning non-taxonomic relationships from web documents for domain ontology construction. Data Knowl. Eng. **64**(3), 600–623 (2008)
16. Sicilia M.-A.: Handbook of metadata, semantics and ontologies. World Scientific (2014)

17. Gruber, T.R.: A translation approach to portable ontology specifications. Knowl. Acquis. **5**, 199–220 (1993)
18. Mizoguchi, R., Vanwelkenhuysen, J., Ikeda, M.: Task ontology for reuse of problem solving knowledge. Very Large Knowl.: Bases Knowl. Build. Knowl. Shar. **46**, 46–59 (1995)
19. Ongenae, F., Claeys, M., Dupont, T., Kerckhove, W., Verhoeve, P., Dhaene, T., De Turck, F.: A probabilistic ontology-based platform for self-learning context-aware healthcare applications. Expert Syst. Appl. **40**(18), 7629–7646 (2013)
20. Yang, Y., Fu, C., Chen, Y., Xu, D., Tang, S.: A belief rule-based expert system for predicting consumer preference in new product development. Knowl.-Based Syst. **94**, 105–113 (2016)
21. Taye, M.M.: Understanding semantic web and ontologies: theory and applications. J. Comput. **2**(6), 182–192 (2010)
22. Neches, R., Fikes, R., Finin, T.W., Gruber, T.R., Patil, R.S., Senator, T.E., Swartout, W.R.: Enabling technology for knowledge sharing. AI Mag. **12**, 36–56 (1991)
23. Reiter, E., Dale, R.: Computational interpretations of the Gricean maxims in the generation of referring expressions. Cognit. Sci. **18**, 233–263 (1995)
24. Pradhan, N., Nathsarma, K., Srinivasa, K., Sukla, L., Mishra, B.: Heap bioleaching of chalcopyrite: a review. Miner. Eng. **21**, 355–365 (2008)
25. Speel, P., Schreiber, A., van Joolingen, W., Beijer, G.: Conceptual Models for Knowledge-Based Systems, in Encyclopedia of Computer Science and Technology. Marcel Dekker Inc., New York (2001)
26. Chabankareh, M., Hezarkhani, A.: Copper potential mapping in Kerman copper bearing belt by using ANFIS method and the input evidential layer analysis. Arab. J. Geosci. **9**(5) (2016). doi:10.1007/s12517-016-2384-z
27. Mann, W.C., Thompson, S.A.: Rhetorical structure theory: toward a functional theory of text organization. Text J. **8**(3), 243–281 (1988)
28. Hunter, J., Gatt, A., Portet, F., Reiter, E., Sripada, G.: Using natural language generation technology to improve information flows in intensive care units. In: Proceedings of 5th Conference on Prestigious Applications of Intelligent Systems, Patras, Greece, 21–25 July 2008
29. Reiter, E., Dale, R.: Building Natural Language Generation Systems. Cambridge University Press, Cambridge (2009)
30. Molina, M., Flores, V.: Generating multimedia presentations that summarize the behavior of dynamic systems using a model-based approach. Expert Syst. Appl. **39**(3), 2759–2770 (2012)
31. Lioma, R., Larsen, B., Lu, W.: Rhetorical relations for information retrieval. In: Proceedings of 35th International ACM SIGIR Conference on Research and Development in Information Retrieval, Oregon, USA (2012)
32. Wang, L., Kim, S.N., Baldwin, T.: The utility of discourse structure in forum thread retrieval. In: Banchs, R.E., Silvestri, F., Liu, T.-Y., Zhang, M., Gao, S., Lang, J. (eds.) AIRS 2013. LNCS, vol. 8281, pp. 284–295. Springer, Heidelberg (2013). doi:10.1007/978-3-642-45068-6_25

Discernibility Matrix and Rules Acquisition Based Chinese Question Answering System

Zhao Han[1,2,3], Duoqian Miao[1,3]([✉]), Fuji Ren[2], and Hongyun Zhang[1]

[1] The College of Electronics and Information Engineering, Tongji University,
Shanghai 201804, China
dqmiao@tongji.edu.cn
[2] The Faculty of Engineering, Tokushima University, Tokushima 770-8506, Japan
[3] The Key Laboratory of Embedded System and Service Computing,
Ministry of Education, Tongji University, Shanghai 200092, China

Abstract. Different from English processing, Chinese text processing starts from word segmentation, and the results of word segmentation will influence the outcomes of subsequent processing especially in short text processing. In this paper, we introduce a novel method for Short Text Information Retrieval based Chinese Question Answering. It is developed from the Discernibility Matrix based Rules Acquisition method. Based on the acquired rules, the matching patterns of the training QA pairs can be represented by the reduced attribute words, and the words can also be represented by the QA patterns. Then the attribute words in the test QA pairs can be used to calculate the matching scores. The experimental results show that the proposed representation method of QA patterns has good flexibility to deal with the uncertainty caused by the Chinese word segmentation, and the proposed method has good performance at both MAP and MRR on the test data.

Keywords: Question Answering · Information Retrieval · Rough Set · Discernibility matrix · Rules acquisition · Short Text Similarity

1 Introduction

Question Answering System (QA System) is one of the most recent research topics in Natural Language Processing (NLP). Most of the existing QA systems are based on one of these two architectures: one is Knowledge based Question Answering (KBQA), and the other is Information Retrieval (IR) based Question Answering (IRBQA). KBQA system generates answering based on the given knowledgebase, while IRBQA searches for the best matching sentence or document from a given list of sentences or documents and returns the matched item as the answering. Because of the difficulty of both knowledgebase construction and text generation, IRBQA is more widely used than KBQA [1,2].

The technology of English Question Answering has been developed well, while the research on Chinese Question Answering still faces a lot of difficulties, especially in Chinese Short Text Question Answering. One of the reasons is that

© Springer International Publishing AG 2017
L. Polkowski et al. (Eds.): IJCRS 2017, Part I, LNAI 10313, pp. 239–248, 2017.
DOI: 10.1007/978-3-319-60837-2_20

Chinese text processing starts from word segmentation, and the results of word segmentation will influence the outcomes of subsequent processing. One of the influences is that the wrong segmentation will reduce the count of the similar words between the question and candidate items, and then reduce the similarity between them. Another is that different word segmentation principles and Chinese abbreviation will also cause the decreasing of the similar words, for example, in some context, the Chinese proper noun *"People's Square"* is not similar with the word *"People"*, while the proper noun *"Baidu Company"* is similar with *"Baidu"*. In English, sometimes this kind of proper nouns can be recognized by capital letters, while in Chinese, all the Chinese characters are without grammatical marker. Since each word of a short sentence text takes a large proportion, the semantic representation of the uncertain word segmentation parts plays an important role in the process of QA matching.

In this paper we will introduce a novel method for Short Text and Information Retrieval based Chinese Question Answering. Based on the Rough Set Theory and Discernibility Matrix based Rules Acquisition method, the matching patterns of the training QA pairs can be represented as rules by the reduced attribute words, and the words can also be represented by the QA patterns. Then the attribute words in the test QA pairs can be used to calculate the matching scores. The experimental results show that the proposed representation method of QA patterns has good flexibility to deal with the uncertainty caused by the Chinese word segmentation, and the proposed method has good performance at both MAP and MRR on the test data.

The remainder of the paper is represented as follows: Sect. 2 introduces related works, and Sect. 3 introduces the training processing of system, such like rules acquisition and attribute vector representation. Section 4 introduces the method of matching QA patterns by a trained QA system. Section 5 describes the experiment details and presents the experimental results and analysis. Section 6 is the conclusion and future work.

2   Related Works

Rough Set Theory [10, 11] is one of the most popular Granular Computing [13, 14] models and can be used to deal with uncertainty problems. In Rough Set Theory, a decision table [12] is defined as $Formula$ (1).

$$DecisionTable = \{U, A = C \cup D, V, f\} \tag{1}$$

In a decision table, U is a finite nonempty set of objects, and A is a finite nonempty set of attributes of the objects. A is divided into two subsets, where one is the set of condition attributes and the other is the set of decision attributes. V is a nonempty set of values of all the attributes, and $f : U \times A \rightarrow V$ is the function that maps an object of U by a attribute of A to a value of V. If there are two objects having the same values of all the condition attributes but their decision attribute values are different, the decision table is inconsistent; otherwise it is consistent.

Based on a decision table, we can get its $POS_c(D)$ by $Formula$ (2) and (3). $POS_C(D)$ is called a positive region of the partition U/D with respective to C, and is a set of all elements of U that can be uniquely classified to blocks of the partition U/D, by means of C. C_*X is called the $C - lower$ region of X, and $C(x)$ is the equivalence class containing an element x.

$$POS_C(D) = \bigcup_{X \in U/D} C_*X \tag{2}$$

$$C_*X = \{x \in U | C(x) \subseteq X\} \tag{3}$$

Sometimes not all the condition attribute are necessary. If a condition attribute $c \in C$ satisfies $Formula$ (4), c is not necessary and can be reduced.

$$POS_{\{C-c\}}(D) = POS_C(D) \tag{4}$$

A lot of Rough Set Theory based methods have been proposed for attribute reduction [3–5]. Our proposed method for QA system is developed from the discernibility matrix theory [6,7]. The classical discernibility matrix is a $|U| \times |U|$ matrix, and its element $M(x, y)$ defined as $Formula$ (5). Based on the discernibility matrix, we can get the discernibility function by $Formula$ (6).

$$M(x, y) = \{a | a \in A, f(x, a) \neq f(y, a)\} \tag{5}$$

$$df(M) = \wedge\{\vee(M(x, y)) | M(x, y) \neq \emptyset\} \tag{6}$$

In traditional IR, the key words are input by users. Different from IR, the input of IRBQA is natural language sentence. The QA system must abstract the key words from the sentence and then match the most related answers. A lot of works have been done for different English and Chinese QA applications [15, 16]. Because of different applications and its corpus or knowledgebase, the method of generating answers is also different, but commonly the QA process is matching the QA pairs by topic similarity. The topic similarity can be measured using the cosine similarity method of word vector representation. In recent years, many word vectorization have been proposed such like VSM [17], LSI [19], LDA [18], Word2Vec [20], and there are also some text similarity related works based on Rough Set method [22,23].

3   Rules Acquisition and Attribute Vectorization

In this section, we will introduce the training processing of our method, including rules acquisition of Chinese QA sentences and vector representations of the attribute words. The attribute word representations are based on the rules, and the representations will be used for matching QA patterns in the testing processing.

3.1   Rules Acquisition of Chinese QA Sentences

Given one question and m labeled candidate items (all the sentences have been segmented into words, the label means whether the item can be used as a answer of the question or not), we first construct a dictionary of all the words of the question and the items. For convenience, we name the item which can match the question as Positive Sentence (PS), and the other Negative Sentence (NS). We name the set of all the PS as Positive Sentence Set (PSS) and the other Negative Sentence Set (NSS). After we get the dictionary, we first remove the words which appear only in the NSS, and also remove some Chinese stopwords. This pre-filtering step will help reduce the dimension and accelerate the following attribute reduction and rules acquisition, and can also make each of the final rule attribute words appear at least once in a PS or the question.

Table 1. Question Answering Matching System (QAMS)

Item/question	w_1	w_2		w_n	Decision label
I_1	v_{11}	v_{12}	...	v_{1n}	v_{1l}
I_2	v_{21}	v_{22}	...	v_{2n}	v_{2l}
...	...	...	...	...	...
I_m	v_{m1}	v_{m2}	...	v_{mn}	v_{ml}
Question	v_{q1}	v_{q2}	...	v_{qn}	v_{ql}

Using the dictionary of n words, we can construct a small Question Answering Matching System (QAMS) for the question and its candidate items, like Table 1. We define this small decision system as $QAMS = \{U = I \cup Q, A = W \cup D, V = 1, 0, f\}$. $I = \{I_1, I_2, \ldots, I_m\}$ is the candidate items set, and Q is a set with only one question in it. $W = \{w_1, w_2, \ldots, w_n\}$ is the word attribute set (the dictionary), and D is the decision attribute set with only the matching label attribute in it. The function $f(u, a)$ is defined as $Formula\,(7)$.

$$f(u \in U, a \in A) = \begin{cases} 1, & \text{if } a \in D \text{ and } u \in PSS \cup Q; \\ & \text{or if } a \in W \text{ and } a \in u \\ 0, & \text{the other} \end{cases} \tag{7}$$

The function $f : U \times A \to V$ means that if an attribute word appears in an item or the question, and the attribute value equals 1, or if the item is a PS or the question, its decision attribute value is 1. Then we need to mining the rules in the $QAMS$. Since for QA system, we only need to concern about the rules for question and its PSS. Then the discernibility matrix of the $QAMS$ is a $x \times y$ matrix, $x = |PSS| + |Q|$, $y = |NSS|$. The values of the QA Discernibility Matrix (QADM) is defined as $Fomular\,(8)$ and (9).

$$Dset(u_p, u_n) = \{a | a \in W, u_n \in NSS, u_p \in PSS \cup Q, f(u_p, a) \neq f(u_n, a)\} \tag{8}$$

$$QADM(u_p, u_n) = \begin{cases} Dset(u_p, u_n), & \text{if } |Dset(u_p, u_n)| > 0 \\ \{a|a \in u_p\}, & \text{the other} \end{cases} \qquad (9)$$

The discernibility function of the $QADM$ is defined as $Fomular$ (10).

$$df(QADM) =$$
$$\wedge \{\vee(QADM(u_p, u_n))|u_n \in NSS, u_p \in PSS \cup Q, QADM(u_p, u_n) \neq \emptyset\} \qquad (10)$$

In the function expression of $QADM$, $\vee(QADM(u_p, u_n))$ is the disjunction of all attributes in $QADM(u_p, u_n)$ and $\wedge\{\vee(QADM(u_p, u_n))\}$ is the conjunction of all $\vee(QADM(u_p, u_n))$. When u_p and u_n is inconsistent, that is to say, all of their attribute words are the same, we will set the value of $QADM$ by the attributes of u_p. The original corpus of QA system is consistent theoretically. However, there are two reasons for this definition: one is that it can avoid the error case of the mislabeled items in the corpus, and the other is that after the pre-filtering step the consistent $QAMS$ may turn to inconsistent.

Table 2. An example of a QAMS

Item/question	w_1	w_2	w_3	w_4	Decision label
I_1	0	0	1	1	1
I_2	1	0	1	0	1
I_3	0	1	1	1	0
I_4	0	1	0	1	0
Question	1	1	1	1	1

A $QAMS$ example is showed in Table 2 and its $QADM$ is showed in Table 3. The example $QAMS$ is with 4 attribute words and 4 candidate items. 2 of the 4 candidate items are PSs. The $QADM$ of it is a 3×2 matrix. Based on $Formula$ (10) we can get the discernibility function, showed in $Formula$ (11). The result of $Formula$ (11) means that a question and its PSs can be discerned from the NSs by the words w_1 and w_2.

$$\begin{aligned} df(M) &= (w_2) \wedge (w_2 \vee w_3) \\ &\wedge (w_1 \vee w_2 \vee w_4) \wedge (w_1 \vee w_2 \vee w_3 \vee w_4) \\ &\wedge (w_1) \wedge (w_1 \vee w_3) \\ &= (w_1) \wedge (w_2) \end{aligned} \qquad (11)$$

If the result is like $(w_1 \vee w_3) \wedge (w_2)$, that means the discernibility rules can be w_1 and w_2, or can be w_3 and w_2.

Table 3. The QADM of the QAMS in Table 2

	I_3	I_4
I_1	$\{w_2\}$	$\{w_2, w_3\}$
I_2	$\{w_1, w_2, w_4\}$	$\{w_1, w_2, w_3, w_4\}$
Question	$\{w_1\}$	$\{w_1, w_3\}$

3.2   Vector Representation of Attribute Word

Given a set of questions and their labeled candidate items, we can get all of their $QAMS$s, reduced attributed words and rules. Based on the reduced attribute words and the acquired rules, each of the attribute words can be represented as list of vectors. The vector unit v is defined as $Formula\,(12)$. $NO.(QADM)$ is the number label of the $QADM$, $Len(df_{QADM})$ is the sum count of all conjunction elements in the final result of the discernibility function, and $NO.(w_{df})$ is the number label of the conjuncted element of the final result in which the word appears. $T(w_{df})$ is the tag whether the word is appeared in the question or candidate items or both of them.

$$v = [NO.(QADM), \quad Len(df_{QADM}), \quad NO.(w_{df}), \quad T(w_{df})] \tag{12}$$

After we trained a set of questions and its labeled candidate items, all the attribute words can be represented like $Formula\,(13)$. In this Formula, θ is the appearance times of the attribute words in all the $QADM$ of the corpus.

$$WV = [v_1, v_2, \ldots, v_\theta] \tag{13}$$

For example, if the $QAMS$ is the second one of the whole training corpus and the word w_1 and w_2 does not appears in other $QAMS$s, based on $Formula\,(11)$ the word w_1 can be represented as $Formula\,(14)$ and the word w_1 can be represented as $Formula\,(15)$. The ellipsis is the cases of the word appearance vectors in other $QAMS$s.

$$WV_{w_1} = [\quad [2,2,1,\{'Q','PSS'\}] \quad ,\ldots] \tag{14}$$

$$WV_{w_2} = [\quad [2,2,2,\{'Q'\}] \quad ,\ldots] \tag{15}$$

The attribute words and the acquired rules can be treated as a kind of QA sentence patterns, and $NO.(QADM)$ can be treated as the QA pattern number. However, the model lacks the topic information of the QA. So when it comes to practical application, it must be used at the same time with some topic similarity model.

4   Method of Matching QA Patterns

We can get a dictionary with all the attribute words represented by $Formula\,(13)$. Then when a test question and an unlabeled candidate item are given, we can get two list of word vector elements from the attribute words appears in the two word sequence: $VL_q = [v_1, v_2, \ldots]$ and $VL_{I_i} = [v_1, v_2, \ldots]$. The next step is to count up the QA pattens and measure their completeness. But before that we must do some preliminary reduction.

At the reduction step, there are two kinds of processing choices. One is that we need to concern the word vector element tag $T(w_{df})$, that means, for example, if a word appears only in the question, and one of its vector tag means it appears only in the NSS in a QA pattern of the train corpus, we must remove it from VL_q. That means we treat strictly that in one QA pattern, the word role of it should not be exchanged. The other processing choice is that we just ignore the tags and we consider that sometimes the words among question and candidate items can be exchanged and will not change the semantic too much.

Table 4. An example of the middle dictionary of the patterns

NO.(QADM)	vlist	Len(df_{QADM})	vlistlength	C_{QADM}
36	{[36, 4,2, {'Q'}], [36, 4,1, {'PSS'}]}	4	2	0.5
53	{ [53, 1,1, {'Q', 'PSS'}] }	1	1	1
...	...	...	...	...
182	{[182, 4,2, {'Q'}] }	4	1	0

Then based on the $NO.(QADM)$ we count up the pattern and its vector elements (the same elements are counted only once). An example of the middle dictionary of the patterns is illustrated in Table 4. Here we define the completeness of a pattern (QADM) as $Formula$ (16).

$$C_{QADM} = \begin{cases} 0, & \text{if } vlistlength - 1 \text{ and } Len(df_{QADM}) \neq 1 \\ \dfrac{vlistlength}{Len(df_{QADM})}, & \text{the other} \end{cases} \quad (16)$$

and the final completeness of the QA pairs is calculated by $Formula$ (17).

$$C(q, I_i) = \sum_{\bigcup QADM|q, I_i} C_{QADM} \quad (17)$$

5   Experiment

The experiment is divided into two parts: one is on the sentence pattern similarity and the other is on the text retrieval. As there are two choice at the reduction step of the Matching method (with vector tags and without tags), we evaluate both in the experiment. The first experiment is comparing the proposed method with the word2vec pattern similarity method, and in the second experiment it is compared with cosine similarity of LDA and LSI model. In the second experiment, the text similarity matching part of our method is the same as LDA baseline.

Both the two experiments use the opensource corpus and toolkits of NLPCC-ICCPOL2016 Shared Task (Evaluation Competition) [8]. The corpus contains a train subset and test subset. The train set contains 8772 question texts, and the test set contains 5997 questions. Each of the question is given a list of candidate items and some of the items can be used as answers to the question. The train set contains 181882 items and the test set contains 122531 items. The baseline models of the experiments are constructed by Gensim Toolkit [9], and the word segmentation of all the Chinese text is completed by the NLPIR (also named as ICTCLAS) tool [21].

In our experiment, the evaluation metrics is the same with the competition: Mean Average Precision (MAP) (see $Formula$ (18) and (19)) and Mean Reciprocal Rank (MRR) (see $Formula$ (20)).

$$MAP = \frac{1}{|Q|} \sum_{i=1}^{|Q|} AveP(C_i, A_i) \tag{18}$$

$$AveP(C_i, A_i) = \begin{cases} 0, & \text{if } min(m,n) = 0 \\ \frac{\sum_{k=1}^{n}(P(k) \cdot rel(k))}{min(m,n)}, & \text{the other} \end{cases} \tag{19}$$

$$MRR = \frac{1}{|Q|} \sum_{i=1}^{|Q|} \frac{1}{rank_i} \tag{20}$$

Here is the explanation of MAP and MRR from the official document [8]: In MAP formula, k is the rank in the sequence of retrieved answer sentences, m is the number of correct answer sentences, and n is the number of retrieved answer sentences. $P(k)$ is the precision at cut-off k in the list. $rel(k)$ equals 1 if the item at rank k is an answer sentence, otherwise it equals 0. In MRR formula, $rank_i$ is the position of the first correct answer in the generated answer set C_i for the Q_i, and if C_i doesn't overlap with the golden answer A_i for Q_i, $\frac{1}{rank_i}$ equals 0.

The experimental results are in Tables 5 and 6. In Table 5, the withtags version of our method has best performance, but the withouttags version is not unsatisfactory. In Table 6, both the two version of our method have improve the performance of LDA baseline, and they all have better performance that LSI baseline model.

Table 5. Results of sentence patterns similarity experiment

	MAP	MRR
W2Vcosine	0.4075	0.4081
DM (withtags)	**0.4520**	**0.4525**
DM (withouttags)	0.2923	0.2924

Table 6. Results of QA retrieval experiment

	MAP	MRR
LDAcosine	0.6386	0.6392
LSIcosine	0.5372	0.5376
DM (withtags)	**0.6464**	**0.6469**
DM (withouttags)	**0.6436**	**0.6440**

The MAP and MRR results of the withtags version of our method are higher than the withouttags version at both of the two experiments. It shows that at this QA corpus, most of the attribute words have fixed roles in QA patterns. So the final rule expressions acquired by the withtags version method can represent more information of the QA patterns.

6   Conclusion

In this paper a novel method for short text and Information Retrieval based Chinese Question Answering is proposed. It has good flexibility to deal with the Chinese QA uncertainty by mining and representing QA pattern, and the proposed method has good performance at both MAP and MRR on the test data. The future work will focus on more QA experiments by other kinds of feature selection and attribute reduction method based on Rough Sets and on other Chinese and English QA corpus.

Acknowledgments. This work is supported by the National Natural Science Foundation of China (61273304, 61673301, 61573255) and the Specialized Research Fund for the Doctoral Program of Higher Education of China (20130072130004).

References

1. Yang, Y., Jiang, P., Ren, F., et al.: Classic Chinese automatic question answering system based on pragmatics information. In: 7th Mexican International Conference on Artificial Intelligence, pp. 58–64. IEEE Computer Society (2008)
2. Hu, H., Ren, F., Kuroiwa, S., Zhang, S.: A question answering system on special domain and the implementation of speech interface. In: Gelbukh, A. (ed.) CICLing 2006. LNCS, vol. 3878, pp. 458–469. Springer, Heidelberg (2006). doi:10.1007/11671299_48
3. Yao, Y., Zhao, Y.: Attribute reduction in decision-theoretic rough set models. Inf. Sci. **178**(17), 3356–3373 (2008)
4. Wang, J., Miao, D.: Analysis on attribute reduction strategies of rough set. J. Comput. Sci. Technol. **13**(2), 189–192 (1998)
5. Lang, G., Miao, D., Yang, T., et al.: Knowledge reduction of dynamic covering decision information systems when varying covering cardinalities. Inf. Sci. **346**, 236–260 (2016)

6. Skowron, A., Rauszer, C.: The discernibility matrices and functions in information systems. Theory Decis. Libr. **11**, 331–362 (1992)
7. Miao, D.Q., Zhao, Y., Yao, Y.Y., et al.: Relative reducts in consistent and inconsistent decision tables of the Pawlak rough set model. Inf. Sci. **179**(24), 4140–4150 (2009)
8. Duan, N.: Overview of the NLPCC-ICCPOL 2016 shared task: open domain chinese question answering. In: Lin, C.-Y., Xue, N., Zhao, D., Huang, X., Feng, Y. (eds.) ICCPOL/NLPCC -2016. LNCS, vol. 10102, pp. 942–948. Springer, Cham (2016). doi:10.1007/978-3-319-50496-4_89
9. Rehurek, R., Sojka, P.: Software framework for topic modelling with large corpora. In: Proceedings of LREC 2010 Workshop on New Challenges for NLP Frameworks, pp. 45–50 (2010)
10. Pawlak, Z.: Rough sets. Int. J. Parallel Prog. **11**(5), 341–356 (1982)
11. Pawlak, Z.: Rough Sets: Theoretical Aspects of Reasoning about Data. Springer Science and Business Media, Heidelberg (2012)
12. Pawlakab, Z.: Rough set approach to knowledge-based decision support. Eur. J. Oper. Res. **99**(1), 48–57 (1995)
13. Bargiela, A., Pedrycz, W.: Toward a theory of granular computing for human-centered information processing. IEEE Trans. Fuzzy Syst. **16**(2), 320–330 (2008)
14. Yao, J.T., Vasilakos, A.V., Pedrycz, W.: Granular computing: perspectives and challenges. IEEE Trans. Cybern. **43**(6), 1977–1989 (2013)
15. Sun, A., Jiang, M., He, Y., et al.: Chinese question answering based on syntax analysis and answer classification. Acta Electronica Sinica **36**(5), 833–839 (2008)
16. Dwivedi, S.K., Singh, V.: Research and reviews in question answering system. Proc. Technol. **10**(1), 417–424 (2013)
17. Salton, G.: A vector space model for automatic indexing. Commun. ACM **18**(11), 613–620 (1975)
18. Blei, D.M., Ng, A.Y., Jordan, M.I.: Latent Dirichlet allocation. J. Mach. Learn. Res. **3**(1), 993–1022 (2003)
19. Papadimitriou, C.H., Tamaki, H., Raghavan, P., Indexing, L.S., et al.: A probabilistic analysis. In: Proceedings of 17th ACM SIGACT-SIGMOD-SIGART Symposium on Principles of Database Systems, pp. 159–168. ACM (1998)
20. Mikolov, T., Sutskever, I., Chen, K., et al.: Distributed representations of words and phrases and their compositionality. In: Advances in Neural Information Processing Systems, vol. 26, pp. 3111–3119 (2013)
21. Zhang, H.P., Yu, H.K., Xiong, D.Y., et al.: HHMM-based Chinese lexical analyzer ICTCLAS. In: Proceedings of 2nd SIGHAN Workshop on Chinese Language Processing, vol. 17, pp. 184–187. Association for Computational Linguistics (2003)
22. Janusz, A., Zak, D., Nguyen, H.S.: Unsupervised similarity learning from textual data. Fundamenta Informaticae **119**(3–4), 319–336 (2012)
23. Janusz, A.: Algorithms for similarity relation learning from high dimensional data. In: Peters, J.F. (ed.) Transactions on Rough Sets XVII, pp. 174–292. Springer, Heidelberg (2014)

Methods Based on Pawlak's Model of Conflict Analysis - Medical Applications

Małgorzata Przybyła-Kasperek[✉]

Institute of Computer Science, University of Silesia,
Będzińska 39, 41-200 Sosnowiec, Poland
malgorzata.przybyla-kasperek@us.edu.pl
http://www.us.edu.pl

Abstract. In the study, issues related to the decision-making process using knowledge that is accumulated in several local knowledge bases are considered. In order to analyze conflicts and to create coalitions of base classifiers, three modifications of Pawlak's model were applied. A system that uses these three modifications was then used for two dispersed sets of medical data. The main aim of this study was to compare the structure of the coalitions that were created. In the paper, the quality of the classification of the system using the proposed modifications was also compared.

Keywords: Decision-making system · Dispersed knowledge · Conflict analysis · Pawlak's model

1 Introduction

The use of dispersed knowledge is very important. When knowledge is collected in independent and separate bases by different units, in order to use all of the available knowledge in the classification process, adequate methods must be used. Such methods should be general enough to cope with many decision tables, in which both the sets of attributes and the sets of objects are not pairwise disjoint or equal.

The author has been dealing with the issues associated with the use of dispersed knowledge for several years. Different approaches to solving this problem have been proposed. Various methods for creating a system's structure have been analyzed - from a static structure [17] through a simple dynamic structure [21] to a complex dynamic structure [19]. It was observed that in a system with dispersed knowledge, an inconsistency of knowledge may occur and method for dealing with this have been proposed [17]. Various methods for fusing local decisions into a global decision have been considered [19,22].

In this article, methods for creating the structure of a dispersed system - coalitions of base classifiers that are based on the Pawlak's conflicts model, are considered. The study is a continuation and extension of the paper [23], in which these methods were proposed for the first time. The paper [23] only contains

© Springer International Publishing AG 2017
L. Polkowski et al. (Eds.): IJCRS 2017, Part I, LNAI 10313, pp. 249–262, 2017.
DOI: 10.1007/978-3-319-60837-2_21

a description and a theoretical analysis of these methods. In this article, the methods have been applied to two medical data sets. These data sets were also considered in the paper [18] but for different approach. The goal of this paper is to experimentally investigate the structure of the coalitions of classifiers that are generated using three methods based on Pawlak's conflicts model. In this article, a comprehensive analysis of the generated coalitions is discussed.

In the study, new methods of creating coalitions of classifiers were used, but the general scheme for operating a dispersed system was taken from the previous work [19]. The general scheme for generating global decisions is as follows. First, each classifier generates a certain vector of ranks that expresses the classification made by the classifier. Then, the structure of the system is created by generating coalitions of classifiers. In this step, new methods are used. For each coalition, a common knowledge is generated. In this step, the method for the elimination of inconsistencies in the knowledge that was proposed in the previous work [19] is used. Then, local decisions are taken. In order to determine the global decisions, a certain method of conflict analysis, which is based on a density algorithm [17], is used.

The main issues that are discussed in this paper are analyzing conflicts and forming coalitions of classifiers. In an article in 1984 [10], Professor Pawlak proposed a model of conflict analysis. This model was then developed in the papers [11–16]. The model provides a simple way to determine the relations between individuals involved in a conflict. It enables an analysis of the strength of units and allows the modeling of the conflict. In this study, modifications of this model were used. In the literature, other approaches to conflict analysis can be found. A brief overview of the various negotiation models that have been proposed in the literature can be found in the paper [9]. Some theoretical models have been proposed for describing, specifying, and reasoning about the key features of negotiating agents [3,25]. Computational models have been suggested for specifying the key data structures of negotiating agents and the processes operating on these structures [4,24]. Many mathematical models of conflict situations have been proposed [6–8]. In these models, a number of different aspects such as risks, consequences and alternatives have been analyzed. In the situation that is considered in the paper, only vectors of ranks are available and it would be difficult to apply such general frameworks since many of the aspects that occur in it are not determined.

The concept of distributed decision making is widely discussed in the paper [26]. The concept of taking a global decision on the basis of local decisions is also used in issues concerning the multiple model approach. Examples of the application of this approach can be found in the literature [1,28]. Moreover, in many other papers [2,27], the problem of using distributed knowledge is considered. This paper describes a different approach to the global decision-making process. We assume that the set of local knowledge bases that contain information from one domain is pre-specified. The only condition that must be satisfied by the local knowledge bases is to have common decision attributes.

In the literature, different fusion methods have been proposed [5,7]. These methods are used to combine the predictions of base classifiers. Fusion methods do not identify the coalitions of classifiers, but simply generate a common decision. Fusion methods are divided into three groups: the abstract level, the rank level and the measurement level. In the paper [22], selected fusion methods in a dispersed system were analyzed.

2   An Overview of Pawlak's Conflict Model and Proposed Modifications

In this section, the basic concepts of the Pawlak's model are given.

It is assumed that the set Ag is the set of agents that are involved in the conflict. An opinion about certain discussed issues is expressed by each agent by assigning one of three values. -1 means that an agent is against the issue, 0 means it is neutral and 1 means it is for the issue. This knowledge can be written in the form of an information system $S = (U, A)$, where the universe U is the set of agents, A is the set of issues and the set of values of $a \in A$ is equal to $V^a = \{-1, 0, 1\}$. The value $a(x)$, where $x \in U, a \in A$ is the opinion of agent x about issue a.

In the first step of conflict analysis, the relationships between agents are determined. For this purpose, the function $\phi_a : U \times U \to \{-1, 0, 1\}$ is defined for each $a \in A$:

$$\phi_a(x, y) = \begin{cases} 1 & \text{if } a(x)a(y) = 1 \text{ or } x = y, \\ 0 & \text{if } a(x)a(y) = 0 \text{ and } x \neq y, \\ -1 & \text{if } a(x)a(y) = -1. \end{cases}$$

Three relations are defined: R_a^+ alliance, R_a^0 neutrality and R_a^- conflict over $U \times U$. These relationships are expressed as follows

$$R_a^+(x, y) \text{ if and only if } \phi_a(x, y) = 1,$$
$$R_a^0(x, y) \text{ if and only if } \phi_a(x, y) = 0,$$
$$R_a^-(x, y) \text{ if and only if } \phi_a(x, y) = -1.$$

Each equivalence class of alliance relation R_a^+ is called a coalition on a.

In order to determine the relations between agents due to a set of attributes, the function of the distance between agents $\rho_B^* : U \times U \to [0, 1]$ for the set of issues $B \subseteq A$ is defined

$$\rho_B^*(x, y) = \frac{\sum_{a \in B} \phi_a^*(x, y)}{card\{B\}},$$

where

$$\phi_a^*(x, y) = \frac{1 - \phi_a(x, y)}{2} = \begin{cases} 0 & \text{if } a(x)a(y) = 1 \text{ or } x = y, \\ 0.5 & \text{if } a(x)a(y) = 0 \text{ and } x \neq y, \\ 1 & \text{if } a(x)a(y) = -1. \end{cases}$$

In the definition, it is assumed that the distance between the agents that are in conflict is greater than the distance between the agents that are neutral. The function of the distance between the agents for the set of all issues $B = A$ is written in short as ρ^*.

The conflict between agents can also be expressed in another way. The conflict function $\rho_B : U \times U \rightarrow [0, 1]$ for the set of issues $B \subseteq A$ is defined as follows:

$$\rho_B(x, y) = \frac{card\{\delta_B(x, y)\}}{card\{B\}},$$

where $\delta_B(x, y) = \{a \in B : a(x) \neq a(y)\}$. When we consider a single attribute in this function, the distance between some agents that are in conflict R_a^- is equal to the distance between the agents that are neutral R_a^0. That means that this function assesses the relationship between agents more restrictively. Agents who are neutral toward some issue (value 0 has been assigned) and all of the agents that are against or for are treated as agents that have opposing goals.

When applying one of the two functions mentioned above, we can define the relations between agents more generally by taking into account a set of attributes. A pair $x, y \in U$ is said to be:

- allied $R^+(x, y)$, if $\rho(x, y) < 0.5$,
- in conflict $R^-(x, y)$, if $\rho(x, y) > 0.5$,
- neutral $R^0(x, y)$, if $\rho(x, y) = 0.5$.

Set $X \subseteq U$ is a coalition if for every $x, y \in X$, $R^+(x, y)$ and $x \neq y$.

The concepts proposed by Pawlak that were discussed above have been applied to the analysis of the relations between the base classifiers. It was assumed that each of the base classifiers made an initial classification that was saved as a vector of ranks. In this vector, one rank was assigned for each decision. More precisely, each classifier is called an agent ag (in this paper, the concepts classifier and agent are used interchangeably). It is assumed that for a classified object x and for each classifier ag_i, a vector of ranks $[r_{i,1}(x), \ldots, r_{i,c}(x)]$, where c is the number of decision classes, is generated. In order to apply the Pawlak's model, an information system should be generated based on these vectors of ranks. The universe in such a system will be equal to the set of classifiers and the set of issues that are considered by the classifiers will be equal to the set of decision classes. Two different methods of defining the function $a : U \rightarrow \{-1, 0, 1\}$, $a \in A$ were considered in this study.

In the first method the function $a : U \rightarrow \{-1, 0, 1\}$ for each $a \in A$ is defined in the following way

$$a(ag) = \begin{cases} 1 & \text{if } r_{ag,a}(x) = 1 \\ -1 & \text{if } r_{ag,a}(x) > 1 \end{cases}$$

In the second method the function $a : U \rightarrow \{-1, 0, 1\}$ for each $a \in A$ is defined in the following way

$$a(ag) = \begin{cases} 1 & \text{if } r_{ag,a}(x) = 1 \\ 0 & \text{if } r_{ag,a}(x) = 2 \\ -1 & \text{if } r_{ag,a}(x) > 2 \end{cases}$$

The first method for defining an information system is more restrictive. Agents are for only to the decisions that received Rank 1. For all other decision values the agents are against. In the second method for defining an information system agent is neutral to the decisions that received Rank 2.

As was described above, in order to determine the coalitions of agents, two functions can be used: the function of distance between agents ρ^* or the conflict function ρ. The first function is less restrictive because the distance between agents which are neutral is smaller than distance between agents being in conflict. Since defining neutrality in an information system does not exist in the first method, both functions generate the same set of coalitions for this system. Thus, three different methods of generating coalitions of classifiers based on Pawlak's model can be distinguished

- *Method 1* - the first method for defining an information system is used,
- *Method 2* - the second method for defining an information system and the function of the distance between the agents are used,
- *Method 3* - the second method for defining an information system and the conflict function are used.

In this study, all three methods of creating coalitions will be considered and compared.

Below, some aspects concerning the organization of a dispersed system, which are taken from the author's previous works [17, 19, 22], will be briefly discussed.

Before defining an information system, a vector of ranks for each classifier must be generated. This is accomplished by generating a vector of probabilities for each classifier using the m_1 nearest neighbor classifier. The vector of ranks is generated based on the vector of probabilities.

After generating the coalitions using one of the methods discussed above, a certain common knowledge for the classifiers from one coalition is generated. For this purpose, a method for the elimination of inconsistencies in the knowledge is used. This method is described in more detail in the paper [17]. The method consists in generating one aggregated decision table that is based on the selected, relevant objects from the decision tables belonging to one coalition. In this method, parameter m_2 occurs, which determines the size of the set of relevant objects. As was described above, the coalitions of classifiers are generated dynamically. That is, for each new case, another set of coalitions is determined. Additionally, new aggregated decision tables are generated for each new object. This is a method that ensures that the aggregated knowledge is relevant to case currently being considered.

Then, a vector of probabilities is generated based on the aggregated decision table. This vector reflects the classification that is made by a coalition. The sum of the probabilities vectors is calculated and the density based algorithm is used to determine the set of decisions that have obtained the highest probability. This is done in the following way. The decision with the largest value of the coordinate of the vector sum is determined and then the set of decisions that is densely located is calculated using the DBSCAN algorithm. This set is the set of global decisions. In the DBSCAN algorithm, parameter ε, which determines the size of the neighborhood, is very significant. This method was also used in the papers [17, 19, 21].

3 Experiments

The aim of the experiments was to compare the structure of the coalitions that are created using three different methods of conflicts analysis that are based on Pawlak's model. The purpose of this comparison was to determine which of the methods captures the relationships between the classifiers in the best way. In the paper, some measures to determine the quality of the created coalitions are proposed. These measures take into account the distances of the vectors of the ranks that were generated by the agents from one coalition and are defined below ($Avg_W, SD_W, Min_W, Max_W$). The relationships between the classifiers are well reflected in the coalitions if the distances of the vectors of ranks that were generated by the agents from one coalition are not too large. An additional objective was to identify some general properties of the considered methods. All of the experiments were performed on a Dell Inspiron N7110 Intel Core i7-2670QM with 8 GB RAM and Windows 7. The algorithms were implemented in C#. For the experiments, the following data from the medical domain, which are in the UCI repository, were used - the Lymphography data set and the Primary Tumor data set. Both data sets were created at the University Medical Centre, Institute of Oncology, Ljubljana, Slovenia. A numerical summary of the data sets is as follows: Lymphography: # training examples - 104; # test examples - 44; # conditional attributes - 18; # decisions - 4; Primary Tumor: # training examples - 237; # test examples - 102; # conditional attributes - 17; # decisions - 22. In the repository, these data are available in a non-dispersed form (one decision table). In order to perform the experiments, some transformations to disperse the data sets were made. These transformations were described in the paper [18]. As a result of the transformations, five different versions of dispersion were obtained (with 3, 5, 7, 9 and 11 decision tables). The following designations are used for these systems: WSD_{Ag1}^{dyn} - 3 decision tables; WSD_{Ag2}^{dyn} - 5 decision tables; WSD_{Ag3}^{dyn} - 7 decision tables; WSD_{Ag4}^{dyn} - 9 decision tables; WSD_{Ag5}^{dyn} - 11 decision tables.

To compare of the structure of coalitions that were created using different methods the following measures were used. To determine the number of coalitions that were created the following measures are used:

- average number of coalitions created for objects from a test set Avg_C
- standard deviation of number of coalitions created for objects from a test set SD_C
- minimum and maximum number of coalitions created for objects from a test set Min_C, Max_C

To determine the number of agents in coalitions that were created, the measures are used:

- average number of agents in coalitions created for objects from a test set Avg_A
- standard deviation of the number of agents in coalitions created for objects from a test set SD_A
- minimum and maximum number of agents in coalitions that are created for objects from a test set Min_A, Max_A

In the proposed methods one agent may be included in many coalitions that are generated for the test object. To determine the number of agents that simultaneously belong to more than one coalition, the measures are used:

- total number of times when one agent has been included in many coalitions r
- average number of times when one agent has been included in many coalitions $\bar{r}$

To determine the distances of vectors of ranks that were generated by agents from one coalition, the measures are used:

- average value of the Euclidean distances between vectors of ranks generated by pairs of agents belonging to the same coalition Avg_W
- standard deviation of the Euclidean distances between vectors of ranks generated by pairs of agents belonging to the same coalition SD_W
- minimum and maximum value of the Euclidean distances between vectors of ranks generated by pairs of agents belonging to the same coalition Min_W, Max_W

Some of these measures are described in more detail in the article [19].

In order to optimize the parameters and to compare the quality of the classification, the following measures are also used:

- estimator of classification error e in which an object is considered to be properly classified if the decision class used for the object belonged to the set of global decisions generated by the system;
- estimator of classification ambiguity error e_{ONE} in which object is considered to be properly classified if only one, correct value of the decision was generated for this object;
- the average size of the global decisions sets $\bar{d}_{WSD_{Ag}^{dyn}}$ generated for a test set.

In the methods that are used in a dispersed system, certain parameters are present: m_1 - the parameter of the method for generating the vectors of ranks for classifiers, m_2 - the parameter of the method for generating the common knowledge for the coalition and ε - the parameter of the DBSCAN algorithm. These parameters were optimized as follows. Firstly, parameters m_1 and m_2 were optimized - values $m_1, m_2 \in \{1, \ldots, 10\}$ were examined. Then, the minimum value of the parameters m_1 and m_2 were chosen, which resulted in the lowest value of the estimator of the classification error on a test set to be reached. The optimum values for these parameters can be chosen unambiguously. Parameter ε was optimized by performing a series of experiments with different values of this parameter that were increased from 0 by the value 0.0001. Then, a graph was created and the points that indicated the greatest improvement in the efficiency of inference were selected. For some sets of data, there were many areas on the graph in which there was a noticeable improvement - a significant decrease in the value of the estimator of classification error was observed. The Lymphography data set is an example of such a set. Therefore, in Table 3, two optimal values of parameter ε are given for each system. It should be noted that the ε parameter had no effect on the coalition's structure. In the rest of the paper, the results that were obtained for the optimal values of the parameter m_1, m_2 and ε are presented.

The main results, which are related to the analysis of the structure of the coalitions are presented in Tables 1 and 2. In the tables, the following information is given: the name of the dispersed system (System); the method that was used to generate the coalitions (Method): *1* - the first proposed method for creating an information system, *2* - the second proposed method for creating an information system with the function of the distance between agents, and *3* - the second proposed method for creating an information system with the conflict function; the measures that are related to the structure of the coalitions: Avg_C, SD_C, Min_C, Max_C, Avg_A, SD_A, Min_A, Max_A, r, $\bar{r}$, Avg_W, SD_W, Min_W and Max_W.

Table 1. Comparison of the coalitions that were generated by Methods 1, 2, and 3 (Lymphography data set)

System	Approach	# coalitions	# agents in coalitions	# joint agents	# distance within coalition
		$Avg_C / SD_C / Min_C / Max_C$	$Avg_A / SD_A / Min_A / Max_A$	$r / \bar{r}$	$Avg_W / SD_W / Min_W / Max_W$
WSD_{Ag1}^{dyn}	1	**1.32**/0.51/1/3	**2.38**/0.74/1/3	6/0.14	**5.97**/4.79/0/18
	2	**1.16**/0.37/1/2	**2.63**/0.66/1/3	2/0.045	**5.33**/3.39/0/12
	3	**1.89**/0.57/1/3	**1.59**/0.69/1/3	0/0	**0.94**/1.53/0/8
WSD_{Ag2}^{dyn}	1	**2.48**/0.50/2/3	**2.02**/1/1/4	0/0	**2.82**/4.96/0/24
	2	**1.57**/0.65/1/3	**3.58**/1.31/1/5	27/0.61	**15.10**/9.92/0/34
	3	**2.82**/0.65/2/4	**1.97**/0.78/1/4	24/0.55	**2.05**/3.24/0/15
WSD_{Ag3}^{dyn}	1	**2.61**/0.65/2/4	**3.15**/1.72/1/6	54/1.23	**14.83**/14.70/0/53
	2	**1.89**/0.86/1/4	**5.12**/1.52/1/7	117/2.66	**24.58**/12.85/0/54
	3	**3.25**/0.86/2/5	**2.67**/1.34/1/6	74/1.68	**4.99**/7.08/0/29
WSD_{Ag4}^{dyn}	1	**3.34**/1.17/2/6	**4.86**/1.84/1/8	319/7.25	**16.71**/12.02/0/54
	2	**2.39**/1.07/1/5	**6.59**/1.45/2/9	296/6.73	**33.33**/15.41/6/72
	3	**3.43**/1.14/2/7	**3.40**/1.61/1/8	118/2.68	**7.25**/8.64/0/36
WSD_{Ag5}^{dyn}	1	**3.61**/1.05/2/7	**3.85**/1.58/1/8	128/2.91	**16.46**/15.09/0/70
	2	**4.07**/0.94/2/7	**3.83**/1.82/1/9	201/4.57	**15.44**/18.25/0/92
	3	**5.43**/1.03/3/8	**2.49**/1.15/1/6	112/2.55	**3.16**/3.93/0/26

Table 2. Comparison of the coalitions that were generated by Methods 1, 2, and 3 (Primary Tumor data set)

System	Approach	# coalitions	# agents in coalitions	# joint agents	# distance within coalition
		$Avg_C/SD_C/$ Min_C/Max_C	$Avg_A/SD_A/$ Min_A/Max_A	$r/\overline{r}$	$Avg_W/SD_W/$ Min_W/Max_W
WSD_{Ag1}^{dyn}	1	1.16/0.36/1/2	2.70/0.51/1/3	13/0.13	190/150/0/740
	2	1.04/0.19/1/2	2.92/0.26/2/3	4/0.04	228/147/11/740
	3	1.18/0.38/1/2	2.69/0.48/1/3	17/0.17	681/412/0/1760
WSD_{Ag2}^{dyn}	1	1.26/0.44/1/2	4.27/1.06/1/5	41/0.40	1671/1188/0/5146
	2	1.19/0.39/1/2	4.60/0.68/2/5	46/0.45	1884/1077/163/5146
	3	1.39/0.53/1/3	4.33/0.68/3/5	105/1.03	3097/1173/474/6520
WSD_{Ag3}^{dyn}	1	1.51/0.71/1/4	5.75/1.42/2/7	171/1.68	1934/1407/25/6862
	2	1.29/0.53/1/3	6.33/0.93/3/7	121/1.19	4377/199/50/1356
	3	2.76/0.96/1/6	4.60/1.11/2/7	582/5.71	3485/2168/157/10084
WSD_{Ag4}^{dyn}	1	1.96/0.82/1/4	7.25/1.45/3/9	531/5.21	2172/1438/46/8354
	2	1.76/0.74/1/4	7.66/1.29/1/9	461/4.52	4396/2748/0/12542
	3	6.38/1.37/3/11	3.44/0.95/1/7	1323/12.97	356/371/0/2476
WSD_{Ag5}^{dyn}	1	1.81/0.74/1/4	8.58/2.41/3/11	466/4.57	2563/1617/146/6104
	2	1.17/0.42/1/3	10.47/0.99/7/11	124/1.22	449/101/180/736
	3	7.41/1.81/3/12	3.73/1.47/1/9	1698/16.65	343/430/0/4096

Based on the results of the experiments given in Tables 1 and 2, the following conclusions can be drawn. For the Lymphography data set, Method 2 created the fewest number of coalitions, but the coalitions were the most numerous. The exception was the dispersed system with eleven classifiers, for this system Method 1 demonstrated such behavior. Method 3 created the greatest number of coalitions, which, however, are the least numerous. When we consider the diversity of the classifiers within a coalition - the distances of the vectors of ranks that were generated by the classifiers from one coalition - it can be observed that the smallest distance was obtained by Method 3, while the largest distance was obtained by Method 2. This means that Method 3 created the most consistent coalitions and Method 2 created coalitions that included classifiers that were the most different from each other. The number of joint agents varied for the different dispersed systems, it was difficult to find some regularity. However, it can be concluded that Method 3 generated a smaller number of joint agents than the other methods.

For the Primary Tumor data set, the differences between the results that were obtained by Methods 1 and 2 compared to the results that were obtained by Method 3 are much more noticeable. This time Methods 1 and 2 had a tendency to generate one coalition that consisted of all of the classifiers (the value of the measure Avg_C is very close to 1). This is a very unfavorable situation because it means that the methods lost the ability to capture the relationships between the classifiers. The first presumption that comes to mind is that the vectors of ranks that were generated by the classifiers had to be very similar. After a thorough analysis, it was found that this was not true - the vectors were very diverse. The methods had lost the ability to capture the relationships between the classifiers because the vectors, for this data set, are very long (22 decision classes) and only few decisions had a Rank 1 or 2. Thus, for both methods of generating an information system, the vast majority of the values in the information system was equal to -1 (that is, the values in the system were compatible with each other, even though the vectors were very different). In the first method for generating the information system, the situation was even worse. The use of the distance function, which reduces the distance between the neutral agents, resulted in a loss of the ability to capture the relationships. For this data set, only Method 3 generated a different result - a larger number of coalitions, which were less numerous. However, in this method, a large number of joint agents was obtained. Simply, one classifier was allied with several other and coalitions that had duplicate classifier were created. It should be noted that despite such a large number of joint agents, the smallest distance within coalitions was obtained by Method 3 for the systems with eleven and nine classifiers.

Some general conclusions can be drawn. Method 3 generally generated more coalitions that are less numerous. Moreover, this method usually produced coalitions with a smaller distance within the coalitions. In the case of data sets that had a large number of decision classes, Methods 1 and 2 did not provide satisfactory results - they lost their ability to capture the relationships between the classifiers.

As was mentioned earlier, the quality of the classification was also analyzed in this study. The results are shown in Tables 3 and 4. In the tables, the following information is given: the method that was used to generate the coalitions (Methods 1, 2 or 3); the name of the dispersed system (System); the optimal parameters values m_1, m_2 and ε (Parameters); the measures that were used to determine the quality of the classifications: e, e_{ONE} and $\overline{d}_{WSD_{Ag}^{dyn}}$; the time t needed to analyze a test set expressed in minutes. In the tables, the best results in terms of the measures e and $\overline{d}_{WSD_{Ag}^{dyn}}$ are bolded.

Based on the results of the experiments given in Tables 3 and 4, the following conclusions can be drawn. It is difficult to say that one method is the best. For the Lymphography data set, Methods 2 and 3 achieved better results than Method 1. For the Primary Tumor data set, the results that were obtained by various methods are similar. The question arises - why are the results comparable despite the fact that the structure of the coalitions that were generated by different methods was so significantly different. The cause lies in the method for generating global decisions. In this method, the structure of the coalitions was not taken into account. This means that both large and small coalitions had the same influence on the final shape of the global decisions. In addition, if one classifier was included in many coalitions, he had the same impact on global decisions in each of them. So, in fact, his voice was counted several times. In a future work, it is planned to use the strength of coalitions in a dispersed system. The ideas proposed in the paper [20] will be used. In these studies, the aim was to examine the structure of

Table 3. Comparison of the classification quality (Lymphography data set)

System	Parameters $m_1/m_2/\varepsilon$	e	e_{ONE}	$\overline{d}_{WSD_{Ag}^{dyn}}$	t
Method 1					
WSD_{Ag1}^{dyn}	1/1/0.0184	0.091	0.477	1.386	0.01
	1/1/0.0019	**0.136**	0.182	**1.045**	0.01
WSD_{Ag2}^{dyn}	9/1/0.0421	0.136	0.682	1.545	0.01
	9/1/0.0006	0.227	0.273	1.045	0.01
WSD_{Ag3}^{dyn}	2/1/0.0291	**0.091**	0.591	**1.500**	0.01
	2/1/0.0006	0.182	0.295	1.114	0.01
WSD_{Ag4}^{dyn}	1/1/0.0356	0.114	0.682	1.568	0.01
	1/1/0.0006	0.159	0.341	1.182	0.01
WSD_{Ag5}^{dyn}	2/1/0.0221	0.205	0.545	1.341	0.03
	2/1/0.0006	0.250	0.500	1.250	0.03
Method 2					
WSD_{Ag1}^{dyn}	3/1/0.0184	**0.045**	0.432	**1.386**	0.01
	3/1/0.0019	**0.136**	0.182	**1.045**	0.01
WSD_{Ag2}^{dyn}	2/1/0.022	0.091	0.659	1.568	0.01
	2/1/0.0004	**0.182**	0.273	**1.091**	0.01
WSD_{Ag3}^{dyn}	1/1/0.0223	0.114	0.614	1.500	0.01
	1/1/0.0004	**0.159**	0.295	**1.136**	0.01
WSD_{Ag4}^{dyn}	1/2/0.0226	**0.091**	0.591	**1.500**	0.03
	1/2/0.0004	0.159	0.341	1.182	0.03
WSD_{Ag5}^{dyn}	2/1/0.031	0.159	0.614	1.455	0.02
	2/1/0.0004	0.227	0.500	1.272	0.02
Method 3					
WSD_{Ag1}^{dyn}	2/1/0.0321	0.068	0.545	1.477	0.01
	2/1/0.0026	0.182	0.227	1.045	0.01
WSD_{Ag2}^{dyn}	1/1/0.0486	**0.091**	0.636	**1.545**	0.01
	1/1/0.0006	0.227	0.273	1.045	0.01
WSD_{Ag3}^{dyn}	1/1/0.0521	0.114	0.545	1.432	0.01
	1/1/0.0011	**0.159**	0.295	**1.136**	0.01
WSD_{Ag4}^{dyn}	1/1/0.0625	0.114	0.568	1.455	0.01
	1/1/0.0009	**0.159**	0.318	**1.159**	0.01
WSD_{Ag5}^{dyn}	2/1/0.0489	**0.159**	0.591	**1.432**	0.06
	2/1/0.0009	**0.227**	0.477	**1.250**	0.06

Table 4. Comparison of the classification quality (Primary Tumor data set)

Method 1					
System	Parameters $m_1/m_2/\varepsilon$	e	e_{ONE}	$\overline{d}_{WSD_{Ag}^{dyn}}$	t
WSD_{Ag1}^{dyn}	1/2/0.00121	**0.392**	0.843	**2.745**	0.01
WSD_{Ag2}^{dyn}	2/2/0.00121	**0.333**	0.853	**3.206**	0.02
WSD_{Ag3}^{dyn}	2/1/0.00021	0.353	0.922	4.000	0.01
WSD_{Ag4}^{dyn}	2/3/0.00021	0.353	0.892	3.706	0.12
WSD_{Ag5}^{dyn}	4/2/0.00021	0.314	0.922	4.294	0.15
Method 2					
WSD_{Ag1}^{dyn}	1/2/0.00121	0.392	0.853	2.755	0.01
WSD_{Ag2}^{dyn}	2/2/0.00121	0.333	0.853	3.225	0.02
WSD_{Ag3}^{dyn}	1/1/0.00021	**0.343**	0.922	**4.333**	0.01
WSD_{Ag4}^{dyn}	3/3/0.00021	0.353	0.892	3.755	0.14
WSD_{Ag5}^{dyn}	1/2/0.00021	0.324	0.922	4.284	0.19
Method 3					
WSD_{Ag1}^{dyn}	2/2/0.00121	**0.392**	0.843	**2.745**	0.01
WSD_{Ag2}^{dyn}	4/2/0.00041	0.343	0.863	3.167	0.03
WSD_{Ag3}^{dyn}	7/1/0.00021	0.353	0.902	4.049	0.03
WSD_{Ag4}^{dyn}	2/3/0.00021	**0.353**	0.892	**3.667**	0.05
WSD_{Ag5}^{dyn}	3/1/0.00021	**0.314**	0.922	**4.275**	0.06

the coalitions that were generated using different modifications of Pawlak's model and to identify some general properties, which are presented above.

As was mentioned earlier, the main aim of this study was to analyze the structure of the clusters that are created using three methods, rather than comparing the quality of the classification. However, in order to set a reference point for the quality of the classification, experiments were conducted in which no method for creating coalitions of classifiers was used. When simply based on the vectors that are generated by the classifiers, the decisions are made by applying the weighted majority vote method. Weights for the classifiers are determined based on the error rate of those classifiers that were estimated by the training set. The results for both sets of data are given in Table 5. In the table, the values of the analogous measures as in Tables 3 and 4 are given.

As can be seen for the Lymphography data set, better results were obtained by Methods 1, 2 and 3 than by not creating coalitions. For the Primary Tumor data set and for some versions of dispersion, better results were obtained without creating coalitions. As was already mentioned, Methods 1 and 2 lost their ability to capture the relationships between the classifiers for this set of data. In addition, the cause of such results is probably that the structure of the coalitions was not taken into account in the method for generating global decisions.

Table 5. Weighted majority vote of individual classifiers

Lymphography data set					Primary Tumor data set				
# decision tables	e	e_{ONE}	Average number of generated decisions	t	# decision tables	e	e_{ONE}	Average number of generated decisions	t
3	0.182	0.205	1.023	0.01	3	0.392	0.804	2.627	0.01
5	0.205	0.250	1.045	0.01	5	0.314	0.794	3.255	0.01
7	0.205	0.318	1.136	0.01	7	0.373	0.892	3.863	0.01
9	0.159	0.318	1.159	0.01	9	0.333	0.892	3.843	0.02
11	0.227	0.500	1.273	0.01	11	0.294	0.912	4.520	0.02

4   Conclusions

In this paper, three different modifications of the conflict analysis method that was proposed by Pawlak were considered. These methods were applied to two medical data sets, which were dispersed in five different ways. The study compared the structure of the coalitions of the classifiers that were obtained using these methods. It was found that Method 3 had the greatest ability to discover the relationships between the classifiers. Methods 1 and 2 had a tendency to generate a small number of coalitions, which consisted of a large number of classifiers. In addition, for data sets with a large number of decision classes, Methods 1 and 2 lost their ability to capture the relationships between the classifiers.

References

1. Bazan, J., Peters, J., Skowron, A., Nguyen, H., Szczuka, M.: Rough set approach to pattern extraction from classifiers. In: Electronic Notes in Theoretical Computer Science, vol. 82, Elsevier Science Publishers (2003)
2. Delimata, P., Suraj, Z.: Feature selection algorithm for multiple classifier systems: a hybrid approach. Fundamenta Informaticae **85**(1–4), 97–110 (2008). IOS Press, Amsterdam
3. Fatima, S., Wooldridge, M., Jennings, N.: A comparative study of game theoretic and evolutionary models of bargaining for software agents. Artif. Intell. Rev. **23**, 185–203 (2005)
4. Kersten, G., Lai, H.: Negotiation support and e-negotiation systems: an overview. Group Decis. Negot. **16**, 553–586 (2007)
5. Kittler, J., Hatef, M., Duin, R.P.W., Matas, J.: On combining classifiers. IEEE Trans. Pattern Anal. Mach. Intell. **20**(3), 226–239 (1998)
6. Kraus, S.: Strategic Negotiations in Multiagent Environments. The MIT Press, Cambridge (2001)
7. Kuncheva, L.: Combining Pattern Classifiers Methods and Algorithms. Wiley, Hoboken (2004)
8. Lai, G., Li, C., Sycara, K., Giampapa, J.A.: Literature review on multi-attribute negotiations. Technical report CMU-RI-TR-04-66, pp. 1–35 (2004)
9. Lopes, F., Novais, A.Q., Mamede, N., Coelho, H.: Negotiation among autonomous agents: experimental evaluation of integrative strategies. Artif. Intell. Rev. **29**, 1–44 (2008)

10. Pawlak, Z.: On conflicts. Int. J. Man-Mach. Stud. **21**, 127–134 (1984)
11. Pawlak, Z.: About Conflicts, pp. 1–72. Polish Scientic Publishers, Warsaw (1987). (in Polish)
12. Pawlak, Z.: Anatomy of conflict. Bull. Eur. Assoc. Theor. Comput. Sci. **50**, 234–247 (1993)
13. Pawlak, Z.: On some issues connected with conflict analysis. Institute of Computer Science Reports, 37/93, Warsaw University of Technology (1993)
14. Pawlak, Z.: An inquiry anatomy of conflicts. J. Inform. Sci. **109**, 65–78 (1998)
15. Pawlak, Z.: Some remarks on conflict analysis. Eur. J. Oper. Res. **166**, 649–654 (2005)
16. Pawlak, Z.: Conflicts and negotations. In: Wang, G.-Y., Peters, J.F., Skowron, A., Yao, Y. (eds.) RSKT 2006. LNCS (LNAI), vol. 4062, pp. 12–27. Springer, Heidelberg (2006). doi:10.1007/11795131_2
17. Przybyła-Kasperek, M., Wakulicz-Deja, A.: Application of reduction of the set of conditional attributes in the process of global decision-making. Fundamenta Informaticae **122**(4), 327–355 (2013)
18. Przybyła-Kasperek, M., Wakulicz-Deja, A.: Global decisions taking on the basis of dispersed medical data. In: Ciucci, D., Inuiguchi, M., Yao, Y., Ślęzak, D., Wang, G. (eds.) RSFDGrC 2013. LNCS (LNAI), vol. 8170, pp. 355–365. Springer, Heidelberg (2013). doi:10.1007/978-3-642-41218-9_38
19. Przybyła-Kasperek, M., Wakulicz-Deja, A.: A dispersed decision-making system - the use of negotiations during the dynamic generation of a systems structure. Inf. Sci. **288**, 194–219 (2014)
20. Przybyła-Kasperek, M., Wakulicz-Deja, A.: The strength of coalition in a dispersed decision support system with negotiations. Eur. J. Oper. Res. **252**, 947–968 (2016)
21. Przybyła-Kasperek, M., Wakulicz-Deja, A.: Global decision-making in multi-agent decision-making system with dynamically generated disjoint clusters. Appl. Soft Comput. **40**, 603–615 (2016)
22. Przybyła-Kasperek, M.: Selected methods of combining classifiers, when predictions are stored in probability vectors, in a dispersed decision-making system. Fundamenta Informaticae **147**(2–3), 353–370 (2016)
23. Przybyła-Kasperek, M.: Directions of use of the Pawlak's approach to conflict analysis. In: Thriving Rough Sets–10th Anniversary - Honoring Professor Zdzislaw Pawlak's Life and Legacy & 35 years of Rough Sets. Studies in Computational Intelligence (2017). ISSN 1860–949X
24. Rahwan, I., Ramchurn, S., Jennings, N., McBurney, P., Parsons, S., Sonenberg, L.: Argumentation-based negotiation. Knowl. Eng. Rev. **18**, 343–375 (2004)
25. Sandholm, T.: Distributed rational decision making. In: Weiss, G. (ed.) MultiAgent Systems a Modern Approach to Distributed Artificial Intelligence, pp. 201–259. MIT Press, Cambridge (1999)
26. Schneeweiss, C.: Distributed Decision Making. Springer, Berlin (2003)
27. Skowron, A., Wang, H., Wojna, A., Bazan, J.: Multimodal classification: case studies. In: Peters, J.F., Skowron, A. (eds.) Transactions on Rough Set. LNCS, vol. Springer, pp. 224–239. 4100, Heidelberg (2006). doi:10.1007/11847465_11
28. Ślęzak, D., Wróblewski, J., Szczuka, M.: Neural network architecture for synthesis of the probabilistic rule based classifiers. In: Electronic Notes in Theoretical Computer Science, vol. 82. Elsevier (2003)

Comprehensive Operational Control
of the Natural and Anthropogenic Territory
Safety Based on Analytical Indicators

Tatiana Penkova(✉), Valeriy Nicheporchuk, and Anna Metus

Institute of Computational Modeling of the Siberian Branch of the Russian
Academy of Science, Krasnoyarsk, Russia
penkova_t@icm.krasn.ru

Abstract. This paper presents an approach of comprehensive operational control of the natural and anthropogenic territory safety based on the integration of Data warehouse, On-line analytical processing and Knowledge engineering technologies. It looks at the description of data warehouse that provides a united informational resource of emergency monitoring. There is a description of OLAP-models that provide a multidimensional analysis and on-line modeling the state of technosphere objects and environment parameters. The authors suggest some criteria of emergency risk assessment using expert knowledge about danger levels. It is demonstrated now some of the proposed solutions could be adopted in territorial decision making support system. Comprehensive operational control allows the authorities to detect threat, prevent emergencies and ensure a comprehensive safety.

Keywords: Operational control · Comprehensive monitoring · Danger level assessment · Analytical indicators · Prevention of emergencies · Territory safety

1 Introduction

Early prevention of natural and anthropogenic emergencies is a major factor for effective territory safety management. To decrease the risk of emergency it has to provide a comprehensive monitoring of current processes, real-time control of the state of technosphere and environment objects and adequate assessment of threats [1, 2]. At present, a lot of control tools are being actively introduced in different areas; a huge amount of data is collected and processed in industrial automated systems [3, 4]. However, as usual, the monitoring systems provide the observation of basic parameters using sensors that do not present the user the powerful analysis tools. Moreover, in many cases the natural and technological processes are considered independently. It does not allow the analyst to assess the situation comprehensively taking into account the influence of many risk factors [5]. Rising of efficiency in applying informational resources and operability of solving analytical tasks require the development of techniques that provide modelling of present conditions and operational assessment of emergency risk based on monitoring data.

© Springer International Publishing AG 2017
L. Polkowski et al. (Eds.): IJCRS 2017, Part I, LNAI 10313, pp. 263–270, 2017.
DOI: 10.1007/978-3-319-60837-2_22

Towards this end, in the paper, it is suggested to apply the approach of comprehensive operational control of the natural and anthropogenic territory safety based on the integration of Data warehouse, On-line analytical processing and Knowledge engineering technologies. The Data warehouse provides the data consolidation from heterogeneous sources and forms a united informational resource for emergency monitoring. The On-line analytical processing presents a technique for multidimensional in-depth data analysis and modelling the state of technosphere objects and environment parameters. The Knowledge engineering technology makes it possible to assess the degree of danger and emergency risks using expert knowledge. The practical importance of this work lies in the implementation of the proposed solutions in the territorial decision making support system of Krasnoyarsk region.

2 Comprehensive Monitoring of the Territory Safety

Krasnoyarsk region is the second largest federal subject of Russia and the third largest subnational governing body by area in the world. Krasnoyarsk region lies in the middle of Siberia and occupies an area of 2.4 million square kilometres. This territory is characterised by heightened level of natural and anthropogenic emergencies which is determined by social-economic aspects, large resource potential, geographical location and climatic conditions. In the territory there are many accident prone technosphere objects including radiation-related objects, chemically-dangerous objects and dangerously explosive objects; hydraulic facilities; critically important objects; and a lot of survival objects. Moreover, the territory is located in seven climatic zones. A number of large-scale natural emergencies, such as flood, forest fire, gale-strength wind and anomalously low temperature are recorded each year [6].

In order to improve the population and territory safety, local authorities take some emergency prevention and mitigation actions. A lot of monitoring systems are being actively introduced within the region. The main core of the regional emergency management is the Center of Emergency Monitoring and Prediction of Krasnoyarsk region (CEMP). Estimation of emergency risk and consequences are major functional tasks of CEMP. One of basic issues that provide early emergency preventing is a comprehensive operational control of the technosphere and environment parameters. Comprehensive operational control of the territory safety is based on consolidation and centralised storage of monitoring data, analytical modelling of the current conditions and operational assessment of the danger level (Fig. 1).

To monitor technosphere and environment parameters there has been developed the specialised data warehouse [7]. The data warehouse provides the integration of information from multiple, distributed and heterogeneous databases and other data sources. The developed data warehouse accumulates the actual data from territorial monitoring systems using on-line reports or special informational packages and from automatic control systems (sensors) directly using export procedures. The comprehensive monitoring covers the following areas: meteorological situation, hydrological situation, snow avalanche situation, seismological situation, radiation situation, municipal facilities, emergencies and other accidents fixed in the territory.

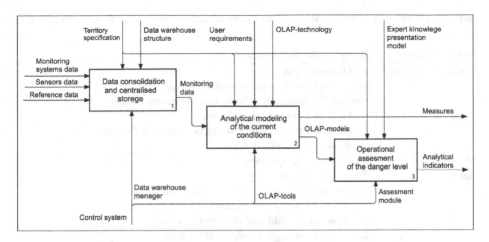

Fig. 1. Comprehensive operational control of the territory safety

For emergency monitoring there has been developed the special structure of centralised data warehouse which combines historical, operational and reference data. Depending on the specific features a domain and taking into account the opportunity to apply the modern data processing techniques the structure of data warehouse includes three principal layers:

- Layer of stationary storage that contains the main part of monitoring data and consists of facts tables and dimensions tables.
- Layer of analytical objects that contains the analytical models which are used for on-line controlling the state of technosphere and environment objects, aggregates tables with interim results and analytical reports.
- Layer of pre-loading processing that provides loading and preliminary processing of monitoring data from heterogeneous operational databases and contains data sources, import and export procedures and temporary tables.

Thus, the centralised data warehouse combines monitoring data from different sources and makes up a united informational resource for comprehensive data processing: analytical modelling and operational assessment of the territory safety.

3 Analytical Modelling of the State of Technosphere and Environment Objects

Analytical modelling of the state of technosphere and environment objects is based on OLAP (On-line Analytical Processing) technology that provides an efficient means to analyse and present data as an easy-to-understand and an easy-to-use data model in form of multidimensional cubes. For analytical processing of monitoring data the set of specific OLAP-models has been developed [8]. Description of OLAP-models sample is represented in Table 1.

Table 1. OLAP-models for modeling of the state of technosphere objects and environment parameters

Monitoring area	OLAP-model characteristic
Controlled events	*OLAP-model:* forest fires *Facts:* fatalities, victims, material damage *Dimensions:* date, place, type, fire-prevention groups *OLAP-model*: municipal accidences *Facts*: adult victims, children victims, material damage *Dimensions*: date, place, type
Meteorological situation	*OLAP-model:* temperature *Facts:* temperature *Dimensions:* date, place, observation point *OLAP-model*: speed and direction of wind *Facts*: speed of wind and direction of wind *Dimensions:* date, place, observation point *OLAP-model*: rainfall *Facts:* rainfall *Dimensions*: date, place, observation point
Hydrological situation	*OLAP-model*: water level of the rivers *Facts*: current water level, crucial water level, exceeding of crucial level *Dimensions*: date, river, observation point *OLAP-model*: water discharge of the hydro power plants *Facts*: minimal acceptable level of discharge, maximal acceptable level of discharge, water discharge level *Dimensions*: date, hydro power plant *OLAP-model*: ice conditions *Facts*: count of ice events, ice event description *Dimensions*: date, river, observation point, freezing-over type
Seismological situation	*OLAP-model*: seismic events *Facts*: depth, magnitude, diameter of the transient cavity, epicenter *Dimensions*: date, place, observation point, seismic event type
Radiation situation	*OLAP-model*: expose dose of gamma-ray *Facts*: exposure dose of gamma-ray *Dimensions*: date, place, observation point
Municipal facilities	*OLAP-model*: pressure of hot water supply *Facts*: current pressure, minimal acceptable pressure, maximal acceptable pressure, departure from minimum, departure from maximum *Dimensions*: date, boiler plants, observation point *OLAP-model*: temperature of hot water supply *Facts*: current temperature, minimal acceptable temperature, maximal acceptable temperature, departure from minimum, departure from maximum. *Dimensions*: date, boiler plants, observation point
State of span	*OLAP-model*: level of snow load *Facts*: level of snow load, maximal acceptable level of snow load *Dimensions*: date, place, observation point

The developed OLAP-modes can be represented as statistical tables or cross-tables. A statistical table represents the analytical processing result as a relational table with data filtration and sorting functions. A cross-table represents the multidimensional cube and provides the tool for intuitive manipulation of monitoring data by applying the such analytical functions as table pivoting, aggregation and detailing, "slicing" and "dicing". In addition, the result of OLAP-modeling can be visualised as a diagram or a map [9]. All these facilities provide the opportunity to discover new analytical relations between parameters and explore the causes of the current conditions.

4 Operational Assessment of the Territory Safety Based on Analytical Indicators

The assessment of the territory safety is based on forming analytical indicators by comparing actual monitoring data with their critical values using expert knowledge about danger levels. The analytical indicator is defined for each OLAP-model according to values of controlled parameters [10]. In order to form analytical indicator the knowledge representation model has been developed which contains the collection of rules with the following construction:

$$ I : M : \text{IF} < (x_1 \sim a_{11}) \,\&\, (x_2 \sim a_{21}) \,\&\ldots\&\, (x_i \sim a_{ij}) \,\&\, (x_n \sim a_{nm}) \text{ THEN } <Q_i > \quad (1) $$

The rule specification is formed by two identifiers: I – is an identifier of unique rule name in knowledge base; M – is an identifier of effected zone – is a pointer to specific OLAP-model. The rule nucleus is interpreted as a cause-effect relation; the antecedent describes the current state and has a logical value: truth or false, the consequent presents one or more operations. In the rule x_i – is a value of i-th parameter of OLAP-model; a_{ij} – is a critical value of i-th parameter for j-th danger level; "$\sim$" symbol is a comparative operation (e.g. >, <, =); Q_j – is an operation to designate analytical indicator value of j-th danger level; $i = \overline{1, n}$, n – is a number of controlled parameters; $j = \overline{1, m}$, m – is a number of analytical indicator values.

The reasoning procedure is a sequential comparison of antecedent of rule with actual data and execution of relevant consequent. In knowledge base there are three values of analytical indicator (danger levels):

- "Green" – the situation is normal – the value of controlled parameter does not exceed the critical value.
- "Yellow" – the situation requires high attention – the value of controlled parameter is approaching to critical value, there is an emergency risk.
- "Red" – the situation is dangerous and requires an immediate reaction – the value of controlled parameter exceeds the critical value.

For each danger level according to geographical and climate specification of the territory as well as according to characteristics of technosphere objects the critical values of controlled parameters have been identified by experts. The example of criteria of emergency risk estimation for Krasnoyarsk region is represented in Table 2.

Table 2. Criteria of emergency risk estimation

Controlled parameter	Condition	Danger level
Emergencies, accidences (E, count)	E = 0	Green
	E > 0, one or more days ago	Yellow
	E > 0 today	Red
Fire hazard class (Class)	Class $\leq$ 3	Green
	Class = 4	Yellow
	Class = 5	Red
Temperature (T, °C)	Else	Green
	30 $\leq$ T < 35 or -40 < T $\leq$ -35	Yellow
	T $\geq$ 35 or T $\leq$ -40	Red
Speed of wind (WS, m/s)	0 < WS < 15	Green
	15 $\leq$ WS < 25	Yellow
	WS $\geq$ 25	Red
Water level of the rivers (RL, m)	0 < RL < Crit$^{1-1}$0%	Green
	Crit-10% $\leq$ RL < Crit	Yellow
	RL $\geq$ Crit	Red
Water discharge of the hydro power plants (HD, m)	Min + 0.5 < HD < Max-0.5	Green
	Min < HD $\leq$ Min + 0.5 or	Yellow
	Max + 0.5 $\leq$ HD < Max	Red
	HD $\leq$ Min or HD $\geq$ Max	
Snow level (SL, m)	Min < SL < Max	Green
	SL < Min or SL > Max	Red
Earthquake, magnitude (M, level of Richter scale)	M < 3	Green
	3 $\leq$ M < 5	Yellow
	M $\geq$ 5	Red
Expose dose of gamma-ray (ED, McR/h)	ED < 20	Green
	20 $\leq$ ED < 40	Yellow
	ED $\geq$ 40	Red
Pressure of hot water supply (hwPr, atmosphere)	Min < hwPr < Max	Green
	hwPr < Min or hwPr > Max	Red
Temperature of hot water supply (hwT, °C)	Min < hwT < Max	Green
	hwT < Min or hwT > Max	Red
Level of snow load (SL, sm)	Else	Green
	SL $\geq$ 70	Yellow
Deformation range of supporting girders (D, mm)	D < 0.4	Green
	0.4 $\leq$ D < 0.6	Yellow
	D $\geq$ 0.6	Red

[a]Critical values (Crit), minimal (Min) and maximal (Max) acceptable values are identified monthly by expert committee based on the analysis of the current situation in the particular territory.

The danger level of monitoring area is identified by analytical indicators values of respective OLAP-models: the monitoring area has the worst danger level among danger levels of constituent OLAP-models. Thus, assessment of controlled parameters based on analytical indicators provides the assessment of the current condition for monitoring areas separately and territory safety as a whole.

5   Implementation of Operational Control Tools

Proposed approach to operational control of the territory safety has been implemented in the automated system of on-line control of natural and anthropogenic emergencies "ESPLA-M". Figures 2 and 3 show the example of hydrological situation visualisation. Figure 1 demonstrates the water discharge of the hydro power plants in form of cross-table. Figure 2 illustrates an overriding of water level in the river on the map. In additional, the monitoring results are automatically published on website of CEMP (http://tcmp.krasn.ru) to display the current state and predicted data about emergencies in region. Developed system is applied successfully in Ministry of Emergency of Krasnoyarsk region as an effective decision-making support tool.

Date	Water discharge	Minimal acceptable level	Maximal acceptable level	Deviation acceptable level
20.01.2017	1220	1150	1300	0
21.01.2017	1210	1150	1300	0
22.01.2017	1100	1150	1300	-50
23.01.2017	1150	1150	1300	0
24.01.2017	1280	1150	1300	0
25.01.2017	1150	1150	1300	0
26.01.2017	1260	1150	1300	0
27.01.2017	1340	1150	1300	40
28.01.2017	1295	1150	1300	0
29.01.2017	1260	1150	1300	0
30.01.2017	1250	1150	1300	0

(Window: ESPLA-M-[Hydrology] — Model Edit Paste Format Window Help — HPP of Krasnoyarsk, HPP Sayno-Shusenska.., HPP of Ust-Ilimsk, HPP Boguchanskaya — Water discharge of hydro power plants — Measure — Query design | SQL-text | Table | Cross-table | Diagramm | Map)

Fig. 2. Visualization of hydrological situation – water discharge of the hydro power plants

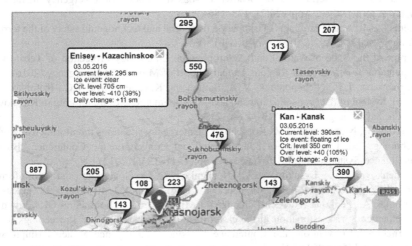

Fig. 3. Visualisation of hydrological situation – water level in the river

6 Conclusion

This paper presents an approach to comprehensive operational control of the natural and anthropogenic territory safety based on the integration of Data warehouse, On-line analytical processing and Knowledge engineering technologies. Unlike in many existing works, proposed approach considers the natural and technological processes comprehensively taking into account the influence of many risk factors. The data warehouse provides a united informational resource through consolidation of monitoring data. The OLAP-technique and data visualisation tools provide the modelling and assessment of the emergency situation and allow us to develop the powerful analytical system instead of traditional monitoring systems which observe only sensor-based basic parameters. Operational assessment tools allow the analyst to get general estimates of the emergency risk and, if it is necessary, to proceed to the investigation of controlled parameters in detail. Implementation of proposed solutions allows the authority to prevent emergency and ensure a comprehensive territory safety.

The future research lies in developing a strategic control approach that provides the assessment of emergency situation by considering the statistical measures of the territory safety and formation of the relevant control recommendations.

The reported study was funded by Russian Foundation for Basic Research according to the research project No. 16-37-00014.

References

1. Beroggi, G., Wallace, W.A.: Operational Risk Management: The Integration of Decision, Communications and Multimedia Technologies. Springer, New York (2012)
2. Bolov, V.R.: Emergency prediction and strategic planning of the future. Nat. Technogen. Risks **3**, 18–24 (2011)
3. Haddow, G., Bullock, J., Coppola, D.P.: Introduction to Emergency Management. CRC Press, Boca Raton (2011)
4. Hernández, J.Z., Serrano, J.M.: Knowledge-based models for emergency management systems. Expert Syst. Appl. **20**(2), 173–186 (2001)
5. Metus, A.M.: Actual problems of estimation of natural and technogenic safety of the territory. Young Sci. **11**, 89–92 (2015). (in Russian)
6. Report of the State of Natural and Anthropogenic Emergency Protection of Territory and Population in Krasnoyarsk Region. Annual Report of Ministry of Emergency (2016)
7. Nozhenkova, L.F., Nicheporchuk, V.V., Badmaeva, K.V., Penkova, T.G., Korobko, A.V., (eds.): System of data consolidation and analysis for emergencies monitoring in Krasnoyarsk region. Saf. Emerg. Probl. **4**, 63–73 (2012)
8. Penkova, T., Nicheporchuk, V., Korobko, A.: Emergency situations monitoring using OLAP technology. In: Proceedings of 35th International Convention the Conference "Business Intelligence Systems (miproBIS)", Croatia, pp. 1941–1946 (2012)
9. Nozhenkova, L.F., Evsukov, A.A., Nozhenkov, A.I.: Governing and geo-informatic modelling methods in OLAP. J. Sib. Fed. Univ. Eng. Technol. **1**, 49–58 (2009). (in Russian)
10. Korobko, A., Penkova, T., Nicheporchuk, V., Mihalev, A.S.: The integral OLAP-model of the emergency risk estimation in the case of Krasnoyarsk region. In: Proceedings of 36th International Convention, the Conference "Business Intelligence Systems (miproBIS)", Croatia, pp. 1456–1461 (2013)

Metaphor Detection Using Fuzzy Rough Sets

Sunny Rai$^{(\boxtimes)}$ and Shampa Chakraverty

Division of Computer Engineering, NSIT, University of Delhi, New Delhi, India
post2srai@gmail.com, apmahs.nsit@gmail.com

Abstract. Recent works in metaphor detection highlight the importance of psychological features such as imageability and concreteness to
identify metaphors in text. However, the aspect of imprecision that is
intrinsic to cognitive concepts is yet to be explored fully. Furthermore,
psychological features give us an approximate indication of whether a
particular textual usage is metaphorical or not. In this paper, we reflect
upon the problem of the inherent vagueness in psychological features and
approximation in classification through the notion of fuzzy rough sets.
We develop a fuzzy-rough rule-based classifier to detect metaphors in
text and evaluate the performance of the proposed model on a dataset of
nominal metaphors. The results indicate the suitability of incorporating
fuzzy-rough sets over SVM and the traditional rough set model.

Keywords: Fuzzy rough sets · Metaphor detection · Conceptual
metaphors · Computational linguistics · Psychological features

1 Introduction

Metaphor is a ubiquitous phenomenon in daily communication. The various
studies on correlation between metaphors and different cognitive aspects such as
sentiment [1] and reasoning [2,3] further highlight the importance of metaphor
processing to achieve a more realistic human computer interaction. In the year
1980, Lakoff and Johnson [4] put forth the idea of *conceptual metaphor*, a medium
to illustrate an abstract concept in target domain through a relatively concrete,
well-defined source domain. Concepts in the well-defined domain are relatively
more intelligible and thus more familiar and easier to imagine. Let us consider
a simple instance of a nominal metaphor:

$$\text{An atom is a solar system.} \qquad \text{(a)}$$

In sentence (a), there is a mapping between the source domain, *solar system* and
the target domain, *atom*. To most humans, astronomical phenomena associated
with concepts, *sun* and *planets* are more familiar and thereby represent concrete concepts. In contrast, sub atomic phenomena associated with *nucleus* and
electrons appear more abstract. This may result from greater familiarity with
astronomical events as compared with sub-atomic events.

© Springer International Publishing AG 2017
L. Polkowski et al. (Eds.): IJCRS 2017, Part I, LNAI 10313, pp. 271–279, 2017.
DOI: 10.1007/978-3-319-60837-2_23

Taking a cue from this contrast in the perception of concepts in source-target domains, prior studies underline the usefulness of psychological features (also known as conceptual features) such as *imageability* [5] and *abstractness* [6] in identifying metaphors. However, the hypothesis that a concrete concept is used metaphorically to explain a relatively abstract concept is not universal. It is possible to generate metaphors by mapping a concrete concept from target domain to a concrete concept in source domain. Examples of this kind of mapping are <*My husband is a gem*> and <*The banyan tree is an umbrella*>. Likewise, a concept in the target domain may be less imageable than the mapped concept in the source domain. Another interesting aspect of psychological features is its dependency on individual's perception and subjective understanding towards a concept. Furthermore, all these features give us an approximate indication of whether a particular usage is metaphorical or not. Thus, we believe that one needs to tackle the orthogonal dimensions of imprecision and approximation while identifying metaphors.

Rough sets [7] is a mathematical theory which deals with approximations in representing concepts while making a decision. In rough set analysis, discretization leads to abrupt transition between intervals and ignores the information to which extent a variable belongs to a certain interval. However, the flow of information in concepts conveyed by human language is vague and gradual. To resolve the problem of abrupt transitions, we use the hybridized concept of Fuzzy rough set [9], which is an amalgamation of Fuzzy sets [8] and Rough sets [7]. It models the impreciseness in data using the concept of approximation like in rough sets and resolves the problem of information loss and abrupt transition due to discretization by incorporating degree of membership as in fuzzy sets. Fuzzy rough sets obviate the need to discretize the data. In this paper, we build a rule-based metaphor classifier using fuzzy rough sets where decisions (metaphor or literal) are crisp sets and relations are fuzzy. Feature engineering is another important aspect of any classification system. We perform feature selection using fuzzy rough *QuickReduct* technique proposed by Jensen and Shen [10] to obtain a subset of informative features called *reduct*. The availability of annotated dataset for rule-based and supervised learning is an ongoing process in the research community. For our experiments, we create a small dataset of nominal metaphors and make it publicly available[1].

The remainder of the paper is organized as follows. We provide a glimpse to the previous work on metaphor detection using psychological features in Sect. 2. We elaborate our proposed application to detect metaphors using Fuzzy rough set theory in Sect. 3. We analyze the applicability of the proposed approach through experiments on a dataset of nominal metaphors in Sect. 4 which is followed by the conclusion.

---

[1] Link: https://goo.gl/jXhSnG.

2 Related Work

In this section, we provide a brief overview of existing work pertinent to the proposed work. Turney et al. [6] showed the utility of psychological feature, *abstractness* by demonstrating its correlation with the context of usage. Bracewell et al. [5] proposed a metaphor detection model by employing imageability peaks and topic modeling. Tsvetkov et al. [12] utilized features such as *imageability* and *abstractness* from MRC Psycholinguistic Database [15]. Gargett and Branden [14] proposed inclusion of sensory features from Affective Norms for English Word (ANEW) [22] to improve the process of metaphor detection. Rai et al. [16] analyzed the usefulness of feature sets namely conceptual, affective and contextual to detect metaphors in an open text.

To the best of our knowledge, there is no existing work which takes into account uncertainties involved in the process of metaphor detection. The above methods adopt a deterministic approach where each feature is assigned a fixed value. The novelty of our approach lies in its ability to capture imprecision in psychological features and approximation in concepts while detecting metaphors.

3 A Model for Metaphor Detection Using Fuzzy Rough Sets

In this paper, we restrict the problem of metaphor detection to nominal metaphors. Nominal metaphors follow the structure of subject-object (S-O) in sentence to explicitly map the source and target domains. We extract psychological features namely *imageability*, *concreteness*, *familiarity* and *meaningfulness* for the subject and object using the MRCP database [15]. Usually, a metaphorical sentence becomes incongruous due to the mapping between seemingly unrelated source and target domains. To measure the degree of incongruity in sentence, we calculate *relatedness* between subject and object. It has been shown that a metaphor is rarely without an emotion [24] thus *affectiveness* for every sentence is also computed (refer Sect. 3.2).

3.1 Problem Representation

Let $T = (\mathbb{U}, \mathcal{A}, \mathcal{D})$ be an information system where $\mathbb{U}$ represents a finite, nonempty set of objects, $\mathcal{A}$ is a finite, nonempty set of attributes such that $\mathbb{U} \longrightarrow V_a, \forall a \in \mathcal{A}$ where V_a represents the range for attributes and $\mathcal{D} = \{d_1, d_2, d_3, ..., d_m\}$ represents a set of decision classes. In our case, the objects are represented as a tuple <subject, object> and $\mathcal{D} = \{M, N\}$ where M represents a class for metaphorical text and N for literal text. In rough set theory, discernibility relation is used to partition data into equivalence classes based on a subset of attributes, $B \subseteq \mathcal{A}$. However, this condition is relaxed in fuzzy rough sets and a similarity relation is used to construct fuzzy tolerance classes as shown in (1) and (2).

$$R_B(x, y) = \mathcal{T}_{a \in B} \{R_a(x, y)\}. \tag{1}$$

where $\mathcal{T}$ is the T-norm. $R_a(x, y)$ is the degree of similarity between x and y with respect to a feature, $a \in B$. For continuous valued attributes, it is defined as (2):

$$R_a(x, y) = 1 - \frac{|V_a(x) - V_a(y)|}{|V_{a_{max}} - V_{a_{min}}|}. \tag{2}$$

where $V_a(x)$ and $V_a(y)$ represent the values of feature, a for x and y respectively. $V_{a_{max}}$ and $V_{a_{min}}$ represent the largest and the smallest values of a. For nominal attributes, the similarity function, $R_a(x, y) = 1$ if $a(x) = a(y)$ else 0.

Let $X \subseteq \mathbb{U}$ be a set of objects. The membership degree of x in the lower approximation of X is defined as (3) and its membership degree in the upper approximation of X is defined as (4).

$$\mu_{\underline{B}X}(x) = \inf_{y \in \mathbb{U}} \mathcal{I}\{R_B(x, y), \mu_X(y)\}. \tag{3}$$

$$\mu_{\overline{B}X}(x) = \sup_{y \in \mathbb{U}} \mathcal{T}\{R_B(x, y), \mu_X(y)\}. \tag{4}$$

where $\mathcal{I}$ is the implicator function and $\mu_X(y)$ is the degree of membership of y in X. The tuple $< \mu_{\underline{B}X}(x), \mu_{\overline{B}X}(x) >$ is called a fuzzy rough set in $\mathbb{U}$. For metaphor detection, we consider all samples to be labeled as either metaphor (M) or non-metaphor(N). Hence, $\mu_X(y)$ is a crisp set. As we can easily verify, (3) and (4) degenerate to (5) and (6) respectively under the condition that $\mu_X(y)$ is crisp.

$$\mu_{\underline{B}X}(x) = \inf_{y \in \mathbb{U}-X} \{1 - R_B(x, y)\}. \tag{5}$$

$$\mu_{\overline{B}X}(x) = \sup_{y \in X} \{R_B(x, y)\}. \tag{6}$$

k-Trimmed Sets. Fuzzy approximations are sensitive to noisy samples and outliers in the training dataset. In order to tackle this, we use the operator, $k - trimmed$ on the set of objects while calculating the approximations. This removes extreme points due to outliers and make the classification robust [17].

Let x be a reference object and $S = \{u_1, u_2, u_3, ..., u_n\}$ be a subset of objects containing few noisy samples. Let $R = \{R_B{}^1, R_B{}^2, ..., R_B{}^k, ..., R_B{}^n\}$ be the ordered set of similarity values between x and the objects in S, arranged in ascending order such that $R_B{}^i < R_B{}^j$ if $i < j$. Given a number k, let $R_1 \subset R$ comprise elements from R_B^{k+1} to R_B^n and let $R_2 \subset R$ comprise elements from R_B^1 to R_B^{n-k-1}. Then, the k-trimmed sets for S are defined by (7) and (8):

$$S_{\min k-trimmed} = \{u_i | R_B(x, u_i) \in R_1\}. \tag{7}$$

$$S_{\max k-trimmed} = \{u_i | R_B(x, u_i) \in R_2\}. \tag{8}$$

Let X_i be the set of objects labeled with decision, $d_i \in \mathcal{D}$ and $x \in X_i$. After k-trimming, the membership degree of x in approximations of X_i are given by (9) and (10).

$$\mu_{\underline{B}X_i}(x) = \inf_{y_k \in (\mathbb{U}-X_i)_{\min k-trimmed}} \{1 - R_B(x, y_k)\}. \tag{9}$$

$$\mu_{\overline{BX_i}}(x) = \sup_{y_k \in (X_i)_{\max k-trimmed}} \{R_B(x, y_k)\}. \tag{10}$$

To illustrate the impact of k-trimmed sets on fuzzy approximations, consider that $x \in M$, $y_1 \in N$ is an outlier similar to x with $R_B(x, y_1) = 0.7$, and $y_2 \in N$ is the second nearest sample with $R_B(x, y_2) = 0.4$. Without trimming, the $\mu_B X_i(x)$ turns out to be as low as $(1 - R_B(x, y_1)) = 0.3$. However, after applying $\min 1 - trimmed$ on set $(\mathbb{U} - X_i)$, the outlier is eliminated and $\mu_B X_i(x) = 1 - R_B(x, y_2) = 0.6$. Similarly, for calculating $\mu_{\overline{BX_i}}(x)$, we ignore the outlier $y_k \in X_i$ which is farthest from x by applying $\max 1 - trimmed$ on set X_i. This makes the approximations of X_i robust against outliers. It may be noted that outliers themselves have a small membership in the lower approximation of their decision class.

3.2   Feature Selection

The feature set, $\mathcal{A}$ comprises the following features:

1. **Conceptual attributes:** It includes imageability, concreteness, familiarity and meaningfulness for S-O.
2. **Derived attributes:** These comprise the difference between conceptual features of S-O, and other linear combinations to represent variations in source and target domains.
3. **relatedness:** It is defined as the cosine of the angle between *word2vec* embeddings [13] for subject and object. These *word2vec* embeddings comprise a set of 50 elements.
4. **affectiveness:** It is the degree of how affective a sentence is *i.e.* capable of expressing an emotion, sentiment or mood. It is calculated using the ANEW database [22].

The total number of extracted features including conceptual and derived ones is 22. Since the dataset is small, having a relatively large feature set may lead to overfitting. In order to reduce the dimensionality of the feature set, we perform feature selection by using the *QuickReduct* technique proposed by Jensen and Shen [10]. *QuickReduct* technique is implemented by fuzzyfing a variable into linguistic variables such as *high_imageability* and *low_imageability*. Thus, the overlap between two linguistic variables such as *high_imageability* and *medium_imageability* is modeled by assigning membership values in both variables. It is necessary to consider the aspect of overlap as it is a region rather than a point where the meaning of words changes from being relevant to irrelevant [23].

3.3   Rule Induction

This step involves generation of If-then rules on the basis of fuzzy approximations derived from instances in training dataset. A rule antecedent is a conjunctive formula comprising an optimized number of attribute assignments. Its consequent

C denotes the class namely *metaphorical* or *literal* on the basis of membership in a certain class. We induce hybrid fuzzy-rough rules for metaphor detection system using the *QuickRules* technique proposed by Jensen et al. [18]. It is to be noted that feature selection through *QuickReduct* [10] is executed as a preprocessing step while inducing fuzzy rough rules through *QuickRules*.

4   Experiments and Results

We used the R package *'RoughSets'* V1.3-0 [11] to perform feature selection and implement a rule based classifier to identify metaphors in text. For our experiments, we created a dataset of 150 sentences with equal number of metaphorical and literal sentences. The dataset is constructed from the list of *Target* sentences present under the title *Stimulus* in [19]. Following pair is one example of metaphorical sentence (b) and its literal counterpart (c) in the dataset:

Insults are razors.   (b)
Insults are hurtful.   (c)

We used 66% of the dataset as training data and the remaining as test data. We selected *Lukasiewicz $T-norm$* by experimental tuning. The *Lukasiewicz* t-norm demonstrated the best results with an accuracy of 86% whereas *min* and *product $T-norm$* give an accuracy of 72% and 70% respectively. We set the value of k equal to 1 for $k-trimmed$ operator used in (9) and (10). We compared the proposed FuzzyRoughSet model (FRSM) with an SVM classifier (kernel=polynomial and C=1) available in *'Kernlab'* V0.9-25 [20] and a rule based classifier, RoughSet Model (RSM) based on traditional Rough Sets by using AQ algorithm [21] for rule induction with (*confidence* = 0.9 and *timeCovered* = 10) in *RoughSets* package. The last method involves an extra discretization step with five intervals to convert real-valued attributes to nominal attributes.

A total of 88 rules were generated for classifying each textual unit as metaphorical or literal. Two of these generated rules are shown below. *O_conc* represents the value for feature *concreteness* of object. Rule1 sums up the idea that low relatedness between subject-object and high concreteness indicate metaphorical text whereas the Rule2 assigns high relatedness and *average concreteness* to literal class.

Rule1 : IF relatedness is around 0.019 & O_conc is around 540 THEN class is M.

Rule2 : IF relatedness is around 0.513 & O_conc is around 405 THEN class is N.

The performance metrics are summarized in Table 1. In the top part of Table 1 without feature reduction, FRSM outperforms RSM in terms of recall, F-score and precision. SVM reports the best results amongst all three, but even for our small dataset, SVM took the longest execution time.

With feature reduction achieved through *Quickreduct*, the performance of all three classifiers improved. The F-score of FRSM increased by 6.03%, that of SVM improved by 2.86% and that of RSM showed a minor increase of 0.65%. After classification with feature reduction, FRSM turns out to be the clear winner. The recall of FRSM is the highest at 96.3% which is 22.23% higher than the recall of RSM and 3.71% higher than that of SVM. The precision of RSM model is slightly higher than the other two models. However, SVM and FRSM show competitive performance in terms of precision. Overall, the F-score of FRSM is 9.74% higher than that of RSM and 1.97% higher than that of SVM.

Table 1. Performance of classification models

FeatureType	Model	A	P	R	F1
Without Feature selection	SVM	80	75.76	92.59	83.34
	RSM	76	77.78	77.78	77.78
	FRSM	80	79.31	85.18	82.14
With Feature selection (*QuickReduct*)	SVM	84	80.64	92.59	86.20
	RSM	78	83.34	74.07	78.43
	FRSM	86	81.25	96.3	88.17

Legends: A-Accuracy; P-Precision; R-Recall; F1-F score

4.1 Discussion

From the reduced feature set, we observed that the difference between conceptual features of subject and object is an important criteria while classifying metaphors. The features, *familiarity* and *meaningfulness* of subject and object are also present in the reduct. So far, these features have received low attention in existing literature. It is noteworthy that FRSM yields a marked improvement in recall. This clearly indicates that combining rough sets with fuzzy sets increased the coverage significantly to pick up more metaphors from the corpus. The experiments in fact, serve as a proof of concept for our idea that metaphor detection needs to take into account imprecision in representing features and also their approximation to real world concepts.

5   Conclusion

The assessment of psychological features are dependent on subjective perception and understanding towards a subject based on one's personal experiences. In this paper, we highlighted the need to model imprecision in psychological features and inclusion of deviations such as mapping between concrete source and concrete target domains while classifying metaphors. We investigated the applicability of fuzzy rough sets in modeling these uncertainties to improve the process of metaphor detection. We employed the $k-trimmed$ sets to reduce approximation errors that may be caused by outliers and noisy data. The results indicate that metaphor detection falls well into the paradigm of approximate computation. In future, we will refine the proposed model to include different kinds of metaphors.

References

1. Nguyen, H.L., Nguyen, T.D., Hwang, D., Jung, J.J.: Kelabteam: a statistical approach on figurative language sentiment analysis in Twitter. In: 9th International Workshop on Semantic Evaluation (SemEval 2015), pp. 679–683 (2015)
2. Thibodeau, P.H., Iyiewaure, P., Boroditsky, L.: Metaphors affect reasoning: measuring effects of metaphor in a dynamic opinion landscape. In: CogSci (2015)
3. Landau, M.E., Robinson, M.D., Meier, B.P.: The Power of Metaphor: Examining its Influence on Social Life. American Psychological Association, Washington, D.C. (2014)
4. Lakoff, G., Johnson, M.: Metaphors We Live By. University of Chicago Press, Chicago (1980)
5. Bracewell, D.B., Tomlinson, M.T., Mohler, M., Rink, B.: A tiered approach to the recognition of metaphor. In: Gelbukh, A. (ed.) CICLing 2014. LNCS, vol. 8403, pp. 403–414. Springer, Heidelberg (2014). doi:10.1007/978-3-642-54906-9_33
6. Turney, P.D., Neuman, Y., Assaf, D., Cohen, Y.: Literal and metaphorical sense identification through concrete and abstract context. In: Empirical Methods in Natural Language Processing, pp. 680–690. ACL (2011)
7. Pawlak, Z.: Rough sets. Int. J. Comput. Inf. Sci. **11**(5), 341–356 (1982)
8. Zadeh, L.A.: Fuzzy sets. Inf. Control **8**(3), 338–353 (1965)
9. Dubois, D., Prade, H.: Rough fuzzy sets and fuzzy rough sets. Int. J. Gen. Syst. **17**(2–3), 191–209 (1990)
10. Jensen, R., Shen, Q.: Fuzzy-rough sets for descriptive dimensionality reduction. In: Fuzzy Systems 2002, FUZZ-IEEE 2002, vol. 1, pp. 29–34 (2002)
11. Riza, L.S., Janusz, A., Bergmeir, C., Cornelis, C., Herrera, F., le, D., Bentez, J.M.: Implementing algorithms of rough set theory and fuzzy rough set theory in the R package roughsets. Inf. Sci. **287**, 68–89 (2014)
12. Tsvetkov, Y., Boytsov, L., Gershman, A., Nyberg, E., Dyer, C.: Metaphor detection with cross-lingual model transfer. In: 52nd Annual Meeting of the Association for Computational Linguistics, pp. 248–258 (2014)
13. Mikolov, T., Chen, K., Corrado, G., Dean, J.: Efficient estimation of word representations in vector space. arXiv preprint arXiv:1301.3781 (2013)
14. Gargett, A., Barnden, J.: Modeling the interaction between sensory and affective meanings for detecting metaphor. In: NAACL HL 2015 (2015), p. 21 (2015)
15. Wilson, M.D.: The MRC psycholinguistic database: machine readable dictionary, V2. Behav. Res. Methods Instrum. Comput. **20**(1), 6–11 (1988)
16. Rai, S., Chakraverty, S., Tayal, D.K.: Supervised metaphor detection using conditional random fields. In: Fourth Workshop on Metaphor in NLP, NAACL-HLT, pp. 18–27 (2016)
17. Hu, Q., Zhang, L., An, S., Zhang, D., Yu, D.: On robust fuzzy rough set models. IEEE Trans. Fuzzy Syst. **20**(4), 636–651 (2012)
18. Jensen, R., Cornelis, C., Shen, Q.: Hybrid fuzzy-rough rule induction and feature selection. In: IEEE International Conference on Fuzzy Systems 2009, FUZZ-IEEE 2009, pp. 1151–1156. IEEE (2009)
19. Thibodeau, P.H., Durgin, F.H.: Metaphor aptness and conventionality: a processing fluency account. Metaphor Symb. **26**(3), 206–226 (2011)
20. Zeileis, A., Hornik, K., Smola, A., Karatzoglou, A.: kernlab- an S4 package for kernel methods in R. J. Stat. Softw. **11**(9), 1–20 (2004)
21. Michalski, R.S., Kaufman, K., Wnek, J.: The AQ family of learning programs: a review of recent developments and an exemplary application. Reports of the Machine Learning and Inference Laboratory, 1051, 91-11 (1991)

22. Bradley, M.M., Lang, P.J.: Affective norms for english words (ANEW): instruction manual and affective ratings. Technical report C-1, the center for research in psychophysiology, University of Florida, pp. 1–45 (1999)
23. Labov, W.: The boundaries of words and their meanings. In: Bailey, C.-J.N., Shuy, R.W. (eds.) New Ways of Analyzing Variation in English. Georgetown University Press, Washington, D.C. (1973)
24. Rentoumi, V., Vouros, G.A., Karkaletsis, V., Moser, A.: Investigating metaphorical language in sentiment analysis: a sense-to-sentiment perspective. ACM Trans. Speech Lang. Process. (TSLP) **9**(3), 6 (2012)

Acr2Vec: Learning Acronym Representations in Twitter

Zhifei Zhang[1,2,3,4], Sheng Luo[3(✉)], and Shuwen Ma[1,2]

[1] Research Center of Big Data and Network Security, Tongji University,
Shanghai 200092, People's Republic of China
[2] Center of Educational Technology and Computing, Tongji University,
Shanghai 200092, People's Republic of China
[3] Department of Computer Science and Technology, Tongji University,
Shanghai 201804, People's Republic of China
tjluosheng@gmail.com
[4] State Key Laboratory for Novel Software Technology, Nanjing University,
Nanjing 210023, People's Republic of China

Abstract. Acronyms are common in Twitter and bring in new challenges to social media analysis. Distributed representations have achieved successful applications in natural language processing. An acronym is different from a single word and is generally defined by several words. To this end, we present *Acr2Vec*, an algorithmic framework for learning continuous representations for acronyms in Twitter. First, a Twitter ACRonym (TACR) dataset is automatically constructed, in which an acronym is expressed by one or more definitions. Then, three acronym embedding models have been proposed: MPDE (Max Pooling Definition Embedding), APDE (Average Pooling Definition Embedding), and PLAE (Paragraph-Like Acronym Embedding). The qualitative experimental results (i.e., similarity measure) and quantitative experimental results (i.e., acronym polarity classification) both show that MPDE and APDE are superior to PLAE.

Keywords: Social media · Acronym · Representation learning · Word embeddings

1 Introduction

Twitter, as a microblogging service, provides a public platform for users to share their opinions towards products, movies, politicians, events and so on. Twitter sentiment analysis has attracted more and more attention due to the rapidly increasing number of tweets [1,2]. Tweets are very short and contain massive misspellings, acronyms and informal words, which brings in new challenges to sentiment analysis [3].

An acronym is an abbreviation formed from the initial components in a phrase or a word and these components are individual letters or parts of words, for example, in most cases "lol" means "laugh out loud" and "yas" means "you

© Springer International Publishing AG 2017
L. Polkowski et al. (Eds.): IJCRS 2017, Part I, LNAI 10313, pp. 280–288, 2017.
DOI: 10.1007/978-3-319-60837-2_24

are stupid". The acronyms can usually convey sentiments, "lol" and "yas" are respectively a positive acronym and a negative one. The labeled training data may not be sufficient to predict the sentiment polarity for such acronyms and labeling enough data is costly and time consuming [4]. The online human-edited definition dictionary for acronyms is an important clue.

Distributed representations for words, phrases and sentences, play an increasingly vital role in building continuous real-valued vectors and these embeddings can be used to measure their similarities [5–7]. The acronyms can be viewed as a special linguistic unit, and the related works about acronym embeddings are seldom reported. Word embeddings can be introduced to address the acronym disambiguation problem [8], but these acronyms are from the formal scientific texts.

In this paper, we firstly automatically construct a *Twitter ACRonym (TACR)* dataset, then propose three acronym embedding methods for *Acr2Vec*, and finally carry out experiments from the perspectives of acronym similarity measure and acronym polarity classification. Code and data are publicly accessible at https://github.com/tjflexic/acr2vec.

2   Related Work

Recent works have studied the word embeddings and applied them in representing acronyms in scientific texts. Polarity classification can be used as a kind of performance measure for embeddings.

2.1   Word Embeddings

Word2Vec [5] provides two model architectures for learning distributed representations of words: continuous bag-of-words model (CBOW) and continuous skip-gram Model (Skip-gram). CBOW predicts one word from its context words, while Skip-gram predicts its context words from one word. Glove [6] is a new global logbilinear regression model that combines the advantages of global matrix factorization and local context window methods. Paragraph Vector [7] represents each document by a dense vector which is trained to predict words in the document.

2.2   Acronym Embeddings

To address the acronym disambiguation problem, Li et al. [8] propose two models for acronym embeddings: TF-IDF based embedding (TBE) and surrounding based embedding (SBE) are proposed. TBE uses the top TF-IDF words' embeddings to represent the topic information of one acronym. SBE represents one acronym by adding its surrounding words' embeddings.

2.3 Polarity Classification

The majority of existing approaches for polarity classification follow Pang et al. [9] and employ machine learning algorithms with more effective features [10]. Turney and Littman [11] infer the semantic orientation of a word from its statistical association with a set of positive and negative paradigm words. Gruhl et al. [12] employ a propagation algorithm that leverages the related word connections to identify the sentiment-bearing slang words from Urban Dictionary. Mohammad et al. [13] construct a Twitter-specific sentiment lexicon by pointwise mutual information (PMI) between each phrase and hashtag/emoticon seed words.

3 Twitter Acronym Dataset

We automatically construct a Twitter ACRonym (TACR) dataset with three steps: collecting, integrating, and correcting acronyms.

3.1 Resources and Tools

We utilize two resources as the original dataset for Twitter acronyms: NetLingo Dictionary[1] (ND) and Slang Dictionary[2] (SD). ND is the largest list of chat acronyms and text shorthand, and SD collects the slang words and acronyms. Besides, we implemented two interfaces to access Acronym Finder[3] (AF) and Urban Dictionary[4] (UD) and to rectify the original dataset.

3.2 Data Integration

In the original dataset, there are totally 913 acronyms in both ND and SD. Given one acronym A, its definition expressions in ND and SD are respectively denoted by D_N and D_S. When D_N is not the same with D_S, the following three cases need to be handled for integrating D_N and D_S:

- Case 1: D_N appears in D_S or D_S appears in D_N, choose a longer one; e.g., "n2m" (D_N: "not to mention -or- not too much"; D_S: "not too much"), we choose the former.
- Case 2: there is a vast majority of repeated words in D_N and D_S, choose a longer one or one with less asterisks; e.g., "figjam" (D_N: "f*** i'm good just ask me"; D_S: "f**k i'm good, just ask me"), we choose the later.
- Case 3: there are barely repeated words in D_N and D_S, choose the both two.

---

[1] http://www.netlingo.com/acronyms.php.
[2] http://www.noslang.com/dictionary/.
[3] http://www.acronymfinder.com/.
[4] http://www.urbandictionary.com/.

Secondly, there exists the one-to-many or many-to-one or many-to-many relation expressions between an acronym and its definition in ND. We split the expressions into several parts and get more acronyms or more definitions.

- Case 4: "or" appears in A, split A into A_1, A_2, $\cdots$;
  e.g., "zmg or zomg" ("oh my god"), we get "zmg" ("oh my god") and "zomg" ("oh my god").
- Case 5: " -or- " or "also seen as" appears in D_N, split D_N into D_{N1}, D_{N2}, $\cdots$;
  e.g., "n2m" ("not to mention -or- not too much"), we get "n2m" ("not to mention" and "not too much").
- Case 6: "or" appears in A and " -or- " appears in D_N, split (A, D_N) into (A_1, D_{N1}), (A_2, D_{N2}), $\cdots$; e.g. "rtm or rtfm" ("read the manual -or- read the f***ing manual"), we get "rtm" ("read the manual" and "read the f***ing manual").

Finally, we restrict the punctuation marks, i.e., a semicolon is used as the separator of several definitions, and a comma is used to join several parts in a single definition, e.g., "nino" is defined as "nothing in, nothing out;no input, no output". Moreover, the words masked with asterisks are substituted by their actual words, e.g., "s**t" is changed to "shit".

3.3   Data Correction

The pre-trained word vectors for Twitter corpus (2B tweets and 27B tokens) using Glove algorithm [6] is available[5]. In order to directly use these word vectors, the tokens contained in all acronym definitions belong to 27B tokens as much as possible. However, typos in definition expressions are not included in these 27B tokens. Thus, AF and UD are used to correct the data. Several examples are given in Table 1. After correcting, the ratio of the number of definition tokens belonging to the 27B tokens to the total number of definition tokens changes from 95.3% to 97.8%.

Table 1. Correct typos in original definitions. "can't", "diliberately", "csae" are not in the Twitter 27B tokens.

Acronym	Original definition	New definition
cw2cu	can't wait to see you	can't wait to see you
troll	person who diliberately stirs up trouble	person who deliberately stirs up trouble
icydk	in csae you didn't know	in case you didn't know

---

[5] http://nlp.stanford.edu/projects/glove/.

4   *Acr2Vec* Framework with Three Acronym Embedding Models

The definition of an acronym A is denoted as a sequence $\{T_1, T_2, \cdots, T_N\}$. The d-dimensional vector for each definition token $T_i(1 \leq i \leq N)$ is denoted by $x_{T_i} = (x_{i1}, x_{i2}, \cdots, x_{id})$.

4.1   Max Pooling Definition Embedding Model (MPDE)

The representation $A = (a_1, a_2, \cdots, a_d)$ for the acronym A is obtained by using max pooling (see Eq. 1) over all the definition token vectors.

$$a_j = \max_{1 \leq i \leq N} x_{ij}, j = 1, 2, ..., d \tag{1}$$

4.2   Average Pooling Definition Embedding Model (APDE)

The representation $A = (a_1, a_2, \cdots, a_d)$ for the acronym A is obtained by using average pooling (see Eq. 2) over all the definition token vectors.

$$a_j = \frac{1}{N} \sum_{1 \leq i \leq N} x_{ij}, j = 1, 2, ..., d \tag{2}$$

4.3   Paragraph-Like Acronym Embedding Model (PLAE)

In the above two models, the representation of an acronym is obtained by global pooling, either max pooling or average pooling, over all the definition token vectors. The paragraph-like acronym embedding model is illustrated in Fig. 1, which is inspired by Paragraph Vector [7].

More precisely, we concatenate the acronym vector with several definition token vectors from an acronym and predict the following token in the given context. Both definition token vectors and acronym vectors are trained by the stochastic gradient descent and backpropagation.

5   Experimental Results

We carry out the qualitative experiment of acronym similarity measure, and the quantitative experiment of acronym polarity classification.

5.1   Datasets

Twitter Acronym Dataset. We automatically construct a Twitter ACRonym (TACR) dataset in Sect. 3. The dataset consists of 7033 acronyms, in which 6717 acronyms have the only one definition.

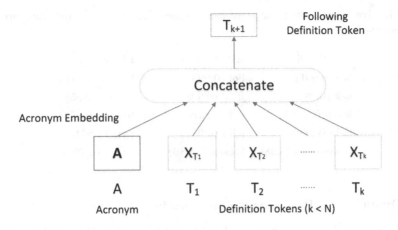

Fig. 1. Paragraph-like acronym embedding model.

Acronym Polarity Dataset. We directly construct a sentiment polarity dataset about definition tokens and acronyms from Sentiment140 lexicon [13] which contains tweet terms with sentiment scores. If one token or acronym from TACR dataset appears in this lexicon, we assign it the positive polarity only when its sentiment score is greater than 0.5 and assign it the negative polarity only when its sentiment score is less than -0.5. The acronym polarity dataset is shown in Table 2.

Table 2. Acronym polarity dataset consists of 1000 definition tokens as training and 766 acronyms as test.

	POS	NEG	Total
Definition tokens	548	452	1000
Acronyms	405	361	766

5.2 Qualitative Performance on *Acr2Vec*

A simple way to investigate the learned embeddings is to find the closest words or acronyms for a user-specified acronym. We list an example (*Acronym: alol (actually laughing out loud)*) in Table 3. The dimension of acronym vectors is $d = 25$.

Moreover, we take the acronyms containing one specific word (e.g., "good" and "shit", their frequencies are approximately equal) as example and plot the acronym embeddings using t-SNE [14] in Fig. 2. The dimension of acronym vectors is set to be 200. The performances of MPDE and APDE are both better than PLAE, because there is not enough acronyms for learning acronym embeddings with PLAE.

Table 3. Five closest words or acronyms for acronym "alol". "Sim" measures the Cosine similarity.

MPDE (Sim)	APDE (Sim)	PLAE (Sim)
llol (0.991)	llol (0.995)	bewbs (0.811)
kek (0.988)	jklol (0.993)	twttr (0.805)
loxen (0.988)	lollerskates (0.989)	bewbz (0.803)
lolin (0.988)	lolin (0.989)	twtr (0.801)
lollerskates (0.988)	loxxen (0.989)	80085 (0.797)

5.3 Quantitative Performance on *Acr2Vec*

The dimension of acronym vectors $d \in \{25, 50, 100, 200\}$. The resulting vectors can be used as features in polarity classification. We classify acronyms into positive or negative. The accuracy *Accu* of acronym polarity classification can be seen as a quantitative evaluation for acronym embeddings. Four common classifiers, such as KNN (Nearest Neighbors, $k = 5$), SVM (Support Vector Machines, $\gamma = 2, C = 1$), RF (Random Forest) and NB (Naive Bayes), and PMI (Pointwise Mutual Information) [11] method are used.

Table 4. Accuracy of Twitter acronym polarity classification. The bold numbers show the best result under four different dimensions.

Model		25	50	100	200
MPDE	PMI	0.5718	0.6332	0.5992	0.6084
MPDE	KNN	0.6371	**0.7102**	0.6997	**0.7037**
MPDE	SVM	0.6645	0.6645	0.6632	0.6632
MPDE	RF	0.6488	0.6658	0.6723	0.6423
MPDE	NB	0.5940	0.6815	0.6593	0.6893
APDE	PMI	0.6305	0.6240	0.6371	0.6097
APDE	KNN	0.6593	0.6932	**0.7089**	0.6984
APDE	SVM	0.6697	0.6658	0.6632	0.6632
APDE	RF	**0.6906**	0.6775	0.6475	0.6645
APDE	NB	0.6462	0.6580	0.6593	0.6828
PLAE	PMI	0.5404	0.5352	0.5379	0.5418
PLAE	KNN	0.5170	0.4883	0.5091	0.4948
PLAE	SVM	0.5444	0.5379	0.5431	0.5496
PLAE	RF	0.5274	0.5078	0.4974	0.5131
PLAE	NB	0.5287	0.5431	0.5352	0.5117

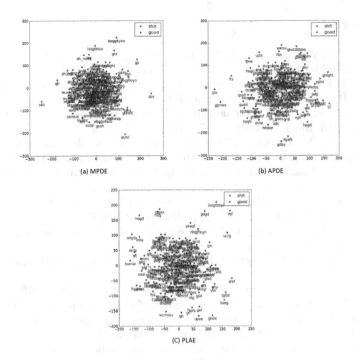

Fig. 2. Acronym embeddings visualization using t-SNE.

In terms of Twitter acronym polarity classification, MPDE and APDE are always better than PLAE, because MPDE and APDE are able to capture better semantics. When the dimension of acronym vectors increases, KNN classifier is better than others. Moreover, PMI is not satisfactory due to noise when computing similarity measure for more acronyms (Table 4).

6   Conclusions

To the best of our knowledge, this is the first work about acronym embeddings in Twitter. We automatically construct a Twitter ACRonym (TACR) dataset and propose an algorithmic framework *Acr2Vec* with three acronym embedding models: MPDE (Max Pooling Definition Embeddings), APDE (Average Pooling Definition Embeddings), and PLAE (Paragraph-Like Acronym Embeddings). The experimental results show that MPDE and APDE achieve almost equal performance, but are always superior to PLAE. Our future work will focus on taking contextual information into account to improve acronym embeddings.

Acknowledgments. This work is partially supported by the National Natural Science Foundation of China (No. 61673301, No. 61573255) and the Open Research Funds of State Key Laboratory for Novel Software Technology (No. KFKT2017B22).

References

1. Jiang, L., Yu, M., Zhou, M., Liu, X., Zhao, T.: Target-dependent Twitter sentiment classification. In: Proceedings of ACL: HLT, pp. 151–160 (2011)
2. Ren, F., Wu, Y.: Predicting user-topic opinions in Twitter with social and topical context. IEEE Trans. Affect. Comput. **4**(4), 412–424 (2013)
3. Kiritchenko, S., Zhu, X., Mohammad, S.M.: Sentiment analysis of short informal texts. J. Artif. Intell. Res. **50**, 723–762 (2014)
4. Wu, F., Song, Y., Huang, Y.: Microblog sentiment classification with contextual knowledge regularization. In: Proceedings of AAAI, pp. 2332–2338 (2015)
5. Mikolov, T., Chen, K., Corrado, G., Dean, J.: Efficient estimation of word representations in vector space. In: Proceedings of ICLR (2013)
6. Pennington, J., Socher, R., Manning, C.: Glove: global vectors for word representation. In: Proceedings of EMNLP, pp. 1532–1543 (2014)
7. Le, Q., Mikolov, T.: Distributed representations of sentences and documents. In: Proceedings of ICML, pp. 1188–1196 (2014)
8. Li, C., Ji, L., Yan, J.: Acronym disambiguation using word embedding. In: Proceedings of AAAI, pp. 4178–4179 (2015)
9. Pang, B., Lee, L., Vaithyanathan, S.: Thumbs up? Sentiment classification using machine learning techniques. In: Proceedings of EMNLP, pp. 79–86 (2002)
10. Wang, S., Manning, C.D.: Baselines and bigrams: simple, good sentiment and topic classification. In: Proceedings of ACL, pp. 90–94 (2012)
11. Turney, P.D., Littman, M.L.: Measuring praise and criticism: inference of semantic orientation from association. ACM Trans. Inf. Syst. **21**(4), 315–346 (2003)
12. Gruhl, D., Nagarajan, M., Pieper, J., Robson, C., Sheth, A.: Multimodal social intelligence in a real-time dashboard system. VLDB J. **19**(6), 825–848 (2010)
13. Mohammad, S., Kiritchenko, S., Zhu, X.: NRC-Canada: building the state-of-the-art in sentiment analysis of tweets. In: Proceedings of SemEval, pp. 321–327 (2013)
14. Van der Maaten, L., Hinton, G.: Visualizing data using t-SNE. J. Mach. Learn. Res. **9**, 2579–2605 (2008)

Attribute Reduction on Distributed Incomplete Decision Information System

Jun Hu$^{(\boxtimes)}$, Kai Wang, and Hong Yu

Chongqing Key Laboratory of Computational Intelligence,
Chongqing University of Posts and Telecommunications, Chongqing 400065, China
hujun@cqupt.edu.cn

Abstract. Attribute reduction is an important issue in rough set theory. This paper mainly studies attribute reduction of distributed incomplete decision information system (DIDIS). Firstly, the definition of rough set in DIDIS is developed. Next, an algorithm for attribute reduction of DIDIS is proposed. In the end, two groups of experiments are conducted to prove the effectiveness of the proposed method. The results show that our method can remove redundant attributes of DIDIS, and does not reduce the classification capability of the system. In addition, the results indicate that the change of data missing rate has weak effect on attribute reduction with the similarity relation, but strong effect on attribute reduction with the tolerance relation.

Keywords: Distributed incomplete decision information system · Attribute reduction · Tolerance relation · Similarity relation · Data missing rate

1 Introduction

In an information system, the missing values of attributes, which we do not know, but exist actually, are ubiquitous. Generally, the data with missing values require related preprocessing for the follow-up data mining. For the processing of centralized incomplete decision information system (CIDIS), researchers carried out extensive researches, and proposed many methods, such as case deletion, imputation, model extension, etc. [1–5]. However, these methods cause certain degree of damage to the original information system.

In order to address the attribute reduction of CIDIS and do not change the original data distribution, many methods have been developed. Meng and Shi constructed a positive region-based attribute reduction algorithm, which is fast and efficient, and could be applied to both consistent and inconsistent incomplete decision systems [6]. Qian et al. proposed a theoretic framework based on tolerance relations, and designed a general heuristic incomplete feature selection algorithm based on this framework, and the algorithm could accelerate the process of feature selection for incomplete data [7]. Sun et al. introduced

© Springer International Publishing AG 2017
L. Polkowski et al. (Eds.): IJCRS 2017, Part I, LNAI 10313, pp. 289–305, 2017.
DOI: 10.1007/978-3-319-60837-2_25

rough entropy-based uncertainty measures to evaluate the roughness and accuracy of knowledge, and proposed a heuristic feature selection algorithm with low computational complexity [8]. Dai et al. introduced another conditional entropy to measure the importance of attributes in incomplete decision system, and constructed three methods to select important attributes from incomplete decision system based on three different kinds of search strategies, but two of them are effective [9]. Zhao and Qin introduced an extended rough set model and neighborhood-tolerance conditional entropy, which can be used to reduce incomplete data with mixed categorical and numerical features [10]. Lu et al. proposed a boundary region-based feature selection algorithm, which can simplify large incomplete decision systems, and select an effective feature subset [11]. All the literatures mentioned above focus on the attribute reduction of incomplete information system which is stored in one place.

To cope with the attribute reduction of information system stored in multiple sites, researchers put forward a lot of methods. For vertically partitioned multi-decision table, Yang and Yang introduced an approximate reduction algorithm based on conditional entropy [12]. Zhou et al. developed secure sum of matrices and secure set union, and studied a privacy preserving attribute reduction algorithm based on discernible matrix for distributed datasets [13]. Ye et al. presented some SMC protocols into efficient privacy preserving attribute reduction algorithm for vertically partitioned data based on semi-trusted third party and commutative encryption [14]. Banerjee and Chakravarty proposed a privacy preserving feature selection algorithm for distributed data using virtual dimension [15]. Hu et al. defined rough set in distributed decision information system, and presented a distributed attribute reduction algorithm [16].

In summary, people have studied attribute reduction of CIDIS and distributed decision information system respectively, but rarely study attribute reduction of distributed decision information system with missing values, called distributed incomplete decision information system (DIDIS). In this paper, attribute reduction of DIDIS based on the tolerance relation and the similarity relation is studied, and the influence of different data missing rates on attribute reduction is illustrated.

This paper is structured as follows: In Sect. 2, some basic concepts of incomplete information system are reviewed. In Sect. 3, the definition of rough set in distributed incomplete decision information system is given. In Sect. 4, we propose an attribute reduction algorithm for distributed incomplete decision information system. In Sect. 5, the experimental results and analysis are presented. In Sect. 6, some conclusions are given.

2 Preliminaries

An incomplete information system refers to the absence of attribute values in an information system, as defined below [17].

Definition 1. *An information system is defined as $IS = (U, A, V, f)$, U is a non-empty finite set of objects, called the universe. A is a non-empty finite set* *of attributes. $V = \cup_{a \in A} V_a$, where V_a is the value of attribute a. $f : U \times A \to V$ is an information function that specifies the value of each object in universe. If there exist $a \in A$ and $x \in U$ such that $f(x, a) = *$ (* indicates a missing attribute value), then the information system is incomplete, otherwise it is complete.*

If the non-empty attribute set A in an incomplete information system is divided into condition attribute set C and decision attribute set D, that is, $A = C \cup D$, an incomplete decision table $IDT = (U, C \cup D, V, f)$ can be obtained. In the following, we do not consider the case where the missing values exist in the decision attribute values.

Kryszkiewicz assumed that the real value of a missing attribute value could be any one from the attribute domain, and introduced a tolerance relation to measure the similarity between objects in an incomplete information system. The tolerance relation is defined as follows [18].

Definition 2. *For an incomplete decision table $IDT = (U, C \cup D, V, f)$ and a subset of condition attribute set $B \subseteq C$, the tolerance relation T is defined as*

$$\forall_{x,y \in U} T(x, y) \Leftrightarrow \forall_{c_j \in B}(c_j(x) = c_j(y) \vee c_j(x) = * \vee c_j(y) = *) \tag{1}$$

The tolerance relation is reflexive and symmetric, but not necessarily transitive. Let $[x]_T^B$ denotes a set of individual object y that satisfy the tolerance relation $T(x, y)$ on B, called the tolerance class of x. Given an arbitrary set $X \subseteq U$, the upper and lower approximation sets of X and the positive region of D with respect to B are defined as follows [18].

Definition 3. *For an incomplete decision table $IDT = (U, C \cup D, V, f)$ and an arbitrary set $X \subseteq U$, the upper approximation $B_T^-(X)$ and the lower approxima-tion $B_-^T(X)$ of X with respect to B are*

$$B_T^-(X) = \{x \in U | [x]_T^B \cap X \neq \emptyset\} \tag{2}$$

$$B_-^T(X) = \{x \in U | [x]_T^B \subseteq X\} \tag{3}$$

Let $U/D = \{d_1, d_2, ..., d_m\}$ be the partition of the universe U defined by D. Then the positive region of D with respect to B is

$$POS_B^T(D) = \bigcup_{i=1}^{m} B_-^T(d_i) \tag{4}$$

Stefanowski and Tsoukiàs assumed that the real value of a missing value is unknown and it is not allowed to compare with missing value, and introduced a similarity relation to measure the similarity between objects in an incomplete information system. The similarity relation is defined as follows [19].

Definition 4. *For an incomplete decision table $IDT = (U, C \cup D, V, f)$ and a subset of condition attribute set $B \subseteq C$, the similarity relation S is defined as*

$$\forall_{x,y \in U} S(x, y) \Leftrightarrow \forall_{c_j \in B}(c_j(x) = c_j(y) \vee c_j(x) = *) \tag{5}$$

The similarity relation S is reflexive and transitive, but not necessarily symmetric. Given an arbitrary object $x \in U$, one can define two sets as below [19].

Definition 5. *The set of objects similar to x and the set of objects to which x is similar are defined respectively as*

$$[x]_B = \{y \in U | S(y, x)\} \tag{6}$$

$$[x]_{\bar{B}} = \{y \in U | S(x, y)\} \tag{7}$$

For convenience, we call $[x]_{\bar{B}}$ as the similarity class of x in the following. Based on $[x]_B$ and $[x]_{\bar{B}}$, Stefanowski and Tsoukiàs defined the upper and lower approximation sets of X and the positive region of D with respect to B [19].

Definition 6. *For an incomplete decision table $IDT = (U, C \cup D, V, f)$ and an arbitrary set $X \subseteq U$, the upper approximation $B_S^-(X)$ and the lower approximation $B_-^S(X)$ of X with respect to B are*

$$B_S^-(X) = \cup\{[x]_B | x \in X\} \tag{8}$$

$$B_-^S(X) = \{x \in U | [x]_{\bar{B}} \subseteq X\} \tag{9}$$

Let $U/D = \{d_1, d_2, ..., d_m\}$ be the partition of the universe U defined by D. Then the positive region of D with respect to B is

$$POS_B^S(D) = \bigcup_{i=1}^{m} B_-^S(d_i) \tag{10}$$

According to the definition above, a positive region is a set of all objects in the universe that can be classified under a given condition attribute set.

3   Rough Set in Distributed Incomplete Decision Information System

Hu et al. presented a definition of rough set in distributed decision information system and proposed an attribute reduction algorithm of distributed decision information system [16]. However, they did not discuss the absence of missing values in distributed decision information system, which will be discussed below.

Let $\Delta = \{S_1, S_2, ..., S_n\}$ be a distributed incomplete decision information system, then there is at least one incomplete decision table $S_i = (U_i, C_i \cup D, V, f)$. There are two generic scenarios of DIDIS. One is instance-distributed, and the other is attribute-distributed. Here we mainly focus on the latter one, where $U_1 = U_2 = ... = U_n$ and $C_i \neq C_j (i \neq j)$.

Definition 7. *Let $\Delta = \{S_1, S_2, ..., S_n\}$ be a distributed incomplete decision information system. Given an arbitrary set $X \subseteq U$, an arbitrary attribute set $B \subseteq C$ where $C = \bigcup_{i=1}^{n} C_i$, $B = \bigcup_{i=1}^{n} B_i$, $B_i \subseteq C_i$, two definitions can be obtained respectively, according to the tolerance relation and the similarity relation.*

Based on tolerance relation T, the upper approximation and the lower approximation of X with respect to B are

$$B_T^-(X) = \{x \in U | \forall_{S_i \in \Delta}([x]_T^{B_i} \cap X \neq \emptyset)\} \tag{11}$$

$$B_-^T(X) = \{x \in U | \exists_{S_i \in \Delta}([x]_T^{B_i} \subseteq X)\} \tag{12}$$

The positive region of Δ with respect to B is

$$POS_B^T(D) = \{x \in U | \exists_{S_i \in \Delta \wedge d_j \in U/D}([x]_T^{B_i} \subseteq d_j)\} \tag{13}$$

where $[x]_T^{B_i}$ is the tolerance class of x produced by the condition attribute set B_i of S_i.

Based on similarity relation S, the upper approximation and the lower approximation of X with respect to B are

$$B_S^-(X) = \cup\{[x]_{B_i} | x \in X, S_i \in \Delta\} \tag{14}$$

$$B_-^S(X) = \{x \in U | \exists_{S_i \in \Delta}([x]_{B_i}^- \subseteq X)\} \tag{15}$$

The positive region of Δ with respect to B is

$$POS_B^S(D) = \{x \in U | \exists_{S_i \in \Delta \wedge d_j \in U/D}([x]_{B_i}^- \subseteq d_j)\} \tag{16}$$

where $[x]_{B_i}^-$ is the set of objects to which x is similar produced by the condition attribute set B_i of S_i.

Theorem 1. *Let* $\Delta = \{S_1, S_2, ..., S_n\}$ *be a distributed incomplete decision information system,* T *is the tolerance relation, the positive region of D with respect to Δ is the union of the positive region generated by each incomplete decision table of Δ. That is,* $POS_C^T(D) = \bigcup\limits_{i=1}^{n} POS_{C_i}^T(D)$.

Proof. Suppose $x \subset POS_\Delta(D)$, there exist $S_i \in \Delta$ and $d_j \in U/D$, $[x]_T^{C_i}$ is the tolerance class of x, such that $[x]_T^{C_i} \subseteq d_j$. That means $x \in POS_{C_i}(D)$, thus $x \in \bigcup\limits_{i=1}^{n} POS_{C_i}(D)$. In the contrary, if $x \in \bigcup\limits_{i=1}^{n} POS_{C_i}(D)$, x must belong to the positive region of an incomplete decision table of Δ. Suppose it is S_i, then there exists $[x]_T^{C_i} \subseteq d_j$. Therefore, $x \in POS_\Delta(D)$. Hence the theorem has been proved.

Theorem 2. *Let* $\Delta - \{S_1, S_2, ..., S_n\}$ *be a distributed incomplete decision information system,* S *is the similarity relation, the positive region of D with respect to Δ is the union of the positive region generated by each incomplete decision table of Δ. That is,* $POS_C^S(D) = \bigcup\limits_{i=1}^{n} POS_{C_i}^S(D)$.

Proof. Suppose $x \in POS_\Delta(D)$, there exist $S_i \in \Delta$ and $d_j \in U/D$, $[x]_{C_i}^-$ is the similarity class of x, such that $[x]_{C_i}^- \subseteq d_j$. That means $x \in POS_{C_i}(D)$, thus $x \in \bigcup\limits_{i=1}^{n} POS_{C_i}(D)$. In the contrary, if $x \in \bigcup\limits_{i=1}^{n} POS_{C_i}(D)$, x must belong to the positive region of an incomplete decision table of Δ. Suppose it is S_i, then there exists $[x]_{C_i}^- \subseteq d_j$. Therefore, $x \in POS_\Delta(D)$. Hence the theorem has been proved.

From above theorems, we know that the positive region of DIDIS can be calculated indirectly through the positive region of each incomplete decision table.

4   Attribute Reduction on Distributed Incomplete Decision Information System

Attribute reduction can effectively delete redundant attributes, improve data quality and speed up the subsequent data mining. In this section, we study the attribute reduction of distributed incomplete decision information system.

Theorem 3. *Let $\Delta = \{S_1, S_2, ..., S_n\}$ be a distributed incomplete decision information system, Φ and Ψ be two subsets of Δ. If $\Phi \subseteq \Psi$, then $POS_\Phi(D) \subseteq POS_\Psi(D)$.*

Proof. The proof comes directly from Theorems 1 or 2, and hence it is omitted here.

According to Theorem 3, if we add a new incomplete decision table to a distributed incomplete decision information system Δ, then the positive region of Δ increases or remains the same. In contrast, if we delete an incomplete decision table from Δ, then the positive region of Δ decreases or is left unchanged.

Definition 8. *Let $\Delta = \{S_1, S_2, ..., S_n\}$ be a distributed incomplete decision information system, if $POS_{\Delta-\{S_i\}}(D) = POS_\Delta(D)$, then S_i is reducible with respect to D in Δ; otherwise S_i is irreducible with respect to D in Δ.*

Theorem 4. *Let $\Delta = \{S_1, S_2, ..., S_n\}$ be a distributed incomplete decision information system, if $POS_{C_i}(D) \subseteq POS_{\Delta-\{S_i\}}(D)$, then S_i is reducible with respect to D.*

Proof. The proof comes directly from Theorems 1 or 2, and hence it is omitted here.

Theorem 5. *Let $\Delta = \{S_1, S_2, ..., S_n\}$ be a distributed incomplete decision information system, if and only if $\exists_{x \in U}(x \in POS_{C_i}(D) \wedge x \notin POS_{\Delta-\{S_i\}}(D))$, then S_i is irreducible with respect to D.*

Proof. The proof comes directly from Theorem 4, and hence it is omitted here.

Definition 9. *Let $\Delta = \{S_1, S_2, ..., S_n\}$ be a distributed incomplete decision information system, C_i is the attribute set of S_i, for any $a \in C_i$, if the positive region of Δ with respect to D stays unchanged when a is deleted from S_i, that is, $POS_\Delta^{S_i-\{a\}}(D) = POS_\Delta(D)$, then a is redundant. Otherwise a is necessary.*

Theorem 6. *Let $\Delta = \{S_1, S_2, ..., S_n\}$ be a distributed incomplete decision information system, a is one condition attribute of S_i. If a is reducible with respect to D in S_i, then a is reducible with respect to D in Δ.*

Proof. If a is reducible with respect to D in S_i, that is, the positive region of S_i remains the same when a is deleted from S_i. According to Theorems 1 or 2, the positive region of Δ stays unchanged. That is, a is reducible with respect to D in Δ.

However, if a is irreducible with respect to D in S_i, it does not mean that a is irreducible with respect to D in Δ.

Definition 10. *Let* $\Delta = \{S_1, S_2, ..., S_n\}$ *be a distributed incomplete decision information system,* $\Theta = \{T_1, T_2, ..., T_m\}$ *is a subsystem of* Δ, *for any* $T_i \in \Theta$, *there exists* $S_j \in \Delta$, *such that* $T_i \subseteq S_j$. Θ *is a reduct of* Δ *with respect to* D *if it satisfies the following two conditions:*

(1) $POS_\Theta(D) = POS_\Delta(D)$;
(2) $\forall a \in T_i,\ POS_\Theta^{T_i - \{a\}}(D) \neq POS_\Theta(D)$.

According to the Definition 9 and Definition 10 presented above, a subsystem Θ of a distributed incomplete decision information system Δ has the same positive region as Δ. If any condition attribute is deleted from Θ, the positive region of Θ decreases. The attribute reduction algorithm of distributed incomplete decision information system is developed as follows.

Algorithm 1. Attribute Reduction of Distributed Incomplete Decision Information System (ARDIDIS)

---

1 **Input:** $\Delta = \{S_1, S_2, \cdots, S_n\}$
2 **Output:** a reduct subsystem Θ
3 Let $\Theta = \Delta$
4 **for** *each incomplete decision table* $S_i \in \Theta$ **do**
5   **for** *each condition attribute* $a \in S_i$ **do**
6   **if** $POS_\Theta^{S_i - \{a\}}(D) = POS_\Theta(D)$ **then**
7   delete a from Θ

8 Return Θ

For a distributed incomplete decision information system, using above algorithm, one can get a reduced subsystem. The following example illustrates how to construct a reduct using ARDIDIS.

As shown in Table 1 is a distributed incomplete decision information system Δ which has two incomplete decision tables, S_1 and S_2. S_1 has three condition attributes $C_1 = \{a_1, a_2, a_3\}$. S_2 has three condition attributes $C_2 = \{a_4, a_5, a_6\}$.

Based on the tolerance relation, attribute reduction for Δ is performed using ARDIDIS, as described below.

For S_1, $[x_0]_T^{C_1} = \{x_0, x_2, x_4\}$, $[x_1]_T^{C_1} = \{x_1, x_3, x_5\}$, $[x_2]_T^{C_1} = \{x_0, x_2, x_3, x_4\}$, $[x_3]_T^{C_1} = \{x_1, x_2, x_3, x_5\}$, $[x_4]_T^{C_1} = \{x_0, x_2, x_4\}$, $[x_5]_T^{C_1} = \{x_1, x_3, x_5\}$.
$U/D = \{\{x_1, x_3, x_5\}, \{x_0, x_2, x_4\}\}$.

Table 1. A distributed incomplete decision information system

U	S_1				S_2			
	a_1	a_2	a_3	D	a_4	a_5	a_6	D
x_0	0	1	0	0	1	*	1	0
x_1	1	0	1	1	0	0	1	1
x_2	*	1	*	0	*	1	0	0
x_3	1	*	1	1	0	0	*	1
x_4	*	1	0	0	1	0	0	0
x_5	1	0	1	1	*	0	1	1

According to Definition 3, $POS_{C_1}^T(D) = \{x_0, x_1, x_4, x_5\}$.

For S_2, $[x_0]_T^{C_2} = \{x_0, x_5\}$, $[x_1]_T^{C_2} = \{x_1, x_3, x_5\}$, $[x_2]_T^{C_2} = \{x_2\}$, $[x_3]_T^{C_2} = \{x_1, x_3, x_5\}$, $[x_4]_T^{C_2} = \{x_4\}$, $[x_5]_T^{C_2} = \{x_0, x_1, x_3, x_5\}$.

$U/D = \{\{x_1, x_3, x_5\}, \{x_0, x_2, x_4\}\}$.

According to Definition 3, $POS_{C_2}^T(D) = \{x_1, x_2, x_3, x_4\}$.

According to Theorem 1, $POS_C^T(D) = POS_{C_1}^T(D) \cup POS_{C_2}^T(D) = \{x_0, x_1, x_2, x_3, x_4, x_5\}$.

We in turn determine which attributes in each incomplete decision table are reducible.

If a_1 is deleted from S_1, then

$[x_0]_T^{C_1-\{a_1\}} = \{x_0, x_2, x_4\}$, $[x_1]_T^{C_1-\{a_1\}} = \{x_1, x_3, x_5\}$, $[x_2]_T^{C_1-\{a_1\}} = \{x_0, x_2, x_3, x_4\}$, $[x_3]_T^{C_1-\{a_1\}} = \{x_1, x_2, x_3, x_5\}$, $[x_4]_T^{C_1-\{a_1\}} = \{x_0, x_2, x_4\}$, $[x_5]_T^{C_1-\{a_1\}} = \{x_1, x_3, x_5\}$. $POS_{C_1-\{a_1\}}^T(D) = \{x_0, x_1, x_4, x_5\}$.

$POS_C^T(D) = \{x_0, x_1, x_2, x_3, x_4, x_5\}$ stays unchanged. That is, a_1 is reducible.

Using the same method to determine the remaining attributes, we found that a_6 can also be reduced. Finally, we obtain a reduct $\{a_2, a_3, a_4, a_5\}$.

Based on the similarity relation, attribute reduction for Δ is performed using ARDIDIS, as described below.

For S_1, $[x_0]_{C_1}^- = \{x_0\}$, $[x_1]_{C_1}^- = \{x_1, x_5\}$, $[x_2]_{C_1}^- = \{x_0, x_2, x_4\}$, $[x_3]_{C_1}^- = \{x_1, x_3, x_5\}$, $[x_4]_{C_1}^- = \{x_0, x_4\}$, $[x_5]_{C_1}^- = \{x_1, x_5\}$.

$U/D = \{\{x_1, x_3, x_5\}, \{x_0, x_2, x_4\}\}$.

According to Definition 6, $POS_{C_1}^S(D) = \{x_0, x_1, x_2, x_3, x_4, x_5\}$.

For S_2, $[x_0]_{C_2}^- = \{x_0\}$, $[x_1]_{C_2}^- = \{x_1\}$, $[x_2]_{C_2}^- = \{x_2\}$, $[x_3]_{C_2}^- = \{x_1, x_3\}$, $[x_4]_{C_2}^- = \{x_4\}$, $[x_5]_{C_2}^- = \{x_1, x_5\}$.

$U/D = \{\{x_1, x_3, x_5\}, \{x_0, x_2, x_4\}\}$.

According to Definition 6, $POS_{C_2}^S(D) = \{x_0, x_1, x_2, x_3, x_4, x_5\}$.

According to Theorem 2, $POS_C^S(D) = POS_{C_1}^S(D) \cup POS_{C_2}^S(D) = \{x_0, x_1, x_2, x_3, x_4, x_5\}$.

We in turn determine which attributes are reducible in each incomplete decision table.

If a_1 is deleted from S_1, then

$[x_0]^-_{C_1-\{a_1\}} = \{x_0, x_4\}$, $[x_1]^-_{C_1-\{a_1\}} = \{x_1, x_5\}$, $[x_2]^-_{C_1-\{a_1\}} = \{x_0, x_2, x_4\}$,
$[x_3]^-_{C_1-\{a_1\}} = \{x_1, x_3, x_5\}$, $[x_4]^-_{C_1-\{a_1\}} = \{x_0, x_4\}$, $[x_5]^-_{C_1-\{a_1\}} = \{x_1, x_5\}$.
$POS^S_{C_1-\{a_1\}}(D) = \{x_0, x_1, x_2, x_3, x_4, x_5\}$.

$POS^S_C(D) = \{x_0, x_1, x_2, x_3, x_4, x_5\}$ stays unchanged, so a_1 can be reduced.

For the remaining attributes, we found that a_2 and a_3 can also be reduced. Finally, we obtain a reduct $\{a_4, a_5, a_6\}$, which is different from the reduct gotten by the tolerance relation.

5   Experimental Studies

In this section, two groups of experiments were conducted. One is to prove the effectiveness of the algorithm developed in the last section, and the other is to analyze the influence of different missing rates on attribute reduction.

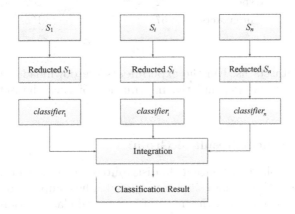

Fig. 1. The experimental framework

To simulate 40 distributed incomplete decision information systems stored in two or three data sites, an incomplete dataset is divided into two or three parts, and a total of 40 splits are performed. Based on the tolerance relation and the similarity relation, all DIDISs are first reduced by ARDIDIS proposed in this paper, and then are trained to obtain the corresponding classifiers. Finally, we get the ensemble result of all classifiers. The experimental framework is shown in Fig. 1. The reason why we conducted experiments on 40 DIDISs is that we expected a static result, such as the average attribute numbers, the mean of integrated classification accuracy, which are showed in the following experimental results.

The classifiers used here are J48 and Naive Bayes (NB) that can handle missing values in weka, and all classification experiments were run in a 10-fold cross validation mode. For the sample to be classified, the integration method is to sum the probability of the same label in different data site, and the predicted label is the label with the largest probability. The calculation method is as follows.

$$\text{predicted\_label} = \arg\max_i(\sum_j x_{ji}) \qquad (17)$$

where the label probability x_{ji} represents the probability of x belonging to label i according to classifier j.

Table 2. Information of datasets

Type of datasets	Datasets	Number of attributes	Number of samples
Incomplete datasets	house_votes_84	16	434
	soybean_large	35	683
	audiology	69	226
Complete datasets	zoo	16	101
	lymphography	18	148
	spect	22	267
	promoters	57	106

The seven datasets used in the experiments are downloaded from the UCI machine learning database, and the information of each dataset is shown in Table 2.

5.1   The Experiment Result of Group 1

(1) Based on the tolerance relation, 40 distributed incomplete decision information systems with two data sites are reduced. The comparison of the average number of attributes and the mean of integrated classification accuracy are shown in Figs. 2 and 3, respectively.

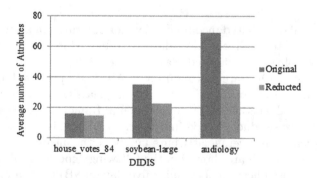

Fig. 2. The average attribute numbers before and after reduction

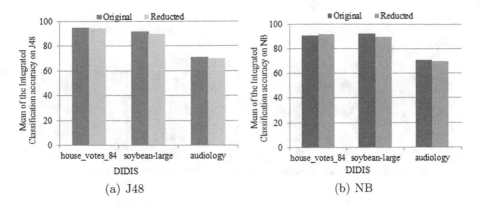

(a) J48   (b) NB

Fig. 3. The mean of integrated classification accuracy before and after reduction

(2) Based on the tolerance relation, 40 distributed incomplete decision information systems with three data sites are reduced. The comparison of the average number of attributes and the mean of integrated classification accuracy are shown in Figs. 4 and 5, respectively.

(3) Based on the similarity relation, 40 distributed incomplete decision information systems with two data sites are reduced. The comparison of the average number of attributes and the mean of integrated classification accuracy are shown in Figs. 6 and 7, respectively.

(4) Based on the similarity relation, 40 distributed incomplete decision information systems with three data sites are reduced. The comparison of the average number of attributes and the mean of integrated classification accuracy are shown in Figs. 8 and 9, respectively.

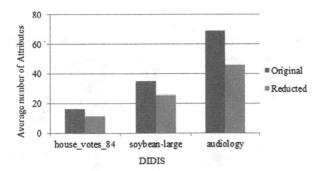

Fig. 4. The average attribute numbers before and after reduction

It can be seen from Figs. 2, 4, 6 and 8 that the conditional attribute set has been reduced to varying degrees, when the tolerance relation or the similarity relation is used. From Figs. 3, 5, 7 and 9, it is found that the integration result

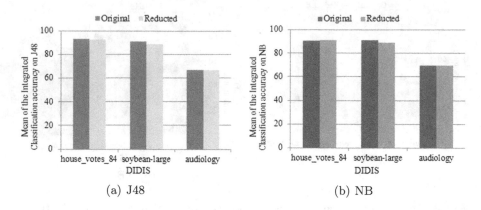

Fig. 5. The mean of integrated classification accuracy before and after reduction

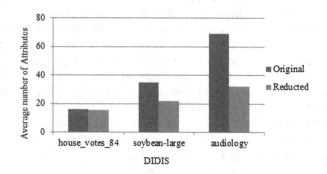

Fig. 6. The average attribute numbers before and after reduction

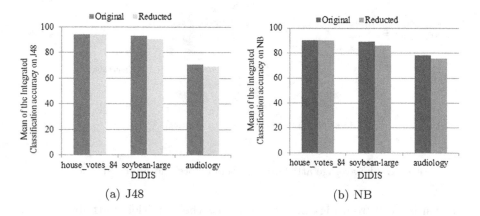

Fig. 7. The mean of integrated classification accuracy before and after reduction

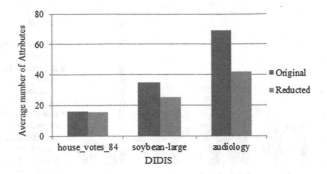

Fig. 8. The average attribute numbers before and after reduction

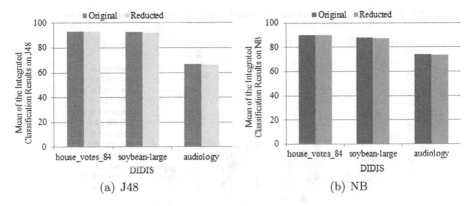

(a) J48   (b) NB

Fig. 9. The mean of integrated classification accuracy before and after reduction

after reduction has little or no difference as the integration result before reduction no matter which classifier is used.

5.2   The Experiment Result of Group 2

To find the influence of different random missing rates on attribute reduction, a complete dataset is randomly deleted at the rates of 5%, 10%, 15%, 20%, 25%, 30%, and then six incomplete datasets can be obtained. Each incomplete dataset is processed in the same way as before.

(1) For all 40 distributed incomplete decision information systems with two data sites, the attribute reduction is performed based on the tolerance relation. The total number of attributes on average after reduction and the total number of attributes of original DIDISs are shown in Fig. 10. Figure 11 shows the results gotten by 40 distributed incomplete decision information systems with three data sites.

From Figs. 10 and 11, we can see that the number of reduced attributes exhibits several kinds of changes as the missing rate increases. First, when the

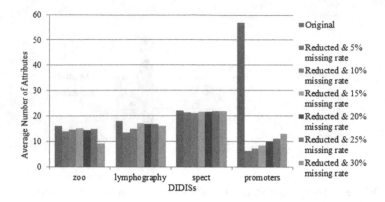

Fig. 10. The average attribute numbers before and after reduction

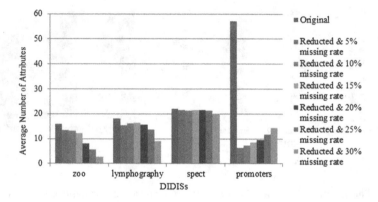

Fig. 11. The average attribute numbers before and after reduction

missing rate is low, the number of attributes that can be reduced decreases gradually with the increase of the missing rate. However, when the missing rate is high, there is no obvious change on the number of attributes that can be reduced by ARDIDIS. Moreover, when the missing rate exceeds a threshold, the number of reduced attributes increases sharply.

The reason why we got above results is that the positive region of DIDIS varies with the increase of the missing rate. When a DIDIS is reduced using the tolerance relation, the size of tolerance class for each sample tends to monotonically increase with the missing rate increasing. When the missing rate does not reach a certain threshold, the tolerance class of each sample does not change or increase, the positive region of DIDIS remains unchanged or does not change much. That is, the classification ability of DIDIS does not change much, but the ability of each attribute to discriminate samples is decreased. Therefore, as the missing rate increases, the number of reduced attributes decreases, and DIDIS needs to retain more attributes to distinguish the samples, which is conforming to the first result. But when the missing rate exceeds a certain threshold, the positive region of DIDIS is reduced a lot due to the fact that the tolerance classes of some samples become very large. In this case, the classification ability of DIDIS is reduced, and the ability of distinguishing the samples of each attribute is also decreased. However, with the increase of the missing rate, the number of reduced attribute may increase or decrease. This analysis is consistent with the second result. If the missing rate becomes so large that the positive region of one or more incomplete decision tables become empty, the number of reduced attributes will increase sharply.

(2) For all 40 distributed incomplete decision information systems with two data sites, the attribute reduction is performed based on the similarity relation. The total number of attributes on average after reduction and the total number of attributes of original DIDISs are shown in Fig. 12. Figure 13 shows the results gotten by 40 distributed incomplete decision information systems with three data sites.

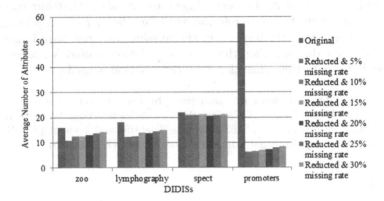

Fig. 12. The average attribute numbers before and after reduction

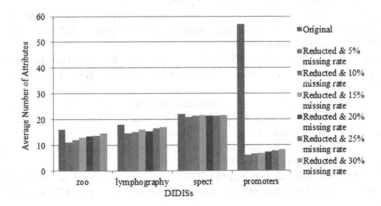

Fig. 13. The average attribute numbers before and after reduction

From Figs. 12 and 13, there is no obvious change rule on the number of reduced attributes when the missing rate increases. That is, similarity class of each sample may increase, decrease or stay unchanged with the increase of the missing rate. As a result, the change of the positive region of DIDIS cannot be predicted. Moreover, with the increasing of the missing rate, the ability of each attribute to distinguish samples may decrease. Compared the attribute reduction using the tolerance relation with the attribute reduction using the similarity relation, the influence of the missing rate is stronger on the former.

6   Conclusions

In order to simplify a distributed incomplete decision information system and keep its classification ability, we proposed an attribute reduction method based on rough set theory. We first proposed a definition of rough set in distributed incomplete decision information system, and then developed an attribute reduction algorithm based on it. The experiment results show that our method is effective no matter the tolerance relation or the similarity relation is applied. In addition, we found that the increase of the missing rate may have larger effect on the attribute reduction when the tolerance relation is used, while less effect on the attribute reduction when the similarity relation is used.

Acknowledgments. This work was supported by the Natural Science Foundation of China (61379114, 61533020, 61472056), the Social Science Foundation of the Chinese Education Commission (15XJA630003), the Scientific and Technological Research Program of Chongqing Municipal Education Commission (KJ1500416).

References

1. Maytal, S.T., Foster, P.: Handling missing values when applying classification models. J. Mach. Learn. Res. **8**, 1625–1657 (2007)
2. Zhang, S.C., Wu, X.D., Zhu, M.L.: Efficient missing data imputation for supervised learning. In: 9th IEEE International Conference on Cognitive Informatics, Beijing, pp. 672–679. IEEE Press (2010)
3. Rahman, M.G., Islam, M.Z.: FIMUS: a framework for imputing missing values using co-appearance, correlation and similarity analysis. Knowl.-Based Syst. **56**, 311–327 (2014)
4. Jordanov, I., Petrov, N.: Sets with incomplete and missing data NN radar signal classification. In: 2014 International Joint Conference on Neural Networks, Beijing, pp. 218–224. IEEE Press (2014)
5. Baitharu, T.R., Pani, S.K.: Effect of missing values on data classification. J. Emerg. Trends Eng. Appl. Sci. **4**, 311–316 (2013)
6. Meng, Z.Q., Shi, Z.Z.: A fast approach to attribute reduction in incomplete decision systems with tolerance relation-based rough sets. Inf. Sci. **179**(16), 2774–2793 (2009)
7. Qian, Y.H., Liang, J.Y., Pedrycz, W., Dang, C.Y.: An efficient accelerator for attribute reduction from incomplete data in rough set framework. Pattern Recogn. **44**(8), 1658–1670 (2011)

8. Sun, L., Xu, J.C., Tian, Y.: Feature selection using rough entropy-based uncertainty measures in incomplete decision systems. Knowl.-Based Syst. **36**, 206–216 (2012)
9. Dai, J.H., Wang, W.T., Tian, H.W., Liu, L.: Attribute selection based on a new conditional entropy for incomplete decision systems. Knowl.-Based Syst. **39**, 207–213 (2013)
10. Zhao, H., Qin, K.Y.: Mixed feature selection in incomplete decision table. Knowl.-Based Syst. **57**, 181–190 (2014)
11. Lu, Z.C., Qin, Z., Zhang, Y.Q., Fang, J.: A fast feature selection approach based on rough set boundary regions. Pattern Recogn. Lett. **36**, 81–88 (2014)
12. Yang, M., Yang, P.: Approximate reduction based on conditional information entropy over vertically partitioned multi-decision tables. Control Decis. **23**, 1103–1108 (2008). (in Chinese)
13. Zhou, Z.Y., Huang, L.S., Ye, Y.: Privacy preserving attribute reduction based on rough set. In: 2009 Second International Workshop on Knowledge Discovery and Data Mining, pp. 202–206. IEEE Press (2009)
14. Ye, M.Q., Hu, X.G., Wu, C.G.: Privacy preserving attribute reduction for vertically partitioned data. In: 2010 International Conference on Artificial Intelligence and Computational Intelligence, Sanya, pp. 315–319. IEEE Press (2010)
15. Banerjee, M., Chakravarty, S.: Privacy preserving feature selection for distributed data using virtual dimension. In: 20th ACM Conference on Information and Knowledge Management, Glasgow, pp. 2281–2284. ACM Press (2011)
16. Hu, J., Pedrycz, W., Wang, G.Y., Wang, K.: Rough sets in distributed decision information systems. Knowl.-Based Syst. **94**, 13–22 (2016)
17. Pawlak, Z.: Information systems theoretical foundations. Inf. Syst. **6**(3), 205–218 (1981)
18. Kryszkiewicz, M.: Rough set approach to incomplete information systems. Inf. Sci. **112**, 39–49 (1998)
19. Stefanowski, J., Tsoukiàs, A.: On the extension of rough sets under incomplete information. In: Zhong, N., Skowron, A., Ohsuga, S. (eds.) RSFDGrC 1999. LNCS, vol. 1711, pp. 73–81. Springer, Heidelberg (1999). doi:10.1007/978-3-540-48061-7_11

The Attribute Reductions Based on Indiscernibility and Discernibility Relations

Keyun Qin[✉] and Sihui Jing

College of Mathematics, Southwest Jiaotong University,
Chengdu 610031, Sichuan, China
keyunqin@263.net, jingsihui1993@163.com

Abstract. Knowledge reduction and knowledge discovery in information systems are important topics of rough set theory. Based on the relative indiscernibility relation and relative discernibility relation of decision systems, the notions of λ reduction and μ reduction are proposed. The judgement theorems for λ consistent set and μ consistent set are provided. The discernibility matrices with respect to λ reduction and μ reduction are obtained and the reduction approaches are presented. Furthermore, the relationships among λ reduction, μ reduction, positive region reduction and assignment reduction are analyzed.

Keywords: Rough set · Indiscernibility and discernibility relation · Reduction

1 Introduction

Rough set theory is a powerful mathematical tool introduced by Pawlak [1] to address imprecise, incomplete or vague information. One fundamental aspect of rough set theory is attribute reduction in information systems, which is selecting those attributes that provide the same information for classification purposes as the entire set of available attributes. As a common technique, attribute reduction has been successfully applied in many fields, such as pattern recognition, machine learning and data mining [2,3].

There are many types of attribute reductions in the area of rough sets. Pawlak [4] proposes the classic attribute reduction, which is intended to preserve a deterministic information with respect to decision attributes of a decision table and is therefore often applied in extracting deterministic decision rules from decision tables. For inconsistent decision tables, Kryszkiewicz proposed assignment reduction and distribution reduction [5,6]. Assignment reduction makes the possible decisions for an arbitrary object in an inconsistent decision table unchanged. In comparison, distribution reduction is a more complete knowledge reduction and is characterized by preserving the class membership distribution for all the objects in an inconsistent decision table. In other words, the distribution reduction preserves not only the deterministic information but also

© Springer International Publishing AG 2017
L. Polkowski et al. (Eds.): IJCRS 2017, Part I, LNAI 10313, pp. 306–316, 2017.
DOI: 10.1007/978-3-319-60837-2_26

the non-deterministic information of an inconsistent decision table. Yao and Zhao [7] thinks that the partition based on the membership distribution vector is a strict requirement, and the decision rules derived from distribution reduction are usually less compact and more complicated. For this reason, Zhang et al. have proposed the maximum distribution reduction [8,9]. It maintains the maximum decision classes for all objects in a decision table unchanged, which is seen as a good compromise between the capability of preserving information with respect to decisions and the compactness of the derived rules. Miao et al. [10] presented three kinds of reductions for inconsistent complete decision systems: region preservation reduction, decision preservation reduction, and relationship preservation reduction. Their main objective was to combine all these reduction approaches into a unified framework. More recently, a relatively systematic study of attribution reduction in inconsistent incomplete decision tables is presented in [11], where five types of discernibility function-based approaches are proposed to identify a specific type of reduction.

Skowron and Rauszer [12] proposed the classical method of discernibility matrix and discernibility function and presented the reduction method for positive region reduction. The discernibility function is a Boolean logical function. This function is reduced by using the distribution and the absorption laws and the reductions are found by looking at the prime implicants of the reduced function. To find other kinds of reductions (assignment reduction, distribution reduction and maximum distribution reduction), Zhang et al. [8,9] have utilized the discernibility matrices with respect to those reductions and have obtained the corresponding discernibility functions. The attribute reduction based on the discernibility matrices has been extensively researched [10,11,13,14]. Although discernibility matrix-based methods can find all of the reductions, the conversion from conjunction normal form to disjunction normal form constitutes an NP-hard problem. When the data set has many attributes, these discernibility matrix-based methods become not feasible because the matrix contains too many candidates. Therefore, heuristic methods are desirable and have been extensively investigated [15–18].

Suppose a finite set of objects are described by a finite set of attributes. With respect to any subset of attributes, one can define a pair of dual indiscernibility and discernibility relations [19–21]. Two objects are considered to be indiscernible or equivalent if and only if they have the same values for all attributes in the set. As a dual relation to indiscernibility, two objects are considered to be discernible if and only if they have different values for at least one attribute. The differences between objects also play a crucial role in data analysis. The similarities of objects lead naturally to their grouping, and the differences lead to group division. It is important to extract similarities of objects by ignoring certain differences in order to form a useful cluster or a high-level concept, and to identify differences among a set of similar objects in order to form sub-concepts. Orłowska [19] investigated the relationships between indiscernibility relation and discernibility relation are analyzed. The notions of indiscernibility reduction, discernibility reduction and indiscernibility-and-discernibility reduction are proposed. This paper is devoted to a further study of the relative reductions. The paper is organized as follows: In Sect. 2, we recall some notions and properties of indiscernibility and discernibility relations. In Sect. 3, the notion of λ reduction for decision tables is proposed. The judgement theorems for λ consistent set are provided and the reduction approaches for λ reduction are presented. The relationships among λ reduction, the positive region reduction and assignment reduction are analyzed. In Sect. 4, μ reduction approach is provided. The paper is completed with some concluding remarks.

2   Indiscernibility and Discernibility Relations

Knowledge representation in the rough set models is realized via information systems, where a set of objects are described by a set of attributes.

Definition 1. *An information system S is the tuple $S = (U, AT, \{V_a | a \in At\}, \{I_a | a \in At\})$, where U is a finite non-empty set of objects, AT is a finite non-empty set of attributes, V_a is a non-empty set of values for an attribute $a \in At$ and $I_a : U \rightarrow V_a$ is an information function. $I_a(x) = v$ means that the object x has the value v on the attribute a.*

Let $S = (U, AT, \{V_a | a \in At\}, \{I_a | a \in At\})$ be an information system and $A \subseteq At$. The indiscernibility relation $Ind(A)$ determined by A is defined by:

$$Ind(A) = \{(x,y) \in U \times U | \forall a \in A(I_a(x) = I_a(y))\}.$$

Clearly, $Ind(A)$ is an equivalence relation and induces a partition $U/A = \{[x]_A | x \in U\}$ of U, where $[x]_A$ is the equivalence class containing x. Based on the indiscernibility relation $Ind(A)$, the lower and upper approximation operators are defined.

Definition 2 [1]. *Let $S = (U, AT, \{V_a | a \in At\}, \{I_a | a \in At\})$ be an information system and $A \subseteq At$. For any $X \subseteq U$, the lower approximation $\underline{A}(X)$ and the upper approximations $\overline{A}(X)$ of X are defined by*

$$\underline{A}(X) = \{x \in U; [x]_A \subseteq X\} \tag{1}$$

$$\overline{A}(X) = \{x \in U; [x]_A \cap X \neq \emptyset\} \tag{2}$$

Given an information system, Zhao et al. [22] (see also [19–21]) proposed the following binary relations to describe the similarity and difference between objects.

Definition 3. *Let $S = (U, AT, \{V_a | a \in At\}, \{I_a | a \in At\})$ be an information system and $A \subseteq At$. Three relations on U are defined by:*
$WInd(A) = \{(x,y) \in U \times U | \exists a \in A(I_a(x) = I_a(y))\};$
$Dis(A) = \{(x,y) \in U \times U | \forall a \in A(I_a(x) \neq I_a(y))\};$
$WDis(A) = \{(x,y) \in U \times U | \exists a \in A(I_a(x) \neq I_a(y))\}.$

$WInd(A)$, $Dis(A)$ and $WDis(A)$ are called weak indiscernibility relation, strong discernibility relation and weak discernibility relation respectively. It is noted that $WInd(A) = U \times U - Dis(A)$ and $WDis(A) = U \times U - Ind(A)$. Thus, theoretically speaking, it is sufficient to discuss $Ind(A)$ and $Dis(A)$. The notions of indiscernibility reduction, discernibility reduction and indiscernibility-discernibility reduction are proposed and the reduction approaches are provided in [22].

A decision table is an information system $S = (U, AT, \{V_a | a \in At\}, \{I_a | a \in At\})$, where $At = C \cup D$, C is a set of conditional attributes, and D is a set of decision attributes. For simplicity, in this paper, we set $D = \{d\}$.

Definition 4. *Let $S = (U, C \cup \{d\}, \{V_a | a \in C \cup \{d\}\}, \{I_a | a \in C \cup \{d\}\})$ be a decision table, and $A \subseteq C$.*

(1) $Pos_A(d) = \cup_{X \in U/d} \underline{A}(X)$ is called the positive region of d with respect to A.

(2) A is called a positive region consistent set if $Pos_A(d) = Pos_C(d)$. A is called a positive region reduction of S if A is a positive region consistent set and B is not a positive region consistent set for each proper subset B of A.

(3) A is called an assignment consistent set if $\overline{A}(X) = \overline{C}(X)$ for each $X \in U/d$. A is called an assignment reduction of S if A is an assignment consistent set and B is not an assignment consistent set for each proper subset B of A.

Positive region reduction and assignment reduction are two typical reductions of decision systems. The reduction approaches have been provided in [8, 9, 12].

For a decision table, Zhao et al. [22] proposed the following decision-relative relations.

Definition 5 [22]. *Let $S = (U, C \cup \{d\}, \{V_a | a \in C \cup \{d\}\}, \{I_a | a \in C \cup \{d\}\})$ be a decision table, and $A \subseteq C$. Four decision-relative relations on U are defined by:*

$Ind_d(A) = \{(x, y) \in U \times U | \forall a \in A(I_a(x) = I_a(y)) \wedge I_d(x) = I_d(y)\}$;
$WInd_d(A) = \{(x, y) \in U \times U | \exists a \in A(I_a(x) = I_a(y)) \wedge I_d(x) = I_d(y)\}$;
$Dis_d(A) = \{(x, y) \in U \times U | \forall a \in A(I_a(x) \neq I_a(y)) \wedge I_d(x) \neq I_d(y)\}$;
$WDis_d(A) = \{(x, y) \in U \times U | \exists a \in A(I_a(x) \neq I_a(y)) \wedge I_d(x) \neq I_d(y)\}$.

Definition 6 [22]. *Let $S = (U, C \cup \{d\}, \{V_a | a \in C \cup \{d\}\}, \{I_a | a \in C \cup \{d\}\})$ be a decision table, and $A \subseteq C$.*

(1) A is called a relative indiscernibility reduction of S if $Ind_d(A) = Ind_d(C)$ and $Ind_d(B) \neq Ind_d(C)$ for each proper subset B of A.

(2) A is called a relative discernibility reduction of S if $Dis_d(A) = Dis_d(C)$ and $Dis_d(B) \neq Dis_d(C)$ for each proper subset B of A.

Qin and Jing [23] noted that there are some errors in the reduction approaches presented in [22]. Furthermore, the reduction approaches for the decision-relative relations $Ind_d(A)$ and $Dis_d(A)$ are provided [23]. For any $x, y \in U$, we define:

$$Dm_d(x, y) = \begin{cases} \{a \in C; I_a(x) \neq I_a(y)\}, & \text{if } I_d(x) = I_d(y), \\ \emptyset, & \text{otherwise.} \end{cases} \tag{3}$$

$$Im_d(x, y) = \begin{cases} \{a \in C; I_a(x) = I_a(y)\}, & \text{if } I_d(x) \neq I_d(y), \\ \emptyset, & \text{otherwise.} \end{cases} \quad (4)$$

Let $F_{Dm} = \wedge\{\vee Dm_d(x, y); Dm_d(x, y) \neq \emptyset\}$, $F_{Im} = \wedge\{\vee Im_d(x, y); Im_d(x, y) \neq \emptyset\}$. F_{Dm} and F_{Im} are called the relative indiscernibility function and relative discernibility function of S respectively.

Theorem 1 [23]. *Let $S = (U, C \cup \{d\}, \{V_a | a \in C \cup \{d\}\}, \{I_a | a \in C \cup \{d\}\})$ be a decision table, and $A \subseteq C$.*

(1) A is a relative indiscernibility reduction of S if and only if $\wedge A$ is a prime implicant of F_{Dm}.

(2) A is a relative discernibility reduction of S if and only if $\wedge A$ is a prime implicant of F_{Im}.

Example 1. We consider the decision table $S = (U, C \cup \{d\}, \{V_a | a \in C \cup \{d\}\}, \{I_a | a \in C \cup \{d\}\})$ presented in [22], where $U = \{o_i; 1 \leq i \leq 8\}$, $C = \{a, b, c, d\}$ is the set of conditional attributes, D is the decision attribute and the information functions are given by the following Table 1:

Table 1. A decision table

	a	b	c	d	e	f	D
o_1	1	1	1	1	1	1	+
o_2	1	0	1	0	1	1	+
o_3	0	0	1	1	0	0	+
o_4	1	1	1	0	0	1	−
o_5	1	0	1	0	1	1	−
o_6	0	0	0	1	1	0	−
o_7	1	0	1	1	1	1	−
o_8	0	0	0	0	1	1	−
o_9	1	0	0	1	0	0	−

It is noted that [23] the relative indiscernibility reductions of S are $\{a, d, e\}$, $\{c, d, e\}$, $\{a, b, c, d\}$ and $\{a, b, d, f\}$. Thus, it seems that the discernibility matrix presented in [22] is unreasonable. Actually, they correspond to the reductions presented in the following two sections.

3   The Reduction Based on λ-Relative Relations

In this section, a kind of decision-relative relation on the universe, called λ-relative relation, is proposed and the λ-reduction approach is presented.

Definition 7. *Let $S = (U, C \cup \{d\}, \{V_a | a \in C \cup \{d\}\}, \{I_a | a \in C \cup \{d\}\})$ be a decision table, and $A \subseteq C$. The λ-relative relation $Ind_d^\lambda(A)$ on U is defined by:*
$$Ind_d^\lambda(A) = \{(x,y) \in U \times U | \forall a \in A (I_a(x) \neq I_a(y)) \vee I_d(x) = I_d(y)\}.$$

Definition 8. *Let $S = (U, C \cup \{d\}, \{V_a | a \in C \cup \{d\}\}, \{I_a | a \in C \cup \{d\}\})$ be a decision table, and $A \subseteq C$.*

(1) A is called a λ-consistent set of S if $Ind_d^\lambda(A) = Ind_d^\lambda(C)$.

(2) A is called a λ-reduction of S if A is a λ-consistent set, and for any proper subset B of A, B is not a λ-consistent set.

For any $x, y \in U$, we define:

$$Dm_d^\lambda(x,y) = \begin{cases} \{a \in C; I_a(x) \neq I_a(y)\}, & \text{if } I_d(x) \neq I_d(y), \\ \emptyset, & \text{otherwise.} \end{cases} \tag{5}$$

Theorem 2. *Let $S = (U, C \cup \{d\}, \{V_a | a \in C \cup \{d\}\}, \{I_a | a \in C \cup \{d\}\})$ be a decision table, and $A \subseteq C$. A is a λ-consistent set of S if and only if for any $x, y \in U$, $A \cap Dm_d^\lambda(x,y) \neq \emptyset$ whenever $Dm_d^\lambda(x,y) \neq \emptyset$.*

Proof. Suppose that A is a λ-consistent set of S and $x, y \in U$ such that $Dm_d^\lambda(x,y) \neq \emptyset$. Then $Ind_d^\lambda(A) = Ind_d^\lambda(C)$. Additionally, $I_d(x) \neq I_d(y)$ and there exists $a \in C$ such that $I_a(x) \neq I_a(y)$. Thus $(x,y) \notin Ind_d^\lambda(C)$. It follows that $(x,y) \notin Ind_d^\lambda(A)$ and thus there exist $b \in A$ such that $I_b(x) \neq I_b(y)$. Consequently, $b \in Dm_d^\lambda(x,y)$ and hence $A \cap Dm_d^\lambda(x,y) \neq \emptyset$.

Conversely, suppose that $A \cap Dm_d^\lambda(x,y) \neq \emptyset$ if $Dm_d^\lambda(x,y) \neq \emptyset$. For any $x, y \in U$, if $(x,y) \notin Ind_d^\lambda(C)$, then $I_d(x) \neq I_d(y)$ and there exists $a \in C$ such that $I_a(x) \neq I_a(y)$. It follows that $Dm_d^\lambda(x,y) \neq \emptyset$ and hence $A \cap Dm_d^\lambda(x,y) \neq \emptyset$. Thus there exists $b \in A$ such that $I_b(x) \neq I_b(y)$. Consequently, we have $(x,y) \notin Ind_d^\lambda(A)$ and thus $Ind_d^\lambda(A) \subseteq Ind_d^\lambda(C)$. On the other hand, $Ind_d^\lambda(C) \subseteq Ind_d^\lambda(A)$ is trivial. It follows that $Ind_d^\lambda(A) = Ind_d^\lambda(C)$ and A is a λ-consistent set of S as required.

Let $F_{Dm}^\lambda = \wedge \{\vee Dm_d^\lambda(x,y); Dm_d^\lambda(x,y) \neq \emptyset\}$. F_{Dm}^λ is called the λ-discernibility function of S. Based on the discernibility function and prime implicant results presented in [12], we have the following corollary.

Corollary 1. *Let $S = (U, C \cup \{d\}, \{V_a | a \in C \cup \{d\}\}, \{I_a | a \in C \cup \{d\}\})$ be a decision table, and $A \subseteq C$. A is a λ-reduction of S if and only if $\wedge A$ is a prime implicant of F_{Dm}^λ.*

Theorem 3. *Let $S = (U, C \cup \{d\}, \{V_a | a \in C \cup \{d\}\}, \{I_a | a \in C \cup \{d\}\})$ be a decision table, and $A \subseteq C$. If A is a λ-consistent set of S, then A is a positive region consistent set.*

Proof. Suppose that $x \in U$ and $x \notin Pos_A(d)$. Then $[x]_A \not\subseteq [x]_d$. It follows that there exists $y \in U$ such that $y \in [x]_A$ and $y \notin [x]_d$. Thus we have $I_d(x) \neq I_d(y)$ and $I_a(x) = I_a(y)$ for each $a \in A$. Consequently, we have $(x,y) \in Ind_d^\lambda(A)$. Because A is a λ-consistent set of S, $(x,y) \in Ind_d^\lambda(C)$. From $I_d(x) \neq I_d(y)$, it follows that $I_a(x) = I_a(y)$ for each $a \in C$, so that $[x]_C = [y]_C$. By $y \notin [x]_d$ and $y \in [x]_C$ we have $[x]_C \nsubseteq [x]_d$ and hence $x \notin Pos_C(d)$. It follows that $Pos_C(d) \subseteq Pos_A(d)$. On the other hand, $Pos_A(d) \subseteq Pos_C(d)$ is trivial. Thus A is a positive region consistent set.

Theorem 4. *Let* $S = (U, C \cup \{d\}, \{V_a | a \in C \cup \{d\}\}, \{I_a | a \in C \cup \{d\}\})$ *be a decision table, and* $A \subseteq C$. *If* A *is a* λ-*consistent set of* S, *then* A *is a assignment consistent set.*

Proof. It is sufficient to prove that $\overline{A}(E) = \overline{C}(E)$ for each $E \in U/d$. By $A \subseteq C$, it follows that $Ind(C) \subseteq Ind(A)$ and hence $[x]_C \subseteq [x]_A$. Consequently, we have $\overline{C}(E) \subseteq \overline{A}(E)$.

On the other hand, if there exists $x \in U$ such that $x \in \overline{A}(E)$ and $x \notin \overline{C}(E)$, then $[x]_A \cap E \neq \emptyset$ and $[x]_C \cap E = \emptyset$. It follows that there exists $y \in U$ such that $y \in [x]_A \cap E$. By $y \in [x]_A$ we can conclude that $I_a(x) = I_a(y)$ for each $a \in A$. Thus we have $(x, y) \in Ind_d^\lambda(A) = Ind_d^\lambda(C)$. By $[x]_{Ind(C)} \cap E = \emptyset$ and $y \in E$ we have $x \notin E$ and hence $I_d(x) \neq I_d(y)$. It follows that, by $(x, y) \in Ind_d^\lambda(C)$, $I_a(x) = I_a(y)$ for each $a \in C$. Thus $y \in [x]_C \cap E$. This is a contradiction with $[x]_C \cap E = \emptyset$.

Example 2. We consider the decision table $S = (U, C \cup \{d\}, \{V_a | a \in C \cup \{d\}\}, \{I_a | a \in C \cup \{d\}\})$, where $U = \{o_i; 1 \leq i \leq 8\}$, $C = \{a, b, c, d\}$ is the set of conditional attributes, D is the decision attribute and the information functions are given by the following Table 2:

Table 2. A decision table

	a	b	c	d	D
o_1	0	0	1	1	0
o_2	1	0	1	2	0
o_3	2	1	2	0	1
o_4	2	1	2	0	2
o_5	1	2	2	1	2
o_6	1	2	2	1	1
o_7	0	1	3	2	1
o_8	0	1	3	2	0

According to (5), the matrix Dm_d^λ is given by the Table 3.
It follows that
$$F_{Dm}^\lambda = \wedge\{\vee Dm_d^\lambda(x, y); Dm_d^\lambda(x, y) \neq \emptyset\}$$
$$= (a \wedge b) \vee (a \wedge c) \vee (a \wedge d) \vee (b \wedge c) \vee (b \wedge d) \vee (c \wedge d).$$
Consequently, the λ-reductions of S are $\{a, b\}$, $\{a, c\}$, $\{a, d\}$, $\{b, c\}$, $\{b, d\}$ and $\{c, d\}$.

Table 3. The matrix Dm_d^λ

	o_1	o_2	o_3	o_4	o_5	o_6	o_7	o_8
o_1	$\emptyset$							
o_2		$\emptyset$						
o_3	$abcd$	$abcd$	$\emptyset$					
o_4	$abcd$	$abcd$		$\emptyset$				
o_5	abc	bcd	abd		$\emptyset$			
o_6	abc	bcd		abd		$\emptyset$		
o_7	bcd	abc		acd	$abcd$		$\emptyset$	
o_8			acd	acd	$abcd$	$abcd$		$\emptyset$

According to [8,9], for assignment reduction, two objects x and y need to be differentiated if $\delta(x) \neq \delta(y)$ where $\delta(x) = \{Y | Y \in U/d \wedge [x]_A \cap Y \neq \emptyset\}$. In this example, $U/d = \{D_1, D_2, D_3\}$, $D_1 = \{o_1, o_2, o_8\}$, $D_2 = \{o_3, o_6, o_7\}$, $D_3 = \{o_4, o_5\}$. Additionally, $\delta(o_1) = \delta(o_2) = \{D_1\}$, $\delta(o_3) = \delta(o_4) = \delta(o_5) = \delta(o_6) = \{D_2, D_3\}$, $\delta(o_7) = \delta(o_8) = \{D_1, D_2\}$. The assignment discernibility matrix is given by Table 4.

Table 4. Assignment discernibility matrix

	o_1	o_2	o_3	o_4	o_5	o_6	o_7	o_8
o_1	$\emptyset$							
o_2		$\emptyset$						
o_3	$abcd$	$abcd$	$\emptyset$					
o_4	$abcd$	$abcd$		$\emptyset$				
o_5	abc	bcd		$\emptyset$				
o_6	abc	bcd			$\emptyset$			
o_7	bcd	abc	acd	acd	$abcd$	$abcd$	$\emptyset$	
o_8	bcd	abc	acd	acd	$abcd$	$abcd$		$\emptyset$

The assignment discernibility function is:
$F_{assign} = c \vee (a \wedge b) \vee (a \wedge d) \vee (b \wedge d)$.

Thus, the assignment reductions are $\{c\}$, $\{a, b\}$, $\{a, d\}$ and $\{b, d\}$. Similarly, it can be computed that the positive region reduction of S are $\{b\}$, $\{c\}$ and $\{a, d\}$. It follows that the λ-reduction, assignment reduction and positive region reduction are different kinds of reductions.

4   The Reduction Based on μ-Relative Relations

Definition 9. Let $S = (U, C \cup \{d\}, \{V_a | a \in C \cup \{d\}\}, \{I_a | a \in C \cup \{d\}\})$ be a decision table, and $A \subseteq C$. The μ-relative relation $Dis_d^\mu(A)$ on U is defined by:
$$Dis_d^\mu(A) = \{(x, y) \in U \times U | \forall a \in A (I_a(x) \neq I_a(y)) \vee I_d(x) \neq I_d(y)\}.$$

Definition 10. Let $S = (U, C \cup \{d\}, \{V_a | a \in C \cup \{d\}\}, \{I_a | a \in C \cup \{d\}\})$ be a decision table, and $A \subseteq C$.

(1) A is called a μ-consistent set of S if $Dis_d^\mu(A) = Dis_d^\mu(C)$.
(2) A is called a μ-reduction of S if A is a μ-consistent set, and for any proper subset B of A, B is not a μ-consistent set.

For any $x, y \in U$, we define:

$$Im_d^\mu(x, y) = \begin{cases} \{a \in C; I_a(x) = I_a(y)\}, & \text{if} \quad I_d(x) = I_d(y), \\ \emptyset, & \text{otherwise.} \end{cases} \quad (6)$$

Theorem 5. Let $S = (U, C \cup \{d\}, \{V_a | a \in C \cup \{d\}\}, \{I_a | a \in C \cup \{d\}\})$ be a decision table, and $A \subseteq C$. A is a μ-consistent set of S if and only if: for any $x, y \in U$, $A \cap Im_d^\mu(x, y) \neq \emptyset$ if $Im_d^\mu(x, y) \neq \emptyset$.

Proof. Suppose that A is a μ-consistent set of S and $x, y \in U$ such that $Im_d^\mu(x, y) \neq \emptyset$. It follows that $Dis_d^\mu(A) = Dis_d^\mu(C)$. Additionally, $I_d(x) = I_d(y)$ and there exists $a \in C$ such that $I_a(x) = I_a(y)$. Thus $(x, y) \notin Dis_d^\mu(C)$. It follows that $(x, y) \notin Dis_d^\mu(A)$ and thus there exist $b \in A$ such that $I_b(x) = I_b(y)$. Consequently, $b \in Im_d^\mu(x, y)$ and hence $A \cap Im_d^\mu(x, y) \neq \emptyset$.

Conversely, suppose that $A \cap Im_d^\mu(x, y) \neq \emptyset$ if $Im_d^\mu(x, y) \neq \emptyset$. For any $x, y \in U$, if $(x, y) \notin Dis_d^\mu(C)$, then $I_d(x) = I_d(y)$ and there exists $a \in C$ such that $I_a(x) = I_a(y)$. It follows that $Im_d^\mu(x, y) \neq \emptyset$ and hence $A \cap Im_d^\mu(x, y) \neq \emptyset$. Thus there exists $b \in A$ such that $I_b(x) = I_b(y)$. Consequently, we have $(x, y) \notin Dis_d^\mu(A)$ and thus $Dis_d^\mu(A) \subseteq Dis_d^\mu(C)$. On the other hand, $Dis_d^\mu(C) \subseteq Dis_d^\mu(A)$ is trivial. It follows that $Dis_d^\mu(A) = Dis_d^\mu(C)$ and A is a μ-consistent set of S as required.

Let $F_{Im}^\mu = \wedge\{\vee Im_d^\mu(x, y); Im_d^\mu(x, y) \neq \emptyset\}$. F_{Im}^μ is called the μ-discernibility function of S.

Corollary 2. Let $S = (U, C \cup \{d\}, \{V_a | a \in C \cup \{d\}\}, \{I_a | a \in C \cup \{d\}\})$ be a decision table, and $A \subseteq C$. A is a μ-reduction of S if and only if $\wedge A$ is a prime implicant of F_{Im}^μ.

5   Concluding Remarks

This paper is devoted to the discussion of attribute reduction approaches of decision tables based on relative indiscernibility relation and relative discernibility relation. The notions of λ reduction and μ reduction are proposed. The discernibility matrices with respect to λ reduction and μ reduction are presented and the reduction approaches are provided. The relationships among λ reduction, μ reduction, positive region reduction and assignment reduction are analyzed. In further research, we will consider the relationships among λ reduction, μ reduction and other kinds of attribute reductions, such as maximum distribution reduction, distribution reduction and relationship preservation reduction.

Acknowledgments. The authors are highly grateful to the anonymous referees for their insightful comments and valuable suggestions which greatly improve the quality of this paper. This work has been partially supported by the National Natural Science Foundation of China (Grant Nos. 61473239, 61372187), and the open research fund of key laboratory of intelligent network information processing, Xihua University (szjj2014-052).

References

1. Pawlak, Z.: Rough sets. Int. J. Comput. Inf. Sci. **11**, 341–356 (1982)
2. Thangavela, K., Pethalakshmi, A.: Dimensionality reduction based on rough set theory: a review. Appl. Soft Comput. **9**, 1–12 (2009)
3. Krawczak, M., Szkatula, G.: An approach to dimensionality reduction in time series. Inf. Sci. **260**, 15–36 (2014)
4. Pawlak, Z.: Rough set approach to knowledge-based decision support. Eur. J. Oper. Res. **99**, 48–57 (1997)
5. Kryszkiewicz, M.: Comparative studies of alternative type of knowledge reduction in inconsistent systems. Int. J. Intell. Syst. **16**(1), 105–120 (2001)
6. Kryszkiewicz, M.: Certain, generalized decision, and membership distribution reducts versus functional dependencies in incomplete systems. In: Kryszkiewicz, M., Peters, J.F., Rybinski, H., Skowron, A. (eds.) RSEISP 2007. LNCS, vol. 4585, pp. 162–174. Springer, Heidelberg (2007). doi:10.1007/978-3-540-73451-2_18
7. Yao, Y.Y., Zhao, Y.: Attribute reduction in decision-theoretic rough set models. Inf. Sci. **178**(17), 3356–3372 (2008)
8. Zhang, W.X., Mi, J.S., Wu, W.Z.: Knowledge reduction in inconsistent information systems. Chin. J. Comput. **26**, 12–18 (2003)
9. Zhang, W.X., Mi, J.S., Wu, W.Z.: Approaches to knowledge reductions in inconsistent systems. Int. J. Intell. Syst. **18**, 989–1000 (2003)
10. Miao, D.Q., Zhao, Y., Yao, Y.Y., Li, H.X., Xu, F.F.: Relative reducts in consistent and inconsistent decision tables of the Pawlak rough set model. Inf. Sci. **179**, 4140–4150 (2009)
11. Meng, Z.Q., Shi, Z.Z.: Extended rough set-based attribute reduction in inconsistent incomplete decision systems. Inf. Sci. **204**, 44–66 (2012)
12. Skowron, A., Rauszer, C.: The discernibility matrices and functions in information systems. In: Slowinski, R. (ed.) Intelligent Decision Support. Handbook of Applications and Advances of the Rough Sets Theory. Kluwer, Dordrecht (1992)
13. Chen, D., Wang, C., Hu, Q.: A new approach to attribute reduction of consistent and inconsistent covering decision systems with covering rough sets. Inf. Sci. **177**(17), 3500–3518 (2007)
14. Qian, Y.H., Liang, J.Y., Li, D.Y., Wang, F., Ma, N.: Approximation reduction in inconsistent incomplete decision tables. Knowl.-Based Syst. **23**(5), 427–433 (2010)

15. Li, M., Shang, C.X., Feng, S.Z., Fan, J.P.: Quick attribute reduction in inconsistent decision tables. Inf. Sci. **254**, 155–180 (2014)
16. Meng, Z.Q., Shi, Z.Z.: A fast approach to attribute reduction in incomplete decision systems with tolerance relation-based rough sets. Inf. Sci. **179**, 2774–2793 (2009)
17. Shen, Q., Chouchoulas, A.: A modular approach to generating fuzzy rules with reduced attributes for the monitoring of complex systems. Eng. Appl. Artif. Intell. **13**(3), 263–278 (2000)
18. Wang, G.Y., Yu, H., Yang, D.: Decision table reduction based on conditional information entropy. Chin. J. Comput. **25**(7), 759–766 (2002)
19. Orłowska, E.: Introduction: what you always wanted to know about rough sets. In: Orłowska, E. (ed.) Incomplete Information: Rough Set Analysis, vol. 13, pp. 1–20. Physica Verlag, Heidelberg (1998)
20. Orłowska, E.: Logic of nondeterministic information. Stud. Log. **44**(1), 91–100 (1985)
21. Vakarelov, D.: A modal logic for similarity relations in Pawlak knowledge representation systems. Fundam. Inform. **15**(1), 61–79 (1991)
22. Zhao, Y., Yao, Y.Y., Luo, F.: Data analysis based on discernibility and indiscernibility. Inf. Sci. **177**(22), 4959–4976 (2007)
23. Qin, K., Jing, S.H.: The attribute reduction of decision systems based on indiscernibility and discernibility. J. Comput. Sci. (submitted)

Stable Rules Evaluation for a Rough-Set-Based Bipolar Model: A Preliminary Study for Credit Loan Evaluation

Kao-Yi Shen[1(✉)], Hiroshi Sakai[2], and Gwo-Hshiung Tzeng[3]

[1] Department of Banking and Finance, Chinese Culture University (SCE),
Taipei, Taiwan
atrategy@gmail.com
[2] Mathematical Sciences Section, Department of Basic Science,
Faculty of Engineering, Kyushu Institute of Technology, Kitakyushu, Japan
sakai@mns.kyutech.ac.jp
[3] Graduate Institute of Urban Planning, College of Public Affairs,
National Taipei University, New Taipei City, Taiwan
ghtzeng@mail.ntpu.edu.tw

Abstract. The modern business environment is full of uncertain and imprecise circumstances that require decision makers (DMs) to conduct informed and circumspect decisions. In this regard, rough set theory (RST) has been widely acknowledged as capable to resolve these complicated problems while relevant knowledge can be extracted—in the form of rules—for decision aids. By using those learned rules, an innovative bipolar decision model that comprises the positive (preferred) and negative (unwanted) rules, can be applied to rank alternatives based on their similarity to the positive and the dissimilarity to the negative ones. However, in some business cases (e.g., personal credit loan), applicants need to provide information (values) on all the attributes, requested by a bank. Sometimes, experienced evaluators (e.g., senior bank staff) might question the validity of some values (direct or indirect evidences) provided by an applicant. In such a case, evaluators may assign additional values to those attributes (regarded as non-deterministic ones) in a bipolar model, to examine the stability of a rule that is supported by questionable instances. How to select those rules with satisfactory stability would be an important issue to enhance the effectiveness of a bipolar decision model. As a result, the present study adopts the idea of stability factor, proposed by Sakai et al. [1], to enhance the effectiveness of a bipolar decision model, and a case of credit loan evaluation, with partially assumed values on several non-deterministic attributes, is illustrated with the discussions of potential application in practice.

Keywords: Rough set theory (RST) · Dominance-based rough set approach (DRSA) · Bipolar decision model · Stability factor · Non-deterministic information systems (NISs)

© Springer International Publishing AG 2017
L. Polkowski et al. (Eds.): IJCRS 2017, Part I, LNAI 10313, pp. 317–328, 2017.
DOI: 10.1007/978-3-319-60837-2_27

1 Introduction

Rough set theory (RST), proposed by Pawlak [2], has been a powerful foundation for modern computational technique on solving vagueness and impreciseness in many real world problems. Although the classical RST has strength in making classifications under impreciseness, certain problems require the RST to deal with decisions that have to consider the preferential characteristic of attributes. Therefore, the eminent dominance-based rough set approach (DRSA) [3–5] and the subsequent variable-consistency dominance-based rough set approach (VC-DRSA) [6, 7] were proposed to enhance the classical RST on decision-making. DRSA or VC-DRSA has been widely adopted for supporting various practical decisions. Examples are evaluating the financial performance (FP) of banks [8], marketing analysis [9], technical analysis for investment aids [10], and the FP improvement planning of insurance companies [11].

The aforementioned applications are mainly based on historical data, where the analyzed information values are generally regarded as deterministic ones. Nevertheless, once the collected data include unknown or unsure values, non-deterministic systems (*NIS*s) [12, 13] or incomplete information systems (*IIS*s) [14, 15] would be needed to resolve the issue of missing or uncertain values of attributes. Take the case of credit loan evaluation for example, most of the information provided by applicants, such as their salaries or bank savings, could be examined by financial institutions with deterministic results; nevertheless, the seniority (as an attribute), sometimes might require the supportive judgments by evaluators to add one or two possible values on this attribute, for some questionable applicants. If one or more extracted decisions rules include this attribute, how to judge the stability of those rules would be a problem. Therefore, the present study attempts to adopt the idea from Sakai *et al.* [1], to evaluate the stability of the selected rules in a bipolar decision model that involve un-deterministic information.

Recently, a hybrid bipolar decision approach, was proposed for ranking alternatives by using the positive and negative decision rules induced from DRSA or VC-DRSA, which evaluates alternatives based on their similarity to the positive rules and the dissimilarity to the negative ones for business analytics [16]. This approach has to set a threshold to select the positive and negative rules to form a bipolar model [17]. The key criterion for a positive/negative rule to be selected, in a bipolar decision model, is based on the support numbers of a rule. Once a rule was selected that include some instances with several questionable values assigned by evaluators, its stability should be examined to ensure that it meets the required stability by DMs.

A simplified case for the credit loan evaluation problem is illustrated with the combination of data—real raw data from applicants and several assumed uncertain attribute values—provided from a branch of Taiwanese bank.

2 Preliminary

This section briefly discusses the two major topics covered in this study: (1) *NIS*s and (2) DRSA and a stability factor for measuring the possible decision rules from a NIS^{DRSA}.

2.1 Non-deterministic Information Systems (*NISs*)

NISs have been proposed to deal with information incompleteness or uncertainty in deterministic information systems (*DISs*). A series of research have established a solid foundation on analyzing *NISs* in various aspects, such as the definability of sets in *NISs* [18, 19], the consistency of objects in *NISs* [20], and the stability factor analysis of decision rules in *NISs* [1]. In this regards, a framework of *Rough Non-deterministic Information System Analysis* (*RNIA*) was proposed [1, 18–22]. For *NIS*, it usually yields more than one *DISs*.

In some types of *DISs*, such as the one from DRSA, it usually comprises a four-tuple information system (*IS*): $DIS^{DRSA} = (U, A, V, f)$. In this type of DIS^{DRSA}, U is a finite set of instances (also termed as objects or observations). A is a finite set of attributes; V denotes a set of finite values of the attributes in A, where f is a total function (i.e., $f : U \times A \rightarrow V$) that maps the value of an instance x (for $x \in U$) on an attribute a_i ($a_i \in A$, $i = 1, \ldots, n$) to a specific attribute value in V.

On the other side, if one or more attributes in the aforementioned DIS^{DRSA} that conform another information function (in which, P denotes a power set for g :

$$U \times A^* \rightarrow P\left(\bigcup_{a^* \in A^*} V_{a^*}\right) \text{ while all } V_{a^*} \in V, \; A \cup A^* = A^{\odot} \text{ and } A \cap A^* = \varnothing), \text{ then}$$

DIS^{DRSA} could be extended into NIS^{DRSA} (for $NIS^{DRSA} = (U, A^{\odot}, V, g)$). Under this circumstance, $f(x, a^*) \subseteq g(x, a^*)$, then this DIS^{DRSA} could be regarded as a derived one from NIS^{DRSA}. Every set $g(x, a^*)$, according the descriptions from *RNIA* [1], is interpreted as that there is a corresponding value in V_{a^*} but the actual value is still unsure or uncertain. In here, the circumstance of a missing or unknown value is not included. Furthermore, only one attribute belongs to the set of decision attribute D in a decision-model-based DIS ($^D a \in D \subseteq A^{\odot}$); the others the condition attributes (i.e., $^C a \in C \subseteq A^{\odot}$). Also, $C \cap D = \varnothing$ and $C \cup D = A^{\odot}$.

Yielded from a typical *DIS*, a decision rule τ is in the form of "**IF** *conditions_satisfied* **THEN** *decision_classified*." Thus, a rule τ can be measured by $SuppR(\tau)$ and $AccuR(\tau)$, defined in Eqs. (1) and (2) respectively.

$$SuppR(\tau) = |consistent(\tau)| / |observations| \tag{1}$$

$$AccuR(\tau) = |consistent(\tau)| / |consistent(\tau^{conditions})| \tag{2}$$

In Eqs. (1) and (2), $|consistnet(\tau)|$ denotes the number of instances that conforms both the *conditions* (antecedents) and the *decision* (consequence) of a rule τ; $|consistnet(\tau^{conditions})|$ indicates the numbers of objects (instances) that at least conform the *conditions* of a rule τ.

In the presence of $g(x, {}^C a^*)$ and $g(x, {}^D a^*)$) while ${}^C a^* \in C$ and ${}^D a^* \in D$) in NIS^{DRSA}, the previous work [1] further defined a set $DD(\tau)$, which denotes a set of derived *DISs* (or termed as $DISs^{DRSA}$ in here) from a τ. And the set of derived $DISs^{DRSA}$ from an instance x is denoted as $DD(\tau^x)$. All the derived $DISs^{DRSA}$ of NIS^{DRSA} are defined as

$DD_{All}(\tau)$. In this study, we discuss a simplified case that most of the attributes $^Ca_i \in C$ (for $i = 1,\ldots,n$) are deterministic, except two condition attribute ($^Ca_k^*$ and $^Ca_l^*$).

2.2 Stability Factor for Measuring DRSA Decision Rules

In the classical DRSA, for any two objects (or called observations) x and y in U, a complete outranking relation regarding an attribute a_1 can be defined as $\succeq_{a_1}$ or $\preceq_{a_1}$. If $x\succeq_{a_1} y$ ($x, y \in U$) holds, it means that "x is at least as good as y regarding the attribute a_1." For any attribute that belongs to A, which categorizes the objects in U into a finite number of classes (e.g., m classes), denoted as $Cl = \{Cl_t : Cl_1, Cl_2,\ldots, Cl_m\}$. For each $x \in U$, object x belongs to only one $Cl_t(Cl_t \in Cl)$. Each Cl has a predefined preferential order; thus, a downward union $Cl_t^{\leq}$ and upward union $Cl_t^{\geq}$ of classes can be defined as Eqs. (3), (4):

$$Cl_t^{\leq} = \bigcup_{s \leq t} Cl_s \tag{3}$$

$$Cl_t^{\geq} = \bigcup_{s \geq t} Cl_s \tag{4}$$

To shorten the descriptions, merely the upward union is discussed; the downward union could be reasoned similarly or refer the previous works [3–5]. For $x, y \in U$, if x dominates y with respect to a partial condition attribute set P (i.e., $P \subseteq C$), it can be denoted as xD_Py to indicate x P-dominates y. Then, for a set of objects that dominate x with regard to P, it can be denoted as $D_P^+(x) = \{y \in U : yD_Px\}$, the P-dominating set. On the other side, a set of objects that are dominated by x with regard to P can be denoted as $D_P^-(x) = \{y \in U : xD_Py\}$ (i.e., the P-dominated set).

The P-lower and P-upper approximations of an upward union can be defined by $\underline{P}(Cl_t^{\geq}) = \{x \in U : D_P^+(x) \subseteq Cl_t^{\geq}\}$ and $\bar{P}(Cl_t^{\geq}) = \{x \in U : D_P^-(x) \cap Cl_t^{\geq} \neq \varnothing\}$. In the DRSA, $\underline{P}(Cl_t^{\geq})$ denotes all of the objects $x \in U$ that should be included in the upward union $Cl_t^{\geq}$ with certainty; the P-upper approximation $\bar{P}(Cl_t^{\geq})$ can be interpreted as all of the objects possibly belong to $Cl_t^{\geq}$ (i.e., uncertainty remains). The boundary region $Bn_P = \bar{P}(Cl_t^{\geq}) - \underline{P}(Cl_t^{\geq})$ can thus be defined. Several famous DRSA algorithms (e.g., DomLEM) can generate DRSA decision rules in five types: (1) certain $D_{\geq}$, (2) possible $D_{\geq}$, (3) certain $D_{\leq}$, (4) possible $D_{\leq}$, and (5) approximate $D_{\geq \leq}$ decision rules.

In this study, after discussions with two senior staffs who are in charge of the credit loan operations in the XY bank, we only presume the existence of two non-deterministic attributes: $^Ca_k^*$, $^Ca_l^*$; all the other attributes are deterministic ones. In the case like a credit loan evaluation problem, a IS collected and organized from applicants will be regarded as the main IS for generating DRSA decision rules at first; DMs or evaluators may assign/add possible values to an observation for those non-deterministic attributes that are questionable. In the next, if a rule τ involves more than one $^Ca^*$ in its conditional parts, then $\Phi_{ini}(\tau)$ is defined as the initial DIS^{DRSA} of τ that comprises of two parts: (1) all the conditional parts with deterministic values and (2) the conditional parts that involve non-deterministic attributes by using those values provided by applicant as the deterministic ones at this stage (extended from the definition of [1]).

Then, $\Phi_{ini}(\tau)$ can yield multiple $\Phi(\tau)$ s to become NIS^{DRSA} by accepting the assigned plausible values (by DMs or evaluators) for those covered observations of a rule τ. Each $\widetilde{\Phi^x}(\tau) \in DD(\tau)$, and $\widetilde{x}_1, \ldots, \widetilde{x}_j, \ldots, \widetilde{x}_n$ denote the n supporting DISs of a possible rule τ where uncertain values co-exist for an observation on a non-deterministic attribute. If τ can meet the following two requirements: (1) $SuppR\left(\widetilde{\tau^x}\right) \geq \alpha$ and (2) $AccuR\left(\widetilde{\tau^x}\right) \geq \beta$, then τ is defined as $(\alpha, \beta)^{stable}$ in $\widetilde{\Phi^x}(\tau)$. In the next, $DD_{All}(\tau)$ means a set of all derived DISs (or DISs^{DRSA} in here) where the rule τ occurs. Then, Eqs. (5), (6) show how to calculate a stability factor for τ.

$$S\left(\tau, (\alpha, \beta)^{stable}\right) = \left\{ \widetilde{\Phi^x}(\tau) \in DD_{All}(\tau) | \tau \text{ is } (\alpha, \beta)^{stable} \text{ in } \widetilde{\Phi^x}(\tau) \right\} \tag{5}$$

$$STF(\tau, \alpha, \beta) = \left| S\left(\tau, (\alpha, \beta)^{stable}\right) \right| \Big/ |DD_{All}(\tau)| \tag{6}$$

There is one more thing that might need attention in here. Since the rules from DRSA have to consider the preferential order of values for a non-deterministic attribute, this requirement has to be considered while calculating $SuppR(\cdot)$ and $AccuR(\cdot)$ to derive a valid stability factor.

3   Bipolar Decision Model Enhanced with Stable Possible Rules

Recently, a hybrid bipolar decision approach was proposed for solving practical problems on ranking or selection [16, 17, 23] in decision science; it can be regarded as a branch of multiple rules-based decision-making (MRDM), which leverages the rules-induction capability of DRSA. However, the critical difference of a bipolar decision, compared with the classical DRSA, begins with dividing the decision attribute D into merely three Cls: positive (POS), neutral (NEU), and negative (NEG). The three Cls have preferential order: $Cl_{POS} \succ Cl_{NEU} \succ Cl_{NEG}$. The essential goal is to explore those influential DRSA rules in two groups: the positive and the negative rules.

In the previous work [23], DMs would need to set a threshold (Ψ) to select the covered rules from the positive and negative groups, to form a bipolar decision model. The threshold is defined as the minimal or required percentage of instances that satisfy the dominance relation of DRSA from the two groups of rules.

$$|O^{POS}|/\varepsilon \geq \Psi \tag{7}$$

$$|O^{NEG}|/\eta \geq \Psi \tag{8}$$

In Eqs. (7), (8), ε and η are the total numbers of the instances that are classified as Cl_{POS} and Cl_{NEG} in a DRSA IS; $|\bullet|$ denotes cardinality. $|O^{POS}|$ and $|O^{NEG}|$ denote the minimal number of instances that should be covered in the positive and negative rules, respectively. DMs would need to rank the two groups of rules, from high to low supports. Suppose that there are n positive and m negative rules in those two groups, they can be ranked from high to low supports, denoted as τ_i^{POS} (for $i = 1,\ldots,i,\ldots n$) and τ_j^{NEG} (for $j = 1,\ldots,j,\ldots m$). And the corresponding support numbers for the two groups of rules are denoted as S_{i-th}^{POS} and S_{j-th}^{NEG} (S_{1-st}^{POS} or S_{1-st}^{NEG} denotes the rule with the highest supports in the positive or negative group). Then τ_{1-st}^{POS} to τ_{k-th}^{POS} rules would be included in the bipolar model if Eq. (9) can be satisfied. Similarly, τ_{1-st}^{NEG} to τ_{l-th}^{NEG} would be selected once Eq. (10) can be satisfied.

$$\sum_{i=1}^{k-th} S_{i-th}^{POS} \geq |O^{POS}| \tag{9}$$

$$\sum_{j=1}^{l-th} S_{j-th}^{NEG} \geq |O^{NEG}| \tag{10}$$

In the previous bipolar model, the support weights of the positive and negative rules for a bipolar model can be obtained by Eqs. (11), (12):

$$w_{i-th}^{POS} = S_{i-th}^{POS} / (|O^{POS}| + |O^{NEG}|) \tag{11}$$

$$w_{j-th}^{NEG} = S_{j-th}^{NEG} / (|O^{POS}| + |O^{NEG}|) \tag{12}$$

However, if any rule among τ_{1-st}^{POS} to τ_{k-th}^{POS} (or τ_{1-st}^{NEG} to τ_{l-th}^{NEG}) that involves $^C a_k^*$ or $^C a_l^*$ with questionable instances, the rule's stability factor should be examined to ensure that rule can be kept in this bipolar model. Take a positive rule for example; if the stability factor of τ_{k-th}^{POS} is lower than the predefined percentage, then $\tau_{(k+1)-th}^{POS}$ should be examined, to see if $\sum_{i=1}^{(k+1)-th} S_{i-th}^{POS} - S_k^{POS} \geq |O^{POS}|$. This idea can be illustrated in Fig. 1 by taking positive rules as an example.

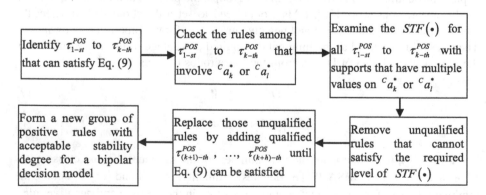

Fig. 1. Conceptual flow of selecting stable (*POS*) rules for a bipolar model

In this regard, $STF(\tau, \alpha, \beta)$ mentioned in Sect. 2 can be used to evaluate those positive and negative rules while a NIS^{DRSA} exists for some decision rules. A simplified case is illustrated in Sect. 4 with discussions.

4 A Brief Illustration Example of Personal Credit Loan Evaluation

To illustrate the proposed idea, a partial set of applicants' data (from a local branch of the *XY* bank in Keelung) that only comprises 40 instances were analyzed to demonstrate the enhanced bipolar model using the stability factor. The two presumed condition attributes are *Job* (occupation, discretized in four *Cls*) and *Seniority* (discretized in two *Cls*: ≥ 2 or < 2 years in current job).

Normally, an applicant has to fill-in all the required information for a bank to approve a credit loan application. Most of the provided information from an applicant can be checked and examined by a bank staff after receiving the application. However, some information is difficult to examine their credibility before making an approval. Take the attribute *Job* (occupation) for example, the *XY* bank divides it into four categories: (1) employees from ordinary companies that do not fit-in the other three categories, (2) an applicant whose salary account is in the *XY* bank, (3) employees from public-listed or top-1500 companies in Taiwan or medical doctors or civil engineering technicians or electronical engineers, and (4) employees from a national/local agency of the government or a public school or a government-owned business (i.e., $4 \succ 3 \succ 2 \succ 1$ from the bank's point of view).

Sometimes, it might not be easy to distinguish an applicant from the second and the fourth categories by the limited information (such as a name card) or indirect evidence provided by the applicant. The staff in charge of such an application might attach additional values for an applicant (instance) on this attribute by his/her own judgments. To illustrate this idea, an *IS* comprises 40 instances were analyzed using DRSA algorithm at first; there are 19 condition attributes (required information by the *XY* bank) and one decision attribute in three *Cls* (*POS*, *NEU*, *NEG*; *POS* indicates acceptance and *NEG* rejection, *NEU* denotes that the bank might consider to approve it with higher interest rate charges).

4.1 Initial Bipolar Model with Deterministic Values

The 40 instances were induced by DRSA algorithm at first before forming a bipolar decision model. There are 26 *POS*, 4 *NEU* and 10 *NEG* instances categorized in the decision attribute. By setting $\Psi = 80\%$, the positive and negative groups have to include at least 21 and 8 instances, respectively. To illustrate the proposed idea, we did not conduct *N*-fold cross validation. Instead, we repeated the rule-induction process for 10 times; the model with the highest re-classification rate 90% (36/40 instances were correctly classified) was adopted. To cover 21 *POS* and 8 *NEG* instances in the decision rules, 6 positive and 5 negative certain rules were selected, and the supporting instances for each rule are shown in Table 1.

Table 1. Selected positive and negative rules with their supporting instances

Rules	Selected decision rules	Supporting instances
PR_1	**IF** $CreditS \geq 1 \wedge CreditLoan \leq 1 \wedge LendR \leq 4$ **then** $D \succeq POS$	5, 9, 10, 11, 12, 16
PR_2	**IF** $Gender \geq 2 \wedge Job \leq 2 \wedge DAccount \leq 1$ **then** $D \succeq POS$	2, *4*, *10*, 14, 20, 22
PR_3	**IF** $Age \geq 2 \wedge CreditS \geq 3 \wedge CCuse \leq 2$ **then** $D \succeq POS$	6, 8, 17, 18, 20
PR_4	**IF** $Job \leq 3 \wedge CreditS \geq 2 \wedge LendR \leq 4$ **then** $D \succeq POS$	2, 3, *10*, 19, *26*
PR_5	**IF** $CreditS \geq 1 \wedge LendR \leq 2$ **then** $D \succeq POS$	3, 5, 21, 27
PR_6	**IF** $Salary \geq 5 \wedge CreditS \geq 2$ **then** $D \succeq POS$	3, 13, 15
NR_1	**IF** $CreditS \leq 1 \wedge DAccount \geq 2$ **then** $D \preceq NEG$	32, 34, 35
NR_2	**IF** $Age \leq 2 \wedge Job \geq 4 \wedge CCuse \geq 3$ **then** $D \preceq NEG$	38, 40
NR_3	**IF** $Age \leq 1 \wedge LendR \geq 7$ **then** $D \preceq NEG$	31
NR_4	**IF** $Job \geq 4 \wedge Position \leq 1$ **then** $D \preceq NEG$	39
NR_5	**IF** $Age \leq 4 \wedge Job \geq 3 \wedge RevolveCredit \geq 2 \wedge LendR \geq 7$ **then** $D \preceq NEG$	37

4.2   Evaluating Stability Factor of Decision Rules

In this case, only the attribute *Job* appeared in the initial bipolar model, and the second one (*Seniority*) was not included. The instances {#4, #10} in PR_2 and {#10, #26} in PR_4 were assumed to be questionable; thus, the two positive rules' certainty might also be questionable. Therefore, those two rules' decision attribute was assumed to be non-deterministic. The newly assumed *NIS*s, exclude the other irrelevant attributes for the two rules, are in Tables 2 and 3, respectively.

Table 2. Assumed *NIS* for the positive rule PR_2

Instances	[1]*Gender*	*Job*	[2]*DAccount*	*Decision* (*Cls*)
#4	{2}	{2, 4}	{1}	{*POS, NEU*}
#10	{2}	{2, 4}	{1}	{*POS, NEU, NEG*}

[1]In the attribute *Gender*, {2} denotes female.
[2]In the attribute *DAccount*, {1} denotes that the applicant has a deposit account in the *XY* bank.

From Table 2, $|DD_{All}(\text{PR\_2})| = 2^3 \times 3 = 24$ (#2, #14, #20, and #22 are all with deterministic values); by setting $\alpha = 0.20$ and $\beta = 0.80$, then $STF(\text{PR\_2}) = 37.50\%$. If DMs may accept lower α (e.g., 0.18) and the same value of β, the new $STF(\text{PR\_2})$ would increase to 87.5%. The 24 pairs (α, β) of the rule PR_2 are shown in Fig. 2.

In other words, based on the proposition from [1], the $(SuppR, AccuR)$ or (α, β) once located partially in the Max/Min (α, β) formed rectangular, it can be regarded as a possible rule, which needs to satisfy $STF(\alpha = 0.18, \beta = 0.8) = 87.5\%$ (STF < 1). This idea is illustrated in Fig. 3. Similarly, from Table 3, $|DD_{All}(\text{PR\_4})| = 2^4 = 16$. If DMs

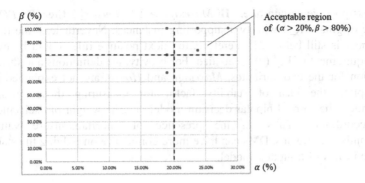

Fig. 2. Plotted 24 pairs of (α, β) of PR_2

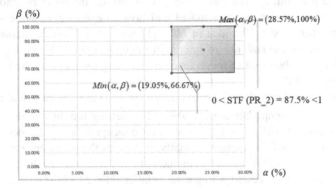

Fig. 3. Min/Max STF region of PR_2

set $\alpha = 0.18$ and $\beta = 0.80$, then $STF(\text{PR\_4}) = 43.75\%$. Once DMs hope to keep stable rules for $STF(\bullet) \geq 80\%$ while $\alpha = 0.18$ and $\beta = 0.80$, PR_4 would have to be removed from the bipoar model.

Table 3. Assumed *NIS* for the positive rule PR_4

Instances	*Job*	[1]*CreditS*	[2]*LendR*	*Decision* (*Cls*)
#10	{2, 4}	{2}	{3}	{*POS, NEU*}
#26	{2, 4}	{2}	{4}	{*POS, NEU*}

[1]In the attribute *CreditS*, {2} denotes a joint credit information score between 600 to 700.
[2]In the attribute *LendR* denotes the amount of loan is a multiple of his/her monthly salary; {3} denotes 7 to 9 times, and {4} denotes 10 to 11 times. This attribute is discretized in 7 *Cls*.

The next positive certain rule: "**IF** *Marriage* $\geq 2 \wedge$ *House* ≤ 2 **then** $D \succeq POS$," will replace the original PR_4 with two supporting instances. Nevertheless, the total covered instances is still below 21; therefore, the next positive rule should be evaluated until the requirement of Eq. (9) is satisfied. For brevity, the definitions and the ways of discretization for the two attributes, *Marriage* and *House*, are not explained in here. After adopting the idea of stability factor for measuring those questionable instances/rules, the formed bipolar decision model and the weight of each rule would change accordingly. Thus, in the presence of uncertain/unsure values for non-deterministic attributes, DMs can have more confidence on judging the stability of the involved rules of a bipolar model.

5   Concluding Remarks

This study is a preliminary work that attempts to discuss the issue of stable/unstable decision rules in a bipolar decision model and how to enhance it, while some questionable observations exist. The idea of *NIS*s [1] has formed a solid theoretical foundation on measuring the stability of uncertain decision rules, which may serve as a bridge on enhancing the result of rough machine learning by adopting the judgments of seasoned experts (DMs).

Three issues may be further discussed in the future. First, the practical meaning of $(\alpha, \beta)^{stable}$ should be comprehended by DMs while setting the thresholds for α and β. How to communicate with DMs on this abstract concept in a bipolar decision model might not be an easy task in practice. Actually, α denotes the occurrence ratio of a rule. Which implies that, if a DM intends to include at least five rules in the positive group (21 observations), the suggested α might be smaller than 23.8% (i.e., 5/21 = 23.8%). Instead, β denotes the consistency of a rule. Although higher α and β both imply that a rule should be more reliable, the actual meaning of reliability delivered by the two thresholds are different.

Second, to begin such a DRSA-based bipolar model by using the information provided by applicants might not be the ideal approach. If a bank tends to be more conservative, it may use the inferior values on those non-deterministic attributes to form the initial bipolar model; it might yield different decision rules. The pros and cons of the two approaches are worthwhile to discuss with practitioners after experimenting several sets of data.

Third, while using this bipolar model on evaluating new alternatives, the degree of fulfillment on each requirement of a new applicant (in those positive/negative rules) could be measured by the fuzzy set technique. As Dubois and Prade [24] stated, fuzzy set and RST have their strength in dealing with *vagueness* and *coarseness*, respectively. The credibility or belongingness of the values in those questionable attributes (from an applicant), could also be handled by measuring their fuzzy degrees; then it would be a different fuzzy-rough approach, which will require the fuzzy judgments of senior staffs.

Finally, this rough-set-based bipolar decision model could accumulate the experience on how to judge those questionable instances (observations) by setting a controlling index: $STF(\bullet)$. Therefore, this enhanced bipolar decision model should be more capable to measure the degree of risky applicants without losing business opportunity; banks could define different charging policies for those somewhat questionable applicants referring the evaluation result by the proposed model. During the discussions with the practitioners, they often mentioned that banks incline to be conservative on credit loan evaluation. However, banks also hope to earn more clients; a decision- support model that could control the acceptable risk level of applicants by setting different charging policies, would be valuable in practice. It is also the hope of this study to work on this direction.

Acknowledgment. We are grateful for the funding support of the Ministry of Science and Technology of Taiwan (R.O.C.) under the grant number MOST-105-2410-H-034-019-MY2. Also, the provided data and opinions from the *XY* bank are appreciated.

References

1. Sakai, H., Okuma, H., Nakata, M., Ślęzak, D.: Stable rule extraction and decision making in rough non-deterministic information analysis. Int. J. Hybrid Intell. Syst. **8**(1), 41–57 (2011)
2. Pawlak, Z.: Rough set theory and its applications to data analysis. Cybern. Syst. **29**(7), 661–688 (1998)
3. Greco, S., Matarazzo, B., Słowiński, R.: Rough sets theory for multicriteria decision analysis. Eur. J. Oper. Res. **129**(1), 1–47 (2001)
4. Greco, S., Matarazzo, B., Słowiński, R.: Rough approximation by dominance relations. Int. J. Hybrid Intell. Syst. **17**(2), 153–171 (2002)
5. Greco, S., Matarazzo, B., Słowiński, R.: Rough sets methodology for sorting problems in presence of multiple attributes and criteria. Eur. J. Oper. Res. **138**(2), 247–259 (2002)
6. Błaszczyński, J., Greco, S., Słowiński, R.: Multi-criteria classification–a new scheme for application of dominance-based decision rules. Eur. J. Oper. Res. **181**(3), 1030–1044 (2007)
7. Inuiguchi, M., Yoshioka, Y., Kusunoki, Y.: Variable-precision dominance-based rough set approach and attribute reduction. Int. J. Approx. Reason. **50**(8), 1199–1214 (2009)
8. Shen, K.Y., Tzeng, G.H.: DRSA-based neuro-fuzzy inference systems for the financial performance prediction of commercial banks. Int. J. Fuzzy Syst. **16**(2), 173–183 (2014)
9. Liou, J.J., Tzeng, G.H.: A dominance-based rough set approach to customer behavior in the airline market. Inf. Sci. **180**(11), 2230–2238 (2010)
10. Shen, K.Y., Tzeng, G.H.: Fuzzy inference-enhanced VC-DRSA model for technical analysis: Investment decision aid. Int. J. Fuzzy Syst. **17**(3), 375–389 (2015)
11. Shen, K.Y., Hu, S.K., Tzeng, G.H.: Financial modeling and improvement planning for the life insurance industry by using a rough knowledge based hybrid MCDM model. Inf. Sci. **375**, 296–313 (2017)
12. Sakai, H., Ishibashi, R., Koba, K., Nakata, M.: Rules and apriori algorithm in non-deterministic information systems. In: Peters, J.F., Skowron, A., Rybiński, H. (eds.) Transactions on Rough Sets IX. LNCS, vol. 5390, pp. 328–350. Springer, Heidelberg (2008). doi:10.1007/978-3-540-89876-4_18
13. Ślęzak, D., Sakai, H.: Automatic extraction of decision rules from non-deterministic data systems: theoretical foundations and sql-based implementation. In: Ślęzak, D., Kim, T.H., Zhang, Y., Ma, J., Chung, K.I. (eds.) DTA 2009. CCIS, vol. 64, pp. 151–162. Springer, Heidelberg (2009). doi:10.1007/978-3-642-10583-8_18
14. Kryszkiewicz, M.: Rough set approach to incomplete information systems. Inf. Sci. **112**(1–4), 39–49 (1998)

15. Kryszkiewicz, M.: Rules in incomplete information systems. Inf. Sci. **113**(3–4), 271–292 (1999)
16. Shen, K.Y., Tzeng, G.H.: Contextual improvement planning by fuzzy-rough machine learning: A novel bipolar approach for business analytics. Int. J. Fuzzy Syst. **18**(6), 940–955 (2016)
17. Shen, K.Y., Tzeng, G.H.: A novel bipolar MCDM model using rough sets and three-way decisions for decision aids. In: 2016 Joint 8th International Conference on Soft Computing and Intelligent Systems (SCIS) and 17th International Symposium on Advanced Intelligent Systems, pp. 53–58. IEEE, August 2016
18. Nakata, M., Sakai, H.: Lower and upper approximations in data tables containing possibilistic information. In: Peters, J.F., Skowron, A., Marek, V.W., Orłowska, E., Słowiński, R., Ziarko, W. (eds.) Transactions on Rough Sets VII: Commemorating the Life and Work of Zdzisław PawlakPart II. LNCS, vol. 4400, pp. 170–189. Springer, Heidelberg (2007). doi:10.1007/978-3-540-71663-1_11
19. Nakata, M., Sakai, H.: Applying rough sets to information tables containing possibilistic values. In: Gavrilova, M.L., Kenneth Tan, C.J., Wang, Y., Yao, Y., Wang, G. (eds.) Transactions on Computational Science II. LNCS, vol. 5150, pp. 180–204. Springer, Heidelberg (2008). doi:10.1007/978-3-540-87563-5_11
20. Sakai, H., Okuma, A.: Basic algorithms and tools for rough non-deterministic information analysis. In: Peters, J.F., Skowron, A., Grzymała-Busse, J.W., Kostek, B., Świniarski, R.W., Szczuka, M.S. (eds.) Transactions on Rough Sets I. LNCS, vol. 3100, pp. 209–231. Springer, Heidelberg (2004). doi:10.1007/978-3-540-27794-1_10
21. Sakai, H., Wu, M., Nakata, M.: Apriori-based rule generation in incomplete information databases and non-deterministic information systems. Fundam. Inform. **130**(3), 343–376 (2014)
22. Sakai, H.: Software tools for RNIA (Rough Non-Deterministic Information Analysis) (2016). http://www.mns.kyutech.ac.jp/~sakai/RNIA/
23. Shen, K.Y.: Compromise between short-and long-term financial sustainability a hybrid model for supporting R&D decisions. Sustainability **9**(3), 375 (pp. 1–17) (2017). doi:10.3390/su9030375
24. Dubois, D., Prade, H.: Rough fuzzy sets and fuzzy rough sets. Int. J. Gen. Syst. **17**(2–3), 191–209 (1990)

On Combining Discretisation Parameters and Attribute Ranking for Selection of Decision Rules

Urszula Stańczyk[1] and Beata Zielosko[2(✉)]

[1] Institute of Informatics, Silesian University of Technology,
Akademicka 16, 44-100 Gliwice, Poland
urszula.stanczyk@polsl.pl
[2] Institute of Computer Science, University of Silesia in Katowice,
Będzińska 39, 41-200 Sosnowiec, Poland
beata.zielosko@us.edu.pl

Abstract. The paper describes research on filtering decision rules with continuous and discretised condition attributes while combining characteristics of these attributes returned from supervised discretisation with their ranking. Numbers of intervals required for partitioning of attributes values imposed their grouping into corresponding categories, and for each group separately ranking procedures with *Relief* algorithm were executed. Information about numbers of bins combined with ranking positions were next exploited for selection of rules induced within rough set approaches. Filtering rules was performed directly by their conditions, or by calculating defined measures based on attribute weights, returning shortened decision algorithms with at least the same or improved classification accuracy.

Keywords: Rule filtering · Decision rules · Continuous attributes · Supervised discretisation · Attribute ranking · CRSA · DRSA

1 Introduction

Pruning rule sets is one of popular post-processing methodologies with the aim of such removal of elements from considered decision algorithms that results in at least the same or possibly increased recognition, but occurring for fewer constituent rules [19,29]. The paper presents research on rule filtering while exploiting two approaches, firstly with selection directed by condition attributes included in rules premises [25], and secondly by evaluation of defined rule quality measures based on importance of variables [28], learned from supervised discretisation and constructed attribute rankings.

Discretisation allows for transforming input continuous space into discrete by grouping values of attributes into ranges called bins. The purposes of such transformation include more general descriptions of recognised concepts, enabling

© Springer International Publishing AG 2017
L. Polkowski et al. (Eds.): IJCRS 2017, Part I, LNAI 10313, pp. 329–349, 2017.
DOI: 10.1007/978-3-319-60837-2_28

techniques working only for nominal variables [10], or improved prediction. Unsupervised discretisation ignores class information, while supervised procedures estimate how loss of knowledge caused by discretisation hurts the ability of recognising classes [18]. Fayyad and Irani's method [11] follows Minimal Description Length (MDL) principle to arrive at optimal numbers of intervals for all features while observing changes of class entropy made by discretisation.

The numbers of bins can be considered as characterisation of attributes with respect to their importance within a classification task, based on discretisation criteria. Higher numbers of bins indicate that for some features more attention is required to study their values in the context of their class labels. On the other hand, for some variables single bins can be found suggesting that these attributes are irrelevant for recognition of classes. Thus established numbers of bins impose grouping of features into corresponding categories. In the research presented this information was combined with attribute ranking, which also can be used to estimate relevance of variables. To emphasize the importance of attribute characterisation by discretisation, for each category of inputs ranking with *Relief* algorithm [16] was obtained separately. These local rankings were merged into one, resulting in the global ranking of features, exploited in selection of rules.

Decision rules were obtained within Dominance-Based Rough Set Approach (DRSA) [13,24] for continuous attributes, and with Classical Rough Set Approach (CRSA) [21,22] for discretised, in the latter case with reduction of features to these with at least two bins found in discretisation. For both rough set approaches exhaustive algorithms [4,12] were induced, and for resulting rule sets filtering of their elements was executed.

The presented study was devoted to two cases of binary authorship attribution [15,17], for a pair of male and a pair of female writers, with balanced classes and stylistic characteristic features. Evaluation of results was obtained by test sets, which were discretised independently on training sets.

Performed experiments show that selection of decision rules driven by condition attributes and calculated measures, based on characterisation by bin numbers and feature ranking, led to construction of optimised rule classifiers, with reduced numbers of constituent rules, and in several cases with increased prediction, in continuous and discrete domain as well.

The text of the paper is organised as follows. Section 2 provides the general research background, and Sect. 3 describes the framework of performed experiments. Section 4 explains executed tests and comments their results, while Sect. 5 gives conclusions and comments on future research.

2   Background Information

The research described in the paper addressed several issues: supervised discretisation and characterisation of continuous characteristic features resulting from it, ranking of attributes, selection of rules from rule sets inferred within rough set approaches, and stylometry as application domain, presented with more details in the following sections.

2.1 Supervised Discretisation

Concepts to be recognised can be described by numeric or nominal attributes, yet not all techniques are capable of processing continuous values of variables. In such situations, either some modifications to methodologies are introduced to adapt them for this kind of data [9,24], or discretisation needs to be performed.

The primary goal of discretisation is partitioning the continuous input space into some number of sub-ranges, corresponding to categories of values for features, established with disregarding class labels in unsupervised approaches, or with taking into account class information in supervised methods [10]. In static algorithms the numbers of intervals are established for all considered attributes independently, while in dynamic discretisation the search is executed simultaneously for all features [18].

Fayyad and Irani's method [11] starts with a single bin assigned for all values of attributes, and in recursive procedures the candidates for cut-points (that is intervals boundaries) for these bins are evaluated by observing class entropy. The number of resulting bins is controlled by exploiting Minimum Description Length principle as a stopping criterion for the search. With this processing some areas of the input continuous space can be partitioned into higher numbers of smaller bins, while for other areas partitioning is rather sparse and bins large.

Numbers of bins found for features reflect interdependencies between their values and class labels for samples. Single bins indicate that no distinction of attribute values is required for undamaged class recognition, thus such features can be treated as irrelevant. On the other hand, fine partitioning into higher numbers of bins means that with lower numbers of ranges class entropy was too degraded and suggests higher importance of some variables, or more complex relationships between these attributes and target concepts. Such reasoning leads to grouping of features into categories that correspond to numbers of bins established for them, and assigning proportional significance to these categories.

2.2 Ranking of Attributes

Rankings belong to approaches serving as estimators of attribute relevance [16], used in feature selection domain to find groups of variables best suited for a studied task. Ranking functions employ statistical measures and calculations referring to information theory, machine learning techniques, or some systematic specialised procedures such as sequential search. The available features are analysed and then ordered in descending order basing on given scores, with the most important variables at the top of the ranking, and the least relevant as the lowest ranking at its bottom.

Relief is one of instance-based ranking algorithms [26], which can be applied for nominal as well as continuous input data. In the original version it worked only for binary classification, but was extended to multiple classes. The pseudocode is listed in Algorithm 1. Within the algorithm all variables are assigned some score reflecting their ability of discerning considered decision classes.

Algorithm 1. Pseudo-code for *Relief*

Input: set of learning instances X, set A of all N attributes, set of classes Cl,
             probabilities of classes $P(Cl)$,
             number of iterations m,
             number k of considered nearest instances from each class;
Output: vector of weights w for all attributes;
begin
for i=1 **to** N **do** $w(i) = 0$ **endfor**
for i=1 **to** m **do**
             choose randomly an instance $x \in X$
             find k nearest hits H_j
             for each class $Cl \neq class(x)$ **do** find k nearest misses $M_j(Cl)$ **endfor**
             for $l = 1$ **to** N **do**

$$w(l) = w(l) - \sum_{j=1}^{k} \frac{diff(l,x,H_j)}{m \times k} + \sum_{Cl \neq class(x)} \frac{\frac{P(Cl)}{1-P(class(x))} \sum_{j=1}^{k} diff(l,x,M_j(Cl))}{m \times k}$$

             endfor
endfor
end {algorithm}

The set of examples is iteratively sampled and for each instance so-called *near-hit H* is found, which is another sample that is its closest neighbour belonging to the same class, and so-called *near-miss M*, the closest neighbour in the other class (or classes if they are multiple). For all tested pairs x_1 and x_2 of instances the distances with respect to attribute a are calculated by the function $diff(a, x_1, x_2)$. For nominal attributes it returns 1 for distinct values and 0 when they are the same, while for numerical attributes normalised actual difference is returned. The results are averaged over contributions from m iterations, with weighting misses by the prior probability of each class.

2.3   Selection of Rules

Rule selection can be performed as pre-processing, when modifications of input data lead to construction of specific rules. If during induction stage some rules are chosen while others immediately rejected, then selection is performed within processing. Filtering in post-processing [19] means discarding rules chosen from the already available set. The last approach can require more resources than others, more processing time, yet it provides possibly the widest context for studying and estimating rule quality, which is the main reason for its popularity.

Analysis of inferred rule sets can be based on inherent rule parameters, such as length, support, strength, included conditions, or some other characteristics. Shorter rules, with fewer conditions in their premise parts, usually possess better generalisation and description properties. Long rules with many conditions often fit to learning samples so closely that they cannot find matching samples in test sets, causing overfitting. Since a rule support specifies a number of training samples for which the rule holds true, rules with high supports describe patterns present in many learning examples, which causes higher probability of finding a match also for unknown samples. While exploiting domain knowledge some preference can be given to selected attributes over others, indicating significance of rules referring to them, or an obtained attribute ranking points out rules with the most relevant features [26].

Yet another way of rule pruning lies in defining and evaluating rule quality measures, which can be divided into objective and subjective categories [29]. Objective measures reflect quality with respect to a fixed dataset, such as a training or a test set, while subjective measures are evaluated accordingly to specific preferences of a user. When estimation of quality is applied to classification rules, the measures become indicators of rule interestingness or attractiveness [27].

2.4 Rough Set Approaches

Rough set theory, invented by Pawlak [21], is used in data mining approaches in cases when knowledge about the universe of discourse and its objects is incomplete and uncertain [7]. In rough set perspective the universe is partitioned into granules of equivalence classes of objects that cannot be discerned basing on values of their attributes. Thus indiscernibility relation plays fundamental part in Classical Rough Set Approach (CRSA), which enables only nominal classification and works only for nominal attributes [20].

Dominance-Based Rough Set Approach (DRSA) is a modification of the classical notion, substituting indiscernibility with dominance relation [13], for tasks of multi-criteria decision making [12]. With this approach granules correspond to dominance cones, constructed as dominating and dominated sets of objects, used to find approximations of upward and downward unions of decision classes. DRSA requires definitions of preference orders for all value sets. Allowing for ordinal properties in sets makes possible both nominal and ordinal classification, and application to continuous valued attributes.

When the knowledge about the types of relationships between condition and decision attributes is incomplete or unavailable, and simple observation of attributes value sets is insufficient for unambiguous definition of preference orders, these preferences can either be discovered [5], established by some search procedures, or arbitrarily assigned. As the former implies additional processing with multiplied numbers of attributes, in the research presented in this paper the latter approach was employed.

2.5 Stylometric Analysis of Texts

Authorship attribution is a task from the domain of stylometric analysis of texts [8], with the fundamental notion of authorial invariants, such groups of characteristic features that allow for unique description and recognition of writing styles [1]. In textual analysis linguistic characteristics and individual preferences of authors are studied [6], leading to quantitative definitions of styles by markers, typically of either lexical or syntactic type [23].

Since stylistic features are characteristic for writers, there are no universal sets and the task of establishing importance of available variables is transferred to the stage of data mining, in which there are employed either some statistical approaches, or machine learning techniques [15,17]. With this attitude recognition of authorship is treated as a classification task.

3   Research Framework

The first stage of presented research was dedicated to preparation of input datasets, for which in the following stages there were executed discretisation and ranking of features. For continuous and discretised sets exhaustive algorithms were inferred with rough set approaches [4,12], and the generated rule sets were then pruned in two ways, by selecting rules with highest ranking attributes, or by evaluation of measures based on weights assigned to attribute ranking positions, which is described in the following sections.

3.1   Input Datasets

Writing styles for male and female writers show different characteristics, thus for experiments two pairs of authors were selected, J. Austen and E. Wharton, and T. Hardy and H. James, famous for their long novels. Their literary works were divided into smaller text samples, for which 17 lexical and 8 syntactic markers were calculated, specifying frequencies of usage for selected function words and punctuation marks, giving the set of 25 features with continuous values.

With construction of training sets as described, evaluation of a classification system by cross-validation would return falsely high results [2]. Therefore, instead test sets were used, based on separate works of compared writers thus assuring independence of samples. For female writers respectively in the training and test sets there were 200 and 90 samples, and for male writers 180 and 60.

3.2   Discretisation Parameters

For all input datasets supervised discretisation by Fayyad and Irani's method returned established numbers of bins for all features, grouping them into three categories, as listed in Table 1 for learning samples. Test samples were discretised separately to maintain their independence [3] and ensure unbiased processing.

For both female and male writer datasets there were found some variables with single bins, which after transformation into discrete domain were rejected as brining zero information. These features in continuous domain were considered as the least important and had lowest weights but were not excluded from considerations. On the other hand, variables with 3 bins were treated as the most important and were assigned the highest positions and weights in the obtained global ranking, as explained in the next section.

Table 1. Categories of condition attributes established by discretisation

Number of intervals	Condition attributes	
	Female writer dataset	Male writer dataset
1	and in with of what from if . !	on of this . , : (
2	but not at this as that by for to , ? (–	but not in with as to if ? ! ; –
3	on ; :	and at that what from by for

3.3 Ranking with *Relief*

To all categories of attributes established by supervised discretisation, yet still working in continuous domain, a ranking algorithm was next applied. As a ranking function based on the same concepts as discretisation (that is referring to entropy) would result in inability to order single bin variables, instead *Relief* algorithm was employed separately for each category. To incorporate characterisation of attributes discovered by supervised discretisation into the obtained attribute ranking, the results from separate categories of attributes were merged to form the global ranking, as shown in Table 2.

To all ranking positions two sets of weights were assigned, spanned over the range of $(0,1]$. For $WR1$ the equation is as follows, with N being the number of considered attributes, and i an attribute ranking position.

$$\forall_{i \in \{1,\ldots,N\}} WR1_i = \frac{1}{i} \qquad (1)$$

The highest ranking attribute had the weight of 1, the second in ranking $1/2$, and so on, to the lowest ranking variable with the weight $1/N$, thus distances between subsequent weights were gradually decreasing.

For $WR2$ set weights were calculated as

$$\forall_{i \in \{1,\ldots,N\}} WR2_i = \frac{N - i + 1}{N}, \qquad (2)$$

thus the assigned weights again were decreasing while following down a ranking, but they were also equidistant, with the range of values divided into N equal parts. The highest and lowest ranking features for both weight sets had the same values of weights assigned, but for all others there were differences. Since for discrete domain the sets of considered features were reduced by rejecting attributes with single bins, thus their weights also differed from those in continuous domain.

3.4 Defined Rule Quality Measures

The first attribute ranking and discretisation-based quality measure $QMWR$ was calculated for r rule as a product of weights assigned to attributes included in the premise part of the rule,

Table 2. *Relief* ranking of condition attributes in continuous domain. Global ranking is composed of local rankings within categories of variables established by discretisation. Columns denote: (a) general position in the attribute ranking, (b) weight $WR1$ for continuous domain, (c) weight $WR2$ for continuous domain, (d) weight $WR1$ for discrete domain, (e) weight $WR2$ for discrete domain, (f) number of bins found within supervised discretisation, (g) local position in the attribute ranking, (h) attribute.

(a)	(b)	(c)	Female writer dataset					Male writer dataset				
			(d)	(e)	(f)	(g)	(h)	(d)	(e)	(f)	(g)	(h)
1	1	1	1	1	3	1	;	1	1	3	1	and
2	1/2	24/25	1/2	15/16		2	:	1/2	17/18		2	for
3	1/3	23/25	1/3	14/16		3	on	1/3	16/18		3	that
4	1/4	22/25	1/4	13/16	2	1	not	1/4	15/18		4	at
5	1/5	21/25	1/5	12/16		2	,	1/5	14/18		5	by
6	1/6	20/25	1/6	11/16		3	–	1/6	13/18		6	what
7	1/7	19/25	1/7	10/16		4	(	1/7	12/18		7	from
8	1/8	18/25	1/8	9/16		5	?	1/8	11/18	2	1	but
9	1/9	17/25	1/9	8/16		6	that	1/9	10/18		2	;
10	1/10	16/25	1/10	7/16		7	as	1/10	9/18		3	?
11	1/11	15/25	1/11	6/16		8	but	1/11	8/18		4	–
12	1/12	14/25	1/12	5/16		9	by	1/12	7/18		5	if
13	1/13	13/25	1/13	4/16		10	for	1/13	6/18		6	not
14	1/14	12/25	1/14	3/16		11	this	1/14	5/18		7	with
15	1/15	11/25	1/15	2/16		12	to	1/15	4/18		8	to
16	1/16	10/25	1/16	1/16		13	at	1/16	3/18		9	as
17	1/17	9/25			1	1	.	1/17	2/18		10	!
18	1/18	8/25				2	in	1/18	1/18		11	in
19	1/19	7/25				3	what			1	1	(
20	1/20	6/25				4	if				2	.
21	1/21	5/26				5	of				3	this
22	1/22	4/25				6	with				4	on
23	1/23	3/25				7	and				5	of
24	1/24	2/25				8	from				6	:
25	1/25	1/25				9	!				7	,

$$QMWR(r) = \prod_{i=1}^{NrCond} Weight(a_i) \tag{3}$$

$$QMWRS(r) = QMWR(r) \cdot Support(r).$$

The weights corresponded to positions in the global feature ranking previously constructed, either from the set $WR1$ or $WR2$, as defined for both continuous and discrete domains in Sect. 3.3. Their usage led respectively to obtaining $QMWR1$

and *QMWR2* measures. With such equation for the measure and most (apart from the highest) weights being fractions, the longer rule, the lower value of the measure became, which reflected typical behaviour of generalisation properties, which are decreasing with increase of rule lengths. Multiplication by rule supports results in *QMWR1S* and *QMWR2S* measures.

The second measure *QMWR1B* explicitly takes into account numbers of bins established by supervised discretisation for all variables,

$$QMWR1B(r) = \prod_{i=1}^{NrCond} NrBin(a_i) \cdot WR1(a_i). \tag{4}$$

The value of this measure also decreased for longer rules, but for short ones including higher ranking features it can achieve values above 1 even without multiplication by support of rules. This multiplication by rule supports results in *QMWR1BS* measure.

3.5 DRSA Rules

Observation of dominance cones offered by DRSA enables operation on features with continuous values, only definitions of preference orders, either assigned arbitrarily or discovered, are required for all attributes. In the research for all sets preference orders were defined arbitrarily basing on performance of minimal cover decision algorithms, induced with DOMLEM implemented in 4eMka software [12]. For female writers for attributes gain type was selected (the higher value the higher class), and for male writers cost type was chosen (the lower value the higher class). Minimal cover decision algorithm for male dataset gave recognition around 50%, and for female writers it was around 75%. Both these algorithms provided rather limited space for research on rule pruning.

On the other hand, exhaustive algorithms, comprised of all rules on examples inferred, for female and male datasets returned very high numbers of rules, 62,383 and 46,191 decision rules respectively. These two algorithms, generated by ALLRULES algorithm implemented in 4eMka, and referred to in the paper also as full algorithms, were denoted as *FC-FAlg* and *MC-FAlg*.

4eMka returns classification results listing three categories of decisions: correct—when all matching rules classify to correct classes, incorrect—when all matching rules classify to incorrect classes, ambiguous—when there are no rules matching, or there are conflicting classifications. In the research ambiguous decisions were treated as incorrect, thus any results list only correct decisions, which accounts for lower classification results for continuous than for discrete datasets, described below, for which conflicts were resolved by simple voting [4]. With all conflicts and cases of no rules matching treated as incorrect classification, all considered sets and subsets of rules could be treated as decision algorithms.

For full algorithms, including all rules on examples, the conflicting rules caused ambiguous decisions, and hard constraints were imposed on support required of rules to arrive at the best performing algorithms, in female case correct recognition of 86.67% of test samples by 17 rules with supports equal or higher than 66, denoted as *FC-BAlg17*, and in male case 76.67% of correct decisions by 80 rules with supports at least 41, denoted as *MC-BAlg80*. These two algorithms were used as points of reference for all tests executed in continuous domain.

3.6   CRSA Rules

For reduced numbers of features in discrete domain rules were induced by RSES System [4], firstly by LEM2 algorithm, but the classification accuracy for female writers was barely above 20%, and for male writers it was even lower. On the other hand, exhaustive algorithms induced for both datasets contained 1,210 rules for female writers and 3,267 for male, denoted as *FD-FAlg* and *MD-FAlg*, with recognition without any hard constraints, but with simple voting in case of conflicts, at the level of 92.22% and 80.00% respectively. Simple voting means that decision is chosen by counting votes casted in favor of each possibility (one matching rule—one vote). By imposing constraints on support the best performing algorithms were found with 58 rules of support equal at least 41 that recognised 98.89% of samples in the female test set, denoted as *FD-BAlg58*, and with 2,181 rules with supports equal or higher than 2, correctly classifying 86.67% for male dataset, denoted as *MD-BAlg2181*.

Comparison of performance of these reference algorithms in continuous and discrete domains brings conclusions that in both cases male writers proved to be more difficult in classification, and respective algorithms were significantly longer than for female writers, providing more space for improvement, and opening for execution of rule filtering.

4   Performed Experiments

In the first stage of research on rule filtering, rules were selected by condition attributes included with following previously constructed rankings, while in the second stage for all rules defined quality measures were calculated and their ordered values led to weighting of rules.

4.1   Selection of Rules by Their Condition Attributes

When the process of rule filtering is driven by an attribute ranking, in the first step some subset of features is selected from the ranking, starting with the highest positions, which customarily are given to the most important variables. Next from the set of available rules such elements are chosen that contain conditions only on attributes present in the subset selected from the ranking. If a rule includes even one condition for a variable that is absent in the considered subsets, the rule is rejected. The results of this processing for continuous case are given in Table 3, and for discrete in Table 4.

The procedure started with a single highest ranking variable, to which in the following steps gradually one by one other, lower and lower ranking, attributes

Table 3. Characteristics of decision algorithms with pruning of rules by condition attributes in continuous domain: N indicates the number of considered attributes, (a) number of bins established in discretisation, (b) number of recalled rules, (c) classification accuracy without constraints [%], (d) constraints on rule support, (e) number of rules satisfying condition on support, (f) maximal classification accuracy [%].

Female						N	Male					
(a)	(b)	(c)	(d)	(e)	(f)		(a)	(b)	(c)	(d)	(e)	(f)
3	5	26.67	25	3	26.67	1	3	6	13.33	14	4	13.33
	12	30.00	16	6	30.00	2		12	18.33	4	10	18.33
	23	34.44	16	7	34.44	3		23	26.67	4	17	26.67
2	60	82.22	31	23	83.33	4		38	40.00	4	28	40.00
	111	84.44	55	27	86.67	5		85	61.67	4	61	63.33
	128	78.89	55	27	86.67	6		123	63.33	4	82	65.00
	157	76.67	55	27	86.67	7		256	70.00	32	31	75.00
	202	71.11	55	27	86.67	8	2	319	65.00	32	33	75.00
	325	67.78	55	27	86.67	9		395	65.00	32	35	75.00
	540	**55.56**	**66**	**11**	**86.67**	10		539	56.67	32	39	75.00
	832	51.11	66	11	86.67	11		675	55.00	32	42	75.00
	1415	37.78	66	12	86.67	12		859	43.33	32	46	75.00
	2201	35.56	66	14	86.67	13		1388	33.33	32	63	75.00
	3038	27.78	66	16	86.67	14		1763	25.00	32	67	75.00
	4235	22.22	66	16	86.67	15		2469	16.67	32	67	75.00
	5709	17.78	66	16	86.67	16		3214	15.00	32	69	75.00
1	7397	13.33	66	16	86.67	17		4347	13.33	34	67	75.00
	10217	5.56	66	16	86.67	18		6314	11.67	35	76	75.00
	13034	5.56	66	16	86.67	19	1	7214	10.00	41	60	75.00
	16020	5.56	66	16	86.67	20		9683	5.00	41	60	75.00
	22227	2.22	66	16	86.67	21		**12832**	**1.67**	**41**	**69**	**76.67**
	28907	0.00	66	16	86.67	22		18882	1.67	41	70	76.67
	38948	0.00	66	16	86.67	23		26965	0.00	41	76	76.67
	50159	0.00	66	16	86.67	24		35014	0.00	41	79	76.67
	62383	0.00	66	17	86.67	25		46191	0.00	41	80	76.67

were added. The process can be stopped once some criterion is satisfied, for example obtaining satisfactory classification accuracy, or, with the goal of observation of occurring trends and general characteristics of constructed algorithms, it can continue till the sets of available features and rules are exhausted. This latter approach was applied in the presented research, thus for both continuous and discrete data tests ended only when all variables were considered and all decision rules were recalled.

For continuous valued features for both datasets in the initial steps, when just few elements were considered, the numbers of rules recalled were relatively low and corresponding classification accuracies rather poor. For female writers in the 5th step recognition reached its highest level, yet as it happened for support of at least 55, lower than for the reference best algorithm *FC-BAlg17*, the number of rules was higher. At the 10th step from the set of rules there were selected 540 elements, reduced to 11 rules with constraints on support to be at least 66, which constitutes the best shortened decision algorithm, with degree of reduction of $6/17 = 35.29\%$. For male writers results were significantly worse, as this dataset proved generally more difficult in classification. The same level of recognition as for the reference best algorithm *MC-BAlg80* was detected at the 21st step, where the algorithm was shortened to 12,832 rules, further reduced to 69 by supports equal at least 41, which meant decreasing the length by $11/80 = 13.75\%$.

For discretised datasets the numbers of features were lower because of rejecting single bin variables from considerations. As can be seen in Table 4, for female writers the required recognition was achieved at the 13th step, when only few variables were left for examination, and the algorithm was shortened to 694 rules, for support equal or higher 41 with 44 rules, which meant reduction by $14/58 = 24.14\%$. For male writer dataset not only very significant reduction of the algorithm was obtained but also noticeable improvement of recognition was observed, the highest reaching 98.33 % with just 35 rules with supports equal at least 22, when only 318 were recalled from the full set, which compared to the reference number of 2181 rules included in *MD-BAlg2181* made quite a contrast.

Thus for both continuous and discrete domains for both datasets rule filtering executed by referring to included condition attributes while following the constructed ranking, combined with characterisation of features by numbers of bins found in discretisation, enabled to filter out some algorithms with undamaged performance, or even increased, but with appreciable reduction of their lengths by rejection of some of constituent rules. It was not possible to achieve this reduction by filtering rules just with respect to their support or length.

4.2   Selection of Rules by Quality Measures

In the second part of performed experiments on rule filtering, the previously defined quality measures were employed. The measures were calculated for all inferred rules, then the rule sets were sorted in descending order with respect to the considered measure, forming in fact rankings of rules. Next, from these rule rankings gradually increasing subsets of rules were retrieved and their performance evaluated by test sets.

Due to construction of measures, if in each processing step a distinctive value of a measure was taken as a single indicator of numbers of rules to be recalled, it would possibly cause unmanageably high numbers of steps. That is why, to reduce processing time needed, some thresholds for values were introduced and for each dataset an arbitrarily set number of steps was executed, 20 for continuous datasets which involved more attributes and rules, and 15 for discrete cases, and only these selected results were presented in the paper. Detailed results for

Table 4. Characteristics of decision algorithms with pruning of rules by discretised condition attributes: N indicates the number of considered attributes, (a) number of bins established in discretisation, (b) number of recalled rules, (c) classification accuracy without constraints [%], (d) minimal support required of rules, (e) number of rules satisfying condition on support, (f) maximal classification accuracy [%].

Female						N	Male					
(a)	(b)	(c)	(d)	(e)	(f)		(a)	(b)	(c)	(d)	(e)	(f)
3	0	0.00	0	0	0.00	1	3	0	0.00	0	0	0.00
	3	28.89	43	2	28.89	2		4	0.00	9	4	0.00
	10	47.78	5	10	47.78	3		9	50.00	28	3	50.00
2	18	66.67	9	15	66.67	4		14	50.00	28	3	50.00
	28	91.11	2	28	91.11	5		31	63.33	2	27	66.67
	48	86.67	11	33	91.11	6		75	63.33	2	55	63.33
	66	92.22	21	31	92.22	7		145	93.33	2	105	93.33
	72	92.22	18	49	92.22	8	2	244	81.67	5	107	93.33
	112	94.44	2	103	94.44	9		**318**	**91.67**	**22**	**35**	**98.33**
	183	88.89	35	32	94.44	10		450	91.67	20	55	98.33
	287	81.11	35	40	92.22	11		495	80.00	20	62	93.33
	435	82.22	41	38	94.44	12		739	78.33	20	80	90.00
	694	**87.78**	**41**	**44**	**98.89**	13		1108	73.33	20	110	85.00
	962	86.67	41	51	98.89	14		1627	75.00	3	854	81.67
	1122	91.11	41	54	98.89	15		1895	75.00	20	173	81.67
	1210	92.22	41	58	98.89	16		2481	78.33	22	165	83.33
						17		2903	81.67	2	1944	86.67
						18		3267	80.00	2	2181	86.67

$QMWR1$ measure are listed in Table 5, the top devoted to continuous domain, and bottom to discrete, and the same convention was used next for Tables 6 and 7, with the results respectively for measures $QMWR1BS$ and $QMWR2S$.

For the first measure $QMWR1$, as there was used its version without support of rules included, more rules were recalled within each step, while for the other two multiplication by support caused immediate exclusion of rules with low support and low values of the calculated product of weights. The processing was stopped when all rules from the reference algorithms were recalled.

It can be observed in Table 5 that for continuous female dataset the required performance was achieved in the 3rd step, after recalling just 94 rules, yet the support was lower than for $FC\text{-}BAlg17$, thus the number of rules in constrained algorithm was higher than in this reference best. Furthermore, in steps 5, 6 and 7 a slight increase of recognition was detected. At the 13th step, in the recalled 537 rules, 11 rules from the best algorithm were present, which was sufficient to give the expected classification accuracy. The remaining rules from this short

Table 5. Characteristics of decision algorithms pruned by measure *QMWR1*: N indicates the processing step, (a) number of recalled rules, (b) classification accuracy without constraints [%], (c) constraints on support, (d) number of rules satisfying condition on support, (e) maximal classification accuracy [%].

Continuous datasets										
Female					N	Male				
(a)	(b)	(c)	(d)	(e)		(a)	(b)	(c)	(d)	(e)
12	30.00	16	6	30.00	1	30	40.00	4	25	40.00
45	80.00	55	13	81.11	2	51	58.33	4	45	58.33
94	83.33	55	23	86.67	3	151	65.00	7	98	65.00
117	80.00	55	23	86.67	4	243	61.67	13	116	66.67
135	78.89	54	25	87.78	5	318	53.33	13	151	65.00
216	76.67	54	25	87.78	6	698	50.00	32	87	71.67
237	74.44	54	25	87.78	7	911	43.33	32	92	71.67
288	72.22	55	28	85.56	8	1139	43.33	27	140	73.33
363	71.11	55	32	84.44	9	1292	43.33	41	55	73.33
398	67.78	55	34	84.44	10	1374	41.67	41	58	73.33
443	63.33	55	35	84.44	11	1867	33.33	41	59	75.00
503	60.00	55	35	84.44	12	2567	21.67	41	62	75.00
537	**55.56**	**66**	**11**	**86.67**	13	3233	20.00	41	64	75.00
546	55.56	66	11	86.67	14	**3878**	**18.33**	**41**	**68**	**76.67**
600	55.56	66	12	86.67	15	4600	15.00	41	70	76.67
645	54.44	66	14	86.67	16	5539	15.00	41	71	76.67
667	54.44	66	14	86.67	17	6194	15.00	41	74	76.67
731	51.11	66	16	86.67	18	7156	11.67	41	76	76.67
901	46.67	66	16	86.67	19	8964	5.00	41	78	76.67
1142	42.22	66	17	86.67	20	9581	5.00	41	80	76.67
Discrete datasets										
Female					N	Male				
(a)	(b)	(c)	(d)	(e)		(a)	(b)	(c)	(d)	(e)
18	64.44	9	15	64.44	1	73	71.67	5	52	73.33
79	92.22	8	62	92.22	2	144	71.67	2	125	81.67
123	95.56	6	99	96.67	3	213	91.67	1	213	91.67
162	91.11	6	123	93.33	4	344	88.33	7	168	90.00
198	88.89	18	79	91.11	5	567	88.33	2	420	91.67
325	88.89	43	35	92.22	6	**664**	**85.00**	**2**	**499**	**93.33**
477	90.00	35	61	96.67	7	856	86.67	2	639	91.67
506	**92.22**	**41**	**50**	**98.89**	8	944	85.00	26	73	91.67
568	93.33	41	51	98.89	9	1199	85.00	2	890	91.67
624	95.56	41	52	98.89	10	1465	85.00	24	123	88.33
709	94.44	41	53	98.89	11	1707	83.33	24	134	90.00
755	96.67	41	55	98.89	12	1912	85.00	22	168	86.67
782	97.78	41	56	98.89	13	2336	80.00	20	236	85.00
830	94.44	41	57	98.89	14	2973	78.33	2	2011	86.67
917	94.44	41	58	98.89	15	3264	80.00	2	2181	86.67

algorithm were retrieved in the following steps, with the final 17th recalled in the set with 1,142 elements. For continuous male dataset the threshold recognition was obtained at 14th step, where 3,878 filtered rules contained 68 with support at least 41, which means than one more rule was rejected from *MC-BAlg80* than in case of filtering by attributes.

For discrete female data no increase in performance was observed, which was not surprising, as it was very high. Filtering by *QMWR1* measure enabled to reject 8 out of 58 rules from the best algorithm *FD-BAlg58*, as in the 8th step with the recalled 506 rules there were 50 with support equal or higher than 41, which made this result worse than for filtering by attributes. The last from 58 rules was filtered with the set of 917 selected elements. For discrete male data again improvement in performance was observed, but the highest recognition was 93.33%, which was lower than the previously detected for filtering by attributes. Since the reference algorithm *MD-BAlg2181* was rather long, most of subsets of selected rules contained fewer elements. The last rule from this reference algorithm was recalled with the set of 3,264 elements, when close to the entire set of rules was selected.

The measure *QMWR1BS*, for which the test results are displayed in Table 6, put emphasis on numbers of bins established in supervised discretisation. Apart from being a factor in construction of the global attribute rankings, also all weights were multiplied by these numbers, and multiplication by rule supports helped to exclude rules with low supports from considerations. Thus at the beginning of processing there were recalled mainly rules with high support values.

In the continuous female case the reduction of rules was at the same level as previously observed, to 11 elements and within this group of tests the fewest rules were selected including all 17 rules from the best reference algorithm *FC-BAlg17*, 658 compared to over a thousand or close to two thousands in other two scenarios. For continuous male, the best algorithm constrained by rule support included 65 rules, which was better than in filtering by attributes and by *QMWR1* measure, as it meant reduction of *MC-BAlg80* by $15/80 = 18.75\%$. For discrete female writers the highest recognition was encountered when 269 were recalled at the 7th step, but the shortened algorithm with constraints on support was the same as for the first measure and contained 50 rules. For discrete male dataset there was detected both shortening of the algorithm as well as increased recognition to 93.33%, but results once again were not as good as in case of filtering by attributes or by *QMWR1* measure, in particular with respect to the length of the algorithm as it contained 546 rules.

With *QMWR2S* measure equidistant weights were assigned to ranking positions. Multiplication by support resulted in selection of rules with mainly higher support values, causing better recognition in the first few steps, which is shown in Table 7. For continuous datasets, for female writers the best performing algorithm was found at the 3rd step, when 34 rules were recalled from the full set *FC-FAlg*. For male writers the same was achieved at the 10th step of selecting 369 rules, which with constraints on support at least 41 left only 60 rules, which was the best overall reduction by $20/80 = 25\%$, the highest obtained for this

Table 6. Characteristics of decision algorithms pruned by measure *QMWR1BS*: N indicates the processing step, (a) number of recalled rules, (b) classification accuracy without constraints [%], (c) constraints on support, (d) number of rules satisfying condition on support, (e) maximal classification accuracy [%].

Continuous datasets

Female					N	Male				
(a)	(b)	(c)	(d)	(e)		(a)	(b)	(c)	(d)	(e)
6	60.00	45	1	60.00	1	4	41.67	51	4	41.67
33	78.89	39	28	78.89	2	11	48.33	43	8	48.33
87	84.44	55	28	85.56	3	28	60.00	34	20	60.00
137	83.33	64	13	85.56	4	34	73.33	34	21	73.33
158	83.33	64	13	85.56	5	55	71.67	32	28	75.00
182	83.33	64	13	85.56	6	92	71.67	32	51	73.33
209	**82.22**	**66**	**11**	**86.67**	7	162	71.67	32	67	71.67
219	80.00	66	11	86.67	8	251	66.67	32	79	71.67
236	80.00	66	11	86.67	9	272	66.67	41	51	73.33
253	81.11	66	12	86.67	10	292	63.33	41	55	73.33
268	81.11	66	15	86.67	11	430	61.67	26	157	75.00
304	74.44	66	16	86.67	12	473	61.67	41	60	75.00
335	73.33	66	16	86.67	13	524	61.67	41	63	75.00
367	72.22	66	16	86.67	14	**632**	**61.67**	**41**	**65**	**76.67**
421	70.00	66	16	86.67	15	833	56.67	41	67	76.67
464	65.56	66	16	86.67	16	1234	45.00	41	69	76.67
523	65.56	66	16	86.67	17	1915	31.67	41	74	76.67
551	65.56	66	16	86.67	18	2645	31.67	41	78	76.67
612	63.33	66	16	86.67	19	3606	23.33	41	78	76.67
658	63.33	66	17	86.67	20	3909	23.33	41	80	76.67

Discrete datasets

Female					N	Male				
(a)	(b)	(c)	(d)	(e)		(a)	(b)	(c)	(d)	(e)
50	91.11	8	48	91.11	1	5	0.00	20	5	0.00
84	93.33	9	73	93.33	2	96	71.67	21	56	73.33
140	92.22	26	59	92.22	3	137	70.00	28	41	71.67
202	91.11	41	41	94.44	4	196	83.33	2	192	83.33
240	91.11	35	60	96.67	5	234	86.67	26	61	86.67
262	91.11	41	49	96.67	6	280	86.67	20	110	88.33
269	**94.44**	**41**	**50**	**98.89**	7	391	90.00	26	74	91.67
280	93.33	41	51	98.89	8	482	90.00	5	358	90.00
346	92.22	41	52	98.89	9	**546**	**93.33**	**1**	**546**	**93.33**
354	92.22	41	53	98.89	10	600	91.67	2	550	91.67
376	92.22	41	54	98.89	11	651	86.67	22	134	90.00
393	93.33	41	55	98.89	12	1091	86.67	2	937	90.00
419	92.22	41	56	98.89	13	1408	83.33	22	185	86.67
507	95.56	41	57	98.89	14	2132	85.00	20	258	85.00
558	94.44	41	58	98.89	15	2927	80.00	2	2047	86.67

dataset in all tested approaches. Also all 80 rules from the reference algorithm *MC-BAlg80* were included in the smallest retrieved set with 2,623 elements.

For the discretised datasets, for female writers also the best algorithm was found at the 3rd step. Within 155 rules recalled there were 46 with support at least 41, which made it second best with respect to reduction of *FD-BAlg58* for this dataset. In case of male writers the highest increase in recognition for all tests with filtering by measures was detected, to 95.00% by 71 rules with supports at least 19, selected with the set of 90 elements in the 4th processing step, which also happened to be second best for this dataset.

4.3 Summary of Test Results

Comparison of experimental results for selection of rules by attributes and by quality measures, brought several conclusions with respect to continuous and discrete datasets. In continuous case for female writers, the maximum shortening of the reference algorithm *FC-BAlg17* was always the same, by 35.29%, and only for filtering by *QMWR1* measure a slight improvement of accuracy was observed. For male writers there was no increase of performance with respect to that of *MC-BAlg80*, and gains with respect to decreased length varied, with the best reduction by 25.00% for *QMWR2S* measure.

In case of discrete datasets, for female writers the highest prediction was the same as for the reference algorithm *FD-BAlg58*, but noticeable reduction of its length was achieved, the highest by 24.13% for filtering by attributes. The reference male algorithm *FD-BAlg2181* was so long that most results offered very high reductions, thus only for the best case the percentage was calculated, for the highest increase in prediction to 98.33% with 35 rules, which made it shortening by 98.39%, again for selection of rules driven by attributes. From all tests with filtering by measures for discrete female dataset the best reduction of the algorithm by 20.69% was discovered for *QMWR2S* measure, which was also the best for male dataset, where reduction of length by 96.74% gave to the algorithm with 71 rules the classification accuracy of 95.00%.

Table 8 displays maximal reduction of length for constructed decision algorithms obtained through all tested approaches for both continuous and discrete domains, for both datasets. The results are given with respect to the reference algorithms, and assume hard constraints imposed on support in order to achieve the highest classification accuracy.

Even though in some cases selection of rules by their condition attributes resulted in better results than filtering by quality measures, in the latter approach several times it was possible to find satisfactory results sooner, at the earlier processing step, or after recalling fewer rules. Therefore, both ways show some merit and prove useful in search for optimal rule classifiers while working in continuous and discrete domains.

5 Conclusions

The paper presents research on rule selection while exploiting characteristics of attributes obtained by supervised discretisation and ranking. Firstly, all available

Table 7. Characteristics of decision algorithms pruned by measure $QMWR2S$: N indicates the processing step, (a) number of recalled rules, (b) classification accuracy without constraints [%], (c) constraints on support, (d) number of rules satisfying condition on support, (e) maximal classification accuracy [%].

Continuous datasets										
Female					N	Male				
(a)	(b)	(c)	(d)	(e)		(a)	(b)	(c)	(d)	(e)
7	38.89	73	5	38.89	1	5	45.00	51	5	45.00
18	83.33	62	14	83.33	2	23	68.33	43	16	68.33
34	**86.67**	**66**	**11**	**86.67**	3	43	68.33	43	27	68.33
54	86.67	66	12	86.67	4	70	71.67	32	51	73.33
57	86.67	66	13	86.67	5	106	71.67	32	66	71.67
61	86.67	66	15	86.67	6	183	70.00	32	80	71.67
74	84.44	66	15	86.67	7	216	70.00	41	51	73.33
97	82.22	66	16	86.67	8	257	66.67	41	55	73.33
154	80.00	66	16	86.67	9	299	66.67	41	56	75.00
343	76.67	66	16	86.67	10	**369**	**63.33**	**41**	**60**	**76.67**
469	71.11	66	16	86.67	11	467	60.00	41	63	76.67
553	64.44	66	16	86.67	12	607	58.33	41	64	76.67
678	54.44	66	16	86.67	13	702	56.67	41	67	76.67
811	46.67	66	16	86.67	14	814	51.67	41	70	76.67
1030	42.22	66	16	86.67	15	953	45.00	41	72	76.67
1160	42.22	66	16	86.67	16	1182	38.33	41	74	76.67
1226	40.00	66	16	86.67	17	1471	31.67	41	76	76.67
1363	40.00	66	16	86.67	18	1748	28.33	41	77	76.67
1494	36.67	66	16	86.67	19	2019	26.67	41	79	76.67
1763	34.44	66	17	86.67	20	2623	25.00	41	80	76.67
Discrete datasets										
Female					N	Male				
(a)	(b)	(c)	(d)	(e)		(a)	(b)	(c)	(d)	(e)
47	90.00	24	43	90.00	1	12	50.03	28	9	50.03
61	92.22	41	36	94.44	2	48	53.33	27	30	71.67
155	**94.44**	**41**	**46**	**98.89**	3	67	81.67	20	58	85.00
171	92.22	41	47	98.89	4	**90**	**70.00**	**19**	**71**	**95.00**
180	94.44	41	48	98.89	5	124	75.00	19	91	91.67
189	92.22	41	49	98.89	6	215	86.67	5	215	86.67
194	92.22	41	50	98.89	7	308	78.33	26	87	88.33
213	95.56	41	51	98.89	8	395	81.67	24	119	88.33
231	93.33	41	52	98.89	9	601	81.67	26	116	86.67
265	95.56	41	53	98.89	10	820	81.67	20	217	83.33
302	97.78	41	54	98.89	11	1405	81.67	21	220	83.33
317	96.67	41	55	98.89	12	1589	78.33	21	226	85.00
318	96.67	41	56	98.89	13	1834	78.33	20	256	83.33
397	94.44	41	57	98.89	14	2227	80.00	23	196	81.67
416	96.67	41	58	98.89	15	2889	80.00	20	267	83.33

Table 8. Length reduction of decision algorithms obtained by filtering driven by condition attributes and measures [%].

		Filtering of decision rules by			
		Condition attributes	Quality measures		
			QMWR1	*QMWR1BS*	*QMWR2S*
Female	Continuous	**35.29**	**35.29**	**35.29**	**35.29**
	Discrete	**24.13**	13.79	13.79	20.69
Male	Continuous	13.75	15.00	18.75	**25.00**
	Discrete	**98.39**	77.12	74.96	96.74

variables were grouped into categories reflecting numbers of bins found for their values by Fayyad and Irani's supervised discretisation algorithm. For each category separately rankings with Relief algorithm were obtained, which were next merged to form the global ranking of features. For two cases of binary authorship attribution exhaustive decision algorithms were inferred within Dominance-Based Rough Set Approach in continuous domain, and with Classical Rough Set Approach in discrete domain. From resulting rule sets elements were then filtered in two ways, directly by referring to condition attributes included in rules, or by evaluation of measures based on attribute rankings and weights assigned to ranking positions. The experimental results show several cases of optimised solutions, and decision algorithms with reduced numbers of constituent rules with the same or increased classification accuracies. In the future research analysis of other ranking strategies for attributes and rules are planned, with filtering of rules induced not only within rough set approaches but also others.

Acknowledgments. In the research there was used RSES system, developed at the Institute of Mathematics, Warsaw University (http://logic.mimuw.edu.pl/~rses/) [4], 4eMka Software developed at the Laboratory of Intelligent Decision Support Systems, Poznań [24], and WEKA workbench [14]. The research was performed at the Silesian University of Technology, Gliwice, within the project BK/RAu2/2017, and at the University of Silesia, Sosnowiec, within the project "Methods of artificial intelligence in information systems".

References

1. Argamon, S., Burns, K., Dubnov, S. (eds.): The Structure of Style: Algorithmic Approaches to Understanding Manner and Meaning. Springer, Berlin (2010). doi:10.1007/978-3-642-12337-5
2. Baron, G.: Comparison of cross-validation and test sets approaches to evaluation of classifiers in authorship attribution domain. In: Czachórski, T., Gelenbe, E., Grochla, K., Lent, R. (eds.) ISCIS 2016. CCIS, vol. 659, pp. 81–89. Springer, Cham (2016). doi:10.1007/978-3-319-47217-1_9

3. Baron, G., Harężlak, K.: On approaches to discretization of datasets used for evaluation of decision systems. In: Czarnowski, I., Caballero, A.M., Howlett, R.J., Jain, L.C. (eds.) Intelligent Decision Technologies 2016. SIST, vol. 57, pp. 149–159. Springer, Cham (2016). doi:10.1007/978-3-319-39627-9_14

4. Bazan, J.G., Szczuka, M.: The rough set exploration system. In: Peters, J.F., Skowron, A. (eds.) Transactions on Rough Sets III. LNCS, vol. 3400, pp. 37–56. Springer, Heidelberg (2005). doi:10.1007/11427834_2

5. Błaszczyński, J., Greco, S., Słowiński, R.: Inductive discovery of laws using monotonic rules. Eng. Appl. Artif. Intell. **25**, 284–294 (2012)

6. Burrows, J.: Textual analysis. In: Schreibman, S., Siemens, R., Unsworth, J. (eds.) A Companion to Digital Humanities. Blackwell, Oxford (2004)

7. Chikalov, I., Lozin, V., Lozina, I., Moshkov, M., Nguyen, H., Skowron, A., Zielosko, B.: Three Approaches to Data Analysis - Test Theory, Rough Sets and Logical Analysis of Data. Intelligent Systems Reference Library, vol. 41. Springer, Heidelberg (2013). doi:10.1007/978-3-642-28667-4

8. Craig, H.: Stylistic analysis and authorship studies. In: Schreibman, S., Siemens, R., Unsworth, J. (eds.) A Companion to Digital Humanities. Blackwell, Oxford (2004)

9. Cyran, K., Stanczyk, U.: Indiscernibility relation for continuous attributes: application in image recognition. In: Kryszkiewicz, M., Peters, J.F., Rybinski, H., Skowron, A. (eds.) RSEISP 2007. LNCS, vol. 4585, pp. 726–735. Springer, Heidelberg (2007). doi:10.1007/978-3-540-73451-2_76

10. Dougherty, J., Kohavi, R., Sahami, M.: Supervised and unsupervised discretization of continuous features. In: Machine Learning Proceedings 1995: Proceedings of the 12th International Conference on Machine Learning, pp. 194–202. Elsevier (1995)

11. Fayyad, U., Irani, K.: Multi-interval discretization of continuous valued attributes for classification learning. In: The 13th International Joint Conference on Artificial Intelligence, vol. 2, pp. 1022–1027. Morgan Kaufmann Publishers (1993)

12. Greco, S., Matarazzo, B., Słowiński, R.: The use of rough sets and fuzzy sets in MCDM. In: Gal, T., Hanne, T., Stewart, T. (eds.) Advances in Multiple Criteria Decision Making, chap. 14, pp. 14.1–14.59. Kluwer Academic Publishers, Dordrecht (1999)

13. Greco, S., Matarazzo, B., Słowiński, R.: Dominance-based rough set approach as a proper way of handling graduality in rough set theory. In: Peters, J.F., Skowron, A., Marek, V.W., Orłowska, E., Słowiński, R., Ziarko, W. (eds.) Transactions on Rough Sets VII. LNCS, vol. 4400, pp. 36–52. Springer, Heidelberg (2007). doi:10.1007/978-3-540-71663-1_3

14. Hall, M., Frank, E., Holmes, G., Pfahringer, B., Reutemann, P., Witten, I.: The WEKA data mining software: an update. SIGKDD Explor. **11**(1), 10–18 (2009)

15. Jockers, M., Witten, D.: A comparative study of machine learning methods for authorship attribution. Lit. Linguist. Comput. **25**(2), 215–223 (2010)

16. Kononenko, I.: Estimating attributes: analysis and extensions of RELIEF. In: Bergadano, F., Raedt, L. (eds.) ECML 1994. LNCS, vol. 784, pp. 171–182. Springer, Heidelberg (1994). doi:10.1007/3-540-57868-4_57

17. Koppel, M., Schler, J., Argamon, S.: Computational methods in authorship attribution. J. Am. Soc. Inf. Sci. Technol. **60**(1), 9–26 (2009)

18. Kotsiantis, S., Kanellopoulos, D.: Discretization techniques: a recent survey. GESTS Int. Trans. Comput. Sci. Eng. **32**(1), 47–58 (2006)

19. Michalak, M., Sikora, M., Wróbel, L.: Rule quality measures settings in a sequential covering rule induction algorithm - an empirical approach. In: Proceedings of the 2015 Federated Conference on Computer Science and Information Systems. ACSIS-Annals of Computer Science and Information Systems, vol. 5, pp. 109–118 (2015)
20. Moshkov, M., Zielosko, B.: Combinatorial Machine Learning - A Rough Set Approach. Studies in Computational Intelligence, vol. 360. Springer, Heidelberg (2011). doi:10.1007/978-3-642-20995-6
21. Pawlak, Z.: Rough sets and intelligent data analysis. Inf. Sci. 147, 1–12 (2002)
22. Pawlak, Z., Skowron, A.: Rough sets and Boolean reasoning. Inf. Sci. 177(1), 41–73 (2007)
23. Peng, R., Hengartner, H.: Quantitative analysis of literary styles. Am. Stat. 56(3), 15–38 (2002)
24. Słowiński, R., Greco, S., Matarazzo, B.: Dominance-based rough set approach to reasoning about ordinal data. In: Kryszkiewicz, M., Peters, J.F., Rybinski, H., Skowron, A. (eds.) RSEISP 2007. LNCS, vol. 4585, pp. 5–11. Springer, Heidelberg (2007). doi:10.1007/978-3-540-73451-2_2
25. Stańczyk, U.: Attribute ranking driven filtering of decision rules. In: Kryszkiewicz, M., Cornelis, C., Ciucci, D., Medina-Moreno, J., Motoda, H., Raś, Z.W. (eds.) RSEISP 2014. LNCS, vol. 8537, pp. 217–224. Springer, Cham (2014). doi:10.1007/978-3-319-08729-0_21
26. Stańczyk, U.: RELIEF-based selection of decision rules. Procedia Comput. Sci. 35, 299–308 (2014)
27. Stańczyk, U.: Measuring quality of decision rules through ranking of conditional attributes. In: Czarnowski, I., Caballero, A.M., Howlett, R.J., Jain, L.C. (eds.) Intelligent Decision Technologies 2016. SIST, vol. 56, pp. 269–279. Springer, Cham (2016). doi:10.1007/978-3-319-39630-9_22
28. Stańczyk, U.: Weighting and pruning of decision rules by attributes and attribute rankings. In: Czachórski, T., Gelenbe, E., Grochla, K., Lent, R. (eds.) ISCIS 2016. CCIS, vol. 659, pp. 106–114. Springer, Cham (2016). doi:10.1007/978-3-319-47217-1_12
29. Wróbel, L., Sikora, M., Michalak, M.: Rule quality measures settings in classification, regression and survival rule induction – an empirical approach. Fundam. Inform. 149, 419–449 (2016)

Induction of Rule for Differential Diagnosis

Shusaku Tsumoto$^{(\boxtimes)}$ and Shoji Hirano

Faculty of Medicine, Department of Medical Informatics, Shimane University,
89-1 Enya-cho, Izumo 693-8501, Japan
{tsumoto,hirano}@med.shimane-u.ac.jp
http://www.med.shimane-u.ac.jp/med_info/tsumoto/index.htm

Abstract. This paper proposes combination of clustering and rule induction in order to acquire rules which is close to differential diagnosis process. First, characterization sets, which are used for exclusive rules are extracted from a dataset and the similarities among characterization sets are calculated. Next, based on the similarities, agglomerative clustering is applied. Then, according to the dendrogram, the classification labels are reformulated and rules for new labels are obtained. Since the dendrogram gives hierarchical structure of classes, each rule for a new label gives a component of hierarchical rules. Finally, combining hierarchical components, rules for differential diagnosis are obtained. The proposed method was evaluated on a medical database and the experimental results show that induced rules as comparable as previously introduced methods.

1 Introduction

Rule mining has been applied to many domains. However, empirical results show that interpretation of extracted rules deep understanding for applied domains [8,9]. One of its reasons is that conventional rule induction methods such as C4.5 [6] cannot reflect the type of experts' reasoning. For example, rule induction methods such as PRIMEROSE [8] induce the following common rule for muscle contraction headache from databases on differential diagnosis of headache:

> [$location = whole$] $\wedge$ [Jolt Headache $= no$] $\wedge$ [Tenderness of M1 $= yes$]
> $\rightarrow$ muscle contraction headache.

This rule is shorter than the following rule given by medical experts.

[Jolt Headache $= no$]
$\wedge$([Tenderness of M0 $= yes$] $\vee$ [Tenderness of M1 $= yes$] $\vee$ [Tenderness of M2 $= yes$])
$\wedge$[Tenderness of B1 $= no$] $\wedge$ [Tenderness of B2 $= no$] $\wedge$ [Tenderness of B3 $= no$]
$\wedge$[Tenderness of C1 $= no$] $\wedge$ [Tenderness of C2 $= no$] $\wedge$ [Tenderness of C3 $= no$]
$\wedge$[Tenderness of C4 $= no$]
$\quad \rightarrow$ muscle contraction headache

S. Tsumoto—This research is supported by Grant-in-Aid for Scientific Research (B) 15H2750 from Japan Society for the Promotion of Science (JSPS).

L. Polkowski et al. (Eds.): IJCRS 2017, Part I, LNAI 10313, pp. 350–361, 2017.
DOI: 10.1007/978-3-319-60837-2_29

where [Tenderness of B1 = no] and [Tenderness of C1 = no] are added.

One of the main reasons why rules are short is that these patterns are generated only by a simple criteria, such as high accuracy or high information gain. The comparative studies [8, 10] suggest that experts should acquire rules not only by a single criteria but by the usage of several measures. For example, the classification rule for muscle contraction headache given in Sect. 1 is very similar to the following classification rule for disease of cervical spine:

[Jolt Headache = no]
$\wedge$([Tenderness of M0 = yes] $\vee$ [Tenderness of M1 = yes] $\vee$ [Tenderness of M2 = yes])
$\wedge$([Tenderness of B1 = yes] $\vee$ [Tenderness of B2 = yes] $\vee$ [Tenderness of B3 = yes]
  $\vee$[Tenderness of C1 = yes] $\vee$ [Tenderness of C2 = yes] $\vee$ [Tenderness of C3 = yes]
  $\vee$[Tenderness of C4 = yes])
  $\rightarrow$ disease of cervical spine

The differences between these two rules are attribute-value pairs, from tenderness of B1 to C4. Thus, these two rules are composed of the following three blocks:

$$A_1 \wedge A_2 \wedge \neg A_3 \rightarrow muscle\ contraction\ headache$$
$$A_1 \wedge A_2 \wedge A_3 \rightarrow disease\ of\ cervical\ spine,$$

where A_1, A_2 and A_3 are given as the following formulae: $A_1 =$ [Jolt Headache = no], $A_2 =$ [Tenderness of M0 = yes] $\vee$ [Tenderness of $M1 = yes$] $\vee$ [Tenderness of M2 = yes], and $A_3 =$ [Tenderness of C1 = no] $\wedge$ [Tenderness of C2 = no] $\wedge$ [Tenderness of C3 = no] $\wedge$ [Tenderness of C4 = no].

The first two blocks (A_1 and A_2) and the third one (A_3) represent the different types of differential diagnosis. The first one A_1 shows the discrimination between muscular type and vascular type of headache. Then, the second part shows that between headache caused by neck and head muscles. Finally, the third formula A_3 is used to make a differential diagnosis between muscle contraction headache and disease of cervical spine. Thus, medical experts first select several diagnostic candidates, which are very similar to each other, from many diseases and then make a final diagnosis from those candidates.

The author previously proposed the solution for this problem in [9, 11, 12] where grouping based on characterization sets and rule induction based on characterization introduced. Experimental evaluation showed that the performance of induced rules are higher than the conventional methods.

However, medical experts pointed out that comprehensibility of induced rules are not so good, because combination of negative and positive terms are not so frequently used in clinical context. Thus, in this paper, in order to acquire more comprehensible rules, we propose combination of clustering and rule induction in order to acquire rules which is close to differential diagnosis process. First, characterization sets, which are used for exclusive rules are extracted from a dataset and the similarities among characterization sets are calculated. Next, based on the similarities, agglomerative clustering is applied. Then, according to the dendrogram, the classification labels are reformulated and rules for new labels are obtained. Since the dendrogram gives hierarchical structure of classes, each rule for a new label gives a component of hierarchical rules. Finally, combining hierarchical components, rules for differential diagnosis are obtained. The proposed method was evaluated on a medical database, the experimental results of which show that induced rules as comparable as previously introduced methods.

2 Probabilistic Rules

In the following sections, we use the following notations introduced by Grzymala-Busse and Skowron [7], which are based on rough set theory [5].

Let U denote a nonempty, finite set called the universe and A denote a nonempty, finite set of attributes, i.e., $a : U \rightarrow V_a$ for $a \in A$, where V_a is called the domain of a, respectively. Then, a decision table is defined as an information system, $A = (U, A \cup \{d\})$, where d is a decision attribute.

The atomic formulae over $B \subseteq A \cup \{d\}$ and V are expressions of the form $[a = v]$, called descriptors over B, where $a \in B$ and $v \in V_a$. The set $F(B, V)$ of formulas over B is the least set containing all atomic formulas over B and closed with respect to disjunction, conjunction and negation. For example, $[location = occular]$ is a descriptor of B. For each $f \in F(B, V)$, f_A denote the meaning of f in A, i.e., the set of all objects in U with property f, defined inductively as follows: (1) If f is of the form $[a = v]$ then, $f_A = \{s \in U | a(s) = v\}$ (2) $(f \wedge g)_A = f_A \cap g_A$; $(f \vee g)_A = f_A \vee g_A$; $(\neg f)_A = U - f_a$.

By the use of the framework above, classification accuracy and coverage, or true positive rate is defined as follows.

Definition 1. *Let R and D denote a formula in $F(B, V)$ and a set of objects which belong to a decision d. Classification accuracy and coverage (true positive rate) for $R \rightarrow d$ is defined as:*

$$\alpha_R(D) = \frac{|R_A \cap D|}{|R_A|} (= P(D|R)), \ \ and \ \kappa_R(D) = \frac{|R_A \cap D|}{|D|} (= P(R|D)),$$

where $|D|$, R_A, $\alpha_R(D)$, $\kappa_R(D)$ and P(S) denote the cardinality of a set D, a meaning of R (i.e., a set of examples which satisfies R), a classification accuracy of R as to classification of D and coverage (a true positive rate of R to D), and probability of S, respectively.

Also, we define partial order of equivalence as follows:

Definition 2. *Let R_i and R_j be the formulae in $F(B, V)$ and let $A(R_i)$ denote a set whose elements are the attribute-value pairs of the form $[a, v]$ included in R_i. If $A(R_i) \subseteq A(R_j)$, then we represent this relation as: $R_i \preceq R_j$.*

Finally, according to the above definitions, probabilistic rules with high accuracy and coverage are defined as:

$$R \xrightarrow{\alpha, \kappa} d \ s.t. \ R = \vee_i R_i = \vee \wedge_j [a_j = v_k], \ \alpha_{R_i}(D) \geq \delta_\alpha \ and \ \kappa_{R_i}(D) \geq \delta_\kappa,$$

where δ_α and δ_κ denote given thresholds for accuracy and coverage, respectively.

3   Characterization Sets

3.1   Characterization Sets

In order to model medical reasoning, a statistical measure, coverage plays an important role in modeling. Let us define a characterization set of D, denoted by $L(D)$ as a set, each element of which is an elementary attribute-value pair R with coverage being larger than a given threshold, δ_κ. That is,

Definition 3. *Let R denote a formula in $F(B,V)$. Characterization sets of a target concept (D) is defined as: $L_{\delta_\kappa}(D) = \{R|\kappa_R(D) \geq \delta_\kappa\}$.*

Then, three types of relations between characterization sets can be defined as follows: (1) Independent type: $L_{\delta_\kappa}(D_i) \cap L_{\delta_\kappa}(D_j) = \phi$, (2) Overlapped type: $L_{\delta_\kappa}(D_i) \cap L_{\delta_\kappa}(D_j) \neq \phi$, and (3) Subcategory type: $L_{\delta_\kappa}(D_i) \subseteq L_{\delta_\kappa}(D_j)$. All three definitions correspond to the negative region, boundary region, and positive region, respectively, if a set of the whole elementary attribute-value pairs will be taken as the universe of discourse.

Tsumoto focuses on the subcategory type in [9] because D_i and D_j cannot be differentiated by using the characterization set of D_j, which suggests that D_i is a generalized disease of D_j. Then, Tsumoto generalizes the above rule induction method into the overlapped type, considering rough inclusion [10]. However, both studies assumes two-level diagnostic steps: focusing mechanism and differential diagnosis, where the former selects diagnostic candidates from the whole classes and the latter makes a differential diagnosis between the focused classes.

The proposed method below extends these methods into multi-level steps. In this paper, we consider the special case of characterization sets in which the thresholds of coverage is equal to 1.0: $L_{1.0}(D) = \{R_i|\kappa_{R_i}(D) = 1.0\}$. It is notable that this set has several interesting characteristics.

Theorem 1. *Let R_i and R_j two formulae in $L_{1.0}(D)$ such that $R_i \preceq R_j$. Then, $\alpha_{R_i} \leq \alpha_{R_j}$.*

Theorem 2. *Let R be a formula in $L_{1.0}(D)$ such that $R = \vee_j[a_i = v_j]$. Then, R and $\neg R$ gives the coarsest partition for a_i, whose R includes D.*

Theorem 3. *Let A consist of $\{a_1, a_2, \cdots, a_n\}$ and R_i be a formula in $L_{1.0}(D)$ such that $R_i = \vee_j[a_i = v_j]$. Then, a sequence of a conjunctive formula $F(k) - \wedge_{i=1}^k R_i$ gives a sequence which increases the accuracy.*

4   Rule Induction

4.1   Rule Induction Process

Figure 1 shows the proposed rule induction method. First, characterization sets for rules are generated from a dataset, and similarities between the sets obtained are calculated. Based on the similarities, agglomerative hierarchical clustering is applied, where the dendrogram is obtained as a hierarchy of decision classes.

Based on this hierarchy, the dataset will be decomposed and classification labels are transformed. For each decomposed dataset, rules for differential diagnosis are induced. Finally, combining rules for a different hierarchy level, rules for total diagnostic process are obtained.

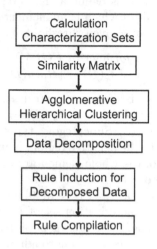

Fig. 1. Rule induction process

4.2   Similarity

Single-Valued Similarity. To measure the similarity between two character-ization sets, we can apply several indices of two-way contigency tables. Table 1 gives a contingency table for two rules, $L_{1.0}(D_i)$ and $L_{1.0}(D_j)$. The first cell a (the intersection of the first row and column) shows the number of matched attribute-value pairs. From this table, several kinds of similarity measures can be defined [2,3]. It is notable that these indices satisfies the property on symmetry.

Table 1. Contingency table for similarity

		$L_{1.0}(D_j)$		Total
		Observed	*Not observed*	
$L_{1.0}(D_i)$	*Observed*	a	b	$a + b$
	Not observed	c	d	$c + d$
Total		$a + c$	$b + d$	$a + b + c + d$

Table 2. A list of similarity measures

(1)	Matching number	a
(2)	Jaccard's coefficient	$a/(a+b+c)$
(3)	χ^2-statistic	$N(ad-bc)^2/M$
(4)	point correlation coefficient	$(ad-bc)/\sqrt{M}$
(5)	Kulczynski	$\frac{1}{2}(\frac{a}{a+b}+\frac{a}{a+c})$
(6)	Ochiai	$\frac{a}{\sqrt{(a+b)(a+c)}}$
(7)	Simpson	$\frac{a}{min\{(a+b),(a+c)\}}$
(8)	Braun	$\frac{a}{max\{(a+b),(a+c)\}}$

$$N = a+b+c+d, \ M = (a+b)(b+c)(c+d)(d+a)$$

In this paper, we focus on the two similarity measures: one is Simpson's measure: $\frac{a}{min\{(a+b),(a+c)\}}$ and the other is Braun's measure: $\frac{a}{max\{(a+b),(a+c)\}}$ (Table 2).

As discussed in Sect. 4, a single-valued similarity becomes low when $L_{1.0}(D_i) \subset L_{1.0}(D_j)$ and $|L_{1.0}(D_i)| \ll |L_{1.0}(D_j)|$. For example, let us consider when $|L_{1.0}(D_i)| = 1$. Then, match number is equal to 1.0, which is the lowest value of this similarity. In the case of Jaccard's coefficient, the value is $1/(1+b)$ or $1/(1+c)$: the similarity is very small when $1 \ll b$ or $1 \ll c$. Thus, these similarities do not reflect the subcategory type. Thus, we should check the difference between $a+b$ and $a+c$ to consider the subcategory type. One solution is to take an interval of maximum and minimum as a similarity, which we call an interval-valued similarity.

For this purpose, we combine Simpson and Braun similarities and define an interval-valued similarity: $\left[\frac{a}{max\{(a+b),(a+c)\}}, \frac{a}{min\{(a+b),(a+c)\}}\right]$. If the difference between two values is large, it would be better not to consider this similarity for grouping in the lower generalization level. For example, when $a+c = 1(a = 1, c = 0)$, the above value will be: $\left[\frac{1}{1+b}, 1\right]$. If $b \gg 1$, then this similarity should be kept as the final candidate for the grouping.

The disadvantage is that it is difficult to compare these interval values. In this paper, the maximum value of a given interval is taken as the representative of this similarity when the difference between min and max are not so large. If the maximum values are equal to the other, then the minimum value will be compared. If the minimum value is larger than the other, the largest one is selected.

5   Example

Let us consider the case of Table 3 as an example for rule induction. For a similarity function, we use a matching number [3] which is defined as the cardinality of the intersection of two the sets. Also, since Table 3 has five classes, k is set to 6. For extraction of taxonomy, the interval-valued similarity is applied.

Table 3. A small example of a database

No.	loc	nat	his	prod	jolt	nau	M1	M2	class
1	occular	per	per	0	0	0	1	1	m.c.h.
2	whole	per	per	0	0	0	1	1	m.c.h.
3	lateral	thr	par	0	1	1	0	0	common.
4	lateral	thr	par	1	1	1	0	0	classic.
5	occular	per	per	0	0	0	1	1	psycho.
6	occular	per	subacute	0	1	1	0	0	i.m.l.
7	occular	per	acute	0	1	1	0	0	psycho.
8	whole	per	chronic	0	0	0	0	0	i.m.l.
9	lateral	thr	per	0	1	1	0	0	common.
10	whole	per	per	0	0	0	1	1	m.c.h.

Definitions. loc: location, nat: nature, his: history,
prod: prodrome, nau: nausea, jolt: Jolt headache,
M1, M2: tenderness of M1 and M2, 1: Yes, 0: No, per: persistent,
thr: throbbing, par: paroxysmal, m.c.h.: muscle contraction headache,
psycho.: psychogenic pain, i.m.l.: intracranial mass lesion, common.:
common migraine, and classic.: classical migraine.

5.1   Grouping

From this table, the characterization set for each concept is obtained as shown
in Fig. 2. Then, the intersection between two target concepts are calculated.

$$
\begin{aligned}
L_{1.0}(m.c.h.) = \quad & \{([loc = occular] \vee [loc = whole]), [nat = per], [his = per], \\
& [prod = 0], [jolt = 0], [nau = 0], [M1 = 1], [M2 = 1]\} \\
L_{1.0}(common) = & \{[loc = lateral], [nat = thr], ([his = per] \vee [his = par]), [prod = 0], \\
& [jolt = 1], [nau = 1], [M1 = 0], [M2 = 0]\} \\
L_{1.0}(classic) = \quad & \{[loc = lateral], [nat = thr], [his = par], [prod = 1], \\
& [jolt = 1], [nau = 1], [M1 = 0], [M2 = 0]\} \\
L_{1.0}(i.m.l.) = \quad & \{([loc = occular] \vee [loc = whole]), [nat = per], \\
& ([his = subacute] \vee [his = chronic]), [prod = 0], \\
& [jolt = 1], [M1 = 0], [M2 = 0]\} \\
L_{1.0}(psycho) = \quad & \{[loc = occular], [nat = per], ([his = per] \vee [his = acute]), \\
& [prod = 0]\}
\end{aligned}
$$

Fig. 2. Characterization sets for Table 3

In the first level, the similarity matrix is generated as shown in Fig. 3.
Since *common* and *classic* have the maximum matching number, these two
classes are grouped into one category, D_6. Then, the characterization of D_6 is
obtained as: $D_6 = \{[loc = lateral], [nat = thr], [jolt = 1], [nau = 1], [M1 = 0],$

	m.c.h.	common	classic	i.m.l.	psycho
m.c.h.	–	[1/8,1/8]	[0,0]	[3/8,3/7]	[2/8,2/4]
common	–	–	[6/8,6/8]	[4/8, 4/7]	[1/7,1/4]
classic	–	–	–	[3/8, 3/7]	0
i.m.l.	–	–	–	–	[2/7, 2/4]

Fig. 3. Interval-valued similarity of two characterization sets (step 2)

	m.c.h.	D_6	i.m.l.	psycho
m.c.h.	–	0	[3/8, 3/7]	[2/8,2/4]
D_6	–	–	[3/7,3/6]	0
i.m.l.	–	–	–	[2/7,2/4]

Fig. 4. Interval-valued similarity of two characterization sets after the first grouping (step 3)

	m.c.h.	D_7	psycho
m.c.h.	–	[0,0]	[2/8,2/4]
D_7	–	[0,0]	[0,0]

Fig. 5. Interval-valued similarity of two characterization sets after the second grouping (step 4)

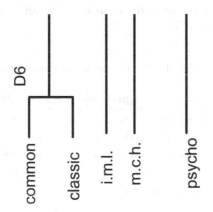

Fig. 6. Grouping by characterization sets

$[M2 = 0]\}$. In the second iteration, the intersection of D_6 and others is considered and the similarity matrix is obtained: as shown in Fig. 4. From this matrix, we have to compare three candidates: $[2/8, 2/4]$, $[3/7, 3/6]$ and $[2/7, 2/4]$. From the minimum values, the middle one: D_6 and i.m.l. is selected as the second grouping. Thus, $D_7 = \{[jolt = 1], [M1 = 0], [M2 = 0]\}$. In the third iteration, the intersection matrix is calculated as Fig. 5 and m.c.h. and psycho are grouped into D_8: $D_8 = \{[nat = per], [prod = 0]\}$. Finally, the dendrogram is given as Fig. 6.

5.2 Data Decomposition

Since classification labels for the first level in the grouping are D_7 and D_8, the original data table is transformed as shown in Table 4.

Table 4. Reformulated table for the first hierarchical level

No.	loc	nat	his	prod	jolt	nau	M1	M2	class
1	occular	per	per	0	0	0	1	1	D8
2	whole	per	per	0	0	0	1	1	D8
3	lateral	thr	par	0	1	1	0	0	D7
4	lateral	thr	par	1	1	1	0	0	D7
5	occular	per	per	0	0	0	1	1	D8
6	occular	per	subacute	0	1	1	0	0	D7
7	occular	per	acute	0	1	1	0	0	D8
8	whole	per	chronic	0	0	0	0	0	D7
9	lateral	thr	per	0	1	1	0	0	D7
10	whole	per	per	0	0	0	1	1	D8

In the same way, for the second to the fourth levels, decomposed tables are obtained as Tables 5, 6 and 7.

Table 5. Reformulated table for the second hierarchical level (D_8)

No.	loc	nat	his	prod	jolt	nau	M1	M2	class
1	occular	per	per	0	0	0	1	1	m.c.h.
2	whole	per	per	0	0	0	1	1	m.c.h.
5	occular	per	per	0	0	0	1	1	psycho.
7	occular	per	acute	0	1	1	0	0	psycho.
10	whole	per	per	0	0	0	1	1	m.c.h.

5.3   Rule Induction

Rule Induction for D_6. First, rule induction is applied to Table 7 and the following rule will be obtained.

$$[prod = 0] \rightarrow common$$
$$[prod = 1] \rightarrow classic$$

Rule Induction for D_7. Second, rule induction is applied to Table 6 and the following rule will be obtained.

$$[loc = lateral] \quad \rightarrow D_6$$
$$[his = par] \qquad \rightarrow D_6$$
$$[nat = per] \qquad \rightarrow i.m.l.$$

Table 6. Reformulated table for the third hierarchical level (D_7)

No.	loc	nat	his	prod	jolt	nau	M1	M2	class
3	lateral	thr	par	0	1	1	0	0	D6
4	lateral	thr	par	1	1	1	0	0	D6
6	occular	per	subacute	0	1	1	0	0	i.m.l.
8	whole	per	chronic	0	0	0	0	0	i.m.l.
9	lateral	thr	per	0	1	1	0	0	D6

Table 7. Reformulated table for the fourth hierarchical level (D_6)

No.	loc	nat	his	prod	jolt	nau	M1	M2	class
3	lateral	thr	par	0	1	1	0	0	common.
4	lateral	thr	par	1	1	1	0	0	classic.
9	lateral	thr	per	0	1	1	0	0	common.

Rule Induction for D_8. Third, rule induction is applied to Table 5 and the following rule will be obtained.

$$[M1 = 1] \rightarrow m.c.h. \ \alpha = 3/4, \kappa = 1.0$$
$$[M2 = 1] \rightarrow m.c.h. \ \alpha = 3/4, \kappa = 1.0$$

It is notable that the above two rules are not deterministic and unless the threshold of accuracy is smaller than 0.5, no rule for psycho is obtained.

Differentiation between D_7 and D_8. Third, rule induction is applied to Table 4 and the following rule will be obtained.

$$[jol1 = 1] \rightarrow D_7 \ \alpha = 1.0, \kappa = 1.0$$
$$[jol1 = 0] \rightarrow D_8 \ \alpha = 1.0, \kappa = 1.0$$
$$[nau = 1] \rightarrow D_7 \ \alpha = 0.8, \kappa = 0.8$$
$$[nau = 0] \rightarrow D_8 \ \alpha = 1.0, \kappa = 0.8$$

Rule Compilation. Rules for each disease is obtained by tracing the hierarchy as follows. After compilation, accuracy and coverage are recalculated.

$$[jolt = 0] \wedge [M1 = 1] \rightarrow m.c.h. \ \alpha = 3/4, \kappa = 1.0$$
$$[jolt = 0] \wedge [M2 = 1] \rightarrow m.c.h. \ \alpha = 3/4, \kappa = 1.0$$
$$[jolt = 1] \wedge [nat = per] \rightarrow m.c.h. \ \alpha = 1.0, \kappa = 1.0$$
$$[jolt = 1] \wedge ([his = per] \vee [loc = lateral]) \wedge [prod = 0]$$
$$\rightarrow common \ \alpha = 1.0, \kappa = 1.0$$
$$[jolt = 1] \wedge ([his = per] \vee [loc = lateral]) \wedge [prod = 1]$$
$$\rightarrow classic \ \alpha = 1.0, \kappa = 1.0$$

The above results can be compared with rules obtained by previously proposed methods. By using methods shown in [12], the following rules will be obtained.

$$\neg([loc = occular] \lor [loc = whole]) \lor \neg[nat = per]$$
$$\lor \neg([his = subacute] \lor [his = chronic])$$
$$\lor \neg[prod = 0] \to \neg i.m.l.$$

$$[nat = thr] \land ([loc = lateral] \lor \neg([his = subacute] \lor [his = chronic]))$$
$$\land [prod = 0] \to common.$$

6   Experimental Results

The above rule induction algorithm is implemented in PRIMEROSE6.0 (Probabilistic Rule Induction Method based on Rough Sets Ver 6.0), and was applied to databases on differential diagnosis of headache, which includes 52119 examples with 45 classes and 147 attributes. In these experiments, δ_α and δ_κ were set to 0.75 and 0.5, respectively. Also, the threshold for grouping is set to 0.8.[1] This system was compared with PRIMEROSE5.0 [12] PRIMEROSE4.5 [10], PRIMEROSE [8] C4.5 [6], CN2 [1], AQ15 [4] with respect to the following points: length of rules, similarities between induced rules and expert's rules and performance of rules.

In this experiment, the length was measured by the number of attribute-value pairs used in an induced rule and Jaccard's coefficient was adopted as a similarity measure [3]. Concerning the performance of rules, ten-fold cross-validation was applied to estimate classification accuracy.

Table 8. Experimental results

Method	Length	Similarity	Accuracy
Headache			
PRIMEROSE6.0	6.5 ± 0.45	0.70 ± 0.15	$89.1 \pm 3.5\%$
PRIMEROSE5.0	8.8 ± 0.27	0.95 ± 0.08	$95.2 \pm 2.7\%$
PRIMEROSE4.5	7.3 ± 0.35	0.74 ± 0.05	$88.3 \pm 3.6\%$
Experts	9.1 ± 0.33	1.00 ± 0.00	$98.0 \pm 1.9\%$
PRIMEROSE	5.3 ± 0.35	0.54 ± 0.05	$88.3 \pm 3.6\%$
C4.5	4.9 ± 0.39	0.53 ± 0.10	$85.8 \pm 1.9\%$
CN2	4.8 ± 0.34	0.51 ± 0.08	$87.0 \pm 3.1\%$
AQ15	4.7 ± 0.35	0.51 ± 0.09	$86.2 \pm 2.9\%$

---

[1] These values are given by medical experts as good thresholds for rules in these three domains.

Table 8 shows the experimental results, which suggest that the performance of PRIMEROSE6 is less than PRIMEROSE5 but outperforms PRIMEROSE4.5 (two-level) and the other four rule induction methods and induces rules very similar to medical experts' ones.

7 Conclusion

In this paper, the characteristics of experts' rules are closely examined, whose empirical results suggest that grouping of diseases is very important to realize automated acquisition of medical knowledge from clinical databases. Thus, we focus on the role of coverage in focusing mechanisms and propose an algorithm for grouping of diseases by using this measure. The above example shows that rule induction with this grouping generates rules, which are similar to medical experts' rules and they suggest that our proposed method should capture medical experts' reasoning. This research is a preliminary study on a rule induction method with grouping and it will be a basis for a future work to compare the proposed method with other rule induction methods by using real-world datasets.

References

1. Clark, P., Niblett, T.: The CN2 induction algorithm. Mach. Learn. **3**, 261–283 (1989)
2. Cox, T., Cox, M.: Multidimensional Scaling, 2nd edn. Chapman & Hall/CRC, Boca Raton (2000)
3. Everitt, B.: Cluster Analysis, 3rd edn. Wiley, London (1996)
4. Michalski, R., Mozetic, I., Hong, J., Lavrac, N.: The multi-purpose incremental learning system AQ15 and its testing application to three medical domains. In: Proceedings of the Fifth National Conference on Artificial Intelligence, pp. 1041–1045. AAAI Press, Menlo Park (1986)
5. Pawlak, Z.: Rough Sets. Kluwer Academic Publishers, Dordrecht (1991)
6. Quinlan, J.: C4.5 - Programs for Machine Learning. Morgan Kaufmann, Palo Alto (1993)
7. Skowron, A., Grzymala-Busse, J.: From rough set theory to evidence theory. In: Yager, R., Fedrizzi, M., Kacprzyk, J. (eds.) Advances in the Dempster-Shafer Theory of Evidence, pp. 193–236. Wiley, New York (1994)
8. Tsumoto, S.: Automated induction of medical expert system rules from clinical databases based on rough set theory. Inf. Sci. **112**, 67–84 (1998)
9. Tsumoto, S.: Extraction of experts' decision rules from clinical databases using rough set model. Intell. Data Anal. **2**(3), 215–227 (1998)
10. Tsumoto, S.: Extraction of hierarchical decision rules from clinical databases using rough sets. Inf. Sci. (2003)
11. Tsumoto, S.: Automated extraction of hierarchical decision rules from clinical databases using rough set model. Expert Syst. Appl. **24**(2), 189–197 (2003). http://dx.doi.org/10.1016/S0957-4174(02)00142-2
12. Tsumoto, S.: Extraction of structure of medical diagnosis from clinical data. Fundam. Inform. **59**(2–3), 271–285 (2004). http://content.iospress.com/articles/fundamenta-informaticae/fi59-2-3-12

Attribute Reduction: An Ensemble Strategy

Suping Xu[1,2], Pingxin Wang[3], Jinhai Li[4], Xibei Yang[1,2(✉)],
and Xiangjian Chen[1]

[1] School of Computer Science and Engineering,
Jiangsu University of Science and Technology, Zhenjiang 212003, Jiangsu,
People's Republic of China
supingxu@yahoo.com, yangxibei@hotmail.com
[2] Intelligent Information Processing Key Laboratory of Shanxi Province,
Shanxi University, Taiyuan 030006, Shanxi, People's Republic of China
[3] School of Mathematics and Physics, Jiangsu University of Science and Technology,
Zhenjiang 212003, Jiangsu, People's Republic of China
[4] Faculty of Science, Kunming University of Science and Technology,
Kunming 650500, Yunnan, People's Republic of China

Abstract. In rough set theory, the heuristic strategy for computing reducts does not take the stability of the selected attributes into account. An unstable reduct may imply the lower adaption to data variations. To fill such a gap, an ensemble strategy is embedded in heuristic algorithm for achieving stable reducts of variable precision fuzzy rough sets. Given an admissible error β, for each looping in the algorithm, a set of attributes will be chosen through considering several admissible errors around the given β, instead of choosing only one attribute by β itself. The main purpose of this replacement is to simulate the sample variations through slight changing of admissible errors over the fixed data. Consequently, the voting ensemble can be used to select an attribute with the maximal frequency of occurrences. The experimental results on eight UCI data sets demonstrate that our ensemble strategy based heuristic approach will improve the stabilities of reducts effectively, while it is unnecessary to add too many attributes for constructing the reducts. This study suggests new trends for considering robust problems in the framework of rough set.

Keywords: Attribute reduction · Ensemble strategy · Stability · Variable precision fuzzy rough sets

1   Introduction

Attribute reduction is one of the most important and fundamental topics in rough set theory. By reducing the number of irrelevant and redundant attributes, attribute reduction can greatly improve the performance of classification learning and effectively decrease the computational complexity in classification tasks. In recent years, attribute reduction has achieved a great success in the fields of

© Springer International Publishing AG 2017
L. Polkowski et al. (Eds.): IJCRS 2017, Part I, LNAI 10313, pp. 362–375, 2017.
DOI: 10.1007/978-3-319-60837-2_30

machine learning [20,22,24], pattern recognition [1,4], decision support [12] and granular computing [21], etc.

Presently, most of the studies on attribute reduction are focused on the following two aspects:

1. **Construction of evaluation criteria.** The evaluation criterion of attributes can be used to measure the qualities of candidate attributes, which has an important influence on finding the results of attribute reduction. To describe the relevance between the decision and condition attributes, a great number of evaluation criteria, such as information entropy [18], consistency [5], and distance [9], have been investigated to select the most optimal candidate attributes. Moreover, aiming at different requirements of practical applications, some combinational and classification-based evaluation criteria are also proposed. For example, in cost-sensitive rough sets and decision-theoretic rough sets, Ju et al. [10,11] designed the evaluation criterion of cost combination which considers decision-cost and test-cost simultaneously, and performed the minimal cost based attribute reduction by decreasing the evaluation criterion of cost combination. In the classification tasks containing discrete and continuous attributes, Hu et al. [7] presented the evaluation criterion of neighborhood decision error rate, and obtained the reduct which can lead to a better classification performance with neighborhood decision error minimization. All the above show that we should construct a reasonable evaluation criterion of attribute reduction to solve some specific problems.

2. **Determination of searching strategies.** The searching strategy of attribute reduction can be used to find a better attribute subset with a certain evaluation criterion. The mainstream searching strategies contain exhaustive algorithms, forward and backward greedy algorithms [8,23,26,27], genetic algorithms [15], etc. Following the above basic strategies, a lot of improved approaches have also been proposed. For example, considering different decision labels may have distinct characteristics of their own, Chen et al. [2,3] introduced the local perspectives into attribute reduction, and obtained a serial of attribute subsets which are most closely related to the specific decision labels. Facing frequent changes in the sample numbers and attribute values, Liu et al. [13,14] presented several incremental searching strategies for decreasing the time consumption in finding attribute subsets. To increase the size of data which can be processed with existing algorithms for attribute reduction, Xu et al. [25] selected the boundary samples which have the larger uncertainty to compute reducts by clustering analysis.

From discussions above, we can see that though a lot of the results about attribute reduction have been obtained, fewer researchers pay much attention to the stability of reduct in rough set theory. In this paper, the stability indicates the variation degree of reduct when data variations happen, i.e., few samples are deleted from the original sample set, and then few new samples are added into the updated sample set. If slight changes of samples will lead to a significant variation of reduct, then the obtained reduct can be considered as an unstable reduct. Obviously, an unstable reduct may bring us unstable learning results and the poor robustness with facing data noise.

Up to now, it has been demonstrated that ensemble strategy is a widely used approach to improve the stability of feature selection. Nevertheless, to the best of our knowledge, how to employ the ensemble strategy to improve the stability of reduct in rough set is still rarely reported. For this purpose, we will simulate sample variations through several slight changes of approximate set in parameterized rough set model. In term of each changed approximate set, we will attempt to add the attribute with maximal significance into the collection of attributes, and then introduce an ensemble voting strategy to select the attribute with the maximal frequency of occurrences in the collection of attributes. In this paper, we adopt variable precision fuzzy rough sets (VPFRS), which can be regarded as the most representative and simplest parameterized rough set model, to verify the effectiveness of our ensemble strategy.

The rest of this paper is organized as follows. Section 2 provides some background materials on VPRS and VPFRS; Sect. 3 introduces the concept of attribute reduction, and then presents the details of our ensemble heuristic algorithm for attribute reduction in VPFRS; Sect. 4 analyzes the effectiveness of our algorithm on 8 UCI data sets from the viewpoints of stabilities and lengths of reducts; Finally, we summarize and set up several issues for future work in Sect. 5.

2   Preliminary Knowledge

In this section, some background materials about variable precision rough sets and variable precision fuzzy rough sets will be provided.

2.1   Variable Precision Rough Sets

In rough set theory, a knowledge representation system can be considered as the 4-tuple $< U, A, V, f >$, in which $U = \{x_1, x_2, \ldots, x_n\}$ is a nonempty finite set of n samples, i.e., the universe of discourse; $A = \{a_1, a_2, \ldots, a_m\}$ is a nonempty finite set of attributes aimed to characterize the samples; V_a is the value domain of attribute a; $f : U \times A \rightarrow V$ is an information function. To be more specific, $< U, A, V, f >$ can also be called a decision system (DS) if $A = AT \cup D$, where AT is the set of condition attributes and D is the decision.

Definition 1. *Given a decision system $DS = < U, AT \cup D, V, f >$, an indiscernibility relation induced by $A \subseteq AT$ is defined as*

$$IND(A) = \{(x_i, x_j) \in U \times U : \forall a \in A, a(x_i) = a(x_j)\}, \tag{1}$$

where $a(x_i)$ is considered as the attribute value of x_i holds on a.

Obviously, $IND(A)$ satisfies reflexive, symmetry and transitivity, and it is an equivalence relation essentially.

Definition 2. *Given a decision system $DS =< U, AT \cup D, V, f >$, $IND(A)$ is an indiscernibility relation induced by $A \subseteq AT$, $\forall X \subseteq U$, $\forall x_i \in U$, the rough inclusion degree of x_i to X in terms of $IND(A)$ is defined as*

$$\psi_X^{IND(A)}(x_i) = \frac{|[x_i]_A \cap X|}{|[x_i]_A|}, \tag{2}$$

where $[x_i]_A = \{x_j \in U : (x_i, x_j) \in IND(A)\}$ is the set of samples in U which satisfy the indiscernibility relation $IND(A)$ with x_i, i.e., the equivalence class generated by x_i, and $|X|$ is the cardinality of a set X.

Definition 3. *Given a decision system $DS =< U, AT \cup D, V, f >$, $IND(A)$ is an indiscernibility relation induced by $A \subseteq AT$, $\forall X \subseteq U$, $\beta \in [0, 0.5)$, the variable precision lower and upper approximations of X in terms of $IND(A)$ are respectively defined as*

$$\underline{IND(A)}^{\beta}(X) = \{x_i \in U : 1 - \psi_X^{IND(A)}(x_i) \leq \beta\}; \tag{3}$$

$$\overline{IND(A)}^{\beta}(X) = \{x_i \in U : 1 - \psi_X^{IND(A)}(x_i) < 1 - \beta\}, \tag{4}$$

where $\psi_X^{IND(A)}(x_i)$ is the rough inclusion degree of x_i to X in terms of $IND(A)$.

The pair $[\underline{IND(A)}^{\beta}(X), \overline{IND(A)}^{\beta}(X)]$ is referred to as the variable precision rough sets of X with respect to the attributes A.

2.2 Variable Precision Fuzzy Rough Sets

Let $U \neq \emptyset$ be a universe of discourse. $F : U \rightarrow [0, 1]$ is a fuzzy set [6] on U. $\forall x_i \in U$, $F(x_i)$ is the membership degree of x_i to F. $F(U)$ is the set of all fuzzy sets on U. R is a fuzzy binary relation, $\forall x_i, x_j, x_k \in U$, R is reflexive if and only if $R(x_i, x_i) = 1$; R is symmetric if and only if $R(x_i, x_j) = R(x_j, x_i)$; R is transitive if and only if $\min_j(R(x_i, x_j), R(x_j, x_k)) \leq R(x_i, x_k)$. In this paper, the fuzzy binary relation R is constructed by the similarity measure.

Definition 4. *Given a decision system $DS =< U, AT \cup D, V, f >$, R_A is a fuzzy binary relation induced by $A \subseteq AT$, $\forall F \in F(U)$, $\forall x_i \in U$, the rough membership degree of x_i to F in terms of R_A is defined as*

$$\psi_F^{R_A}(x_i) = 1 - \frac{|R_A(x_i) \cap (\neg F)|}{|R_A(x_i)|}, \tag{5}$$

where $R_A(x_i)$ is the fuzzy set such that $\forall x_j \in U$, $R_A(x_i)(x_j) = R_A(x_i, x_j)$, and $|F| = \sum_{x_i \in U} F(x_i)$ is the cardinality of a fuzzy set F.

Definition 5. *Given a decision system $DS =< U, AT \cup D, V, f >$, R_A is a fuzzy binary relation induced by $A \subseteq AT$, $\forall F \in F(U)$, $\beta \in [0, 0.5)$, the variable precision fuzzy lower and upper approximations of F in terms of R_A are respectively defined as*

$$\underline{R_A}^{\beta}(F) = \{x_i \in U : 1 - \psi_F^{R_A}(x_i) \leq \beta\}; \tag{6}$$

$$\overline{R_A}^{\beta}(F) = \{x_i \in U : 1 - \psi_F^{R_A}(x_i) < 1 - \beta\}, \tag{7}$$

where $\psi_F^{R_A}(x_i)$ is the rough membership degree of x_i to F in terms of R_A.

The pair $[\underline{R_A}^\beta(F), \overline{R_A}^\beta(F)]$ is referred to as the variable precision fuzzy rough sets of F with respect to the attributes A.

3   Attribute Reduction

In this section, we will introduce the concept of attribute reduction, and then present the details of the traditional heuristic algorithm and our proposed ensemble heuristic algorithm.

3.1   Heuristic Algorithm

Definition 6. *Given a decision system DS $=< U, AT \cup D, V, f >$, R_A is a fuzzy binary relation induced by $A \subseteq AT$, $U/IND(D) = \{d_1, d_2, \ldots, d_p\}$ is the partition induced by the decision D, $\beta \in [0, 0.5)$, the approximate quality of $U/IND(D)$ is defined as*

$$\gamma^\beta(A, D) = \frac{\left| \bigcup_{i=1}^p R_A^\beta(d_i) \right|}{|U|}, \tag{8}$$

where $|X|$ is the cardinality of a set X, $\forall d_i \in U/IND(D)$, d_i is a decision class.

$\gamma^\beta(A, D)$ reflects the approximation abilities of the granulated space induced by the attributes A to characterize the decision D, and it is obvious that $0 \leq \gamma^\beta(A, D) \leq 1$ holds.

Definition 7. *Given a decision system DS $=< U, AT \cup D, V, f >$, $\forall A \subseteq AT$, A is referred to as a reduct of AT if and only if*

1. $\gamma^\beta(A, D) = \gamma^\beta(AT, D)$;
2. $\forall A' \subset A$, $\gamma^\beta(A', D) \neq \gamma^\beta(AT, D)$.

By Definition 7, we can see that a reduct of AT is a minimal subset of AT, which preserves the unchange of approximate quality. However, in practice, the criteria of reduct are much too strict in Definition 7. To expand the application scope of attribute reduction, some researchers [7,8,17,24] have introduced the threshold ε to control the change of approximate quality for relaxing the criteria of reduct, and considered A as an ε-approximate reduct of AT with the following conditions:

1. $\gamma^\beta(A, D) \geq (1 - \varepsilon) \cdot \gamma^\beta(AT, D)$;
2. $\forall A' \subset A$, $\gamma^\beta(A', D) < (1 - \varepsilon) \cdot \gamma^\beta(AT, D)$.

The above conditions show that ε is aimed at eliminating redundant attributes as much as possible, while maintaining the change of approximate quality in a smaller range. In general, ε is recommended to be $[0, 0.1]$. Specifically, if $\varepsilon = 0$, then ε-approximate reduct is actually the traditional definition of attribute reduction in Definition 7, from which we can conclude that ε-approximate reduct is a generalization of attribute reduction.

Let $DS =< U, AT \cup D, V, f >$ be a decision system, suppose that $A \subseteq AT$, $\forall a_i \in A$, we define a coefficient

$$Sig_{in}^{\beta}(a_i, A, D) = \gamma^{\beta}(A, D) - \gamma^{\beta}(A \backslash \{a_i\}, D) \tag{9}$$

as the significance of a_i in A relative to decision D. $Sig_{in}^{\beta}(a_i, A, D)$ reflects the change of approximate quality if a_i is eliminated from A. Accordingly, we can also define

$$Sig_{out}^{\beta}(a_i, A, D) = \gamma^{\beta}(A \cup \{a_i\}, D) - \gamma^{\beta}(A, D), \tag{10}$$

where $a_i \in AT \backslash A$, $Sig_{out}^{\beta}(a_i, A, D)$ measures the change of approximate quality if a_i is introduced into A. By $Sig_{in}^{\beta}(a_i, A, D)$ and $Sig_{out}^{\beta}(a_i, A, D)$, a forward heuristic attribute reduction algorithm can be designed as follows.

Algorithm 1. Heuristic Algorithm (HA)

Inputs: $DS =< U, AT \cup D, V, f >$, admissible error β,

　　　　approximate quality threshold ε.

Outputs: An ε-approximate reduct A.

1. $A \leftarrow \emptyset$;

2. For each $a_i \in AT$, compute $Sig_{in}^{\beta}(a_i, AT, D)$;

3. $A \leftarrow a_j$, where $Sig_{in}^{\beta}(a_j, AT, D) = \max\{Sig_{in}^{\beta}(a_i, AT, D) : \forall a_i \in AT\}$, compute $\gamma^{\beta}(A, D)$;

4. **While** $\gamma^{\beta}(A, D) < (1 - \varepsilon) \cdot \gamma^{\beta}(AT, D)$

　　(1) For each $a_i \in AT \backslash A$, compute $Sig_{out}^{\beta}(a_i, A, D)$;

　　(2) $A \leftarrow A \cup \{a_j\}$, where $Sig_{out}^{\beta}(a_j, A, D) = \max\{Sig_{out}^{\beta}(a_i, A, D) : \forall a_i \in AT \backslash A\}$;

　　(3) Compute $\gamma^{\beta}(A, D)$;

　　End While

5. For each $a_i \in A$, if $\gamma^{\beta}(A \backslash \{a_i\}, D) \geq (1 - \varepsilon) \cdot \gamma^{\beta}(AT, D)$, **then** $A \leftarrow A \backslash \{a_i\}$;

6. **Return** A.

In Algorithm 1, Step 3 is used to find the first attribute with maximal approximate quality, that is to say, the approximate quality of first selected attribute should be closest to the raw approximate quality $\gamma^{\beta}(AT, D)$. For each looping in Step 4, the aim is also to find an attribute with maximal significance and then add this attribute into reduct.

3.2   Ensemble Heuristic Algorithm

For Algorithm 1, the key is to find the attribute with maximal significance. By Eqs. (9) and (10), we can see that the computation of such significance is based on the given admissible error β. Nevertheless, if samples in data vary, then the attribute with maximal significance may also be changed. Such case tells us that the criterion used in Algorithm 1 may not be suitable for data variations. The ensemble mechanism [16] is a feasible way to improve the stability of feature subset in feature selection. It attempts to find a set of candidate attributes through different varied data, and then adopts voting strategy to select an attribute with the maximal frequency of occurrences. However, in real-world applications, the changing trend of data is impossible to know in advance. Therefore, we will use the slight changes of admissible error β to simulate data variations, and the changes of admissible error β will cause the changes of approximate set in VPFRS, that is to say, several admissible errors which are close to the given β will be used to obtain a set of candidate attributes, and then we will make voting mechanism applicable.

By the proposed ensemble criterion for selecting attributes, our ensemble heuristic algorithm to compute reduct can be designed as follows.

Algorithm 2. Ensemble Heuristic Algorithm (EHA)

Inputs: $DS =< U, AT \cup D, V, f >$, admissible error β,

approximate quality threshold ε, margin α, stepsize ω.

Outputs: An ε-approximate reduct A.

1. $A \leftarrow \emptyset, T \leftarrow \emptyset$;

2. **For** $k = -\alpha$ to α

   (1) $\beta' = \beta + \omega \cdot k$;

   (2) For each $a_i \in AT$, compute $Sig_{in}^{\beta'}(a_i, AT, D)$;

   (3) $T \leftarrow T \cup \{a_j\}$, where $Sig_{in}^{\beta'}(a_j, AT, D) = \max\{Sig_{in}^{\beta'}(a_i, AT, D) : \forall a_i \in AT\}$;

  End For

3. Find attribute v_i with the maximal frequency of occurrences in T;

4. $A \leftarrow v_i$, compute $\gamma^{\beta}(A, D)$;

5. **While** $\gamma^{\beta}(A, D) < (1 - \varepsilon) \cdot \gamma^{\beta}(AT, D)$

   (1) $T \leftarrow \emptyset$;

   (2) **For** $k = -\alpha$ to α

     [1] $\beta' = \beta + \omega \cdot k$;

     [2] For each $a_i \in AT \backslash A$, compute $Sig_{out}^{\beta'}(a_i, A, D)$;

     [3] $T \leftarrow T \cup \{a_j\}$, where $Sig_{out}^{\beta'}(a_j, A, D) = \max\{Sig_{out}^{\beta'}(a_i, A, D) : \forall a_i \in AT \backslash A\}$;

End For

(3) Find attribute v_i with the maximal frequency of occurrences in T;

(4) $A \leftarrow A \cup \{v_i\}$, compute $\gamma^\beta(A, D)$;

End While

6. For each $a_i \in A$, **if** $\gamma^\beta(A \backslash \{a_i\}, D) \geq (1-\varepsilon) \cdot \gamma^\beta(AT, D)$, **then** $A \leftarrow A \backslash \{a_i\}$;

7. Return A.

4   Experiments

In this section, we will analyze the effectiveness of our ensemble heuristic algorithm on 8 UCI data sets, and the stabilities and lengths of reducts will be compared.

4.1   Data Sets

To evaluate the performances of our EHA, 8 real-world data sets from UCI machine learning repository [19] have been employed in this paper. Table 1 summarizes some detailed statistics of these data sets used in our experiments.

Table 1. Characteristics of the experimental data sets

ID	Data sets	Samples	Attributes	Decision classes
1	Climate Model Simulation Crashes	540	20	2
2	Forest Fires	523	27	4
3	Glass	214	9	6
4	Lymphography	98	18	3
5	Parkinsons	195	23	7
6	Seeds	210	7	3
7	Wdbc	569	30	2
8	Wine	178	13	3

4.2   Configuration

In this paper, the reducts obtained by Algorithms 1 and 2 will be compared. For a given data set, we will compare two attribute reduction algorithms (HA and EHA) on 6 different admissible errors β of VPFRS such that $\beta = \{0.05, 0.10, 0.15, 0.20, 0.25, 0.30\}$. In Algorithm 2, margin α and stepsize ω

are set to be 2 and 0.01, respectively. That is to say, to release the influence generated by data variations, through considering 5 admissible errors (i.e., $\beta - 0.01 \cdot 2$ to $\beta + 0.01 \cdot 2$) around the original given β, we iteratively select the most significant attributes with a voting strategy. Note that, to our best knowledge, no theoretical bases have been reported to specify the threshold ε for controlling the change of approximate quality. Therefore, we conducted some experiments to determine $\varepsilon = 0.1$ for achieving the more reasonable length of reduct.

Furthermore, all the experiments have been carried out on a workstation equipped with a Intel Core i3-3240 CPU (3.40 GHz) and 4.00 GB memory. The programming language is Matlab R2014b.

4.3   Experimental Results and Discussions

To describe the stability of reduct when data is changed, we break all samples into t groups with the same size, denoted by $U_1, U_2, \ldots, U_t$, and then combine $t-1$ groups of them in turn to compute reducts. For example, firstly, $U_2 \cup U_3 \cup \ldots \cup U_t$ is used to compute reduct A_1, and then $U_1 \cup U_3 \cup \ldots \cup U_t$ is used to compute reduct $A_2, \ldots$, finally, $U_1 \cup U_2 \cup U_3 \cup U_{t-1}$ is used to compute reduct A_t. From the above, we can see that the degree of data variations is $1 - \frac{|\{U \backslash U_i\} \cap \{U \backslash U_j\}|}{|\{U \backslash U_i\}|}$, where $1 \leq i, j \leq t$ and $i \neq j$. The stability of reduct can be defined as

$$ReductStability = \frac{2}{t \cdot (t-1)} \sum_{i=1}^{t-1} \sum_{j=i+1}^{t} \frac{|A_i \cap A_j|}{|A_i \cup A_j|}, \tag{11}$$

where A_i is the reduct on $U \backslash U_i$. The bigger the value of $ReductStability$, the better the stability. Specially, the stability is perfect when $ReductStability = 1$. For each data set in Table 1, t is set to be 5, and the degree of data variations is 25%. Meanwhile, the above process of data partition will be repeated randomly 5 times, and the mean value of 5 experimental results is recorded.

Tables 2, 3, 4, 5, 6, 7, 8 and 9 demonstrate the comparisons of reduct stabilities between Algorithms 1 and 2 in terms of the 8 UCI data sets, respectively. The better performance is highlighted in boldface, and the similar performance is marked with boldface and underline. From Tables 2, 3, 4, 5, 6, 7, 8 and 9, it is not difficult to observe that the stabilities of reducts generated by our Algorithm 2 (EHA) are bigger than the stabilities of reducts generated by Algorithm 1 (HA) in the majority of admissible errors β of VPFRS. In all the 48 stability comparisons (8 data sets × 6 admissible errors), the performance of our Algorithm 2 is better than that of Algorithm 1 at 60.42% cases, and Algorithm 2 achieves roughly equivalent performance with Algorithm 1 at 31.25% cases. Moreover, there are only 8.33% cases that, compared with the traditional heuristic attribute reduction algorithm, our ensemble heuristic attribute reduction algorithm is a decline in the stabilities of reducts.

From Tables 10, 11, 12, 13, 14, 15, 16 and 17, we can see that the difference between the lengths of reducts generated by Algorithm 1 and those generated by Algorithm 2 is little. For some admissible errors in the given data set, the lengths

Table 2. Stability of reduct on Climate Model Simulation Crashes

Admissible error β	0.05	0.10	0.15	0.20	0.25	0.30
Algorithm 1	0.5610	0.7288	0.5180	0.2376	**1.0000**	**1.0000**
Algorithm 2	**0.6352**	**0.7783**	**0.6834**	**0.3009**	**1.0000**	**1.0000**

Table 3. Stability of reduct on Forest Fires

Admissible error β	0.05	0.10	0.15	0.20	0.25	0.30
Algorithm 1	0.8035	0.6684	0.6180	0.5320	0.4794	0.4113
Algorithm 2	**0.8272**	**0.7176**	**0.6302**	**0.5786**	**0.5586**	**0.4557**

Table 4. Stability of reduct on Glass

Admissible error β	0.05	0.10	0.15	0.20	0.25	0.30
Algorithm 1	0.5180	**0.6786**	**0.6619**	0.6135	0.7127	**0.6796**
Algorithm 2	**0.5320**	**0.6776**	**0.6623**	**0.6458**	**0.7356**	**0.6835**

Table 5. Stability of reduct on Lymphography

Admissible error β	0.05	0.10	0.15	0.20	0.25	0.30
Algorithm 1	**0.4833**	**0.4967**	**0.4348**	0.3351	0.3277	**0.2825**
Algorithm 2	**0.4833**	**0.4967**	**0.4394**	**0.3830**	**0.3486**	**0.2744**

Table 6. Stability of reduct on Parkinsons

Admissible error β	0.05	0.10	0.15	0.20	0.25	0.30
Algorithm 1	**0.7699**	**0.7995**	**0.7274**	0.6390	**0.6950**	0.7313
Algorithm 2	**0.7789**	**0.8022**	**0.7234**	**0.6737**	0.6796	**0.7448**

Table 7. Stability of reduct on Seeds

Admissible error β	0.05	0.10	0.15	0.20	0.25	0.30
Algorithm 1	**0.6283**	0.6417	0.6393	0.5437	0.6320	**0.5927**
Algorithm 2	0.5907	**0.6653**	**0.6570**	**0.5710**	**0.6820**	**0.5863**

of reducts generated by Algorithm 2 are even shorter than those of Algorithm 1. Therefore, we can conclude that our ensemble strategy based heuristic algorithm is effective in improving the stability of reduct when facing sample variations, and compared with the traditional heuristic algorithm, it will not add large numbers of attributes into reduct.

Table 8. Stability of reduct on Wdbc

Admissible error β	0.05	0.10	0.15	0.20	0.25	0.30
Algorithm 1	0.5969	0.4629	0.4083	**0.4857**	0.4690	**0.2900**
Algorithm 2	**0.6177**	**0.5146**	**0.4947**	0.4695	**0.4957**	0.2767

Table 9. Stability of reduct on Wine

Admissible error β	0.05	0.10	0.15	0.20	0.25	0.30
Algorithm 1	0.4705	0.4517	0.5252	0.4560	<u>0.5120</u>	<u>0.3970</u>
Algorithm 2	**0.5355**	**0.4639**	**0.5437**	**0.4788**	<u>0.5150</u>	<u>0.4010</u>

Table 10. Length of reduct on Climate Model Simulation Crashes

Admissible error β	0.05	0.10	0.15	0.20	0.25	0.30
Algorithm 1	5.0000	4.6800	4.2800	2.7200	1.0000	1.0000
Algorithm 2	5.0000	4.6800	4.1600	2.9200	1.0000	1.0000

Table 11. Length of reduct on Forest Fires

Admissible error β	0.05	0.10	0.15	0.20	0.25	0.30
Algorithm 1	18.3200	15.9600	14.3600	12.3200	10.3200	8.4000
Algorithm 2	18.2400	16.0000	14.4400	12.4000	10.2000	8.2400

Table 12. Length of reduct on Glass

Admissible error β	0.05	0.10	0.15	0.20	0.25	0.30
Algorithm 1	5.0800	5.2400	5.8000	5.6000	5.1200	5.0000
Algorithm 2	5.0800	5.2400	5.8000	5.6400	5.1200	5.0000

Table 13. Length of reduct on Lymphography

Admissible error β	0.05	0.10	0.15	0.20	0.25	0.30
Algorithm 1	4.9200	4.8800	4.9200	4.9600	4.8000	3.8000
Algorithm 2	4.9200	4.8800	5.0400	5.1600	4.8000	3.9200

Table 14. Length of reduct on Parkinsons

Admissible error β	0.05	0.10	0.15	0.20	0.25	0.30
Algorithm 1	13.4000	14.0400	12.4000	11.5600	11.0800	10.6800
Algorithm 2	13.5600	14.1600	12.3200	11.5600	10.9200	10.5600

Table 15. Length of reduct on Seeds

Admissible error β	0.05	0.10	0.15	0.20	0.25	0.30
Algorithm 1	4.7200	4.0400	3.6800	3.4000	3.0800	2.8400
Algorithm 2	4.6800	4.0400	3.7200	3.4800	3.1200	2.8800

Table 16. Length of reduct on Wdbc

Admissible error β	0.05	0.10	0.15	0.20	0.25	0.30
Algorithm 1	11.0400	8.2400	6.2000	4.2800	3.1200	2.6000
Algorithm 2	11.1600	8.2800	6.3200	4.3600	3.1600	2.6400

Table 17. Length of reduct on Wine

Admissible error β	0.05	0.10	0.15	0.20	0.25	0.30
Algorithm 1	5.3600	4.9200	4.0400	3.9600	3.3600	2.9600
Algorithm 2	5.4400	4.9200	4.0800	3.9600	3.3600	2.9600

5 Conclusions

Traditional heuristic algorithm ignores the stability of selected attributes in attribute reduction, which may cause the lower adaption to data variations and the unstable classification performances. To remedy this deficiency, we have developed an ensemble voting strategy based heuristic algorithm for obtaining stable reducts in variable precision fuzzy rough sets. Such voting is based on a set of candidate attributes obtained by several admissible errors instead of only one. The experimental results demonstrate that our ensemble heuristic algorithm is effective in improving the stabilities of reducts without adding large numbers of attributes in reducts.

The following topics deserve our further investigations.

1. We have only studied approximate quality based attribute reduction in this paper, and some other measures, such as conditional entropy, combination entropy, classification error rate, etc., will be further applied to our ensemble heuristic approach.

2. Attribute reduction or feature selection can be considered as the first step of data processing, and classification performances of different classifiers based on our stable reducts will be further explored.

Acknowledgments. This work is supported by the Natural Science Foundation of China (Nos. 61572242, 61503160, 61502211), Macau Science and Technology Development Foundation (No. 081/2015/A3), Postgraduate Innovation Foundation of Jiangsu Province (No. KYLX16_0505), Postgraduate Research Innovation Foundation of Jiangsu University of Science and Technology (No. YCX15S-10), Qing Lan Project of Jiangsu Province of China, Open Project Foundation of Intelligent Information Processing Key Laboratory of Shanxi Province (No. 2014002).

References

1. An, S., Shi, H., Hu, Q.H., Li, X.Q., Dang, J.W.: Fuzzy rough regression with application to wind speed prediction. Inf. Sci. **282**, 388–400 (2014)
2. Chen, D., Tsang, E.C.C.: On the local reduction of information system. In: Yeung, D.S., Liu, Z.-Q., Wang, X.-Z., Yan, H. (eds.) ICMLC 2005. LNCS, vol. 3930, pp. 588–594. Springer, Heidelberg (2006). doi:10.1007/11739685_61
3. Chen, D.G., Zhao, S.Y.: Local reduction of decision system with fuzzy rough sets. Fuzzy Sets Syst. **161**, 1871–1883 (2010)
4. Dai, J.H., Xu, Q.: Attribute selection based on information gain ratio in fuzzy rough set theory with application to tumor classification. Appl. Soft Comput. **13**, 211–221 (2013)
5. Dash, M., Liu, H.: Consistency-based search in feature selection. Artif. Intell. **151**, 155–176 (2003)
6. Dubois, D., Prade, H.: Rough fuzzy sets and fuzzy rough sets. Int. J. Gen. Syst. **17**, 191–209 (1990)
7. Hu, Q.H., Pedrycz, W., Yu, D.R., Lang, J.: Selecting discrete and continuous features based on neighborhood decision error minimization. IEEE Trans. Syst. Man Cybern. Part B: Cybern. **40**, 137–150 (2010)
8. Hu, Q.H., Zhang, L., Chen, D.G., Pedrycz, W., Yu, D.R.: Gaussian kernel based fuzzy rough sets: model, uncertainty measures and applications. Int. J. Approx. Reason. **51**, 453–471 (2010)
9. Ho, T.K., Basu, M.: Complexity measures of supervised classification problems. IEEE Trans. Pattern Anal. Mach. Intell. **24**, 289–300 (2002)
10. Ju, H.R., Li, H.X., Yang, X.B., Zhou, X.Z., Huang, B.: Cost-sensitive rough set: a multi-granulation approach. Knowl.-Based Syst. **123**, 137–153 (2017)
11. Ju, H.R., Yang, X.B., Yu, H.L., Li, T.J., Yu, D.J., Yang, J.Y.: Cost-sensitive rough set approach. Inf. Sci. **355–356**, 282–298 (2016)
12. Li, H.X., Zhou, X.Z.: Risk decision making based on decision-theoretic rough set: a three-way view decision model. Int. J. Comput. Intell. Syst. **4**, 1–11 (2011)
13. Liu, D., Li, T.R., Zhang, J.B.: A rough set-based incremental approach for learning knowledge in dynamic incomplete information systems. Int. J. Approx. Reason. **55**, 1764–1786 (2014)
14. Liu, D., Li, T.R., Zhang, J.B.: Incremental updating approximations in probabilistic rough sets under the variation of attributes. Knowl.-Based Syst. **73**, 81–96 (2015)

15. Liu, J.B., Min, F., Liao, S.J., Zhu, W.: A genetic algorithm to attribute reduction with test cost constraint. In: 6th International Conference on Computer Sciences and Convergence Information Technology, pp. 751–754. IEEE press, New York (2011)
16. Li, Y., Si, J., Zhou, G.J., Huang, S.S., Chen, S.C.: FREL: a stable feature selection algorithm. IEEE Trans. Neural Netw. Learn. Syst. **26**, 1388–1402 (2015)
17. Ślęzak, D.: Approximate entropy reducts. Fundam. Inform. **53**, 365–390 (2002)
18. Sun, L., Xu, J.C., Tian, Y.: Feature selection using rough entropy-based uncertainty measures in incomplete decision systems. Knowl.-Based Syst. **36**, 206–216 (2012)
19. UCI Machine Learning Repository. http://archive.ics.uci.edu/ml/
20. Vluymans, S., D'eer, L., Saeys, Y., Cornelis, C.: Applications of fuzzy rough set theory in machine learning: a survey. Fundam. Inform. **142**, 53–86 (2015)
21. Wang, B.L., Liang, J.Y., Qian, Y.H.: Determining decision makers' weights in group ranking: a granular computing method. Int. J. Mach. Learn. Cybern. **6**, 511–521 (2015)
22. Wang, R., Chen, D.G., Kwong, S.: Fuzzy-rough-set-based active learning. IEEE Trans. Fuzzy Syst. **22**, 1699–1704 (2014)
23. Xu, S.P., Yang, X.B., Song, X.N., Yu, H.L.: Prediction of protein structural classes by decreasing nearest neighbor error rate. In: 2015 International Conference on Machine Learning and Cybernetics, pp. 7–13. IEEE Press, New York (2015)
24. Xu, S.P., Yang, X.B., Tsang, E.C.C., Mantey, E.A.: Neighborhood collaborative classifiers. In: 2016 International Conference on Machine Learning and Cybernetics, pp. 470–476. IEEE Press, New York (2016)
25. Xu, S.P., Yang, X.B., Yu, H.L., Yu, D.J., Yang, J.Y., Tsang, E.C.C.: Multi-label learning with label-specific feature reduction. Knowl.-Based Syst. **104**, 52–61 (2016)
26. Yang, X.B., Qi, Y.S., Song, X.N., Yang, J.Y.: Test cost sensitive multigranulation rough set: model and minimal cost selection. Inf. Sci. **250**, 184–199 (2013)
27. Yang, X.B., Qi, Y., Yu, H.L., Song, X.N., Yang, J.Y.: Updating multigranulation rough approximations with increasing of granular structures. Knowl.-Based Syst. **64**, 59–69 (2014)

On Importance of Rows for Decision Tables

Hassan AbouEisha, Mohammad Azad[✉], and Mikhail Moshkov

Mathematical and Computer Sciences and Engineering Division,
King Abdullah University of Science and Technology,
Thuwal 23955-6900, Saudi Arabia
{hassan.aboueisha,mohammad.azad,mikhail.moshkov}@kaust.edu.sa

Abstract. In this paper, we propose a method for the evaluation of importance of rows for decision tables. It is based on indirect information about changes in the set of reducts after removing the considered row from the table. We also discuss results of computer experiments with decision tables from UCI Machine Learning Repository.

Keywords: Decision table · Canonical form · Test · Reduct · Characteristic function

1 Introduction

In this paper, we discuss a way to evaluate the importance of rows for decision tables (importance of objects for datasets) which is based on the study of changes in the set of reducts [3, 4] if we remove the considered row from the decision table. Unfortunately, the problem of constructing the set of reducts for a given decision table is too complicated: the number of reducts can grow exponentially depending on the size of the decision table. However, we can obtain useful indirect information about the set of reducts in polynomial time depending on the size of the input decision table.

We associate a given decision table T with n conditional attributes a characteristic function f_T with n variables that describes the set of tests (superreducts) for T [2]. This is a monotone Boolean function for which the set of lower units correspond to the set of reducts for T. This function can be described not only by the set of lower units but also by the set of upper zeros U_T which can be constructed for T in polynomial time depending on the size of the input decision table. Note that upper zeros correspond to maximal subsets of attributes which are not tests. For a given row r of the table T, we construct the table $T(r)$ obtained from T by the removal of the row r. We find the cardinality of the symmetric difference of the sets U_T and $U_{T(r)}$, $|(U_T \cup U_{T(r)}) \setminus (U_T \cap U_{T(r)})|$, which is considered as the importance of the row r for the table T.

In [2], a way to find the set of upper zeros U_T for the characteristic function f_T was proposed for decision tables with binary attributes. It was used in creation of classifiers. In this paper, we extend it to arbitrary decision tables with categorical attributes, and use it in the evaluation of the importance of rows.

L. Polkowski et al. (Eds.): IJCRS 2017, Part I, LNAI 10313, pp. 376–383, 2017.
DOI: 10.1007/978-3-319-60837-2_31

The created technique can be useful for analysis of decision tables with categorical attributes. It will allow us to point to rows (objects) that have the greatest influence on the formation of the set of reducts. We apply this technique to a number of decision tables from the UCI Machine Learning Repository [1] and find the importance of rows for these tables.

The paper consists of fours sections. In Sect. 2, we consider the main notions, and discuss a way to find the set of upper zeros of the characteristic function and to calculate the importance of rows. Section 3 discusses the experimental results, and Sect. 4 contains short conclusions.

2   Main Notions and Tools

In this section, we consider the main notions, and discuss how to construct the set of upper zeros of the characteristic function for a decision table and how to evaluate the importance of a row.

2.1   Decision Tables, Tests and Reducts

A *decision table* is a rectangular table T whose elements belong to the set $\omega = \{0, 1, 2, \ldots\}$ of nonnegative integers. Columns of this table are labeled with attributes $f_1, \ldots, f_n$. Rows of the table are pairwise different, and each row is labeled with a number from ω (a decision).

A *test for* T is a subset of attributes (columns) such that at the intersection with these columns any two rows with different decisions are different. A *reduct for* T is a test for T for which each proper subset is not a test. It is clear that each test has a reduct as a subset.

2.2   Characteristic Functions

Let T be a decision table with n columns labeled with attributes $f_1, \ldots, f_n$. There exists a one-to-one correspondence between E_2^n, where $E_2 = \{0, 1\}$, and the set of subsets of attributes from T. Let $\bar{\alpha} \in E_2^n$ and $i_1, \ldots, i_m$ be indices of elements from $\bar{\alpha}$ which are equal to 1. Then the set $\{f_{i_1}, \ldots, f_{i_m}\}$ corresponds to the tuple $\bar{\alpha}$.

Let us associate a *characteristic function* $f_T : E_2^n \rightarrow E_2$ with the table T. For $\alpha \in E_2^n$ we have $f_T(\bar{\alpha}) = 1$ if and only if the set of attributes corresponding to $\bar{\alpha}$ is a test for T.

We consider now some notions related to monotone Boolean functions. We define a partial order $\leq$ on the set E_2^n where n is a natural number. Let $\bar{\alpha} = (\alpha_1, \ldots, \alpha_n)$, $\bar{\beta} = (\beta_1, \ldots, \beta_n) \in E_2^n$. Then $\bar{\alpha} \leq \bar{\beta}$ if and only if $\alpha_i \leq \beta_i$ for $i = 1, \ldots, n$. The inequality $\bar{\alpha} < \bar{\beta}$ means that $\bar{\alpha} \leq \bar{\beta}$ and $\bar{\alpha} \neq \bar{\beta}$. Two tuples $\bar{\alpha}$ and $\bar{\beta}$ are *incomparable* if both relations $\bar{\alpha} \leq \bar{\beta}$ and $\bar{\beta} \leq \bar{\alpha}$ do not hold. A function $f : E_2^n \rightarrow E_2$ is called a *monotone Boolean function* if, for every tuples $\bar{\alpha}, \bar{\beta} \in E_2^n$, if $\bar{\alpha} \leq \bar{\beta}$ then $f(\bar{\alpha}) \leq f(\bar{\beta})$.

A tuple $\bar{\alpha} \in E_2^n$ is called an *upper zero* of the monotone Boolean function f if $f(\bar{\alpha}) = 0$ and, for any tuple $\bar{\beta}$ such that $\bar{\alpha} < \bar{\beta}$, we have $f(\bar{\beta}) = 1$. For any $\bar{\alpha} \in E_2^n$, the equality $f(\bar{\alpha}) = 0$ holds if and only if there exists an upper zero $\bar{\beta}$ of f such that $\bar{\alpha} \leq \bar{\beta}$. A tuple $\bar{\alpha} \in E_2^n$ is called a *lower unit* of the monotone Boolean function f if $f(\bar{\alpha}) = 1$ and $f(\bar{\beta}) = 0$ for any tuple $\bar{\beta}$ such that $\bar{\beta} < \bar{\alpha}$. For any $\bar{\alpha} \in E_2^n$, the equality $f(\bar{\alpha}) = 1$ holds if and only if there exists a lower unit $\bar{\beta}$ of f such that $\bar{\beta} \leq \bar{\alpha}$. So the set of upper zeros allows us to describe completely the set of lower units of a monotone Boolean function.

We omit the proof of the following simple statement.

Lemma 1. *For any decision table T, the characteristic function f_T is a monotone Boolean function which does not equal to 0 identically and for which the set of lower units coincides with the set of tuples corresponding to reducts for the table T.*

2.3   Canonical Forms of Decision Tables

Let us associate a decision table $\tau(T)$ with the decision table T. The table $\tau(T)$ has n columns labeled with attributes $f_1, \ldots, f_n$. The first row of $\tau(T)$ is filled by 1. The set of all other rows coincides with the set of all rows of the kind $l(\bar{\delta}_1, \bar{\delta}_2)$ where $\bar{\delta}_1$ and $\bar{\delta}_2$ are arbitrary rows of T labeled with different decisions, and $l(\bar{\delta}_1, \bar{\delta}_2)$ is the row containing at the intersection with the column f_i, $i = 1, \ldots, n$, the number 0 if $\bar{\delta}_1$ and $\bar{\delta}_2$ have different numbers at the intersection with the column f_i, and the number 1 otherwise. The first row of $\tau(T)$ is labeled with the decision 1 . All other rows are labeled with the decision 2.

We denote by $C(T)$ the decision table obtained from $\tau(T)$ by the removing all rows $\bar{\sigma}$ for each of which there exists a row $\bar{\delta}$ of the table $\tau(T)$ that is different from the first row and satisfies the inequality $\bar{\sigma} < \bar{\delta}$. The table $C(T)$ will be called the *canonical form of the table T*.

Lemma 2. *For any decision table T, $f_T = f_{C(T)}$.*

Proof. One can show that $f_T = f_{\tau(T)}$. Let us prove that $f_{\tau(T)} = f_{C(T)}$. It is not difficult to check that $f_{C(T)}(\bar{\alpha}) = 0$ if and only if there exists a row $\bar{\delta}$ of $C(T)$ labeled with the decision 2 for which $\bar{\alpha} \leq \bar{\delta}$. Similar statement is true for the table $\tau(T)$.

It is clear that each row of $C(T)$ is also a row in $\tau(T)$, and equal rows in these tables are labeled with equal decisions. Therefore if $f_{\tau(T)}(\bar{\alpha}) = 1$ then $f_{C(T)}(\bar{\alpha}) = 1$.

Let $f_{C(T)}(\bar{\alpha}) = 1$. We will show that $f_{\tau(T)}(\alpha) = 1$. Let us assume the contrary. Then there exists a row $\bar{\sigma}$ from $\tau(T)$ which is labeled with the decision 2 and for which $\bar{\alpha} \leq \bar{\sigma}$. From the description of $C(T)$ it follows that there exists a row $\bar{\delta}$ from $C(T)$ which is labeled with the decision 2 and for which $\bar{\sigma} \leq \bar{\delta}$. But in this case $\bar{\alpha} \leq \bar{\delta}$ which is impossible. Hence $f_{\tau(T)}(\alpha) = 1$ and $f_{\tau(T)} = f_{C(T)}$. $\square$

Proposition 1. *For any decision table T, the set of rows of the table $C(T)$ with the exception of the first row coincides with the set of upper zeros of the function f_T.*

Proof. Let $\bar{\alpha}$ be an upper zero of the function f_T. Using Lemma 2 we obtain $f_{C(T)}(\bar{\alpha}) = 0$. Therefore there exists a row $\bar{\delta}$ in $C(T)$ which is labeled with the decision 2 and for which $\bar{\alpha} \leq \bar{\delta}$. Evidently, $f_{C(T)}(\bar{\delta}) = 0$. Therefore $f_T(\bar{\delta}) = 0$. Taking into account that $\bar{\alpha}$ is an upper zero of the function f_T we conclude that the inequality $\bar{\alpha} < \bar{\delta}$ does not hold. Hence $\bar{\alpha} = \bar{\delta}$ and $\bar{\alpha}$ is a row of $C(T)$ which is labeled with the decision 2.

Let $\bar{\delta}$ be a row of $C(T)$ different from the first row. Then $f_{C(T)}(\bar{\delta}) = 0$, and by Lemma 2, $f_T(\bar{\delta}) = 0$. Let $\bar{\delta} < \bar{\sigma}$. We will show that $f_T(\bar{\sigma}) = 1$. Let us assume the contrary. Then by Lemma 2, $f_{C(T)}(\bar{\sigma}) = 0$. Therefore there exists a row $\bar{\gamma}$ of $C(T)$ which is labeled with the decision 2 and for which $\bar{\sigma} \leq \bar{\gamma}$ and $\bar{\delta} < \bar{\gamma}$. But this is impossible since any two different rows of $C(T)$ which are labeled with 2 are incomparable. Hence $f_T(\bar{\sigma}) = 1$, and $\bar{\delta}$ is an upper zero of f_T.   □

This proposition gives us an efficient way to construct the set U_T of upper zeros of the function f_T. We construct in polynomial time depending on the size of T the canonical form $C(T)$ of T. By Proposition 1, the set U_T coincides with the set of rows of the table $C(T)$ with the exception of the first row.

2.4 Importance of Rows

The idea of evaluation of row importance is the following. We construct the canonical form $C(T)$ of the table T and the set U_T of upper zeros of the characteristic function f_T corresponding to the table T. We remove a row r from the decision table T. As a result, we obtain new decision table $T(r)$. We construct the canonical form $C(T(r))$ of the table $T(r)$ and the set $U_{T(r)}$ of upper zeros of the characteristic function $f_{T(r)}$ corresponding to the table $T(r)$. The cardinality $|(U_T \cup U_{T(r)}) \setminus (U_T \cap U_{T(r)})|$ of the symmetric difference of the sets U_T and $U_{T(r)}$ will be considered as the *importance of the row r for the table T*.

Example 1. Let T be the decision table depicted in Fig. 1 and r_4 be the fourth row of T. We construct tables $C(T)$, $T(r_4)$, and $C(T(r_4))$ (see Fig. 1)

As a result, we have $U_T = \{(0, 0, 1), (1, 1, 0)\}$ and $U_{T(r_4)} = \{(0, 0, 1), (0, 1, 0)\}$. The symmetric difference of the sets U_T and $U_{T(r_4)}$ is equal to $\{(0, 1, 0), (1, 1, 0)\}$. Therefore the importance of the row r_4 for the table T is equal to 2.

Of course, it would be better to compare the sets of reducts of the tables T and $T(r)$ directly. Unfortunately, there are no efficient algorithms for the construction of the set of reducts. So instead of the comparison of the sets of reducts directly, we compare the sets U_T and $U_{T(r)}$ which describe completely the sets of reducts for the tables T and $T(r)$, respectively. In particular, the importance of the row r for the table T is equal to 0 if and only if the tables T and $T(r)$ have the same sets of reducts.

3 Experimental Results

We did experiments with 10 decision tables from UCI ML Repository [1]. Some preprocessing steps were done before the actual experiments. We removed conditional attributes which have unique value for each row. Each group of identical

$$T = \begin{array}{|ccc|c|} \hline f_1 & f_2 & f_3 & \\ \hline 1 & 1 & 1 & 0 \\ 1 & 0 & 0 & 0 \\ 0 & 0 & 1 & 1 \\ 0 & 0 & 0 & 0 \\ \hline \end{array} \qquad C(T) = \begin{array}{|ccc|c|} \hline f_1 & f_2 & f_3 & \\ \hline 1 & 1 & 1 & 1 \\ 0 & 0 & 1 & 2 \\ 1 & 1 & 0 & 2 \\ \hline \end{array}$$

$$T(r_4) = \begin{array}{|ccc|c|} \hline f_1 & f_2 & f_3 & \\ \hline 1 & 1 & 1 & 0 \\ 1 & 0 & 0 & 0 \\ 0 & 0 & 1 & 1 \\ \hline \end{array} \qquad C(T(r_4)) = \begin{array}{|ccc|c|} \hline f_1 & f_2 & f_3 & \\ \hline 1 & 1 & 1 & 1 \\ 0 & 0 & 1 & 2 \\ 0 & 1 & 0 & 2 \\ \hline \end{array}$$

Fig. 1. Decision table T and tables $C(T)$, $T(r_4)$, and $C(T(r_4))$

rows was replaced with a single row labeled with the most common decision for this group. Missing values for an attribute were replaced with a most common value for this attribute. Table 1 contains information about the considered decision tables including the number of rows, the number of conditional attributes, and the existence of important rows – rows for which the importance is greater than zero.

Table 1. Characteristics of decision tables

Decisiontable	Rows	Attrs	Has important rows?
BALANCE-SCALE	625	4	No
BREAST-CANCER	266	9	Yes
CARS	1728	6	No
HAYES-ROTH-DATA	69	4	No
HOUSE-VOTES-84	279	16	Yes
LYMPHOGRAPHY	148	18	Yes
SOYBEAN-SMALL	47	35	Yes
SPECT-TEST	169	22	Yes
TIC-TAC-TOE	958	9	No
ZOO-DATA	59	16	Yes

For the decision tables BREAST-CANCER, HOUSE-VOTES-84, SPECT-TEST, and ZOO-DATA, we show the results of experiments in the form of range of importance in the left column and the number of rows with importance in this range in the right column.

The decision tables LYMPHOGRAPHY and SOYBEAN-SMALL were not changed during the preprocessing steps. For these tables, for each row with non-zero importance, we show the number of row and its importance.

For the decision table HOUSE-VOTES-84, we have 15 rows with non-zero importance and 264 rows with zero importance (see Table 2).

Table 2. Importance of rows for HOUSE-VOTES-84

Range of importance	No. of rows
0	264
1 to 5	14
14	1

For the decision table SPECT-TEST, there are 18 rows with non-zero importance and 151 rows with zero importance (see Table 3).

Table 3. Importance of rows for SPECT-TEST

Range of importance	No. of rows
0	151
1 to 5	14
6 to 10	3
34	1

For the decision table ZOO-DATA, there are 44 rows with zero importance and 15 rows with non-zero importance (see Table 4).

Table 4. Importance of rows for ZOO-DATA

Range of importance	No. of rows
0	44
1 to 5	11
9	1
12	1
13	1
20	1

For the decision table BREAST-CANCER, there are 262 rows with zero importance and 4 rows with non-zero importance (see Table 5).

For the decision table LYMPHOGRAPHY, there are 41 rows with zero importance and 107 rows with non-zero importance (see Table 6).

For the decision table SOYBEAN-SMALL, there are 3 rows with zero importance and 44 rows with non-zero importance (see Table 7).

Each of the considered tables has rows that are not important (rows with zero importance). If a row is not important, it does not mean that it does not

Table 5. Importance of rows for BREAST-CANCER

Range of importance	No. of rows
0	262
1 to 5	4

Table 6. Importance of rows for LYMPHOGRAPHY

Row No.	Importance of row	Row No.	Importance of row	Row No.	Importance of row	Row No.	Importance of row
146	29	32	7	144	3	21	1
46	26	35	7	7	2	25	1
113	22	41	7	11	2	28	1
75	21	71	7	13	2	34	1
60	17	94	6	18	2	40	1
88	17	131	6	31	2	42	1
10	14	6	5	33	2	43	1
39	14	90	5	45	2	52	1
69	14	97	5	53	2	58	1
9	12	118	5	57	2	67	1
89	12	121	5	63	2	77	1
147	12	17	4	73	2	82	1
81	11	24	4	79	2	83	1
12	10	78	4	98	2	84	1
122	10	107	4	99	2	85	1
16	9	111	4	102	2	91	1
29	9	128	4	103	2	104	1
72	9	138	4	117	2	108	1
96	9	142	4	127	2	112	1
105	9	5	3	129	2	115	1
114	9	27	3	135	2	126	1
116	9	48	3	141	2	133	1
30	8	51	3	143	2	134	1
50	8	92	3	145	2	136	1
56	8	110	3	1	1	139	1
86	8	120	3	19	1	148	1
26	7	124	3	20	1		

Table 7. Importance of rows for SOYBEAN-SMALL

Row No.	Importance of row	Row No.	Importance of row	Row No.	Importance of row	Row No.	Importance of row
4	20	42	11	45	7	18	3
17	17	1	9	3	6	23	3
25	17	7	9	14	5	31	3
26	17	9	9	38	5	43	3
12	15	24	9	44	5	19	2
30	13	34	9	47	5	21	2
41	13	5	8	8	4	37	2
2	11	27	7	11	4	15	1
22	11	29	7	16	4	20	1
28	11	32	7	33	4	36	1
39	11	35	7	10	3	46	1

contain important information: the information contained in the row is "covered" by the information of other rows. If row is important, it means that it contains some unique information relative to other rows, and it deserves special attention, especially if its importance is relatively high (as for the row No. 146 in the decision table LYMPHOGRAPHY which importance is equal to 29).

4 Conclusions

In this paper, we proposed a method for the evaluation of importance of rows for decision tables. This allows us to understand how a given row affects the formation of the set of reducts. In the future, we are planning to consider not only the cardinality of the symmetric difference of the sets U_T and $U_{T(r)}$ but also other measures of difference of these sets.

Acknowledgements. Research reported in this publication was supported by King Abdullah University of Science and Technology (KAUST).

References

1. Lichman, M.: UCI Machine Learning Repository. University of California, Irvine, School of Information and Computer Sciences (2013). http://archive.ics.uci.edu/ml
2. Moshkov, M., Zielosko, B.: Combinatorial Machine Learning - A Rough Set Approach, Studies in Computational Intelligence, vol. 360. Springer, Heidelberg (2011)
3. Pawlak, Z.: Rough Sets - Theoretical Aspects of Reasoning About Data. Kluwer Academic Publishers, Dordrecht (1991)
4. Skowron, A., Rauszer, C.: The discernibility matrices and functions in information systems. In: Słowiński, R. (ed.) Intelligent Decision Support: Handbook of Applications and Advances of the Rough Sets Theory, pp. 331–362. Kluwer Academic Publishers, Dordrecht (1992)

Assignment Reduction of Relation Decision Systems

Guilong Liu[✉]

School of Information Science, Beijing Language and Culture University,
Beijing 100083, China
liuguilong@blcu.edu.cn

Abstract. Assignment reduction is a special reduction type of attribute reduction. It is first studied in decision tables and the reduction approaches are then extended to ordered decision systems. This paper continues to consider such a reduction type in relation decision systems. We propose a new discernibility matrix. Based on the matrix, we give the corresponding reduction algorithm. As special case, we derive respectively the assignment reduction algorithms for decision tables and ordered decision systems.

Keywords: Assignment reduction · Discernibility matrix · Relation decision system · Relative set · Ordered decision system

1 Introduction

Attribute reduction has long been an active research topic with machine learning, pattern recognition and data mining. Rough sets [12,13] have been used to develop attribute reduction algorithms by finding condition attribute reduction in decision tables. In fact, the attribute reduction of decision tables is one of the most important applications of rough sets in databases. Now much work [1,7,9–11,19] has been done on attribute reduction for decision tables.

Pawlak was the first to study attribute reduction for decision tables. Skowron and Rauszer [14,15] first proposed the discernibility matrix based attribute reduction approaches for decision tables. In order to obtain reduction sets, they transform the discernibility function from its conjunctive normal form (CNF) into the disjunctive normal form (DNF), the minimal reduction set of attributes can then be obtained. Now the discernibility matrix based attribute reduction becomes one of the most important attribute reduction methods.

Zhang et al. [20] were the first to study assignment reduction in decision tables. Xu and Zhang [18] extended their research work and proposed an assignment reduction algorithm in ordered information systems. This paper continues to consider such a reduction type and gives an assignment reduction algorithm

G. Liu—This work is supported by the National Natural Science Foundation of China (No. 61272031).

L. Polkowski et al. (Eds.): IJCRS 2017, Part I, LNAI 10313, pp. 384–391, 2017.
DOI: 10.1007/978-3-319-60837-2_32

in relation decision systems. Since the concept of relation decision systems is a common generalization of decision tables and ordered information systems. Our algorithm is also a common extension of their algorithms. In the process of the discernibility matrix based reduction, a difficult step is to find a discernibility matrix, this paper proposes a new discernibility matrix for assignment reduction.

The remainder of the paper is organized as follows. In Sect. 2, we briefly recall some basic concepts and notations of binary relations, relation decision systems and ordered decision systems. Section 3 studies the assignment reduction for relation decision systems and gives a corresponding algorithm. In Sect. 4, as an application of our algorithm, we give an assignment reduction algorithm for decision tables. Section 5 obtains an assignment reduction algorithm for ordered decision systems. Finally, Sect. 6 concludes the paper.

2   Preliminaries

This section reviews briefly the fundamental notation and notions of relations and relation decision systems.

Let U be a universal set and $P(U)$ be the power set of U. Suppose that R is an arbitrary relation on U, the left and right R-relative sets for an element x in U are defined as [2,5,6]

$$l_R(x) = \{y|y \in U, yRx\} \text{ and } r_R(x) = \{y|y \in U, xRy\},$$

respectively. Recall the following terminology [8]: (1) R is reflexive if $x \in r_R(x)$ for each $x \in U$; (2) R is symmetric if $l_R(x) = r_R(x)$ for each $x \in U$; (3) R is transitive if $x \in r_R(y)$ implies that $r_R(x) \subseteq r_R(y)$; and (4) R is an equivalence relation if R is reflexive, symmetric and transitive.

Definition 2.1 [3,4,16,17]. Let U be a universal set and A be a family of arbitrary binary relations on U, then (U, A) is called a relation system. In addition, if $A = C \cup D$, and $C \cap D = \emptyset$, then $(U, C \cup D)$ is called a relation decision system, C is called a condition attribute set, and D is called the decision attribute set. If $R_C = \cap_{R \in C} R \subseteq R_D = \cap_{d \in D} d$, then $(U, C \cup D)$ is called consistent; otherwise, $(U, C \cup D)$ is called inconsistent.

If both C and D consist of equivalence relations, then $(U, C \cup D)$ is just a decision table. In fact, a decision table is one of the most important examples of relation decision systems. Thus a relation decision system is a significant generalization of decision tables.

Definition 2.2 [18]. Let (U, A) be a relation system.

(1) If the domain of $a \in A$ is ordered according to a decreasing or increasing preference, then a is called a criterion.
(2) If each attribute $a \in A$ is a criterion, then (U, A) is called an ordered information system(OIS).

(3) If (U, A) is an ordered information system, $A = C \cup D$ and $C \cap D = \emptyset$. Then (U, A) is called an ordered decision system.

For ordered decision systems, we always assume that the domain of each $a \in A$ is ordered according to an increasing preference, for a decreasing preference, we have similar results.

Let $(U, C \cup D)$ be a relation decision system, from now on, we always assume that $U = \{x_1, x_2, \cdots, x_n\}$ is a non-empty finite universal set, $A = \{a_1, a_2, \cdots, a_m\}$ is a non-empty finite condition attribute set and D is a non-empty finite decision attribute set. For the sake of simplicity, we always assume $D = \{d\}$ in the sequel. With every $\emptyset \neq B \subseteq A$, we associate a relation $R_B = \{(x, y) | x, y \in U, (x, y) \in R \text{ for each } R \in B\}$.

3   An Assignment Reduction Algorithm for Relation Decision Systems

This section studies an assignment reduction algorithm for relation decision systems. Let $(U, C \cup D)$ be a relation decision system, denote

$$\delta_C(x) = \{r_{R_D}(y) | r_{R_D}(y) \cap r_{R_C}(x) \neq \emptyset\}.$$

Proposition 3.1. Let $(U, C \cup D)$ be a relation decision system.

(1) If $r_{R_D}(y) \in \delta_C(x)$, then $r_{R_D}(y) \neq \emptyset$ and $r_{R_C}(x) \neq \emptyset$.
(2) If $B \subseteq C$ and $r_{R_B}(x) \subseteq r_{R_B}(y)$, then $\delta_B(x) \subseteq \delta_B(y)$ for $x, y \in U$.
(3) If $E \subseteq F \subseteq C$, then $\delta_F(x) \subseteq \delta_E(x)$ for each $x \in U$.

Proof. Straightforward.

Zhang et al. [20] studied the assignment reduction for decision tables, Xu and Zhang [18] extended their approaches to the ordered decision systems. Now we begin to consider this reduction type in relation decision systems. We first give the definition of the assignment reduction for relation decision systems.

Definition 3.1. Let $(U, C \cup D)$ be a relation decision system with $B \subseteq C$. B is called an assignment reduction of C if B satisfies the following conditions:

(1) $\delta_C(x) = \delta_B(x)$ for each $x \in U$.
(2) For any $\emptyset \neq B' \subset B$, $\delta_C(x) \neq \delta_{B'}(x)$ for some $x \in U$.

In order to obtain an assignment reduction algorithm for a relation decision system $(U, C \cup D)$, we define the corresponding discernibility matrix $M = (m_{ij})_{n \times n}$ as follows.

$$m_{ij} = \begin{cases} \{R | R \in C, (x_i, x_j) \notin R\}, & r_{R_D}(y) \notin \delta_C(x_i), x_j \in r_{R_D}(y) \text{ for some } y \in U. \\ \emptyset, & otherwise \end{cases}$$

We have the following lemma.

Lemma 3.1. Let $(U, C \cup D)$ be a relation decision system. If $r_{R_D}(y) \notin \delta_C(x_i)$ and $x_j \in r_{R_D}(y)$ for some $y \in U$, then $m_{ij} \neq \emptyset$.

Proof. If $m_{ij} = \emptyset$, then $(x_i, x_j) \in R$ for each $R \in C$, that is, $x_i R_C x_j$. Since $r_{R_D}(y) \notin \delta_C(x_i)$, we have $r_{R_C}(x_i) \cap r_{R_D}(y) = \emptyset$, however, $x_j \in r_{R_C}(x_i) \cap r_{R_D}(y)$, this is a contradiction.   □

Theorem 3.1. Let $(U, C \cup D)$ be a relation decision system with $\emptyset \neq B \subseteq C$. Then the following conditions are equivalent.

(1) $\delta_C(x) = \delta_B(x)$ for each $x \in U$.
(2) If $m_{ij} \neq \emptyset$, then $B \cap m_{ij} \neq \emptyset$.

Proof. (1) $\Rightarrow$ (2): Suppose that $m_{ij} \neq \emptyset$ and $m_{ij} \cap B = \emptyset$, by the definition of the discernibility matrix, we assume $r_{R_D}(y) \notin \delta_C(x_i)$ and $x_j \in r_{R_D}(y)$. Note that $B \cap m_{ij} = \emptyset$ implies $x_i R_B x_j$, that is, $x_j \in r_{R_B}(x_i)$. By condition (1), $r_D(y) \notin \delta_B(x_i)$, so $r_{R_D}(y) \cap r_{R_B}(x_i) = \emptyset$. This is a contradiction to $x_j \in r_{R_D}(y) \cap r_{R_B}(x_i)$.
    (2) $\Rightarrow$ (1): Since $B \subseteq C$, we have $R_C \subseteq R_B$, thus $\delta_C(x_i) \subseteq \delta_B(x_i)$ for each $x_i \in U$. Now we need to show $\delta_B(x_i) \subseteq \delta_C(x_i)$.
    Suppose that $r_{R_D}(y) \notin \delta_C(x_i)$, then $r_{R_C}(x_i) \cap r_{R_D}(y) = \emptyset$. If $x_j \in r_{R_D}(y)$, by Lemma 3.1, $m_{ij} \neq \emptyset$, using condition (3), $m_{ij} \cap B \neq \emptyset$, that is, $(x_i, x_j) \notin R_B$, so $x_j \notin r_{R_B}(x_i)$ and $r_{R_B}(x_i) \cap r_{R_D}(y) = \emptyset$. Hence, $r_{R_D}(y) \notin \delta_B(x_i)$, this proves $\delta_B(x_i) \subseteq \delta_C(x_i)$ and $\delta_B(x_i) = \delta_C(x_i)$.   ⊓

By using Theorem 3.1, we have the following corollary.

Corollary 3.1. Let $(U, C \cup D)$ be a relation decision system with $\emptyset \neq B \subseteq C$, then B is an assignment reduction of C if and only if it is a minimal subset satisfying $m_{ij} \cap B \neq \emptyset$ for any $m_{ij} \neq \emptyset$.
    According to Corollary 3.1, we propose an assignment reduction algorithm for a relation decision system $(U, C \cup D)$ as follows.

(1) Compute a discernibility matrix $M = (m_{ij})_{n \times n}$.
(2) Transform the discernibility function f from its CNF $f = \prod(\sum m_{ij})$ into a DNF $f = \sum_{t=1}^{s}(\prod B_t), (B_t \subseteq C)$.
(3) $Red(C) = \{B_1, B_2, \cdots, B_s\}$ and $Core(C) = \cap_{t=1}^{s} B_t$.

End the algorithm.
We illustrate the algorithm introduced previously with a simple example

Example 3.1. Let $(U, C \cup D)$ be a relation decision system, $U = \{1, 2, 3, 4, 5\}$, $C = \{R_1, R_2, R_3, R_4\}$, and $D = \{d\}$, where $R_1 = \{(2, 1), (2, 3), (2, 4), (3, 2), (4, 2), (4, 5), (5, 2), (5, 5)\}$, $R_2 = \{(1, 4), (2, 1), (2, 3), (2, 4), (4, 1), (4, 2), (4, 5), (5, 2), (5, 4)\}$, $R_3 = \{(2, 1), (2, 3), (4, 2), (4, 5), (5, 2), (5, 3), (5, 5)\}$, $R_4 = \{(2, 1), (2, 3), (2, 4), (4, 2), (4, 5), (5, 2), (5, 5)\}$, and $d = \{(1, 2), (2, 1), (2, 3), (2, 4), (3, 1), (3, 5), (4, 4), (4, 5), (5, 1), (5, 3), (5, 4)\}$.

By direct computation, all relative sets are shown in Table 1.

Table 1. Relative sets

i	1	2	3	4	5
$r_D(i)$	$\{2\}$	$\{1,3,4\}$	$\{1,5\}$	$\{4,5\}$	$\{1,3,4\}$
$r_C(i)$	$\emptyset$	$\{1,3\}$	$\emptyset$	$\{2,5\}$	$\{2\}$
$\delta_C(i)$	$\emptyset$	$\{r_{R_D}(2), r_{R_D}(3), r_{R_D}(5)\}$	$\emptyset$	$\{r_{R_D}(1), r_{R_D}(3), r_{R_D}(4)\}$	$\{r_{R_D}(1)\}$

(1) We first compute the 5×5 discernibility matrix $M = (m_{ij})_{5 \times 5}$

$$
M = \begin{pmatrix}
C & C & C & C & C \\
\emptyset & C & \emptyset & \{R_3\} & C \\
C & \{R_2, R_3, R_4\} & C & C & C \\
\{R_1, R_3, R_4\} & \emptyset & C & C & \emptyset \\
C & \emptyset & \{R_1, R_2, R_4\} & \{R_1, R_3, R_4\} & \{R_2\}
\end{pmatrix}.
$$

(2) We then transform the discernibility function

$$f = (R_1 + R_3 + R_4)R_3(R_2 + R_3 + R_4)(R_1 + R_3 + R_4)(R_1 + R_2 + R_4)(R_1 + R_3 + R_4)R_2$$

from its CNF into a DNF
$$f = R_2 R_3.$$

(3) Thus $\{R_2, R_3\}$ is a unique assignment reduction of C.

4　An Application to Decision Tables

In this section, we consider the assignment reduction algorithm for decision tables as a special case. Let $(U, C \cup D)$ be a decision table, then both C and D consist of equivalence relations on U, thus $r_C(x) = l_C(x) = [x]_C$ is an equivalent class of $x \in U$. The following definition comes from Zhang et al. [20].

Definition 4.1. Let $(U, C \cup D)$ be a decision table with $\emptyset \neq B \subseteq C$. B is called an assignment reduction of C if B satisfies the following conditions:

(1) $\delta_C(x) = \delta_B(x)$ for each $x \in U$.
(2) For any $\emptyset \neq B' \subset B$, $\delta_C(x) \neq \delta_{B'}(x)$ for some $x \in U$.

The corresponding discernibility matrix $M = (m_{ij})_{n \times n}$ becomes as follows.

$$
m_{ij} = \begin{cases} \{a | a \in C, a(x_i) \neq a(x_j)\}, & [y]_D \not\subseteq \delta_C(x_i), D(x_j) = D(y) \text{ for some } y \in U \\ \emptyset, & otherwise \end{cases}
$$

The following example illustrates our algorithm.

Example 4.1. Let $(U, C \cup D)$ be a decision table as shown in Table 2. Where $U = \{x_1, x_2, x_3, x_4, x_5, x_6\}$, $C = \{a_1, a_2, a_3, a_4, a_5\}$ and $D = \{d\}$.

Table 2. A decision table

U	a_1	a_2	a_3	a_4	a_5	d
x_1	1	0	1	1	1	1
x_2	1	0	1	1	1	2
x_3	0	0	0	0	1	1
x_4	1	1	1	0	1	1
x_5	2	1	2	0	1	2
x_6	0	1	2	0	0	2

(1) We first compute the 6×6 discernibility matrix $M = (m_{ij})_{6 \times 6}$

$$M = \begin{pmatrix} \emptyset & \emptyset & \emptyset & \emptyset & \emptyset & \emptyset \\ \emptyset & \emptyset & \emptyset & \emptyset & \emptyset & \emptyset \\ \emptyset & \{a_1, a_3, a_4\} & \emptyset & \emptyset & \{a_1, a_2, a_3\} & \{a_2, a_3, a_5\} \\ \emptyset & \{a_2, a_4\} & \emptyset & \emptyset & \{a_1, a_3\} & \{a_1, a_3, a_5\} \\ \{a_1, a_2, a_3, a_4\} & \emptyset & \{a_1, a_2, a_3\} & \{a_1, a_3\} & \emptyset & \emptyset \\ C & \emptyset & \{a_2, a_3, a_5\} & \{a_1, a_3, a_5\} & \emptyset & \emptyset \end{pmatrix}$$

(2) We then transform the discernibility function

$$f = (a_2 + a_4)(a_1 + a_3)(a_2 + a_3 + a_5)$$

from its CNF into a DNF

$$f = a_1 a_2 + a_2 a_3 + a_3 a_4 + a_1 a_4 a_5.$$

(3) Thus, $\{a_1, a_2\}, \{a_2, a_3\}, \{a_3, a_4\}$ and $\{a_1, a_4, a_5\}$ are the four assignment reduction sets.

5 An Application to Ordered Information Systems

This section will give an assignment reduction algorithm for ordered decision systems. Since an ordered decision system is a special case of relation decision systems, we can apply the previous result to an ordered decision system.

Let $(U, C \cup D)$ be an ordered decision system with $B \subseteq C$, we denote $R_B = \{(x, y) | a(x_i) \leq a(y), \forall a \in B\}$ and $R_D = \{(x, y) | a(x_i) \leq a(y), \forall a \in D\}$. Clearly, R_B and R_D are dominance relations on U.

Definition 4.2. Let $(U, C \cup D)$ be an ordered decision system with $B \subseteq C$. B is called an assignment reduction of C if B satisfies the following conditions:

(1) $\delta_C(x) = \delta_B(x)$ for each $x \in U$.
(2) For any $\emptyset \neq B' \subset B$, $\delta_C(x) \neq \delta_{B'}(x)$ for some $x \in U$.

We present its assignment reduction algorithm via the following example.

Table 3. An ordered decision system

U	a_1	a_2	a_3	a_4	d
x_1	3	2	2	2	3
x_2	1	2	1	3	2
x_3	3	1	2	2	3
x_4	2	0	1	1	0
x_5	0	1	2	0	2

Example 5.1. Let $(U, C \cup D)$ be an ordered decision system as shown in Table 3. Where $U = \{x_1, x_2, x_3, x_4, x_5\}$, $C = \{a_1, a_2, a_3, a_4\}$ and $D = \{d\}$. We note that each attribute can be viewed as a dominance relation on U via

$$(x_i, x_j) \in R \text{ if and only if } R(x_i) \leq r(x_j) \text{ for } R \in \{a_1, a_2, a_3, a_4, d\}.$$

Thus $(U, C \cup D)$ is a relation decision system. The algorithm of Sect. 3 can be used to compute the assignment reduction.

(1) We first compute the 6×6 discernibility matrix $M = (m_{ij})_{5 \times 5}$

$$M = \begin{pmatrix} \emptyset & \emptyset & \emptyset & \emptyset & \emptyset \\ \{a_4\} & \emptyset & \{a_2, a_4\} & \emptyset & \emptyset \\ \emptyset & \emptyset & \emptyset & \emptyset & \emptyset \\ \emptyset & \emptyset & \emptyset & \emptyset & \emptyset \\ \emptyset & \emptyset & \emptyset & \emptyset & \emptyset \end{pmatrix}.$$

(2) We then transform the discernibility function $f = a_4(a_2 + a_4)$ from its CNF into a DNF $f = a_4$.

(3) Thus $\{a_4\}$ is a unique assignment reduction of C.

6   Conclusions

A relation decision system is a natural and important extension of decision tables. In this paper, the assignment reduction theory based on general binary relations has been established. We obtained an assignment reduction algorithm for relation decision systems. The algorithm can find all reduction sets for a relation decision system. As special cases, we derived the corresponding assignment reduction algorithms for decision tables and ordered information systems. That is, we provide a unified assignment reduction algorithm for decision tables and ordered information systems. Our future work will concentrate on real applications of the proposed algorithms.

References

1. Inuiguchi, M., Yoshioka, Y., Kusunoki, Y.: Variable-precision dominance-based rough set approach and attribute reduction. Int. J. Approx. Reason. **50**, 1199–1214 (2009)
2. Liu, G.L.: Using one axiom to characterize rough set and fuzzy rough set approximations. Inf. Sci. **223**, 285–296 (2013)
3. Liu, G.L., Li, L., Yang, J.T., Feng, Y.B., Zhu, K.: Attribute reduction approaches for general relation decision systems. Pattern Recogn. Lett. **65**, 81–87 (2015)
4. Liu, G.L., Hua, Z., Zou, J.Y.: A unified reduction algorithm based on invariant matrices for decision tables. Knowl.-Based Syst. **109**, 84–89 (2016)
5. Liu, G.L., Sai, Y.: Invertible approximation operators of generalized rough sets and fuzzy rough sets. Inf. Sci. **180**, 2221–2229 (2010)
6. Liu, G.L., Hua, Z., Chen Z.H.: A general reduction algorithm for relation decision systems and its applications. Knowl.-Based Syst. (in press). http://dx.doi.org/10.1016/j.knosys.2016.11.027
7. Liu, J.N.K., Hua, Y., He, Y.: A set covering based approach to find the reduct of variable precision rough set. Inf. Sci. **275**, 83–100 (2014)
8. Grassmann, W.K., Tremblay, J.P.: Logic and Discrete Mathematics, A computer Science Perspective. Prentice-Hall, Upper Saddle River (1996)
9. Mi, J.S., Wu, W.Z., Zhang, W.X.: Approaches to knowledge reduction based on variable precision rough set model. Inf. Sci. **159**, 255–272 (2004)
10. Mieszkowicz-Rolka, A., Rolka, L.: Variable precision rough sets in analysis of inconsistent decision tables. In: Rutkowski, L., Kacprzyk, J. (eds.) Advances in Soft Computing. Physica-Verlag, Heidelberg (2003)
11. Mieszkowicz-Rolka, A., Rolka, L.: Variable precision fuzzy rough sets. In: Peters, J.F., Skowron, A., Grzymała-Busse, J.W., Kostek, B., Świniarski, R.W., Szczuka, M.S. (eds.) Transactions on Rough Sets 1. LNCS, vol. 3100, pp. 144–160. Springer, Heidelberg (2004). doi:10.1007/978-3-540-27794-1_6
12. Pawlak, Z.: Rough sets. Int. J. Comput. Inf. Sci. **11**, 341–356 (1982)
13. Pawlak, Z.: Rough Sets: Theoretical Aspects of Reasoning about Data. Kluwer Academic Publishers, Boston (1991)
14. Skowron, A.: Boolean reasoning for decision rules generation. In: Komorowski, J., Raś, Z.W. (eds.) ISMIS 1993. LNCS, vol. 689, pp. 295–305. Springer, Heidelberg (1993). doi:10.1007/3-540-56804-2_28
15. Skowron, A., Rauszer, C.: The discernibility matrices and functions in information systems. In: Slowinski, R. (ed.) Intelligent Decision Support, Handbook of Applications and Advances of the Rough Sets Theory, pp. 331–362. Springer, Heidelberg (1992). doi:10.1007/978-94-015-7975-9_21
16. Wang, C.Z., Wu, C.X., Chen, D.G.: A systematic study on attribute reduction with rough sets based on general binary relations. Inf. Sci. **178**(9), 2237–2261 (2008)
17. Wang, C.Z., He, Q., Chen, D.G., Hu, Q.H.: A novel method for attribute reduction of covering decision systems. Inf. Sci. **254**, 181–196 (2014)
18. Xu, W.H., Zhang, W.X.: Knowledge reductions in inconsistent information systems based on dominance relation. Comput. Sci. (In Chin.) **33**(2), 182–184 (2006)
19. Ziarko, W.: Variable precision rough set model. J. Comput. Syst. Sci. **46**, 39–59 (1993)
20. Zhang, W.X., Mi, J.S., Wu, W.Z.: Approaches to knowledge reductions in inconsistent systems. Int. J. Intell. Syst. **18**, 989–1000 (2003)

Automatically Determining the Popularity of a Song

Costin Chiru[(⊠)] and Oana-Georgiana Popescu

Department of Computer Science and Engineering,
University Politehnica of Bucharest,
313 Splaiul Independentei, Bucharest, Romania
costin.chiru@cs.pub.ro, oana.popescu28@gmail.com

Abstract. The purpose of this paper is to identify a connection, if such a connection exists, between the sequence of sounds and the lyrics of a melody and its popularity with the help of machine learning techniques. The melody popularity will be quantified as the number of views and number of "like" votes on the YouTube platform, where users can upload, view and vote videos. This analysis will reveal whether the two indicators from the YouTube platform are more influenced by the words or sounds of the songs. This work may help the producers from the music industry since the popularity of a melody (determined by analyzing a large set of songs) might be a very important aspect to be considered when deciding whether to make and launch a musical product or not.

Keywords: Machine learning · Data mining · Songs' popularity · SVM · KNN · Logistic regression · Fourier transform · YouTube

1 Introduction

Nowadays, music is part of people's lives and is present in various actions that we do: from relaxation, to learning, to promoting various products to attract buyers, and to many others. Socially, the music manages to bring together people who share the same musical preferences, through the existence of concerts where listeners gather, communicate and have the pleasant feeling of belonging to a group. However, even when one listens music in solitude, the effect is similar, because unconsciously, the feeling of loneliness fades away due to the feeling that someone is present through the song.

It is not clear when or why music appeared, but there is evidence of its presence since Paleolithic, when our ancestors were building whistles from animal bones. What makes music different from other sounds that we hear in nature is the organization of sounds in a certain form and the expression of attitudes and feelings through it.

What makes a song pleasant or not to a person is related to a complex combination of micro-emotions related to the history of his/her personal experiences. Neurology highlights the influence that music has on people: "During periods of intense perceptual engagement, such as being enraptured by music, activity in the prefrontal cortex, which generally focuses on introspection, shuts down" [1]. Therefore, it happens that the person listening to music to feel in a parallel universe during these intense moments, this condition being rarely achieved and being similar to a state of deep meditation.

© Springer International Publishing AG 2017
L. Polkowski et al. (Eds.): IJCRS 2017, Part I, LNAI 10313, pp. 392–406, 2017.
DOI: 10.1007/978-3-319-60837-2_33

Another study [2] in which the neuroscientists monitored muscle movement and the physical states of the people who made effort while listening to music, led to the conclusion that music distracts the brain from the sensation of pain felt because of doing exercises, so the body becomes more resistant to effort under the action of music. Thus, this study has contributed to the therapeutic effect of music: "music makes strenuous physical activities less exhausting" [2].

Different studies have shown what happens to the human brain when a melody is liked by that person and what are the levels of relaxation and concentration that are reached during listening to music, but why a song is perceived as pleasant remains unknown and thus it attracts the curiosity and interest of researchers on this topic.

The current paper aims to identify a connection between a song's lyrics and music and its popularity to establish, using machine learning methods, if the two evident elements of a melody determine people appreciate a melody. In this context, the popularity will be evaluated using the YouTube platform through the number of views and number of "like" votes associated to each melody by users.

The study from this paper may help the producers from the music industry, the popularity of a melody, determined by analyzing a large set of songs from the same genre, representing an index to consider before launching a musical product.

The musical genres are very different in terms of sounds that compose the songs' lyrics and melody, but also the groups of listeners have their own characteristics: age, education level, social environment, etc. To reduce the variability, we restricted our analysis to a single musical genre: the pop-dance music. We chose this genre because its songs are more common, and artists are promoted on radio, television, these songs easily reaching the listeners.

The pop music has its origins in the 1950s in UK and US and derives mainly from the "rock and roll" music genre. It is a music genre that encourages the dance due to the energetic rhythm and melodic line that are produced by the electric guitar, piano or organ and drums. The favorite subjects of this genre are love, freedom, sorrow and success.

An element that explains the popularity of this genre is that the public can easily remember the melody and the lyrics, as they have a simple and repeatable structure. It is a music genre that is constantly changing in an attempt to satisfy a constantly wider audience so that to give possibility to people to express and find themselves through pop songs. Because this music is trying to cover general preferences of the masses of people, this kind of music sells very well and is a reference for the affective mood and trends of the population, especially young people, to whom it is directed to.

Another characteristic of the pop music refers to the fact that the use of technology and songs recording is preferred at the expense of live music. This way, they can be easily played on commercial radios to attract large audiences, making it a higher probability the listener's personality to be reflected to some extent in the atmosphere created by song, which further stirs psychologically reactions.

As already mentioned, the popularity of songs is evaluated starting from the YouTube platform. YouTube has become a social network for sharing videos of various types: tutorials, commercials, music, shows, movies, etc., having over a billion unique users and daily displaying hundreds of millions of hours of video[1]. The resources loaded on the platform receive an almost immediate reaction of users and thus, an important indicator in determining the popularity of a song is the success it enjoys on YouTube.

The next section will present a brief description of similar applications, to highlight the existing approaches and to set the expectation regarding the results accuracy. In Sect. 3 we will describe how we gathered the data required for this experiment and how we extracted the sounds frequencies of the songs. The next section explains the algorithms used to create the models for predicting songs popularity, while Sect. 5 shows the results of these algorithms. The paper will end with our final conclusions and with the next steps that can be undertaken to extend the presented research.

2 Similar Applications

A similar application for establishing if a song will become popular amongs listeners is "ScoreAHit"[2], developed by the member of the MIR team of the University of Bristol. The project aimed to predict which songs will be part of the weekly list of the most popular songs in the UK. The prediction is based only on information extracted from the melody of the songs, and to determine whether a song will become a hit or not are considered 23 predictors including: the loudness of the song, the state that the song induces, if the song may be danced or not, how energetic it is, the length, the time signature and the tempo of the song [3].

De Bie and his colleagues extracted all the songs from the official UK top 40 singles charts over the past 50 years, computed the predictors weights based on the success that the songs had, and finally, for a new song they could compute a score using the learnt weights that was used to classify it as being a hit or not.

The application had an accuracy of 60%, being applied on pop songs from 1960 to 2010, without considering the artist popularity, the lyrics, the song advertising, or other social factors.

Another project having the same purpose was "Hit Song Science" (HSS)[3], which was an application from Polyphonic HMI, a subsidiary of a Spanish company specialized in the analysis of mathematic and physics as a means for solving complex business problems.HSS appeared in 2002 and tried to find out a mathematical model for each song which became popular, and based on these models to build clusters of songs. Thus, the application computes for new songs how close they are to different clusters using statistics, providing a score on the scale from 1 to 10 of how popular the song will become.

The authors did not provide information about the product's accuracy and suggested that their product should be used together with the advertising plan of the music producers to successfully predict the songs' popularity. However, in 2008, their article

---

[1] https://www.youtube.com/yt/press/en-GB/statistics.html [accessed: February 2nd, 2017].

[2] http://www.scoreahit.com [accessed: February 2nd, 2017].

[3] http://polyphonichmi.blogspot.ro/p/about-company.html [accessed: February 2nd, 2017].

[4] presented an experiment realized on 32,000 songs from various musical genre, using three different kinds of predictors: a generic one using information from the song melody extracted in the form of bag-of-frames; aspecific acoustic predictor developed by Sony for the successful songs; and a human predictor based on manually annotated songs, using a set of 632 labels, out of which 3 contained information about the song popularity and thus receiving higher weights.

The purpose of the experiment was the classification of the song in one of three classes of popularity (low, medium and high), this information being extracted from hit charts and records of music history. For classification were used two different algorithms: a random one and the Support Vector Machines (SVM) algorithm using the Radial-Basis Function (RBF) kernel. Since the data was unbalanced, the authors used F-score instead of accuracy and reported values in the range of 40–50%: for the human data, the results had an F-score of 41% for low popularity, 37% for medium one and 3% for high popularity. For the acoustic predictors, the F-score varied from 0 to 74% in the case of generic predictors and to 76% for the specific ones.

When comparing the accuracy of SVM and the random algorithms, the results were not satisfactory. Thus, Pachet and Roy [4] concluded that the principle on which the previously built application was based was not correct and that the predictors that were considered were not enough to categorize the songs based on their popularity.

3 Data Acquisition

The prediction of the success of different songs with the help of machine learning algorithms requires a large data set for determining whether there is any connection between the song's popularity and its melody and lyrics. The results provided by the machine learning algorithms depend entirely on the chosen data set and its diversity. Therefore, in this section, we will detail the process of obtaining the data set by extracting the song lyrics and melody, along with the mechanism of extracting the information related to the sounds of the melody.

The first step in obtaining the data was to identify the names of dance-pop music artists, both famous and less renown, having a list of songs that have enjoyed different degrees of popularity. These names were extracted from the Wikipedia list of dance-pop artists[4]. The next step consisted in extracting the list of songs belonging to each artist and afterwards were retrieved the lyrics and melody for each song. Finally, we extracted the main frequencies from the melody of each song.

3.1 Lyrics Retrieval

Since we were unable to find an open-source database containing songs lyrics, we identified the LyricsMania[5] platform that can be easily browsed using a web crawler for retrieving the songs and their lyrics for the previously extracted artists. The structure

---

[4] https://en.wikipedia.org/wiki/List_of_dance-pop_artists [accessed: February 2nd, 2017].

[5] http://www.lyricsmania.com/ [accessed: February 2nd, 2017].

of the website is very friendly, having a page for each artist, where one can find the list of songs of that artist, along with links to web pages containing the lyrics of each song.

Using a Python crawler and considering the above structure, we managed to build a set of documents, each containing the lyrics of a single song. However, the data about artists and lyrics that are available on the LyricsMania platform are input by the users of the site and therefore the obtained set of lyrics required a cleaning step to eliminate errors, such as: incomplete lyrics, duplicate lyrics or lyrics of several songs grouped under a single song. Moreover, using the Python package PyEnchant[6] to detect words that are not in English, we filtered out the songs that didn't have English lyrics, in order not to influence the accuracy of the algorithms.

3.2   Extraction of the Main Frequencies from the Songs' Melody

Before explaining how we extracted the frequencies from the songs' melody, we need to introduce a couple of concepts from the domain of signal and sounds processing. A signal represents a quantity of information (called amplitude) that varies in time or space, such as: the phone signal, the light wave, the audio of a song, etc. The sound is a variation in air pressure over time and it is called acoustic or musical signal when it comes to music. The human ear perceives only the sounds having frequencies between 20 Hz–20 kHz [5]. The sampling frequency is the number of discrete signal values (samples) per second of the sound and is measured in hertz.

After obtaining the lyrics corpus, we extracted the frequencies with the highest amplitude from every analysed song using the Time Fourier Transform. To obtain this information, we used audio files in the Waveform Audio File Format (WAV) format, having a sampling frequency of 44.1 kHz[7], the frequency generally used for high-quality audio files to allow the reconstruction of the continuous signal from the discreet one with very high fidelity. According to the Nyquist–Shannon sampling theorem [6], for this sampling frequency, the musical sounds have a frequency up to 22 kHz, and cover the entire range of frequencies that the human ear can hear. A second from the signal extracted from a WAV file is presented in Fig. 1.

The Fourier transform is a function for decomposing a signal into a sum of simple sinusoidal functions (sine and cosine functions). For sound waves, Fourier transform gives the frequencies of the sounds that make up that wave. In this research, we applied discrete Fourier transform signal (DFT) as the sound signal requiring decomposition was sampled in the WAV file. DFT transforms the representation of the original signal from the domain of discrete time to the one of discrete frequencies. According to [7], if the sampling frequency is fs, then the domain of the definition for the signal representation obtained after DFT is [0, fs].

---

[6] https://pythonhosted.org/pyenchant/ [accessed: February 2nd, 2017].

[7] http://www.fon.hum.uva.nl/praat/manual/sampling_frequency.html [accessed: February 2nd, 2017].

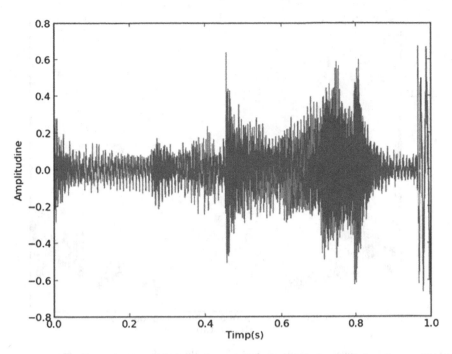

Fig. 1. A second from the original signal from the WAV file, before applying discrete Fourier transform

In this research, we used the C libraries libsndfile[8], for reading the WAV files, and fftw[9], for applying the Fast Fourier Transform which is the faster way of computing the DFT.

After applying DFT we obtained the chart of sound intensity depending on the frequency, which is symmetrical to the central point - 0.5 * fs (see Fig. 2). The first half of the graph, corresponding to the frequencies from the [0, 0.5 * fs] interval, represents the frequency spectrum for the sampled signal for which the DFT was applied, and the second half of the graph is the mirror on the X axis of the first half, adding redundant information [7].

Since the magnitude represents the sound intensity, we extracted, for every second of every song, the frequency with the maximum magnitude, this frequency having the largest weight of all sounds frequencies that are heard in a second. If multiple such frequencies where detected (having the maximum magnitude), only the one with the highest frequency was retained, as the human ear perceives louder the sounds with higher frequencies than the ones with lower frequencies. For example, for the signal from Figs. 1 and 2, the predominant sound frequency was identified to be the one of 344 Hz (see Fig. 3).

---

[8] http://www.mega-nerd.com/libsndfile/ [accessed: February 2nd, 2017].
[9] http://www.fftw.org [accessed: February 2nd, 2017].

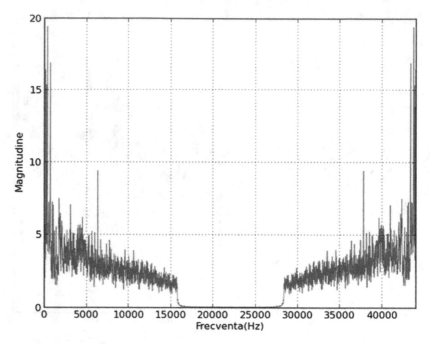

Fig. 2. The frequency spectrum obtained after applying DFT on the sound from Fig. 1

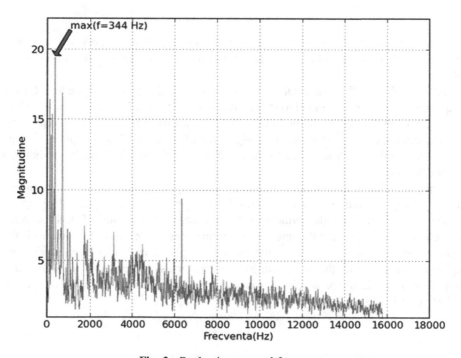

Fig. 3. Predominant sound frequency

3.3 Extracting the Number of Views and Number of "Like" Votes on the YouTube Platform

The next thing to do, after extracting the frequencies from the melody of the songs, was to obtain the data that reflects the degree of popularity of each song from the YouTube platform. To extract this information, we used the available YouTube API for visualizing, adding, deleting or modifying the content from the platform. With the help of this API, we searched the analysed songs on the YouTube platform and from the list of results we selected the first video, along with its ID. Next, we used this ID to obtain the number of views and number of "like" votes. We also interrogated the duration of each song and eliminated the ones having more than five minutes, as these might have been different mixes of multiple songs.

We have chosen to consider the first video from the list returned by the API because this list was ordered by the songs popularity on the YouTube platform, and by choosing it, we hoped to obtain the official version of the analysed song. However, we are aware that the popular songs might be uploaded to YouTube multiple times (different versions from different concerts or even by different singers) which might lead to some errors when the official version of the song is not the most popular one.

A different approach that we investigated was to consider all the versions of a song and to average the results among them. We didn't choose this option from two different reasons: on one hand this would introduce a source of errors, since there might be different singers (or even wannabe singers) who upload their version of the song, leading to a large deviation in terms of number of views and number of "like" votes of the different versions of the analysed song, and thus to less precise results. On the other hand, analysing all the versions of a song would greatly increase the required computation of the application, thus leading to a very large running time.

After extracting the information from YouTube, the data had to be cleaned to eliminate the answers that were returned in the case that no video was available for a given song.

4 Used Algorithms

In this section, we will present the algorithms that were used to determine the influence of lyrics and melody of a song on its popularity.

Machine learning algorithms are applied in more and more areas as they are able to learn from the examples that they see in many activities such as: scientific experiments, fraud detection, medical diagnostics, business processes, etc. The purpose of these algorithms is to identify a pattern or different connections between the characteristics (features) of the training examples, which are called predictors, to classify, diagnose or estimate a value for a new case whose value is unknown.

Two main tasks can be seen in the context of machine learning: classification, where the predictors are combined to generate a binary value (positive/negative) of the target function; and regression, where a continuous function is required as the output of the algorithm. Even though the output of the two task is different, their purpose is similar: to find a model able to map the training example so that to predict the value of the target for a new example. For this task, two kinds of algorithm may be used: parametric and non-parametric [8]. The parametric models are trying to detect a set of weights (w_i) for the available predictors (x_i), as in (1), so that to minimize the error (J (w)), usually computed as the root-mean-square error, between the estimated value (f(x, w)) and the real one (y), as shown in (2).

$$f(x; w) = w_0 + w_1 x_1 + \ldots + w_d x_d = w_0 + x^T w \tag{1}$$

$$J(w) = \frac{1}{n} \sum_{i=1}^{n} (y_i - f(x_i; w))^2 \tag{2}$$

The non-parametric approaches require storing and computing with the entire data set. They are based on the locality assumption, considering that examples having similar values for the predictors should have similar values for the target also. Due to this fact, the non-parametric methods are more flexible, as they do not imply anything about the distribution of the data that is modelled in comparison to the parametric models which are restricted to specific forms that are chosen before actually seing the data. On the other hand, once fitted the parametric models are much more efficient in terms of storage and computation, as they do not require the data anymore, as opposed to the non-parametric methods that have to use all the data all the time to do the required computation.

In the current research, we decided to use algorithms from both categories, and thus we ended up with Logistic Regression and SVM from the category of parametric methods and with K-Nearest Neighbors (KNN) from the class of non-parametric approaches.

4.1   Logistic Regression

Logistic Regression is a model that uses the probabilistic function from (3) to model the transition of the training example from one class to another. In this formula, w_0 is called the bias, while w represents a set of weights that are applied on the different dimensions of the input vector (one weight per dimension). During training, the best values of w_0 and w are computed based on the evidence from the labeled samples.

$$p(x) = \frac{1}{1 + e^{-(w_0 + x^T * w)}} \tag{3}$$

Logistic Regression is mostly used for classification and thus, for a new example (x), it computes the probability of this example to belong to one of the two classes. To decide to which class the example belongs, its computed probability is compared to 0.5: if $p(x) < 0.5$, then x belongs to the negative class; otherwise it belongs to the positive one. This model is very used in practice, as it is very simple and, based on the probability function that it uses, gives very good results in practice [9].

If the logistic regression has to chose between multiple classes, then the "one versus all" technique may be used in order to do the discrimination. In the case of regression, as for the current research, the logistic function maps the training examples as good as possible and for a new test example it outputs the value of the logistic function in that point.

4.2 Support Vector Machines (SVM)

SVM, developed by Vapnik [10], was initially designed to solve classification problems and afterwards it was successfully extended for regression problems. In the case of classification with two classes, if the data is linearly separable, SVM finds a hyperplane that divides the training examples in the two classes. From the infinity of available hyperplanes, SVM chooses the one which maximizes the distance to any of the examples from the two classes. However, most of the times, the data is not linearly separable and thus it has to be translated from the initial space in a different one, with the help of kernels, so that in the new space to be linearly separable.

Kernels are special functions that compute the distance between two vectors as their product in the new space, but using their coordinates from the initial space. These distances are afterwards used as weights to obtain the class of a new instance by determining to which degree the samples from the training set should contribute to the classification of this new instance.

This way, kernels optimize the computation and allow the data to become linearly separable. The most popular kernel functions are polinomials, sigmoid and Gaussian, also called RBF. In this paper, we used the RBF kernels, having the formula presented in (4), where w and y represent two multi-dimensional vectors, $\|x-y\|^2$ represents the squared Euclidean distance between them, while γ is a parameter that is chosen by the user.

$$K(x, y) = e^{-\gamma\|x-y\|^2} \tag{4}$$

In the case of regression, the algorithm is called Support Vector Machines Regression. Being given the training data $D = \{(y_i, t_i)|i = 1, 2, .., n\}$, where y_i are the training points and t_i are the targets for y_i, the purpose of SVM Regression is to find a function g(y) which approximates the relation that exists between the data from the training set and to use this function to compute the target t for a new testing point y. For finding g(y), the algorithm defines a loss function L(t, g(y)) that is minimized. An example of such a loss function is the Vapnik function (5) that is called "epsilon-insensitive loss function" [11], where $\varepsilon > 0$ is a constant controlling the acceptable noise for the regression.

$$L(t, g(y)) = \begin{cases} 0, & if \quad |t - g(y)| \leq \varepsilon \\ |t - g(y)| \quad - & \varepsilon, \; otherwise \end{cases} \tag{5}$$

The regression algorithm ignores the errors, as long as they are lower than ε but penalizes larger errors with the help of the loss function.

4.3 K-Nearest Neighbors (KNN)

In the case of classification, the KNN algorithm identifies the closest neighbors of the test example, and then, using the "majority" voting, it identifies the predominant class and attributes this class to the new instance. Fir regression, the algorithms determines the closest k neighbors and computes the mean of their values. The obtained value is the value of the testing point. This method may be improved starting from the idea that the influence of the neighbors is not equal. Thus, the influence of the neighbors may be weighted by the distance to the testing point. To compute the distance between different points, different metrics may be used [12]: Euclidian Distance, Manhattan Distance, Minkowski Distance, Chebyshev Distance, etc.

Since the classic version of this algorithm (to iterate through all the training set and compute all the distances) is very slow and computational intense, some improvements were developed. One possible option is to use kd-tree and binary search [13]. Another option is to use an approximation of the KNN algorithm, called Locality-sensitive hashing [14] that uses hash functions to probabilistically group similar examples.

The key element of the KNN algorithm is the parameter K that establishes the number of neighbors that are analysed in order to predict the class/value of the new sample. The alue of this parameter highly influences the prediction quality and thus it should be carefully chosen. One method for determining the value of K is through cross-validation.

5 Obtained Results

In this section, we will present the results that we obtained by applying the previously described algorithms on the extracted data set of songs for determining their popularity based on the number of views and the number of "like" votes. For this, we used the available algorithms implementation from the Python scikit-learn library[10].

For SVM, the regression is not penalizing points which have an error smaller than an imposed value, epsilon, and for this research we set the value of epsilon at 100 views. In the case of the KNN algorithm, we considered 10 neighbours (K = 10) and averaged their values to predict the value of the test case, as this proved to lead to the best results.

Since we wanted to predict the number of views and the number of "like" votes based on the lyrics and the main frequency from the songs' melody, we did in total six different experiments, trying to predict each thing (views or "like" votes) using each predictor on its own and also their combination.

5.1 Predicting the Number of Views

Before applying the learning algorithms, we analysed the songs distribution based on their number of views. Since the interval of views was very large – from 20 views to 0.4 billion – we decided to eliminate the extremes and only consider the songs having between 1000 and 0.15 billion (around 7,500 songs). For this dataset, we extracted the words from the lyrics, in a bag-of-words fashion, along with their frequencies of appearance, and the main frequency from the melody of the songs. These were the features used for all the machine learning algorithms. Furthermore, we divided the

---

[10] http://scikit-learn.org/ [accessed: February 2nd, 2017].

dataset in two classes: popular songs, with more than 1 million views, and unpopular songs, having less than 1 million views.

To evaluate the accuracy of the used algorithms, we used 10-folds cross-validation, along with the "Root Mean Squared Error" (RMSE) as in (6), where y represents the real value of the number of views, y' is its estimation and n is the number of testing examples.

$$Error = \sqrt{\frac{1}{n}\sum_{i=1}^{n}(y_i - y_i')^2} \qquad (6)$$

The results of applying SVM (using both linear regression and RBF kernels) and KNN for predicting the songs' number of views are presented in Table 1. In these experiments, Logistic Regression obtained results that were much worse than the ones presented in Table 1 and thus they were ignored.

Table 1. The average error of the learning algorithms for predicting the songs' number of views in million of views

Predictors	Average error for SVM using Liniar regression		Average error for SVM using RBF kernels		Average error for KNN	
	Unpopular songs (< 1 million views)	Popular songs (> 1 million views)	Unpopular songs (< 1 million views)	Popular songs (> 1 million views)	Unpopular songs (< 1 million views)	Popular songs (> 1 million views)
The frequencies of the words from the songs' lyrics	9.46	28.35	9.79	**28.29**	5.22	30.78
The main frequency from the songs' melody	0.90	31.77	**0.88**	31.78	5.89	30.38
Both predictors	1.61	31.57	0.89	31.78	5.57	30.46

The errors presented in Table 1 had values of millions. However, to compute the real average error, one should divide the value of the error by the available range of the interval. For example, in the case of popular songs, the best results were obtained using SVM with RBF kernel considering only the songs' lyrics as predictors. In this case, the average error was 28.29 million. In order to compute the real error, we should divide this value by 0.1 billion, obtaining an error rate of 28.29%. The best results for unpopular songs were obtained using SVM with RBF kernel and considering only the main frequency from the songs' melody as predictor.

As it can be seen in Table 1, the best results were obtained using SVM with RBF kernel. Furthermore, the melody line has a higher weight in estimating the number of views for the unpopular songs, while the lyrics are more important for the popular songs.

When combining the two predictors, the results did not improve. In the case of the KNN algorithm, the results were similar, worse than for SVM, no matter what combination of predictors was used (only lyrics, only melody's main frequency, or both).

However, the large error obtained for unpopular songs led to the conclusion that estimating the number of views cannot be done only using these two predictors. Other important factors for determining the number of views of a song could be the artist popularity or the advertising campaign of that song, which might make listeners curious and willing to visit YouTube to hear the song, even though afterwards they will not like it.

5.2   Predicting the Number of "Like" Votes

In this section, we will present the results of applying the same methodology for estimating the number of "like" votes of songs on the YouTube platform. In this case, we selected for analysis the songs having between 100 and 100,000 "like" votes, representing about 6,000 songs. Again, we divided the dataset in two classes: popular, having over 10,000 votes and unpopular, with less than 10,000 votes. As in the previous experiment, we used 10-fold cross-validation and RMSE to estimate the quality of the estimation.

The obtained results are presented in Table 2, where the error is given in thousands votes. Again, to compute the real error rate, one should divide the value from the table to the maximum value of the interval (10,000 in the case of unpopular songs, and 100,000 for the popular ones).

Table 2. The average error of the learning algorithms for predicting the number of "like" votes in thousands of votes

Predictors	Average error for SVM using Liniar regression		Average error for SVM using RBF kernels		Average error for KNN		Average error for logistic regression	
	Unpopular songs (< 10,000 likes)	Popular songs (> 10,000 likes)	Unpopular songs (< 10,000 likes)	Popular songs (> 10,000 likes)	Unpopular songs (< 10,000 likes)	Popular songs (> 10,000 likes)	Unpopular songs (< 10,000 likes)	Popular songs (> 10,000 likes)
Words freq. from the lyrics	5.47	17.44	3.85	16.58	**2.03**	19.63	7.54	22.58
Main freq.	3.80	17.57	3.88	17.57	3.05	18.40	7.10	24.17
Both	6.41	17.11	3.88	**16.16**	2.87	18.37	5.83	20.26

Table 2 shows that for the popular songs the results obtained by the SVM with RBF kernels are the best, while the ones obtained by the Logistic Sigmoid are the worst. From the two predictors, the one having more importance seems to be the songs' lyrics. However, when combined with the main frequency of the song's melody, it led to the best result obtained in the current research, having an error of 16.16 * 1,000/100,000 = 16.16%. In other words, SVM with RBF kernels achieve an 83.84% accuracy in predicting the number of "like" votes of popular songs, when using as predictors both the song's lyrics and main frequency from its melody.

In the case of unpopular songs, KNN obtained the best results, with an error rate of 2.03* 1,000/10,000 = 20.3%. Thus, the best accuracy in the case of unpopular songs is of almost 80% and is obtained by KNN when using only the lyrics of the song as predictor. Again, the results obtained by the Logistic Regression proved to be the worst.

In conclusion, we may say that the song's lyrics are the most useful features in identifying whether a song will be successful or not. However, in the case of popular songs, the quality of the results may be improved if the main frequency of the song's melody is also used. In this case, the algorithm that worked best was SVM with RBF kernels. For unpopular songs, KNN had the biggest accuracy.

Compared to the results reported by the similar applications presented in Sect. 2 (at most 60% accuracy), the errors obtained when estimating the number of "like" votes that will be received by songs is considered to be small enough to be acceptable in predicting the success of such songs using the presented algorithms.

6 Conclusions and Further Development

The use of machine learning algorithms for building models for predicting the popularity of songs highlighted an important issue: the song popularity, measured as the number of views on YouTube, does not depend only on the lyrics and the melody of the song, but also on the artist popularity, on the advertise for promoting the song through means that arouse people's curiosity to listen the song at least once, and on other social aspects.

Considering the number of "like" votes on this platform, both the lyrics and the melody of a song contribute to its success. The accuracy of estimating this success was higher when considering both predictors in the case of popular songs, while for non-popular ones, the lyrics alone proved to give the best estimation. The minimum value of accuracy is achieved at the boundary between popular and unpopular songs, because the algorithms can not establish a fixed boundary between the degrees of popularity.

The best predictions were made by the SVM algorithm using the RBF kernel and estimating the error based on the magnitude order of the data. The only exception was made by the KNN algorithm that generated the best estimations for the number of "like" votes received by unpopular songs.

In this paper, we only considered the English songs belonging to the pop music. We intend to extend this research by also considering other musical genres, as well as analysing songs written in other languages.

During this research, we have seen that the popularity of the artist is very important for estimating the success of a song and thus, in the future, we will also consider this aspect as a predictor. Other possible predictors that might be used in the next version of the current application include how the song is advertised and the musical instruments that are used in the song. In the same time, not all the words from the songs' lyrics are relevant for the estimation and thus we plan to use feature selection for eliminating some of these useless words. Also, we plan on investigating the influence of the mood (s) triggered by the song on the number of views and the number of "like" votes by estimating the emotions expressed in the song's lyrics.

Finally, another issue that we intend to address in a future study is the comparison of the lyrics of songs that are popular in different languages, as this may facilitate the identification of feelings and sentiments that are common among different civilizations, using methods based on machine learning and data mining.

Acknowledgments. This work has been funded by University Politehnica of Bucharest, through the "Excellence Research Grants" Program, UPB – GEX. Identifier: UPB–EXCELENȚĂ–2016 Aplicareametodelor de învățareautomatăînanalizaseriilor de timp (Applying machine learning techniques in time series analysis), Contract number 09/26.09.2016.

References

1. Berger, J.: How music hijacks our perception of time, a composer details how music works its magic on our brains. Nautilus, 23 January 2014. http://nautil.us/issue/9/time/how-music-hijacks-our-perception-of-time
2. Fritz, T.H., Hardikar, S., Demoucron, M., Niessen, M., Demey, M., Giot, O., Li, Y., Haynes, J.D., Villringer, A., Leman, M.: Musical agency reduces perceived exertion during strenuous physical performance. Proc. Natl. Acad. Sci. **110**(44), 17784–17789 (2013)
3. Brown, M.: Pop hit prediction algorithm mines 50 years of chart toppers for data. Wired, 19 December 2011. http://www.wired.co.uk/article/song-prediction-algorithm
4. Pachet, F., Roy, P.: Hit song science is not yet a science. In: Proceedings of ISMIR 2008, USA, pp. 355–360 (2008)
5. Schroeder, M., Rossing, T.D., Dunn, F., Hartmann, W.M., Campbell, D.M., Fletcher, N.H.: Springer Handbook of Acoustics, pp. 747–748. Springer, Heidelberg (2007). ISBN 978-0387304465
6. Nyquist, H.: Certain topics in telegraph transmission theory. Trans. AIEE. **47**, 617–644 (1928)
7. FFT Tutorial: University of Rhode Island Department of Electrical and Computer Engineering, Communication Systems Course. http://www.phys.nsu.ru/cherk/fft.pdf
8. Bishop, C.M.: Pattern Recognition and Machine Learning. Springer, Heidelberg (2006)
9. Shalizi, C.R.: Advanced Data Analysis from an Elementary Point of View. Cambridge University Press, Cambridge (2013)
10. Vapnik, V.: The Nature of Statistical Learning Theory, 2nd edn. Springer, New York (2001)
11. Farag, A., Mohamed, R.M.: Regression using support vector machines: basic foundations. Technical report, CVIP Laboratory, University of Louisville, pp. 1–5 (2004)
12. Kouser, K., Sunita, A.: A comparative study of K means algorithm by different distance measures. In: International Journal of Innovative Research in Computer and Communication Engineering, vol. 1, Ranchi, India (2013)
13. Moore, A. W.: An introductory tutorial on kd-tree. Technical report No. 209, Computer Laboratory, University of Cambridge (1991)
14. Dasgupta, A., Kumar, R., Sarlós, T.: Fast locality-sensitive hashing. In: Proceedings of the 17th ACM SIGKDD International Conference on Knowledge Discovery and Data Mining, pp. 1073–1081. ACM, August 2011

iPDO: An Effective Feature Depth Estimation Method for 3D Face Reconstruction

Xun Gong[1], Xinxin Li[2(✉)], Shengdong Du[1], and Yang Zhao[1]

[1] School of Information Science and Technology, Southwest Jiaotong University,
Chengdu 611756, People's Republic of China
xgong@swjtu.edu.cn
[2] Jincheng College of Sichuan University, Chengdu 611731,
People's Republic of China
xinxinli@foxmail.com

Abstract. We present a 3D face modeling approach under uncontrolled conditions. In the heart of this work is an efficient and accurate facial landmark depth estimation algorithm. The objective function is formulated by similarity transformation among face images. In this method, pose parameters and depth values are optimized iteratively. The estimated 3D landmarks then are taken as control points to deform a generic 3D face shape into a specific face shape. Test results on synthesized images show that the proposed methods can obtain landmarks depth both effectively and efficiently. Whats' more, the 3D faces generated from real-world photos are rather realistic based on a set of landmarks.

Keywords: 3D face reconstruction · Depth estimation · Pose estimation

1 Introduction

3D face reconstruction from images has dawn increasing attentions in virtual reality and natural human-computer interaction areas. Considerable methods have been developed. Such as Shape-from-Shading (SFS), 3D Morphable Models (3DMM) [1], Structure-from-Motion (SFM) [2], etc. Most existing 3D face modeling methods from one image depend heavily on prior models, e.g., 3DMM suffers from three limitations: limited range, limited scale and cant run automatically [3]. Recently, Kemelmacher et al. build a shape basis directly from the photos [3] and create a entire head based on it [4]. And another impressive work is an unconstrained 3D face reconstruction algorithm proposed by Roth et al. [5].

The problem of extracting the shape and motion parameters from a 2D image sequence is known as a Structure-from-Motion (SFM) problem. A similarity transform based method is proposed to derive the 3D structure of a human face from a group of face images under the framework of SFM [6]. Sun et al. [7] proposed Nonlinear Least-Squares (NLS) model-based methods for estimation.

© Springer International Publishing AG 2017
L. Polkowski et al. (Eds.): IJCRS 2017, Part I, LNAI 10313, pp. 407–417, 2017.
DOI: 10.1007/978-3-319-60837-2_34

SFMs performance degrades drastically when tracking errors caused by self-occlusion or image noise. Yang et al. [8] propose a reliable point selection method to evaluate the reliability of corresponding points obtained by optical flow.

Our previous research [9] reveals that we can get a more accurate 3D face reconstruction with more precise depth information of facial landmarks. So this paper mainly focuses on depth estimation under the framework of SFM. Landmarks Quasi-3D (Q-3D, named as their real 3D coordinates are unattainable) coordinates are formed by combining the known 2D coordinates with estimated depth value. Compared to the existing depth estimation methods [6,7], main contributions of this paper can be summarized as follows:

(1) We propose an iterative pose and depth optimization method (iPDO) which can ensure a precise depth estimation of face landmark.
(2) We provide an integration strategy for features' depth estimation from multiple non-frontal-view images.

2   Face Surface Reconstruction

Like some conventional methods [8,10], our method also works in a coarse-to-fine way. Based on a set of salient landmarks on 2D images, their corresponding 3D positions are computed at first. These estimated 3D landmarks are then taken as control points to create a specific facial shape. The problem of iPDO can be formulated as: given one near-frontal face image I_0 and n non-frontal-view images $(I_1, \cdots, I_n)$, compute a sparse 3D-face shape from the input images by estimating the depth value of all landmarks.

2.1   A Generic Framework of Depth Estimation from Two Images

First of all, we discuss how to compute the landmarks depth from two images. One is a near-frontal image I_0 while the other I_i is non-frontal view, $1 \leq i \leq n$. This is a problem of minimizing the sum of the distances between a translated shape and a shape on I_i. Let s_0 and s_i denote the 2D shape containing k landmarks on these two images, respectively, hence

$$s_0 = \left(\boldsymbol{p}_0^T \cdots \boldsymbol{p}_t^T \cdots \boldsymbol{p}_k^T\right)^T \in \Re^{2k}, 1 \leq t \leq k. \tag{1}$$

$$s_i = \left(\boldsymbol{q}_0^T \cdots \boldsymbol{q}_t^T \cdots \boldsymbol{q}_k^T\right)^T \in \Re^{2k}, 1 \leq t \leq k. \tag{2}$$

And $\boldsymbol{p}_t, \boldsymbol{q}_t, (1 \leq t \leq k)$ are the 2D coordinates of the t-th feature point on I_0 and I_i respectively. s_0 can be transformed into a shape s_0' that is close to s_i. With a scalar factor σ, a rotation matrix $\boldsymbol{R}(\alpha, \beta, \gamma)$ and a translation vector $t = [\Delta x, \Delta y]^T$, under scaled-orthographic camera model we have

$$s_0' = \left(\boldsymbol{p}_0'^T \cdots \boldsymbol{p}_t'^T \cdots \boldsymbol{p}_k'^T\right)^T \in \Re^{2k}, \tag{3}$$

$$\begin{bmatrix} \boldsymbol{p}'_t \\ z'_t \end{bmatrix} = \sigma \cdot [\boldsymbol{R}\ t] \cdot [\boldsymbol{p}_t^T, z_t, 1]^T, \tag{4}$$

with z_t the Z-coordinate of the t-th landmark on the frontal image I_0, and z'_t is the Z-coordinate on $\boldsymbol{s}'_0$. Obviously, z_t is unknown. Hence, in total, there are $k + 5$ unsolved parameters $(\alpha, \beta, \gamma, \Delta x, \Delta y, z_1, \cdots, z_k)$ which can be solved by:

$$min(d(\boldsymbol{s}'_0, \mathbf{s}_i)) = min \left\| \boldsymbol{s}'_0 - \mathbf{s}_i \right\|_2. \tag{5}$$

For simplicity, let $\boldsymbol{w}$ denotes the rotation angles α, β, γ in the following sections. Given an initial value of depth value of all landmarks $\boldsymbol{z}^0 = \left\{ z_1^0, \cdots, z_k^0 \right\}$, Particle Swarm Optimization algorithm (PSO) [11] is adopted to optimize all unknown parameters. Generally, scholars are willing to use the corresponding Z-coordinates on a generic face model as the initial value $\boldsymbol{z}'_0$ [7].

The initial values always play an important role. Differ from existing methods [6,7], we use a linear model SLMO (a sparse linear model combining with an optimization) [12] to estimate $\boldsymbol{z}'_0$ from the frontal face image I_0 at first. The feature positions obtained by SLMO are far more accurate than values on a generic face. Without any iteration, SLMO can run quickly in a single step. A Two-Stage Estimation (TSE) method is outlined as Algorithm 1.

Algorithm 1. A Two-Stage Estimation (TSE) method

Input:
   two sets of 2D landmarks $\boldsymbol{s}_0$ and $\boldsymbol{s}_i$
Output:
   The estimated Z-coordinate $\boldsymbol{z} = \left\{ \boldsymbol{z}_1, \cdots, \boldsymbol{z}_k \right\}$ of all landmarks.
 1: Obtain an initial value $\boldsymbol{z}^0$ of the landmarks depth by SLMO algorithm, which estimates depth from $\boldsymbol{s}_0$.
 2: *Step 1*: Fix the depth value $\boldsymbol{z}^0$, optimize $\boldsymbol{w}$ and $\boldsymbol{z}$ by solving (5), then get $\boldsymbol{w}^0$ and $\boldsymbol{z}^0$.
   Step 2: Fix the pose & translation parameters, i.e., $\boldsymbol{w}^0$ and $\boldsymbol{t}^0$, then compute Z-coordinate of all landmarks by optimizing (5) again.

The main difference of TSE from existing methods, obviously, is the use of depth value $\boldsymbol{z}^0$ that estimated by SLMO as an initialization.

2.2   Basic Idea of iPDO

As aforementioned, in order to get accurate estimation for both pose parameters $\boldsymbol{w}$ and the depth values $\boldsymbol{z}$, TSE computes these values separately. From the scaled-orthographic camera model in (4), we can see clearly that pose estimation and depth estimation have mutual effect.

To assess the effect influence of $\boldsymbol{w}$ to $\boldsymbol{z}$, we conduct a simulation as a guide of algorithm design (details of test settings can refer to Sect. 3). During this simulation, we project a 3D face to 2D plane to create two face images, one is frontal and the other is with 20° yaw and 20° pitch angles. On the one hand, we use sub-step *step 1*, stage 2 of TSE to estimate the pose angles. And on the other hand the known angles (20°, 20°, 0°) are input directly to sub-step *step 2*, stage 2 of TSE. Besides TSE, NLS [7] is also tested. Test results are shown in Fig. 1, where 'Avg. Face' means the error of use the landmark vertexes of a 3D generic face, and '*-r' means input the real angles (20°, 20°, 0°) to the estimation algorithms while '*-e' means using the estimated angles. '*-mid' is the middle value between '*-r' and '*-e'. So, in a sense, NLS-r is the ground-truth to NLS-e while TSE-r is the ground-truth to TSE-e. Test result shown in Fig. 1 tells us that we can get a more accurate depth estimation result by more accurate pose angles. We may not reach to the ground-truth due to the existence of pose estimation errors, but compromised performance might be achievable.

A feasible way to improve the accuracy of w is to input relative accurate depth values. Hence, we intuitively propose to reform Algorithm 2 into an iterative version, i.e., an iterative pose and depth optimization method:

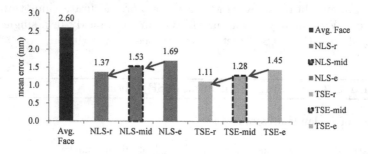

Fig. 1. Depth estimation error of different strategies, using real pose angles or the estimated pose angles.

Algorithm 2. An Iterative Pose and Depth Optimization (iPDO) method

---

Input:

 two sets of 2D landmarks s_0 and s_i, maximum iteration number N, convergence threshold τ.

Output:

 Quasi-3D (Q-3D) of all landmarks, which is formed by concatenating the known s_0 and their estimated depth values z^i.

1: Obtain an initial value of the landmarks depth by SLMO based on s_0, denoted as z_0. Set an indicator $i = 0$.

2: *Step 1*: Fix z^i, optimize w and t by solving (5), then get w^i, t^i.

 Step 2: Fix w^i and t^i, update Z-coordinate of all landmarks by optimizing (5) again, then get z^i. Set $i = i + 1$.

3: If $i > N$ or $\left\| z^i - z^{i-1} \right\|_2 < \tau$, then exit. Otherwise, go to Stage 2.

2.3 Depth Fusion and Dense 3D Face Modeling

When n non-frontal-view face image of a subject are available, then n depth values of each landmark can be obtained via iPDO. Therefore, an integration method is needed to fuse these values into a reasonable one. Here, we propose to use a normal distribution model to exclude the outliers. For the t-th landmark, we get a Z-coordinate set $\Omega = \{z_{t,1}, \cdots, z_{t,n}\}$, from which we can extracted a new set with n elements:

$$\Sigma = \{z_{t,i} \in \Omega : \bar{z}_t - 3\sigma_t < z_{t,i} < \bar{z}_t + 3\sigma_t\}, 1 \leq i \leq n \quad (6)$$

where, $\bar{z}_t$, σ_t are the mean and standard deviation of the Z-coordinate of the t-th landmark. $\bar{z}_t$ and σ_t are computed from a training 3D face set. Then, with Σ, we can get the final integrated Z-coordinate of the t-th landmark:

$$z_t = \begin{cases} mean(\Sigma), & if \Sigma \neq \phi \\ z_t^0, & if \Sigma = \phi \end{cases} \quad (7)$$

where, 'mean' is the mean function while z_t^0 is the depth value of the t-th landmark estimated by SLMO.

With the Q-3D coordinates of the key landmarks, we can deform a generic 3D facial shape to make a specific 3D face for input images. Here, we adopt the commonly used Radial Basis Functions (RBFs) as a global tool for deformation. RBFs builds a smooth interpolation function $f(v)$ based on offsets of the landmarks. And for the rest ten thousands of non-feature vertices v_i on the generic face mesh, their displacement d_i can be computed by $f(v)$ straightly. More details please refer to literature [13].

3 Experiments and Analysis

We conduct experiments on two 3D face databases, one is the Bosphorus database [14] that is also adopted by Sun [7] and the other is SWJTU 3D face database (shorted as SWJTU-3D) collected by ourselves.

3.1 Experiment Configuration

Bosphorus database (shorted as BS) consists of 105 subjects with up to 54 face scans per subject. Each scan has been manually labelled for 22 facial landmark points. The training set is composed of 115 3D face scans with neutral pose & expression while a testing set is composed of five non-frontal-view face images (P_R_D, P_R_SD, P_R_SU, P R_U, Y R_R10) and one corresponding frontal-view face image.

SWJTU-3D consists of 450 persons with 6 models per subject, where 76 facial landmarks are manually labeled. This database is split into a testing and a training set of 225 models each. For SWJTU-3D, we synthesize images by projecting 3D faces of testing set under different views: (10,10,0), (10,20,0), (10,30,0), (20,10,0), (20,20,0), (30,30,0).

For quantitative comparison, we use the mean error $e(\boldsymbol{z}^e, \boldsymbol{z}^g)$ to measure the error between estimated depth value and its ground-truth, i.e.,

$$e(\boldsymbol{z}^e, \boldsymbol{z}^g) = \frac{1}{k} \sum_{t=1}^{k} |z_t^e - z_t^g|, \tag{8}$$

with the real depth values $\boldsymbol{z}^g$ on a 3D face, which is deemed as the ground-truth, and the estimated depth values $\boldsymbol{z}^e$. We also use the correlation coefficient $c(\boldsymbol{z}^e, \boldsymbol{z}^g)$, i.e., the correlation coefficient of two depth vectors:

$$c(\boldsymbol{z}^e, \boldsymbol{z}^g) = \frac{1}{k-1} \sum_{t=1}^{k} \left(\frac{z_t^g - \bar{z}^g}{\sigma^g} \right) \left(\frac{z_t^e - \bar{z}^e}{\sigma^e} \right) \tag{9}$$

where, $\bar{z}^g$ and σ^g are the mean and standard deviation of $\boldsymbol{z}^g$. $\bar{z}^e$ and σ^e are the mean and standard deviation of $\boldsymbol{z}^e$.

3.2 Experimental Results

(1) Depth Estimation Evaluation. In order to investigate the generalization of our algorithm for face images of different poses, methods are evaluated by a frontal image and one synthesized image under various angles (SWJTU-3D database is used). GA (Genetic Algorithm) [6] and NLS (Nonlinear Least-Squares) [7] are also tested for comparing purposes.

To give a comparable test according to the relative literatures [7], we evaluate depth accuracy on BS database. Data of GA and NLS come from the original studies. As shown in Table 1, we know that the proposed TSE and iPDO outperforms GA (Genetic Algorithm) [6], NLS (Nonlinear Least-Squares) [7] under different profile images. Test on simulated images in Fig. 2 shows that the Euclidean distance between the estimated Z-coordinate of iPDO and their ground-truth are as close as to 1.3 mm.

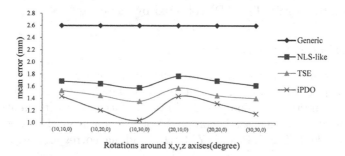

Fig. 2. Depth estimation error of different methods (on SWJTU-3D). The non-frontal images used are in different viewpoint. The numbers in the parentheses are the angles around X, Y, Z axis, respectively.

Table 1. Depth value estimation comparison under the BS database.

	GA [6]	NLS1_SR [7]	TSE	iPDO
PR_D	0.1962	0.8916	0.9685	**0.9686**
PR_SD	0.2787	0.8655	0.9673	**0.9674**
PR_SU	0.5568	0.8454	0.9656	**0.9657**
PR_U	0.7283	0.8573	0.9675	**0.9677**
YR_R10	0.5128	0.9016	0.9674	**0.9674**
$\mu + std$	0.4546	0.8723	0.9671	**0.9672**
$\mu - std$	±0.2408	±0.0236	±0.0011	**±0.0011**

The effectiveness of using multiple images is validated in Fig. 3. We can see that, iPDO can perform better with more images. Running time of these algorithms is listed in Table 2. Without any coding optimization, iPDO costs 1.72 s on a MacBook Pro. with a 2.7 GHz CPU and 4G of RAM.

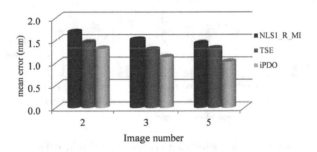

Fig. 3. Depth estimation error of using multiple images. 3 different methods are tested.

Table 2. Time costs of different methods.

Methods	GA	NLS1_SR	NLS2	SLMO	TSE	iPDO
Time (s)	50.09	0.10	3.0	0.03	0.53	1.72

(2) Pose Estimation Evaluation. As pose estimation is an important step for both NLS-like and our TSE algorithm. In this test, with simulated images of SWJTU-3D, we will investigate carefully how the pose estimation performance would affect the depth estimation. The non-frontal image we used here is (20°, 20°, 0°) around X and Y axis respectively.

The mean error $e(z^e, z^g)$ and $c(z^g, z^e)$ of the estimated depth with different strategies are listed in Table 3 where '-r' means input the real angles (20°, 20°, 0°) to the estimation algorithm. While '-e' means using the estimated angles w.

So NLS-like-r is the ground-truth of NLS-like-e while TSE-r is the ground-truth of TSE-e. We can see that depth error of TSE-r is lower than TSE-e and the mean error is close to 1 mm while the correlation coefficient is up to 1.0. This result tells us that the proposed iPDO is reasonable since it can improve the estimation results by further updating the pose angles.

Table 3. Depth estimation accuracy comparison of different strategies, using real angles or the estimated ones

	Avg. face	NLS-like-r	NLS-like-e	TSE-r	TSE-e
$e(z^e, z^g)$	2.5988	1.3719	1.6899	**1.1140**	1.4511
$\sigma(z^e, z^g)$	0.8118	0.0297	0.1451	**0.0241**	0.1369
$c(z^g, z^e)$	0.9688	0.9999	0.9982	**1.0000**	0.9985

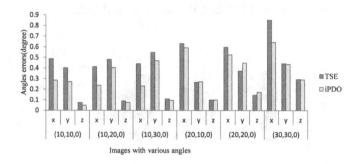

Fig. 4. Angle estimation errors of TSE and iPDO.

Then, we compare the errors of the estimated angle by the proposed TSE and iPDO, respectively. As shown in Fig. 4, the rotation anlges estimated by iPDO is evidently more accurate than that of TSE.

(3) 3D Face Reconstruction Evaluation. With the estimated Q3D landmarks, now we can evaluate our 3D face modeling method described in Sect. 2.3. At first, we create synthesized images by rendering each 3D face of the SWJTU3D database into two images, one is frontal and the other is non-frontal of $(20°, 20°, 0°)$. The captured 3D models in the database can be regarded as the ground-truth. For quantity evaluation, we map the 3D faces into range images [15] and use correlation coefficient $c(I_e, I_g)\epsilon[0,1]$ to measure the similarity of two range images (I_e and I_g).

The Q-3D obtained by iPDO & TSE has been substantiated by the previous results, i.e., Q-3D coordinates obtained by iPDO are much closer to the real values than other methods. Here, 3 tests are contrived: (a) only use 2D coordinates (x, y) of landmarks on synthesized images; (b) use 3D coordinates (x, y, z) of landmarks directly on the testing 3D faces; (c) use estimated Q-3D landmarks.

Test (b) can be regarded as the ideal results. A sparse morphable model SRSD [16] is also compared. The results shown in Fig. 5 reveal that the use of Q-3D reduces the error in face modeling considerably.

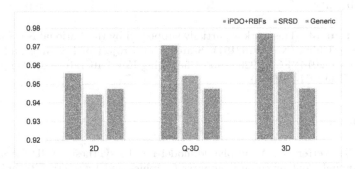

Fig. 5. A comparison of different reconstruction accuracy using the similarities of range image.

Three reconstructed 3D faces from real-word images are demonstrated in Fig. 6. Two subject is from the IMM database [17] and the last one is our group member. We can see that Q-3D features indeed are helpful to accurately recover the shape in Z-axis direction. Note that here we use 3 images for reconstruction. We also can use just 2 uncontrolled images as inputs.

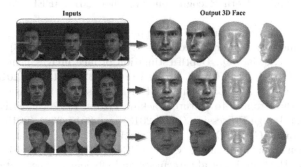

Fig. 6. 3D face reconstructed from 2 images. The left are the inputted images while the right is different views of the 3D models.

4   Conclusions

Pose estimation and depth estimation have mutual effect in 3D face reconstruction. However, most existing methods handle them simultaneously. We put forward a pose and depth optimization method, which optimizes pose parameters and depth values separately and iteratively. In order to handle multiple images, we also propose an integrated method. There are a number of potential improvements and challenges going forward. In the next work, it would be interesting to exploit other cues such as knowledge of pose and profile contours to resolve metric ambiguity.

Acknowledgment. This work is partially supported by the National Natural Science Foundation of China (No. 61202191), State's Key Project of Research and Development Plan (No. 2016YFC0802209) and Chongqing Key Laboratory of Computational Intelligence (CQ-LCI-2013-06).

References

1. Blanz, V., Vetter, T.: A morphable model for the synthesis of 3D faces. In: The 26th Annual Conference on Computer Graphics and Interactive Techniques, pp. 187–194. ACM Press/Addison-Wesley Publishing Co., Los Angeles (1999)
2. Torresani, L., Hertzmann, A., Bregler, C.: Non-rigid structure-from-motion: estimating shape and motion with hierarchical priors. IEEE Trans. Pattern Anal. Mach. Intell. **30**(5), 878–892 (2008)
3. Shu, L., Linda, S., Ira, K.: Internet-based morphable model. In: IEEE International Conference on Computer Vision, pp. 3256–3263. IEEE Computer Society (2015)
4. Liang, S., Shapiro, L.G., Kemelmacher-Shlizerman, I.: Head reconstruction from internet photos. In: Leibe, B., Matas, J., Sebe, N., Welling, M. (eds.) ECCV 2016. LNCS, vol. 9906, pp. 360–374. Springer, Cham (2016). doi:10.1007/978-3-319-46475-6_23
5. Roth, J., Tong, Y., Liu, X.: Unconstrained 3D face reconstruction. In: IEEE Computer Vision and Pattern Recognition, pp. 2606–2615. IEEE Computer Society (2015)
6. Koo, H., Lam, K.: Recovering the 3D shape and poses of face images based on the similarity transform. Pattern Recogn. Lett. **29**(6), 712–723 (2008)
7. Sun, Z., Lam, K., Gao, Q.: Depth estimation of face images using the nonlinear least-squares model. IEEE Trans. Image Process. **22**(1), 17–30 (2013)
8. Yang, C., Chen, J., Xia, C., et al.: A SFM-based sparse to dense 3D face reconstruction method robust to feature tracking errors. In: 20th IEEE International Conference on Image Processing (ICIP 2013), pp. 3617–3621 (2013)
9. Gong, X., Wang, G., Li, X., et al.: A statistical two-step method for 3D face reconstruction from single image. Chin. J. Electron. **20**(4), 671–675 (2011)
10. Le, V., Tang, H., Cao, L., et al.: Accurate and efficient reconstruction of 3D faces from stereo images. In: 17th IEEE International Conference on Image Processing (ICIP 2010), pp. 4265–4268 (2010)
11. Kennedy, J., Eberhart, R.: Particle swarm optimization. In: IEEE International Conference on Neural Networks, Perth, WA, pp. 1942–1948 (1995)
12. Gong, X., Wang, G.: Example-based learning for depth estimation of facial landmarks and its application in face modeling. Chin. J. Electron. **19**(4), 676–680 (2010)
13. Gong, X., Wang, G.: Realistic face modeling based on multiple deformations. J. Chin. Univ. Posts Telecommun. **14**(4), 110–117 (2007)

14. Savran, A., Alyüz, N., Dibeklioğlu, H., Çeliktutan, O., Gökberk, B., Sankur, B., Akarun, L.: Bosphorus database for 3D face analysis. In: Schouten, B., Juul, N.C., Drygajlo, A., Tistarelli, M. (eds.) BioID 2008. LNCS, vol. 5372, pp. 47–56. Springer, Heidelberg (2008). doi:10.1007/978-3-540-89991-4_6
15. Gong, X., Luo, J., Fu, Z.: Normalization for unconstrained pose-invariant 3D face recognition. In: Sun, Z., Shan, S., Yang, G., Zhou, J., Wang, Y., Yin, Y.L. (eds.) CCBR 2013. LNCS, vol. 8232, pp. 1–8. Springer, Cham (2013). doi:10.1007/978-3-319-02961-0_1
16. Blanz, V., Mehl, A., Vetter, T., et al.: A statistical method for robust 3D surface reconstruction from sparse data. In: Proceeding of the 2nd International Symposium on 3D Data Processing, Visualization, Thessaloniki, Greece, pp. 293–300. IEEE Computer Society (2004)
17. Nordstrom, M.M., Larsen, M., Sierakowski, J., et al.: The IMM face database - an annotated dataset of 240 face images. Technical Richard Petersens Plads, Building 321 (2004)

Proposal of Dominance-Based Rough Set Approach by STRIM and Its Applied Example

Yuichi Kato[1]([✉]), Takahiro Itsuno[1], and Tetsuro Saeki[2]

[1] Shimane University, 1060 Nishikawatsu-cho, Matsue City, Shimane 690-8504, Japan
ykato@cis.shimane-u.ac.jp
[2] Yamaguchi University, 2-16-1 Tokiwadai, Ube City, Yamaguchi 755-8611, Japan
tsaeki@yamaguchi-u.ac.jp

Abstract. The conventional rough sets theory is used for inducing if-then rules hidden behind a dataset called the decision table which has some condition attributes and a decision attribute. Each attribute is considered in principle as a nominal scale. The conventional rough sets theory also extends its method in order to apply to the table with an ordinal scale which is used for rating the preference of users, and proposes a dominance-based rough set approach (DRSA) for the conventional rule induction methods. This paper also proposes a DRSA by STRIM named DOMSTRIM with a consistency index of dominance, applies it to a real-world dataset of a questionnaire survey and confirms the usefulness of DOMSTRIM by comparing with the conventional method DOMLEM.

1 Introduction

The Rough Sets theory was introduced by Pawlak [1] and used for inducing if-then rules from a dataset called the decision table. Each data in the decision table is a sample consisting of the tuple of condition attributes' values and the decision attribute value and each attribute of the sample in principle takes values on a nominal scale with a finite set. The induced if-then rules simply and clearly express the structure of rating and/or knowledge hiding behind the decision table. Such rule induction methods are needed for disease diagnosis systems, discrimination problems, decision problems, and other aspects, and consequently, many effective methods and algorithms for the rule induction by rough sets have been reported [2–6]. Among the conventional methods for inducing if-then rules, VPRS (Variable Precision Rough Set) [4] and the methods developing VPRS [6] are best used although many methods have been proposed. We also proposed a rule induction method named STRIM (Statistical Test Rule Induction Method) [7–12] by expanding and developing the notion of VPRS into a statistical model since the attributes and the sample data in the decision table should be recognized as random variables and their outcomes from the population of interest respectively.

The conventional rough sets theory also expanded and developed its methods in order to deal with the dataset on ordinal scales since there were many cases

© Springer International Publishing AG 2017
L. Polkowski et al. (Eds.): IJCRS 2017, Part I, LNAI 10313, pp. 418–431, 2017.
DOI: 10.1007/978-3-319-60837-2_35

gathered from questionnaire surveys which rated objects from the population, for example, by the degree of preference, satisfaction and so on, that is, by ordinal scales. Such expansions were called Dominance-based Rough Set Approach (DRSA) [13] and DRSA developed the algorithm LEM2 [3] into DOMLEM [14] and VC-DRSA (Variable Consistency DRSA) [15], which can be utilized in a free software named jMAF [16].

In this paper, we also present the proposal of DRSA by STRIM named DOM-STRIM. Specifically, we apply STRIM to a real-world dataset with regard to Rakuten Travel presented by Rakuten Inc. [17] and analyze the dataset on the nominal scales. From this analysis, we first extract the principal variables and structures constructing the degree of satisfaction obtained from rating the leisure facility. Based on this knowledge obtained, we construct the model of DRSA by STRIM, that is, DOMSTRIM, conduct the rule induction by DOMSTRIM and not only show the results reasonable coordinating with our common sense but also confirm the preprocessing by STRIM to be useful. Furthermore, we propose a consistency index of dominance which confirms the order relation of the induced if-then rule set. At last, we analyze the same dataset by applying it to jMAF [16] and show the results difficult to understand the meanings of them comparing with those by DOMLEM.

2   Conventional Rough Sets and DRSA

In this section, we briefly summarize the conventional rough sets theory [1–6] and its Dominance-based Rough Set Approach (DRSA) [13–15]. Rough Sets theory is used for inducing if-then rules from a decision table S. S is conventionally denoted $S = (U, A = C \cup \{D\}, V, \rho)$. Here, $U = \{u(i)|i = 1, ..., N\}$ is a sample set, A is an attribute set, $C = \{C(j)|j = 1, ..., M_C\}$ is a condition attribute set, $C(j)$ is a member of C and a condition attribute, and D is a decision attribute. V is a set of attribute values denoted by $V = \bigcup_{a \in A} V_a$ and is characterized by an information function $\rho \colon U \times A \to V$ (see Table 1).

Table 1. An example of a decision table S.

U	$C(1)$	...	$C(j)$	...	$C(M_C)$	D
$u(1)$	...	...	$\rho(u(1), C(j))$	...	...	$\rho(u(1), D)$
...	...	...	...	...	...	...
$u(i)$	...	...	$\rho(u(i), C(j))$	...	...	$\rho(u(i), D)$
...	...	...	...	...	...	...
$u(N)$	...	...	$\rho(u(N), C(j))$	...	...	$\rho(u(N), D)$

Rough Sets theory focuses on the following equivalence relation and equivalence set of indiscernibility: $I_C = \{(u(i), u(j)) \in U^2 | \rho(u(i), a) = \rho(u(j), a), \forall a \in C\}$. I_C is an equivalence relation in U and derives the quotient set

$U/I_C = \{[u_i]_C | i = 1, 2, ..., |U| = N\}$. Here, $[u_i]_C = \{u(j) \in U | (u(j), u_i) \in I_C, u_i \in U\}$. $[u_i]_C$ is an equivalence set with the representative element u_i.

Let X be any subset of U then X can be approximated like $C_*(X) \subseteq X \subseteq C^*(X)$ by use of the equivalence set. Here,

$$C_*(X) = \{u_i \in U | [u_i]_C \subseteq X\}, \tag{1}$$
$$C^*(X) = \{u_i \in U | [u_i]_C \cap X \neq \emptyset\}. \tag{2}$$

$C_*(X)$ and $C^*(X)$ are called the lower and upper approximations of X by C respectively. The pair of $(C_*(X), C^*(X))$ is usually called a rough set of X by C.

Specifically, we let $X = D_d = \{u(i) | \rho(u(i), D) = d\}$ and define a set of $u(i)$ as $U(CP) = \{u(i) | u^{C=CP}(i)\}$, meaning that the condition part of $u(i)$ denoted by $u^C(i)$ satisfies $CP = \bigwedge_j (C(j_k) = v_{C(j_k)})$, where $\bigwedge$ is conjunction. If $U(CP) \subseteq D_d$, then CP can be used as the condition part of the if-then rule of $D = d$, with necessity. That is, the following expression of if-then rules with necessity is obtained:

$$\text{Rule}(d, k) : \text{ if } CP(d, k) = \bigwedge_j (C(j) = v_{j_k}) \text{ then } D = d, (k = 1, 2, ...). \tag{3}$$

In the same way, $C^*(X)$ derives the condition part CP of the if-then rule of $D = d$ with possibility.

The conventional rough sets theory in principle handles attributes of nominal scales. However, when questionnaire surveys rating objects are executed, ordinal scales, for example, {"Dissatisfied(DS)," "Somewhat dissatisfied(SD)," "Neither satisfied nor dissatisfied(NN)," "Satisfied(ST)," and "Very Satisfied(VS)"} are often used. Here, there is an ordinal relation $DS < SD < NN < ST < VS$ with regard to the degree of satisfaction to the object. The conventional methods studying such cases where the condition and decision attributes consist of an ordinal scale are called Dominance-based Rough Set Approach (DRSA) [13–15].

Specifically, DRSA replaces the above equivalence relation with a dominance relation denoted by yD_Px meaning that for $\forall a \in P \subseteq C$, $\rho(y, a) \geq \rho(x, a)$, that is, that y dominates x with respect to a set of attributes $P \subseteq C$. This dominance relation derives the following two sets: $D_P^+(x) = \{y \in U | yD_Px\}$ and $D_P^-(x) = \{y \in U | xD_Py\}$. Here, $D_P^+(x)$ is a set of objects (samples) dominating x and $D_P^-(x)$ is a set of objects (samples) dominated by x. By use of those expressions, the lower approximation by (1) can be replaced with the following two expressions:

$$P_*(D_d^\geq) = \{x \in U | D_P^+(x) \subseteq D_d^\geq\}, \tag{4}$$
$$P_*(D_d^\leq) = \{x \in U | D_P^-(x) \subseteq D_d^\leq\}, \tag{5}$$

where

$$D_d^\geq = \{y \in U | \rho(y, D) \geq d\}, \tag{6}$$
$$D_d^\leq = \{y \in U | \rho(y, D) \leq d\}. \tag{7}$$

The expressions (4) and (5) derive if-then rules with necessity corresponding to (3) as follows:

$$\text{Rule}^{\geq}(d, k): \text{ if } CP^{\geq}(d, k) = \bigwedge_j (C(j) \geq v_{j_k}) \text{ then } D \geq d, \tag{8}$$

$$\text{Rule}^{\leq}(d, k): \text{ if } CP^{\leq}(d, k) = \bigwedge_j (C(j) \leq v_{j_k}) \text{ then } D \leq d. \tag{9}$$

Let us call (8) and (9) at-least rules and at-most rules by lower approximations respectively.

In the same way, the upper approximation by (2) can be replaced the following two expressions:

$$P^{*}(D_{\bar{d}}^{\geq}) = \{x \in U | D_P^{+}(x) \bigcap D_{\bar{d}}^{\geq} \neq \emptyset\}, \tag{10}$$

$$P^{*}(D_{\bar{d}}^{\leq}) = \{x \in U | D_P^{+}(x) \bigcap D_{\bar{d}}^{\leq} \neq \emptyset\}. \tag{11}$$

The expressions (10) and (11) analogously derive if-then rules with possibility corresponding to (8) and (9).

3 Conventional STRIM

In this section, we briefly summarize STRIM (Statistical Test Rule Induction Method) [7–12]. STRIM considers the decision table shown in Table 1 to be a sample dataset obtained from an input-output system including a rule box, as shown in Fig. 1, and hypotheses regarding the decision attribute values, as shown Table 2. A sample $u(i)$ consists of its condition attributes values $u^C(i)$ and its decision attribute $u^D(i)$. $u^C(i)$ is the input into the rule box, and is transformed into the output $u^D(i)$ using the rules (generally unknown) contained in the rule box and the hypotheses. In contrast, $u(i) = (u^C(i), u^D(i))$ is measured by an observer, as shown in Fig. 1. The existence of NoiseC and NoiseD makes missing values in $u^C(i)$, and changes $u^D(i)$ to create another value of $u^D(i)$, respectively. Those noises bring the system closer to a real-world system. One of the features of STRIM is to have the data generation model shown in Fig. 1 though the conventional rough sets methods do not.

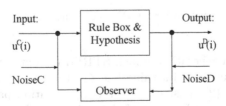

Fig. 1. Rough sets system contaminated with noise. Rule box contains if-then rules $Rule(d, k)$: if $CP(d, k)$ then $D = d$ $(d = 1, 2, ...)$.

Table 2. Hypotheses with regard to the decision attribute value.

Hypothesis 1	$u^C(i)$ coincides with $CP(d,k)$, and $u^D(i)$ is uniquely determined as $D = d$ (uniquely determined data)
Hypothesis 2	$u^C(i)$ does not coincide with any $CP(d,k)$, and $u^D(i)$ can only be determined randomly (indifferent data)
Hypothesis 3	$u^C(i)$ coincides with several $CP(d,k)$ ($d = d1, d2, ...$), and their outputs of $u^C(i)$ conflict with each other. Accordingly, the output of $u^C(i)$ must be randomly determined from the conflicted outputs (conflicted data)

Line No.	Algorithm to induce if-then rules by STRIM with a reduct function
1	int main(void) {
2	int rdct_max[|CV|]={0,...,0}; //initialize maximum value of C(j)
3	int rdct[|CV|]={0,...,0}; //initialize reduct results by D=l
4	int rule[|C|]={0,...,0}; //initialize trying rules
5	int tail=-1; // initial vale set
6	input data; // set decision table
7	for (di=1; di<=|D|; di++) {// induce rule candidates every D=l
8	attribute_reduct(rdct_max)
9	set rdct[ck] ; // if (rdct_max[ck]==0) {rdct[ck]=0; }else {rdct[ck]=1; }
10	rule_check(rcdct, redct_max, tail, rule); // the first stage process
11	}// end of di
12	arrange rule candidates // the second stage
13	}// end of main
14	int attribute_reduct(int rdct_max[]) {
15	make contingency table for D=l vs. C(j)
16	Test H0(j,l);
17	if H0(j,l) is rejexted then set rdct_max[j,l]=jmax else rdct_max[j,l]=0; // jmax:the attribute vale of the maximum frequency
18	}// end of attribute_reduct
19	int rule_check(int rdct[], int rdct_max[], int tail,int rule[]) {// the first stage process
20	for (ci=tail+1; cj<|C|; ci++) {
21	for (cj=1; cj<=rdct[ci]; cj++) {
22	rule[ci]=rdct_max[cj]; // a trying rule sets for test
23	count frequency of the trying rule; // count n1, n2,...
24	if (frequency>=N0) {//sufficient frequency ?
25	if (|z|>3.0) {//sufficient evidence ?
26	add the trying rule as a rule candidate
27	}// end of if |z|
28	rule_check(ci,rule)
29	}// end of if frequency
30	}// end of for cj
31	rule[ci]=0; // trying rules reset
32	}// end of for ci
33	}// end of rule_check

Fig. 2. An algorithm for STRIM including a reduct function.

Based on the data generation model, STRIM (1) extracted significant pairs of a condition attribute and its value like $C(j) = v_{j_k}$ for rules of $D = d$ by the local reduct [11], (2) constructed a trying condition part of the rules like $CP(d, k) = \bigwedge_j (C(j_k) = v_j)$ by use of the reduct results, and (3) investigated whether $CP(d, k)$ caused a bias at n_d in the frequency $f = (n_1, n_2, ..., n_{M_D})$ or not, where $n_m = |U(CP(d,k)) \cap U(m)|$ $(m = 1, ..., |V_D| = M_D)$, $U(CP(d,k)) = \{u(i)|u^{C=CP(d,k)}(i)\}$ and $U(m) = \{u(i)|u^{D=m}(i)\}$, which means satisfying $u^D(i) = m$ }. Specifically, STRIM used a statistical test method specifying a null hypothesis $H0$: f does not have any bias and its alternative hypothesis $H1$: f has a bias, and a proper significance level, and tested $H0$ by use of the sample dataset, that is, the decision table and the proper test statistics, for example,

$$z = \frac{(n_d + 0.5 - np_d)}{(np_d(1 - p_d))^{0.5}},$$ (12)

where $p_d = P(D = d)$, $n = \sum_{j=1}^{M_D} n_j$. z obeys the standard normal distribution under a proper condition [18] and is considered to be an index of the bias of f. (4) If $H0$ is rejected, and then the assumed $CP(d,k)$ becomes a candidate for the rules in the rule box. (5) After repeating the processes from (1) to (4) and obtaining the set of rule candidates, STRIM arranged their rule candidates and induced the final results (see literatures [7-12] for details).

Figure 2 shows an algorithm for STRIM including a reduct function. Line No. (LN) 8 and 9 are the reduct part of the above (1), and (2) is executed at LN 10 and the dimension rule[] is used for the trying condition part of rules, (3) is executed at LN 25 in the function rule_check(), (4) is executed at LN 26 and (5) is from LN 7 to LN 11 and LN12.

4   Example of STRIM Applying to a Real-World Dataset

Rakuten Inc. presents an open dataset of Rakuten Travel [17]. This dataset contains about 6,200,000 questionnaire surveys of rating $A = \{ C(1) = $ "Location," $C(2) = $ "Room," $C(3) = $ "Meal," $C(4) = $ "Bath (Hot Spring)," $C(5) = $ "Service," $C(6) = $ "Amenity," $D = $ "Overall" } of about 130,000 travel facilities by use of a set of categorical values $V_a = \{ DS(1), SD(2), NN(3), ST(4), VS(5) \}$, $\forall a \in A$, that is, $|V_{a=D}| = M_D = |V_{a=C(j)}| = M_{C(j)} = 5$. We constructed a decision table of $N = 10,000$ questionnaire surveys by randomly selecting 2,000 samples, each of $D = m$ $(m = 1, ..., 5)$ from about 400,000 surveys of the 2013–2014 dataset since there were heavily biases with respect to the frequency of $D = m$. We applied the STRIM summarized in Sect. 3 to this decision table and obtained Table 3. This table, for example, means the following:

(1) $CP(d = 5, k = 1)$ stands for the rule stating that if $C(3) = VS(5) \bigwedge C(5) = VS(5)$ then $D = VS(5)$, and its accuracy and coverage are 0.876 and 0.639 respectively.

(2) This rule causes the frequency $f = (11, 12, 9, 146, 1258)$ and the bias at $D = 5$ is $z = 64.08$ calculated by (12) corresponding to the p-value = 0.0.

From Table 3 we can see, for example, the following:

(1) In order to gain the high evaluation at "Overall(D)," "Meal($C(3)$)" must be rated $VS(5)$ and then "Service($C(5)$)" or "Amenity($C(6)$)" can be $VS(5)$ (see $CP(5, 1)$ and $CP(5, 2)$).

Table 3. Rule induction results for Rakuten Travel dataset by STRIM.

$CP(d,k)$	$C(1)C(2)$ ...$C(6)$	D	p-value(z)	Accuracy	Coverage	$f = (n_1, n_2, n_3, n_4, n_5)$
(5,1)	005050	5	0.0 (64.08)	0.876	0.629	(11, 12, 9, 146, 1258)
(5,2)	005005	5	0.0 (58.31)	0.915	0.486	(17, 6, 5, 62, 972)
(1,1)	000010	1	0.0 (57.78)	0.766	0.639	(1277, 346, 40, 4, 1)
(4,1)	040040	4	0.0 (40.37)	0.719	0.348	(16, 37, 90, 695, 129)
(3,1)	030030	3	0.0 (38.12)	0.633	0.392	(73, 203, 784, 170, 9)
(2,1)	020000	2	3.0E-168 (27.62)	0.494	0.348	(303, 695, 351, 51, 6)

(2) Reversely, if "Service($C(5)$)" $= DS(1)$ then "Overall(D)" $= DS(1)$ (see $CP(1,1)$).

Table 3 gives us information of the rating structure of users and/or strategies for improving the facilities.

5   Studies from an Ordinal Scale and Proposal of DOMSTRIM

In Sect. 4, the rule induction by STRIM was once executed for the Rakuen Travel dataset regarding their attribute as a nominal scale. In this section, we study the same dataset taking an ordinal scale of $DS(1) < SD(2) < NN(3) < ST(4) < VS(5)$ into account and propose a DOMSTRIM which develops STRIM into a dominance-based rough set approach (DRSA). Specifically, for example, let a dataset satisfying the condition part of (8) denote with $U(CP^{\geq}(d,k)) = \{x \in U | CP^{\geq}(d,k) = \bigwedge_j (\rho(x, C(j)) \geq v_{j_k}\}$. Then the dataset can be rewritten by the decomposition of those satisfying (3) as follows:

$$U(CP^{\geq}(d,k)) = \sum_{i \geq d} U(CP(i, k_i)). \tag{13}$$

In the same way,

$$D_{\overline{d}}^{\geq} = \sum_{i \geq d} D_i. \tag{14}$$

On the other hand, STRIM induced if-then rules satisfying $U(CP(i,k)) \subseteq D_i$ within proper errors corresponding to (3) of the lower approximation. Accordingly, $U(CP(i,k)) \subseteq D_i$ induced by STRIM satisfies $\sum_{i=d} U(CP(i, k_i)) \subseteq \sum_{i=d} D_i$ within proper errors and also constructs one of the if-then rules satisfying (8) within proper errors, which shows STRIM handling a nominal scale to be easily developed into a model of DRSA.

Taking the above consideration and Table 3 showing the results: if $CP(d,k) = \bigwedge_j (C(j) = d)$ then $D = d$ ($d = 1, ..., 5$) into account, it is proper for Rakuten

Table 4. Part of rule candidates for Rakuten Travel dataset by DOMSTRIM: at-least rule candidates.

Trying $CP^{\geq}(d,k)$	$C(1)C(2)$ $...C(6)$	$D^{\geq}$	p-value(z)	Accuracy	Coverage	$f = (n^{<}, n^{\geq})$
(5,1)	005050	5	0.0(64.1)	0.876	0.629	(178, 1258)
(5,2)	000050	5	0.0(64.0)	0.764	0.788	(488, 1576)
(5,3)	050050	5	0.0(63.7)	0.889	0.608	(152, 1215)
(4,1)	040040	4	0.0(61.8)	0.931	0.756	(224, 3024)
(4,2)	044040	4	0.0(61.3)	0.970	0.674	(83, 2694)
(5,4)	055050	5	0.0(60.8)	0.942	0.505	(62, 1009)
(5,5)	000055	5	0.0(60.0)	0.881	0.547	(148, 1093)
(4,3)	400044	4	0.0(58.5)	0.933	0.674	(193, 2695)
(3,1)	033033	3	0.0(52.0)	0.967	0.775	(159, 4650)
(3,2)	033333	3	0.0(51.8)	0.978	0.732	(98, 4394)
(3,3)	033330	3	0.0(51.7)	0.968	0.763	(151, 4575)
(3,4)	333033	3	0.0(51.6)	0.970	0.754	(140, 4522)
(3,5)	333030	3	0.0(51.1)	0.956	0.789	(220, 4731)
(2,1)	022222	2	0.0(37.7)	0.987	0.801	(87, 6410)
(2,2)	022022	2	1.1E-299(37.0)	0.980	0.826	(134, 6606)
(2,3)	020000	2	1.16E-78(18.7)	0.880	0.942	(1018, 7536)
...	...	...	...	...	...	...

dataset to specify the following model for (8): if $CP^{\geq}(d,k) = \bigwedge_j (C(j) \geq d)$ then $D \geq d$. Moreover, in the case $D \geq 2$ (the case of $D \geq 1$ is self-evident), Table 3 shows that the condition part of trying rules should be constructed by combinations of $C(j) \geq d$ ($j = 2, 3, 5$, and 6) (the constructing strategy for rule candidates). However, we constructed the condition of trying rules by all the combinations of $C(j) \geq d$ ($j = 1, ..., 6$) to extensively search for the condition part. Table 4 corresponding to Table 3 shows part of the candidates by the searching procedures. For example, trying $CP^{\geq}(5,1)$ shows that if $CP^{\geq}(5,1) = C(3) \geq 5 \bigwedge C(5) \geq 5$ then $D \geq 5$, and that the accuracy can be calculated as $1,258/(178 + 1,258) = 0.876$, the coverage is 0.629 and the bias of the rule is 64.1 calculated by use of the expression corresponding to (12). We can further see the following:

(1) $U(CP^{\geq}(5,1)) \subseteq U(CP^{\geq}(5,2))$
(2) $U(CP^{\geq}(5,3)) \subseteq U(CP^{\geq}(5,2))$
(3) The z of $CP^{\geq}(5,1)$ is the greatest among those of $CP^{\geq}(5,1)$, $CP^{\geq}(5,2)$ and $CP^{\geq}(5,3)$. Accordingly $CP^{\geq}(5,1)$ should represent their candidates.

This kind of procedure for inducing dominance rules is called DOMSTRIM named after DOMLEM [14].

Table 5. Results for Rakuten Travel dataset by DOMSTRIM: (a) at-least rules: $CP^{\geq}(d,k)$, (b) at-most rules: $CP^{\leq}(d,k)$.

(a)

$CP^{\geq}(d,k)$	$C(1)C(2)$ ...$C(6)$	$D^{\geq}$	p-value(z)	accuracy	coverage	$f = (n^{<}, n^{\geq})$
(2,1)	022222	2	1.05E-299(37.6)	0.987	0.801	(87, 6410)
(3,1)	033033	3	0.00(52.0)	0.967	0.775	(159, 4650)
(4,1)	040040	4	0.0(61.8)	0.931	0.756	(224, 3024)
(5,1)	005050	5	0.0(64.1)	0.876	0.628	(178, 1258)
(5,2)	005005	5	0.0(58.3.)	0.915	0.486	(90, 972)

(b)

$CP^{\leq}(d,k)$	$C(1)C(2)$ ...$C(6)$	$D^{\leq}$	p-value(z)	accuracy	coverage	$f = (n^{\leq}, n^{>})$
(4,1)	044040	4	0.0(38.2)	0.987	0.826	(6607, 90)
(4,2)	040044	4	0.0(37.9)	0.984	0.835	(6681, 108)
(3,1)	030030	3	0.0(49.1)	0.956	0.729	(4371, 202)
(3,1)	003030	3	0.00(47.9)	0.950	0.711	(4268, 223)
(2,1)	000020	2	0.0(54.7)	0.867	0.653	(2610, 301)
(2,2)	020000	2	0.0(47.5)	0.836	0.596	(2384, 468)
(1,1)	000010	1	0.0(58.3)	0.915	0.486	(90, 972)

Table 5(a) shows the end arrangement of Table 4. $CP^{\geq}(2,1) =$ "022222" is seen in Table 5(a) and Table 4. It should be noted that $CP^{\geq}(2,2) =$ "022022" in Table 4 was constructed by the above constructing strategy for rule candidates ($C(j) \geq d$ ($j = 2, 3, 5$, and 6)) and the z of $CP^{\geq}(2,2)$ was just less than that of $CP^{\geq}(2,1)$. As another example, there is $CP^{\geq}(2,3) =$ "020000" in Table 4 which can be easily derived from $CP(2,1) =$ "020000" in Table 3 by use of the principle of DRSA. DOMSTRIM selected $CP^{\geq}(2,1) =$ "022222" as their representative in Table 5 based on the principle of selecting one of the most biased among their inclusion relation. The above mentioned strategy for rule candidates is proved to be sufficiently proper. The same circumstances happened with regard to $CP^{\geq}(3,1)$ in Table 5(a). $CP^{\geq}(5,1)$, $CP^{\geq}(5,2)$ and $CP^{\geq}(4,1)$ in Table 5(a), however, coincide with those derived from Table 3 by use of the principle of DRSA. Table 5(b) also shows the results of the at-most rules without the self-evident case of $D \leq 5$ corresponding to (9) by use of the same inducing procedures of the at-least rules corresponding to (8). Furthermore, we have the same consideration as those in the case of Table 5(a).

Table 5 (a) (b) including the knowledge from Table 3, for example, indicates the following:

(1) In order to get more than "Satisfied (ST)" at $D =$ "Overall," we should get more than "Satisfied (ST)" at $C(2) =$ "Room" and $C(5) =$ "Service" (see $CP^{\geq}(4,1)$).

(2) The reason why $D =$ "Overall" stays less than "Somewhat dissatisfied (SD)" shows that it is highly possibly that $C(5) =$ "Service" or $C(2) =$ "Room" stay less than "Somewhat dissatisfied (SD)" (see $CP^{\leq}(2,1)$ and $CP^{\leq}(2,2)$).

From the above considerations, DOMSTRIM which at first analyzes the decision table recognizing its attributes as a nominal scale and then reuses the results for inducing if-then rules based on DRSA recognizing them an ordinal scale, is found to be very effective for the rule induction and useful for marketing strategies.

6   Proposal of Consistency Index for Dominance

The rules induced by DOMSTRIM satisfy the relation: $D_{\bar{r}}^{\geq} \supset D_{\bar{s}}^{\geq}$ for $r < s, \forall r, s \in TT = \{1, ..., M_D\}$, and $U(CP^{\geq}(r,k)) \subseteq D_{\bar{r}}^{\geq}$ and $U(CP^{\geq}(s,k)) \subseteq D_{\bar{s}}^{\geq}$ are held within admissible errors. Accordingly, the inclusion relation: $U(CP^{\geq}(r,k_r)) \supset U(CP^{\geq}(s,k_s))$ should be held within some proper errors. One of the degrees holding this condition named Consistency Index of at-least Dominance denoted with $CID^{\geq}$ is formulated as follows:

$$CID^{\geq} = \frac{|U(CP^{\geq}(r,k)) \cap U(CP^{\geq}(s,k))|}{|U(CP^{\geq}(s,k))|}. \tag{15}$$

Table 6(a) shows each $CID^{\geq}$ calculated by (15) for Table 5(a). For example, $U(CP^{\geq}(2,1))$ includes $U(CP^{\geq}(3,1))$ and $U(CP^{\geq}(4,1))$ by 99.7 [%] and 99.8

Table 6. Consistency Index for Dominance (CID) against results of Rakuten Travel dataset by DOMSTRIM: (a) Consistency Index of at-least Dominance $(CID^{\geq})$, (b) Consistency Index of at-most Dominance $(CID^{\leq})$.

(a)

$CP^{\geq}(d,k)$	(2,1)	(3,1)	(4,1)	(5,1)	(5,2)
(2,1)	1	0.997	0.998	1	1
(3,1)	–	1	0.992	0.999	1
(4,1)	–	–	1	0.997	0.999

(b)

$CP^{\leq}(d,k)$	(4,1)	(4,2)	(3,1)	(3,2)	(2,1)	(2,2)	(1,1)
(4,1)	1	0.967	0.986	0.989	0.982	0.989	0.993
(4,2)	–	1	0.990	0.980	0.983	0.992	0.993
(3,1)	–	–	1	0.938	0.960	0.983	0.982
(3,2)	–	–	–	1	0.960	0.952	0.984
(2,1)	–	–	–	–	1	0.915	1
(2,2)	–	–	–	–	–	1	0.951

[%] respectively. Figure 3(a) illustrates the inclusion relations for Table 6(a) to easily see their relations by the values in the figure which corresponds to those in italic in the table. In the same way, Consistency Index of at-most Dominance denoted with $CID^{\leq}$ is formulated as follows:

$$CID^{\leq} = \frac{|U(CP^{\leq}(r,k)) \cap U(CP^{\leq}(s,k))|}{|U(CP^{\leq}(r,k))|},$$ (16)

and each $CID^{\leq}$ is shown in Table 6(b) for Table 5(b) and illustrated in Fig. 3(b).

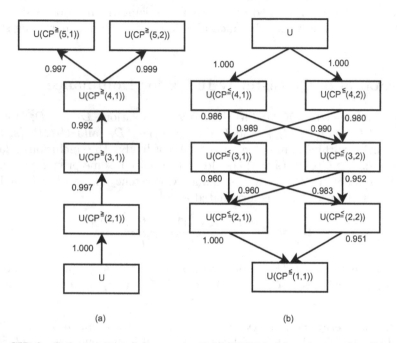

(a)   (b)

Fig. 3. CID for Rakuten Travel dataset by DOLSTRIM: (a) at-least rules, (b) at-most rules.

Each $CID^{\geq}$ and $CID^{\leq}$ shown in Table 6 shows high degrees of inclusion relations. Table 6 confirms not only the validity of the results for the rule induction by DOMSTRIM in Table 5 but also the consistency of Rakuten Travel dataset rated by the ordinal scale since the consistent rule set with high degrees of Consistency Index of Dominance (CID) is never derived from inappropriate rule induction methods and/or the inconsistent dataset.

7   Examinations by DOMLEM

The open and free software jMAF [16] implementing DOMLEM [14,15] was applied for the Rakuten Travel dataset specifying the condition to induce the at-least rules of $CP^{\geq}(d,k)$ and the at-most rules of $CP^{\leq}(d,k)$ with accuracy (consistency level) of more than 0.8. The software induced 119 $CP^{\geq}(d,k)$s consisting of those of the number of 42, 39, 29 and 9 for $d = 5, 4, 3$ and 2 respectively. The parts of rules are shown in Table 7 which presents us with rules of long rule lengths of five or six, while $CP^{\geq}(5,1)$ and $CP^{\geq}(5,2)$ in Table 5(a) induced by DOMSTRIM are two. In the same way, the software induced 94 $CP^{\leq}(d,k)$s consisting of the numbers 56, 20, 17 and 1 for $d = 1, 2, 3$ and 4 respectively. The software seemed to induce $CP^{\geq}(d,k)$s or $CP^{\leq}(d,k)$s satisfying the specified accuracy of (8) or (9) by just changing the condition part of the rules. As a result, the software seemed to induce a large number of rules without the arrangement like DOMSTRIM and the index like CID proposed by DOMSTRIM, and had difficulty presenting any knowledge and/or information for the dataset and any strategies for the marketing to compare with those by DOMSTRIM.

Table 7. Examples of results against Rakuten Travel dataset by jMAF in the case of at-least rules with accuracy of more than 0.8.

No.	Induced rules
1	(C1 >= 4) & (C2 >= 2) & (C3 >= 4) & (C5 >= 5) & (C6 >= 5) =>(D >= 5) |CERTAIN, AT_LEAST, 5|
2	(C1 >= 5) & (C2 >= 5) & (C3 >= 4) & (C4 >= 5) & (C6 >= 5) =>(D >= 5) |CERTAIN, AT_LEAST, 5|
3	(C1 >= 4) & (C2 >= 5) & (C3 >= 2) & (C4 >= 3) & (C5 >= 4) & (C6 >= 5) =>(D >= 5) |CERTAIN, AT_LEAST,5|
4	(C1 >= 5) & (C2 >= 5) & (C4 >= 4) & (C5 >= 2) & (C6 >= 5) =>(D >= 5) |CERTAIN, AT_LEAST, 5|
5	(C1 >= 4) & (C2 >= 4) & (C3 >= 4) & (C4 >= 4) & (C5 >= 4) & (C6 >= 5) =>(D >- 5) |CERTAIN, AT_LEAST, 5|
6	(C2 >= 5) & (C3 >= 3) & (C4 >= 5) & (C5 >= 5) & (C6 >= 3) =>(D >= 5) |CERTAIN, AT_LEAST, 5|
7	(C2 >= 2) & (C3 >= 5) & (C4 >= 5) & (C5 >= 5) & (C6 >= 2) =>(D >= 5) |CERTAIN, AT_LEAST, 5|
8	(C1 >= 5) & (C2 >= 4) & (C3 >= 4) & (C5 >= 5) & (C6 >= 2) =>(D >= 5) |CERTAIN, AT_LEAST, 5|
9	(C1 >= 5) & (C2 >= 4) & (C4 >= 2) & (C5 >= 5) & (C6 >= 4) =>(D >= 5) |CERTAIN, AT_LEAST, 5|
...	...

8   Conclusions

The conventional rough sets theory is used for inducing if-then rules from a dataset called the decision table which is assumed, in principle, to consist of attributes of a nominal scale, and has developed various kinds of methods and algorithms for it [1–6]. The theory also has expanded the methods and algorithms to be able to handle a dataset of an ordinal scale, which is called DRSA, and DOMLEM and jMAF implementing DOMLEM are well known [13–16].

We also proposed STRIM for inducing if-then rules statistically expanding VPRS [4] of the conventional method and confirmed its validity and usefulness by a simulation experiment [7–12]. In this paper, we also expanded STRIM to be able to handle such a dataset of an ordinal scale through the rule induction process from Rakuten Travel dataset which was a typical real-world dataset of an ordinal scale. Specifically, we first induced rules from the dataset recognizing its attributes as a nominal scale and extracted their pairs of the condition attribute and its value connecting to each decision attribute value of their rules. This process was a kind of reduct process for DRSA. We then decided the form of the at-least and/or at-most rules based on the results from the first step and applied STRIM expanded for handing such ordinal datasets. We called this expanded method DOMSTRIM named after DOMLEM. Furthermore, we proposed a Consistency Index of Dominance (CID ($CID^{\geq}$ and $CID^{\leq}$)) to confirm the validity of rules induced by DRSA. Lastly, we confirmed that the induced rule set was found to be reasonable coordinating with our common sense and useful for the marketing strategy comparing with those by jMAF.

Acknowledgements. We truly thank Rakuten Inc. for presenting Rakuten Travel dataset [17].

References

1. Pawlak, Z.: Rough sets. Internat. J. Inform. Comput. Sci. **11**(5), 341–356 (1982)
2. Skowron, A., Rauser, C.M.: The discernibility matrix and functions in information systems. In: Słowiński, R. (ed.) Intelegent Decision Support, pp. 331–362. Kluwer Academic Publishers, Berlin (1992)
3. Grzymala-Busse, J.W.: LERS – a system for learning from examples based on rough sets. In: Słowiński, R. (ed.) Intelligent Decision Support, pp. 3–18. Kluwer Academic Publishers, Berlin (1992)
4. Ziarko, W.: Variable precision rough set model. J. Comput. Syst. Sci. **46**, 39–59 (1993)
5. Shan, N., Ziarko, W.: Data-based acquisition and incremental modification of classification rules. Comput. Intell. **11**(2), 357–370 (1995)
6. Błaszczynski, J., Słowinski, R., Szela, M.: Sequential covering rule induction algorithm for variable consistency rough set approaches. Inf. Sci. **181**, 987–1002 (2011)
7. Matsubayashi, T., Kato, Y., Saeki, T.: A new rule induction method from a decision table using a statistical test. In: Li, T., Nguyen, H.S., Wang, G., Grzymala-Busse, J., Janicki, R., Hassanien, A.E., Yu, H. (eds.) RSKT 2012. LNCS (LNAI), vol. 7414, pp. 81–90. Springer, Heidelberg (2012). doi:10.1007/978-3-642-31900-6_11
8. Kato, Y., Saeki, T., Mizuno, S.: Studies on the necessary data size for rule induction by STRIM. In: Lingras, P., Wolski, M., Cornelis, C., Mitra, S., Wasilewski, P. (eds.) RSKT 2013. LNCS (LNAI), vol. 8171, pp. 213–220. Springer, Heidelberg (2013). doi:10.1007/978-3-642-41299-8_20

9. Kato, Y., Saeki, T., Mizuno, S.: Considerations on rule induction procedures by STRIM and their relationship to VPRS. In: Kryszkiewicz, M., Cornelis, C., Ciucci, D., Medina-Moreno, J., Motoda, H., Raś, Z.W. (eds.) RSEISP 2014. LNCS, vol. 8537, pp. 198–208. Springer, Cham (2014). doi:10.1007/978-3-319-08729-0_19

10. Kato, Y., Saeki, T., Mizuno, S.: Proposal of a statistical test rule induction method by use of the decision table. Appl. Soft Comput. **28**, 160–166 (2015)

11. Kato, Y., Saeki, T., Mizuno, S.: Proposal for a statistical reduct method for decision tables. In: Ciucci, D., Wang, G., Mitra, S., Wu, W.-Z. (eds.) RSKT 2015. LNCS, vol. 9436, pp. 140–152. Springer, Cham (2015). doi:10.1007/978-3-319-25754-9_13

12. Kitazaki, Y., Saeki, T., Kato, Y.: Performance comparison to a classification problem by the second method of quantification and STRIM. In: Flores, V., Gomide, F., Janusz, A., Meneses, C., Miao, D., Peters, G., Ślęzak, D., Wang, G., Weber, R., Yao, Y. (eds.) IJCRS 2016. LNCS, vol. 9920, pp. 406–415. Springer, Cham (2016). doi:10.1007/978-3-319-47160-0_37

13. Greco, S., Matarazzo, B., Słowinski, R.: The use of rough sets and fuzzy sets in MCDM. In: Gal, T., Stewart, T.J., Hanne, T. (eds.) Multicriteria Decision Making, pp. 14-1–14-59. Kluwer Academic Publishers, Berlin (1999)

14. Greco, S., Matarazzo, B., Slowinski, R., Stefanowski, J.: An algorithm for induction of decision rules consistent with the dominance principle. In: Ziarko, W., Yao, Y. (eds.) RSCTC 2000. LNCS, vol. 2005, pp. 304–313. Springer, Heidelberg (2001). doi:10.1007/3-540-45554-X_37

15. Greco, S., Matarazzo, B., Slowinski, R., Stefanowski, J.: Variable consistency model of dominance-based rough sets approach. In: Ziarko, W., Yao, Y. (eds.) RSCTC 2000. LNCS, vol. 2005, pp. 170–181. Springer, Heidelberg (2001). doi:10.1007/3-540-45554-X_20

16. http://idss.cs.put.poznan.pl/site/139.html

17. http://rit.rakuten.co.jp/opendataj.html

18. Walpole, R.E., Myers, R.H., Myers, S.L., Ye, K.: Probability and Statistics for Engineers and Scientists, pp. 187–190. Eighth edition, Pearson Prentice Hall (2007)

Regularization and Shrinkage in Rough Set Based Canonical Correlation Analysis

Ankita Mandal and Pradipta Maji[✉]

Biomedical Imaging and Bioinformatics Lab Machine Intelligence Unit,
Indian Statistical Institute, Kolkata, India
{amandal,pmaji}@isical.ac.in

Abstract. The modern technology has enabled very high dimensional multimodal data streams to be routinely acquired, which results in very high dimensional feature spaces (p) as compared to number of training samples (n). In this regard, the paper presents a new feature extraction algorithm to address the 'small n and large p' problem associated with multimodal data sets. It judiciously integrates both regularization and shrinkage with canonical correlation analysis (CCA). While the diagonal elements of covariance matrices are increased using regularization parameters, the off-diagonal elements are decreased by shrinkage parameters. The theory of rough sets is used to find out the optimum regularization parameters of CCA. The effectiveness of the proposed method, along with a comparison with other methods, is demonstrated on three pairs of modalities of two real life data sets.

1 Introduction

Simultaneous analysis of different omics data may provide a better understanding of the biological systems. Such an analysis enables a true understanding on the relationships between these different types of variables. Multimodal data such as transcriptomics, proteomics or metabolomics data contain more information and help to create linkages between attributes within each type of data. There exist many approaches to deal with these high throughput data [10,16,17,29,30].

Canonical correlation analysis (CCA) [12] is a popular exploratory statistical method, which allows the analysis of the relationships that exist between two sets of variables. The best linear transformation for two multidimensional data sets, which gives the maximum correlation between them can be achieved by using CCA. CCA has been successfully applied to many important fields of biomedical sciences [10,16,17,25,29,30]. It extracts those relevant features from both data types, which provide more insight into biological experimental hypotheses.

Let p and q be the number of features of two multivariate data sets X and Y respectively, where the number of samples in both X and Y is n. The modern technology has enabled more directions on data streams, which ensues in very high dimensional feature spaces p and q. On the other hand, the number of

This work is partially supported by the Department of Electronics and Information Technology, Government of India (PhD-MLA/4(90)/2015-16).

L. Polkowski et al. (Eds.): IJCRS 2017, Part I, LNAI 10313, pp. 432–446, 2017.
DOI: 10.1007/978-3-319-60837-2_36

training samples n is usually limited. When $n \ll (p, q)$, the features in X and Y tend to be highly collinear, which leads to ill-conditioned of the covariance matrices C_{xx} and C_{yy} of X and Y, respectively. In effect, their inverses are no longer reliable, resulting in an invalid computation of CCA [8].

There are two ways to overcome this problem. The first possible approach has been introduced in [7], which is a regularized version of CCA. In regularized CCA (RCCA) [6,28], the diagonal elements of C_{xx} and C_{yy} have to be increased using a grid search optimization. On the other hand, off-diagonal elements remain constant. This method is computationally expensive and the results depend on the range of regularization parameters provided by the user. The second alternative method of regularization algorithm is based on the optimal estimates of the correlation matrices [1]. This algorithm is known as fast RCCA (FRCCA), because it is computationally inexpensive and relatively fast to estimate the results. In FRCCA, shrinkage coefficients [24] are estimated to invert the C_{xx} and C_{yy}. The procedure used to obtain the minimum mean squared error estimator of a correlation matrix [24] can be applied to estimate any correlation matrix. It is not limited to intra-set correlation matrices such as C_{xx} and C_{yy}; it can also be applied to find the minimum mean squared error estimator of C_{xy} [1]. These shrinkage coefficients reduce the values of off-diagonal elements of C_{xx} and C_{yy}, where the values of diagonal elements remain same. However, CCA, RCCA and FRCCA all are unsupervised in nature and fail to take complete advantage of available class label information [1,5]. To incorporate the class information, some supervised version of RCCA have been introduced, termed as supervised RCCA (SRCCA) [5,15,20]. It includes available class label information to select maximally correlated features.

One of the main problems in omics data analysis is uncertainty. Rough set theory [23] is an effective paradigm to deal with uncertainty, vagueness, and incompleteness. It provides a mathematical framework to capture uncertainties associated with the data [2]. In this context, a feature extraction algorithm, termed as CuRSaR [19], has been introduced, which judiciously integrates the merits of SRCCA and rough sets. It extracts the maximally correlated features from two multidimensional data sets. To compute the relevance and significance of the extracted features, rough hypercuboid approach of [18] is used. However, the CuRSaR fails to produce the optimal set of relevant and significant features.

To deal with the singularity issue of covariance matrices, RCCA increases the diagonal elements, whereas FRCCA decreases the off-diagonal elements of covariance matrices. If both can be done concurrently, it is expected to give better results. In this regard, the paper presents a new feature extraction algorithm, which integrates the advantages of both RCCA and FRCCA to handle the ill-conditioned of the covariance matrices. The diagonal elements of covariance matrices are increased by using regularization parameters, whereas the off-diagonal elements are decreased by using shrinkage parameters. It also integrates the merits of rough hypercuboid approach to extract maximally correlated and most relevant and significant features. The effectiveness of the proposed method, along with a comparison with other methods, is demonstrated on several real life data sets.

2   Basics of Canonical Correlation Analysis, Rough Sets and Rough Hypercuboid Approach

This section presents the basic concepts in the theories of CCA, rough sets and rough hypercuboid approach.

2.1   Canonical Correlation Analysis

CCA [12] is used to extract latent features, which are maximally correlated between two multidimensional variables $X \in \mathbb{R}^{p \times n}$ and $Y \in \mathbb{R}^{q \times n}$. Here n is the number of samples, p and q are the number of features of X and Y, respectively. CCA obtains two directional basis vectors $w_x \in \mathbb{R}^p$ and $w_y \in \mathbb{R}^q$ such that the correlation between $X^T w_x$ and $Y^T w_y$ is maximum. The correlation coefficient ρ is given as

$$\rho = \max_{w_x, w_y} \frac{w_x{}^T C_{xy} w_y}{\sqrt{w_x{}^T C_{xx} w_x w_y{}^T C_{yy} w_y}} \qquad (1)$$

where $C_{xy} \in \mathbb{R}^{p \times q}$ is the cross-covariance matrix of X and Y, while $C_{xx} \in \mathbb{R}^{p \times p}$ and $C_{yy} \in \mathbb{R}^{q \times q}$ are covariance matrices of X and Y, respectively. To calculate the basis vectors w_x and w_y, eigenvectors of $\Sigma \Sigma^T$ and $\Sigma^T \Sigma$ are needed, where matrix $\Sigma \in \mathbb{R}^{p \times q}$ is given as follows:

$$\Sigma = C_{xx}^{-1/2} C_{xy} C_{yy}^{-1/2}. \qquad (2)$$

The t-th pair of basis vectors is given by

$$w_{xt} = C_{xx}^{-1/2} \xi_{xt}; \quad \text{and} \quad w_{yt} = C_{yy}^{-1/2} \xi_{yt}; \qquad (3)$$

and the t-th pair of canonical variables is as follows:

$$\mathcal{U}_t = w_{xt}^T X; \quad \text{and} \quad \mathcal{V}_t = w_{yt}^T Y. \qquad (4)$$

where ξ_{xt} and ξ_{yt} are the orthonormalized eigenvectors of $\Sigma \Sigma^T$ and $\Sigma^T \Sigma$, respectively with corresponding eigenvalue ρ_t.

2.2   Rough Sets

An approximation space or information system is a pair $<\mathbb{U}, \mathbb{A}>$ [23], where the universe of discourse $\mathbb{U} = \{O_1, \cdots, O_t, \cdots, O_n\}$ be a non-empty set, and $\mathbb{A}$ is a family of attributes known as knowledge in the universe. $<\mathbb{U}, \mathbb{A}>$ is called a decision table if the set $\mathbb{A} = \mathbb{C} \cup \mathbb{D}$, where $\mathbb{C} = \{\mathcal{A}_1, \cdots, \mathcal{A}_t, \cdots, \mathcal{A}_m\}$ and $\mathbb{D}$ are condition and decision attribute sets, respectively. $\mathbb{V}$ is the value domain of $\mathbb{A}$ and f is an information function $f : \mathbb{U} \times \mathbb{A} \to \mathbb{V}$. Any subset $\mathcal{R}$ of knowledge $\mathbb{A}$ defines an equivalence or indiscernibility relation $IND(\mathcal{R})$ on $\mathbb{U}$

$$IND(\mathcal{R}) = \{(O_i, O_j) \in \mathbb{U} \times \mathbb{U} | \forall a \in \mathcal{R}, f(O_i, a) = f(O_j, a)\}. \qquad (5)$$

If $(O_i, O_j) \in \mathcal{IND}(\mathcal{R})$, then O_i and O_j are indiscernible by attributes from $\mathcal{R}$. The partition of $\mathbb{U}$ generated by $\mathcal{IND}(\mathcal{R})$ is denoted as

$$\mathbb{U}/\mathcal{IND}(\mathcal{R}) = \{[O_i]_{\mathcal{R}} : O_i \in \mathbb{U}\} \tag{6}$$

where $[O_i]_{\mathcal{R}}$ is the equivalence class containing O_i. The elements in $[O_i]_{\mathcal{R}}$ are indiscernible or equivalent with respect to knowledge $\mathcal{R}$. Equivalence classes, also termed as information granules, are used to characterize arbitrary subsets of $\mathbb{U}$. The equivalence classes of $\mathcal{IND}(\mathcal{R})$ and the empty set $\emptyset$ are the elementary sets in the approximation space $<\mathbb{U}, \mathbb{A}>$.

Given an arbitrary set $\beta \subseteq \mathbb{U}$, in general, it may not be possible to describe β precisely in $<\mathbb{U}, \mathbb{A}>$. One may characterize β by a pair of lower and upper approximations, defined as follows [23]:

$$\underline{\mathcal{R}}(\beta) = \bigcup\{[O_i]_{\mathcal{R}} \mid [O_i]_{\mathcal{R}} \subseteq \beta\}; \quad \text{and} \tag{7}$$

$$\overline{\mathcal{R}}(\beta) = \bigcup\{[O_i]_{\mathcal{R}} \mid [O_i]_{\mathcal{R}} \cap \beta \neq \emptyset\}. \tag{8}$$

Hence, the lower approximation $\underline{\mathcal{R}}(\beta)$ is the union of all the elementary sets which are subsets of β, and the upper approximation $\overline{\mathcal{R}}(\beta)$ is the union of all the elementary sets which have a non-empty intersection with β. The tuple $<\underline{\mathcal{R}}(\beta), \overline{\mathcal{R}}(\beta)>$ is the representation of an ordinary set β in the approximation space $<\mathbb{U}, \mathbb{A}>$ or simply called the rough set of β. The lower (respectively, upper) approximation $\underline{\mathcal{R}}(\beta)$ (respectively, $\overline{\mathcal{R}}(\beta)$) is interpreted as the collection of those elements of $\mathbb{U}$ that definitely (respectively, possibly) belong to β. A set β is said to be definable or exact in $<\mathbb{U}, \mathbb{A}>$ iff $\underline{\mathcal{R}}(\beta) = \overline{\mathcal{R}}(\beta)$. Otherwise β is indefinable and termed as a rough set. $\mathcal{BND}_{\mathcal{R}}(\beta) = \overline{\mathcal{R}}(\beta) \setminus \underline{\mathcal{R}}(\beta)$ is called a boundary set.

Definition 1. *An information system $<\mathbb{U}, \mathbb{A}>$ is called a decision table if the set $\mathbb{A} = \mathbb{C} \cup \mathbb{D}$, where $\mathbb{C}$ and $\mathbb{D}$ are condition and decision attribute sets, respectively. The dependency between $\mathbb{C}$ and $\mathbb{D}$ can be defined as [23]*

$$\gamma_{\mathbb{C}}(\mathbb{D}) = \frac{|\mathcal{POS}_{\mathbb{C}}(\mathbb{D})|}{|\mathbb{U}|} \tag{9}$$

where $\mathcal{POS}_{\mathbb{C}}(\mathbb{D}) = \bigcup \underline{\mathbb{C}}(\beta_i)$ is termed as positive region of $\mathbb{D}$ with respect to $\mathbb{C}$, β_i is the ith equivalence class induced by $\mathbb{D}$ and $|\cdot|$ denotes the cardinality of a set.

Definition 2. *Given $\mathbb{C}, \mathbb{D}$ and an attribute $\mathcal{A} \in \mathbb{C}$, the significance of the attribute $\mathcal{A}$ is defined as [23]:*

$$\sigma_{\mathbb{C}}(\mathbb{D}, \mathcal{A}) = \gamma_{\mathbb{C}}(\mathbb{D}) - \gamma_{\mathbb{C} - \{\mathcal{A}\}}(\mathbb{D}). \tag{10}$$

2.3   Rough Hypercuboid Approach

Let $\mathbb{U}/\mathbb{D} = \{\beta_1, \cdots, \beta_i, \cdots, \beta_c\}$ be c equivalence classes or information granules of $\mathbb{U}$ generated by the equivalence relation induced from the decision attribute set $\mathbb{D}$. The hypercuboid equivalence partition matrix of the condition attribute $\mathcal{A}_t$ is denoted by $\mathbb{H}(\mathcal{A}_t) = [h_{ij}(\mathcal{A}_t)]_{c \times n}$ [18,22], where c and n are the number of classes and total number of samples, respectively and

$$h_{ij}(\mathcal{A}_t) = \begin{cases} 1 \text{ if } \mathcal{L}_i \leq O_j(\mathcal{A}_t) \leq \mathcal{U}_i \\ 0 \text{ otherwise.} \end{cases} \tag{11}$$

The tuple $[\mathcal{L}_i, \mathcal{U}_i]$ represents the interval of the ith class β_i according to the decision attribute set $\mathbb{D}$. The set $\beta_i \subseteq \mathbb{U}$ can be approximated using only the information contained within $\mathcal{A}_t$ by constructing the $\mathcal{R}$-lower and $\mathcal{R}$-upper approximations of β_i [18]:

$$\underline{\mathcal{R}}(\beta_i) = \{O_j | h_{ij}(\mathcal{A}_t) = 1 \text{ and } v_j(\mathcal{A}_t) = 0\}; \tag{12}$$

$$\overline{\mathcal{R}}(\beta_i) = \{O_j | h_{ij}(\mathcal{A}_t) = 1\}; \tag{13}$$

$$\text{where } v_j(\mathcal{A}_t) = \min\{1, \sum_{i=1}^{c} h_{ij}(\mathcal{A}_t) - 1\} \tag{14}$$

and equivalence relation $\mathcal{R}$ is induced from attribute $\mathcal{A}_t$. The boundary region of β_i is then defined as

$$\mathcal{BND}_{\mathcal{R}}(\beta_i) = \overline{\mathcal{R}}(\beta_i) \setminus \underline{\mathcal{R}}(\beta_i) = \{O_j | h_{ij}(\mathcal{A}_t) = 1 \text{ and } v_j(\mathcal{A}_t) = 1\}. \tag{15}$$

Hence, the dependency between condition attribute $\mathcal{A}_t$ and decision attribute $\mathbb{D}$, which is the relevance of $\mathcal{A}_t$, can be determined as follows [18]:

$$\gamma_{\mathcal{A}_t}(\mathbb{D}) = 1 - \frac{1}{n} \sum_{j=1}^{n} v_j(\mathcal{A}_t) \tag{16}$$

whereas the significance of the attribute $\mathcal{A}_t$ with respect to the condition attribute set $\mathbb{C}$ is given by [18]:

$$\sigma_{\mathbb{C}}(\mathbb{D}, \mathcal{A}_t) = \frac{1}{n} \sum_{j=1}^{n} \left[v_j(\mathbb{C} - \{\mathcal{A}_t\}) - v_j(\mathbb{C}) \right]. \tag{17}$$

3   Proposed Method

This section presents a new feature extraction algorithm, integrating judiciously the advantages of both RCCA and FRCCA to take care of the singularity problem of covariance matrices. The proposed method also incorporates the available class label information to make it supervised. Prior to describing the proposed method for multimodal data analysis, some important analytical formulations are reported next.

Suppose $\mathcal{X} \in \mathbb{R}^{p \times n}$ and $\mathcal{Y} \in \mathbb{R}^{q \times n}$ be two multidimensional variables with n unique samples. The number of features p and q of $\mathcal{X}$ and $\mathcal{Y}$, respectively, are larger than n, that is, $n \ll (p, q)$, which make the covariance matrices C_{xx}

and C_{yy} ill-conditioned. That means, the inverses of C_{xx} and C_{yy} do not make any sense [8]. To overcome this problem, RCCA [6,28] has been introduced, where regularization is done by a grid search optimization [9]. This is done by adding small positive quantities, also called regularization parameters, to the diagonals of C_{xx} and C_{yy}, which make them invertible [11]. The regularization parameters, r_x and r_y, vary within a range $[r_{min}, r_{max}]$, where $r_{min} \leqslant r_x, r_y \leqslant r_{max}$. The optimal parameter set of r_x and r_y is selected for which the Pearson's correlation is maximum, that is

$$\max_{r_x, r_y} \frac{w_x{}^T C_{xy} w_y}{\sqrt{w_x{}^T [C_{xx} + r_x I] w_x \, w_y{}^T [C_{yy} + r_y I] w_y}}. \tag{18}$$

In [1], another alternative method, named FRCCA, has been proposed to make covariance matrix invertible. Here, shrinkage parameters s_x and s_y are used to handle the singularity problem of covariance matrices C_{xx} and C_{yy}, respectively. The shrinkage parameter s_{xy} is also used to find the minimum mean squared error estimator of cross-covariance matrix C_{xy}. So,

$$[\tilde{C}_{xx}]_{ij} = (1 - s_x)[C_{xx}]_{ij}; \quad [\tilde{C}_{yy}]_{ij} = (1 - s_y)[C_{yy}]_{ij}; \quad \text{where } i \neq j$$

$$\text{and} \quad [\tilde{C}_{xy}]_{ij} = (1 - s_{xy})[C_{xy}]_{ij}. \quad \forall \, i, j \tag{19}$$

The best estimator of the shrinkage parameters s_x, s_y and s_{xy}, which minimize the risk function of the mean squared error, are denoted by

$$s_x = \frac{\sum_{i \neq j} \hat{V}([C_{xx}]_{ij})}{\sum_{i \neq j} [C_{xx}^2]_{ij}}; \quad s_y = \frac{\sum_{i \neq j} \hat{V}([C_{yy}]_{ij})}{\sum_{i \neq j} [C_{yy}^2]_{ij}}; \quad \text{and} \quad s_{xy} = \frac{\sum_i \sum_j \hat{V}([C_{xy}]_{ij})}{\sum_i \sum_j [C_{xy}^2]_{ij}}; \tag{20}$$

where $\hat{V}([C_{xx}]_{ij})$, $\hat{V}([C_{yy}]_{ij})$ and $\hat{V}([C_{xy}]_{ij})$ are the unbiased empirical variance of $[C_{xx}]_{ij}$, $[C_{yy}]_{ij}$ and $[C_{xy}]_{ij}$, respectively. On the other hand, (2) can be rewritten as,

$$\Sigma = \tilde{C}_{xx}{}^{-1/2} \tilde{C}_{xy} \tilde{C}_{yy}{}^{-1/2}. \tag{21}$$

However, CCA, RCCA and FRCCA all are unsupervised in nature, that is, they do not incorporate the information of class label even if it is given. In this context, a new method, named SRCCA, has been proposed in [5], which is a supervised version of CCA. SRCCA chooses the optimal regularization parameters r_x and r_y by using grid search optimization and some feature evaluation measures such as t-test [14], Wilcoxon rank sum test [26], and Wilk's lambda test [13].

To make both C_{xx} and C_{yy} invertible, RCCA adds regularization parameters to the diagonal elements of these matrices. On the other hand, FRCCA reduces the values of off-diagonal elements of these matrices using shrinkage parameters to take care of this singularity issue. In the proposed method, both of these are done simultaneously to deal with the singularity problem. Here, regularization parameters $\mathfrak{r}_x$ and $\mathfrak{r}_y$ vary within a range $[\mathfrak{r}_{min}, \mathfrak{r}_{max}]$, where common differences are d_x and d_y for $\mathfrak{r}_x$ and $\mathfrak{r}_y$, respectively and $\mathfrak{r}_{min} \leqslant \mathfrak{r}_x, \mathfrak{r}_y \leqslant \mathfrak{r}_{max}$. And the shrinkage parameters s_x, s_y and s_{xy} can be computed by using (20). Hence, to address this singularity issue, the covariance and cross-covariance matrices can be formulated as

$$[\tilde{C}_{xx}]_{ij} = \begin{cases} (1 - s_x)[C_{xx}]_{ij}; & \text{where } i \neq j \\ [C_{xx}]_{ij} + (\mathfrak{r}_x + k d_x); & \text{where } i = j \end{cases} \qquad (22)$$

$$[\tilde{C}_{yy}]_{ij} = \begin{cases} (1 - s_y)[C_{yy}]_{ij}; & \text{where } i \neq j \\ [C_{yy}]_{ij} + (\mathfrak{r}_y + l d_y); & \text{where } i = j \end{cases} \qquad (23)$$

$$\text{and} \quad [\tilde{C}_{xy}]_{ij} = (1 - s_{xy})[C_{xy}]_{ij}; \qquad \forall \, i, j \qquad (24)$$

where $\forall k \in \{1, 2, \cdots, t_x\}$ and $\forall l \in \{1, 2, \cdots, t_y\}$. The parameters t_x and t_y denote the number of possible values of $\mathfrak{r}_x$ and $\mathfrak{r}_y$, respectively. As $\mathfrak{r}_x$ and $\mathfrak{r}_y$ vary within a range with arithmetic progression, there exists a relation between the first and the k-th and l-th eigenvalues of $\tilde{C}_{xx}$ and $\tilde{C}_{yy}$, respectively [19]. Let us assume that, Λ_x and Λ_y be the diagonal matrices, where diagonal elements are the eigenvalues of $\tilde{C}_{xx}$ and $\tilde{C}_{yy}$, respectively and the corresponding orthonormal eigenvectors are in the columns of Ψ_x and Ψ_y, respectively. The theoretical analysis, reported in [19], gives assistance to compute Σ_{kl} as follows:

$$\Sigma_{kl} = \Psi_x (\Lambda_x + (k - 1) d_x I)^{-1/2} \Psi_x^T \tilde{C}_{xy} \Psi_y (\Lambda_y + (l - 1) d_y I)^{-1/2} \Psi_y^T. \qquad (25)$$

As non-zero eigenvalues of $\Sigma_{kl} \Sigma_{kl}^T$ are same as non-zero eigenvalues of $\Sigma_{kl}^T \Sigma_{kl}$ [4], one of the matrices is enough to compute the eigenvector of $\Sigma_{kl} \Sigma_{kl}^T$ or $\Sigma_{kl}^T \Sigma_{kl}$ [19]. Hence, the t-th pair of basis vectors and canonical variables can be determined using (3) and (4), where $\forall t \in \{1, 2, \cdots, \mathcal{D}\}$ and $\mathcal{D} = \min(p, q)$.

The concept of hypercuboid equivalence partition matrix of rough hypercuboid approach [18] is used to compute both the relevance and significance of an extracted feature. The regularization parameters are optimized through computing the relevance and significance measures [19]. To solve this problem, the following greedy algorithm is used. At first, covariance matrices and cross-covariance matrix have to be computed. Then, determine the values of $\tilde{C}_{xx}$, $\tilde{C}_{yy}$ and $\tilde{C}_{xy}$ using (22), (23) and (24), respectively. The eigenvalue-eigenvector pairs of covariance matrices have to be computed next. Then, the basis vectors and canonical variables have to be calculated for (k, l)-th regularization parameters of $\mathfrak{r}_x$ and $\mathfrak{r}_y$ where $\forall k \in \{1, 2, \cdots, t_x\}$ and $\forall l \in \{1, 2, \cdots, t_y\}$. $\mathcal{D}$ number of features $\{\mathcal{A}_{kl}\}$ corresponding to (k, l)-th pair of regularization parameters can be extracted next as follows: $\mathcal{A}_t = \mathcal{U}_t + \mathcal{V}_t$, where $\forall t \in \{1, 2, \cdots, \mathcal{D}\}$ and $\mathcal{D} = \min(p, q)$. Then the relevance of all features for (k, l)-th regularization parameters of $\mathfrak{r}_x$ and $\mathfrak{r}_y$ have to be calculated by using

$$R(\mathcal{k}, \ell) = \sum_{\mathcal{A}_{t \mathcal{k}\ell} \in \mathbb{S}} \gamma_{\mathcal{A}_{t \mathcal{k}\ell}}(\mathbb{D}) \tag{26}$$

and the significance among these features is as follows

$$S(\mathcal{k}, \ell) = \sum_{\mathcal{A}_{t \mathcal{k}\ell} \neq \mathcal{A}_{\tilde{t} \mathcal{k}\ell} \in \mathbb{S}} \sigma_{\{\mathcal{A}_{t \mathcal{k}\ell}, \mathcal{A}_{\tilde{t} \mathcal{k}\ell}\}}(\mathbb{D}, \mathcal{A}_{t \mathcal{k}\ell}) + \sigma_{\{\mathcal{A}_{t \mathcal{k}\ell}, \mathcal{A}_{\tilde{t} \mathcal{k}\ell}\}}(\mathbb{D}, \mathcal{A}_{\tilde{t} \mathcal{k}\ell}). \tag{27}$$

where $\gamma_{\mathcal{A}_t}(\mathbb{D})$ is the relevance of a feature or condition attribute $\mathcal{A}_t$ with respect to the class labels or decision attribute $\mathbb{D}$ and $\sigma_{\{\mathcal{A}_t, \mathcal{A}_{\tilde{t}}\}}(\mathbb{D}, \mathcal{A}_t)$ is the significance of the feature $\mathcal{A}_t$ with respect to the feature set $\{\mathcal{A}_t, \mathcal{A}_{\tilde{t}}\}$ [19]. Finally, the objective function $J(\mathcal{k}, \ell)$ is calculated using

$$J(\mathcal{k}, \ell) = \frac{R(\mathcal{k}, \ell)}{\mathcal{D}} + \frac{S(\mathcal{k}, \ell)}{\mathcal{D}(\mathcal{D} - 1)}. \tag{28}$$

The regularization pair, for which the objective function gives maximum value, has to be selected as optimal pair.

4 Experimental Results and Discussion

This section compares the performance of the proposed feature extraction algorithm with that of some existing CCA based algorithms, namely, principal component analysis (PCA), CCA, RCCA, FRCCA, several variants of SRCCA using t-test (SRCCA$_{TT}$) [5], Wilcoxon rank sum test (SRCCA$_{WR}$) [5], and Wilks's lambda test (SRCCA$_{WL}$) [5] and CuRSaR [19]. The regularization parameters $\mathfrak{r}_\chi$ and $\mathfrak{r}_y$ are varied within $[0.0, 1.0]$ with 0.1 as common difference.

In the current research work, the multimodal data sets, named BRCA and OV, are used with three different modalities, namely, gene expression, protein expression, and DNA methylation. The data sets are downloaded from TCGA. The BRCA data set contains a total number of 204 breast invasive carcinoma samples, whereas, OV data set has 379 ovarian serous cystadenocarcinoma samples. Both BRCA and OV data set grouped into two categories: 189 samples of infiltrating ductal carcinoma and 15 samples of infiltrating lobular carcinoma for BRCA data and 51 samples of grade 2 and 328 samples of grade 3 ovarian serous cystadenocarcinoma. Both data sets contain expressions of 17 814 genes and β values of 27 578 methylated DNAs. While BRCA data has expression of 142 proteins, OV data has expression of 222 proteins. 2000 top-ranked features, based on their variances, are taken from both gene and methylation data in the current study.

To evaluate the performance of different algorithms, both support vector machine (SVM) [27] and nearest neighbor algorithm (NNA) [3] are used. To compute the classification accuracy and F1 score of different approaches 10-fold cross-validation [3] is performed. The classification accuracy is defined as [3]

$$\text{accuracy} = \frac{\text{TP+TN}}{\text{TP+FP+TN+FN}}; \tag{29}$$

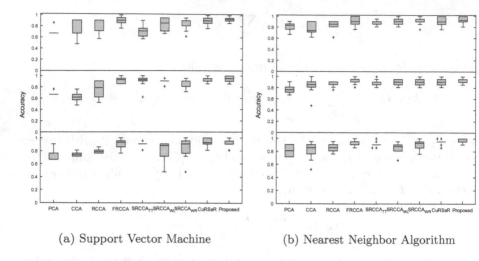

(a) Support Vector Machine   (b) Nearest Neighbor Algorithm

Fig. 1. Box and whisker plots for classification accuracy on BRCA (top: gene-DNA methylation; middle: gene-protein; and bottom: protein-DNA methylation)

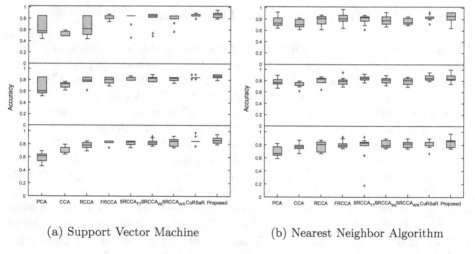

(a) Support Vector Machine   (b) Nearest Neighbor Algorithm

Fig. 2. Box and whisker plots for classification accuracy on OV (top: gene-DNA methylation; middle: gene-protein; and bottom: protein-DNA methylation)

where TP, FP, TN, and FN represent the number of true positive, false positive, true negative, and false negative samples, respectively. Similarly, the F1 score is defined as follows:

$$\text{F1 score} = \frac{2 \times \text{precision} \times \text{recall}}{\text{precision} + \text{recall}}; \tag{30}$$

where precision and recall (sensitivity) are given by

$$\text{precision} = \frac{TP}{TP+FP}; \quad \text{and} \quad \text{recall} = \frac{TP}{TP+FN}. \tag{31}$$

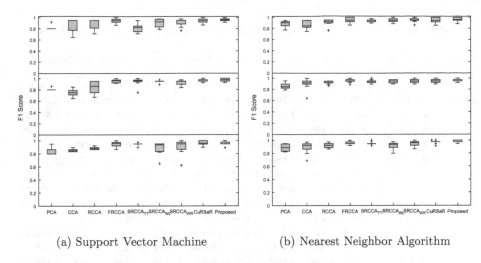

(a) Support Vector Machine   (b) Nearest Neighbor Algorithm

Fig. 3. Box and whisker plots for F1 score on BRCA (top: gene-DNA methylation; middle: gene-protein; and bottom: protein-DNA methylation)

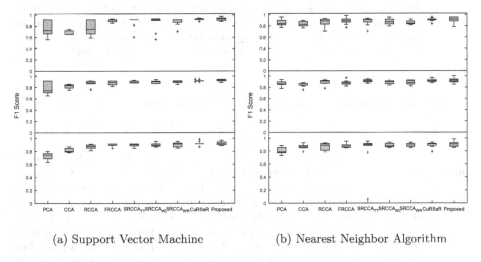

(a) Support Vector Machine   (b) Nearest Neighbor Algorithm

Fig. 4. Box and whisker plots for F1 score on OV (top: gene-DNA methylation; middle: gene-protein; and bottom: protein-DNA methylation)

For each training set, a set of correlated features is first generated and then both SVM and NNA are trained with this feature set. The correlated features which are selected for the training set are used to generate test set. Finally, the class label of the test sample is predicted using the SVM and NNA. Twenty five top-ranked correlated features are selected for the analysis.

The box and whisker plots, tables of means, standard deviations, and p-value computed through paired-t (one-tailed) test are used to study the performance of different algorithms and the proposed algorithm. Figures 1, 2 and 3, 4 show

Table 1. Classification accuracy of the SVM for proposed and other methods

Data sets	Different algorithms	Gene-protein			Protein-DNA Methy.			Gene-DNA Methy.		
		Mean	StdDev	p-value	Mean	StdDev	p-value	Mean	StdDev	p-value
BRCA	PCA	0.676	0.030	1.29E-08	0.710	0.079	1.61E-05	0.686	0.060	3.01E-06
	CCA	0.624	0.082	1.20E-06	0.748	0.039	1.48E-07	0.786	0.162	1.56E-02
	RCCA	0.752	0.165	9.15E-04	0.790	0.033	2.67E-05	0.814	0.132	1.41E-02
	FRCCA	0.914	0.054	1.84E-02	0.910	0.069	8.39E-02	0.900	0.073	3.31E-02
	SRCCA$_{TT}$	0.900	0.106	8.88E-02	0.900	0.035	6.03E-02	0.705	0.105	3.55E-05
	SRCCA$_{WL}$	0.900	0.035	1.59E-02	0.810	0.140	1.22E-02	0.833	0.113	9.56E-03
	SRCCA$_{WR}$	0.876	0.075	8.06E-03	0.852	0.163	6.06E-02	0.852	0.109	2.43E-02
	CuRSaR	0.919	0.039	5.54E-02	0.929	0.064	3.39E-01	0.867	0.160	3.31E-02
	Proposed	**0.952**	0.050		**0.938**	0.055		**0.933**	0.046	
OV	PCA	0.677	0.149	1.93E-03	0.595	0.080	4.58E-07	0.654	0.171	8.00E-04
	CCA	0.715	0.050	5.56E-05	0.695	0.055	4.00E-05	0.515	0.046	2.51E-09
	RCCA	0.787	0.068	4.55E-03	0.774	0.052	5.53E-03	0.667	0.164	1.13E-03
	FRCCA	0.792	0.059	4.30E-05	0.828	0.032	3.84E-02	0.823	0.044	2.28E-03
	SRCCA$_{TT}$	0.821	0.034	5.81E-03	0.813	0.042	2.46E-02	0.792	0.126	7.27E-02
	SRCCA$_{WL}$	0.823	0.046	2.28E-03	0.828	0.051	1.66E-02	0.787	0.146	8.55E-03
	SRCCA$_{WR}$	0.813	0.042	9.38E-03	0.828	0.062	6.70E-02	0.797	0.092	2.64E-02
	CuRSaR	0.851	0.026	6.91E-02	0.859	0.054	4.61E-01	0.851	0.026	1.99E-01
	Proposed	**0.864**	0.036		**0.862**	0.049		**0.864**	0.051	

Table 2. Classification accuracy of the NNA for proposed and other methods

Data sets	Different algorithms	Gene-protein			Protein-DNA Methy.			Gene-DNA Methy.		
		Mean	StdDev	p-value	Mean	StdDev	p-value	Mean	StdDev	p-value
BRCA	PCA	0.771	0.074	3.22E-05	0.810	0.081	2.67E-05	0.810	0.074	8.09E-04
	CCA	0.833	0.144	3.69E-02	0.814	0.132	3.93E-03	0.771	0.105	4.70E-04
	RCCA	0.857	0.045	7.48E-03	0.852	0.061	1.00E-03	0.838	0.088	1.89E-02
	FRCCA	0.914	0.054	2.60E-01	0.938	0.045	8.39E-02	0.905	0.084	4.79E-02
	SRCCA$_{TT}$	0.900	0.052	8.39E-02	0.910	0.042	7.48E-03	0.890	0.045	7.63E-02
	SRCCA$_{WL}$	0.890	0.055	6.03E-02	0.857	0.081	1.98E-03	0.905	0.063	2.61E-02
	SRCCA$_{WR}$	0.905	0.055	1.06E-01	0.905	0.074	1.21E-02	0.914	0.070	2.60E-01
	CuRSaR	0.910	0.061	1.35E-01	0.948	0.042	1.72E-01	0.924	0.060	4.79E-02
	Proposed	**0.929**	0.046		**0.957**	0.035		**0.929**	0.064	
OV	PCA	0.677	0.149	3.41E-03	0.692	0.075	1.31E-03	0.759	0.090	3.97E-02
	CCA	0.726	0.050	2.46E-04	0.772	0.053	1.36E-02	0.726	0.072	1.71E-04
	RCCA	0.808	0.068	1.16E-01	0.782	0.083	4.72E-02	0.782	0.083	9.97E-02
	FRCCA	0.797	0.070	5.49E-04	0.805	0.061	4.06E-02	0.808	0.092	7.31E-02
	SRCCA$_{TT}$	0.841	0.050	1.90E-01	0.759	0.216	1.65E-01	0.797	0.082	1.87E-01
	SRCCA$_{WL}$	0.810	0.065	2.99E-02	0.813	0.051	7.72E-02	0.790	0.091	2.61E-02
	SRCCA$_{WR}$	0.797	0.060	4.77E-02	0.818	0.052	1.22E-01	0.762	0.057	7.25E-03
	CuRSaR	**0.854**	0.050	5.00E-01	0.821	0.065	2.04E-01	0.838	0.055	4.65E-01
	Proposed	**0.854**	0.073		**0.844**	0.074		**0.841**	0.092	

Table 3. F1 score of the SVM for proposed and other methods

Data sets	Different algorithms	Gene-protein			Protein-DNA Methy.			Gene-DNA Methy.		
		Mean	StdDev	p-value	Mean	StdDev	p-value	Mean	StdDev	p-value
BRCA	PCA	0.806	0.018	5.57E-09	0.828	0.051	2.04E-05	0.812	0.038	3.33E-06
	CCA	0.753	0.063	2.10E-06	0.855	0.025	2.10E-07	0.867	0.113	2.03E-02
	RCCA	0.840	0.119	1.72E-03	0.883	0.021	4.17E-05	0.885	0.094	1.98E-02
	FRCCA	0.952	0.030	1.99E-02	0.949	0.039	8.72E-02	0.944	0.041	3.38E-02
	SRCCA$_{TT}$	0.941	0.070	9.40E-02	0.947	0.020	8.74E-02	0.813	0.076	5.90E-05
	SRCCA$_{WL}$	0.946	0.020	2.03E-02	0.887	0.098	1.91E-02	0.902	0.071	1.30E-02
	SRCCA$_{WR}$	0.931	0.045	9.22E-03	0.909	0.115	7.49E-02	0.914	0.070	3.14E-02
	CuRSaR	0.956	0.022	5.93E-02	0.960	0.036	3.41E-01	0.919	0.115	3.38E-02
	Proposed	**0.974**	0.027		**0.965**	0.032		**0.962**	0.027	
OV	PCA	0.793	0.110	2.36E-03	0.731	0.057	4.92E-07	0.765	0.139	1.83E-03
	CCA	0.823	0.035	3.43E-05	0.814	0.034	1.34E-05	0.679	0.039	2.66E-09
	RCCA	0.878	0.045	5.04E-03	0.871	0.034	6.05E-03	0.776	0.130	1.91E-03
	FRCCA	0.882	0.038	1.00E-04	0.904	0.021	4.75E-02	0.901	0.026	3.02E-03
	SRCCA$_{TT}$	0.898	0.019	4.27E-03	0.895	0.027	2.82E-02	0.876	0.100	9.75E-02
	SRCCA$_{WL}$	0.899	0.025	1.20E-03	0.902	0.029	1.26E-02	0.860	0.131	9.61E-02
	SRCCA$_{WR}$	0.895	0.025	9.70E-03	0.901	0.037	5.31E-02	0.881	0.069	3.90E-02
	CuRSaR	0.918	0.014	9.02E-02	**0.923**	0.030	5.03E-01	0.918	0.016	2.70E-01
	Proposed	**0.925**	0.020		0.922	0.027		**0.923**	0.029	

Table 4. F1 score of the NNA for proposed and other methods

Data sets	Different algorithms	Gene-protein			Protein-DNA Methy.			Gene-DNA Methy.		
		Mean	StdDev	p-value	Mean	StdDev	p-value	Mean	StdDev	p-value
BRCA	PCA	0.861	0.051	4.85E-05	0.890	0.050	3.75E-05	0.886	0.053	1.25E-03
	CCA	0.900	0.099	4.73E-02	0.891	0.087	6.97E-03	0.863	0.070	6.64E-04
	RCCA	0.922	0.026	9.08E-03	0.918	0.036	1.59E-03	0.909	0.056	2.96E-02
	FRCCA	0.952	0.031	2.51E-01	0.966	0.025	1.00E-01	0.944	0.050	4.49E-02
	SRCCA$_{TT}$	0.945	0.029	9.05E-02	0.949	0.023	9.07E-03	0.939	0.026	1.10E-01
	SRCCA$_{WL}$	0.940	0.031	6.70E-02	0.918	0.050	2.79E-03	0.947	0.037	3.41E-02
	SRCCA$_{WR}$	0.947	0.030	1.14E-01	0.947	0.042	1.35E-02	0.952	0.040	3.03E-01
	CuRSaR	0.950	0.034	1.40E-01	0.970	0.025	1.72E-01	0.958	0.034	4.49E-02
	Proposed	**0.960**	0.026		**0.975**	0.020		**0.959**	0.039	
OV	PCA	0.793	0.110	3.63E-03	0.806	0.052	1.10E-03	0.853	0.057	4.00E-02
	CCA	0.838	0.035	3.56E-04	0.867	0.035	1.97E-02	0.837	0.046	2.54E-04
	RCCA	0.891	0.044	1.66E-01	0.870	0.056	5.37E-02	0.867	0.069	1.27E-01
	FRCCA	0.879	0.040	6.24E-04	0.885	0.035	4.78E-02	0.884	0.057	6.36E-02
	SRCCA$_{TT}$	0.908	0.027	2.33E-01	0.814	0.269	1.73E-01	0.878	0.070	2.22E-01
	SRCCA$_{WL}$	0.887	0.037	3.32E-02	0.889	0.028	7.46E-02	0.874	0.056	2.34E-02
	SRCCA$_{WR}$	0.881	0.036	5.08E-02	0.893	0.030	1.43E-01	0.856	0.037	8.62E-03
	CuRSaR	0.913	0.029	4.68E-01	0.892	0.040	1.94E-01	**0.908**	0.031	5.77E-01
	Proposed	**0.914**	0.043		**0.907**	0.042		0.905	0.054	

the box and whisker plots for classification accuracy and F1 score, respectively for both data sets. On the other hand, the means and standard deviations and p-values of accuracy and F1 score for all the methods are reported in Tables 1, 2, 3, and 4. The best mean values are marked in bold in these tables. The experimental results are presented on three pairs of modalities, namely, gene-protein, gene-DNA methylation, and protein-DNA methylation. All the results, presented in Figures 1, 2, 3 and 4 and Tables 1, 2, 3, and 4, establish the fact that the proposed method attains the best mean classification accuracy in all the cases, irrespective of the pairs of modalities of both data sets, and classifiers used. On the other hand, the proposed method achieves best mean F1 score in 4 cases out of total 6 cases on OV data. Whereas, the proposed method attains the best mean F1 score in all the cases of BRCA data, irrespective of the pairs of modalities, and classifiers used. The results reported in Figs. 1, 2, 3 and 4, and Tables 1, 2, 3, and 4, demonstrate that the proposed algorithm performs significantly better than other algorithms in 60 cases out of total 96 cases on OV data set, considering 0.05 as the level of significance. In remaining 34 cases, it is better but not significant. There are only 2 cases where CuRSaR performs better than the proposed algorithm. On the other hand, the proposed algorithm performs significantly better than other algorithms in 66 cases on BRCA data and remaining 30 cases it is better but not significant.

5   Conclusion and Future Directions

This paper presents a new feature extraction algorithm, which takes care of small n large p problem associated with multimodal data analysis. Now-a-days, this small n large p problem becomes a common issue in genetics research, medical studies, risk management, and other fields. When $n \ll p$, the features become highly collinear, which leads to ill-conditioned of the covariance matrix. The proposed method deals with this singularity issue and performs better than all other existing methods. The effectiveness of the proposed algorithm, along with a comparison with other algorithms, has been demonstrated considering three different modalities, namely, gene expression, protein expression, and DNA methylation on both data sets. Recently, a new supervised RCCA, termed as FaRoC [21], has been proposed, where only required number of relevant, significant, and nonredundant features are extracted sequentially. In effect, it is computationally less expensive. Hence, in near feature, the current framework will be combined with this new sequential feature generation technique.

References

1. Cruz-Cano, R., Lee, M.T.: Fast regularized canonical correlation analysis. Comput. Stat. Data Anal. **70**, 88–100 (2014)
2. Dubois, D., Prade, H.: Rough fuzzy sets and fuzzy rough sets. Int. J. Gen Syst **17**(2–3), 191–209 (1990)

3. Duda, R.O., Hart, P.E.: Pattern Classification and Scene Analysis. Wiley, Hoboken (1973)
4. Gladwell, G.M.L.: On isospectral spring - mass systems. Inverse Probl. **11**(3), 591–602 (1995)
5. Golugula, A., Lee, G., Master, S.R., Feldman, M.D., Tomaszewski, J.E., Speicher, D.W., Madabhushi, A.: Analysis, supervised regularized canonical correlation: integrating histologic and proteomic measurements for predicting biochemical recurrence following prostate surgery. BMC Bioinform. **12**, 483 (2011)
6. Gonzalez, I., Dejean, S., Martin, P.G.P., Baccini, A.: CCA: an R package to extend canonical correlation analysis. J. Stat. Softw. **23**(12), 1–14 (2008)
7. Gonzalez, I., Dejean, S., Martin, P.G.P., Goncalves, O., Besse, P., Baccini, A.: Highlighting relationships between heterogeneous biological data through graphical displays based on regularized canonical correlation analysis. J. Biol. Syst. **17**(2), 173–199 (2009)
8. Gou, Z., Fyfe, C.: A canonical correlation neural network for multicollinearity and functional data. Neural Netw. **17**(2), 285–293 (2004)
9. Guo, Y., Hastie, T., Tibshirani, R.: Regularized linear discriminant analysis and its application in microarrays. Biostatistics **8**(1), 86–100 (2007)
10. Hassan, M., Boudaoud, S., Terrien, J., Karlsson, B., Marque, C.: Combination of canonical correlation analysis and empirical mode decomposition applied to denoising the labor electrohysterogram. IEEE Trans. Biomed. Eng. **58**(9), 2441–2447 (2011)
11. Hoerl, A.E., Kennard, R.W.: Ridge regression: biased estimation for nonorthogonal problems. Technometrics **12**(1), 55–67 (1970)
12. Hotelling, H.: Relations between two sets of variates. Biometrika **28**(3/4), 321–377 (1936)
13. Hwang, D., Schmitt, W.A., Stephanopoulos, G., Stephanopoulos, G.: Determination of minimum sample size and discriminatory expression patterns in microarray data. Bioinformatics **18**, 1184–1193 (2002)
14. Jafari, P., Azuaje, F.: An assessment of recently published gene expression data analyses: reporting experimental design and statistical factors. BMC Med. Inform. Decis. Making **6**, 27 (2006)
15. Lee, G., Singanamalli, A., Wang, H., Feldman, M.D., Master, S.R., Shih, N.N.C., Spangler, E., Rebbeck, T., Tomaszewski, J.E., Madabhushi, A.: Supervised Multi-View Canonical Correlation Analysis (sMVCCA): integrating histologic and proteomic features for predicting recurrent prostate cancer. IEEE Trans. Med. Imaging **34**(1), 284–297 (2015)
16. Li, M., Liu, Y., Feng, G., Zhou, Z., Hu, D.: OI and fMRI signal separation using both temporal and spatial autocorrelations. IEEE Trans. Biomed. Eng. **57**(8), 1917–1926 (2010)
17. Lin, Z., Zhang, C., Wu, W., Gao, X.: Frequency recognition based on canonical correlation analysis for SSVEP-based BCIs. IEEE Trans. Biomed. Eng. **53**(12), 2610–2614 (2006)
18. Maji, P.: A rough hypercuboid approach for feature selection in approximation spaces. IEEE Trans. Knowl. Data Eng. **26**(1), 16–29 (2014)
19. Maji, P., Mandal, A.: Multimodal omics data integration using max relevance-max significance criterion. IEEE Trans. Biomed. Eng. (2016). doi:10.1109/TBME.2016.2624823
20. Maji, P., Mandal, A.: Rough hypercuboid based supervised regularized canonical correlation for multimodal data analysis. Fundamenta Informaticae **148**(1–2), 133–155 (2016)

21. Mandal, A., Maji, P.: FaRoC: fast and robust supervised canonical correlation analysis for multimodal omics data. IEEE Trans. Cybern. (2017). doi:10.1109/TCYB.2017.2685625
22. Paul, S., Maji, P.: μHEM for identification of differentially expressed miRNAs using hypercuboid equivalence partition matrix. BMC Bioinform. **14**(1), 266 (2013)
23. Pawlak, Z.: Rough Sets: Theoretical Aspects of Reasoning about Data. Kluwer Academic Publishers, Dordrecht (1991)
24. Schafer, J., Strimmer, K.: A shrinkage approach to large-scale covariance matrix estimation and implications for functional genomics. Stat. Appl. Genet. Mol. Biol. **4**(1), 32 (2005)
25. Sweeney, K.T., McLoone, S.F., Ward, T.E.: The use of ensemble empirical mode decomposition with canonical correlation analysis as a novel artifact removal technique. IEEE Trans. Biomed. Eng. **60**(1), 97–105 (2013)
26. Thomas, J.G., Olson, J.M., Tapscott, S.J., Zhao, L.P.: An efficient and robust statistical modeling approach to discover differentially expressed genes using genomic expression profiles. Genome Res. **11**(7), 1227–1236 (2001)
27. Vapnik, V.: The Nature of Statistical Learning Theory. Springer, New York (1995)
28. Vinod, H.D.: Canonical ridge and econometrics of joint production. J. Econometrics **4**(2), 147–166 (1976)
29. Wu, G.R., Chen, F., Kang, D., Zhang, X., Marinazzo, D., Chen, H.: Multiscale causal connectivity analysis by canonical correlation: theory and application to epileptic brain. IEEE Trans. Biomed. Eng. **58**(11), 3088–3096 (2011)
30. Yamanishi, Y., Vert, J.P., Kanehisa, M.: Protein network inference from multiple genomic data: a supervised approach. Bioinformatics **20**, i363–i370 (2004)

Temporal Relations of Rough Anti-patterns in Software Development

Łukasz Puławski[✉]

Institute of Informatics, University of Warsaw, Banacha 2, 02-097 Warszawa, Poland
Lukasz.Pulawski@mimuw.edu.pl

Abstract. Design anti-patterns are common wrong solutions in software, whose frequency has been proven to be correlated with poor system quality. This paper investigates temporal relations between different types of anti-patters, i.e. how the appearance of one type of anti-pattern in the source code increases the probability that different anti-pattern will appear shortly after in its neighbourhood. The notion of *rough anti-pattern* used to model the vagueness of anti-patterns allows us to reformulate the question and establish if certain *rough* patterns tend to be temporally correlated. The proposed framework was used to build a classifier, which can be employed to predict the appearance of some anti-patterns by looking at the temporal relations between other anti-patterns. The experiments conducted on two large open-source projects suggest that a few common anti-patterns tend to be temporally dependent on others, whereas a few others do not.

Keywords: Spatio-temporal patterns · Software design anti-patterns · Mining software repositories · Rough sets · Pattern recognition

1 Introduction

Recently a lot of research has been aimed at the analysis of the structure and evolution of software systems. There are journals and conferences dedicated to the matter, such as [2–4], to name a few. The variety of specific research goals includes identification of certain a-priori defined sub-structures (generally called *software patterns*) in the system construction or design [13]. These may be frequently occurring good or bad solutions for some matter, named respectively: *design patterns* and *anti-patterns* [10,18]. Both have important practical applications: e.g. reverse engineering or software quality analysis [27,45].

The second popular research topic is *software evolution*, which covers the attempts to understand temporal phenomena that happen during long-term software development and maintenance. Specifically, it may refer to the evolution of certain design patterns and anti-patterns along with the software in which they appear.

One area poorly explored in to-date research is the phenomena of the co-occurrence of various types of design patterns and anti-patterns, which can be

© Springer International Publishing AG 2017
L. Polkowski et al. (Eds.): IJCRS 2017, Part I, LNAI 10313, pp. 447–464, 2017.
DOI: 10.1007/978-3-319-60837-2_37

formulated as a research question if certain groups of patterns appear statistically more often "close" to one another in the system structure. The notion of closeness can be understood in many ways e.g. by overlapping [22] or presence in a common file [29]. In this paper an attempt is made to combine the topics of software evolution and software patterns co-existence by looking at the matter of co-evolution of different patterns along with the system development and maintenance. Conceptually it entails an investigation how the "lives" of two patterns are correlated to each another. Formal definition of this research question is given in Sect. 3.4.

The formal graph-based models are frequently used to represent the structure of the software system under analysis as well as the sub-structures. The methods of their construction may vary and include reconstruction by *static code analysis (SCA)* [9,27,40], tracing the execution of the program while it is running [23,33] and other methods [17,28,43]. Given that the structure of a software system as well as the structure of the searched software pattern is represented in the form of a graph, a naive approach of identifying all occurrences of the pattern can be based on classical sub-graph isomorphism problem. One of the issues is the fact that software patterns are not always formally defined strict structures, but rather vague concepts. To tackle that matter a notion of *rough software pattern* is used. It is conceptually based on the notion of a rough set (see [37]). Formal definitions are given in Sect. 3.

This allows us to reformulate the previously mentioned research question and analyze how often the structures that fall under the rough software pattern definition co-evolve during the development of the software system.

1.1   Remainder of This Paper

Section 2 describes the domain of software development and conceptually describes the goal of this research. Section 3 provides a formal definition of all concepts and describes the proposed method for finding co-evolution patterns in the software development process. Section 4 describes the experiments that were conducted to validate the method proposed in this paper and provides a brief summary of the results. Section 6 contains concluding remarks and outlines a possible application of this research and its potential further extensions. Related work is discussed in Sect. 5.

1.2   Contributions of This Paper

This paper introduces a simple framework for the identification of spatio-temporal patterns in the software that is being developed. The proposed method allows one to identify temporal relations between occurrences of pre-defined static patterns in software. The solution has been experimentally validated on data gathered from two popular open-source projects: it was applied to the identification of temporal dependencies between a few common anti-patterns. Since anti-patterns are vague concepts, this paper uses a novel approach to their definition, inspired by the rough-set theory. It introduces the notion of *rough design pattern* in the domain of software analysis.

2   Software Development

2.1   Software Structure

The development of software system is a process in which software developers modify the source code files that all together constitute the *source code* of the system. The contents of the files have certain semantics that represent a formal structure of a program in a particular programming language. In this research we will assume that the structure of a software is a labeled multi-graph, where nodes represent implemented logical elements of the source code and edges represent different dependencies between them. The elements will be called *software entities*. Since this research is based on programs written in Java, the software entities are *packages, classes* and *methods* and the types of dependencies are *calling, returning, declaring, containing* or *extending*. The formal definition of the dependencies is given in the following list:

– Entity e_1 is calling e_2 (equivalently: e_1 is dependent on e_2 by *calling*) iff either e_2 is method and the source code of the body of e_1 contains a direct invocation of e_2 or e_2 is a class and the body of e_1 contains a direct invocation of some method defined in e_2.
– Entity e_1 is returning entity e_2 (e_1 is dependent on e_2 by *returning*) iff e_1 is a method with the return type e_2.
– Entity e_1 is declaring entity e_2 (e_1 is dependent on e_2 by *declaring*) iff either e_2 is class and the body of e_1 contains a variable of type e_2 or e_1 is method and its header contains a formal parameter of type represented by e_2.
– Entity e_1 is containing entity e_2 (e_1 is dependent on e_2 by *containing*) iff the complete source code of e_2 is contained in the source code of e_1.
– Entity e_1 is extending e_2 (e_1 is dependent on e_2 by *extending*) iff both e_1 and e_2 are classes and e_1 is a direct subclass of e_2.

The comments in code excerpt from Listing 1.1 explains the concept of software entity and inter-entity relations.

Listing 1.1. Code excerpt with exemplary software entities and their inter-relations

```
1  //Entity pkg
2  package pkg;
3  //Entity SuperClass contained in pkg
4  class SuperClass {
5  //SuperClass contains superMethod
6  //superMethod returns String
7  public String superMethod() { return null;}
8  }
```

```
 9
10   // SubClass extends SuperClass
11   class SubClass extends SuperClass {
12     //SubClass contains InnerClass
13     class InnerClass {
14
15     //InnerClass declares SuperClass
16     private SuperClass field;
17
18     //InnerClass contains innerMethod
19     //InnerClass#innerMethod calls SuperClass#superMethod()
20     public String innerMethod() { return field.superMethod()}
21   }
```

The unique identification of software entities is important because during software evolution the structure of the source code changes and, when looking at it at two different points in time, we need to know what fragments of it were changed and what remained intact. In this research, software entities are uniquely identified by their local name and the identifier of the software entity they are contained in. That is: 1. The packages are identified by their name, 2. non-nested classes are identified by their name and the name of the package they belong to, 3. nested classes are identified by their name and the identifier of the class they belong to, 4. methods are identified by their name and the identifier of the class they belong to[1]. For example, in the code excerpt Listing 1.1 the method innerMethod in InnerClass is technically identified by '(pkg, Subclass, SuperClass, innerMethod)'.

2.2 Software Metrics

Source code metrics are well-known tools for static code analysis. They measure the complexity of source code units and thus provide the information about potentially ill-structured parts of the code, which may be error-prone or hard to maintain [32]. Formally, each metric is a real-valued function defined on the set of all possible source code units of some kind. $NCSS$ (Non-Commenting Source Statements) is a good example here. This metric is applicable to any source code entity and the value of it is defined as the number of the lines of the code that define the entity, excluding the lines that are empty or commented out. In this research we will formally define the function $Metr$ that encodes the values of many metrics on all software entities present in the analyzed software source code: Let M be the set of source code metrics and V the set of entities of the system. $Metr : V \times M \to \Re \cup \{\bot\}$ is given by:

---

[1] Please note that one consequence of such an assumption is that overloaded methods are not discerned from each other. The motivation for this simplification comes from the fact that typically, if a class contains overloaded methods, they functionally represent the same operation but, due to technical reasons, depend on different arguments (see [8]).

$$Metr(e, m) = \begin{cases} m(e) & \text{if } m \text{ is applicable to } e, \\ \bot & \text{otherwise.} \end{cases} \qquad (1)$$

2.3 Software Snapshot

Let $DT = \{calling, declaring, returning, containing, extending\}$ denote the set of all possible types of inter-software-entity dependencies, $Metr$ be defined as above on some fixed set of software metrics M, V denote the set of software entities present in the software source code. Let $E \subseteq V \times V \times DT$ denote the set of actual inter-software-entity dependencies, such that $(e_1, e_2, t) \in E$ iff entity e_1 depends on entity e_2 by t as defined above in this section. The triple

$$SSN = (V, E, Metr) \qquad (2)$$

is called *software snapshot* and it represents the structure and the properties of the source code of the system. Please note that (V, E) can be treated as an edge-labeled multi-graph and $Metr$ can be technically treated as a vertex labeling, with the labels in the form of vectors built from the values of metrics. This allows us to treat SSN as a multi-graph with labeled edges and nodes and, consequently, use graph-theoretical concepts such as sub-graph or sub-graph-isomorphism in further deliberations. Most notions introduced later in this paper will be based on such an understanding of SSN.

2.4 Software Evolution

During the software development process, engineers perform modifications to the source code, usually with use of *Source Code Management System (SCM)*. It usually is a central server which stores the current version of all the source code files and all past modifications. It allows the developers to apply their changes to a common source code base in a transactional manner. Such modifications are called *commits*. A commit has a unique identifier, called *revision*, which might be just a subsequent number in a sequence. Moreover, it contains the information about time-stamp, the information about the author, a short textual message entered by him/her and a list of modifications applied to many files managed by the SCM. Technically, the commit also contains information about the commit(s) it directly follows, so it is possible to arrange the commits into partial order. According to common practice [14], the main line of development contains commits that can be linearly-ordered in such a way. Therefore we can look at the software evolution as a sequence of states of the system source code indexed by revisions.

Until now we only considered the structure of a software system at a given point in time and defined the SSN to represent it. Given the sequence of revisions $R = (r_1, \ldots, r_n)$ we can define a sequence of software snapshots $(SSN^r)_{r \in R}$ such that $SSN^{r_i} = (V^{r_i}, E^{r_i}, Metr^{r_i})$ represents the structure of the software system at revision r_i. With R representing the revisions in the main development line of a system, $(SSN^r)_{r \in R}$ will be called *software evolution*.

2.5 Design Patterns and Anti-patterns

As already stated in Sect. 1, in software engineering, a *design pattern* is a frequently used, universal resolution of commonly occurring problems in software
design [18]. This concept is not strictly formalized - it is rather an idea how to
approach certain problems. A *Factory method* is an exemplary design pattern
that moves the operation of creating an object to a dedicated, separated method
to be used instead of the constructor. As regards programs written in Java, one
could expect that a factory method FM of class C has the following properties: 1. The method returns type C and calls the constructor of C, 2. No other
methods call any constructor of C. This trivial heuristic can be further enhanced
to apply to more sophisticated situations when e.g. C has many constructors,
there are more factory methods, etc. Please note that these properties can be
expressed within the *software snapshot* structure described above. Therefore a
straight-forward method for finding the occurrences of factory method patterns
for class C represented by SSN vertex c, can be formulated as finding all such
sub-graphs of SSN that: 1. Have a single vertex fm that represents the factory
method. 2. For any vertex con, that represents a C constructor (i.e.: c is containing con, con does not have a return type in header, c and con have the same
name), if some entity m is calling con, then $m = fm$.

A *design anti-pattern* is a dual concept to the design pattern. It is a frequently
used, wrong resolution of certain types of problems in software design, which
has well-known disadvantages [10,11]. *God Class* can be given as an example:
it is a practice of implementing too much unrelated functionality in a single
class, which violates a good principle in object oriented programming that a
class should have single responsibility [31]. Similarly, this vague concept can be
heuristically modeled within SSN, for example as a sub-graph which represents
a class with many methods contained in it, such that many other entities are
calling them.

Software patterns are introduced to the source code during software evolution. Since all changes are tracked by SCM, we can precisely identify when each
particular occurrence of the pattern was introduced, and how it was modified.
Conceptually, we can assign each pattern the time when it was present. This
allows us to state the research question of this paper: If appearance of certain
software patterns indicates that some other patterns will appear closely in the
future.

3   Finding Anti-patterns

This section describes the process of finding the software patterns in the SSN,
finding their temporal existence in the software evolution and analyzing the
spatio-temporal relations between them.

3.1 Raw Data Fetching

The process of building SSN for the system is done according to the following
procedure: source code files are firstly parsed and translated into the forest of

abstract syntax tree (AST). Secondly the ASTs are traversed and the logical structure of (V, E) is built. Lastly the values of the source code metrics for each elements of V are evaluated by the source code analysis tool. The metrics used in this research are: *Boolean expression complexity, Data abstraction, Fan out, Cyclomatic complexity and NPath Complexity, NCSS - Non Commenting Source Statements* and their formal definition of can be found in [1].

The process of extracting V and E from the ASTs just follows the definition of this structure outlined in Sect. 2.1.

3.2 Software Pattern Matching

Let $\mathcal{P}(SSN)$ denote the set of all sub-graphs[2] of SSN. $C \subseteq \mathcal{P}(SSN)$ is a *definable pattern* iff there is a reference graph $R_C = (V_{R_C}, E_{R_C})$ and a function[3] $Metr_C : V_{R_C} \times M \rightarrow P(\Re \cup \{\bot\})$, such that for any sub-graph $S = (V_S, E_S)$ the following conditions are equivalent:

- (V_S, E_S) is isomorphic to R_C where the isomorphism is given by $i : V_{R_C} \rightarrow V_S$ and the following condition holds: $\forall v \in V_{R_C}, m \in MMetr(i(v), m) \in Metr_C(v, m)$,
- graph induced by S by adding vertex-labeling from $Metr$ is an element of C.

Conceptually it means that the properties of C can be expressed by inter-software-entity relations and the values of their software metrics.

Not all patterns are definable, but for each pattern C there is a maximal definable pattern $\overline{C}$ and a minimal definable pattern $\underline{C}$ such that the former is a subset and the latter is a super-set of C. The fact that $\overline{C}$ and $\underline{C}$ exist is straightforward, based on the following observations: 1. An empty set is clearly definable by an empty graph and an arbitrary function $Metr_C$. 2. A complete $\mathcal{P}(SSN)$ is clearly definable by a reference graph $(V, \{\emptyset\})$ and a $Metr_C$ function with a constant value $\Re \cup \{\bot\}$. 3. $\mathcal{P}(SSN)$ is finite and all its elements are ordered by set-theoretical inclusion.

We will call $\overline{C}$ the *upper bound,* $\underline{C}$ the *lower bound* of C and $\overline{C} \setminus \underline{C}$ will be called the *boundary region* of C. The pair $(\overline{C}, \underline{C})$ will be called the *rough pattern* for C.

Software patterns are examples of non-definable concepts. Therefore instead of fine-tuning existing algorithms for software pattern identification (see [16]) against different source code repositories, this paper proposes to formally define more universal and less accurate upper and lower bounds of software patterns and use them to mine knowledge about software structure and evolution. Such an approach is closer to the actual expertise of software engineers who are not always certain if a given structure is or is not a software (anti-)pattern. In the proposed method, such cases should be considered as an element in the boundary region.

---

[2] Please recall from Sect. 2.3 that we can treat SSN as a labeled multi-graph.

[3] Please note different symbols: $\mathcal{P}(X)$ denotes the set of sub-graphs of X, while $P(Y)$ denotes the power-set of Y.

In the experimental validation a rough patterns have been defined for a few simple design anti-patterns and tuned by an expert against the source code of two open-source projects: *Struts 1.3*, one of the most popular web framework 10 years ago and *Wildfly 10* - a currently popular web application server. The proposed very simple definitions of upper and lower bound were correlated with expert classification of the identified instances, so that: 1. All instances identified by expert were part of the upper bound of the respective pattern (1.0 recall), 2. the lower bound of the respective pattern contain only instances identified by the expert (1.0 precision).

3.3   Pattern Instance

We will discern two notions considered in the context of SSN: the *pattern* and the *pattern instance*. The former is a concept described by some specification, whereas the latter is the occurrence of this pattern in *SSN*. For example, the pattern is a concept '*a class with cyclomatic complexity over 100 calls a method with less than 2 lines of code*', whereas its instance in *SSN* is each sub-graph $PI = (V_{PI}, E_{PI}, Metr_{PI})$ of *SSN* such that: 1. $V_{PI} = \{c, m\}$ where c, m are class and method respectively. 2. $Metr(c, Cyclomatic) > 100$ and $Metr(m, NCSS) < 2$ 3. $(c, m, calling) \in E$, 4. E_{PI} and $Metr_{PI}$ are respective subsets of E and $Metr$ induced by V_{PI}. Formally, the pattern is an arbitrary subset of the set of sub-graphs of *SSN* and each element of it is the pattern's instance.

Please note that the notion of a rough pattern is defined for the pattern and not for the pattern instance. In fact, in the context of some *SSN* we can associate the lower bound of the pattern P with some subset of instances of P. The upper bound is more problematic to grasp, but we can conceptually associate it with the set of substructures of *SSN* that in terms of definable patterns are indiscernible from instances of P.

3.4   Overlapping and Distance Between Patterns

Given two instances of patterns we will define two notions that enable to answer a question how "close" they are one to each other in the software structure. Let $PI_1 = (V_1, E_1, Metr_1), PI_2 = (V_2, E_2, Metr_2)$ be two instances of some patterns. Let $D \subseteq DT$ be a subset of dependencies. The *overlapping* of and the *distance* between PI_1 and PI_2 are respectively given by:

$$Ov(PI_1, PI_2) = \frac{|V_1 \cap V_2|}{|V_1 \cup V_2|} \tag{3}$$

$$d(PI_1, PI_2, D) = min_{v_1 \in V_1, v_2 \in V_2} dist(v_1, v_2, (V, E \cap (V \times V \times D))) \tag{4}$$

where $dist(a, b, G)$ is the distance between vertices a and b measured as the shortest path between them in the multi-graph G.

Conceptually the overlapping measures how much two pattern instances share common vertices and the distance measures the shortest path between some two vertices from both instances, such that the path can only be constructed with edges with labels from D.

Please note that the definition of distance relies on the sets of vertices of SSN. Theoretically it means that we can evaluate the formula at any revision r as long as SSN^r contains all vertices from both pattern instances. This yields a notion of *distance at revision r*:

$$d^r(PI_1, PI_2, D) = min_{v_1 \in V_1, v_2 \in V_2} dist(v_1, v_2, (V^r, E^r \cap (V^r \times V^r \times D))) \quad (5)$$

This enables us to tell how "close" two pattern instances are in the entire software evolution, even if they never appear together in a single revision. Analogous statement also applies to the overlapping: Since Ov function can be evaluated at any revision in which all entities from PI_1 and PI_2 are present (in fact it is constant), the overlapping can be defined for two pattern instances which are present in different revisions in a similar fashion. These important observations enable us to describe a spatio-temporal relation between software patterns. The formal definition is explained in the following paragraphs.

3.5 Closeness of Pattern Instances

We will consider the closeness of two pattern instances in two alternative variants: we will say that two pattern instances PI_1, PI_2 are *close*:

- if their overlapping is greater than 0.4 or
- if their distance is at most 2 at the maximum revision r such that $d^r(PI_1, PI_2, DT)$ is defined.

The threshold values given in the above definition are just parameters that were tuned during the experimental validation of the proposed framework (results presented in Sect. 4.3). The former definition will be called *overlapping-closeness* whereas the latter - the *distance-closeness*.

3.6 Pattern Instance Lifespan

Again, the above considerations define the pattern instance in a single software snapshot. We will now define the temporal aspect of it: Let P be a pattern, PI be its instance present in some SSN^r. If for some other r' $SSN^{r'}$ contains a sub-graph PI' isomorphic to PI, such that PI' satisfies P then we say that r' belongs to the *lifespan* of PI. The set of all revisions that belong to the lifespan of PI will be denoted by $\mathcal{L}(PI)$. Conceptually the lifespan is the time in which particular pattern instance, built from specific, named software entities, was present in the system. The specificity of the entities is guaranteed by the isomorphism condition and the fact that all software entities in the SSN are uniquely identified by their name and the identifier of the containing software entity (refer back to Sect. 2.1 for details).

Clearly, each lifespan can be expressed as a set-theoretical sum of maximum continuous intervals of revisions from R, where R is the linearly-ordered set of all revisions in the evolution of the observed software. For a given pattern P, the set of all such intervals in all distinct instances of P will be called the *occurrences of P* and denoted by $Occ(P)$.

3.7 Temporal Pattern Relations

Given two such intervals $l_1(PI_1)$ and $l_2(PI_2)$ of two different pattern instances of two different patterns P_1 and P_2, we can name a temporal relation between them in the Allen algebra [6] and define the relative occurrences of pattern: for a fixed interval $l_1(PI_1)$ from the lifespan of a fixed pattern P_1 and a fixed Allen's algebra relation A, $Occ_{l_1(PI_1),A}(P_2)$ denotes the set of such maximum revision intervals $l_2(PI_2)$ in a lifespan of some instance of P_2 which satisfy the following condition: PI_1 is close to PI_2 and $l_1(PI_1)$ is related to $l_2(PI_2)$ by relation A. The set $Occ_{l_1(PI_1),A}(P_2)$ will be called *occurrences of P_2 relative to $l_1(PI_1)$ by A*. The example depicted in Fig. 1 shows two pattern instances PI and PI' that are in $<$ (*takes place before*) temporal relation, since PI can only be observed in revision Rev_n and PI' can be observed not later than in revision Rev_1 which *takes place before Rev_n*. The software entities denoted with squares in the diagram are uniquely identified, therefore we can map the neighbourhood of PI, which is observed only in Rev_n, to past revision as well, because the software entities that constitute the neighborhood are partially present in them.

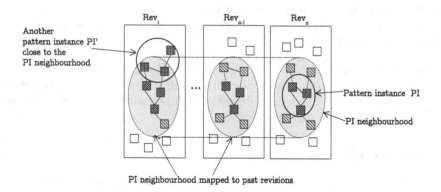

Fig. 1. The concept of spatio-temporal relation between pattern instances

3.8 Classification of Temporal Pattern Relations

The above definitions allow us to describe a method of construction of the decision table that encodes the facts about temporal relations between different instances of predefined software patterns. Conceptually, each row in this table corresponds to a single continuous interval for some pattern P related to some instance PI, the decision for it is marked as P and the remaining attributes encode the temporal Allen's relation to some other interval of some other pattern. Each attribute is denoted by a pair (A, P), where A is some Allen's relation and P is a pattern. Therefore the number of attributes is the half the number of Allen's algebra relations multiplied by the number of studied software patterns. The half comes from the fact that each of Allen's relation has its inverse. The formal construction of the decision table is described in the following procedure:

Let PT be a finite set of pre-defined known software patterns.

Let $\mathcal{A} = \{<, m, o, s, d, f\}$ denote the subset of non-inversed Allen's algebra relations.

- For each $P \in PT$ create a row for each element $l(PI) \in Occ(P)$
- Set the symbolic decision of the row to 'P'
- For each $A \in \mathcal{A}$ and $P_1 \in PT$ set the value of attribute (A, P_1) to the power of $Occ_{l(PI), A}(P_1)$

Please note that $\mathcal{A}$ does not contain equality relation. Therefore, there is no such attribute that expresses the relation between $l(PI)$ and itself. This guarantees that the condition attributes and the decision are not trivially dependent. Conceptually each condition attribute represents the "strength" of a particular spatio-temporal relation observed in the analyzed software evolution (the "strength" is related to the number of such observed relations to $l(PI)$). Therefore, the fact that we can construct a good-quality classifier on such a table can be interpreted as a proof for the existence of actual spatio-temporal relations. A more detailed analysis of the results can lead to further statements: e.g. that certain types of patterns (decision classes in the table) do not tend to be spatio-temporally related to others.

4   Experimental Validation

The framework of modeling and identifying co-evolution of design anti-patterns described in the previous sections has been experimentally validated in two configurations, derived from the rough pattern concept: based on the lower bound and upper bound definitions respectively. The following paragraphs describe particular definitions of the two and their application to the data-sets built from the evolution of Struts and Wildfly mentioned in Sect. 3.2. The data was gathered from the software development process done on the main branch which lasted at least one year and consisted of respectively 953 and 1641 significant commits. The source code of the analyzed systems had approximately 2500 and 4500 classes respectively. The number of different anti-pattern instances found in these systems is given in Table 1.

4.1   Definition of Anti-patterns

Here are some of the examples of design anti-patterns experimentally validated in this research. The *YoYo* anti-pattern is present in the source code when a logic is spread over excessively large inheritance structure. The lower bound of YoYo consist of substructures with at least a 7-element set of classes in a common inheritance hierarchy with more than 10 calls between different inheritance levels. For the upper bound the threshold values were set to 6 and 8 respectively.

Anemic entity is a class that does not implement any logic and only stores excessive portion of information. The lower bound of it contains classes with more than 8 attributes no non-trivial methods, such as accessors. The definition of upper bound required the class to have at least 7 attributes and allowed at most one non-trivial method. A *Circular dependency* pattern is a situation when there is a cycle of method calls between classes from different packages. We will say that class c_1 implicitly calls class c_2 (denoted by $c_1 \mapsto c_2$) iff $E \cap (V \times V \times \{calling\})$ contains an element that represents a call from c_1 or some entity transitively contained in c_1 to a method of c_2. The lower bound of circular dependency was defined as a structure with three nodes representing classes (c_1, c_2, c_3), such that $c_1 \mapsto c_2 \wedge c_2 \mapsto c_3 \wedge c_3 \mapsto c_1 \wedge c_2 \mapsto c_1$. The upper bound consisted of class pairs (c_1, c_2) such that $c_1 \mapsto c_2 \wedge c_2 \mapsto c_1$.

Similar definitions have been given for *BaseBean, Dependency hell, God class* (see [10]).

4.2   Occurrences and Co-occurrences of Patterns

The Table 1 presents the power of $Occ(P)$ for particular patterns for both lower-bound-based and upper-bound-based definitions.

Table 1. Power of $Occ(P)$ sets for the data used in the experimental validation

Pattern	Struts		Wildlfly	
	Upper bound	Lower bound	Upper bound	Lower bound
AnemicEntity	3	1	13	7
BaseBean	51	38	65	41
Blob	36	25	52	22
CircularDependency	4	0	22	11
DependencyHell	13	7	114	80
GodClass	34	25	40	22
YoYo	19	15	23	10

The data about the evolution of these patterns was encoded in the decision table according to the procedure described in Sect. 3.8. A C4.5 tree classifier was then trained and tested on disjoint sets of data acquired in this way. Please note that such a classifier applied in the ongoing software development process can output the prediction of appearance of some anti-pattern instances. In other words it can warn about a high chance of appearance of some anti-patterns in some areas in the source code in the near future. The results presented in the following section can be read in such a manner.

4.3   Results

This section provides an excerpt of experimental results conducted in this research.

Temporally Unrelated Patterns. The first observation is that certain types of anti-patterns appear not to be temporally related to others. Table 2 shows the best classification quality factors for such patterns achieved in all configurations of the experiment.

Table 2. Patterns that were poorly temporally correlated with others.

	Precision	Recall
AnemicEntity	0.0	0.0
Blob	0.32	0.68
GodClass	0.42	0.28

Temporally Related Patterns. The second observation is that some patterns tend to have strong-to-moderate temporal correlation with others. Specific results are shown in Table 3.

Table 3. Patterns that were strongly or moderately temporally correlated with others.

	Precision	Recall
DependecyHell	0.93	0.88
YoYo	0.72	0.85
BaseBean	0.54	0.77
CircularDependency	0.69	0.51

Difference Between Upper and Lower Bound. The third observation is related to the use of rough pattern definition. It concerns the question how the change of the lower-bound definition of the patterns to the upper-bound influences prediction quality. Since the upper bound of any pattern can contain more elements, the number of pattern instances that are close one to each other can increase and, consequently, a greater number of temporal relations can be observed. Table 4 shows the actual comparison. In general, precision slightly improves, while recall may worsen insignificantly for the patterns that are strongly or moderately temporally correlated with others.

Table 4. Difference in prediction quality for upper and lower bound of rough pattern.

	Lower-bound		Upper-bound	
	Precision	Recall	Precision	Recall
DependecyHell	0.93	0.88	0.94	0.92
YoYo	0.72	0.85	0.87	0.89
BaseBean	0.54	0.77	0.54	0.77
CircularDependency	0.69	0.51	0.82	0.48

5   Related Work

Software Pattern Mining Techniques. Arguably most existing methods for this matter fall under a common scheme: software structure is represented in some formalized model that reduces the search space, the specification of a pattern is expressed in terms of this model, so that some kind of search scan is possible. The models used for representations include: untransformed AST directly parsed from the source code [23,24], a collection of logic predicates [7,24,26], various graphs, most similar to the model used in this research [35,36, 39,42] or traces of execution of the running program [23,24]. Some of the models also contain information about software metric values [20,30].

Vague Software Patterns. The majority of the research to-date treats software patterns as crisp concepts. Still little effort was put to represent them as vague notions. In [40], later extended in [44], the patterns are described in first-order-logic predicates and the method allows to relax predefined descriptions of patterns in order to detect their "variants". [34] suggests a method for coping with the vagueness of the pattern which is based on two ideas: 1. Having multiple formal descriptions of a single pattern and 2. Assigning a fuzzy value to each individual description, which measures the accuracy of a match. In such an approach the individual matches can then be aggregated into a single "global" match. [20] uses a machine learning algorithm to find descriptions of certain patterns based on the values of the software metrics of its constituents.

Software entities that form an instance of design pattern may also be related to other elements that should be irrelevant for the pattern (e.g. additional methods in the class that do not play any role for a particular pattern). [15] uses such additional information to build a machine-learning classifier that allows to discern false-positives in a set of potential instances of design patterns on the basis of such additional structures. [12,42] suggest an algorithm in which structure of the software and the patterns are given as graphs and the method of approximate finding instances of the patterns is based on the graph similarity measures (see [5]).

A method for modeling vagueness of a software pattern proposed in this paper is based on the concept of a rough set. To author's best knowledge only a very few similar approaches have been published to date. In [38] the authors introduce a similar approximate model which can be used to match design documentation with the actual source code. Yet, it is not applied to mine temporal patterns in software evolution.

[9,13] provide a survey of existing design pattern mining techniques.

Temporal Patterns in Software Evolution. In [19] the authors propose the use of a formal model to describe static patterns in the object oriented software and apply a temporal logic to extend it so that it is also capable of describing temporal patterns in software evolution. The expressive power of the proposed language is shown on a few examples of temporal phenomena that can be useful in the software engineering. Similar languages, also built on the basis of the temporal logic, can be found in [25,41]. Yet, none of them is used to build a predictor of spatio-temporal patterns similar to the one described in this paper.

6   Conclusions and Future Work

6.1   Spatio-Temporal Patterns in Software Development

The paper has presented a formal framework for definition and reasoning about spatio-temporal patterns in software development process. The spatial aspects concern the definition and the detection of static software patterns, whereas the temporal - the relation between static patterns lifespan defined by Allen's algebra relations. The experiments identified that certain common anti-patterns can be put into three categories: 1. the ones that tend to be highly temporally related to other patterns (*Dependency hell* and *YoYo*), 2. the ones that are only moderately temporally related (*Base bean, Circular dependency*) and 3. the ones that do not appear to be temporally related to others (*Anemic entity, Blob, God class*).

6.2   Rough Software Patterns

The work defines the *software snapshot* - a simple multi-graph-based model to represent the structure of the software system. In order to cope with the vagueness of software design (anti-)patterns and actual expert uncertainty, the notion of rough design pattern has been proposed. It allows to define the lower and upper bound of a software pattern, such that both are definable in terms of the software snapshot structure. The experimental validation has shown that: 1. The model is sufficient to resemble the classification of instances of a few popular anti-patterns provided by a software engineering expert. 2. The method of anti-pattern prediction described in Sect. 3.8 used with upper-bound definition pattern tends to have a higher precision and almost a constant recall, all together having a better accuracy.

6.3   Future Work

The proposed method for the prediction of the appearance of future anti-patterns described in this paper can be applied in he ongoing software development process: it can indicate the chance of appearance of anti-patterns in certain areas of the source code (see Sect. 3.8). To author's best knowledge no other method of this kind has been published to date, but the experimental results appear to show much better classification quality than state-of-the-art solutions for a similar problem of *defect prediction* (see [21]).

This paper presents preliminary work on identifying spatio-temporal relations between vague software patterns. The temporal aspect is modeled by a few Allen's algebra relations, but further extension of the proposed framework can include simple sequential patterns or generalized temporal patterns. As regards the spatial aspects, a pre-defined set of definitions of patterns provided by an expert used in this work, can be replaced by a set of frequently occurring software structures which can be mined by a machine-learning algorithm.

References

1. http://checkstyle.sourceforge.net/config_metrics.html. Accessed June 2016
2. The 14th Working Conference on Mining Software Repositories, February 2017
3. International Conference on Software Analysis, Evolution and Reengineering, February 2017
4. International Conference on Software Maintenance and Evolution, February 2017
5. Aggarwal, C.C., Wang, H.: Managing and Mining Graph Data. Springer, Heidelberg (2010)
6. Allen, J.F.: Maintaining knowledge about temporal intervals. Commun. ACM **26**(11), 832–843 (1983)
7. Antoniol, G., Fiutem, R., Cristoforetti, L.: Design pattern recovery in object-oriented software. In: Proceedings of 6th International Workshop on Program Comprehension, IWPC 1998, p. 153+. IEEE Computer Society, Washington, DC (1998)
8. Arnold, K., Gosling, J., Holmes, D.: The Java Programming Language, 4th edn. Addison-Wesley Professional, Boston (2005)
9. Bernardi, M.L., Cimitile, M., Di Lucca, G.: Design pattern detection using a DSL-driven graph matching approach. J. Softw. Evol. Process **26**(12), 1233–1266 (2014)
10. Brown, W.J., Malveau, R.C., McCormick, H.W., Mowbray, T.J.: AntiPatterns: Refactoring Software, Architectures, and Projects in Crisis, 1st edn. Wiley, New York (1998)
11. Bugen, D.: Software Design, 2nd edn. Pearson Education, London (2003)
12. Cichý, M., Jakub'ık, J.: Design patterns identification using similarity scoring algorithm with weighting score extension. In: Proceedings of 2008 Conference on Knowledge-Based Software Engineering: Proceedings of 8th Joint Conference on Knowledge-Based Software Engineering, pp. 465–473. IOS Press, Amsterdam (2008)
13. Dong, J., Zhao, Y., Peng, T.: A review of design pattern mining techniques
14. Driessen, V. (2010). https://datasift.github.io/gitflow/IntroducingGitFlow.html

15. Ferenc, R., Beszedes, A., Fulop, L., Lele, J.: Design pattern mining enhanced by machine learning. In: Proceedings of 21st IEEE International Conference on Software Maintenance, ICSM 2005, pp. 295–304. IEEE Computer Society, Washington, DC (2005)

16. Fontana, F.A., Dietrich, J., Walter, B., Yamashita, A., Zanoni, M.: Preliminary catalogue of anti-pattern and code smell false positives. Technical report RA-5/15, Poznan University of Technology (2015)

17. Funkhouser, O., Etzkorn, L., Hughes, W.: A lightweight approach to software validation by comparing UML use cases with internal program documentation selected via call graphs. Softw. Qual. J. **16**(1), 131–156 (2008)

18. Gamma, E., Helm, R., Johnson, R., Vlissides, J., Patterns, D.: Elements of Reusable Object-Oriented Software, 1st edn. Addison-Wesley Professional, Boston (1994)

19. Gómez, V.U., Kellens, A., Brichau, J., D'Hondt, T.: Time warp, an approach for reasoning over system histories. In: Proceedings of Joint International and Annual ERCIM Workshops on Principles of Software Evolution (IWPSE) and Software Evolution (Evol) Workshops, IWPSE-Evol 2009, pp. 79–88. ACM, New York (2009)

20. Gueheneuc, Y.G., Sahraoui, H., Zaidi, F.: Fingerprinting design patterns. In: Proceedings of 11th Working Conference on Reverse Engineering, WCRE 2004, pp. 172–181. IEEE Computer Society, Washington, DC (2004)

21. He, P., Li, B., Liu, X., Chen, J., Ma, Y.: An empirical study on software defect prediction with a simplified metric set. Inf. Softw. Technol. **59**(C), 170–190 (2015)

22. M. Heričko, S. Beloglavec. A composite design-pattern identification technique. Informatica **29** (2005)

23. Heuzeroth, D., Holl, T., Hogstrom, G., Lowe, W.: Automatic design pattern detection. In: 11th IEEE International Workshop on Program Comprehension, pp. 94–103. IEEE, May 2003

24. Heuzeroth, D., Mandel, S., Lowe, W.: Generating design pattern detectors from pattern specifications. In: Proceedings of 18th IEEE International Conference on Automated Software Engineering, pp. 245–248. IEEE Computer Society (2003)

25. Hindle, A., German, D.M.: SCQL: a formal model and a query language for source control repositories. In: Proceedings of 2005 International Workshop on Mining Software Repositories, MSR 2005, vol. 30, pp. 1–5. ACM, New York (2005)

26. Huang, H., Zhang, S., Cao, J., Duan, Y.: A practical pattern recovery approach based on both structural and behavioral analysis. J. Syst. Softw. **75**(1–2), 69–87 (2005)

27. Jaafar, F., Gueheneuc, Y.G., Hamel, S., Khomh, F.: Mining the relationship between anti-patterns dependencies and fault-proneness. In: 2013 20th Working Conference on Reverse Engineering (WCRE), pp. 351–360. IEEE, October 2013

28. Kim, S., Pan, K., Whitehead, E.E.J.: Memories of bug fixes. In: Proceedings of 14th ACM SIGSOFT International Symposium on Foundations of Software Engineering, SIGSOFT 2006/FSE-2014, pp. 35–45. ACM, New York (2006)

29. Kim, S., Zimmermann, T., Whitehead, E.J., Zeller, A.: Predicting faults from cached history. In: Proceedings of 29th International Conference on Software Engineering, ICSE 2007, pp. 489–498. IEEE Computer Society, Washington, DC, May 2007

30. Lanza, M., Marinescu, R.: Object Oriented Metrics in Practice Using Software Metrics to Characterize, Evaluate, and Improve the Design of Object Oriented Systems. Springer, Berlin (2006)

31. Martin, R.C.: Agile Software Development: Principles, Patterns, and Practices. Prentice Hall PTR, Upper Saddle River (2003)

32. McCabe, T.J.: A complexity measure. In: Proceedings of 2nd International Conference on Software Engineering, ICSE 1976, p. 407+. IEEE Computer Society Press, Los Alamitos (1976)
33. Nayrolles, M., Moha, N., Valtchev, P.: Improving SOA antipatterns detection in service based systems by mining execution traces. In: 2013 20th Working Conference on Reverse Engineering (WCRE), pp. 321–330. IEEE, October 2013
34. Niere, J., Schäfer, W., Wadsack, J.P., Wendehals, L., Welsh, J.: Towards pattern-based design recovery. In: Proceedings of 24th International Conference on Software Engineering, ICSE 2002, pp. 338–348. ACM, New York (2002)
35. Oruc, M., Akal, F., Sever, H.: Detecting design patterns in object-oriented design models by using a graph mining approach. In: 2016 4th International Conference in Software Engineering Research and Innovation (CONISOFT), pp. 115–121. IEEE, April 2016
36. Park, C., Kang, Y., Wu, C., Yi, K.: A static reference flow analysis to understand design pattern behavior. In: Proceedings of 11th Working Conference on Reverse Engineering, WCRE 2004, pp. 300–301. IEEE Computer Society, Washington, DC (2004)
37. Pawlak, Z.: Some issues on rough sets. In: Peters, J., Skowron, A., Grzymała-Busse, J., Kostek, B., Świniarski, R., Szczuka, M. (eds.) Transactions on Rough Sets I. Lecture Notes in Computer Science, vol. 3100, pp. 1–58. Springer, Heidelberg (2004). doi:10.1007/978-3-540-27794-1_1
38. Peters, J., Ramanna, S.: Approximation space for software models. In: Peters, J., Skowron, A., Grzymała-Busse, J., Kostek, B., Świniarski, R., Szczuka, M. (eds.) Transactions on Rough Sets I. Lecture Notes in Computer Science, vol. 3100, pp. 338–355. Springer, Berlin Heidelberg (2004). doi:10.1007/978-3-540-27794-1_16
39. Seemann, J., von Gudenberg, J.W.: Pattern-based design recovery of Java software. In: Proceedings of 6th ACM SIGSOFT International Symposium on Foundations of Software Engineering, SIGSOFT 1998/FSE-6, pp. 10–16. ACM, New York (1998)
40. Stencel, K., Wegrzynowicz, P.: Detection of diverse design pattern variants. In: 2008 15th Asia-Pacific Software Engineering Conference, pp. 25–32. IEEE, December 2008
41. Torres Carbonell, J.J., Parets-Llorca, J.: A formalisation of the evolution of software systems. In: Kopacek, P., Moreno-Díaz, R., Pichler, F. (eds.) EUROCAST 1999. LNCS, vol. 1798, pp. 435–449. Springer, Heidelberg (2000). doi:10.1007/10720123_38
42. Tsantalis, N., Chatzigeorgiou, A., Stephanides, G., Halkidis, S.T.: Design pattern detection using similarity scoring. IEEE Trans. Softw. Eng. 32(11), 896–909 (2006)
43. Wedel, M., Jensen, U., Göhner, P.: Mining software code repositories and bug databases using survival analysis models. In: Proceedings of 2nd ACM-IEEE International Symposium on Empirical Software Engineering and Measurement, ESEM 2008, pp. 282–284. ACM, New York (2008)
44. Wegrzynowicz, P., Stencel, K.: Relaxing queries to detect variants of design patterns. In: 2013 Federated Conference on Computer Science and Information Systems (FedCSIS), pp. 1571–1578. IEEE (2013)
45. Zhu, L., Babar, M.A., Jeffery, R.: Mining patterns to support software architecture evaluation. In: Proceedings of 4th Working IEEE/IFIP Conference on Software Architecture, WICSA 2004, pp. 25–34. IEEE, June 2004

Temporal Prediction Model for Social Information Propagation

Fei Teng[(✉)], Rong Tang, Yan Yang, Hongjie Wang, and Rongjie Dai

School of Information Science and Technology, Southwest Jiaotong University,
Chengdu 610031, China
fteng@swjtu.edu.cn

Abstract. Prediction of information propagation is an important issue
in research of social network. Recent researches can be divided into graph
or non-graph approaches. Most of non-graph approaches use regression analysis and probability model, seldomly considering clustering
features of social time series. In clustering-based temporal prediction
model, every cluster center is treated as a propagation pattern, and so
that the prediction can be realized through classification to find out
the nearest-neighbor pattern. Prediction performance may be influenced
by clustering performance based on clustering approaches. This paper
proposes a new model Scaling Clustering based Temporal Prediction
Model (SCTPM), which is applicable for predicting propagation pattern
of social information. Through 10-fold cross-validation experiments on
twitter and phrase datasets, SCTPM obtains lower prediction bias and
variance than the existing clustering-based models.

Keywords: Prediction model · Time series · Clustering · Propagation
pattern · Social information

1 Introduction

In Web2.0, social network provides convenient way for users to post and access
information. In September 2016, twitter users produce about 58 million tweets
and twitter search engine conducts 2.1 billion queries everyday [1]. Social network
is a platform for information exchange and sharing, the information on which
owns flu-like propagation characteristic [2]. Information attention is a measure
of heat of social information, which can be visually described as information
propagation trend over time. Figure 1 shows an example of time series of information propagation trend (twitter tag). On June 11, 2009, on the eve of Iran
Election, the tag IranElection appeared on the twitter and caused wide attention
and discussion of campaign results. Attention of IranElection reached the peak
on June 21 at 2:00, and then follows slow decline [21].

This work is supported by the Natioanl Science Foundation of China (Nos. 61572407
and 61603313), the Project of National Science and Technology Support Program
(No. 2015BAH19F02).

© Springer International Publishing AG 2017
L. Polkowski et al. (Eds.): IJCRS 2017, Part I, LNAI 10313, pp. 465–476, 2017.
DOI: 10.1007/978-3-319-60837-2_38

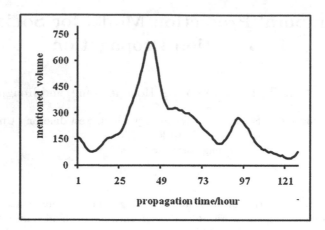

Fig. 1. Temporal propagation trend of IranElection during 128 h starting from 7:00 June 19, 2009.

Prediction of social information propagation is an important issue, which has practical significance such as better placing of content to maximize click-through rates of media content [3] and beforehand determining bandwidth reservation [4]. Traditional predictive models can be divided into graph and non-graph approaches [5]. These approaches' target is to predict how a specific information propagation would expand in a given social network. Some recent works use clustering-based methods to predict propagation trend. The main idea of these works is that propagation trends may be classified into a few number of patterns, so that we can use clustering methods to find out these patterns and then predict the propagation trend according to the nearest-neighbor pattern. Note that the clustering patterns vary with different clustering methods, which are determined by distance measures. As a result, the first goal of this paper is to explore how the distance measure affects prediction performance.

In this paper, we firstly compare clustering performance between KSC [6] and Kmeans. KSC outperforms Kmeans as a good clustering method for social time series, because KSC uses the scaling distance to measure distance between different time series. Secondly, we propose a new model SCTPM including 3 steps: KSC clustering, nearest-neighbor classification and scaling the nearest-neighbor cluster center. Thirdly, we evaluate prediction performance on twitter and phrase datasets, and the results show SCTPM outperforms the existing algorithms by achieving lower prediction bias and prediction variance.

The rest of paper is organized as follows. Section 2 discusses related works. SCTPM and some related definitions are introduced in Sect. 3. Section 4 validates the model on 2 social datasets and analyzes the experiment results. Section 5 concludes this study and presents prospects towards information propagation prediction.

2 Related Work

Recent researches of information propagation prediction can be divided into graph or non-graph approaches [5,7–9]. These approaches use regression analysis, probability model and classification to predict how the information propagation process would expand in social network.

The paper mainly focus on non-graph prediction approaches. Non-graph prediction approaches depend on information propagation characteristics like influence of information publishers [10–12], user forwarding behaviors [13,14] and information popularity. Research of predicting information popularity is a important target because information popularity can be visually represented by social time series like Fig. 1. Based on both the intrinsic attractiveness of a video and the influence from the underlying propagation structure, Li et al. [15] presents SoVP model to predict video views. Kong and Mao [16] analyze dynamic evolution process of previous forum posts and then present a multiple dynamic factors based model to predict popularity of posts. Mazloom et al. [17] propose engagement parameters based model to predict brand-related user post popularity and obtain better prediction accuracy than using visual and textual features.

These researches of predicting information popularity above seldomly consider clustering features of social time series. Taking every cluster center as a propagation pattern, Zhou et al. [18] present a clustering-based temporal prediction model (CTPM) to predict propagation patterns for predictive objects. But Zhou et al. lack the analysis on the relationship between clustering methods and prediction performance. The goal of the paper is to explore how prediction performance is influenced by clustering methods, which are based on distance measures. Yang and Leskovec [6] present KSC or IKSC (Incremental KSC) clustering method based on distance invariant to scaling and translation of time series [19]. KSC is a proper clustering method for social time series and attracts several researchers to do related researches. Han et al. [20] present WKSC to reduce time complexity of KSC based on Discrete Haar Wavelet Transform (DHWT). Combined with KSC and hierarchical clustering, Zhou et al. [18] presents TSC to address the problem of clustering number setting. The paper adopts KSC clustering method, because KSC produces a unique cluster center by scaling for every cluster member, which may be helpful to obtain fine-grained prediction results.

3 Scaling Clustering Based Temporal Prediction Model

This section firstly gives several related terms and then introduces CTPM and SCTPM. Finally, we analyze time complexity of CTPM using Kmeans and SCTPM using KSC.

Given $A_{(1,n)} = [x_1, x_2, \cdots, x_n]$ is a social time series where x_i represents mentioned volume during ith hour, so n continuous volumes build a propagation trend.

Temporal variation of attention of social information can be classified into a few number of propagation patterns. These patterns can be represented as cluster centers using clustering methods.

Introduction to CTPM. CTPM represents Clustering based Temporal Prediction Model. Clustering for social time series observes that propagation pattern before time t is associated with that after t, demonstrated by CTPM [18]. As shown in Algorithm 1, the model includes 2 steps: clustering and nearest-neighbor classification. Firstly the model conducts clustering to acquire cluster centers and every center represents a propagation pattern. Secondly taking propagation pattern as an individual class, the model proceeds with nearest-neighbor classification for predictive objects. Finally, the subsequence of nearest-neighbor propagation pattern is treated as the prediction result.

Algorithm 1. Clustering based Temporal Prediction Model (CTPM)

Input: time series set *items*, cluster number K, predictive object $x_{(1,\beta)}$ with known length β, predictive length γ, clustering algorithm *clusteringAlg*
Output: the final prediction result $\mu_{i^*(\beta,\beta+\gamma)}$
1: $\{\mu_{1(1,\beta+\gamma)}, \ldots, \mu_{K(1,\beta+\gamma)}\} \leftarrow clusteringAlg(items, K, \beta + \gamma)$
2: **for** $i = 1$ to K **do**
3:     $t_i \leftarrow d_1(x_{(1,\beta)}, \mu_{i(1,\beta)})$
4: **end for**
5: $i^* \leftarrow argmin_{i=1,\ldots,K} t_i$
6: **return** $\mu_{i^*(\beta+1,\beta+\gamma)}$

Analysis of Time Complexity for CTPM Using Kmeans. In clustering step, time complexity of every iteration of Kmeans is $O(NKL)$ where N denotes the number of clustering samples, K denotes the number of cluster centers and $L = \beta+\gamma$. In classification step, the complexity of computing $d_1(item1, item2)$ is $O(\beta)$, where d_1 is Euclidean distance, so the complexity of complete classification is $O(K\beta)$ for every predictive object. Conclusively the complexity of CTPM using Kmeans is $O(TNKL)$, where T denotes iteration times.

Introduction to SCTPM. SCTPM denotes Scaling Clustering based Temporal Prediction Model. Based on CTPM, we propose SCTPM using KSC by adding a process of scaling the prediction result. As shown in Fig. 2, the model contains 3 flows: KSC clustering, nearest-neighbor classification and scaling the nearest-neighbor cluster center. First, KSC clustering can produce clustering centers as propagation patterns. Next, nearest-neighbor classification can find out the nearest-neighbor propagation pattern for predictive objects. Finally, scaling process can restore prediction results from cluster centers because KSC cluster centers are eigenvectors.

Based on 3 flows above, we develop detailed steps of SCTPM in Algorithm 2. First, the model conducts KSC clustering to obtain cluster centers $\{\mu_1, \cdots, \mu_K\}$.

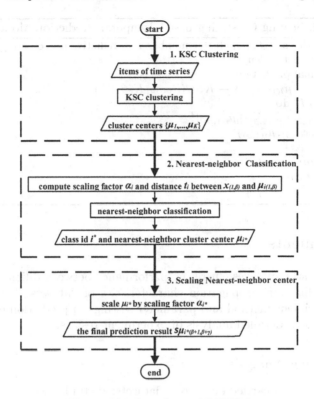

Fig. 2. The flow chart of SCTPM.

Next, the model computes scaling factor α_i and distance t_i between predictive object $x_{(1,\beta)}$ and $\mu_{i(1,\beta)}$, where β is propagation length. Then, the model proceeds with nearest-neighbor classification for $x_{(1,\beta)}$ to acquire class id i^*. After that, the model scales the prediction result μ_{i^*} by scaling factor α_{i^*} to obtain the final prediction result $s\mu_{i^*}$. μ_{i^*} and $s\mu_{i^*}$ are a cluster center and a scaled cluster center respectively, both identified as i^*. Finally, as the subsequence of $s\mu_{i^*}$, $s\mu_{i^*(\beta+1,\beta+\gamma)}$ can be considered as propagation pattern of $x_{(1,\beta)}$ during γ hours after time β.

Analysis of Time Complexity for SCTPM. In clustering step, time complexity of every iteration of KSC is $O(max(NL^2, KL^3))$ where N denotes the number of clustering samples, K denotes the number of cluster centers and $L = \beta + \gamma$ [6]. In classification step, the complexity of computing $d_2(item1, item2)$ is $O(\beta)$, where d_2 is defined in Eq. 3, so the complexity of complete classification is $O(K\beta)$ for every predictive object. Conclusively the complexity of SCTPM is $O(T * max(NL^2, KL^3))$, where T denotes iteration times.

Algorithm 2. Scaling Clustering based Temporal Prediction Model (SCTPM)

Input: time series set *items*, cluster number K, predictive object $x_{(1,\beta)}$ with known length β, predictive length γ

Output: the final prediction result $s\mu_{i^*(\beta,\beta+\gamma)}$

1: $\{\mu_{1(1,\beta+\gamma)}, \ldots, \mu_{K(1,\beta+\gamma)}\} \leftarrow KSC(items, K, \beta + \gamma)$
2: **for** $i = 1$ to K **do**
3:     $\alpha_i \leftarrow x_{(1,\beta)} * \mu_{i(1,\beta)}^T / \|\mu_{i(1,\beta)}\|^2$
4:     $t_i \leftarrow d_2(x_{(1,\beta)}, \mu_{i(1,\beta)})$
5: **end for**
6: $i^* \leftarrow argmin_{i=1,\ldots,K} t_i$
7: $s\mu_{i^*} \leftarrow \mu_{i^*} * \alpha_{i^*}$
8: **return** $s\mu_{i^*(\beta+1,\beta+\gamma)}$

4   Experiments

This section firstly analyzes clustering performance between different clustering methods and find out propagation characteristics of datasets. Then we introduce the experiment method and parameter settings in prediction experiments. Finally we present detailed analysis of experiment results.

4.1   Clustering Analysis

The experiments are carried on 2 open datasets: 1000 phrases and 1000 twitter tags, both from Stanford University. Every item exhibits a propagation pattern during 128 h, whose highest peak appears at 43-th hour [21].

The clustering performance may impact prediction performance. The silhouette value is a measure of how similar an object is to its own cluster (cohesion) compared to other clusters (separation). The higher the value, the better the clustering model. KSC clustering performance is appropriate. In Table 1, twitter items with silhouette > 0 occupy about 88.3% and phrase items occupy about 92.2%. Every item's silhouette is shown in Fig. 3. Besides that, KSC can lessen clustering error of 95.6% phrase items and 97.6% twitter items respectively, compared with Kmeans. The experiment results exactly is consistent with the conclusion that KSC is a better clustering algorithm for social temporal datasets [6].

Propagation characteristics of dataset may be another factor influencing the final prediction result. Twitter presents propagation patterns with richer variation characteristics than phrase items. Combined with Table 1 and Fig. 5, nearly 34% twitter items and 8.1% phrase items exhibit rich propagation patterns with several peaks. About 66% twitter items and 91.9% phrases show monotonous propagation patterns with just only single peak. Besides that, variation trend of variance of dataset attention is consistent with variation trend of dataset attention. As shown in Fig. 4, the variance of dataset attention is highest on time 43 and then follows decline. The attention of twitter dataset is more discrete than that of phrase dataset, because the variance of twitter attention is much higher than that of phrase attention.

Table 1. KSC clustering statistics. n_c: number of cluster members, p_1: percentage between n_c and $Total$, n_s: number of items with silhouette > 0, p_2: percentage between n_s and n_c.

	Cluster	C1	C2	C3	C4	C5	C6	$Total$
Phrase	n_c	284	208	167	141	119	81	1000
	p_1	28.4%	20.8%	16.7%	14.1%	11.9%	8.1%	100.0%
	n_s	284	202	167	132	90	47	922
	p_2	100%	97.1%	100%	93.6%	75.6%	58%	92.2%
Twitter	n_c	361	164	136	135	109	95	1000
	p_1	36.1%	16.4%	13.6%	13.5%	10.9%	9.5%	100.0%
	n_s	361	140	85	123	87	87	883
	p_2	100%	85.37%	62.5%	91.11%	79.82%	91.58%	88.3%

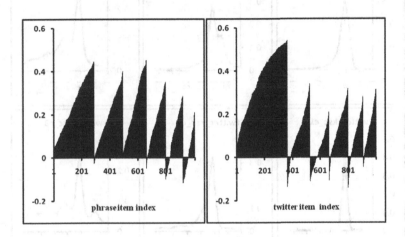

Fig. 3. Silhouettes of phrase and twitter items.

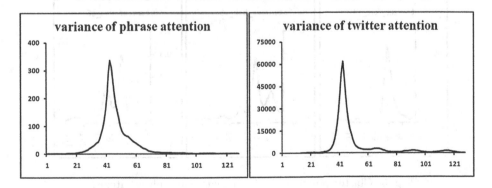

Fig. 4. Variance of phrase and twitter attention.

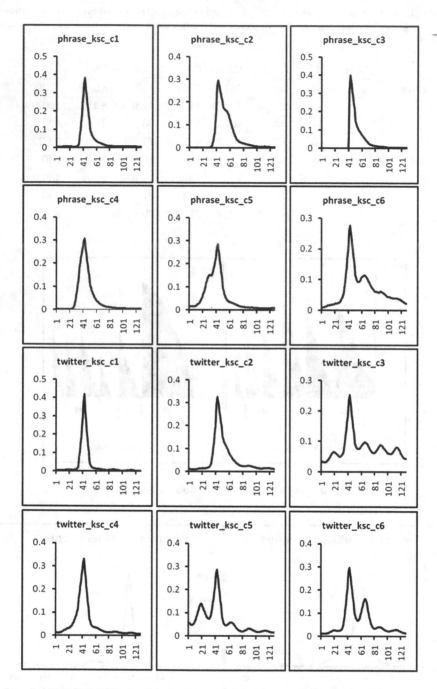

Fig. 5. Cluster centers of KSC on twitter and phrase items.

4.2   SCTPM Experiments

10-fold Cross-validation Experiments. To maintain reliability of experimental results under lower quantity of samples, we adopt 10-fold cross-validation experiments. We firstly split original dataset into 10 subsamples and next select single subsample with 100 items as test set and others with 900 items as training set. We then conduct 10 times of cross-validation experiments and each subsample can be treated as test set one time.

Parameter Settings. β is assigned from $\{43, 64\}$ while γ is assigned from $\{12, 24, 48\}$. Because peak appears at time 43 and time 64 is half of whole (128) propagation length. Prediction performance may be influenced by the predictive length, so we assign successively 12, 24 and 48 to γ to conduct comparison experiments.

Prediction performance is measured by prediction accuracy and precision. Accuracy is how close a measured value is to the actual value. Precision is how close the measured values are to each other.

Given prediction difference PD denotes difference between the predictive propagation pattern and the real pattern. PD_{CTPM} and PD_{SCTPM} represent PD from CTPM and SCTPM, based on Euclidean distance (d_1) and scaling distance (d_2) [19] respectively (See Eqs. 1, 2 and 3).

Given prediction bias PB denotes PD average of every hour and the lower the PB, the higher the prediction accuracy. Given prediction variance PV denotes PD variance average of every hour and the lower the PV, the higher the prediction precision.

Both PB and PV are defined in Eq. 4, where n is the items' number (1000 in this paper), γ is the predictive length.

$$PD_{CTPM} = d_1(x_{(\beta+1,\beta+\gamma)}, \mu_{i*(\beta+1,\beta+\gamma)}). \tag{1}$$

$$PD_{SCTPM} = d_2(x_{(\beta+1,\beta+\gamma)}, s\mu_{i*(\beta+1,\beta+\gamma)})* \parallel x_{(\beta+1,\beta+\gamma)} \parallel. \tag{2}$$

$$d_2(x, y) = \min_{\alpha, q} \frac{\parallel x - \alpha y_{(q)} \parallel}{\parallel x \parallel}, \alpha = \frac{xy^T}{\parallel y \parallel^2}. \tag{3}$$

$$PB = \frac{\sum_{i=1}^{n} PD_i}{n * \gamma}, PV = \frac{\sum_{i=1}^{n} (PD_i - \overline{PD})^2}{n * \gamma} \tag{4}$$

Comparison Experiments. We conduct SCTPM using KSC and CTPM using Kmeans respectively to compare prediction performance by counting PB and PV. The experiment is associated with **2** prediction models, **2** datasets, β with **2** candidates, γ with **3** candidates and **10-fold** cross-validation. Therefore there are **120** groups of experiments for SCTPM and CTPM respectively.

4.3   Analysis of PB and PV

There are 4 factors affecting PB or PV like β, γ, dataset and prediction model, as shown in Figs. 6 and 7. The coordinates of horizontal axis are represented by $Dataset\_\beta\_\gamma$ and P denotes phrase dataset while T denotes twitter dataset.

(1) *Taking β as the variable.* PB or PV is higher under $\beta = 43$ than that under $\beta = 64$ when γ is fixed. Combined with variance of dataset attention in Fig. 4, attention variance after time 43 is higher than that after time 64 and higher attention variance can increase PB or PV.
(2) *Taking γ as thse variable.* PB follows decline trend as γ increases. The variance of dataset attention mainly presents descending trend after time 43 or 64 and lower attention variance can reduce PB.
(3) *Taking dataset as the variable.* PB or PV from sst twitter is higher than that from phrase. Because twitter exhibits rich propagation patterns with several peaks while phrase presents monotonous ones with just one peak. The more the peaks, the higher the attention variance.
(4) *Taking prediction model as the variable.* SCTPM using KSC outperforms CTPM using Kmeans in terms of PB or PV, observing that PB or PV from SCTPM is lower than that from CTPM. Because KSC produces a unique prediction pattern for every predictive object by scaling process while Kmeans without scaling just only outputs fixed K(number of cluster) prediction patterns for all predictive objects. Thus SCTPM obtains fine-grained prediction results while CTPM represents coarse-grained ones.

In summary, CTPM can obtain poor prediction performance especially for social propagation trend with rapid dynamics while SCTPM is suitable for predicting trend with rapid or monotonous changes.

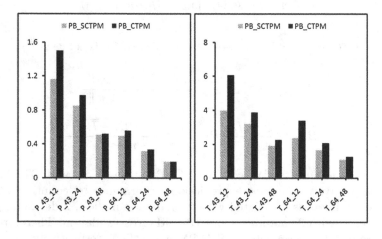

Fig. 6. PB statistics of SCTPM and CTPM

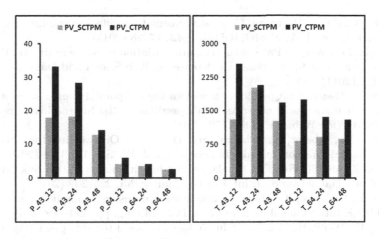

Fig. 7. *PV* statistics of SCTPM and CTPM

5   Conclusion

This paper studies a clustering-based temporal prediction model to predict the propagation of social time series. We firstly compare clustering performance between KSC and Kmeans because prediction performance can be influenced by clustering methods depending on distance measures. Secondly we propose a new model SCTPM including 3 steps: KSC clustering, nearest-neighbor classification and scaling the nearest-neighbor cluster center. KSC clustering can produce cluster centers as propagation patterns and then nearest-neighbor classification can find out the nearest-neighbor propagation pattern for predictive objects. Finally scaling process can restore prediction results from cluster centers because KSC cluster centers are eigenvectors. After 10-fold cross-validation experiments on CTPM using Kmeans and SCTPM using KSC, results show that SCTPM obtains lower prediction bias and prediction variance than CTPM. The superiority of SCTPM comes from the fact that KSC produces a unique prediction pattern for every predictive object while Kmeans only outputs fixed K prediction patterns for all predictive objects. In future, we would like to present upper and lower limits of time series of prediction results.

References

1. Statistics of Twitter. http://www.statisticbrain.com/twitter-statistics/
2. Wang, H., Li, Y., Feng, Z., Feng, L.: ReTweeting analysis and prediction in microblogs: an epidemic inspired approach. J. China Commun. **10**(3), 13–24 (2013)
3. Backstrom, L., Kleinberg, J., Kumar, R.: Optimizing web traffic via the media scheduling problem. In: Proceedings of 15th ACM SIGKDD International Conference on Knowledge Discovery and Data Mining, pp. 89–98 (2009)
4. Wang, Z., Sun, L., Chen, X.: Propagation-based social-aware replication for social video contents. In: Proceedings of 20th ACM International Conference on Multimedia, pp. 29–38 (2012)

5. Guille, A., Hacid, H., Favre, C., et al.: Information diffusion in online social networks: a survey. J. ACM SIGMOD Rec. **42**, 17–28 (2013)
6. Yang, J., Leskovec, J.: Patterns of temporal variation in online media. In: Proceedings of 4th ACM International Conference on Web Search and Data Mining, pp. 177–186 (2011)
7. Guille, A., Hacid, H.: A predictive model for the temporal dynamics of information diffusion in online social networks. In: Proceedings of 21st International Conference on World Wide Web, pp. 1145–1152 (2012)
8. Galuba, W., Aberer, K., Chakraborty, D., et al.: Outtweeting the Twitterers-predicting information cascades in microblogs. J. WOSN. **10**, 3–11 (2010)
9. Wu, J., Zhang, G., Ren, Y.: A balanced modularity maximization link prediction model in social networks. J. Inf. Process. Manag. **53**, 295–307 (2017)
10. Yang, J., Leskovec, J.: Modeling information diffusion in implicit networks. In: 2010 IEEE International Conference on Data Mining, pp. 599–608 (2010)
11. Wang, F., Wang, H., Xu, K.: Diffusive logistic model towards predicting information diffusion in online social networks. In: 2012 32nd International Conference on Distributed Computing Systems Workshops, pp. 133–139 (2012)
12. Li, J., Peng, W., Li, T., et al.: Social network user influence sense-making and dynamics prediction. J. Expert Syst. Appl. **41**, 5115–5124 (2014)
13. Yang, Z., Guo, J., Cai, K., et al.: Understanding retweeting behaviors in social networks. In: Proceedings of 19th ACM International Conference on Information and Knowledge Management, pp. 1633–1636 (2010)
14. Cao, J., Wu, J., Shi, W., et al.: Sina microblog information diffusion analysis and prediction. J. Chin. J. Comput. **37**(4), 779–790 (2014)
15. Li, H., Ma, X., Wang, F., et al.: On popularity prediction of videos shared in online social networks. In: Proceedings of 22nd ACM International Conference on Information and Knowledge Management, pp. 169–178 (2013)
16. Kong, Q., Mao, W.: Predicting popularity of forum threads based on dynamic evolution. J. Chin. J. Softw. **25**(12), 2767–2776 (2014)
17. Mazloom, M., Rietveld, R., Rudinac, S., et al.: Multimodal popularity prediction of brand-related social media posts. In: Proceedings of 2016 ACM on Multimedia Conference, pp. 197–201 (2016)
18. Zhou, X., Xu, K., Zhang, L., et al.: Spreading measurement and time series clustering analysis of social networks. J. Small MicroComput. Syst. China **36**, 1545–1552 (2015)
19. Chu, K.K.W., Wong, M.H.: Fast time-series searching with scaling and shifting. In: Proceedings of 18th ACM SIGMOD-SIGACT-SIGART Symposium on Principles of Database Systems, pp. 237–248 (1999)
20. Han, Z., Chen, N., Le, J., et al.: An efficient and effective clustering algorithm for time series of hot topics. J. Chin. J. Comput. **35**(11), 2337–2347 (2012)
21. Volume Time Series of Memetracker Phrases and Twitter Hashtags. http://snap.stanford.edu/data/volumeseries.html

Characteristic Sets and Generalized Maximal Consistent Blocks in Mining Incomplete Data

Patrick G. Clark[1], Cheng Gao[1], Jerzy W. Grzymala-Busse[1,2(✉)], and Teresa Mroczek[2]

[1] Department of Electrical Engineering and Computer Science, University of Kansas, Lawrence, KS 66045, USA
patrick.g.clark@gmail.com, {cheng.gao,jerzy}@ku.edu
[2] Department of Expert Systems and Artificial Intelligence, University of Information Technology and Management, 35-225 Rzeszow, Poland
tmroczek@wsiz.rzeszow.pl

Abstract. Mining incomplete data using approximations based on characteristic sets is a well-established technique. It is applicable to incomplete data sets with a few interpretations of missing attribute values, e.g., lost values and "do not care" conditions. Typically, probabilistic approximations are used in the process. On the other hand, maximal consistent blocks were introduced for incomplete data sets with only "do not care" conditions, using only lower and upper approximations. In this paper we introduce an extension of the maximal consistent blocks to incomplete data sets with any interpretation of missing attribute values and with probabilistic approximations. Additionally, we present results of experiments on mining incomplete data using both characteristic sets and maximal consistent blocks, using lost values and "do not care" conditions. We show that there is a small difference in quality of rule sets induced either way. However, characteristic sets can be computed in polynomial time while computing maximal consistent blocks is associated with exponential time complexity.

Keywords: Incomplete data · Lost values · "Do not care" conditions · Characteristic sets · Maximal consistent blocks · MLEM2 rule induction algorithm · Probabilistic approximations

1 Introduction

We report results of experiments on incomplete data sets, using two interpretations of missing attribute values: lost values and "do not care" conditions [3]. A lost value, denoted by "?", is interpreted as a value that we do not know since it was erased or not inserted into the data set. Rules are induced from existing, specified attribute values. "Do not care" conditions are interpreted as any attribute value. For example, if an attribute is the hair color, and possible values are blond, dark and red, a "do not care" condition is interpreted as any of these three colors.

© Springer International Publishing AG 2017
L. Polkowski et al. (Eds.): IJCRS 2017, Part I, LNAI 10313, pp. 477–486, 2017.
DOI: 10.1007/978-3-319-60837-2_39

For incomplete data sets special kinds of approximations: singleton, subset and concept should be used [3]. In this paper we consider probabilistic approximations, an extension of lower and upper approximations. Such approximations are defined using a probability denoted by α. If $\alpha = 1$, the probabilistic approximation is lower, if α is a positive number, slightly greater than 0, the probabilistic approximation is upper. Such approximations were usually used for completely specified data sets [8,10–17]. Probabilistic approximations were extended to incomplete data sets in [5]. First experimental results on such approximations were reported in [1,2].

Maximal consistent blocks were introduced for incomplete data sets with only "do not care" conditions, using only lower and upper approximations [9]. The main objective of this paper is to extend the definition of maximal consistent blocks to arbitrary interpretation of missing attribute values. Additionally, the obvious question is what a better choice for data mining is: characteristic sets or maximal consistent blocks. We conducted experiments on data sets with two interpretations of missing attribute values, lost values and "do not care" conditions. As a result, we show that there is a small difference in quality of rule sets induced from approximations based on characteristic sets or on maximal consistent blocks. However, characteristic sets can be computed in polynomial time while computing maximal consistent blocks is associated with exponential time complexity.

2   Incomplete Data Sets

An example of incomplete data set is presented in Table 1. A *concept* is a set of all cases with the same decision value. In Table 1 there are two concepts, the set $\{1, 2, 3, 4\}$ of all cases with flu and the other set $\{5, 6, 7, 8\}$.

Table 1. An incomplete data set

	Attributes			Decision
Case	Temperature	Headache	Cough	Flu
1	Normal	?	Yes	Yes
2	*	Yes	No	Yes
3	*	No	*	Yes
4	High	?	Yes	Yes
5	High	No	No	No
6	*	No	Yes	No
7	High	*	?	No
8	Normal	*	No	No

We use notation $a(x) = v$ if an attribute a has the value v for the case x. The set of all cases will be denoted by U. In Table 1, $U = \{1, 2, 3, 4, 5, 6, 7, 8\}$.

For complete data sets, for an attribute-value pair (a, v), a *block* of (a, v), denoted by $[(a, v)]$, is the following set

$$[(a, v)] = \{x | x \in U, a(x) = v\}.$$

For incomplete decision tables the definition of a block of an attribute-value pair must be modified in the following way [3,4]:

- If for an attribute a and a case x, $a(x) = ?$, then the case x should not be included in any blocks $[(a, v)]$ for all values v of attribute a,
- If for an attribute a and a case x, $a(x) = *$, then the case x should be included in blocks $[(a, v)]$ for all specified values v of attribute a.

For the data set from Table 1, all of blocks of attribute-value pairs are

$[(Temperature, normal)] = \{1, 2, 3, 6, 8\}$,
$[(Temperature, high)] = \{2, 3, 4, 5, 6, 7\}$,
$[(Headache, no)] = \{3, 5, 6, 7, 8\}$,
$[(Headache, yes)] = \{2, 7, 8\}$,
$[(Cough, no)] = \{2, 3, 5, 8\}$,
$[(Cough, yes)] = \{1, 3, 4, 6\}$.

3 Characteristic Sets and Maximal Consistent Blocks

For a case $x \in U$ the *characteristic set* $K_B(x)$ is defined as the intersection of the sets $K(x, a)$, for all $a \in B$, where B is a subset of the set A of all attributes and the set $K(x, a)$ is defined in the following way:

- If $a(x)$ is specified, then $K(x, a)$ is the block $[(a, a(x))]$ of attribute a and its value $a(x)$,
- If $a(x) = ?$ or $a(x) = *$, then $K(x, a) = U$.

For the data set from Table 1, the characteristic sets are
$K_A(1) = \{1, 3, 6\}$,
$K_A(2) = \{2, 8\}$,
$K_A(3) = \{3, 5, 6, 7, 8\}$,
$K_A(4) = \{3, 4, 6\}$,
$K_A(5) = \{3, 5\}$,
$K_A(6) = \{3, 6\}$,
$K_A(7) = \{2, 3, 4, 5, 6, 7\}$,
$K_A(8) = \{2, 3, 8\}$.

The *B-characteristic relation* $R(B)$ is a relation on U defined for $x, y \in U$ as follows:

$$(x, y) \in R(B) \ if \ and \ only \ if \ y \in K_B(x).$$

We say that $R(B)$ is *implied* by its B-characteristic sets $K_B(x)$, $x \in U$. The B-characteristic relation $R(B)$ is reflexive but—in general—does not need to be symmetric or transitive. For the data set from Table 1, $R(A) = \{(1, 1), (1, 3), (1, 6), (2, 2), (2, 8), (3, 3), (3, 5), (3, 6), (3, 7), (3, 8), (4, 3), (4, 4), (4, 6), (5, 3), (5, 5), (6, 3), (6, 6), (7, 2), (7, 3), (7, 4), (7, 5), (7, 6), (7, 7), (8, 2), (8, 3), (8, 8)\}$.

Let X be a subset of U. The set X is *consistent* with respect to B if $(x, y) \in R(B)$ for any $x, y \in X$. If there does not exist a consistent subset Y of U such that X is a proper subset of Y, the set X is called a *maximal consistent block* of B. For data sets in which all missing attribute values are "do not care" conditions, an idea of a maximal consistent block of B was defined in [9]. Note that in our definition the maximal consistent blocks of B are defined for arbitrary interpretations of missing attribute values. Following [9], we will denote the set of all maximal consistent blocks of B by $\mathscr{C}(B)$. For Table 1, the set of all maximal consistent blocks of A is $\mathscr{C}(A) = \{\{1\}, \{2, 8\}, \{3, 5\} \{3, 6\}, \{3, 7\}, \{3, 8\}, \{4\}\}$.

4   Probabilistic Approximations

For incomplete data sets there exist a number of different definitions of approximations [3]. In this paper we will use only *concept* approximations.

4.1   Probabilistic Approximations Based on Characteristic Sets

Let B be a subset of the set A of all attributes. A B-probabilistic approximation of the set X with the threshold α, $0 < \alpha \leq 1$, based on characteristic sets and denoted by B-$appr_\alpha^{CS}(X)$, is defined as follows

$$\cup \{K_B(x) \mid x \in X, \ Pr(X|K_B(x)) \geq \alpha\},$$

where $Pr(X|K_B(x)) = \frac{|X \cap K_B(x)|}{|K_B(x)|}$ is the conditional probability of X given $K_B(x)$ [5]. A-probabilistic approximations of X with the threshold α will be denoted by $appr_\alpha^{CS}(X)$.

Table 2. Conditional probabilities $Pr([(Flu, yes)]|K_A(x))$

x	1	2	3	4
$K_A(x)$	$\{1, 3, 6\}$	$\{2, 8\}$	$\{3, 5, 6, 7, 8\}$	$\{3, 4, 6\}$
$P(\{1, 2, 3, 4\} \mid K_A(x))$	0.667	0.5	0.2	0.667

For Table 1 and both concepts, all conditional probabilities $P(X|K_A(x))$ are presented in Tables 2 and 3. All distinct probabilistic approximations based on characteristic sets are

Table 3. Conditional probabilities $Pr([(Flu, no)]|K_A(x))$

x	5	6	7	8
$K_A(x)$	$\{3, 5\}$	$\{3, 6\}$	$\{2, 3, 4, 5, 6, 7\}$	$\{2, 3, 8\}$
$P(\{5, 6, 7, 8\} \mid K_A(x))$	0.5	0.5	0.5	0.333

$appr^{CS}_{0.2}(\{1, 2, 3, 4\}) = U,$

$appr^{CS}_{0.5}(\{1, 2, 3, 4\}) = \{1, 2, 3, 4, 6, 8\},$

$appr^{CS}_{0.667}(\{1, 2, 3, 4\}) = \{1, 3, 4, 6\},$

$appr^{CS}_{1}(\{1, 2, 3, 4\}) = \emptyset,$

$appr^{CS}_{0.333}(\{5, 6, 7, 8\}) = \{2, 3, 4, 5, 6, 7, 8\},$

$appr^{CS}_{0.5}(\{5, 6, 7, 8\}) = \{2, 3, 4, 5, 6, 7\},$

$appr^{CS}_{1}(\{5, 6, 7, 8\}) = \emptyset.$

If for some β, $0 < \beta \leq 1$, a probabilistic approximation $appr^{CS}_{\beta}(X)$ is not listed above, it is equal to the probabilistic approximation $appr^{CS}_{\alpha}(X)$ with the closest α to β, $\alpha \geq \beta$. For example, $appr^{CS}_{0.4}(\{1, 2, 3, 4\}) = appr^{CS}_{0.5}(\{1, 2, 3, 4\})$.

4.2 Probabilistic Approximations Based on Maximal Consistent Blocks

By analogy with the definition of a B-probabilistic approximation based on characteristic sets, a B-probabilistic approximation of the set X with the threshold α, $0 < \alpha \leq 1$, based on maximal consistent blocks and denoted by $B\text{-}appr^{MCB}_{\alpha}(X)$, is defined as follows

$$\cup\{Y \mid Y \in \mathscr{C}(B),\ Pr(X|Y) \geq \alpha\},$$

where $Pr(X|Y) = \frac{|X \cap Y|}{|Y|}$ is the conditional probability of X given Y. A-probabilistic approximations of X, based on maximal consistent blocks, with the threshold α will be denoted by $appr^{MCB}_{\alpha}(X)$.

For Table 1 and the concept $[(Flu, yes)]$, all conditional probabilities $Pr([(Flu, yes)]|Y)$, where $Y \in \mathscr{C}(A)$, are presented in Table 4. Conditional probabilities $Pr([(Flu, no)]|Y)$, where $Y \in \mathscr{C}(A)$, may be computed in an analogous way. All distinct probabilistic approximations based on maximal consistent blocks are

$appr^{MCB}_{0.5}(\{1, 2, 3, 4\}) = U,$

Table 4. Conditional probabilities $Pr([(Flu, yes)]|Y)$

Y	{1}	{2, 8}	{3, 5}	{3, 6}	{3, 7}	{3, 8}	{4}
$P(\{1, 2, 3, 4\} \mid Y)$	1	0.5	0.5	0.5	0.5	0.5	1

$$appr_1^{MCB}(\{1, 2, 3, 4\}) = \{1, 4\},$$

$$appr_{0.5}^{MCB}(\{5, 6, 7, 8\}) = \{2, 3, 5, 6, 7, 8\},$$

$$appr_1^{MCB}(\{5, 6, 7, 8\}) = \emptyset.$$

5 Definability

Any union of characteristic sets $K_B(x)$ is called B-*globally definable* [7]. An A-globally definable set is called *globally definable*. Let T be a set of attribute-value pairs, where all involved attributes are distinct and are members of a set B. Such set T is called B-*complex*. A block of a B-complex T, denoted by $[T]$, is the set $\cap\{[t]|t \in T\}$. Any union of blocks of B-complexes is called B-*locally definable* [7]. A-locally definable set is called *locally definable*.

Rules are expressed by attribute-value pairs, so any set X may be described by rules if it is locally definable, as was explained in [6]. As follows from [6], maximal consistent blocks for incomplete data sets with only "do not care" conditions are locally definable, so corresponding approximations are also locally definable. However, in general, for arbitrary incomplete data sets, maximal consistent blocks are not locally definable. For example, for the data set from Table 1, sets {1} and {4}, maximal consistent blocks, are not locally definable. Indeed, case 1 occurs in only two blocks: [(Temperature, normal)] and [(Cough, yes)], and the intersection of these two sets is {1, 3, 6}. Similarly, case 4 occurs also in only two blocks: [(Temperature, high)] and [(Cough, yes)], while the intersection of these two sets is {3, 4, 6}. Thus none of the sets: {1}, {4} and {1, 4} can be expressed by rules. From the point of rule induction the set $\{1, 4\} = appr_1^{MCB}(\{1, 2, 3, 4\})$ is useless.

6 Experiments

Our experiments were conducted on nine data sets obtained from the University of California at Irvine *Machine Learning Repository*. For any data set, a corresponding incomplete data set was created by a random replacement of specified values by question marks (lost values), until an entire row of a data set was full of "?"s. Such a data set was removed from experiments, we used only data sets with at least one specified value for any row. For any incomplete data set with "?"s, another incomplete data set was created by replacing all "?"s by "*"s ("do not care" conditions).

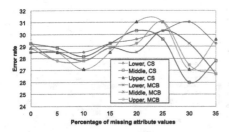

Fig. 1. Number of rules for the *breast cancer* data set

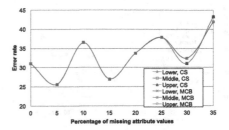

Fig. 2. Error rate for the *echocardiogram* data set with lost values

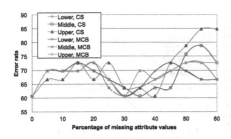

Fig. 3. Error rate for the *global climate* data set with lost values

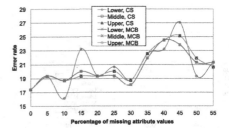

Fig. 4. Error rate for the *hepatitis* data set with lost values

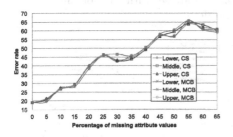

Fig. 5. Error rate for the *image segmentation* data set with lost values

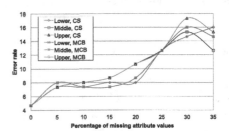

Fig. 6. Error rate for the *iris* data set with lost values

Our main objective was to compare the quality of two approaches to rule induction, based on characteristic sets and maximal consistent blocks, respectively, in terms of an error rate. Note that due to computational complexity, our experiments were restricted to only some percentage of missing attribute values and to some type of incomplete data sets. Results of our experiments, presented in Figs. 1, 2, 3, 4, 5, 6, 7, 8, 9, 10, 11 and 12, are restricted to only three data sets with "do not care" conditions, due to excessive computational complexity. In Figs. 1, 2, 3, 4, 5, 6, 7, 8, 9, 10, 11 and 12, "Lower" means a lower approximation ($\alpha = 1$), "Middle" means a middle probabilistic approximation ($\alpha = 0.5$), and "Upper" means an upper approximation ($\alpha = 0.001$). Additionally, "CS" means a characteristic set and "MCB" means a maximal consistent block.

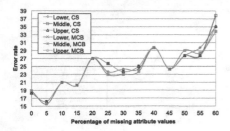

Fig. 7. Error rate for the *lymphography* data set with lost values

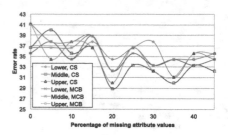

Fig. 8. Error rate for the *postoperative patient* data set with lost values

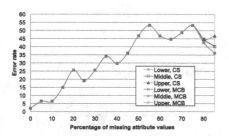

Fig. 9. Error rate for the *small soybean* data set with lost values

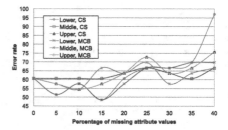

Fig. 10. Error rate for the *global climate* data set with "do not care" conditions

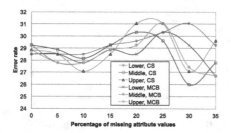

Fig. 11. Error rate for the *echocardiogram* data set with "do not care" conditions

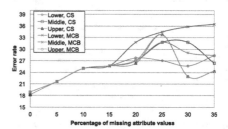

Fig. 12. Error rate for the *lymphography* data set with "do not care" conditions

For a comparison of the two approaches to rule induction, based on characteristic sets and maximal consistent blocks, we used the Friedman rank sum test combined with multiple comparisons, with a 5% level of significance. For all twelve possibilities, presented in Figs. 1, 2, 3, 4, 5, 6, 7, 8, 9, 10, 11 and 12, for only one possibility (presented in Fig. 8 for *postoperative patient* with lost values) the null hypothesis of nonsignificant differences between the six methods is rejected: methods based on characteristic sets combined with middle approximations are better than methods based on maximal consistent blocks with upper approximations.

Thus, we may conclude that there is a small difference in quality of rule sets induced by characteristic sets and maximal consistent blocks. Taking into account computational complexity, it is better to apply data mining to characteristic sets than to maximal consistent blocks.

Originally, maximal consistent blocks were introduced for incomplete data sets with "do not care" conditions [9]. For such data sets rule induction is much more time consuming than for data sets with lost values.

7   Conclusions

In experiments reported in this paper, we compared quality of rule sets induced from characteristic sets and maximal consistent blocks. Results of our experiments show that there is a small difference in quality of rule sets induced using both approaches. Taking into account computational complexity, it is better to apply data mining to characteristic sets than to maximal consistent blocks.

References

1. Clark, P.G., Grzymala-Busse, J.W.: Experiments on probabilistic approximations. In: Proceedings of the 2011 IEEE International Conference on Granular Computing, pp. 144–149(2011)
2. Clark, P.G., Grzymala-Busse, J.W.: Rule induction using probabilistic approximations and data with missing attribute values. In: Proceedings of the 15-th IASTED International Conference on Artificial Intelligence and Soft Computing ASC 2012, pp. 235–242 (2012)
3. Grzymala-Busse, J.W.: Rough set strategies to data with missing attribute values. In: Notes of the Workshop on Foundations and New Directions of Data Mining, in Conjunction with the Third International Conference on Data Mining, pp. 56–63 (2003)
4. Grzymala-Busse, J.W.: Three approaches to missing attribute values—a rough set perspective. In: Proceedings of the Workshop on Foundation of Data Mining, in Conjunction with the Fourth IEEE International Conference on Data Mining, pp. 55–62 (2004)
5. Grzymala-Busse, J.W.: Generalized parameterized approximations. In: Proceedings of the 6-th International Conference on Rough Sets and Knowledge Technology, pp. 136–145 (2011)
6. Grzymala-Busse, J.W., Mroczek, T.: Definability in mining incomplete data. In: Proceedings of the 20-th International Conference on Knowledge Based and Intelligent Information and Engineering Systems, pp. 179–186 (2016)
7. Grzymala-Busse, J.W., Rzasa, W.: Local and global approximations for incomplete data. In: Proceedings of the Fifth International Conference on Rough Sets and Current Trends in Computing, pp. 244–253 (2006)
8. Grzymala-Busse, J.W., Ziarko, W.: Data mining based on rough sets. In: Wang, J. (ed.) Data Mining: Opportunities and Challenges, pp. 142–173. Idea Group Publishing, Hershey (2003)

9. Leung, Y., Li, D.: Maximal consistent block technique for rule acquisition in incomplete information systems. Inf. Sci. **153**, 85–106 (2003)
10. Pawlak, Z., Skowron, A.: Rough sets: some extensions. Inf. Sci. **177**, 28–40 (2007)
11. Pawlak, Z., Wong, S.K.M., Ziarko, W.: Rough sets: probabilistic versus deterministic approach. Int. J. Man-Mach. Stud. **29**, 81–95 (1988)
12. Ślęzak, D., Ziarko, W.: The investigation of the bayesian rough set model. Int. J. Approx. Reason. **40**, 81–91 (2005)
13. Wong, S.K.M., Ziarko, W.: INFER—an adaptive decision support system based on the probabilistic approximate classification. In: Proceedings of the 6-th International Workshop on Expert Systems and their Applications, pp. 713–726 (1986)
14. Yao, Y.Y.: Probabilistic rough set approximations. Int. J. Approx. Reason. **49**, 255–271 (2008)
15. Yao, Y.Y., Wong, S.K.M.: A decision theoretic framework for approximate concepts. Int. J. Man-Mach. Stud. **37**, 793–809 (1992)
16. Ziarko, W.: Variable precision rough set model. J. Comput. Syst. Sci. **46**(1), 39–59 (1993)
17. Ziarko, W.: Probabilistic approach to rough sets. Int. J. Approx. Reason. **49**, 272–284 (2008)

Rough Sets in Incomplete Information Systems with Order Relations Under Lipski's Approach

Michinori Nakata[1]($\boxtimes$), Hiroshi Sakai[2], and Keitarou Hara[3]

[1] Faculty of Management and Information Science,
Josai International University, 1 Gumyo, Togane, Chiba 283-8555, Japan
nakatam@ieee.org
[2] Faculty of Engineering, Department of Mathematics and Computer Aided Sciences,
Kyushu Institute of Technology, Tobata, Kitakyushu 804-8550, Japan
sakai@mns.kyutech.ac.jp
[3] Department of Informatics, Tokyo University of Information Sciences,
4-1 Onaridai, Wakaba-ku, Chiba 265-8501, Japan
hara@rsch.tuis.ac.jp

Abstract. Rough sets and rule induction based on them are described in incomplete information tables where attribute values are ordered. We apply possible world semantics to an incomplete information table, as Lipski did in incomplete databases. The set of possible tables on a set of attributes is derived from the original incomplete information table. Rough sets, a pair of lower and upper approximations, are obtained from every possible table. An object is certainly included in an approximation when it is in the approximation in all possible tables, while an object is possibly included in an approximation when it is in the approximation in some possible tables. From this, we obtain certain and possible approximations. The actual approximation is greater than the certain one and less than the possible one. Finally, we obtain the approximation in the form of interval sets. There exists a gap between rough sets and rule induction from them. To bridge rough sets and rule induction, we give expressions that correspond to certain and possible approximations. The expressions consist of a pair of an object and a rule that the object supports. Consequently, four types of rule supports: certain and consistent, certain and inconsistent, possible and consistent, and possible and inconsistent supports, are obtained from the expressions. The formulae can be applied to the case where not only attributes used to approximate but also attributes approximated have a value with incomplete information. The results give a correctness criterion of rough sets and rule induction based on them in incomplete ordered information systems, as the results of Lipski's work are so in incomplete databases.

Keywords: Rough sets · Rule induction · Incomplete information systems · Ordered domains · Possible world semantics

© Springer International Publishing AG 2017
L. Polkowski et al. (Eds.): IJCRS 2017, Part I, LNAI 10313, pp. 487–506, 2017.
DOI: 10.1007/978-3-319-60837-2_40

1   Introduction

Rough sets, proposed by Pawlak [21], give successful results as a tool for data analysis. The rough sets are defined by using classes obtained from an indiscernibility relation. The indiscernibility relation is derived from two objects being indiscernible when data values characterizing them are symbolically equal. The essential elements are lower and upper approximations that correspond to inclusion and intersection, respectively. These approximations are defined under obtaining complete information for objects and existing no order between values specifying the objects. As a matter of fact, it is common that data from the real world contains incomplete information [19, 20]. Also, data values are used aligning in some order; for example, in ascending or descending order, in dominance order, in preference order, in alphabetical order, and so on. For example, suppose that data values 17, around 30, 22, and 40 are obtained as ages of four persons. These data values are aligned in ascending order like 17, 22, around 30, and 40 from the viewpoint of youngness and "around 30" is not a value with complete information. Such a situation frequently occurs in the real data. So, we describe rough sets and how rules are derived from them in incomplete information tables with ordered domains.

For existing order between data values, Greco et al. proposed rough sets based on dominance relations [7]. And also Greco et al. dealt with incomplete information by fixing indiscernibility of a missing value with another one [6], as Kryszkiewicz dealt with the missing value in incomplete information systems without ordered domains [11]. Lots of authors adopt a similar treatment for the missing value [4, 15, 22, 28, 31, 33]. Qian et al. fix the order of a value having incomplete information with another value by comparing possible minimum and maximum that the values can take [23], which is used by some authors [3, 14, 30]. Yang and Dou fix a degree with which a missing value is indiscernible with another value [32].

Fixing indiscernibility or order of a value having incomplete information with another value is questionable. This is because we cannot definitely know whether it may be actually equal to another one or not without additional information. There exist two possibilities for a value with incomplete information. One possibility is that it may be equal to another value; namely the values may be indiscernible. The other possibility is that the two values may be not equal to each other; namely, they may be discernible. Fixing indiscernibility means to take into account only one possibility, but to neglect the other possibility. This treatment generates information loss and creates poor results [16, 29].

Such a situation also occurs for fixing order of a value having incomplete information with another value. For example, suppose we have two values x with complete information and y with incomplete information where x is 5 and the actual value of y is one in $\{2, 4, 5, 7, 9\}$. There exists two possibilities for order of x and y, If the actual value of y is 7 or 9, we obtain $x < y$, otherwise $x \geq y$. We cannot know which possibility is true without additional information. Two possibilities should be taken into account. Therefore, fixing order of a value having incomplete information with another value generates loss of information and creates poor results, as is shown in incomplete information systems with no ordered domains [16, 29].

Lipski proposed an approach dealing with incomplete information [12, 13]. Lipski's approach is based on possible world semantics and deals with all possibilities that a value with incomplete information has. The approach does not fix both indiscernibility and order of a value having incomplete information with another value, although it seems to have difficulty of computational complexity. This is because the number of possibilities grows exponentially, as the number of values with incomplete information increases. However, we can undoubtedly know properties of operations to incomplete information under Lipski's approach. From this, results of Lipski's approach are used as a correctness criterion of handling incomplete information in the field of databases [1, 2, 5, 9, 10, 18, 34]. Therefore, we describe properties of rough sets and rule induction from them under Lipski's approach. The results of this paper give a correctness criterion of rough sets and rule induction based on them in incomplete information tables with ordered domains.

The paper is organized as follows. In Sect. 2, an approach based on classes obtained from order relations is briefly addressed in complete information tables with ordered domains, called complete ordered information systems. The descriptions are based on Greco et al. [7]. In Sect. 3, we describe an approach based on possible world semantics in incomplete information tables with ordered domains, called incomplete ordered information systems. Rough sets are formulated from the viewpoint of both certainty and possibility, as Lipski dealt with incomplete information. To induce rules from lower and upper approximations, we gives expressions whose element is a pair of an object and a rule that the object supports. By using the expressions, we clarify what rules objects support and how they do the rules. In Sect. 4, we give conclusion and future work.

2   Rough Sets by Classes from Order Relations in Complete Ordered Information Systems

A data set obtained from some observations is represented as a table, called an information table. In the information table each row represents an object and each column an attribute with an ordered domain. When information is complete, a mathematical model of an information table with ordered domains is called a complete ordered information system. The complete ordered information system is a quardple expressed by $(U, AT, \{Dom(a_i) \mid a_i \in AT\}, \{I_{a_i} \mid a_i \in AT\})$ where $Dom(a_i)$ is the set of values that attribute a_i can have; namely, the domain of a_i, and I_{a_i} is the order relation imposed on a_i. A non-empty finite set of objects, called the universe, is denoted by U. A non-empty finite set of attributes is denoted by AT. The relationship of U and AT is such that for every $a_i \in AT$ $a_i : U \rightarrow Dom(a_i)$ with order relation I_{a_i}.

Greco et al. proposed expressions of rough sets in complete information systems with ordered domains [7]. Suppose order of any two values in $Dom(a_i)$ is derived from order relation I_{a_i} that is equal to ascending order relation $I_{\overline{a_i}}^{\geq}$ or descending order relation $I_{\overline{a_i}}^{\leq}$ whose element is pair (o, o') of objects o and o':

$$I_{\overline{a_i}}^{\geq} = \{(o, o') \in U \times U : a_i(o) \geq a_i(o')\}, \tag{1}$$

$$I_{\overline{a_i}}^{\leq} = \{(o, o') \in U \times U : a_i(o) \leq a_i(o')\}, \tag{2}$$

where $a_i(o)$ denotes the value of object o for attribute a_i. From $I_{\overline{a_i}}^{\geq}$ and $I_{\overline{a_i}}^{\leq}$, we obtain ascending classe $C_{\overline{a_i}, y_j}^{\geq}$ and descending class $C_{\overline{a_i}, y_j}^{\leq}$ where $C_{\overline{a_i}, y_k}^{\geq}$ is the set of objects with $a_i(o) \geq y_k$ and $C_{\overline{a_i}, y_k}^{\leq}$ is the set of objects with $a_i(o) \leq y_k$, respectively, where y_k is in V_{a_i} with $|V_{a_i}| = n$ where $V_{a_i} \subseteq Dom(a_i)$ is the set of values that actually occur for attribute a_i.

$$C_{\overline{a_i}, y_k}^{\geq} = \{o \in U : (o, o') \in I_{\overline{a_i}}^{\geq} \wedge a_i(o') = y_k\}, \tag{3}$$

$$C_{\overline{a_i}, y_k}^{\leq} = \{o \in U : (o, o') \in I_{\overline{a_i}}^{\leq} \wedge a_i(o') = y_k\}. \tag{4}$$

Formula (3) means that objects with $a_i(o) \geq y_k$ belong to the same class $C_{\overline{a_i}, y_k}^{\geq}$; namely, they are indiscernible in being greater than or equal to y_k for a_i. Formula (4) means that objects with $a_i(o) \leq y_k$ belong to the same class $C_{\overline{a_i}, y_k}^{\leq}$; namely, they are indiscernible in being less than or equal to y_k for a_i. When elements in V_{a_i} are linearly ordered; namely, for $y_1 \leq y_2 \leq \cdots \leq y_n$, $U = C_{\overline{a_i}, y_1}^{\geq} \supseteq C_{\overline{a_i}, y_2}^{\geq} \supseteq \cdots \supseteq C_{\overline{a_i}, y_n}^{\geq}$ and $C_{\overline{a_i}, y_1}^{\leq} \subseteq C_{\overline{a_i}, y_2}^{\leq} \subseteq \cdots \subseteq C_{\overline{a_i}, y_n}^{\leq} = U$.

Lower approximation $\underline{a_j}(C_{\overline{a_i}, y_k}^{\geq})$ and upper approximation $\overline{a_j}(C_{\overline{a_i}, y_k}^{\geq})$ of $C_{\overline{a_i}, y_k}^{\geq}$ by $a_j \in AT$ are:

$$\underline{a_j}(C_{\overline{a_i}, y_k}^{\geq}) = \{o \in U : C_{\overline{a_j}, a_j(o)}^{\geq} \subseteq C_{\overline{a_i}, y_k}^{\geq}\}, \tag{5}$$

$$\overline{a_j}(C_{\overline{a_i}, y_k}^{\geq}) = \{o \in U : C_{\overline{a_j}, a_j(o)}^{\leq} \cap C_{\overline{a_i}, y_k}^{\geq} \neq \emptyset\}, \tag{6}$$

Lower approximation $\underline{a_j}(C_{\overline{a_i}, y_k}^{\leq})$ and upper approximation $\overline{a_j}(C_{\overline{a_i}, y_k}^{\leq})$ of $C_{\overline{a_i}, y_k}^{\leq}$ by $a_j \in AT$ are:

$$\underline{a_j}(C_{\overline{a_i}, y_k}^{\leq}) = \{o \in U : C_{\overline{a_j}, a_j(o)}^{\leq} \subseteq C_{\overline{a_i}, y_k}^{\leq}\}, \tag{7}$$

$$\overline{a_j}(C_{\overline{a_i}, y_k}^{\leq}) = \{o \in U : C_{\overline{a_j}, a_j(o)}^{\geq} \cap C_{\overline{a_i}, y_k}^{\leq} \neq \emptyset\}. \tag{8}$$

The following properties hold [6]:

$$\underline{a_j}(C_{\overline{a_i}, y_k}^{\geq}) \subseteq C_{\overline{a_i}, y_k}^{\geq} \subseteq \overline{a_j}(C_{\overline{a_i}, y_k}^{\geq}), \tag{9}$$

$$\underline{a_j}(C_{\overline{a_i}, y_k}^{\leq}) \subseteq C_{\overline{a_i}, y_k}^{\leq} \subseteq \overline{a_j}(C_{\overline{a_i}, y_k}^{\leq}). \tag{10}$$

Also, complementarity holds [6]:

$$\underline{a_j}(C_{\overline{a_i}, x_k}^{\geq}) = U - \overline{a_j}(C_{\overline{a_i}, y_{k-1}}^{\leq}), k = 2, \ldots, n, \tag{11}$$

$$\underline{a_j}(C_{\overline{a_i}, x_k}^{\leq}) = U - \overline{a_j}(C_{\overline{a_i}, y_{k+1}}^{\geq}), k = 1, \ldots, n-1, \tag{12}$$

$$\overline{a_j}(C_{\overline{a_i}, x_k}^{\geq}) = U - \underline{a_j}(C_{\overline{a_i}, y_{k-1}}^{\leq}), k = 2, \ldots, n, \tag{13}$$

$$\overline{a_j}(C_{\overline{a_i}, x_k}^{\leq}) = U - \underline{a_j}(C_{\overline{a_i}, y_{k+1}}^{\geq}), k = 1, \ldots, n-1. \tag{14}$$

We induce rules from lower and upper approximations. When an object is included in an approximation, the object consistently or inconsistently supports a rule.

- When $o \in \underline{a_j}(C^{\geq}_{\overline{a_i},y_k})$, o consistently supports a rule "If $a_j \geq a_j(o)$, then $a_i \geq y_k$" where $k = 2, \ldots, n$.
- When $o \in \overline{a_j}(C^{\geq}_{\overline{a_i},y_k}) \setminus \underline{a_j}(C^{\geq}_{\overline{a_i},y_k})$, o inconsistently supports a rule "If $a_j \geq a_j(o)$, then $a_i \geq y_k$" where $k = 2, \ldots, n$. The degree of consistency, called the accuracy of the rule, is $|C^{\geq}_{a_j,a_j(o)} \cap C^{\geq}_{\overline{a_i},y_k}|/|C^{\geq}_{a_j,a_j(o)}|$.
- When $o \in \underline{a_j}(C^{\leq}_{\overline{a_i},y_k})$, o consistently supports a rule "If $a_j \leq a_j(o)$, then $a_i \leq y_k$" where $k = 1, \ldots, n - 1$.
- When $o \in \overline{a_j}(C^{\leq}_{\overline{a_i},y_k}) \setminus \underline{a_j}(C^{\leq}_{\overline{a_i},y_k})$, o inconsistently supports a rule "If $a_j \leq a_j(o)$, then $a_i \leq y_k$" where $k = 1, \ldots, n - 1$. The degree of consistency is $|C^{\leq}_{a_j,a_j(o)} \cap C^{\leq}_{\overline{a_i},y_k}|/|C^{\leq}_{a_j,a_j(o)}|$.

Thus far, the formulae are described for a single attribute. We express formulae for a set of attributes. Order relations on set A of attributes are:

$$I^{\geq}_A = \{(o,o') \in U \times U : A(o) \geq A(o')\} = \cap_{a \in A} I^{\geq}_a,$$
$$I^{\leq}_A = \{(o,o') \in U \times U : A(o) \leq A(o')\} = \cap_{a \in A} I^{\leq}_a,$$

where $A(o) \geq A(o')$ and $A(o) \leq A(o')$ are equal to $\wedge_{a \in A}(a(o) \geq a(o'))$ and $\wedge_{a \in A}(a(o) \leq a(o'))$, respectively. Classes derived from $I^{\geq}_A$ and $I^{\leq}_A$ are:

$$C^{\geq}_{A,Y_k} = \{o \in U : (o,o') \in I^{\geq}_A \wedge A(o') = Y_k\} = \cap_{h=1,m} C^{\geq}_{\overline{a_h},y_{h,k}},$$
$$C^{\leq}_{A,Y_k} = \{o \in U : (o,o') \in I^{\leq}_A \wedge A(o') = Y_k\} = \cap_{h=1,m} C^{\leq}_{\overline{a_h},y_{h,k}},$$

where $A = \{a_1, \ldots a_m\}$ with $m \leq |AT|$, $Y_k = \{y_{1,k}, \ldots, y_{m,k}\}$, and $A(o) = Y_k$ is equal to $\wedge_{h=1,m}(a_h(o) = y_{h,k})$. Lower approximation $\underline{B}(C^{\geq}_{A,Y_k})$ and upper approximation $\overline{B}(C^{\geq}_{A,Y_k})$ of $C^{\geq}_{A,Y_k}$ by $B \subseteq AT$ are:

$$\underline{B}(C^{\geq}_{A,Y_k}) = \{o \in U : C^{\geq}_{B,B(o)} \subseteq C^{\geq}_{A,Y_k}\} = \cap_{h=1,m} \underline{B}(C^{\geq}_{\overline{a_h},y_{h,k}}),$$
$$\overline{B}(C^{\geq}_{A,Y_k}) = \{o \in U : C^{\leq}_{B,B(o)} \cap C^{\geq}_{A,Y_k} \neq \emptyset\} = \cap_{h=1,m} \overline{B}(C^{\geq}_{\overline{a_h},y_{h,k}}),$$

Lower approximation $\underline{B}(C^{\leq}_{A,Y_k})$ and upper approximation $\overline{B}(C^{\leq}_{A,Y_k})$ of $C^{\leq}_{A,Y_k}$ by B are:

$$\underline{B}(C^{\leq}_{A,Y_k}) = \{o \in U : C^{\leq}_{B,B(o)} \subseteq C^{\leq}_{A,Y_k}\} = \cap_{h=1,m} \underline{B}(C^{\leq}_{\overline{a_h},y_{h,k}}),$$
$$\overline{B}(C^{\leq}_{A,Y_k}) = \{o \in U : C^{\geq}_{B,B(o)} \cap C^{\leq}_{A,Y_k} \neq \emptyset\} = \cap_{h=1,m} \overline{B}(C^{\leq}_{\overline{a_h},y_{h,k}}).$$

Note that complementarity holds for these approximations if $|A| = 1$; namely, a single attribute, otherwise it does not hold.

3 Rough Sets Based on Possible World Semantics in Incomplete Ordered Information Systems

Incomplete information is expressed by a set of values that an object can take for an attribute. A missing value that means existing but unknown at present is expressed by the set of all elements in the domain. Therefore, for $a_i \in AT$ $a_i : U \rightarrow 2^{Dom(a_i)}$. We describe rough sets on the basis of Lipski's work using possible world semantics [12]. Suppose we focus on set A of attributes. The set of possible tables on A is obtained from the original incomplete ordered information table. A possible table is a candidate on A of the actual table. In a possible table, the value that an object has for each attribute in A is one of possible values that the object has for the attribute in the original incomplete ordered information table. Set pt_A of possible tables on A is:

$$pt_A = \{t : \forall o \in U \ \forall a_i \in A \ a_i(o)^t = e \wedge e \in a_i(o)\}, \tag{15}$$

where $a_i(o)^t$ and $a_i(o)$ are values of attribute a_i for object o in possible table t and in the original incomplete ordered information table, respectively. Every possible table has complete information on A, called a complete information table on A. The formulae in complete information systems can be applied to every possible table on A. Therefore, rough sets, lower and upper approximations, are derived for each possible table by using the formulae described in the previous section.

Example 1. Let an information table be as follows:

U	a_1	a_2	a_3
1	$\{x\}$	$\{1, 2, 4\}$	$\{a, c\}$
2	$\{y, z\}$	$\{1, 3\}$	$\{c\}$
3	$\{x, y\}$	$\{1\}$	$\{a\}$
4	$\{y\}$	$\{1\}$	$\{b\}$
5	$\{y\}$	$\{3\}$	$\{c\}$
6	$\{z\}$	$\{2\}$	$\{c\}$

Order relations: $z > y > x$, $3 > 2 > 1$, and $c > b > a$ are imposed on a_1, a_2 and a_3, respectively. When we focus on attributes a_1 and a_3, the following eight possible tables are obtained on $\{a_1, a_3\}$:

t_1

U	a_1	a_2	a_3
1	$\{x\}$	$\{1, 2, 4\}$	$\{a\}$
2	$\{y\}$	$\{1, 3\}$	$\{c\}$
3	$\{x\}$	$\{1\}$	$\{a\}$
4	$\{y\}$	$\{1\}$	$\{b\}$
5	$\{y\}$	$\{3\}$	$\{c\}$
6	$\{z\}$	$\{2\}$	$\{c\}$

t_2

U	a_1	a_2	a_3
1	$\{x\}$	$\{1, 2, 4\}$	$\{c\}$
2	$\{y\}$	$\{1, 3\}$	$\{c\}$
3	$\{x\}$	$\{1\}$	$\{a\}$
4	$\{y\}$	$\{1\}$	$\{b\}$
5	$\{y\}$	$\{3\}$	$\{c\}$
6	$\{z\}$	$\{2\}$	$\{c\}$

t_3

U	a_1	a_2	a_3
1	$\{x\}$	$\{1, 2, 4\}$	$\{a\}$
2	$\{y\}$	$\{1, 3\}$	$\{c\}$
3	$\{y\}$	$\{1\}$	$\{a\}$
4	$\{y\}$	$\{1\}$	$\{b\}$
5	$\{y\}$	$\{3\}$	$\{c\}$
6	$\{z\}$	$\{2\}$	$\{c\}$

t_4

U	a_1	a_2	a_3
1	$\{x\}$	$\{1,2,4\}$	$\{c\}$
2	$\{y\}$	$\{1,3\}$	$\{c\}$
3	$\{y\}$	$\{1\}$	$\{a\}$
4	$\{y\}$	$\{1\}$	$\{b\}$
5	$\{y\}$	$\{3\}$	$\{c\}$
6	$\{z\}$	$\{2\}$	$\{c\}$

t_5

U	a_1	a_2	a_3
1	$\{x\}$	$\{1,2,4\}$	$\{a\}$
2	$\{z\}$	$\{1,3\}$	$\{c\}$
3	$\{x\}$	$\{1\}$	$\{a\}$
4	$\{y\}$	$\{1\}$	$\{b\}$
5	$\{y\}$	$\{3\}$	$\{c\}$
6	$\{z\}$	$\{2\}$	$\{c\}$

t_6

U	a_1	a_2	a_3
1	$\{x\}$	$\{1,2,4\}$	$\{c\}$
2	$\{z\}$	$\{1,3\}$	$\{c\}$
3	$\{x\}$	$\{1\}$	$\{a\}$
4	$\{y\}$	$\{1\}$	$\{b\}$
5	$\{y\}$	$\{3\}$	$\{c\}$
6	$\{z\}$	$\{2\}$	$\{c\}$

t_7

U	a_1	a_2	a_3
1	$\{x\}$	$\{1,2,4\}$	$\{a\}$
2	$\{z\}$	$\{1,3\}$	$\{c\}$
3	$\{y\}$	$\{1\}$	$\{a\}$
4	$\{y\}$	$\{1\}$	$\{b\}$
5	$\{y\}$	$\{3\}$	$\{c\}$
6	$\{z\}$	$\{2\}$	$\{c\}$

t_8

U	a_1	a_2	a_3
1	$\{x\}$	$\{1,2,4\}$	$\{c\}$
2	$\{z\}$	$\{1,3\}$	$\{c\}$
3	$\{y\}$	$\{1\}$	$\{a\}$
4	$\{y\}$	$\{1\}$	$\{b\}$
5	$\{y\}$	$\{3\}$	$\{c\}$
6	$\{z\}$	$\{2\}$	$\{c\}$

Set $pt_{\{a_1,a_3\}}$ of possible tables on $\{a_1, a_3\}$ is:

$$pt_{\{a_1,a_3\}} = \{t_1, \cdots, t_8\}.$$

Lower $\underline{a_1}(C^{\geq}_{a_3,b})^{t_i}$ and upper approximation $\overline{a_1}(C^{\geq}_{a_3,b})^{t_i}$ of $C^{\geq}_{a_3,b}$ for a_1 are:

$$\underline{a_1}(C^{\geq}_{a_3,b})^{t_1} = \{o_2, o_4, o_5, o_6\},$$

$$\overline{a_1}(C^{\geq}_{a_3,b})^{t_1} = \{o_2, o_4, o_5, o_6\},$$

$$\underline{a_1}(C^{\geq}_{a_3,b})^{t_2} = \{o_2, o_4, o_5, o_6\},$$

$$\overline{a_1}(C^{\geq}_{a_3,b})^{t_2} = \{o_1, o_2, o_3, o_4, o_5, o_6\},$$

$$\underline{a_1}(C^{\geq}_{a_3,b})^{t_3} = \{o_6\},$$

$$\overline{a_1}(C^{\geq}_{a_3,b})^{t_3} = \{o_2, o_3, o_4, o_5, o_6\},$$

$$\underline{a_1}(C^{\geq}_{a_3,b})^{t_4} = \{o_6\},$$

$$\overline{a_1}(C^{\geq}_{a_3,b})^{t_4} = \{o_1, o_2, o_3, o_4, o_5, o_6\},$$

$$\underline{a_1}(C^{\geq}_{a_3,b})^{t_5} = \{o_2, o_4, o_5, o_6\},$$

$$\overline{a_1}(C^{\geq}_{a_3,b})^{t_5} = \{o_2, o_4, o_5, o_6\},$$

$$\underline{a_1}(C^{\geq}_{a_3,b})^{t_6} = \{o_2, o_4, o_5, o_6\},$$

$$\overline{a_1}(C^{\geq}_{a_3,b})^{t_6} = \{o_1, o_2, o_3, o_4, o_5, o_6\},$$

$$\underline{a_1}(C^{\geq}_{a_3,b})^{t_7} = \{o_2, o_6\},$$

$$\overline{a_1}(C^{\geq}_{a_3,b})^{t_7} = \{o_2, o_3, o_4, o_5, o_6\},$$

$$\underline{a_1}(C^{\geq}_{a_3,b})^{t_8} = \{o_2, o_6\},$$

$$\overline{a_1}(C^{\geq}_{a_3,b})^{t_8} = \{o_1, o_2, o_3, o_4, o_5, o_6\},$$

where $C^{\geq}_{a_3,b} = \{o_2, o_4, o_5, o_6\}$ for possible tables t_1, t_3, t_5, and t_7, and $C^{\geq}_{a_3,b} = \{o_1, o_2, o_4, o_5, o_6\}$ for the other possible tables.

$$\underline{a_1}(C^{\leq}_{a_3,b})^{t_1} = \{o_1, o_3\},$$

$$\overline{a_1}(C^{\leq}_{a_3,b})^{t_1} = \{o_1, o_2, o_3, o_4, o_5\},$$

$$\underline{a_1}(C^{\leq}_{a_3,b})^{t_2} = \emptyset,$$

$$\overline{a_1}(C^{\leq}_{a_3,b})^{t_2} = \{o_1, o_2, o_3, o_4, o_5\},$$

$$\underline{a_1}(C^{\leq}_{a_3,b})^{t_3} = \{o_1\},$$

$$\overline{a_1}(C^{\leq}_{a_3,b})^{t_3} = \{o_1, o_2, o_3, o_4, o_5\},$$

$$\underline{a_1}(C^{\leq}_{a_3,b})^{t_4} = \emptyset,$$

$$\overline{a_1}(C^{\leq}_{a_3,b})^{t_4} = \{o_1, o_2, o_3, o_4, o_5\},$$

$$\underline{a_1}(C^{\leq}_{a_3,b})^{t_5} = \{o_1, o_3\},$$

$$\overline{a_1}(C^{\leq}_{a_3,b})^{t_5} = \{o_1, o_3, o_4, o_5\},$$

$$\underline{a_1}(C^{\leq}_{a_3,b})^{t_6} = \emptyset,$$

$$\overline{a_1}(C^{\leq}_{a_3,b})^{t_6} = \{o_1, o_3, o_4, o_5\},$$

$$\underline{a_1}(C^{\leq}_{a_3,b})^{t_7} = \{o_1\},$$

$$\overline{a_1}(C^{\leq}_{a_3,b})^{t_7} = \{o_1, o_3, o_4, o_5\},$$

$$\underline{a_1}(C^{\leq}_{a_3,b})^{t_8} = \emptyset,$$

$$\overline{a_1}(C^{\leq}_{a_3,b})^{t_8} = \{o_1, o_3, o_4, o_5\},$$

where $C^{\leq}_{a_3,b} = \{o_1, o_3, o_4\}$ for possible tables t_1, t_3, t_5, and t_7, and $C^{\geq}_{a_3,b} = \{o_3, o_4\}$ for the other possible tables.

There may exist an object that is included in an approximation in all possible tables. The object is certainly an element of the approximation. The set of such objects is called the certain approximation. Certain approximations, sets of objects that certainly belong to approximations, are:

$$Ca_j(C^{\geq}_{a_i,y_k}) = \{o \in U : \forall t \in pt_{\{a_i,a_j\}} \; o \in \underline{a_j}(C^{\geq}_{a_i,y_k})^t\}, \tag{16}$$

$$C\overline{a_j}(C^{\geq}_{a_i,y_k}) = \{o \in U : \forall t \in pt_{\{a_i,a_j\}} \; o \in \overline{a_j}(C^{\geq}_{a_i,y_k})^t\}, \tag{17}$$

$$Ca_j(C^{\leq}_{a_i,y_k}) = \{o \in U : \forall t \in pt_{\{a_i,a_j\}} \; o \in \underline{a_j}(C^{\leq}_{a_i,y_k})^t\}, \tag{18}$$

$$C\overline{a_j}(C^{\leq}_{a_i,y_k}) = \{o \in U : \forall t \in pt_{\{a_i,a_j\}} \; o \in \overline{a_j}(C^{\leq}_{a_i,y_k})^t\}, \tag{19}$$

where $\underline{a_j}(C^{\geq}_{a_i,y_k})^t$, $\overline{a_j}(C^{\geq}_{a_i,y_k})^t$, $\underline{a_j}(C^{\leq}_{a_i,y_k})^t$, and $\overline{a_j}(C^{\leq}_{a_i,y_k})^t$ are approximations in possible table t.

There may exist an object that is included in an approximation in some possible tables. The object is possibly an element of the approximation. The set of such objects is called the possible approximation. Possible approximations, sets of objects that possibly belong to approximations, are:

$$Pa_j(C^{\geq}_{a_i,y_k}) = \{o \in U : \exists t \in pt_{\{a_i,a_j\}}\ o \in \underline{a_j}(C^{\geq}_{a_i,y_k})^t\}, \qquad (20)$$

$$P\overline{a_j}(C^{\geq}_{a_i,y_k}) = \{o \in U : \exists t \in pt_{\{a_i,a_j\}}\ o \in \overline{a_j}(C^{\geq}_{a_i,y_k})^t\}, \qquad (21)$$

$$Pa_j(C^{\leq}_{a_i,y_k}) = \{o \in U : \exists t \in pt_{\{a_i,a_j\}}\ o \in \underline{a_j}(C^{\leq}_{a_i,y_k})^t\}, \qquad (22)$$

$$P\overline{a_j}(C^{\leq}_{a_i,y_k}) = \{o \in U : \exists t \in pt_{\{a_i,a_j\}}\ o \in \overline{a_j}(C^{\leq}_{a_i,y_k})^t\}. \qquad (23)$$

Proposition 1

$$Ca_j(C^{\geq}_{a_i,y_k}) \subseteq C^{\geq}_{a_i,y_k} \subseteq C\overline{a_j}(C^{\geq}_{a_i,y_k}),$$

$$Pa_j(C^{\geq}_{a_i,y_k}) \subseteq C^{\geq}_{a_i,y_k} \subseteq P\overline{a_j}(C^{\geq}_{a_i,y_k}),$$

$$Ca_j(C^{\leq}_{a_i,y_k}) \subseteq C^{\leq}_{a_i,y_k} \subseteq C\overline{a_j}(C^{\leq}_{a_i,y_k}),$$

$$Pa_j(C^{\leq}_{a_i,y_k}) \subseteq C^{\leq}_{a_i,y_k} \subseteq P\overline{a_j}(C^{\leq}_{a_i,y_k}).$$

Proposition 2

$$Ca_j(C^{\geq}_{a_i,y_k}) \subseteq Pa_j(C^{\geq}_{a_i,y_k}),$$

$$C\overline{a_j}(C^{\geq}_{a_i,y_k}) \subseteq P\overline{a_j}(C^{\geq}_{a_i,y_k}),$$

$$Ca_j(C^{\leq}_{a_i,y_k}) \subseteq Pa_j(C^{\leq}_{a_i,y_k}),$$

$$C\overline{a_j}(C^{\leq}_{a_i,y_k}) \subseteq P\overline{a_j}(C^{\leq}_{a_i,y_k}).$$

From Propositions 1 and 2,

$$Ca_j(C^{\geq}_{a_i,y_k}) \subseteq Pa_j(C^{\geq}_{a_i,y_k}) \subseteq C^{\geq}_{a_i,y_k} \subseteq C\overline{a_j}(C^{\geq}_{a_i,y_k}) \subseteq P\overline{a_j}(C^{\geq}_{a_i,y_k}),$$

$$Ca_j(C^{\leq}_{a_i,y_k}) \subseteq Pa_j(C^{\leq}_{a_i,y_k}) \subseteq C^{\leq}_{a_i,y_k} \subseteq C\overline{a_j}(C^{\leq}_{a_i,y_k}) \subseteq P\overline{a_j}(C^{\leq}_{a_i,y_k}).$$

Example 2. In information table T of Example 1, certain lower and upper approximations of $C^{\geq}_{a_3,b}$ are:

$$Ca_1(C^{\geq}_{a_3,b}) = \{o_6\},$$

$$C\overline{a_1}(C^{\geq}_{a_3,b}) = \{o_2, o_4, o_5, o_6\},$$

$$Ca_1(C^{\leq}_{a_3,b}) = \emptyset,$$

$$C\overline{a_1}(C^{\leq}_{a_3,b}) = \{o_1, o_3, o_4, o_5\}.$$

Possible lower and upper approximations are:

$$Pa_1(C^{\geq}_{a_3,b}) = \{o_2, o_4, o_5, o_6\},$$

$$P\overline{a_1}(C^{\geq}_{a_3,b}) = \{o_1, o_2, o_3, o_4, o_5, o_6\},$$

$$Pa_1(C^{\leq}_{a_3,b}) = \{o_1, o_3\},$$

$$P\overline{a_1}(C^{\leq}_{a_3,b}) = \{o_1, o_2, o_3, o_4, o_5\}.$$

The following relationships between approximations hold:

Proposition 3

$$Ca_j(C^{\geq}_{\overline{a_i},y_k}) = U - P\overline{a_j}(C^{\leq}_{\overline{a_i},y_{k-1}}), k = 2, \ldots, n,$$

$$Pa_j(C^{\geq}_{\overline{a_i},y_k}) = U - C\overline{a_j}(C^{\leq}_{\overline{a_i},y_{k-1}}), k = 2, \ldots, n,$$

$$Ca_j(C^{\leq}_{\overline{a_i},y_k}) = U - P\overline{a_j}(C^{\geq}_{\overline{a_i},y_{k+1}}), k = 1, \ldots, n-1,$$

$$Pa_j(C^{\leq}_{\overline{a_i},y_k}) = U - C\overline{a_j}(C^{\geq}_{\overline{a_i},y_{k+1}}), k = 1, \ldots, n-1,$$

$$C\overline{a_j}(C^{\geq}_{\overline{a_i},y_k}) = U - Pa_j(C^{\leq}_{\overline{a_i},y_{k-1}}), k = 2, \ldots, n,$$

$$P\overline{a_j}(C^{\geq}_{\overline{a_i},y_k}) = U - Ca_j(C^{\leq}_{\overline{a_i},y_{k-1}}), k = 2, \ldots, n,$$

$$C\overline{a_j}(C^{\leq}_{\overline{a_i},y_k}) = U - Pa_j(C^{\geq}_{\overline{a_i},y_{k+1}}), k = 1, \ldots, n-1,$$

$$P\overline{a_j}(C^{\leq}_{\overline{a_i},y_k}) = U - Ca_j(C^{\geq}_{\overline{a_i},y_{k+1}}), k = 1, \ldots, n-1.$$

By using certain and possible approximations, lower and upper approximations are:

$$\underline{a_j}^{\bullet}(C^{\geq}_{\overline{a_i},y_k}) = [Ca_j(C^{\geq}_{\overline{a_i},y_k}), Pa_j(C^{\geq}_{\overline{a_i},y_k})], \tag{24}$$

$$\overline{a_j}^{\bullet}(C^{\geq}_{\overline{a_i},y_k}) = [C\overline{a_j}(C^{\geq}_{\overline{a_i},y_k}), P\overline{a_j}(C^{\geq}_{\overline{a_i},y_k})], \tag{25}$$

$$\underline{a_j}^{\bullet}(C^{\leq}_{\overline{a_i},y_k}) = [Ca_j(C^{\leq}_{\overline{a_i},y_k}), Pa_j(C^{\leq}_{\overline{a_i},y_k})], \tag{26}$$

$$\overline{a_j}^{\bullet}(C^{\leq}_{\overline{a_i},y_k}) = [C\overline{a_j}(C^{\leq}_{\overline{a_i},y_k}), P\overline{a_j}(C^{\leq}_{\overline{a_i},y_k})]. \tag{27}$$

As is shown in these formulae, approximations are expressed by interval sets. The lower bound of an approximation is a set of objects that certainly belongs to the approximation. The upper bound of an approximation is a set of objects that possibly belongs to the approximation.

Proposition 4

$$\underline{a_j}^{\bullet}(C^{\geq}_{\overline{a_i},y_k}) \subseteq \overline{a_j}^{\bullet}(C^{\geq}_{\overline{a_i},y_k}),$$

$$\underline{a_j}^{\bullet}(C^{\leq}_{\overline{a_i},y_k}) \subseteq \overline{a_j}^{\bullet}(C^{\leq}_{\overline{a_i},y_k}).$$

Example 3. By using approximations that are described in Example 2, lower and upper approximations of $C^{\geq}_{a_3,b}$ and $C^{\leq}_{a_3,b}$ by a_1 are:

$$\underline{a_1}^{\bullet}(C^{\geq}_{a_3,b}) = [\{o_6\}, \{o_2, o_4, o_5, o_6\}],$$

$$\overline{a_1}^{\bullet}(C^{\geq}_{a_3,b}) = [\{o_2, o_4, o_5, o_6\}, \{o_1, o_2, o_3, o_4, o_5, o_6\}],$$

$$\underline{a_1}^{\bullet}(C^{\leq}_{a_3,b}) = [\emptyset, \{o_1, o_3\}],$$

$$\overline{a_1}^{\bullet}(C^{\leq}_{a_3,b}) = [\{o_1, o_3, o_4, o_5\}, \{o_1, o_2, o_3, o_4, o_5\}].$$

Proposition 5

$$\underline{a_j}^{\bullet}(C^{\geq}_{\overline{a_i},y_k}) = U - \overline{a_j}^{\bullet}(C^{\leq}_{\overline{a_i},y_{k-1}}), k = 2,\dots,n,$$

$$\underline{a_j}^{\bullet}(C^{\leq}_{\overline{a_i},y_k}) = U - \overline{a_j}^{\bullet}(C^{\geq}_{\overline{a_i},y_{k+1}}), k = 1,\dots,n-1,$$

$$\overline{a_j}^{\bullet}(C^{\geq}_{\overline{a_i},y_k}) = U - \underline{a_j}^{\bullet}(C^{\leq}_{\overline{a_i},y_{k-1}}), k = 2,\dots,n,$$

$$\overline{a_j}^{\bullet}(C^{\leq}_{\overline{a_i},y_k}) = U - \underline{a_j}^{\bullet}(C^{\geq}_{\overline{a_i},y_{k+1}}), k = 1,\dots,n-1.$$

This proposition shows that the complementarity holds in incomplete ordered information systems, as it holds in complete ordered information systems in the previous section.

There exists a gap between rule induction and approximations. For example, $o_2 \in \overline{Ca_1}(C^{\geq}_{a_3,b})$, but $a_1(o_2) = \{y, z\}$; namely, o_2 supports a rule with $a_1 \geq y$ or $a_1 \geq z$. We cannot know from the approximations which rule and how o_2 supports. Considering such a situation, we use the expressions whose element is a pair of an object and the rule that the object supports.

First, in the case of possible table t that is a complete ordered information table on $\{a_i, a_j\}$, we describe the expressions as follows:

$$\underline{r_{a_j}}(C^{\geq}_{\overline{a_i},y_k})^t = \{(o \in U, a_j \geq a_j(o) \rightarrow a_i \geq y_k) : C^{\geq}_{a_j,a_j(o)} \subseteq C^{\geq}_{\overline{a_i},y_k}\}, \quad (28)$$

$$\overline{r_{a_j}}(C^{\geq}_{\overline{a_i},y_k})^t = \{(o \in U, a_j \geq a_j(o) \rightarrow a_i \geq y_k) : C^{\leq}_{a_j,a_j(o)} \cap C^{\geq}_{\overline{a_i},y_k} \neq \emptyset\}, \quad (29)$$

$$\underline{r_{a_j}}(C^{\leq}_{\overline{a_i},y_k})^t = \{(o \in U, a_j \leq a_j(o) \rightarrow a_i \leq y_k) : C^{\leq}_{a_j,a_j(o)} \subseteq C^{\leq}_{\overline{a_i},y_k}\}, \quad (30)$$

$$\overline{r_{a_j}}(C^{\leq}_{\overline{a_i},y_k})^t = \{(o \in U, a_j \leq a_j(o) \rightarrow a_i \leq y_k) : C^{\geq}_{a_j,a_j(o)} \cap C^{\leq}_{\overline{a_i},y_k} \neq \emptyset\}. \quad (31)$$

We apply the expressions to every possible table.

Example 4. In each possible tables obtained in Example 1, we derive pairs of an object and the rule that it supports by using the above formulae (28) and (29).

$$\underline{r_{a_1}}(C^{\geq}_{a_3,b})^{t_1} = \{(o_2, a_1 \geq y \rightarrow a_3 \geq b), (o_4, a_1 \geq y \rightarrow a_3 \geq b),$$
$$(o_5, a_1 \geq y \rightarrow a_3 \geq b), (o_6, a_1 \geq z \rightarrow a_3 \geq b)\},$$

$$\overline{r_{a_1}}(C^{\geq}_{a_3,b})^{t_1} = \{(o_2, a_1 \geq y \rightarrow a_3 \geq b), (o_4, a_1 \geq y \rightarrow a_3 \geq b),$$
$$(o_5, a_1 \geq y \rightarrow a_3 \geq b), (o_6, a_1 \geq z \rightarrow a_3 \geq b)\},$$

$$\underline{r_{a_1}}(C^{\geq}_{a_3,b})^{t_2} = \{(o_2, a_1 \geq y \rightarrow a_3 \geq b), (o_4, a_1 \geq y \rightarrow a_3 \geq b),$$
$$(o_5, a_1 \geq y \rightarrow a_3 \geq b), (o_6, a_1 \geq z \rightarrow a_3 \geq b)\},$$

$$\overline{r_{a_1}}(C^{\geq}_{a_3,b})^{t_2} = \{(o_1, a_1 \geq x \rightarrow a_3 \geq b), (o_2, a_1 \geq y \rightarrow a_3 \geq b),$$
$$(o_3, a_1 \geq x \rightarrow a_3 \geq b), (o_4, a_1 \geq y \rightarrow a_3 \geq b),$$
$$(o_5, a_1 \geq y \rightarrow a_3 \geq b), (o_6, a_1 \geq z \rightarrow a_3 \geq b)\},$$

$$\underline{r_{a_1}}(C^{\geq}_{a_3,b})^{t_3} = \{(o_6, a_1 \geq z \rightarrow a_3 \geq b)\},$$

$$\underline{r_{a_1}}(C_{a_3,b}^{\geq})^{t_3} = \{(o_2, a_1 \geq y \rightarrow a_3 \geq b), (o_3, a_1 \geq y \rightarrow a_3 \geq b),$$
$$(o_4, a_1 \geq y \rightarrow a_3 \geq b), (o_5, a_1 \geq y \rightarrow a_3 \geq b),$$
$$(o_6, a_1 \geq z \rightarrow a_3 \geq b)\},$$

$$\underline{r_{a_1}}(C_{a_3,b}^{\geq})^{t_4} = \{(o_6, a_1 \geq z \rightarrow a_3 \geq b)\},$$

$$\overline{r_{a_1}}(C_{a_3,b}^{\geq})^{t_4} = \{(o_1, a_1 \geq x \rightarrow a_3 \geq b), (o_2, a_1 \geq y \rightarrow a_3 \geq b),$$
$$(o_3, a_1 \geq y \rightarrow a_3 \geq b), (o_4, a_1 \geq y \rightarrow a_3 \geq b),$$
$$(o_5, a_1 \geq y \rightarrow a_3 \geq b), (o_6, a_1 \geq z \rightarrow a_3 \geq b)\},$$

$$\underline{r_{a_1}}(C_{a_3,b}^{\geq})^{t_5} = \{(o_2, a_1 \geq z \rightarrow a_3 \geq b), (o_4, a_1 \geq y \rightarrow a_3 \geq b),$$
$$(o_5, a_1 \geq y \rightarrow a_3 \geq b), (o_6, a_1 \geq z \rightarrow a_3 \geq b)\},$$

$$\overline{r_{a_1}}(C_{a_3,b}^{\geq})^{t_5} = \{(o_2, a_1 \geq z \rightarrow a_3 \geq b), (o_4, a_1 \geq y \rightarrow a_3 \geq b),$$
$$(o_5, a_1 \geq y \rightarrow a_3 \geq b), (o_6, a_1 \geq z \rightarrow a_3 \geq b)\},$$

$$\underline{r_{a_1}}(C_{a_3,b}^{\geq})^{t_6} = \{(o_2, a_1 \geq z \rightarrow a_3 \geq b), (o_4, a_1 \geq y \rightarrow a_3 \geq b),$$
$$(o_5, a_1 \geq y \rightarrow a_3 \geq b), (o_6, a_1 \geq z \rightarrow a_3 \geq b)\},$$

$$\overline{r_{a_1}}(C_{a_3,b}^{\geq})^{t_6} = \{(o_1, a_1 \geq x \rightarrow a_3 \geq b), (o_2, a_1 \geq z \rightarrow a_3 \geq b),$$
$$(o_3, a_1 \geq x \rightarrow a_3 \geq b), (o_4, a_1 \geq y \rightarrow a_3 \geq b),$$
$$(o_5, a_1 \geq y \rightarrow a_3 \geq b), (o_6, a_1 \geq z \rightarrow a_3 \geq b)\},$$

$$\underline{r_{a_1}}(C_{a_3,b}^{\geq})^{t_7} = \{(o_2, a_1 \geq z \rightarrow a_3 \geq b), (o_6, a_1 \geq z \rightarrow a_3 \geq b)\},$$

$$\overline{r_{a_1}}(C_{a_3,b}^{\geq})^{t_7} = \{(o_2, a_1 \geq z \rightarrow a_3 \geq b), (o_3, a_1 \geq y \rightarrow a_3 \geq b),$$
$$\{(o_4, a_1 \geq y \rightarrow a_3 \geq b), (o_5, a_1 \geq y \rightarrow a_3 \geq b),$$
$$\{(o_6, a_1 \geq z \rightarrow a_3 \geq b)\},$$

$$\underline{r_{a_1}}(C_{a_3,b}^{\geq})^{t_8} = \{(o_2, a_1 \geq z \rightarrow a_3 \geq b), (o_6, a_1 \geq z \rightarrow a_3 \geq b)\},$$

$$\overline{r_{a_1}}(C_{a_3,b}^{\geq})^{t_8} = \{(o_1, a_1 \geq x \rightarrow a_3 \geq b), (o_2, a_1 \geq z \rightarrow a_3 \geq b),$$
$$(o_3, a_1 \geq y \rightarrow a_3 \geq b), (o_4, a_1 \geq y \rightarrow a_3 \geq b),$$
$$(o_5, a_1 \geq y \rightarrow a_3 \geq b), (o_6, a_1 \geq z \rightarrow a_3 \geq b)\}.$$

By using the above formulae (30) and (31).

$$\underline{r_{a_1}}(C_{a_3,b}^{\leq})^{t_1} = \{(o_1, a_1 \leq x \rightarrow a_3 \leq b), (o_3, a_1 \leq x \rightarrow a_3 \leq b)\},$$

$$\overline{r_{a_1}}(C_{a_3,b}^{\leq})^{t_1} = \{(o_1, a_1 \leq x \rightarrow a_3 \leq b), (o_2, a_1 \leq y \rightarrow a_3 \leq b),$$
$$(o_3, a_1 \leq x \rightarrow a_3 \leq b), (o_4, a_1 \leq y \rightarrow a_3 \leq b),$$
$$(o_5, a_1 \leq y \rightarrow a_3 \leq b)\},$$

$$\underline{r_{a_1}}(C_{a_3,b}^{\leq})^{t_2} = \emptyset,$$

$$\overline{r_{a_1}}(C_{a_3,b}^{\leq})^{t_2} = \{(o_1, a_1 \leq x \rightarrow a_3 \leq b), (o_2, a_1 \leq y \rightarrow a_3 \leq b),$$
$$(o_3, a_1 \leq x \rightarrow a_3 \leq b), (o_4, a_1 \leq y \rightarrow a_3 \leq b),$$
$$(o_5, a_1 \leq y \rightarrow a_3 \geq b)\},$$

$$\underline{r_{a_1}}(C_{a_3,b}^{\leq})^{t_3} = \{(o_1, a_1 \leq x \rightarrow a_3 \leq b)\},$$

$$\overline{r_{a_1}}(C^{\leq}_{a_3,b})^{t_3} = \{(o_1, a_1 \leq x \rightarrow a_3 \leq b), (o_2, a_1 \leq y \rightarrow a_3 \geq b),$$
$$(o_3, a_1 \leq y \rightarrow a_3 \leq b), (o_4, a_1 \leq y \rightarrow a_3 \leq b)\},$$
$$(o_5, a_1 \leq y \rightarrow a_3 \geq b)\},$$

$$\underline{r_{a_1}}(C^{\leq}_{a_3,b})^{t_4} = \emptyset,$$

$$\overline{r_{a_1}}(C^{\leq}_{a_3,b})^{t_4} = \{(o_1, a_1 \leq x \rightarrow a_3 \leq b), (o_2, a_1 \leq y \rightarrow a_3 \leq b),$$
$$(o_3, a_1 \leq y \rightarrow a_3 \leq b), (o_4, a_1 \leq y \rightarrow a_3 \leq b)\},$$
$$(o_5, a_1 \leq y \rightarrow a_3 \leq b)\},$$

$$\underline{r_{a_1}}(C^{\leq}_{a_3,b})^{t_5} = \{(o_1, a_1 \leq x \rightarrow a_3 \leq b), (o_3, a_1 \leq x \rightarrow a_3 \leq b)\},$$

$$\overline{r_{a_1}}(C^{\leq}_{a_3,b})^{t_5} = \{(o_1, a_1 \leq x \rightarrow a_3 \leq b), (o_3, a_1 \leq x \rightarrow a_3 \leq b),$$
$$(o_4, a_1 \leq y \rightarrow a_3 \leq b), (o_5, a_1 \leq y \rightarrow a_3 \leq b)\},$$

$$\underline{r_{a_1}}(C^{\leq}_{a_3,b})^{t_6} = \emptyset,$$

$$\overline{r_{a_1}}(C^{\leq}_{a_3,b})^{t_6} = \{(o_1, a_1 \leq x \rightarrow a_3 \leq b), (o_3, a_1 \leq x \rightarrow a_3 \leq b),$$
$$(o_4, a_1 \leq y \rightarrow a_3 \leq b), (o_5, a_1 \leq y \rightarrow a_3 \leq b)\},$$

$$\underline{r_{a_1}}(C^{\leq}_{a_3,b})^{t_7} = \{(o_1, a_1 \leq x \rightarrow a_3 \leq b)\},$$

$$\overline{r_{a_1}}(C^{\leq}_{a_3,b})^{t_7} = \{(o_1, a_1 \leq x \rightarrow a_3 \leq b), (o_3, a_1 \leq y \rightarrow a_3 \leq b),$$
$$(o_4, a_1 \leq y \rightarrow a_3 \leq b), (o_5, a_1 \leq y \rightarrow a_3 < b)\},$$

$$\underline{r_{a_1}}(C^{\leq}_{a_3,b})^{t_8} = \emptyset,$$

$$\overline{r_{a_1}}(C^{\leq}_{a_3,b})^{t_8} = \{(o_1, a_1 \leq x \rightarrow a_3 \leq b), (o_3, a_1 \leq y \rightarrow a_3 \leq b),$$
$$(o_4, a_1 \leq y \rightarrow a_3 \leq b), (o_5, a_1 \leq y \rightarrow a_3 \leq b)\}.$$

Second, in the case of incomplete ordered information tables, expressions whose element is a pair of an object and the rule that it supports are:

$$Cr_{a_j}(C^{\geq}_{a_i,y_k}) = \{(o \in U, a_j \geq a_j(o) \rightarrow a_i \geq y_k) :$$
$$(\exists t \in pt_{\{a_i,a_j\}}\ (o, a_j \geq a_j(o) \rightarrow a_i \geq y_k) \in \underline{r_{a_j}}(C^{\geq}_{a_i,y_k})^t) \wedge$$
$$(\forall t \in pt_{\{a_i,a_j\}}\ (o, a_j \geq a_j(o) \rightarrow a_i \geq y_k) \in \underline{r_{a_j}}(C^{\geq}_{a_i,y_k})^t \vee$$
$$(\exists x \in V_{a_j}\ x \leq a_j(o) \wedge (o, a_j \geq x \rightarrow a_i \geq y_k) \in \underline{r_{a_j}}(C^{\geq}_{a_i,y_k})^t))\}, \quad (32)$$

$$C\overline{r_{a_j}}(C^{\geq}_{a_i,y_k}) = \{(o \in U, a_j \geq a_j(o) \rightarrow a_i \geq y_k) :$$
$$(\exists t \in pt_{\{a_i,a_j\}}\ (o, a_j \geq a_j(o) \rightarrow a_i \geq y_k) \in \overline{r_{a_j}}(C^{\geq}_{a_i,y_k})^t) \wedge$$
$$(\forall t \in pt_{\{a_i,a_j\}}\ (o, a_j \geq a_j(o) \rightarrow a_i \geq y_k) \in \overline{r_{a_j}}(C^{\geq}_{a_i,y_k})^t \vee$$
$$(\exists x \in V_{a_j}\ x \leq a_j(o) \wedge (o, a_j \geq x \rightarrow a_i \geq y_k) \in \overline{r_{a_j}}(C^{\geq}_{a_i,y_k})^t))\}, \quad (33)$$

$$Cr_{a_j}(C^{\leq}_{a_i,y_k}) = \{(o \in U, a_j \leq a_j(o) \rightarrow a_i \leq y_k) :$$
$$(\exists t \in pt_{\{a_i,a_j\}}\ (o, a_j \leq a_j(o) \rightarrow a_i \leq y_k) \in \underline{r_{a_j}}(C^{\leq}_{a_i,y_k})^t) \wedge$$
$$(\forall t \in pt_{\{a_i,a_j\}}\ (o, a_j \leq a_j(o) \rightarrow a_i \leq y_k) \in \underline{r_{a_j}}(C^{\leq}_{a_i,y_k})^t \vee$$
$$(\exists x \in V_{a_j}\ x \geq a_j(o) \wedge (o, a_j \leq x \rightarrow a_i \leq y_k) \in \underline{r_{a_j}}(C^{\leq}_{a_i,y_k})^t))\}, \quad (34)$$

$$Cr_{\overline{a_j}}(C^{\leq}_{\overline{a_i},y_k}) = \{(o \in U, a_j \leq a_j(o) \to a_i \leq y_k) :$$
$$(\exists t \in pt_{\{a_i,a_j\}} \ (o, a_j \leq a_j(o) \to a_i \leq y_k) \in \overline{r_{a_j}}(C^{\leq}_{\overline{a_i},y_k})^t) \wedge$$
$$(\forall t \in pt_{\{a_i,a_j\}} \ (o, a_j \leq a_j(o) \to a_i \leq y_k) \in \overline{r_{a_j}}(C^{\leq}_{\overline{a_i},y_k})^t \vee$$
$$(\exists x \in V_{a_j} \ x \geq a_j(o) \wedge (o, a_j \leq x \to a_i \leq y_k) \in \overline{r_{a_j}}(C^{\leq}_{\overline{a_i},y_k})^t))\}, \quad (35)$$

$$Pr_{a_j}(C^{\geq}_{\overline{a_i},y_k}) = \{(o, a_j \geq a_j(o) \to a_i \geq y_k) :$$
$$\exists t \in pt_{\{a_i,a_j\}} \ (o, a_j \geq a_j(o) \to a_i \geq y_k) \in r_{a_j}(C^{\geq}_{\overline{a_i},y_k})^t\}, \quad (36)$$

$$Pr_{\overline{a_j}}(C^{\geq}_{\overline{a_i},y_k}) = \{(o, a_j \geq a_j(o) \to a_i \geq y_k) :$$
$$\exists t \in pt_{\{a_i,a_j\}} \ (o, a_j \geq a_j(o) \to a_i \geq y_k) \in \overline{r_{a_j}}(C^{\geq}_{\overline{a_i},y_k})^t\}, \quad (37)$$

$$Pr_{a_j}(C^{\leq}_{\overline{a_i},y_k}) = \{(o, a_j \leq a_j(o) \to a_i \leq y_k) :$$
$$\exists t \in pt_{\{a_i,a_j\}} \ (o, a_j \leq a_j(o) \to a_i \leq y_k) \in r_{a_j}(C^{\leq}_{\overline{a_i},y_k})^t\}, \quad (38)$$

$$Pr_{\overline{a_j}}(C^{\leq}_{\overline{a_i},y_k}) = \{(o, a_j \leq a_j(o) \to a_i \leq y_k) :$$
$$\exists t \in pt_{\{a_i,a_j\}} \ (o, a_j \leq a_j(o) \to a_i \leq y_k) \in \overline{r_{a_j}}(C^{\leq}_{\overline{a_i},y_k})^t\}, \quad (39)$$

where it is taken into account that for $Cr_{a_j}(C^{\geq}_{\overline{a_i},y_k})^t$ and $Cr_{\overline{a_j}}(C^{\geq}_{\overline{a_i},y_k})^t$, if $(o, a_j \geq u \to a_i \geq y_k)$ is an element and $v \geq u$ with $u \in V_{a_j}$ and $v \in V_{a_j}$, then $(o, a_j \geq v \to a_i \geq y_k)$ can be regarded as an element, while for $Cr_{a_j}(C^{\leq}_{\overline{a_i},y_k})^t$ and $Cr_{\overline{a_j}}(C^{\leq}_{\overline{a_i},y_k})^t$, if $(o, a_j \leq u \to a_i \leq y_k)$ is an element and $v \leq u$, then $(o, a_j \leq v \to a_i \leq y_k)$ can be regarded as an element.

Proposition 6

$$Cr_{a_j}(C^{\geq}_{\overline{a_i},y_k}) \subseteq Cr_{\overline{a_j}}(C^{\geq}_{\overline{a_i},y_k}),$$
$$Pr_{a_j}(C^{\geq}_{\overline{a_i},y_k}) \subseteq Pr_{\overline{a_j}}(C^{\geq}_{\overline{a_i},y_k}),$$
$$Cr_{a_j}(C^{\geq}_{\overline{a_i},y_k}) \subseteq Pr_{a_j}(C^{\geq}_{\overline{a_i},y_k}),$$
$$Cr_{\overline{a_j}}(C^{\geq}_{\overline{a_i},y_k}) \subseteq Pr_{\overline{a_j}}(C^{\geq}_{\overline{a_i},y_k}),$$
$$Cr_{a_j}(C^{\leq}_{\overline{a_i},y_k}) \subseteq Cr_{\overline{a_j}}(C^{\leq}_{\overline{a_i},y_k}),$$
$$Pr_{a_j}(C^{\leq}_{\overline{a_i},y_k}) \subseteq Pr_{\overline{a_j}}(C^{\leq}_{\overline{a_i},y_k}),$$
$$Cr_{a_j}(C^{\leq}_{\overline{a_i},y_k}) \subseteq Pr_{a_j}(C^{\leq}_{\overline{a_i},y_k}),$$
$$Cr_{\overline{a_j}}(C^{\leq}_{\overline{a_i},y_k}) \subseteq Pr_{\overline{a_j}}(C^{\leq}_{\overline{a_i},y_k}).$$

Example 5. Results in Example 4 are replaced by using the above formulae (32)–(35). From expressions that correspond to certain approximations of $C^{\geq}_{a_3,b}$ and $C^{\leq}_{a_3,b}$,

$$Cr_{\overline{a_1}}(C^{\geq}_{a_3,b}) = \{(o_6, a_1 \geq z \to a_3 \geq b)\},$$
$$Cr_{\overline{a_1}}(C^{\geq}_{a_3,b}) = \{(o_2, a_1 \geq z \to a_3 \geq b), (o_4, a_1 \geq y \to a_3 \geq b),$$
$$(o_5, a_1 \geq y \to a_3 \geq b), (o_6, a_1 \geq z \to a_3 \geq b)\}.$$

$$Cr_{\underline{a_1}}(C_{a_3,b}^{\leq}) = \emptyset,$$
$$\overline{Cr_{a_1}}(C_{a_3,b}^{\leq}) = \{(o_1, a_1 \leq x \rightarrow a_3 \leq b), (o_3, a_1 \leq x \rightarrow a_3 \leq b),$$
$$(o_4, a_1 \leq y \rightarrow a_3 \leq b), (o_5, a_1 \leq y \rightarrow a_3 \leq b)\}.$$

By using the above formulae (36)–(39), from expressions that correspond to possible approximations of $C_{a_3,b}^{\geq}$ and $C_{a_3,b}^{\geq}$,

$$Pr_{\underline{a_1}}(C_{a_3,b}^{\geq}) = \{(o_2, a_1 \geq y \rightarrow a_3 \geq b), (o_2, a_1 \geq z \rightarrow a_3 \geq b),$$
$$(o_4, a_1 \geq y \rightarrow a_3 \geq b), (o_5, a_1 \geq y \rightarrow a_3 \geq b),$$
$$(o_6, a_1 \geq z \rightarrow a_3 \geq b)\},$$
$$\overline{Pr_{a_1}}(C_{a_3,b}^{\geq}) = \{(o_1, a_1 \geq x \rightarrow a_3 \geq b), (o_2, a_1 \geq y \rightarrow a_3 \geq b),$$
$$(o_2, a_1 \geq z \rightarrow a_3 \geq b), (o_3, a_1 \geq x \rightarrow a_3 \geq b),$$
$$(o_3, a_1 \geq y \rightarrow a_3 \geq b), (o_4, a_1 \geq y \rightarrow a_3 \geq b),$$
$$(o_5, a_1 \geq y \rightarrow a_3 \geq b), (o_6, a_1 \geq z \rightarrow a_3 \geq b)\},$$
$$Pr_{\underline{a_1}}(C_{a_3,b}^{\leq}) = \{(o_1, a_1 \leq x \rightarrow a_3 \leq b), (o_3, a_1 \leq x \rightarrow a_3 \leq b)\},$$
$$\overline{Pr_{a_1}}(C_{a_3,b}^{\leq}) = \{(o_1, a_1 \leq x \rightarrow a_3 \leq b), (o_2, a_1 \leq y \rightarrow a_3 \leq b),$$
$$(o_3, a_1 \leq x \rightarrow a_3 \leq b), (o_3, a_1 \leq y \rightarrow a_3 \leq b),$$
$$(o_4, a_1 \leq y \rightarrow a_3 \leq b), (o_5, a_1 \leq y \rightarrow a_3 \leq b)\}.$$

How do objects support rules? This is classified into four types: certain and consistent, certain and inconsistent, possible and consistent, and possible and inconsistent supports.

- When $(o, a_j \geq a_j(o) \rightarrow a_i \geq y_k)$ belongs to $Cr_{a_j}(C_{a_i,y_k}^{\geq})$, object o certainly and consistently supports rule $a_j \geq a_j(o) \rightarrow a_i \geq y_k$.
- When $(o, a_j \geq a_j(o) \rightarrow a_i \geq y_k)$ belongs to $\overline{Cr_{a_j}}(C_{a_i,y_k}^{\geq}) \backslash Cr_{a_j}(C_{a_i,y_k}^{\geq})$, object o certainly and inconsistently supports rule $a_j \geq a_j(o) \rightarrow a_i \geq y_k$.
- When $(o, a_j \geq a_j(o) \rightarrow a_i \geq y_k)$ belongs to $Pr_{a_j}(C_{a_i,y_k}^{\geq}) \backslash Cr_{a_j}(C_{a_i,y_k}^{\geq})$, object o possibly and consistently supports rule $a_j \geq a_j(o) \rightarrow a_i \geq y_k$.
- When $(o, a_j \geq a_j(o) \rightarrow a_i \geq y_k)$ belongs to $\overline{Pr_{a_j}}(C_{a_i,y_k}^{\geq}) \backslash Pa_j(C_{a_i,y_k}^{\geq}) \backslash \overline{Cr_{a_j}}(C_{a_i,y_k}^{\geq})$, object o possibly and inconsistently supports rule $a_j \geq a_j(o) \rightarrow a_i \geq y_k$.
- When $(o, a_j \leq a_j(o) \rightarrow a_i \leq y_k)$ belongs to $Cr_{a_j}(C_{a_i,y_k}^{\leq})$, object o certainly and consistently supports rule $a_j \leq a_j(o) \rightarrow a_i \leq y_k$.
- When $(o, a_j \leq a_j(o) \rightarrow a_i \leq y_k)$ belongs to $\overline{Cr_{a_j}}(C_{a_i,y_k}^{\leq}) \backslash Cr_{a_j}(C_{a_i,y_k}^{\leq})$, object o certainly and inconsistently supports rule $a_j \leq a_j(o) \rightarrow a_i \leq y_k$.
- When $(o, a_j \leq a_j(o) \rightarrow a_i \leq y_k)$ belongs to $Pr_{a_j}(C_{a_i,y_k}^{\leq}) \backslash Cr_{a_j}(C_{a_i,y_k}^{\leq})$, object o possibly and consistently supports rule $a_j \leq a_j(o) \rightarrow a_i \leq y_k$.
- When $(o, a_j \leq a_j(o) \rightarrow a_i \leq y_k)$ belongs to $\overline{Pr_{a_j}}(C_{a_i,y_k}^{\leq}) \backslash Pa_j(C_{a_i,y_k}^{\leq}) \backslash \overline{Cr_{a_j}}(C_{a_i,y_k}^{\leq})$, object o possibly and inconsistently supports rule $a_j \leq a_j(o) \rightarrow a_i \leq y_k$.

Note that an object has more than one types of rule supports.

Example 6. From the results of Example 5, we obtain four types of rule supports. From the expressions for $C_{a_3,b}^{\geq}$ rule supports are as follows:

- From $Cr_{a_1}(C_{a_3,b}^{\geq})$, object o_6 certainly and consistently supports rule $a_1 \geq z \to a_3 \geq b$.
- From $\overline{Cr_{a_1}}(C_{a_3,b}^{\geq}) \setminus Cr_{a_1}(C_{a_3,b}^{\geq})$, object o_2 certainly and inconsistently supports rule $a_1 \geq z \to a_3 \geq b$, and also o_4 and o_5 do $a_1 \geq y \to a_3 \geq b$.
- From $Pr_{a_1}(C_{a_3,b}^{\geq}) \setminus Cr_{a_1}(C_{a_3,b}^{\geq})$, o_2, o_4, and o_5 possibly and consistently $a_1 \geq y \to a_3 \geq b$, where $a_1 \geq y \to a_3 \geq b$ includes $a_1 \geq z \to a_3 \geq b$.
- From $\overline{Pr_{a_1}}(C_{a_3,b}^{\geq}) \setminus Pr_{a_1}(C_{a_3,b}^{\geq}) \setminus \overline{Cr_{a_1}}(C_{a_3,b}^{\geq})$, o_1 and o_3 possibly and inconsistently rule $a_1 \geq x \to a_3 \geq b$, where $a_1 \geq x \to a_3 \geq b$ includes $a_1 \geq y \to a_3 \geq b$.

From the expressions for $C_{a_3,b}^{\leq}$ rule supports are as follows:

- From $Cr_{a_1}(C_{a_3,b}^{\leq})$, there is no object that certainly and consistently supports a rule.
- From $\overline{Cr_{a_1}}(C_{a_3,b}^{\leq}) \setminus Cr_{a_1}(C_{a_3,b}^{\leq})$, objects o_1 and o_3 certainly and inconsistently support rule $a_1 \leq x \to a_3 \leq b$, and also o_4 and o_5 certainly and inconsistently support rule $a_1 \leq y \to a_3 \leq b$.
- From $Pr_{a_1}(C_{a_3,b}^{\leq}) \setminus Cr_{a_1}(C_{a_3,b}^{\leq})$, o_1 and o_3 possibly and consistently support rule $a_1 \leq x \to a_3 \leq b$.
- From $\overline{Pr_{a_1}}(C_{a_3,b}^{\leq}) \setminus Pr_{a_1}(C_{a_3,b}^{\leq}) \setminus \overline{Cr_{a_1}}(C_{a_3,b}^{\leq})$, o_2 and o_3 possibly and inconsistently support rules $a_1 \leq y \to a_3 \leq b$.

Thus far, the formulae are described for a single attribute. Formulae for sets A and B of attributes can be expressed as follows. Certain approximations are:

$$C\underline{B}(C_{A,Y_k}^{\geq}) = \{o \in U : \forall t \in pt_{A \cup B} \; o \in \underline{B}(C_{A,Y_k}^{\geq})^t\},$$
$$C\overline{B}(C_{A,Y_k}^{\geq}) = \{o \in U : \forall t \in pt_{A \cup B} \; o \in \overline{B}(C_{A,Y_k}^{\geq})^t\},$$
$$C\underline{B}(C_{A,Y_k}^{\leq}) = \{o \in U : \forall t \in pt_{A \cup B} \; o \in \underline{B}(C_{A,Y_k}^{\leq})^t\},$$
$$C\overline{B}(C_{A,Y_k}^{\leq}) = \{o \in U : \forall t \in pt_{A \cup B} \; o \in \overline{B}(C_{A,Y_k}^{\leq})^t\}.$$

Possible approximations are:

$$P\underline{B}(C_{A,Y_k}^{\geq}) = \{o \in U : \exists t \in pt_{A \cup B} \; o \in \underline{B}(C_{A,Y_k}^{\geq})^t\},$$
$$P\overline{B}(C_{A,Y_k}^{\geq}) = \{o \in U : \exists t \in pt_{A \cup B} \; o \in \overline{B}(C_{A,Y_k}^{\geq})^t\},$$
$$P\underline{B}(C_{A,Y_k}^{\leq}) = \{o \in U : \exists t \in pt_{A \cup B} \; o \in \underline{B}(C_{A,Y_k}^{\leq})^t\},$$
$$P\overline{B}(C_{A,Y_k}^{\leq}) = \{o \in U : \exists t \in pt_{A \cup B} \; o \in \overline{B}(C_{A,Y_k}^{\leq})^t\}.$$

Lower and upper approximations are:

$$\underline{B}^{\bullet}(C_{A,Y_k}^{\geq}) = [C\underline{B}(C_{A,Y_k}^{\geq}), P\underline{B}(C_{A,Y_k}^{\geq})],$$

$$\overline{B}^{\bullet}(C_{A,Y_k}^{\geq}) = [C\overline{B}(C_{A,Y_k}^{\geq}), P\overline{B}(C_{A,Y_k}^{\geq})],$$

$$\underline{B}^{\bullet}(C_{A,Y_k}^{\leq}) = [C\underline{B}(C_{A,Y_k}^{\leq}), P\underline{B}(C_{A,Y_k}^{\geq})],$$

$$\overline{B}^{\bullet}(C_{A,Y_k}^{\leq}) = [C\overline{B}(C_{A,Y_k}^{\leq}), P\overline{B}(C_{A,Y_k}^{\leq})].$$

Expressions whose element is a pair of an object and the rule that it supports are:

$$C\underline{r_B}(C_{A,Y_k}^{\geq}) = \{(o \in U, B \geq B(o) \to A \geq Y_k) :$$

$$(\exists t \in pt_{A \cup B} \ (o, B \geq B(o) \to A \geq Y_k) \in \underline{r_B}(C_{A,Y_k}^{\geq})^t) \wedge$$

$$(\forall t \in pt_{A \cup B} \ (o, B \geq B(o) \to A \geq Y_k) \in \underline{r_B}(C_{A,Y_k}^{\geq})^t \vee$$

$$(\exists X \in V_B \ X \leq B(o) \wedge (o, B \geq X \to A \geq Y_k) \in \underline{r_B}(C_{A,Y_k}^{\geq})^t))\},$$

$$C\overline{r_B}(C_{A,Y_k}^{\geq}) = \{(o \in U, B \geq B(o) \to A \geq Y_k) :$$

$$(\exists t \in pt_{A \cup B} \ (o, B \geq B(o) \to A \geq Y_k) \in \overline{r_B}(C_{A,Y_k}^{\geq})^t) \wedge$$

$$(\forall t \in pt_{A \cup B} \ (o, B \geq B(o) \to A \geq Y_k) \in \overline{r_B}(C_{A,Y_k}^{\geq})^t \vee$$

$$(\exists X \in V_B \ X \leq B(o) \wedge (o, B \geq X \to A \geq Y_k) \in \overline{r_B}(C_{A,Y_k}^{\geq})^t))\},$$

$$C\underline{r_B}(C_{A,Y_k}^{\leq}) = \{(o \in U, B \leq B(o) \to A \leq Y_k) :$$

$$(\exists t \in pt_{A \cup B} \ (o, B \leq B(o) \to A \leq Y_k) \in \underline{r_B}(C_{A,Y_k}^{\leq})^t) \wedge$$

$$(\forall t \in pt_{A \cup B} \ (o, B \leq B(o) \to A \leq Y_k) \in \underline{r_B}(C_{A,Y_k}^{\leq})^t \vee$$

$$(\exists X \in V_B \ X \geq B(o) \wedge (o, B \leq X \to A \leq Y_k) \in \underline{r_B}(C_{A,Y_k}^{\leq})^t))\},$$

$$C\overline{r_B}(C_{A,Y_k}^{\leq}) = \{(o \in U, B \leq B(o) \to A \leq Y_k) :$$

$$(\exists t \in pt_{A \cup B} \ (o, B \leq B(o) \to A \leq Y_k) \in \overline{r_B}(C_{A,Y_k}^{\leq})^t) \wedge$$

$$(\forall t \in pt_{A \cup B} \ (o, B \leq B(o) \to A \leq Y_k) \in \overline{r_B}(C_{A,Y_k}^{\leq})^t \vee$$

$$(\exists X \in V_B \ X \geq B(o) \wedge (o, B \leq X \to A \leq Y_k) \in \overline{r_B}(C_{A,Y_k}^{\leq})^t))\},$$

$$P\underline{r_B}(C_{A,Y_k}^{\geq}) = \{(o, B \geq B(o) \to A \geq Y_k) :$$

$$\exists t \in pt_{A \cup B} \ (o, B \geq B(o) \to A \geq Y_k) \in \underline{r_B}(C_{A,Y_k}^{\geq})^t\},$$

$$P\overline{r_B}(C_{A,Y_k}^{\geq}) = \{(o, B \geq B(o) \to A \geq Y_k) :$$

$$\exists t \in pt_{A \cup B} \ (o, B \geq B(o) \to A \geq Y_k) \in \overline{r_B}(C_{A,Y_k}^{\geq})^t\},$$

$$P\underline{r_B}(C_{A,Y_k}^{\leq}) = \{(o, B \leq B(o) \to Y \leq Y_k) :$$

$$\exists t \in pt_{A \cup B} \ (o, B \leq B(o) \to A \leq Y_k) \in \underline{r_B}(C_{A,Y_k}^{\leq})^t\},$$

$$P\overline{r_B}(C_{A,Y_k}^{\leq}) = \{(o, B \leq B(o) \to A \leq Y_k) :$$

$$\exists t \in pt_{A \cup B} \ (o, B \leq B(o) \to A \leq Y_k) \in \overline{r_B}(C_{A,Y_k}^{\leq})^t\}.$$

4   Conclusion and Future Work

On the basis of possible world semantics, we have described rough sets and rule induction based on them in incomplete information systems with ordered domains. Incomplete information are expressed by a set of possible values, which contains a missing value as a special case. The set of possible tables on a set of attributes is derived from an incomplete ordered information table, as Lipski dealt with it on the whole set of attributes on the basis of possible world semantics. A possible table on a set of attributes is a complete table on the set. Therefore, rough sets, a pair of lower and upper approximations, in each possible table are derived by applying formulae used in complete ordered information tables.

When an object belongs to a certain approximation, the object belongs to the approximation in all possible tables. When an object belongs to a possible approximation, the object belongs to the approximation in some possible tables. The certain approximation is the lower bound of the approximation. The possible approximation is the upper bound of the approximation. The approximations are expressed by an interval set. In the approximations, complementarity holds, as is so in complete ordered information systems.

There is a gap between approximations and rule induction. To bridge the gap, we have introduced expressions whose element is a pair of an object and a rule that it supports. Supports of rules induced from the expressions are classified in four types: certain and consistent, certain and inconsistent, possible and consistent, and possible and inconsistent supports. We do not impose any restriction on attributes for occurrence of incomplete information. Therefore, formulae described in this paper have the generality that not only attributes used in approximations but also those approximated have a value with incomplete information. These results should be used as a correctness criterion in rule induction based on rough sets from incomplete ordered information tables, as is so in the field of incomplete database.

In Lipski's approach the number of possible tables grows exponentially, as the number of values with incomplete information increases. However, some work reports that Lipski's approach is released from the exponential order problem in incomplete information tables without order relations [25–27]. One of future work is to examine the exponential order problem of Lipski's approach in incomplete ordered information systems.

Another topic is definability problem. We have two types of definability in incomplete information systems without order relations [17,24]. One is certain definability. A set of objects is certainly definable, if the set is definable in all possible tables. The other is possible definability. A set of objects is possibly definable, if the set is definable in some possible tables. The two types of definability can be also obtained by using possible classes [17]. These definitions are valid in incomplete ordered information systems. Furthermore, the definability problem of interval sets is pointed out by Hu and Yao [8], because approximations are expressed by interval sets. This is another future work.

Acknowledgment. The authors wish to thank the anonymous reviewers for their valuable comments.

References

1. Abiteboul, S., Hull, R., Vianu, V.: Foundations of Databases. Addison-Wesley Publishing Company, Boston (1995)
2. Bosc, P., Duval, L., Pivert, O.: An initial approach to the evaluation of possibilistic queries addressed to possibilistic databases. Fuzzy Sets Syst. **140**, 151–166 (2003)
3. Chen, Z., Shi, P., Liu, P., Pei, Z.: Criteria reduction of set-valued ordered decision system based on approximation quality. Int. J. Innov. Comput. Inf. Control **9**(6), 2393–2404 (2013)
4. Du, W.S., Hu, B.Q.: Dominance-based rough set approach to incomplete ordered information systems. Inf. Sci. **346–347**, 106–129 (2016)
5. Grahne, G.: The Problem of Incomplete Information in Relational Databases. LNCS, vol. 554. Springer, Heidelberg (1991). doi:10.1007/3-540-54919-6
6. Greco, S., Matarazzo, B., Słowinski, R.: Handling missing values in rough set analysis of multi-attribute and multi-criteria decision problems. In: Zhong, N., Skowron, A., Ohsuga, S. (eds.) RSFDGrC 1999. LNCS, vol. 1711, pp. 146–157. Springer, Heidelberg (1999). doi:10.1007/978-3-540-48061-7_19
7. Greco, S., Matarazzo, B., Slowinski, R.: Rough sets theory for multicriteria decision analysis. Eur. J. Oper. Res. **129**, 1–47 (2001)
8. Hu, M., Yao, Y.: Definability in incomplete information tables. In: Flores, V., Gomide, F., Janusz, A., Meneses, C., Miao, D., Peters, G., Ślęzak, D., Wang, G., Weber, R., Yao, Y. (eds.) IJCRS 2016. LNCS, vol. 9920, pp. 177–186. Springer, Cham (2016). doi:10.1007/978-3-319-47160-0_16
9. Imielinski, T.: Incomplete information in logical databases. Data Eng. **12**, 93–104 (1989)
10. Imielinski, T., Lipski, W.: Incomplete information in relational databases. J. ACM **31**, 761–791 (1984)
11. Kryszkiewicz, M.: Rules in incomplete information systems. Inf. Sci. **113**, 271–292 (1999)
12. Lipski, W.: On semantics issues connected with incomplete information databases. ACM Trans. Database Syst. **4**, 262–296 (1979)
13. Lipski, W.: On databases with incomplete information. J. ACM **28**, 41–70 (1981)
14. Luo, C., Li, T., Chen, H., Liu, D.: Incremental approaches for updating approximations in set-valued ordered information systems. Knowl.-Based Syst. **50**, 218–233 (2013)
15. Luo, G., Yang, X.: Limited dominance-based rough set model and knowledge reductions in incomplete decision system. J. Inf. Sci. Eng. **26**, 2199–2211 (2010)
16. Nakata, M., Sakai, H.: Applying rough sets to information tables containing missing values. In: Proceedings of 39th International Symposium on Multiple-Valued Logic, pp. 286–291. IEEE Computer Society Press (2009)
17. Nakata, M., Sakai, H.: Twofold rough approximations under incomplete information. Int. J. Gen. Syst. **42**, 546–571 (2013)
18. Paredaens, J., De Bra, P., Gyssens, M., Van Gucht, D.: The Structure of the Relational Database Model. Springer, Heidelberg (1989)
19. Parsons, S.: Current approaches to handling imperfect information in data and knowledge bases. IEEE Trans. Knowl. Data Eng. **8**, 353–372 (1996)

20. Parsons, S.: Addendum to current approaches to handling imperfect information in data and knowledge bases. IEEE Trans. Knowl. Data Eng. **10**, 862 (1998)
21. Pawlak, Z.: Rough Sets: Theoretical Aspects of Reasoning about Data. Kluwer Academic Publishers, Dordrecht (1991)
22. Qi, Y., Sun, H., Yang, X., Song, Y., Sun, Q.: Approches to approximate distribution reduct in incomplete ordered decision system. J. Inf. Comput. Sci. **3**(3), 189–198 (2008)
23. Qian, Y.H., Liang, J.Y., Song, P., Dang, C.Y.: On dominance relations in disjunctive set-valued ordered information systems. Int. J. Inf. Technol. Decis. Mak. **9**(1), 9–33 (2010)
24. Sakai, H., Okuma, A.: Basic algorithms and tools for rough non-deterministic information analysis. In: Peters, J.F., Skowron, A., Grzymała-Busse, J.W., Kostek, B., Świniarski, R.W., Szczuka, M.S. (eds.) Transactions on Rough Sets I. LNCS, vol. 3100, pp. 209–231. Springer, Heidelberg (2004). doi:10.1007/978-3-540-27794-1_10
25. Sakai, H., Ishibashi, R., Koba, K., Nakata, M.: Rules and apriori algorithm in non-deterministic information systems. In: Peters, J.F., Skowron, A., Rybiński, H. (eds.) Transactions on Rough Sets IX. LNCS, vol. 5390, pp. 328–350. Springer, Heidelberg (2008). doi:10.1007/978-3-540-89876-4_18
26. Sakai, H., Liu, C., Zhu, X., Nakata, M.: On NIS-apriori based data mining in SQL. In: Flores, V., et al. (eds.) IJCRS 2016. LNCS, vol. 9920, pp. 514–524. Springer, Cham (2016). doi:10.1007/978-3-319-47160-0_47
27. Sakai, H., Wu, M., Nakata, M.: Apriori-based rule generation in incomplete information databases and non-deterministic information systems. Fundam. Inform. **130**(3), 343–376 (2014)
28. Shao, M., Zhang, W.: Dominance relation and rules in an incomplete ordered information system. Int. J. Intell. Syst. **20**, 13–27 (2005)
29. Stefanowski, J., Tsoukiàs, A.: On the extension of rough sets under incomplete information. In: Zhong, N., Skowron, A., Ohsuga, S. (eds.) RSFDGrC 1999. LNCS, vol. 1711, pp. 73–81. Springer, Heidelberg (1999). doi:10.1007/978-3-540-48061-7_11
30. Wang, H., Guan, Y., Huang, J., Shen, J.: Decision rules acquisition for inconsistent disjunctive set-valued ordered decision information systems. Math. Prob. Eng. **2015**, Article ID 936340, 8 p. (2015)
31. Wei, L., Tang, Z., Wang, R., Yang, X.: Extensions of dominance-based rough set approach in incomplete information system. Autom. Control Comput. Sci. **42**(5), 255–263 (2008)
32. Yang, X., Dou, H.: Valued dominance-based rough set approach to incomplete information system. In: Gavrilova, M.L., Tan, C.J.K. (eds.) Transactions on Computational Science XIII. LNCS, vol. 6750, pp. 92–107. Springer, Heidelberg (2011). doi:10.1007/978-3-642-22619-9_5
33. Yang, X., Yang, J., Wu, C., Yu, D.: Dominance-based rough set approach and knowledge reductions in incomplete ordered information system. Inf. Sci. **178**, 1219–1234 (2008)
34. Zimányi, E., Pirotte, A.: Imperfect information in relational databases. In: Motro, A., Smets, P. (eds.) Uncertainty Management in Information Systems: From Needs to Solutions, pp. 35–87. Kluwer Academic Publishers, Dordrecht (1997)

A Measure of Inconsistency for Simple Decision Systems over Ontological Graphs

Krzysztof Pancerz[✉]

Chair of Computer Science, Faculty of Mathematics and Natural Sciences, University of Rzeszów, Prof. S. Pigonia Str. 1, 35-310 Rzeszów, Poland
kpancerz@ur.edu.pl

Abstract. Rough sets are an appropriate tool to deal with rough (ambiguous, imprecise) concepts in the universe of discourse. A general idea of rough sets is to approximate a given set of objects of interest by other sets of objects, called elementary sets, forming basic knowledge granules. Approximation can be either exact or rough. In the paper, we show that adding information on semantic relations between decision attribute values in a form of an ontological graph enables us to make a quantitative assessment of basic knowledge granules approximating a given set of objects. We focus on semantic relations fundamental in linguistics, called paradigmatic semantic relations. Based on approximation, the whole universe of objects can be divided into three disjoint regions, the positive region, the negative region, and the boundary region. The assessment measure has a fuzzy character, i.e., 0 for granules included in the negative region, 1 for granules included in the positive region, and between 0 and 1 for granules included in the boundary region. It is a measure of inconsistencies existing in simple decision systems over ontological graphs.

Keywords: Rough sets · Knowledge granules · Decision systems over ontological graphs · Semantic relations

1 Introduction

Effective data mining requires incorporating background (domain) knowledge connected with data semantics into the mining processes [28]. This background knowledge is useful in case of both nominal and numeric attribute values. The background knowledge delivers important information about different aspects of data. Some of the significant aspects are relations between attribute values, especially, semantic relations. Data mining with background knowledge has been extensively studied in the past. Over time, different forms of the background knowledge have been used, for example:

- preference order of attribute values (cf. [8]),
- concept hierarchies like attribute value taxonomies (cf. [32,33]), attribute value ontology (cf. [11]),
- ontologies and semantic nets (cf. [2,24]).

© Springer International Publishing AG 2017
L. Polkowski et al. (Eds.): IJCRS 2017, Part I, LNAI 10313, pp. 507–522, 2017.
DOI: 10.1007/978-3-319-60837-2_41

In case of attribute value ontology, the partial order of concepts generated by the narrower/broader meaning of concepts is only considered. In case of ontologies, the background knowledge is expressed as a set of concepts together with relationships defined among them comprising the vocabulary from a given area (cf. [17]) and these relationships may lead to non-hierarchical structures with concepts.

In [18], we proposed to incorporate ontologies into information systems (understood as Pawlak's knowledge representation systems [21]). In the classic information systems, there is a lack of semantics explaining the meaning of data, i.e., with each attribute describing objects of interest, only a set of its values is associated. In order to cover the meaning of data, simple information systems over ontological graphs were defined. In this case, values of a given attribute are concepts from the domain described by this attribute. The domain is modeled using an ontology. The ontology is represented by means of the graph structure, called the ontological graph. In such a graph, each node represents one concept from the ontology, whereas each edge represents a relation between two concepts. It is assumed that the ontological graph represents the whole domain of a given attribute, i.e., only concepts present in the ontological graph can become attribute values. In the next papers, e.g. [19,20], simple decision systems over ontological graphs were also considered. It is worth noting that we can consider some hybrid information/decision systems, where ontological graphs are associated with selected attributes only, for example, either condition attributes or a decision attribute. In general, ontology can model various semantic relations between concepts. At the beginning, our attention is focused on those fundamental relations considered in linguistics, called paradigmatic semantic relations (or paradigmatic relations shortly), i.e., synonymy, antonymy, hyponymy, hyperonymy, meronymy, and holonymy (cf. [14]). Such relations are, among others, distinguished in WordNet [6] - a large lexical database of English as well as in the project called Wikisaurus [1] aiming at creating a thesaurus of semantically related terms. Synonymy concerns concepts with the meaning that is the same as, or very similar to, the meaning of other concepts. Antonymy concerns concepts which have the opposite meaning to the other ones. Hyponymy/hyperonymy determines the narrower/broader meaning of concepts. Hyponymy concerns more specific concepts than the other ones. Hyperonymy concerns more general concepts than the other ones. Meronymy and holonymy define part/whole relations. Meronymy concerns concepts that denote parts of the wholes that are denoted by other concepts. Holonymy concerns concepts that denote the wholes whose parts are denoted by other concepts. However, research in knowledge engineering, linguistics, logic, cognitive psychology has recognized a variety of taxonomies of different types of semantic relations, e.g. [3,4,13,26,27]. A comprehensive review of the literature concerning semantic relations is given in [16]. As the authors noticed, almost every new attempt to analyze semantic relations leads to a new list of relations.

Rough sets are an appropriate tool to deal with rough (ambiguous, imprecise) concepts in the universe of discourse. A general idea of rough sets is to approximate a given set of objects of interest by other sets of objects, called elementary sets, forming basic granules of knowledge. In the original Pawlak's rough sets, basic granules are induced by an indiscernibility relation on attribute values (cf. [21]). However, the notion of rough sets can be generalized using an arbitrary binary relation on attribute values (cf. [29]). Approximation can be either exact or rough. Rough set methods were also supported by the background knowledge, for example, Dominance-Based Rough Set Approach (DRSA) [7], DAG-Decision Systems [12], knowledge reduction for decision tables with attribute value taxonomies [30].

Several examples indicating problems of applying rough sets to decision systems over ontological graphs were considered in [19]. An influence of taking into consideration both semantics of condition attribute values and semantics of decision attribute values on defining rough sets was shown. As it was noticed, dealing with semantic relations enriches our look at approximations (lower and upper) of sets defined in decision systems. In [20], we showed that adding information on semantics of decision attribute values (expressed in ontological graphs) enables us to determine qualitatively the accuracy of approximation. The qualitative assessment of approximation is treated as some additional characteristic of rough sets. According to Pawlak and Skowron, each rough set can be characterized numerically (quantitatively) by the coefficient called the accuracy of approximation (see, for example, [22]).

In this paper, we propose another approach taking benefit from adding information on semantics of decision attribute values. We use information on semantic relations between decision attribute values in the form of ontological graphs to make a quantitative assessment of basic knowledge granules approximating a given set X of objects in the whole universe U of objects. The proposed measure is a kind of degree to which the assessed granule belongs to the set X. Based on approximation of the set X, the whole universe U can be divided into three disjoint regions, the positive region $POS(X)$, the negative region $NEG(X)$, and the boundary region $BND(X)$. $POS(X)$ encompasses granules entirely included in X, $NEG(X)$ encompasses granules not included in X at all, and $BND(X)$ encompasses granules only partially included in X. The existence of the boundary region is a sign of inconsistency in a simple decision system over ontological graphs. Therefore, the proposed assessment enables us to measure inconsistencies existing in simple decision systems over ontological graphs. The measure has a fuzzy character, i.e., 0 for granules included in $NEG(X)$, 1 for granules included in $POS(X)$, and between 0 and 1 for granules included in $BND(X)$.

On the one hand, the presented approach differs from the approach based on a rough membership function proposed by Pawlak and Skowron (cf. [22]). The Pawlak's rough membership function is a kind of conditional probability. It does not depend on decision attribute values adopted by the objects included in a given basic knowledge granule. The value of the membership function is interpreted as degree to which the basic knowledge granule is included in the set

X. On the other hand, the presented approach is strictly connected with one of the fundamental notions of rough sets, namely a generalized decision function (cf. [22,25]) that is used to define measures for inconsistent decision systems.

In our approach, the value of the measure for granules covered by the boundary region depends on decision attribute values adopted by the objects included in granules as well as on semantic distances between these values. The more dispersion of decision attribute values for a given granule, according to semantic distances between them, the lower the degree to which the assessed granule belongs to the set X.

The rest of the paper is organized as follows. Theoretical background for the proposed approach is presented in Sect. 2. Section 3 describes a new approach for assessment of basic knowledge granules describing rough sets in simple decision systems over ontological graphs. Finally, Sect. 4 consists of some conclusions and directions for the further work.

2   Theoretical Background

Theoretical background for the proposed approach is given in this section. A series of notions is recalled.

2.1   Binary Relations, Basic Knowledge Granules and Rough Sets

Let U be a non-empty set of objects. U is called a universe. Any subset $R \subseteq U \times U$ is called a binary relation on U. A binary relation $R \subseteq U \times U$ is an equivalence relation if and only if it is reflexive, symmetric, and transitive.

Let a non-empty set U and a family $\Pi = \{G_1, G_2, \ldots, G_k\}$ of non-empty subsets of U, i.e., $G_i \subseteq U$ and $G_i \neq \emptyset$ for $i = 1, 2, \ldots, k$, be given. The family Π is called:

- a partition of U if and only if $G_i \cap G_j = \emptyset$ for any $i, j = 1, 2, \ldots, k$, $i \neq j$, and $\bigcup_{i=1}^{k} G_i = U$,

- a covering of U if and only if $\bigcup_{i=1}^{k} G_i = U$.

A given equivalence relation defines uniquely some partition of U, whereas, in general case, any binary relation defines uniquely some covering of U. It is worth noting that every partition is a covering but not every covering is a partition.

From a practical point of view, it is better to describe objects from the universe using a data structure called a decision system. A decision system is a data table containing rows labeled by objects of interest (from the universe), columns labeled by attributes (features of objects) and entries of the table representing attribute values. A set of attributes is partitioned into two classes of attributes, called condition and decision attributes, respectively. Condition attributes describe the objects in terms of available information. Decision attributes (in many cases, one decision attribute) partition these objects into groups (the so-called decision classes). Formally, a decision system DS is a tuple

$$DS = (U, C, D, \{V_a\}_{a \in C \cup D}, f_{inf}, f_{dec}),$$

where:

- U is the nonempty, finite set of objects,
- C is the nonempty, finite set of condition attributes,
- D is the nonempty, finite set of decision attributes,
- $\{V_a\}_{a \in C \cup D}$ is the family of sets of condition and decision attribute values,
- $f_{inf} : C \times U \rightarrow \bigcup_{c \in C} V_c$ is the information function such that $f_{inf}(c, u) \in V_c$
  for each $c \in C$ and $u \in U$.
- $f_{dec} : D \times U \rightarrow \bigcup_{d \in D} V_d$ is the decision function such that $f_{dec}(d, u) \in V_d$ for
  each $d \in D$ and $u \in U$.

Let $DS = (U, C, D, \{V_a\}_{a \in C \cup D}, f_{inf}, f_{dec})$ be a decision system and $\Pi = \{G_1, G_2, \ldots, G_k\}$ be a finite covering of U. The elements of Π are called elementary sets. Each elementary set forms a basic granule of knowledge about U. The elements of Π will be further called basic knowledge granules. Let $\Pi = \{G_1, G_2, \ldots, G_k\}$ be a fixed covering of U, and $X \subseteq U$. We define the lower approximation of X as follows

$$\underline{\Pi}(X) = \bigcup_{i=1,2,\ldots,k, G_i \subseteq X} G_i.$$

The lower approximation $\underline{\Pi}(X)$ is the union of all basic knowledge granules from Π which are subsets of X. The lower approximation $\underline{\Pi}(X)$ is called the positive region $POS_\Pi(X)$ of X. Hence,

$$POS_\Pi(X) = \underline{\Pi}(X).$$

We define the upper approximation of X as follows

$$\overline{\Pi}(X) = \bigcup_{i=1,2,\ldots,k, G_i \cap X \neq \emptyset} G_i.$$

The boundary region $BND_\Pi(X)$ of X is defined as:

$$BND_\Pi(X) = \overline{\Pi}(X) - \underline{\Pi}(X).$$

The negative region $NEG_\Pi(X)$ of X is defined as:

$$NEG_\Pi(X) = U - \overline{\Pi}(X).$$

One can see that basic knowledge granules can be divided into three disjoint groups:

- basic knowledge granules included in the positive region $POS_\Pi(X)$, called positive basic knowledge granules,
- basic knowledge granules included in the boundary region $BND_\Pi(X)$, called boundary basic knowledge granules,
- basic knowledge granules included in the negative region $NEG_\Pi(X)$, called negative basic knowledge granules.

In general, the notion of rough sets can be considered using an arbitrary binary relation on attribute values (cf. [29]). A special case is an equivalence relation considered in the original Pawlak's definition of rough sets. Let $DS = (U, C, D, \{V_a\}_{a \in C \cup D}, f_{inf}, f_{dec})$ be a decision system. Each subset $B \subseteq C$ of condition attributes determines an equivalence relation on U, called an indiscernibility relation IR_B, defined as

$$IR_B = \{(u, v) \in U \times U : \underset{a \in B}{\forall} f_{inf}(a, u) = f_{inf}(a, v)\}.$$

The indiscernibility relation IR_B defines a covering (partition) $\Pi_{IR_B}(U) = \{G_1, G_2, \ldots, G_k\}$ including basic knowledge granules which are equivalence classes of IR_B.

2.2   Decision Systems over Ontological Graphs

We introduced simple information systems over ontological graphs in [18]. Next, simple decision systems over ontological graphs were considered (see, for example, [19,20]).

An ontology specifies the concepts and relationships among them comprising the vocabulary from a given area (cf. [17]). Formally, an ontology can be represented by means of graph structures. In our approach, a graph representing the ontology $\mathcal{O}$ is called an ontological graph. Let $\mathcal{O}$ be a given ontology. An ontological graph is defined as

$$OG = (\mathcal{C}, E, \mathcal{R}, \rho),$$

where:

- $\mathcal{C}$ is the nonempty, finite set of nodes representing concepts in the ontology $\mathcal{O}$,
- $E \subseteq \mathcal{C} \times \mathcal{C}$ is the finite set of edges representing semantic relations between concepts from $\mathcal{C}$,
- $\mathcal{R}$ is the family of semantic descriptions (in a natural language) of types of relations (represented by edges) between concepts,
- $\rho : E \to \mathcal{R}$ is the function assigning a semantic description of the relation to each edge.

Let $OG = (\mathcal{C}, E, \mathcal{R}, \rho)$ be an ontological graph. We will use the following notation:

- $[c_i, c_j]$ - a simple path in OG between $c_i, c_j \in \mathcal{C}$,
- $\mathcal{E}([c_i, c_j])$ - a set of edges from E belonging to the simple path $[c_i, c_j]$,
- $\mathcal{P}(OG)$ - a set of all simple paths in OG.

In ontological graphs used by us, semantic relations are paradigmatic relations which hold between concepts belonging to the same grammatical category. WordNet and Wikisaurus, mentioned in Sect. 1, distinguish the following paradigmatic relations between concepts: synonymy, antonymy, hyponymy/hyperonymy, meronymy/holonymy. For simplicity, we use the following labels of paradigmatic relations:

- $R_\sim$ - synonymy, $(u, v) \in R_\sim$ is read "u is a synonym of v",
- $R_\leftrightarrow$ - antonymy, $(u, v) \in R_\leftrightarrow$ is read "u is an antonym of v",
- $R_\lhd$ - hyponymy, $(u, v) \in R_\lhd$ is read "u is a hyponym of v",
- $R_\rhd$ - hyperonymy, $(u, v) \in R_\rhd$ is read "u is a hyperonym of v",
- $R_\subset$ - meronymy, $(u, v) \in R_\subset$ is read "u is a meronym of v",
- $R_\supset$ - holonymy, $(u, v) \in R_\supset$ is read "u is a holonym of v".

A simple decision system over ontological graphs is a tuple

$$SDS^{OG} = (U, C, D, \{OG_a\}_{a \in C \cup D}, f_{inf}, f_{dec}),$$

where:

- U is the nonempty, finite set of objects,
- C is the nonempty, finite set of condition attributes,
- D is the nonempty, finite set of decision attributes,
- $\{OG_a\}_{a \in C \cup D}$ is the family of ontological graphs associated with condition and decision attributes,
- $f_{inf} : C \times U \to \bigcup_{c \in C} \mathcal{C}_c$ is the information function such that $f_{inf}(c, u) \in \mathcal{C}_c$ for each $c \in C$ and $u \in U$, $\mathcal{C}_c$ is the set of concepts from the graph OG_c
- $f_{dec} : D \times U \to \bigcup_{d \in D} \mathcal{C}_d$ is the decision function such that $f_{dec}(d, u) \in \mathcal{C}_d$ for each $d \in D$ and $u \in U$, $\mathcal{C}_d$ is the set of concepts from the graph OG_d.

Binary relations over the set U of objects in a simple decision system over ontological graphs can be defined on the basis of relations over value sets of attributes determined for each attribute separately. Let $OG_a = (\mathcal{C}_a, E_a, \mathcal{R}, \rho_a)$ be an ontological graph associated with the attribute a, and τ_1, τ_2 be two fixed positive integer values, where $\tau_1 < \tau_2$. If we consider semantic relations, like synonymy, antonymy, hyponymy/hyperonymy, then the relations over the value set of a can be as follows (cf. [18–20]):

- An exact meaning relation

$$EMR_a = \{(v_1, v_2) \in \mathcal{C}_a \times \mathcal{C}_a : v_1 = v_2\}.$$

- A synonymous meaning relation

$$SMR_a = \{(v_1, v_2) \in \mathcal{C}_a \times \mathcal{C}_a : (v_1, v_2) \in E_a \text{ and } \rho_a((v_1, v_2)) = R_\sim\}.$$

- An antonymous meaning relation

$$AMR_a = \{(v_1, v_2) \in \mathcal{C}_a \times \mathcal{C}_a : (v_1, v_2) \in E_a \text{ and } \rho_a((v_1, v_2)) = R_{\leftrightarrow}\}.$$

- A hyperonymous meaning relation $HprMR_a$ is a set of all pairs $(v_1, v_2) \in \mathcal{C}_a \times \mathcal{C}_a$ for which there exists $v_3 \in \mathcal{C}_a$ such that:

$$\underset{[v_1,v_3] \in \mathcal{P}(OG_a)}{\exists} \quad \underset{e \in \mathcal{E}([v_1,v_3])}{\forall} \quad \rho_a(e) \in \{R_{\sim}, R_{\lhd}\}.$$

and

$$\underset{[v_2,v_3] \in \mathcal{P}(OG_a)}{\exists} \quad \underset{e \in \mathcal{E}([v_2,v_3])}{\forall} \quad \rho_a(e) \in \{R_{\sim}, R_{\lhd}\}$$

Moreover, let $d_1 = card(\{e' \in \mathcal{E}([v_1, v_3]) : \rho_a(e') = R_{\lhd}\})$ and $d_2 = card(\{e' \in \mathcal{E}([v_2, v_3]) : \rho_a(e') = R_{\lhd}\})$. We distinguish three types of a hyperonymous meaning relation:

- A far hyperonymous meaning relation $FHprMR_a$ if

$$max(d_1, d_2) > \tau_2.$$

- A middle-far hyperonymous meaning relation $MHprMR_a$ if

$$\tau_1 < max(d_1, d_2) \le \tau_2$$

- A close hyperonymous meaning relation $CHprMR_a$, otherwise.

It is worth noting that the values of τ_1 and τ_2 can be chosen according to the size of the graph OG_a (especially, according to the depth of the hierarchy generated by the hyponymy/hyperonymy relations).

2.3   Fuzzy Sets

Fuzzy sets were introduced by Zadeh [31]. A fuzzy set F in a universe of discourse X is defined as a set of pairs $(\mu_F(x), x)$, where $\mu_F : X \to [0, 1]$ is a membership function of F and $\mu_F(x) \in [0, 1]$ is the grade of membership of $x \in X$ in F.

3   Assessment of Basic Knowledge Granules

In this section, we propose to use some measure to assess basic knowledge granules describing rough sets in simple decision systems over ontological graphs according to values of a decision attribute. The assessment measure has a fuzzy character. It enables us to characterize inconsistencies existing in simple decision systems over ontological graphs.

Let $SDS^{OG} = (U, C, D, \{OG_a\}_{a \in C \cup D}, f_{inf}, f_{dec})$, be a simple decision system over ontological graphs and $\Pi_R = \{G_1, G_2, \dots, G_k\}$ be a covering of U (a family of basic knowledge granules induced by the binary relation R). For a basic knowledge granule $G \in \Pi_R$, we define the set $Dec_d(G)$ of all decision attribute values adopted by the objects included in G as

$$Dec_d(G) = \{f_{dec}(d, u) : u \in G\}.$$

Let us assume that the approximated set is a set X_d^v of objects such that the decision attribute d has a distinguished value v, i.e.:

$$X_d^v = \{u \in U : f_{dec}(d, u) = v\}.$$

A fuzzy set $F(X_d^v)$ in Π_R is defined as:

$$\mu_{F(X_d^v)}(G) = \begin{cases} 1 & \text{if } G \in POS_{\Pi_R}(X_d^v), \\ \underset{u \in G}{Op} \ sem(v, f_{dec}(d, u)) & \text{if } G \in BND_{\Pi_R}(X_d^v), \\ 0 & \text{if } G \in NEG_{\Pi_R}(X_d^v). \end{cases}$$

where Op is an aggregation operator (e.g., minimum, arithmetic average, maximum, etc.), and

- $sem(v, f_{dec}(d, u)) = 1$ if and only if $(v, f_{dec}(d, u)) \in EMR_d$ or $(v, f_{dec}(d, u)) \in SMR_d$,
- $sem(v, f_{dec}(d, u)) = 0.9$ if and only if $(v, f_{dec}(d, u)) \in CHprMR_d$,
- $sem(v, f_{dec}(d, u)) = 0.5$ if and only if $(v, f_{dec}(d, u)) \in MHprMR_d$,
- $sem(v, f_{dec}(d, u)) = 0.1$ if and only if $(v, f_{dec}(d, u)) \in FHprMR_d$,
- $sem(v, f_{dec}(d, u)) = 0$ if and only if $(v, f_{dec}(d, u)) \in AMR_d$.

Instead of a minimum, one can use a t-norm and instead of a maximum, an s-norm. They are more general cases (cf. [9]). It is worth noting that the selection of fuzzy values for a semantic distance sem is arbitrary. One can use another strategy.

It was mentioned in Sect. 1 that we can deal with hybrid decision systems (see Example 1) such that only some of their attributes have ontological graphs associated with them. To focus on the presented approach, we will consider in Example 1, a simple decision system over ontological graphs in the form

$$SDS^{OG} = (U, C, D, \{V_c\}_{c \in C}, \{OG_d\}_{d \in D}, f_{inf}, f_{dec}),$$

where:

- U is the nonempty, finite set of objects,
- C is the nonempty, finite set of condition attributes,
- D is the nonempty, finite set of decision attributes,
- $\{V_c\}_{c \in C}$ is the family of sets of condition attribute values,
- $\{OG_d\}_{d \in D}$ is the family of ontological graphs associated with decision attributes,
- $f_{inf} : C \times U \to \bigcup_{c \in C} V_c$ is the information function such that $f_{inf}(c, u) \in V_c$ for each $c \in C$ and $u \in U$.

- $f_{dec} : D \times U \to \bigcup_{d \in D} \mathcal{C}_d$ is the decision function such that $f_{dec}(d, u) \in \mathcal{C}_d$ for each $d \in D$ and $u \in U$, $\mathcal{C}_d$ is the set of concepts from the graph OG_d.

Example 1. Let us consider the simple decision system over ontological graphs

$$SDS^{OG} = (U, C, D, \{V_c\}_{c \in C}, \{OG_d\}_{d \in D}, f_{inf}, f_{dec})$$

describing students, where:

- $U = \{u_1, u_2, \ldots, u_{12}\}$,
- $C = \{c_g, c_{mp}, c_{bc}, c_h\}$,
- $D = \{d\}$,
- the ontological graph associated with the decision attribute d is shown in Fig. 1,
- the condition attribute value sets, as well as both the information function f_{inf} and the decision function f_{dec}, can be obtained from Table 1.

The meaning of attributes (condition and decision) is as follows:

- c_g - gender,
- c_{mp} - abilities in mathematics and physics,
- c_{bc} - abilities in biology and chemistry,
- c_h - abilities in humanities,
- d - field of study.

Table 1. The simple decision system over ontological graphs describing students

U/A	c_g	c_{mp}	c_{bc}	c_h	d
Description	Gender	Abilities in mathematics and physics	Abilities in biology and chemistry	Abilities in humanities	Field of study
u_1	Male	Good	Medium	Low	Physics
u_2	Male	Good	Medium	Low	Astronomy
u_3	Female	Medium	Good	Medium	Astronomy
u_4	Male	Medium	Medium	Good	Finance
u_5	Female	Medium	Good	Medium	Chemistry
u_6	Male	Good	Medium	Low	Physics
u_7	Female	Medium	Good	Medium	Biochemistry
u_8	Female	Medium	Good	Medium	Law
u_9	Male	Low	Medium	Good	Law
u_{10}	Female	Medium	Medium	Good	Law
u_{11}	Female	Medium	Medium	Good	Administration
u_{12}	Male	Medium	Medium	Good	Economy

The field of study is depicted as a consequence of a gender as well as selected abilities of students. We have the following relationship:

$$conditions(gender, selectedabilities) \rightarrow decision(fieldofstudy).$$

As it is expected, there are some inconsistencies in this relationship.

The ontological graph OG_d associated with the decision attribute d describes fields of studies (see Fig. 1). For simplicity, it is a small part of a real ontological graph describing fields of studies and it is depicted as a hierarchy of classes in Protege. Protege [15] is a free, open source, platform-independent environment for creating and editing ontologies and knowledge bases. A covering (partition) including basic knowledge granules induced by the indiscernibility relation IR_C has the form $\Pi_{IR_C} = \{G_1, G_2, G_3, G_4, G_5\}$, where:

- $G_1 = \{u_1, u_2, u_6\}$,
- $G_2 = \{u_3, u_5, u_7, u_8\}$,
- $G_3 = \{u_4, u_{12}\}$,
- $G_4 = \{u_9\}$,
- $G_5 = \{u_{10}, u_{11}\}$.

For simplicity, we assume $\tau_1 = 1$ and $\tau_2 = 2$ to determine the kind of a hyperonymous meaning relation $HprMR_a$ (see Sect. 2.2).

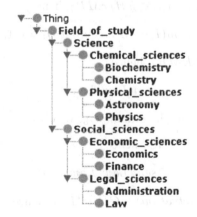

Fig. 1. The ontological graph describing fields of studies (a hierarchy of classes in Protege) associated with the decision attribute

One can see that the decision system describing students is inconsistent with respect to the partition Π_{IR_C}. Let us use a measure defined by us to assess inconsistencies. Two sets of objects, X_d^{Law} and $X_d^{Physics}$, for approximation by basic knowledge granules, will be considered as examples. Assignment of basic knowledge granules from Π_{IR_C} to regions on account of approximated sets of objects is shown in Table 2.

Table 2. Assignment of basic knowledge granules to regions on account of approximated sets of objects

X	$POS_{\Pi_{IR_C}}(X)$	$BND_{\Pi_{IR_C}}(X)$	$NEG_{\Pi_{IR_C}}(X)$
X_d^{Law}	G_4	$G_2 \cup G_5$	$G_1 \cup G_3$
$X_d^{Physics}$	$\emptyset$	G_1	$G_2 \cup G_3 \cup G_4 \cup G_5$

For granules from boundary regions, we have:

- $Dec_d(G_1) = \{Physics, Astronomy\}$,
- $Dec_d(G_2) = \{Astronomy, Chemistry, Biochemistry, Law\}$,
- $Dec_d(G_5) = \{Law, Administration\}$.

In case of the set X_d^{Law} and the granule G_2, we obtain:

- for u_3, $(Law, Astronomy) \in FHprMR_d$, hence

$$sem(Law, Astronomy) = 0.1,$$

- for u_5, $(Law, Chemistry) \in FHprMR_d$, hence

$$sem(Law, Chemistry) = 0.1,$$

- for u_7, $(Law, Biochemistry) \in FHprMR_d$, hence

$$sem(Law, Biochemistry) = 0.1,$$

- for u_8, $(Law, Law) \in EMR_d$, hence

$$sem(Law, Law) = 1.$$

In case of the set X_d^{Law} and the granule G_5, we obtain:

- for u_{10}, $(Law, Law) \in EMR_d$, hence

$$sem(Law, Law) = 1,$$

- for u_{11}, $(Law, Administration) \in CHprMR_d$, hence

$$sem(Law, Administration) = 0.9.$$

In case of the set $X_d^{Physics}$ and the granule G_1, we obtain:

- for u_1, $(Physics, Physics) \in EMR_d$, hence

$$sem(Physics, Physics) = 1,$$

- for u_2, $(Physics, Astronomy) \in CHprMR_d$, hence

$$sem(Physics, Astronomy) = 0.9,$$

– for u_6, $(Physics, Physics) \in EMR_d$, hence

$$sem(Physics, Physics) = 1.$$

If we take a minimum (one of the worst cases) as an aggregation operator, we obtain assessment of basic knowledge granules on account of approximated sets of objects as in Table 3. If we take an arithmetic average (some of average cases) as an aggregation operator, we obtain assessment of basic knowledge granules on account of approximated sets of objects as in Table 4.

Table 3. Assessment of basic knowledge granules on account of approximated sets of objects in case of a minimum operator

X	G_1	G_2	G_3	G_4	G_5
X_d^{Law}	0.00	0.10	0.00	1.00	0.90
$X_d^{Physics}$	0.90	0.00	0.00	0.00	0.00

Table 4. Assessment of basic knowledge granules on account of approximated sets of objects in case of an arithmetic average operator

X	G_1	G_2	G_3	G_4	G_5
X_d^{Law}	0.00	0.33	0.00	1.00	0.95
$X_d^{Physics}$	0.97	0.00	0.00	0.00	0.00

In our approach, we can also adopt other measures. Several similarity measures between two concepts have been proposed, especially for semantic nets organized hierarchically (see, for example, [10,23]). The measure defined in [10] utilizes information from the hierarchical net, in our case, ontological graph. Concepts at upper levels of the hierarchy have more general semantics and less similarity between them, while concepts at lower levels have more concrete semantics and stronger similarity. The similarity between two concepts v and v' is considered to be governed by the length of the shortest path as well as the depth of the subsumer (cf. [10]):

$$s(v, v') = f_1(l)f_2(h),$$

where l is the length of the shortest path between v and v' in the ontological graph and h is the depth of the subsumer in the hierarchy.

In general, functions f_1 and f_2 are nonlinear. For the function f_1:

– if the path length decreases to zero, the similarity will monotically increase toward 1,
– if the path length increases infinitely, the similarity will monotically decrease toward 0.

The depth is measured by counting the closest level from subsumers to the top of hierarchy (the root concept). The function f_2 should be selected to satisfy the fact that concepts at lower levels of the hierarchy are more similar than at higher levels.

In [10], the following component functions have been defined:

- $f_1(l) = e^{-\alpha l}$,
- $f_2(h) = \frac{e^{\beta h} - e^{-\beta h}}{e^{\beta h} + e^{-\beta h}}$,

where α is a constant and β is a smoothing factor.

4   Conclusions

We have shown how to measure inconsistencies in simple decision systems over ontological graphs if the ontological graphs include paradigmatic relations fundamental in linguistics (i.e., synonymy, antonymy, hyponymy, hyperonymy). One of the challenging problems is to define measures enabling us to make a quantitative assessment of basic knowledge granules in case of other paradigmatic semantic relations (e.g., meronymy/holonymy) or any other semantic relations, especially those non-hierarchical. Meronymy/holonymy relations are also hierarchical ones. The proposed measure can be helpful to consider decision systems over ontological graphs in terms of the Variable Precision Rough Set Model (VPRSM) [34]. Moreover, we plan to consider simple decision systems over ontological graphs in the context of generalized decision functions, especially for the decision reduct and decision rule generation.

References

1. The Wikisaurus Homepage: http://en.wiktionary.org/wiki/Wiktionary: Wikisaurus
2. Bloehdorn, S., Hotho, A.: Ontologies for machine learning. In: Staab, S., Studer, R. (eds.) Handbook on Ontologies, pp. 637–661. Springer, Heidelberg (2009)
3. Brachman, R.: What IS-A is and isn't: an analysis of taxonomic links in semantic networks. Computer **16**(10), 30–36 (1983)
4. Chaffin, R., Herrmann, D.J.: The nature of semantic relations: a comparison of two approaches. In: Evens, M. (ed.) Relational Models of the Lexicon: Representing Knowledge in Semantic Networks, pp. 289–334. Cambridge University Press, New York (1988)
5. Dubois, D., Prade, H.: Rough fuzzy sets and fuzzy rough sets. Int. J. Gen. Syst. **17**(2–3), 191–209 (1990)
6. Fellbaum, C. (ed.): WordNet - An Electronic Lexical Database. MIT Press, Cambridge (1998)
7. Greco, S., Matarazzo, B., Słowiński, R.: Rough sets theory for multicriteria decision analysis. Eur. J. Oper. Res. **129**(1), 1–47 (2001)
8. Greco, S., Matarazzo, B., Slowinski, R.: The use of rough sets and fuzzy sets in MCDM. In: Gal, T., Stewart, T.J., Hanne, T. (eds.) Multicriteria Decision Making: Advances in MCDM Models, Algorithms, Theory, and Applications, pp. 397–455. Springer, Boston (1999). doi:10.1007/978-1-4615-5025-9_14

9. Klement, E.P., Mesiar, R., Pap, E.: Triangular Norms. Kluwer Academic Publishers, Dordrecht (2000)
10. Li, Y., Bandar, Z., Mclean, D.: An approach for measuring semantic similarity between words using multiple information sources. IEEE Trans. Knowl. Data Eng. **15**(4), 871–882 (2003)
11. Lukaszewski, T., Józefowska, J., Lawrynowicz, A.: Attribute value ontology - using semantics in data mining. In: Maciaszek, L.A., Cuzzocrea, A., Cordeiro, J. (eds.) Proceedings of the 14th International Conference on Enterprise Information Systems, pp. 329–334. Wroclaw, Poland (2012)
12. Midelfart, H., Komorowski, J.: A rough set framework for learning in a directed acyclic graph. In: Alpigini, J.J., Peters, J.F., Skowron, A., Zhong, N. (eds.) RSCTC 2002. LNCS, vol. 2475, pp. 144–155. Springer, Heidelberg (2002). doi:10.1007/3-540-45813-1_18
13. Milstead, J.L.: Standards for relationships between subject indexing terms. In: Bean, C.A., Green, R. (eds.) Relationships in the Organization of Knowledge, pp. 53–66. Kluwer Academic Publishers, Dordrecht (2001)
14. Murphy, M.L. (ed.): Semantic Relations and the Lexicon: Antonymy, Synonymy, and other Paradigms. Cambridge University Press, Cambridge (2003)
15. Musen, M., et al.: The protege project: a look back and a look forward. AI Matters **1**(4), 4–12 (2015)
16. Nastase, V., Nakov, P., Séaghdha, D.O., Szpakowicz, S.: Semantic Relations Between Nominals. Morgan & Claypool Publishers, San Rafael (2013)
17. Neches, R., Fikes, R., Finin, T., Gruber, T., Patil, R., Senator, T., Swartout, W.: Enabling technology for knowledge sharing. AI Mag. **12**(3), 36–56 (1991)
18. Pancerz, K.: Toward information systems over ontological graphs. In: Yao, J.T., Yang, Y., Słowiński, R., Greco, S., Li, H., Mitra, S., Polkowski, L. (eds.) RSCTC 2012. LNCS, vol. 7413, pp. 243–248. Springer, Heidelberg (2012). doi:10.1007/978-3-642-32115-3_29
19. Pancerz, K.: Semantic relationships and approximations of sets: an ontological graph based approach. In: Proceedings of the 6th International Conference on Human System Interaction (HSI'2013), pp. 62–69. Sopot, Poland (2013)
20. Pancerz, K.: Toward qualitative assessment of rough sets in terms of decision attribute values in simple decision systems over ontological graphs. In: Peters, J.F., Skowron, A., Ślęzak, D., Nguyen, H.S., Bazan, J.G. (eds.) Transactions on Rough Sets XIX. LNCS, vol. 8988, pp. 83–94. Springer, Heidelberg (2015). doi:10.1007/978-3-662-47815-8_6
21. Pawlak, Z.: Rough Sets. Theoretical Aspects of Reasoning about Data. Kluwer Academic Publishers, Dordrecht (1991)
22. Pawlak, Z., Skowron, A.: Rudiments of rough sets. Inf. Sci. **177**, 3–27 (2007)
23. Rada, R., Mili, H., Bicknell, E., Blettner, M.: Development and application of a metric on semantic nets. IEEE Trans. Syst. Man Cybern. **19**(1), 17–30 (1989)
24. Ristoski, P., Paulheim, H.: Semantic web in data mining and knowledge discovery: a comprehensive survey. Web Semant.: Sci. Serv. Agents World Wide Web **36**, 1–22 (2016)
25. Ślęzak, D.: Normalized decision functions and measures for inconsistent decision tables analysis. Fundam. Informaticae **44**(3), 291–319 (2000)
26. Storey, V.C.: Understanding semantic relationships. VLDB J. **2**, 455–488 (1993)
27. Winston, M.E., Chaffin, R., Herrmann, D.: A taxonomy of part-whole relations. Cogn. Sci. **11**(4), 417–444 (1987)
28. Witten, I.H., Frank, E.: Data Mining: Practical Machine Learning Tools and Techniques. Morgan Kaufmann, Burlington (2005)

29. Yao, Y., Wong, S.: Generalization of rough sets using relationships between attribute values. In: Wang, P. (ed.) Proceedings of the 2nd Annual Joint Conference on Information Sciences, pp. 30–33. Wrightsville Beach, NC, USA (1995)
30. Ye, M., Wu, X., Hu, X., Hu, D.: Knowledge reduction for decision tables with attribute value taxonomies. Knowl.-Based Syst. **56**, 68–78 (2014)
31. Zadeh, L.: Fuzzy sets. Inf. Control **8**, 338–353 (1965)
32. Zhang, J., Honavar, V.: Learning decision tree classifiers from attribute value taxonomies and partially specified data. In: Fawcett, T., Mishra, N. (eds.) Proceedings of the 20th International Conference on Machine Learning (ICML 2003), pp. 880–887. Washington D.C., USA (2003)
33. Zhang, J., Kang, D.K., Silvescu, A., Honavar, V.: Learning accurate and concise naïve bayes classifiers from attribute value taxonomies and data. Knowl. Inf. Syst. **9**(2), 157–179 (2006)
34. Ziarko, W.: Variable precision rough set model. J. Comput. Syst. Sci. **46**(1), 39–59 (1993)

A Rough View on Incomplete Information in Games

Georg Peters[1,2(✉)]

[1] Department of Computer Science and Mathematics,
Munich University of Applied Sciences, Lothstrasse 34, Munich, Germany
georg.peters@cs.hm.edu
[2] Australian Catholic University, Sydney, Australia

Abstract. In both game theory and in rough sets, the management of missing and contradicting information is regarded as one of the biggest challenges with significant practical relevance. In game theory, a distinction is made between imperfect and incomplete information. Imperfect information is defined when a player cannot identify the decision node it is presently at. Incomplete information refers to a lack of knowledge about the future actions of one's opponent, e.g., due to missing information about its payoffs. In rough set theory, missing and contradicting information in decision tables has been extensively researched and has led to the definition of lower and upper approximations of sets. Although game theory and rough sets have already addressed missing and contradicting information thoroughly little attention has been given to their relationship. In the paper, we present an example how games with imperfect information can be interpreted in the context of rough sets. In particular, we further detail Peters' recently proposed mapping of a game with incomplete information on a rough decision table.

Keywords: Missing and contradicting information · Incomplete information · Game theory · Rough set theory

1 Introduction

Motivation. In game theory [3] as well as in rough set theory [12] the role of information, in particular missing and contracting information, is of crucial importance. Therefore, extensive research has been directed at the role of information in both areas. While game theory deals with two or more players who develop strategies competing and striving for their individual maximum payoffs, in rough set theory a classic decision table is assumed. This table consists of a set of records of actions. Each record is defined by its attributes and their values and leads to a certain result. Such a decision table can be interpreted as one player who has a portfolio of actions; it plays 'nature' that comprises of a set of attributes. Although both, game theory and rough sets, face similar challenges regarding the management of information, little attention has been given to a discussion of their relationship to each other so far.

© Springer International Publishing AG 2017
L. Polkowski et al. (Eds.): IJCRS 2017, Part I, LNAI 10313, pp. 523–534, 2017.
DOI: 10.1007/978-3-319-60837-2_42

Due to a high number of applications and models in economics [10,15], game theory is often associated with economic analysis. However, game theory is also applied in a diverse range of further areas, including, e.g., in biology [6], computer science [2,5] or political science [11] besides many others. In connection with rough sets, Herbert and Yao [8,9] proposed game-theoretic rough sets. In game-theoretic rough sets game theory is applied to rough sets to optimize the distribution of objects in the lower approximations and boundaries. Hence, game theory is used as an optimization method in game-theoretic rough sets like in several other domains. In contrast to this, Xu and Yao [18], for example, integrate rough concepts into game theory by proposing a two-person games with rough payoffs.

Recently, Peters [14] outlined an introductory perspective from rough sets on games with imperfect and incomplete information. He also proposed to distinguish between irrelevant, weak and strong boundaries depending on their impact on missing information in games. However, a detailed and extensive discussion about the relationship of game theory and rough set theory, especially with respect to information, would be much desirable but is still missing. It could possible enrich both fields in many ways. First, new perspectives from game theory on rough sets may enrich rough sets. Second, established methods to manage information developed in game theory may possibly be applied to rough sets. Of course, the same applies vice versa, i.e., a rough perspective and respective rough methods could possibly enrich game theory.

Objective. Therefore, as a next step towards this directions, the objective of the paper is to further discuss and detail the relationship of games and rough sets. In particular, we focus on incomplete information in extensive-form games and rough sets by presenting an illustrate example.

Structure. The remainder of the paper is organized as follows. In the next section, we provide some introductional and notational remarks and then briefly discuss missing information in games. In Sect. 3, we transform a game with incomplete information into a rough decision table. Subsequently, we discuss an example how games can be interpreted from a rough set perspective. In Sect. 4 we show how the concept of roughness can be used as an indicator for the degree of incomplete information in games. The paper ends with a conclusion in Sect. 5.

2   Missing Information in Games

In this section, we provide some introductional and notational remarks on games and rough sets first. Then we review imperfect and incomplete information and their relationship to each other.

2.1   Introductional and Notational Remarks

Games. For the sake of simplicity, but without loss of generality, we assume a two player game with the players R and S. Furthermore, we limit ourselves in our example to two-way decisions at any decision node of a player. The decision nodes are numbered sequentially for player R ($D_{R1}, \ldots$) and player S ($D_{S1}, \ldots$); the attributes at the nodes are denoted by $R_1, \ldots$ and $S_1, \ldots$, respectively. At each decision node, a player can decide to go 'up' or 'down' the decision tree. To illustratively symbolize these two possibilities we represent the strategies by up arrows ($\uparrow$) and down arrows ($\downarrow$) as depicted in Fig. 1. A star ($*$) indicates that it is irrelevant which decision a player takes since all lead to the same payoff. The strategies of the players are indicated by lower cases of the corresponding letters of the player R ($r_1, \ldots$) and S ($s_1, \ldots$), respectively. They consist of the single actions taken at each decision node. E.g., assuming player S has two decision nodes one strategy would be $s_1 = \{\uparrow, \uparrow\}$. This means that the player moves up at both nodes, D_{S1} and D_{S2}. The payoffs for the players R and S are denominated as $C_i = (c_{Ri}, c_{Si})$. Missing information, e.g., about the payoff an opponent receives and its strategy, is denoted by a question mark ($?$).

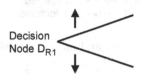

Decision
Node D_{R1}

Fig. 1. Notational remarks

Rough Sets. For a rough decision table, we use the notations as presented by Grzymala-Busse [4]: U is the set of all cases, A the set of all attributes and B a nonempty subset of A. The set of all attribute values is denoted by V while the mapping $\rho: U \times A \rightarrow V$ represents an information function.

2.2   Imperfect and Incomplete Information

Missing and contradicting information is one of the biggest challenges in decision theory as well as in game theory. For example, Akerlof [1] pointed out the important role and significant implications of asymmetric information for markets. Furthermore, in particular in games theory, imperfect information and incomplete information are distinguished while these terms seems to be often used more vaguely in some other areas.

Imperfect Information. Imperfect information is related to the indistinguishability of decision nodes for a player. For example in Fig. 2, player S cannot distinguish between its decision nodes D_{S1} and D_{S2} (indicated by the vertical fine dashed line in the figure). Both nodes form a single information set I for the player: $I_{S1} = \{D_{S1}, D_{S2}\}$. Obviously, imperfect information is related to a past decision of its player's opponent; the player has no information how the opponent decided at a former node (in our case, whether player R moved up or down at node D_{R1}).

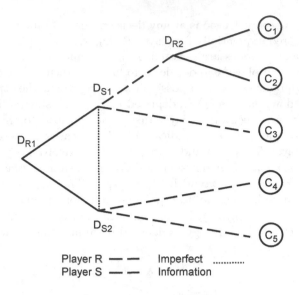

Fig. 2. Imperfect and incomplete information

Incomplete Information. In contrast to imperfect information, incomplete information is related to a future decision of a player's opponent. To illustrate this, we consider the subgame in Fig. 2 staring at node D_{S1}. Let us assume that player S knows that it is at D_{S1} (perfect information) and that its payoffs are as follows: $c_{S1} > c_{S3} > c_{S2}$. Let us further assume that player S knows the payoffs of player R, i.e., player S has complete information. Obviously, player S would decide to go up when player R decided to go up at D_{R2}. This is the case for $c_{R1} > c_{R2}$. However, for $c_{R1} < c_{R2}$ player R would go down at node D_{R2} and player S would receive a payoff of c_{S2}. To avoid this, player S would decide to move down at D_{S2} and obtain the higher payoff c_{S3} instead.

Now consider the case that the payoffs of player R are unknown for player S. Apparently, an evaluation as discussed above is no longer possible for player S. It cannot select a sure strategy that will optimize its payoff since it faces incomplete information.

Harsanyi Transformation. Harsanyi [7] showed that, under some assumptions, a game with incomplete information can be transformed into a game with imperfect information. He proposed to interpret the original game as several subgames where each subgame represents a different possible payoff structure. Therefore, each subgame has complete information. To determine which subgame is played Harsanyi introduced a new player 'nature', which selects the particular subgame that will be played.

3   Relationship of Incomplete Information in Games and Rough Sets

In this section, we concentrate on games with incomplete information and transform such games into a rough decision tables. We also show how rough methods, in particular the roughness observed in a rough decision table, can be interpreted as an indicator for the degree of incomplete information in the original extensive-form game.

3.1   Transforming a Game with Incomplete Information into a Rough Decision Table

To illustrate the representation of a game with incomplete information as rough decision table let us consider the extensive-form game of the players R and S as depicted in Fig. 3.

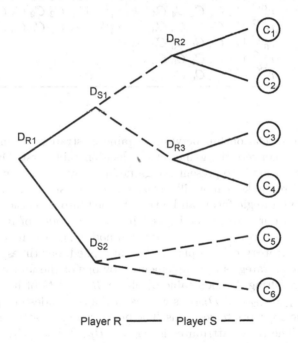

Fig. 3. Game of players R and S in extensive form

The corresponding game in strategic form is given in Table 1. The table shows the entire set of strategies of player R in the left subtable (indicted by a superscript EG for entire game: r^{EG}) and its minimum representation in the right subtable (indicted by a superscript MG for minimum game: r^{MG}).

Let us consider the entire game first. When player R selects one of the strategies $r_5^{EG} - r_8^{EG}$ it moves down at node D_{R1} and faces no further own decision.

Therefore, its decisions prepared for the nodes D_{R2} and D_{R3} are irrelevant for the outcome of the game in this case. Hence, the game can be reduced. In the minimum game, the original strategies $r_5^{EG} - r_8^{EG}$ melt down to one strategy r_5^{MG}. In this strategy, the corresponding decisions at the nodes D_{R2} and D_{R3} are marked by stars ($*$) indicating that they irrelevant.

Table 1. Game of players R and S in strategic form

	Entire Game					Minimum Game			
	Player S					Player S			
	s_1	s_2	s_3	s_4		s_1	s_2	s_3	s_4
	↑↑	↑↓	↓↑	↓↓		↑↑	↑↓	↓↑	↓↓
	r_1^{EG} ↑↑↑	C_1	C_1	C_3	C_3	r_1^{MG} ↑↑↑ C_1	C_1	C_3	C_3
	r_2^{EG} ↑↑↓	C_1	C_1	C_4	C_4	r_2^{MG} ↑↑↓ C_1	C_1	C_4	C_4
Player	r_3^{EG} ↑↓↑	C_2	C_2	C_3	C_3 ⇒	r_3^{MG} ↑↓↑ C_2	C_2	C_3	C_3
R	r_4^{EG} ↑↓↓	C_2	C_2	C_4	C_4	r_4^{MG} ↑↓↓ C_2	C_2	C_4	C_4
	r_5^{EG} ↓↑↑	C_5	C_6	C_5	C_6	r_5^{MG} ↓ $**$ C_5	C_6	C_5	C_6
	r_6^{EG} ↓↑↓	C_5	C_6	C_5	C_6				
	r_7^{EG} ↓↓↑	C_5	C_6	C_5	C_6				
	r_8^{EG} ↓↓↓	C_5	C_6	C_5	C_6				

To discuss the relationship between a game in strategic form and a rough decision table we convert the game into a decision table first. Our motivation for this transformation is to present the game in a way that is common in rough sets and, therefore, make it more illustrative and accessible for the reader.

The game in strategic form can be transformed into a decision table for one of the players, in our case player R, as follows. The nodes of its opponent, in our case player S, are considered to be its own nodes, i.e., the nodes of player R. Therefore, each strategy r_i^{MG} of player R is multiplied four times. Then, each of the four obtained strategies is complemented by one of the four strategies s_j of player S. The resulting decision table of player R consists of its original set of three nodes (D_{R1}, D_{R2} and D_{R3}) as well as of the two nodes (D_{S1} and D_{S2}) of player S and the appropriate decisions. The nodes represent attributes in a rough decision table. The set of attributes is $A_R = \{B_R, B_S\} = \{R_1, R_2, R_3, S_1, S_2\}$ consisting of the two subsets B_R and B_S of the original attributes of the players R and S, respectively. The possible actions (move up ($\uparrow$) or down ($\downarrow$)) in the game are attribute values in the rough decision table with the set of attribute values $V = \{\uparrow, \downarrow\}$. Note, that the subset of attributes B_S consist of the original actions of player S. However, these actions are treated as part of the attribute set of player R in the obtained decision table now (see Table 2).

In real life applications games can get big which possibly leads to decision tables with large numbers of attributes. In such cases, like, e.g., often observed in bioinformatics, one would possibly face dimensionality scalability, i.e., the challenge of dealing with many attributes [16]. However, a detailed discussion, including an examination if rough sets could be applied to reduce the number of attributes (see, e.g., Wang and Miao [17]), would go beyond the focus of our paper.

Table 2. Entire decision tables (ET) of player R

Player ▷	Complete information		Incomplete information						Payoff
			Partial		Partial		Total		
	ET_1		ET_2		ET_3		ET_4		
	R	S	R	S	R	S	R	S	
r_1^{ET}	↑↑↑	↑↑	↑↑↑	↑?	↑↑↑	?↑	↑↑↑	??	C_1
r_2^{ET}	↑↑↑	↑↓	↑↑↑	↑?	↑↑↑	?↓	↑↑↑	??	C_1
r_3^{ET}	↑↑↑	↓↑	↑↑↑	↓?	↑↑↑	?↑	↑↑↑	??	C_3
r_4^{ET}	↑↑↑	↓↓	↑↑↑	↓?	↑↑↑	?↓	↑↑↑	??	C_3
r_5^{ET}	↑↑↓	↑↑	↑↑↓	↑?	↑↑↓	?↑	↑↑↓	??	C_1
r_6^{ET}	↑↑↓	↑↓	↑↑↓	↑?	↑↑↓	?↓	↑↑↓	??	C_1
r_7^{ET}	↑↑↓	↓↑	↑↑↓	↓?	↑↑↓	?↑	↑↑↓	??	C_4
r_8^{ET}	↑↑↓	↓↓	↑↑↓	↓?	↑↑↓	?↓	↑↑↓	??	C_4
r_9^{ET}	↑↓↑	↑↑	↑↓↑	↑?	↑↓↑	?↑	↑↓↑	??	C_2
r_{10}^{ET}	↑↓↑	↑↓	↑↓↑	↑?	↑↓↑	?↓	↑↓↑	??	C_2
r_{11}^{ET}	↑↓↑	↓↑	↑↓↑	↓?	↑↓↑	?↑	↑↓↑	??	C_3
r_{12}^{ET}	↑↓↑	↓↓	↑↓↑	↓?	↑↓↑	?↓	↑↓↑	??	C_3
r_{13}^{ET}	↑↓↓	↑↑	↑↓↓	↑?	↑↓↓	?↑	↑↓↓	??	C_2
r_{14}^{ET}	↑↓↓	↑↓	↑↓↓	↑?	↑↓↓	?↓	↑↓↓	??	C_2
r_{15}^{ET}	↑↓↓	↓↑	↑↓↓	↓?	↑↓↓	?↑	↑↓↓	??	C_4
r_{16}^{ET}	↑↓↓	↓↓	↑↓↓	↓?	↑↓↓	?↓	↑↓↓	??	C_4
r_{17}^{ET}	↓ **	↑↑	↓ **	↑?	↓ **	?↑	↓ **	??	C_5
r_{18}^{ET}	↓ **	↑↓	↓ **	↑?	↓ **	?↓	↓ **	??	C_6
r_{19}^{ET}	↓ **	↓↑	↓ **	↓?	↓ **	?↑	↓ **	??	C_5
r_{20}^{ET}	↓ **	↓↓	↓ **	↓?	↓ **	?↓	↓ **	??	C_6

Table 2 consists of four different subtables. Each of these subtables is an entire[1] decision tables (ET for entire decision table) representing a different degree of incomplete information. Table ET_1 shows the strategies of player R when it has complete information about the payoffs and, therefore, the actions of

---

[1] 'Entire' in a sense of the minimum game as depicted in Table 1.

player S. The tables $ET_2 - ET_4$ contain R's strategies when it faces incomplete information. This lack of knowledge of player R is indicated by question marks (?) in Table 2. In table ET_2 player R has no knowledge about the decision of player S at node D_{S1}. In ET_3 no information is given about the moves of player S at node D_{S1} and in table ET_4 player R does not know anything about the decisions of player S at any of its nodes, i.e., at the nodes D_{S1} and D_{S2}.

Table 3. Minimum decision tables (MT) of player R

Player ▷	Complete information		Incomplete information						Payoff
			Partial		Partial		Total		
	$MT_{min,1}$		$MT_{min,2}$		$MT_{min,3}$		$MT_{min,4}$		
	R	S	R	S	R	S	R	S	
r_1^{MT}	↑↑ *	↑ *	↑↑ *	↑ *	↑↑ *	?*	↑↑ *	?*	C_1
r_2^{MT}	↑↓ *	↑ *	↑↓ *	↑ *	↑↓ *	?*	↑↓ *	?*	C_2
r_3^{MT}	↑ * ↑	↓ *	↑ * ↑	↓ *	↑ * ↑	?*	↑ * ↑	?*	C_3
r_4^{MT}	↑ * ↓	↓ *	↑ * ↓	↓ *	↑ * ↓	?*	↑ * ↓	?*	C_4
r_5^{MT}	↓ **	* ↑	↓ **	*?	↓ **	* ↑	↓ **	*?	C_5
r_6^{MT}	↓ **	* ↑	↓ **	*?	↓ **	* ↓	↓ **	*?	C_6

The number of strategies shown in Table 2 can be reduced. The corresponding reduced set of strategies is depicted in Table 3 (MT for minimum decision table). Note, that player R overwrites unknown actions of player S, i.e., decisions that are marked by a question mark (?) in case they are irrelevant from its perspective (indicated by a star (*)). For example, r_1^{MT} in MT_4 is ↑↑ *?*. Although player R does not know the decision of player S at node D_{S2} it is indicated by a star (*) since it is irrelevant for player R whatever decision player S makes at this node.

4   Roughness of Games

In the subsequent sections, we discuss the concept of the roughness of a game. This could be applied to the entire decision tables as depicted in Table 2 as well as to the minimum decision tables as shown in Table 3. However, for the sake of simplicity we only apply it to the entire decision tables as shown in Table 2. We think that this table is easier and more intuitive to understand as an introductory example.

4.1   Rough Analyses of the Game with Imperfect Information

The decision tables $ET_1 - ET_4$ in Table 2 can be treated like normal rough decision tables, i.e., the methods developed for rough decision tables can be directly applied to the tables. For example, we can determine lower approximations and the boundaries of the corresponding sets. Note, in our case, the sets equal the payoffs of the players ($C_i = (c_{Ri}, c_{Si})$). We obtain for the subtable $ET_1 - ET_4$:

- Table ET_1 represents the case where player R has complete information. From a rough set perspective, this is indicated by the non-existence of any boundary. All strategies of player R, $r_1^{ET} - r_{20}^{ET}$, are assigned to lower approximations of the payoffs $C_1 - C_6$ (in rough set terms these are the sets $C_1 - C_6$).
- In table ET_2, the strategies r_{17}^{ET} and r_{18}^{ET} are indiscernible since they have identical attribute values of $\downarrow ** \uparrow$. However, they lead to different payoffs. In the case of r_{17}^{ET}, the payoff C_5 is obtained and the strategy r_{18}^{ET} leads to a payoff of C_6. Hence, the strategies r_{17}^{ET} and r_{18}^{ET} belong to the boundaries of C_5 and C_6. The same applies to r_{19}^{ET} and r_{20}^{ET}. They have identical attribute values, but the payoffs are different (C_5 and C_6, respectively). So, they also belong to the boundaries of C_5 and C_6. The remaining indiscernible strategies lead to identical payoffs. Therefore, they do not contradict each other and consequently belong to the lower approximations of the corresponding payoffs. E.g., the strategies r_1^{ET} and r_2^{ET} are indiscernible but lead to the same payoff of C_1. Hence, they are assigned to the lower approximation of the set C_1.
- Like in the case of ET_2, in table ET_3 we observe several indiscernible strategies that lead to different payoffs. The strategies r_1^{ET} and r_3^{ET} are indiscernible but lead to payoffs of C_1 and C_3; r_2^{ET} and r_4^{ET} are indiscernible but lead to C_1 and C_3; r_5^{ET} and r_7^{ET} are indiscernible but lead to C_1 and C_4; r_6^{ET} and r_8^{ET} are indiscernible but lead to C_1 and C_4; r_9^{ET} and r_{11}^{ET} are indiscernible but lead to C_2 and C_3; r_{10}^{ET} and r_{12}^{ET} are indiscernible but lead to C_2 and C_3; r_{13}^{ET} and r_{15}^{ET} are indiscernible but lead to C_2 and C_4; and finally, r_{14}^{ET} and r_{16}^{ET} are indiscernible but lead to C_2 and C_4. Only the four remaining strategies, $r_{17}^{ET} - r_{20}^{ET}$ belong to lower approximations: r_{17}^{ET} and r_{19}^{ET} are indiscernible but lead to the same payoff C_5 and r_{18}^{ET} and r_{20}^{ET} are indiscernible and also lead to a same payoff, in this case C_6. Hence, they are non-contradictory and, therefore, assigned to the lower approximations of the corresponding sets.
- In the case of totally incomplete information in table ET_4, all strategies belong to boundaries: $r_1^{ET} - r_4^{ET}$ to the boundaries of C_1 and C_2; $r_5^{ET} - r_8^{ET}$ to the boundaries of C_1 and C_4; $r_9^{ET} - r_{12}^{ET}$ to the boundaries of C_2 and C_3; $r_{13}^{ET} - r_{16}^{ET}$ to the boundaries of C_2 and C_4; $r_{17}^{ET} - r_{20}^{ET}$ to the boundaries of C_5 and C_6.

The memberships to the lower approximations (indicated by an underline $\underline{C_i}$) and boundaries (indicated by a hat $\widehat{C_i}$) of $C_1 - C_6$ of the strategies for $ET_1 - ET_4$ are summarized in Table 4.

As we can see from Table 4, the number of boundary objects is minimal for ET_1 which represents complete information and maximal in the case of totally incomplete information. As we discuss in the next section, this leads to the interpretation of the roughness of a set as indicator for the degree of incomplete information in a game.

Table 4. Lower approximations and boundaries

Lower approximation	Boundary
ET_1	
$\underline{C_1} = \{r_1^{ET}, r_2^{ET}, r_5^{ET}, r_6^{ET}\}$	$\widehat{C_1} = \emptyset$
$\underline{C_2} = \{r_9^{ET}, r_{10}^{ET}, r_{13}^{ET}, r_{14}^{ET}\}$	$\widehat{C_2} = \emptyset$
$\underline{C_3} = \{r_3^{ET}, r_4^{ET}, r_{11}^{ET}, r_{12}^{ET}\}$	$\widehat{C_3} = \emptyset$
$\underline{C_4} = \{r_7^{ET}, r_8^{ET}, r_{15}^{ET}, r_{16}^{ET}\}$	$\widehat{C_4} = \emptyset$
$\underline{C_5} = \{r_{17}^{ET}, r_{19}^{ET}\}$	$\widehat{C_5} = \emptyset$
$\underline{C_6} = \{r_{18}^{ET}, r_{20}^{ET}\}$	$\widehat{C_6} = \emptyset$
ET_2	
$\underline{C_1} = \{r_1^{ET}, r_2^{ET}, r_5^{ET}, r_6^{ET}\}$	$\widehat{C_1} = \emptyset$
$\underline{C_2} = \{r_9^{ET}, r_{10}^{ET}, r_{13}^{ET}, r_{14}^{ET}\}$	$\widehat{C_2} = \emptyset$
$\underline{C_3} = \{r_3^{ET}, r_4^{ET}, r_{11}^{ET}, r_{12}^{ET}\}$	$\widehat{C_3} = \emptyset$
$\underline{C_4} = \{r_7^{ET}, r_8^{ET}, r_{15}^{ET}, r_{16}^{ET}\}$	$\widehat{C_4} = \emptyset$
$\underline{C_5} = \emptyset$	$\widehat{C_5} = \{r_{17}^{ET}, r_{19}^{ET}\}$
$\underline{C_6} = \emptyset$	$\widehat{C_6} = \{r_{18}^{ET}, r_{20}^{ET}\}$
ET_3	
$\underline{C_1} = \emptyset$	$\widehat{C_1} = \{r_1^{ET}, r_2^{ET}, r_5^{ET}, r_6^{ET}\}$
$\underline{C_2} = \emptyset$	$\widehat{C_2} = \{r_9^{ET}, r_{10}^{ET}, r_{13}^{ET}, r_{14}^{ET}\}$
$\underline{C_3} = \emptyset$	$\widehat{C_3} = \{r_3^{ET}, r_4^{ET}, r_{11}^{ET}, r_{12}^{ET}\}$
$\underline{C_4} = \emptyset$	$\widehat{C_4} = \{r_7^{ET}, r_8^{ET}, r_{15}^{ET}, r_{16}^{ET}\}$
$\underline{C_5} = \{r_{17}^{ET}, r_{19}^{ET}\}$	$\widehat{C_5} = \emptyset$
$\underline{C_6} = \{r_{18}^{ET}, r_{20}^{ET}\}$	$\widehat{C_6} = \emptyset$
ET_4	
$\underline{C_1} = \emptyset$	$\widehat{C_1} = \{r_1^{ET}, r_2^{ET}, r_5^{ET}, r_6^{ET}\}$
$\underline{C_2} = \emptyset$	$\widehat{C_2} = \{r_9^{ET}, r_{10}^{ET}, r_{13}^{ET}, r_{14}^{ET}\}$
$\underline{C_3} = \emptyset$	$\widehat{C_3} = \{r_3^{ET}, r_4^{ET}, r_{11}^{ET}, r_{12}^{ET}\}$
$\underline{C_4} = \emptyset$	$\widehat{C_4} = \{r_7^{ET}, r_8^{ET}, r_{15}^{ET}, r_{16}^{ET}\}$
$\underline{C_5} = \emptyset$	$\widehat{C_5} = \{r_{17}^{ET}, r_{19}^{ET}\}$
$\underline{C_6} = \emptyset$	$\widehat{C_6} = \{r_{18}^{ET}, r_{20}^{ET}\}$

4.2 Roughness with Respect to Incomplete Information

In rough sets, the ratio of the cardinalities of the lower and upper approximations was originally defined as roughness [13]. We use a small common variation of the definition of the roughness ρ and take the quotient of the numbers of objects in boundaries to all objects as indicator for the roughness. When we apply roughness to the transformed game as depicted in the Tables 2 and 4 we obtain results as shown in Table 5.

Note, that we apply the concept of roughness to the minimal game as depicted in Table 1. Alternatively, we could also use the entire game (see Table 1). However, the entire game consists of four strategies $r_5^{EG} - r_8^{EG}$ that can be considered as one strategy r_5^{MG} with two irrelevant decisions. Therefore, we think that, generally, the minimal game should be taken. However, as discussed above, we do not strictly follow this rule in all places of our paper: we take Table 2 instead of Table 3 since we think that, in this particular case, taking Table 2 is more illustrative and easier to understand than an example based on Table 3.

Table 5. Roughness with respect to incomplete information

	ET_1	ET_2	ET_3	ET_4
Number of boundary strategies	0	4	16	20
Number of strategies	20	20	20	20
Incomplete information roughness ρ	0.0	0.2	0.8	1.0

The roughness observed in table ET_1 is $\rho = 0.0$ which indicates that information is complete for player R. In contrast to this, the roughness recorded in table ET_4 equals $\rho = 1.0$ revealing totally incomplete information from the perspective of player R. Of particular interest are the tables ET_2 and ET_3 which both represent games with partly incomplete information for player R. The roughnesses differ significantly with $\rho = 0.2$ for ET_2 and $\rho = 0.8$ for ET_3. These differences can be comprehended when we take a look on the original game in Fig. 3. Table ET_2 represents a game with missing information for player R about the payoffs C_5 and C_5 of player S, i.e., player R has no information about the decision of player S at node D_{S2}. Table ET_3 is related to missing information at node D_{S1}, i.e., player R does not know how player S decides at this node.

Obviously, the remaining subtree starting at D_{S1} is more complex in comparison to the subtree beginning at D_{S2}. While the latter subtree directly leads to two consequences (C_5 and C_6), the subtree starting at D_{S1} requires a further decision of player R either at D_{R1} or at D_{R2} depending on the decision taken by player S. Therefore, with respect to information, ET_2 is superior to ET_3 which is also observed in a lower roughness in subtable ET_2 in comparison to ET_3.

5   Conclusion

In the paper, we presented an example how an extensive-form game with incomplete information can be transformed into a rough decision table. Thus, it is possible to directly apply well-established methods from rough sets to this table, and, therefore, also to the underlying game. In our example, we illustrated this for the roughness. We showed that the observed roughness is an indicator for the degree of incomplete information in the original game. Obviously, further methods from rough set theory could also be applied to the rough decision table and interpreted in the context of the original game. However, also, vice versa, rough sets could possibly draw from the rich portfolio, in particular with respect to information, that has been developed in game theory. Therefore, it would be desirable to discuss the relationship of game theory and rough sets more intensively, including a more formal comparison that goes beyond the presented example. Both fields could possibly mutually benefit from each other.

References

1. Akerlof, G.A.: The market for "lemons": quality uncertainty and the market mechanism. Q. J. Econ. **84**(3), 488–500 (1970)
2. Apt, K.R., Grädel, E. (eds.): Lectures in Game Theory for Computer Scientists. Cambridge University Press, Cambridge (2011)
3. Fudenberg, D., Tirole, J.: Game Theory. MIT Press, Cambridge (1991)
4. Grzymala-Busse, J.: Rough set theory with applications to data mining. In: Negoita, M.G., Reusch, B. (eds.) Real World Applications of Computational Intelligence. Studies in Fuzziness and Soft Computing, vol. 179, pp. 221–244. Springer, Heidelberg (2005). doi:10.1007/11364160_7
5. Halpern, J.Y.: Computer science and game theory: a brief survey (2007). arXiv preprint: arXiv:cs/0703148
6. Hammerstein, P., Selten, R.: Game theory and evolutionary biology. In: Handbook of Game Theory with Economic Applications, vol. 2, pp. 929–993. Elsevier (1994)
7. Harsanyi, J.C.: Games with incomplete information played by "Bayesian" players, I–III. Manag. Sci. **14**, 159–183 (Part I), 320–334 (Part II), 486–502 (Part III) (1967/1968)
8. Herbert, J.P., Yao, J.T.: Game-theoretic risk analysis in decision-theoretic rough sets. In: Wang, G., Li, T., Grzymala-Busse, J.W., Miao, D., Skowron, A., Yao, Y. (eds.) RSKT 2008. LNCS, vol. 5009, pp. 132–139. Springer, Heidelberg (2008). doi:10.1007/978-3-540-79721-0_22
9. Herbert, J.P., Yao, J.T.: Game-theoretic rough sets. Fundam. Inform. **108**(3–4), 267–286 (2011)
10. Kreps, D.M.: Game Theory and Economic Modelling. Oxford University Press, Oxford (1990)
11. Morrow, J.D.: Game Theory for Political Scientists. Princeton University Press, Princeton (1994)
12. Pawlak, Z.: Rough sets. Int. J. Comput. Inf. Sci. **11**, 341–356 (1982)
13. Pawlak, Z.: Rough Sets: Theoretical Aspects of Reasoning About Data. Kluwer Academic Publishers, Dordrecht (1991)
14. Peters, G.: A rough perspective on information in extensive form games. In: Flores, V., et al. (eds.) IJCRS 2016. LNCS, vol. 9920, pp. 145–154. Springer, Cham (2016). doi:10.1007/978-3-319-47160-0_13
15. Tirole, J.: The Theory of Industrial Organization. MIT Press, Cambridge (1988)
16. Wang, B., Li, R., Perrizo, W.: Big Data Analytics in Bioinformatics and Healthcare. IGI Global, Hershey (2014)
17. Wang, J., Miao, D.: Analysis on attribute reduction strategies of rough set. J. Comput. Sci. Technol. **13**(2), 189–192 (1998)
18. Xu, J., Yao, L.: A class of two-person zero-sum matrix games with rough payoffs. Int. J. Math. Math. Sci. **2010**, Article ID 404792, 22 p. (2010). doi:10.1155/2010/404792

A Proposal of Machine Learning by Rule Generation from Tables with Non-deterministic Information and Its Prototype System

Hiroshi Sakai[1]($\boxtimes$), Michinori Nakata[2], and Junzo Watada[3]

[1] Graduate School of Engineering, Kyushu Institute of Technology,
Tobata, Kitakyushu 804-8550, Japan
sakai@mns.kyutech.ac.jp

[2] Faculty of Management and Information Science, Josai International University,
Gumyo, Togane, Chiba 283-0002, Japan
nakatam@ieee.org

[3] Department of Computer and Information Sciences, Universiti Teknologi
PETRONAS, 32610 Seri Iskandar, Perak Darul Ridzuan, Malaysia
junzo.watada@gmail.com

Abstract. A logical framework on *Machine Learning by Rule Generation* (MLRG) from tables with non-deterministic information is proposed, and its prototype system in SQL is implemented. In MLRG, the certain rules defined in *Rough Non-deterministic Information Analysis* (RNIA) are obtained at first, and each uncertain attribute value is estimated so as to cause the certain rules as many as possible, because the certain rules show us the most reliable information. This strategy is similar to the maximum likelihood estimation in statistics. By repeating this process, a standard table and the rules in its table are learned (or estimated) from a given table with non-deterministic information. Even though it will be hard to know the actual unknown values, MLRG will give a plausible estimation value.

Keywords: Machine learning by rule generation · Uncertainty · NIS-Apriori algorithm · SQL · Prototype

1 Introduction

The management of information incompleteness in tables [3,5,7–13,20] is still a very important issue in rough sets, data mining, machine learning, and soft computing. We followed *Nondeterministic Information Systems* (NISs) [9,10] and the missing values [5], and proposed the framework of *Rough Non-deterministic Information Analysis* (RNIA) [12,13]. Table 1 is an exemplary NIS Φ_{salary}, where each attribute value is given as a set or a missing value ?. We see that there is an actual value in each set but we do not know which is the actual value. We have characterized the rules in such NISs, and we are applying them to the several issues connected with information incompleteness.

© Springer International Publishing AG 2017
L. Polkowski et al. (Eds.): IJCRS 2017, Part I, LNAI 10313, pp. 535–551, 2017.
DOI: 10.1007/978-3-319-60837-2_43

Table 1. An exemplary NIS Φ_{salary}.

Object	Age	Depart(ment)	Smoke	Salary
$x1$	$\{young\}$	$\{first\}$	$\{yes\}$	$\{low\}$
$x2$	$\{young, senior\}$	$\{first, second, third\}$	$\{yes\}$	$\{low\}$
$x3$	$\{senior\}$	$\{second\}$	$\{yes, no\}$	$\{high\}$
$x4$	$\{young, senior\}$	$\{second\}$	$\{no\}$	$\{high\}$
$x5$	$\{young\}$	?	$\{yes, no\}$	$\{high\}$
$x6$	$\{senior\}$	$\{third\}$	$\{no\}$	$\{high\}$

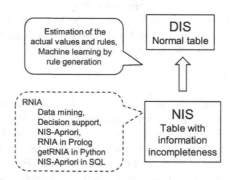

Fig. 1. A research map with respect to RNIA.

In RNIA, the *Apriori* algorithm [1] is extended to the *NIS-Apriori* algorithm [12,13], and it generates the certain rules and the possible rules. These rules with modality are defined by using all possible tables derived from NIS [12,13], and there may be a huge number of possible tables. For example, there are more than 10^{100} possible tables in the Mammographic data set in UCI machine learning repository [4]. Even though the definition of the certain rules and the possible rules is natural, it seemed hard to realize a rule generator for these rules due to the huge number of possible tables.

However, the NIS-Apriori algorithm affords a solution to this problem. Since it employs the mathematical property shown in [12,13], it does not depend upon the number of all possible tables. Furthermore, the NIS-Apriori algorithm is *sound* and *complete* [14] for the certain rules and the possible rules. Recently, we are considering a software tool in SQL [16] in order to handle the large size data sets. Some actual execution logs including the Mammographic data set are in the web page [17].

Figure 1 shows the research map, where the block with the broken lines shows previous research and the block with the solid line does the purpose in this paper. We are applying the NIS-Apriori algorithm to machine learning (or estimating

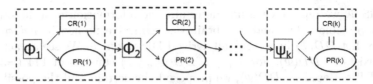

CR(i): A set of certain rules in NIS Φi,
PR(i): A set of possible rules in NIS Φi,
CR(1)⊂CR(2)⊂ ::: ⊂CR(k)=PR(k)⊂PR(k-1)⊂ ::: ⊂PR(1),

DIS ψ$_k$: Estimated DIS from Φ1,
CR(k)=PR(k): Learned rules from Φ1.

Fig. 2. A chart on machine learning by rule generation [15].

the actual attribute values) from NIS. The idea is the following: We obtain the certain rules in NIS Φ_i by using the NIS-Apriori algorithm, and we change Φ_i to NIS Φ_{i+1} so as to cause the obtained certain rules as many as possible [15]. By repeating this procedure, we finally obtain a standard table *Deterministic Information System* (DIS). Figure 2 shows a chart on *Machine Learning by Rule Generation* (MLRG).

As far as we know, the system based on the NIS-Apriori algorithm is unique, so a software tool on MLRG is also unique. Of course, it will be hard to know the unknown actual values, but MLRG will give a plausible estimation value. This paper is organized as follows: Sect. 2 surveys the framework of RNIA, and Sect. 3 proposes MLRG. Section 4 presents an experimental example, and Sect. 5 investigates some procedures in SQL. Section 6 concludes this paper.

2   Background of Rules in NISs and NIS-Apriori Based Rule Generation

This section briefly reviews RNIA, and describes how NIS-Apriori algorithm solves the computational problem for handling non-deterministic information.

2.1   RNIA and Rule Generation

At first, we clarify the rules in DIS. A pair $[A, val_A]$ of an attribute A and an attribute value val_A is called a *descriptor*. For a fixed decision attribute *Dec* and a set *CON* of attributes, an implication $\tau : \wedge_{A \in CON}[A, val_A] \Rightarrow [Dec, val]$ is (a candidate of) a *rule*, if τ satisfies the next two constraints for two given threshold values $0 < \alpha, \beta \leq 1.0$.

(1) $support(\tau)\,(=N(\tau)/|OB|) \geq \alpha$,
(2) $accuracy(\tau)\,(=N(\tau)/N(\wedge_{A \in CON}[A, val_A])) \geq \beta$.

Here, $N(*)$ means the number of the objects satisfying the formula $*$, and OB means a set of all objects.

In NIS Φ, we replace each non-deterministic information or a missing value ? with a possible value, and we obtain one DIS. We named it a *derived DIS* from NIS. Let $DD(\Phi)$ be a set of all derived DISs from Φ. We see an actual DIS ψ^{actual} exists in $DD(\Phi)$. For Φ_{salary}, $DD(\Phi_{salary})$ consists of 144 ($=3^2 \times 2^4$) derived DISs. Based on $DD(\Phi)$, we proposed the certain and the possible rules below:

Definition 1 [12,13].

(1) τ is a certain rule, if τ is a rule in each $\psi \in DD(\Phi)$,
(2) τ is a possible rule, if τ is a rule at least one $\psi \in DD(\Phi)$.

The above two types of rules follow the modal concepts [8] by Lipski. Since a certain rule τ is also a rule in an actual DIS ψ^{actual}, this τ is the most reliable. Every certain rule is not influenced by the information incompleteness. On the other hand, a possible rule may be a rule in an actual DIS ψ^{actual}. These two types of rules will be one example of three way decision [20] by Yao.

Even though the definition of rules seems natural, we need to handle a huge number of DISs. For this computational problem, we defined two sets for a descriptor $[A, val]$ below:

$inf([A, val]) = \{x : object \mid \text{the value of } x \text{ for A is a singleton set } \{val\}\}$,
$sup([A, val]) = \{x : object \mid \text{the value of } x \text{ for A is a set including } val\}$,
$inf(\wedge_{A \in CON}[A, val_A]) = \cap_{A \in CON} inf([A, val_A])$,
$sup(\wedge_{A \in CON}[A, val_A]) = \cap_{A \in CON} sup([A, val_A])$.

For example, $inf([age, young]) = \{x1, x5\}$ and $sup([age, young]) = \{x1, x2, x4, x5\}$ hold in Φ_{salary}. The actual equivalence class is between two sets. For $minsupp(\tau)$ ($=min_{\psi \in DD(\Phi)}\{support(\tau) \text{ by } \psi\}$) and $minacc(\tau)$ ($=min_{\psi \in DD(\Phi)}$ $\{accuracy(\tau) \text{ by } \psi\}$), we have the following which do not depend upon the number of $DD(\Phi)$.

$$\begin{aligned}
&\tau : \wedge_{A \in CON}[A, val_A] \Rightarrow [Dec, val], \\
&minsupp(\tau) = |inf(\wedge_{A \in CON}[A, val_A]) \cap inf([Dec, val])|/|OB|, \\
&minacc(\tau) = \frac{|inf(\wedge_{A \in CON}[A, val_A]) \cap inf([Dec, val])|}{|inf(\wedge_{A \in CON}[A, val_A])| + |OUTACC|}, \\
&OUTACC = \{sup(\wedge_{A \in CON}[A, val_A]) \setminus inf(\wedge_{A \in CON}[A, val_A])\} \\
&\quad \setminus inf([Dec, val]).
\end{aligned} \qquad (1)$$

The $OUTACC$ means a set of objects, from which we can obtain an implication $\tau' : \wedge_{A \in CON}[A, val_A] \Rightarrow [Dec, val']$ ($val \neq val'$, the same condition part and the different decision). Similarly, we can calculate $maxsupp(\tau)$ and $maxacc(\tau)$. We can also prove that there exists $\psi_{min} \in DD(\Phi)$ which makes both $support(\tau)$ and $accuracy(\tau)$ the minimum. There exists $\psi_{max} \in DD(\Phi)$ which makes both $support(\tau)$ and $accuracy(\tau)$ the maximum. Based on these results, we have the chart in Fig. 3 and Theorem 1.

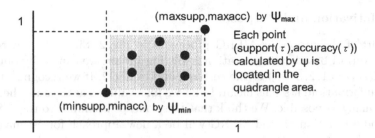

Fig. 3. For every implication τ, each point $(support(\tau), accuracy(\tau))$ by $\psi \in DD(\Phi)$ is located in a rectangle area.

Theorem 1 [12,13]. *For an implication τ, we have the following.*

(1) τ is a certain rule, if and only if $minsupp(\tau) \geq \alpha$ and $minacc(\tau) \geq \beta$.
(2) τ is a possible rule, if and only if $maxsupp(\tau) \geq \alpha$ and $maxacc(\tau) \geq \beta$.

Even though the certain rules and the possible rules depend upon $DD(\Phi)$, it is enough to examine two points ψ_{min} and ψ_{max}. Based on Theorem 1, we can escape from the exponential order problem. Without Theorem 1, it will be hard to handle rules in NISs like Mammographic data set, which has more than 10^{100} derived DISs.

2.2 NIS-Apriori Algorithm and Its Implementation

In order to handle the certain rules and the possible rules in NISs, we adjusted *Apriori* algorithm [1] to NISs, and named it *NIS-Apriori* algorithm [13]. NIS-Apriori algorithm consists of two phases, namely the certain rule generation phase and the possible rule generation phase. We employ *minsupp* and *minacc* values in certain rule generation, and we do *maxsupp* and *maxacc* values in possible rule generation. Since we can calculate *minsupp*, *minacc*, *maxsupp*, and *maxacc* by using *inf* and *sup* information, the NIS-Apriori algorithm is independent from the number of derived DISs.

Recently, we implemented the NIS-Apriori algorithm in SQL [16], and opened the execution logs [17], for example Lenses, Car Evaluation, Mammographic, Credit Card Approval, Congressional Voting data sets in UCI machine learning repository [4].

The analysis on the computational complexity of the NIS-Apriori algorithm is still in progress. This algorithm consists of two phases, and the Apriori algorithm is applied to each phase. Therefore, we figure out that the computational complexity of the NIS-Apriori algorithm is more than twice the complexity of the Apriori algorithm.

3   Machine Learning by Rule Generation in NISs

This section proposes the framework of MLRG including two strategies for learning by rule generation, and applies RNIA to realizing the MLRG process.

3.1   Motivation and Purpose

The chart of the proposing MLRG process is in Fig. 2. Since the environment for NIS-Apriori based rule generation is getting better, we can easily obtain the sets $CR(i)$ $(i = 1, 2, 3, \cdots)$ of the certain rules in Fig. 2. If we recognize them as reliable information, it seems natural that we fix a value so as to cause the reliable rules as many as possible. We think that this concept is similar to the maximum likelihood estimation [2] and MLRG will be a new approach for estimating one DIS from NIS. In this paper, we propose this framework and realize a software tool for MLRG.

3.2   Some Properties on CR(i) and PR(i)

Let us consider Fig. 2, then we easily have the properties in the following.

Proposition 1. *In Fig. 2, $CR(i) \subset PR(i)$ holds in every Φ_i.*

Proof. In Φ_i, $\tau \in CR(i)$ is a rule in each $\psi \in DD(\Phi_i)$. So, τ satisfies the condition of the possible rule, namely $\tau \in PR(i)$.

Proposition 2. *In Fig. 2, $CR(i) \subset CR(i + 1)$ holds.*

Proof. In Φ_i and Φ_{i+1} in Fig. 2, $DD(\Phi_{i+1}) \subset DD(\Phi_i)$ holds, because some unfixed attribute values in $DD(\Phi_i)$ are fixed in $DD(\Phi_{i+1})$. Let $minsupp(\tau, i)$ be $minsupp(\tau)$ and $minacc(\tau, i)$ be $minacc(\tau)$ in Φ_i. Since $minsupp(\tau, i)$ is the minimum value in $DD(\Phi_i)$ and $minsupp(\tau, i+1)$ is the minimum value in $DD(\Phi_{i+1})$, clearly $minsupp(\tau, i) \leq minsupp(\tau, i + 1)$ and $minacc(\tau, i) \leq minacc(\tau, i + 1)$ hold. So, if τ is a certain rule in Φ_i, we have $\alpha \leq minsupp(\tau, i) \leq minsupp(\tau, i+1)$ and $\beta \leq minacc(\tau, i) \leq minacc(\tau, i + 1)$. This means τ is also a certain rule in Φ_{i+1}, namely $CR(i) \subset CR(i + 1)$.

Proposition 3. *In Fig. 2, $PR(i + 1) \subset PR(i)$ holds.*

Proof. In Φ_i and Φ_{i+1} in Fig. 2, $DD(\Phi_{i+1}) \subset DD(\Phi_i)$ holds. Let $maxsupp(\tau, i)$ and $maxacc(\tau, i)$ be $maxsupp(\tau)$ and $maxacc(\tau)$ in Φ_i, respectively. Then, clearly $maxsupp(\tau, i + 1) \leq maxsupp(\tau, i)$ and $maxacc(\tau, i + 1) \leq maxacc(\tau, i)$ hold. Therefore, if τ is a possible rule in Φ_{i+1}, we have $\alpha \leq maxsupp(\tau, i + 1) \leq maxsupp(\tau, i)$ and $\beta \leq maxacc(\tau, i + 1) \leq maxacc(\tau, i)$. This means τ is also a possible rule in Φ_i, namely $PR(i + 1) \subset PR(i)$.

Therefore, for the fixed threshold values α and β, we have the following inclusion relation in Fig. 2. The uncertainty is sequentially reduced, and finally we have one DIS ψ_k.

$$CR(1) \subset CR(2) \subset \cdots \subset CR(k) = PR(k) \subset \cdots \subset PR(2) \subset PR(1). \quad (2)$$

3.3   The Framework of MLRG and Two Strategies

In NIS Φ_i, we fix some attribute values, and have a new NIS Φ_{i+1}. Since there is the inclusion relations in formula (2), we finally have the rules $CR(k) (= PR(k))$ in DIS ψ_k. We named this process MLRG. So, the most important issue on MLRG is how we fix some attribute values.

For this issue, we employ the certain rules in Φ_i. Let $\tau_1, \tau_2, \cdots, \tau_m$ be the certain rules in $CR(i)$. The order of each τ_i is defined such that the first priority is *minacc* (descending order) and the second priority is *minsupp* (descending order). By using the ordered certain rules, we propose the next two strategies.

(Strategy 1) (Positive Unification) *In an object x, a value is assigned to the unfixed value so as to cause a higher ordered certain rule.*

(Strategy 2) (Contradiction Prevention) *In an object x, a value is assigned so as not to contradict a higher ordered certain rule.*

Two strategies try to support the obtained certain rules in Φ_i much more. We may see this strategy as that we locally find a functional dependency between attributes and we reinforce its dependency much more. These strategies will also take the similar role of the maximum likelihood estimation in statistics. Each parameter is estimated so as to cause the likelihood function to the maximum in statistics, and each value is estimated so as to support the higher ordered certain rules in MLRG.

Remark 1. In the prototype system based on two strategies, we use only the certain rules with one condition, namely the certain rules in the form of $[A, val_A] \Rightarrow [Dec, val]$ for simplicity. We do not consider the certain rules in the form of $p_1 \wedge p_2 \Rightarrow q$ and $p_1 \wedge p_2 \wedge p_3 \Rightarrow q$. (The current system by NIS-Apriori algorithm generates rules with maximally three conditions.)

Remark 2. Two strategies employ the certain rules with one condition in Φ_i. Without the background of certain rule generation in RNIA, we can consider neither two strategies nor MLRG.

4   An Example of MLRG

For simplicity, we present an example of MLRG, and we describe the details of the prototype system in the next section.

We employ NIS Φ_{salary} in Fig. 4 in this section. This Φ_{salary} consists of 6 objects, 4 attributes, age: {young, senior}, depart(ment): {first, second, third}, smoke: {yes, no}, and salary: {low, high}. Non-deterministic information is expressed by a list like {*young, senior*}. The decision attribute is 'salary'. There are 144 $(= 2^4 \times 3^2)$ derived DISs in Φ_{salary}.

Figure 5 shows $CR(1)$ $(support(\tau) \geq 0.3$ and $accuracy(\tau) \geq 0.6)$ in Fig. 2, and Fig. 6 does $PR(1)$ $(support(\tau) \geq 0.3$ and $accuracy(\tau) \geq 0.6)$ in Fig. 2. In this case, each rule occasionally consists of one condition, however generally NIS-Apriori algorithm generates the rules with maximally three conditions.

```
mysql> select * from `table 1`;
+--------+---------------+--------------------+---------+--------+
| object | age           | depart             | smoke   | salary |
+--------+---------------+--------------------+---------+--------+
|      1 | young         | first              | yes     | low    |
|      2 | [young,senior]| [first,second,third]| yes    | low    |
|      3 | senior        | second             | [yes,no]| high   |
|      4 | [young,senior]| second             | no      | high   |
|      5 | young         | ?                  | [yes,no]| high   |
|      6 | senior        | third              | no      | high   |
+--------+---------------+--------------------+---------+--------+
6 rows in set (0.00 sec)
```

Fig. 4. The original data set of Φ_{salary}.

```
mysql> select * from c1_rule;
+-----------+------------+--------+--------+------------+---------+--------+
| Crule_num | att1       | val1   | deci   | deci_value | minsupp | minacc |
+-----------+------------+--------+--------+------------+---------+--------+
| c1        | age        | senior | salary | high       | 0.333   | 0.667  |
| c2        | depart     | second | salary | high       | 0.333   | 0.667  |
| c3        | smoke      | no     | salary | high       | 0.333   | 1.000  |
| 0         | end_attrib | NULL   | NULL   | NULL       | NULL    | NULL   |
+-----------+------------+--------+--------+------------+---------+--------+
4 rows in set (0.00 sec)
```

Fig. 5. $CR(1)$: three certain rules satisfying $support(\tau) \geq 0.3$ and $accuracy(\tau) \geq 0.6$ in each of 144 derived DISs.

```
mysql> select * from p1_rule;
+-----------+------------+--------+--------+------------+---------+--------+
| Prule_num | att1       | val1   | deci   | deci_value | maxsupp | maxacc |
+-----------+------------+--------+--------+------------+---------+--------+
| p1        | age        | senior | salary | high       | 0.500   | 1.000  |
| p2        | age        | young  | salary | high       | 0.333   | 0.667  |
| p3        | age        | young  | salary | low        | 0.333   | 0.667  |
| p4        | depart     | first  | salary | low        | 0.333   | 1.000  |
| p5        | depart     | second | salary | high       | 0.500   | 1.000  |
| p6        | depart     | third  | salary | high       | 0.333   | 1.000  |
| p7        | smoke      | no     | salary | high       | 0.667   | 1.000  |
| p8        | smoke      | yes    | salary | low        | 0.333   | 1.000  |
| 0         | end_attrib | NULL   | NULL   | NULL       | NULL    | NULL   |
+-----------+------------+--------+--------+------------+---------+--------+
9 rows in set (0.00 sec)
```

Fig. 6. $PR(1)$: eight possible rules satisfying $support(\tau) \geq 0.3$ and $accuracy(\tau) \geq 0.6$ in at least one derived DIS.

The set of rules in DIS ψ^{actual} is a superset of $CR(1)$ and a subset of $PR(1)$. By using MLRG, we estimate ψ^{actual} and the rules in ψ^{actual}. Let us see Fig. 7. The step1 ('salary', 6, 0.3, 0.6) command (the decision attribute is 'salary', the number of objects is 6, $minsupp \geq 0.3$, and $minacc \geq 0.6$) generates 3 certain rules in Fig. 5, then fixes some attribute values based on two strategies. The step2

```
mysql> call step1('salary',6,0.3,0.6);
Query OK, 0 rows affected (0.37 sec)

mysql> call step2('salary',6,0.1,0.3);
Query OK, 0 rows affected (0.33 sec)

mysql> select * from estimated_dis;
+--------+--------+--------+-------+--------+
| object | age    | depart | smoke | salary |
+--------+--------+--------+-------+--------+
|      1 | young  | first  | yes   | low    |
|      2 | young  | first  | yes   | low    |
|      3 | senior | second | no    | high   |
|      4 | senior | second | no    | high   |
|      5 | young  | second | no    | high   |
|      6 | senior | third  | no    | high   |
+--------+--------+--------+-------+--------+
6 rows in set (0.00 sec)
```

Fig. 7. An execution of machine learning by rule generation and an estimated DIS.

```
mysql> select * from rule1;
+------------+--------+--------+------------+---------+----------+
| att1       | val1   | deci   | deci_value | support | accuracy |
+------------+--------+--------+------------+---------+----------+
| age        | senior | salary | high       | 0.500   | 1.000    |
| age        | young  | salary | low        | 0.333   | 0.667    |
| depart     | first  | salary | low        | 0.333   | 1.000    |
| depart     | second | salary | high       | 0.500   | 1.000    |
| smoke      | no     | salary | high       | 0.667   | 1.000    |
| smoke      | yes    | salary | low        | 0.333   | 1.000    |
| end_attrib | NULL   | NULL   | NULL       | NULL    | NULL     |
+------------+--------+--------+------------+---------+----------+
7 rows in set (0.00 sec)
```

Fig. 8. The estimated rules ($CR(3) = PR(3)$) satisfying $support(\tau) \geq 0.3$ and $accuracy(\tau) \geq 0.6$ in the estimated DIS ψ^{actual}.

('salary', 6, 0.1, 0.3) command (the decision attribute is 'salary', the number of objects is 6, $minsupp \geq 0.1$, and $minacc \geq 0.3$) does the similar procedure. In order to find more certain rules, we loosened the constraints to $support(\tau) \geq 0.1$ and $accuracy(\tau) \geq 0.3$. After the step1 and step2 commands, one DIS (a table estimated_dis in Fig. 7) is estimated from Φ_{salary} with 144 derived DISs. In this case, the MLRG process terminates in the three steps below, and 6 rules in Fig. 8 are estimated.

$$CR(1) \subset CR(2) \subset CR(3) = PR(3) \subset PR(2) \subset PR(1). \tag{3}$$

In $CR(1)$, there are three certain rules in Fig. 5, and new three rules are learned by the process in Fig. 7. On the other hand, in $PR(1)$ there are eight possible rules in Fig. 6, and two possible rules are removed by the process in Fig. 7.

5   SQL Procedures in MLRG

We have implemented SQL procedures, step1, step2, step3, pstep, apri, and other translation procedures. The arguments in each procedure except the translation are ('decision_attribute', number_of_objects, support, accuracy).

5.1   NRDF Format

In data sets, we usually have the csv format. This is very familiar, however the name of the attribute and the number of all attributes may be different in each data set. For handling various types of data sets uniquely, it is useful to employ another unified format. Otherwise, the program is depending upon the number of the attributes and the name of the attribute.

```
mysql> select * from nrdf1 where object=5;
+--------+--------+--------+------+
| object | attrib | value  | det  |
+--------+--------+--------+------+
|      5 | age    | young  |   1  |
|      5 | depart | first  |   3  |
|      5 | depart | second |   3  |
|      5 | depart | third  |   3  |
|      5 | salary | high   |   1  |
|      5 | smoke  | no     |   2  |
|      5 | smoke  | yes    |   2  |
+--------+--------+--------+------+
7 rows in set (0.00 sec)
```

Fig. 9. The NRDF format of the object 5.

We employ the NRDF format [18], which is the extended RDF (resource description framework) format. The RDF format may be called as the EAV (entity-attribute-value) format [6,19]. The NRDF format employs 4 attributes, *object*, *attrib*, *value*, and *det*. Figure 9 shows a part of the NRDF format of Φ_{salary}. In order to specify non-deterministic information, we added the 4th column *det*. The value of *det* means the number of possible values. If $det = 1$, this means that the value is deterministic. Otherwise, we know the value is non-deterministic, and see the number of values by *det*.

(Merit 1 of using the NRDF format) *Even though we need to prepare a translation program to each csv file, we can handle any data set uniformly after this translation.*

This NRDF format is useful for managing MLRG process in Fig. 2. Namely, we at first prepare a table nrdf1 in the NRDF format, and we sequentially revise the tables to nrdf2, nrdf3, $\cdots$ in each step. If $det = 1$ holds for each tuple, each value for non-deterministic information is estimated, and we stop the process of MLRG.

(Merit 2 of using the NRDF format) *By using the tables $nrdf_i$ in the NRDF format, we can control the process of MLRG.*

5.2 SQL Procedure step1

The role of step1 is below:

(step1-1) An execution of certain rule generation by using the table nrdf1, and a generation of some data tables.
(step1-2) A generation of the table nrdf2 from the table nrdf1.

After certain rule generation in step1-1, we have some tables. The step1 command copies nrdf1 to nrdf2, and employs two strategies, namely the positive unification strategy and the contradiction prevention strategy, for revising nrdf2.

```
mysql> select * from cll_revise where object=b;
+-----+--------+--------+--------+------+--------+--------+------+
| num | object | attrib1 | value1 | det1 | attrib2 | value2 | det2 |
+-----+--------+--------+--------+------+--------+--------+------+
|   7 |      5 | smoke  | no     |    2 | salary | high   |    1 |
|   8 |      5 | depart | second |    3 | salary | high   |    1 |
+-----+--------+--------+--------+------+--------+--------+------+
2 rows in set (0.00 sec)

mysql> select * from `table 1` where object=5;
+--------+-------+---------------------+--------+--------+
| object | age   | depart              | smoke  | salary |
+--------+-------+---------------------+--------+--------+
|      5 | young | [first,second,third] | [yes,no] | high |
+--------+-------+---------------------+--------+--------+
1 row in set (0.00 sec)

mysql> select * from nrdf2 where object=5;
+--------+--------+--------+-----+
| object | attrib | value  | det |
+--------+--------+--------+-----+
|      5 | age    | young  |   1 |
|      5 | depart | second |   1 |
|      5 | salary | high   |   1 |
|      5 | smoke  | no     |   1 |
+--------+--------+--------+-----+
4 rows in set (0.00 sec)
```

Fig. 10. Some tables generated by the step1 command and the revised table nrdf2.

```
mysql> select * from nrdf1 where object=2;
+--------+--------+--------+------+
| object | attrib | value  | det  |
+--------+--------+--------+------+
|      2 | age    | senior |    2 |
|      2 | age    | young  |    2 |
|      2 | depart | first  |    3 |
|      2 | depart | second |    3 |
|      2 | depart | third  |    3 |
|      2 | salary | low    |    1 |
|      2 | smoke  | yes    |    1 |
+--------+--------+--------+------+
7 rows in set (0.00 sec)

mysql> select * from nrdf2 where object=2;
+--------+--------+--------+-----+
| object | attrib | value  | det |
+--------+--------+--------+-----+
|      2 | age    | young  |   1 |
|      2 | depart | first  |   2 |
|      2 | depart | third  |   2 |
|      2 | salary | low    |   1 |
|      2 | smoke  | yes    |   1 |
+--------+--------+--------+-----+
5 rows in set (0.00 sec)
```

Fig. 11. The revision of the object 2 in the table nrdf2.

We focus on the revision on the object 5 in Fig. 10. This is an example of Strategy 1, which tries to cause the higher ordered certain rules as many as possible. There are two certain rules with one condition related to the object 5 (a table c11_revise). As for [smoke, no] in the object 5, the attribute value is not fixed, since $det1 = 2$. So, the step1 command removes the tuples (5, smoke, yes, 2) and (5, smoke, no, 2) from nrdf2, and newly adds (5, smoke, no, 1) to nrdf2. As for [depart, second], the step1 command does the same procedure. Each value of the object 5 is fixed in the table nrdf2 in Fig. 10.

Then, we show an example of Strategy 2, which tries to reduce the contradiction to the higher ordered certain rules. This Strategy 2 is applied after the application of the procedure on Strategy 1. In an object x, if the condition part in x matches a certain rule τ and $det > 1$, we know the tuple of x contradicts τ, because the revision by Strategy 1 is finished. (If Strategy 1 was applied, every det is changed to $det = 1$.) In this case, we fix the attribute values so as not to contradict τ. In Figs. 5 and 11, the certain rule with one condition [depart, second] $\Rightarrow$ [salary, high] in $CR(1)$ contradicts [depart, second] $\Rightarrow$ [salary, low] in the object 2. So, the step1 command removes (2, depart, second, 3) from nrdf2, and revises other two tuples to (2, depart, first, 2) and (2, depart, third, 2). Similarly, since the certain rule [age, senior] $\Rightarrow$ [salary, high] in $CR(1)$ contradicts the implication [age, senior] $\Rightarrow$ [salary, low] in the object 2, the step1 command adds (2, age, young, 1) to nrdf2 after removing (2, age, young, 2) and (2, age, senior, 2).

5.3 SQL Procedure pstep

In MLRG, we sequentially reduce the threshold values for obtaining new certain rules with one condition, and we change the table nrdf_n to the next table nrdf_{n+1}. However, each certain rule is defined as an implication of a definite object [12,13], so some parts of non-deterministic information may not be changed, even if we employ the lower threshold values. For solving this problem, we define a procedure pstep. The role of the procedure pstep is below:

(pstep-1) An execution of possible rule generation in RNIA, and a generation of some data tables.
(pstep-2) A generation of the table pnrdf from the current table nrdf_n.

Since a possible rule is defined as an implication of any object [12,13], we usually have the table nrdf_{n+1}, where $\det = 1$ for any object, after executing the pstep procedure. For example, the step1 command employs three certain rules in Fig. 5 for revising the table nrdf1. On the other hand, the pstep command does eight possible rules in Fig. 6 for revising the table nrdf1. Actually, the estimated_dis in Fig. 7 was obtained after applying the pstep command in the first step. So, we can intentionally terminate MLRG process by using the procedure pstep. However, the application of the pstep command means the use of possible information from NIS. There will be the volatility risk of the possible rules. We may have inconsistent possible rules like $p \Rightarrow q_1$ and $p \Rightarrow q_2$. Thus, we should consider the application of the procedure pstep after the procedure step2 or step3.

5.4 SQL Procedure apri

The procedure apri simulates the Apriori algorithm in DISs. The following is the overview of the series of the SQL procedures in the implemented procedure apri.

```
delimiter //
create procedure apri
begin
create table condi(); /* Generate a table of the specified conditions,
            decision attribute, objects, α, β */
create table deci(); /* Generate a table of the decision */
create table con1(); /* Generate a table of the condition */
create table rule1(); /* Generate a table of the rules satisfying
            support ≥ α and accuracy ≥ β */
create table rest1(); /* Generate a table of the rules satisfying
            support ≥ α and accuracy < β */
create table con20(),create table con21(),create table con2();
            /* Generate a table of the condition part,
            whose element is p₁ ∧ p₂ from rest1 */
create table con2_infc0(),create table con2_infc();
            /* Generate a table of inf (=sup) information */
```

```
create table rule21(),create table rule2(); /* Generate a table of
            rule2 satisfying support ≥ α and accuracy ≥ β */
create table rest2(); /* Generate a table of rest2 satisfying
            support ≥ α and accuracy < β */
create table con30(),create table con31(),create table con3();
            /* Generate a table of the condition part,
            whose element is p₁ ∧ p₂ ∧ p₃ from rest2 */
create table con3_inf0(),create table con3_infc();
            /* Generate a table of inf (=sup) information */
create table rule31(),create table rule3(); /* Generate a table of
            rule3 satisfying support ≥ α and accuracy ≥ β */
end //
```

The procedure apri generates rules in the forms of $p_1 \Rightarrow q$, $p_1 \wedge p_2 \Rightarrow q$, and $p_1 \wedge p_2 \wedge p_3 \Rightarrow q$. The details of this apri are in the web page [17]. In Fig. 8, the procedure apri generated 6 rules in the form of $p_1 \Rightarrow q$ from the estimated DIS ψ^{actual}.

```
mysql> select count(*) from nrdf1 where det>1;
+----------+
| count(*) |
+----------+
|      784 |
+----------+
1 row in set (0.00 sec)

mysql> call step1('a1',435,0.3,0.6);
Query OK, 0 rows affected (1 min 2.98 sec)

mysql> select count(*) from nrdf2 where det>1;
+----------+
| count(*) |
+----------+
|      398 |
+----------+
1 row in set (0.00 sec)

mysql> call step2('a1',435,0.1,0.3);
Query OK, 0 rows affected (1 min 39.94 sec)

mysql> select count(*) from nrdf3 where det>1;
+----------+
| count(*) |
+----------+
|        0 |
+----------+
1 row in set (0.00 sec)
```

Fig. 12. The MLRG process of the Congressional Voting data set.

5.5 Implementation of MLRG Procedures in SQL

Since each procedure is implemented as a stored procedure in SQL, each procedure will be applicable to any SQL system. The text file size of all procedures is about 53 KB, and we employed windows desktop PC (3.30 GHz).

Figure 12 shows the MLRG process on the Congressional Voting data set in UCI machine learning repository. It consists of 435 objects, the decision attribute 'a1', 16 condition attributes, and 392 missing values ?. The decision attribute value is either democrat or republic. Each attribute value for other attribute is either yes or no, so we replaced each missing values with a set $\{democrat, republic\}$ or a set $\{yes, no\}$, and generated NIS $\Phi_{congress}$. The number of $DD(\Phi_{congress})$ is $2^{392} \doteqdot 10^{100}$.

The step1 command at first generated $CR(1)$ satisfying $support(\tau) \geq 0.3$ and $accuracy(\tau) \geq 0.6$ in each of about 10^{100} derived DISs. In this step, about a half of the unfixed values are fixed. The number of the unfixed values is 199 (=398/2) in the middle of Fig. 12. Then, the step2 command generated certain rules with one condition satisfying $support(\tau) \geq 0.1$ and $accuracy(\tau) \geq 0.3$ in each of all derived DISs. In this step, each missing value is fixed, and one DIS ψ^{actual} is estimated. The details of the execution logs including the logs of Mammographic data set are in [17].

6 Concluding Remarks and Discussion

This paper briefly described the framework of MLGR. In real life, if we recognize the proper and attractive property (namely, certain rules), we will take an action (namely, the recovery of non-deterministic information) to support the recognized proper and attractive property as much as possible. Intuitively, MLRG takes such a strategy, and we see the estimated DIS ψ^{actual} and the rules in ψ^{actual} will be reasonable.

We have also implemented a software tool on NIS-Apriori based rule generation in SQL, and applied it to MLGR. We know data recovery by using the functional dependency in a standard table. In a table with uncertainty, we generate the ordered certain rules by the *minacc* value and the *minsupp* value, and make use of the concept on the maximum likelihood estimation in statistics. Then, the plausible value for non-deterministic information is estimated.

As for this prototype, we have the following consideration.

(1) Since SQL has the high versatility, NIS-Apriori in SQL and MLRG in SQL will offer the useful environment for analyzing tables with uncertainty.
(2) It is necessary to clarify the relation between the threshold values and the estimated DIS. If we specify the higher threshold values in the procedure step1, we have less certain rules with one condition and we may need several steps for terminating MLRG process. On the other hand, if we specify the lower threshold values, we have lots of certain rules with one condition and MLRG process will easily terminate. We need to consider what is the proper

threshold values for MLRG process. Furthermore, if we employ the procedure pstep with the lower threshold values, MLRG process will terminate in the first step. Each non-deterministic information is estimated by using the ordered possible rules. However in possible rule generation, we consider only one DIS from several possible tables, so there is a very big volatility. We may have two contradictory rules like $p \Rightarrow q1$ and $p \Rightarrow q2$. So, there is a tradeoff between the steps of the termination and the quality of the estimated DIS. We have not touched this issue yet.

(3) In this prototype, we faithfully simulated the MLRG process, so the procedures in SQL may have meaningless parts. It is necessary to brush up this software tool.

Acknowledgment. The authors would be grateful to the anonymous referees for their useful comments. This work is supported by JSPS (Japan Society for the Promotion of Science) KAKENHI Grant Number 26330277.

References

1. Agrawal, R., Srikant, R.: Fast algorithms for mining association rules in large databases. In: Proceedings of VLDB 1994, pp. 487–499. Morgan Kaufmann (1994)
2. Aldrich, J.: R.A. Fisher and the making of maximum likelihood 1912–1922. Stat. Sci. **12**(3), 162–176 (1997)
3. Clark, P., Grzymala-Busse, J.: Mining incomplete data with many attribute-concept values and "do not care" conditions. In: Proceedings of IEEE Big Data 2015, pp. 1597–1602 (2015)
4. Frank, A., Asuncion, A.: UCI machine learning repository. School of Information and Computer Science, University of California, Irvine (2010). http://mlearn.ics.uci.edu/MLRepository.html
5. Grzymala-Busse, J.: Data with missing attribute values: generalization of indiscernibility relation and rule induction. Trans. Rough Sets **1**, 78–95 (2004)
6. Kowalski, M., Stawicki, S.: SQL-based heuristics for selected KDD tasks over large data sets. In: Proceedings of FedCSIS 2012, pp. 303–310 (2012)
7. Kryszkiewicz, M.: Rules in incomplete information systems. Inf. Sci. **113**(3–4), 271–292 (1999)
8. Lipski, W.: On databases with incomplete information. J. ACM **28**(1), 41–70 (1981)
9. Orłowska, E., Pawlak, Z.: Representation of nondeterministic information. Theor. Comput. Sci. **29**(1–2), 27–39 (1984)
10. Pawlak, Z.: Systemy Informacyjne: Podstawy Teoretyczne (in Polish) WNT (1983)
11. Sahri, Z., Yusof, R., Watada, J.: FINNIM: iterative imputation of missing values in dissolved gas analysis dataset. IEEE Trans. Ind. Inform. **10**(4), 2093–2102 (2014)
12. Sakai, H., et al.: Rules and apriori algorithm in non-deterministic information systems. Trans. Rough Sets **9**, 328–350 (2008)
13. Sakai, H., Wu, M., Nakata, M.: Apriori-based rule generation in incomplete information databases and non-deterministic information systems. Fundam. Inform. **130**(3), 343–376 (2014)
14. Sakai, H., Wu, M.: The completeness of NIS-Apriori algorithm and a software tool getRNIA. In: Mori, M. (ed.) Proceedings of International Conference on AAI 2014, pp. 115–121. IEEE (2014)

15. Sakai, H., Liu, C.: A consideration on learning by rule generation from tables with missing values. In: Mine, T. (ed.) Proceedings of International Conference on AAI 2015, pp. 183–188. IEEE (2015)
16. Sakai, H., Liu, C., Zhu, X., Nakata, M.: On NIS-Apriori based data mining in SQL. In: Flores, V., et al. (eds.) IJCRS 2016. LNCS (LNAI), vol. 9920, pp. 514–524. Springer, Cham (2016). doi:10.1007/978-3-319-47160-0_47
17. Sakai, H.: Execution logs by RNIA software tools (2016). http://www.mns.kyutech.ac.jp/~sakai/RNIA
18. Ślęzak, D., Sakai, H.: Automatic extraction of decision rules from non-deterministic data systems: theoretical foundations and SQL-based implementation. In: Ślęzak, D., Kim, T.H., Zhang, Y., Ma, J., Chung, K.I. (eds.) DTA 2009. CCIS, vol. 64, pp. 151–162. Springer, Heidelberg (2009). doi:10.1007/978-3-642-10583-8_18
19. Swieboda, W., Nguyen, S.: Rough set methods for large and spare data in EAV format. In: Proceedings of IEEE RIVF 2012, pp. 1–6 (2012)
20. Yao, Y.Y.: Three-way decisions with probabilistic rough sets. Inf. Sci. **180**, 314–353 (2010)

Rough Set Analysis of Classification Data with Missing Values

Marcin Szeląg[1](✉), Jerzy Błaszczyński[1], and Roman Słowiński[1,2]

[1] Institute of Computing Science, Poznań University of Technology,
60-965 Poznań, Poland
{mszelag,jblaszczynski,rslowinski}@cs.put.poznan.pl
[2] Systems Research Institute, Polish Academy of Sciences, 01-447 Warsaw, Poland

Abstract. In this paper, we consider a rough set analysis of non-ordinal and ordinal classification data with missing attribute values. We show how this problem can be addressed by several variants of Indiscernibility-based Rough Set Approach (IRSA) and Dominance-based Rough Set Approach (DRSA). We propose some desirable properties that a rough set approach being able to handle missing attribute values should possess. Then, we analyze which of these properties are satisfied by the considered variants of IRSA and DRSA.

Keywords: Rough set · Indiscernibility-based rough set approach · Dominance-based rough set approach · Missing values

1 Introduction

In data mining concerning classification problems, it is quite common to have missing values for attributes describing objects [12]. To cope with the problem of missing values, several approaches have been proposed. The usual approach is to assume that some value(s) can represent correctly the missing one. Then, the missing values are replaced in some way by so-called representative values. In this case, the question is how to avoid data distortion [12].

Rough set approach to handling missing values avoids making changes in the data. The problem is addressed by a proper definition of the relation employed to form granules of knowledge.

In this work, we consider both Indiscernibility-based Rough Set Approach (IRSA), in which value sets of attributes describing objects are not supposed to be ordered, and Dominance-based Rough Set Approach (DRSA), which takes into account an order in the value sets of attributes, monotonically related with the order of decision classes. We focus on the following types of IRSA:

- classical rough set approach (CRSA) proposed by Pawlak [16],
- Variable Consistency Indiscernibility-based Rough Set Approach (VC-IRSA) proposed by Błaszczyński et al. [2,3],

and on the following types of DRSA:

© Springer International Publishing AG 2017
L. Polkowski et al. (Eds.): IJCRS 2017, Part I, LNAI 10313, pp. 552–565, 2017.
DOI: 10.1007/978-3-319-60837-2_44

- classical Dominance-based Rough Set Approach (CDRSA) proposed by Greco et al. [8,9,17],
- Variable Consistency Dominance-based Rough Set Approach (VC-DRSA) proposed by Błaszczyński et al. [2,3].

Adaptations of the classical rough set model [16] to handling missing values, were presented in [6,7,10,11,14,19]. Proposals of handling missing values in dominance-based rough set approaches were given in [1,5–7,13,15,20]. We review all these approaches and analyze their properties, refining and extending the research results presented in [1,4].

The rest of this paper is structured as follows. Section 2 reminds basics of IRSA and DRSA. In Sect. 3, we present ways of handling missing values in IRSA and DRSA. We also propose a list of desirable properties that IRSA and DRSA adapted to handle missing values should possess. After characterizing variants of IRSA and DRSA coping with missing values, we discover non-dominated variants with respect to these properties. Section 4 concludes the paper.

2 Basics of IRSA and DRSA

Classification data analyzed by IRSA and DRSA concern a finite universe U of objects described by attributes from a finite set A. Moreover, A is divided into disjoint sets of condition attributes C and decision attributes Dec. The value set of $q \in C \cup Dec$ is denoted by V_q, $q(x) \in V_q$ denotes evaluation of object $x \in U$ on attribute q, and $V_C = \prod_{q=1}^{|C|} V_q$ is called C-evaluation space. For simplicity, we assume that $Dec = \{d\}$. Values of attribute d are class labels.

Decision attribute d makes a partition of set U into n disjoint sets of objects, called *decision classes*. We denote this partition by $\mathcal{X} = \{X_1, \ldots, X_n\}$.

2.1 Basics of IRSA

In IRSA, the value sets of attributes are not considered to be ordered, and thus *indiscernibility relation* is employed. Object y is considered to be indiscernible with object x (denoted by yIx) if and only if (iff) $q(y) = q(x)$ for each $q \in C$. Given an object $x \in U$,

$$I(x) = \{y \in U : yIx\} \tag{1}$$

denotes a set (granule) of objects indiscernible with referent x.

Given a non-ordinal classification problem, two objects $x, y \in U$ are said to be *inconsistent* with respect to (w.r.t.) indiscernibility relation, if they are indiscernible but they are assigned to different decision classes. In order to handle such inconsistency, one calculates lower approximations of considered classes.

CRSA. In CRSA [16], *lower approximation* of class $X_i \in \mathcal{X}$ is defined as

$$\underline{X_i} = \{x \in U : I(x) \subseteq X_i\}, \tag{2}$$

and *upper approximation* of class $X_i \in \mathcal{X}$ is defined as

$$\overline{X_i} = \{x \in U : I(x) \cap X_i \neq \emptyset\}. \tag{3}$$

VC-IRSA. In VC-IRSA [2,3], *probabilistic lower approximation* of class $X_i \in \mathcal{X}$ is defined using an *object consistency measure*. We employ cost-type measure ϵ_{X_i}:

$$\epsilon_{X_i}(x) = \frac{|I(x) \cap \neg X_i|}{|\neg X_i|}, \tag{4}$$

where $\neg X_i = U \setminus X_i$. Then,

$$\underline{X_i} = \{x \in X_i : \epsilon_{X_i}(x) \leq \theta_{X_i}\}, \tag{5}$$

where threshold $\theta_{X_i} \in [0,1]$. In the following, we will denote this version of VC-IRSA by ϵ-VC-IRSA.

In [3], we introduced some *monotonicity properties* required from an object consistency measure. For IRSA, relevant properties are: $(m1)$ – monotonicity w.r.t. growing set of attributes, and $(m2)$ – monotonicity w.r.t. growing set of objects (class). As proved in [3], ϵ_{X_i} has both property $(m1)$ and property $(m2)$.

2.2   Basics of DRSA

In DRSA, it is supposed that value sets of condition attributes, as well as decision classes, are ordered. Then, it is often meaningful to consider *monotonicity constraints* (*monotonic relationships*) between ordered class labels and values of attributes expressed on ordinal or cardinal (numerical) scales [8,9,17]. In order to make a meaningful representation of classification decisions, one has to consider the *dominance relation* D in the C-evaluation space. Let us denote by $\succeq_q$ the *weak preference relation* over U confined to single attribute $q \in C$:

$$y \succeq_q x \Leftrightarrow \begin{cases} q(y) \text{ is not missing,} \\ q(x) \text{ is not missing,} \\ q(y) \text{ is at least as good as } q(x). \end{cases} \tag{6}$$

Then, classically (i.e., when there are no missing attribute values), given $x, y \in U$, object y is said to *dominate* object x, denoted by yDx, iff $y \succeq_q x$ for each $q \in C$. Moreover, y is said to *be dominated* by x, denoted by $y \, \mathcal{Q} \, x$, iff $x \succeq_q y$ for each $q \in C$. Let us observe that, classically, yDx iff $x \, \mathcal{Q} \, y$.

Dominance relations D and $\mathcal{Q}$ are partial preorders, i.e., they are reflexive, transitive, and not necessarily complete. For any object $x \in U$, two types of dominance cones can be defined in the C-evaluation space. Positive dominance cone with the origin in x w.r.t. relation D:

$$D^+(x) = \{y \in U : yDx\}, \tag{7}$$

and negative dominance cone with the origin in x w.r.t. relation D:

$$D^-(x) = \{y \in U : xDy\}. \tag{8}$$

In DRSA, if $1 \leq i < j \leq n$, then class X_i is considered to be worse than X_j. Moreover, rough approximations concern unions of classes: upward unions $X_i^{\geq} = \bigcup_{t \geq i} X_t$, and downward unions $X_i^{\leq} = \bigcup_{t \leq i} X_t$, where $i = 1, \ldots, n$.

CDRSA. In CDRSA [8,9,17], *lower approximations* of unions of classes $X_i^{\geq}$, $X_i^{\leq}$, $i = 1, \ldots, n$, are defined using strict inclusion relation:

$$\underline{X_i^{\geq}} = \{x \in U : D^+(x) \subseteq X_i^{\geq}\}, \quad \underline{X_i^{\leq}} = \{x \in U : D^-(x) \subseteq X_i^{\leq}\}. \tag{9}$$

Moreover, *upper approximations* of unions of classes $X_i^{\geq}$, $X_i^{\leq}$ are defined as

$$\overline{X_i^{\geq}} = \{x \in U : D^-(x) \cap X_i^{\geq} \neq \emptyset\}, \quad \overline{X_i^{\leq}} = \{x \in U : D^+(x) \cap X_i^{\leq} \neq \emptyset\}. \tag{10}$$

VC-DRSA. Definition (9) appears to be too restrictive in practical applications. This explains the interest in VC-DRSA [2,3] which is a probabilistic extension of CDRSA. We use *object consistency measures* $\epsilon_{X_i^{\geq}} : U \to [0,1]$, $\epsilon_{X_i^{\leq}} : U \to [0,1]$, introduced in [2,3]:

$$\epsilon_{X_i^{\geq}}(x) = \frac{|D^+(x) \cap \neg X_i^{\geq}|}{|\neg X_i^{\geq}|}, \quad \epsilon_{X_i^{\leq}}(x) = \frac{|D^-(x) \cap \neg X_i^{\leq}|}{|\neg X_i^{\leq}|}. \tag{11}$$

Then, *probabilistic lower approximations* of $X_i^{\geq}$, $X_i^{\leq}$, $i = 1, \ldots, n$, are defined as

$$\underline{X_i^{\geq}} = \{x \in X_i^{\geq} : \epsilon_{X_i^{\geq}}(x) < \theta_{X_i^{\geq}}\}, \quad \underline{X_i^{\leq}} = \{x \in X_i^{\leq} : \epsilon_{X_i^{\leq}}(x) \leq \theta_{X_i^{\leq}}\}, \tag{12}$$

where $\theta_{X_i^{\geq}}, \theta_{X_i^{\leq}} \in [0,1)$. In the following, we will denote this version of VC-DRSA by ϵ-VC-DRSA.

As proved in [3], $\epsilon_{X_i^{\geq}}$, $\epsilon_{X_i^{\leq}}$ have monotonicity properties $(m1)$, $(m2)$, and $(m4)$ (monotonicity w.r.t. dominance relation), sufficient in practical applications.

3   Different Ways of Handling Missing Values in IRSA and DRSA

In the following, a missing attribute value is denoted by $*$. We assume that each object $x \in U$ has at least one known value, i.e., for each $x \in U$ there exists $q \in C$ such that $q(x) \neq *$. Moreover, we use symbol X to denote an approximated set of objects. In IRSA, X denotes a single decision class $X_i \in \mathcal{X}$. In DRSA, X denotes a union of decision classes $X_i^{\geq}$ or $X_i^{\leq}$, $i \in \{1, \ldots, n\}$.

3.1   Adaptations of IRSA to Handle Missing Values

Handling of missing attribute values requires a proper adaptation of IRSA by redefinition of the indiscernibility relation I. Once we fix this definition, we can proceed by calculating rough approximations of decision classes, and then inducing decision rules from data structured in the rough set way.

The approaches resulting from different definitions of the indiscernibility relation are denoted by CRSA-mv_j and ϵ-VC-IRSA-mv_j, and the respective indiscernibility relations are denoted by I_j, where j stands for the version id. When these approaches are described jointly, we use denotation IRSA-mv_j.

It is important to underline that due to missing values, considered indiscernibility relation I_j may miss some properties, like symmetry or transitivity. For this reason, in the following, we employ generalized definitions of rough approximations proposed in [18], where indiscernibility relation is only assumed to be reflexive (so it may be not symmetric and/or not transitive). According to [18],

$$I_j^{-1}(x) = \{y \in U : xI_jy\} \tag{13}$$

denotes the set (granule) of objects with which x is indiscernible (to which x is similar). Then, in CRSA-mv_j, *generalized lower approximation* of class $X_i \in \mathcal{X}$ is defined as

$$\underline{X_i} = \{x \in U : I_j^{-1}(x) \subseteq X_i\}. \tag{14}$$

Generalized upper approximation of class $X_i \in \mathcal{X}$ is defined as

$$\overline{X_i} = \bigcup_{x \in X_i} I_j(x). \tag{15}$$

Let us remark that if I_j is symmetric, then $I_j^{-1}(x) = I_j(x)$, and then, definitions (14) and (2) are equivalent [18].

Analogously, ϵ-VC-IRSA is adjusted to the case of I_j, possibly being not symmetric, by redefining object consistency measure ϵ_{X_i}, given by (4), in the following way:

$$\epsilon_{X_i}(x) = \frac{|I_j^{-1}(x) \cap \neg X_i|}{|\neg X_i|}. \tag{16}$$

IRSA-mv_1 employs the indiscernibility relation defined in [6,7], which we denote by I_1. This relation is considered as a directional statement where a subject is compared to a referent which cannot have missing values. Subject y is considered to be indiscernible with referent x iff for each $q \in C$, $q(x) \neq *$, and either $q(y) = q(x)$ or $q(y) = *$. Thus, it is not true that xI_1x when object $x \in U$ has some missing attribute values (i.e., I_1 is, in general, not reflexive). Nevertheless, it is still interesting to see consequences of adapting IRSA by using relation I_1.

Note that in [6,7], lower approximation of class X_i was not defined using (14), and moreover, some properties considered in these papers (like rough inclusion or complementarity), were defined with respect to subset U_C of the universe U, where U_C is composed of all objects from U which have no missing value. Thus, we have to verify if these properties hold also for U.

IRSA-$mv_{1.5}$ [19] can be considered as an improvement over IRSA-mv_1. It defines a reflexive and transitive similarity relation without imposing that a referent cannot have missing values. In this approach, subject y is considered to be indiscernible with referent x iff $q(y) = q(x)$ for each $q \in C$ such that $q(y) \neq *$. Let us remark that this approach is treating missing values as "lost" ones (see, e.g., [10,11]).

IRSA-mv_2 [6,7,14,19] employs a reflexive and symmetric tolerance relation. In this approach, subject y is considered to be indiscernible with referent x iff for each $q \in C$ there is $q(y) = q(x)$, or $q(y) = *$, or $q(x) = *$. Note that this approach is treating missing values as "do not care" ones (see, e.g., [10,11]).

IRSA-mv_3 is a new approach which is an indiscernibility-based counterpart of DRSA-mv_3 proposed in [1]. In this approach, subject y is considered to be indiscernible with referent x iff $q(y) = q(x)$ for each $q \in C$ such that $q(x) \neq *$.

3.2   Desirable Properties of IRSA Adapted to Handle Missing Values

We consider the following desirable properties of IRSA-mv_j, $j = 1, 1.5, 2, 3$:

1. Property S (reflecting symmetry of indiscernibility relation): IRSA-mv_j has property S iff $yI_jx \leftrightarrow xI_jy$, for any $x, y \in U$.
2. Property R (reflecting reflexivity of indiscernibility relation): IRSA-mv_j has property R iff xI_jx, for any $x \in U$.
3. Property T (reflecting transitivity of indiscernibility relation): IRSA-mv_j has property T iff $yI_jx \wedge xI_jz \Rightarrow yI_jz$, for any $x, y, z \in U$.
4. Property B (robustness): given $x \in U$, let $C^x = \{q \in C : q(x) \neq *\}$; IRSA-$mv_j$ has property B iff for each $x \in \underline{X}$, $I_j^{-1'}(x) \cap \neg X \subseteq I_j^{-1}(x) \cap \neg X$, where $I_j^{-1'}(x)$ is a set of objects such that in C^x-evaluation space, object x is indiscernible with them.
5. Property P (reflecting precisiation of data): IRSA-mv_j has property P iff the lower approximation of any $X \subseteq U$ does not shrink when any missing attribute value is replaced by some non-missing value.
6. Property RI (rough inclusion): IRSA-mv_j has property RI iff $\underline{X} \subseteq X \subseteq \overline{X}$, for any $X \subseteq U$.
7. Property C (complementarity): IRSA-mv_j has property C iff $\underline{X} = U \setminus \overline{\neg X}$, for any $X \subseteq U$.
8. Property M_1 (monotonicity w.r.t. growing set of attributes): IRSA-mv_j has property M_1 iff the lower approximation of any $X \subseteq U$ does not shrink when set P is extended by new attributes.
9. Property M_2 (monotonicity w.r.t. growing set of objects): IRSA-mv_j has property M_2 iff the lower approximation of any $X \subseteq U$ does not shrink when this set is augmented by new objects.
10. Property MT (transitivity of membership to lower approximation): IRSA-mv_j has property MT iff for any $X \subseteq U$ and for any $x, y \in U$ it is true that $x \in \underline{X} \wedge y \in X \wedge xI_jy \Rightarrow y \in \underline{X}$.

Comparing to the list of desirable properties introduced in [4], we propose new property B which postulates that an object x, belonging to the lower approximation of class X_i when considering all condition attributes, should also belong to this approximation when considering only these attributes, for which evaluation of x is not missing. Moreover, we modify definition of property MT to reflect definition of generalized lower approximation given by (14) (for CRSA-mv_j), and by (5), (16) (for ϵ-VC-IRSA-mv_j).

The properties of IRSA-mv_j, $j = 1, 1.5, 2, 3$, are summarized in Table 1, where **T** and F denote presence and absence of a given property, respectively. Moreover, in case of two symbols $\cdot/\cdot$, the first (resp. the second) one concerns only CRSA (resp. only ϵ-VC-IRSA).

Table 1. Properties of IRSA-mv_j, $j = 1, 1.5, 2, 3$

Property/Approach	IRSA-mv_1	IRSA-$mv_{1.5}$	IRSA-mv_2	IRSA-mv_3
S	F	F	T	F
R	F	T	T	T
T	T	T	F	T
B	F	T	T	F
P	F	F	T	F
RI	F	T	T	T
C	F/T	T	T	T
M_1	T	T	T	T
M_2	T	T	T	T
MT	T	T	F	T

According to Table 1, IRSA-$mv_{1.5}$ and IRSA-mv_3 dominate IRSA-mv_1, which has the least number of desirable properties; IRSA-mv_3 is dominated by IRSA-$mv_{1.5}$. Thus, taking into account the considered properties, we can conclude that there are two non-dominated approaches: IRSA-$mv_{1.5}$ and IRSA-mv_2.

3.3   Adaptations of DRSA to Handle Missing Values

Handling of missing attribute values requires a proper adaptation of DRSA by redefinition of the dominance relations D and $\mathcal{D}$. Once we fix these definitions, we can proceed by calculating rough approximations of unions of decision classes, and then inducing decision rules from data structured in the rough set way.

In this sub-section, we review several ways of adapting DRSA to missing values known from the literature, and we propose some new adaptations. All of them are based on specific definitions of dominance relations.

The approaches, resulting from different definitions of the dominance relations, are denoted by CDRSA-mv_j and ϵ-VC-DRSA-mv_j, and the respective dominance relations are denoted by D_j and $\mathcal{C}_j$, where j stands for the version id. When these approaches are described jointly, we use denotation DRSA-mv_j.

It is important to underline that due to missing values, an approach employing dominance relation D_j may miss some properties, like transitivity. Moreover, it may be the case that yD_jx while not $x\,\mathcal{C}_j\,y$ (lack of a specific kind of symmetry). For this reason, in the following, we employ generalized definitions of rough approximations formulated in [20], related to generalized definitions of rough approximations proposed for IRSA in [18]. These generalized definitions are valid for the case when considered relations D_j and $\mathcal{C}_j$ are reflexive (regardless of their being transitive or satisfying $yD_jx \Leftrightarrow x\,\mathcal{C}_j\,y$).

According to [20], for any object $x \in U$, apart from dominance cones $D_j^+(x)$ and $D_j^-(x)$, two more types of dominance cones in the C-evaluation space should be considered. Positive dominance cone with the origin in x w.r.t. relation $\mathcal{C}_j$:

$$\mathcal{C}_j^+(x) = \{y \in U : x\,\mathcal{C}_j\,y\}, \tag{17}$$

and negative dominance cone with the origin in x w.r.t. relation $\mathcal{C}_j$:

$$\mathcal{C}_j^-(x) = \{y \in U : y\,\mathcal{C}_j\,x\}. \tag{18}$$

Let us observe that, when the description of objects has no missing values, $\mathcal{C}_j^+(x) = D_j^+(x)$ and $\mathcal{C}_j^-(x) = D_j^-(x)$. Then, according to [20], in CDRSA-mv_j:

- *generalized lower approximation* of $X_i^{\geq}$, $i \in \{1, \ldots, n\}$, is defined as

$$\underline{X_i^{\geq}} = \{x \in U : \mathcal{C}_j^+(x) \subseteq X_i^{\geq}\}, \tag{19}$$

  where $\mathcal{C}_j^+(x)$ is read as "the set of objects that x is dominated by";
- *generalized upper approximation* of $X_i^{\geq}$, $i \in \{1, \ldots, n\}$, is defined as

$$\overline{X_i^{\geq}} = \{x \in U : D_j^-(x) \cap X_i^{\geq} \neq \emptyset\}, \tag{20}$$

  where $D_j^-(x)$ is read as "the set of objects that x dominates";

- *generalized lower approximation* of $X_i^{\leq}$, $i \in \{1, \ldots, n\}$, is defined as

$$\underline{X_i^{\leq}} = \{x \in U : D_j^-(x) \subseteq X_i^{\leq}\}, \tag{21}$$

  where $D_j^-(x)$ is read as "the set of objects that x dominates";
- *generalized upper approximation* of $X_i^{\leq}$, $i \in \{1, \ldots, n\}$, is defined as

$$\overline{X_i^{\leq}} = \{x \in U : \mathcal{C}_j^+(x) \cap X_i^{\leq} \neq \emptyset\}, \tag{22}$$

  where $\mathcal{C}_j^+(x)$ is read as "the set of objects that x is dominated by".

Note that when yD_jx implies $x\,\mathcal{C}_j\,y$, and vice versa (presence of a specific kind of symmetry), then:

- the lower approximation of a union of classes $X_i^{\geq}$ defined by (19) is identical to the lower approximation of the same union defined by (9);
- the upper approximation of a union of classes $X_i^{\leq}$ defined by (22) is identical to the upper approximation of the same union defined by (10).

Analogously, ϵ-VC-DRSA is generalized by redefining object consistency measures $\epsilon_{X_i^{\geq}}$, $\epsilon_{X_i^{\leq}}$, given by (11), in the following way:

$$\epsilon_{X_i^{\geq}}(x) = \frac{|\mathcal{D}_j^+(x) \cap \neg X_i^{\geq}|}{|\neg X_i^{\geq}|}, \qquad \epsilon_{X_i^{\leq}}(x) = \frac{|D_j^-(x) \cap \neg X_i^{\leq}|}{|\neg X_i^{\leq}|}. \qquad (23)$$

DRSA-mv_1 employs two dominance relations defined in [6,7], which we denote by D_1 and $\mathcal{D}_1$. These relations are considered as directional statements where subject y is compared to referent x which cannot have missing values:

- subject y *dominates* referent x (denoted by yD_1x) iff for each $q \in C$, $q(x) \neq *$, and either $y \succeq_q x$ or $q(y) = *$;
- subject y *is dominated by* referent x (denoted by $y \, \mathcal{D}_1 \, x$) iff for each $q \in C$, $q(x) \neq *$, and either $x \succeq_q y$ or $q(y) = *$.

In view of the above definitions of D_1 and $\mathcal{D}_1$, neither xD_1x nor $x \, \mathcal{D}_1 \, x$ (i.e., D_1, $\mathcal{D}_1$ are not reflexive), in general. Nevertheless, it is still interesting to see consequences of adapting DRSA to handle missing values by using relations D_1 and $\mathcal{D}_1$. Note that in [6,7], lower approximations of unions of classes $X_i^{\geq}$ and $X_i^{\leq}$ were not defined using (19) and (21), and moreover, some properties considered in these papers (like rough inclusion or complementarity), were defined with respect to $U_C \subseteq U$, where U_C is composed of all objects from U which have no missing value. Thus, we have to verify if these properties hold also for U.

DRSA-$mv_{1.5}$ [20] can be considered as an improvement over DRSA-mv_1. In this approach, the authors propose two relations (called in [20] *similarity dominance relations*), which we denote by $D_{1.5}$ and $\mathcal{D}_{1.5}$:

- subject y *dominates* referent x (denoted by $yD_{1.5}x$) iff $y \succeq_q x$ for each $q \in C$ such that $q(y) \neq *$;
- subject y *is dominated by* referent x (denoted by $y \, \mathcal{D}_{1.5} \, x$) iff $x \succeq_q y$ for each $q \in C$ such that $q(y) \neq *$.

Taking into account the semantics of missing values considered in [10,11], it can be said that DRSA-$mv_{1.5}$ treats missing values as "lost" values.

DRSA-mv_2 was first proposed in [6,7], and extended in [5] to handle imprecise evaluations on attributes and imprecise assignments to decision classes, both modeled by intervals. When considering missing values only, each object is assigned to a single class, and each missing attribute value corresponds to an interval spanning over entire value set of this attribute. This implies the following definitions of so-called *possible dominance relations*, denoted by D_2 and $\mathcal{D}_2$:

- subject y *dominates* referent x (denoted by yD_2x) iff for each $q \in C$, $y \succeq_q x$, or $q(y) = *$, or $q(x) = *$;

- subject y *is dominated by* referent x (denoted by $y \, \mathcal{D}_2 \, x$) iff for each $q \in C$, $x \succeq_q y$, or $q(y) = *$, or $q(x) = *$.

Taking into account the semantics of missing values considered in [10, 11], it can be said that DRSA-mv_2 treats missing values as "do not care" values.

In DRSA-$mv_{2.5}$ [13], two dominance relations (called in [13] *generalized extended dominance relations*) are defined as in DRSA-mv_2, only with additional condition that the ratio of the number of "common" attributes (i.e., attributes for which both x and y have simultaneously a non-missing value) and the number of all attributes in set C is not less than a given user-defined threshold $\lambda \in [0,1]$. We denote these relations by $D_{2.5}$ and $\mathcal{D}_{2.5}$. The additional condition was introduced to restrict the dominance relations used in DRSA-mv_2 to pairs of objects that have at least one, or more, "common" attribute(s).

In DRSA-mv_3 [1], we employ dominance relations D_3 and $\mathcal{D}_3$, defined as:

- subject y *dominates* referent x (denoted by yD_3x) iff $y \succeq_q x$ for each $q \in C$ such that $q(x) \neq *$;
- subject y *is dominated by* referent x (denoted by $y \, \mathcal{D}_3 \, x$) iff $x \succeq_q y$ for each $q \in C$ such that $q(x) \neq *$.

DRSA-mv_4 uses the concept of a *lower-end dominance relation* introduced in [5]. Resulting dominance relations D_4 and $\mathcal{D}_4$ are defined as:

- subject y *dominates* referent x (denoted by yD_4x) iff for each $q \in C$, $y \succeq_q x$, or $q(x) = *$, or $q(x) = \inf(V_q)$;
- subject y *is dominated by* referent x (denoted by $y \, \mathcal{D}_4 \, x$) iff for each $q \in C$, $x \succeq_q y$, or $q(y) = *$, or $q(y) = \inf(V_q)$,

where $\inf(V_q)$ denotes the worst value in V_q (if no such value exists, $\inf(V_q) = -\infty$).

DRSA-mv_5 uses the concept of an *upper-end dominance relation* introduced in [5]. Resulting dominance relations D_5 and $\mathcal{D}_5$ are defined as:

- subject y *dominates* referent x (denoted by yD_5x) iff for each $q \in C$, $y \succeq_q x$, or $q(y) = *$, or $q(y) = \sup(V_q)$;
- subject y *is dominated by* referent x (denoted by $y \, \mathcal{D}_5 \, x$) iff for each $q \in C$, $x \succeq_q y$, or $q(x) = *$, or $q(x) = \sup(V_q)$,

where $\sup(V_q)$ denotes the best value in V_q (if there is no such value, $\sup(V_q) = \infty$).

In DRSA-mv_6 [15], the authors define so-called *new extended dominance relation*, which we denote by D_6. It is an α-cut of fuzzy dominance relation $\widetilde{D}$, such that $\widetilde{D}(y,x)$ reflects a possibility of yDx, for $y, x \in U$. Threshold $\alpha \in [0,1]$ is a parameter estimated using decision-theoretic rough set model. This approach assumes that the value set of each attribute is discrete. Relation $\widetilde{D}$ is defined as

$$\widetilde{D}(y,x) = \prod_{q \in C} \widetilde{\succeq}_q(y,x), \tag{24}$$

where *fuzzy weak preference relation* over U confined to single attribute $q \in C$

$$\widetilde{\succeq_q}(y,x) = \begin{cases} 0, & \text{if } q(y) \neq *, q(x) \neq *, \text{not } y \succeq_q x \\ 1, & \text{if } q(y) \neq *, q(x) \neq *, y \succeq_q x \\ \frac{|\{v:v\in V_q, v \text{ is not worse than } q(x)\}|}{|V_q|}, & \text{if } q(y) = *, q(x) \neq * \\ \frac{|\{v:v\in V_q, q(y) \text{ is not worse than } v\}|}{|V_q|}, & \text{if } q(y) \neq *, q(x) = * \\ \frac{1}{2} + \frac{1}{2|V_q|}, & \text{if } q(y) = *, q(x) = * \end{cases}$$

(25)

Then,

$$D_6 = \{(y,x) \in U \times U : \widetilde{D}(y,x) \geq \alpha\} \cup \{(x,x) : x \in U\}, \tag{26}$$

where threshold $\alpha \in [0,1]$. Moreover, once can define dominance relation $\mathcal{D}_6$ as

$$\mathcal{D}_6 = \{(y,x) \in U \times U : \widetilde{\mathcal{D}}(y,x) \geq \alpha\} \cup \{(x,x) : x \in U\}, \tag{27}$$

where fuzzy dominance relation $\widetilde{\mathcal{D}}$, reflecting for a pair $(y,x) \in U \times U$ the possibility of $y \mathcal{D} x$, is defined as

$$\widetilde{\mathcal{D}}(y,x) = \prod_{q\in C} \widetilde{\succeq_q}(x,y). \tag{28}$$

3.4 Desirable Properties of DRSA Adapted to Handle Missing Values

We consider the following desirable properties of DRSA-mv_j, where $j = 1, 1.5, 2, 2.5, 3, \ldots, 6$:

1. Property S (reflecting a specific kind of symmetry): DRSA-mv_j has property S iff $y D_j x \Leftrightarrow x \mathcal{D}_j y$, for any $x, y \in U$.
2. Property R (reflecting reflexivity of dominance relations): DRSA-mv_j has property R iff $x D_j x$ and $x \mathcal{D}_j x$, for any $x \in U$.
3. Property T (reflecting transitivity of dominance relations): DRSA-mv_j has property T iff $y D_j x \wedge x D_j z \Rightarrow y D_j z$, and $y \mathcal{D}_j x \wedge x \mathcal{D}_j z \Rightarrow y \mathcal{D}_j z$, for any $x, y, z \in U$.
4. Property B (robustness): let $C^x = \{q \in C : q(x) \neq *\}$; DRSA-$mv_j$ has property B iff the following two conditions hold simultaneously:
   - for each $x \in X_i^\geq$, $\mathcal{D}_j^{+\prime}(x) \cap \neg X_i^\geq \subseteq \mathcal{D}_j^{+}(x) \cap \neg X_i^\geq$, where $\mathcal{D}_j^{+\prime}(x)$ is a positive dominance cone with the origin in x w.r.t. relation $\mathcal{D}_j$, defined in the C^x-evaluation space,
   - for each $x \in X_i^\leq$, $D_j^{-\prime}(x) \cap \neg X_i^\leq \subseteq D_j^{-}(x) \cap \neg X_i^\leq$, where $D_j^{-\prime}(x)$ is a negative dominance cone with the origin in x w.r.t. relation D_j, defined in the C^x-evaluation space.
5. Property P (reflecting precisiation of data): DRSA-mv_j has property P iff the lower approximation of any $X \subseteq U$ does not shrink when any missing attribute value is replaced by some non-missing value.
6. Property RI (rough inclusion): DRSA-mv_j has property RI iff $\underline{X} \subseteq X \subseteq \overline{X}$, for any $X \subseteq U$.

7. Property C (complementarity): DRSA-mv_j has property C iff $\underline{X} = U \setminus \overline{\neg X}$, for any $X \subseteq U$.
8. Property M_1 (monotonicity w.r.t. growing set of attributes): DRSA-mv_j has property M_1 iff the lower approximation any $X \subseteq U$ does not shrink when set P is extended by new attributes.
9. Property M_2 (monotonicity w.r.t. growing union of classes): DRSA-mv_j has property M_2 iff for any $X \subseteq U$, the lower approximation of X does not shrink when this set is augmented by new objects.
10. Property M_3 (monotonicity w.r.t. super-union of classes): DRSA-mv_j has property M_3 iff given any two upward unions of classes $X_i^{\geq}, X_k^{\geq}$, with $1 \leq i < k \leq n$, there is $\underline{X_i^{\geq}} \supseteq \underline{X_k^{\geq}}$, and, moreover, given any two downward unions of classes $X_i^{\leq}, X_k^{\leq}$, with $1 \leq i < k \leq n$, there is $\underline{X_i^{\leq}} \subseteq \underline{X_k^{\leq}}$.
11. Property M_4 (monotonicity w.r.t. dominance relation): $\overline{\text{DRSA-}mv_j}$ has property M_4 iff the following two conditions hold simultaneously:
    - for any $X_i^{\geq} \subseteq U$, with $i \in \{1, \ldots, n\}$, and for any $x, y \in U$ such that $x \, \mathcal{C}_j \, y$, it is true that $(x \in \underline{X_i^{\geq}} \wedge y \in X_i^{\geq} \Rightarrow y \in \underline{X_i^{\geq}})$;
    - for any $X_i^{\leq} \subseteq U$, with $i \in \{1, \ldots, n\}$, and for any $x, y \in U$ such that $x D_j y$, it is true that $(x \in \underline{X_i^{\leq}} \wedge y \in X_i^{\leq} \Rightarrow y \in \underline{X_i^{\leq}})$.

Comparing to the list of desirable properties introduced in [1], we propose new property B which postulates that an object x, belonging to the lower approximation of any union of classes when considering all condition attributes, should also belong to this approximation when considering only these attributes, for which evaluation of x is not missing. Moreover, we modify definition of property M_4 to reflect definitions of generalized lower approximations.

Note that there is a correspondence between the above properties M_1, M_2, M_3, and M_4, and monotonicity properties (m1), (m2), (m3), and (m4), introduced in [3]. However, in VC-DRSA-mv_j, it may happen that for some $k \in \{1, \ldots, 4\}$, (mk) is satisfied while M_k is not satisfied.

The properties of DRSA-mv_j, $j = 1, 1.5, 2, 2.5, 3, \ldots, 6$, are summarized in Table 2, where **T** and F denote presence and absence of a given property, respectively. Moreover, in case of two symbols $\cdot/\cdot$, the first one reflects only CDRSA-mv_j while the second one reflects only ϵ-VC-DRSA-mv_j.

According to Table 2, DRSA-$mv_{2.5}$ is the least attractive due to lack of many important properties (R, T, P, RI, M_1, and M_4). DRSA-mv_1 is dominated by: DRSA-$mv_{1.5}$, DRSA-mv_3, DRSA-mv_4, and DRSA-mv_5. DRSA-mv_3 is dominated by: DRSA-$mv_{1.5}$, DRSA-mv_4, and DRSA-mv_5. DRSA-mv_6 is dominated by: DRSA-mv_2, DRSA-mv_4, and DRSA-mv_5. The only non-dominated approaches are DRSA-$mv_{1.5}$, DRSA-mv_2, DRSA-mv_4, and DRSA-mv_5.

4 Conclusions

We considered different ways of dealing with missing attribute values in ordinal and non-ordinal classification data when analyzed using Indiscernibility-based

Table 2. Properties of DRSA-mv_j, $j = 1, 1.5, 2, 2.5, 3, \ldots, 6$

Prop./Approach	DRSA-mv_1	DRSA-$mv_{1.5}$	DRSA-mv_2	DRSA-$mv_{2.5}$	DRSA-mv_3	DRSA-mv_4	DRSA-mv_5	DRSA-mv_6
S	F	F	T	T	F	T	T	T
R	F	T	T	F	T	T	T	T
T	T	T	F	F	T	T	T	F
B	F	T	T	T	F	F	F	F
P	F	F	T	F	F	F	F	F
RI	F	T	T	F	T	T	T	T
C	T	T	T	T	T	T	T	T
M_1	T	T	T	F	T	T	T	T
M_2	T	T	T	T	T	T	T	T
M_3	T/F	T/F	T/F	T/F	T/F	T/F	T/F	T/F
M_4	T	T	F	F	T	T	T	F

Rough Set Approach (IRSA) or Dominance-based Rough Set Approach (DRSA). Moreover, we proposed some desirable properties for IRSA and DRSA that a rough set approach capable of dealing with missing attribute values should possess. We analyzed which of these properties are satisfied by the considered rough set approaches resulting from different definitions of indiscernibility or dominance relations, suitable for the case of missing values. Based on this analysis, we uncovered some non-dominated, with respect to desirable properties, indiscernibility-based and dominance-based rough set approaches. These are:

- in IRSA: IRSA-$mv_{1.5}$ and IRSA-mv_2,
- in DRSA: DRSA-$mv_{1.5}$, DRSA-mv_2, DRSA-mv_4, and DRSA-mv_5.

Our future work will focus on experimental comparison of non-dominated variants uncovered in this paper. One of them, called DRSA-mv_2, was already compared with respect to classification performance against some other ordinal and non-ordinal classifiers. The results reported in [1] show that DRSA-mv_2-based rule classifier performs better than other well known methods like: Naive Bayes, SVM, Ripper, or C4.5 when the share of missing values in a data set is below 20%.

Acknowledgment. The first author acknowledges financial support from the Poznań University of Technology, grant no. 09/91/DSMK/0609.

References

1. Błaszczyński, J., Słowiński, R., Szeląg, M.: Induction of ordinal classification rules from incomplete data. In: Yao, J.T., Yang, Y., Słowiński, R., Greco, S., Li, H., Mitra, S., Polkowski, L. (eds.) RSCTC 2012. LNCS (LNAI), vol. 7413, pp. 56–65. Springer, Heidelberg (2012). doi:10.1007/978-3-642-32115-3_6
2. Błaszczyński, J., Greco, S., Słowiński, R., Szeląg, M.: Monotonic variable consistency rough set approaches. In: Yao, J.T., Lingras, P., Wu, W.-Z., Szczuka, M., Cercone, N.J., Ślezak, D. (eds.) RSKT 2007. LNCS (LNAI), vol. 4481, pp. 126–133. Springer, Heidelberg (2007). doi:10.1007/978-3-540-72458-2_15
3. Błaszczyński, J., Greco, S., Słowiński, R., Szeląg, M.: Monotonic variable consistency rough set approaches. Int. J. Approximate Reason. **50**(7), 979–999 (2009)

4. Błaszczyński, J., Słowiński, R., Szeląg, M.: Rough set approach to classification of incomplete data. Research Report RA-22/2013, Poznań University of Technology (2013)
5. Dembczyński, K., Greco, S., Słowiński, R.: Rough set approach to multiple criteria classification with imprecise evaluations and assignments. Eur. J. Oper. Res. **198**(2), 626–636 (2009)
6. Greco, S., Matarazzo, B., Słowinski, R.: Handling missing values in rough set analysis of multi-attribute and multi-criteria decision problems. In: Zhong, N., Skowron, A., Ohsuga, S. (eds.) RSFDGrC 1999. LNCS (LNAI), vol. 1711, pp. 146–157. Springer, Heidelberg (1999). doi:10.1007/978-3-540-48061-7_19
7. Greco, S., Matarazzo, B., Słowiński, R.: Dealing with missing data in rough set analysis of multi-attribute and multi-criteria decision problems. In: Zanakis, S., et al. (eds.) Decision Making: Recent Developments and Worldwide Applications, pp. 295–316. Kluwer, Dordrecht (2000)
8. Greco, S., Matarazzo, B., Słowiński, R.: Rough sets theory for multicriteria decision analysis. Eur. J. Oper. Res. **129**(1), 1–47 (2001)
9. Greco, S., Matarazzo, B., Słowiński, R.: Granular computing for reasoning about ordered data: the dominance-based rough set approach. In: Pedrycz, W., et al. (eds.) Handbook of Granular Computing, Chap. 15. Wiley, Chichester (2008)
10. Grzymala-Busse, J.W., Hu, M.: A comaprison of several approaches in missing attribute values in data mining. In: Ziarko, W., Yao, Y. (eds.) RSCTC 2000. LNAI, vol. 2005, pp. 378–385. Springer, Berlin (2001). doi:10.1007/3-540-45554-X_46
11. Grzymala-Busse, J.W.: Mining incomplete data - a rough set approach. In: Yao, J.T., et al. (eds.) RSKT 2011. LNCS, vol. 6954, pp. 1–7. Springer, Berlin (2011). doi:10.1007/978-3-642-24425-4_1
12. Hastie, T., Tibshirani, R., Friedman, J.: The Elements of Statistical Learning. Springer, Berlin (2009)
13. Hu, M.L., Liu, S.F.: A rough analysis method of multi-attribute decision making for handling decision system with incomplete information. In: Proceedings of 2007 IEEE International Conference on Grey Systems and Intelligent Services, 18–20, November 2007, Nanjing, China (2007)
14. Kryszkiewicz, M.: Rough set approach to incomplete information systems. Inf. Sci. **112**, 39–49 (1998)
15. Liang, D., Yang, S.X., Jiang, C., Zheng, X., Liu, D.: A new extended dominance relation approach based on probabilistic rough set theory. In: Yu, J., Greco, S., Lingras, P., Wang, G., Skowron, A. (eds.) RSKT 2010. LNCS (LNAI), vol. 6401, pp. 175–180. Springer, Heidelberg (2010). doi:10.1007/978-3-642-16248-0_28
16. Pawlak, Z.: Rough Sets. Theoretical Aspects of Reasoning about Data. Kluwer Academic Publishers, Dordrecht (1991)
17. Słowiński, R., Greco, S., Matarazzo, B.: Rough set methodology for decision aiding. In: Kacprzyk, J., Pedrycz, W. (eds.) Handbook of Computational Intelligence, Chap. 22, pp. 349–370. Springer, Berlin (2015). doi:10.1007/978-3-662-43505-2_22
18. Słowiński, R., Vanderpooten, D.: A generalized definition of rough approximations based on similarity. IEEE Trans. Knowl. Data Eng. **12**(2), 331–336 (2000)
19. Stefanowski, J., Tsoukias, A.: Incomplete information tables and rough classification. Comput. Intell. **17**(3), 545–566 (2001)
20. Yang, X., Yang, J., Wu, C., Yu, D.: Dominance-based rough set approach and knowledge reductions in incomplete ordered information system. Inf. Sci. **178**(4), 1219–1234 (2008)

The Optimal Estimation of Fuzziness Parameter in Fuzzy C-Means Algorithm

Hsun-Chih Kuo[1] and Yu-Jau Lin[2(✉)]

[1] Department of Statistics, National Chengchi University, Taipei City, Taiwan, ROC
seankuo@nccu.edu.tw
[2] Department of Applied Mathematics, Chung Yuan Christian University,
Taoyuan City, Taiwan, ROC
yujaulin@cycu.edu.tw

Abstract. The fuzziness parameter m is an extra parameter that facilitates the iterative formulas of Fuzzy c-means (FCM). However, the parameter m, commonly set to be 2.0, is an important factor that effects the effectiveness of FCM. In literatures, the statistical study of m is so far not available. Viewing m as a random variable, we propose a novel idea to optimize the fuzziness parameter m. For the model selection, a modified cluster validity index is defined as the optimal function of m and improve the effectiveness of FCM. Then the simulated annealing algorithm is applied to approximate its estimate.

Keywords: Fuzzy c-means · Xie-Beni index · Simulated annealing · Markov chain

1 Introduction

Clustering methods [3] can be roughly divided into two groups: hierarchical and classification methods. Classification method aims to find the best partition of data into c clusters in such a way that one criterion is optimized. Here we consider the fuzzy classification and use the Fuzzy C-Means (FCM) algorithm [1,2,6,7]. In addition to the specification of the number c of clusters in the data set, FCM method requires to choose the fuzziness parameter m, an important factor that influences the effectiveness of FCM. Note that the study of m has not been completely investigated in literatures. Pal and Bezdek [4] suggested $m \in [1.5, 2.5]$, and Yu et al. [10] proposed a theoretical upper bound for m to prevent the sample mean from being the unique optimizer of an FCM objective function. Wu [8] showed that the parameter m influenced the robustness of FCM and $m \in [1.5, 4]$. For a large theoretical upper bound, they suggested the implementation of the FCM with a suitable large m value. Also, the value $m = 4$ is recommended for FCM when the data contains noise and outliers. In practical use purpose, m is commonly fixed to 2. This choice allows an easy computation of the membership values.

© Springer International Publishing AG 2017
L. Polkowski et al. (Eds.): IJCRS 2017, Part I, LNAI 10313, pp. 566–575, 2017.
DOI: 10.1007/978-3-319-60837-2_45

2   Methodology

2.1   The FCM Algorithm

For a given number of c clusters and the fuzzifier $m > 1$, the FCM algorithm is an iterative procedure that minimizes the objective function

$$J(c) = \sum_{k=1}^{c} \sum_{i=1}^{N} u_{ki}^{m} d^2(x_i, a_k), \tag{1}$$

where $d(x_i, a_k)$ is the distance (dissimilarity) between the cluster center a_k, $k = 1, 2, \cdots, c$ and the data x_i, $i = 1, 2, \cdots, N$(number of sample size), and u_{ki} denotes the fuzzy membership value of object x_i to the cluster k that satisfies the following conditions

$$0 \leq u_{ki} \leq 1 \text{ and } \sum_{k=1}^{c} u_{ik} = 1 \tag{2}$$

FCM algorithm is then minimized (1) by the following iterative equations.

$$a_k = \frac{\sum_{i=1}^{N} u_{ki}^{m} x_i}{\sum_{i=1}^{N} u_{ki}^{m}} \tag{3}$$

$$u_{ki} = \frac{1}{\sum_{j=1}^{c} \left(\frac{d(x_i, a_k)}{d(x_i, a_j)} \right)^{\frac{1}{m-1}}} \tag{4}$$

Fuzzy partitioning is carried out through an iterative optimization (minimizing) of the objective function $J(c)$ by alternatively updating the membership μ_{ij} and the cluster center a_k.

2.2   The XB Index

Among the existing validity indices to evaluate the goodness of clustering according to a given number of clusters, the Xie–Beni (XB) index [9] is a credible fuzzy-validity criterion based on a validity function which identifies overall compact and separate fuzzy c-partitions. This function depends upon the data set, geometric distance measure, and distance between cluster centroids and fuzzy partition, irrespective of any fuzzy algorithm used. For evaluating the goodness of the data partition, both cluster compactness and intercluster separation should be taken into account. For FCM algorithm with $m = 2.0$, the XB index can be shown to be

$$\text{XB}(c) = \frac{J(c)}{N d_{\min}} \tag{5}$$

where $d_{\min}$ is the minimum distance between cluster centroids. The more separate the clusters are, the larger $d_{\min}$ and the smaller $\text{XB}(c)$.

2.3 The Parameter m as a Random Variable

The following numerical example shows that different values of m yield to different models according to XB index. To demonstrate the class clustering, we generate a pseudo dataset from 4 clusters centered at $(5, 5)$, $(5, -5)$, $(-5, 5)$ and $(-5, -5)$, each has 12 observations and they follow the two dimensional independent normal distribution. A realization of simulated data, denoted by D_1, is shown in Fig. 1. Each elements of the same cluster are marked with the same color points. Visually, the number of clusters are likely to be 4 and possibly 3.

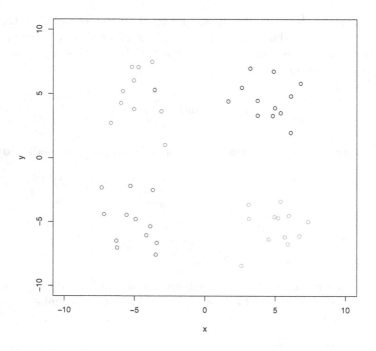

Fig. 1. The scatter plot of data set D_1

Table 1 lists the summary of the model suggested by XB indices.

We see, when $m = 6.0$, the suggested cluster number by XB index is $c = 3$. But it is incorrect. This implies that XB index is somehow not perfect since it depends on m.

Different from the classical analysis, our novel idea is to view the fuzziness parameter m as a random variable in the XB index. That is, given the data, XB index consists of two parameter m and c.

$$\text{XB}(c, m) = \frac{J(c)}{Nd_{\min}} \tag{6}$$

Next, we apply the simulated annealing algorithm to find the maximum likelihood estimator of m.

Table 1. Different values of m yield to different models.

m	c (suggested by XB)	Correct or not
2.0	4	Yes
3.0	4	Yes
4.0	4	Yes
5.0	4	Yes
6.0	3	No
7.0	3	No

2.4 Simulated Annealing Algorithm

The simulated annealing algorithm (SA) [5] which employs a probabilistic procedure can approximate the minimizer m of an optimal function. It originally simulates the process of slow cooling of molten metal to achieve the minimum function value in a minimization problem. The cooling phenomenon of the molten metal is simulated by introducing a temperature like parameter and cooling it down using the concept of Boltzmann's probability distribution. The Boltzmann's probability distribution implies that the energy E of a system in thermal equilibrium at temperature T is distributed probabilistically according to the relation $P(E) = e^{-E/kT}$, where $P(E)$ denotes the probability of achieving the energy level E, and k is called the Boltzmann's constant [5]. SA's major advantage over other methods is an ability to avoid becoming trapped at local minima. The algorithm employs a random search for which not only accepts changes that decrease objective function but also some changes that increase it. The latter are accepted with probability $p = e^{-\triangle F/t_n}$, where $\triangle F = F_n - F_{n-1}$ is the increase or the decrease in objective function value and F_n is a control parameter, which by analogy with the original application is known as the system "temperature" irrespective of the objective function involved.

3 The Estimation of m

The theoretical distribution of m is so far not available since m depends on the data and the corresponding objective functions. For example, if the optimal function is to minimize $J(c, m) = J(c)$ in (1), we consider m as a random variable that has the probability density function $f(m|c)$ of the form

$$m \sim f(m|c) \propto e^{-J(c,m)}$$

We see that the estimate, so called maximum likelihood estimate in statistics, of maximizing a probability density function with kernel $e^{-J(c,m)}$ is equivalent the optimal estimate of minimizing $J(c, m)$.

We define the cluster validity function as the objective function of m in our analysis.

$$G(k) = \frac{\mathrm{XB}(k, m)}{\min_{i \neq k}\{\mathrm{XB}(k, m)\}} \tag{7}$$

In determining the number of clusters c, the model with minimum $\mathrm{XB}(c, m)$ is preferred. However, It's difficult to optimize both the number of cluster c and the fuzziness parameter m together in the same procedure since the problem of choosing best c has been a hard problem in classification. Given a likely c, the new validity function $G(k)$ in (7) can differentiates the best model between other clusters.

With vague information when $m = 2.0$ in dataset D_1, the preferred model can be identified to be 4. We emphasize the difference between the best and the second best models in terms of XB index by taking the ratio of them. Since small $\mathrm{XB}(c, m)$ indicates a better number of cluster c, the minimum of $G(c, m)$ is desired. And SA, the general procedure in optimizing an objective function with different initial values of cluster center a_k and μ_{ij}, can approximate the fuzziness parameter m as a sequence of Markov chain that ultimately converges to its minimizer.

3.1   Simulation Study

Using the data used in the numerical example, we see the *correct* model $c = 4$, and we wish to estimate m given the data and possible clusters $(2, 3, 4, 5)$. According to XB index, the best model $c^* = 4$. Then the minimizer m^* of objective function $G_4(m)$ is the estimate.

$$G_4(m) = \frac{\mathrm{XB}(4, m)}{\min\{\mathrm{XB}(2, m), \mathrm{XB}(3, m), \mathrm{XB}(5, m)\}} \tag{8}$$

We propose the following algorithm: start from $m = 2.0$. The number of clusters is firstly determined by the one, say c^*, with minimum XB index among possible clusters. Note that $\hat{c}$ is a ball park figure. Next, SA is applied to locate the estimate of $\hat{m}$ of the cluster validity function $G_4(m)$. That is,

$$G_4(\hat{m}) = \min_{m>1} G_4(m, c^*).$$

Finally, set $m = \hat{m}$, proceed FCM and double check XB indices for possible models to ensure c^* is the cluster with smallest XB index. If not, run the above procedure again until the estimate $\hat{m}$ agrees with the indicator XB.

FCM algorithm

(a) Pre-set the cluster number c and the fuzziness parameter m.
(b) Set initial values of cluster center a_k and fuzziness membership u_{ki}, $i = 1, 2, \cdots, N$(number of sample size), $k = 1, 2, \cdots, c$.
(c) $u_{ki} = \dfrac{1}{\sum_{j=1}^{c} \left(\frac{d(\mathbf{x}_1, a_k)}{d(x_i, a_j)}\right)^{\frac{1}{m-1}}}$
(d) $a_k = \dfrac{\sum_{i=1}^{N} u_{ki}^m x_i}{\sum_{i=1}^{N} u_{ki}^m}$
(e) $J(c) = \sum_{k=1}^{c} \sum_{i=1}^{N} u_{ki}^m d^2(x_i, a_k) < \epsilon = 10^{-4}$, stop;

else, go to Step (b).
SA algorithm

1 Set the starting values of $m^{(0)} = 2.0$.
2 Calculate $XB(k, m^{(0)})$, $k = 1, 2, \cdots, c$, by FCM algorithm and $XB(c, m)$ in (6) and determine the one with smallest XB index as the preferred number of clusters, say c^*.
3 At state j, propose a candidate $m^* \sim N(m^{(j)}, 0.05^2)$.
4 Let u follow uniform distribution$(0, 1)$.
5 Accept the candidate m^* as the next state value of Markov chain $\{m^{(j)}\}_{j=1,2,\ldots}$ with probability

$$\alpha_1 = e^{\frac{(-1)}{T_j}\left(G(m^*) - G(m^{(j-1)})\right)}.$$

That is

$$m^{(j+1)} = \begin{cases} m^* & \text{if } u < \alpha \\ m^{(j)} & \text{otherwise.} \end{cases}$$

where $T_j = \dfrac{100}{j \log(j)}$, $G(m) = G(m, c^*)$ is defined in (7).
6 If $j < n_2$, say $n_2 = 20,000$, then go to Step 3.
7 Calculate $XB(2,\hat{m})$, $XB(3, \hat{m})$, $XB(4, \hat{m})$ and $XB(5,\hat{m})$. If c^* is the one with smallest XB index, then STOP; otherwise set $j = 0$ and $m^{(0)}$ and go to Step 2.

$$\hat{m} - m^{(n_2)} \text{is the minimier of } G(m)$$

$$\hat{c} = c^* \text{is the number of clusters.}$$

8 The cluster center a_k, $k = 1, 2, \cdots, \hat{c}$ can be obtained by FCM with $m = \hat{m}, c = \hat{c}$.

4   The Numerical Experiment

We apply our proposed method to the data with obvious clusters and see how well it performs. To make comparisons, we simulate data based on the statistical distribution of data set D_1 in Sect. 2.3.

The Data Scheme (I): Standard Derivation $\sigma = 1.5$

Three data sets, D_2, D_3, D_4, are simulated from the same target distribution as D_1 in Fig. 1, each has 12 observations and they follow the 2 dimensional independent normal distribution with same standard deviation $\sigma = 1.5$, $N_2(\mu_i = (5, 5), (-5, -5), (5, -5), (-5, 5), \sigma)$. Together with the time series plots of m in applying SA algorithm, the scatter plots of the three data sets are shown in Fig. 2.

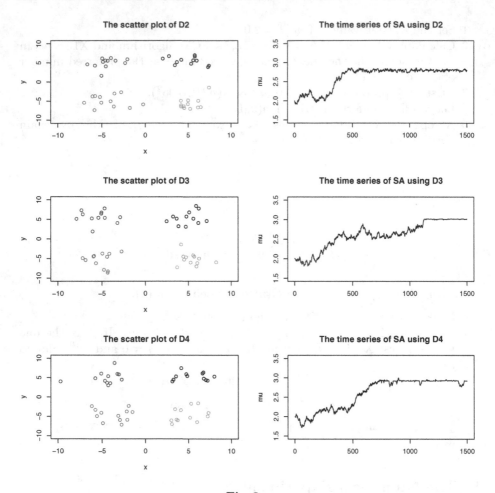

Fig. 2. .

The Data Scheme (II): $\sigma = 1.0, 1.0, 1.2, 1.8$

Four data sets, D_5, D_6, D_7, D_8, are simulated from 4 clusters, the same mean points as D_1, each has 12 observations and they follow the 2 dimensional independent normal distribution with standard deviations $\sigma = 1.0, 1.0, 1.2, 1.8$ $N_2(\mu_i = (5,5), (-5,-5), (5,-5), (-5,5), \sigma)$. The scatter plots and the time series plots of m given by SA algorithm using the data sets are shown in Fig. 3.

The Data Scheme (III): $c = 2, 3$

Two data sets, D_9, D_{10}, are simulated from 2 and 3 clusters, each has 12 observations and they follows the 2 dimensional independent normal distributions with same standard deviation $\sigma = 1.5$, $N_2(\mu_i = (5,5), (-5,5), \sigma = 1.5)$ and

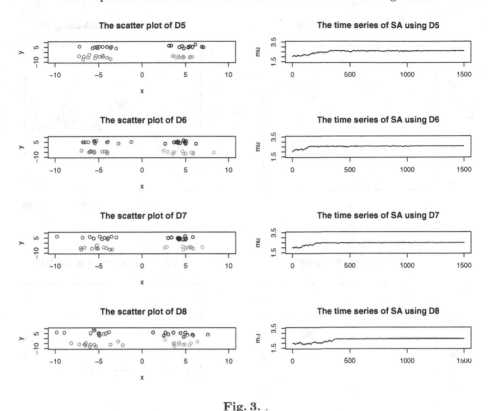

Fig. 3. .

$N_2(\mu_i = (5,5), (-5, -5), (-5,5), \sigma = 1.5)$, respectively. The scatter plots of the data sets and the time series plots of m are shown in Fig. 4.

4.1 Concluding Remarks

As seen the the time series plots of m given by SA algorithm, their Markov chains converge. For example in D_1, starting from $m = 2.0$, the last 10 realizations of $m^{(j)}_{j=1,2,\cdots,1500}$ are

2.7847	2.7912	2.7912	2.7644	2.7832
2.8023	2.7930	2.7930	2.8007	2.7822

The sequence of Markov chains of m given by SA algorithm using the data set D_1 are getting close to a fixed point $\hat{=}2.7822$. And the suggested number of clusters indicates the correct model is $c = 4$ with cluster centers $(5.91, 5.09)$, $(4.92, -6.12)$, $(-4.69, 5.17)$, $(-5.04, -5.41)$.

Repeated numerical experiments using data sets $D_i, i = 1, 2, \cdots, 10$, show that our proposed work well. The suggested clusters $\hat{c}$ by XB indices are as good

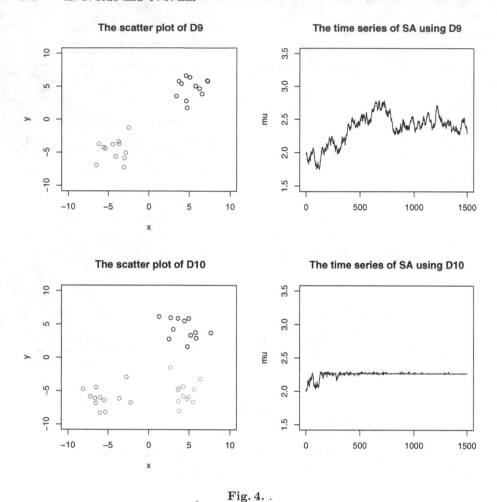

Fig. 4. .

Data	c	$\hat{c}$	$\hat{m}$
D_1	4	4	2.7822
D_2	4	4	3.0219
D_3	4	4	2.5896
D_4	4	4	2.6703
D_5	4	4	2.6221
D_6	4	4	2.5525
D_7	4	4	2.4842
D_8	4	4	2.4221
D_9	2	2	2.2946
D_{10}	3	3	2.5525

as expected. The SA estimates of m are eventually convergent. The estimates $\hat{m}$ range from 2.1 to 3.0. See the following table for the summary.

Since the optimal estimates of m are not far from the commonly used value, 2.0, the cluster centers computed by FCM are about the same.

5   Conclusion

Fuzzy c-means is a common, fast and useful method of clustering classification. In applying FCM algorithm, the fuzziness parameter m, originally designed to facilitate the iterative formulas of FCM, is usually set to be 2.

In this paper, we first show that m indeed an important factor in determining the cluster validity. We then view m as a random variable and apply SA algorithm to approximate the optimal estimate of m based on the modified XB index.

Even though the results of our numerical experiments are not surprising, our approach is novel. We successfully delete the effect due to the extra parameter m by finding its minimizer and thus guarantee the effectiveness of FCM. Furthermore, the statistical distribution of m can be possibly available by the Markov chain Monte Carlo in the future.

References

1. Bezdek, J.C.: Numerical taxonomy with fuzzy sets. J. Math. Biol. **1**, 57–71 (1974)
2. Bezdek, J.C.: Pattern Recognition with Fuzzy Objective Function Algorithms. Plenum Press, New York (1981)
3. Gath, I., Geva, A.B.: Unsupervised optimal fuzzy clustering. IEEE Trans. Pattern Anal. Mach. Intell. **11**, 773–781 (1989)
4. Pal, N.R., Bezdek, J.C.: On cluster validity for fuzzy c-means model. IEEE Trans. Fuzzy Syst. **1**, 370–379 (1995)
5. Wang, X.Y., Garibaldi, J.M.: Simulated annealing fuzzy clustering in cancer diagnosis. Informatica **29**, 61–70 (2005)
6. Wang, W., Zhang, Y.: On fuzzy cluster validity indices. Elsevier Fuzzy Sets Syst. **158**, 2095–2117 (2007)
7. Wu, K.L., Yang, M.S.: A cluster validity index for fuzzy clustering. Pattern Recogn. Lett. **26**, 1275–1291 (2005)
8. Wu, K.L.: Analysis of parameter selections for fuzzy c-means. Elsevier Pattern Recogn. **45**, 407–415 (2012)
9. Xie, X.L., Beni, G.A.: A validity measure for fuzzy clustering. IEEE Trans. Pattern Anal. Mach. Intell. **13**, 841–847 (1991)
10. Yu, J., Cheng, Q., Huang, H.: Analysis of the weighting exponent in the FCM. IEEE Trans. Syst. Man Cybern. B **34**, 634–639 (2004)

Supercluster in Statics and Dynamics: An Approximate Structure Imitating a Rough Set

Ivan Rodin[✉] and Boris Mirkin

National Research University Higher School of Economics,
Moscow, Russian Federation
ivvrodin@gmail.com, bmirkin@hse.ru

Abstract. We present a new method for cluster analysis that finds a composite "supercluster" consisting of two non-overlapping parts: a tight core and a less connected shell. We expand this approach to data that changes over time by assuming that the core is unchangeable, while the shell depends on the time period. We define a data recovery approximation model of a dynamic supercluster, and present a suboptimal algorithm for finding superclusters.

Keywords: Supercluster · Rough sets · Dynamic clusters · Approximation model

1 Introduction

The idea that a cluster as a set of similar objects is not necessarily quite homogeneous is not uncommon in data analysis. A most explicit expression of that is the concept of fuzzy cluster [1]. Next come less arbitrary membership functions formalising the idea that a cluster should have a deep-down core and shell around it, differently expressed in concepts of rough set cluster [2,3], shadowed set [4,5] and layered cluster [6]. Of these by far most popular is the concept of rough cluster and rough k-means partition [7,8]. According to the original message of the rough set theory [9], a rough cluster's core is referred to as lower approximation, whereas the shell as boundary. A rough k-means partition must satisfy the following conditions [8]:

- An object cannot be simultaneously member of a cluster's lower approximation and the same cluster's boundary region.
- If an object is member of a cluster's lower approximation it cannot belong to any other cluster, neither to its lower approximation nor to its boundary region.
- If an object is not a member of any lower approximation it must belong to the boundary regions of at least two clusters.

This paper relates to a less restrictive concept of a single rough cluster rather than rough partition so that the last condition in this list is not applicable

© Springer International Publishing AG 2017
L. Polkowski et al. (Eds.): IJCRS 2017, Part I, LNAI 10313, pp. 576–586, 2017.
DOI: 10.1007/978-3-319-60837-2_46

anymore. Another difference comes from a different type of input data involved in the definition. We consider rough clusters in networks rather than entity-to-feature tables. One more feature of our approach is that we focus on dynamic data rather than static ones. This latter feature leads us to consider a special type of rough cluster, what we call a supercluster. A dynamic supercluster has its core unvaried over time while its shell can change according to temporal nature of the data.

The next section defines and analyzes the concept of supercluster within a data-recovery framework [10]. A local optimization algorithm for building a supercluster and supercluster set is given in Sect. 3. Section 4 describes results of application of the algorithm to two dynamic network datasets that we derived ourselves: (a) interrelations between main characters of a modern saga novel [11], (b) intercitations between a circle of specialists in cluster analysis, participants to an IFCS biennial conference series.

2 Dynamic Supercluster Model

2.1 Static Data

Let I be a set of elements and $A = \{a_{ij}\}$ a given similarity index matrix over I. Our goal is to define a subset $U \subseteq I$, consisting of two disjoint parts $U = R \cup S$, where S represented by a 1/0 vector s_i is the shell, with intensity λ, R represented by 1/0 vector r_i is the core with intensity $\lambda + \mu$ where $\lambda, \mu > 0$. As usual, $s_i = 1$, or $r_i = 1$, if and only if $i \in S$, or $i \in R$. A data-recovery model of supercluster is:

$$a_{ij} = \lambda s_i s_j + (\lambda + \mu) r_i r_j + e_{ij} \tag{1}$$

where residuals e_{ij} are small. The products $s_i s_j$ and $r_i r_j$ correspond to binary matrices showing whether elements belong to core/shell or not. Then a most approximate supercluster $U = R \cup S$ can be found as that minimizing the summary square error e_{ij}:

$$\Delta = \sum_{i,j=1}^{N} e_{ij}^2 = \sum_{i,j=1..N} [a_{ij} - \lambda s_i s_j - (\lambda + \mu) r_i r_j]^2 \to \min \tag{2}$$

Remark 1: Hereinafter we consider symmetric $a(i, j)$ matrix. If original matrix A is asymmetric, we can symmetrize it: $A \to (A + A^T)/2$. As shown in [10] this transformation does not change the minimum of function Δ. All diagonal elements are set to be equal to zero.

Consider the first order necessary conditions of minimality of function Δ:

$$\frac{\partial \Delta}{\partial \lambda} = -2 \sum_{i,j} (a_{ij} - \lambda s_i s_j - (\lambda + \mu) r_i r_j)[-s_i s_j - r_i r_j] = 0 \tag{3}$$

and

$$\frac{\partial \Delta}{\partial \mu} = -2 \sum_{i,j} (a_{ij} - \lambda s_i s_j - (\lambda + \mu) r_i r_j) r_i r_j = 0 \tag{4}$$

Equations (3) and (4) imply that the intensities are just average within core and shell similarities:

$$\lambda + \mu = \frac{\sum_{i,j} a_{ij} r_i r_j}{\sum_{i,j} r_i r_j} \tag{5}$$

$$\lambda = \frac{\sum_{i,j} a_{ij} s_i s_j}{\sum_{i,j} s_i s_j} \tag{6}$$

The condition that S and R do not intersect, so that $s_i r_i = 0$, is taken into account when deriving the above.

Substituting these into 2, we obtain

$$\Delta = \sum_{i,j} \left[(a_{ij})^2 - 2a_{ij}(\lambda s_i s_j - (\lambda + \mu) r_i r_j) + \lambda^2 s_i s_j + (\lambda + \mu)^2 r_i r_j \right]$$

$$+ 2\lambda(\lambda + \mu) r_i r_j s_i s_j$$

$$= C - 2(\lambda + \mu) \sum_{i,j} \left(a_{ij} - \frac{\lambda + \mu}{2} \right) r_i s_j - 2\lambda \sum_{i,j} \left(a_{ij} - \frac{\lambda}{2} \right) s_i s_j = C - g^2 \tag{7}$$

Here $C = \sum_{i,j} a_{ij}^2$ is the similarity data scatter and g^2 the contribution of the supercluster to the data scatter that should be maximized to minimize the square error criterion.

2.2   Supercluster at Dynamic Data

Let us consider the case at which the similarity matrix a_{ij}^t changes over time $t = 1..T$. We define a dynamic supercluster $U_t = R \cup S_t$ so that its core $R = (r_i)$ does not change over time, whereas its shells $S_t = (s_i^t)$ may vary at different time periods.

Consider the least squares approximation criterion for obtaining the best dynamic supercluster:

$$\Delta = \sum_{t=1}^{T} \sum_{i,j=1}^{N} e_{ij}^t = \sum_{t=1}^{T} \sum_{i,j=1}^{N} \left[a_{ij}^t - \lambda^t s_i^t s_j^t - (\lambda^t + \mu^t) r_i r_j \right]^2 \to \min \tag{8}$$

We suppose that average values of core and shell intensities may change depending on time period. Indeed, the fact that the average link between core elements may change over time is compatible with the assumption that the core is constant. The changes in core intensity $\lambda^t + \mu^t$ may follow corresponding changes in similarities a_{ij}^t over time.

Consider again the first order optimality conditions – this time for the criterion (8):

$$\frac{\partial \Delta}{\partial \lambda^t} = -2 \sum_{i,j} (a_{ij}^t - \lambda s_i^t s_j^t - (\lambda^t + \mu^t) r_i r_j)[-s_i^t s_j^t - r_i r_j] = 0 \tag{9}$$

$$\frac{\partial \Delta}{\partial \mu^t} = -2 \sum_{i,j} (a_{ij}^t - \lambda^t s_i^t s_j^t - (\lambda^t + \mu^t) r_i r_j) r_i r_j = 0 \tag{10}$$

It is easy to see, that these equations are similar to Eq. (9)–(10) for the static case. This means that the optimal λ^t and μ^t for a single period t satisfy similar equations:

$$\lambda^t + \mu^t = \frac{\sum_{i,j} a_{ij}^t r_{ij}}{\sum_{i,j}^t r_{ij}} \tag{11}$$

$$\lambda^t = \frac{\sum_{i,j} a_{ij}^t s_i^t s_j^t}{\sum_{i,j} s_i^t s_j^t} \tag{12}$$

Equations (11)–(12) refer to the average intensities in core and shell parts in period t $(t = 1, 2, ..., T)$. For derivation of other parameters, let us return to Eq. (8). We denote the constant summary data scatter by $C = \sum_t \sum_{i,j} (a_{ij}^t)^2$. Therefore,

$$\Delta$$

$$= \sum_t \sum_{i,j} \left[(a_{ij}^t)^2 - 2a_{ij}^t (\lambda^t s_i^t s_j^t - (\lambda^t + \mu^t) r_i r_j) + (\lambda^t)^2 s_i^t s_j^t + (\lambda^t + (\mu^t)^2) r_i r_j \right]$$

$$+ 2\lambda^t (\lambda^t + \mu^t) r_i r_j s_i^t s_j^t$$

$$= C - 2\sum_t (\lambda^t + \mu^t) \sum_{i,j} \left(a_{ij}^t - \frac{\lambda^t + \mu^t}{2} \right) r_i r_j - 2\sum_t \lambda^t \sum_{i,j} \left(a_{ij}^t - \frac{\lambda^t}{2} \right) s_i^t s_j^t \tag{13}$$

Equation (13) can be represented in a shorter form:

$$\Delta = \sum_t \sum_{i,j} a_{ij}^t - g^2 = C - g^2 \tag{14}$$

where data scatter C is constant and g^2 the contribution of the supercluster to the data scatter:

$$g^2 = 2\sum_t (\lambda^t + \mu^t) \sum_{i,j} \left(a_{ij}^t - \frac{\lambda^t + \mu^t}{2} \right) r_i r_j + 2\sum_t \lambda^t \sum_{i,j} \left(a_{ij}^t - \frac{\lambda^t}{2} \right) s_i^t s_j^t \tag{15}$$

Equations (11)–(12) lead us to the following equations relating the optimal intensity values: (a) $(\lambda^t + \mu^t) \sum_{i,j}^t r_i r_j = \sum_{i,j} a_{ij}^t r_i r_j$; (b) $\lambda^t \sum_{i,j}^N s_i^t s_j^t = \sum_{i,j} a_{ij}^t s_i^t s_j^t$. We will use these formulas to simplify (15):

$$g^2 = \sum_t \left[(\lambda^t + \mu^t)^2 |R|^2 + (\lambda^t)^2 |S^t|^2 \right] \tag{16}$$

This formula shows how the approximate supercluster relates to the optimal intensities λ^t, μ^t, and to core and shell sizes $|R|$ and $|S^t|$. Minimizing the least-squares criterion is equivalent to maximizing g^2.

3   Building Superclusters

Our method for finding dynamic superclusters is based on AddRemAdd(j) algorithm from [10], that finds an approximate cluster which is homogeneous, that is, has no explicitly defined core and shell parts.

AddRemAdd(j) involves the following quantities: the average similarity between any $i \in I$ and a cluster $S \subset I$ defined as $a(i, S) = \sum_{j \in S} a_{ij}/|S|$ and the average within-cluster similarity defined by $a(S) = \sum_{i \in S} a(i, S)/|S|$. These are easily computed for the starting singleton cluster $S = \{j\}$ and easily updated as the S changes with entities being added to or removed from S. One more parameter usually applied with this algorithm is the similarity shift, a real subtracted from each entry of similarity matrix A as part of data preprocessing. The greater the shift value, the smaller the number of positive entries in A after the preprocessing stage. In the absence of other information, the similarity shift value is usually taken as the average of all entries in A. As mentioned above, we make all the diagonal entries equal to 0 as a result of preprocessing.

A pseudocode for AddRemAdd(j) is as follows.

Algorithm 1. AddRemAdd(j)

Input   : Similarity matrix $A = (a_{ij})$ and initial singleton cluster $S = \{j\}$.
Output: Cluster S containing j, its intensity equal to the average within-cluster similarity λ, and contribution to the data scatter g^2

1 **Initialization** Set N-dimensional vector z to have all its elements equal to -1, except for $z_j = 1$; the number of elements in cluster $n = 1$; the average within-cluster similarity $\lambda = 0$, the contribution $g^2 = 0$, and define $a(i, S) = a_{ij}$ for each element $i \in I$.

2 **Selection** Find i^* maximizing $a(i, S)$.

3 **Test**

4 **if** $\left(z_{i*}a(i, S) < z_{i*}\frac{\lambda}{2}\right)$ **then**

5 | $z_{i*} \leftarrow -1 \cdot z_{i*}$

6 | $n \leftarrow n + z_{i*}$

7 | $\lambda \leftarrow \dfrac{(n - z_{i*}(n - z_{i*} - 1)\lambda + 2z_{i*}a(i*, S)(n - z_{i*}))}{n(n - 1)}$

8 | $a(i, S) = [(n - z_{i*}a(i, S) + z_{i*}a_{ii*})]/n$

9 | $g2 = \lambda^2 n^2$

10 | Go to 2.

11 **end**

12 **else**

13 | Output: S, λ, $g2$

14 **end**

After applying AddRemAdd(j) for all $j \in I$, we take, as the final output, the result corresponding to the maximum g^2. We refer to the AddRemAdd(j) with this postprocessing step as ARA algorithm. This algorithm utilizes no ad hoc parameters, except for the similarity shift value, so the cluster sizes are determined by the process of clustering itself.

Our algorithm for building a dynamic supercluster involves 3 main steps:

1. *Base supercluster construction.* At this step we build an initial approximation of the core R. For each period we find a single cluster with ARA algorithm.

Thus obtained T clusters then are averaged according to the α-majority rule. Any item i belongs to the α-majority if it is present in αT sets or more. The greater the α threshold, the less elements will be present in the core. The α value is given by the user. By default we set $\alpha = 2/3$, gradually decreasing it if there are no elements in the α-majority set. After thus defining initial R, we define the initial shells at each period t as the set-theoretic differences of the single clusters found in the beginning, and the R. We extract basic shell as a set of elements which presented in basic single cluster and which are not included in core. Then initial values of parameters λ^t and μ^t are found according to Eq. (11)–(12).

2. *Core optimization.* We calculate an aggregate similarity matrix as the weighted sum of matrices A^t with weights taken from (13). We define the similarity shift as $\sum_t (0.5\lambda^t + 0.5\mu^t)$ and then apply the ARA algorithm to obtain the final version of supercluster's core.

3. *Shells optimization.* At this step we assume that the core is found so that shells are looked at by using the ARA algorithm applied on the set $I\backslash R$.

After extracting a dynamic supercluster, its absolute and relative contributions to the data scatter are found: g^2 and $g^2/\sum_{t,i,j}(a_{ij}^t)^2$, respectively.

Algorithm 2. Building a dynamic supercluster

Input : Similarity matrices $A^t = (a_{ij}^t)$, majority threshold α

Output: Core R, the average similarity between its elements $\lambda^t + \mu^t$, shells S^t, the average similarity values λ^t, contribution of the model to the original data scatter g^2

1 **I. Build a base dynamic supercluster:**
2 **for** $t = 1..T$ **do**
3 $\quad$ Build a single cluster U^t by using $ARA(I, A^t, \frac{\lambda^t}{2}) \Rightarrow U^t$
4 **end**
5 Define $\tau(i)$ — the number of periods t at which i is included in U^t
6 **if** $\tau(i) \geq \alpha T$ **then**
7 $\quad$ $R \to R \cup \{i\}$
8 **end**
9 **for** $t = 1..T$ **do**
10 $\quad$ $S^t = U^t \backslash R$
11 $\quad$ $\lambda^t = \frac{\sum_{i,j} a_{ij}^t s_{ij}^t}{\sum_{i,j} s_{ij}^t}$
12 $\quad$ $\mu^t = \frac{\sum_{i,j} a_{ij}^t r_{ij}}{\sum_{i,j} r_{ij}} - \lambda^t$
13 **end**
14 **II. Core optimization:**
15 Calculate the weighted similarity matrix:
$$B = 2\sum_t (\lambda^t + \mu^t)\left(A^t - \frac{\lambda^t + \mu^t}{2}\right) + 2\sum_t \lambda^t \left(A^t - \frac{\lambda^t}{2}\right)$$
16 Updated core: $ARA(I, B, \sum_t \frac{\lambda^t + \mu^t}{2}) \Rightarrow R$
17 **II. Shells optimization:**
18 **for** $t = 1..T$ **do**
19 $\quad$ $ARA(I\backslash R, A^t, \frac{\lambda^t}{2}) \Rightarrow S^t$
20 **end**

After a dynamic supercluster is found, one can apply the same procedure for finding one more supercluster by restricting its core to be part of the residual set $I - R$. This process of sequential supercluster extraction can be repeated as many times as necessary.

4   Application

We apply the dynamic supercluster algorithm to two self-developed dynamic network data, as described in the follow-up sections.

4.1   IFCS Network Superclusters

We have taken names of 42 researchers who have been active at the biennial meetings of the International Federation of Classification Societies for a two-decade period from 1997 to 2016. And used Google Scholar query system to find intercitation data. For example, a query *Murtagh author: "Mirkin"* returns a list of publications (co)-authored by Boris Mirkin, in which F. Murtagh was referred to. The matrix of intercitations is available from the authors upon a personal request.

Then we divide data in 10 biennial periods from 1997 to 2016 and form an intercitation matrix for each of the periods. These ten similarity matrices have been taken as the input to our Superclustering algorithm.

Results are presented in the table below Table 1.

Table 1. Superclusters found at the IFCS intercitation subnetwork.

n	Core	Number of shell participants	Contribution, %
1	P. Groenen, J. Meulman, R. Tibshirani, T. Hastie, G. McLachlan	10	10.0
2	F. de Carvalho, C. Hennig, B. Mirkin, F. Murtagh, V. Makarenkov	13	2.7
3	V. Batagelj, A. Ferligoj, H. Kiers, I. Van Mechelen	9	2.8
4	W. Gaul, A. Geyer-Schulz	11	1.7
5	E. Diday, A. Raftery, R. Rocci, M. Vichi	12	1.4

4.2   The Structure of a Novel's Plot

In order to provide another example, we created an English language corpus based on first four books from a series of popular epic fantasy novels "A Song of Ice and Fire" [11]. To construct our network data, we divided each chapter in 2 to 7 equally-sized parts, depending on the size of the chapter. Each part was then taken to the corpus as a single document. Then, the set of all documents was divided into groups of 50 sequential documents, forming 14 time periods.

We take the list of characters of that novel as a set of objects and score the co-occurence of characters on the book pages. Let $D_\tau(w_i)$ be a set of documents in period τ where character w_i appears. Then we say that concept w_i "refers" to concept w_j in time period τ with confidence $C_\tau(w_i, w_j)$, where $C_\tau(w_i, w_j) = \frac{|D_\tau(w_i) \cap D_\tau(w_j)|}{|D_\tau(w_i)|} \in [0; 1]$. In other words, confidence $C_\tau(w_i, w_j)$ shows the conditional probability of occurrence of concept w_j in document where w_i occurred. After calculating all possible $D_\tau(w_i)$ and $C_\tau(w_i, w_j)$ we can build a dynamic reference graph as described in [12]. The work also provides visualization of such graphs (Fig. 1).

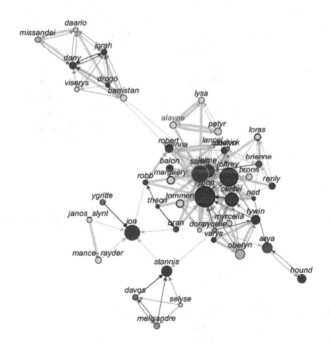

Fig. 1. Visualization of ASOIAF reference graph for 11-th period (end of third book)

For this dataset we present only one supercluster, as other superclusters appeared to be less interpretable, which probably correctly reflects the structure of a literary work.

The core of this dynamic supercluster has a contribution of 8.97% and consists of 6 characters—four of them are members of the House Lannister which rule the kingdom during all four books (Cersei, Joffrey, Tommen, Tyrion), another 2 characters are from the House Tyrell, the second powerful family in the kingdom after the second book (Margaery, Loras). The core of supercluster really shows strong connection between the two houses and their exceptional significance for the plot.

Shells for each period also show groups of strongly-connected characters: in 10 periods out of 14 all characters from the shell are located in the same geographical area and mutually interact between each other (Table 2).

List of all entities from both datasets is presented in (Table 3).

Table 2. Shells for ASOIAF supercluster

#	Shell	g^2, %	#	Shell	g^2, %	#	Shell	g^2, %
1	Jorah Dany Viserys Drogo	8.89	6	Sansa Hound	5.38	11	Sansa Lancel Olenna	5.41
2	Jorah Dany Viserys Drogo	8.57	7	Ned Catelyn Lysa Hoster Edmure	15.42	12	Theon Asha Balon Euron Victarion	18.62
3	Ned Robert Renly Varys Pycelle Barristan	10.15	8	Varys Pycelle Balon Lancel	5.12	13	Jaime Lancel Olenna	11.16
4	Ned Catelyn Robb Theon Petyr Hoster Edmure	11.34	9	Bronn Doran Podrick	5.92	14	Pycelle High Sparrow	17.49
5	Catelyn Renly Brienne	3.28	10	Theon Balon Euron Victarion	7.09			

Table 3. List of entities used in work:

IFCS-Citations:	Batagelj, Vladimir; Bertrand, Patrice Bodjanova, Slavka; Braak, Cajo ter; De Carvalho, Francisco De Assis Tenhorio; Ferligoj, Anuška; Geyer-Schulz, Andreas; Gorban, Alexander N; Groenen, Patrick J.F.; Hastie, Trevor; Hennig, Christian; Hruschka, Harald; Jajuga, Krzysztof; Kiers, Henk; Kuntz, Pascale; Lausen, Berthold; Leisch, Friedrich; Makarenkov, Vladimir; McLachlan, Geoff; Meulman, Jacqueline; Mirkin, Boris; Murtagh, Fionn; Palumbo, Francesco; Riani, Marco; Rocci, Roberto; Steinley, Doug; Tibshirani, Robert; Van Mechelen, Iven; Paula Brito; Gilles Celeux; Renato Coppi; Frank Klawonn; Rudolf Kruse; Verde, Rosanna; Vermunt, Jeroen; Vichi, Maurizio; Wolfgang A. Gaul; Wojtek J Krzanowski; Gilbert Saporta; Edvin Diday; Adrian Raftery
ASOIAF-RefGraph:	Ned Catelyn Robb Jon Sansa Bran Arya Hodor Theon Roose Ramsay Tywin Cersei Jaime Joffrey Myrcella Tommen Tyrion Lancel Hound Bronn Dany Viserys Jorah Missandei Daario Lysa Robert Stannis Selyse Shireen Melisandre Davos Renly Brienne Asha Balon Victarion Euron

5 Conclusions and Future Work

The approximation model of cluster structure imitating static and dynamic rough sets was presented in the paper. We have retrieved parameters of the model and proposed an suboptimal iterative algorithm for building superclusters. We have verified our approach on two dynamic network data sets. The proposed algorithm finds satisfactory superclusters with core elements that are strongly connected within all time periods and shells showing local trends of each period.

Although the presented approach showed its effectiveness on our data sets, much work remains to be done. First it is necessary to test the scalability of the algorithm—our approach needs to be verified on the larger amounts of data. Another open question is the question of algorithm's applicability to other types of data. One of possible areas of research is the analysis of images, in particular, changes in temperature maps. In this scope superclusters may find its applications for the analysis and detection of upwellings. Finally, we are also planning to integrate the algorithm for finding superclusters with our dynamic network visualization software.

References

1. Bezdek, J.C., et al.: Fuzzy Models and Algorithms for Pattern Recognition and Image Processing, vol. 4. Springer Science & Business Media, New York (2006)
2. Ho, T.B., Nguyen, N.B.: Nonhierarchical document clustering based on a tolerance rough set model. Int. J. Intell. Syst. **17**(2), 199–212 (2002)
3. Lingras, P.: Rough set clustering for web mining. In: Proceedings of the 2002 IEEE International Conference on Fuzzy Systems, Fuzzy Systems, 2002, FUZZ-IEEE 2002, vol. 2, pp. 1039–1044 (2002)
4. Pedrycz, W.: Knowledge-Based Clustering: From Data to Information Granules. Wiley, Hoboken (2005)
5. Zhou, J., Pedrycz, W., Miao, D.: Shadowed sets in the characterization of rough-fuzzy clustering. Pattern Recogn. **44**(8), 1738–1749 (2011)
6. Mirkin, B., Muchnik, I.: Layered clusters of tightness set functions. Appl. Math. Lett. **15**(2), 147–151 (2002)
7. Lingras, P., West, C.: Interval set clustering of web users with rough k-means. J. Intell. Inf. Syst. **23**(1), 5–16 (2004)
8. Peters, G., Crespo, F., Lingras, P., Weber, R.: Soft clustering-fuzzy and rough approaches and their extensions and derivatives. Int. J. Approx. Reason. **54**(2), 307–322 (2013)
9. Pawlak, Z.: Rough Sets: Theoretical Aspects of Reasoning About Data, vol. 9. Springer Science & Business Media, Dordrecht (2012)
10. Mirkin, B.: Clustering: A Data Recovery Approach. CRC Press, Boca Raton (2012)
11. Martin, G.R.R.: A Song of Ice and Fire, Books 1–4. Bantam, New York (2011)
12. Rodin, I., et al.: Visualization of dynamic reference graphs. In: Proceedings of the 10th Workshop on Graph-Based Methods for Natural Language Processing, NAACL, vol. 16 (2016)

Integration of Gene Expression and Ontology for Clustering Functionally Similar Genes

Sushmita Paul[(⊠)]

Department of Bioscience and Bioengineering, Indian Institute of Technology
Jodhpur, Jodhpur, India
sushmitapaul@iitj.ac.in

Abstract. Clustering functionally similar genes helps in understanding
the mechanism of a biological pathway. It also provides information of
those genes whose biological importance is previously not known. Clustering of genes is highly dependent on the similarity or dissimilarity criterion. Usually, microarray gene expression data is used to cluster genes.
However, a microarray data may contain noise that may lead to unde-
sired results. Therefore, incorporating gene ontology information may
improve the clustering solutions. In this regard, an integrated dissimilarity measure is introduced for grouping functionally similar genes. It
is comprised of city block distance and gene ontology based semantic
dissimilarity. While, the city block distance is used to compute distance
between two gene expression vectors, gene ontology based semantic dissimilarity measure is used for incorporating biological knowledge. The
importance of the integrated dissimilarity measure is shown by incorporating it in different c-means clustering algorithms including rough-fuzzy
clustering algorithms. In this work it has been shown that incorporation
of integrated dissimilarity measure increases the functional similarity of
cluster of genes as compared to the methods that are based on either
type of dissimilarity measure. It is also observed that the rough-fuzzy
clustering algorithm performs better with the new dissimilarity measure
compared to different c-means clustering algorithms.

Keywords: Genes · Co-expressed genes · Rough sets · Gene ontology ·
Functionally similar genes · City-block distance

1 Introduction

Clustering functionally similar genes is important to understand the role of
individual gene in a pathway. It also reveals about the co-expression and co-
regulation patterns of genes. A lot of insight can be gained for the genes whose
information is previously unknown. Functionally similar genes often are organized in clusters in the genome. Expression analyses showed strong positive
correlations among the closely located genes, indicating that they may be controlled by common regulatory element(s). In fact, experimental evidence demonstrated that clustered gene loci form an operon-like gene structure and that they

© Springer International Publishing AG 2017
L. Polkowski et al. (Eds.): IJCRS 2017, Part I, LNAI 10313, pp. 587–598, 2017.
DOI: 10.1007/978-3-319-60837-2_47

are transcribed from common promoter. Existence of co-expressed genes is also demonstrated using expression profiling analysis in [10]. Several gene clusters have been experimentally shown by RT-PCR [4]. These findings suggest that members of a gene cluster, which are at a close proximity on a chromosome, are highly likely to be processed as co-transcribed units. Expression data of genes can be used to detect clusters of genes as it is suggested that co-expressed genes are co-transcribed, so they should have similar expression pattern. However, a microarray gene expression data may contain noise that may lead to misleading results.

It has been demonstrated in [15] that the quality of generated clusters is always relative to a certain distance measure. Different distance measures may lead to different clustering results. Several similarity or dissimilarity measures such as Euclidean distance, Jaccard index, Pearson correlation coefficient, and city block distance (CBD) are used in various clustering algorithms based on expression vector of genes. To avoid the problem of noise in microarray gene expression data one may integrate prior biological knowledge information so that more functionally relevant genes get grouped. In this regard, several studies have developed or used microarray gene expression data and gene ontology (GO) based semantic dissimilarity. In those works Pearson correlation distance [9] is computed using microarray expression data and it is integrated with GO based semantic dissimilarity. However, the Pearson correlation only measures linear relationship. This integrated dissimilarity measure is used with different c-means clustering algorithms but not with rough-fuzzy clustering algorithms. It has been shown that rough-fuzzy clustering algorithm can perform better than K-means [8], fuzzy c-means algorithms [5] as they can handle the issue of noise as well as overlapping boundary [13]. However, no work has been conducted using integrated dissimilarity measure in rough-fuzzy clustering algorithm.

In this regard, this paper presents a new integrated dissimilarity measure for grouping functionally similar genes. It is developed by integrating city block distance (CBD) and gene ontology (GO) semantic dissimilarity. While, the CBD measure is used in this paper for computing gene expression vector based dissimilarity, GO based dissimilarity measure is used to incorporate biological knowledge in the clustering algorithm. It has been shown that rough-fuzzy clustering algorithm can overcome the issues of noise and overlapping boundaries but no work has demonstrated the impact of integrated dissimilarity measure with rough-fuzzy c-means algorithms. The effectiveness of integrated approach along with different types of c-means clustering algorithms is shown on several gene expression microarray data. It has been observed that the rough-fuzzy c-means algorithm along with proposed integrated dissimilarity measure generates more clusters of functionally related genes.

2   Proposed Dissimilarity Measure

This section describes the proposed integrated dissimilarity measure. It is developed by integrating microarray gene expression data and gene ontology (GO) based semantic dissimilarity. The distance between two gene expression vectors is calculated using city block distance (CBD). While, Du et al. [6] GO based semantic dissimilarity is used for incorporating biological knowledge.

City Block Distance. The CBD, also known as the Manhattan distance or taxi distance, is closely related to the Euclidean distance. Whereas the Euclidean distance corresponds to the length of the shortest path between two points, the CBD is the sum of distances along each dimension. The distance between two objects x_i and x_j is defined as follows:

$$CBD(x_i, x_j) = \sum_{k=1}^{m} |x_{ik} - x_{jk}| \tag{1}$$

where m is the number of features of the objects x_i and x_j. As for the Euclidean distance, the expression data are subtracted directly from each other, and therefore should be made sure that they are properly normalized. There are many variants of the CBD. The normalized range-normalized CBD (NRNCBD) is defined as follows:

$$\mathcal{N}(x_i, x_j) = \frac{1}{m} \times \sum_{k=1}^{m} \left[\frac{|x_{ik} - x_{jk}|}{|k_{max} - k_{min}|} \right], \tag{2}$$

where k_{max} and k_{min} denote the maximum and minimum values along the kth feature, respectively.

Gene Ontology Based Semantic Dissimilarity. The gene ontology (GO) project aims to build tree structures and controlled vocabularies, also called ontologies, which describe gene products in terms of their associated biological processes (BPs), molecular functions (MFs), or cellular components (CCs).

When biological entities are described using a common schema such as an ontology, they can be compared by means of their annotations. This type of comparison is called semantic similarity since it assesses the degree of relatedness between two entities by the similarity in meaning of their annotations. To quantify similarity between two genes, many information content-based measures have been developed [11,17]. In the present work, the Du et al. semantic similarity measure [6] is used to measure the functional dissimilarity between a pair of genes. The functional similarity between a pair of genes based on gene annotation information from heterogeneous data sources is computed as follows.

Definition 1. *Given two genes x_1 and x_2, and their annotated GO terms $GO_1 = \{go_{11}, go_{12}, \cdots, go_{1m}\}$ and $GO_2 = \{go_{21}, go_{22}, \cdots, go_{2\acute{m}}\}$, respectively, for the ontology O, the functional similarity between x_1 and x_2 is defined as follows:*

$$Sim(x_1, x_2) = \frac{\sum_{i=1}^{m} Sim(go_{1i}, GO_2) + \sum_{j=1}^{\acute{m}} Sim(go_{2j}, GO_1)}{m + \acute{m}}.$$

The value of similarity $Sim(x_1, x_2)$ ranges from zero to one, nearer the value to one higher the functional similarity between the pair of genes.

In this work, functional dissimilarity is computed as follows: $DISSim(x_1, x_2) = 1 - Sim(x_1, x_2)$. Nearer the value to zero higher the functional similarity between the pair of genes. Whereas, if its one that means no similarity between the genes.

Integrated Dissimilarity Measure. To generate group of functionally similar genes average of both distance measures is computed. The integrated distance between two genes x_i and x_j can be calculated as follows:

$$d(x_i, x_j) = \mathcal{N}(x_i, x_j) + DISSim(x_i, x_j) \tag{3}$$

The following properties can be derived for the proposed dissimilarity measure:

1. $0 \leq d(x_i, x_j) \leq 1$.
2. $d(x_i, x_j) = d(x_j, x_i)$.
3. $d(x_i, x_i) = 0$.
4. $d(x_i, x_j) \leq d(x_i, x_k) + d(x_k, x_j)$.

The proposed integrated dissimilarity measure is incorporated into different c-means clustering algorithm including rough-fuzzy clustering algorithm.

2.1   Selection of Initial Cluster Prototypes

A limitation of any c-means algorithm is that it can only achieve a local optimum solution that depends on the initial choice of the cluster prototypes. Consequently, computing resources may be wasted in that some initial centers get stuck in regions of the input space with a scarcity of data points and may therefore never have the chance to move to new locations where they are needed. To overcome this limitation, the proposed study begins with the selection of c distinct genes from the given gene expression data set using the NRNCBD, which enables the algorithm to converge to an optimum or near optimum solutions [15].

The main steps for selection of initial genes as mentioned in [15] are as follows:

1. For each gene x_i, calculate $\mathcal{N}(x_i, x_j)$ between itself and the gene x_j, $\forall_{j=1}^{n}$.
2. Calculate similarity score between two genes x_i and x_j as follows:

$$S(x_i, x_j) = \begin{cases} 1 \text{ if } \mathcal{N}(x_i, x_j) \leq \lambda \\ 0 \text{ otherwise.} \end{cases} \tag{4}$$

3. For each gene x_i, calculate total number of similar genes of x_i as

$$N(x_i) = \sum_{j=1}^{n} S(x_i, x_j). \tag{5}$$

4. Sort n genes according to their values of $N(x_i)$ such that $N(x_1) > N(x_2) > \cdots > N(x_n)$.
5. If $N(x_i) > N(x_j)$ and $\mathcal{N}(x_i, x_j) \leq \lambda$, then x_j cannot be considered as an initial cluster center, resulting in a reduced set of genes to be considered for c initial cluster centers v_i, $i = 1, 2, \cdots, c$. Also, the λ is a user defined parameter.
6. Stop.

3 Gene Expression Data Sets Used

In this work, publicly available three gene expression data sets are used to compare the performance of different clustering methods along with proposed dissimilarity measure. This section gives a brief description of the following three gene expression data sets, two of which are downloaded from Gene Expression Omnibus (www.ncbi.nlm.nih.gov/geo/).

1. **Cho Data Set:** This data set contains gene expression profile of yeast genome during mitotic cell cycle. The number of genes and time points of this data are 5575 and 17, respectively [2].
2. **GDS759:** This data set is related to analysis of gene expression in temperature sensitive pre-mRNA splicing factor mutants prp17 null, prp17-1, and prp22-1 at various time points following a shift from the permissive temperature of $23\,^{\circ}C$ to the restrictive temperature of $37\,^{\circ}C$. The number of genes and time points of this data are 6350 and 24, respectively [18].
3. **GDS2347:** It contains the analysis of wild type W303 cells across two cell cycles, a length of 2 h after synchronization with alpha factor. The number of genes and time points are 6228 and 13, respectively [16].

4 Results and Discussions

In this section, the performance of the proposed dissimilarity measure is demonstrated. The dissimilarity measure is incorporated with hard c-means (HCM) [8], fuzzy c-means (FCM) [5], rough-fuzzy c-means (RFCM) [12], and robust rough-fuzzy c-means (rRFC-M) [13], The performance of the proposed dissimilarity measure over only normalized range normalized city block distance or Gene ontology based dissimilarity measure is also presented. The results are reported on three microarray gene expression data sets, namely, Cho data set, GDS759, and GDS2347. Gene expression vectors are used for only those genes whose gene ontology information is also available. For each data set, the number of clusters c is decided by using the CLICK [19] algorithm. Each gene data set is pre-processed by standardizing each feature or time point to zero mean and unit variance. The values of two fuzzifiers are set to 2.0, that is, $\acute{m}_1 = 2.0$ and $\acute{m}_2 = 2.0$. All the results are reported using gene ontology based functional annotation ratio. This evaluation criterion quantify the functional similarity among a set of genes.

4.1   Optimum Clustering Solutions

The threshold λ [15] plays an important role to generate the initial cluster centers. It controls the degree of dissimilarity among the genes present in microarray data. In effect, it has a direct influence on the performance of the initialization method used. Also, the performance of the rough-fuzzy clustering algorithm depends on the weight parameter ω [12,13].

Let $\Phi = \{\lambda, \omega\}$ be the set of parameters and $\Phi^\star = \{\lambda^\star, \omega^\star\}$ is the set of optimal parameters. To find out the optimum set $\Phi^\star$, containing optimum values of $\lambda^\star$ and $\omega^\star$, the Davies-Bouldin (DB) cluster validity index [3] is used here. DB index [3] is designed to identify sets of clusters that are compact and well separated. DB index minimizes

$$\text{DB} = \frac{1}{c} \sum_{i=1}^{c} \max_{i \neq k} \left\{ \frac{S(v_i) + S(v_k)}{d(v_i, v_k)} \right\} \tag{6}$$

for $1 \leq i, k \leq c$. The DB index minimizes the within-cluster distance $S(v_i)$ and maximizes the between-cluster separation $d(v_i, v_k)$. Therefore, for a given data set and c value, the higher the similarity values within the clusters and the between-cluster separation, the lower would be the DB index value. A good clustering procedure should make the value of DB index as low as possible.

For three gene microarray data sets, the value of λ is varied from 0.0 to 0.15, while the value of ω is varied from 0.51 to 0.99. The optimum values of $\lambda^\star$ and $\omega^\star$ for each microarray data set and for two rough-fuzzy clustering algorithms [12,13] are obtained using the following relation:

$$\Phi^\star = \arg\min_{\Phi} \{\text{DB}\}. \tag{7}$$

While for HCM and FCM only λ parameter is considered. The optimum values of λ and ω for the rough-fuzzy clustering algorithms [12,13] as well as HCM and FCM with NRNCBD distance for three data sets, namely, Cho data set, GDS759, and GDS2347 are mentioned in Table 1.

Table 1. Optimum parameter values of different clustering algorithms

Methods algorithm	Cho data set		GDS759		GDS2347	
	λ	ω	λ	ω	λ	ω
HCM	1.00	-	0.92	-	0.93	-
FCM	0.96	-	0.91	-	0.85	-
RFCM	1.00	0.99	0.98	0.51	0.98	0.75
rRFCM	1.00	0.95	0.97	0.99	0.98	0.55

4.2 Importance of Integrated Dissimilarity Measure

This section describes about the importance of the integrated dissimilarity measure in terms of functional consistency of a gene cluster. In order to evaluate the functional consistency of the gene clusters produced by different algorithms, the biological annotations of the gene clusters are considered in terms of the GO. The annotation ratios of each gene cluster in three GO ontologies are calculated using the GO Term Finder [1]. The GO term is searched in which most of the genes of a particular cluster are enriched. The annotation ratio, also termed as cluster frequency, of a gene cluster is defined as the number of genes in both the assigned GO term and the cluster divided by the number of genes in that cluster. A higher value of annotation ratio indicates that the majority of genes in the cluster are functionally more closer to each other, while a lower value signifies that the cluster contains much more noises or irrelevant genes. After computing the annotation ratios of all gene clusters for a particular ontology, the sum of all annotation ratios is treated as the final annotation ratio. A higher value of final annotation ratio represents that the corresponding clustering result is better than other, that is, the genes are better clustered by function, indicating a more functionally consistent clustering result [20].

Here, the importance of proposed integrated dissimilarity measure is shown over dissimilarity measure based on only either type of dissimilarity measure. Table 2 presents the comparative results of different types of dissimilarity measures, in term of final annotation ratio or cluster frequency, for the MF, BP, and

Table 2. Comparative performance of different c-means algorithms and distance measures

Methods algorithm	Distance measure	Cho data set			GDS759			GDS2347		
		MF	BP	CC	MF	BP	CC	MF	BP	CC
IICM	NRNCBD	6.062	7.329	11.322	1.812	4.462	6.826	0.857	0.995	1.530
	Integrated	**15.682**	**23.380**	11.380	7.938	14.404	**10.056**	**2.036**	**2.666**	1.632
	GO distance	12.692	23.193	14.035	**8.256**	**15.174**	9.599	1.639	2.210	**2.656**
FCM	NRNCBD	4.511	5.542	8.076	1.953	2.333	5.090	0.123	0.778	1.386
	Integrated	**16.798**	**19.770**	**14.053**	**11.946**	13.628	6.455	**1.986**	**2.465**	1.678
	GO distance	-	-	-	7.274	**15.211**	**11.161**	1.649	2.387	**2.548**
RFCM	NRNCBD	2.958	5.979	5.360	2.214	2.566	4.631	0.272	0.556	1.140
	Integrated	**9.598**	**23.230**	**12.397**	2.144	2.841	4.296	1.644	1.972	1.712
	GO distance	-	-	-	**7.274**	**15.211**	**11.161**	1.649	**2.387**	**2.548**
rRFCM	NRNCBD	4.868	6.050	6.487	1.149	2.858	4.558	0.433	0.783	1.472
	Integrated	**13.460**	**25.130**	**17.283**	**17.069**	**21.179**	**9.801**	**1.477**	**2.697**	**2.371**
	GO distance	-	-	-	-	-	-	1.220	1.999	1.871

CC ontologies on three data sets. From the table it is seen that the integrated dissimilarity measure performs better than city block distance alone and gene ontology based distance alone. The dissimilarity measures are incorporated in to different c-means clustering algorithms. Out of 36 cases the integrated dissimilarity measure performs better in 24 cases. On the other hand, the HCM and FCM algorithms generates more functionally consistent clustering results with integrated dissimilarity measure in most of the cases. Only in three cases in each of the HCM and FCM algorithms the ontology based dissimilarity measure performs better. The RFCM algorithm performs better with GO based dissimilarity measure in most of the cases. The sign '-' indicates that the algorithm could not generate desired number of clusters. Using only GO based distance in few cases the clustering algorithms generate co-incident clusters. Therefore, they are not further studied. The rRFCM algorithm always generates better result with integrated dissimilarity measure. From the results it is seen that incorporation of integrated dissimilarity measure drastically improves the performance of clustering algorithms.

4.3   Comparative Performance Analysis of Different Clustering Algorithms

In this section performance of different c-means clustering algorithm is shown in terms of annotation ratio or cluster frequency. Table 3 represents the performance of different clustering algorithms along with integrated dissimilarity measure. From the table it is seen that the rRFCM generates more number of functionally consistent clusters. Out of nine cases the rRFCM algorithm along with integrated dissimilarity measure performs better than other clustering algorithms in six cases. Only in one case and two cases the FCM and HCM, respectively performs better.

Table 3. Performance of different clustering algorithms

Methods/ algorithms	Cho data set			GDS759			GDS2347		
	MF	BP	CC	MF	BP	CC	MF	BP	CC
HCM	15.682	23.380	11.380	7.938	14.404	**10.056**	**2.036**	2.666	1.632
FCM	**16.798**	19.770	14.053	11.946	13.628	6.455	1.986	2.465	1.678
RFCM	9.598	23.230	12.397	2.144	2.841	4.296	1.644	1.972	1.712
rRFCM	13.460	**25.13**	**17.283**	**17.069**	**21.179**	9.801	1.477	**2.697**	**2.371**

4.4   Qualitative Performance Analysis

The Eisen plot gives a visual representation of the clustering result. In Eisen plot [7], the expression value of a gene at a specific time point is represented

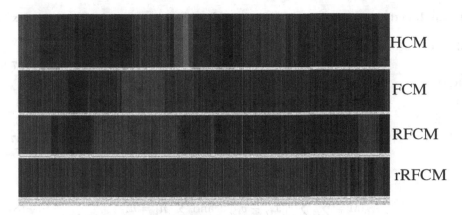

Fig. 1. Eisen plots of different clusters for Cho yeast data set generated by HCM, FCM, RFCM, and rRFCM

by coloring the corresponding cell of the data matrix with a color similar to the original color of its spot on the microarray. The shades of red color represent higher expression level, the shades of green color represent low expression level and the colors towards black represent absence of differential expression values. In the present representation, the genes are ordered before plotting so that the genes that belong to the same cluster are placed one after another. The cluster boundaries are identified by white colored blank rows.

The gene clusters produced by the HCM, FCM, RFCM, SOM, and rRFCM algorithms on Cho yeast data set are visualized by TreeView software, which is available at http://rana.lbl.gov/EisenSoftware and the plots for one data sets are reported in Fig. 1 as examples. From the Eisen plots presented in Fig. 1, it is evident that the expression profiles of the genes in a cluster are similar to each other and they produce similar color pattern, whereas the genes from different clusters differ in color patterns. Also, the results obtained by both RFCM and rRFCM algorithms are more promising than that by both HCM and FCM algorithms.

4.5   Performance of Clustering Algorithms in Terms of Cluster Validity Indices

The expression data of clustering solutions is used to evaluate the performance of different clustering algorithms in terms of some standard cluster validity indices. Table 4 presents the performance of different c-means algorithms for optimum values of λ and ω in terms of Davies Bouldin Index [3] and β Index [14].

The β index [14] is defined as the ratio of total variation and within-cluster variation, and is given by

$$\beta = \frac{N}{M}; \text{ where } N = \sum_{i=1}^{c} \sum_{j=1}^{n_i} ||x_{ij} - \overline{v}||^2;$$

Table 4. Performance of different clustering algorithms in terms of DB and β index

Methods/algorithms	DB index			β index		
	Cho Data	GDS759	GDS2347	Cho Data	GDS759	GDS2347
HCM	6.0862	1.0004	1.0000	0.000002	0.000003	0.000001
FCM	12.9881	1.0003	0.9999	0.000001	0.000001	0.000004
RFCM	4.8820	1.0004	0.9999	0.000001	0.000002	0.000003
rRFCM	**4.3548**	**1.0003**	**0.9999**	**0.000022**	**0.000011**	**0.000007**

$$M = \sum_{i=1}^{c} \sum_{j=1}^{n_i} ||x_{ij} - v_i||^2; \text{ and } \sum_{i=1}^{c} n_i = n; \tag{8}$$

n_i is the number of objects in the ith cluster ($i = 1, 2, \cdots, c$), n is the total number of objects, x_{ij} is the jth object in cluster i, v_i is the mean or centroid of ith cluster, and $\overline{v}$ is the mean of n objects. For a given data set and c value, the higher the homogeneity within the clusters, the higher would be the β value. The value of β also increases with c.

The results and subsequent discussions are presented with respect to DB index and Beta index. The results establish the fact that the rRFCM algorithm performs equal or better than other c-means clustering algorithms.

5   Conclusion

In this paper importance of dissimilarity measure in a clustering algorithm has been demonstrated. Application of only one type of distance measure may not generate desired results as that of integrated dissimilarity measure. Here, microarray gene expression data based distance as well as Gene Ontology based distance measures are integrated and their importance over individual type of distance measure is shown. It has been observed that integrated dissimilarity measure generates more functionally similar gene clusters. The effectiveness of the integrated dissimilarity measure is shown on different gene expression data sets. It has been observed that the integrated dissimilarity measure along with rRFCM algorithm performs better than any other clustering algorithm.

Acknowledgements. The author wants to acknowledge Dr. Pradipta Maji of Indian Statistical Institute, Kolkata, India for his valuable suggestions.

References

1. Boyle, E.I., Weng, S., Gollub, J., Jin, H., Botstein, D., Cherry, J.M., Sherlock, G.: GO: term finder open source software for accessing gene ontology information and finding significantly enriched gene ontology terms associated with a list of genes. Bioinformatics **20**, 3710–3715 (2004)
2. Cho, R.J., Campbell, M.J., Winzeler, E.A., Steinmetz, L., Conway, A., Wodicka, L., Wolfsberg, T.G., Gabrielian, A.E., Landsman, D., Lockhart, D.J., Davis, R.W.: A genome-wide transcriptional analysis of the mitotic cell cycle. Mol. Cell **2**(1), 65–73 (1998)
3. Davies, D.L., Bouldin, D.W.: A cluster separation measure. IEEE Trans. Pattern Anal. Mach. Intell. **1**, 224–227 (1979)
4. de Jong, S., Boks, M.P.M., Fuller, T.F., Strengman, E., Janson, E., de Kovel, C.G.F., Ori, A.P.S., Vi, N., Mulder, F., Blom, J.D., Glenthj, B., Schubart, C.D., Cahn, W., Kahn, R.S., Horvath, S., Ophoff, R.A.: A gene co-expression network in whole blood of schizophrenia patients is independent of antipsychotic-use and enriched for brain-expressed genes. PLOS One **7**(6), 1–10 (2012)
5. Dembele, D., Kastner, P.: Fuzzy C-means method for clustering microarray data. Bioinformatics **19**(8), 973–980 (2003)
6. Du, Z., Li, L., Chen, C.F., Yu, P.S., Wang, J.Z.: G-SESAME: web tools for go-term-based gene similarity analysis and knowledge discovery. Nucleic Acids Res. **37**, W345–W349 (2009)
7. Eisen, M.B., Spellman, P.T., Patrick, O., Botstein, D.: Cluster analysis and display of genome-wide expression patterns. Proc. Natl. Acad. Sci. USA **95**(25), 14863–14868 (1998)
8. Heyer, L.J., Kruglyak, S., Yooseph, S.: Exploring expression data: identification and analysis of coexpressed genes. Genome Res. **9**(11), 1106–1115 (1999)
9. Kustra, R., Zagdanski, A.: Incorporating gene ontology in clustering gene expression data. In: 19th IEEE Symposium on Computer-Based Medical Systems (CBMS 2006), pp. 555–563 (2006)
10. Li, J., Bushel, P.R.: EPIG-Seq: extracting patterns and identifying co-expressed genes from RNA-Seq data. BMC Genomics **17**(1), 255 (2016)
11. Lin, D.: An information-theoretic definition of similarity. In: Proceedings of 15th International Conference on Machine Learning, pp. 296–304 (1998)
12. Maji, P., Pal, S.K.: RFCM: a hybrid clustering algorithm using rough and fuzzy sets. Fundam. Informaticae **80**(4), 475–496 (2007)
13. Maji, P., Paul, S.: Rough-fuzzy clustering for grouping functionally similar genes from microarray data. IEEE/ACM Trans. Comput. Biol. Bioinform. **10**(2), 286–299 (2013)
14. Pal, S.K., Ghosh, A., Shankar, B.U.: Segmentation of remotely sensed images with fuzzy thresholding and quantitative evaluation. Int. J. Remote Sens. **21**(11), 2269–2300 (2000)
15. Paul, S., Maji, P.: City block distance and rough-fuzzy clustering for identification of co-expressed microRNAs. Mol. BioSyst. **10**(6), 1509–1523 (2014)
16. Pramila, T., Miles, S., GuhaThakurta, D., Jemiolo, D., Breeden, L.L.: Conserved homeodomain proteins interact with MADS box protein Mcm1 to restrict ECB-dependent transcription to the M/G1 phase of the cell cycle. Genes Dev. **16**(23), 3034–3045 (2002)
17. Resnik, P.: Using information content to evaluate semantic similarity in a taxonomy. In: Proceedings of 14th International Joint Conference on Artificial Intelligence, pp. 448–453 (1995)

18. Sapra, A.K., Arava, Y., Khandelia, P., Vijayraghavan, U.: Genome-wide analysis of pre-mRNA splicing: intron features govern the requirement for the second-step factor, Prp17 in Saccharomyces cerevisiae and Schizosaccharomyces pombe. J. Biol. Chem. **279**(50), 52437–52446 (2004)
19. Shamir, R., Sharan, R.: CLICK: a clustering algorithm for gene expression analysis. In: Proceedings of the 8th International Conference on Intelligent Systems for Molecular Biology (2000)
20. Wang, H., Wang, Z., Li, X., Gong, B., Feng, L., Zhou, Y.: A robust approach based on Weibull distribution for clustering gene expression data. Algorithms Mol. Biol. **6**(1), 14 (2011)

Multi-view Clustering Algorithm Based on Variable Weight and MKL

Peirui Zhang, Yan Yang$^{(\boxtimes)}$, Bo Peng, and Mengjiao He

School of Information Science and Technology, Southwest Jiaotong University,
Chengdu 610031, People's Republic of China
yyang@swjtu.edu.cn

Abstract. Compared with Single-view clustering, Multi-view clustering analysis exploits more hidden information. Multiple kernel learning (MKL) performs its superiority in heterogeneous sources and solves the problem of selection of kernel functions. Many existing multi-view literatures based on MKL consider instances in each view equally and overlook the difference among them. In this paper, a multi-view clustering algorithm based on variable weight and MKL (called MVMKC) is proposed. MVMKC improves clustering quality with more-refined analyses on data. To be specific, it uses an improved weighted Gaussian kernel rather than the traditional combined kernel function. Meanwhile, variable weights are introduced to measure the contribution of instance in different views. Experimental results on real-world datasets demonstrate the effectiveness of the proposed approach.

Keywords: Multi-view clustering · Variable weight · Multiple Kernel Learning (MKL) · Weighted Gaussian kernel

1 Introduction

Multi-view data appears in various fields and increases at a rapid rate. It describes observation from different perspectives and consists of multiple feature sets. However, single view dataset regards the collection of all feature sets as a whole. The traditional clustering algorithms cannot handle dataset with more than one views. Therefore, multi-view clustering is put forward to deal with this kind of data, which aims at obtaining a better cluster results by analyzing the multi-view information and studying the similarities and dissimilarities between different views.

Although there are a lot of clustering methods, the traditional clustering algorithms could not solve the clustering problem of multi-view data well. Commonly multi-view clustering algorithms are divided into three categories:

Y. Yang—This work is supported by the Natioanl Science Foundation of China (Nos. 61572407 and 61603313), the Project of National Science and Technology Support Program (No. 2015BAH19F02).

L. Polkowski et al. (Eds.): IJCRS 2017, Part I, LNAI 10313, pp. 599–610, 2017.
DOI: 10.1007/978-3-319-60837-2_48

(1) Clustering after combining the views [1,2]: it combines the information from different views and clusters it. (2) Clustering based on common subspace [3]: this method projects data to a subspace and an algorithm is applied on this subspace. (3) Clustering based on ensemble learning [4]: every view is clustered to get a cluster result and combine those results to be a matrix, and an ensemble method is used on this matrix. (4) Clustering based on MKL.

For multi-view datasets, each variable is described in multiple views at the same time but the contribution of each view is different. Therefore, it is effective to take the differences among the views into consideration in the clustering process. But the traditional algorithms treat every view as a whole and ignore the differences among the variables in this view. Taking this into account, we weight the variables in different views to extract the effective information about the variables more effectively.

With the development of Support Vector Machine(SVM), the kernel technique [5] has obtained wide applications. Kernel function transforms the inner product of the high-dimensional space into the kernel function calculation of the low-dimensional space, which subtly solves the problem of "dimension disaster" in the high-dimensional feature space. However, different kernel functions have their unique characteristics; moreover some multi-view datasets are constituted by multiple sources or heterogeneous data. Single kernel function does not accurately represent all the charactistics. Hence, MKL (Multiple Kernel Learning) [6] is put forward, which intergrates multiple base kernels instead of single kernel. For multi-view data, the general method is a linear combination of kernel matrixes obtained by kernel transformation on every view. It enhances the interpretability of the decision function and improve the performance.

The rest of this paper is organized as follows. Section 2 reviews related work. In Sect. 3 we propose MVMKC algorithm, while Sect. 4 gives experimental results and analysis. Finally, we draw a conclusion in Sect. 5.

2   Related Work

In recent publications, many cluster methods have been introduced to learn the multi-view data. Bickel and Scheffer first proposed the concept of multi-view clustering [7] in 2004. Then many well-known algorithms have been utilized to cluster multi-view data. A variety of multi-view clustering methods based on co-training have been developed in succession. Such as co-training was combined with spectral clustering for multi-view data [2]. In 2007, a non-redundant multi-view clustering algorithm [8] is adopted to emphasize the difference between different views and reduced the redundant information. A method based on Canonical Correlation Analysis (CCA) [9] was introduced by Chaudhuri et al. in 2009, which extracted the common information of the two views by CCA before cluster. He et al. applied Non-negative Matrix Factorization (NMF) to learn latent features for multi-view clustering [10].

In order to effectively combine the information of those different views, MKL technology was introduced in multi-view clustering algorithms. Tzortzis and

Likas published a kernel-based weighted multi-view clustering [11] in 2012. In 2014, Guo et al. developed an improved MKL and combined it with multi-view spectral clustering [12]. MKL [13] was utilized by Nazarpour and Adibi to reduce the input dimensionality and improve the classification accuracy. Fu et al. presented a group based non-sparse Localized MKL algorithm [14] to make the best of useful kernels in 2016.

Variable weighting clustering is an important part of cluster analysis, and it focus on the study that how to update the weights automatically. Huang et al. proposed a W-k-means clustering algorithm [15] that can automatically update weight values during the K-means clustering process. Locally Adaptive Clustering (LAC) algorithm [16] was presented that it weighted variables of each cluster. An entropy weighting K-means (EWKM) [17] is adopted to automatically compute the weights of all dimensions in each cluster. A constrained locally weighted scheme [18] was utilized to capture the local correlation structures.

3 Multi-view Clustering Algorithm Based on Variable Weight and MKL (MVMKC)

Inspired by the MVKKM algorithm [11], this paper presents MVMKC algorithm and the detailed description is as follows.

3.1 Kernel Function

The core idea of the kernel function is to map the variables from low dimensional space to high-dimensional space through an inner product. It is not difficult to determine the kernel function by satisfying the Mercer theorem.

Theorem 1. *Mercer kernel.*

Suppose X is a set of samples in the input space: $x_k \in \mathbb{R}^N (k = 1, 2, \ldots, K)$, and by using a non-linear mapping ϕ to map X, a set of vectors $\phi(x_1)$, $\phi(x_2)$, $\phi(x_k), \cdots, \phi(x_K)$ in high-dimensional space (also called feature space) H could be obtained. Thus the dot product form of input space could be represented by Mercer in feature space [19]:

$$K(x_i, x_j) = \phi(x_i) \cdot \phi(x_j). \tag{1}$$

All of these samples are represented by a kernel matrix: $K_{ij} = K(x_i, x_j)$, which is the basic SVM technology.

The commonly used kernel functions are shown as follow:

Linear kernel. The linear kernel is the simplest kernel function. It is given by a sum of inner product and an optional constant.

$$K(x_i, x_j) = x_i \cdot x_j + c. \tag{2}$$

Polynomial kernel. The Polynomial kernel is a non-stationary kernel. Polynomial kernels are well suited for problems where all the training data is normalized.

$$K(x_i, x_j) = (x_i \cdot x_j + 1)^d. \tag{3}$$

Gaussian kernel. The Gaussian kernel is an example of radial basis function kernel.

$$K(x_i, x_j) = exp\left(-\frac{\|x_i - x_j\|^2}{2\sigma^2}\right) \tag{4}$$

here $\sigma > 0$ is the width of the Gaussian kernel function.

These different kernels may correspond to different datasets come from multiple sources, such as they have different representations or different feature subsets, or they contains a lot of heterogeneous information. So only a single kernel function can't achieve ideal result. For instance, the input space is composed of two vector spaces: the first vector follows Gaussian distribution, while the second vector is subject to polynomial distribution. In this case, only one kernel function becomes inadequate. If we mix the two kinds of kernel functions, the effect would be better than a single one.

3.2   Weighted Gaussian Kernel

Most combination kernel functions are summed by many independent kernel functions, information in different views are different. In order to describe this difference and extract as much useful messages as possible, here designs a weighted Gaussian kernel [20], which integrates the advantage of Gaussian kernel and Polynomial kernel. The formula is as follow:

$$K(x, y) = \left[exp\left(-\frac{\|x - y\|^2}{2\sigma^2}\right) + R\right]^d$$
$$\forall R \geq 0, d \geq 0, d \in N. \tag{5}$$

According to the binomial theorem, the above formula is expanded as follow:

$$K(x, y) = \left[exp\left(-\frac{\|x - y\|^2}{2\sigma^2}\right) + R\right]^d$$
$$= \sum_{s=0}^{d} \binom{d}{s} R^{d-s} exp\left(-\frac{s\|x - y\|^2}{2\sigma^2}\right)$$
$$= R^d + \sum_{s=1}^{d} \binom{d}{s} R^{d-s} exp\left(-\frac{\|x - y\|^2}{2\sigma^2/s}\right). \tag{6}$$

It is obvious that weighted Gaussian kernel is a combination of d Gaussian kernels with different widths, that the widths are changed from σ^2 to σ^2/s.

Weight R^{d-s} is used to reflect the importance of the $d - s$ kernel and enlarge the linear translation of distance between points. In this way, we expand the difference between points so instances of nuance could be clustered preferably.

3.3   MVMKC Algorithm

Different with traditional Gaussian kernel function, we develop weighted Gaussian kernel to calculate the distance and update objective function. It adapts for different datasets by adjusting parameters and increases the distance between variables so as to separate them easily. In addition, we introduce the weight of each variable in different views to measure the importance of them.

Firstly, Kernel Principal Component Analysis (KPCA) is used to reduce dimension and the datasets are normalized. Then MVMKC is imported. Finally clustering centroids and variable weight matrix are updated. The algorithm flow is shown in the following Fig. 1:

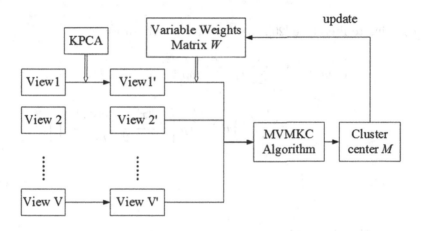

Fig. 1. The flow chart of MVMKC

Now given a multi-view dataset with V views and N samples: $X = \{x_i\}_{i=1}^{N}$, $x_i = \{x_i^{(v)}\}_{v=1}^{V}$, x_i is the ith sample, and $x_i \in \mathbb{R}^{d(v)}$ prensents the ith sample in the vth view. The dataset would be partitioned into K disjoint clusters $C_1, C_2, \ldots, C_K$ and $\{m_k\}_{k=1}^{K}$ is the kth cluster centroid. δ_{ik} is the indicator variable with $\delta_{ik} = 1$ if $x_i \in m_k$ and otherwise $\delta_{ik} = 0$. The objective function based on K-means and kernel is as follow:

$$\min J(w, m_k) = \sum_{v=1}^{V} \sum_{i=1}^{N} w_{i,v} \sum_{k=1}^{K} \delta_{ik} \left\| \phi^{(v)}(x_i^{(v)}) - \phi^{(v)}(m_k^{(v)}) \right\|^2$$

$$s.t. w_{i,v} \geq 0, \prod_{v=1}^{V} w_{i,v} = 1 \tag{7}$$

where $w_{i,v}(i = 1, 2, \ldots, N; v = 1, 2, \ldots, V)$ is a vector of variable weights, in which rows represent all variables and columns represent weight values of one variable in different views. i.e. $\prod_{v=1}^{V} w_{i,v} = 1(i = 1, 2, \ldots, N)$.

And Euclidean distance in the feature space is expanded as follow [21]:

$$\left\|\phi^{(v)}(x_i^{(v)}) - \phi^{(v)}(m_k^{(v)})\right\|^2 = (\phi^{(v)}(x_i^{(v)}) - \phi^{(v)}(m_k^{(v)})) \cdot (\phi^{(v)}(x_i^{(v)}) - \phi^{(v)}(m_k^{(v)}))$$
$$= \phi^{(v)}(x_i^{(v)}) \cdot \phi^{(v)}(x_i^{(v)}) + \phi^{(v)}(m_k^{(v)}) \cdot \phi^{(v)}(m_k^{(v)}) - 2\phi^{(v)}(x_i^{(v)}) \cdot \phi^{(v)}(m_k^{(v)}). \tag{8}$$

As $K(x_i, x_j) = \phi(x_i) \cdot \phi(x_j)$, the above equation is converted to:

$$J(w, m_k) = \sum_{v=1}^{V} \sum_{i=1}^{N} w_{i,v} \sum_{k=1}^{K} \delta_{ik} \left[K(x_i^{(v)}, x_i^{(v)}) + K(m_k^{(v)}, m_k^{(v)}) \right.$$
$$\left. - 2K(x_i^{(v)}, m_k^{(v)}) \right]. \tag{9}$$

According to literature [20], the objective is written as:

$$\min J(w, m_k) = \sum_{v=1}^{V} \sum_{i=1}^{N} w_{i,v} \sum_{k=1}^{K} 2\delta_{ik} \left[(1 + R)^d - R^d \right.$$
$$\left. - \sum_{s=1}^{d} \binom{d}{s} R^{d-s} exp\left(-\frac{\left\| x_i^{(v)} - m_k^{(v)} \right\|^2}{2\sigma^2/s} \right) \right].$$
$$s.t. w_{i,v} \geq 0, \prod_{v=1}^{V} w_{i,v} = 1. \tag{10}$$

3.4   Algorithm Derivation

An iterative algorithm is advanced to update the cluster center m_k and weight value $w_{i,v}$.

Before making a calculation, we define that:

$$H_i^v = \sum_{k=1}^{K} 2\delta_{ik} \left[(1 + R)^d - R^d - \sum_{s=1}^{d} \binom{d}{s} R^{d-s} exp\left(-\frac{\left\| x_i^{(v)} - m_k^{(v)} \right\|^2}{2\sigma^2/s} \right) \right]. \tag{11}$$

$$D^v = exp\left(-\frac{\left\| x_i^{(v)} - m_k^{(v)} \right\|^2}{2\sigma^2} \right). \tag{12}$$

The first step is to update m_k, when $w_{i,v}$ is fixed, according to [22], cluster center m_k is calculated as follow:

$$m_k = \frac{\sum_{v=1}^{V} \sum_{i=1}^{N} w_{i,v}\delta_{ik}(D^v + R)^d * D^v * x_i^{(v)}}{\sum_{v=1}^{V} \sum_{i=1}^{N} w_{i,v}\delta_{ik}(D^v + R)^d * D^v}. \tag{13}$$

The most important step is to calculate weight $w_{i,v}$. We incorporate the constraints into objective function and construct the Lagrangian expression:

$$L = \sum_{v=1}^{V} \sum_{i=1}^{N} w_{i,v}H_i^v + \lambda(\prod_{v=1}^{V} w_{i,v} - 1). \tag{14}$$

Setting the derivative of the Lagrangian to zero yields, the $w_{i,v}$ can be obtained as follow:

$$w_{i,v} = \frac{(\prod_{v'=1}^{V} H_i^{v'})^{\frac{1}{V}}}{H_i^v}. \tag{15}$$

Determining the clustering center m_k and weight $w_{i,v}$, the sample is divided into the nearest cluster by comparing the distance between it to all clusters:

if

$$\sum_{v=1}^{V} w_{i,v} \left\| \phi^{(v)}(x_i^{(v)}) - \phi^{(v)}(m_k^{(v)}) \right\|^2 < \sum_{v=1}^{V} w_{i,v} \left\| \phi^{(v)}(x_i^{(v)}) - \phi^{(v)}(m_l^{(v)}) \right\|^2. \tag{16}$$

$\forall l \neq k$,   then $x_i \in C_k$.

The above two formulas (14) and (15) are worked cyclically, until objective function converges. The specific process of algorithm MVMKC is as shown below.

Algorithm 1. (MVMKC Algorithm)

Input:
    Multi-view dataset X; The number of views V; The number of clusters K;
    The parameters R, d
Output:
    Clustering centroids M, cluster labels C, variable weights W
Initial The cluster centroids M, $w_{i,v} = 1$;
    Obtain a new dataset by using KPCA and normalization;
Repeat
    1) Fix W and C, update M according formula (13)
    2) Fix M and C, update W according formula (15)
    3) Fix W and M, update C according formula (16)
Untill eq.(10) convergence
End

---

4 Experiment

In order to demonstrate the performance of MVMKC algorithm, we conducted a comparative experiment on several data sets.

4.1 Experiment Setting

Data Sets. In this experiment, seven real world datasets are used to test the effect of algorithm. They are Digits, Animal, SenseIT, CiteSeer, Texas, Wisconsin, and Washington. The information aggregation of the six multi-view clustering datasets used in the experiment is as Table 1 shown.

Table 1. Detail information of datasets

Dataset	Digits	Animal	SenseIT	CiteSeer	Texas	Wisconsin	Washington
Instances	2000	2594	1000	3312	187	265	230
Views	6	3	2	2	2	2	2
Clusters	10	6	3	6	5	5	5

Digits is a multi-view dataset that consists of features of handwritten numerals ($'0' -' 9'$) corresponding to 200 samples.

Animal is constituted by 2594 samples selected from 30475 samples, mainly divided into 6 types, and three views are RGSIFT, SURF and LSS separately.

SenseIT describes a wireless sensor network, which consists of two different types of sensors to send three types of vehicle signals to intelligent transportation systems.

CiteSeer is a link dataset with 3312 scientific publications. Each publication is described by a 0/1-valued word vector indicating the absence/presence of the corresponding word from the dictionary.

Texas, Washington and Wisconsin are three sub datasets of WebKB dataset. And each item is described by web text and web link.

Baseline Algorithms. In addition, five methods are taken as baseline algorithms. They are RMKMC [23], MVKKM and MVSPec [11], RMSC [24] and TWkmeans [25]. RMKMC is a robust clustering method aims on large-scale data with heterogeneous representations. MVKKM and MVSpec are multi-view kernel K-means and spectral clustering methods. TWkmeans is a multi-view clustering method based on two-level variable weighting automatically.

Evaluating Indicators. We adopt two metrics as standard evaluation: RI (Rand Index) [26] and F-measure [27].

RI (Rand Index) evaluates the fitting degree of two partition and is defined by:

$$RI = \frac{N_a + N_B}{N}. \tag{17}$$

N_a is the number of object pairs that co-occur in a cluster and co-occur in a class. N_b is the number of object pairs that do not co-occur in a cluster and do not co-occur in a class. And N is the total number of object pairs.

F-measure is commonly used in information retrieval. And its formula is as follows:

$$F = \frac{2 * p * r}{p + r} \tag{18}$$

where, p is precision and r is recall rate.

4.2   Results

In the experiment, we set the parameters $d = 4, R = 0.6$, and maximum iteration number is set to 50 empirically. Considering influence of the initial clustering centroids and parameters setting, all algorithms are run 30 times and took the average. And the comparison results of 5 baseline algorithms and MVMKC are shown in the following tables. Tables 2 and 3 are the results of F-measure and RI respectively.

Table 2. F-measure of 6 algorithms on 7 datasets

Dataset	RMKMC	MVKKM	MVSpec	RMSC	TWkmeans	MVMKC
digits	0.5032	0.3873	0.3811	0.679	**0.7449**	0.4818
Animal	0.2811	0.2556	0.2556	0.2314	0.2395	**0.3477**
SenseIT	0.4391	0.4515	0.4466	0.5078	0.4501	**0.5955**
CiteSeer	0.3193	0.2825	0.3445	0.2686	0.2535	**0.4801**
Texas	0.4478	0.4747	0.4191	0.369	0.5535	**0.8919**
Wisconsin	0.5013	0.4018	0.3675	0.2969	0.5146	**0.6009**
Washington	0.4856	0.5701	0.4757	0.3613	0.514	**0.7149**

In this part, MVMKC algorithm is compared with the other 5 algorithms in order to prove the effectiveness of MVMKC algorithm. The closer the evaluation index values to 1, the better the clustering effect. This is due to MVMKC weights variables respectively and lower the intersection between different variables. One the other hand, the advantage of MKL technique is embedded in the comparison of MVKKM and MVSpec.

In order to analyze the convergence of the MVMKC algorithm, F-measure, RI and objective function value is recorded during the iterative process. Figure 2 displays the change course over iteration times on 3Source dataset. It is noted that MVMKC algorithm achieves convergence through about 10 iterations.

Table 3. RI of 6 algorithms on 7 datasets

Dataset	RMKMC	MVKKM	MVSpec	RMSC	TWkmeans	MVMKC
digits	0.8863	0.8659	0.6752	0.9353	**0.9448**	0.5995
Animal	0.6688	0.687	0.7174	0.7205	0.414	**0.7406**
SenseIT	0.5936	0.5865	0.5914	0.6467	0.5421	**0.6047**
CiteSeer	0.751	0.384	0.7605	0.7301	0.7092	**0.7981**
Texas	0.6559	0.6364	0.6513	0.6261	0.4716	**0.6577**
Wisconsin	0.7271	0.5098	0.6665	0.6157	0.5206	**0.7322**
Washington	0.714	0.655	0.7062	0.6519	0.5022	**0.7235**

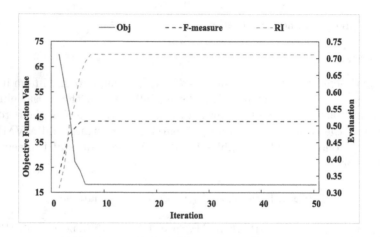

Fig. 2. Proof of convergence of MVMKC

5   Conclusion

This paper presents MVMKC, an innovative multi-view clustering algorithm based on variable weights and MKL. It uses a weighted Gaussian kernel function and forms a new kernel function to calculate the distance. Meanwhile, it computes weights of variables and updates them automatically. So it achieves a superior clustering effect by reducing the influence between variables.

Experiment on seven datasets shows that MVMKC outperforms the other five algorithms significantly on F-measure and RI. But MVMKC is not good at processing data with high number views. We will devote ourselves to this problem.

References

1. Cheng, Y., Zhao, R.: Multiview spectral clustering via ensemble. In: IEEE International Conference on Granular Computing, pp. 101–106 (2009)

2. Kumar, A., Rai, R., Daume, H.: Co-regularized multi-view spectral clustering. Adv. Neural Inf. Process. Syst. **24**, 1413–1421 (2011)
3. Blaschko, M.B., Lampert, C.H.: Correlational spectral clustering. In: IEEE Conference on Computer Vision and Pattern Recognition, pp. 1–8 (2008)
4. Kumar, A., Daume, H.: A co-training approach for multi-view spectral clustering. Int. Conf. Mach. Learn. **44**(4), 393–400 (2011)
5. Ajzerman, M.A., Braverman, E.M., Rozonoehr, L.I.: Theoretical foundations of the potential function method in pattern recognition learning. Autom. Remote Control. Doc2 **25**(6), 821–837 (1964)
6. Gonen, M., Alpaydin, E.: Multiple kernel learning algorithms. J. Mach. Learn. Res. **12**, 2211–2268 (2011)
7. Bickel, S., Scheffer, T.: Multi-view clustering. In: International Conference on Data Mining, pp. 19–26 (2004)
8. Cui, Y., Fern, X.Z., Dy, J.G.: Non-redundant multi-view clustering via orthogonalization. In: International Conference on Data Mining, pp. 133–142 (2007)
9. Chaudhuri, K., Kakade, S.M., Livescu, K., et al.: Multi-view clustering via canonical correlation analysis. In: International Conference on Machine Learning, pp. 129–136 (2009)
10. He, M., Yang, Y., Wang, H.: Learning latent features for multi-view clustering based on NMF. In: International Joint Conference on Rough Sets, LNAI9920, pp. 459–469 (2016)
11. Tzortzis, G., Likas, A.: Kernel-based weighted multi-view clustering. IEEE Int. Conf. Data Min. **5**(1), 675–684 (2012)
12. Guo, D., Zhang, J., Liu, X., et al.: Multiple kernel learning based multi-view spectral clustering. In: International Conference on Pattern Recognition, pp. 3774–3779 (2014)
13. Nazarpour, A., Adibi, P.: Two-stage multiple kernel learning for supervised dimensionality reduction. Pattern Recogn. **48**(5), 1854–1862 (2015)
14. Fu, G., Wang, Q., Bai, D., et al.: Group based localized multiple kernel algorithm with lp-norm. Int. J. Innov. Comput. Inf. Control **12**, 1835–1849 (2016)
15. Huang, J.Z., Ng, M.K., Rong, H., et al.: Automated variable weighting in k-means type clustering. IEEE Trans. Pattern Anal. Mach. Intell. **27**(5), 657–668 (2005)
16. Domeniconi, C., Gunopulos, D., Ma, S., et al.: Locally adaptive metrics for clustering high dimensional data. Data Min. Knowl. Disc. **14**(1), 63–97 (2007)
17. Jing, L., Ng, M.K., Huang, J.Z.: An entropy weighting k-means algorithm for subspace clustering of high-dimensional sparse data. IEEE Trans. Knowl. Data Eng. **19**(8), 1026–1041 (2007)
18. Cheng, H., Hua, K.A., Vu, K.: Constrained locally weighted clustering. VLDB Endow. **1**(1), 90–101 (2008)
19. Burges, C.J.C.: Geometry and invariance in kernel based methods. In: Advances in Kernel Methods. MIT Press (1998)
20. Tian, J., Zhao, L.: Weighted gaussian kernel with multiple widths and support vector classifications. In: IEEE International Symposium on Information Engineering and Electronic Commerce, pp. 79–382 (2009)
21. Filippone, M., Camastra, F., Masulli, F., et al.: A survey of kernel and spectral methods for clustering. Pattern Recogn. **41**(1), 176–190 (2008)
22. Ferreira, M.R.P., de Carvalho, F.D.A.T., Simoes, E.C.: Kernel-based hard clustering methods with kernelization of the metric and automatic weighting of the variables. Pattern Recogn. **51**, 310–321 (2016)
23. Xiao, C., Nie, F., Huang, H.: Multi-view k-means clustering on big data. In: International Joint Conference on Artificial Intelligence, pp. 2598–2604 (2013)

24. Xia, R., Pan, Y., Du, L., Yin, J.: Robust multi-view spectral clustering via low-rank and sparse decomposition. Artif. Intell. **3**, 2149–2155 (2011)
25. Chen, X., Xu, X., Huang, J., Ye, Y.: TW-K-means: automated two-level variable weighting clustering algorithm for multi-view data. IEEE Trans. Knowl. Data Eng. **25**(4), 932–944 (2013)
26. Rand, W.M.: Objective criteria for the evaluation of clustering methods. J. Am. Stat. Assoc. **66**(336), 846–850 (1971)
27. Yang, Y., Jin, F.: Mohamed, K: Survey of clustering validity evaluation. Appl. Res. Comput. **25**(6), 1630–1629 (2008)

An Overlapping Clustering Approach with Correlation Weight

Yingge Xu, Yan Yang[✉], Hongjun Wang, and Jie Hu

School of Information Science and Technology, Southwest Jiaotong University,
Chengdu 610031, People's Republic of China
yyang@swjtu.edu.cn

Abstract. Overlapping clustering works on the hypothesis that one object belongs to one or more clusters. It tolerates intersection among clusters and discovers overlapping information hidden in observed data as well. Most overlapping clustering methods dedicate to studying the strategy of discovering overlapping observations, and ignore the correlation of overlapping observation and different clusters. In this paper, an Overlapping Clustering approach with Correlation Weight (called OCCW) is proposed. Correlation weights are assigned to those clusters that one observation belongs to along with the multi-assignment procedure in our approach. Experiments on multi-label datasets, subsets of movie recommendation dataset and text dataset demonstrate that the proposed algorithm has a better performance compared with several existing approaches.

Keywords: Overlapping clustering · Correlation weight · Multi-assignment

1 Introduction

Clustering is a process of detecting structures hidden in observed data, so that observations within one cluster are similar to each other but are dissimilar to objects in other clusters. Clustering plays an important role in various fields, including data mining, machine learning and statistics. Almost all kinds of clustering methods assume that each observation should belong to one cluster exactly and finally make a clear distinction among different clusters.

In practice, however, overlapping data is ubiquitous in many application domains, ranging from information retrieval to disease diagnosis, market analysis and personalized recommendation. With the evolution of Internet and information technology, overlapping phenomena are especially apparent in topic detection, recommended system and social network. For example, in topic detection,

This work is supported by the Natioanl Science Foundation of China (Nos. 61572407 and 61603313), the Project of National Science and Technology Support Program (No. 2015BAH19F02).

L. Polkowski et al. (Eds.): IJCRS 2017, Part I, LNAI 10313, pp. 611–619, 2017.
DOI: 10.1007/978-3-319-60837-2_49

a fair number of news and articles are related to several subjects. In social networks, one person may participate in several social hubs. In this case, clustering analysis with conventional algorithms may result in some deviation with the reality. For this reason, overlapping clustering, which allows overlaps among clusters, becomes a research hotspot and makes a lot of sense and practicability.

The relationship of overlapping observation to multiple clusters is distinct and exerts different influence on the evolution of clusters. Most existing approaches dedicate to studying the strategy of discovering overlapping observation and ignore the correlation of overlapping observation and different clusters.

In this paper, we propose a new Overlapping Clustering approach with Correlation Weight (called OCCW). Here weight is used to indicate the closeness degree of one observation and those overlapping clusters that it belongs to. And its influence could be reflected by the image of the observation in overlapping region. Experiments on Multi-label datasets, subsets of movie recommendation dataset and text dataset illustrate the effectiveness of our approach.

The rest of this paper is organized as follows: Sect. 2 provides some major works relevant to overlapping clusters. Section 3 presents the overlapping clustering approach with correlation weight we propose. Section 4 describes comparative experiments and results on overlapping datasets and thereafter conclusions are shown.

2   Related Work

In this section, we give a brief introduction to literatures on overlapping clustering.

2.1   Overlapping Clustering

The first overlapping partition method is proposed by Jardine and Sibson early in 1971, which introduces the idea of overlapping to mathematical taxonomy [1]. Shepard and Arabie put forward a famous additive clustering model leading to overlapping clusters [2]. Thereafter researches on overlapping clustering are mostly on the basis of hierarchical model [3,4] and graph theory [5,6]. With the evolution of Internet and information technology, overlapping clustering has set off a research boom in academia once again. One category method among is generative model based, conducting EM-type alternating optimization procedure. Banerjee et al. addressed MOC (Model-based Overlapping Clustering) under the inspiration of probabilistic relational models applied in the gene microarray data [7]. Fu and Banerjee provided a MMMs (Multiplicative Mixture Models) in the view of additive mixture models and further illustrate kernelized MMMs as a general model [8]. One kind approach to identify non-disjoint clusters is partitioning-based, in which Cleuziou has made great contributions [9–11]. Baadel et al. developed an overlapping algorithm having a good adaptation to different datasets, which uses the maximum distance allowed in K-means to assign objects to a given cluster as the global threshold [12]. Besides, Another category is rough set based. Yu provided a three-way decision strategy for over-lapping clustering based on the decision-theoretic rough set model [13].

2.2 Partitioning Overlapping Clustering

The simplest and most fundamental method of cluster analysis is partitioning, which organizes the objects of a set into several groups or clusters. Partitional methods are the most widely used and even in many complex methods. Hence, it makes a lot of sense and has better practicability to extend partitional method to overlapping clustering. If we regard center of the cluster that observation belongs to as its image, clustering analysis is to find the best image for each observation in the dataset. From this viewpoint, Cleuziou proposed a new objective criterion and extended an overlapping version of classical K-means algorithm (called OKM) [9]. To optimize the framework, Cleuziou puts forward a weighted overlapping K-means algorithm (called WOKM) by importing local feature weight [10].

3 Overlapping Clustering with Correlation Weight

In this section, we discribe overlapping clustering approach with correlation weight on defects of partitioning overlapping clustering.

3.1 Motivation

Let X be a set of n observations represented by n-dimensional feature vectors $x_i = \{x_{i1}, x_{i2}, \cdots, x_{id}\}$ where $X = \{x_1, x_2, \cdots, x_n\}$. The aim of overlapping clustering is to find a coverage $\{\pi_j\}_{j=1}^k$ of k non-disjoint covers centering on v_j, $j = 1, 2, \cdots, k$ respectively.

First, OKM [9] proceeds optimization process by minimizing the sum of distances between observation x_i and its corresponding image x_i^*. The image of observation x_i is acquired by the gravity center of clusters representatives to which it belongs to:

$$x_i^* = \frac{\sum_{v_j \in \mathbb{A}_i} v_j}{\mid A_i \mid}. \tag{1}$$

In formula (1), A_i is the cluster set of observation x_i belongs to. Obviously, this formulation treats those clusters that one object belongs to *equally*, and ignores the distinction of correlation degree, which is not in accordance with actual situations. This is the first motivation of OCCW algorithm.

More generally, WOKM [10] imports local feature weight ω_{jp} which denotes the important of the pth attribute in cover π_j. Then ω_{jp} is transferred to sample feature weight λ_{ip} to guide multi-assignment. The optimization of WOKM is performed by multi-assignment, representative updating and weight updating in turn, which results in a *high time complexity* $O(t \cdot n \cdot d \cdot k \lg k)$, where t denotes the number of iterations. This is the other motivation of OCCW algorithm.

3.2   OCCW Algorithm

Considering different effect of clusters that one observation is assigned to, we propose an overlapping clustering approach with correlation weight. The quality of OCCW approach is measured by the sum of squared error between all observations in dataset and its corresponding image, which can be expressed by the following formula:

$$J(\{\pi_j\}_{j=1}^{k}) = \sum_{i=1}^{n} \| x_i - \phi(x_i) \|^2 . \tag{2}$$

Here, $\phi(x_i)$ indicates the image of observation x_i. For the above analysis, we introduce membership weight ω_{ij} to indicate the correlation degree of observation x_i and cover π_j. Hence, the image of observation x_i could be viewed as the weighted gravity center of clusters it belongs to.

$$\phi(x_i) = \sum_{v_j \in \mathbb{A}_i} \omega_{ij} v_j, s.t. \sum_{v_j \in \mathbb{A}_i} \omega_{ij} = 1. \tag{3}$$

First of all, we illustrate the update of the image by combining multi-assignment procedure.

1. Find the nearest cluster representative

$$h = \arg\min_{j;j=1,2,\cdots,k} \| x_i - v_j \|^2,$$

and set $A_i = \{h\}$, $\phi(x_i) = v_h$, $\omega_{ih} = 1$.

2. Find the next nearest cluster representative

$$h' = \arg\min_{j;j=1,2,\cdots,k\backslash\{A_i\}} \| x_i - v_j \|^2,$$

set $A_i' = A_i \cup \{h'\}$, compute correlation weight between observation x_i and cluster π_j

$$\omega_{ih'} = \frac{1/ \| x_i - v_h' \|^2}{\sum_{l \in \mathbb{A}_i'}(1/ \| x_i - v_l \|^2)},$$

and the latent image

$$\phi'(x_i) = \omega_{ih'}(\phi(x_i) - v_h') + v_h'.$$

3. If $\| x_i - \phi'(x_i) \|^2 < \| x_i - \phi(x_i) \|^2$, update correlation weight of clusters in A_i in proportion, set $A_i = A_i'$, $\phi(x_i) = \phi'(x_i)$, and continue to step 2; otherwise output A_i and ω_i.

The update formula of $\phi(x_i)$ during multi-assignment is derived based on vector space model. With the limitation of space, the derivation process is omitted.

Different with membership degree in FCM algorithm [14], membership weight in OCCW is assigned from the nearest cluster to the farthest, and the process is terminated when $\| x_i - x_i^* \|^2$ is larger than the present assignment. This technique provides two advantages including: (a) Ignore the influence of clusters that have a small correlation degree with observation x_i; (b) In this way, membership weight could be calculated along with multi-assignment procedure, so the time complexity of OCCW algorithm is $O(t \cdot n \cdot k \lg k)$.

Next, with k covers and correlation information obtained by multi-assignment procedure, the update of cluster representative, which is similar to that of K-means algorithm is a convex optimization problem. According to formula (2) and (3), it is convenient to obtain

$$v_j = \frac{1}{\sum_{x_i \in \pi_j} \omega_{ij}^2} \sum_{x_i \in \pi_j} \omega_{ij}(x_i - \sum_{v_l \in \mathbb{A}_i \setminus \{v_j\}} \omega_{il} v_l). \tag{4}$$

That is to say, cluster representative is the weighted average belonging to the cluster with the consideration of correlation.

It is noted that, in the final of OCCW, a post-processing is necessary to convert weight matrix to label matrix. The procedure of OCCW algorithm is shown as Table 1.

Table 1. Algorithm OCCW discription

Algorithm OCCW

Input: Dataset X; Number of Clusters k; Convergence threshold ε;
Output: A non-disjoint coverage $\{\pi_j\}_{j=1}^k$.
Method:
1) Choose k observations in X as the initial cluster representatives;
2) Repeat;
   3) Calculate the image for each $x_i \in \mathbb{X}$ starting from the nearest to the farthest according to formula (3) and assign it to the cluster while gaining a better image;
   4) Update cluster representatives according to formula (4);
5) Until convergence;
6) Convert weight matrix to label matrix.

---

4   Experiments

To illustrate the performance of OCCW approach, we conduct comparison experiments with MOC [7], OKM [9] and WOKM [10].

4.1   Datasets and Evaluation Standard

Three types of datasets are used: multi-label datasets [15], movie recommendation dataset [16] and text dataset [17].

For multi-label datasets, the *emotions* dataset classifies songs by 6 kinds of emotions: *happy, sad, calm, surprised, quiet* and *angry*; the *scene* dataset is categorized by image scene: *beach, sunset, fallfoliage, field, mountain* and *urban*.

For movie recommendation data, MovieLens dataset contains 100,000 ratings (1–5) from 943 users on 1682 movies [18]. And each movie could be denoted as a vector of 943 user ratings. Based on the user ratings, we can cluster movies in terms of their genres. The corresponding genre information of these movies is extracted from the Internet Movie Database (IMDB) collection. We create two subsets of rating matrix from MovieLens dataset: *movie_taa*: 517 movies containing *thriller, action* and *adventure*; *movie_afc*: 526 movies containing *animation, family* and *comedy*.

For text data, 3source is a multi-view dataset which collects 948 news articles covering 416 distinct news stories by three well-known online news sources: BBC, Reuters and The Guardian. Each story was manually annotated with one or more of the six topical labels: *business, entertainment, health, politics, sport* and *technology*. Here we only use the 169 news data reported by all three sources.

Table 2 gives statistics of the mentioned datasets. The quantity *cardinality* is the average number of labels one instance has in the dataset.

Table 2. Detail information of datasets

Dataset	Instances	dimensions	Clssses	Cardinality
Emotions	593	72	6	1.87
Scene	2407	294	6	1.07
Movie_taa	517	943	3	1.44
Movie_afc	526	943	3	1.16
3source	169	9944	6	1.12

To measure the clustering performance, we take F-measure and Rand Index as evaluation standard. F-measure is the harmonic mean of precision and recall.

$$P = \frac{Number\,of\,Correctly\,Identified\,Pairs}{Number\,of\,Identified\,Pairs}. \tag{5}$$

$$R = \frac{Number\,of\,Correctly\,Identified\,Pairs}{Number\,of\,True\,Pairs}. \tag{6}$$

$$F_\beta = \frac{(\beta^2+1)P*R}{\beta^2 P + R}. \tag{7}$$

In above formula, P is precision rate, R is recall rate and β is a weight parameter to balance the two. $\beta > 1$ means giving more weight to recall, whereas $\beta < 1$ means giving more weight to precision. Here, excessive or lacking overlaps both are not what we expect, so we define $\beta = 1$ weighting precision and recall equally.

4.2   Experiment Results

Table 3 lists the results including: precision (P), recall (R), F-measure (F_1), Rand Index (RI) and CPU time (T). In order to evaluate the clustering result better, we conduct repeated experiments 10 times and take the average as final results. It's worth mentioning that Euclidean distance is used for multi-label datasets and I-divergence with Laplace smoothing [19] is used for movie recommendation dataset and text dataset in our experiments.

Table 3. Experiment results of four algorithms

Dataset		Emotions	Scene	Movie_taa	Movie_afc	3source
P	MOC	0.5021	**0.4438**	0.6452	0.8129	0.2789
	OKM	0.4850	0.2155	0.6479	0.8119	0.2897
	WOKM	0.4932	0.2289	0.6515	0.8137	0.2833
	OCCW	**0.5091**	0.3191	**0.6541**	**0.8163**	**0.3233**
R	MOC	0.2110	0.4132	0.6946	0.5284	0.8910
	OKM	**0.5129**	**0.9415**	0.8489	0.9038	**0.9573**
	WOKM	0.5076	0.8333	0.8523	0.9112	0.9282
	OCCW	0.3957	0.8087	**0.8739**	**0.9418**	0.9455
F_1	MOC	0.3972	0.4280	0.6690	0.6405	0.4248
	OKM	0.4986	0.3507	0.7349	0.8554	0.4448
	WOKM	**0.5002**	0.3591	0.7384	0.8597	0.4363
	OCCW	0.4453	**0.4576**	**0.7482**	**0.8746**	**0.4819**
RI	MOC	0.5294	**0.7866**	0.5539	0.5228	0.3230
	OKM	0.5136	0.3264	0.6026	0.7542	0.3295
	WOKM	0.5217	0.4532	**0.6301**	0.7686	0.3476
	OCCW	**0.5352**	0.6295	0.6182	0.7828	0.4295
T	MOC	10	3493	93	46	12
	OKM	4	366	5	**10**	**17**
	WOKM	25	894	36	49	672
	OCCW	**2**	**25**	**4**	14	74

Firstly, it is noted that OCCW gains the best F-measure on five datasets and the best Rand Index on three datasets. That is to say, our OCCW approach can detect structure hidden in overlapping data more precisely.

From the result of *scene* dataset, MOC approach fails to find overlapping observations therein and gets a good ranking.

The last measure in Table 3, CPU time, shows the running time of the four algorithms under the same experimental conditions. Compared with OKM and WOKM, our OCCW approach achieves convergence in a relatively short time.

5   Conclusions

In overlapping clustering, it is possible that one observation is close to several clusters at the same time but in different extents. This paper proposes a new overlapping clustering approach called OCCW. It imports a correlation weight to distinguish the closeness degree of clusters that one observation belongs to. It is a trade off between crisp and fuzzy clustering. Experiments on several overlapping datasets illustrate its better performance. In our Experiment, we find that OCCW approach is sensitive to initial cluster representatives. And as it takes a rough treatment on correlation weight, in the future we may consider the scale of clusters into overlapped weight to develop more robust methods.

References

1. Jardine, N., Sibson, R.: Mathematical taxonomy. J. Syst. Zool. **15**, 188–189 (1974)
2. Shepard, R.N., Arabie, P.: Additive clustering: representation of similarities as combination of discrete overlapping properties. J. Psychol. Rev. **86**(2), 87–123 (1979)
3. Diday, E.: Orders and overlapping clusters by pyramids. J. Technical report 730, INRIA (1984)
4. Gama, F., Segarra, S., Ribeiro, A.: Hierarchical overlapping clustering of network data using cut metrics. IEEE Trans. Sig. Infor. Process. Netw. 1–13 (2016, submitted). arXiv:1611.01393v1 [cs.SI] 4 Nov 2016
5. Gregory, S.: An algorithm to find overlapping community structure in networks. In: Kok, J.N., Koronacki, J., Lopez de Mantaras, R., Matwin, S., Mladenič, D., Skowron, A. (eds.) PKDD 2007. LNCS, vol. 4702, pp. 91–102. Springer, Heidelberg (2007). doi:10.1007/978-3-540-74976-9_12
6. Whang, J.J., Gleich, D.F., Dhillon, I.S.: Overlapping community detection using neighborhood-inflated seed expansion. IEEE Trans. Knowl. Data Eng. **28**(5), 1272–1284 (2016)
7. Banerjee, A., Krumpelman, C., Ghosh, J., Basu, S., Mooney, R.J.: Model-based overlapping clustering. In: Eleventh ACM SIGKDD International Conference on Knowledge Discovery and Data Mining, pp. 532–537 (2005)
8. Fu, Q., Banerjee, A.: Multiplicative mixture models for overlapping clustering. In: IEEE International Conference on Data Mining, pp. 791–796 (2008)
9. Cleuziou, G.: An extended version of the k-means method for overlapping clustering. In: International Conference on Pattern Recognition, pp. 1–4 (2008)
10. Cleuziou, G.: Two variants of the OKM for overlapping clustering. In: Guillet, F., Ritschard, G., Zighed, D.A., Briand, H. (eds.) Advances in Knowledge Discovery and Management, pp. 149–166. Springer, Heidelberg (2009)
11. Cleuziou, G.: Osom: a method for building overlapping topological maps. Pattern Recogn. Lett. **34**(3), 239–246 (2013)
12. Baadel, S., Thabtah, F., Lu, J.: MCOKE: multi-cluster overlapping k-means extension algorithm. Int. J. Comput. Electr. Autom. Control Inf. Eng. **9**(2), 427–430 (2015)
13. Yu, H., Wang, Y.: Three-way decisions method for overlapping clustering. In: Yao, J.T., Yang, Y., Słowiński, R., Greco, S., Li, H., Mitra, S., Polkowski, L. (eds.) RSCTC 2012. LNCS, vol. 7413, pp. 277–286. Springer, Heidelberg (2012). doi:10.1007/978-3-642-32115-3_33

14. Bezdek, J.C.: Selected applications in classifier design. In: Bezdek, J.C. (ed.) Pattern Recognition with Fuzzy Objective Function Algorithms, vol. 22, no. 1171, pp. 203–239. Plenum Press, New York (1981)
15. Mulan. http://mulan.sourceforge.net/datasets-mlc.html
16. GroupLens. http://grouplens.org/datasets/movielens/
17. Insight Project Resources. http://mlg.ucd.ie/datasets/3sources.html
18. Harper, F.M., Konstan, J.A.: The movielens datasets: history and context. ACM Trans. Interact. Intell. Syst. 5(4), 1–20 (2015)
19. Ghosh, J.: Clustering with bregman divergences. J. Mach. Learn. Res. 6(4), 1705–1749 (2004)

Software and Systems for Rough Sets

A Metadata Diagnostic Framework for a New Approximate Query Engine Working with Granulated Data Summaries

Agnieszka Chądzyńska-Krasowska[1], Sebastian Stawicki[2],
and Dominik Ślęzak[2(✉)]

[1] Polish-Japanese Academy of Information Technology,
Koszykowa 86, 02-008 Warsaw, Poland
[2] Institute of Informatics, University of Warsaw,
Banacha 2, 02-097 Warsaw, Poland
slezak@mimuw.edu.pl

Abstract. This paper refers to a new database engine that acquires and utilizes granulated data summaries for the purposes of fast approximate execution of analytical SQL statements. We focus on the task of creation of a relational metadata repository which enables the engine developers and users to investigate the collected data summaries independently from the engine itself. We discuss how the design of the considered repository evolved over time from both conceptual and software engineering perspectives, addressing the challenges of conversion and accessibility of the internal engine contents that can represent hundreds of terabytes of the original data. We show some scenarios of a usage of the obtained metadata repository for both diagnostic and analytical purposes. We pay a particular attention to the relationships of the discussed scenarios with the principles of rough sets – one of the theories that hugely influenced the presented solutions. We also report some empirical results obtained for relatively small fragments (100×2^{16} rows each) of data sets coming from two organizations that use the considered new engine.

Keywords: Big data · Approximate query · Data granulation · Metadata · Data visualization · Software tools · Business analytics

1 Introduction

There is a growing need to explore big data sets. Most companies address this challenge by scaling out resources. However, this strategy is increasingly cost-prohibitive and inefficient for large and distributed data. On the other hand, people are realizing that the tasks of data exploration could be successfully performed in at least partially approximate fashion. This way of thinking opens new opportunities to seek for a balance between the speed, resource consumption and accuracy of computations. This is particularly true for the case of an approach referred in this paper – a new engine that produces high value approximate answers to SQL statements by using the summaries of the input data.

© Springer International Publishing AG 2017
L. Polkowski et al. (Eds.): IJCRS 2017, Part I, LNAI 10313, pp. 623–643, 2017.
DOI: 10.1007/978-3-319-60837-2_50

The considered new engine captures knowledge in a form of single- and multi-column data summaries. It collects chunks of data and builds summaries for each chunk separately. Unlike in standard databases, the query execution mechanisms do not assume any access to the original chunks. For a given query received from an external tool, each subsequent data operation scheduled within the execution plan is performed as a transformation of summaries representing its input into summaries representing its output. It has been already shown in the market that the engine allows its users to achieve approximate – yet accurate enough – analytical insights 100–1000 times faster than other solutions[1].

The aim of this paper is to introduce an analytical diagnostic framework that lets the engine users and developers understand its behavior and set up expectations with respect to its efficiency in practical usage scenarios. The fundamental assumption is that these goals can be achieved by providing the analysts with sufficiently convenient way to work with the contents of data summary structures captured by the engine. Thus, we focus on the task of creation of a relational metadata repository which makes it possible to easily access and investigate the collected data summaries independently from the engine itself.

The layout of the designed repository needs to reflect two important aspects: (1) modularity of the captured knowledge structures with respect to their particular focuses (e.g.: modeling domains of single columns, modeling frequencies of column values and ranges, modeling data-driven dependencies and co-occurrences of values of different columns, etc.) and (2) modularity of the captured knowledge structures with respect to granularity of ingestion of the original data (i.e.: making sure that the contents of knowledge structures collected independently for different chunks of data can be flexibly queried together).

The developed relational metadata schema satisfies the above requirements and, actually, goes beyond our original expectations. It has become a great means for elucidation to the customers who use the considered new engine within their complex applications. It can be helpful for the users to better understand the quality and performance characteristics of query execution processes. Moreover, one may wish to explore the metadata tables directly to do basic analytics, e.g., approximately visualize demographics of particular data columns. Finally, one can also work with data summaries in their relational form while prototyping new algorithms, before implementing them within the engine.

The paper is organized as follows. In Sect. 2, we outline the architecture of the considered engine, referring also to our earlier developments and to some inspirations taken from the theory of rough sets. In Sect. 3, we discuss how our vision of a metadata repository evolved over time. In Sect. 4, we show how one can work with the proposed metadata model, for the purposes of fast data visualization, prototyping machine learning algorithms running on summaries and diagnosing whether the captured structures are enough to approximate column domains. In Sect. 5, we conclude the paper with final remarks.

---

[1] One of the current deployments of the considered new engine assumes working with 30-day periods, wherein there are over 10 billions of new data rows coming every day and ad-hoc analytical queries are required to execute in 2 s.

2   The New Approximate Query Engine

There are several ways to develop approximate SQL solutions. In most approaches, the results are estimated by executing queries on data samples [1]. One of advantages of such approaches is their ability to adapt statistical apparatus to deliver confidence intervals for approximate outcomes of simple queries. However, for truly big data sets, good-quality samples need to be large too which limits query acceleration possibilities. Moreover, the complexity of producing reliable confidence intervals grows quite quickly for more complicated select statements. The second category of approximate query methods is based on summaries (histograms, sketches, etc.) [2]. The approach considered in this paper drops into the latter category, as it forms granulated data summaries expressed by means of enhanced histograms. There is a long tradition of using histograms within standard database optimizers. In the literature, a lot of effort has been also spent on the task of updating histogram structures while loading new data. This is one of the aspects where the considered new engine is different. This is because it builds separate summaries for each subsequently collected chunks of table rows – so called *packrows*. Therefore, summaries of the newly buffered packrows do not interfere with the previously captured knowledge structures.

The foundations of the engine considered in this paper partially relate to our earlier relational database software, currently available in the market as *Infobright DB*[2]. During load, Infobright DB clusters the incoming data into 2^{16}-row packrows, additionally decomposing each packrow onto *data packs* gathering values of particular columns. The contents of data packs are described by simple summaries accessible independently from the underlying data packs. Infobright DB combines the ideas taken from modern database technologies and the theory of rough sets [3], by means of using summaries to classify data packs as irrelevant, relevant or partially relevant to particular queries. All together, the loaded data tables are processed according to the four following principles: storing data in data packs, creating approximate summaries for each of data packs, conducting approximate computations on summaries, and, whenever there is no other way to finish query execution, iteratively accessing the contents of some of data packs. As it was summarized in [4], Infobright DB is known as the first successful rough-set-based commercial development in the database industry.

When compared to Infobright DB, the solution considered in this paper operates with the data at the same level of packrow/data pack granulation but it captures their slightly richer summaries and – what is the fundamental difference – it does not need to access the actual data at all during the query execution. For each original data pack, its histogram contains information about dynamically derived range-based bars and *special values* that differ from neighboring values of the corresponding column by means of their frequencies in the corresponding packrow. Another stored structures include information about the most significant *gaps*, i.e., the areas where there are no values occurring. Finally, the engine

---

[2] Formerly known as *Brighthouse* and *Infobright Community/Enterprise Edition*.

summarizes packrow-specific co-occurrences of values belonging to bars representing pairs of columns. The engine intelligently decides what to store based on the algorithms that rank the significance of detected co-occurrences.

Figure 1 illustrates the components of one-dimensional representation of the ingested data chunks. Besides histogram ranges, special values and gaps, there is also stored basic domain information including the greatest common divisor (gcd) and the dictionary with distinct values occurring for a given column within a given packrow (stored only if the number of distinct values is low enough). The way of deriving ranges has a lot in common with the task of data discretization/quantization [5]. As the captured granular representations should be as compact as possible to achieve fast query execution, the number of ranges needs to be significantly lower than the number of original distinct values. Algorithm 1 combines two standard discretization approaches that, up to now, yield the best quality of approximate queries executed in the considered engine.

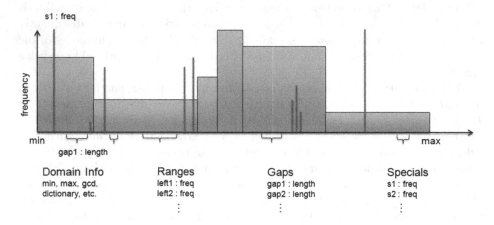

Fig. 1. Types of knowledge captured by the engine for a single original data pack.

For the same reason as above, the engine can store information only about a limited number of special values, gaps and co-occurrence ratios (also referred to as tau-ratios) which reflect local column interdependencies. Every ratio $\tau_t(x, y)$ is defined as the data-derived probability $p_t(x, y)$ of the occurrence of a pair of values or ranges x and y over two columns in a packrow t, divided by the product of marginal probabilities $p_t(x)$ and $p_t(y)$. The ranking functions identify the pairs of values/ranges with tau-ratios that maximally differ from the unity. The tau-ratios are used in approximate data operations such as, e.g., the `where`-related filtering which is implemented by following the methods of belief propagation in graphical models [6]. However, those methods need to refer also to tau-ratios that were not selected to be stored. Such ratios are represented as the averaged defaults calculated at the three hierarchy levels (one level for not stored pairs of ranges and two specific levels for not stored pairs of special values).

Algorithm 1. Histogram construction method

Input: $list$: sorted list of values v of column c in packrow t of table T;
$max\_no\_of\_buckets$: maximum number of equal-length buckets (8 by default);
$max\_no\_of\_bars$: maximum number of resulting histogram bars (64 by default);
Output: $cuts$: the list of cut-points between bars describing c in packrow t;

 1: **begin**
 2: **if** the number of distinct values in the list $\leq max\_no\_of\_bars$ **then**
 3:     add to $cuts$ all elements of $list$ except max($list$);
 4: **else**
 5:     split [min($list$), max($list$)] onto $max\_no\_of\_buckets$ intervals of equal length;
 6:     remove intervals which do not contain any elements of $list$;
 7:     shift intervals' right and left sides to their closest leftmost elements of $list$;
 8:     add all intervals' right sides except max($list$) to $cuts$;
 9:     $no\_of\_waiting\_buckets \leftarrow$ the number of intervals;
10:     $no\_of\_undefined\_bars \leftarrow max\_no\_of\_bars$;
11:     **for all** intervals sorted by the number of elements of $list$ that they contain **do**
12:         $\# \leftarrow$ the number of elements of $list$ contained in the considered interval;
13:         **if** $\# \leq \lfloor no\_of\_undefined\_bars \, / \, no\_of\_waiting\_buckets \rfloor$ **then**
14:             add to $cuts$ all elements of $list$ contained in the considered interval;
15:         **else**
16:             $\# \leftarrow \lfloor no\_of\_undefined\_bars \, / \, no\_of\_waiting\_buckets \rfloor$;
17:             split the considered interval onto $\#$ bars with roughly uniform supports;
18:             and cut-points between the obtained bars to $cuts$;
19:         **end if**
20:         $no\_of\_waiting\_buckets \leftarrow no\_of\_waiting\_buckets - 1$;
21:         $no\_of\_undefined\_bars \leftarrow no\_of\_undefined\_bars - \#$;
22:     **end for**
23: **end if**
24: **end**

As mentioned in Sect. 1, the considered new approximate query mechanisms do not access the original packrows. For a given query, each consecutive operation scheduled within the execution plan (such as filtering, joining, grouping, etc.) is performed as a transformation of histograms/special values/gaps/tauratios representing its input into the analogous structures that are estimated to represent its output. Once this kind of representation of the final query outcome is reached, the engine translates it into the standard SQL statement result format. Prior to that stage, information being transformed throughout query execution stages is highly condensed and therefore it requires only a fraction of resources of traditional database solutions to produce the results.

Among further directions for improving the considered new engine, it is worth investigating relationships between the accuracy of captured knowledge structures and the accuracy of SQL query results that can be produced using those structures [7]. Yet another source of inspiration refers to the area of granular computing. If one interprets data ingestion as information granulation, then the final stage of translating the query result summaries into the final approximate results can be interpreted as a kind of information degranulation. The literature contains a number of useful approaches that can be potentially adapted within the engine for both granulation and degranulation purposes [3].

3   Towards the Design of Metadata Repository

In this section, we discuss how to provide the users with a possibility to work directly with granulated data summaries captured by the considered approximate query engine. We show the evolution of our ideas with this respect, starting from converting internal engine's files into CSV format, then to XML and finally to the contents of a relational metadata model. We also refer to a tool – called *metaviewer* – which was developed in order to visualize descriptions of particular packrows basing on their XML versions and which, after all, turned out not flexible enough to conduct all useful aspects of metadata analytics.

3.1   Extracting Metadata from the Engine

The considered engine stores granulated data summaries in files accessible by approximate query execution methods via internal interfaces. In order to follow the modularity design principles, different aspects of the captured knowledge are collected within their dedicated structures and stored separately. Histogram ranges and special values that approximate the actual data distributions are stored in separation from gaps that model the domain itself. Co-occurrence ratios are stored in yet another units, as they are potentially used in different parts of query execution processes. This modularity makes it possible to use, replace or disable each of summary types without affecting the other ones.

The I/O operations are always an important issue in the high performance systems and may influence the execution speed significantly. Thus, the discussed granulated data summaries are stored in concise binary formats. Although the unit and functional Q&A tests were prepared to check the correctness of each data summary type, one could not avoid situations when the access to the stored structures is required to debug or trace their influence to the other parts of the approximate query execution path. Therefore, it was necessary to prepare a kind of diagnostic tool facilitating the access to the stored structures independently from the engine operations. In its first design, the tool aimed at translating a single data summary structure from its binary format to a more readable CSV-like format. Examples of such translation are presented in Table 1.

3.2   Initial Designs for Metadata Visualization

Conversion of binary contents to CSV significantly simplified the tasks of accessing summaries stored on disk for debugging purposes. However, to examine the issues reported during the new engine production tests, a more general view was needed, e.g., to combine the actual data distributions (histogram ranges and special values) with information about the column domains (gaps). To meet

Table 1. A fragment of raw information captured for a single original chunk of rows (packrow). Each table refers to its different aspect stored as a separate unit, i.e.: (a) bars and special values, (b) gaps, (c) tau-ratios.

a) ranges and special values representation

pack_min:1 - *minimal value in the pack*
pack_max:15861 - *maximal value in the pack*
pack_gcd:1 - *greatest common divisor for values in the pack*

	left border	right border	count	width	frequency	list of special values × their frequencies within each range
0	l:1	r:204	cnt:2989	w:204	avg_cnt:14.652	sv:151 × 2, 142 × 4, 299 × 7, (...)
1	l:205	r:432	cnt:3010	w:228	avg_cnt:13.2018	sv:73 × 266, 113 × 306, 134 × 367, (...)
2	l:433	r:963	cnt:12666	w:531	avg_cnt:23.8531	sv:105 × 462, 83 × 568, 157 × 613, (...)
3	l:964	r:967	cnt:1	w:4	avg_cnt:0.25	sv: none
4	l:968	r:981	cnt:3	w:14	avg_cnt:0.214286	sv: none
5	l:982	r:984	cnt:2	w:3	avg_cnt:0.666667	sv: none
6	l:985	r:1082	cnt:2100	w:98	avg_cnt:21.4286	sv:144 × 1055, 765 × 1056, (...)
(...)	(...)	(...)	(...)	(...)	(...)	(...)

b) gaps representation

	left border	right border	size
0	l:72	r:81	size:10
1	l:119	r:141	size:23
2	l:189	r:199	size:11
3	l:209	r:218	size:10
4	l:223	r:228	size:6
5	l:235	r:260	size:26
6	l:381	r:387	size:7
7	l:421	r:427	size:7
8	l:434	r:435	size:2
9	l:438	r:439	size:2
10	l:446	r:448	size:3
11	l:450	r:451	size:2
12	l:457	r:461	size:5
13	l:463	r:465	size:3
14	l:477	r:478	size:2
15	l:487	r:490	size:4
16	l:502	r:503	size:2
17	l:508	r:509	size:2
18	l:520	r:521	size:2
(...)	(...)	(...)	(...)

c) tau-ratio representation

Default tau: 0.69003
Default tau minus: 0.692418

first entity code	second entity code	tau values (with additional defaults in the case of pairs of bars)
6	3	1.90752, 0.613704
13	7	12.096, 8.69155
19	3	0.0550151, 0.0550151
2	3	2.76967, 1.0241
8	22	6.9184, 6.9184
19	10	7.56932, 7.56932
19	16	7.07605, 7.07605
(...)	(...)	(...)
103	89	19.6471
96	87	0.254706
65	87	3.25763
90	101	9.69591
78	87	0.00171537
81	87	2.28507
61	146	48.2593
(...)	(...)	(...)

such needs, a higher level diagnostic tool was prepared. First, the set of available output formats was extended with XML to allow portability and flexibility in using data summary structures by external visualization tools. Examples of translation of the binary format to XML are shown in Table 2. Second, the XML summary representations were used as an input to a new *metaviewer* tool in order to support visualization of packrow representations.

One-dimensional charts produced by metaviewer for single data packs take a form analogous to Fig. 1. Multi-dimensional interdependencies between two selected columns, over a single packrow, are visualized as in Fig. 2. The areas marked with rectangles of different brightness represent strengths of stored co-occurrences of values dropping into pairs of histogram ranges. (In particular, white rectangles denote tau-ratios equal to 0 which means that the corresponding combinations of values did not occur together in the considered packrow.) The background area corresponds to pairs for which tau-ratios are not captured. The

Table 2. The same information as in Table 1, now transformed into XML.

a) XML for ranges and special values

```
<packkn>
<pack_meta>
<min>1</min>
<max>15861</max>
<gcd>1</gcd>
</pack_meta>
  <bars>
   <bar>
    <left>1</left>
    <right>204</right>
    <width>204</width>
    <count>2989</count>
    <avg_count>
      14.652
    </avg_count>
   </bar>
   <bar>
    <left>205</left>
    <right>432</right>
    <width>228</width>
    <count>3010</count>
    <avg_count>
      13.2018
    </avg_count>
   </bar>
   (...)
  </bars>
  <special_values>
   <special_value>
    <value>2</value>
    <count>151</count>
   </special_value>
   (...)
  </special_values>
</packkn>
```

b) XML for gaps

```
<packkn>
 <gaps>
  <gap>
   <left>72</left>
   <right>81</right>
   <size>10</size>
  </gap>
  <gap>
   <left>119</left>
   <right>141</right>
   <size>23</size>
  </gap>
  <gap>
   <left>189</left>
   <right>199</right>
   <size>11</size>
  </gap>
  <gap>
   <left>209</left>
   <right>218</right>
   <size>10</size>
  </gap>
  <gap>
   <left>223</left>
   <right>228</right>
   <size>6</size>
  </gap>
  <gap>
   <left>235</left>
   <right>260</right>
   <size>26</size>
  </gap>
  (...)
 </gaps>
</packkn>
```

c) XML for tau-ratios

```
<packkn>
 <default_tau>
   0.69003
 </default_tau>
 <default_tau_minus>
   0.692418
 </default_tau_minus>
 <bar_taus>
  <bar_tau>
   <code1>6</code1>
   <code2>3</code2>
   <tau_value>
     1.90752
   </tau_value>
   <tau_wave_value>
     0.613704
   </tau_wave_value>
  </bar_tau>
  (...)
 </bar_taus>
 <sv_taus>
  <sv_tau>
   <code1>103</code1>
   <code2>89</code2>
   <tau_value>
     19.6471
   </tau_value>
   <from_kn_minus>
     0
   </from_kn_minus>
  </sv_tau>
  (...)
 </sv_taus>
</packkn>
```

stored co-occurrences of pairs of special values are marked with circles. This kind of visualization can help to understand the collected knowledge and, to some extent, simulate the specifics of query execution.

The visualization layer was implemented in Python, with a use of package *matplotlib*[3] allowing to explore and save the plots using a mouse or keyboard. We consider Python a good choice for prototyping and creating general purpose scripts. It would not be a good decision to use it while developing the core approximate query engine (which was written entirely in C/C++). However, it is perfect for diagnostic methods discussed in this paper.

3.3 Relational Schema for Metadata Contents

The metaviewer tool described briefly in Subsect. 3.2 was intended to visualize the combined data from low level summary chunks for one-dimensional and two-dimensional dependencies inferred during the load process. However, its focus

---

[3] https://pypi.python.org/pypi/matplotlib.

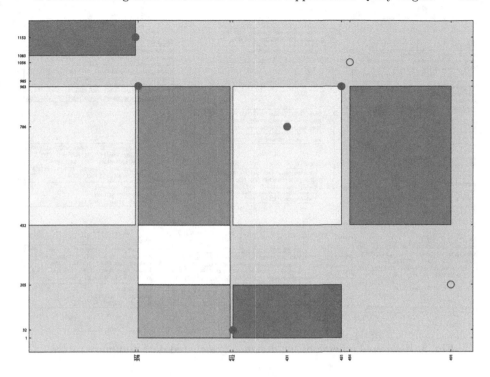

Fig. 2. An example of the output from metaviewer for two columns over a single packrow. Each of the axis corresponds to a single column.

was limited only to single packrows. In order to enable the developers and analysts a more flexible access to the gathered knowledge structures, we designed a relational metadata repository that stores particular aspects of granulated summaries in separate – but well-integrated – tables. Figure 3 illustrates complete layout of the proposed metadata model. The descriptions of the most important tables in the proposed metadata schema can be found in Table 3. Let us also refer to Table 4 for some examples of the metadata table contents.

In Sect. 4, we show some examples of practical SQL-based usage of metadata tables. Herein, let us concentrate on technical aspects of filling them with appropriate contents using a publicly available free software. We have already outlined that our metaviewer tool simplifies the access to the engine's data summaries that correspond to a single packrow. A single storage unit contains a summary that can be further successfully represented in a relational form. Metaviewer gives us a choice between CSV and XML formats. The latter one seems to be more flexible to convert to the contents of relational metadata tables because of its structure and description of the contained information.

As already mentioned, metaviewer was created using Python. We use this language also to populate the proposed metadata tables. Most of Python's implementations contain a read-eval-print loop (*REPL*) which lets use it as a command

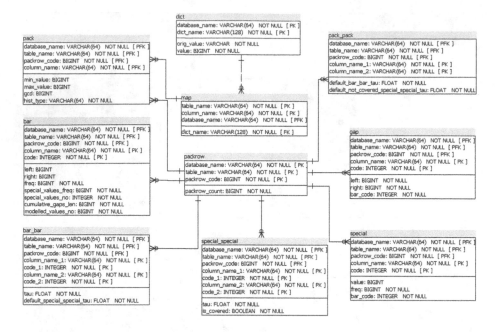

Fig. 3. Relational schema of the designed granulated data summary tables.

interpreter making it easier to prepare final solution for a given task. For the purpose of XML parsing we chose *lxml*[4] – a feature-rich binding for C libraries *libxml2* and *libxslt*. We used *ElementTree API* to access summaries in their form prepared by metaviewer and transform them to a kind of preliminary relational form. Then, we employed package *Pandas*[5] which supports expressive data structures designed to work with tabular/relational data. Separate metaviewer-specific summary units corresponding to different columns and packrows were parsed from XML and loaded to table-like structures. The features of Pandas, including SQL-like filtering operations, facilitated the overall process of combining and joining information from single storage units to produce the final form of CSV files containing an integrated metadata representation of the whole original data, ready to be loaded into the proposed metadata tables.

As a result, we reach a framework complying the fundamental ideas developed for databases over 50 years ago. Namely, we provide the granular-summary-related metadata of a relational database in a relational form itself. This kind of approach has been promoted particularly in the area of data warehousing, wherein metadata information is maintained at every step of system management, including conceptual models, ETL parameters, OLAP cube specifications, etc. [8]. In practice, every new solution aimed at enhancing standard database methodology implies a need of collecting new aspects of metadata [9].

---

[4] https://pypi.python.org/pypi/lxml.
[5] https://pypi.python.org/pypi/pandas.

Table 3. Description of the contents of the proposed metadata tables and their columns. Columns in the category **all tables** are included into all considered metadata tables in order to easily specify particular packrows.

Table/Column	Description of contents
All tables	Columns identifying specific packrows in all considered metadata tables
database_name	Database name
table_name	Table name
packrow_code	Packrow identifier
table *packrow*	Basic information about specific packrows
packrow_count	The number of original rows collected within the packrow (2^{16} by default)
table *pack*	Information about values in data packs
column_name	Column name
min_value	Minimum value occurring in the data pack
max_value	Maximum value occurring in the data pack
gcd	Greatest common divisor for all values in the data pack
hist_type	Histogram type
table *bar*	Information about particular bars
column_name	Column name
code	Bar identifier (unique in the data pack)
left	Minimum value in the bar
right	Maximum value in the bar
freq	Number of rows with values contained within the bar's range
special_values_freq	Number of rows with special values in the bar
special_values_no	Number of special values in the bar
cumulative_gaps_len	Cumulative length of gaps in the bar
modeled_values_no	Number of unique values which can be generated
table *special*	Information about special values
column_name	Column name
code	Special value identifier (unique in the data pack)
value	Value
freq	Number of rows with the special value
bar_code	Identifier of the bar containing the special value
table *gap*	Information about gaps
column_name	Column name
code	Gap identifier (unique in the data pack)
left	Left border of the gap
right	Right border of the gap
bar_code	Identifier of the bar which contains the gap
table *pack_pack*	Co-occurrence ratios not present in tables *bar_bar* and *special_special*
column_name_1	The first column in the pair
column_name_2	The second column in the pair
default_bar_bar_tau	Default ratio for pairs of bars not present in table *bar_bar*
default_not_covered_special_special_tau	Default ratio for pairs of special values not present in table *special_special* and whose "parents" (bars they belong to) are not present in table *bar_bar*
table *bar_bar*	Information about co-occurrence ratios at the level of pairs of bars
column_name_1	The first column in the pair
code_1	First column's bar identifier
column_name_2	The second column in the pair
code_2	Second column's bar identifier
tau	Ratio for the pair of bars
default_special_special_tau	Default ratio for pairs of special values belonging to the considered pair of bars that are not present in table *special_special*
table *special_special*	Information about co-occurrence ratios for pairs of special values
column_name_1	The first column in the pair
code_1	First column's special value identifier
column_name_2	The second column in the pair
code_2	Second column's special value identifier
tau	Ratio for the pair of special values
is_covered	Does the pair of special values belong to a pair of bars in table *bar_bar*

Table 4. Example of the contents loaded into the relational metadata repository.

database_name	table_name	packrow_code	column_name	min_value	max_value	gcd	hist_type
dbname	tabname	0	col1	7	11093	1	Ranges
dbname	tabname	0	col2	1	15861	1	Ranges
(...)	(...)	(...)	(...)	(...)	(...)	(...)	(...)

pack relational table

database_name	table_name	packrow_code	column_name	code	left	right	freq	special_values_freq	special_values_no	cumulative_gaps_len	modeled_values_no
dbname	tabname	0	col1	0	NULL	NULL	0	0	1	0	1
dbname	tabname	0	col1	1	7	59	3661	3661	2	51	2
dbname	tabname	0	col1	2	60	108	4024	4024	4	45	4
dbname	tabname	0	col1	3	109	230	5287	5274	5	116	6
dbname	tabname	0	col1	4	231	377	3652	3608	4	136	11
dbname	tabname	0	col2	0	NULL	NULL	0	0	1	0	1
dbname	tabname	0	col2	1	1	204	2989	2308	8	44	160
dbname	tabname	0	col2	2	205	432	3010	2031	9	56	172
(...)	(...)	(...)	(...)	(...)	(...)	(...)	(...)	(...)	(...)	(...)	(...)

bar relational table

database_name	table_name	packrow_code	column_name	code	left	right	bar_code
dbname	tabname	0	col1	0	8	58	1
dbname	tabname	0	col1	1	60	65	2
dbname	tabname	0	col1	2	67	77	2
dbname	tabname	0	col1	3	79	104	2
dbname	tabname	0	col1	4	106	107	2
dbname	tabname	0	col2	0	72	81	1
dbname	tabname	0	col2	1	119	141	1
dbname	tabname	0	col2	2	189	199	1
(...)	(...)	(...)	(...)	(...)	(...)	(...)	(...)

gap relational table

database_name	table_name	packrow_code	column_name_1	code_1	column_name_2	code_2	tau	default_special_special_tau
dbname	tabname	0	col1	8	col2	13	1.69969988	1.69969988
dbname	tabname	0	col1	36	col2	16	5.00550365	5.00550365
dbname	tabname	0	col1	1	col2	2	2.75356102	2.75356102
dbname	tabname	0	col1	19	col2	12	0	0
(...)	(...)	(...)	(...)	(...)	(...)	(...)	(...)	(...)

bar_bar relational table

4   Working with Metadata Tables

In this section, we discuss several examples of the usage of the developed meta-data repository. From a logical viewpoint, the contents of the original binary files, as well as their CSV, XML and relational metadata formats are equivalent to each other. The binary files are surely the best input to automatized approximate query processes. On the other hand, the metadata tables provide the users with the most flexible means for accessing and analyzing granulated representations of the original data independently from the considered engine. One can use, e.g., standard *PostgreSQL* environment to work with histogram frequencies and ranges, special values, gaps, as well as bar-to-bar and value-to-value co-occurrences, per each database, table, column and packrow. Using simple SQL, one can check which pairs of columns are most correlated by means of their tau-ratios (by querying tables *bar_bar* and *special_special*), what is the degree of repeatability of special values in different data packs of the same column (by querying table *special*), whether values of particular data columns evolve from packrow to packrow (by querying tables *pack* and *gap*), etc.

4.1   Data Demographics

Let us start with examples of simple operations displaying the data in a sum-marized form. One can realize that the outcomes of such operations can be used both by the approximate query engine users and developers – as an independent diagnostic/verification methodology – or by data analysts who basically want to explore the data fully independently from the engine.

The discussed examples of SQL statements will contain the following section that allows to focus on metadata contents corresponding to a given column (over its all data pack granular summaries aggregated together):

```
[condition identifying a single column]
database_name = 'database_name'
and       table_name = 'table_name'
and       column_name = 'column_name'
```

For instance, the following query sums frequencies of special values:

```
select    value, sum(freq) sum_freq, count(*) pack_cnt
from      special
where     [condition identifying a single column]
group by value
order by value;
```

When combined with a similar query over histograms, one can obtain a high-level visualization of the overall domain of a given column. Figure 4 illustrates a plot of the tabular output from the appropriate select statement. Needless to say, such output can be produced hundreds times faster than in the case of analogous queries executed over the original data table.

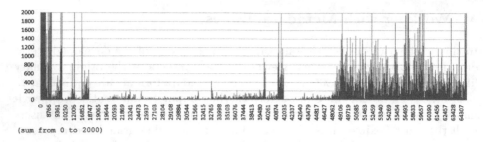

(sum from 0 to 2000)

Fig. 4. Column characteristics obtained using SQL over metadata tables.

The next two examples refer to use cases mentioned at the beginning of Sect. 4. The following query verifies how often the ranking algorithms identify the same special values within different chunks of the ingested data. Figure 5 shows a typical result for a foreign key column, over a small data subset (100×2^{16} rows) obtained from one of customers using the considered engine.

```
select    value, count(*) packrow_count
from      special
where     [condition identifying a single column]
group by value
order by value;
```

Figure 6 illustrates the result of the following query for the same column.

```
select    right_value + 1, left_bound,
          coalesce(lead(left_value, 1)
          over (partition by packrow_code order by code) - 1,
          (select max(max_value) from pack
           where [condition identifying a single column]
           and packrow_code = gap.packrow_code)) right_bound,
          packrow_code
from      gap
where     [condition identifying a single column]
union
select    min_value, left_value, gap.packrow_code
from
(select   min_value, packrow_code from pack
where     [condition identifying a single column)) pack
inner join
(select   min(left_value) -1 left_value, packrow_code
from      gap
where     [condition identifying a single column]
group by packrow_code) gap
on        gap.packrow_code = pack.packrow_code
order by packrow_code, left_bound;
```

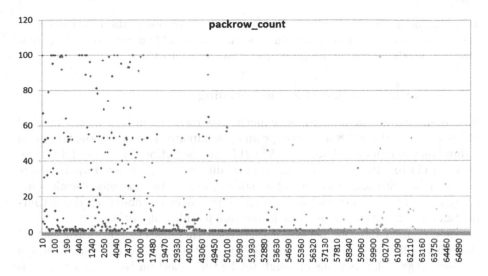

Fig. 5. Re-occurrence of the same special values in different data packs.

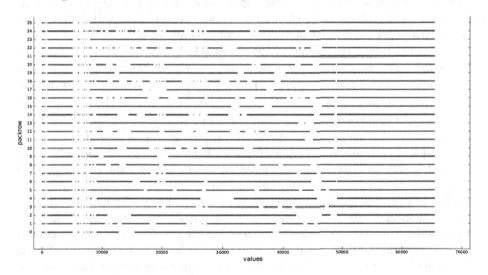

Fig. 6. Evolution of column values occurring in subsequent data packs.

From the perspective of data analysts, the above metadata queries reflect the repeatability of particular column values for data rows ingested by the considered engine over time. From the perspective of the engine developers and administrators, the outcomes of such "meta-queries" provide useful hints with regards to the credibility of the results of potential approximate SQL statements over the most meaningful values (represented as special values in Fig. 5), as well as, e.g., potential selectivity of approximate statements with filters over particular columns (whereby selectivity grows proportionally with the growth of empty areas visible in Fig. 6). However, the most important observation is that everyone can think about his/her own queries that can quickly derive completely new kinds of insights from the proposed metadata repository.

4.2   Towards Granular Machine Learning

In this subsection, we refer to our experiments reported in [10], where we used SQL over metadata tables to prototype an approximate approach to the minimum redundancy maximum relevance ($mRMR$) feature selection [11]. We did it for two reasons: (1) to extend the current functionality of the considered approximate query engine with some elements of scalable granular-style machine learning and (2) to extend the current engine's testing environment by comparing the outputs of standard and granular versions of machine learning algorithms.

Before going into the details, let us recall that feature selection is one of the most well-known areas of rough set applications. Thus, it is our intension to develop granular versions of rough set feature selection techniques too. It is also worth considering analogous re-implementations of rough-set-based machine learning approaches, e.g., in the field of decision tree induction [5], as well as many other methods of knowledge discovery and representation [12]. Nevertheless, in this paper we restrict ourselves to an example of mRMR.

The considered feature selection algorithm is based on the measure of mutual information. For packrow t and data columns a and b, such measure could be defined as $I_t(a,b) = \sum_{x,y} p_t(x,y) \log \frac{p_t(x,y)}{p_t(x)p_t(y)}$, for x and y denoting the ranges/values occurring on a and b, respectively. However, as the engine stores only a limited number of tau-ratios of the form $\tau_t(x,y) = \frac{p_t(x,y)}{p_t(x)p_t(y)}$, for some combinations of x and y we need to rely on default ratios available in metadata tables. There are three possibilities with this respect: (1) default ratios gathered in column *default_bar_bar_tau* (table *pack_pack*) for the case of pairs of histogram ranges whose ratios are not stored by the engine, (2) default ratios in column *default_not_covered _special_special_tau* (table *pack_pack*) for the case of pairs of special values whose tau-ratios are not stored neither for themselves nor for their "parents" (histogram ranges that they belong to) and (3) default ratios in column *default_special_special_tau* (table *bar_bar*) for the case of pairs of special values whose tau-ratios are not stored but the corresponding ratios for their "parents" are stored by the engine. Further, the overall mutual information is approximated as the average of the quantities $I_t(a,b)$ derived over particular packrows of the given data table. Certainly, such approximations are not guaranteed to be equal to the actual values of mutual information that would be computed from the original data. However, in our experiments, we were mainly interested in observing whether such quickly approximated measures could drive the feature selection process similarly to thorough computations.

In mRMR, attributes are added to the resulting set iteratively by examining their mutual information relationships with both the decision attribute and conditional attributes that were added in previous steps. Table 5 shows the results of one of our experiments conducted over the already-mentioned data set of 100×2^{16} network events, wherein the decision attribute corresponds to the number of bytes transmitted in every event and the stopping criterion is turned off, so all attributes are added step by step. The first column reports an order of selecting attributes according to the exact computations over the original data. The second column corresponds to calculations over a random sample consisting of 15% of data rows. The third column shows how mRMR behaves when fed with mutual information approximations derived from metadata tables. In this case, the sample-based approach seems to yield an order that is slightly closer to that obtained over the original data. However, the differences are minor and – most importantly – granular calculations have a huge advantage with regards to their speed when compared to both standard and sampled runs.

Table 5. mRMR attribute rankings for a data table describing network events.

Rank	Standard	Sampled	Approximated
1	p_element	p_element	p_element
2	trans_type	trans_type	Service
3	s_address	s_address	trans_type
4	Service	d_class	d_address
5	d_address	Service	s_vrf
6	s_port	s_port	s_port
7	Server	d_port	s_address
8	d_port	Server	d_port
9	Protocol	s_class	Protocol
10	s_class	d_address	Monitor
11	d_class	Protocol	d_class
12	s_vrf	s_vrf	s_class
13	Monitor	d_interface	d_interface
14	d_interface	Monitor	s_interface
15	s_interface	s_interface	m_address
16	m_address	m_address	Server

4.3   Approximating Column Domains

As outlined in Sect. 2, the engine conducts query execution as a chain of transformations of granulated data summaries that aim at modeling characteristics of intermediate results corresponding to subsequent execution stages. Once the summary of a query output is calculated, the engine translates it into the standard SQL result format which – as already discussed – could be interpreted as a stage of degranulation. This stage is particularly difficult for high-cardinality columns, e.g., in the case of involving them into **group by** operations. Then, at the end, the engine needs to replace the codes of histogram ranges with their actual values. This is quite problematic because information about the actual values is only partial, so there is a risk that the final result will include non-existing values or will omit some values that should be included.

Let us recall that the engine stores the most significant gaps and the greatest common divisors of values observed in the original data packs. Referring to the theory of rough sets again, we can say that special values whose frequencies were not pushed down to zero during query execution constitute a kind of domain's *positive region*, i.e., these are values that should contribute to the query result. On the other hand, gaps, greatest common divisors, dictionaries (if available) and zeroed frequencies can be used to define the domain's *negative region*, i.e., values that should not contribute to the result. For every data pack, our metadata repository actually encodes one more type of information – the cardinality of *upper approximation* (derivable as the sum of values of column *modeled_values_no* over all histogram bars describing a given data pack), i.e., the number of column values (including those potentially not existing) that might be potentially generated from the given data pack during the degranulation process.

The metadata-related case study discussed in this subsection refers to a slightly modified interpretation of lower approximation of the column domains. Thanks to the analysis of approximate query results, it turned out that there are two kinds of values that should not be included: (1) values existing in the original data that do not satisfy the query conditions and (2) values that did not exist in the original data at all but were produced from histogram ranges under the assumption of locally uniform distributions. As the first category seems to be less harmful for the user perception of final query results, the considered diagnostic task is to compute lower approximations as the sets of column values – gathered from all data packs – which occurred for sure in the original data and, then, compare them with the actual sets of all distinct column values.

The following query shows how to derive the above-discussed cardinality of lower approximation of the column domain from the metadata tables. It is based on observation that, besides special values, the original data must have included also the borders of histogram ranges and gaps. (This is how the knowledge capture algorithms work during the phase of original data ingestion.)

```
select count(distinct v) cnt from
(select database_name, table_name, column_name, min_value v
from pack
where [condition identifying a single column]
union
select database_name, table_name, column_name, right_value v
from bar
where [condition identifying a single column]
union
select database_name, table_name, column_name, left_value - 1 v
from gap
```

```
where [condition identifying a single column]
union
select database_name, table_name, column_name, right_value + 1 v
from gap
where [condition identifying a single column]
union
select database_name, table_name, column_name, value v
from special
where [condition identifying a single column]);
```

Table 6. Cardinalities of lower and upper approximations of column domains.

Database	Column	Lower approximation	Upper approximation	Real count distinct
database 1	s_port	13121	62648	40945
database 1	d_port	9298	64184	43001
database 1	s_address	5155	~4000000000	19035
database 1	d_address	3409	~4000000000	17072
database 1	load_time	15989	36277	17568
database 1	real_time	14199	1400000000	20376
database 1	monitor	1026	1050	1050
database 1	d_name	883	1788	1788
database 2	d_port	8622	65270	64844
database 2	s_port	9273	65356	64855
database 2	s_address	6461	~4000000000	173989
database 2	d_address	6158	~4000000000	191293
database 2	p_element	1016	11093	1214
database 2	packets	6772	191208	7166
database 2	d_class	2091	9212	5747
database 2	s_class	1990	9267	5524

Table 6 shows the results obtained for the already-referred 100×2^{16} fragments of data sets coming from two companies (labeled as *database 1* and *database 2*), whereby columns *lower approximation* and *real count distinct* report the results of the above query and the actual number of distinct values in the original data, respectively. One can see that for many cases these outcomes are quite similar to each other (e.g.: 1026 versus 1050 for data column *monitor* in *database 1*), or at least of the same order of magnitude (e.g.: 2091 versus 5747 for data column *d_class* in *database 2*). This means that if the engine – during query processing – could dynamically gather together the borders of gaps and histogram ranges corresponding to all data packs (of course excluding those data fragments which are filtered out during the previous query execution stages) and then pick the elements of such constructed sets while generating the final outcomes, then the overall approximate query accuracy may be significantly improved.

Moreover, for those of data columns for which the differences between real count distinct scores and their lower approximations are bigger, it seems to be important to estimate the real scores, so at least the cardinalities of distinct values (though not necessarily particular values) are produced in a correct way. This is because otherwise those cardinalities might be over-generated, potentially at the level reported in column *upper approximation* in Table 6. Such observations – achieved by the analysis conducted over the proposed metadata tables – can be very useful for further enhancements of the considered engine.

5   Conclusions

We designed and developed a relational metadata repository enabling the developers and users of a new approximate database engine to investigate the collected granulated data summaries independently from the engine itself. We discussed how the proposed repository characteristics evolved over time from both conceptual and software engineering perspectives. We showed several scenarios of a usage of the repository for both diagnostic and analytical purposes. We also reported empirical results obtained for relatively small fragments (100×2^{16} rows each) of data sets coming from companies using the considered engine.

References

1. Mozafari, B., Niu, N.: A handbook for building an approximate query engine. IEEE Data Eng. Bull. **38**(3), 3–29 (2015)
2. Cormode, G., Garofalakis, M.N., Haas, P.J., Jermaine, C.: Synopses for massive data: samples, histograms, wavelets, sketches. Found. Trends Databases **4**(1–3), 1–294 (2012)
3. Pawlak, Z., Skowron, A.: Rough sets: some extensions. Inf. Sci. **177**(1), 28–40 (2007)
4. Ślęzak, D., Synak, P., Wojna, A., Wróblewski, J.: Two database related interpretations of rough approximations: data organization and query execution. Fund. Inf. **127**(1–4), 445–459 (2013)
5. Nguyen, H.S.: Approximate boolean reasoning: foundations and applications in data mining. In: Peters, J.F., Skowron, A. (eds.) Transactions on Rough Sets V. LNCS, vol. 4100, pp. 334–506. Springer, Heidelberg (2006). doi:10.1007/11847465_16
6. Neapolitan, R.E.: Learning Bayesian Networks. Prentice Hall, Upper Saddle River (2003)
7. Chądzyńska-Krasowska, A., Kowalski, M.: Quality of histograms as indicator of approximate query quality. In: Proceedings of FedCSIS 2016, pp. 9–15 (2016)
8. Kimball, R.: The Data Warehouse Lifecycle Toolkit. Wiley, Hoboken (2008)
9. Pagani, I., Liolios, K., Jansson, J., Chen, I.A., Smirnova, T., Nosrat, B., Markowitz, V.M., Kyrpides, N.: The Genomes OnLine Database (GOLD) v. 4: status of genomic and metagenomic projects and their associated metadata. Nucleic Acids Res. **40**(Database–Issue), 571–579 (2012)

10. Chądzyńska-Krasowska, A., Betliński, P., Ślęzak, D.: Scalable machine learning with granulated data summaries: a case of feature selection. In: Proceedings of ISMIS 2017 (2017)
11. Peng, H., Long, F., Ding, C.: Feature selection based on mutual information criteria of max-dependency, max-relevance, and min-redundancy. IEEE Trans. Pattern Anal. Mach. Intell. **27**(8), 1226–1238 (2005)
12. Ganter, B., Meschke, C.: A formal concept analysis approach to rough data tables. In: Peters, J.F., Skowron, A., Sakai, H., Chakraborty, M.K., Slezak, D., Hassanien, A.E., Zhu, W. (eds.) Transactions on Rough Sets XIV. LNCS, vol. 6600, pp. 37–61. Springer, Heidelberg (2011). doi:10.1007/978-3-642-21563-6_3

Scalable Maximal Discernibility Discretization for Big Data

Michal Czolombitko$^{(\boxtimes)}$ and Jaroslaw Stepaniuk

Faculty of Computer Science, Bialystok University of Technology,
Wiejska 45A, 15-351 Bialystok, Poland
{m.czolombitko,j.stepaniuk}@pb.edu.pl
http://www.wi.pb.edu.pl

Abstract. Discretization of numerical (continuous) attributes is one of the most important data preprocessing tasks in knowledge discovery and data mining. Some of data mining techniques require discretized data. The article aim is to demonstrate that discretization methods based on the discernibility measure to evaluate cuts can be parallelized in Big Data platform Apache Spark. We thus propose a distributed implementation of one of the most well-known discretizers based on rough set methodology. The experimental results in terms of scalability, speedup and sizeup are quite promising.

Keywords: Discretization of attributes · Rough sets · Apache Spark

1 Introduction

Data in all domains is getting bigger. The growth of capacity of data storage systems, reduction of their prices and usage of computers in almost every sphere of life has caused an increase in amount of data that are collected [4]. Since the massive data can be stored in cloud platforms, mining large datasets so called Big Data is a hot topic. Big Data creates many new challenges, like data storage, data preprocessing, analysis and visualization.

Objects can be described by continuous or discrete attributes. Some of data mining techniques require discretized data. The goal of the discretization process is to reduce continuous-valued attribute into a smaller set of nominal values. Other phases of data mining depend on this operation, e.g., removing superfluous attributes or decision rules generation. Clearly, we can see that discretization is one of the most important tasks of data preprocessing. Unfortunately, standard discretization techniques are not prepared to deal with big datasets, because of its volume and variety. In [17] a parallel Chi2-based algorithm based on MapReduce model was proposed. Experiments have been done by using different size of data sets on the different nodes. In [9] an implementation of Fayyads's and Irani's discretizer using computation engine Apache Spark was presented. Nevertheless, the set of cuts isn't optimal because discretization of every attribute is considered separately.

© Springer International Publishing AG 2017
L. Polkowski et al. (Eds.): IJCRS 2017, Part I, LNAI 10313, pp. 644–654, 2017.
DOI: 10.1007/978-3-319-60837-2_51

Rough set theory was introduced by Pawlak in early 1980's as a methodology to deal with incomplete and uncertain information (for more details see e.g. [8,11]). In [7]an approach based on rough sets and approximate Boolean reasoning to discretization was proposed. In [6] an incremental global merging algorithm of discretization attributes - SDMNS based on counting sort was proposed. They used some parameters to achieve balance between number of cuts and classification accuracy.

Apache Spark [1] improves over MapReduce model in several key dimensions: it is much faster, it offers much more operations on data and it provides multiple types of computations, e.g., SQL queries, text processing, and machine learning, data streaming. Application programming interface is centered on a data structure called the resilient distributed dataset (RDD), representing a collection of data distributed across many computing nodes that can be manipulated in parallel. RDD API offers two types of operations: transformations and actions. *Transformations* build a new RDD from a previous one and *actions* compute a result based on an RDD.

In recent years there has been research work combining MapReduce and rough set theory but only a few works which used computing engine Apache Spark. In [15] parallel method for computing rough set approximations was proposed. The authors continued their work and proposed in [16] three strategies based on MapReduce to compute approximations in incomplete information systems. In [13] method for computing core based on finding positive region was proposed. They also presented a parallel algorithm for attribute reduction in [14]. However, authors used MapReduce model only for splitting data set and parallelization of computation using one of traditional reduction algorithm.

This paper is organized as follows. Problem of optimal discretization of continuous attributes is presented in Sect. 2. A distributed implementation of the discretizers based on discernibility measure is proposed in Sect. 3. Results of experiments and analysis are presented in Sect. 4. Conclusions and future work are discussed in Sect. 5.

2   Optimal Discretization of Continuous Attributes

In this section we discuss the optimal discretization problem (see e.g. [7]).

Let $DT = (U, A \cup \{d\})$ be a decision table, where U is a set of objects, A is a set of condition attributes and d is a decision attribute and $\{v_1^a, ..., v_n^a,\}$ is a list of sorted values of attribute a, where $v_1^a < ... < v_n^a$. The set C_a of all potential cuts on attribute a can be computed as:

$$C_a = \left\{ \left(a, \frac{v_1^a + v_2^a}{2} \right), ..., \left(a, \frac{v_{n-1}^a + v_n^a}{2} \right) \right\} \tag{1}$$

Value of potential cut is middle value between two values which discerns objects from different classes. More precisely only so called boundary cuts are used.

Definition 1. *The cut* $\left(a, \frac{v_{i-1}^a + v_i^a}{2}\right)$, *where* $1 < i < n+1$, *is called the boundary cut if and only if there are at least two objects* $x, y \in U$ *such that* $a(x) = v_{i-1}^a$, $a(y) = v_i^a$ *and* $d(x) \neq d(y)$.

The set of cuts $C = \bigcup_{a \in A} C_a$ determines a global discretization of the whole decision table.

Definition 2. *Two objects* $x, y \in U$ *are discernible by* A *if and only if there is an attribute* $a \in A$ *such that* $a(x) \neq a(y)$.
Two objects $x, y \in U$ *are discernible by* C *if and only if there is an attribute* $a \in A$ *and a cut* $(a, c) \in C_a$ *such that* $(a(x) - c)(a(y) - c) < 0$.

Definition 3. *A set of cuts* C *is consistent with* $DT = (U, A \cup \{d\})$ *if and only if for any pair of objects* $x, y \in U$ *such that* $d(x) \neq d(y)$, *the following condition holds: IF* x, y *are discernible by* A *THEN* x, y *are discernible by* C.

Definition 4. *A consistent set* C *of cuts is* DT-*optimal if and only if* C *contains a smallest number of cuts among* DT-*consistent sets of cuts.*

Definition 5 [7]. *The optimal discretization problem is defined as follows:*
Input: A decision table DT.
Find: DT-*optimal set of cuts.*

Theorem 1. *The problem of optimal discretization (finding minimal and consistent set of cuts) is NP-hard.*

Let us recall, that the class P consists of all polynomial-time solvable decision problems and NP is the class of all nondeterministic polynomial-time solvable decision problems. The result from Theorem 1 means that we can not expect a polynomial time searching algorithm for optimal discretization, unless $P = NP$. Thus, we can only propose approximation algorithms as a tool for coping with the intractable problem of optimal discretization (especially for Big Data). Approximation algorithm based on maximal discernibility heuristic is discussed in the next section.

3   Apache Spark Implementation

The standard algorithm for discretization consists of four main steps: sorting data for an attribute a, selection of values for cuts, evaluating cuts and splitting/merging objects. Process of discretization was shown in Fig. 1. All of those phases are repeated for each of the subsets until condition for stop is not fulfilled. One of the critical operations is sorting. It has to be done in the optimal way in order to reduce cost of the computations e.g. using counting sort [6].

Internal conflict [7] of the set $X \subset U$ can be defined as:

$$conflict(X) = \frac{1}{2} card(\{(x, y) \in X \times X : d(x) \neq d(y)\}) \tag{2}$$

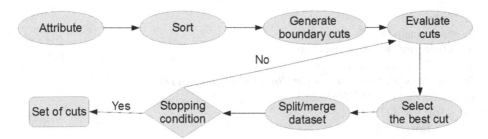

Fig. 1. Process of discretization

Discernibility measure of the cut (a, c) according to the subset X which splits the set of objects X into $X_L = \{x \in X : a(x) < c\}$ and $X_R = \{x \in X : a(x) > c\}$ can be computed by:

$$disc((a, c), X) = conflict(X) - conflict(X_L) - conflict(X_R) \qquad (3)$$

The discernibility measure can be also computed by [7]:

$$disc((a, c), X) = \sum_{i \neq j} card(\{x \in X_L : d(x) = i\}) \cdot card(\{x \in X_R : d(x) = j\}), \qquad (4)$$

where the summation is over all the different pairs (i, j) of decision classes.

Our approach is based on the MD heuristics using $DTree$ structure. [7]. In every iteration the cut that separates the maximal number of objects from different decision classes is selected. Then, the decision table is split according to the chosen cut and in every decision subtable cuts are searched separately. These steps are repeated until all objects with the different decisions will be discerned. Memory complexity of this method is $O(card(U) \cdot card(A))$.

The main concept of the proposed algorithm rests in cumulating the information about class distribution using shared variables. Spark provides two types of those variables: broadcast variables and accumulators.

Broadcast variables allow to keep on every node read-only variable necessary to realize tasks. Creating broadcast variables is useful when tasks across multiple stages need the same data. Using broadcast variables can reduce cost of communication between nodes. The broadcasted data cannot be modified during computations.

The second type of shared variables available in Spark - accumulators allow to raise partial computation from every node. They can be numeric types but also collections.

Using both of these shared variables made it possible to implement the MD-discretization algorithm for a Big Data.

BigData MD-Discretization
Input: decision table - $DT = (U, A \cup d)$
Output: Set of pairs $<attribute, cut>$ as the semi-optimal solution

1: $Cuts \leftarrow \emptyset$
2: stack.push(DT)
3: **while not** stack.empty() **do**
4:      $DT' \leftarrow stack.pop()$
5:      $b\_classDistribution \leftarrow getClassDistribution(DT')$
6:      $attrVal \leftarrow DT'.flatmap\{$
7:      **for** $u \in DT'$ **do**
8:          **for** $a \in A$ **do**
9:              $v_c[d(u)] \leftarrow 1$
10:             $emit << a, a(u) >, v_c >$
11:         **end for**
12:     **end for**
13:     $\}$
14:     $unique \leftarrow attrVal.reduceByKey()\{emit(<< a, a(u) >, \sum v_c >\}$
15:     $sorted \leftarrow unique.sortByKey()$
16:     $b\_first \leftarrow unique.firstElemPart()$
17:     $bc \leftarrow sorted.getBoundaryCuts()$
18:     $attr \leftarrow bc.map()\{<< attr, cut >, v_c >=>< attr, < cut, v_c >>\}$
19:     $bestCut \leftarrow attr.getBestCut()$
20:     $Cuts \leftarrow Cuts \cup \{bestCut.max()\}$
21:     $(DT'_L, DT'_R) \leftarrow split(DT, bestCut)$
22:     **if** $isCut(DT'_L)$ **then**
23:         $stack.push(DT'_L)$
24:     **else if** $isCut(DT'_R)$ **then**
25:         $stack.push(DT'_R)$
26:     **end if**
27: **end while**

Input to the algorithm is a decision table DT and the output is the set of semi-optimal cuts - $Cuts$. Sample decision table was shown in Table 1. In the beginning, a set of cuts $Cuts$ is initialized as an empty set and whole decision table is pushed on ancillary stack. Lines 4–26 are repeated until stack is not empty.

Table 1. Sample decision table

U	a	b	d
x_1	0.8	2	0
x_2	1	0.5	1
x_3	1.3	3	1
x_4	1.4	1	0
x_5	1.4	2	1
x_6	1.6	3	1
x_7	1.3	1	0

In line 4 the decision subtable DT' is taken for computation. In the broadcast variable $b\_classDistribution$ the class distribution in the DT' which is needed later to calculate the number of pairs of objects with different decisions discerned by cut is stored. Next in lines 7–13 pairs $<key, value>$ are emitted where key is a pair (the attribute, its value for the object u) and $value$ is a vector v_c. Length of the vector v_c is equal to the number of decisions in whole dataset. First, each element of this vector is initialized to the value 0 and then value on index represented the decision value is set as 1. The pair $<key, value>$ represents the value of continuous attribute according to the decision for the object.

Next step is to reduce the number of pairs $<key, value>$ by aggregating them by key in the line 14 of the algorithm. The new set contains pairs $<key, value>$ where key is the same like before the operation, but $\sum v_c$ is a sum of vectors v_c corresponding to the key. Pair $<key, value>$ represents now the decision distribution according to value of the continuous attribute. In the line 15 pairs are sorted by the key. To avoid loss of potential cuts on borders of data partitions in the broadcast variable b_first are stored first pairs from every partition. Output of those operations for the sample decision Table 1 was shown in the first line of Fig. 2. Data is split on partitions which are process on computing nodes. In every partition first column represents continuous attribute, second - value of this attribute, and third class distribution for the value of this attribute.

Thereafter in line 17, the set of potential cuts is generated. Output from this procedure are pairs $<key, value>$ where key is a pair (the attribute, the value of the potential cut) and $value$ is the decision distribution to the left of the cut. Similar approach to capture the class distribution was proposed in decision-tree-based algorithm, called SPRINT [10]. The boundary cut is generated if it separates objects from the different classes according to the Definition 1. To generate all potential cuts in this operation broadcast variable b_first is used. Additionally, accumulators are used to store the number of the objects according to attribute on each partition. The final result is stored in the broadcast variable. Sample process of generating boundary cuts was shown in the first two lines in Fig. 2.

To begin the evaluation of each potential cut, we change the mapping of pairs $<key, value>$ in line 18 of the algorithm. The key is an attribute and a $value$ is a pair: the cut and decision class distribution on the left of the cut. In operation of computing the number of pairs discern by the cut, additionally stored in broadcast variables are used: number of the objects according to attribute on each partition ($accumLeft$) and class distribution in decision subtable ($bClassDistr$) Process of evaluation of cuts using discernibility measure was shown in Fig. 2 in the second and third lines.

In lines 19–20 the best cut is chosen which discerns the biggest number of pairs of objects with different decisions. For the sample decision table in first iteration will be chosen cut $(b, 1.5)$ because it discerns 7 pairs of objects with different decision classes. After this operation decision subtable DT' is split correspondingly to chosen cut on subtables DT'_L and DT'_R. If in this subtables are potential cuts, they are pushed on the stack.

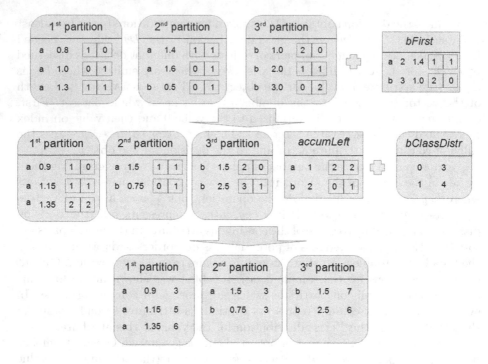

Fig. 2. Generating boundary cuts and process of evaluation

In implementation of this algorithm we used Apache Spark but it can be implemented on any parallel computation system with available shared memory or communications between nodes.

4   Experimental Results

The proposed algorithm of discretization was running on the Apache Spark computation engine [1] connected to YARN-based system for parallel processing of big datasets. In the experiments, Apache Spark 2.0.1 version was used. All the computing nodes have eight 3.4 GHz cores processors and 16 GB of memory. All files were stored in HDFS. Each file was merged on blocks and each of those blocks was replicated three times. A limitation of the proposed method is the size of the available free disk space in distributed file system for files and temporary data.

In this paper, we present the results of the conducted experiments using datasets epsilon created for Pascal Large Scale Learning Challenge in 2008 [2] and KDDCup-99 from the machine learning data repository, University of California at Irvine [3].

The dataset epsilon consists of five hundred thousand objects. Each object is described by two thousand conditional attributes and one decision attribute.

All conditional attributes are continuous. Epsilon is artificial dataset created for competitions included in LibSVM repository. This database was used for generating datasets consisting of $62.5 \cdot 10^5$ to $1 \cdot 10^6$ of objects.

The data set KDDCup-99 consists of almost five million objects. Each object is described by forty one conditional attributes and one decision attribute. There are 23 decisions in this highly imbalanced dataset. Seven nominal conditional attributes were removed from dataset. Information gathered in this dataset can be used to build a network intrusion detector. This database was used for generating datasets consisting approximately of $625 \cdot 10^5$ to $10 \cdot 10^6$ of objects.

New datasets were created by randomly choosing rows from whole dataset with preservation of original decision class proportion.

4.1 Scalability

Scalability is the capability of the system to handle growing work by its enlarging. For example, if amount data to process is growing, additional computing nodes are added to distributed system.

Scaleup analysis studies the stability of the system when the system and dataset size grow in each step of experiment. The scaleup coefficient is defined as follows [12]:

$$Scaleup(DT, n) = \frac{t_{DT_{1,1}}}{t_{DT_{n,n}}} \tag{5}$$

where $t_{DT_{1,1}}$ is the computational time for dataset DT on one node, and $t_{DT_{n,n}}$ is the computational time for n times larger dataset DT on n nodes. If we achieve value near 1 we can say the system is scalable. In fact there is always additional cost for e.g. communication between nodes or sending data.

Figure 3 shows that the scalability of algorithm for KDDCup-99 dataset can depend on the number of decision classes. The least numerous class in this set has only two objects. Scalability of algorithm for this dataset stabilizes on value about 0.6. For the epsilon dataset scalability of the proposed parallel algorithm stabilizes when the number of the nodes is equal 6. We can say the proposed algorithm is scalable as an iterative method.

4.2 Speedup

In speedup tests, the dataset size is constant and the number of nodes grows in each step of experiment. To measure speedup we used one fourth of KDDCup-99 and epsilon datasets in each step of this experiment. The speedup given by the n-times larger system is measured as [12]:

$$Speedup(n) = \frac{t_n}{t_1} \tag{6}$$

where n is the number of computing nodes in cluster, t_1 is the computation time on one node, and t_n is the computation time on n nodes.

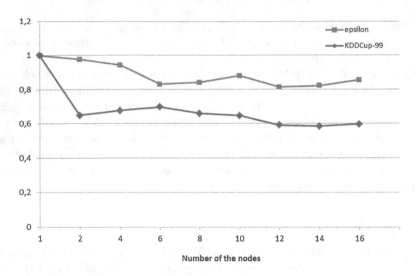

Fig. 3. Scaleup

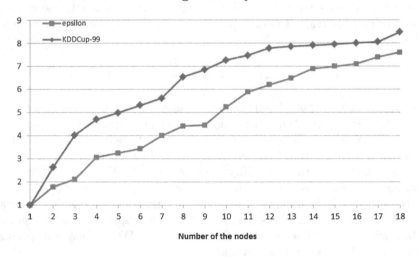

Fig. 4. Speedup

The ideal parallel system with n nodes provides n times speedup (Fig. 4).

Figure 3 shows that with the growth of the number of nodes, the speed performs better.

4.3   Sizeup

In sizeup tests, the number of nodes is constant, and the dataset size grows in each step of experiment. Sizeup measures how much time is needed for calculations when the size of dataset is n times larger than the original dataset. Sizeup is defined as follows [12]:

$$Sizeup(DT) = \frac{t_{DT_n}}{t_{DT_1}} \tag{7}$$

where t_{DT_1} is execution time for a given dataset DT, and t_{DT_n} is execution time n times larger dataset than DT.

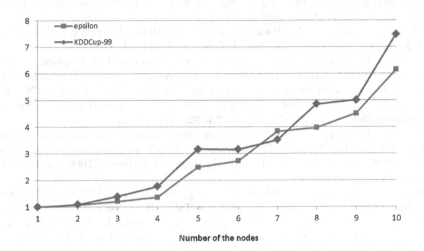

Fig. 5. Sizeup

Figure 5 shows the sizeup experiments results on twenty nodes. Results shows that the proposed algorithm copes well with the growing amount of data.

5   Conclusions and Future Research

In this paper, discretization of continuous attributes for large datasets based on rough set theory is studied. A parallel multivariate attribute discretization algorithm is proposed, which used the distributed computational engine Apache Spark and the discernibility measure of a cut. It is worth noting that a interesting element of the paper is concurrent searching optimal cuts on every conditional attribute. It can guarantee to find semi-optimal, consistent and minimal set of cuts. The results of the experiments show that the proposed method is efficient for large data, and it is a useful method for data preprocessing for big datasets. Our future research work will focus on applications of distributed in-memory computing for decision rule induction.

Acknowledgements. This research was partially supported by the grant S/WI/3/2013 of the Polish Ministry of Science and Higher Education. The experiments were performed using resources co-financed with the European Union funds as a part of the "Centre for Modern Education of the Bialystok University of Technology" project (Operational Programme Development of Eastern Poland).

References

1. Apache Spark: lightning-fast cluster computing. http://spark.apache.org/
2. Pascal Large Scale Learning Challenge. http://largescale.ml.tu-berlin.de
3. UCI Repository of Machine Learning Databases, University of California, Department of Information and Computer Science, Irvine, CA. http://archive.ics.uci.edu/ml/datasets/KDD+Cup+1999+Data
4. Chen, C.P., Zhang, C.-Y.: Data-intensive applications, challenges, techniques and technologies: a survey on big data. Inf. Sci. **275**, 314–347 (2014)
5. Czolombitko, M., Stepaniuk, J.: Attribute reduction based on MapReduce model and discernibility measure. In: Saeed, K., Homenda, W. (eds.) CISIM 2016. LNCS, vol. 9842, pp. 55–66. Springer, Cham (2016). doi:10.1007/978-3-319-45378-1_6
6. Jiang, F., Sui, Y.: A novel approach for discretization of continuous attributes in rough set theory. Knowl.-Based Syst. **73**, 324–334 (2015)
7. Nguyen, H.S.: Approximate boolean reasoning: foundations and applications in data mining. In: Peters, J.F., Skowron, A. (eds.) Transactions on Rough Sets V. LNCS, vol. 4100, pp. 334–506. Springer, Heidelberg (2006). doi:10.1007/11847465_16
8. Pawlak, Z., Skowron, A.: Rudiments of rough sets. Inf. Sci. **177**(1), 3–27 (2007)
9. Ramírez-Gallego, S., García, S., Mouriño-Talín, H., Martínez-Rego, D., Bolón-Canedo, V., Alonso-Betanzos, A., Benítez, J.M., Herrera, F.: Data discretization: taxonomy and big data challenge. WIREs Data Mining Knowl. Discov. **6**, 5–21 (2015). doi:10.1002/widm.1173
10. Shafer, J.C., Agrawal, R., Mehta, M.: SPRINT: a scalable parallel classifier for data mining. In: Proceedings of the 22th International Conference on Very Large Databases, Mumbai (Bombay), India, pp. 544–555. Morgan Kaufmann Publishers Inc., San Francisco (1996)
11. Stepaniuk, J.: Rough-Granular Computing in Knowledge Discovery and Data Mining. Springer, Heidelberg (2008)
12. Xu, X., Jäger, J., Kriegel, H.P.: A fast parallel clustering algorithm for large spatial databases. Data Mining Knowl. Discov. **3**, 263–290 (1999). Springer
13. Yang, Y., Chen, Z.: Parallelized computing of attribute core based on rough set theory and MapReduce. In: Li, T., Nguyen, H.S., Wang, G., Grzymala-Busse, J., Janicki, R., Hassanien, A.E., Yu, H. (eds.) RSKT 2012. LNCS, vol. 7414, pp. 155–160. Springer, Heidelberg (2012). doi:10.1007/978-3-642-31900-6_20
14. Yang, Y., Chen, Z., Liang, Z., Wang, G.: Attribute reduction for massive data based on rough set theory and MapReduce. In: Yu, J., Greco, S., Lingras, P., Wang, G., Skowron, A. (eds.) RSKT 2010. LNCS, vol. 6401, pp. 672–678. Springer, Heidelberg (2010). doi:10.1007/978-3-642-16248-0_91
15. Zhang, J., Li, T., Ruan, D., Gao, Z., Zhao, C.: A parallel method for computing rough set approximations. Inf. Sci. **194**, 209–223 (2012)
16. Zhang, J., Wong, J., Pan, Y., Li, T.: A parallel matrix-based method for computing approximations in incomplete information systems systems. IEEE Trans. Knowl. Data Eng. **27**, 326–339 (2015)
17. Zhang, Y., Yu, J., Wang, J.: Parallel implementation of Chi2 algorithm in MapReduce framework. In: Zu, Q., Hu, B., Gu, N., Seng, S. (eds.) HCC 2014. LNCS, vol. 8944, pp. 890–899. Springer, Cham (2015). doi:10.1007/978-3-319-15554-8_83

Hardware Supported Rule-Based Classification on Big Datasets

Maciej Kopczynski, Tomasz Grzes, and Jaroslaw Stepaniuk(✉)

Faculty of Computer Science, Bialystok University of Technology, Wiejska 45A,
15-351 Bialystok, Poland
{m.kopczynski,t.grzes,j.stepaniuk}@pb.edu.pl
http://www.wi.pb.edu.pl

Abstract. In this paper we propose a combination of capabilities of the Field Programmable Gate Arrays based device and PC computer for data processing resulting in classification using previously generated decision rules. Solution is focused on big datasets. Presented architecture has been tested in programmable unit on real datasets. Obtained results confirm the significant acceleration of the computation time using hardware supported operations in comparison to software implementation.

Keywords: Rough sets · FPGA · Hardware · Decision rules

1 Introduction

The rough sets' theory was developed in the eighties of the twentieth century by Prof. Z. Pawlak and is an useful tool for data analysis. A lot of rough sets algorithms were implemented in scientific and commercial tools for data processing.

Data processing efficiency problem is arising with increase of the amount of data. Commonly used term is Big Data processing. Unfortunately, there is no precise definition for Big Data. In [14] can be found, that "Big Data usually includes data sets with sizes beyond the ability of commonly used software tools to capture, curate, manage, and process data within a tolerable elapsed time". In this paper, datasets that are called big are these, which cannot be processed in tolerable time by existing scientific software tools, such as RSES package. Existing software limitations in both commercial and scientific areas lead to the search for new possibilities.

Field Programmable Gate Arrays (FPGAs) are the digital integrated circuits which function is not determined during the manufacturing process, but can be programmed by engineers any time. One of the main features of FPGAs is the possibility of evaluating any boolean function. That's why they can be used for supporting rough sets calculations.

At the moment there are some hardware implementation of specific rough set methods. The idea of sample processor generating decision rules from decision tables was described in [13]. In [10] authors presented architecture of rough set

© Springer International Publishing AG 2017
L. Polkowski et al. (Eds.): IJCRS 2017, Part I, LNAI 10313, pp. 655–668, 2017.
DOI: 10.1007/978-3-319-60837-2_52

processor based on cellular networks described in [12]. In [3] a concept of hardware device capable of minimizing the large logic functions created on the basis of discernibility matrix was developed. More detailed summary of the existing ideas and hardware implementations of rough set methods can be found in [4].

None of the above solutions is complete, i.e. creates a system making it possible to solve each problem from a wider class of basic problems related to rough sets. Our aim is to create such a system. Authors are working on fully operational System-on-Chip (SoC) including central processing unit based on Altera NIOS II core implemented in Stratix III FPGA and co-processor for rough sets calculations. Authors have been working on hardware rough sets implementations since 2013. Authors' ideas related to hardware implementations of basic rough sets operations can be found in [17]. Preliminary works related to design concepts of first solutions devoted to reducts and cores calculation can be found in [1]. Implementation of sequential hardware units performing reduct calculation for small datasets (around 100 object with dozen of attributes) was presented in [5]. Paper [6] contains description of different hardware approaches to core calculation. These solutions were still focused on small datasets. In [7] redesign of previously introduced core calculation unit was presented. Modified design can process datasets consisting of millions of objects. Papers [8,9] introduce hardware supported implementation of LEM2 rules generation algorithm. Described solution is able to process datasets that contain millions of object.

2 Introductory Information

Below are the descriptions of the algorithm for hardware supported classification, data preprocessing algorithm for hardware unit, as well as datasets used for experiments.

2.1 Algorithm for Hardware Supported Classification

This section describes pseudocode for rule-based data classification algorithm called **HC** (**H**ardware **C**lassification).

Let $DT_{training} = (U_{training}, A \cup \{d\})$ be a decision table, where $U_{training}$ is a non-empty training set of objects, A is a set of condition attributes and d is a decision attribute. Let GR be a set of decision rules generated from $DT_{training}$.

Example 1. Let $A = \{a, b, c\}$ and $V_d = \{0, 1\}$. For example, $GR = \{r_1, \dots, r_7\}$, where:

r_1 : **if** $a = 1$ & $b = 1$ **then** $d = 1$, r_2 : **if** $b = 1$ & $c = 0$ **then** $d = 1$,
r_3 : **if** $a = 0$ & $b = 2$ **then** $d = 1$, r_4 : **if** $b = 2$ & $c = 0$ **then** $d = 1$,
r_5 : **if** $a = 0$ & $b = 1$ **then** $d = 1$, r_6 : **if** $a = 1$ & $b = 0$ **then** $d = 0$,
r_7 : **if** $a = 1$ & $c = 0$ **then** $d = 0$.

In this paper, in experiments we used decision rules generated by LEM2 algorithm (**L**earning from **E**xamples **M**odule - version **2**). LEM2 was presented by Grzymala-Busse in [2]. Authors' previous papers focused on hardware implementation of LEM2 can be found in [8,9]. HC algorithm uses input dataset decomposition that allows for processing fixed-size data parts by hardware modules. Further details on system architecture are presented in Sect. 3. Algorithm part supported by hardware module is prefixed with [H] in pseudocode. This is module for creating set of objects fulfilling conditional part of the rule. Authors avoided diving into hardware details, because pseudocode would become hardly understandable. Details are included in Sect. 3.2.

HC Algorithm (Hardware Classification Algorithm)
INPUT: dataset $DT = (U, A)$, precomputed rules set GR
OUTPUT: classification result CR
1: **for** $x \in U$ **do**
2:    $CR[x] \leftarrow \emptyset$
3: **end for**
4: **for** $x \in U$ **do**
5:    **for** $vd \in$ every value of d **do**
6:       $RCA[x][vd] \leftarrow 0$
7:    **end for**
8: **end for**
9: **for** $x \in U$ **do**
10:    **for** $r \in GR$ **do**
11:       **if** [H] r satisfies x **then**
12:          $RCA[x][d(r)] = RCA[x][d(r)] + 1$
13:       **end if**
14:    **end for**
15: **end for**
16: **for** $x \in U$ **do**
17:    $CR[x] \leftarrow$ find vd with maximum value in $RCA[x]$
18: **end for**

Input of the algorithm is dataset DT and precomputed decision rules set GR. Output is classification result vector CR. First loop in line 1 prepares vector CR by fulfilling it by empty values for every object contained in DT. Loops in lines 4 and 5 initialize rules counting array RCA with 0 values. Each row of this array corresponds to given object in DT, while each column is mapped to subsequent decision class. Loops in lines 9 and 10 are main loops iterating over all objects (denoted as x) and all rules (denoted as r). If conditional part of processed rule r satisfies conditional attributes of selected object x, then given cell (decision part of rule $d(r)$) of RCA array is incremented by 1 in line 12. Rule satisfaction checking is supported by hardware module in line 11. Last loop of the algorithm in line 16 is responsible for final assignment of decision class for every object in input dataset. Result is stored in CR. Assignment is based of finding decision class that has highest value in RCA in terms of satisfied rules for given object x.

Figure 1 presents idea of HC algorithm. Possible ties in classification are broken by choosing first decision, that comes from matching rule. This fact is true for both types of implementation.

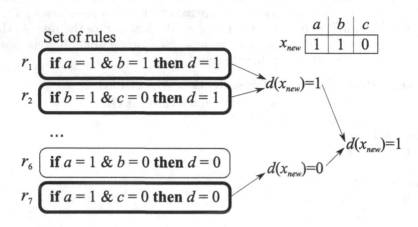

Fig. 1. Idea of HC algorithm

Description of subsequent dataset processing performed by hardware unit is shown in Sect. 2.2.

2.2   Hardware Dataset Processing in Proposed Algorithm

Input dataset for classification is divided by control software into fixed-size parts which are subsequently processed by calculations supporting hardware unit. General pseudocode for such processing is shown below:

HC Algorithm dataset processing
INPUT: dataset $DT = (U, A)$, precomputed rules set GR
OUTPUT: rules counting array RCA
1: **for** $cnt \leftarrow 0$ **to** $m - 1$ **do**
2:     $RAM_{set} \leftarrow \{x \in U : x_{cnt \cdot n}$ **to** $x_{(cnt+1) \cdot n - 1}\}$
3:     $RCA \leftarrow$ store rules satisfaction on objects in RAM_{set}
4: **end for**

Input of the hardware control algorithm is dataset DT and precomputed rules set GR. Output is corresponding part of rules counting array RCA. Loop in lines 1 to 4 is responsible for choosing parts of input dataset DT. Dataset is divided into m parts, where each of them have the fixed size of n objects. Selected part denoted as RAM_{set}, is loaded into internal FPGA's RAM memory (more details in Sect. 3.1) in line 2. Line 3 is responsible for storing partial results RCA.

2.3 Data to Conduct Experimental Research

In this paper, we present the results of the conducted experiments using two datasets: Poker Hand Dataset (created by Robert Cattral and Franz Oppacher) and data about children with insulin-dependent diabetes mellitus type 1 (created by Jarosław Stepaniuk).

First dataset was obtained from UCI Machine Learning Repository [11]. Each of 1 000 000 records is an example of a hand consisting of five playing cards drawn from a standard deck of 52. Each card is described using two attributes (suit and rank), for a total of 10 conditional attributes. There is one decision attribute that describes the "Poker Hand". Decision attribute describes 10 possible combinations of cards in descending probability in the dataset: nothing in hand, one pair, two pairs, three of a kind, straight, flush, full house, four of a kind, straight flush, royal flush.

Diabetes mellitus is a chronic disease of the body's metabolism characterized by an inability to produce enough insulin to process carbohydrates, fat, and protein efficiently. Twelve conditional (physical examination results) and one decision attribute (microalbuminuria) describe the database. The database consisting of 107 objects is shown at the end of the paper [15]. An analysis can be found in Chap. 6 of the book [16].

The Poker Hand database was used for creating smaller datasets consisting of 1 000 to 1 000 000 of objects by selecting given number of first rows of original dataset. Diabetes database was used for generating bigger datasets consisting of 1 000 to 1 000 000 of objects. New datasets were created by multiplying the rows of original dataset. Numerical values were discretized and each attributes value was encoded using four bits for both datasets. Every single object was described on 44 bits for Poker Hand and 52 bits for Diabetes. To fit to memory boundaries in both cases, objects descriptions had to be extended to 64 bits words by filling unused attributes with 0's. Thus prepared hardware units doesn't have to be reconfigured for different datasets until these datasets fit into configured and compiled unit.

3 System Architecture and Hardware Realization

Startix III FPGA contains processor control unit implemented as NIOS II embedded core. Softcore processor supports hardware block responsible for data classification. Hardware calculation block is synthesized together with NIOS II inside the FPGA chip. Development board provides other necessary for SoC elements like memories for storing data and programs or communication interfaces to exchange data and transmit calculation results.

3.1 Softcore Control Unit

Hardware modules are controlled by software executed in softcore processor. Main goal of this implementation is:

- read and write data to hardware module,
- prepare input dataset,
- perform operations on binary sets,
- control overall operation.

Initially preprocessed on PC dataset as well as precomputed rules are stored on Secure Digital card in binary version. In the first step of operation, dataset and rules are copied from SD card to DDR2 RAM module on development board. Results of subsequent operations and currently processed parts of dataset are stored in FPGA built-in RAM memories (MLAB, M9k and M144k).

MLAB blocks are synchronous, dual-port memories with configurable organization 32×20 or 64×10. Dual-port memories can be read and written simultaneously what makes operations faster. M9k and M144k are also synchronous, dual-port memory blocks with many possible configurable organizations. These blocks give a wide possibility of preparing memories capable of storing almost every type of the objects (words) – from small ones to big ones.

3.2   Hardware Implementation

Hardware implementation, created after analysis of the HC algorithm described in Sect. 2.1, was focused on assigning objects fulfilling conditional part of processed rule to decision class related to rule. Hardware block was implemented as combinational unit, what means that all calculations are performed in one clock cycle. Nature of performed operation gives possibility of using them for parallel computing systems.

Prepared hardware unit was called *rComparator*. It's purpose is to check if conditional part of rule fulfills conditional attributes of processed objects. This operation is performed on many objects at one time. Results in terms of decision class is stored in register corresponding to each processed object. Below is the description of prepared module.

Diagram of *rComparator* module is shown on Fig. 2. Inputs of this module are:

- **PDATR** (**P**art of **DAT**a **R**egister) - contains fixed-size part of dataset for processing,
- **CPRDR** (**C**onditional **P**art of **R**ule **D**efined **R**egister) - defines which conditional part of the rule is defined on input,
- **CPRVR** (**C**onditional **P**art of **R**ule **V**alue **R**egister) - contains values of conditional parts of the rule,

Outputs of the module is **OSRR** (**O**bject **S**atisfied by **R**ule **R**egister) that describes which objects fulfill conditional part of processed rule.

Single comparator block (CB) for *rComparator* module is shown on Fig. 3. This block is used to compare the values from CPRVR register with selected object from dataset.

rComparator is designed as a combinational circuit and thus does not need a clock signal for proper work. Amount of time needed to obtain correct results

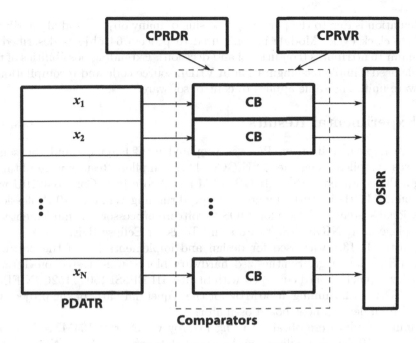

Fig. 2. *rComparator* module

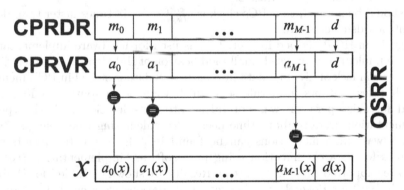

Fig. 3. *rComparator* primary building block, where M is a number of conditional attributes

depends only on propagation time of logic blocks inside the FPGA. This property allows to significantly increase the speed of calculations because the time of propagation in contemporary FPGAs usually do not exceed 10 ns. However, for the proper cooperation with external control blocks, as well as to perform other parts of the HC algorithm, hardware module must be controlled by the clock.

Main design principle of presented solution assumes, that each of described modules process fixed-size part of dataset. Results of calculations are stored using software implemented inside NIOSII softcore processor. Biggest impact on time of calculation is due to the parallel processing of many objects and all attributes in single clock cycle. Module is configured to process 64 objects described by maximum 16 attributes (conditional and decision). Extending possibilities of this module needs simple reconfiguration in VHDL source code and recompilation of hardware unit. The same applies to control software.

4   Experimental Results

Software implementation on PC was prepared in C language and the source code was compiled using the GNU GCC 4.8.1 compiler. Results were obtained using a PC equipped with an 16 GB RAM and 2-core Intel Core i5 4210U with maximum 2.4 GHz in Turbo mode clock speed running Windows 10 Professional operational system. Software for NIOS II softcore processor was implemented in C language using NIOS II Software Build Tools for Eclipse IDE.

Quartus II 13.1 was used for design and implementation of the hardware using VHDL language. Synthesized hardware blocks were tested on TeraSIC DE-3 development board equipped with Stratix III EP3SL150F1152C2N FPGA chip. FPGA clock running at 50 MHz for the sequential parts of the project was derived from development board oscillator.

Timing results were obtained using LeCroy waveSurfer 104MXs-B (1 GHz bandwidth, 10 GS/s) oscilloscope for small datasets. Hardware time counter was introduced for bigger datasets.

It should be noticed, that PCs clock is $\frac{clk_{PC}}{clk_{FPGA}} = 48$ times faster than development boards clock source.

Algorithm HC described in Sect. 2.1 was used for hardware implementation. Software implementation used small modification of HC algorithm, which differs from above in lack of dividing data into parts - all data is stored in PC's memory. In both cases, authors used rule sets which were precomputed on PC. Time needed for this operation was not taken into consideration in both types of implementation. Details about time needed for calculating rules using software and hardware implementations can be found in [8,9]. Presented results show the times for data classification using pure software implementation (t_S) and hardware supported classification (t_H). Results are shown in Table 1 for Diabetes and in Table 2 for Poker Hand datasets. Calculations were carried out on two sizes of rule sets. For Diabetes it were 33 and 66 rules, while for Poker Hand it were 222 and 444 rules. 33 rules for Diabetes dataset were generated using 107 objects (original size of set) using LEM2 algorithm. 66 rules set was created by simple duplication of rules. 222 rules for Poker Hand dataset were generated using first 500 objects from original dataset, while 444 rules set was created, similar to Diabetes, by duplication of rules. Last two columns in both tables describe the speed-up factor without (C) and with (C_{clk}) taking clock speed difference between PC and FPGA into consideration. k denotes thousands and M stands for millions.

In this case, one hardware execution unit was used, that consumed 19 335 of 113 600 Logical Elements (LEs) total available. This number includes also resources used by NIOS II softcore processor.

Table 1. Comparison of execution time between hardware and software implementation for Diabetes dataset using HC algorithm

Objects —	Software - t_S [ms]	Hardware - t_H [ms]	$C = \frac{t_S}{t_H}$ —	$C_{clk} = 48\frac{t_S}{t_H}$ —
33 rules				
1k	2.24	1.02	2.20	105.50
2k	3.72	1.73	2.16	103.45
5k	8.63	3.65	2.36	113.37
10k	17.11	7.50	2.28	109.50
20k	33.48	15.77	2.12	101.92
50k	84.39	42.17	2.00	96.05
100k	162.64	74.23	2.19	105.16
200k	329.14	156.35	2.11	101.05
500k	818.78	385.63	2.12	101.92
1M	1 640.48	775.32	2.12	101.56
66 rules				
1k	4.69	2.10	2.23	107.12
2k	7.73	3.50	2.21	106.15
5k	17.92	8.69	2.06	98.97
10k	34.90	16.65	2.10	100.58
20k	69.72	29.67	2.35	112.80
50k	176.34	75.13	2.35	112.66
100k	326.62	144.74	2.26	108.32
200k	682.81	321.20	2.13	102.04
500k	1 682.33	821.65	2.05	98.28
1M	3 344.27	1 548.64	2.16	103.66

Figures 4 and 5 present graphs showing the relationship between the number of objects and execution time for hardware and software solution for respectively Diabetes and Poker Hand datasets. Both axes on graphs use logarithmic scale.

Presented results show increase in the speed of data processing. Hardware module execution time compared to the software implementation is about 2.2 times faster for Diabetes dataset and 2 for Poker Hand dataset. If we take clock speed difference between PC and FPGA under consideration, these results are much better - speed-up factor is about 100 for Diabetes dataset and about 90 for Poker Hand dataset.

Speed-up factors are slightly different for two datasets. The reason for this is difference in number of attributes (12 conditional for Diabetes and 10 for Poker Hand) for processing data by software solution. It is worth to notice, that for hardware module it doesn't matter what is the width in bits of single object from dataset, unless it fits in assumed memory boundary. Hardware processing

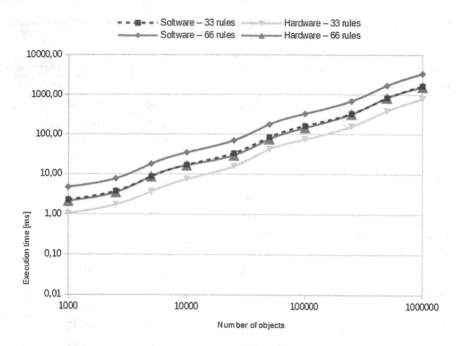

Fig. 4. Relation between number of objects and calculation time for hardware and software implementation using HC algorithm for Diabetes dataset

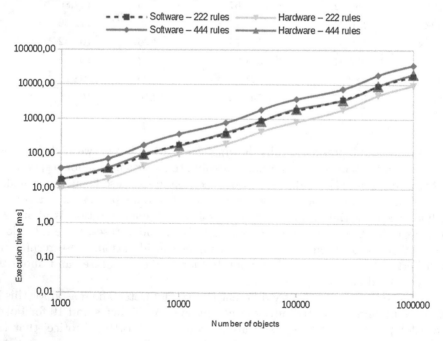

Fig. 5. Relation between number of objects and calculation time for hardware and software implementation using HC algorithm for Poker Hand dataset

Table 2. Comparison of execution time between hardware and software implementation for Poker Hand dataset using HC algorithm

Objects —	Software - t_S [ms]	Hardware - t_H [ms]	$C = \frac{t_S}{t_H}$ —	$C_{clk} = 48\frac{t_S}{t_H}$ —
222 rules				
1k	17.86	9.79	1.82	87.53
2k	34.53	18.89	1.83	87.75
5k	86.06	44.29	1.94	93.27
10k	179.19	95.90	1.87	89.69
20k	374.31	190.03	1.97	94.55
50k	894.84	434.73	2.06	98.80
100k	1 802.77	826.75	2.18	104.67
200k	3 671.71	1 878.11	1.96	93.84
500k	8 971.25	4 824.35	1.86	89.26
1M	17 299.41	9 397.91	1.84	88.36
444 rules				
1k	37.47	17.82	2.10	100.92
2k	70.90	39.22	1.81	86.77
5k	172.97	94.86	1.82	87.52
10k	367.85	167.50	2.20	105.41
20k	780.79	406.09	1.92	92.29
50k	1 842.87	875.34	2.11	101.05
100k	3 776.56	1 960.15	1.93	92.48
200k	7 417.72	3 545.18	2.09	100.43
500k	18 695.86	9 150.04	2.04	98.08
1M	35 873.84	19 736.88	1.82	87.24

unit takes the same time to finish the calculation for every object size, because it always performs the same type of operation. Differences between hardware solutions comes from the nature of data and number of loops iterations.

Let comparison of attribute's value between two objects or iterating over dynamic list of elements be an elementary operation. k denotes number of conditional attributes, n is the number of objects in dataset and m is the number of rules. Computational complexity of software implementation of the classification operation is $\Theta(knm)$ according to HC algorithm shown in Sect. 2.1. Using hardware implementation, complexity of rules generation is $\Theta(nm)$. The k is missing, because our solution performs comparison between all attributes in $\Theta(1)$ - all values on attributes in object and rule are compared in single clock cycle. Additionally, *rComparator* module performs comparisons between single rule and many objects at a time.

Many real datasets are built of tens or hundreds of attributes, so it is impossible to create a single hardware structure capacious enough to process all attributes at once. In such case decomposition must be done in terms of attributes, thus the computational complexity of software and hardware implementation will be almost the same, but in terms of time needed for data processing, hardware implementation will be still much faster than software implementation. The reason for this is that most comparison and counting operations are performed by the hardware block in parallel in terms of objects and attributes.

5   Conclusions

The hardware implementation is the main direction of using data processing methods in real time solutions. As it was presented, performing classification using hardware implementations gives us an acceleration in comparison to software solution, what is very important in case of big datasets. It can be noticed, that speed-up factor remains constant with growing datasets. Number of rules has linear impact on execution time for both hardware and software implementations.

Presented solution deals with the problem of massive data classification. In contrast to most of "big data papers", that deal with the problem of learning decision models from big training data sets, this paper is more related to big testing data sets. This type of problem is very important in practice. One of the examples are cases of real-time monitoring systems that must classify massive amounts of constantly incoming new cases. Of course, way to using presented in this paper solution in industrial environment is long, but it was shown, that this direction of development is very promising.

Hardware classification unit was not optimized for performance in this paper. Processing time can be substantially reduced by increasing FPGA clock frequency, modifying control unit and introducing triggering on both edges of clock signal. Big impact on increasing processing speed can be achieved by redesigning hardware module for processing multiple rules at a time (similar to objects).

Future research will be focused on optimization of presented solution: different sizes of hardware classification unit will be checked, as well as results related to performing the calculations in parallel by multiplying hardware modules. Using FPGA-based solutions it is relatively easy, because multiplication of execution modules needs only few changes in VHDL source code. Most time-consuming part will be design and implementation of parallel execution control unit.

It is worth noticing that current solution is focused only on data processing aspect in terms of classification. Reader should be aware, that possible bottlenecks could be related to sending data for processing and retrieving its results between hardware module and data source. This is also aspect that should be examined in further research plans.

Acknowledgements. The present study was supported by a grant S/WI/3/2013 from Bialystok University of Technology and founded from the resources for research by Ministry of Science and Higher Education.

References

1. Grześ, T., Kopczyński, M., Stepaniuk, J.: FPGA in rough set based core and reduct computation. In: Lingras, P., Wolski, M., Cornelis, C., Mitra, S., Wasilewski, P. (eds.) RSKT 2013. LNCS (LNAI), vol. 8171, pp. 263–270. Springer, Heidelberg (2013). doi:10.1007/978-3-642-41299-8_25
2. Grzymala-Busse, J.W.: Rule Induction, Data Mining and Knowledge Discovery Handbook, pp. 249-265. Springer, New York (2010)
3. Kanasugi, A., Yokoyama, A.: A basic design for rough set processor. In: The 15th Annual Conference of Japanese Society for Artificial Intelligence (2001)
4. Kopczyński, M., Stepaniuk, J.: Rough sets and intelligent systems - professor Zdzisław Pawlak in memoriam, intelligent systems reference library. In: Skowron, A., Suraj, Z. (eds.) Hardware Implementations of Rough Set Methods in Programmable Logic Devices, pp. 309–321. Springer, Heidelberg (2013)
5. Kopczyński, M., Grześ, T., Stepaniuk, J.: FPGA in rough-granular computing : reduct generation. In: The 2014 IEEE/WCI/ACM International Joint Conferences on Web Intelligence, WI 2014, vol. 2, pp. 364–370. IEEE Computer Society, Warsaw (2014)
6. Kopczynski, M., Grzes, T., Stepaniuk, J.: Generating core in rough set theory: design and implementation on FPGA. In: Kryszkiewicz, M., Cornelis, C., Ciucci, D., Medina-Moreno, J., Motoda, H., Raś, Z.W. (eds.) RSEISP 2014. LNCS, vol. 8537, pp. 209–216. Springer, Cham (2014). doi:10.1007/978-3-319-08729-0_20
7. Kopczyński, M., Grześ, T., Stepaniuk, J.: Core for large datasets: rough sets on FPGA. Fundam. Inform. **147**, 241–259 (2016)
8. Kopczyński, M., Grześ, T., Stepaniuk, J.: Rough sets based LEM2 rules generation supported by FPGA. Fundam. Inform. **148**, 107–121 (2016)
9. Kopczynski, M., Grzes, T., Stepaniuk, J.: Hardware supported rough sets based rules generation for big datasets. In: Saeed, K., Homenda, W. (eds.) CISIM 2016. LNCS, vol. 9842, pp. 91–102. Springer, Cham (2016). doi:10.1007/978-3-319-45378-1_9
10. Lewis, T., Perkowski, M., Jozwiak, L.: Learning in hardware: architecture and implementation of an FPGA-based rough set machine. In: 25th EUROMICRO Conference (EUROMICRO 1999), euromicro, vol. 1, p. 1326 (1999)
11. Lichman, M.: UCI Machine Learning Repository. University of California, School of Information and Computer Science, Irvine, CA (2013). http://archive.ics.uci.edu/ml
12. Muraszkiewicz, M., Rybinski, H.: Towards a parallel rough sets computer. In: Ziarko, W.P. (ed.) Rough Sets, Fuzzy Sets and Knowledge Discovery, pp. 434–443. Springer, London (1994)
13. Pawlak, Z.: Elementary rough set granules: toward a rough set processor. In: Pal, S.K., Polkowski, L., Skowron, A. (eds.) Rough-Neurocomputing: Techniques for Computing with Words, Cognitive Technologies, pp. 5–14. Springer, Berlin (2004)
14. Snijders, C., Matzat, U., Reips, U.-D.: Big data: big gaps of knowledge in the field of internet science. Int. J. Internet Sci. **7**, 1–5 (2012)

15. Stepaniuk, J.: Knowledge discovery by application of rough set models. In: Polkowski, L., Tsumoto, S., Lin, T.Y. (eds.) Rough Set Methods and Applications, New Developments in Knowledge Discovery in Information Systems, pp. 137–233. Physica-Verlag, Heidelberg (2000)
16. Stepaniuk, J.: Rough-Granular Computing in Knowledge Discovery and Data Mining. Springer, Heidelberg (2008)
17. Stepaniuk, J., Kopczyński, M., Grześ, T.: The first step toward processor for rough set methods. Fundam. Inform. **127**, 429–443 (2013)

Introducing NRough Framework

Sebastian Widz(✉)

Systems Research Institute, Polish Academy of Sciences,
ul. Newelska 6, 01-447 Warsaw, Poland
widz@nrough.net

Abstract. In this article we present the new machine learning framework called *NRough*. It is focused on rough set based algorithms for feature selection and classification i.e. computation of various types of decision reducts, bireducts, decision reduct ensembles and rough set inspired decision rule induction. Moreover, the framework contains other routines and algorithms for supervised and unsupervised learning. *NRough* is written in C# and compliant with .NET Common Language Specification (CLS). Its architecture allows easy extendability and integration.

Keywords: Rough sets · Approximate decision reducts · Bireducts · .NET · C#

1 Introduction

Interest in machine learning tools and algorithms has been huge in recent years and is still growing. There is a wide range of applications on the market that use various machine learning routines. There is however still only a few solutions compatible with the Microsoft .NET framework that can provide machine learning algorithms. Those that exist are rather focused on numerical rather than symbolic methods and so far none of these has included rough set [1] based algorithms.

Machine learning models that are based on mathematically sophisticated methods may achieve high accuracy but they are hardly understandable by users who expect not only accurate results but also easy yet meaningful explanation how these results were obtained. Models relaying on symbolic, e.g., rule based methods may be less accurate but more intuitive and understandable for humans [2]. In both cases, feature subset selection leads to an increase of interpretability and practical usefulness of machine learning models.

Symbolic methods focus on finding relationships in data, typically reported in a form of rules in a feature-value language. The rules are built with a use of basic logical operators. Examples include the rule induction methods such as learning if-then rules [3] or decision trees [4].

Rough sets have proven to be a successful tool in feature selection (see e.g. [5]). The rough set approach is based on *decision reducts* – irreducible subsets of features, which determine specified decision classes in (almost) the same

© Springer International Publishing AG 2017
L. Polkowski et al. (Eds.): IJCRS 2017, Part I, LNAI 10313, pp. 669–689, 2017.
DOI: 10.1007/978-3-319-60837-2_53

degree as the original set of features. Determining decisions can be interpreted analogously to, e.g., functional or multi-valued dependencies in relational databases. Subsets of features providing exactly the same degree of determination as the original set are often referred as *crisp* decision reducts, in opposite to *approximate* decision reducts [6] where some controlled decrease of determination is allowed. By specifying a threshold for allowed decrease of determination, one can address the balance between decision model's simplicity and accuracy. Indeed, it is easier to search for smaller subsets of features yielding simpler submodels under loosened constraints for decision determination, although too weak constraints may also cause poorer accuracy. However, even relatively less accurate sub-models may lead towards very accurate final model, if the processes of sub-models' design are appropriately synchronized.

NRough is a set of libraries written in C# programming language focusing on rough sets and other symbolic machine learning methods. It contains a number of algorithms for searching approximate decision reducts and constructing decision models. All presented algorithms has been successfully used in our previous research and proven their value. The framework is aimed to be used by researchers who can extend it and test their methods against already implemented models. The second user group are developers and system integrators who can include described routines in their applications.

NRough can be downloaded from *GitHub* Repository [7] as well as from its dedicated website [8] in a form of a Microsoft Visual Studio solution containing source code for all described libraries. The sources include unit test code that presents use case examples as well as unit testing procedures.

We present the framework's key features as well as formal definitions behind implemented algorithms in Sect. 2. We describe data representation, approximate decision reducts and decision reduct classifier ensembles in this section. Moreover, we list other supervised and unsupervised machine learning algorithms included in *NRough*. Finally, we list included features related to model evaluation. Next, in Sect. 3 we describe the architecture of our solution. We put licensing information in Sect. 4. In Sect. 5 we describe other rough set based frameworks. The last Sect. 6 concludes this paper and includes draft of a road map as well as a direction in which we would like the framework to evolve.

2   Key Features

NRough framework contains a number of algorithms for searching approximate decision reducts and constructing decision models based on the rough set theory. Moreover, we added a number of decision rule based classifiers known from machine learning. Last but not least, the framework contains routines for classifier validation and results presentation. Below, we present the list of implemented features starting with data representation description.

2.1   Data Representation

We follow data representation in a form of a decision table which is a well known structure in the rough sets domain. *Decision table* is a tuple $\mathbb{A} = (U, A \cup \{d\})$, where U is a finite set of objects, A is a finite set of attributes and $d \notin A$ is a distinguished decision attribute. We refer to elements of U using their ordinal numbers $i = 0, ..., |U| - 1$ as well as by unique record identifier (if such exists in the data set). We treat attributes $a \in A$ as functions $a : U \to V_a$, where V_a denotes the set of values of a. Values $v_d \in V_d$ correspond to decision classes that we want to describe using the values of attributes in A. The framework internally encodes attribute values using *signed long* base type which allows generic approach for data access and avoiding boxing/unboxing from origin types i.e. faster computations. Internal values can be however converted to their original typed values using a dictionary lookup methods. There are no restrictions about input types, that are automatically recognized during data loading.

Decision tables can be loaded from text files (including comma delimited files and RSES 1.0 format [9]) as well as from the System.Data.DataTable instance which is often used in .NET to store SQL query results. The framework includes a number of filters to manipulate the data such as removal of selected attributes or records based on a given user criteria. Filter concept is also used to define more sophisticated data manipulations such as numeric value discretization.

One of the key concepts in rough sets theory is the definition of indiscernibility relation. For any subset of attributes $B \subseteq A$ and the universe of objects $x \in U$ we are able to define an information vector $B(x) = [a_{i_1}(x), \ldots, a_{i_{|B|}}(x)]$ where $a_{i_j}(x)$ are values of attributes $a_{i_j} \in B$ and $j = 1, \ldots, |B|$. We can also denote the set of all *B-information* vectors, which will then occur in $\mathbb{A}$, as $V_B = \{B(x) : x \in U\}$. Each subset $B \subseteq A$ partitions the space U onto so called *equivalence classes* that can be enumerated as $v_1, \ldots, v_{|V_B|}$. For such division we get the partition space denoted as $U/B = \{E_1, \ldots, E_t\}$ where $E_t \subseteq U$ for $t = 1, \ldots, |V_B|$. Each equivalence class is defined as $E_t = \{x \in U : B(x) = v_t\}$. *NRough* utilizes this concept in a form of a dedicated data structure which is used in many scenarios like calculating functions *information entropy, majority* or *relative gain* functions to name a few. The *majority* function is used in many ways by framework algorithms e.g. for approximate decision reducts computation as well as for decision tree pre-pruning or branch split calculation.

Last but not least, the library contains a number of benchmark data sets taken from UCI repository [10]. These data can be accessed with a predefined methods loading the data into memory including their meta data.

2.2   Approximate Decision Reducts

Attribute selection plays an important role in knowledge discovery. It establishes the basis for more efficient classification, prediction and approximation models. Attribute selection methods originating from the theory of rough sets aim at searching for so called decision reducts – irreducible subsets of attributes that satisfy predefined criteria for keeping *enough* information about decision classes. *NRough* contains a number of algorithms for computing *approximate* decision reducts (as well as *crisp* decision reducts when approximation threshold is set to 0). All reduct computation algorithms are based on heuristic approach and many utilize parallel computing.

We define an (F, ε)-approximate decision reduct [11] where F is a measure $F(d|\cdot) : 2^{|A|} \to \Re$ which evaluates the degree of influence $F(d|B)$ of subset $B \subseteq A$ in d. Below we present the definition as well as the general routine for computing (F, ε)-approximate decision reducts as Algorithm 1 called (F, ε)-REDORD [11]).

Definition 1. *Let $\varepsilon \in [0, 1)$ and $\mathbb{A} = (U, A \cup \{d\})$ be given. We say that $B \subseteq A$ is an (F, ε)-approximate decision reduct, iff it is an irreducible subset of attributes satisfying the following condition:*

$$F(B) \geq (1 - \varepsilon)F(A) \tag{1}$$

Algorithm 1. Modified (F, ε)-REDORD using *Reach* and *Reduce* operations

---

Input: $\varepsilon \in [0, 1)$, $\mathbb{A} = (U, A \cup \{d\})$, $\sigma : \{1, ..., n\} \to \{1, ..., n\}$, $n = |A|$
Output: $B \subseteq A$
1: $B \leftarrow \emptyset$
2: **for** $i = 1 \to n$ **do**   //*Reach*
3:      **if** $F(B \cup \{a_{\sigma(i)}\}) < (1 - \varepsilon)F(A)$ **then**
4:          $B \leftarrow B \cup \{a_{\sigma(i)}\}$
5:      **else**
6:          **break**
7:      **end if**
8: **end for**
9: **for** $j = |B| \to 1$ **do**   //*Reduce*
10:      **if** $F(B \setminus \{a_{\sigma(i)}\}) \geq (1 - \varepsilon)F(A)$ **then**
11:          $B \leftarrow B \setminus \{a_{\sigma(i)}\}$
12:      **end if**
13: **end for**
14: **return** B

The framework defines three types of F measures: $\gamma(B)$ [1] which is based on so called *positive region*, Majority $M(B)$ [11] and Relative Gain $R(B)$ [12]. Other user defined measures can be used with (F, ε)-approximate reduct computation algorithm.

$$M(B) = \frac{1}{|U|} \sum_{E \in U/B} \max_{k \in V_d} |X_k \cap E| \tag{2}$$

$$R(B) = \frac{1}{|V_d|} \sum_{E \in U/B} \max_{X \in U/\{d\}} \frac{|X \cap E|}{|X|} \tag{3}$$

$$\gamma(B) = \frac{1}{|U|}|POS(B)| = \frac{1}{|U|} \sum_{E \in U/B : P(X|E)=1} |E| \tag{4}$$

In [13] it was shown how to compute approximate decision reducts over a universe of weighted objects and that two different weighting schemes lead to an unified way of computing $M(B)$ and $R(B)$ measures that is for $\mathbf{1} : U \to \{1\}$ we have $M_{\mathbf{1}}(B) = M(B)$ and for $r(u) = \frac{1}{|\{x \in U : d(x)=d(u)\}|}$ we obtain $M_r(B) = R(B)$.

Definition 2. *Let $\varepsilon \in [0, 1)$, $\mathbb{A} = (U, A \cup \{d\})$ and $\omega : U \to [0, +\infty)$ be given. We say that $B \subseteq A$ is an (ω, ε)-approximate decision reduct, iff it is an irreducible subset of attributes satisfying the following condition:*

$$M_\omega(B) \geq (1 - \varepsilon)M_\omega(A) \tag{5}$$

$$M_\omega(B) = \frac{1}{|U|_\omega} \sum_{E \in U/B} \max_{k \in V_d} |X_k \cap E|_\omega \tag{6}$$

$$|Y|_\omega = \sum_{u \in Y} \omega(u) \tag{7}$$

Moreover the framework contains algorithms for computing decision bireducts and their derivatives γ-bireducts and relative-bireducts [14]. Below we present definitions as well as pseudo code as Algorithm 2. In [15] we showed relationships between (F, ε)-approximate decision reducts and different types of bireducts.

Definition 3. *Let $\mathbb{A} = (U, A \cup \{d\})$ be a decision system. A pair (B, X), where $B \subseteq A$ and $X \subseteq U$, is called a decision bireduct, iff B discerns all pairs $i, j \in X$ where $d(i) \neq d(j)$, and the following properties hold:*

1. *There is no $C \subsetneq B$ such that C discerns all pairs $i, j \in X$ where $d(i) \neq d(j)$;*
2. *There is no $Y \supsetneq X$ such that B discerns all pairs $i, j \in Y$ where $d(i) \neq d(j)$.*

Definition 4. *Let $\mathbb{A} = (U, A \cup \{d\})$ be a decision system. A pair (B, X), where $B \subseteq A$ and $X \subseteq U$, is called a decision γ-bireduct, iff B discerns all pairs $i \in X, j \in U$ where $d(i) \neq d(j)$, and the following properties hold:*

1. *There is no $C \subsetneq B$ such that C discerns all pairs $i \in X, j \in U$ where $d(i) \neq d(j)$;*
2. *There is no $Y \supsetneq X$ such that B discerns all pairs $i \in Y, j \in U$ where $d(i) \neq d(j)$.*

In [16] we presented the new definition of so called generalized majority decision function, which can be treated as an extension to well known generalized decision function. We also showed the definition of generalized approximate majority decision reducts. The pseudo code is presented as Algorithm 3. An interesting extension in to use so called *exceptions* which on one hand allow further feature reduction in the main model and on the other hand store details about outlayers. Both definitions are implemented in *NRough*.

Algorithm 2. Decision bireduct calculation for a decision system $\mathbb{A} = (U, A \cup \{d\})$

Input: $\mathbb{A} = (U, A \cup \{d\})$, $\sigma : \{1, ..., n+m\} \to \{1, ..., n+m\}$, $m = |A|$, $n = |U|$
Output: $(B \subseteq A, X \subseteq U)$
1: $B \leftarrow A$; $X \leftarrow \emptyset$
2: **for** $i = 1 \to n+m$ **do**
3:     **if** $\sigma(i) \leq n$ **then**
4:         **if** $B \setminus \{a_{\sigma(i)}\} \Rightarrow_X d$ **then**
5:             $B \leftarrow B \setminus \{a_{\sigma(i)}\}$
6:         **end if**
7:     **else**
8:         **if** $B \Rightarrow_{X \cup \{\sigma(i)-n\}} d$ **then**
9:             $X \leftarrow X \cup \{\sigma(i) - n\}$
10:        **end if**
11:    **end if**
12: **end for**
13: **return** (B, X)

Definition 5. *For any decision table $\mathbb{A} = (U, A \cup \{d\})$ and approximation threshold $\varepsilon \in [0, 1)$ one can consider generalized approximate majority decision function $m_d^\varepsilon : 2^U \to 2^{V_d}$ that is taking the following form:*

$$m_d^\varepsilon(E) = \{k : |X_k \cap E| \geq (1-\varepsilon)\max_j |X_j \cap E|\} \tag{8}$$

Definition 6. *Let $\mathbb{A} = (U, A \cup \{d\})$ be given. We say that $B \subseteq A$ is a m_d^ε-decision superreduct, if and only if the following condition holds:*

$$\bigvee_{x,y \in U} m_d^\varepsilon([x]_A) \neq m_d^\varepsilon([y]_A) \Rightarrow \exists_{a \in B} a(x) \neq a(y) \tag{9}$$

We say that B is a m_d^ε-decision reduct, if and only if it is a m_d^ε-superreduct and none of it proper subsets satisfy the above condition.

2.3   Approximate Decision Reduct Classifier Ensembles

Approximate decision reducts usually include less attributes than classical reducts. On the other hand, they may generate if-then rules that make mistakes even within the training samples. For noisy data sets it is to some extent desirable. Nevertheless, some methods for controlling those mistakes should be considered. For example, if the goal is to construct a classification model based on several approximate decision reducts, then – by following ideas taken from machine learning [17] – one may wish to assure that if-then rules generated by different reducts do not repeat the same mistakes on the training data. For this purpose, we can consider a mechanism aiming at diversification of importance of particular objects while searching for different approximate reducts. The same

---

Algorithm 3. Generalized Majority Decision Reduct

Input: $\mathbb{A} = (U, A \cup \{d\})$, $\varepsilon \in [0, 1)$, $\sigma : \{1, ..., n\} \to \{1, ..., n\}$, $n = |A|$
Output: $B \subseteq A$

1: **for all** $E_A \in U/A$ **do**
2:     $d(x) \leftarrow m_d^\varepsilon(E_A)$
3: **end for**
4: $B \leftarrow A$
5: **for** $i = 1 \to n$ **do**
6:     $B \leftarrow B \setminus \{a_{\sigma(i)}\}$
7:     $stop \leftarrow 0$
8:     **for all** $E_B \in U/B$ **do**
9:         **for all** $(x_1, x_2) \in E_B$ **do**
10:             **if** $d(x_1) \cap d(x_2) = \varnothing$ **then**
11:                 $stop \leftarrow 1$
12:                 **break**
13:             **else**
14:                 $d(x_1) \leftarrow d(x_1) \cap d(x_2)$
15:                 $d(x_2) \leftarrow d(x_1)$
16:             **end if**
17:         **end for**
18:         **if** $stop = 1$ **then**
19:             $B \leftarrow B \cup \{a_{\sigma(i)}\}$
20:             **break**
21:         **end if**
22:     **end for**
23: **end for**
24: **return** B

---

mechanisms are used in classifier ensemble methods. These methods perform usually better than their components used independently [18,19]. Combining classifiers is efficient especially if they are substantially different from each other. In fact, the feature subsets applied in ensembles can be relatively smaller than in case of a single feature subset approach, if we can guarantee that combination of less accurate classifier components (further referred as weak classifiers) will lead back to satisfactory level of determining decision or preserving information about decision.

NRough includes several mechanisms for approximate decision reduct classifier ensembles learning. One method is based on well known Adaptive Boosting algorithm [20]. In *NRough* we introduced an *AdaBoost* version which use decision rules derived from approximate decision reducts [21] - the pseudo code is presented in Algorithm 5.

When a reduct ensemble is used to create decision rules one can consider a weak classifier output combination method. We implemented several voting mechanisms described in [22]. We present different voting options in Table 1 in the way compliant with (ω, ε)-approximate decision reducts. The voting weights are presented in a slightly changed form where

$$X_E^\omega = \operatorname*{argmax}_{X \in U/\{d\}} |X \cap E|_\omega \tag{10}$$

Algorithm 4. Generalized Majority Decision Reduct with exceptions

---

Input: $\mathbb{A} = (U, A \cup \{d\})$, $\phi \in [0, 1)$, $\varepsilon \in [0, 1)$, $\sigma : \{1, ..., n\} \to \{1, ..., n\}$, $n = |A|$
Output: $B \subseteq A$

1: **for all** $E_A \in U/A$ **do**
2:     $d(x) \leftarrow m_d^{\phi,0}(E_A)$
3: **end for**
4: $B \leftarrow A$, $c \leftarrow |U|$
5: **for** $i = 1 \to n$ **do**
6:     $B \leftarrow B \setminus \{a_{\sigma(i)}\}$
7:     $stop \leftarrow 0$
8:     SHUFFLE(E_B)
9:     **for all** $E_B \in U/B$ **do**
10:         **for all** $(x_1, x_2) \in E_B$ **do**
11:             **if** $d(x_1) \cap d(x_2) = \varnothing$ **then**
12:                 $c \leftarrow c - |E_B|$
13:                 **if** $c < (1 - \phi) * |U|$ **then**
14:                     $stop \leftarrow 1$
15:                     **break**
16:                 **else**
17:                     SAVEEXCEPTIONRULE(E_B)
18:                 **end if**
19:             **else**
20:                 $d(x_1) \leftarrow d(x_2) \leftarrow d(x_1) \cap d(x_2)$
21:             **end if**
22:         **end for**
23:         **if** $stop = 1$ **then**
24:             $B \leftarrow B \cup \{a_{\sigma(i)}\}$
25:             **break**
26:         **end if**
27:     **end for**
28: **end for**
29: **return** B

Table 1. Six options of weighting decisions by if-then rules, corresponding to the consequent coefficient types plain, ω-confidence and ω-coverage, and antecedent coefficient types single and ω-support. $|E|_\omega$ denotes the support of a rule's left side. X_E^ω is defined by formula (10).

	Single	ω-support
Plain	1	$|E|_\omega/|U|_\omega$
ω-confidence	$|X_E^\omega \cap E|_\omega/|E|_\omega$	$|X_E^\omega \cap E|_\omega/|U|_\omega$
ω-coverage	$(|X_E^\omega \cap E|_\omega/|X_E^\omega|_\omega)/(|E|_\omega/|U|_\omega)$	$|X_E^\omega \cap E|_\omega/|X_E^\omega|_\omega$

Algorithm 5. AdaBoost with (ω, ε)-Approximate Reducts as Weak Classifier

---

Input: $\mathbb{A} = (U, A \cup \{d\})$, $n = |A|$, $\varepsilon \in [0, 1)$, integer T specifying number of iterations
Output: Approximate Reduct Ensemble $S = \{r_1, ..., r_s\}$, $s \leq T$
Initialize: $\omega_i = 1/n$ for $i = 1, 2, 3, ..., n$

1: Calculate error threshold $\epsilon_0 = 1 - M_\omega(\emptyset)$;
2: **for** $t = 1 \rightarrow T$ **do**
3:     Generate permutation σ
4:     Create (ω, ε)-approximate decision reduct r_t based on permutation σ
5:     Generate decision rules based on conditional attributes from reduct r_t
6:     Classify training examples
7:     Calculate the error ϵ_t
8:     **if** $\epsilon_t > \epsilon_0$ **or** $\epsilon_t = 0$ **then**
9:         Break
10:    **end if**
11:    Calculate weak classifier confidence α_t
12:    Update and normalize object weights ω
13: **end for**
14: Normalize α
15: **return** S

Another introduced method for decision reduct diversification is based on decision reduct hierarchical clustering where a distance between reducts is based on binary vectors created according to Formula 11. Figure 1 presents an example of a dendrogram created based on hierarchical clustering of approximate decision reducts. By choosing a cut level we create a number of reducts groups. From each group a single reduct is selected and used as a base for creating a weak classifier. Weak classifiers together form a classifier ensemble.

$$\vec{v_B}[k] = \begin{cases} 1, & \text{if} \quad d(x_k) = \underset{X \in U/\{d\}}{\text{argmax}} |X \cap E| \\ 0, & \text{otherwise} \end{cases} \tag{11}$$

The framework also includes selection mechanisms which allow to select from a reduct pool those reducts that meet a user defines criteria e.g. contain least number of features, generate least number of decision rules etc.

2.4   Other Machine Learning Algorithms

Except rough sets inspired classifiers the framework includes a number of decision rule induction algorithms. These algorithms can be combined with rough set based feature selection methods defined in the previous section. Current implementation includes the following routines:

Decision lists generation routine based on feature subsets and a given decision table.
Majority voting based on a feature subset and a given decision table [23].

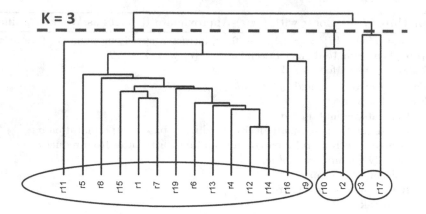

Fig. 1. Dendrogram created based on hierarchical clustering of 18 approximate decision reducts.

Decision trees (C4.5 [24], **ID3** [25]) implementation supporting numerical and nominal attributes types. The impurity functions can be easily exchanged with one another and include *information entropy, gini index, majority* function or other user defined methods. Decision tree base class include **pruning** option - current implementation includes an *error based pruning* and a *reduced error pruning* [26]. We also introduce a new pre-pruning method based on the *majority* function.

Random forest implementation with option to select ensemble size, base decision tree type and data sampling method.

1R rule inducer which, as suggested in [27], could be used to calculate data set baseline accuracy.

Constant decision classifier which classifies all object as majority decision from training data set.

The framework includes a set of unsupervised algorithms based on **Hierarchical clustering** [28] with different *linkage* and *distance* methods. Model construction algorithms that work only with nominal data can utilize a number of numerical attribute discretization methods, both supervised and unsupervised. **Supervised** include hierarchical methods based on *information entropy* [29,30] and *majority* function. **Unsupervised** include *equal width* and *equal frequency* binning. Most of implemented algorithms can work with weighted instances.

2.5   Model Evaluation

Proper evaluation and error estimation is crucial in constructing and comparing decision models. One of the key features in *NRough* is decision model evaluation. Currently the framework provides the following evaluation methods [31]: *k-fold n-repeated cross validation* (CV), *leave-one-out* CV, *bootstrap* with *out-of-the-bag* testing and finally *n-repeated hold out*.

Each evaluation test can return detailed information about experiment results in a form of a formatted table which can be saved as a .CSV or .TEX file. Additionally, results can be presented in a graphical form using an interface to *R* environment [32] - the graphical presentation as well as the latex tabular output are still under development but the working code is available in the repository and can be customized according to your need. The *classification result* class interface contains information such as *error* and *accuracy* rates, *balanced accuracy* (useful for testing imbalanced data sets), *error standard deviation, confidence, coverage, f-score, recall* and *precision* as well as classification *confusion table*. If model definition allows it, there is possibility to include information about complexity e.g. size of a decision tree, number of rules, average length of rules, etc.

3 Architecture

NRough is a Microsoft .NET based framework written in C# programming language. The source code is CLS compliant which enables to use it in other .NET languages. Currently the framework is provided as a set of libraries targeting .NET 4.6.1 and 64 bit architecture.

The libraries have the following structure:

NRough.Core Contains generic data structures and extensions methods.
NRough.Data Responsible for data handling. It defines the *decision table* interface and *equivalence class* collection as well as routines for providing meta data and interface to data filtering.
NRough.MachineLearning Contains approximate decision reduct computation algorithms as well as other described machine learning models and routines.
NRough.Math Contains special functions used across other modules e.g. statistical functions or distance metrics used in clustering.
NRough.Tests.* Contains a set of test fixtures which except unit testing purpose serve as a code sample repository. Each of the above listed libraries has its own unit test library e.g. NRough.Data is tested by NRough.Tests.Data.

The framework is currently dependent on the following external libraries (except standard .NET): Math.NET.Numerics [33], NUnit [34] and R.NET [35].

4 License

NRough libraries are provided under *GNU Lesser General Public License ver. 3* (GNU LGPLv3). This means that provided source can be used for research, commercial and non-commercial purposes without any charges as long as GNU LGPLv3 restrictions are satisfied. Copyright and license notices must be preserved. Contributors provide an express grant of patent rights. However, a larger work using the licensed work through interfaces provided by the licensed work may be distributed under different terms and without source code for the larger work. The source code is provided "as is" without warranty of any kind, express or implied. In no event shall the authors or copyright holders be liable for any claim, damages or other liability. Complete license can be found in [36].

5   Other Frameworks

Let us focus on other rough set related frameworks developed by various researches. First of all, let us mention LERS - a system for Learning from Examples based on Rough Sets [37]. LERS contained two rules' induction algorithms (LEM1 and LEM2) that could cope with inconsistent data. LERS contained also a number of algorithms for handling missing data and numerical attribute discretization. Its performance was comparable with AQ15 and C4.5 algorithms.

Secondly let us mention more complete GUI-based systems: Rough Set Exploration System (RSES) [9] and ROSETTA [38] (a toolkit for analyzing tabular data within a framework of rough sets). Both solutions shared the same computational kernel developed at the Group of Logic, Institute of Mathematics, University of Warsaw, Poland and finally ROSE2 (Rough Sets Data Explorer) [39] which is a software implementing basic elements of the rough set theory and rule discovery techniques. It was created at the Laboratory of Intelligent Decision Support Systems of the Institute of Computing Science in Poznan, Poland. RSES, ROSETTA as well as ROSE2 contained many different algorithms ranging from data preprocessing, filtering, discretization, rule induction, to classification and feature selection.

All mentioned above solutions are according to authors knowledge no longer maintained. These solutions were based on Java or C++ and its source code was not open. More recently, there were several attempts to revive RSES in a form of an open source Java based library distributed under GNU GPL license called *RSESLib* [40].

Last but not least we need to mention *RoughSets* [41] and *RapidRoughSets* [42] packages as a most recent development in rough sets domain. The former package contains the core computational methods for rough and fuzzy sets based on already mentioned R statistical software. The latter package is the GUI extension based on *RapidMiner* software.

In .NET domain there were so far, according to authors knowledge, no attempts to publish a machine learning framework containing rough set based algorithms. We would like to mention Microsoft Azure Machine Learning [43] which is a cloud based service integrating many different solutions resulting in a platform worth considering for system integrators. Its is however a commercial solution. We also would like to mention Accord.NET framework [44] which is an open source machine learning framework focusing on numerical methods as well as on machine vision. This framework could complement some general machine learning routines not yet implemented in *NRough*.

6   Conclusions and Future Work

We have created *NRough* framework based on our experience and research focused on approximate decision reducts done over past few years. In the beginning presented methods had been developed separately, but recently the whole source code went through major refactoring process resulting in presented solution. We have added other machine learning routines to the framework for two reasons: First to combine well known proven machine learning algorithms with rough sets, secondly, in order to be able to compare their performance against rough set inspired classifiers.

The whole framework was so far developed by a single person and there is still much to be done. First of all the framework needs strong API documentation and more examples. We are planning to add this in the nearest future and publish it on-line Secondly, we would like to add more rough set related algorithms in order to create a comprehensive library of different decision reduct computation routines. Thirdly, we are planning to extend the approximate decision reduct selection and diversification criteria. Last but not least, there are some development tasks to complete like graphical presentation methods using *R* interface. Moreover the framework is currently targeting .NET version 4.6.1 which allows to compile it only on Windows platform. We plan to extend its compatibility *.NET Core* to be able to use it on *Linux* and *OSX* platforms, but so far .NET Core lacks some important functionality so we are waiting for its new releases.

Appendix NRough Code Samples

———— Sample 1: 10-fold cross validation of C4.5 decision tree ————

```
1  //load data
2  var data = DecisionTable.Load("data.txt", FileFormat.CSV);
3
4  //create 10-fold 25-repeated cross validation
5  var cv = new CrossValidation(data, 10, 25);
6
7  //create C4.5 decision tree and run cv evaluation
8  var c45 = new DecisionTreeC45();
9  var result = cv.Run<DecisionTreeC45>(c45);
10
11 //output result
12 Console.WriteLine("Train Error: {0}", result.Error);
```

———— Sample 2: Random forest based on C4.5 decision trees ————

```
1  //load data from a CSV file
2  var data = DecisionTable.Load("german.data", FileFormat.CSV);
3  DecisionTable train, test;
4  var splitter = new DataSplitterRatio(data, 0.8);
5  splitter.Split(out train, out test);
6  //Initialize and Learn Random Forest
7  var forest = new DecisionForestRandom<DecisionTreeC45>();
```

```
 8  forest.Size = 500;
 9  forest.Learn(train, train
10      .SelectAttributeIds(a => a.IsStandard).ToArray());
11  //Validate on test data set
12  var result = Classifier.Default.Classify(forest, test);
13  //Output the results
14  Console.WriteLine(result);
```

___ *Sample 3: Generate (F, ε)-approximate decision reducts using reduct factory* ___

```
 1  //load data
 2  var data = Data.Benchmark.Factory.Golf();
 3  //set parameters for reduct factory
 4  var parm = new Args();
 5  parm.SetParameter(ReductFactoryOptions.DecisionTable, data);
 6  parm.SetParameter(ReductFactoryOptions.ReductType,
 7      ReductTypes.ApproximateDecisionReduct);
 8  parm.SetParameter(ReductFactoryOptions.FMeasure,
 9      (FMeasure) FMeasures.Majority);
10  parm.SetParameter(ReductFactoryOptions.Epsilon, 0.05);
11  //compute reducts
12  var reducts =
13      ReductFactory.GetReductGenerator(parm).GetReducts();
14  //output reducts and attributes
15  foreach (IReduct reduct in reducts)
16      Console.WriteLine(reduct.Attributes.ToArray().ToStr());
```

_____ *Sample 4: Generate (ω, ε)-decision reducts using reduct factory* _____

```
 1  //load benchmark data
 2  var data = Data.Benchmark.Factory.Zoo();
 3
 4  //set object weights using r(u) weighting scheme
 5  data.SetWeights(new WeightGeneratorRelative(data).Weights);
 6
 7  //split data into training and testing sets
 8  DecisionTable train, test;
 9  var splitter = new DataSplitterRatio(data, 0.8);
10  splitter.Split(out train, out test);
11
12  //set parameters for reduct factory
13  var parm = new Args();
14  parm.SetParameter(ReductFactoryOptions.DecisionTable, train);
15  parm.SetParameter(ReductFactoryOptions.ReductType,
16      ReductTypes.ApproximateDecisionReduct);
17  parm.SetParameter(ReductFactoryOptions.FMeasure,
18      (FMeasure)FMeasures.MajorityWeighted);
19  parm.SetParameter(ReductFactoryOptions.Epsilon, 0.05);
20
21  //compute reducts
22  var reductGenerator = ReductFactory.GetReductGenerator(parm);
23  var reducts = reductGenerator.GetReducts();
```

```
24
25  //select 10 reducts with least number of attributes
26  var bestReduct = reducts
27      .OrderBy(r => r.Attributes.Count).Take(10);
28
29  //create decision rules based on reducts
30  var decisionRules = new ReductDecisionRules(bestReducts);
31
32  //when test instance is not recognized
33  //set output as unclassified
34  decisionRules.DefaultOutput = null;
35
36  //classify test data
37  var result = Classifier.DefaultClassifer
38      .Classify(decisionRules, test);
39
40  //output accuracy and coverage
41  Console.WriteLine("Accuracy: {0}", result.Accuracy);
```

Sample 3: Boosting (ω, ε)-decision reduct based classifier

```
1   //load training and testing DNA (spieces) data sets
2   var train = Data.Benchmark.Factory.Dna();
3   var test = Data.Benchmark.Factory.DnaTest();
4
5   //set weights
6   var weightGen = new WeightGeneratorConstant(train,
7       1.0 / (double)train.NumberOfRecords);
8   train.SetWeights(weightGen.Weights);
9
10  //create parameters for reduct factory
11  var parm = new Args();
12  parm.SetParameter(ReductFactoryOptions.ReductType,
13      ReductTypes.ApproximateDecisionReduct);
14  parm.SetParameter(ReductFactoryOptions.FMeasure,
15      (FMeasure)FMeasures.MajorityWeighted);
16  parm.SetParameter(ReductFactoryOptions.Epsilon, 0.05);
17  parm.SetParameter(ReductFactoryOptions.NumberOfReducts, 100);
18  parm.SetParameter(ReductFactoryOptions.ReductComparer,
19      ReductRuleNumberComparer.Default);
20  parm.SetParameter(ReductFactoryOptions.SelectTopReducts, 1);
21
22  //create weak classifier prototype
23  var prototype = new ReductDecisionRules();
24  prototype.ReductGeneratorArgs = parm;
25
26  //create ada boost ensemble
27  var adaBoost = new AdaBoost<ReductDecisionRules>(prototype);
28  adaBoost.Learn(train,
29      train.SelectAttributeIds(a => a.IsStandard).ToArray());
30
```

```
31  //classify test data set
32  var result = Classifier.Default.Classify(adaBoost, test);
33
34  //print result header & result
35  Console.WriteLine(ClassificationResult.TableHeader());
36  Console.WriteLine(result);
```

Sample 4: (F, ε)-decision reduct ensemble using hierarchical clustering diversification

```
1   //load training and testing DNA (spieces) data sets
2   var train = Data.Benchmark.Factory.Dna();
3   var test = Data.Benchmark.Factory.DnaTest();
4
5   //create reduct diversification
6   var reductDiversifier
7       = new HierarchicalClusterReductDiversifier();
8   reductDiversifier.Data = train;
9   reductDiversifier.Distance = ReductDistance.Hamming;
10  reductDiversifier.Linkage = ClusteringLinkage.Average;
11  reductDiversifier.NumberOfReducts = 10;
12
13  //create parameters for reduct factory
14  var parm = new Args();
15  parm.SetParameter(ReductFactoryOptions.ReductType,
16      ReductTypes.ApproximateDecisionReduct);
17  parm.SetParameter(ReductFactoryOptions.FMeasure,
18      (FMeasure)FMeasures.MajorityWeighted);
19  parm.SetParameter(ReductFactoryOptions.Epsilon, 0.05);
20  parm.SetParameter(ReductFactoryOptions.NumberOfReducts, 100);
21  parm.SetParameter(ReductFactoryOptions.Diversify,
22      reductDiversifier);
23
24  var rules = new ReductDecisionRules();
25  rules.ReductGeneratorArgs = parm;
26  rules.DecisionIdentificationMethod
27      = RuleQualityMethods.Confidence;
28  rules.RuleVotingMethod = RuleQualityMethods.Coverage;
29
30  //classify test data set and show results
31  var result = Classifier.Default.Classify(rules, test);
32  Console.WriteLine(result);
```

Sample 5: Generate bireducts using class hierarchy

```
1   //load training data set
2   var train = Data.Benchmark.Factory.Dna();
3
4   //generate 100 permutations based on attributes and objects
5   var permGenerator =
6       new PermutationGeneratorAttributeObject(train, 0.5);
7   var permutations = permGenerator.Generate(100);
8
```

```
9    //setup gamma-bireduct generator
10   //generate bireducts based on permutations
11   var bireductGammaGenerator = new BireductGammaGenerator();
12   bireductGammaGenerator.DecisionTable = train;
13   bireductGammaGenerator.Permutations = permutations;
14   var bireducts = bireductGammaGenerator.GetReducts();
15
16   //for each bireduct show its attributes and supported objects
17   foreach (var bireduct in bireducts)
18   {
19       Console.WriteLine(
20           bireduct.Attributes.ToArray().ToStr());
21
22       Console.WriteLine(
23           bireduct.SupportedObjects.ToArray().ToStr());
24   }
```

—————— *Sample 8: Compute Generalized Majority Decision Reducts* ——————

```
1    //load training data set
2    var train = Data.Benchmark.Factory.Dna();
3
4    //setup reduct factory parameters
5    Args parms = new Args();
6    parms.SetParameter(ReductFactoryOptions.DecisionTable, train);
7    parms.SetParameter(ReductFactoryOptions.ReductType,
8        ReductTypes.GeneralizedMajorityDecision);
9    parms.SetParameter(ReductFactoryOptions.WeightGenerator,
10       new WeightGeneratorMajority(train));
11   parms.SetParameter(ReductFactoryOptions.Epsilon, 0.05);
12   parms.SetParameter(ReductFactoryOptions.PermutationCollection,
13       new PermutationCollection(10,
14       train.SelectAttributeIds(a => a.IsStandard)
15           .ToArray()));
16
17   //generate reducts
18   var reductGenerator = ReductFactory.GetReductGenerator(parms);
19   var reducts = reductGenerator.GetReducts();
```

—— *Sample 9: Compute Generalized Majority Decision Reducts with exceptions* ——

```
1    //load training and test data sets
2    var train = Data.Benchmark.Factory.Dna();
3    var test = Data.Benchmark.Factory.DnaTest();
4
5    //setup reduct factory parameters
6    Args parms = new Args();
7    parms.SetParameter(ReductFactoryOptions.DecisionTable, train);
8    parms.SetParameter(ReductFactoryOptions.ReductType,
9        ReductTypes.GeneralizedMajorityDecision);
10   parms.SetParameter(ReductFactoryOptions.WeightGenerator,
11       new WeightGeneratorMajority(train));
```

```
12  parms.SetParameter(ReductFactoryOptions.Epsilon, 0.05);
13  parms.SetParameter(ReductFactoryOptions.PermutationCollection,
14      new PermutationCollection(10,
15          train.SelectAttributeIds(a => a.IsStandard)
16              .ToArray()));
17  parms.SetParameter(ReductFactoryOptions.UseExceptionRules,
18      true);
19
20  //generate reducts with exceptions
21  var reductGenerator = ReductFactory.GetReductGenerator(parms);
22  var reducts = reductGenerator.GetReducts();
23
24  foreach (var reduct in reducts) {
25      var r = reduct as ReductWithExceptions;
26      foreach (var exception in r.Exceptions) {
27          Console.WriteLine(exception.Attributes
28              .ToArray().ToStr());
29          Console.WriteLine(exception.SupportedObjects
30              .ToArray().ToStr());
31      }
32  }
33
34  var rules = new ReductDecisionRules(reducts);
35  rules.DecisionIdentificationMethod
36      = RuleQualityMethods.Confidence;
37  rules.RuleVotingMethod = RuleQualityMethods.SingleVote;
38  rules.Learn(train, null);
39
40  //classify test data set
41  var result = Classifier.Default.Classify(rules, test);
42
43  //show results
44  Console.WriteLine(result);
```

Sample 10: Decision table discretization

```
1   var data = Data.Benchmark.Factory.Vehicle();
2
3   DecisionTable train, test;
4   var splitter = new DataSplitterRatio(data, 0.8);
5   splitter.Split(out train, out test);
6
7   var tableDiscretizer = new TableDiscretizer(
8       new IDiscretizer[]
9       {
10          //try to discretize using Fayyad MDL Criterion
11          new DiscretizeFayyad(),
12
13          //in case Fayyad MDL is to strict
14          //use standard entropy and 5 buckets
15          new DiscretizeEntropy(5)
```

```
16  });
17
18  tableDiscretizer.FieldsToDiscretize = train
19      .SelectAttributeIds(a => a.IsStandard && a.CanDiscretize());
20
21  var filter = new DiscretizeFilter();
22  filter.TableDiscretizer = tableDiscretizer;
23  filter.Compute(train);
24
25  foreach(int attributeId in tableDiscretizer.FieldsToDiscretize)
26  {
27      var fieldDiscretizer = filter
28          .GetAttributeDiscretizer(attributeId);
29
30      Console.WriteLine("Attribute {0} was discretized with {1}",
31          attributeId, fieldDiscretizer.GetType().Name);
32      Console.WriteLine("Computed Cuts: {0}",
33          fieldDiscretizer.Cuts.ToStr());
34  }
35
36  var trainDisc = filter.Apply(train);
37  var testDisc = filter.Apply(test);
```

References

1. Pawlak, Z., Skowron, A.: Rudiments of rough sets. Inf. Sci. **177**(1), 3–27 (2007)
2. Widz, S., Ślęzak, D.: Rough set based decision support - models easy to interpret. In: Peters, G., Lingras, P., Ślęzak, D., Yao, Y. (eds.) Rough Sets: Selected Methods and Applications in Management and Engineering, pp. 95–112. Springer, Heidelberg (2012)
3. Agrawal, R., Imielinski, T., Swami, A.N.: Mining association rules between sets of items in large databases. In: Buneman, P., Jajodia, S. (eds.) Proceedings of the 1993 ACM SIGMOD International Conference on Management of Data, Washington, D.C., 26–28 May 1993, pp. 207–216. ACM Press (1993)
4. Rokach, L., Maimon, O.: Data Mining with Decision Trees: Theory and Applications. World Scientific, Singapore (2014)
5. Świniarski, R.W., Skowron, A.: Rough set methods in feature selection and recognition. Pattern Recogn. Lett. **24**(6), 833–849 (2003)
6. Nguyen, H.S., Ślęzak, D.: Approximate reducts and association rules - correspondence and complexity results. In: Zhong, N., Skowron, A., Ohsuga, S. (eds.) RSFD-GrC 1999. LNCS, vol. 1711, pp. 137–145. Springer, Heidelberg (1999). doi:10.1007/978-3-540-48061-7_18
7. Widz, S.: NRough framework git repository (2017). https://www.github.org/nrough/
8. Widz, S.: NRough framework website (2017). http://www.nrough.net
9. Bazan, J.G., Szczuka, M.S.: The rough set exploration system. In: Peters, J.F., Skowron, A. (eds.) Transactions on Rough Sets III. LNCS, vol. 3400, pp. 37–56. Springer, Heidelberg (2005)

10. Lichman, M.: UCI machine learning repository (2013)
11. Ślęzak, D.: Rough sets and functional dependencies in data: foundations of association reducts. In: Gavrilova, M.L., Tan, C.J.K., Wang, Y., Chan, K.C.C. (eds.) Transactions on Computational Science V. LNCS, vol. 5540, pp. 182–205. Springer, Heidelberg (2009). doi:10.1007/978-3-642-02097-1_10
12. Ślęzak, D., Ziarko, W.: The investigation of the Bayesian rough set model. Int. J. Approximate Reason. **40**(1–2), 81–91 (2005)
13. Widz, S., Ślęzak, D.: Attribute subset quality functions over a universe of weighted objects. In: Kryszkiewicz, M., Cornelis, C., Ciucci, D., Medina-Moreno, J., Motoda, H., Raś, Z.W. (eds.) RSEISP 2014. LNCS, vol. 8537, pp. 99–110. Springer, Cham (2014). doi:10.1007/978-3-319-08729-0_9
14. Stawicki, S., Ślęzak, D., Janusz, A., Widz, S.: Decision bireducts and decision reducts - a comparison. Int. J. Approximate Reason. **84**, 75–109 (2017)
15. Stawicki, S., Widz, S.: Decision bireducts and approximate decision reducts: comparison of two approaches to attribute subset ensemble construction. In: 2012 Federated Conference on Computer Science and Information Systems (FedCSIS), pp. 331–338. IEEE (2012)
16. Widz, S., Stawicki, S.: Generalized majority decision reducts. In: 2016 Federated Conference on Computer Science and Information Systems (FedCSIS), pp. 165–174. IEEE (2016)
17. Kuncheva, L.I., Diez, J.J.R., Plumpton, C.O., Linden, D.E.J., Johnston, S.J.: Random subspace ensembles for fMRI classification. IEEE Trans. Med. Imaging **29**(2), 531–542 (2010)
18. Breiman, L.: Bagging predictors. Mach. Learn. **24**(2), 123–140 (1996)
19. Kuncheva, L.I.: Combining Pattern Classifiers: Methods and Algorithms. Wiley, Hoboken (2014)
20. Freund, Y., Schapire, R.E.: Experiments with a new boosting algorithm. In: Saitta, L. (ed.) ICML, pp. 148–156. Morgan Kaufmann, Burlington (1996)
21. Widz, S.: Boosting approximate reducts. In: Techniki informacyjne: teoria i zastosowania: wybrane problemy, Instytut Badań Systemowych PAN, vol. 5, no. 17, pp. 129–148 (2015)
22. Ślęzak, D., Widz, S.: Is it important which rough-set-based classifier extraction and voting criteria are applied together? In: Szczuka, M., Kryszkiewicz, M., Ramanna, S., Jensen, R., Hu, Q. (eds.) RSCTC 2010. LNCS, vol. 6086, pp. 187–196. Springer, Heidelberg (2010). doi:10.1007/978-3-642-13529-3_21
23. Kohavi, R.: The power of decision tables. In: Lavrac, N., Wrobel, S. (eds.) ECML 1995. LNCS, vol. 912, pp. 174–189. Springer, Heidelberg (1995). doi:10.1007/3-540-59286-5_57
24. Quinlan, J.R.: C4.5: Programs for Machine Learning. Elsevier, Amsterdam (2014)
25. Quinlan, J.R.: Induction of decision trees. Mach. Learn. **1**(1), 81–106 (1986)
26. Quinlan, J.R.: Simplifying decision trees. Int. J. Man-Mach. Stud. **27**(3), 221–234 (1987)
27. Holte, R.C.: Very simple classification rules perform well on most commonly used datasets. Mach. Learn. **11**(1), 63–90 (1993)
28. Gurrutxaga, I., Arbelaitz, O., Martín, J.I., Muguerza, J., Pérez, J.M., Perona, I.: SIHC: a stable incremental hierarchical clustering algorithm. In: ICEIS, vol. 2, pp. 300–304 (2009)
29. Fayyad, U.M., Irani, K.B.: Multi-interval discretization of continuous-valued attributes for classification learning. In: Thirteenth International Joint Conference on Artificial Intelligence, vol. 2, pp. 1022–1027. Morgan Kaufmann Publishers (1993)

30. Kononenko, I.: On biases in estimating multi-valued attributes. In: 14th International Joint Conference on Articial Intelligence, pp. 1034–1040 (1995)
31. Friedman, J., Hastie, T., Tibshirani, R.: The Elements of Statistical Learning: Data Mining, Inference, and Prediction. Springer Series in Statistics. Springer, Heidelberg (2009)
32. R Development Core Team: R: A Language and Environment for Statistical Computing. R Foundation for Statistical Computing, Vienna, Austria (2008). ISBN 3-900051-07-0
33. Rüegg, C., Marcus, C.: Math.NET numerics (2017). https://numerics.mathdotnet.com/. Accessed 11 Feb 2017
34. Poole, C., Prouse, R., Busoli, S., Colvin, N.: NUnit framework (2017) https://www.nunit.org/. Accessed 11 Feb 2017
35. Perraud, J.M.: R.NET github repository (2017). https://github.com/jmp.75/rdotnet. Accessed 11 Feb 2017
36. Free Software Foundation: Gnu lesser general public license. https://www.gnu.org/licenses/lgpl-3.0.en.html. Accessed 11 Feb 2017
37. Grzymala-Busse, J.W.: LERS-a data mining system. In: Maimon, O., Rokach, L. (eds.) Data Mining and Knowledge Discovery Handbook, pp. 1347–1351. Springer, Heidelberg (2005)
38. Komorowski, J., Øhrn, A., Skowron, A.: Case studies: public domain, multiple mining tasks systems: ROSETTA rough sets. In: Handbook of Data Mining and Knowledge Discovery, pp. 554–559. Oxford University Press, Inc. (2002)
39. Prędki, B., Słowiński, R., Stefanowski, J., Susmaga, R., Wilk, S.: ROSE - software implementation of the rough set theory. In: Polkowski, L., Skowron, A. (eds.) RSCTC 1998. LNCS, vol. 1424, pp. 605–608. Springer, Heidelberg (1998). doi:10.1007/3-540-69115-4_85
40. Wojna, A.: RSESLib. (2017). http://rseslib.mimuw.edu.pl/. Accessed 11 Feb 2017
41. Riza, L.S., Janusz, A., Bergmeir, C., Cornelis, C., Herrera, F., Ślęzak, D., Benítez, J.M., et al.: Implementing algorithms of rough set theory and fuzzy rough set theory in the R package "roughsets". Inf. Sci. **287**, 68–89 (2014)
42. Janusz, A., Stawicki, S., Szczuka, M., Ślęzak, D.: Rough set tools for practical data exploration. In: Ciucci, D., Wang, G., Mitra, S., Wu, W.-Z. (eds.) RSKT 2015. LNCS, vol. 9436, pp. 77–86. Springer, Cham (2015). doi:10.1007/978-3-319-25754-9_7
43. Barga, R., Fontama, V., Tok, W.H., Cabrera-Cordon, L.: Predictive Analytics with Microsoft Azure Machine Learning. Springer, Heidelberg (2015)
44. Souza, C.R.: The Accord.NET framework, SãoCarlos, Brazil (2014). http://accord-framework.net. Accessed 11 Feb 2017

Author Index

Printed in the United States
By Bookmasters